# THE HISTORIANS' HISTORY OF THE WORLD

HUME

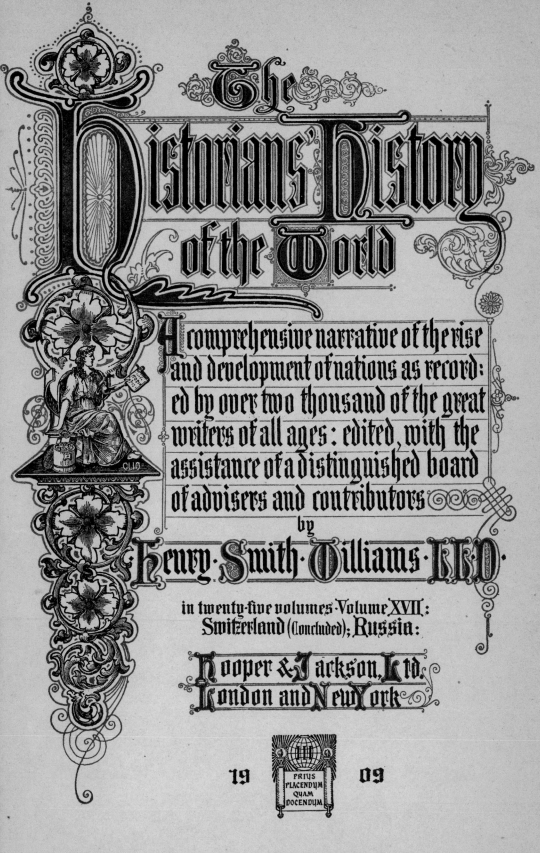

# The Historians' History of the World

A comprehensive narrative of the rise and development of nations as recorded by over two thousand of the great writers of all ages : edited, with the assistance of a distinguished board of advisers and contributors

by

## Henry Smith Williams LL.D.

in twenty-five volumes · Volume XVII :
Switzerland (Concluded) ; Russia :

### Hooper & Jackson, Ltd.
### London and New York

19    09

PRIUS PLACENDUM QUAM DOCENDUM

909
W72
v. 17

2038

VOLUME XVII

SWITZERLAND (CONCLUDED); RUSSIA

# Contributors, and Editorial Revisers

Prof. Adolf Erman, University of Berlin.

Prof. Joseph Halévy, College of France.

Prof. Thomas K. Cheyne, Oxford University.

Prof. Andrew C. McLaughlin, University of Chicago.

Prof. David H. Müller, University of Vienna.

Prof. Alfred Rambaud, University of Paris.

Capt. F. Brinkley, Tokio.


Prof. Eduard Meyer, University of Berlin.

Dr. James T. Shotwell, Columbia University.

Prof. Theodor Nöldeke, University of Strasburg.

Prof. Albert B. Hart, Harvard University.

Dr. Paul Brönnle, Royal Asiatic Society.

Dr. James Gairdner, C.B., London.


Prof. Ulrich von Wilamowitz Möllendorff, University of Berlin.

Prof. H. Marczali, University of Budapest.

Dr. G. W. Botsford, Columbia University.

Prof. Julius Wellhausen, University of Göttingen.

Prof. Franz R. von Krones, University of Graz.

Prof. Wilhelm Soltau, Zabern University.


Prof. R. W. Rogers, Drew Theological Seminary.

Prof. A. Vambéry, University of Budapest.

Prof. Otto Hirschfeld, University of Berlin.

Dr. Frederick Robertson Jones, Bryn Mawr College.

Baron Bernardo di San Severino Quaranta, London.

Dr. John P. Peters, New York.


Prof. Adolph Harnack, University of Berlin.

Dr. A. S. Rappoport, School of Oriental Languages, Paris.

Prof. Hermann Diels, University of Berlin.

Prof. C. W. C. Oman, Oxford University.

Prof. W. L. Fleming, Louisiana State University.

Prof. I. Goldziher, University of Budapest.

*Printed in the United States.*          Prof. R. Koser, University of Berlin.

# CONTENTS

## VOLUME XVII

### SWITZERLAND (*Concluded*)

### RUSSIA

## CHAPTER V

## CHAPTER VI

## CHAPTER VII

## CHAPTER VIII

# SWITZERLAND (Concluded)

## CHAPTER V

### THE EIGHTEENTH CENTURY

> There is an evil worse than war and that is the debasement of peoples. The wounds of war may be healed, but moral degradation leads nations to the tomb. During the peace that followed the battle of Villmergen up to the time of the French revolution Switzerland suffered more calamities than in all the wars against Burgundy and Austria. For during the eighty years of repose during which the swords of the Winckelrieds, the Fontanas, the Halhwyls, and the Erlachs were tarnishing, the rust of egoism and of pride succeeded in eating away the tablets on which was engraven the loyal union of the ancient Swiss; and like a corpse the old confederation was rotting away. In vain degenerate sons decorated pompously the corpse of the achievements of their ancestors, that they might conceal the fact that the spirit which animated it aforetime had left it.—ZSCHOKKE.[b]

### THE CONSPIRACY OF HENTZI; THE INSURRECTION AT FRIBOURG

THE outward peace enjoyed by the confederacy during the eighteenth century (the last of its existence in its primitive form) was contrasted by incessant inward disturbances. The first of these which claims our attention is the conspiracy of Hentzi at Bern. Here, as in most towns of the confederacy, a more and more formal and regular aristocracy had grown up by degrees in the course of centuries. From time immemorial the powers of government had been held by the avoyer and council. For the protection of the burghers against the encroachments of the council, and of that body against the influence of the multitude, an assembly of two hundred of the most respectable burghers was formed, the members of which were annually elected.

The most important acts, which imposed duties on every burgher, not only for himself but for his posterity, were often brought before the whole body of citizens, and even country people; the more so as at that time a few villages constituted the whole domain of Bern. The continual aggrandisement of the state rendered obsolete the fundamental laws of its constitution, which became imperceptibly modified in proportion as political emergencies appeared to require alterations. When the power of Bern was doubled by the conquest of the Vaud, the assembly of the burghers ceased to be thought of. The dignities of the state became hereditary in those families which had once obtained a seat in the great council. It is true that the other burghers remained eligible to public functions; but it was rarely indeed, and generally by means of intermarriages, that a new family raised itself to the rank of the rulers *de facto*.

The administration of these ruling families was, in general, not devoid of wisdom and equity; and, in fact, the principal subject of complaint was that participation in state affairs had ceased to be open to all. It was, however, precisely this system of aristocratic exclusion which was felt so insupportably by many of those who were subjected to it, that so early as 1710 attempts were made to break it up. These were renewed with increased vigour, in 1743, by six-and-twenty burghers, who combined to petition the council for the revival of a greater equality of rights in favour of the general body of citizens. These adventurous men incurred the censure of the authorities, and were placed under arrest in their houses or banished.

Amongst the exiles was Samuel Hentzi, a man of no ordinary talent and spirit. He had fixed on Neuchâtel as the place of his banishment, the term of which was shortened by the favour of the authorities. On his return, the embarrassed state in which he found his domestic economy, and the ill success of his efforts to obtain a lucrative office, may have mingled with other motives in inducing him to take the lead in a desperate undertaking of a little band of malcontents, who, without money, arms, or even unity of purpose, dreamed of overturning a government strong in its own resources, and sure of support from the whole Helvetic body, and of instituting equality of rights among all burghers, and appointment to all offices by lot. Yet, with all their root-and-branch work, the conspirators had no idea of remedying the real defects of the state, of satisfying the prevalent and increasing discontents of the Vaud, or of procuring an extension of political rights to the whole people: for, in the plan of a constitution annexed to their mediated manifesto, exclusive regard was paid to the burghers at Bern; and the rest of the people would hardly have been bettered by their accession to the dignities which had hitherto been engrossed by the ruling families. .The 13th of July, 1749, was fixed for the execution of the plans of the conspirators; but many of their own number had opened their eyes by this time to the utter impossibility of success, produced by the disunion and imprudence of their colleagues — to the passion and cupidity of some, and the atrocious hopes of murder and plunder entertained by others.

No man felt more sensibly the criminal views of his party than the only man of ability and public spirit among them, Hentzi. He would not betray those with whom he had long pursued the same object; but he made an attempt to save himself by flight from further participation in their plans and foreseen destiny. It was too late: a betrayer had already done his work. Hentzi and other leaders of the party were taken and beheaded during the first exasperation of the government. Sentence of death was also pronounced upon some who had made their escape; others were imprisoned or banished, but soon afterwards pardoned. On embarking with her two sons to quit the Helvetic territory, the wife of Hentzi exclaimed, "I would rather see these children sink in the Rhine-stream than they should not one day learn to avenge the murder of their father." However, when the sons came to manhood, they displayed more magnanimity than their mother; and one of them, who rose to distinction in the service of the Netherlands, requited with good offices to the burghers of his native town the unmerited misfortunes which they had brought upon his family.

In Fribourg — where, in olden times, equality of rights for all burghers had been settled as a principle — an aristocracy, no less close than in Bern, had formed itself since the middle of the seventeenth century. A few houses, under the denomination of secret families, had contrived to exclude, not only the country people, but a large proportion likewise of the town burghers, from all participation in public affairs; and, in 1684, admission into the number of these secret families was rendered wholly impossible. From thenceforwards, constantly increasing discontent displayed itself both in town and country. Several very moderate proposals for alleviating the pressure of this oligarchy were rejected with such haughtiness by the government that disaffection swelled into revolt.

In 1781 Peter Nicholas Chenaux of la Tour de Trême, John Peter Raccaud, and an advocate of Gruyères of the name of Castellaz, formed a league for the achievement of a higher degree of freedom. First they endeavoured to work upon the people by fair promises. Then Chenaux, at the head of a select band of fifty or sixty, undertook to terrify the government into a compromise. But the gates being closed on the party, and the walls manned with armed burghers, this undertaking ended in open revolt. The toll of alarm-bells summoned up the country people from every hill and valley in the canton to assist in the coercion of the domineering capital. A body of nearly three thousand men encamped before the walls of Fribourg, and further aid was hourly expected. The terrified burghers instantly called for the armed intervention of Bern, and the latter town detached a part of its guard without delay. Three hundred dragoons marched upon Fribourg, and were to be followed by fourteen hundred foot. The burghers of Fribourg now thought themselves strong enough to meet force with force. The garrison made a sally from the town, and on the first sight of the Bernese flag, not to mention the heavy artillery, the malcontents solicited an armistice. The surrender of their arms and of the ringleaders was demanded as preliminary to all negotiation. The people refused the latter of these conditions, but fled panic-struck on the first attack, without making any resistance.

The whole affair would have ended without bloodshed, had not the leader Chenaux been murdered in his flight by Henry Rosier, himself one of the popular party. The two remaining heads of the insurgents got clear off: Chenaux's corpse was delivered to the public executioner, and his head fixed on a spear above the Romont gate. Sentence of death was passed on Castellaz and Raccaud, the two fugitives. Several others were visited with less degrees of punishment: new reinforcements from Bern, Solothurn, and Lucerne secured the town from any recurrence of tumult, and their ambassadors strove to promote the restoration of tranquillity. It was ordered to be proclaimed, from all the pulpits, that the council was well disposed to protect the old and well attested rights of its loving subjects, as well as to hear, with its never-failing graciousness, every suitable and respectful representation. Three days were allotted to each commune to lay their complaints and wishes before the government, through delegates. But when months elapsed without the popular grievances having obtained a hearing, the loss of Chenaux began to be appreciated. Multitudes assembled round his tomb weeping and praying: pilgrimages, as if to the tomb of a saint, were made thither with banners, and with crucifixes. Vainly were these demonstrations of feeling stigmatised by the government as crime against the state, by the bishop as impious profanations. They were neither to be checked by posting sentinels, nor fulminating excommunications. They were the last sad consolation of the people — the last substitute for hopes that were already given up.

## DISORDERS AT GENEVA (1707-1782 A.D.)

Shortly after the establishment of Genevan independence, it had been decreed by the general assembly, for the better suppression of hostile attempts against their hard-won freedom, that whoever should propose a change in the government of Geneva should be considered to deserve capital punishment. This did not, however, hinder alterations being made, at different times, in various parts of the constitution. So early as the middle of the sixteenth century, the laws were revised and improved. The advantageous situation of the town and the long duration of peace promoted the increase of wealth in Geneva and the rise of many families to opulence. These families aimed at separating themselves from their fellow citizens, even in their places of habitation, by settling in the upper part of the town, near the council-house, while the other burghers inhabited the lower town. The principal families already regarded themselves as a standing patriciate; and even the name of patrician came into use in the acts of council.

The year 1707 witnessed an effort of the inferior burghers to wrest from the principal families a part of their usurped power, and to introduce amendments in the constitution. In this emergency, the council invoked the mediation of Bern and Zurich, received a confederate garrison, and maintained itself by force of arms and by execution of its principal antagonists. A renewal of the disturbances which had been quelled by such violent measures was produced, in 1714, by the imposition of an arbitrary tax by the council for the enlargement and completion of the fortifications of the town. This stretch of power occasioned great discontent among the burghers; bitter attacks and censures on the government appeared in print; and the more strictly these were prohibited, they obtained the more eager perusal and credence.

One of the arch-promoters of the rising storm was Michael Ducrest, a Genevan burgher and noble, an officer in the army, and a member of the great council. This man opposed himself with extraordinary vehemence to the building of the new fortifications, and heaped offensive charges on the partisans of the measure. The government condemned him to recant, and, on his evading compliance by flight, a penal sentence was pronounced against him. New attempts which he made to excite disturbance were followed by a sentence of perpetual imprisonment. This sentence could not be put in execution, as Ducrest had taken refuge under a foreign jurisdiction, where he set at defiance the council of Geneva, and provoked that body to such a degree by his writings and intrigues against them, that sentences more and more severe were heaped upon his head, until at length the most offensive of his writings was torn by the hangman, and his effigy was suspended from the gallows. His person, however, enjoyed impunity till 1744, when he was taken into custody in the territory of Bern. The government of Geneva did not thirst for his blood, and was content with his perpetual imprisonment. Even in this situation he contrived to mix in Hentzi's conspiracy, was confined in the castle of Aarburg, and closed, in extreme old age, as a state prisoner, a life which he had spent in incessant labours in the cause of democracy.

Meanwhile Geneva continued to be agitated by party manœuvres and popular discontents. In the year 1734 a body of eight hundred burghers addressed themselves to the heads of the government, desiring the curtailment of the projected fortifications, and the repeal of the tax levied for that object. The council only replied by preparations for defence: firearms were transported to the council hall; barricades erected in the approaches thither as well as in those to the upper town, where the principal class of burghers lived, and the garrison kept in readiness to act on the first signal. All this apparatus was regarded with mistrust by the burghers, who were still farther provoked by reports of the approach of Bernese troops, and by the removal of a part of the town artillery to the upper regions, while two and twenty other pieces were spiked. The multitude made themselves masters of the city guard, pointed field-pieces on the road by which the troops from Bern were expected, and tumultuously demanded the convocation of the burgher assembly, the sovereign authority of Geneva. The council contrived to win over the members of this body so far that they voted unanimously the completion of the fortifications and the continuance of the tax for ten years. The declaration of an amnesty and improvement of the criminal and judicial administration formed the rest of their business. The burghers laid down their arms and returned to their ordinary vocations; so that an embassy which arrived from Zurich and Bern found Geneva in a state of apparent tranquillity.

Permanent ill-will was fostered only against the syndic Trembley, commander of the garrison and conductor of the defensive preparations of the council. Whatever this person had done by the instructions of the council was laid to his individual account, and added to the mass of dark imputations which were heaped on him, as the head of an already obnoxious family. He plumed himself on the favour of the confederate ambassadors, and forfeited thus the last chance of retrieving himself in the public opinion. The remembrance of the armed intervention of Zurich and Bern, in 1707, was too recent to admit of their ambassadors doing any good to Trembley's cause through the medium of pacific intercession. The departure of these embassies removed the only screen of the syndic: he demanded his dismission, which was refused him, in order to deprive him of his functions more ignominiously. No resistance or artifice of a powerful connection could save him: the tumults were renewed with increased fury; and the question soon ceased to regard the person or party of Trembley, and became that of the triumph of the aristocratic or democratic principle at Geneva. In 1737, the council ventured several arrests, and the consequence was that the whole body of burghers rushed to arms, and the council was defeated, not without bloodshed. A garrison from Bern and Zurich was thrown into the town: the ambassadors of these cantons, in concert with the French ambassadors, undertook the office of mediators, and in 1738 framed a constitution which set limits to the assumptions of the council and the principal families, and was gratefully and all but unanimously accepted as a fundamental law by the burghers.

After four-and-twenty years of repose and prosperity, occasion was given to new political movements at Geneva by a subject of a nature purely speculative. It pleased more than one government about this time to apply the doom of fire, which had been visited by inquisitors on the ill-fated victims of their zealotry, to certain of the more remarkable works of the human intellect — a proceeding highly calculated to draw the eyes of the reading public on productions which seemed worthy of such signal condemnation. On the first appearance of that work of Rousseau which opened views so novel and so striking on the moral and still more on the physical education of man, the parliament of Paris had the work burned by the hangman, and sentenced Rousseau to imprisonment, which he only escaped by flight. Both of these decisions were immediately repeated by the council of Geneva [1762], which improved on them by launching a like condemnatory sentence against the *Contrat Social* of the same author. It was in vain that Rousseau's connections demanded a copy of the sentence against him: their reiterated demands, though supported by a large body of burghers, were rejected by the council. The popular party, which vindicated the right of the burgher assembly to

JEAN JACQUES ROUSSEAU
(1712–1778)

bring up representations or remonstrances against the council on any subject under discussion, distinguished themselves by the name of representatives. Their claims were met by asserting a *droit négatif*, or right of rejection, on the strength of which the council pretended that nothing that should not have been previously consented to by themselves could come before the general assembly. The partisans of the council were called negatives.

The tranquillity of Geneva was once more disturbed to such a degree by passionate discourses, party writings, and manœuvres that the ambassadors of Zurich, Bern, and France again interfered, and pronounced themselves in favour of the council. The representatives rejected their decision, the ambassadors left Geneva, French troops advanced on the town, and all trade and intercourse were suspended. But the French ministry speedily became lukewarm in the cause of the negatives. The latter, when they found themselves abandoned by all foreign aid, apprehending what might ensue, patched up a peace with the representatives. By a compact closed in March, 1768, the burghers acquired valuable rights, and even a third party, that of the so-called *natifs* or *habitans* (old inhabitants, excluded by birth from taking part in public affairs), obtained extended franchises, and was flattered with a prospect of participation in all the rights of citizenship.

But on recovery from the first panic, reciprocal hatred soon revived. The negatives were vexed at having made such important sacrifices, and aimed at resuming all their former ascendency. Moreover they found a favourable hearing in the French court, which had long viewed with an evil eye the trade and wealth of Geneva, desired to raise the neighbouring Versoix to a commercial town, and hoped, by encouraging tumult and disorder at Geneva, either to annihilate its industry and opulence, or ultimately to bring it under the sovereignty of France. French emissaries therefore aided the negatives in spiriting the natifs up against the representatives, by promising to confer on them the franchises withheld by the latter. But the representatives flew

[1782 A.D.]

to arms, took possession of the gates, and speedily succeeded in disarming the unpractised and undisciplined mob of natifs. Well aware by what manœuvres the natifs had been led to revolt, they prudently abstained from taking any vindictive measures against them; but, on the contrary, imparted to them, in 1781, that equality of rights which had been promised by the negatives, and endeavoured thus to win them over permanently to the common cause.

The council, on the other hand, impelled by French influence, declared the newly conferred rights illegally extorted, and invoked the mediation of Bern and Zurich. But, betwixt representative stubbornness and negative assumption, the ambassadors of these towns could exert but limited influence. They essayed to put an end to disputes by amicable arrangements, but were baffled by the intrigues of the French court, which was resolved to recognise no democratical system on its frontiers, and soon proceeded to open force in support of its secret policy. The first act of aggression was to garrison Versoix; a measure which gave just offence to Zurich and Bern, who thereupon renounced all adhesion to the mediation of 1738, and left the Genevans to their own discretion. France also declared she would mix no more in the affairs of Geneva; the government was overthrown and a new constitution established.

Zurich and Bern now declared formally and coldly that they could not acknowledge a government erected by revolt. Still more indignation was exhibited by France and Savoy, who entered into a league for the coercion of the town. Bern, too, joined this league in 1782, that the destiny of Geneva, that *point d'appui* of her own dominion, might not be trusted altogether to the caprices of foreign powers. On the appearance of the allied troops before the gates of Geneva, the burghers, unaware of the bad state of their defences, swore to bury themselves in the ruins of their native town rather than yield. But when the cannon of the besiegers was advanced up to their walls, and the alternative of desperate resistance or surrender was offered, the disunited city opened her gates without stroke of sword, after the principal heads of the representative party had taken to flight.

Mortal dread accompanied the victorious troops as they entered Geneva. Many had reason to tremble for their lives, their liberty, and possessions. No punishments, however, were inflicted, excepting only the banishment of the principal popular leaders; but the rights of the burghers were almost entirely annihilated by the arbitrary arrangements of the victors; the government was invested by them with almost unlimited power, and proceeded under their auspices to prohibit all secret societies, military exercises, books and pamphlets on recent events, and to re-inforce the garrison by twelve hundred men under foreign leaders. Thus the town was reduced to utter subjection, and depopulated by exile and emigration. From thenceforwards commerce and enterprise fell into decay; and for seven long years a forced, unnatural calm dwelt in Geneva.

During these years the government was conducted with much mildness, the administration of justice was impartial, that of the public revenues incorrupt, art and industry were encouraged to the utmost. But nothing could win the lost hearts of the people back to the government. The iniquity of the so-called *règlement* of 1782, the destruction of their franchises, and the disarming of their persons, had wounded irrecoverably the feelings of the burghers. The malcontents increased daily in number; and even many former negatives now disowned their party, which had gone greater lengths than they had ever wished or expected. At length, on the death of Vergennes, the

French minister, and arch enemy of Genevan independence, the spirit of freedom awoke with all its ancient strength in Geneva, and the burghers arose to break their slavish fetters. But the recital of the subsequent occurrences must be postponed until we come to notice the train of events fired by the French Revolution.

## TUMULTS IN NEUCHÂTEL

The little principality of Neuchâtel, the succession of which had descended in the same line since the era of the second Burgundian monarchy, came, in 1707, into the hands of the king of Prussia, as next heir to the ancient house of Chalons. In 1748, Frederick II displayed that love of economy which distinguished all his measures, by farming out certain parts of the public revenue arising from tithes, ground rents, and the crown lands ; from the former administration of which many of the inhabitants had enjoyed considerable profits. The loss of these, of course, was felt as a grievance by the losers; but what was viewed with more concern by the mass of the inhabitants was the prospect of still further innovations. Accordingly five communes of the Val de Travers transmitted their remonstrances through a delegate to Berlin; and their example was soon afterwards followed throughout the principality.

The arrival of two commissaries, despatched by the king to Neuchâtel, was viewed with discontent as an encroachment on its immunities. Shortly after their coming, an attempt was made to put in execution the proposed financial system, of which the only result was to provoke a tumultuous popular movement. On the 7th of January, 1767, the burgher assembly of Neuchâtel passed a resolution of exclusion from the rights of citizenship, against all who should farm or guarantee the farming of the revenues. On this the royal commissary, Von Derschau, brought a suit before the council of Bern, against the town of Neuchâtel; and the advocate-general, Gaudot, who had formerly been a popular favourite, much to the surprise of his fellow-citizens, seceded to the royal side, and thenceforwards gave his active assistance to the commissary.

The cause was decided at Bern (with some limitations) in the royal favour. With regard to the resolutions of the Neuchâtel burghers, already referred to, it was decreed that they should be cancelled in the presence of the burgher assembly, and a public apology made to the vice-governor. The costs of the whole process to be paid by the town. Gaudot, who had attacked the civic immunities both by word and writing, naturally became an object of popular indignation. By way of compensation, however, he received a lucrative government office, along with the functions of procurator-general, from which another man had been removed who possessed the popular favour. He returned to Neuchâtel from Bern with the royal plenipotentiaries. These and the vice-governor advised him to take up his residence in the castle; but, in spite of their recommendations, Gaudot thought fit to repair to his own residence. The same evening, clamour and disturbance took place around the house, which the magistrates were forced to protect by military force.

The next morning the mob returned in increased numbers, and was still further exasperated by missiles being thrown down upon them. A carriage, escorted by servants in the royal livery, which had been sent by the king's commissary for Gaudot, was knocked to pieces by the infuriated multitude. Gaudot and his nephew now imprudently fired from the windows, and their shots took effect, fatally for themselves. The exasperated populace forced its way into the house; Gaudot was killed by three shots, and the mob dispersed after the deed, with cries of "Long live the king!" The chief actors in this tragedy escaped, and could be executed only in effigy. The whole affair was ultimately compromised by the benevolent moderation of the great Frederick; and terms of pacification were accepted by the communes, which provided alike against arbitrary government and popular turbulence.

On this occasion, Frederick displayed more generosity than would have been shown by any cantonal government; and his conduct seemed to justify the general reflection, which must often occur to the student of Swiss history that when administrative abuses are introduced into a monarchy, it only requires a well-disposed and enlightened prince to crush the gang of official oppressors and extortioners; because such a prince is powerfully backed in such measures by the public opinion. Whereas, when the majority of the ruling class in misnamed republics is corrupted so far as to speculate on the profits of malversation, it generally takes care to recruit its ranks with new accomplices; or, at all events, only to promote to public offices such men as will at least shut their eyes to public abuses. The magnanimity of Frederick was but ill repaid to his successor by the tumults which ensued in Neuchâtel on the commencement of the French Revolution; and we have lately seen the same misunderstandings, as in the last century, arise between the now canton of Neuchâtel and its Prussian sovereign.

## ARISTOCRACY AND DEMOCRACY

The democratical cantons, where the assembled population exercised the supreme power in their *landsgemeinde*, held the lowest station, in almost every respect, amongst the confederates. Narrowness of mind and ignorant hatred of all innovation withstood every proposal of improvement; while passion and prejudice, aided by the artifices of demagogues, often occasioned acts of crying injustice. Judicial proceedings were in the highest degree arbitrary; confession of crimes was extracted by torture, which, indeed, was often employed when nothing more remained to confess. Capital punishment, even for minor offences, was by no means rare. Public offices, particularly that of bailiff or land-vogt, were commonly conferred not on the worthiest but on the highest bidder; and the proceeds of this ignominious traffic went to the public treasury. Was it to be wondered at if these functionaries in their turn set justice up to auction in their bailiwicks, and endeavoured to recover their advances to the government by every sort of oppression of its subjects?

Mental cultivation was extremely neglected in these cantons, scientific establishments were rare, and those for education were, for the most part, in the hands of the capuchins; whose *esprit de corps* was at least on one occasion beneficial, by preventing the admission of the jesuits into the canton of Schwytz in 1758. Elsewhere, however, similar influences produced worse effects. In Glarus, so late as 1780, an unfortunate servant girl was executed as a witch, on the charge of having lamed the leg of a child by magic, and having caused it to vomit pins. Credulous souls were even found to believe the affirmation that the girl had administered pin-seed through the medium of a magical cake, which had afterwards borne its fruit within the body of the child. The political relations of these cantons, in the period now before us, were of little importance.

The constitutions of the aristocratical cantons had all of them this circumstance in common, that not only the capital towns assumed the rule of the whole canton, but the burghers of those towns themselves were divided into ruling and non-ruling families, of which the former monopolised admission. to all places of honour. But the governments of these cantons deserve to be treated of more at length.

Bern, which, in the first period after its foundation, had no domains of any importance outside its walls, possessed in that immediately preceding the French revolution a territory containing more than 400,000 inhabitants. This considerable tract of land was administered by 250 ruling families, of which, however, only about sixty were in actual possession of the government; and these again were divided into so-called great and small families, and did not easily suffer others to rise to an equality with them. The sovereign power resided in 299 persons, of whom the great council was composed. A little council or senate of five-and-twenty formed the executive. The rural districts and the Pays de Vaud were governed by land-vogts or bailiffs. It was chiefly there that discontent prevailed against the Bernese government. The nobles of the Pays de Vaud were rendered wholly insensible to the real and solid advantages secured to them by that government, by resentment of their exclusion from all public employments. The peasants of that district, for the most part subjects or bondsmen of the nobles, sighed under the weight of feudal oppression and its accustomed offspring, poverty, neglected culture, mental and moral abortion.

## Davel

A singular attempt at revolt was made in 1723 by Major Daniel Abraham Davel, a well-intentioned man, of excellent character, but a decided political and religious enthusiast, possessed with the idea that he was called by inspiration to emancipate the Vaud from Bern. He assembled the regiment of militia which he commanded, under the pretext of a review, and with these troops, who were altogether ignorant of his real design, and unprovided with stores or ammunition, he surprised the town of Lausanne at a point of time when all the Bernese land-vogts had gone to Bern for the annual installation. Davel offered his aid for the restoration of independence to the hastily assembled town council. He found, however ,no kindred spirit in that body; and the cautious citizens put him off with fair words till a force was under arms sufficient to crush him. Meanwhile his troops had discovered the real object of their commander, and shrank from him in surprise and consternation. He himself was arrested, cruelly tortured for the discovery of accomplices, of whom he had none, and lastly beheaded.

A certain contempt of scholastic acquirements seemed the prevailing tone at Bern; and school education naturally came to deserve the low esteem which it met with. Accordingly those patrician youths who did not serve in the army remained for the most part unemployed until they obtained places under government. The establishment of what was called the "exterior state" afforded but a superficial substitute for more solid attainments, and initiated youth only too early in the petty intrigues and jealousies of faction. This institution, which was also known by the name of the "shadow state," was intended to give the youth of the ruling families opportunities for acquainting themselves with the forms at least of public business, and of acquiring an unembarrassed address, so important for republicans. It parodised the dignities and offices of the state, the election of avoyers, councillors, and senators, had its secretaries and functionaries of all ranks, and distributed by lot 120 vogtships, which for the most part took their names from ruined castles.

Without any sufficient evidence, some would refer to the era of the

Burgundian war the origin of this institution, which received the sanction of government in 1687, and for which a council-house, far more splendid than that which belonged to the actual government, was built in 1729. The seal of this "exterior state" bore an ape astride on a lobster, and looking at himself in a mirror. These and similar traits of humour seem to owe their descent to an era exceedingly remote from the measured formality of later times.

The government of Lucerne, which with Solothurn and Fribourg formed the remaining pure Swiss aristocracies, consisted of a little council of six-and-thirty members, which, reinforced by sixty-four others, held the sovereign authority. With regard to intellectual cultivation, the most contradictory features were observable at Lucerne. On the one hand, learning, enlightenment, and patriotism were hereditary distinctions of some families; while, on the other hand, the mass was imbued with ignorant fanaticism. On the one hand, the encroachments of the papacy were resisted with inflexible firmness; while, on the other hand, the clergy kept possession of a highly mischievous influence in the state. On the one hand, a series of saints' days and holidays was abolished, as being dedicated to dissoluteness more than devotion; while, on the other hand, we are horror-struck by the burning of a so-called heretic. In 1747, a court, consisting of four clergymen, sentenced Jacob Schmidli, a man of blameless life, to be strangled, and then burned with his books and writings, because he had not only read the Bible for his private edification, but had explained and recommended it to others as the sole true basis of religion. His wife, his six children, and seventy-one other persons were banished, his house was burned to the ground by the hands of the public executioner, and a monument raised on its former site, to perpetuate the ignomy (query: of the victim or of his judges?).

The appearance of two pamphlets in 1769, on the question "whether removal or restriction of the monastic orders might not be found beneficial to the Catholic cantons?" excited terrible uproar at Lucerne, where certain classes were constantly scenting danger to church or state from some quarter. The town and county clergy, and the bigots in the council, were rejoiced to get so good an opportunity to persecute the holders of free principles, and raised a deplorable howl, as if the canton were on the verge of destruction. The whole population was plunged in consternation and astonishment by thundering sermons and rigorous prohibitions of the obnoxious work. Free-thinkers were fulminated against by name from the pulpits, and Schinznach, which had witnessed the formation of the Helvetic society, was denounced as the focus and headquarters of heresy.

This society, which aimed at the diffusion of useful knowledge, public spirit, and union throughout the Helvetic body, without reference to varieties of religion, rank, or political system, was founded by a knot of patriotic and instructed men, in the pious hope of arresting the decline of the confederation. At its commencement it consisted of no more than nine members, but added to its numbers with astonishing rapidity. The society was soon viewed with an evil eye by the cantonal governments, which dreaded all independence of feeling and action in the people. At Bern, political dangers were anticipated from it, as symptoms of refractoriness were exhibited shortly after its formation by the nobles in the Vaud; while at Lucerne it was regarded as a conspiracy for shaking off the Catholic religion, and assisting the supposed ambition of Bern to gain ascendency over the whole confederation.

The aristo-democratical governments next come under our notice, and in these, as in most of the purely aristocratical, the metropolis had obtained unlimited power over the whole canton. In these, however, particular families did not engross the sovereign power; the collective body of citizens had maintained themselves by means of the regulations of their guilds in the possession of considerable influence over the public affairs. Accordingly the magistracy favoured the monopolies which enriched the metropolitan traders, and imposed restraints on the industry and invention of the surrounding country. Thence the subjects of these towns were much more harshly governed than those of the aristocratical cantons. Their ancient charters fell into oblivion, and were withdrawn as far as possible from public inspection; they were not only excluded from civil and military, but even from ecclesiastical functions; and the exercise of many branches of industry, and the sale of their productions in the towns, was wholly cut off by corporation privileges. Moreover, since the commencement of the century of which we are treating, no mode of acquiring the rights of burghers remained open; they were only conferred on extremely rare occasions to reward eminent merit; or when the times became troublesome to conciliate influential burghers. Hence that discontent and disaffection which broke out at the close of the century found a principal focus in the heart of the mixed aristocracies.

In the larger cantons the public administration was for the most part incorrupt; and that of justice was liable on the whole to fewer complaints than in many other European countries. The pay of public servants, with few exceptions, was extremely moderate. Men who had devoted their whole lives to public affairs, and who had filled the highest offices in the state, lost more than they gained by the bounty of their country. At Zurich, the expenses of the government were wholly defrayed without the imposition of taxes, properly so called, from the revenues and interests of the national lands and capital, from ground-rents, tithes, the salt monopoly, and the produce of the premium paid by the several guilds of traders in return for their exclusive privileges. The same description is applicable to the government of Bern, excepting that here the course of justice was tedious and expensive. The superior financial resources of the latter canton enabled her to execute more for public ends than Zurich. Bern invested considerable sums in foreign securities, particularly in the English funds; and, besides, amassed a treasure amounting to some millions of dollars, which became, as we shall presently see, and as Mably had predicted, the booty of rapacious and powerful neighbours.

Very different was the condition of the free or common bailiwicks, particularly those of the democratical cantons; here most of the land-vogts sought by every species of extortion to indemnify themselves for the sums for which they had in fact bought their places from the general assemblies of their respective cantons. Many made an open traffic of justice; took presents from both parties; helped delinquents to evade deserved punishment who could pay for exemption, and exacted contributions from the wealthier class whenever and wherever they could. Even farther than in the German domains of Switzerland were abuses of this kind carried in the Italian bailiwicks, and most of all in those of the Grisons. The inevitable tendency of such treatment was to debase the popular character in those districts, and its effects have left unequivocal traces even to this day.

In those towns of which the constitution was grounded on corporate bodies, the privileges of the burghers and their guilds received progressive extensions. Propositions were made which would hardly have been conceivable in monarchical states, and could only, in fact, take place where

[1780 A.D.]

particular classes had to decide upon the destiny of the rest of their fellow-countrymen. In Bâle it was several times proposed, under the pretext of protection to agriculture, that the exercise of certain manufactures should be prohibited altogether in the rural part of the canton.ᶜ

## FEDERAL RELATIONS OF THE SWISS STATES

The federal bond which united the various cantons and their allies was very loose, and far different from that which fastened together the united provinces of Holland, or even from the federal compact of the United States of North America. There was not in Switzerland any permanent sovereign body, no standing federal magistrate equally acknowledged by all, no central government having its own establishment, its own treasury, its own servants, civil and military. The general diets could not decide upon any important question, unless it had been previously debated and decided on in the councils of each of the cantons, who were applied to by their own deputies for fresh instructions at every new case which was brought before the diet. The cantons were not even each allied to all. The eight older cantons had among them a federal compact for their common defence, and even of these eight the first five only, *viz.* Zurich, Schwyz, Uri, Unterwalden, and Lucerne, were bound to enter into no other alliance without each other's consent; while the other three, Glarus, Zug, and Bern, were at liberty to form alliances with other states or foreign princes, provided such alliances contained nothing prejudicial to the federal bond. The eight cantons were also bound, by the convention of Stanz, to assist one another in supporting the form of government established in each of them.

The five junior cantons, *viz.* Fribourg, Solothurn, Bâle, Schaffhausen, and Appenzell, had no federal bond with the whole of the rest, nor among themselves, but every one of them was allied to some one or more of the others. The three forest cantons alone were allied to every one of the other cantons. By these means, however, the guarantee of common defence was secured to each; for, as any canton attacked had the right of calling some other cantons to its assistance, and as these were entitled to call others, all would be brought in to take a part, in virtue of their particular bonds.

The general diets of the confederation were either ordinary or extraordinary. The ordinary diets met once a year at Frauenfeld in Thurgau, instead of Baden, where, until the treaty of Aarau in 1712, they had been accustomed to meet. The deputy from Zurich presided: he brought forward the matters to be discussed, collected the votes, framed the resolutions, etc. Each canton or associate had one vote and questions were decided by a simple majority. The sittings were held with closed doors, and at the end of the session the deputy of Zurich drew up a statement of the decisions of the diet, of which he sent a copy round to each canton. The principal business of the diet was to hear appeals from the common bailiwicks, and to inspect the accounts and inquire into the conduct of the bailiffs.

Extraordinary diets were assembled at the request of any particular canton, or of any of the foreign ministers in case of urgent business. In such a case the canton of Zurich summoned the other cantons to send their deputies to Frauenfeld, or any other place fixed upon, acquainting them at the same time with the nature of the subjects which were to be discussed, in order that the cantonal governments might give instructions to their deputies accordingly. The foreign minister, at whose request an extraordinary diet was convoked, was bound to pay the expenses of the deputies who were thus called from their homes at an unexpected season.

The partial diets were held by the Protestant cantons at Aarau, and by the Catholic ones at Lucerne. There was no fixed time for their meeting, but they were summoned as the occasion required it.

A regulation, called the "defensionale," was, as we have seen, agreed upon at a general diet held at Baden in 1668, for providing against sudden emergencies, such as an attack from foreign powers, when the proceedings of the diet would have proved too slow for the common safety. In such a case deputies were to be named by all the members of the Helvetic body, and invested with full powers to direct the military force of the nation, which was to be raised by contingents from the militia of each state. This body consisted of 9600 men for the thirteen cantons, 1400 for the associates, and 2400 for the subject bailiwicks — in all 13,400 men; which number, however, might be doubled and trebled if required.

The militia of each canton consisted of all the males from sixteen to sixty years of age, and these received military instruction at certain periods. Only one-third of the whole, however, consisting of the youngest and strongest, were enrolled into regiments, the other two-thirds supplying them with recruits if necessary. The regiments were divided into fusileers and electionaries, the fusileers being all young unmarried men, who were considered as always ready to march at a moment's notice; the electionaries were composed of the married men, of an age and size proper for service, and these were called out after the fusileers. When in active service they received regular pay; but every man was bound to provide his own uniform, arms, and accoutrements.

The Swiss, it is well known, furnished troops to several European powers, according to certain treaties or capitulations, as they were called, agreed upon between those powers and the various cantons. The chief power having Swiss troops in its service was France, who had retained them ever since the treaty made between the Swiss and Louis XI. Under Louis XIV the number of Swiss troops in the French service amounted to 28,000 men; but, in 1790, at the beginning of the French Revolution, there were not more than 15,000, who were divided into twelve regiments. Six Swiss regiments were in the service of Holland, four were serving in Piedmont, four at Naples, and four in Spain: the pope had also a small body guard of Swiss. There has been considerable misconception abroad upon this subject; the cantons have been represented as selling their countrymen as if they were cattle, while the truth is that the men were not sold, but enlisted of their own accord for a certain period of time, receiving the bounty money.[d]

Agriculture was advanced by the cultivation of clover and of other artificial grasses, and by the consequent increase of pasturage and manure. Many districts which had formerly been regarded as unfruitful were thus rendered remarkable for fertility. The processes of manuring, and many other processes in Swiss cultivation, became a model for foreign agriculturists. Arts and manufactures were extended more and more widely. In the canton of Bern, in the Thurgau, and elsewhere, industry was employed on native materials in the linen manufacture; in Zurich, St. Gall, and Appenzell, in working up imported wool in spinning, weaving, and cotton printing. Silk manufactures occupied Zurich and Bâle, and the latter town enriched itself by its riband manufacture. Trade in all its branches throve at Geneva; where a wholesale watch manufacture was conducted, and from whence watchmaking was soon spread through the district of Neuchâtel, where it suggested many other mechanical processes.

[1780 A.D.]

Intellectual culture and social refinements marched abreast with commercial wealth. Not only the towns were embellished with architectural structures, but in the Emmenthal, and around the lakes of Zurich and Geneva, arose new and splendid edifices which bespoke increasing opulence. In Neuchâtel, which a century before had been inhabited by shepherds, the villages assumed the appearance of towns; and the wealthy marts of England or the Netherlands were recalled to the mind of the traveller by the principal street of Winterthur. Intercourse with other states in trade or in foreign services naturalised new wants and desires, yet many still adhered to the old usages and manners. In whole districts, especially in the democratic cantons, public opinion imperiously set limits to the advance of luxury. In other places sumptuary laws maintained a struggle with the various arts of invention; and a wholesome state of simplicity was preserved in Zurich, St. Gall, and Bâle, in which celibacy became a rarity.c

Although in political matters dissentions prevailed, yet in intellectual and scientific life a sense of the unity of the fatherland was beginning to arise, notably in the reformed towns, where intellectual life had made great strides since the success of the war of Toggenburg. Men began to study their own position, learnt to know the individuality of Switzerland, and drew thence the hope of a brighter future. The pioneers of the movement were Scheuchzer of Zurich, and Haller of Bern. J. J. Scheuchzer (1672–1733), physician and naturalist, made himself famous by various journeys into the Swiss Alps, wrote the first natural history of Switzerland, and also completed a large map of Switzerland, by which labours he put new life into patriotism.

Albrecht von Haller (ob. 1777), the great poet and naturalist, by unrivalled industry acquired an extensive and learned education; he also possessed a strong poetic vein, and a warm and patriotic heart. Among his poems which appeared in 1732, Die Alpen (The Alps) made a great impression by its poetic depth and the novelty of its ideas. Full of indignation at the depravity of the time, and yearning for natural and unspoiled conditions, he there depicts with vigorous touches the life of nature and of men in the Alps, the simple, beautiful customs of the Alpine folk, with a patriotic warmth and enthusiasm before unknown. In another poem, Der Mann der Welt (The Man of the World), he laments the degeneration of his fatherland; in a third, Die verdorbenen Sitten (Demoralisation), in contradistinction to the good old times, he apostrophises the decay of his own day, exclaiming— "O Helvetia, once the land of heroes, how is it possible that the men whom we now behold could have descended from thy former inhabitants?" By his poems and his researches in natural science Haller became so famous in other lands that he received a number of honourable calls; yet he declined them all: he wanted to devote his powers to his beloved country, and from 1753 until his end he served her as a government official with affectionate devotion and self-sacrifice.e

Eloquence and daring imagination conferred European celebrity on Lavater. Rousseau promulgated truths in education and in politics which will not be lost for future generations, whatever alloy of paradox or perverse misapplication they might suffer from himself or his followers. The bitterness of religious and political dissension which had long prevailed in so many odious forms began to decline, and the personal worth of men began to be estimated by less absurd criteria than their speculative opinions. Old prejudices vanished, or at all events were mitigated, and even if the recognition of principles more enlightened was with many a matter of fashion and imitation, still those may be deemed fortunate whose existence falls on a period in which truth and liberal sentiments find favour and adoption.

On the whole, the century was not worse than those which had preceded it. Even if the forms of government favoured many abuses, a more extended spirit of activity prevailed amongst the people than in previous generations; and though it is true that no extraordinarily great actions were performed, it is also true that no great occasion called for their performance. It cannot

J. C. LAVATER
(1741–1801)

be denied that too much jealousy prevailed between the cantons, and that more reliance was often placed on strangers than on fellow confederates. But Germany, which united might have given law to Europe, had been even more distracted by like errors, reduced to a mere battle-field for foreigners, and robbed of its most valuable dependencies.[c]

Seldom during the eighteenth century did the confederates act together. Only once did the confederation appear as a unit toward the outside. That was in 1777, when an alliance was concluded with France which well expressed the subserviency of the Swiss at this period to that country. The members of the diet convened at Solothurn went through a humiliating ceremony. They appeared in a body at the ambassador's hotel, followed him to church and thence to the place of the deliberations. By this treaty the Helvetic body was bound to render a levy of six thousand men to France in case her territory was invaded, and in return the king of France promised the Swiss help in danger and to maintain the privileges accorded them by his predecessors.[af]

### SWITZERLAND FEELS THE SHOCK OF THE FRENCH REVOLUTION

The Swiss government, as well as that large portion of their subjects who were contented with their condition, and desired no alteration in it, were startled out of a state of perfect tranquillity by the first shock of the French revolution. The shifting of the whole political scenery of Europe surrounded them with entirely new embarassments. They resembled steersmen tolerably capable of guiding their bark safely through the tempests of their native lakes; but who found themselves now on unknown seas without chart or compass. The situation of the Swiss regiments engaged in the French service afforded the first reason for disquietude; the next was the apprehension of infection from the principles predominant in France. Alarming political movements soon began in the interior; and the solution of the problems which were set before Swiss politicians by the progress of events in the neighbouring countries was the more difficult the more various were the views, wants, and relations of the cantons, and the lands which were subject to them.

It was in the latter districts, as might have been expected, that the new ideas gained the greatest currency, and that the first attempts were made for their realisation. Educated and thinking men in the subject towns and territories brooded resentfully on their exclusion from all public posts and dignities. In those cantons where trade and manufactures were most cultivated, it was regarded as an intolerable hardship by the enterprising and wealthy rural proprietor, that he was hindered by oppressive regulations from purchasing the requisite raw materials, or from disposing of the products of his industry in any quarter except to a wholesale dealer of the capital. Similar resentments were excited by corporate privileges. Nevertheless, in the German regions of Switzerland, a longer time elapsed before the new modes of thinking, and the comparisons which they suggested, set the public mind in motion. This took place much sooner in the west, where the French language and neighbourhood made communication easier; above all, in Geneva, where nothing but an auspicious hour was waited for to burst asunder a yoke imposed by foreigners.

A rise in the price of bread, which was imputed to the government, gave occasion to the long prepared explosion. On the 26th of February, 1789, the burghers assailed the garrison with everything which could be turned into a weapon of offence. Fire-engines with boiling water supplied the place of artillery: the garrison was put to the rout, and the power of the government overturned the more easily, as its foreign props had now ceased to support it. The ruling class was compelled to throw itself wholly on the citizens, to restore the ancient liberties of the town, and to recall the banished heads of the representatives. But the hour was come for the ruin of Genevan independence. The country people and habitans of the town now demanded an equality of rights with the burghers, on the model of republican France; and the latter power was induced to second their wishes, by the suggestions of the ex-representative Clavière. The malcontents were kept for a while in check by troops from Bern and Zurich; but, on the withdrawal of these in 1792, the country people, habitans and natifs, flew to arms, made themselves masters of the town, deposed the government, and established, on the model of France, a national convention, with committees of general safety and of public welfare.

A show of moderation and tranquillity lasted some time longer; but distrust and exasperation received continual new aliment, and the disinterested friends of peace could hardly prevent some furious outbreak. Many votes were gained to a proposed new constitution, by the hope of securing order and repose; and in the beginning of 1794 it was adopted by a large majority. In April, syndics and council were again installed in their former functions, and the event was announced to Zurich and Bern with expressions of hope and confidence. Bern, however, could not resolve, on the instant, to give the name of confederates to these newly re-established authorities; and what had been done had no effect in mitigating the violence of those who put themselves forwards as the organs of the multitude, which they first set in motion for their own purposes, and then were forced, in turn, to flatter its passions, in order to continue popular favourites. Meanwhile, the price of necessaries rose, while trade and industry stagnated; and the repeated demands for so-styled free-will offerings to the public were answered by supplies more and more sparing.

In order to crush, at a stroke, all resistance, and to furnish themselves with the necessary stores and ammunition, the party of terrorists made a nocturnal seizure of the arsenal in July, 1794, occupied all the posts in war-like array; and filled the prisons of the town, and even the corn-magazine, with nearly six hundred men, whom they chose to designate as aristocrats;

and amongst whom were a number of the most respectable members of the magistracy, merchants, and men of letters. Of eight of the prisoners first examined, a revolutionary tribunal contented itself with sentencing one to death; but the clamour and threats of the multitude worked on these unsteady judges to retract their verdict, and extend the same condemnation to all the others. The doom of four of these was commuted for banishment by the general assembly; but a band of wretches again collected, stormed the prisons, and the bloody tribunal now sentenced their victims to be shot; and afterwards endeavoured to excuse itself on the plea that this had only been done to prevent worse atrocities. More executions followed, which included several persons who had actively promoted revolution. Numbers were banished, in order to secure the ruling party a majority in the general assembly. The large sums required by a revolutionary government for the payment of public officers, and the armed force of the populace, were defrayed by imposing heavy contributions on the possessors of property; indifferentists being made to pay double, aristocrats a treble amount.

Party spirit, however, cooled by degrees; approximations and concessions took place between all classes of citizens, who felt, in common, the general ruin of public and private happiness; and the disappointment of all the hopes which had formerly found indulgence. In 1796, a return to the old constitution was agreed upon, on condition of equality of rights being conceded to the old and new burghers, and the town and country inhabitants. The exiles returned home, and all rejoiced that they could again breathe freely. For two years more, the little republic dragged on an infirm existence; till it was finally united with France in 1798, and forced to partake, for fifteen years, the destinies of that country.

Of the men who had at different times been banished for political offences from Switzerland, many had taken refuge in the French metropolis, and endeavoured to persuade the republican statesmen that their enemies were equally those of France. [Notable among them was La Harpe of Vaud, who published a treatise on the situation of the Pays de Vaud and demanded its restoration from Bern.] Their representations found the easier audience, as Switzerland was already regarded with greedy eyes by their hearers. " At an early period of the Revolution," observes an English writer,[i] " the views of France were directed towards Switzerland, as well from its importance as a barrier on her eastern frontier, as from its central position between the German Empire and Italy. The reduction, therefore, of Switzerland, was a favourite object of the republican rulers, and was only suspended by the dread of adding its people to the host of enemies who menaced France on all sides; they accordingly temporised under the mask of friendship, and succeeded in preserving the neutrality of the Helvetic confederacy, by fomenting the national antipathy to the house of Austria. Yet even during this specious display of friendship, their agents industriously spread disaffection, and prepared the mine which was ready to explode on the first favourable opportunity: such an opportunity presented itself at the conclusion of the treaty of Campo Formio, which left the Swiss without an ally on the Continent. At this period the French Republic had acquired a colossal strength. The king of Sardinia, deprived of half his territory, was the vassal of France; the pope, and the king of Naples, owed the possession of a precarious sceptre to the forbearance of the directory; Prussia pertinaciously maintained her close connection with the new republic; and Austria, vanquished by the genius of Bonaparte, had concluded a dishonourable peace.

" But the French rulers were not content with planting the tricoloured flag on the summit of Mont Blanc, on the left bank of the Rhine, and at the mouth of the Scheldt, and with establishing the limits of their empire by the natural boundaries of the Pyrenees, the Alps, the Mediterranean and the ocean. With a view to secure their territories against the future aggressions of the continental powers, they purposed to form a series of dependent republics along the line of their frontiers, as a kind of outwork, to remove the point of attack. At the extremities of this line they had already established the Ligurian and Batavian republics; the Cisalpine soon followed. A connecting link of this chain was Switzerland, which covered the most vulnerable parts of the French territory; and, from its natural strength and central position, formed the citadel of Europe."

Besides these motives, acknowledged by the French themselves, their rapacity was stimulated by the treasures known to exist at Bern and elsewhere, the amount of which, as usual, was enormously exaggerated. What was required, in short, was not a motive but a pretext for intermeddling with the internal regulations of the Helvetic body. That body had with the utmost caution avoided giving offence; had recognised every successive form of government in France; and had turned out of their territories the unfortunate French *émigrés* who had fled thither for refuge from the rage of their own countrymen.

The triumphs of Napoleon in Italy were concluded by the construction of the Cisalpine Republic. The Swiss subjects of the Valteline, Chiavenna, and Bormio, were tempted to desire participation in the freedom thus established on their borders; and Napoleon offered the Grisons the alternative of conceding equal rights to these districts, or of seeing them included in the new Cisalpine state. Parties ran so high on this proposal, that no friendly understanding was possible; and when the term allowed for reply elapsed without any being given, Napoleon put his threat into effect, and confiscated all property belonging to the Grisons contained in the above-mentioned districts.

Such was the first encroachment on the ancient limits of Switzerland: shortly afterwards the bishopric of Bâle was annexed to France. Great consternation was caused by these proceedings in the confederation; but still more serious evils were at hand. In the canton of Bâle the peasantry murmured loudly against the town: in the Aargau several towns advanced tumultuous claims against Bern, for the recovery of their old and chartered rights; and the Pays de Vaud reclaimed its freedom with more impatience than ever. It was said besides, that a French army was already marching on Switzerland; ostensibly to support the claims of the malcontents, but really to make themselves masters of the land for their own purposes. Bern and Fribourg hastily levied forces for the coercion of their turbulent dependencies; and a diet of the confederacy was summoned at Aarau. Much was said and nothing done at this meeting, as the cantonal governments neither trusted each other nor their subjects. The members of the diet renewed the original league of the cantons, as if urged by the presentiment of its coming dissolution. The oath had hardly been taken, when a messenger from Bâle brought the intelligence that the mansions of the land-vogts were in flames; that a large body of peasantry had entered the town, and that all the subject districts had declared themselves free.

The spectacle of feebleness and fear in the authorities, combined with dogged resistance to the wishes of the people, of course diffused, instead of quelling, the spirit of revolt. As in the thirteenth and succeeding century, the prerogatives of the nobles had been forced to yield to the claims of a class of burghers and of shepherds, so soon as the example of the Lombard towns, and the growth of public prosperity, had excited independence of feeling; so likewise, in the times of which we are treating, it had ceased to be within the power of a privileged class to contend with success against the claims of the so-called third order, encouraged as it was by the example of France. Some districts, indeed, took no part in the prevalent agitations, and pertinaciously adhered to the accustomed order of things; others, more distinguished for enlightenment and enterprise, demanded an equality of rights in town and country; others, again, required the restoration of ancient franchises: some regarded nothing as attainable but by French interference; while nobler minds retained an insurmountable abhorrence for the agency of strangers in the internal affairs of their country.

It became more and more evident that the policy of the French directory led them to foment intestine discord in Switzerland. For several years past it had been observed, that foreign emissaries set themselves to work upon the public opinion. A person of the name of Mengaud made his appearance at Bâle, under the unusual and equivocal title of commissary, and set his seal on the papers of the French embassy: this individual not only made no secret of his intelligence with the malcontents in Switzerland, but affected to display it ostentatiously. He went to Bern on the 10th of October, 1797, where he demanded, in a note addressed to the government, the dismissal of the English ambassador Wickham, who had certainly exerted himself openly against France, but had done so as the envoy of a power at war with that country. Bern referred the demand of Mengaud to the then directing canton, as a matter which concerned the whole confederacy.

Wickham relieved for the moment the embarassment of the Helvetic body, while he deprived the French directory of a present pretence for violence, by taking his departure on a tour into Germany; but he left an able diplomatist behind him in the person of his secretary Talbot. Mengaud was received at Zurich and Bern with undisguised aversion, and no diplomatic visits were paid him at either of these places. In the month of November, an embassy from the latter town had been sent to Paris; which, though admitted to an audience of the director Barras, soon received a rude dismissal homewards.

Great were the hopes infused into the disaffected party by the promises of Mengaud, and other subordinate agents of France; and proportional fears were excited amongst the friends of the old system, including the greater number of public functionaries. In order to increase their uneasiness, Mengaud threatened the diet of the confederation in January, 1798, with the entrance of French troops into Switzerland, should Austria be suffered to occupy the Grisons. He travelled to the place of meeting at Aarau, with tricoloured flags flying from his carriage; and, on his arrival there, hung out an immense banner in front of his house. The triumphant revolutionists of Bâle had already formed a tricoloured flag of their own, by the addition of green to their formal cantonal colours, black and white, and their delegate at Paris, Ochs, had hastily sketched what he called an Helvetic constitution, on the model of that of the French Republic. This document was printed in Italian, French, and German, and distributed by Mengaud, not in official quarters only, but throughout the whole population of the cantons.

## FRENCH TROOPS IN SWITZERLAND

In the mean time, a division of the French army, under Menard, appeared on the western frontier; and the Pays de Vaud, protected by it, declared its

[1798 A.D.]

independence of Bern. The Bernese government saw the necessity of trying the force of arms on its subjects; and the command of the forces having been declined by councillor Erlach of Spiez, who had hitherto been one of the strongest assertors of aristocracy, it was conferred on Colonel Rudolf Weiss, who had, till then, sustained the character of a champion of the opposite system; and had contributed, by a published work,*g* to the favourable temper of the partisans of Robespierre towards the Swiss confederation. An unusual delegation of full powers placed in his hands the whole military government of the Vaud. The new commander held conferences with the leaders of the malcontents; published a treatise *h* intended to conciliate them, but intermixed conciliation with menace. Chillon was recovered by surprise from the insurgents, and the German troops of Bern were moved on the frontiers of the Vaud.

Meanwhile, General Menard was already on the lake of Geneva, with ten thousand men of the conquering army of Italy; and to him the insurgent leaders, alarmed for their own safety, addressed themselves. Menard replied, that he was instructed to give them aid and protection; and threatened Colonel Weiss that he would repel force with force, if the former should persist in drawing troops around a territory already declared independent, and in arming the communes against each other. Without taking any measures of defence — without even attempting to maintain himself on the high grounds — Weiss withdrew to the neighbourhood of Yverdun. It happened, accidentally, that two French hussars were shot on the outposts of the Bernese army, because they had not immediately answered the challenge of the sentinels. This incident was taken up by Menard, and afterwards by the directory, as an infringement of the law of nations, and the commencement of hostilities.

The revolution of Bâle, and the entrance of French troops into the Pays de Vaud, rendered it impossible for reflecting men any longer to doubt that sweeping social changes were inevitable. Yet the Swiss democracies would not be persuaded that anyone could shake their constitutions, or force on them a new species of freedom. The numerous friends of things as they were still hoped to steer themselves through the crisis without any great sacrifices, by mere dint of tenacity and delay. Many, moreover, flattered themselves with the notion that the plans of France were levelled at no wider mark than the Vaud; and were prompted by a petty feeling of jealousy towards Bern [the stronghold of the aristocracy], to see nothing in the affair but a mortification to that envied canton.

It could hardly be conceived at Bern, that the French should have advanced without meeting any resistance up to Yverdun, while the headquarters of Colonel Weiss were withdrawn behind Avenche. He was instantly dismissed from his command, which was transferred to General Erlach of Hindelbank; but the evil effects of exorbitant discretionary powers had been so sensibly felt, that the opposite extreme was now adopted. Meanwhile, the leading statesmen of Bern, had, at length, became convinced that concessions must be made to the people. Fifty-two members were added to the great council from amongst the burghers, citizens of the minor towns, and rural inhabitants. It was resolved to introduce, within a year's time, a new constitution; in which admission to every public function should be open to all, and due proportion should be observed in the emoluments of all public services. These resolutions were laid before the directory, together with a demand for the withdrawal of the French troops. The government also stooped to make a like communication to Mengaud, to acquaint him with the actual political system of Bern, and inform him of the wish of that canton to preserve peace with France. Mengaud made just such an answer as ought to have been expected from him. He demanded a prompt and complete change of the old political system, declared that further delays could not be suffered by the majesty of the French Republic; and designated the persevering defenders of the existing order as a handful of inveterate tyrants.

Disregarding their own positive engagements, the French, on the 8th of February, took possession of the town of Bienne. Yet the confederates still hoped to conciliate France, and were encouraged in this illusion by General Brune, who now commanded the French troops, reinforced by several thousand men, and fixed his headquarters at Payerne. This subtle leader, who, without having performed a lengthened' public career, was, to borrow a diplomatic expression, *rompu dans les affaires*, proposed, with artful blandishments, and with hinted hopes of peaceful adjustment, an armistice of fourteen days; during which the discipline and enthusiasm of the Bernese army had time to abate, indecision and distrust to increase, and recruits to join the French army.

Meanwhile, General Schauenburg had collected a division of troops on the frontiers of Solothurn and Bern, equal in strength to that of Brune. The latter announced, on the 26th of February, that he had received full powers to treat from the executive directory. He proposed his ultimatum to the Swiss delegates, that without farther delay they should introduce a provisional government, take measures for the establishment of a new constitution, with securities for freedom and equality, liberate all prisoners for political offences, and withdraw their own troops, as well as those of the other cantons. On the due fulfilment of these conditions, the French troops should be drawn off likewise; and should not again enter the Swiss territory, unless the government called for their assistance.

On the very day when Brune had given his insolent ultimatum, Erlach entered the great council at Bern, accompanied by eighty of his officers, who were members, like himself, of that body. In a moment of unusual resolution, he was invested with full powers to commence hostilities on the close of the armistice. However, two days afterwards, the delegates returned from Brune's encampment at Payerne. Erlach and his brothers in arms were no longer present in council; the rest of that body were paralysed by the imminent and gigantic danger; and the full powers which had just been given the general were taken away. The same evening, Erlach received instructions *not* to attack the French, which fired his troops with anger and suspicion, and tended to confirm the belief in the treachery of their leaders, already widely prevalent in the army. Brune's ultimatum, in all its principal features, was accepted. The delegates of Zurich, Wyss, and Tscharner sought a conference with him, when he renewed his former offers in cold and peremptory language; but now added a novel stipulation to them, namely, that, even after the confederate troops were disbanded, his should remain till the new constitution should be established. It was affirmed, truly or otherwise, that he granted, without difficulty, an extension of the truce for twenty-four hours; notwithstanding which, the delegates, on their return, saw his troops already in motion for the attack. Orders for the commencement of hostilities had also been forwarded from the council of war at Bern to the army, and two hours afterwards, retracted.

In obedience to the first of these contradictory instructions, the Bernese colonel Gross had given notice to the French outposts that the truce would come to an end at ten in the evening of the 1st of March; but when he with-

[1798 A.D.]

drew his former announcement on the arrival of counter-orders, Schauenburg would admit no further parley. He had already attacked, without warning, the old castle of Dornach, in the neighbourhood of Bâle, which sustained a siege of twenty-four hours. The attack of a Bernese division near Vingels was repulsed with loss, and the French surprised the Bernese posts at Lengnau, which they carried after an obstinate resistance. The town of Solothurn capitulated, on Schauenburg's appearance before it. The passage across the Aar now lay open to the French troops. Fribourg was attacked and taken, though a stand was made by the Bernese garrison.

Erlach was now compelled to withdraw his troops behind the Aar and the Sense; though it was not without extreme reluctance that the men of Bern abandoned Morat. On the 3rd of March, Brune destroyed one of the finest monuments of Swiss courage and union, the Ossuary of Morat; and the French, among whom were many natives of Burgundy, honoured the bones of their ancestors with a grave, after an interval of more than three hundred years. Now at length, Bern, Solothurn, and Fribourg proclaimed a levy *en masse* of the able-bodied men within their territories. The Bernese army was in a dreadful state of confusion; particularly that division which stood directly opposed to Brune, in which the distrust and exasperation of the soldiers were at their highest pitch. Officers were dismissed by their soldiers, and others put in their place. Colonels Stettler and Ryhiner were bayonetted and shot before the very gates of Bern; and Colonels Crusez and Goumoens fell beneath the sabre-strokes of their own dragoons. Nevertheless, the troops were again assembled under command of Grafenried, who was admirably supported by his officers, and repulsed the French in every attempt to charge them at the point of the bayonet. Eighteen cannons were taken from the enemy, and their loss in men besides was very considerable.

### The Capitulation of Berne ; the Constitution Unitaire (1798 A.D.)

The native troops had now fully recovered spirit and confidence; but just as Grafenried prepared to cross the Sense at Neueneck, the decisive intelligence arrived that Bern was in the hands of the enemy! Early on the 5th, an attack had been made by Schauenburg on Solothurn. His force was far numerically superior to the Bernese; his horse artillery terrified the native militia by its novelty, and his cavalry was nearly eight-fold that of Bern in numbers. At Fraubrunnen, the French turned the left flank of the Bernese: in the Grauholz and at Breitenfeld their militia under Erlach offered a brave resistance, armed with scythes and other agricultural implements. Men, women, and even children mixed, and fell in the mortal struggle. On its unsuccessful issue, ensued the capitulation of Bern.

All was lost: the armed bands of the peasantry dispersed in every direction with loud accusations of treason against their officers, many of whom were slain by their own men. Amongst these was the general Erlach, an illustrious name in the annals of Bern. That unfortunate commander, and the avoyer Steiger, when the fortune of the day was decided, retreated towards the Oberland, whither they knew that arms and money had already been despatched by the government, and where they still hoped to offer an effective resistance. But Erlach was murdered in the way by the enraged fugitives, who breathed nothing but revenge for their imaginary betrayal, and it was only by chance that Steiger did not meet a similar fate.

Even public extremity could not restore public spirit. Every little canton treated, armed, and cared for itself exclusively, totally regardless of the rest.

Wherever the authorities had, till then, withheld freedom from their subjects, they no longer delayed to grant it; but bestowed emancipation with so ill a grace, as to indicate how gladly they would have refused it, had they dared.

France now assumed a tone of direct command, and proclaimed the dissolution of the Helvetic body, and the establishment of a *constitution unitaire,* embracing the whole of Switzerland under one uniform system of government. This system announced a perfect equality of rights between the inhabitants of the towns and of the villages, assigned the nomination of judges, magistrates, and legislators, to the people in their primary assemblies, and entrusted to the government the choice of executive functionaries. The founders of this new Helvetic republic next proceeded to the more material objects of their mission. They levied large contributions on the towns, appropriated the treasures amassed at Bern, Zurich, Solothurn, and Fribourg, and carried off many members of council and other persons, as hostages for the further payments exacted from those places.

But the people of Uri, Nidwalden, Schwyz, and Glarus, were resolved not to deliver up their old independence so easily, and organised a heroic, though a useless, resistance under their brave leader Aloys Reding. The most brilliant and the most sanguinary struggle took place at Rothenthurm, in the neighbourhood of the battle-field of Morgarten. These Alpine shepherds combated with a spirit and success which showed them not unworthy of their forefathers. Thrice were the attacks of regular troops, four times their number, repulsed, with serious loss on the side of the enemy. But the vigour of this peasant militia was exhausted by their very successes, and they were, finally, compelled to accept terms from the invaders, and to bow beneath the yoke of the Helvetic Republic. Thus ended the old Swiss confederation, after enduring for a term of nearly five centuries. "It fell," says an enlightened native historian,[1] "not exactly for want of strength in the bands which held it together; for, without any stronger bond of union the old confederates won their freedom, crushed or repelled the force of mighty antagonists, and rendered themselves poweful and fomidable. The Swiss succumbed in the last unfortunate struggle, because the feeling of duty, the lofty faith in their country and its fortunes, had become chilled in the bosoms of the many, and because the democratical cantons thought of none but themselves."

While the well-instructed friends of their country regretted the rude violence with which every link in the system of society, from the Alps to the Jura, had been totally torn away from its ancient holdings, they could not fail to perceive the ultimate benefits educible from the general convulsion. The former aggregation of little states had been productive of estrangement and enmity; the cantons had been proved powerless, even for self-defence; separately too poor for public enterprises; collectively incapable of any combined action. But now an opportunity seemed to be given to the Swiss people of becoming one great family, enjoying equal rights. The mass of the people, however, was not penetrated by such ideas, and only deplored the breach made in their old habits and usages. They had, indeed, demanded freedom and independence, but not this melting up into an uniform mass. They would have preferred that every petty district, nay, every single valley, should become a free and independent canton, ruling itself in its own assemblies, according to its own pleasure, and only connected by federal ties with the rest of the Swiss people. The whole subsequent march of events tended only to increase the desire for a subdivided federative system of this kind,

---

[1] Ludwig Meyer.

[1798 A.D.]

and the aversion for the newly established order. The new general government, called an executive directory, after its prototype at Paris, resided at Aarau without inspiring either respect or confidence, dependent on its sole protectors, the French plenipotentiaries. In the senate and the great council, composed of delegates from all the cantons, the conflicting opinions of parties caused an incessant wordy warfare. Out of doors the same parties abandoned parliamentary weapons, and asserted their discordant creeds with arms in their hands. New and old laws and regulations were perpetually coming in collision. While the state was often without the most indispensable means for its maintenance, and even for the daily pay of its functionaries, the French plenipotentiaries, leaders, and subalterns, rioted in shameless superfluities at the cost of the country, and sent to France the surplus of their plunder.

The discontents of the people were considerably aggravated by the murmurs and manœuvres of the ci-devant authorities; of the monks who apprehended the abolition of all monasteries; of the priests who had suffered diminution of the stipends, and of the traders and artisans in the towns who no longer enjoyed the sweets of corporations and monopolies. They trusted to the approaching renewal of war between France and Austria, and prepared to support the emperor for the expulsion of the French. When the whole population was summoned, in July, 1798, to take the oath of allegiance to the newly formed constitution, disturbances and revolts took place in many districts.[c]

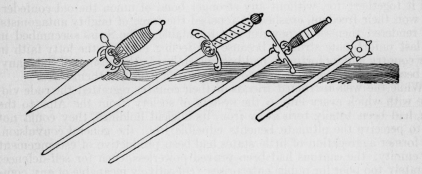

# CHAPTER VI

## SWITZERLAND SINCE 1798

### CHANGES OF CONSTITUTIONS AND ADMINISTRATIONS

WAR with France was at length renewed by the emperor of Austria, and a division of his army entered the Grisons. A signal defeat sustained by the French troops near Stockach, in Swabia, the victorious advance of the Austrian army into Switzerland, and the removal of the seat of the Helvetic government from Lucerne to Bern, seemed to inspire the conflicting parties with renewed animation and fury. Swiss fought against Swiss under the banners of France and Austria; tumults and revolts took place on account of the French conscription or in favour of the Austrian invasion; battles were fought between foreign armies in the valleys, on the Alps, and on the banks of the lakes; and horse and man clambered over heights which had formerly been only known to the chamois hunter. The Grisons and the mountainous lands as far as the St. Gotthard were alternately won and lost by French and Germans. The victorious banners of Austria were carried on the left as far as Zurich and the St. Gotthard, on the right up to the banks of the Rhine, supported by the Russians under Suvarov. Switzerland had never sustained such desolating inroads since the times of the Romans, Alamanni, and Burgundians.

Many of the old superseded members of the government now looked forward to the speedy restoration of their authority, which they here and there attempted to recover with the assistance of the Austrian bayonets: even the new abbot of St. Gall resumed the exercise of his feudal rights, such as they had existed before the recent emancipation which had been granted to the

26

people. The effects of this iniquitous resumption did not fail soon to be felt by the proud prelate himself; Zurich and Schaffhausen, too, were soon forced to acknowledge that the people did not wish to be replaced in its state of subjection. The decisive and brilliant victory of Masséna near Zurich, and the destruction of Suvarov's army, which had marched over the Alps from Italy, restored the Helvetic constitution throughout the whole country. Parties now supplanted and succeeded each other in quick succession, so that none could remain long at the helm or consult for the public benefit.

First of all, the legislative councils dissolved the executive directory, and substituted for it an executive committee; then, in its turn, this executive committee dissolved the councils, convoked a new legislature, and styled itself an executive council. Twelve months afterwards a general Helvetic diet was assembled at Bern for the formation of a new and improved constitution: this, like the former deliberative bodies, was arbitrarily deposed from its functions, and a newest-of-all constitution established, in October, 1801. Alois Reding, the victor of Rothenthurm, as the foremost Swiss landammann, was placed at the head of the senate; but as he possessed neither the confidence of the French rulers nor that of those who detested all recurrence to the old state of things, a new act of arbitrary power deposed him from the presidency of the council.

These continual changes of administration were looked upon with absolute indifference by the Swiss people, who only sighed at the total interruption of law and order, the increase of taxes, and the lawless acts of the French soldiery. The Valais more particularly suffered by the military tyranny to which it was subjected. The object of France was to separate it from Switzerland, in order to keep a route open across the Alps into Italy.

In the same degree as popular consideration ceased to attend the ever-changing but equally odious aspects of the new government, individual opinions and wild fancies obtained prevalence. Mystical views were propagated in Appenzell; and the anabaptists reared their heads once more in Bern and Zurich. The quiet of the former town and its neighbourhood was suddenly disturbed by a swarm of fanatics from Amsoldingen. Two years before, a quack doctor and fanatic, by name Antony Unternerer, had fixed his abode in that village. A certain flow of language, combined with prepossessing manners and the profuse employment of benedictory formulas in human diseases, as well as in those of cattle, had gained for this fellow the confidence of the multitude. He held meetings in which particular parts of the New Testament were interpreted in a new and peculiar manner; and his adherents ceased their attendance on the ordinary divine service. Unternerer addressed a summons in writing to the supreme tribunal of Bern, to appear, with all its prisoners and their keepers, in the cathedral church on the morning of Good Friday, when the Saviour of the world would ascend the pulpit and hold his judgment. He also summoned all his disciples to meet at Bern on the same day. Many of them had already remained during several days assembled together; and, anticipating the coming judgment, had transferred their worldly possessions to others. Curiosity drew a multitude together from all quarters. Unternerer himself was announced as Saviour by his adherents; and seditious projects peeped out under the mantle of fanaticism. However, such a wholesome effect was produced by the arrest of the ringleader, the consignment of his most conspicuous followers to the lunatic hospital, and the billetting of dragoons in the houses of others, that the poor enthusiasts soon came to their senses, lamenting the error of their ways and the transfer of their properties.

THE EVACUATION OF SWITZERLAND; THE NOMINATION OF DEPUTIES
(1802–1803 A.D.)

The Peace of Amiens, betwixt France and the other belligerent powers in consequence of which the French garrisons were drawn home out of Switzerland, afforded opportunity to the party and provincial spirit to show itself with new vigour.   On the 12th of July Montrichard, the French resident in Switzerland, communicated in an extra-official note to the Helvetic land-ammann, Dolder, that he had received commands from the minister of war to hold himself, with the troops under his orders, in readiness for instant return to France.   The landammann laid this note before the then executive council, who were considerably embarrassed by its import, and addressed themselves to Montrichard and to the Swiss ambassador at Paris, to petition for a postponement of the measure.   But shortly afterwards, Boizot, secretary of the Helvetic embassy, arrived from Paris with Talleyrand's note, which fixed for the approaching 20th of July the complete evacuation of Switzerland.   It was now out of the question for the heads of the Helvetic government to oppose themselves to a measure invoked by the wishes of a large majority.   Accordingly the executive council did its best to assume an unconstrained and easy attitude; and with all expedition voted its liveliest thanks to the first consul for his purpose of withdrawing his troops from Switzerland, which they hailed as the highest proof of his benevolence and respect for the independence of the Helvetic nation.

The reply of the French minister was couched in terms of disinterested delicacy, which almost seemed ironical.   He talked of the French troops as the battalions which the first consul had consented to leave in Switzerland on the conclusion of peace.   He based the proposed measure on the confidence entertained by the first consul in the virtues of the Helvetic people, who were now better agreed, as he said, on the principles of political organisation, and in whose attachment the government would find sufficient securities for the maintenance of order and tranquillity.   "The Helvetic government could regard this resolution but as a pledge of the consul's confidence in its friendly intentions and policy, and of his disinclination to meddle with the internal affairs of other nations."

It is impossible to assign with any certainty the motives by which this ambiguous language and conduct were dictated.   The first consul may have meant to give a popular example of moderation and respect for the faith of treaties; or he may have designed a covert chastisement for the feeble attempts at independence made by the Helvetic government and its refusal of unconditional acquiescence in the projected separation of the Valais; or he may have wished to extort an express prayer for the stay of his troops, or to revive the struggle of parties, and compel the Helvetic government to throw itself into the arms of France, and urge him, as though against his will, to assume the part of arbiter and ruler; or, finally, perhaps, the best solution of his conduct may be found by supposing the combination of all or most of these motives.

Conformably with the system thus enforced upon them, the executive council made known to the Swiss people the departure of the French troops, as a gracious boon  the offer of which they had eagerly accepted.   In effect, the removal of these troops was performed with such celerity that none were left behind but the sick in the hospitals and a handful of men here and there to guard whatever French property was not of a movable description.

The news of the retreat of the French troops and the ill-concealed uneasiness of the government flew through the country with wonderful rapidity, and everywhere roused the concealed but numerous enemies of the existing order, who had hitherto lurked inactively, as it were in scattered cantonments. The Valais declared itself independent. Uri, Schwyz, and Unterwalden took up arms against the Helvetic government. The town of Zurich, likewise, threw off allegiance to it — an example which was speedily followed by Schaffhausen and Bâle. A general levy took place in the Aargau against Bern: the helpless Helvetic government fled for refuge to Lausanne, while a diet was held in Schwyz for the restoration of the old league. The feeble body of troops in the pay of the government were driven from the interior of the country, and followed their employers into the Vaud: everywhere the opposite factions prepared for active hostilities; the towns planned the destruction of the general government; the peasants armed for their freedom against the pretensions of the towns; and the Pays de Vaud arrayed itself in defence of Helvetic unity. Blood had already flowed, and civil war appeared inevitable, when Napoleon turned his eyes again upon Switzerland, and commanded peace in a tone which was not apt to meet with resistance.

"Inhabitants of Switzerland" (such were the terms of a declaration addressed by him through General Rapp to the cantons of the Helvetic Republic): "you have presented, during two years, a melancholy spectacle. Sovereign power has alternately been seized by opposite factions, whose transitory and partial sway has only served to illustrate their own incapacity and weakness. If you are left to yourselves any longer, you will cut one another to pieces for years, without any prospect of coming to a rational understanding. Your intestine discord never could be terminated without the effective interposition of France. I had resolved not to mix in your affairs; but I cannot and will not view with indifference those calamities to which I now perceive you exposed. I retract my former resolution. I offer myself as your mediator, and will exert my mediation with that energy which becomes the powerful nation in whose name I speak. Five days after reception of the present declaration, the senate shall assemble at Bern to nominate three deputies to be sent to Paris, and each canton will also be admitted to send delegates thither. All citizens who have held public employments during the last three years may also appear at Paris to deliberate by what means may best be effected the restoration of concord and the reconciliation of parties. Every rational man must perceive that my purposed mediation is a blessing conferred on Switzerland by that providence which, amidst so many concurring causes of social dissolution, has always preserved your national existence and independence. It would be painful to think that destiny had singled out this epoch, which has called to life so many new republics, as the hour of destruction to one of the oldest commonwealths in Europe."

The Helvetic senate instantly replied to this announcement by declaring that it received, with lively gratitude, this new proof of the friendly dispositions of the first consul, and would conduct itself in all points in conformity with his wishes. In a proclamation addressed to the Helvetic people, after some allusion to the mighty and uplifted arm of the mediator, it recommended union, tranquillity, and calm expectation. The cantonal diets met to elect deputies to Paris. The several communes also were permitted to despatch delegates thither at their own expense. The mandate of Napoleon and the presence of his soldiers induced conflicting parties to suspend their hostilities, and tacitly, at least, to acquiesce in his mediation, as they could come to no agreement with each other.

On the 10th of December, 1803, Swiss delegates were received in the office of foreign affairs at Paris, to hear a note of Bonaparte read, in which he addressed them as president of the French and Cisalpine republics, and laid down the basis of his intended mediation. "A federal constitution," he said, "is a point of prime necessity for you. Nature herself has adapted Switzerland for it. What you want is an equality of rights among the cantons, a renunciation of all family privileges, and the independent federative organisation of each canton. The central constitution may be easily arranged afterwards. The main points for your people are neutrality, promotion of trade, and frugal administration: this is what I have always said to your delegates when they asked my advice; but the very men who seemed to be the best aware of its truth turned out to be the most obstinately wedded to their privileges. They attached themselves, and looked for support, to the enemies of France. The first acts of your insurgents were to appeal to the privileged orders, annihilate equality, and insult the French people. No party shall triumph; no counter-revolution take place. In case of violation of neutrality, your government must decide upon making common cause with France."

On the 12th, Bonaparte received a select number of the Swiss deputation to whom he further addressed himself as follows: "The only constitution fit for Switzerland, considering its small extent and its poverty, is such a one as shall not involve an oppressive load of taxation. Federalism weakens larger states by splitting their forces, while it strengthens small ones by leaving a free range to individual energies." He added, with an openness peculiar to great characters, and unequivocally indicative of good-will, "When I make any demand of an individual, he does not often dare to refuse it; but if I am forced to apply myself to a crowd of cantonal governments, each of them may declare itself incompetent to answer. A diet is called: a few months' time is gained; and the storm blows over."

Almost every word of the first consul during these negotiations has historical value. Most of his expressions wear a character of greatness; all of them afford a clue to the system on which he acted. One or two passages, taken at random here and there, will suffice for a specimen: "It is the democratic cantons which distinguish you, and draw on you the eyes of the world. It is they which do not allow the thought of melting you up with other states to gain any coherence or consistency. The permission to settle wherever they please, in pursuit of their vocation, must be extended to all natives of Switzerland. The small cantons are said to be averse to this principle; but who on earth would ever think of troubling them by settling amongst them? France will re-open a source of profit in favour of these poorer cantons, by taking additional regiments into her pay. France will do this, not because she needs additional troops but because she feels an interest in attaching these democracies."

## THE ACT OF MEDIATION (1813 A.D.); CABALS FOLLOW NAPOLEON'S FALL

The Act of Mediation, which resulted from these conferences, restored the old federative system; but not without introducing very considerable improvements. The amnesty announced by it precluded all persecutions, and the new agitations necessarily arising from them. All servitude and all privilege were abolished; while equality of rights and freedom of industry were established. The mischievous freedom formerly enjoyed by the several cantons of entering into hostilities or alliances against each other was quite put an end to. In future, they could only use their arms against the common

[1813 A.D.]

enemy; and the objects of the whole league could no longer be frustrated by the humours of its individual members.

The dissolution of the Helvetic general government followed naturally on the completion of the above-mentioned arrangements; and soon afterwards Napoleon recalled his troops from Switzerland. The people, in almost every part of the country, returned quietly to their usual occupations, and tendered their allegiance to the new order of things. In the canton of Zurich alone several communes refused the oaths; complaining of the difficulties newly thrown in the way of the redemption of tithes, ground-rent, and other burdens. They would listen to no friendly representations; but committed acts of violence on unoffending funtionaries, set fire to the castle of Wadenschwyl, and finally took to arms. The prolonged disorders of former years had accustomed them to lawless self-defence; but the insurrection was soon suppressed by the aid of the neighbouring cantons, combined with the well-affected part of the Zurichers.

The ringleader John James Willi, shoemaker in the village of Horgen, and others of his more conspicuous comrades, were punished with death. The less distinguished rioters suffered imprisonment, and forty-two offending communes were visited with a war-tax of above 200,000 florins. It was well that the first flame of revolt was speedily extinguished, before it had time to spread itself through the country. Parties remained everywhere unreconciled; and each imagined nothing to be required for their predominance but the fall of the new order of things. The friends of Helvetic unity still murmured at the cantonal partition of the country. The monasteries murmured as they felt their existence threatened; and Pancrace, the *ci-devant* abbot of St. Gall, openly stigmatised the inhabitants of that district as contumacious vassals of the empire. Many of the country people murmured, who wished for *Landsgemeinde*, on the model of the original cantons. Many patrician and city families murmured that their privileges were swept away, and the peasantry no longer their subjects. The majority of the people, however, wished for nothing but peace and quiet, and decidedly adhered to the existing order of things, and the rights which they had acquired under that order.

Thus the peace of the country remained for the most part undisturbed; and a series of comparatively prosperous years followed. The energies of the Swiss had been awakened by the years of revolution and of civil war, and displayed themselves in a hitherto unprecedented degree. They no longer stood apart from each other as formerly, like strangers; but had been made better acquainted by the storms of social collision. The concerns of each canton were now interesting to all. Journals and newspapers, which had formerly been suppressed by timid governments, instructed the people in useful knowledge, and drew its attention to public affairs. The Swiss of all cantons formed societies for the furtherance of objects of common utility, for the encouragement of various arts and sciences, and for the maintenance of concord and patriotism. The canal of the Linth formed a lasting monument of this newly reawakened public spirit.

Since the people had ceased to be viewed as in a state of perpetual infancy a new impulse was given to trade and industry, which were now no longer cramped and confined, as formerly, by corporate restrictions and monopolies. The participation in public affairs allowed to all free citizens enforced a mild and equitable conduct on the governments. Schools were increased and improved throughout the country; the military force was newly organised; and, on the whole, a greater number of laudable objects were provided for in the space of ten years than had been thought of in the previous century.

When the throne of Napoleon sank under the power of the allies, the public-spirited part of the Swiss nation fondly imagined that the hour was come in which their country's honour and independence might be established on a firmer footing than ever. To preserve the benefits gained to the land by his act of mediation was the wish of a large majority of the people. If the Swiss had sometimes felt, along with others, the iron arm of that formidable despot (who had, however, spared them more than any neighbouring population), yet his gift of a constitution had become deservedly dear to them. It had dried up innumerable sources of discord. Under it a fellow-feeling, never before experienced, had been diffused in the same degree as individual pride had been humbled. The cessation of a state of subjection, wherever it had before existed, had decupled the number of confederates, and all restraints on free communication betwixt one canton and another had been removed.

The cantons sent their contingents for the protection of the frontiers, voted extraordinary imposts for their maintenance, and a diet was assembled at Zurich with unanimous instructions from its constituents. This body declared with one voice its resolution "to observe a conscientious and impartial neutrality with regard to all the high belligerent powers," expressing, at the same time, its full anticipation that "the same would be acknowledged upon their part." It addressed itself as follows to the confederates: "The great and only end of all our endeavours is to maintain this neutrality by every means in our power; to protect our country's freedom and independence; to preserve its soil inviolate, and to defend its constitution." The senate of Bern expressed itself as follows: "Our object is to guard the pacific borders of our country inviolate from the march of foreign armies; we are unanimously resolved, however, at all events, to maintain tranquillity, order, and security in our canton by all the means which stand in our power."

Such was the general sense of the Swiss people. Not such, however, was the sense of the great families in the once dominant towns of the confederation. Many of these wished to see their country invaded by foreign armies, by aid of which they hoped to restore the old league of the thirteen cantons, with all its hated appendages of sovereignty and servitude, which had vanished from the face of the land in 1798.

The Swiss delegates were received in a friendly manner by the emperor of Austria and the king of Prussia; but no direct recognition of their neutrality was vouchsafed to them. The satellites of these monarchs gave them distinctly to understand that Switzerland was regarded and would be treated as nothing else than as a limb of the French system. A large Austrian force was collected on the frontiers, particularly in the neighbourhood of Bâle; yet many still believed that a determined vindication of neutrality would not be put down by violence. In the meantime, the Swiss delegates were stopped at Fribourg in Brisgau on their return homewards from Frankfort, and their letters were intercepted. A general enervation seemed to have spread itself over the conduct of the affairs of the confederation at this crisis. There is no ground for supposing that the men who led their forces and presided in their governments acted the part of secret conspirators against the order of things which they professed to defend. But when the overwhelming powers of the allies came pouring in upon them; when these were joined by kings who owed their crowns to Napoleon; when even the French ambassador dissuaded reinforcement of the frontier cordon — when, in short, the ancient state of things renewed its sway on every side, while a decided popular will showed itself nowhere, opposition was in a manner overwhelmed by the force of circumstances.

[1813 A.D.]

A proclamation, couched in terms of mildness and of amity, was issued by Prince Schwarzenberg, the Austrian commander-in-chief; and at the same time Count Capo d'Istria declared, on his arrival in Zurich, that the monarchs could not recognise a neutrality which, in the existing situation of Switzerland, must be nothing more than nominal. The armies of the allied powers hoped to find none but friends there. Their majesties pledged themselves solemnly not to lay down their arms until they should have secured the restoration to Switzerland of the territories wrested from her by France — a pledge which we shall presently see was adhered to but indifferently. They disclaimed all wish to meddle with her internal constitution; but at the same time could not allow her to remain under foreign influence. They would recognise her neutrality from that day in which she became free and independent.

The Austrian army marched over the Rhine on the 21st of December, 1813, through the territories of Bâle, Aargau, Solothurn, and Bern, into France. During the first months of the following year the burdens and even the dangers of war were felt very severely in the northern and western parts of Switzerland, particularly in Bâle, which received much annoyance from the obstinate defence of Hüningen, and the hostile disposition of the commander of that place. Geneva, too, while she welcomed in anticipation the new birth of her ancient independence, saw herself suddenly surrounded with the actual horrors of warfare, and threatened with a regular siege. The continual passage of large bodies of troops brought malignant fevers and maladies in their train, and it became more and more difficult to supply them with provisions.

On the entrance of the Austrian troops, Bern set the example of abolishing the Act of Mediation, and reclaimed the restoration of the predominance which she had previously enjoyed in the Helvetic body. The example was followed first by Solothurn and Fribourg, and then by Lucerne. In Zurich, too, the diet declared the Act of Mediation, by virtue of which it was sitting, null and void, and drew up a plan for a new confederation of the nineteen cantons. But this was not enough for some of the men in power at that time, who demanded nothing short of the restoration of the old league of the thirteen cantons, and had already summoned the Pays de Vaud and the Aargau to return under the government of Bern. These cantons, however, resolutely rejected the proposal.

The diet, which was again convoked at Zurich and consisted of delegates newly elected by all the nineteen cantons, was now the only feeble bond which kept the Helvetic body together. Interested voices were raised on every side for annihilating or mutilating the last constructed cantons, which for sixteen years had enjoyed the boon of freedom and independence. Zug demanded a part of its former subject lands from the Aargau; Uri, the Valle Levantina from the canton of Ticino; Glarus, the district of Sargans from the canton of St. Gall; the prince abbot Pancrace, his former domains and sovereignties in the Thurgau; Schwyz and Glarus combined to demand compensation for their privileges over the districts of Utznach, Gaster, Wesen, and Ersatz; Unterwalden, Uri, and Schwyz united in a similar demand for compensation for the sovereign rights which had formerly been possessed by them in Aargau, Thurgau, St. Gall, and on the Ticino.

In these cabals and commotions Zurich, Bâle, and Schaffhausen displayed the least of prejudice or passion; while the Aargau and the Vaud showed themselves worthy of their freedom by the spirited resolution of their people. In the lands and towns of Bâle, Solothurn, and Zurich it was proposed to espouse the cause and rally round the standard of the Aargau. Bern, however, avoided open hostilities, and even offered to recognise the independence of the Vaud on certain conditions, which were rejected by the latter. Aargau now made menacing demonstrations, and a dangerous ferment showed itself in the Oberland. Here, as in many other places, the jealousy and suspicion of the various parties came into play, in proportion as discussion was broached on the limits to be assigned to the rights of the people and their governments. News was daily received of scattered plots and insurrections, of imprisonments and banishments, in various places. The town of Solothurn called for the protection of a Bernese garrison against the threatened attacks of its own people. Swiss troops were precipitately despatched to the banks of the Ticino to prevent the breaking out of civil war; while other troops were sent into the canton of St. Gall to put an end to a scene of absolute confusion.

While Switzerland was thus given up to a state of such disquietude that blood had already flowed in more than one district, and the gaols of several towns were filled with prisoners, the plenipotentiaries of the great powers were sitting in congress at Vienna, to establish the peace of Europe on a durable foundation. The allies had already allowed the addition to the Helvetic body of Geneva, as well as of the Valais, and the Prussian principality of Neuchâtel. Swiss delegates made their appearance with equal promptitude in the imperial metropolis on the Danube, as they had done eleven years before in the capital of France.

But the politics of Europe moved no faster at Vienna than those of Switzerland did at the diet of Zurich. No settlement of Swiss affairs had been made, when the sudden news of Napoleon's landing from Elba and his triumphal march through France awakened European diplomacy once more from its slumbers. The diet called to arms the half contingent of fifteen thousand men for the defence of the frontiers. Two battalions of the Vaud were detached hastily to Geneva, and the same canton received as friends and comrades the troops of Bern, against which it had taken up arms a month before. The most important elements of discord seemed to have disappeared — the most inveterate enemies to be reconciled.

On the 20th of March, 1815, the definitive arrangements of the allied powers were promulgated. The existing nineteen cantons were recognised, and the increase of their number to two-and-twenty confirmed, by the accession of Geneva, Neuchâtel, and the Valais. The canton of Vaud received back the Dappenthal, which had been taken from it by France. Bienne and the bishopric of Bâle were given to Bern by way of compensation for its former sovereign rights over the Vaud. One moiety of the customs received in the Vale Levantina was assigned to Uri; the prince abbot Pancrace and his *ci-devant* functionaries were indemnified with 8000 florins yearly. A decision was also given on the indemnification of those Bernese who had possessed jurisdictions in the Pays de Vaud, and on many other points in dispute. The complaints of the Grisons alone were disregarded — Chiavenna, the Valtellina, and Bormio, which had now become the property of Austria, were neither restored nor was any compensation for them given, notwithstanding the clause to the contrary in Prince Schwarzenberg's proclamation.

The cantons now remodelled their respective constitutions in the midst of agitations of all kinds. Those in which the supreme power is assigned to the *Landsgemeinde* for the most part removed the restrictions on the popular prerogative, which had been introduced by the Act of Mediation, and approximated anew to pure democracy. In the city cantons the capitals recovered, though in various modifications and proportions, a preponderance in the system of representation. Even in these privileged places, however,

[1817-1823 A.D.]

many friends of the public weal remained true to the conviction tried and proved by past experience (and about to receive after no long period additional confirmation from the march of events) — that participation of the lesser towns and rural districts in public functions was a requisite condition for the permanence of tranquillity; and that the members introduced from these remoter parts of the country would form vigorous roots of the slender stem of authority, and fix them wide and deep in a republican soil.

## SWITZERLAND DEVELOPS ALONG NEW LINES

In 1817, the confederates were led by the invitation of the emperor Alexander into a signal deviation from the policy of their forefathers. They entered into a close alliance with Austria, Russia, and Prussia; and allowed themselves to be mixed up with the system of the great powers, by giving their adhesion to the Holy Alliance, unmindful of the lessons left by the Swiss of old times.

On the conclusion of the War of Liberation from Napoleon, an opinion which the allied powers had encouraged by their promises became prevalent through great part of Germany — that the efforts of the people should be requited by the grant of representative constitutions. The realisation of this object was pursued by open and secret means, which soon aroused attention and mistrust on the part of the governments. Investigations were set on foot, followed up by penal inflictions; and many of the accused parties made their escape into Switzerland. A similar course was taken by some Italians, on the suppression of the Piedmontese revolts and the abortive revolution of Naples. Natives of France, moreover, who had given offence to their government, either by republican principles or by adherence to the cause of Napoleon, in like manner sought a place of refuge in Switzerland. These occurrences did not fail to give umbrage to several cabinets, which was increased by the friendly welcome and assistance afforded to the fugitives from Greece. It never seemed to occur to foreign potentates what a blessing in the vicissitudes of European affairs was the existence of a land to which political victims of all parties might resort as an inviolable sanctuary.

The year 1823, that of the French invasion of Spain under Louis XVIII, seemed an epoch of especially unfriendly dispositions in more than one European court against Switzerland. There were personages who would willingly have used these dispositions to effect some limitation of Helvetic independence; but their influence was either insufficient for that purpose in the cabinets to which they belonged, or Europe seemed as yet not ripe for success in such an experiment. Meanwhile the remonstrances and demands of continental powers afforded matter of anxious consultation to the Helvetic diet; and their usual subjects of discussion were increased by two new topics — foreign police and surveillance of the press.

It was resolved that both these points touched the prerogatives of the separate cantons, and therefore did not admit of decision at any general diet. An invitation was accordingly issued to the governments of all the cantons, exhorting them to adopt vigorous measures, in order that nothing might find its way into newspapers and journals inconsistent with proper respect to friendly governments. With regard to foreign police it was proposed to take measures for preventing the entrance or residence of such strangers as had left their country on account of crimes or efforts at disturbance of the public repose; and for providing that no foreigners should be admitted except such as could show certificates or passports from their respective governments.

In many of the cantons these demands were met by a ready alacrity not only to urge their execution in their full extent but even to improve on them by subjecting discussion of domestic as well as of foreign affairs to strict surveillance. On the other hand, in more enlightened parts of the confederacy, it was thought that public discussion and the old right of sanctuary should be guarded from every species of encroachment. The diets continued to busy themselves with deliberations on both subjects. Returning tranquillity diminished the uneasiness of the cabinets; and, by consequence their inquisitive and minute attention to Switzerland. Individuals lost the importance which had formerly been ascribed to them, and the sojourn of strangers in Switzerland again became freer. The press occasioned more prolonged discussions at the diets and in several of the councils; but in the midst of these it obtained more and more freedom, and in some districts shook off all its former restrictions.

During these years an interest in church affairs diffused itself amongst laymen, as well as amongst theologians by profession. In the educated classes religious indifferentism became less frequent; while the genuine spirit of tolerance made progress. This tendency, like every other widely extended mental movement, had its questionable as well as its pleasing features. Shocking ebullitions of fanaticism are reported to have taken place in Zurich, Bern, and other cantons. A footing was gained in Fribourg and the Valais by the revived order of Jesuits; and the friends of human improvement could not regard without anxiety their influence in ecclesiastical matters and in education.[b]

### REACTION AND REFORM; EFFECTS OF THE REVOLUTION OF JULY

The reaction making itself manifest throughout Europe in the third decade of the nineteenth century appeared also in the individual cantons of Switzerland and in its general government. The same disparity between the rights of the nobility and those of the people which existed in northern Germany was to be found here. As we have seen, the cantons for the most part had an aristocratic government in which a few favoured families, the patricians, had so decided a preponderance that there was hardly a shadow of representation of the people. As at an earlier period in other countries there had been a distinction between *Stadt* and *Amt* (city and subject land), so at this time in Switzerland the same distinction was still made between *Stadt* and *Landschaft* (city and rural district). The citizens belonging to the latter were permitted to send but a few members to the "great council" of a canton.

With such privileges in the hands of the patrician families the administration of the state was as bad as possible. Offices were apportioned more according to birth than merit, the finances were not always managed in the interests of the state. The evils of the administration of justice had become proverbial. Federal laws for the regulation of domestic intercourse and commerce were not thought of. The diet which met at one of the three leading places *(Vororte)* — Bern, Zurich, and Lucerne — did not fall behind the German diet in reactionary sentiment, adhered closely to the system of Metternich and sent its men as mercenaries to France and Naples that it might provide appointments as officers for the young patricians.

The younger generation, such as was growing up at the universities and elsewhere, would not content itself with such republics. Everywhere the opposition of the liberals was becoming active against the rule of the oligarchies. Since the uprisings in northern Germany, especially, the demand for constitutional reforms became still more general. Societies were formed and the liberal press did not tire in proclaiming the principles of the new era; political equality, abolition of all privileges, equal representation for all the citizens of a canton, freedom of the press, etc. Bern, at that time the chief place *(Vorort,* capital), whose government was the most aristocratic of all, September 22nd, 1830, sent a circular letter to the governments of the cantons urging them to proceed against the press and to hold fast to the old constitutions. This only fanned the flame. In the months of October and November assemblies of the notables and of the people were held in almost all the cantons, the principles of new constitutions were determined upon, and in a few weeks the governments were forced to accept them.

Already before the revolution of July, in May, 1830, the oligarchal-ultramontane government in Ticino was overthrown and a different one erected on a democratic basis. The new constitution was accepted by the people in March, 1831. Events took a similar course in Zurich, where it was chiefly a matter of the relation of the rural districts *(Landschaft)* to the too powerful city; in Aargau, St. Gall, Lucerne, Solothurn, Fribourg — where the hierarchical aristocracy, supported by the Jesuits and congregationalists *(Congre-gisten)* who had been driven out of France, mustered out soldiers but was

PLACE DE LA PALUD, LAUSANNE

overthrown together with everything belonging to it; in Vaud — where, acting with the hot-bloodedness of Frenchmen, the people called out to the great councillors *(Gross-räthe)* of Lausanne, "Down with the tyrants!" and established a radical constitution; in Schaffhausen and in Bern — where the deposed government for a time had the mad plan to maintain itself by help of the discharged Swiss soldiers of Charles X; in Bâle—where bloody encounters twice occurred, and where for the adjustment of the quarrel federal troops had to take station, the great council of the city consented rather to a separation from the rural districts than conform to their demands. Thus there were formed here in 1832 the two half-cantons, Bâle (city) and rural Bâle (with its government at Liestal). Similar desires for separation also showed themselves in Schwyz and Valais, but they were laid aside after embittered conflicts. On the other hand, the old constitution remained in force in Uri, Unterwalden, Zug, Geneva, Glarus, the Grisons, and Appenzell. In Neuchâtel the liberal party would no longer recognise the king of Prussia as the sovereign, but was suppressed in 1831 by the energy of the Prussian general Von Pfuel; and the movement ended in a victory for the existing government.

## SIEBENER KONKORDAT; DISPUTES OVER ASYLUM AND RELIGION

The party which in 1831 had secured a more liberal form of government in a majority of the cantons strove also to achieve reforms in the federal constitution. At the diet of 1832 it obtained the appointment of a commission which was to revise the federal statutes and present its conclusions to an extraordinary session of the diet of 1833. The liberal cantons, Bern, Aargau, Thurgau, St. Gall, Solothurn, Zurich, and Lucerne, concluded the agreement of the Seven (Siebener Konkordat) for the preservation and attainment of popular sovereignty. On the other hand the conservative party, Uri, Schwyz, Unterwalden, Valais, Neuchâtel, and the city of Bâle, united in the league of Sarnen (Sarner-Bund). In conjunction with the neutral party these succeeded in 1833 in balking federal revision. As a result their hopes and demands increased. Armed bands from Schwyz and the city of Bâle, July 30th, 1833, entered Outer Schwyz and rural Bâle to compel the submission of these seceding districts. The consequence was that Schwyz and Bâle city were occupied by federal troops and the league of Sarnen was declared annulled. The separation of Bâle into two independent cantons was recognised and the reunion of Schwyz was declared — this, however, with complete equality of rights.

The gathering of many fugitives from Germany, Poland, and Italy, who found an asylum in republican Switzerland but who at times abused hospitality, brought on complications with foreign powers. The most active among these revolutionists was Giuseppe Mazzini of Genoa, who in spite of total lack of any promise of success was continually setting on foot new attempts at insurrection, to keep his Italian fellow countrymen in practice. "Young Italy" which he founded at that time caused an inroad of about four hundred men under General Romarino into Savoy in order from this point to revolutionise Piedmont and the rest of Italy. After the occupation of several villages the undertaking foundered because of the indifference of the people. From this time on Switzerland in the eyes of the outside world appeared as the hearth of radicalism, especially as Mazzini wished to extend his activity to the whole of Europe and for the republicanisation of this continent founded "Young Europe." Now it rained diplomatic notes. The neighbouring powers complained of the abuse of the right of asylum and held out the prospect of the most hostile measures, if Switzerland would not expel the participants of the Italian raid and keep a better watch over the rest. Louis Philippe went farthest in severity toward Switzerland and even threatened her with war if she would not expell Louis Napoleon, who had returned from America, and was living in Arenenberg as a citizen of Thurgau. The latter left Switzerland for England of his own accord.

Even more important were the consequences of the religious conflicts. The calling of Doctor Strauss from Würtemberg to the University at Zurich in 1839 roused the rural population to arms and caused the fall of the liberal government at Zurich; this did not again secure supremacy till 1845. More significant was the question of the convents. In a conference at Baden in

1834 seven cantons had determined upon the subjection of the church to the authority of the state and the employment of the convents for purposes of general usefulness. Most violent was the quarrel over this matter in the canton Aargau, whose radical government finally, in 1841, closed all the convents, among others the wealthy one of Muri, and took possession of the property for " purpose of instruction and benevolence." Among the bigoted Catholics there was great excitement over this. It led to a victory of the ultramontane party in Lucerne and Valais in 1844. This party called the Jesuits to Lucerne to take charge of the instruction of youth.

In this affair the wealthy farmer Joseph Leu and Sigwart Müller showed themselves especially active. The Jesuits had also established themselves in Fribourg and Schwyz. To expel them from Switzerland was the aim of all the liberal cantons. The expedition of the free lances *(Freischaren)* of 1845 under the leadership of Ochsenbein of Bern met with failure. The government of Lucerne, still more embittered by the murder of Leu, assumed a terrorising attitude, demanded the punishment of the free lances, and restoration of the convents of the Aargau; and when no attention was paid to these demands concluded with Schwyz, Uri, Unterwalden, Zug, Fribourg, and Valais a separate league *(Sonderbund)* for mutual protection against external and internal enemies. This league within a league was not to be endured; and, since the liberal cantons were in the majority, they decided at the diet in Bern, in July, 1847, upon the dissolution of the Sonderbund, as being contrary to the Pact of Federation *(Bundesvertrag)* and upon the expulsion of the Jesuits. As the fanatics of Lucerne failed to obey the diet, orders were given for federal action against the cantons of the Sonderbund. The federal army was mustered in and the experienced general Dufour of Geneva was placed at its head.*c*

## THE SONDERBUND WAR (1847 A.D.)

Europe had followed with an attentive eye the events we have just related. Peoples were preoccupied with them, courts saw in them a source of serious anxiety. All, taking the Vienna congress as their point of view, desired a federative, neutral, and peaceable Switzerland. From this point of view the cause of the Sonderbund seemed to them to have justice on its side. But everywhere, owing to diversified interests, the language differed. "A fine country and a good people," said King Louis Philippe, "but it is in a bad way. Let us keep from interfering. To hinder others so doing is to render them a great service." Guizot nevertheless proposed to occupy himself in Swiss affairs in a conference to be held at Paris or in London, but he was unsuccessful. Once Austrian troops on the one hand, French on the other, drew near Switzerland, but they were speedily recalled to their cantonments. Metternich would willingly have taken the lead, had he not known that France could not leave Austria to interfere alone. Thenceforth, of the two powers, one contented itself with secretly aiding the Sonderbund by relays of arms and money, the other with lavishing encouragements on the seven cantons through its ambassador.

Prussia hesitated, recommending Neuchâtel prudence. Czar Nicholas could not understand an intervention unless the powers had sixty thousand men behind them. Great Britain would not interfere at all. Under the ministry of Lord Palmerston, a young statesman named Peel, son of the illustrious minister of that name, joined the Bear Club at Bern where radicals met. At Rome, the French ambassador, Rossi, an ancient deputy of the

Geneva diet, was charged to solicit Pius IX to recall the Jesuits from Lucerne. It was thought both in London and Paris that the best means of restoring peace to Switzerland was to take from the radicals their principal grievance and their flag. The holy father contented himself with letting the Swiss know that he would remain passive in the strife (*passive se habere decrevit*).

Switzerland, under these circumstances, was persuaded that the moment had come frankly to declare to Europe her intention of being sole interpreter of her Pact of Alliance; to have done with the questions that agitated her; and to constitute herself on the basis of an enlarged and equitable democracy, which would soon see her the first on the road towards which all European peoples were proceeding. She knew the states which lavished advice on her to be torn by a revolutionary spirit and incapable of uniting against her in a common resolution. It was under the influence of this thought that Ochsenbein opened the confederation diet on the 5th of July, 1847.

Although only the son of a hotel keeper, without instruction in the classics, but gifted with prompt and pleasing intelligence, he presented himself unembarrassed before an assembly wherein the heads of the two parties dividing Switzerland were sitting, and at which the majority of ministers from foreign powers assisted. Frankness characterised his discourse. Foreseeing a European crisis — "Our modern world," said he, "rests on worm-eaten columns, on institutions that have for support only the powers of habit and interests, a construction that the slightest storm will make a ruin. Well, this storm approaches; the colossus is quite aware of it. He sleeps a dangerous sleep." Descending from these heights to questions of the moment, the president of the diet proclaimed the right of the majority, whom Switzerland had always recognised. When this majority had been declared, he courteously invited all the cantons to join with it. Callame, a Neuchâtel deputy, exposed in language firm and untouched by passion the gravity of events that had given place to a separate alliance, and demanded that they should leave those who had concluded it the time to convince themselves that it was no longer necessary.

In reality, the vote of the majority meant a declaration of war. The diet adjourned so as to give the parties time either to unite or to finish their preparations for hostilities. It reassembled on the 18th of October. Two delegates, envoys of peace, were sent from each of the Sonderbund cantons, but they met with scant welcome: one-half wanted war.

### Colonel Dufour is Made Commander of the Army

On the 29th of October the deputies from the seven cantons left Bern, and on the 4th of November it was decided that the decree ordering the dissolution of their alliance should be executed by arms. The diet put on foot fifty thousand men, and entrusted the command, with the rank of general, to Colonel Dufour, of Geneva. No name in the army was more respected, none had more weight. Dufour did not belong to either side. In sympathy he was conservative, but was none the less a man of progress. He had been in the wars and published writings on military science, fruits of a long and wide experience. No chief knew as he did the canton militia, over whose manœuvres he had for a number of years presided in the camp at Thun, as chief instructor of the engineering corps. To these warlike qualities he united the virtues of a man of peace. He was occupied in the elaboration, on a plan he had conceived, of the fine map of Switzerland which bears his name, when he was called to quit the pursuits of the student for the field of battle. He comprehended the danger to his country. He clearly perceived his duty, and he thought only of accomplishing it.

In accepting the first command he made what he considered necessary stipulations, demanding a sufficient number of troops and absolute power. All this he obtained, though not without some resistance. He was given 100,000 men and 260 field pieces. This army he distributed into seven divisions. In the choice of superior officers, he exacted that he alone should judge of their capacity without any regard to political opinion; this was the way both to get excellent officers and to prepare for what he considered to be his duty — the quieting of hatreds after the struggle. In a short time there was no longer question of politics in the army. Addressing once his heads of divisions, "I shall never depart," he said, "from the laws of moderation and humanity. A stranger to political agitation and faithful to my military duties, I shall try to establish order and discipline in the federal troops, to make public and private property respected, to protect the Catholic religion in her ministers, her temples, and her religious establishments — in a word, to do everything to soften the inevitable evils of war. If violence be used, let it not come from us. After fighting, spare the vanquished; however strong one may be, relieve the despair of the enemy. then we can congratulate ourselves after the fight on never having forgotten that it was between confederates."

These instructions being made known, the general resolved to trust nothing to chance, and to make no offensive movement unless sure of the superiority of his forces; this he recognised as the surest way towards a speedy ending with the least bloodshed. Soon the confidence he inspired began to show itself. The city of Bâle, long undecided, sent him excellent artillery. Neuchâtel and Appenzell alone continued to take no part in the war. The promptitude with which the army got under arms, well ordered, well clothed, and well equipped, astonished foreigners. The redivision of troops was necessitated by the situation. The country occupied by the Sonderbund formed three distinct masses — Fribourg, the original cantons, and Valais. Dufour proposed to attack them separately, and to begin with Fribourg.

### Preparations of the Sonderbund

The powers held exaggerated ideas of the Sonderbund forces. It could hardly put on foot more than thirty thousand regular troops. The *Landsturm*, it is true, meant a more considerable number of men, but not having received sufficient organisation could not be compared to the excellent reserves of the large cantons, and did not give the help expected of them. Far from one another, the separatist states could only with difficulty lend one another aid. The original cantons tried nevertheless to keep their ways open by means of boldness in offensive actions. Even before the diet began its campaign, the men of Uri seized the St. Gotthard passes (November 3rd); threw themselves across the Levantina, surprised three thousand Ticinese encamped at Airolo, and drove them as far as the Moesa bridge. But arrived at this point, they found themselves face to face with Grisons and Ticino militia, superior to them in number, who stopped their progress. The expedition had no other result than that of holding back two thousand excellent soldiers from the places where decisive blows were to be struck. Another attempt, made from Lucerne, to penetrate into Catholic Aargau and to free Fribourg, by means of a diversion, had no better success.

## The Capitulations of Fribourg and Lucerne End the Sonderbund

Without taking much account of these movements, Dufour occupied himself only in concentrating his forces so as to surround the Sonderbund states, on all their accessible frontiers. His provisions were assured, his hospital organised. Immediately upon the rupture being announced, Colonel Ochsenbein, who presided over the diet, left office to put himself entirely at the disposition of the general-in-chief. The general placed him at the head of the Bernese reserves, which composed his seventh division and which he assimilated with the active troops. He stationed them first on the Lucerne frontier, and when he arranged to draw near Fribourg, he called Ochsenbein to advance towards that capital, in order to make the enemy think he would attack from the eastern side. However, twenty thousand men and fifty-four artillery pieces, under colonels Rilliet, Burkhard, and Donatz, advanced from the north and west by different routes, and kept their movements secret that they might arrive on the same day at the gate of Fribourg. On the 13th the town was surrounded. An experienced leader, Colonel Maillardoz, had raised defences all round, and they had prepared to attack these exteriors forts when the Fribourg government, recognising the impossibility of resistance, gave up the town, dismissed the troops, and renounced the Sonderbund. The taking of Fribourg would not have cost the federal army a single man if through a mistake a Vaudois troop had not rushed under fire from the Bertigny redoubt, which resulted in seven killed and a large number wounded.

As soon as Fribourg had capitulated the general confided to Colonel Rilliet the care of occupying the military cantonments and watching the entrance of Valais. He himself hastened to Aarau, to prepare for the investment of Lucerne. Two rivers, the Emme and the Reuss, protected this town. The bridges on these rivers had been broken or fortified. The ground on which it was foreseen that the most serious engagements would be delivered was the labyrinth which stretches from the Reuss to the Lake of Zug; bristling with wooded hills, where passage had been stopped by barricades and mines had been laid in the defiles. It was necessary to attack these strong positions, because they served as a link between Schwyz and Lucerne, and success on this point was decisive, whilst elsewhere it was not so. The leader whom the five cantons had put in charge of their militia, Ulrich de Salis-Soglio, understood this, and went to these places. The forces he could dispose of were some twenty thousand regulars and a similar body of the *Landsturm*. Salis had learned warfare in fighting Napoleon. A sincere Protestant, he had nevertheless devoted himself to a cause which had his political sympathies, but of which he despaired.

A resolution being taken to force his entrenchments, Dufour set five divisions of his army on the march from the various points they occupied, giving them Lucerne as object. Ochsenbein's reserves went down the Emme valley, overcoming a lively resistance. The Burkhard and Donatz divisions approached the Emme and the Reuss between the bridges of Wolhusen and Gislikon, at the same time that colonels Ziegler and Gmur at the head of some odd thousands of men attacked Salis in his intrenched camps. Ziegler mastered the Gislikon bridge and the Honau defiles. Gmur, after having received on his march the submission of Zug, scaled the heights of Meyers Kappel. Everything made for success. Victory was hotly disputed, but the Schwyzers were in the end thrown back towards Immensee, whence they fell back on Art and Goldau. Troops from the other cantons turned to Lucerne. The separation of Schwyz with its allies was accomplished. On every hand the federal troops marched simultaneously on that capital. The gates were opened to them by a convention, and on the 24th of November Dufour made his entry. On the following days the Waldstätte and the Valais made their submission. Twenty-five days after the decree of execution the task of the army was complete — the Sonderbund no longer existed.[d]

The diet now debated the draft constitution drawn up by Kern of Thurgau and Druey of Vaud, which in the summer of 1848 was accepted by fifteen and a half cantons, the minority consisting of the three forest cantons, Valais, Zug, Ticino, and Appenzell (Tuner Rhodes), and it was proclaimed on September 12th.

From 1848 onwards the cantons continually revised their constitutions, always in a democratic sense, though after the Sonderbund War Schwyz and Zug abolished their Landsgemeinde. The chief point was the introduction of the *referendum*, by which laws made by the cantonal legislature may (facultative referendum) or must (obligatory referendum) be submitted to the people for their approval; and this has obtained such general acceptance that Fribourg alone does not possess the referendum in either of its two forms, Ticino having accepted it in its optional form in 1883. It was therefore only natural that attempts should be made to revise the federal constitution of 1848 in a democratic and centralising sense, for it had been provided that the federal assembly, on its own initiative or on the written request of fifty thousand Swiss electors, could submit the question of revision to a popular vote. In 1866 the restriction of certain rights to Christians only was swept away; but the attempt at final revision in 1872 was defeated by a small majority, owing to the efforts of the anti-centralising party. Finally, however, another draft was better liked, and on April 19th, 1874, the new constitution was accepted by the people. This constitution is that now in force, and is simply an improved edition of that of 1848. The federal tribunal (now of nine members only)

A SWISS FINIAL

was fixed (by federal law) at Lausanne, and its jurisdiction enlarged, especially in constitutional disputes between cantons and the federal authorities, though jurisdiction in administrative matters (*e.g.*, educational, religious, election, commercial) is given to the federal council — a division of functions which is very anomalous, and does not work well.

A system of free elementary education was set up, and many regulations were made on ecclesiastical matters. A man settling in another canton was, after a residence of three months, only, given all cantonal and communal rights, save a share in the common property (an arrangement which as far as possible kept up the old principle that the "commune" is the true unit out of which cantons and the confederation are built), and the membership of the "commune" carries with it cantonal and federal rights. The referendum was introduced in its "facultative" form — *i.e.*, all federal laws must be submitted to popular vote on the demand of thirty thousand Swiss electors or of eight cantons. If the revision of the federal constitution is demanded by one of the two houses of the federal assembly or by fifty thousand Swiss citizens, the question of revision must be submitted to a popular vote, as also the draft of the revised constitution — these provisions, contained already in the constitution of 1848, forming a species of "obligatory referendum." It was supposed that this plan would lead to radical and sweeping changes, but as a matter of fact there have been (1874-1886) about one hundred and seven federal laws and resolutions passed by the assembly, of which ninteeen were by the referendum submitted to popular vote, thirteen being rejected, while six only were accepted — the rest becoming law, as no referendum was demanded. There has been a very steady opposition to all schemes aiming at increased centralisation. By the constitutions of 1848 and 1874 Switzerland has ceased to be a mere union of independent states joined by a treaty, and has become a single state with a well-organized central government.

This new constitution inclined rather to the Act of Mediation than to the system which prevailed before 1798. A status of "Swiss citizenship" was set up, closely joined to cantonal citizenship: a man settling in a canton not being his birthplace got cantonal citizenship after two years, but was excluded from all local rights in the "commune" where he might reside. A federal or central government was set up, to which the cantons gave up a certain part of their sovereign rights, retaining the rest. The federal legislature (or assembly) was made up of two houses — the council of states (*Stände Rat*), composed of two deputies from each canton, whether small or great (forty-four in all), and the national council (*National Rat*), made up of deputies (now 145 in number) elected for three years, in the proportion of one for every twenty thousand souls or fraction over ten thousand, the electors being all Swiss citizens. The federal council or executive (*Bundesrat*) consisted of seven members elected by the federal assembly; they are jointly responsible for all business, though for the sake of convenience there are various departments, and their chairman is called the president of the confederation. The federal judiciary (*Bundesgericht*) is made up of eleven members elected by the federal assembly for three years; its jurisdiction is chiefly confined to civil cases, in which the confederation is a party (if a canton, the federal council may refer the case to the federal tribunal), but takes in also great political crimes — all constitutional questions, however, being reserved for the federal assembly. A federal university and a polytechnic school were to be founded; the latter only has as yet been set up (1887) and is fixed at Zurich. All military capitulations were forbidden in the future. Every canton must treat Swiss citizens who belong to one of the Christian confessions like their own citizens, for the right of free settlement is given to all such, though they acquired no rights in the "commune." All Christians were guaranteed the exercise of their religion, but the Jesuits and smiliar religious orders were not to be received in any canton. German, French, and Italian were recognised as national languages.

The constitution as a whole marked a great step forward; though very many rights were still reserved to the cantons, yet there was a fully organised central government. Almost the first act of the federal assembly was to exercise the power given them of determining the home of the federal authorities, and on Novembber 28th, 1848, Bern was chosen, though Zurich still ranks as the first canton in the confederation. By this early settlement of

[1891 A.D.]

disputes Switzerland was protected from the genezal revolutionary movement of 1848.

The federal constitution of 1848 set up a permanent federal executive, legislature, and tribunal, each and all quite distinct from and independent of any cantonal government. This system was a modified revival of the state of things that had prevailed from 1798 to 1803, and was an imitation of the political changes that had taken place in the cantonal constitutions after 1830. Both were victories of the centralist or radical party, and it was therefore but natural that this party should be called upon to undertake the federal government under the new constitution, a supremacy that it has kept ever since. To the centralists the council of states (two members from each canton, however large or small) has always been a stumbling-block, and they have mockingly nicknamed it "the fifth wheel of the coach." In the other house of the federal legislature, the national council (one member per twenty thousand, or fraction of over ten thousand of the entire population), the radicals have always since its creation in 1848 had a majority. Hence, in the congress formed by both houses sitting together, the radicals have had it all their own way. This is particularly important as regards the election of the seven members of the federal executive which is made by such a congress. Now the federal executive (federal council) is in no sense a cabinet — *i.e.*, a committee of the party in the majority in the legislature for the time being. In the Swiss federal constitution the cabinet has no place at all. Each member of the federal executive is elected by a separate ballot, and holds office for the fixed term of three years, during which he cannot be turned out of office, while as yet but a single instance has occurred of the rejection of a federal councillor who offered himself for re-election.

Further, none of the members of the federal executive can hold a seat in either house of the federal legislature, though they may appear and speak (but not vote) in either, while the federal council as such has not necessarily any common policy, and never expresses its views on the general situation (though it does as regards particular legislative and administrative measures) in anything resembling the "speech from the throne" in England. Thus it seems clear that the federal executive was intended by the federal constitution of 1848 (and in this respect that of 1874 made no change) to be a standing committee of the legislature as a whole, but not of a single party in the legislature, or a "cabinet," even though it had the majority. Yet this rule of a single political party is just what has taken place. Between 1848 and the end of 1899, thirty-six federal councillors were elected (twenty-three from German-speaking, eleven from French-speaking, and two from Italian-speaking Switzerland, the canton of Vaud heading the list with seven). Now of these thirty-six two only were not radicals, *viz.* M. Ceresole (1870–75) of Vaud, who was a Protestant liberal-conservative, and Herr Zemp (elected in 1891), a Romanist conservative; yet the conservative minority is a large one, while the Romanists form about two-fifths of the population of Switzerland. But, despite this predominance of a single party in the federal council, no true cabinet system has come into existence in Switzerland, as members of the council do not resign even when their personal policy is condemned by a popular vote, so that the resignation of Herr Welti (a member of the federal council from 1866 to 1891), in consequence of the rejection by the people of his railway policy, caused the greatest amazement and consternation in Switzerland.

The chief political parties in the federal legislature are the right, or conservatives (whether Romanists or Protestants), the centre (now often called "liberals," but rather answering to the whigs of English political language), the left (or radicals), and the extreme left (or the socialists). In the council of states there is always a federalist majority, since in this house the smaller cantons are on an equality with the greater ones, each indifferently having two members. But in the national council (147 elected members) there has always been a radical majority over all other parties, the numbers of the various parties after the triennial elections of 1899 being roughly as follows: radicals, 86; socialists, 9; Centre, 19; and the Right, 33. The socialists long worked under the wing of the radicals, but now in every canton (save Geneva) the two parties have quarrelled, the socialist vote having largely increased. In the country the anti-radical opposition is made up of the conservatives, who are strongest in the Romanist, and especially the forest cantons, and of the "federalists" of French-speaking Switzerland. There is no doubt that the people are really anti-radical, though occasionally led away by the experiments made recently in the domain of state socialism: they elect, indeed, a radical majority, but very frequently reject the bills laid before them by their elected representatives.

From 1885 onwards Switzerland had some troubles with foreign powers owing to her defence of the right of asylum for fugitive German socialists, despite the threats of Prince Bismarck, who maintained a secret police in Switzerland, one member of which, Wohlgemuth, was expelled in 1889, to the prince's huge but useless indignation. From about 1890, as the above troubles within and without gradually subsided, the agitation in the country against the centralising policy of the radicals became more and more strongly marked. By the united exertions of all the opposition parties, and against the steady resistance of the radicals, an amendment was introduced in 1891 into the federal constitution, by which fifty thousand Swiss citizens can by the "initiative" compel the federal legislature and executive to take into consideration some point in the federal constitution which, in the opinion of the petitioners, requires reform, and to prepare a bill dealing with it which must be submitted to a popular vote. Great hopes and fears were entertained at the time as to the working of this new institution, but both have been falsified, for the initiative has as yet only succeeded in inserting (in 1893) in the federal constitution a provision by which the Jewish method of killing animals is forbidden. On the other hand, it has failed (in 1894) to secure the adoption of a socialist scheme by which the state was bound to provide work for every able-bodied man in the country, and (also in 1894) to carry a proposal to give to the cantons a bonus of two francs per head of the population out of the rapidly growing returns of the customs duties.

The great rise in the productiveness of these duties has tempted the Swiss people of late years to embark on a course of state socialism, which may be also described as a series of measures tending to give more and more power to the central federal government at the expense of the cantons. So, in 1890, the principle of compulsory universal insurance against sickness and accidents was accepted by a popular vote, in 1891 likewise that of a state or federal bank, and in 1898 that of the unification of the cantonal laws, civil and criminal, into a set of federal codes. In each case the federal government and legislature were charged with the preparation of laws carrying out in detail these general principles. But in 1897 their proposals as to a federal bank were rejected by the people, while at the beginning of 1900 the suspicion felt as to the insurance proposals elaborated by the federal authorities was so keen that a popular demand for a popular vote was signed by 115,000 Swiss citizens, the legal minimum being only 30,000: they were rejected (20th of May, 1900) on a popular vote by a two to one majority. The preparation of the federal codes has progressed quietly, drafts being framed by experts and then submitted for criticism to special commissions and public opinion. But this method, though the true one to secure the evolving of order out of chaos, takes time.

By a popular vote in 1887 the federal authorities were given a monopoly of alcohol, but a proposal to deal similarly with tobacco has been very ill received (though such a monopoly would undoubtedly produce a large amount), and would pretty certainly be refused by the people if a popular vote were ever taken upon it. In 1895 the people declined to sanction a state monopoly of matches, even though the unhealthy nature of the work was strongly urged, and have also resolutely refused on several occasions to accept any projects for the centralising of the various branches of military administration, etc. Among other reforms which have recently been much discussed in Switzerland are the introduction of the obligatory referendum (which hitherto has applied only to amendments to the federal constitution) and the initiative (now limited to piecemeal revision of the federal constitution) to all federal laws, etc., and the making large federal money grants to the primary schools (managed by the several cantons). The former scheme is an attempt to restrain important centralising measures from being presented as laws (and as such exempt from the compulsory referendum), and not as amendments to the federal constitution, while the proposed school grant is part of the radical policy of buying support for unpopular measures by lavish federal subventions, which it is hoped will outweigh the dislike of the cantons to divest themselves of any remaining fragments of their sovereignty.[e]

In recent years arbitration treaties have been concluded with Great Britain, France, Austria, Italy, and other countries. In May, 1906, the celebrated Simplon tunnel was formally opened by the president and by the king of Italy. In 1907 proposals were made to build an electric railway up the Matterhorn. Later, in the same year, the canton of Geneva voted to discontinue the connection between church and state.[a]

# BRIEF REFERENCE–LIST OF AUTHORITIES BY CHAPTERS

[The letter *a* is reserved for Editorial Matter.]

CHAPTER I. SWITZERLAND TO THE FOUNDING OF THE CONFEDERATION (earliest times to 1291 A.D.)

*b* STRABO, *Geographica.* — *c* JOHN WILSON, *History of Switzerland* (in the "Cabinet Cyclopædia"). — *d* FERDINAND KELLER, *Pfahlbauten.* — *e* FREDERIC TROYON, *Habitations lacustres.* — *f* VICTOR GROSS, *Les Proto-helvètes.* — *g* ELISÉE RECLUS, *The Lacustrian Cities of Switzerland* (in Smithsonian Report for 1861). — *h* G. O. MONTELIUS, *Die Chronologie der Pfahlbauten in Mittheilungen der Anthropologischen Gesellschaft in Wien. Vol. XXX.* — *i* JOHN LUBBOCK, *Prehistoric Times.* — *j* T. STUDER, *Pfahlfan Bevölkering in Zeit fur Ethr. Verband*, 1885. — *k* RUDOLF VIRCHOW, in letter prefixed to V. Gross, *Les Proto-helvètes.* — *l* ROBERT MUNRO, *The Lake Dwellings of Europe.* — *m* A. VIEUSSEUX, *The History of Switzerland.* — *n* MICHAEL STETTLER, *Annales.* — *o* JOHANN VON MÜLLER, *Geschichte der Schweizerischen Eidgenossenschaft.* — *p* ALEXANDRE DAGUET, *Histoire de la Confédération Suisse.*

CHAPTER II. THE RISE OF THE SWISS CONFEDERATION (1288–1402 A.D.)

*c* E. A. FREEMAN, *The Historical Geography of Europe.* — *d* A. RILLIET, *Les Origines de la Confédération Suisse.* — *e* J. DIERAUER, *Geschichte der Schweizerischen Eidgenossenschaft.* — *f* W. A. B. COOLIDGE, *History of Switzerland* in *Encyclopædia Britannica.* — *g* K. DÄNDLIKER, *Histoire du Peuple Suisse.* — *k* J. VON MÜLLER, *Geschichte der Schweizerischen Eidgenossenschaft.* — *l* G. MEYER VON KNONAU, *Die Sage von der Befreiung der Waldstätte*, in *Sweizer Oeffentliche Vorträge.* — *m* A. HUBER, *Die Waldstätte, Uri, Sweiz, Unterwalden, etc.* — *n* R. VON RADEGG, *Capella Eremitana.* — *o* JOHN OF WINTERTHUR, *Chronikon Vitodurani* in W. Oechsli's *Anfänge der Schweizerischen Eidgenossenschaft.* — *p* W. OECHSLI, *Quellenbuch zur Schweizer Geschichte.* — *q* A. VIEUSSEUX, *The History of Switzerland.* — *r* J. WILSON, *History of Switzerland.* — *s* J. VULLIEMIN, *Histoire de la Confédération Suisse.*

CHAPTER III. THE CONFEDERATION AT THE HEIGHT OF ITS POWER (1402–1516 A.D.)

*b* W. A. B. COOLIDGE, Switzerland, in *Encyclopædia Britannica* — *c* A. VIEUSSEUX, *The History of Switzerland.* — *d* VULLIEMIN, *Histoire de la Confédération Suisse.* — *e* A. DAUGET, *Histoire de la Confédération Suisse.* — *f* A. MORIN, *Précis de l'Histoire.* — *g* WILSON. — *h* P. VERRI, *Storia di Milano.* — *i* F. GUICCIARDIN, *Historia di Milano.*

CHAPTER IV. THE SIXTEENTH AND SEVENTEENTH CENTURIES

*b* A. VIEUSSEUX, *The History of Switzerland.* — *c* J. K. L. GIESELER, *Compendium of Ecclesiastical History.* — *d* J. WILSON, *History of Switzerland.* — *e* J. STRICKLER, *Grundniss der Schweizer-Geschichte.* — *f* MAGUENOT, *Abrége de l'Histoire de la Suisse.* — *g* DAGUET, *Histoire de la Confédération.*

CHAPTER V. THE EIGHTEENTH CENTURY

*b* JOHANN HEINRICH DANIEL ZSCHOKKE, *Des Schweizerlandes Geschichte.* — *c* J. WILSON, *History of Switzerland.* — *d* A. VIEUSSEUX, *The History of Switzerland.* — *e* K. DÄNDLIKER, *History of Switzerland.* — *f* A. DAGUET, *Histoire de la Confédération.* — *g* R. WEISS, *Coup d'œil sur les rélations politiques entre la république Française et le corps Helvétique* (1793). — *h* R. WEISS, *Réveillez-vous, Suisses, le danger approche.* — *i* W. COXE, *A History of the House of Austria.*

CHAPTER VI. SWITZERLAND SINCE 1798

*b* J. WILSON, *History of Switzerland.* — *c* W. MÜLLER, *Politische Geschichte der neuesten Zeit.* — *d* VULLIEMIN, *Histoire de la Confédération Suisse.* — *e* W. A. B. COOLIDGE, article on Switzerland in *Encyclopædia Britannica.*

# A GENERAL BIBLIOGRAPHY OF SWISS HISTORY

BASED ON THE WORKS QUOTED, CITED, OR CONSULTED IN THE PREPARATION OF
THE PRESENT WORK; WITH CRITICAL AND BIOGRAPHICAL NOTES

**Adams,** F. O., and C. D. **Cunningham,** The Swiss Confederation, London, 1889. — **Ah,** J. J. von, Die Bundesbriefe der altern Eidgenossen, Einsiedeln, 1891. — **Alt,** F. N. dé, Histoire de la Suisse, Fribourg, 1750–1755, 10 vols.

*François Joseph Nicholas,* baron of Alt, the son of an ancient patrician family of Fribourg, Switzerland, was born in 1689, and died in 1771. His history, which was admirably planned, would have greater value for the general student if much of the extraneous matter and all the violent Catholic partisanship were eliminated.

**Amtliche Sammlung der Akten aus der Zeit der Helvetischen Republik,** 2 vols., translated by J. Strickler, Bern, 1886–1890, 4 vols. — **Amtliche Sammlung der ältern eidgenössichen Abschiede 1245–1798,** 1839–1856, 8 vols. Reports of the old Federal diets, containing an enormous amount of historical matter. — **Anshelm,** Berner-Chronik, Bern, 1825–1833, 6 vols. — **Arx,** J. von, Geschichte von St. Gallen, St. Gallen, 1810, 2 vols. — **Aubigné,** T. A. d', Histoire Universelle 1550–1601, Geneva, 1626, 3 vols.

*Théodore Agrippa d'Aubigné,* one of the most notable characters of the sixteenth century, was born at St. Maury, near Pons, February 8th, 1550, of an old and noble family which had embraced the religion of the Calvinists. The young d'Aubigné neglected none of the educational opportunities afforded him by his father, and at the age of six was already able to read Latin, Greek and Hebrew. At thirteen he escaped from the restraints of his tutor to take part in the siege of Orléans. After his father's death he won reputation as a warrior under the prince of Condé, and later entered the service of the king of Navarre. In the wars of Henry IV for the recovery of his kingdom, d'Aubigné further distinguished himself; but he was finally obliged by the enmity of the queen-mother to retire from the court. During his exile he composed the history of his time, a work remarkable for its fearless frankness. The first two volumes were printed without opposition; but the third was condemned on account of its merciless criticisms. D'Aubigné, however, caused it to be printed, thereby incurring the burning of all three volumes; the confiscation of all his goods, and the savage persecution of his later years, until his death at Geneva, April 29, 1630.

**Bachtold,** J., and F. **Vetter,** Bibliotek alterer Schriftwerke der deutschen Schweiz, Frauenfeld, 1882–1884, 5 vols. — **Baker,** T. G., The Model Republic, London, 1895. — **Baebler,** J. J., Die alten eidgenössischen Bünde, St. Gall., 1848. — **Baumgartner,** G. J., Die Schweiz in ihren Kämpfen und Umgestaltungen, 1830–1850, Zurich, 1853–66, 4 vols.; Erlebnisse auf dem Felde der Politik, Schaffhausen, 1844; Geschichte Spaniens zur Zeit der französichen Revolution, Berlin, 1861; Geschichte des Schweiz Freistaats und Kantons St. Gallen, Zurich, 1868, 2 vols. — **Berchtold,** J., Histoire du canton de Fribourg, Fribourg, 1841–1845. — **Berthold,** de Constance, continuator of the Chronicon de sex œtatibus mundi. — **Blochmann,** C. J., Heinrich Pestalozzi, Leipsic, 1846. — **Bloesch,** E., Rapport sur les affaires communales Berne, 1851. — **Blumer,** J. J., Staats- und Rechtsgeschriften der Schweiz. Demokratien, St. Gallen, 1850–59, 3 vols.; Handbuch des schweiz. Bundesstaatsrechts, Schaffhausen, 1877–87, 13 vols. — **Bluntschli,** J. K., Geschichte des schweiz. Bundesrechts, Stuttgart, 1875, 2 vols.; Staats- und Rechtsgeschichte der Stadt und Landschaft Zurich, Zurich, 1838, 2 vols. — **Böhmer,** J. F., Regesta Karolorum, Frankfort, 1833. — **Bonivard,** F., Les Chroniques de la Genève, Geneva, 1831, 2 vols.

*François Bonivard*, to whom we owe the vivid pictures of the agitations which marked the beginning of the sixteenth century, was born of Savoyard parents, in 1493, at Seyssel. At seventeen he became prior of St. Victor, a community of Benedictines near Geneva. Revolutionist at heart, he entered into the struggle against the duke of Savoy, who in 1519 imprisoned him and confiscated his priory. He died in 1570, aged seventy-seven years, after a troubled youth and a melancholy old age as pensioner in the city where he had once been a man of mark. He left behind him the invaluable chronicle of his time, written half in Latin, half in the quaint French of his day, in a style at once rude and naïve, familiar and vigorous, and brimming with picturesque imagery and lively metaphor.

**Bonnechose,** É. de, Les Réformateurs avant la Réforme, Paris, 1860, 3rd edition, 2 vols. —**Brandstetter,** J. L., Repertorium über die Zeit und Sammelschriften der Jahre 1812–1890, Bâle, 1892. — **Bulletin** official du Directoire Helvétique, 3 vols. — **Bullinger,** H., Reformationsgeschichte, Frauenfeld, 1838–40, 3 vols.

*Henry Bullinger* was born at Bremgarten in 1504 and died at Zurich in 1575. After a preliminary course at Emmerich, his father having refused him the means necessary to continue his education, he made money by singing in the streets and in 1520 he recommenced his studies at Cologne, with the idea of joining the community of the Chartreux. But his resolution and his religion as well were changed by his association with Zwingli, whose doctrine he embraced and whose successor he became. In addition to his history of the Reformation and numerous theological writings he edited the complete works of Zwingli.

**Burckhardt,** Der Kirchenschatz des Münsters zu Basel, Bâle, 1867.

**Cæsar,** J., De bello gallico.—**Casus S. Galli.** By Ekkehard IV. Translated by G. Meyer von Knonau, Leipsic, 1878. —**Chambrier,** F. de, Histoire de Neuchâtel et Valangin jusqu'à l'avènement de la maison de Prusse, Neuchâtel, 1840.

*Frédéric de Chambrier*, the real founder of the Academy of Neuchâtel, was a man of wide culture and varied resources. In his *Histoire* he follows faithfully, century by century, the progress of the little but proud and independent people of Neuchâtel, handling his character analyses with skill and persisting in a style at once simple and dignified.

**Chauffour-Kestner,** Etudes sur les Reformateurs du XVI Siècle. —**Cherbuliez,** A., De la Democratie en Suisse, Geneva, 1843. —**Chronique d'Edlibach.** — **Chronica de Berno.** — **Chronique Anonyme.** — **Chronique des chanoines de Neuchâtel,** Michaud, 1839. — **Chronik des Hans Fründ,** Chur, 1875. —**Colton,** J. M., Annals of Switzerland, New York, 1897. — **Coxe,** W., A History of the House of Austria, London, 1807. — **Crétineau,** Joly J., Histoire du Sonderbund, Paris, 1850, 2 vols. — **Curti,** T., Geschichte der Schweizerischen Volksgesetzgebung, Zurich, 1885.

**Daguet,** A., Biographie de Guillimann, Fribourg, 1843 ; Les barons de Forell, Lausanne, 1873 ; Histoire de la Confédération Suisse, Geneva, 1880, 2 vols.

*Alexander Daguet*, Swiss historian and professor was born at Fribourg, March 12, 1816, of a family of poor nobles. Since 1866 he has held the chair of history and pedagogy at the Academy of Neuchâtel. He has edited successively numerous educational journals and figures among the authors of the publications of the Société de la Suisse romande. In his own country and abroad he has gained innumerable distinctions. He is the founder of several literary and historical societies, and the honoured member of many more.

**Dändliker,** C., Ursachen und Vorspiel der Burgunderkriege, Zurich, 1876 ; Geschichte der Schweiz, Zurich, 1884–88, 3 vols.; A short history of Switzerland, translation by E. Salisbury, London, 1899.

*Chas. Dändliker*, Swiss historian, was born at Staffa, May 6, 1849. He studied at Zurich and Munich and in 1871 was called to the chair of history at the Pedagogical Institute, Küssnacht, where he is still instructor. In 1887 he was named professor extraordinary in Swiss history at the University of Zurich. His history of Switzerland has been translated into English.

**Dawson,** W. H., Social Switzerland, London, 1897. —**Der Schweizerische Republikaner,** Zurich, Lucern, Bern, 1798–9, 3 vols. —**Dierauer,** J., Geschichte der schweizerischen Eidgenossenschaft, Gotha, 1887, 2 vols. —**Dottain,** E., La question suisse, éclaircissements historiques, Paris, 1860. —**Droz,** N., Instruction civique, Geneva and Lausanne, 1885 ; Die Schweiz im 19ten Jahrhundert, Lausanne, 1899.

*Numa Droz*, minister of foreign affairs for the Swiss Confederation, was born January 7, 1844, of a humble family of watchmakers. In 1864 he turned his attention to politics and became editor of a radical instrument, *Le National Suisse*. During the elections of 1869 he obtained a high place in the grand council, thanks to his facile elocution and his ardent liberalism. He was in 1882 one of the negotiators of the Franco-Swiss treaty. His writings are distinguished for clearness of presentation, beauty of style, and substantialness of matter.

**Dubs,** J. Das öffentliche Recht der Eidgenossenschaft, Zürich, 1855, 2 vols. —**Dufour,** G. H., Der Sonderbundskrieg, Bâle, 1882.

**Eckhardus,** Jr. (monk of St. Gall) St. Galler Kloster-Chronik, Leipsic, 1891. —**Egli,** S. E., Die schlacht bei Kappel, Zurich, 1873. —**Elgger,** C. von, Kriegswesen und Kriegskunst der schweizerischen Eidgenossenschaft, Lucerne, 1873. — **Escher,** H., Die Glaubensparteien in der Eidgenossenschaft, Frauenfeld, 1882. — **Etterlin von Lucerne,** Petermann, Kronica von der löblichen Eydtgnoschaft, Bâle, 1507.

*Petermann Etterlin,* captain of Lucernois in the wars of Burgundy, was the first to give to the world a veritable Swiss chronicle. A good deal of fiction is mixed with his facts, but we glean from his writings many interesting details of the scenes in which he was an actor.

**Fassbind,** T., Geschichte von Schwyz, Schwyz, 1832–1838, 5 vols. — **Feddersen,** Geschichte der Schweizerischen Regeneration, Zurich, 1867. — **Fetscherin,** W., Die eidgenössischen Abschiede aus den Jahren 1814 bis 1848. — **Fiala,** F., Archives pour l'histoire de la Réformation en Suisse, 1868–69, 2 vols. — **Fleury,** J., Franc-Comtois et Suisse, Besançon, 1869.

*Jean Fleury,* professor of French literature at St. Petersburg, member of numerous societies of savants in France, England, and Russia, was born at Vasteville, Feb. 14, 1816. He has published a considerable quantity of political, literary, pedagogical, and other papers, besides numerous books on a variety of subjects.

**Forel,** F., Introduction de Regeste des documents de la Suisse romande, Lausanne, 1862. — **Freeman,** E. A., "The Landsgemeinde of Ury and Appenzell," in *History of Federal government,* London, 1863. — **Froment,** A., Acts et gestes merveilleux de la cité de Genève, 1548.

*Froment* was a continuator of the chronicles of Bonivard and of Jeanne de Jussie. —**Furrer,** P., Geschichte von Wallis, Sitten, 1850–1854, 4 vols.

**Galiffe,** J. B. G. (fils) Genève historique et archéologique, Geneva, 1869–72, 2 vols. — **Galiffe,** J. A., (père) Notices généalogiques. — **Gaullier,** E. H. La Suisse en 1847, Geneva, 1848. — **Gaullier,** E. H. A., and **Schaub,** C., La Suisse historique et pittoresque, Geneva, 1855–6, 2 vols.; Les armoiries et les couleurs de la Confédération et des cantons suisses, Geneva and Bâle, 1879. — **Gelpke,** Kirchengeschichte der Schweiz, Bern, 1856–1861, 2 vols. — **Gingins la Sarra,** F. de, Épisodes des Guerres de Bourgogne, Lausanne, 1850. — **Gisi,** W., Quellenbuch zur Schweizergeschichte, Berne, 1869. — **Grandpierre,** L., Mémoires politiques, Neuchâtel, 1877. — **Gelzer,** H., Die zwei ersten Jahrhunderte der Schweizergeschichte, Bâle, 1840; Die zwei letzten Jahrhunderte der Schweizergeschichte, Aarau and Thun, 1838–39. — **Gregory** of Tours, Historia Francorum. — **Grasser,** J. J., Schweizerisch Heldenbuch, Basel 1624. — **Grote,** G., Seven letters on the recent politics of Switzerland, London, 1847. — **Guérard,** Polyptyque d'Irminon, Paris, 1844, 2 vols. — **Guillimann de Fribourg,** F., De rebus helvetiorum, 1598.

*François Guillimann* (or more properly Vuillemain), a distinguished savant, was born at Romont, a canton of Fribourg. He taught at Solothurn, afterwards became professor of history at Fribourg and historiographer to the emperor Rudolf II. His death is variously placed at 1612 and 1623. Besides numerous poems he has left us valuable historical works.

**Gut,** Der Überfall in Nidwalden, Stanz, 1862. — **Guye,** P. H., Die Schweiz in ihrer politischen Entwickelung als Föderativ-Staat, Bonn, 1877.

**Haller,** C. L. von, Geschichte der Wirkungen und Folgen des österreichischen Feldzugs in der Schweiz, Weimar, 1801; Histoire de la Réforme protestante dans la Suisse occidentale, Lausanne, 1828.

*Charles Louis von Haller,* grandson of the great Albert von Haller, was born at Bern in 1768 and died at Solothurn May 17, 1854. In 1806 he was elected member of the two councils and was ejected from both in 1821 when it became known that he had embraced Catholicism. He sojourned for a time in France, but returned in 1830 to Solothurn, where he died at an advanced age.

**Haller,** C. L. de, Helvetischen Annalen. — **Heer,** J., Jahrbuch des Historie-Vereins des Cantons Glarus; Heft, 1865. — **Hegel,** C., Stadtchroniken, Leipsic, 1862–64, 19 vols.; Scriptores rerum Germanicarum, Munich, 1885.

*Charles Hegel,* an eminent German historian, son of the celebrated philosopher, was born at Nuremburg June 7, 1813; since 1856 he has been professor of history at the University of Erlangen.

**Heierli,** J., Urgeschichte der Schweiz, Bern, 1901.

*Jacque Heierli,* Swiss litterateur, was born October 11, 1853, at Herisan (Appenzell); he devoted himself to pedagogy and has made the whole of the north of Europe the field of his researches.

**Henne,** A., Schweizerchronick, St. Gallen, 1840. — **Henne-am-Rhyn,** O., Geschichte von St. Gallen, 1863; Geschichte des Schweizervolkes, Leipsic, 1865, 3 vols.— **Hermann le Paralytique** (monk of Reichenau), Chronicon de sex ætatibus mundi, Bâle, 1529.

*Hermann of Reichenau,* surnamed the Paralytic on account of a contraction of the limbs, was the son of a count of Wehringen, born in 1013. In spite of his physical affliction he was possessed of unusual intelligence, and he became at an early age the most learned man of his day. He embraced the monastic life. He became abbot of Reichenau, where he died in 1054. He continued his chronicle up to the day of his death, after which it was continued by Berthold de Constance.

**Herminijard,** A. L., Correspondance des Réformateurs, Bâle, 1546; Harlem, 1868. — **Heusler,** A., Der Bauernkrieg von 1653, in der Landschaft Basel. (Bâle, 1864); Verfassungsgeschichte der Stadt Basel, Bâle, 1860. — **Hidber,** B., Schweizerisches Urkundenregister, Bern, 1863–1877, 2 vols.

*Basil Hidber,* Swiss historian, born at Mels, November 23, 1817 ; professor of natural history at the University of Bern.

**Hilty,** C., Vorlesungen über die Helvetik, Bern, 1878 ; Die Bundes Verfassung der schweizerischen Eidgenossenschaft, Bern, 1891.

*Charles Hilty,* Swiss jurisconsult, born at Werdenberg, February 28, 1833 ; called in 1873 to the chair of common (public) and federal law in the University of Bern.

**Hisely,** J. J., Cartulaire de Hautcrest ; sur l'origine et le développment des libertés des Waldstätt, Uri, Schwyz, et Unterwalden, Lausanne, 1839 ; Histoire du comte de Gruyère, Lausanne, 1855. — **Hodler,** Geschichte des Sweizervolkes, neuere Zeit., 1865. — **Herzog,** J. A., Das Referendum in der Schweiz, Berlin, 1885. — **Hottinger,** J. J., Das Wiedererwachen der wissenschaftlichen Bestrebungen in der Schweiz während der Mediations und Restaurations-epoche ; Vorlesungen über die Geschichte des Untergangs der alten Eidgenossenschaft, Zurich, 1844 ; Vorlesungen über den Untergang der schweizerischen Eidgenossenschaft, Zurich, 1866 ; Geschichte der Eidgenossen, Zurich, 1825–1827, 2 vols.

*Johann Jacob Hottinger,* born in 1783, professor of Greek at Zurich, must not be con-founded with Jean Jacques Hottinger, also a professor at Zurich, who died in 1819.

**Hug,** L., and **Stead,** P., The story of Switzerland, New York, 1890. — **Hutten,** U. von, Œuvres complètes, Berlin, 1822–1825, 5 vols.

**Imhof,** J. (Bourcard Leu) Die Jesuiten in Luzern. — **Istria,** Dora d', Switzerland, London, 1858, 2 vols.

**Jahn,** H. A., Chronik des Cantons Bern, Bern, 1857; Der Keltische Alterthum der Schweiz, Bern, 1860.

*Henry Albert Jahn,* Swiss historian and archæologist, professor at Bern, formerly secretary of the department of the interior, was born at Bern, October 9, 1811.

**Johannes Vitoduranus,** Chronicon, Zurich, 1856. — **Jovius,** P., Historiæ sui temporis, Bâle, 1567, 2 vols. — **Jullien,** Histoire de Genève, 1865. — **Jussie,** Jeanne de, Levain de calvinisme, 1605.

A religious abbess of the convent of St. Claire, whence she was driven in 1535, together with the other members of the community, to seek refuge at Annecy, where she later became abbess. She has pictured for us in all its crudity the conflict of popular passions in the most primitive style, and in language, which is in itself an index to the comedy, the tragedy, and the overwhelmingly gross superstition of her day and generation.

**Justinger,** C., Bernerchronik, Bern, 1871.

**Keller,** A., Die kirchlich politischen Fragen bei der Eidg. Bundesrevision von 1871. — **Klingenberger,** Chronik, Gotha, 1861.—**Königshofen,** J. von, Chronique helvetique.—**Königs-hoven,** von Strasbourg, J. T., Chronicum latinum, Strasburg, 1678.

*Jacques Twinger Königshoven,* better known under the name of Twinger, a celebrated chronicler of the 14th century, was born at Strasburg in 1346, of rich and influential parents. At the age of thirty-six he changed his condition of citizen for the ecclesiastical state and died in 1420, aged seventy-four years.

**Kopp,** J. E., Urkunden zur Geschichte der Eidgenössischen Bunde, 1835 ; Geschichte der Eidgenössischen Bunde, Leipsic and Berlin, 1844-52, 11 vols.

**Laharpe,** F. C., Mémoires, Bern, 1864. — **Liebenau,** T. von, Blicke in die Geschichte Engelbergs, 1876 ; Die Schlacht bei Sempach, Luzern, 1886 ; Indicateur de l'histoire suisse, 1876 ; Die Böcke von Zurich, Stanz., 1876. — **Lavater,** J. C., Letter to the French Directory, London, 1799. — **Lütolf,** Die Glaubensboten der Schweiz, Luzern, 1871.

**Mallet,** J., Considérations sur la Révolution, Brussels, 1793. — **Mallet-Dupan,** J., Mém-oires historiques et littéraires, Geneva, 1779–1782, 5 vols.— **Mallet,** P. H., Histoire des Suisses ou Helvétiens, Geneva, 1803, 4 vols.

*Paul Henri Mallet,* an eminent historian, was born at Geneva in 1730, of a family remark-able for the number of great men it has produced. He held the position of professor of history in several universities, and was a member of the academies of Upsala, Lyons, Cassel, and the Celtic Academy. He died of a paralytic stroke in the city of his birth, February 8, 1807.

**Marsauche,** L., La Confédération Helvétique, Neuchâtel, 1890. — **Matile,** G. A., Monu-ments de l'histoire de Neuchâtel, Musée historique, 3 vols. — **May de Romainmotier,** E., Histoire militaire des Suisses, Bern, 1772, 2 vols.

*E. M. de Romainmotier* was born at Bern in 1734, and became known to the world chiefly through the military history. This, though a somewhat mediocre production as a literary work, contains important facts not to be found elsewhere.

**McCracken,** W. D., Rise of the Swiss Republic, New York, 1901. — **Mémoires et Documents** publiés par la Société de la Suisse romande, Lausanne. — **Meyer von Knonau,** Gerold, Eidg. Abschiede ; St. Gallische Geschichtsquellen, St. Gall, 1870–81, 5 vols.; Die Sage

von der Befreiung der Waldstätte, Bâle, 1873. — **Meyer,** H., Die Denare und Bractealen in
der Schweiz, Zurich, 1858–60 ; Geschichte der XI^e und XXI^e Legion, Mittheilungen de
Zürich, Zurich, 1853. — **Meyer,** J., Geschichte des schweiz. Bundesrechts, Zurich, 1849–1852,
2 vols. — **Meyer von Knonau,** Ludwig, Handbuch der Geschichte der schweizerischen Eidgenossenschaft, Zurich, 1843, 2 vols.

*Louis Meyer von Knonau* was born at Zurich September 12, 1769. He studied history,
law, and philology at Halle, where he became an ardent disciple of Professor Wolf. He filled
various diplomatic offices with firmness and intelligence, retired to private life in 1839, and died
September 6, 1841. His history of the confederation is one of the most accurate and complete
at the disposition of the student. His son, Gerold, born March 2, 1804, followed in his father's
footsteps and devoted himself to public life. The government confided to his care the
archives of Zurich and charged him with the publication of the documents of the federal diet.
He died November 1, 1858.

**Miles,** H., Chronik, St. Gall., 1902. — **Mohr,** T. von, Die Regesten der Benedictiner-Abtei
Einsiedeln, Chur., 1848. — **Mommsen,** T., Römische Geschichte, Berlin, 1885, 5 vols. ; Inscrip-
tiones Confœderationis helveticæ, Mitt. d. antiq. Ges., Zurich, vols. 10 and 15.

*Theodor Mommsen,* an eminent historian, was born Nov. 30, 1817, at Garding, Schleswig,
of a Danish family. He was displaced in 1852 from the chair of law at Leipsic for partisanship
in political events, but was immediately called to that of the University of Zurich. During the
Franco-Prussian War he was among the bitterest enemies of France.

**Monnard,** C., Histoire de la Confédération suisse, Zurich, 1847–1853, 5 vols.

*Charles Monnard* was born in 1790, and died at Bonn in 1865. His chief labour was the
continuation of the history of Switzerland by J. von Müller. His classic style is apt to strike
us of to-day as too stilted, but it is easily overlooked in the appreciation due to his solid merit,
his simple modesty, his generous and liberal spirit.

**Moor,** Theodore, Historisch-chronologischer Wegweiser, Chur., 1873 ; Wegweiser durch
da Curratien, 1873. — **Morel,** G., Mémoires et documents de la Soc. d'histoire de la Suisse
romande; Die Regesten der Benedictiner-Abtei Einsiedeln.—**Morell,** C., Die helvetische
Gesellschaft.— **Morf,** H., in Dittes Pädagogium for 1878.— **Morin,** A., Précis de l'histoire politique de la Suisse, Genève and Paris, 1856-75.— **Müller, J.** von, Der Geist der Ahnen oder die
Einheitsbestrebungen in der Schweiz vor der helvetischen Revolution, Zurich, 1874; Geschichte
der schweizerischen Eidgenossenschaft, 1841–1847, 7 vols. ; Indicateur d'antiquités suisses, 1875 ;
Schweizergeschichte, Lausanne, 1795–1801, 11 vols. ; Der Geschichten Schweizerischer Eidgenossenschaft, Leipsic and Zurich, 1805–16, 5 vols.— **Müller-Friedberg,** Schweizerische Annalen,
1830, 6 vols. — **Muralt,** C., Schweizergeschichte mit durchganziger Quellenangabe, Bern, 1885.

**Nayler,** F. H., History of Helvetia, London, 1801, 2 vols. — **Nisard, M.,** Études sur la
renaissance, Paris, 1855. — **Nuscheler,** A., Die Siechenhäuser in der Schweiz, Zurich, 1866.

**Ochs,** Geschichte der Stadt und Landschaft Basel, Bâle, 1796–1822, 8 vols. — **Ochsenbein,**
Die Kriegsgründe und Kriegsbilder des Burgunderkrieges, 1876. — **Oe,** Die Anfänge der
schweizerischen Eidgenossenschaft, Zurich, 1891. — **Oechsli,** W., Lehrbuch für den Geschichts-
unterricht, Zurich, 1885 ; Quellenbuch zur Schweizergeschichte, Zurich, 1886 ; Die Anfänge
der schweizerischen Eidgenossenschaft, Zurich, 1891.

*William Oechsli,* born October 6, 1851, at Riesbach, was destined by his family to the
ministry; but he deserted theology for history, and after exhaustive study at Heidelberg,
Berlin, and Paris, he was called in 1887 to the professorship of Swiss history in the Zurich
Polytechnical Institute.

**Orelli,** A. von, Das Staatsrecht der schweizerischen Eidgenossenschaft, Fribourg, 1885.

**Pierrefleur,** P. de, Mémoires.

*The Memoirs of Pierre de Pierrefleur,* grand banneret of Orbe, present an accurate picture
of the progress of the Reformation. Modestly and without recrimination, though himself an
ardent Catholic, he endeavours accurately to reproduce day by day the scenes which pass before
his eyes — truth without passion, simplicity without grossness his chief object. Moderation is
the keynote of this recital from the lips of the pious and honourable knight of Orbe. Unfortunately, the original chronicle having been lost, we are obliged to content ourselves with extracts.

**Peyssonel,** C. C., de, Discours sur l'alliance de la France avec les Suisses et les Grisons,
Paris, 1790. — **Pfyffr,** C., Sammlung kleiner Schriften, Zurich, 1866. — **Pirkheimer,** W.,
Historia belli Suitensis sive Helvetici, Tiguri, 1735. — **Planta,** P. C. von, Die Schweiz in ihrer
Entwicklung zum Einheitsstaate. — **Pupikofer,** Geschichte des Thurgaus, Bischoffzell, 1830. —
**Pury,** S. de, Chronique des chanoines de Neuchâtel, Neuchâtel, 1839.

**Rahn,** J. N., Geschichte der bildenden Künste in der Schweiz, Zurich, 1876. — **Rambert,**
E., Les Alps suisses, Geneva, 1875.

*Eugene Rambert,* born in 1830, first turned his studies in the direction of theology, but at
twenty-four he was appointed to the chair of French literature at Lausanne, which he
occupied until the Confederation called him to the Polytechnical School. His sojourn at
Zurich lasted twenty-one years, when, in 1881, he returned to his own canton. He was not

long, however, to breathe his native air, his laborious career being suddenly cut short in 1886. His works are numerous and varied, but all are remarkable for great power, authority, and calm.

**Rauchenstein,** H., Der Feldzug Cæsars gegen die Helvetier, Zurich, 1882. — **Relatio Conflictus Laupensis.** — **Reportorium** der Abschiede der Eidgenössischen Tagsatzungen, 1803–1848, 3 vols. (Additional reports of the old federal diets). — **Rilliet,** A., Les Origines de la Confédération suisse, Geneva, 1868. — **Rochholz,** Eidgenössische Liederchronik, Bern, 1835. — **Rodt,** E. von, Die Feldzüge der Schweizer gegen Karl den Kühnen. Geschichte des bernischen Kriegswesens, Schaffhausen, 1843–1844, 2 vols. — **Roget,** Amédée, Les Suisses et Genève, Geneva, 1864; Histoire du peuple de Genève, Geneva, 1870–83, 7 vols. — **Rossel,** V., Histoire littéraire de la Suisse romande, Bern, 1887–91, 2 vols. — **Rovéréa,** F. de, Mémoires, Bern. — **Ruchat,** A., Histoire de la Réformation en Suisse, Lausanne, 1727–28.

*Abraham Ruchat,* the father of Swiss (French) history, was born in 1678 of a peasant family. Educated in Germany and Holland, he returned to Switzerland to become professor of history at the University of Lausanne. The *Histoire de la Réformation en Suisse* was but a part of a projected general history of Switzerland which was never completed. Ruchat says of his labours : " I have been tempted nine times to give up the enterprise and live in peace ; but the desire to serve my country has ever reinvested me with courage. I seek not glory, but truth and the public good. I have always endeavoured to write as though some day I were to be called to account for the products of my pen."

**Sarnen,** Livre blanc de Sarnen, in Les Origines de la Confédération suisse, by A. Rilliet, Geneva, 1868. — **Schilling,** D. (the younger), Luzerner Chronik, Luzern, 1862. — **Schreiber,** H. Loriti Glareanus, Fribourg, 1878. — **Schuler,** M., Geschichte des Landes Glarus ; Thaten und Sitten der Eidgenossen, Zurich, 1856, 7 vols. — **Secrétan,** E., Galérie suisse, Biographies Nationales, Lausanne, 1874. — **Seehausen,** R., Schweizer Politik während des dreissigjährigen Krieges, Halle, 1882. — **Segesser,** P. von, Eidgenössische Abschiede, Staats- und Rechtsgeschichte von Luzern, Lucerne, 1839–1856, 17 vols. — **Simmler,** J., Vom Regiment der löblichen Eidgenossenschaft, Zurich, 1576. — **Steiger,** R. de, Coup d'œil général sur l'histoire militaire des Suisses, Lausanne, 1869. — **Steinauer,** Geschichte des Freistaates Schwyz, Einsiedeln, 1861. — **Stettler,** M., Annales oder Beschreibung der vornehmeten Geschichten, Bern, 1626, 2 vols. — **Studer,** H., Till-Eulenspiegel im Lande des Tell, Zurich, 1900. — **Strickler,** J., Lehrbuch der Schweizergeschichte, Zurich, 1874, Aktensammlung der helvetischen Republik, Frauenfeld, 1899; Die Quellen zur Reformationsgeschichte, 1884. — **Stumpf,** J., Swiss Chronicle, Zurich, 1547.

**Tageblatt der Gesetze und Dekrete der gesetzgebenden Räthe der Helvetischen Republik,** Bern, 1800, 6 vols. — **Tillier,** J. A. von, Geschichte der Eidgenossen während der Zeit des sogeheissenen Fortschrifts, Bern, 1853–1855, 3 vols.; Geschichte der Eidgenossenschaft während der sogenannten Restaurationsepoche, Zurich, 1848–1850, 3 vols.; Geschichte der Eidgenossen während der Herrschaft der Vermittlungsakte, Zurich, 1845–1846, 2 vols.; Geschichte des Freistaates Bern, Bern, 1838–1839, 5 vols.; Geschichte der helvetischen Republik, Bern, 1843, 3 vols. — **Tschudi,** A., Chronicon Helveticum, Basel, 1734–1736, 2 vols.

The most complete of the early Swiss chronicles and the basis of Müller's history.

**Vaucher,** P., Esquisses d'histoire Suisse, Lausanne, 1882. — **Vieusseux,** A., History of Switzerland, London, 1846. — **Vincent,** J. M., State and Federal Government of Switzerland, Baltimore, 1891. — **Vischer,** W., Geschichte det Schwäbischen Städtebünde, Götingen, 1861. — **Vita S. Galli,** Translated by A. Potthast in Die Geschichtschreiber der deutschen Vorzeit, Vol. 1, Berlin, 1857. — **Vögeli,** Vaterländische Geschichte, Zurich, 1872. — **Vogelin,** A. and **Escher,** Geschichte der schweizerischen Eidgenossenschaft, Zurich, 1854, 4 vols. — **Vulliemin,** L., Histoire de la Confédération suisse, Lausanne, 1875–1876, 2 vols.

*Louis Vulliemin* was the founder of the *Société d'histoire de la Suisse romande,* together with Felix Chavannes the poet and F. de Gingins the historian. Imaginative, ardent, patriotic, variously gifted, Vulliemin devoted all his talent to his country's use, and merits the eternal gratitude of Switzerland.

**Wattenwyl,** Geschichte der Stadt und Landschaft Bern, Schaffhausen, 1867–1872, 2 vols. — **Weidmann, Father,** Geschichte der Landschaft St. Gallen, St. Gall, 1834. — **Wild,** K., Auszüge aus handschriftlichen chroniken und aus den Rathsprotokollen der Stadt und Republik St. Gallen, St. Gall, 1847. — **Wilson,** J., History of Switzerland, London, 1832. — **Wirth,** Statistik der Schweiz, Zurich, 1871–75, 3 vols. — **Wittekind** (monk of Corvey), Chronique. — **Wyss,** G. von, Geschichte der Historiographie in der Schweiz, Zurich 1895. — Indicateur d'histoire de Soleure, Solothurn, 1866.

*J. G. von Wyss,* Swiss historian, born at Zurich March 31st, 1816, is the son of the burgomaster David von Wyss. He was appointed president of the *Société d'histoire suisse* in 1854, and is universally recognised as among the most learned of the historians of the century.

**Zellweger,** J. K., Geschichte des Appenzellischen Volkes, Trogen, 1830 ; Chronologische Uebersicht der Schweizergeschichte, Zurich, 1887 ; Geschichte der diplomatischen verhältnisse der Schweiz mit Frankreich, Bern, 1848. — **Zschokke,** J. H., Histoire de la lutte des cantons démocratiques, Geneva and Paris 1823 ; History of the Invasion of Switzerland by the French, translated by J. Aiken, London, 1803.

# A CHRONOLOGICAL SUMMARY OF THE HISTORY OF SWITZERLAND

## BEFORE THE ROMAN CONQUEST

**Before 3000 B.C.** (Stone Age.) The lake-dwellers, the earliest people of which traces remain in what is now Switzerland, live in primitive huts built on piles in the shallow waters of various lakes. They do not know the use of metal; use stone axe-heads, fixed in stag's horn and wood hafts, flint arrow-heads, etc.

**3000-1000 B.C.** (Bronze Age.) The lakemen learn to manipulate metal; advance in skill and mental culture; make artistically shaped bronze spear-heads, swords, etc.

**1000-100 B.C.** (Iron Age.) The lakemen substitute iron for bronze and achieve greater beauty and perfection of workmanship. Their weapons and implements become gradually identical with those of historic times. In their later days they come into contact with Gauls and Romans.

**107 B.C.** The Helvetians, one of the chief of the tribes then inhabiting Switzerland, led by the clan of the Tigurini and under command of their chief Diviko, joined the Cimbri and Teutones in a raid into southern Gaul. The allies defeat the Romans, under the consul Lucius Cassius, at Agen, and overrun Gaul.

**102 B.C.** The barbarians are defeated by the Romans under the consul Marius near Aquæ Sextiæ and one clan of the Helvetians, that of the Toygeni, is annihilated.

**101 B.C.** Another division of the invading barbarians is cut to pieces by the forces of Marius and his colleague Catullus, near Vercelli. The Helvetian clan of the Tigurini alone escapes.

**60 B.C.** The Helvetians prepare for a second migration into Gaul. A powerful chief, Orgetorix, promises to secure free passage through the lands of the Allobroges and Ædui. He is accused of treason and dies, by suicide or murder.

**58 B.C.** The Helvetians, accompanied by the Boii and neighboring tribes, begin the march. Julius Cæsar checks the Helvetians at the Rhone, and destroys the Tigurini at return home. the Arar (Saône). At Bibracte Cæsar defeats the Helvetians. Their remnants

## UNDER ROMAN DOMINION

**57 2.3.** Cæsar's lieutenant, Sergius Galba, subdues the Helvetian Veragri and Seduni. Helvetia is made a Roman province.

**52 B.C.** The Helvetians take part in the revolt of Vercingetorix.

**43 B.C.** Romans settle at Noviodunum (Nyon) and in various other parts of Helvetia.

**27 B.C.** Helvetia is made part of Belgica, one of the provinces of Gaul, and comes more directly under Roman control.

**15 B.C.** Rhætia (the Grisons) is subjugated by armies under Drusus and Tiberius Nero and made a Roman province.

**A.D. 69** Aulus Cæcina lays waste Helvetia and massacres large numbers of the inhabitants. Claudius Corius, a Helvetian deputy, by his eloquence saves the people from complete destruction. Aventicum (Avenches) becomes a Roman city of .mportance. Roman civilisation makes much progress in Helvetia, especially in the western portion. Under the Romans military roads and fortresses are built.

## FROM THE GERMAN INVASIONS THROUGH THE CARLOVINGIANS

**260** Hordes of Alamanni devastate Switzerland. They partially destroy Aventicum.

**300** Christianity makes some converts in Switzerland.

**305** Alamanni again overrun Switzerland.

**406** The Alamanni conquer eastern Switzerland.

**409** The Burgundians march toward the Rhine and approach Switzerland.

**443** The Burgundians settle in western Switzerland, receiving "Sabaudia" (Savoy) from the Romans.

496 The Franks subjugate the Alamanni, acquiring eastern Switzerland.
493 The Goths conquer Rhætia.
500 King Gondebaud rules in Burgundy. His laws become part of Swiss institutions.
524 The Franks, under Clodomir, capture Geneva.
534 The Franks subjugate the Burgundians, bringing western Switzerland into their power.
536 Rhætia is given up to the Franks by the Goths.
570 The Langobardi invade southern Switzerland.
574 The Frankish king Gontran checks the incursions of the Langobardi.
610 The Culdee monks, led by Columbanus and Gallus, spread Christianity in Switzerland.
687 The Carlovingians begin their rule over the Franks. They foster religious establishments in Switzerland.
768 Charlemagne ascends the Frankish throne. He givs an impetus to religion, education, and industry in Switzerland; founds schools and churches and increases their wealth.
774 The Franks gain possession of the Italian valleys of Switzerland till then held by the Langobardi.
843 By the Treaty of Verdum western or Burgundian Switzerland falls to Lothair, eastern or German Switzerland (Alamannia) with Rhætia to Ludwig the German. Feudalism is becoming well established in Switzerland. The church owns large estates and the bishops are powerful. Arts and sciences progress in the monasteries of St. Gall, Reichenau, and Pfäffers.
853 Ludwig the German founds the Fraumünster at Zurich.

### TIME OF BURGUNDIAN AND ALAMANNIAN RULERS

888 Rudolf I is crowned king of Upper Burgundy and begins to rule over western Switzerland.
917 Count Burkhard of Rhætia is made duke of Alamannia (Swabia). He rules over eastern Switzerland.
919 Burkhard I, duke of Alamannia, defeats Rudolf II of Upper Burgundy at Winterthur.
920 Alamannia is formally incorporated with Germany. Eastern Switzerland thus becomes a part of Germany.
922 Rudolf II of Upper Burgundy marries Burkhard's daughter Bertha who brings to Burgundy the upper Aargau.
930 Rudolf II acquires Arelat (Cisjurane Burgundy) as the result of a raid into Italy with Hugo of Provence. Thus the kingdom of Burgundy is reunited and Switzerland, as an important part of this kingdom, attains prominence.
937 Rudolf II of Burgundy dies. Good Queen Bertha, his widow, rules beneficently as regent for her son Conrad.
940 Conrad is placed under the guardianship of Otto I of Germany. Beginning of German influence in western Switzerland.
950 Conrad defeats the Hungarians that invade Switzerland.
962 Queen Bertha founds a religious house at Payerne. (Traditional.)
990 Ekkehard II of St. Gall, the most famous man of learning of his time, dies.
992 The serfs rise against the nobles of Aargau and Thurgau.
993 Rudolf III of Burgundy. Switzerland is turned over more and more to the clergy and the great nobles.
1016 Rudolf III abdicates in favor of Henry II of Germany. Henry is opposed by the nobles of Burgundy in several battles in Switzerland.
1022 The distinguished scholar Notker III of St. Gall dies.

### FROM THE UNION OF SWITZERLAND UNDER THE GERMAN EMPERORS TO THE FOUNDING OF THE SWISS CONFEDERATION

1032 Conrad II of Germany defeats the Burgundians at Morat and Neuchâtel.
1033 He is crowned king of Burgundy and thus adds western Switzerland to Germany.
1038 Burgundy, Alamannia, and Rhætia fall to Henry III. All Switzerland is hereby reunited as part of Germany. St. Gall is a leader in learning. The abbeys of Zurich, Rheinau, and Einsiedeln and the bishoprics of Coire, Constance, and Bâle attain great eminence.
1045 Henry III of Germany by assuming the crown of Lombardy secures possession of all the territories of Switzerland not already within his dominions (Italian Switzerland). He is frequently at Bâle and Solothurn. He holds imperial diets at Zurich and lavishes gifts on her religious foundations.

1057 Rudolf of Rheinfelden begins his rule as duke of Alamannia and governor of Burgundy, thus controlling all Switzerland.

1077 Rudolf is elected king by the opponents of Henry IV. Switzerland is drawn into the struggle between Henry IV and Pope Gregory VII.

1080 Rudolf is slain and his army defeated at Mersburg. The Guelf-Zähringen faction wars against Frederick of Hohenstaufen for the possession of Alamannia. Many monasteries, castles, and towns are destroyed in Switzerland.

1090 Berthold II of Zähringen inherits the possessions of the Rheinfeldens in Switzerland.

1097 Berthold II surrenders his claims to the dukedom of Alamannia. He receives as recompense the imperial bailiwick of Zurich, and is made duke of that portion of Alamannia lying in what is now Switzerland.

1114 The people of Schwyz resist the encroachments of the monks of Einsiedeln. Henry V decides in favour of Einsiedeln.

1127 Conrad of Zähringen is created rector of Burgundy by the emperor Lothair. Most of the territories comprising modern Switzerland are now under the rule of the house of Zähringen. This family governs benevolently throughout the century.

1140 Arnold of Brescia finds asylum at Zürich.

1144 In the quarrel of Einsiedeln and Schwyz, Conrad III decides in favour of Einsiedeln.

1146 Bernard of Clairvaux preaches the crusade at Zurich. Many Swiss join the crusade.

1152 The Waldstätte are placed under an interdict by the bishop of Constance.

1173 By inheritance of the possessions of the house of Lenzburg in Aargau and in the forest states the house of Hapsburg gains in wealth and power.

1177 Berthold IV of Zähringen founds the free city of Fribourg.

1186 Berthold V. succeeds. He develops the policy of walling in strong cities to offset the power of the nobles. He fortifies Burgdorf, Moudon, Yverdon, Laupen, and Schaffhausen.

1190 Berthold V defeats the rebellious nobles at Avenches and in the Grindelwald.

1191 Berthold V founds the city of Bern.

1209 Franciscan monks begin to enter Switzerland.

1211 Berthold V is defeated by Count Thomas of Savoy, who seizes Moudon.

1215 Dominicans begin to enter Switzerland.

1218 Berthold V dies childless. With him the house of Zähringen and the rectorate of Burgundy ends. Switzerland reverts to Germany. Bern, Solothurn, Zurich, and other towns become immediately dependent on the emperor, and gain in freedom. Many nobles become subject to the empire alone and increase in power. The houses of Savoy, Kyburg (inheritors of the lands of the Zähringens), and Hapsburg become most prominent. Religious orders flourish.

1231 The people of Uri obtain their first charter from King Henry, which nominally places them directly under the empire.

1240 The community of Schwyz is given a charter from the empire by Frederick II. Savoy extends her dominion to include Vaud and other portions of Southern Switzerland.

1245-1250 The people of Switzerland take sides in the struggle between Guelfs and Ghibellines. Risings occur in the Waldstätte against the house of Hapsburg which has gained authority in middle and eastern Switzerland. The expulsion of oppressive bailiffs (referred to this period by modern investigators from its former position in 1307-08).

1250 Lucerne enters into alliance with Schwyz and Obwalden.

1254 The *antiqua confederatio*, the earliest league of the Waldstätte, is formed (uncertain date).

1255 Pierre of Savoy is acknowledged suzerain of Bern; later of Morat and Bâle.

1264 Pierre of Savoy is acknowledged suzerain of Geneva. The greatness of the house of Habsburg is founded through the inheritance of the possessions of the Kyburgs.

1266 Zurich with the aid of Rudolf of Habsburg defeats Ulrich of Regensburg. Rudolf gains in influence with several Swiss towns.

1267 Pierre of Savoy defeats an army sent against him by Rudolf of Habsburg at Löwenburg. Peace between Habsburg and Savoy.

1273 Rudolf of Habsburg besieges Bâle. He is chosen emperor of Germany. Bâle submits, Rudolf inherits the possessions of his cousins in the Waldstätte.

1275 Rudolf of Habsburg is consecrated emperor by Pope Gregory at Lausanne.

1277 Rudolf acquires Fribourg. He now holds in Switzerland territories equivalent to the modern cantons of Aar, Zug, Thurgau, Bern, and Lucerne, the towns of Sursee, Sempach, and Winterthur, the convent of Säckingen, and the wardenship of Waldstätte.

1288 Rudolf twice unsuccessfully besieges Bern.

1289 The Bernese suffer loss in an Austrian ambuscade at the Schosshalde and Bern compelled to make peace.

1291 The men of Uri, Schwyz, and Unterwalden (the three Waldstätte) form the Everlasting League (*Ewige Bund*), for the defence of their common rights and interests.

The Waldstätte form a temporary alliance with Zurich. In the struggle for the imperial throne between Adolf of Nassau and Albert, duke of Austria, the confederates with Zurich and Bâle side against Albert. War ensues. The territories of the bishop of Constance and the abbot of St. Gall are laid waste.

1292 The Austrians defeat the men of Zurich before Winterthur. Zurich is forced to make peace with Albert and her alliance with the forest states is annulled.

1294 The first Landsgemeinde of which record remains is held in Schwyz.

1297 Adolf of Nassau as king of Germany confirms the charter of 1240 to Schwyz and the same charter to Uri.

1298 The Bernese defeat the Austrian nobles at Dornbühl. Albert, duke of Austria, ascends the German throne and strengthens the power of Austria in Switzerland.

## THE FOURTEENTH CENTURY

1307 Werner Stauffacher of Schwyz, Walter Fürst of Uri, and Arnold of the Melchthal in Unterwalden, with thirty companions take an oath on the Rütli to free the country from oppressors. William Tell shoots the Austrain bailiff Gessler. (These events are now regarded as legendary.)

1308 The expulsion of the bailiffs. (This event some historians now regard as merely traditional and refer it to the period 1245-50.) King Albert is murdered. Bern concludes a league with Solothurn.

1309 Henry VIII confirms the charters of Schwyz and Uri, and grants liberties to Unterwalden, placing all three under direct imperial jurisdiction. The confederates renew their alliance with Zurich.

1314 The men of Schwyz capture the abbey of Einsiedeln because of a quarrel over pasture land. Frederick of Austria places the Waldstätte under the ban of the empire. The Waldstätte conclude alliances with Glarus, Ursern, Art, and Interlaken. Louis of Bavaria, rival of Frederick for the German throne, declares the ban removed. The confederates take his side in the struggle for the throne.

1315 Duke Leopold of Austria, brother of Frederick, moves against the Waldstätte. The Swiss vanquish the Austrians at Morgarten. Leopold is slain. The three forest districts renew the Everlasting League of 1291.

1316 Louis of Bavaria recognises the new league, declares the political rights of the house of Austria forfeit in the forest districts, and confirms their several charters.

1318 Truce with Austria. The Habsburgs surrender all jurisdiction over the Waldstätte, but their rights merely as landowners are recognized. Risings against Austria in western Switzerland. Leopold besieges the free town of Solothurn, but soon withdraws. (Traditional rescue of the Austrians at the bridge by the men of Solothurn.)

1323 Bern and other Burgundian towns enter into an alliance with the forest districts for protection against Austria and the aristocracy.

1328 Lucerne revolts from Austria.

1332 Lucerne (fourth of the "old" places) joins the league.

1336 Civic revolution in Zurich places Rudolf Brun at the head of the city government and gives power to the craft-guilds.

1339 The Bernese with men from the forest districts defeat the nobles at Laupen.

1350 Massacre of Austrian conspirators at Zurich. The men of Zurich destroy the castle of Rapperschwyl, Zurich thereby incurs the enmity of Austria.

1351 Zurich (fifth of the "old" places) for protection against Austria enters the league. First regulations as to the aid that the confederates owe to each other, first federal rights and establishment of the circle of confederate defence. Duke Albert of Austria unsuccessfully besieges Zurich.

1352 Zug and Glarus (sixth and seventh of the "old" places) enter the league. The duke of Austria renews war on Zurich. By the terms of the peace of Brandenburg, Zug and Glarus are again brought into subjection to Austria.

### THE CONFEDERATION OF THE EIGHT OLD PLACES

1353 Bern (completing the eight "old places) enters the league, adding greatly to its strength.

1354 Zurich is besieged by the forces of Austria and the empire.

1355 Peace is declared at Regensburg (Ratisbon).

1361 Charles IV recognises the confederation of eight states as a lawful union for the preservation of the public peace (*Landfriedensverbindung*).

1364 Zug is freed from Austrian rule by the men of Schwyz.

1367 The Gotteshausbund (league of God's house) is formed in the Engadine.

1368 The Peace of Thorberg adjusts matters between Austria and the confederates. Zug rejoins the league as a permanent member.

1370 The Parson's Ordinance (*Pfaffenbrief*) abolishes special exemption of the clergy and provides for the preservation of peace among the confederates.

1375 Enguerrand de Coucy to assert claims to lands in Aargau invades Switzerland with a horde of irregulars in the Guglerkrieg, or English War. De Coucy is routed in the Entlebuch and at Freibrunnen.

1382 Rudolf of Kyburg, of the Habsburg line, is defeated by Bern and Solothurn, in the Kyburg War.

1384 Bern and Solothurn take Thun, Burgdorf, and other places from Rudolf of Kyburg. The Kyburgs are forced to accept citizenship in Bern.

1385 The Swiss cities join the league of the south German towns. The men of Lucerne demolish Rotenburg, the residence of the Austrian bailiff.

1386 The forest districts come to the aid of Lucerne against Austria. The Swiss defeat the Austrians in spite of great odds in the battle of Sempach (Arnold Winkelried).

1388 The men of Glarus aided by a few from Schwyz defeat the Austrians at Näfels. Glarus is delivered from Austria.

1389 The confederates are secured in their conquests by a seven years' truce with Austria. Glarus permanently rejoins the league.

1393 Schöno's attempt to deliver Zurich to Austria fails. By the Sempach Ordinance (*Sempacher Brief*) the confederates are drawn closer together by provision for an army and for the preservation of order.

1394 The truce with Austria is prolonged for twenty years. The Swiss Confederacy is recognised and political dependence on Habsburg is practically at an end. The country hereafter is commonly known as *Die Schweiz* (Switzerland).

1395 Formation of the Upper (Grey) League in the western Grisons.

## THE FIFTEENTH CENTURY

1402 Revolt of the people of Appenzell and St. Gall against the abbot of St. Gall.

1403 The Appenzellers defeat the abbot's forces at Vögelinseck.

1405 The abbot's troops, assisted by an Austrian army, are defeated in the battle of the Rheinthal or Stoss.

1408 The Appenzellers are beaten at Bregenz.

1411 Appenzell is placed under the protection of the Swiss League (save Bern).

1412 The truce of the league with Austria is prolonged for fifty years. During the first half of the century the league increases its territory, not giving political rights, however, to the acquired lands.

1414 The council of Constance is convened. Switzerland is visited by great numbers of ecclesiastics and great nobles.

1415 Duke Frederick of Austria helps John XXIII escape from Constance. The emperor Sigismund places Frederick under the ban. By Sigismund's order the confederates conquer the Austrian Aargau. Bern receives the lion's share. The first common bailiwicks (*Freie Amter*) are established. Uprising of the Valais against the baron von Raron, a despotic ruler.

1416 Lucerne, Uri, and Unterwalden form an alliance with Upper Valais.

1417 Uri and Upper Valais take the Val d'Ossola from Savoy.

1422 The attempts of Uri and the confederates to acquire territory to the south of the Alps receive a check in their defeat by the Milanese at Arbedo.

1424 The Grey League is formally renewed.

1436 The league of the Ten Jurisdictions is formed in the eastern Grisons. Conflicting claims over the territories left by Frederick, count of Toggenburg, cause dissension between Zurich and Schwyz. The other confederates take sides with Schwyz.

1440 The men of Zurich invade Schwyz but are compelled to retreat. Felix Hämmerlin, humanist, furthers the new learning at Zurich.

1442 Zurich allies itself with Austria and resists federal jurisdiction. Civil war (the Old Zurich War) breaks out.

1443 The Zurich troops are defeated at Sankt Jacob on the Sihl. Stüssi, the burgomaster of Zurich is slain.

1444 Zurich is besieged by the confederates. Charles VII of France sends to her aid wild bands of the Armagnacs under command of the dauphin Louis. They slaughter the confederates, who make a heroic defence at Sankt Jacob on the Birs before Bâle.

1450 Peace is concluded. Zurich is forced to renounce her alliance with Austria.

1452 The Swiss League concludes treaty of friendship with France. A new class of allies, the associate districts (*Zugwandte Orte*), begins to gather round the league.

1458 The league forms an alliance with Rapperschwyl. Sigismund, duke of Austria, irritated by its loss declares war.

1460 The confederates overrun the Austrian Thurgau. This results in the second accession of common bailiwicks. The art of printing is established at Bâle. Founding of the University of Bâle. Material and artistic culture flourishes.

1461 Sigismund gives up Thurgau which comes under the protection of the confederates.

1463 The confederates renew the French treaty with Louis XI.

1467 Zurich purchases Winterthur from Sigismund. The league makes a treaty of friendship with Philip the Good, duke of Burgundy.

1468 The Swiss lay siege to Waldshut. Sigismund buys them off.

1469 Sigismund obtains the protection and financial aid of Charles the Bold of Burgundy. He gives as security Alsace, the Waldshut, and the Black Forest. The alliance of Charles with Sigismund violates the treaty of 1467 and incenses the Swiss. Charles the Bold commits the mortgaged lands to Peter von Hagenbach, as *vogt*. His severity is complained of by the Swiss.

1470 Louis XI of France makes a treaty with the Swiss to secure their neutrality.

1471 The three leagues of the Grisons confirm an earlier alliance.

1473 Sigismund becomes the ally of Louis, who aims to reconcile Sigismund and the Swiss and turn them against Charles the Bold.

1474 The confederates attempt in vain to get redress from Charles the Bold for the wrongs done by Hagenbach to their friends in Alsace. As the result of the efforts of Louis XI, the Everlasting Compact (*Ewige Richtung*) is signed at Constance. By it Sigismund renounces all Austrian claims on the lands of the confederates and they agree to support him. The freedom of the Swiss Confederation from the Habsburgs is now formally established. The Swiss and Sigismund join a league of the Alsatian and Rhine cities. Hagenbach is put to death with the connivance of Bern. The confederates at the instance of Sigismund declare war against Charles. Bern takes the lead in westward aggression. Héricourt is taken by the confederates.

1475 Further successes of the Swiss. Bern captures sixty towns in Vaud, fighting against Savoy, which has joined Charles the Bold. Bern and Upper Valais form an alliance and the latter prevents the passage of the Milanese troops of Savoy. The emperor and Louis desert the confederates.

1476 Charles the Bold captures Granson and has the garrison executed by two of their own comrades. The Swiss gain a glorious victory in the battle of Granson and retake the town. Rich spoils and revenge. Charles besieges Morat. In the battle of Morat the Swiss decisively defeat the Burgundians. By intervention of Louis XI an arrangement is made with Savoy by which for the first time French-speaking districts become connected with the confederation. Savoy loses Fribourg, Granson, Morat, Orbe, Echallens, and Aigle. Bern profits most.

1477 The Swiss and the troops of René, duke of Lorraine, defeat Charles the Bold at the battle of Nancy. The foundation of Swiss nationality is firmly laid by these victories, and the fame of Swiss arms is world-wide; but internal jealousies arise. Riots in various states. The band of the Mad Life. Zurich, Bern, Lucerne, Fribourg, and Solothurn form a separate league and a perpetual treaty (*Burgrecht*).

1478 The men of Zurich, Lucerne, Uri, and Schwyz defeat the Milanese at the battle of Giornico. Switzerland expands toward the south.

1480 Fribourg and Solothurn seek admission to the league. This demand is opposed by the rural members and supported by the towns belonging to the separate league of the Burgrecht.

1481 The Compact of Stanz (*Stanzer Verkomnis*) prevents disruption. Nicholas von der Fluhe aids to an understanding. Fribourg and Solothurn (the ninth and tenth members) are admitted to the confederation. The separate league of the towns is dissolved. Dangerous societies are forbidden. The compact concentrates the government of the confederation.

1489 Hans Waldmann, burgomaster of Zurich, attempts to subordinate the peasants. He is overthrown and executed.

1490 Insurrection against the federal government in St. Gall is put down.

1496 The Swiss refuse to obey the imperial chamber, objecting to taxation without representation. They refuse to join the Swabian League.

1497 The confederates conclude a perpetual league with the Grey League of the Grisons.

1498 The confederates conclude a perpetual league with the League of God's House (*Gotteshausbund*) of the Grisons.

1499 The Swiss go to the support of their allies in the Grisons against the emperor Maximilian and the Swabian League. Successes of the Swiss at Triesen, at Bruderholz near Bâle, at Calven, at Schwaderloo, and at Frastenz. The Swiss Confederation by the peace of Bâle secures freedom from German imperial regulations and rises to the rank of an allied state of the empire, having practical independence. The Swiss establish their rights in the Thurgau. The league of Ten Jurisdictions in the Grisons confirms an alliance with the Swiss League.

1500 Swiss mercenaries engaged by Louis Sforza surrender Novara to the French rather than fight the Swiss in the French army of Louis XII. By the help of the Swiss Milan becomes a property of France. The practice of Swiss serving in foreign armies has now become frequent.

## THE SIXTEENTH CENTURY

1501 Bâle and Schaffhausen (the eleventh and twelfth members) are admitted to the confederation.
1510 Schinner, bishop of Sitten, induces Swiss troops to aid in the expulsion of the French from Italy.
1512 The Swiss conquer Milan and drive the French out of Italy; declare Maximilian duke of Milan. In return the confederates receive Ticino and the Grisons leagues get the Valtellina, Cleves, and Bormio.

### THE CONFEDERATION OF THIRTEEN STATES

1513 Appenzell is admitted to the confederation, thus completing the confederation of Thirteen States. The Swiss defeat the French at Novara.
1515 Francis I defeats the Swiss at Marignano, breaking the Swiss power in northern Italy.
1516 The Swiss League concludes a treaty of Perpetual Peace with France. Hans Holbein at Bâle wins great reputation as a painter. His work marks the further advance of humanism in Switzerland.
1519 Ulrich (Huldreich) Zwingli preaches the Reformation at Zurich.
1521 Twelve states of the confederation (Zurich being restrained by Zwingli) conclude an alliance with France.
1522 The diet at Lucerne forbids the clergy to preach unauthorised doctrines.
1523 Zwingli's teaching is sanctioned by the council at two "disputations" at Zurich. Zurich pushes forward the work of the Reformation, but is not supported by the other confederates. The first ecclesiastics are publicly married.
1524 Under Zwingli's leadership Zurich dissolves the monasteries. The forest states prevail on the diet at Lucerne to pronounce for the old faith. Religious riots occur in the Thurgau. The monastery of Ittingen is burned down. The Reformation progresses in eastern Switzerland.
1525 The mass is discontinued at Zurich. The temporal rights of the Grossmünster are turned over to the state. The Carolinum, a school for humanists, founded by Zwingli and Zurich, is made a nursery of culture. Lausanne concludes an alliance with Fribourg and Bern. The disorders caused by the anabaptists are checked. The Swiss mercenaries are defeated with the French at Pavia.
1526 The disputation at Baden, Eck, and Faber, representing the Catholics, decides in favour of the old faith. Several executions follow. Geneva forms alliances with Bern and Fribourg.
1527 Evangelical coburghership of Zurich and Constance (*Evangelisches Burgrecht*). Execution of Max Wehrli, the Catholic bailiff in the Thurgau. Troubles in Toggenburg and St. Gall widen the breach between Catholics and Evangelicals.
1528 Bern joins Zurich and Constance in favour of religious freedom and is followed by Bâle, Schaffhausen, St. Gall and Mülhausen. The confederation is in danger of breaking up.
1529 Lucerne, Uri, Schwyz, Unterwalden, and Zug form the Christian Alliance (*Christliche Vereinigung*), and ally themselves with Austria. First war of Kappel. The Austrian alliance is annulled and religious parity for each member of the confederation is declared by the first Peace of Kappel.
1530 Genoa with confederate aid secures freedom from Savoy.
1531 Second war of Kappel. The Catholic members of the confederation advance on Zurich. Near Kappel the men of Zurich are defeated and Zwingli is slain. Second Peace of Kappel. The Reformation in Switzerland is considerably checked. Catholic reaction. The league is now completely split into Catholics and evangelicals.
1532 William Farel begins to preach the Reformation in Geneva.
1535 The Reformation is successfully planted in Geneva by Farel.
1536 Bern conquers Vaud and Lausanne and takes them from Savoy. Calvin comes to Geneva. The first Helvetic confession is published.
1538 By influence of the papal party Calvin is exiled from Geneva.
1541 Calvin returns to Geneva and there establishes a theoretic government, the *consistorium*. He enters upon a harsh rule, imprisoning and executing his opponents.
1548 Constance is captured by the Austrians in the war of Smalkalden and is cut off from the Swiss Confederation.

1549 Calvin's theological disputes with the Zurich reformers are partly settled by the Compromise of Zurich (*Consensus Tigurinus*).

1553 Michael Servetus is burned at he stake at Geneva at the instance of Calvin.

1555 Calvin expels from Geneva many who uphold municipal liberty and replaces them by foreigners. The city gains the name of the "Protestant Rome." Evangelicals driven out of Locarno take refuge in Zurich.

1559 Calvin founds the University of Geneva.

1564 Calvin dies. Théodore de Bèze succeeds him as head of the church. Emanuel Philibert, duke of Savoy, supported by the Catholic members of the league, demands back the districts seized by Bern in 1536. The Treaty of Lausanne restores several of them. The counter-Reformation (Catholic reaction) makes itself strongly felt in Switzerland. It is furthered by Carlo Borromeo, archbishop of Milan, and at Lucerne by Ludwig Pfyffer, the "Swiss king."

1565 The Catholic states of Switzerland ally themselves with Pope Pius IV.

1566 The second Helvetic Confession is published as a basis for union between the Calvinists and the Zurich reformers.

1574 The Catholic reaction advances by the establishment of the Jesuits at Lucerne.

1580 A papal nuncio comes to Lucerne. Borromeo founds at Milan the "Collegium Helveticum" for the education of Swiss priests.

1581 The Capuchins become active in Switzerland for the Catholic reaction.

1582 The Protestants object to the introduction of the Gregorian calendar.

1586 The Golden or Borromean League for support of Catholicism is formed by the seven Catholic members of the confederation (Uri, Schwyz, Unterwalden, Lucerne, Zug, Freiburg, Solothurn).

1588 The reformed states form a separate league with Strasburg.

1597 Appenzell is divided into two parts, "Inner Rhodes," Catholic, and "Outer Rhodes," Protestant.

## THE SEVENTEENTH CENTURY

1602 The Duke of Savoy attempts to get hold of Geneva (the "Escalade").

1620 Massacre of Protestants in the Valtellina. The valley is won for the Catholics. The Swiss Confederation remains nominally neutral in the Thirty Years' War, but various members become involved from time to time.

1622 The Austrians conquer the Prätigau.

1624 French troops take the Valtellina.

1629 The Valtellina is taken by the imperial troops.

1632 The Baden Compromise adjusts the religious status of the "common bailiwicks."

1635 The French once more capture the Valtellina.

1637 George Jenatsch with help of the Spaniards drives the French out of the Valtellina.

1639 The independence of the Grisons is established.

1648 By the Treaty of Westphalia the Swiss Confederation is formally separated from Germany and recognized as independent. Religious divisions continue to cripple the energy of the confederation. Poverty, a result of the Thirty Years' War, causes discontent.

1653 The Peasants' War breaks out in Bern, Solothurn, Lucerne, and Bâle because of the oppression of the governing class. The peasants form a league of Sumiswald. They are defeated at Wohlenschwyl.

1654 The Protestant Swiss intercede for the Waldenses. They win the friendship of Oliver Cromwell, who pays great honor to their envoys.

1655 Protestant fugitives from Schwyz find refuge in Zurich.

1656 The first Villmergen War results. Christopher Pfyffer of Lucerne with a body of Catholics defeats the Protestants at Villmergen. A treaty is concluded which provides for the individual sovereignty of each member of the confederation in religious matters.

1663 The confederation makes a treaty with Louis XIV of France, by which Protestant Swiss mercenaries are taken into the king's pay.

1668 As the result of encroachments by Louis in the Franche-Comté the confederates provide for joint action against outside enemies by putting into execution the agreement known as the Defensionale. French Protestant refugees find shelter in Switzerland.

## THE EIGHTEENTH CENTURY

1707 Pierre Fatio at the head of a committee of the council at Geneva demands a more liberal government.

1712 The abbot of St. Gall by his oppressions rouses the people of Toggenburg to insurrection. The second Villmergen War (or war of Toggenburg) between Catholics and Protestants from these troubles. The Catholics are defeated at Villmergen. The Treaty of Aarau assures the " common bailiwicks " religious liberty and gives advantages to the Protestants.

1715 The Catholic members of the confederation by the Truckli Bund agree to put France in the position of guarantor of the confederation. A period of decline. The con-.federation has little unity. Unsatisfactory relations of the classes.

1723 The conspiracy of Davel to free Vaud from the oppression of Bern is crushed.

1729 The " *Harten* " (hard ones) opponents of the government, and the " *Linden* " (soft ones) at Zug struggle for supremacy.

1732 The " Harten " gain a victory over the " Linden " in the Outer Rhodes of Appenzell.

1737 The democrats win a victory for liberal government in Geneva.

1744 Demands for a more liberal government are made in Bern.

1749 Hentzi's conspiracy attempts in vain to overthrow the oligarchy at Bern.

1748 Discontents of the common people cause disorder in Neuchâtel.

1755 Popular uprisings in the Leventina are crushed by the government of Uri.

1762 The Helvetic Society is founded and fosters aspirations for liberty. Rousseau, then a citizen of Geneva, publishes the *Contrat Social*. These books are publicly burned by order of the city government. The popular party wins in the Outer Rhodes of Appenzell.

1764 The " Harten " are victorious in Zug.

1768 Armed intervention of France, Zurich, and Bern in Geneva to suppress popular revolts of the " natives." Disorders occur in the patriciate of Lucerne.

1770 The " natives " rise in revolt in Geneva.

1777 All of the thirteen states of the confederation join in making a new alliance with France. Political disturbances occur in Zurich.

1780 The meetings of the Helvetic Society are forbidden.

1781 Anarchy in Geneva. Pastor Waser is executed at Zurich for opposition to the city government. France, Bern, and Sardinia intervene. Emigration from Geneva. Insurrection at Fribourg under Chenaux.

1784 Joseph Suter, a popular leader in the Inner Rhodes of Appenzell, is executed.

1789 The French Revolution begins to find sympathizers in Switzerland.

1790 Exiles from Vaud and Fribourg organise the Helvetic Club at Paris to spread the new ideas in Switzerland. The club stirs up risings in the western part·of the confederation. Lower Valais rises against the oppressive rule of the upper districts.

1792 Porrentruy defies the prince-bishop of Bâle; with the help of the French drives out the imperial troops; forms the Rauracian Republic. This afterward becomes the French department of Mont Terrible. Geneva is saved from France by a force from Zurich and Bern. Massacre of the Swiss guards at the Tuileries by the Paris mob. The diet of Aarau orders the recall of the Swiss regiments.

1793 A reign of terror begins in Geneva because of uprising of the " natives."

1794 The revolutionary party assumes control in Geneva. Arrests and murders. Demands for greater freedom are made at Stäfa in the territory of Zurich.

1795 A reaction sets in in Geneva. The insurrection at Stäfa is suppressed.

1797 Bonaparte incorporates the Italian bailiwicks of the Valtellina with the Cisalpine Republic. La Harpe calls on the Directory to protect the liberties of Vaud against the oppression of Bern.

## THE HELVETIC REPUBLIC

1798 French troops in response occupy Mülhausen, Bienne, and part of the lands of the prince-bishop of Bâle. Insurgents open the prison of Chillon. Another French army enters Vaud and the Lemanic Republic is proclaimed there. The French occupy Fribourg and solothurn; defeat the Bernese after fierce fighting at Neueneck; take Bern, the stronghold of the aristocratic party, and pillage the treasury. The Revolution triumphs over the Confederation. By order of the Directory, the Helvetic Republic, one and indivisible, is proclaimed. Peter Ochs of Bâle supplies a constitution. Ten of the thirteen members of the old confederation accept the new government. Twenty-three " cantons," or administrative districts, are created. The forest districts rebel. Their resistance, headed by Alois Reding, of Schwyz, is put down after desperate conflicts at Schindellegi, Morgarten, and at Rothenthurm. An insurrection of the mountaineers of Upper Valais against the French is bloodily repressed. The French put down an insurrection in Nidwald with great bloodshed. (The days of terror of Nidwald end.)

1799 Zurich, the forest cantons, and Rhætia become the scene of the struggle of the Austrian and Russians against the French in the wars of the Coalition.

## THE NINETEENTH CENTURY

1802 Strife between the centralists and the federalists. Bonaparte withdraws the French troops. The Helvetian government is driven from Bern. Bonaparte convenes Swiss statesmen at Paris in the *consulta,* and acts as mediator. The Frickthal, the last Austrian possession in Switzerland, is given to the Helvetic Republic by Bonaparte.

### THE CONFEDERATION OF NINETEEN CANTONS

1803 Napoleon's Act of Mediation is made the constitution of "Switzerland." This name for the first time is used as the official name of the country. The thirteen members of the old confederation are set up again and six new cantons are added. There are to be no more privileged classes or subject lands. Switzerland enjoys ten years of peace and prosperity.
1804 Insurrection breaks out at Horgen in the canton Zurich.
1806 Neuchâtel is given to Marshal Berthier.
1810 Valais, which has been a separate republic, is made into the French department of the Simplon. The Swiss Society of the Public Good is founded. Pestalozzi and Fellenberg work out an educational system.
1813 Austrian and Russian troops, supported by the reactionary party, enter Switzerland; the diet abolishes the constitution of 1803.
1814 "The long diet" at Zurich attempts to adjust party differences. Bern heads a party anxious to restore the old order. Zurich and the majority stand out for the nineteen cantons of Napoleon. The allies enter Switzerland.

### THE LEAGUE OF TWENTY-TWO STATES

1815 The Swiss diet accepts the decisions of the congress of Vienna and a new constitution, the Federal Pact, is adopted. The league of States (*Staatenbund*) is made to include twenty-two members. The sovereign rights of each canton are recognised. The federal diet exercises supreme sovereignty only in purely national concerns. The great powers at the congress of Vienna guarantee the neutrality of Switzerland. Switzerland is freed from subserviency to France. New aristocracies make themselves felt.
1817 Switzerland becomes a party to the Holy Alliance.
1819 The Helvetic Society again takes up political reforms.
1823 Freedom of the press is restricted under influence of the great powers. Intellectual reaction and ultra-montanism become noticeable and cause dissensions.
1830 The July revolution in Paris finds an echo in Switzerland. Twelve cantons reform their constitutions in a democratic sense. Popular demonstrations at the assembly of Uster.
1831 The aristocracy of Bern submits to liberal reforms.
1832 The cantons Zurich, Bern, Lucerne, Solothurn, St. Gall, Aargau, and Thurgau agree to united action looking toward reform (*Siebener Concordat*). They are opposed by the reactionary cantons, Uri, Schwyz, Unterwalden, Valais, and Neuchâtel which form the league of Sarnen (Sarner Bund).
1833 Bâle is divided into a rural (Baselland) and an urban (Baselstadt) half-canton because of the desire of the rural population for proportional representation the Diet.
1834 Political refugees to Switzerland increase to such an extent that measures are taken by the diet to prevent abuse of the privilege of asylum.
1835 Religious tumults in Aargau.
1836 Difficulties with France over tariff regulations. Religious tumults in the Bernese Jura.
1838 The Society of the Grütli is founded at Geneva.
1839 Reaction in Zurich against radicals and freethinkers. (Strauss' *Life of Jesus*).
1840 Clericals revolt against the radicals in Aargau.
1841 They are put down. Eight monasteries in Aargau are suppressed. The quarrel provokes disputes in the diet.
1843 The diet effects a compromise in the religious quarrel in Aargau by which four instead of eight of the monasteries are suppressed. The seven Catholic cantons, Uri, Schwyz, Unterwalden, Lucerne, Zug, Fribourg, and Valais hereupon form a separate league, the Sonderbund.
1844 The Sonderbund declares for the reopening of all the monasteries in Aargau. The

clericals in Lucerne, the Vorort, give high posts to Jesuits. Parties of free-lances attempt to capture the city.

1845 The attack on Lucerne is renewed but is unsuccessful. The radicals gain control in Zurich.

1846 The radicals become the majority in Bern and Geneva.

1847 The radicals get a majority in St. Gall. The diet in which the radicals are now in the majority declares the Sonderbund contrary to the Federal Pact. The diet resolves to revise the pact and asks the cantons to expel the Jesuits. The attempt to enforce the decree leads to the Sonderbund War. This is quickly ended by the defeat of the rebellious Catholic cantons at Gislikon, largely because of the good generalship of Dufour.

## SWITZERLAND AS A FEDERAL STATE

1848 A new constitution is accepted by the majority of the cantons. Switzerland becomes a federal state (*Bundesstaat*). A central government is organised consisting of a council of states (*Ständerath*), a national council (*National Rath*) and a federal council or executive (*Bundesrath*). German, French, and Italian are recognised as national languages. Bern is chosen the national capital.

1855 The federal polytechnic school is opened at Zurich. Improvements in the educational system are introduced.

1856 A royalist conspiracy in Neuchâtel is put down and causes a dispute between Switzerland and the king of Prussia, the overlord of Neuchâtel.

1857 Neuchâtel is definitely ceded to Switzerland.

1859 Switzerland posts troops on the Italian frontier to preserve neutrality in the Italian War and puts an end to foreign enlistments.

1860 The Swiss government protests against the cession of Nice and Savoy to France.

1861 French troops occupy the Vallée de Dappes.

1862 The question of the frontiers in the Vallée de Dappes is arranged with France by mutual cession of territory.

1864 The convention of Geneva introduces humanitarian reforms in warfare. Election riots at Geneva lead to bloodshed.

1865 International social science congress meets at Bern.

1866 Restrictions on religious liberty of Jesuits, etc., are removed. An attempt is made to revise the constitution in a democratic sense but fails.

1867 An international congress of workmen is held at Lausanne.

1869 The construction of the St. Gotthard tunnel is decided upon.

1871 Switzerland shelters French refugees of the Franco-German War though insisting on the maintenance of neutrality. The growth in power of the "old Catholics" causes disturbances in western Switzerland (the struggle against Ultramontanism). The Alabama Arbitration Commission meets in Geneva.

1872 An attempt at revision of the constitution is defeated by a small majority.

1873 Abbé Mermillod, appointed by the pope "apostolic vicar" of Geneva, is banished from Switzerland. The see of Bishop Lachat of Bâle is suppressed by several cantons because he upholds the doctrine of papal infallibility.

## SWITZERLAND UNDER THE CONSTITUTION OF 1874

1874 A new constitution, a revision of that of 1848, is accepted by the people. The referendum hereby becomes a part of the machinery of the federal government as it had already been part of that of most of the cantons. The new constitution increases centralisation in the government. The international postal congress meets at Bern and lays the foundation for the international postal union.

1876 Religious and political differences cause an armed encounter in Ticino.

1877 A law regulating the working hours in factories is passed, marking an advance in labour legislation.

1878 James Fazy, noted statesman, dies.

1879 Legislation puts an end to dissensions over the financiering of the St. Gotthard railway.

1882 The St. Gotthard railway is opened.

1883 Mermillod is appointed bishop of Lausanne.

1884 Bishop Lachat is made apostolic vicar of Ticino. An international conference is held at Bern to secure the protection of copyright.

1887 Alcohol is made a state monopoly.

1888 The creation of a see at Lugano excites the opposition of the radicals. An important law for the protection of patents is passed.

1889 Bismarck's spy Wohlgemuth is expelled. Germany protests. Difficulties arising out of the Swiss custom of granting political asylum are settled.

1890 Religious riot at Ticino. The principal compulsory insurance against sickness and accident is accepted by popular vote.

1891 The federal constitution is amended so that fifty thousand citizens by the "initiative" can compel the federal authorities to prepare and submit to the people any reform in the constitution demanded by the petitioners. The establishment of a state or federal bank is approved by the people. The purchase of the Central Railway by the confederation is rejected by popular vote.

1893 The killing of animals in Jewish fashion is prohibited by exercise of the initiative

1894 An attempt by the initiative to secure the adoption for the government of a socialist scheme to provide employment fails.

1896 A National exhibition is held at Geneva. Labour riots directed against the employment of Italians cause many of these to leave Zurich. The eighteenth international congress on copyright meets at Bern and takes steps for copyright reform in Germany and Great Britain.

1897 The national council adopts a bill authorising the confederation to purchase the five principal railroads when the terms of the concessions expire. The proposals of the government as to a federal bank are rejected by the people. An international congress for the protection of labour is held at Zurich. It votes in favour of the prohibition of Sunday labour except under special conditions, for the restriction of unhealthful trades and night-work, for the betterment of the conditions of employment for women and for a working day of eight hours by legal enactment.

1898 The government authorises the construction of the Simplon tunnel. The people vote for the unification of the cantonal laws civil and criminal into a set of federal codes. The principle of the purchase by the confederation of the principal railroads is approved by popular vote. The empress Elizabeth of Austria is assassinated by an Italian anarchist in Geneva. Expulsion of anarchists follows.

1899 The scheme for the establishment of the "double initiative" is launched. The law for the compulsory insurance of working men against sickness and accident is passed by the legislature.

1900 This proposal, however, is rejected by the people by a large majority. The proposals for proportional representation in the national council and for the election of the federal council by the people (the "double initiative") are rejected by popular vote.

## THE TWENTIETH CENTURY

1901 On representation of the Turkish government the federal council suppresses publications of the party of Young Turkey criticising the sultan for the Armenian massacres. Public opinion condemning the action of the council as a violation of the right of asylum finds expression in many places. Anti-Russian demonstrations are made at Geneva and Bern by socialists. The socialist movement gains in strength.

1902 Difficulties with Italy over the publication in an anarchist organ at Geneva of an article reflecting on the murdered king Humbert causes the temporary withdrawal of the diplomatic representatives of the two countries. A general strike in Geneva leads to disturbances which are put down by troops. The federal council issues a decree suppressing such religious congregations or orders as have not been authorised by law. The radical democratic majority in the national council is considerably strengthened.

1903 A new protective tariff is adopted by popular vote. The Zionist congress at Bâle votes to investigate Great Britain's offer of land in East Africa for Jewish colonisation.

1904 Arbitration treaty concluded with Great Britain, and new commercial treaties arranged with Germany and Italy. Construction of the Simplon tunnel hindered by discovery of hot springs.

1905 The north and south headings of the Simplon tunnel meet on February 24th. Arbitration treaties ratified with France, Austria, Italy, Belgium, Sweden, and Norway.

1906 Official inauguration of the Simplon tunnel by the president and the king of Italy, May 19th.

1907 The government petitioned to conduct a plébiscite prohibiting the sale of absinthe (Feb.). Proposals to build electric railway up the Matterhorn; and general railway activity. Strikes at Vevey, involving the calling out of the militia; agreement arrived at in April. People of Geneva vote for a separation of church and state.

# PART XXI

# THE HISTORY OF RUSSIA

BASED CHIEFLY UPON THE FOLLOWING AUTHORITIES

R. BELL, R. N. BESTUZHEV–RIUMIN, V. A. BILBASOV, A. BRÜCKNER, A. DE
HAXTHAUSEN, E. HERMANN, N. M. KARAMZIN, W. K. KELLY, N. I.
KOSTOMAROV, M. KOVALEVSKI, A. LEROY-BEAULIEU, P. MÉRIMÉE, NESTOR,
A. RAMBAUD, T. SCHIEMANN, J. H. SCHNITZLER, A. A. SCHUMAKR, N. K.
SHILDER, G. M. SOLOVIEV, P. STRAHL, N. TURGENIEV, D. M. WALLACE

TOGETHER WITH A STUDY OF

## THE INTELLECTUAL DEVELOPMENT OF RUSSIA

BY

## A. S. RAPPOPORT

WITH ADDITIONAL CITATIONS FROM

ALEXANDER II, A. ALISON, R. N. BAIN, T. VON BERNHARDI, A. J. BEVERIDGE,
CATHERINE II, A. P. DE CUSTINE, T. DELORD, J. ECKHARDT, A. DE
FERRAND, I. GOLIKOV, P. DE LA GORCE, R. GOSSIP, A. N. KURO-
PATKIN, LEO, M. LÉVESQUE, C. A. DE LOUVILLE, H. MARTIN, MAURICIUS,
A. MIKHAILOVSKI-DANILEVSKI, H. NORMAN, PROCOPIUS, C. C. DE RULHI-
ÈRE, F. SCHLOSSER, P. DE SÉGUR, P. SHCHEBALSKI, F. H. SKRINE,
STORCK, H. TYRRELL, VOLTAIRE

# INTRODUCTION

## THE INTELLECTUAL DEVELOPMENT OF RUSSIA

WRITTEN SPECIALLY FOR THE PRESENT WORK

BY DR. A. S. RAPPOPORT

Author of "Russian History," "The Curse of the Romanovs," etc., etc.

"RUSSIA evolves very slowly, like an empire that is not of yesterday and that has ample time before it," is one of Nietzsche's remarks before his reason had hopelessly gone adrift in the vast ocean of insanity. This remark of the German poet-philosopher is true enough. What Nietzsche, however, did not know or did not say is that one can hardly speak of any evolution, as far as general civilisation, intellectual culture, and development are concerned, of Russia as a whole. Only a small minority, the so-called *intelligentia*, has evolved intellectually, not Russia itself. Here lies the fundamental difference between Russia and the rest of Europe.

There is a vast gulf, ever broadening, between the Russian intelligentia and the *moujiks*. Thought and culture, nay even civilisation, seem to be limited to a select few. The bulk of the people has not only failed to advance from a state in which it was surprised by Jenghiz Khan, but it has actually retrograded to a more savage condition. Revolutions have passed over their heads without in the least affecting them. "The Russian masses," says Leroy-Beaulieu (*The Empire of the Czars*), "have not felt the breath of either the Renaissance, or the Reformation, or the Revolution. All that has been done in Europe or America for the last four centuries, since the time of Columbus and Luther, Washington and Mirabeau, is, as far as Russia is concerned, non-existent."

The people never think, or at least have not yet left that crude state of barbarism which precedes the dawn of civilisation; the first rays of thought have scarcely tinted with orient hues the dark horizon of ignorance and superstition of the Russian population; the great events have failed to stir its mental inertia. I am, however, far from maintaining that the fault lies with the nature and national character of the people. The rich nature, the subtle spirit of the Slav, his power of adaptation and imitation make him not only accessible to western civilisation and culture but also capable of producing something which bears the impress of the peculiarity of the Slavonic genius. The intelligentia is now giving ample proof corroborating this statement. The Russian intelligentia has passed the phases of growing and changing and doubting and has reached a condition of maturity, asserting its manhood and right. Before examining the intellectual development of the Russian intelligentia and the point it has reached, as compared with western Europe, we must try to find out the causes that first produced that gulf between the few and the many, and the circumstances that were instrumental in widening it.

It is a mistake to imagine that the very first foundations of Russian intellectual development were laid by Peter the Great and that Russia, although behind western Europe in culture and civilisation, is still in her youthful vigour and freshness and will soon overtake the old world. There was a time, at the beginning of the eleventh century, when the Slavonic countries under the rule of the Norman conquerors were on the same level of civilisation as western Europe. The foundations were laid before the Norman invasion and very frequent were the relations between this people in the east and those in the north of Europe. Long before the ninth century, Kiev was known to the inhabitants of Scandinavia. Many a jarl sought refuge there and many a merchant ship found its way to the shores of Russia. On the road along which the commercial connection between the East Sea and Byzantium developed were situated the towns of Smolensk, Tchernigov, Pereiaslavl (cf. V. der Bruggen, *Wie Russland Europäisch Wurde*, p. 22). When the Norman princes, the varangians, as they were called by the Slavonic nations, conquered these towns and subdued one tribe after the other, the existing civilisation developed rapidly under the protection of the new rulers. Forth from Byzantium and Greece, from Italy, Poland, and Germany, with which countries the descendants of Rurik kept up a connection, western influence came to the north. Learned monks came from Byzantium, architects, artisans, and merchants from Greece, Italy and Germany, and were instrumental in spreading the languages, customs and ideas of the west. Not only did the *kniazi* (princes) of Kiev build churches and edifices after the model of Greek and Italian art, but they established schools to which Vladimir compelled his nobles and boyars to send their children. The commercial relations with the west and the south were very vivid and frequent, and on the market places of Kiev and Novgorod a motley crowd of Normans and Slavs, Hungarians, Greeks, Venetians, Germans, Arabs, and Jews were to be seen.

The intellectual culture of the time had not yet, one must admit, penetrated the masses of the Slavonic tribes. Yet the Normans, as the propagators of culture, speedily and easily merged into one with the conquered tribes, much easier perhaps than the Normans who came with William the Conqueror amalgamated with Britons and Saxons in England. Had the Tatar invasion not taken place, it is highly probable that the intellectual development of Russia would have followed the same lines as that of western Europe. The commercial and intellectual relations with the rest of Europe, so eagerly sought after and cultivated by the Norman princes, would have continued and brought the Slav countries in increasingly closer contact with the west and under the influence of all the currents that were destined to traverse Europe later on. The Renaissance and the revival of learning which shed their light upon the dark mediæval age (and only a few rays of which found their way to Russia by way of Poland at a much later period) would have made themselves felt in Russia. This was, however, not to happen. The Mongolian invasion had actually cut off Russia from Europe, and brought it under the Tatar influence. The Norman civilisation, which was in a nascent state, was crushed; the threads connecting Russia with Europe were cut off. The wave of Mongolian invasion had inundated the flat land situated between Europe and Asia, carried away and destroyed every vestige of western influence. Kiev, Moscow, Tver, Riazan, Tchernigov, and Smolensk were conquered by the hordes of the Great Khan, who from his seat somewhere in the heart of China or in the centre of Asia sent down his generals and tax collectors.

Hundreds of thousands of Mongols came to Russia, mixed with the Slavs, and influenced habits, customs, civilisation, social life, administration and even language. The influence was a very far-reaching and deep one; Mongolism has penetrated Russian life to a much higher degree than a Russian would care to admit or western Europeans have realised. Greater and greater became the gulf between the Russian and the Romance and Teutonic worlds. But that gulf might have been bridged over and Russia might have been saved, when the dawn of better and happier days broke in, by another power: the influence of the church. Here again, however, owing to circumstances, this in many respects civilising agent was powerless.

In spite of all the reproaches hurled at the church, it must be admitted that it had all the education in its hands. In Russia, however, the case was different. From the very beginning, ever since Christianity was introduced, ever since Vladimir had accepted baptism in Kiev, the Russian people as Christians were divided into two distinct groups. Whilst the enthusiastic adherents of the new religion endeavoured to introduce the piety of Byzantium, the mass of the people, although nominally Christian, remained heathen in reality and has remained so up to the present. This was due to two reasons. Vladimir had accepted the Greek form of worship with its asceticism. Asceticism and monasticism, a retirement from the world, became the Christian ideal. This ideal was too high, too unattainable and too foreign for reality and for daily life, whilst on the other hand the perfect Christians considered the life of the world as sinful and dangerous. Thus the clergy sought retirement in cloisters and monasteries and the mass, whilst accepting the ceremonies of Byzantium, had learned nothing of its eithical teachings. The gulf thus arising between clergy and people was also due to another reason. The first members of the clergy were Greeks, monks coming from Byzantium, who spoke a language incomprehensible to the Slavs. The Russian bishops, who gradually took the place of the learned eastern monks, and who could communicate with the people, were still too ignorant themselves. And then suddenly the Tatar invasion came. Connection with Byzantium was cut off. The influx of the Greek clergy and Byzantine learning had ceased too early, before the Russians had had time to acquire some amount of knowledge to replace it. Thus whilst the intellectual development of the mass took place very slowly, the intellectual level of the clergy sank rapidly. The consequence was that when the Russian clergy met the people they were both on the same intellectual level; the priests had nothing to teach and had no prestige. This also explains, psychologically, the origin of so many religious sects in Russia. Having no respect and no admiration for the ignorant priest, addicted to drink, the peasant goes his own way when he suddenly feels a craving for religious ideals.

Thus the Mongolian invasion had cut off Russia from Europe and whilst the latter was passing through the phases of transition, approaching slowly but gradually the times of light and learning, Russia stood still. The Europe of the Renaissance was not a *creatio ex nihilo*. It was the result of a slow process of development. The barbarians who had built their realms on the ruins of the ancient worlds, Hellas and Rome, had taken over the classical heritage left to them after the disappearance of the Roman Empire. Rude and barbarous, however, these new conquerors had no understanding for the value of the heritage and destroyed many of its richest treasures. Worlds of intellectual culture were lost. But slowly the age of understanding dawned and the former barbarians brought forth many of the treasures which they had relegated to the lumber-room, added many of their own, and blended them into one whole. The result was the Græco-Roman, Romance, and Teutonic civilisation. Crusades, Arabian civilisation passing by way of Spain, scholasticism, Reformation, Renaissance, revival of learning, the discovery of new worlds, the spread of commerce, scientific inventions and discoveries, stimulating the desire for learning and creating impulses in every new direction — all these new and stirring events were so many phases through which European society and European life passed before they reached the state of modern development. Many were the streams and cross-currents that traversed Europe separately before they united and continued the more rapid advance of a new life and civilisation. All this was lacking in Russia. Russia missed during its Mongolian period, the time of general transition. None of the forces which, although invisibly, were steadily furrowing the European soil and preparing it for the influx of fresh air and new light, were at work in Russia. The phase of transition had not yet commenced. That period of constant change, of mingled decadence and spiritual growth, that ceaseless blending of the old and the new, unnoticed at the time but clearly distinguished from the distance of later ages, was lacking in Russia. There was no pope, no powerful church, and consequently no Reformation and no spirit of individualism — no feudalism, no knights, no Crusades and no acquaintance with foreign lands, no spread of commerce, and no widening of the mental horizon of the people. There were no learned monks copying Greek and Latin manuscripts, paving the way for scholasticism and modern thought. There was even no language in which the treasures of the ancient world could be communicated to the Slavs. Few people could write, few even count properly.

There were no schools and the attempts to establish some such institutions during the seventeenth century failed. A school was founded at Moscow under Alexis, but here only a foreign language or two were taught. Its aim was to train translators for the government. There was no art, nor technical science. There were no medical men. The two or three foreign practitioners were considered as sorcerers.

Towards the end of the seventeenth century therefore Russia had absolutely no culture of her own. All that the Normans had established had been wiped out. The Byzantine influence had no effect. And when after a struggle extending over three centuries the czardom of Moscow had thrown off the shackles of the Great Khan, liberated itself from thraldom and laid the foundations of the great empire of Russia, it had only established, on the ruins of the old Mongolian, a new state which was Mongolian and Tatar in its essence and spirit, in its customs and institutions, and had little or nothing in common with the rest of Europe.

Moscow was the inheritor of Mongolism, the Czar was spiritually, and even physically, a descendant of Mongol princes. Ivan IV married a Mongolian princess, his son married a sister of the Mongol Godunov. They had actually taken over the inheritance of the khans of Kiptchak. It was in this barren soil that Peter sowed the seed of European culture. What happened?

Peter was undoubtedly great and deserves this title. He was one of the great makers of history. But though great in his plans, great in what he wished to accomplish, he was not great in what he really attained. He only saw the superficiality of European civilisation. He introduced it like some foreign product, like some fashionable article, like some exotic plant, without first asking whether the national soil was propitious for its cultivation. He, at the utmost, created a hot-house atmosphere where his plants could vegetate, and they remained what they originally were: exotic. He failed to see that civilisation is the product of a long process of evolution, the natural product of the social and national conditions, drawing its life and sap from the inner forces of the people. Instead of making use of these inner forces of his people, he endeavoured to introduce civilisation by his power of will. He only had an eye for the effects but not for the causes that were working as the hidden springs.

In France, in England, in Germany, in all western Europe, civilisation, the moral and intellectual evolution, was a natural phenomenon, the effect of previous causes. In Russia, civilisation was the outcome of a sudden revolution, the slavish, reluctant and half-hearted compliance with the commands of an individual will. The former was natural, the latter artificial. An evolution is a slow change, an unconscious and imperceptible process, finding a state prepared for innovation, a soil, furrowed and fertile, ready to receive the seed and to bring forth fruit. A revolution, on the other hand, is a radical, sudden change which seldom succeeds and, in most cases, calls forth reactions. In Western Europe there was, as we have see above, a time of transition from the barbarous to the civilised state. The morning of the Renaissance had dawned upon mediæval Europe and tinted with orient colours the sombre sky. The first rays appeared on the horizon of the Italian poets, dissipating the darkness here and there. The sun gradually rose higher and higher, penetrated the houses of the people and woke them (who had been lulled to sleep by the mysterious whisperings of superstition) from their prolonged slumbers. They awoke, opened their windows and allowed the light of the morning to penetrate into their dark abodes. Not so in Russia. There the people were suddenly awakened, dragged out from the utter darkness, without any transition, into the broad midday of an artificial light. They opened their eyes, but the light was too strong, too glaring; so they shut them again. Peter wanted to jump over three centuries and catch up with Europe. He established a fleet without Russian sailors, an administration with foreign administrators, an academy of science in a land without elementary schools. He began a race with Europe but his people could not follow him. He borrowed everything from Europe and instead of giving his people a chance to develop naturally and freely, he crushed the spirit of independence and introduced a knout civilisation. Everything had to be done by order. He forced his people to swallow Europeanism. The bulk of his subjects, however, could not digest it. The consequence was that they could not follow the few, and remained far behind them. The gulf therefore between the few, who form the present intelligentia, and the great mass — a gulf which was but narrow towards the end of the sixteenth century when by way of Poland and Livonia a glimpse of the western sun penetrated into Russia — suddenly widened considerably. Thus the origin of the striking phenomenon which Russia offers in her intellectually high developed intelligentia and her uneducated, ignorant masses is to be sought in Russia's past, in the absence of a period of transition, and in Peter's misunderstanding the process of European civilisation, in his admiration for the effects, but utter ignorance of the causes that brought about these effects.

There is, however, yet another factor — a factor which, whilst accounting for the existence of an intelligentia, or a coterie of intellectuals, and of an utterly ignorant mass, will also throw some light upon the intellectual development of this very intelligentia and explain the reasons which compelled it to choose certain channels by which it sends forth the currents of its thoughts. This factor is the despotic government of the czars. If Russia's unhappy past and Peter's good intentions but great blunders produced the present state of intellectual development in that country, the government of the Reformer's successors has done its very best to preserve this condition.

The continuous policy of the Russian government to civilise by means of the knout has on the one hand brought about the result that not Russia but only a few Russians evolved intellectually and, on the other, it has given a certain direction to the thought and intellectual productions of these few. Even during the reign of Peter I or Catherine II, when the spirit of civilisation began to move its wings, independent thought has had to sustain a fierce struggle against authority. In the most civilised countries of western Europe ever and anon a cross-current of reaction traverses the stream of intellectual evolution: narrow-minded zealots, hypocritical bigots, false patriots, literary Gibeonites, gossiping old women arrayed in the mantles of philosophers, do their best to put fetters on the independent thought of man, to nip the free and natural intellectual development in the very bud by forcing it under the iron grip of tradition and authority. In western Europe, however, reactionary tendencies of the lovers of darkness are only exceptions, and will lead thought for a while into a side channel, but cannot stop the triumphant march onwards. Not so in Russia.

In the empire of the czar thought is almost a crime and every means is employed to keep it within the boundaries prescribed by the governing power. To overstep these boundaries, to develop itself freely, and I might say naturally, is to declare war against authority, to revolt. The history of evolution of thought in Russia is therefore almost identical with the revolutionary movement. If whilst working on the construction of the temple with the right hand, the left has to wield the sword against a sudden attack of the enemy, the edifice can rise only very slowly. Renan says (in his *Future of Science*) that the great creations of thought appear in troublous times and that neither material ease nor even liberty contributes much to the originality and the energy of intellectual development. On the contrary the work of mind would only be seriously threatened if humanity came to be too much at its ease. Thank God! exclaims the Breton philosopher, that day is still far distant. The customary state of Athens, he continues, was one of terror; the security of the individual was threatened at every moment, to-day an exile, to-morrow he was sold as a slave. And yet in such a state Phidias produced the Propylæa statues, Plato his dialogues and Aristophanes his satires. Dante would never have composed his cantos in an atmosphere of studious ease. The sacking of Rome did not disturb the brush of Michael Angelo. In a word, the most beautiful things are born amid tears and it is in the midst of struggle, in the atmosphere of sorrow and suffering that humanity develops itself, that the human mind displays the most energy and activity in all directions. But Renan was an individualist and aristocratic in his teachings; he seems to have in view only the individual, nay, the genius. Suffering and oppression, physical, intellectual and moral, are schools where the strong gather more strength and come forth triumphant, but where the weaker are destroyed. What is true for the *élite*, for the very limited number of the chosen few, does not hold good for humanity at large, which is not strong enough to think when it is hungry, to fight against opposing forces and to hurl down the barriers erected against the advance of thought. Few indeed are those who can carry on the struggle to a successful issue. The Russian government, with its Mongolian traditions of autocracy, threw the great nation, which remained behind Peter's forward march, back into complete indifference and apathy, into a state of submissive contentment, where, like a child, it kissed the rod that punished it, sometimes cried like a child, and is lulled to sleep by the whisperings of mystic superstition and the vapours of *vodki*.

Had not the populace a terrifying example in the martyrs of Russian thought? A terrible destiny awaited him who dared to step beyond the line traced by the hand of the government, who ventures to look over the wall erected by imperial ukase. "The history of Russian thinkers," says Alexander Herzen (*Russland's Sociale Zustände*, page 136), "is a long list of martyrs and a register of convicts." Those whom the hand of the imperial government has spared died in the prime of youth, before they had time to develop, like blossoms hurrying to quit life before they could bear fruit. A Pushkin and a Lermontov fell in the prime of youth, one thirty-eight and the other twenty-seven years old, victims of the unnatural state of society. Russia's Beaumarchais, Griboiedov, found a premature end in Persia in his thirty-fifth year; Kolzov, the Russian Burns, Bielinski, the Russian Lessing, died in misery, the latter at the age of thirty-eight. Czerncevski was torn from his literary activity and sent to Siberia. Dobrolubov sang his swan-song in his twenty-fifth year. Chaadaev, the friend of Schelling, was declared mad by order of the government. If such measures have kept the people in a state of ignorance and still lowered the already low level of civilisation, the autocratic rule has further, as it was unable to crush it, caused the intelligentia to turn its thoughts into a certain direction.

If we follow the development of the Russian intelligentia we notice at once that all the currents of its intellectual life are, at the present time at least, converging into one centre, swelling the stream, that is already running high, to a vast and mighty ocean, which is sending its waters, through many channels, all over Europe. This centre is literature. Since the foundation of the Academy of Science by Peter the Great Russian achievements in the domains of science, technical education, art, sculpture, music, painting, history and philosophy have been very small.

In science and art the Russians have produced nothing of importance, nothing original. Mendeleev, Lobatshevski, Pirogov, Botkin, Soloviev are a few scientific names of some eminence but they are few as compared with Europe and America. Many others, who are known to the western world as Russians, are in reality Germans or Armenians. The great historian, Karamzin, was of Tatar extraction. In the domain of art Vereshchagin was a Russian, but Ainasowski was an Armenian, Brulov a Prussian and Antokolski a Jew (cf. Brüggen, *Das heutige Russland*, p. 182).

Russia has had no Spinoza and no Kant, no Newton and no Spencer. Since the foundation of the University of Moscow in 1755, some semblance of Russian philosophy has appeared but a Soloviev and a Grote, a Troitski and a Preobrajenski have only introduced the philosophy of Germany, France, and England into Russia, but not worked out their own philosophical systems. Thus, whilst Russian scientists, technicians, artists and even musicians have to go abroad to complete their education, Russian philosophers borrow from Hegel or Descartes, from Locke or Comte. This is, however, not the case with Russian literature. Russia has quickened her development in the realm of literature. Her decades were centuries. Rapidly she has lived through phases of growth and evolution, of achievement and reflection which have filled long periods in other people's lives. The peaks of Russian creative power in this domain, the productions of Pushkin and Turgeniev, of Lermontov, Dostoievski and Tolstoi proudly face the heights of literary western Europe.

Whilst, however, the Russian genius of the intelligentia centred its force in literature, this literature bears the unmistakable trait, that distinguishes it from European literature, of having a tendency to teach and of taking a moral aspect. Russian literature on the whole has not entered the sphere of artistic interest; it has always been a pulpit whence the word of instruction came forth. With very few exceptions, like Merejkovski and Andreev, the Russian author is not practising art for art's sake (*l'art pour l'art*), but is pursuing a goal, is accomplishing a task.

The Russian literature is a long cry of revolt, a continuous sigh•or an admonition. Taine says, somewhere, when speaking of Stendhal and Balzac: "They love art more than men—they are not writing out of sympathy for the poor, but out of love for the beautiful." This is just what the Russian modern author is not doing. The intellectual and instructive moments predominate over the emotional and artistic.

This state of Russia's intellectual development is explained by what has been stated above. It is due to the sudden introduction of western manners and civilisation, followed by a powerful foreign influence on the one hand, and the social and political state of the country on the other. When Peter had suddenly launched Russia—which was floating like some big hulk between Asia and Europe—towards the west, the few who helped him in this endeavour came under the complete influence of western thought and manners. St. Petersburg soon became a Versailles in miniature. Voltaire, Diderot, and the encyclopædists governed and shaped Russian thought and Russian society. But not only France—Germany too, and England, Byron and his individualism, had gained great sway in Russia. The independence of Russian thought and its intellectual development only dates from about 1840. When it awoke at that time, when it became conscious of itself, it felt that it had a great work, a great mission, to fulfil. Surrounded on one side by a people that were ignorant, ready to sink lower and lower; opposed, on the other, by a government that did its best to check individualism and independence in every possible way—the Russian intelligentia felt its great responsibility.

Surrounded by a population whose mental development was on a very low level, the atmosphere was and still is not propitious for the cultivation of art or science, whilst the Russian author had no time simply to admire the beautiful in nature, but was compelled to look round and try what good he could do. Thus Russian genius concentrated itself in literature as the best vehicle to expose the state of Russian society. The Russian writer became an apostle. He was not anxious to be artistic, to shape his style and to be fascinating, but to give as true a picture of Russian life as he possibly could, to show the evil and to suggest the remedy.

Such, in broad lines, was, and still is, the state which the few, whom we termed the Russian intelligentia, have reached in their intellectual development. In a moment of strength the Russian genius has attained itself, with self-asserting individuality. Its task is great, its obstacles are manifold, but it fights valiantly and moves on steadily. This only applies to the few. When the day of political freedom will dawn for Russia, then and then only the great evolution and the intellectual development of Russia itself, of the Russian people as a whole, will begin. On the day when civil and religious despotism, that everywhere crushes individuality, ceases, then the genius of the Russian people will spread its pinions, and the masses will awake from their inertia to new life, like the gradual unfolding of spring into summer.

# CHAPTER I

## LAND AND PEOPLE AND EARLY HISTORY

### [To 1054 A.D.]

#### EXTENT, CONFIGURATION, AND CLIMATE

To arrive at a just appreciation of Russia's genius we must have a knowledge of the soil that nourishes her, the peoples that inhabit her, and the history through which she has passed. Let us begin with nature, soil, and climate.

The first fact that strikes us in regard to the Russian empire is its vastness.[1] Its colossal dimensions are so out of proportion to the smallness of the greatest among European states, that, to bring them within the sphere of human imagination, Alexander von Humboldt, one of the greatest scientists of his century, makes the statement that the portion of the globe under Russia's dominion is greater than the entire surface of the moon at its full.

The territories of that vast empire acknowledge no limits; its vast plains stretch toward the heart of the old continent, as far as the huge peaks of central Asia; they are stopped between the Black and the Caspian seas by the great wall of the Caucasus, whose foot is planted below the sea-level, and the height of whose summits exceeds by eight hundred feet that of Mont Blanc.

In lakes Ladoga and Onega, in the northwest, Russia possesses the greatest lakes in Europe; in Lake Baikal, in Siberia, the greatest in Asia; in the Caspian and Aral seas, the greatest in the world. Her rivers equal her plains in proportion: the Obi, the Yenisei, the Amur, in Asia; the Dnieper, the Don, the Volga, in Europe. The central artery of Russia is the Volga — a river that, in its winding course of nearly twenty-four hundred miles, is not altogether European. Nine tenths of the Russian territory are as yet nearly empty of inhabitants, and nevertheless the population, according to the census of 1897, taken over all the empire except Finland, numbered 129,000,-000; and the annual increase is very nearly two million.

[1] According to recent computations the Russian Empire covers an area of 8,660,000 square miles — about one sixth of the land surface of the globe.

Europe is distinguished from other regions of the globe by two characteristics which make her the home of civilisation: her land is cut into by the seas — "cut into bits," as Montesquieu says; she is, according to Humboldt, "an articulated peninsula"; her other distinctive advantage is a temperate climate which, in great measure the result of her configuration, is duplicated nowhere under the same latitude. Russia alone, adhering solidly to Asia by her longest dimension, bordered on the north and northwest by icy seas which permit to the borders few of the advantages of a littoral, is one of the most compact and eminently continental countries of the globe.

She is deprived of the even, temperate climate due to Europe's articulated structure, and has a continental climate — nearly equally extreme in the rigour of its winters and the torrid heat of its summers. Hence the mean temperature varies.

The isothermal lines extend in summer toward the pole; in winter they sink southward: so that the greater part of Russia is included in January in the rigid, in July in the torrid zone. Her very vastness condemns her to extremes. The bordering seas are too distant or too small to serve her as reservoirs of warmth or basins of coolness. Nowhere else in the Occident are to be found winters so long and severe, summers so burning. Russia is a stranger to the great influences that moderate the climate of the rest of Europe — the gulf stream and the winds of the Sahara. The long Scandinavian peninsula, stretching between Russia and the Atlantic, deflects from her coasts the great warm current flowing from the New World to the Old. In place of the gulf stream and the African deserts it is the polar snows of Europe, and Siberia, the frozen north of Asia, that hold the predominating influence over Russia. The Ural range, by its insignificant elevation and its perpendicularity to the equator, is but an inconsiderable barrier to these influences. In vain does Russia extend south into the latitude of Pau and Nice; nowhere this side the Caucasus will she find a rampart against the winds of the north. The conformation of the soil, low and flat, leaves her open to all the atmospheric currents — from the parching breath of the central Asian deserts to the winds of the polar region.

This lack of mountains and inland seas deprives Russia of the necessary humidity brought to the rest of Europe by the Atlantic and laid up for it in the store-houses of the Alps. The ocean breezes reach her only when empty of refreshing vapours; those of Asia are wrung dry long before they touch her confines. The further the continent stretches, the greater its poverty of rain. At Kazan the rainfall is but half that of Paris. Hence the lack, over an enormous southern region, of the two principal elements of fertility — warmth and moisture; hence in part those wide, woodless, arid, un-European steppes in the southeast of the empire.

### THE SIMILARITY OF EUROPEAN AND ASIATIC RUSSIA

One whole formed of two analogous halves, Russia is in nowise a child of Europe; but that is not to say that she is Asiatic — that we can shelve her among the dormant and stationary peoples of the far East. Far from it: Russia is no more Asiatic than she is European. But in all physical essentials of structure, climate, and moisture, she is opposed to historical, occidental Europe; in all these she is in direct relation with the bordering countries of Asia. Europe proper naturally begins at the narrowing of the continent between the Baltic and the Black seas.

In the southeast there is no natural barrier between Russia and Asia;

therefore the geographers have in turn taken the Don, the Volga, the Ural, or again the depression of the Obi, as boundaries. Desert steppes stretch from the centre of the old continent into Russia by the door left open between the Ural chain and the Caspian. From the lower course of the Don to the Aral Sea, all these low steppes on both banks of the Volga and the Ural rivers form the bed of an old, dried-up sea, whose borders we can still trace, and whose remnants constitute the great salt lakes known as the Caspian and the Aral seas. By a hydrographical accident which has had an enormous influence upon the character and destinies of the people, it is into one of these closed Asiatic seas that the Volga, the great artery of Russia, empties, after turning its back upon Europe almost from its very source.

To the north of the Caspian steppes, from latitude 52° to the uninhabitable polar regions, the longest meridional chain of mountains of the old continent forms a wall between Russia and Asia. The Russians in olden days called it the "belt of stone," or "belt of the world"; but, despite the name, the Ural indicates the end of Asia on the one side, only to mark its recommencement, almost unaltered, on the European slope. Descending gradually by terraces on the European side, the Ural is less a chain than a plateau crowned with a line of slight elevations. It presents principally low ridges covered with forests, like those of the Vosges and the Jura. So greatly depressed is the centre that along the principal passes between Russia and Siberia (from Perm to Iekaterinburg, for example) the eye looks in vain for the summits; in constructing a railroad through the pass the engineers had no long tunnels to build, no great difficulties to surmount. At this high altitude, where the plains are snow-bound during six or seven months, no peak attains the limit of eternal snows, no valley enbosoms a glacier.

In reality the Ural separates neither the climates, nor the fauna and flora. Extending almost perpendicularly from north to south, the polar winds blow almost equally unhindered along both sides; on both, the vegetation is the same. It is not till the heart of Siberia is reached — the upper Yenisei and Lake Baikal — that one finds a different soil, a new flora and fauna. The upheaval of the Ural failed to wipe out the resemblance and the unity of the two regions it divides. Instead of a wall between the Russias, it is merely a store-house of mineral wealth. In the rocks, of eruptive or metamorphic origin, are veins of metals not found in the regular strata of the great plains. It no more separates one from the other than does the river of the same name; and when one day Siberia shall boast a denser population, the Ural will be regarded as the axis, the backbone of the two great halves of the empire.

### THE DUALISM OF NORTH AND SOUTH

Unity in immensity is Russia's chief characteristic. From the huge wall of the Caucasus to the Baltic this empire, in itself greater than all the rest of Europe, in its numerous provinces presents perhaps less variety of climate than west European countries whose area is ten or twelve times less. This is on account of the flat uniformity. And yet, underlying this homogenity of climate and configuration, nature has marked with special characteristics and a distnct individuality a number of regions which, divided into two groups, embrace all European Russia. Equally flat, with a climate nearly equally extreme, these two great zones, notwithstanding their similarity, present a remarkable contrast in soil, vegetation, moisture, and most other physical and economic conditions. One is the forest region, the other the woodless zone of the steppes; they divide the empire into almost equal halves.

From the opposition, from the natural dualism of the steppe and the forest, has sprung the historical antagonism and the now-ended strife between the two halves of Russia — the struggle between the sedentary north and the nomad south; between the Russian and the Tatar; between the Muscovite state laid in the forest region, and the free Cossacks, children of the steppes. The forest region, though ceaselessly diminished by cutting, still remains the more extensive. Occupying the entire north and centre, it grows wider from east to west, from Kazan to Kiev.

Beyond the polar circle no tree can withstand the intensity and permanence of the frost. On both sides of the Ural, in the neighbourhood of Siberia, stretch vast boggy plains *(toundras)*, perpetually frost-bound, and clothed with moss. In these latitudes no cultivation is possible, no pasturage but lichens is to be obtained, no animal but the reindeer can exist. Hunting and fishing are the sole occupations of the [few inhabitants who make their dwelling in these lands of ice.

The soil of the wooded plains, at least in the northwest, from the White Sea to the Niemen and the Dnieper, is low, swampy, and peaty, intersected by arid sandy hills. The Valdai Hills, the highest plateau, scarcely attain the height of one thousand feet. This region is rich in springs and is the source of all the great rivers. The flatness of the land prevents the rivers from assuming a distinctly marked course, and as no ridge intervenes, their waters at the thaw run together and form enormous swamps; or, travelling slowly down undefined slopes, form at the bottom vast lakes like the Ladoga, a veritable inland sea, or strings of wretched little pools, like the eleven hundred lakes in the government of Archangel.

The population, though scattered over wide expanses and averaging less than fifteen to the square mile, fails to wring from the unfriendly soil a sufficient nourishment. Wheat will not thrive; barley, rye, and flax alone flourish. A multitude of small industries eke out the livelihood for which agriculture is insufficient.

The augmentation of the scattered population is scarcely perceptible having, so to speak, reached the point of saturation. Russia can hope for an increase of wealth and population in this desolate northland only upon the introduction into it of industrial pursuits, as in the case of Moscow and the Ural regions.

Russian civilisation finds a great, though by no means insurmountable obstacle in the extremes of temperature. It must be remembered that Europe enjoys a temperate climate unparalleled in her fairest colonies, while other continents, for analagous reasons, labour under much the same disadvantages as Russia. The climate of the northern portion of the United States greatly resembles that of south Russia, while New York, Pennsylvania, and the New England states pass through the same extremes of temperature as the steppes of the Black Sea.

### THE SOIL OF THE BLACK LANDS AND THE STEPPES

The Black Lands, one of the largest and most fertile agricultural tracts in the world, occupy the upper part of the woodless zone at its juncture with the forest and lake district. Obtaining moisture and shelter from the latter, the Black Lands enjoy much more favourable climatic conditions than the steppes of the extreme south. They derive their name *(tchernoziom)* from a stratum of black humus, of an average depth of from one and a half to five feet, consisting partly of loam, partly of oily clay mixed with organic substances. It dries rapidly and is thereupon reduced to a fine dust; but it absorbs moisture with equal promptitude, and after a rain takes on the appearance of a coal-black paste. The formation of this wonderfully fertile layer is attributed to the slow decomposition of the steppe grasses, accumulated during many centuries.

The *tchernoziom* circles like a belt across European Russia, from Podolia and Kiev on the southwest beyond Kazan in the northeast; after the interruption of the Ural ridge it reappears in Siberia in the southern part of Tobolsk. The trees disappear altogether as we advance southwards, till not even a bush is to be seen. Nothing is visible to the eye but hundreds of miles of fertile black soil, a limitless field stretching beyond the horizon. As a consequence of its fertility this portion of Russia is most populous; the population increases steadily, as railways are constructed and as agriculture gains upon the surrounding steppes.

Between the Black Lands and the southern seas lie the steppes proper wherein the dead level of the country, the absence of all arboreal vegetation, and the summer droughts attain their maximum. These great plains, covering over half a million miles of Europe, include many different qualities of soil, destined to as many different ends.

The sandy, stony, saline steppes will forever be unfit for cultivation. The fertile steppes which occupy the greater part of the space between the Black Lands and the Black Sea and the sea of Azov consist of a layer of black vegetable mould ready for cultivation and teeming with fertility. The grass, growing five or six feet high, in rainy seasons even higher, accounts in some measure for the absence of woods: its rapid luxuriant growth would smother young trees.

The virgin steppe with its rank vegetation — the steppe of history and poetry — diminishes day by day, and will soon disappear before the agricultural invasion. The legendary Ukraine has almost lost its wild beauty; Gogol's steppe, like Cooper's prairie, will soon be but a memory — lost in the black belt. The long delay in opening up these grassy plains is due as well to the lack of water and wood as to the lack of workers. The lack of water is difficult to remedy, hence the plains are bound to experience alternately good and bad years; hence, also, the frequent famines in lands which otherwise might be regarded as the storehouse of the empire.

Perhaps an even greater drawback is the lack of trees; thereby the population is deprived both of fuel and of materials for building. Stalks of the tall steppe-grasses and the dung of the flocks, which otherwise would go to the soil, supply it with a fuel that would not suffice for a dense population. The introduction of railroads and the opening of coal mines will, however, remedy little by little these evils, by supplying fuel and restoring the manure to the soil. The proximity to the estuaries of the great rivers and to the Black Sea renders the position of these steppes especially favourable to trade with Europe.

The Ural-Caspian depression is as truly a desert as the Sahara. It contains but few oases. These saline steppes sink in part below the sea level, like the Caspian itself, whose ancient basin they formed, and which now, narrowed and sunk, lies about eighty-five feet below the Black Sea's surface. This region is of all European Russia the barest, the driest, and the most exposed to extreme seasons. It is decidedly Asiatic in soil, climate, flora, fauna, and inhabitants. This barren steppeland, covering three hundred thousand square miles, has less than a million and a half inhabitants. It is good for nothing but pasturage; and is therefore overrun with nomad Asiatic tribes.

We cannot consider as Russian in character the Caucasus and the southern coast of the Crimea; these present an entirely different aspect, and are as varied as the real Russia is monotonous. In the valleys of the Caucasus appear again forests — absent from the centre of the empire southwards — dense and vigorous, not thin and scattered and monotonous as in the north. Here fruit-trees thrive, and all varieties of plant life for which Russia seeks in vain over her wide plains, from the shores of the ice-bound north to the Black Sea — the vine, which on the banks of the Don finds but a precarious existence; the mulberry-tree; the olive. Few are the fruits that cannot prosper in the hanging gardens of the Crimea suspended above the sea, or in Transcaucasia where, not content with having introduced successfully the cultivation of cotton and the sugar cane, the Russian merchants are anxious to establish tea plantations.

COSTUME WORN BY COSSACK OF THE
UKRAINE

### DIVERSITY OF RACES

The number of diverse races is accounted for by the configuration of Russia. Lacking defined boundaries to east and west, Russia has been open always to invasion — she has been the great highway of emigration from Asia into Europe. The strata of human alluvions have nowhere been more numerous, more mingled, more broken or inharmonious than on this flat bed, where each wave, pushed by the one behind it, encountered no obstacle other than the wave which had preceded. Even since historical times it is difficult to enumerate the peoples who have followed one another upon Russian soil — who have there formed empires more or less durable: Scythian, Sarmatian, Goth, Avar, Bulgarian, Hungarian, Chazar, Petcheneg, Lithuanian, Mongol, Tatar; without counting the previous migrations of the Celts and Teutones, or of peoples whose very names have perished, but among whom even the most obscure have left upon the population some impression whose origin to-day it is impossible to trace.

While the configuration of Russia has left her open to every invader, the structure of her soil forbade the development of the invaders into organised nations independent of one another. Instead of being the consequence of slow development by physical causes, this multiplicity of races and tribes is an historical heritage. Without considering the glacial regions of the north, uninhabitable save for hunters and fishers, or the sandy and saline steppes of the southeast, where wander only pastoral nomads, this complexity of races and tribes, far from being a result of adaptation to the soil — far from being in harmony with physical conditions, is directly opposed to them. Far from having a tendency to race diversion, the natural conditions made for unity and harmony. The absence of boundaries made it impossible for the different tribes to isolate themselves.

In the immense quadrilateral comprised between the glacial ocean and the Black Sea, between the Baltic and the Ural, there is not a single mountain — not a single dividing line.    Over this even surface the different tribes have been obliged to scatter at random — just as the waters have flowed together, having no ridge to separate them, no banks to contain them.    Thus, while custom, religion, and language prevented their mingling, they were yet obliged to live side by side: to invade one another, to mingle one with another without loss of individuality, as the rivers which flow together without confounding their waters.    Exhausted in the effort to spread over too large expanses, or broken up into fragments, all these races have the more easily submitted to the domination of one rule;   and under this domination they have been the more rapidly unified and mingled.    From this fusion, begun centuries ago under the Christian empire and the Muscovite sovereignty, have sprung the Russian people — that mass of about 129,000,000 souls, which, compared with other peoples, resembles the sea devouring its own shores, a sea dotted with islands which it swallows one by one.

Out of the seeming chaos of Russian ethnology emerge definitely three principal elements — Finn, Tatar, and Slav, which last has to-day to a great extent absorbed the other two.    Not counting the three millions of Jews in the west, the seven or eight hundred thousand Rumanians in Bessarabia, the eight or nine hundred thousand Germans of the Baltic provinces and the southern colonies; without counting the Kalmucks of the steppe of the lower Volga, the Circassians, the Armenians, the Georgians, and the whole babel of the Caucasus — all the races and tribes which have invaded Russia in the past and all which inhabit her to-day can be traced to one of these three races.    As far back as history goes, are to be found upon Russian soil, under one name or another, representatives of all these three groups; and their fusion is not yet so complete that we cannot trace their origin, their distinctive characteristics, or their respective original dominions.

The Finnish tribe seems in olden times to have occupied the most extensive territory in what is to-day called Russia.    It is manifestly foreign to Aryan or European stock, whence, with the Celts and Latins, Germans and Slavs, most of the European peoples have sprung.    Ethnological classifications usually place the Finns in a more or less comprehensive group known variously as Turanian, Mongolian, and Mongoloid.

The Mongols, properly so called, with the Tatars are usually arranged beside the Finns in the Ural-Altaic group; which, on the other hand, rejects the. Chinese and other great nations of oriental Asia.    This classification appears to be the most reasonable; but it must be noticed that this Ural-Altaic group is far from presenting the same homogeneousness as the Aryan or Semitic group.    The relationship between the numerous branches is far less fundamental than between Latin and German; it is probably far more remote than that between the Brahman or Gheber of India and the Celt of Scotland or Brittany; at bottom it is perhaps less close than between the Indo-European and the Semite.

### The Finns

The Finnish race, which outside of Hungary is almost entirely comprised within European Russia, numbers five or six millions, divided into a dozen different tribes.    To the Hungarian family in the north belongs the only Finnish people which ever played an important rôle in Europe, or arrived at a high state of civilisation — the Magyars of Hungary.    In the northwest we find the Finns properly so called; they are subdivided into two or three tribes, the Suomi, as they designate themselves, constituting the only tribe in the whole empire that possesses a national spirit, a love of country, a history, and a literature; also the only one that has escaped the slow absorption by which their kindred have been swallowed up. They form five-sixths of the population of the grand duchy of Finland — a population almost wholly rural. A Swedish element mingled with German and Russian is predominant in the cities.

St. Petersburg is, truth to tell, built in the midst of Finnish territory; the immediate surroundings only are russified, and that quite recently:

A TATAR

(Russian)

even half a century ago Russian was not understood in the hamlets lying at the very gates of the capital. To this Finnish branch belong the Livs, a tribe nearly extinct, which has given its name at Livonia; also the Lapps — the last, physically the ugliest, morally the least developed, of all the branches of this tribe.

The race is almost infinitely subdivided; its members profess all the religions from Shamanism to Mohammedanism, from Greek orthodoxy to Lutheranism. They are nomadic, like the Lapp; pastoral, like the Bashkir; sedentary and agricultural like the Esth and the Finn. They have adopted the customs and spoken the language of each and all, have been ruled by peoples of different origins, have been russified after having been partially tatarised — all these influences contributing to break up the race into insignificant fragments. As numerous as their Hungarian kindred, the Finns of the Russian Empire are far from being able to claim an equal political significance.

Is it true that the alliance with the Finns is for Russia an irremediable cause of inferiority? It is doubtful. In their isolation and disruption, hampered by the thankless soil upon which they dwell, the Finns have been unable to achieve an original development; as compensation, they have everywhere manifested a singular facility of assimilation with more developed races with which they have come in contact; they allowed themselves easily to be overwhelmed by a civilisation which they themselves were unable to originate: if they possessed no blood-ties with Europe, they placed no obstacles in the way of annexation by her. Their religion is the best proof. The majority have long been Christians; and it is principally Christianity which has led the way to their fusion with the Slavs and their assimilation into civilised Europe. From Hungary to the Baltic and the Volga, they have accepted with docility the three principal historical forms of Christianity; the most modern, Protestantism, has thriven better among the Finnish and Esthonic tribes than among the Celtic, Iberian, and Latin peoples.

If we seek in language an unmistakable sign of race and intelligence, it must be admitted that certain Finns — the Suomi of Finland like the Magyars of Hungary — have brought their agglutinated languages to a perfection which for power, harmony, and wealth of expression well bears comparison with our most complex flexional languages. If it is true that the Finns are related to the Mongols, they have certainly the virtues of that race, which holds its own so well in its struggle with Europe: they possess the same stability, patience, and perseverance; hence perhaps the fact that to every country and every state which has felt their influence the Finns have communicated a singular power of resistance, a remarkable vitality.

### ETHNOLOGICAL DISTRIBUTION OF RELIGIONS

The Finn has become Christian; the Turk or Tatar, Moslem; the Mongol, Buddhist: to this ethnological distribution of religion there are few exceptions. Hereto are attributable the causes of the widely different destinies of these three groups — particularly the neighbouring Finns and Tatars. It is religion which has prepared the one for its European existence; it is religion which has made that existence impossible for the other. Islam has given the Tatar a higher and more precocious civilisation; it has inspired him to build flourishing cities like the ancient Sarai and Kazan, and to found powerful states in Europe and Asia; it has achieved for him a brilliant past, while exposing him to a future full of difficulties: while saving him from absorption into Europe, it has left him completely outside the gate of modern civilisation.

It is the Tatars who have given to the Russians the name of Mongols, to which the Tatars themselves have but a questionable right. In any case the title is not applicable to the true Russians, who have at most but a drop or two of Mongol blood in their veins, and less of Tatar than the Spaniards have of Moorish or Arab.

At the same time with the process of absorption and assimilation of the Finnish element, another process has for centuries been going on — an inverse process of secretion and elimination of the Tatar and Moslem elements which Russia found herself unable to assimilate. After their submission a great number of Tatars left Russia, being unwilling to become the subjects of the infidels whose masters they had been. Before the progress of Christianity they spontaneously retreated to the lands still dominated by the law of the prophet. After the destruction of the Khanates of Kazan and Astrakhan, they tended to concentrate in the Crimea and the neighbouring straits — in what up to the eighteenth century was known as Little Tartary; after the conquest of the Crimea by Catherine II they took their way still farther toward the empire of their Turkish brethren. Even in our own time, after the war of Sebastopol and after the conquest of the Caucasus, the emigration of the Tatars and the Nogaians began again on an enormous scale, together with that of the Circassians. In the Crimea the Tatar population, already diminished by one-half in the time of Catherine II, is to-day scarcely one-fifth of what it was at the time of the annexation to Russia. The introduction of obligatory military service in the year 1874 drove them out in large numbers. By defeat and voluntary exile have the Tatars been reduced to insignificant groups in a country where, formerly, they reigned for centuries — in some parts of which even they were the sole inhabitants.[b]

## THE SLAVS

As to the Slavs, who form the nucleus of the Russian population, it is now generally recognised that they migrated to Russia from the neighbourhood of the Carpathian Mountains. The Byzantine annalists of the sixth and the beginning of the seventh centuries, speaking of the Slavs, whom they called Sklaboi, a name appearing as early as the end of the fifth century, distinguish two branches of them: the Ants, living from the Danube to the mouth of the Dnieper; and the Slavs, properly so named, living northeast of the Danube and as far to the east as the source of the Vistula, and on the right bank of the Dniester. In this, their statement agrees with that of Jornandes,[l] the historian of the Goths. Some Russian scholars suppose

that before coming to the Danube the Slavs lived near the Carpathians, whence they invaded the Byzantine empire. These encroachments, beginning as far back as the third century, resulted in the penetration of the Slavs into southern Austria and the Balkan peninsula. Byzantine annalists of the sixth and seventh centuries, Procopius and the emperor Maurice, who had to fight the Slavs in person, speak of them as being ever on the move: "They live in woods and on the banks of rivers, in small hamlets, and are always ready to change their abode." At the same time these Byzantine annalists describe this people as exceedingly fond of liberty. "From the remotest period," says Procopius,[d] "the Slavs were known to live as democracies; they discussed their wants in popular assemblies or folkmotes." "The Slavs are fond of liberty," writes the emperor Maurice[e]; "they cannot bear unlimited rulers, and are not easily brought to submission." The same language is used also by the emperor Leo.[f] "The Slavs," says he, "are a free people, strongly opposed to any subjection." If the Byzantine historians do not speak of the invasion of the Slavs into the limits of the empire during the second part of the seventh

A FINNISH COSTUME

century, it is because their migration took at this time another direction: from the Carpathians they moved toward the Vistula and the Dnieper.

During the ninth century, the time of the founding of the first principalities, the Dnieper, with its numerous affluents on both sides, formed the limit of the Slavonic settlements to the east. This barrier was broken only by the Viatitchi, stretching as far to the northeast as the source of the Oka. On the north the Slavs reached the great Valdai plateau from which Russia's largest rivers descend, and the southern part of the great lake region, that of Ilmen.[c]

There is no indication that the race is deficient in genius. It was the Slavs who opened the way to the west by two great movements which inaugurated the modern era — the Renaissance and the Reformation; by the discovery of the laws that govern the universe, and the plea for liberty of thought. The Pole Copernicus was the herald of Galileo; the Czech, John Huss, the precursor of Luther. Poland and Bohemia, the two Slav peoples most nearly connected with the west by neighbourhood and religion, can cite a long list of men distinguished in letters, science, politics, and war. Ragusa alone could furnish an entire gallery of men talented along all lines. There where remoteness from the west and foreign oppression have made study impossible and prevented single names from becoming widely known, the people have manifested their genius in songs which lack none of the qualities inherent in the most splendid poetry of the west. In that popular impersonal literature which we admire so frankly in the *romanceros* of Spain, the ballads of Scotland and Germany, the Slav, far from yielding the palm to the Latin or the Teuton, perhaps excels both. Nothing more truly poetical exists than the *pesmes* of Servia or the *doumas* of Little Russia; for, by a sort of natural compensation, it is among the Slavs least initiated into western culture that popular poetry has flowered most freely.

A WOMAN OF YAKUTSK

In temperament and character the Slavs present an ensemble of defects and qualities which unite them more nearly with the Latins and Celts than with their neighbours the Germans. They are characterised by a vivacity, a warmth, a mobility, a petulance, an exuberance not always found to the same degree among even the peoples of the south. Among the Slavs of purer blood these characteristics have marked their political life with a mobile, inconstant, and anarchical spirit which has rendered extremely difficult their national existence and which, taken with their geographical position, has been the great obstacle in the way of their civilisation. The distinguishing faculty of the race is a certain flexibility and elasticity of temperament and character which render it adaptable to the reception and the reproduction of all sorts of diverse ideas; the imitative faculty of the Slavs is well known. This gift is everywhere distributed among them; this Slav malleability, peculiar alike to Pole and Russian, is perhaps fundamentally but a result of their historical progress and of their geographical position. But lately entered in at the gate of civilisation, and during long years inferior to the neighbouring races, they have always gone to school to the others; instead of living by their own invention, they have lived by borrowing, and the imitative spirit has become their ruling faculty, having been for them the most useful as well as the most widely exercised.

In the west the Slavs fell under the influence of Rome; in the east, under that of Byzantium: hence the antagonism which during long centuries has set strife in the midst of the two chief Slavonic nations. United by their common origin and the affinity of their languages, they are, however, separated by the very elements of civilisation — religion, writing, and calendar; therein lies the secret of the moral and material strife between Russia and Poland — a strife which, after having nearly annihilated the one, actually cost the other its life; as though from the Carpathian to the Ural, on those vast even plains, there was not room at one time for two separate states.

In the northwest, on the banks of the Niemen and Dvina, appears a strange group, incontestably of Indo-European origin yet isolated amidst the peoples of Europe; harking back to the Slavs, yet forming a parallel branch rather than offshoot — the Letto-Lithuanian group. Shut away in the north by marshy forests, restricted by powerful neighbours, the Lithuanian group long remained closed to all outer influences, whether of East or West. Last of all the peoples of Europe to accept Christianity, its language even to-day is the nearest of European tongues to the Sanskrit. The bone of contention among the Germans, the Poles, and the Russians, who each in turn obtained a footing among them and left an influence on their religion, they found themselves divided into Protestants, Catholics, and Orthodox.

Mixed with Poles and Russians, menaced on both sides with complete absorption, the Lithuanians and the Samogitians, their brothers by race and language, still number in ancient Lithuania nearly two million souls, Catholics for the most part; they formed the majority of the population of Vilna and Kovno. In Prussia some two hundred thousand Lithuanians constitute the representatives of the ancient population of oriental Prussia, whose name is derived from a people of that race which kept its language intact up to the seventeenth century.

The second existing group of this family, the Letts, crossed probably with Finns, number more than a million souls; they inhabit chiefly Courland, Vitetesk and Livonia; but, converted, subjected, and made slaves of by the Teutonic kinghts, they still live under the dominion of the German barons of the Baltic provinces, with whom they have nothing in common but their religion — Lutheranism. Like the Finnish tribes outside of Finland, the Letts and Lithuanians, scanty in number and widely scattered, are incapable of forming by themselves a nation or a state. Out of this intermixture of races by the assimilation of the ruder by the more civilised, was formed a new people — a homogenous nation. In fact, contrary to popular prejudice there is in Russia something more than an intermixture of diverse races — there is what we to-day call a "nationality" — as united, as compact, and as self-conscious as any nation in the world. Russia, notwithstanding all her various races, is yet no incoherent mass, no political conglomeration or mosaic of peoples. She resembles France in her national unity rather than Turkey or Austria.

If Russia must be compared to a mosaic, let it be to one of those ancient pavements whose scheme is a single substance of solid color edged with a border of diverse forms and shades — most of Russia's original alien populations being relegated to her borders and forming around her a sort of belt of uneven width.

It is in the centre of Russia that is found that uniformity of much more marked among the Russians than among all other peoples of Europe; from one end of the empire to the other the language presents fewer dialects and less localisms than most of our western languages. The cities all look alike; the peasants have the same customs, the same manner of life. The nation resembles the country, having the same unity, almost the same monotony as the plains which it peoples.

### The Great Russians and the Little Russians

There are, however, two principal types, almost two peoples, speaking two dialects and wholly separated from each other: the Great Russians and the Little Russians. In their qualities and in their defects they represent in Russia the eternal contrast of north and south. Their history is no less diversified than their nature; the first have their centre at Moscow, the second at Kiev. Stretching, the one to the northeast, the other to the southwest, these two unequal halves of the nation do not precisely correspond to the two great physical zones of Russia. This is due partly to nature, partly to history, which has hindered the development of the one and fostered that of the other. The southern steppes, open to every invasion, long arrested the expansion of the Little Russians, who for centuries were shut up in the basins of the Dnieper, the Bug, and the Dniester; while the Great Russians spread freely in the north and east and established themselves in the enormous basin of the Volga; masters of nearly all the forest regions and of the great Ural Lake, they took possession of the Black Belt and the steppes along the Volga and the Don.

The White Russian inhabits Mohilev, Vitebsk, Grodno, Minsk — a region possessing some of the finest forests in Russia, but whose soil is marshy and unwholesome. United politically with the Little Russian, the two have been classed under the name Western Russians. Subjected at an early date by Lithuania, whose dialect became its official language, White Russia was with the greater part of Little Russia united to Poland, and was for centuries the object of strife between that nation and the Muscovite czars, from the effects of which strife she still bleeds. Of the three Russian tribes this is perhaps the purest in blood; but thanks to the sterility of the soil and the remoteness of the sea, she has remained the poorest and least advanced in civilisation.

The Great Russians are the most vigorous and expansive element of the Russian nation, albeit the most mixed. Finnish blood has left its traces in their physique; Tatar dominion in their character. Before the advent of the Romanovs they formed alone the Muscovite Empire, and their czars took the title "Sovereign of all the Russias" long before Alexis, father of Peter the Great, justified this title by the annexation of the Ukraine. Hence Great Russia, under the name Muscovite, has been considered by certain foreigners the true, the only Russia. This is an error; since the Great Russian, the product of the colonisation of central Russia by the western Russians before the invasion of the Tatars antidates the state and even the village of Moscow. If, therefrom has emerged the Muscovite autocracy, it is impossible to cut the ties that bind it to the great Slav republic of the world whose name is still the active symbol of liberty — Novgorod.

Least Slav of all the peoples that pretend to the name, the Great Russian has been the coloniser of the race. His whole history has been one long struggle against Asia; his conquests have contributed to the aggrandisement of Europe. Long the vassal of the Tatar khans, he never forgot under Asiatic domination his European origin; and in the farthest limits of Muscovy the very name Asiatic is an insult to the peasant.

Conqueror over Asia, influenced morally and physically by all the populations assimilated or subjugated by him in his march from the Dnieper to the Ural, the Great Russian lost something of his independence, his pride, his individuality; but he gained in stability and solidity.

In spite of the obvious evidences of his mixed blood, the Great Russian is in perfect harmony with the Caucasian race by the exterior characteristics which distinguish it — his stature, his complexion, the colour of his hair and eyes. He is apt to be tall, his skin is white, his eyes are very often blue; his hair is usually blond, light chestnut, or red. The long heavy beard so dear to the heart of the moujik and which all the persecutions of Peter the Great failed to induce him to dispense with, is in itself a mark of race, as nothing could be smoother than the chin of the Mongol, the Chinese, or the Japanese.

The Little Russians dwelling in the south have brown or dark chestnut hair, and are of purer race, dwelling nearer to the Occident; they pride themselves upon their comparatively unmixed blood, their more temperate climate, their less dreary land; they are a more imaginative, more dreamy, more poetic people than their neighbours of the north. It is in Little Russia that the Zaparogians belong, the most celebrated of those Cossack tribes which in the Ukraine or the southern steppes played so important a rôle between the Poles, the Tatars, and the Turks, and whose name will ever remain in Russia the synonym of freedom and independence. Even to-day the Zaparogian, with his liberal or democratic tradition, remains the more or less conscious and avowed ideal of the majority of the Little Russians. Another reason, in the history of the Ukraine, which makes for democratic instincts in the Little Russians is the foreign origin and denaturalisation of a great part of the higher classes among the Poles and Great Russians. From this double motive the Little Russian is perhaps more susceptible to political aspirations, more accessible to revolutionary seduction than his brother of Great Russia.

Of the Cossacks of to-day only those of the Black Sea transplanted to the Kuban between the sea of Azov and the Caucasus are Little Russians; the Cossacks of the Don and the Ural are Great Russians.[b]

## SOCIAL AND POLITICAL ORGANISATION

It is extremely difficult to draw an approximately correct picture of the life of the Russian Slavs even in its barest outlines. Among the widely scattered tribes there was hardly more than one element tending towards union — that of language. Frequent contact with the populations living on their borders and wedged in between them, must of itself have produced considerable modifications in their mode of life.

The entire social organisation of the early Slavs, like that of all other Aryan and non-Aryan peoples, was based upon kinship or descent from a common ancestor.[a] Even in the Varangian period we can discover traces of this primeval organisation in clans among a few tribes. In time of peace these clans were in the habit of meeting together in order to discuss common affairs. The chronicler [h] uses the expression "came together" when he wants to speak of decisions taken in common. This practice seems to have been known to all Slavonic peoples. Among the Russian Slavs these folkmotes were known under the name of vetché, and they remained to the end of their existence a necessary part of the political institutions, not only in the northern city republics, Novgorod and Pskov, but also in nearly all the principalities of Russia, with the exception of one of the latest founded, Moscow.

Among these tribes we also find native princes or clan chieftains (kniaz), and it is also certain that as early as the ninth century there were among the Russian Slavs private owners of tracts of land who occupied an advantageous position as compared with the great bulk of the members of the community, and from whom the latter nobles (boyars) were descended. But on the whole the village community formed the nucleus of the entire political and economic organisation of the eastern or Russian Slavs. It was a world complete in itself, self-sufficient and independent both economically and juridically. The community was the possessor of the soil, which was periodically redistributed among its component members; the separate patriarchal families, and the assembly of the heads of the families was the body that judged and decided all things pertaining to the community. It is thus that we are to understand the apparently contradictory reports of the Byzantine writers, who say, on the one hand, that the Slavs know of no government and do not obey any individual, and on the other hand speak of a popular government that has existed from ancient times, that discusses all things in common, and that has many petty princes at its head.

It is self-evident that a government adapted to the requirements of a village community must assume a different character as soon as the settlement gains in extent and assumes the character of a city. And cities grew up quite early in northern and southwestern Russia. Toward the end of the ninth century Kiev had a wide fame as a large and populous city. Constantine Porphyrogenitus also knows of Novgorod, Smolensk, Linbetch, Tchernigov, Vishgorod, and Vititchev; in the time of Igor more than twenty cities can be named. The question as to the origin of Russian cities has called forth much debate and an extensive literature.

The chief difficulty lies in a proper understanding of the so-called Bavarian geographer, a writer of the ninth or tenth century, who counts, in his description of the northern Slavs, some twenty peoples with more than 3,760 cities. These latter he calls now *civitates*, now *urbes*, without indicating that there is any distinction of meaning to be attached to these terms, so that we are left to conclude that both names denote settlements. The present consensus of opinion as to those old Russian cities is as follows:

The old word *grad*, (now *gorod*, city) denoted any space surrounded by a palisade or earthworks. Thus there were wooden and earthen cities built for protection in time of war, and every community had its city. But in the regions that offered a natural protection by their inaccessible and swampy character the need for these cities was not so urgent, so that the wooded and marshy north had fewer cities than the open south. Numerous remains of these ancient earth piles enable us to recognise the position and wide extension of these old Slavonic settlements. Sometimes they are circular in form, others consist of a double angular trench with outlying earthworks. These are to be distinguished from the wooden cities, which were originally built for trading purposes, and only later were fenced in and enclosed, so that they could also serve for protective purposes. They were built in favourable situations, adjacent to some trade route. The more complex social relations that grew up in them demanded a more thorough organisation of social and political life, for which the village community did indeed furnish the basis, but which, in the long run, was found to be inadequate. The questions of general interest to the city were settled in the first place by the vetché, which greatly resembled the village gathering of the family elders.

But the need of a power which should decide all questions that might arise while the vetché was in abeyance, was more pressing in the cities, and favoured the development of the power — originally very limited, — of the *kniazes* or princes, who were elective and whose dignity was neither hereditary nor lifelong. The prince did not even have a permanent military following; his dignity was of a purely personal nature. It is certain that not he but the vetché had the power to make laws. Our information concerning the political organisation of the earliest period of Russian history is very scanty, and we know more of what it lacked than of what it possessed. What strikes us most is the absence of a military organisation. In times of danger, those who could defend themselves took up arms, the remainder fled to places of safety.

Nor can we discern with certainty any social differentiation into classes. On the other hand we know that a thriving trade was being carried on in the ninth century along the route which led from the gulf of Finland through Lake Ilmen to the Dvina and down the Dnieper to the Black Sea and thence to Greece. The oldest wooden cities lay along the famous route of the Varangians to the Greek Empire, along which amidst many dangers, the raw products of the north were exchanged for the finished commodities of the

NATIVE OF YAKUTSK

south. It is owing to these dangers that the trader had also to be a warrior, and it is into those ancient trade relations — peaceful intercourse enforced by warlike means — that we are to look for the most important arms of the old Russian state. Who discovered this trade route? We see no compelling reason to deny the honour to the Slavs, although it is established beyond doubt that even before the middle of the ninth century the Northmen reached Byzantium along this route. On the other hand, the marauding and trading expeditions which were carried on by Russians in the tenth century and earlier to the sea of Azov, the Caspian, and further still to the Caucasus and the shores of Persia, emanated from Scandinavians, and not from Slavs.

### RELIGION

The religious conceptions of the Russian Slavs were but little developed. All other Aryan peoples, including the western Slavs, excel them in this respect. There was neither a distinct priestly class, nor were there images of the gods, nor were there distinct types of gods. The Arabian travellers almost unanimously ascribe sun worship to the eastern Slavs, and Byzantine writers before the ninth century tell of a belief in a supreme being who rules the universe. It is now generally accepted that this supreme god was called Svarog and was a personification of heaven and light, while sun and fire were regarded as his children. Perun, the thunder god, and Veles, god of herds, both mentioned by the oldest chronicler, must be brought in relation to the sun. But it is highly probable that these two gods were taken over by the Slavs from their Varangian rulers. Water also was regarded as sacred, and, like the forest, it was filled with animate beings which must be propitiated with sacrifices, since they had relations to human beings. Water, fire, and earth were related to death. The *russalki*, shades of the dead, swam about in the water, and the bodies of the dead were given up to the flames in order to make easier their passage to the realm of the dead (*rai*). The

[862 A.D.]

slaves, as well as the wife and the domestic animals were burned on the funeral pyre, and cremation was preceded by a feast and games in honour of the dead. But burial also was common.g

We find the Russian Slavs about the middle of the ninth century split up into numerous tribes, settled on the soil and engaged chiefly in hunting and agriculture. A continental people, everywhere confining itself to the inland country, leaving the sea-borders to non-Slavonic tribes. Politically they were in the midst of the transition from the clan organisation to the village community, without any central authority, without any military organisation, and but little able to resist the inroads from north, south, and east, of populations who lived by plunder.a  The primitive condition of their political organisation, their extreme subdivision into tribes and cantons, the endless warfare of canton with canton, delivered them up defenceless to every invader. While the Slavs of the south paid tribute to the Chazars, the Slavs of Ilmen, exhausted by internecine conflicts, decided to call in the Varangians. "Let us seek," they said, "a prince who will govern us and reason with us justly. Then," continues Nestor,h "the Tchud, the Slavs (of Novgorod), the Krivitchi, and other confederate tribes said to the Varangian princes: 'Our land is great and has everything in abundance, but it lacks order and justice; come and take possession and rule over us.'"

## THE VARANGIAN PERIOD (862–1054 A.D.)

To the elements that have obtained a permanent foothold on the soil of modern Russia and affected the Slavs in a greater or less degree, a new one must now be added in the Varango-Russians. The brave inhabitants of Sweden and Norway, who were known in western Europe under the name of Northman or Normans, directed their first warlike expeditions against their Slavonian and Finnish neighbours. The flotillas of the vikings were directed to the shores of the Baltic, and austrvegr — the eastern route — was the name they gave to the journey into the country of the Finns and Slavs on the gulf of Finland and further inland. Gardar was the name they gave to the Slavo-Finnish settlements, Holmgardar was their name for Novgorod, Kaenungardar for Kiev. Mikligardar, for Constantinople, shows that the Normans first learned to know that city through the eastern Slavs. The Slavs, on the other hand, called those Scandinavians by a name given to them by the Finns — Rus. The Scandinavians who sent their surplus of fighting men to Russia and were destined to found the Russian state, lived — as we learn from the form of the names that have come down to us — in Upland, Södermanland, and Östergötland, that is, on the east coast of Sweden north of Lake Mälar. In these lands and throughout the Scandinavian north, men who were bound to military chiefs by a vow of fidelity were called vaeringr (pl. vaeringjar, O. Sw. Warung), a name changed by the eastern Slavs into variag. It was these Russo-Varangians who founded the state of Old Russia.g

At the call of the Slavs of Novgorod and their allies, three Varangian brothers, Rurik, Sineus, and Truvor (Scand. Hrurekr, Sikniutr, Thorwardr), gathered together their kindred and armed followers, or drujina, and established themselves on the northern frontiers of the Slavs: Sineus to the northeast, on the White Lake; Rurik, the eldest, in the centre, on Lake Ladoga near the Volkhov River, where he founded the city of Ladoga; and Truvor to the northwest, at Izborsk, near Lake Pskov. The year 862 is usually assigned as the date in which the Varangians settled in Russia, and it is the official year for the founding of the Russian empire; but it is more probable that they had come before that date.

Shortly after their settlement the two younger brothers died and Rurik became sole chief of all the Varangian bands in northern Russia and assumed the title of grand-prince. He now became so powerful that he was able to subject Novgorod, which he made the capital of an empire stretching from the lakes in the north to the sources of the Dnieper in the south.*a* The country drained by that river was also occupied by Varangians, but independently of Rurik. Two chiefs by the name of Askold and Dir (Scand. Höskaldr and Dyri) wrested Kiev from the Chazars and ruled over the Polians, the most civilized tribe of the eastern Slavs. In 865 they led against Byzantium an expedition which consisted of at least two hundred ships, and according to Venetian accounts of three hundred and sixty ships, to which would correspond an army of about fourteen thousand warriors. A tempest arose and destroyed the fleet in the sea of Marmora. The barbarians attributed their disaster to the wonder-working virgin, and it is reported that Askold embraced Christianity. This expedition has a two-fold importance: (1) it gives us the *first* certain date in Russian history; and (2) it introduced the seeds of Christianity into Russia. In the following year, 866, the patriarch Photius established a bishopric at Kiev.

After the death of his brothers Rurik reigned till his death in 879, when he was succeeded, not by his son Igor (Scand. Ingvarr), but by the eldest member of his family Oleg (Scand. Helge). In 882 he set out from Novgorod with an army composed of Varangians and the subject Slavo-Finnish tribes — Tchuds, Merians, Vesians, Ilmen Slavs, and Krivitchi — sailed down the upper Dnieper, took Smolensk, freed the Radimichi and the Severians from the yoke of the Chazars and incorporated them in his empire, and finally reached Kiev. Askold and Dir were then got rid of by an act of treachery, and Kiev was made the capital of an empire embracing nearly all the eastern Slavs.

### The Treaty with Constantinople

But Kiev was only one of the stages in the southward progress of the Varangians. The great city of the east, Constantinople, was the glittering prize that dazzled their eyes and was ever regarded as the goal of their ambition. Accordingly, in 907, Oleg sailed with a fleet of two thousand boats and eighty thousand men, and reached the gates of Constantinople. The frightened emperor was obliged to pay a large ransom for the city and to agree to a treaty of free commercial intercourse between the Russians and the Greeks. A particular district in the suburbs of the city was assigned as the place of residence for Russian traders, but the city itself could be visited by no more than fifty Russians simultaneously, who were to be unarmed and accompanied by an imperial officer.*g a*

Oleg's Varangian guard, who seem to have been also his council, were parties with him to this treaty, for their assent appears to have been requisite to give validity to an agreement affecting the amount of their gains as conquerors. These warriors swore to the treaty by their gods Perun and Volos, and by their arms, placed before them on the ground: their shields, their rings, their naked swords, the things they loved and honoured most. The gorged barbarian then departed with his rich booty to Kiev, to enjoy there an uncontested authority, and the title of Wise Man or Magician, unanimously conferred upon him by the admiration of his Slavonic subjects.

## The First Written Document of Russian History (911 A.D.)

Three years after this event, in 911, Oleg sent ambassadors to Constantinople to renew the treaty of alliance and commerce between the two empires. This treaty, preserved in the old chronicle of Nestor, is the first written monument of Russian history, for all previous treaties were verbal. It is of value, as presenting to us some customs of the times in which it was negotiated.

Here follow some of the articles that were signed by the sovereigns of Constantinople and of Kiev respectively:

II. "If a Greek commit any outrage on a Russian, or a Russian on a Greek, and it be not sufficiently proved, the oath of the accuser shall be taken, and justice be done.

III. "If a Russian kill a Christian, or a Christian kill a Russian, the assassin shall be put to death on the very spot where the crime was committed. If the murderer take to flight and be domiciliated, the portion of his fortune, which belongs to him according to law, shall be adjudged to the next of kin to the deceased; and the wife of the murderer shall obtain the other portion of the estate which, by law, should belong to him.

IV. "He who strikes another with a sword, or with any other weapon, shall pay three litres of gold, according to the Russian law. If he have not that sum, and be affirms it upon oath, he shall give the party injured all he has, to the garment he has on.

V. "If a Russian commit a theft on a Greek, or a Greek on a Russian, and he be taken in the act and killed by the proprietor, no pursuit shall be had for avenging his death. But if the proprietor can seize him, bind him, and bring him to the judge, he shall take back the things stolen, and the thief shall pay him the triple of their value.

X. "If a Russian in the service of the emperor, or travelling in the dominions of that prince, shall happen to die without having disposed of his goods, and has none of his near relations about him, his property shall be sent to Russia to his heirs; and, if he have bequeathed them by testament, they shall be in like manner remitted to the legatee."

The names of Oleg's ambassadors who negotiated this treaty of peace, show that all of them were Northmen. From this we may conclude that the government of the country was as yet wholly in the hands of the conquerors.

### THE REIGN OF IGOR

Igor, the son of Rurik, who was married to a Scandinavian princess named Olga (Helga), was nearly forty years of age when he succeeded Oleg in 913. He ascended the throne under trying circumstance, for the death of the victor revived the courage of the vanquished and the Drevlians raised the standard of revolt against Kiev; but Igor soon quelled them, and punished them by augmenting their tribute. The Uglitches, who dwelt on the southern side of the Dnieper, contended longer for their liberty against the voyevod Sveneld, whom Igor had despatched against them. One of their principal towns held out a siege of three years. At last they too were subdued and made tributary.

Meanwhile new enemies, formidable from their numbers and their thirst for pillage, showed themselves on the frontiers of Russia: these were the Petchenegs, famous in the Russian, Byzantine, and Hungarian annals, from

the tenth to the twelfth century. They were a nomad people, of the Turcoman stock, whose only wealth consisted in their lances, bows and arrows, their
flocks and herds, and their swift horses, which they managed with astonishing
address. The only objects of their desires were fat pastures for their cattle,
and rich neighbours to plunder. Having come from the east they established
themselves along the northern shores of the Black Sea. Thenceforth occupying the ground between the Greek and the Russian empires, subsidised by
the one for its defence, and courted by the other from commercial motives —
for the cataracts of the Dnieper and the mouths of the Danube were in the
hands of those marauders — the Petchenegs were enabled for more than two
hundred years to indulge their ruling propensity at the expense of their neighbours. Having concluded a treaty with Igor, they remained for five years
without molesting Russia; at least Nestor does not speak of any war with
them until 920, nor had tradition afforded him any clue to the result of that
campaign.

The reign of Igor was hardly distinguished by any important event until
the year 941, when, in imitation of his guardian, he engaged in an expedition
against Constantinople. If the chroniclers do not exaggerate, Igor entered
the Black Sea with ten thousand barks, each carrying forty men. The imperial
troops being at a distance, he had time to overrun and ravage Paphlagonia,
Pontus, and Bithynia. Nestor speaks with deep abhorrence of the ferocity
displayed by the Russians on this occasion; nothing to which they could
apply fire or sword escaped their wanton lust of destruction, and their prisoners were invariably massacred in the most atrocious manner — crucified,
impaled, cut to pieces, buried alive, or tied to stakes to serve as butts for the
archers. At last the Greek fleet encountered the Russian as it rode at anchor
near Pharos, prepared for battle and confident of victory. But the terrible
Greek fire launched against the invaders struck them with such dismay that
they fled in disorder to the coasts of Asia Minor. Descending there to pillage,
they were again routed by the land forces, and escaped by night in their barks,
to lose many of them in another severe naval defeat. By the confession of
the Russian chronicles, Igor scarcely took back with him a third part of his
army.

Instead of being discouraged by these disasters, Igor prepared to revenge
them. In 944 he collected new forces [which included a large number of
Scandinavians collected for this special purpose by Igor's recruiting agents],
took the Petchenegs into his pay, exacting hostages for their fidelity, and again
set out for Greece. But scarcely had he reached the mouths of the Danube
when he was met by ambassadors from the emperor Romanus, with an offer
to pay him the same tribute as had been exacted by Oleg. Igor halted and
communicated this offer to his chief men, whose opinions on the matter are
thus reported by Nestor: "If Cæsar makes such proposals," said they, "is
it not better to get gold, silver, and precious stuffs, without fighting? Can we
tell who will be the victor, and who the vanquished? And can we guess what
may befall us at sea? It is not solid ground that is under our feet, but the
depths of the waters, where all men run the same risks."

In accordance with these views Igor granted peace to the empire on the
proposed conditions, and the following year he concluded with the emperor a
treaty, which was in part a renewal of that made by Oleg.[1] Of the fifty

[1 This treaty was not so favourable to the Russians as the one concluded with Oleg — a
result, evidently, of the former defeat. Another point of importance is that it makes mention
of Russian Christians, to whom there is no allusion in the treaty of 911. From this we may
conclude that Christianity had spread largely during this interval.g]

names attached on the part of Russia to this second treaty, three are Slavonic, the rest Norman.

Igor, being now advanced in years, was naturally desirous of repose, but the insatiable cupidity of his comrades in arms forced him to go to war. From the complaints of his warriors it appears that the Russian, like the German princes, furnished their faithful band with clothing, arms, horses, and provisions. "We are naked," Igor's companions and guards said to him, "while the companions of Sveneld have beautiful arms and fine clothing. Come with us and levy contributions, that we may be in plenty with thee." It was customary with the grand prince to leave Kiev every year, in November, with an army, and not to return until April, after having visited his cities and received their tributes. When the prince's magazine was empty, and the annual contributions were not sufficient, it became necessary to find new enemies to subject to exactions, or to treat as enemies the tribes that had submitted. To the latter expedient Igor now resorted against the Drevlians. Marching into their country he surcharged them with onerous tributes, besides suffering his guards to plunder them with impunity. His easy success in this rapacious foray tempted him to his destruction. After quitting the country of his oppressed tributaries, the thought struck him that more might yet be squeezed out of them. With this view he sent on his army to Kiev, probably because he did not wish to let his voyevods or lieutenants share the fruit of his contemplated extortions, and went back with a small force among the Drevlians, who, driven to extremity, massacred him and the whole of his guard near their town of Iskorost.[i]

## THE REGENCY OF OLGA

Olga, Igor's widow, assumed the regency in the name of her son Sviatoslav, then of tender age. Her first care was to revenge herself upon the Drevlians. In Nestor's narrative it is impossible to separate the historical part from the epic. The Russian chronicler recounts in detail how the Drevlians sent two deputations to Olga to appease her and to offer her the hand of their prince; how she caused their death by treachery, some being buried alive, while others were stifled in a bath-house; how she besieged their city of Iskorost and offered to grant them peace on payment of a tribute of three pigeons and three sparrows for each house; how she attached lighted tow to the birds and then sent them off to the wooden city, where the barns and the thatched roofs were immediately set on fire; how, finally, she massacred part of the inhabitants of Iskorost and reduced the rest to slavery.

But it was this vindictive barbarian woman that was the first of the ruling house of Rurik to adopt Christianity.[d] We have seen before how Christianity was planted in Kiev under the protection of Askold and Dir, and how the converts to the new religion were specially referred to in the commercial treaty between Oleg and the Byzantine emperor. There existed a Christian community at Kiev but it was to Constantinople that Olga went to be baptised in the presence of the patriarch and the emperor. She assumed the Christian name of Helena, and after her death she was canonised in the Russian church. On her return she tried also to convert her son Sviatoslav, who had by this time become the reigning prince, but all her efforts were unavailing. He dreaded the ridicule of the fierce warriors whom he had gathered about himself. And no doubt the religion of Christ was little in consonance with the martial character of this true son of the vikings. The chronicle of Nestor gives the following embellished account of Olga's conversion:[a]

### Nestor Tells of the Baptism of Olga

In the year 948 Olga went to the Greeks and came to Tsargorod (Constantinople). At that time the emperor was Zimischius,[1] and Olga came to him, and seeing that she was of beautiful visage and prudent mind, the emperor admired her intelligence as he conversed with her and said to her: "Thou art worthy to reign with us in this city." When she heard these words she said to the emperor: "I am a heathen, if you wish me to be baptised, baptise me yourself; otherwise I will not be baptised." So the emperor and patriarch baptised her. When she was enlightened she rejoiced in body and soul, and the patriarch instructed her in the faith and said to her: "Blessed art thou among Russian women, for thou hast loved light and cast away darkness; the sons of Russia shall bless thee unto the last generation of thy descendants." And at her baptism she was given the name of Helena, who was in ancient times empress and mother of Constantine the Great. And the patriarch blessed Olga and let her go.

OLGA

After the baptism the emperor sent for her and said to her: "I will take thee for my wife."

She answered: "How canst thou wish to take me for thy wife when thou thyself hast baptised me and called me daughter? for with the Christians this is unlawful and thou thyself knowest it."

And the emperor said: "Thou hast deceived me, Olga," and he gave her many presents of gold and silver, and silk and vases and let her depart, calling her daughter.

She returned to her home, going first to the patriarch to ask his blessing on her house and saying unto him: "My people are heathen and my son, too; may God preserve me from harm!"

And the patriarch said: "My faithful daughter, thou hast been baptised in Christ, thou hast put on Christ, Christ shall preserve thee as he preserved Enoch in the first ages, and Noah in the Ark, as he preserved Abraham from Abimelech, Lot from the Sodomites, Moses from Pharaoh, David from Saul, the three young men from the fiery furnace, and Daniel from the lions; thus shall he preserve thee from the enemy and his snares!" Thus the patriarch blessed her and she returned in peace to her own land and came to Kiev.

Olga lived with her son Sviatoslav and she repeatedly tried to induce him to be baptised, but he would not listen to her, for if any one then wished to be baptised it was not forbidden, but people mocked at him. And Olga often said, "My son, I have learned wisdom and rejoice; if thou knewest it, thou too wouldst rejoice." But he paid no heed to her, saying: "How

---

[1 According to another Ms., Constantine, son of Lev.]

should I alone adopt a strange faith, my droujina (followers, men-at-arms) would mock at me." She said: "If thou art baptised, all will do likewise," but he would not listen to his mother and persisted in the heathen customs, not knowing that who does not hearken to his mother shall fall into misfortune, for it is written, he that does not hearken to his father or mother, let him die the death.[1] And he was angered against his mother. However, Olga loved her son Sviatoslav, and said: "God's will be done! If God wills to have mercy on my race and on the Russian land, he will put into their hearts to turn to God, even as He did unto me." And having thus said, she prayed for her son and for the people night and day, and she brought up her son until he was grown to be a man.

### SVIATOSLAV; THE VICTORY OF NORTH OVER SOUTH

Sviatoslav assumed the reins of government in 964, and he ruled only till 972, but this short period was filled with warlike expeditions. He crushed the power of the Volga Bulgarians and of the Chazars, and he incorporated the Viatitchi in the empire — thus destroying the danger ever menacing from the east, and uniting all the Slavs under one dominion. In 968 he marched — at the instigation of the Greek emperor, who furnished him the means — with an army of sixty thousand men against the Bulgarians of the Danube, conquered Pereiaslavl (the location of which is unknown) and Durostorus (the modern Silistria), and began to form the project of erecting for himself a new empire on the ruins of the Bulgarian power, when tidings reached him of a raid of the Petchenegs against Kiev and of the imminent danger to his mother and children who were beleaguered in that town. Leaving garrisons in the conquered towns he hurried back by forced marches and drove the Petchenegs back into the steppe. He divided his Russian dominions among his three young sons, giving Kiev to Iaropolk, the land of the Drevlians to Oleg, and Novgorod to Vladimir; while he himself went back to Bulgaria, for "Pereiaslavl is dear to him, where all good things meet, fine stuffs, wine, fruits, and gold from Greece, silver and horses from Bohemia and Hungary, furs, wax, honey, and slaves from Russia."

In 970 he conquered Bulgaria and crossed the Balkans with an army of thirty thousand men. Defeated before Arcadipole (the present Lüle Burpas), his barbarian followers gave way to their plundering instincts, ravaged Macedonia, and scattered in all directions, while the emperor John Tzimiskes was making extensive preparations for their annihilation. Thus the year 971 was spent. In March of the next year the Russian garrison was almost annihilated at Pereiaslavl, which the Greeks took by storm, and only a small remnant reached Sviatoslav. In this hour of need Sviatoslav exhibited a tremendous energy. By recalling his roving bands he soon found himself at the head of sixty thousand men, and a pitched battle was fought. Twelve times the victory wavered from one side to the other, but finally their lack of cavalry and their inferior armament decided the day against the Russians, and they were forced back upon Drster. For three months they held the town against a regular siege, until, reduced in numbers by hunger and numerous sorties, Sviatoslav decided on a last desperate effort to break through the Greek lines. The battle is described in great detail by the Byzantine historians, in whom Sviatoslav's bravery excited admiration. Fifteen thousand Russians were left on the field, the survivors were forced

---

[1] *Ex. XXI, 17.*

back into Durostorus. Surrounded on all sides, Sviatoslav sued for peace, and Tzimiskes granted an honourable retreat to a foe so gallant and withal dangerous. He renewed with him the old treaties, undertook to supply his army with provisions on its retreat, and also to induce the Petchenegs to grant a free passage into Russia. But at the rapids of the Dnieper these sons of the steppe surprised Sviatoslav and killed him, and only a small remnant of his force, led by the voyevod Svenedl, reached Kiev.[g][a]

Sviatoslav's overthrow was, after all, a fortunate event for the Russian empire. Kiev was already a sufficiently eccentric capital; had Sviatoslav established the seat of government on the Danube, his successor would have gone still further; and Rurik, instead of being the founder of a mighty empire, would have been nothing more than the principal leader of one of those vast but transient irruptions of the northern barbarians, which often ravaged the world without leaving behind any permanent trace of their passage. But in the Greek emperor Tzimiskes, Sviatoslav met with a hero as pertinacious as himself, and with far more talent, and the Russians, driven back within the limits of Russia, were compelled to establish themselves there.[i]

VLADIMIR I

(Died 1015)

Sviatoslav's death seems to have left no perceptible influence on the destinies of Russia, for his three young sons were in the undisputed possession of authority while he and his warriors were fighting for a new empire in the Balkan peninsula. But his division of Russia among his sons, as if it were his private estate, soon showed its mischievous effects. In 977 civil war broke out between Iaropolk, who was at Kiev, and Oleg, who was in the Drevlian country. The latter was defeated in battle, and in his flight met death by the breaking down of a bridge thronged with fugitives. His territory was thereupon annexed by Iaropolk to his own dominions.

Vladimir, prince of Novgorod, the youngest of the three brothers, now became alarmed for his own safety and fled across the sea to seek refuge among the Scandinavian Varangians. After two years he returned with a numerous force of Norse adventurers, expelled from Novgorod the voyevods whom Iaropolk had installed there during his absence, and led his army against Kiev. On his march he conquered Polotsk on the Dvina, an independent Varangian principality, killing its prince by the name of Rogvolod (Scand. Rangvaldr) and forcing his daughter Rogneda to marry him. Iaropolk, betrayed by his chief men, surrendered Kiev without offering any resistance and finally delivered his own person into the hands of Vladimir, by whose order he was put to death. Vladimir now became sole ruler of Russia.

The victory of Vladimir over Iaropolk was achieved with the aid of Northmen and Novgorodians. It was, therefore, a victory of the Russian north over the Russian south, of Novgorod, where paganism was still unshaken, over Kiev, which was permeated with Christian elements. Vladimir was brought up in Novgorod, and during his two years' stay in Sweden he must have become still more strongly impregnated with heathen ideas. Accordingly we find that no sooner was he firmly seated on his throne at Kiev than he tried to restore the heathen worship to more than its pristine strength among the Russian Slavs. Statues of the gods were erected: Perun, Dashbog, Stribog, Simargla, Mokosh — all of them, with the exception of Perun, known to us hardly more than by name. Human sacrifices were introduced, and two Christians, a father and his son, who resisted this blood-tax, were killed by a fanatical mob — the first and only Christian martyrs on Russian soil. One is tempted to assume that the Russian Slavs had originally no representations of the gods, and that it was their Norse princes who introduced them — at any rate there is no mention of images before the arrival of the latter; while the mode of worship introduced by Vladimir bears a bloody character, quite alien to the eastern Slavs. It is evident that he is making a last effort to impart to the colourless paganism of his subjects a systematic character which would enable it to resist the growing new religion.

But the circumstances of this prince soon underwent a change. His Norse auxiliaries, whose rapacity he could not satisfy, he was soon obliged to dismiss. According to northern sagas he was even involved in a war with Sweden, the stronghold of heathenism. His new capital was in constant commercial intercourse with Byzantium, and the reports that reached him of its gorgeous worship made a deep impression on the imagination of the barbarian. But if he was to accept the religion of the Cæsars, he was determined to do it not as a suppliant, but as a conqueror.*g a* In what follows we give in full the circumstantial account of Nestor.

### NESTOR'S ACCOUNT OF VLADIMIR'S CONVERSION

In the year 987, Vladimir called together his boyars and the elders of the town, and said to them: "Behold, the Bulgarians have come to me saying: Receive our law; then came Germans and they praised their laws; after them came the Jews, and finally came the Greeks, blaming all other laws, but praising their own, and they spoke at great length, from the creation of the world, of the history of the whole world; they speak cunningly, and it is wonderful and pleasing to hear them; they say that there is another world, and that whosoever receives their faith, even though he die shall live to all eternity; but if he receive another law he shall burn in another world amidst flames. What think ye of it, and what will you answer?"

And the boyars and elders answered, "Thou knowest, prince, that nobody finds fault with his own, but on the contrary praises it; if thou desirest to test this matter deeply, send some of thy men to study their various faiths and see how each one serves God." And the speech pleased the prince and all the people; ten wise and good men were chosen and were told to go first to the Bulgarians and study their faith. So they went, and coming saw infamous doings, and how the people worshipped in their mosques, and they returned to their own country. And Vladimir said to them: "Go now to the Germans, and observe in the same manner, and afterwards go to the Greeks." They came to the Germans, and after having watched their church services, they went on to Tsargorad (Constantinople) and came to the emperor; the emperor asked them what brought them there, and they told him all that had happened. When he had heard it, he was glad and did them great honour from that day. The next day he sent to the patriarch saying: "There have come certain Russians to study our faith, prepare the church and thy clergy, and array thyself in thy episcopal robes that they may see the glory of our God." When the patriarch heard this, he called together his clergy and they celebrated the service as for a great festival, and they burned incense and the choirs sang. And the emperor went with the Russians into the church and they were placed in a spacious part so that they might see the beauty of the church and hear the singing; then they explained to them the archiepiscopal service, the ministry of the deacons and the divine office. They were filled with wonderment and greatly admired and praised the service. And the emperors Basil and Constantine called them and said, "Return now to your country." And they bade them farewell, giving them great gifts and showing them honour.

When they returned to their own country, the prince assembled the boyars and elders and said to them: "These are the men whom we have sent; they have returned, let us listen to what they have seen." And he said: "Speak before the droujina." And they said : " First we went to the Bulgarians and we observed how they worship in their temples, they stand without girdles, they sit down and look about them as though they were possessed by the demon, and there is no gladness amongst them, but only sorrow and a great stench; their religion is not a good one. We then went to the Germans, and we saw many services celebrated in their temples, but we saw no beauty there. Then we came to the Greeks, and they took us where they worship their God, and we no longer knew whether we were in heaven or on earth, for there is nothing like it on earth, nor such beauty, and we know not how to tell of it; we only know that it is there, that God dwells among men, and their service surpasses that of any other land. We can never forget its beauty, for as every man when he has tasted sweetness cannot afterwards endure bitterness, so can we no longer dwell here." The boyars answered: "If the Greek religion were evil, then thy grandmother Olga, who was wiser than all men, would not have adopted it." And Vladimir replied: "Where then shall we be baptised?" They answered: "Where thou wilt." And the year passed by.

In the year 988 Vladimir marched with his troops against Kherson, a Greek town, and the inhabitants shut themselves up in the town. So Vladimir established himself on the other side of the town, in the bay, at an arrow's throw from the town. And the people of Kherson fought hard against him, but he blockaded the town and they were exhausted, and Vladimir said to them: "If you do not surrender I will stay three years if necessary." But they would not listen to him.

Then Vladimir ranged his men in battle array and commanded them to build a trench towards the town. And a man of Kherson, by name Anastasius, threw out an arrow, on which he had inscribed: "To the east of thee lie springs, the waters of which come into the town through pipes; dig there and thou shalt intercept the water." When Vladimir heard this he looked up to heaven and said: "If this comes to pass I will be baptised." He commanded his soldiers to dig above the pipes, and he cut off the water, and the people, exhausted by thirst, surrendered.

So Vladimir with his droujina entered into the town. And he sent messengers to Basil and Constantine, saying: "Behold I have conquered your famous town. I have heard that you have a maiden sister; if you will not give her to me, I will do with your capital even as I have done with this town." The emperors were grieved when this message was brought to them and sent back the following answer: "It is not meet to give a Christian maiden in marriage to a heathen. If thou art baptised thou shalt receive what thou askest, and the kingdom of heaven besides, and thou shalt be of the same faith as we, but if thou wilt not be baptised we cannot give thee our sister."

When he heard this, Vladimir said to the emperor's messengers, "Tell your emperor thus: I will be baptised, for I have already inquired into your religion, and your faith and rites please me well as they have been described to me by the men whom we have sent." And when the emperors heard these words they rejoiced and persuaded their sister, who was named Anna, and sent to Vladimir saying: "Be baptised and we will send thee our sister." Vladimir answered: "Let them come with your sister to baptise me." When the emperors heard this they sent their sister with some dignitaries and priests; and she did not want to go and said: "I am going like a slave to the heathen, it would be better for me to die." But her brothers persuaded her saying: "It is through thee that God shall turn the hearts of the Russian people to repentance, and thou shalt save the land of Greece from a cruel war; seest thou not how much harm the Russians have already done to the Greeks? And now if thou goest not they will do more harm." And they persuaded her with difficulty. So she took ship, kissed her parents, and weeping went across the sea to Kherson.

When she arrived, the people of Kherson came out to greet her, led her into the town, and took her to the palace. By the will of God Vladimir's eyes were then sore and he could not see anything, he was greatly troubled. And the czarina [1] went unto him saying: "If thou desirest to be delivered from this malady, be baptised as quickly as possible, or otherwise thou wilt not be cured." When Vladimir heard this he said: "If this is accomplished, truly the God of the Christians is great:" and he was baptised. The bishop of Kherson after having announced it to the people, baptised Vladimir together with the czarina's priests, and as soon as he laid his hands on him, he saw. When Vladimir perceived how quickly he was healed, he glorified God, saying: "Now only do I know the true God." And when his droujina saw it, many were also baptised. Vladimir was baptised in the church of St. Basil, which is in Kherson in the midst of the town, where the people hold their market.

After the baptism Vladimir was wedded to the czarina. And when he had been baptised the priests expounded to him the Christian faith. After this Vladimir with the czarina and Anastasius and the priests of Kherson took the relics of St. Clement and St. Theba, his disciple, as well as the sacred vessels and relics, and he built a church on an eminence in the middle of the town, which had been raised with the earth taken from the trench, and this church still exists. As a wedding present to the czarina he gave back Kherson to the Greeks, and himself returned to Kiev. When he came there he commanded all the idols to be overthrown, some to be chopped in pieces, others cast into the flames. Then Vladimir had the following proclamation made throughout the town. "Whosoever to-morrow, rich or poor, mendicant or artisan, does not come to the river to be baptised, will be as an alien to me," When the people heard these words, they came joyfully saying: "If this faith were not good, the prince and the boyars would not have adopted it." The next day Vladimir came with the czarina's priests and those of Kherson to the banks of the Dnieper, and an innumerable multitude of people were assembled and they went into the water, some up to their necks, others to their breasts; the younger ones stood on the banks, men held their children in their arms, the adults were quite in the water, and the priests stood repeating

[1 In the original Nestor always calls thus the sister of the emperors.]

the prayers. And there was joy in heaven and on earth to see so many souls saved. When they were baptised the people returned to their homes and Vladimir rejoiced that he and his people knew God. He ordered that churches and priests should be established in all the towns, and that the people should be baptised throughout all the towns and villages; then he sent for the children of the chief families and had them instructed in book learning. Thus was Vladimir enlightened with his sons and his people, for he had twelve sons. And he henceforth lived in the Christian faith.[h]

### The Death of Vladimir the Christian

The chronicler then goes on to describe the changes wrought in Vladimir's character by his conversion: how this prince, who had hitherto been an oriental voluptuary and maintained in several places numerous harems with hundreds of wives, suddenly changed into the faithful husband of his Christian wife; and how he who had murdered his brother (whose wife he appropriated) and the father and brother of another of his wives, now became fearful of punishing offenders and criminals lest he commit a sin, so that it became the duty of his priests to admonish him to enforce justice and punish the guilty. All this, whether true or false, shows in what deep veneration the founder of Russian Christianity was held by subsequent generations.

On the other hand, his acceptance of Christianity does not seem to have diminished his love of war, which in those days, surrounded as the agricultural Russians were by semi-nomadic and marauding tribes, was indeed a social necessity. Throughout his reign he was engaged in suppressing revolts, reconquering territory lost during the reign of the weak Iaropolk — Galicia or Red Russia had then been lost to Poland — and punishing Lithuanians, Volga Bulgarians, and Petchenegs. To secure the southern frontier against these last, he erected a line of fortifications at strategical points and transplanted a large number of colonists from the north to the borders of the steppe.[a]

Vladimir died in 1015, leaving a large number of heirs by his numerous wives. From the division that he made among them of his states we learn what was the extent of Russia at that epoch. To Iaroslav he gave Novgorod; to Iziaslav, Polotsk; to Boris, Rostov; to Gleb, Murom — these last two principalities being in the Finn country; to Sviatoslav, the country of the Drevlians; to Vsevolod, Vladimir in Volhynia; to Mstislav, Tmoutarakan[1]; to his nephew Sviatopolk, the son of his brother and victim Iaropolk, the principality of Tourov, in the country of Minsk, founded by a Varangian named Tour, who, like Askold and Rogvolod, was not of the blood of princes.[j]

This division of the territories of the state among the heirs of the prince was in entire accord with the ideas of the Norse conquerors, who regarded their conquests as their private property. It was, moreover, dictated by the economic conditions of the time. Money being but rarely employed and all payments being made in service and in kind, it was indispensable, in making provision for the members of the ruling house, to supply them with territories and subjects. The immense extent of Russia, the lack of adequate means of communication, and its subdivision among a large number of tribes without any national cohesion, were further reasons for the introduction of this system of government.[a]

[1 An antiquarian inquiry instituted by Catherine in 1794 resulted in proving that Tmoutarakan was situated on the isle of Taman, forming a key to the confluence of the sea of Azov with the Black Sea.[k]]

## SVIATOPOLK IS SUCCEEDED BY IAROSLAV (1019 A.D.)

Sviatopolk, who claimed a divided parentage between Vladimir and Iaropolk — being the son of the widow of the latter, who on the murder of her husband was forced to live with the former, she being already pregnant — was at Kiev when the news of Vladimir's death arrived.   He had long indulged in a project for seizing the throne, which was favoured in its formation by the increasing imbecility of his father, whose death now ripened it into action. His ambitious schemes embraced a plan for securing the sole monarchy, by obtaining the grand princedom first, and then by artifice or treachery to put his brothers out of the way, so that he might thus reorganise under the one head the divided and independent governments.   The moment had now arrived when this violent scheme was to be put into execution.   His brother Boris, who was employed with the army against the Petchenegs, was the first object of his hate and fear, because his good qualities had so strongly recommended him, that he was the most popular of the brothers, and the most likely to gain the ascendency through the will of the people.   There was but one sure method to get rid of this formidable rival, and Sviatopolk did not hesitate to adopt it.   When the intelligence of his father's decease reached Boris, he declared that the throne devolved properly upon the elder brother, and rejected the unanimous offer of the soldiery to assist in placing him upon it.   This noble insensibility to the general wish alienated his troops, and exposed him to the designs of his treacherous rival.   The assassins who were commissioned to despatch him found easy access to his tent, and having first slain a faithful Russian who threw himself before the person of his master, they soon effected their horrible purpose.

Two other brothers met a similar fate.   Gleb was informed by letter that his father was ill, and desired his return.   On his way he was so injured by a fall from his horse as to be forced to continue his journey in a litter.   In this state he learned that Sviatopolk had issued orders for his murder, which, tempted probably by the reward, were carried into effect by his own cook, who stabbed him with a knife in the breast.   Both Gleb and Boris were afterwards sainted, which appears to have been the last compliment paid by the Russians to their ill-used princes.   These villainies alarmed a third brother, who fled to Hungary; but the emissaries of the triumphant assassin seized him in his flight, brought him back to the capital, and put him to death.

The way to the throne was now tolerably well cleared.   Sviatopolk I found no further difficulty in assuming the government of Kiev, and calling in such of the tributary provinces as his recent excesses either terrified into submission or reduced within his control.   But the most powerful opponent yet remained to be subjugated.

Iaroslav, prince of Novgorod, alarmed and outraged by the cruelties of his brother, and apprehending that, unless they were speedily arrested, they would spread into his own principality, determined to advance upon Kiev and make war on the usurping fratricide.   The Novgorodians, to whom he was greatly endeared by the wisdom and mildness of his sway, entered so warmly into the expedition, that the tyrant was driven out of Kiev without much cost of blood, and obliged to flee for refuge to his father-in-law, the duke of Poland. At that period Poland was resting from the ruinous effects of a disastrous and straggling campaign in Germany which had considerably reduced her power, and curtailed her means of satisfying the ambition of her restless ruler.   The representations of Sviatopolk rekindled the ardour of the Poles, who, animated as much by the desire of recovering those provinces which

Vladimir had formerly wrested from Miecelsas, as by the prospect of ulterior aggrandisement, readily fell into the proposals of the exiled prince to make an attempt for his restoration to the throne. Boleslav at the head of a powerful force, advanced into Russia. Iaroslav, however, apprised of the movements of the enemy, met them on the banks of the Bug, prepared for battle. The army of Boleslav lay at the opposite side. For some time the invader hesitated to ford the river under the fire of the Russian soldiers; and might, probably, have returned as he came, had not a petty occurrence excited his impetuosity, and urged him forward.

IAROSLAV I
(Died 1054)

A Russian soldier one day, while both armies lay inactive within sight of each other, stood upon the bank of the river, and with gesticulations and bold language mimicked the corpulent size and gait of the Polish duke. This insult roused the spirit of Boleslav, who, plunging into the water, and calling on his men to follow, landed in the face of the Russians at the head of his intrepid troops. A long and well-contested action took place, and tardily closed in favour of the Poles, who, flushed with victory, pursued the fugitives to the walls of the capital. Sviatopolk was now reinstated in his throne, and Iaroslav, disheartened by defeat, made his way to Novgorod, where, doubtful even of the fidelity of his own people, he prepared to cross the Baltic in order to get beyond the reach of his brother. The Novgorodians, however, were faithful, and proved their attachment to his person by taking down the rigging of the vessels which had been got in readiness for his departure, and by levying contributions amongst themselves for the purpose of enabling him to procure auxiliary troops to assist in the recovery of the grand principality.

In the meantime, Sviatopolk was unconsciously facilitating his own downfall. After the Poles had helped him to re-establish himself, he began to feel the oppressive superiority of their presence, and plotted a base design to remove them. He instigated the inhabitants and the soldiery to conspire against the strangers, and massacre them in the midst of their security. Boleslav discovered the plot before it had time to be carried into execution; and, disgusted at a design so cruel and treacherous, he resolved to take ample revenge. The capital was plundered of its accumulated wealth by the incensed Poles, who, but for the moderation of their leader, would have burned it to ashes; and, loaded with treasures, they returned towards the Russian frontiers. Sviatopolk was artful enough to turn the whole transaction to the discredit of his ally, and thus to rouse the courage of his followers, who were easily persuaded to take the field against Boleslav. The belligerents met on the banks of the Bug before the Poles had passed the boundaries. The battle that ensued terminated in the discomfiture of

[1019 A.D.]

Sviatopolk, who now returned with broken fortunes to the capital which he had so lately entered with acclamations of triumph. This was the opportunity for Iaroslav to appear with his followers. The usurper's troops were so reduced by his late disasters, that he was forced to seek assistance from the Petchenegs, the hereditary enemies of the country; and they, tempted by hopes of booty, flocked to his standard to resist the approach of Iaroslav. The armies met on a plain near the place where Boris had been assassinated by the command of the fratricide. The coincidence was fortunate, for Iaroslav, taking a prudent advantage of the circumstance, employed all his eloquence in describing to his soldiers the righteousness of the cause in which they were engaged against a second Cain, the shedder of a brother's blood. His oration, concluding with a fervent prayer to the Almighty to nerve his arm, and direct his sword, so that he might be made the instrument of reparation in so just a fight, wrought powerfully upon the assembled army, and excited them to an unexampled display of bravery. The advantage of numbers was on the opposite side; but such was the courage exhibited by the Novgorodians, that after a desperate battle, which lasted throughout the whole day, they succeeded in putting the enemy completely to flight. Sviatopolk took to horse and fled, but died in a wretched condition on the road.

The zeal and bravery of the Novgorodians were not forgotten by Iaroslav when he ascended the throne and concentrated the sole dominion in himself. His first attention was directed to the revision of the ill-constructed laws of their city, and to the grant of certain franchises, which had the effect of procuring unanimity amongst the inhabitants, and of establishing the peaceful arts and commercial interests of the place upon a sure and solid foundation. He at once evinced a capacity for legislation beyond the abilities of his most distinguished predecessors, and set about the labours of improvement in so vigorous a temper, and with so much aptitude for his objects, that the happiest results sprang up under his administration in all parts of the empire.

But it was not in the destiny of the age in which he lived to permit such extensive benefits to progress without interruption. His brother Mstislav, the seventh son of Vladimir, a warrior distinguished in his wars against the Kossoges, discontented with the enlarged authority that the grand princedom vested in the hands of Iaroslav, transmitted to him a petition praying of him to cede to him a part of the fraternal appanage which he governed. Iaroslav partially assented to the request, by granting to his brother the small territory of Murom. This grant was insufficient to satisfy Mstislav, who immediately equipped an army and proceeded to wage an offensive war against the monarch. In this war the invader was successful, but he was not ungenerous in his triumph; for when he had vanquished the grand prince, he restored to him so large a portion of his possessions that the empire became equally divided between them. In this league of amity the brothers continued to govern for seven years, during the remainder of the life of Mstislav; and at his death the colossal empire, with all its appanages, reverted to the hands of Iaroslav.

It is in this part of his reign, and in this memorable period in the annals of the nation, that we find the first development of justice in Russian legislation, and the first application of philosophy to the management of public affairs. Although Iaroslav's career commenced with war, and although he extended his arms into Finland, Livonia, Lithuania, and Bulgaria, and even penetrated into Byzantium, yet it was not by war that the glory of his name or the ability of his rule was to be accomplished. His wars could hardly claim the merits of conquests; and in some instances they terminated in such vague conclusions, that they resembled drawn battles on which much treasure had been lavished in vain. In Greece he was routed. He was driven before the soldiers of Sviatopolk, and forced to surrender at his own gates to the victorious Mstislav. His utmost successes amounted to preservation against aggression; and so indifferent was he to the barbarian mode of elevating the empire by wanton and hazardous expeditions into the neighbouring countries, that on most of those occasions he entrusted the command of his army to his lieutenants. It is necessary to explain that part of his character, in order that the loftiness of his nature may be the more clearly understood.

At this period the Russian Empire comprehended those enormous tracts that lie between the Volga and the lower Danube, and stretch from the Black Sea to the Baltic. This accumulation of territory was not the work of a progressive political system; it was not accomplished by the growth of a powerful government or by the persevering pursuit of co-operating interests, and the increasing circles of acquisition were in a constant state of dismemberment, separation, and recall. The surface of the land from the days of Rurik was overrun by revolutions. The marauder, legalised by his tribe, haunted the forest and devastated the populous places, carrying away with him plunder, or usurping authority wherever he remained. The feudal system, introduced by the Scandinavians as a provision for trouble-some leaders, was carried to excess. The nominal head was disavowed and resisted at will; and the subordinate governments made war upon each other, or joined in schemes of rapine, with impunity. The maintenance of each fief seemed to depend upon civil war; and the office of the grand prince was not so much to govern the dominions he possessed, as to keep, if he could, the dominion he was called upon to govern.

Russia, combining these gigantic outlines of territory, was now, for the second time, united under one head; but, for the first time, under a head that could discern her necessities, and provide for them. Her civilisation was in progress, but it wanted the impetus of knowledge, and the control of law. The reign of the sword had done its work: what was required was the reign of justice and wisdom to improve and consolidate the triumphs and acquisitions of the barbarian era. In Iaroslav, Russia found a prince whose genius was adapted to her critical circumstances. He effectually raised her from obscurity, and placed her for a time amongst the family of European states. He made her church independent, increased the privileges of the people, facilitated the means of instruction, and elevated her national dignity by contracting domestic alliances with the most powerful countries. His sister was queen of Poland; his three daughters-in-law were Greek, German, and English princesses; and the queens of Norway, Hungary, and France were his daughters. But these were the least memorable evidences of his greatness. He gave Russia a code of laws, which was more valuable to her than the highest connections, or the most ambitious accessions of dominion.

### IAROSLAV'S CODE OF LAWS

This code must be judged in reference to the times in which it was enacted and in comparison with the formless mass of confused precedents it super-seded. The existence of commercial cities in Russia so far back as the invasion of Rurik, may be accepted as presumptive proof that there were not wanting some regulations to render individuals amenable to the common good. But these were merely the rude precepts of the hunting and agricultural nations matured into a stronger form, and adapted to the wants of the commercial community. When the Scandinavians subjugated the aborigines, the languages, customs, and laws of both fell into still greater confusion by admixture. When each was imperfect, it was unlikely that a forcible intermixture would have improved either, or led to the harmonious union of both. It is to be observed, too, that none of the nations that made up the population possessed written laws; so that whatever notions of legislation they entertained, were constantly liable to the fluctuations of capricious opinion, and were always subject to the interpretation of the strong over the weak. Where there were no records there was but little responsibility, and even that little was diminished by the character of the rulers and the lawlessness of the ruled. The exclusive attention of the princes being of necessity confined to the most effectual methods of preserving their sovereignties, of enlarging their domains, and of exacting tributes, it was natural that the unsystematic and crude usages that prevailed should fall into further contempt, and, instead of acquiring shape and consistency from experience, become still more oppressive, dark, and indecisive.

It was this matter of incongruities that Iaroslav cast out; supplying its place with a series of written laws, in which some sacrifices were made to popular customs, but which, on the whole, was an extraordinary boon to a people that, like mariners at sea without a compass, were tossed about in a tumult of uncertainty and perplexity. Had Iaroslav been a mere soldier, like the majority of his predecessors, he would have employed his talents in the field, and directed the enormous physical means at his command to the purposes of a wild and desolating ambition. But his policy was in advance of the heathen age: it restrained boundless licentiousness, created immunities, protected life and property, bestowed rewards, enacted punishments, established safeguards and facilities for trade, and expounded and confirmed those distinctions of ranks in which a community on a large scale recognises the elements of its permanency. He had the magnanimity to forego vulgar conquests for the higher conquest of prejudices and ancient habits. The people, probably fatigued with the restlessness of their mode of life, and yearning after repose and settlement, rendered now more necessary by the rapid increase of their numbers, received his laws with gratitude.

A short outline of the leading provisions of these laws will form a curious and valuable commentary upon the character of the grand prince, and the actual state of the people at this period (1018). The first article of the code empowers the friends of a murdered man to take satisfaction upon the murderer; constituting the law as the public avenger only in cases where there are no friends to take their vengeance in kind. In the event of there being no relatives to take the revenge into their own hands, the law goes on to enact that the assassin shall pay into the public treasury a certain fine, according to the rank of his victim. Thus, for the murder of a boyar, or thane of the prince, the mulct was fixed at the highest penalty of eighty grivnas;[1] for a page of the prince, his cook, or other domestics, for a merchant, for the sword-bearer of a boyar, and for every free Russian, without distinction of origin, forty grivnas; for a woman, half the usual fine: no fine for killing a slave; but if killed without sufficient cause, the value to be paid to the master: for a serf belonging to a boyar or free Russian, five grivnas to the owner; for the superintendent of a village, an artisan, schoolmaster, or nurse, twelve grivnas; for a female servant, six grivnas to the master, and twelve to the state.

---

[1] A copper coin, of the value, as near as we can ascertain, of about $4\frac{1}{2}d.$ of English money.

From these penalites a correct estimate may be formed of the principles upon which the social fabric was erected. In all these provisions the rich were favoured above the poor, the strong above the weak. The life of a woman, because her utility in a barbarous community was rated according to its menial value, was fixed at half the worth of a man's, to be proportioned according to her station. The murder of a slave was not visited with any penalty whatever; the exception constituting, in fact, the privilege to kill a slave at pleasure. Slavery was carried to extremity in Russia. Prisoners of war and their posterity were condemned to perpetual slavery; the poverty of the soil, and the oppression of its lords, forced many to sell their freedom for limited periods; insolvent debtors became slaves by law; and all freemen who married slaves unconditionally, participated in their servitude.

Yet, degrading as these institutions must be considered, it appears that the rights of the person were scrupulously maintained. Thus this code enumerates penalties for striking a blow, describes the different degrees of the offence, and regulates the responsibility accordingly. The distinctions drawn between the different modes of striking are singular, and help to show that, ill as the Russians could appreciate public liberty, they had a jealous sense of that individual respect which, in modern Europe, is called the point of honour. The penalty for striking a blow with the scabbard or handle of a sword, with the fist, a stick, cup, or goblet, was twelve grivnas — equal to the fine for murdering an artisan or a schoolmaster. If the blow was struck with a club, which, we presume, was considered a plebeian weapon, the penalty was only three grivnas. But the most characteristic penalty was that of twelve grivnas for pulling a man by the beard, or knocking out a tooth. The origin of this law may be easily traced to the Goths and Germans, who were rigid in the preservation of their hair, to which they attached extraordinary importance. In the same spirit was the enactment that prohibited the making use of a horse without the permission of the owner, and that visited with imprisonment for life the crime of horse-stealing. This legal protection of the horse is still preserved in the Saxon laws.

The prevailing tendency of the code was to secure to each man his lawful property, and to arm him with the means of protection. Yet it must be remarked as a strange inconsistency, in the midst of this anxiety to erect safeguards around property, that fraudulent debtors were granted a direct escape from liability to consequences. It was enacted, that if one man lent money to another, and the latter denied the loan, the ordeal should not apply; the oath of the defendant being deemed a sufficient release from the debt. This law was the more unaccountable in a country where the legal interest of money was forty per cent., — a circumstance calculated to increase the motives to dishonesty.

Another enactment makes a distinction between the Varangians and Slavs, which illustrates the fact that the latter had always been more advanced in civilisation than the former. By this enactment, a Koblegian or a Varangian was compelled to take an oath where such a test was required, but a Slavonian was exempted. It would therefore appear, if the conclusion may be safely ventured upon, that judicial combats, which formed the final appeal when a defendant in a cause acquitted himself in the first instance by a solemn oath, were not adopted amongst the Slavs, who were satisfied with a public examination of facts, and an adjudication, without the sacred or the physical test. It is sufficient, however, for the great uses of historical inquiry, to know that a difference so remarkable between two branches of the people was recognised and confirmed by law.

One of the most important declarations of the code was that which divided the population into three classes — the nobles, the freemen, and the slaves. Of these three, the slaves alone were left unprotected. The freemen, who were fenced in from the encroachments of the nobles, were composed of the citizens, the farmers, the landholders, and hired servants. They were sub-classified into centuries, each of which elected a head, who filled an office equivalent to that of a tribune. The civil magistracy, thus created, had a separate guard of their own, and were placed, in virtue of their office, on an equality with the boyars. The city of Novgorod, which maintained, under a nominal princedom, the spirit of a republic, exhibited these municipal franchises in a more complete form than any of the Russian cities; all of which, however, possessed similar privileges, more or less modified according to their relative importance, or the circumstances under which their charters were granted. The chief of the Novgorodian republic was a prince of the blood; the title of his office was that of Namestnick. He took no share in the deliberations of the people, nor does it appear that he even possessed a veto upon their decisions. His oath of instalment bound him as the slave rather than the governor of the city; for it pledged him to govern agreeably to the constitution as he found it; to appoint none but Novgorodian magistrates in the provinces, and even those to be previously approved of by the Posadnick or mayor; to respect strictly the exclusive rights possessed by the citizens sitting in judgment on their own order, of imposing their own taxes, and of carrying on commerce at their own discretion; to interdict his boyars from acquiring landed property within the villages dependent on Novgorod, and to oblige them to travel at their private cost; to discourage immigration; and never to cause a Novgorodian to be arrested for debt. A princedom, accepted on such restrictive conditions, was but the shadow of a sceptre, as the municipal union of the legislative and judicial abundantly proved. The first officer was the Posadnick, or mayor, chosed by election for a limited time; the next was the Tisiatski, or tribune, who was a popular check upon the prince and mayor; and the rest of the functionaries consisted of the senate, the city assembly, and the boyars, all of whom were elective. By the electoral system, the people preserved a constant guard over the fidelity of their representatives in the senate, and their officers of justice; so that, while the three grades propounded by law were kept widely apart, and socially distinguished, the prerogatives of each were rigidly protected against innovation from the other two. All that this little republic required to render its security perfect, was liberty. It was based upon a system of slavery, and sustained its dominion more by fear than righteousness. Nor was it independent of control, although all its domestic concerns were uninterruptedly transacted within its own confines. It was an appanage of the grand princedom; but on account of its fortunate geographical position on the northern and north-western frontiers, which were distant from the capital — a circumstance that delegated to Novgorod the defence of those remote boundaries — it acquired a degree of political importance that preserved it for four centuries against the cupidity of the succession of despots that occupied the throne. The removal of the seat of empire from Kiev to Vladimir, and finally to Moscow, by drawing the centre nearer to Novgorod, diminished its power by degrees, and finally absorbed it altogether.

One of the enactments of the code of Iaroslav will show what advances had been made towards the segregation of the people into different orders, and how much the government partook, or was likely to partake, of a mixed form, in which a monarchical, an hereditary, and a representative estate were combined. It made the prince the heir-at-law of every freeman who died without male issue, with the exception of the boyars and officers of the royal guard. By this regulation the prerogative of the crown was rendered paramount, while the hereditary rights of property were preserved unconditionally to the families of the nobles alone. A class of rich patricians was thus formed and protected, to represent, by virtue of birth, the interests of property; while commerce and popular privileges were fully represented in the assembly of the elected senators. The checks and balances of this system were pretty equal; so that, if the constitution of which these outlines were the elements, had been allowed to accumulate strength and to become consolidated by time, it would at last have resolved itself into a liberal and powerful form; the semi-savage usages with which it was encrusted would have dropped away, and wiser institutions have grown up in their stead.

So clearly were the popular benefits of the laws defined, that the code regulated the maximum demand which the proprietor of the soil might exact from his tenant; and it neither enforced taxation, nor recognised corporal punishment, nor in the composition of a pecuniary mulct admitted any distinction between the Varangians and the Slavs, who formed the aristocracy and the democracy. The prince neither possessed revenue nor levied taxes. He subsisted on the fines he imposed for infractions of law, on the tributes he received from his estates, on the voluntary offerings of the people, and the produce of such property as had fallen to the private title of the sovereignty. Even the tribute was not compulsory; it was rather a right derived from pre-scription. The only dependence of the lords of fiefs was in that they were compelled to render military service when required to the grand prince; and it was expected that they should come numerously attended, well armed, and provisioned. The tribute was the mark of conquest, and was not considered to imply taxation.

But while the monarchical principle was thus kept within proscribed limits, the power of the democracy was not sufficiently curbed: over both there was a check, but the hands of the prince were bound too tightly. His dominion was despotic, because he was surrounded by men devoted to his will; but the dominion of the people was boundless, because opinion was only in its rickety infancy, and the resistance to the offending prince lay in the demonstration of physical superiority instead of moral combination. They never hesitated to avail themselves of their numerical advantage. They even carried it to extravagance and licentiousness; and so much did they exult in their strength, that they regulated the hours at which the sovereign was permitted to enjoy relaxation, punished the obnoxious heads of the church by summary eject-ment, and in several instances, taking the charter of law into their own keep-ing, deposed their princes. The checks, therefore, established in Iaroslav's wise convention between the government and the constituency were over-borne by the rudeness of the times.

That the period had arrived when laws were necessary to the settlement of the empire, was sufficiently testified by the circumstances, external and domestic, in which the people were placed. The adoption of Christianity had partially appeased the old passion for aggression against Constantinople, which, having now become the metropolis of their religion, was regarded with some degree of veneration by the Russians. A war of plundering Byzan-tium, therefore, could not be entertained with any prospect of success. The extension of the empire under Vladimir left little to be coveted beyond the frontiers, which spread to the east, north and south as far as even the wild grasp of the lawless tribes of the forests could embrace. To the west, the

Russians had ceased to look for prey, since Boleslav, by his easy conquest of Kiev, had demonstrated the strength of Poland. Having acquired as much as they could, and having next, in the absence of warlike expeditions abroad, occupied themselves with ruthless feuds at home, they came at length to consider the necessity of consulting the security of possessions acquired at so much cost, and so often risked by civil broils. This was the time for a code of laws. But unfortunately there still existed too many remains of the barbarian era, to render the introduction of legal restraints a matter easy of accomplishment. The jealousy of Greek superiority survived the admission of the Greek religion. The longing after power still inspired the petty chiefs; and hopeless dreams of larger dominion wherewith to bribe the discontented, and provide for the hirelings of the state, still troubled the repose of the sovereign. The throne stood in a plain surrounded by forests, from whence issued, as the rage propelled them, hordes of newly reclaimed savages, pressing extraordinary demands, or threatening with ferocious violence the dawning institutions of civilisation. In such a position, it was not only impossible to advance steadily, but to maintain the ground already gained.

## Iaroslav Dies (1054 A.D.)

Could the character of Iaroslav, the legislator, have been transmitted through his successors, the good of which he laid the seeds, might have been finally cultivated to maturity. But his wisdom and his virtues died with him. Nor, elevated as he was in moral dignity above the spirit of his countrymen, can it be said that he was free from weaknesses that marred much of the utility of his best measures. One of his earliest errors was the resignation of Novgorod to his son Vladimir, who had no sooner ascended the throne of the republican city, than, under the pretext of seeking satisfaction for the death of a Russian who had been killed in Greece, he carried arms into the Byzantine empire. The folly of this wild attempt was abundantly punished in the sequel; fifteen thousand men were sacrificed on the Grecian plains, and their chief hunted back disgracefully to his own territories. Yet this issue of one family grant did not awaken Iaroslav to the danger of partitioning the empire. Before his death he divided the whole of Russia amongst his sons, making, however, the younger sons subordinate to the eldest, as grand prince of Kiev, and empowering the latter to reduce the others to obedience by force of arms whenever they exhibited a disposition to dispute his authority.

This settlement, enforced with parting admonitions on his death-bed, was considered by Iaroslav to present a sufficient security against civil commotion and disputes about the succession. But he did not calculate upon the ungovernable lust for power, the jealousy of younger brothers, and the passion for aggrandisement. His injunctions were uttered in the amiable confidence of Christianity; they were violated with the indecent impetuosity of the barbarian nature.

With the death of Iaroslav, and the division of the empire, a new period of darkness and misrule began. The character of the legislator, which influenced his own time, was speedily absorbed in the general confusion. Iaroslav's name was held in reverence, but the memory of his excellence did not awe the multitudes that, upon his decease, sprang from their retirement to revive the disastrous glories of domestic warfare. Much as he had done for the extension of Christianity, he had failed in establishing it in the hearts of the people. He was an able theologian, and well acquainted with the church ordinances, agenda, and other books of the Greek religion, many of which he caused to be translated into the Russian language, and distributed in copies over the country. So strong an interest did he take in the cultivation of the doctrines of the church, that he established a metropolitan at Kiev, in order to relieve the Russian people and their priests from the inconveniences of attending the residence of the ecclesiastical head at Constantinople, and also with a desire to provide for the more prompt and certain dissemination of the principles of faith. But the value of all these exertions expired with their author. He did much to raise the fame and consolidate the resources of the empire; but the last act of his political career, by which he cut away the cord that bound the rods, had the effect of neutralising all the benefits he meditated to accomplish, as well as those that he actually effected, for his country. His reign was followed by a period of savage anarchy that might be said to have resolved the half-civilised world into its original elements.[k]

## CHAPTER II

## THE PERIOD OF THE PRINCIPALITIES

### [1054-1224 A.D.]

#### THE CHARACTER OF THE PRINCIPALITIES

THE period extending from the year of Iaroslav's death (1054) to the year of the appearance of the Tatars (1224) is one of the most troublous and confused epochs in the history of Russia. As the Scandinavian custom of partition continued to prevail over the Byzantine idea of political unity, the national territory was constantly divided.

The princely anarchy of oriental Europe finds a parallel in the feudal anarchy of the Occident. Pogodine enumerates for this period sixty-four principalities which enjoyed a more or less protracted existence; two hundred and ninety-three princes who during these two centuries contended over Kiev and other Russian domains; eighty-three civil wars in which the entire country was concerned. Foreign wars helped to augment the enormous mass of historical facts. The chronicles mention against the Polovtsi alone eighteen campaigns, while these barbarians invaded Christian territory forty-six times.

The ancient names of the Slav tribes have entirely disappeared, or are preserved only in the names of towns — as, for instance, that of the Polotchanes in Polotsk; that of the Severians in Novgorod-Seversk. The elements in the composition of Russia were thus rather principalities than peoples. No more is said of the Krivitchi or of the Drevlians; we hear only of Smolensk or of Volhinia. These little states were dismembered at each new division among the children of a prince; they were then reconstituted, to be again divided into appanages. In spite of all these vicissitudes, however, some among them had an uninterrupted existence due to certain topographical and ethnographical conditions. Setting aside the distant principality of

Tmoutorakan, established almost at the foot of the Caucasus in the midst of Turkish and Circassian tribes and counting eight different princes, the following are, from the eleventh to the thirteenth centuries, the principal divisions of Russia:

(1) The principality of Smolensk, which occupied the important territory which is in a manner the central point of the orographic system of Russia; it comprises the old forest of Okov, where the three greatest rivers of Russia, the Volga, the Dnieper, and the Dvina, have their rise. Hence the political importance of Smolensk, which is attested by the many wars undertaken against her; hence also her commercial prosperity. It is noticeable that all her towns were built on some one of the three rivers; all the commerce of ancient Russia thus passed through her bounds. Besides Smolensk it is necessary to cite Mozhaisk, Viasma, and Toropets, the capital of a secondary principality, the domain of two famous princes — Mstislav the Brave and Mstislav the Bold.

LAPLANDER

(2) The principality of Kiev, which was *Rus* — Russia in the strict sense of the term. Its situation on the Dnieper, the proximity of Greece, the fertility of its Black Lands, long assured to this state the supremacy over all other Russian principalities. To the south it was bordered by the Nomad tribes of the steppe. Against the inroads of these tribes the princes of Kiev were obliged to construct frontier fortresses; though frequently they ceded them lands and took them into their pay, constituting them into veritable military colonies. The principality of Pereiaslavl was a dependency of Kiev; Vishgorod, Bielgorod, Tripoli, and Torlshok were at different times constituted into appanages for princes of the same family.

(3) The two principalities of Tcheringov with Starodub and Lubetz and of Novgorod-Seversk with Putivl, Kursk and Briansk, which extended along the tributaries flowing into the Dnieper from the left — the Soj and the Desna swelled by the Seim. Tcheringov, extending towards the upper Oka, had thus one foot in the basin of the Volga; its princes, the Olgovitchi, were the most redoubtable rivals of those of Kiev. As for the princes of Seversk, they were ceaselessly occupied with wars against their dangerous rivals on the south, the Polovtsi. It is the exploits of a prince of Seversk against these barbarians which form the subject of a *chanson de geste* — The *Song of Igor*.

(4) The duplex principality of Riazan and Murom, another state whose existence was maintained at the expense of ceaseless war against the nomads.

[1054 A.D.]

The principal towns were Riazan, Murom, Pereiaslavl-Riazanski, on the Oka; Kolomna, at the junction of the Moskva with the Oka; and Pronsk, on the Pronia. The upper Don bounded it on the west. This principality was established in the midst of Finnish tribes — the Muromians and the Meshtseraks. The warlike character and the rude and coarse habits attributed to the people of the principality doubtless resulted not less from the assimilation of the aborigines by the Russian race than from the continuous brutal strife of the inhabitants with the nomads.

(5) The principalities of Suzdal — with their metropolitan towns of Tver, Suzdal, Rostov, Iuriev-Polski, and Vladimir on the Kliasma; of Iaroslavl and Pereiaslavl-Zaliesski — which were established on the Volga and the Oka, in the densest of the northern forests, surrounded by Finnish tribes — Mouromians, Merians, Vesses, and Tcherimisses. Though situated at the extreme limit of the Russian world, these principalities nevertheless exercised great influence over it. We shall see their princes now reducing Novgorod and the Russia of the lakes to a certain political dependence, the consequence of a double economical dependence; then victoriously intervening in the quarrels of the Russia of the Dneiper. The Suzdalians were of the same character as the Riazanians — rude and warlike. The characteristics of a new nationality were already noticeable among these two peoples. That which differentiated them from the Kievans and the Novgorod-Severskans, who, like themselves, were occupied in the great struggle against the barbarians, was that the Russians of the Dneiper, sometimes mingling their blood with that of their enemies, became fused with Turkish tribes, nomadic and essentially mobile, while the Russians of the Oka and the Volga united with Finnish tribes, agricultural and essentially sedentary. This difference between the two foreign elements which entered into the blood of the Slavs, without doubt contributed to that marked difference in character between the two branches of the Russian race. During the period from the eleventh to the thirteenth centuries, as colonization advanced, from the basin of the Dnieper to the basin of the Volga, the divisions of Little Russia and Great Russia were formed.

(6) The principalities of Kiev, Tchernigov, Novgorod-Seversk, Riazan, Murom, and Suzdal, which formed the marches of Russia on the borders of the steppe with its devastating hordes — constituting its frontier states. On the confines of the northwest, opposite the Lithuanians, the Letts and the Tchuds, the same rôle devolved on the principality of Polotsk, occupying the basin of the Dvina, and on the republican principalities of Novgorod and Pskov on the lakes of Ilmen and Peipus. The principality of Minsk was attached to that of Polotsk. It was situated in the basin of the Dnieper and, owing to that circumstance, its possession was frequently disputed by the grand princes of Kiev. The towns of Torzhok, Volok-Lamski, Izborsk, and Veliki Luki belonged to Novgorod; at times they were the capitals of individual states.

Southwestern Russia comprehended (1) in the fan-shaped territory formed by the Pripet and its tributaries — Volhinia, with Vladimir in Volhinia, Lutsk, Turov, Brest, and even Lublin, which is unquestionably Polish; (2) in the basins of the San, the Dniester, and the Pripet — Galicia proper, or Red Russia, whose ancient inhabitants, the white Croats, seem to have originated in the Danubian Slavs. Its principal towns were Galitch, founded by Vladimirko about 1444; Peremishl; Terebovlia, and Svenigorodka. The near neighbourhood of Hungary and Poland contributed to these two principalities distinctive characteristics, as well as a more advanced civilisation.

In the epic songs Galicia, the land of the hero Dvorik Stepanovitch, is a country of fabulous wealth. *The Narrative of the Expedition of Igor* gives an exalted idea of the power of its princes: "Iaroslav Osmomysl of Galicia," cries the poet addressing one of them, "high art thou seated upon thy golden throne! With thy iron regiments thou guardest the Carpathian mountains, thou shuttest the gates of the Danube, thou barrest the way to the king of Hungary; at will thou openest the gates of Kiev, and thine arrows reach far into the distance."

## THE UNITY OF THE PRINCIPALITIES

The disposition of these fifteen or sixteen principalities confirms what has been previously stated concerning the essential unity of the configuration of the Russian soil. None of the river-basins forms a closed or isolated region; no line of heights establishes between them barriers or political frontiers. The greater number of the Russian principalities belonged to the basin of the Dnieper, but pushed their limits everywhere beyond. Kiev, with Pereiaslavl, is the only one strictly confined within it; but Volhinia puts the basin of the Dnieper in communication with those of the Bug in the south and of the Vistula; Polotsk connects it with the basins of the Niemen and the Dvina, Novgorod-Seversk with that of the Don, Tchernigov and Smolensk with that of the Volga. Between these principalities, watercourses everywhere establish communications. Russia, though divided into appanages, was already making toward a great united empire. The lack of cohesion among nearly all the states and their frequent dismemberments prevented their becoming actual nationalities. The principalities of Smolensk, of Tchernigov, of Riazan never possessed that definite historical existence so characteristic of the duchy of Brittany or the county of Toulouse in France, the duchies of Saxony, Swabia, or Bavaria in Germany.

The interests of the princes and their ambition to provide an appanage for each of their children, necessitated at the death of every sovereign a fresh distribution of Russian territory. Yet a certain cohesion was evident in the midst of these vicissitudes. There was visible a unity of race and language, the more marked, notwithstanding differences of dialect, in that the Russian Slavs, excepting in the southwest, were surrounded everywhere by entirely dissimilar peoples — Lithuanians, Tchuds, Finns, Turks, and Magyars. There was also unity of religion; the Russians were differentiated from nearly all their neighbours in that, in contradistinction to the Slavs of the west, the Poles, Czechs, and Moravians, they represented a distinct form of Christianity, acknowledging no tie with Rome and rejecting Latin as the church language.

There was also a unity of historical development, since hitherto the Russian Slavs had all followed the same destiny, had equally accepted Greek civilisation, submitted to Varangian conquest, and pursued in common certain great enterprises, such as the expeditions against Byzantium and the wars with the nomads. There was finally political unity, as among all — in Galicia as in Novgorod, by the Dnieper as in the forests of Suzdal — the same family sat upon all the thrones. All the Russian princes were descended from Rurik, from St. Vladimir, and from Iaroslav the Great. The civil wars which desolated the country affirmed anew this unity. No state in Russia could regard the rest as outsiders, when the princes of Tchernigov and Suzdal were seen to take up arms solely to decide which among them was the eldest — which held the right to the title of grand prince and to the throne of Kiev. There were descendants of Rurik who governed successively the most distant states in

[1054 A.D.]

Russia, and who, having reigned at Tmoutarakan on the straits of Ienikale, at Novgorod the Great, at Toropetz in the country of Smolensk, finished by obtaining recognition of their right to reign over Kiev.[b]

### THE THEORY OF SUCCESSION

If the question be asked why the Russian state continued undivided throughout the two hundred years of the Varangian period, our answer is that it was due solely to the fact that during the greater part of this period the grand princes left one son and heir. Whenever the case was otherwise, as after the death of Sviatoslav and Vladimir, the brothers straightway entered upon a struggle for mastery that did not terminate until all but one were destroyed. That one then became undisputed master, for no one dared dispute the possession of power with the descendants of Rurik.

A KORIAK

The theory of succession in the Rurik family was as follows: the grand prince of Kiev was lord paramount of Russia. He disposed of all vacant principalities, and was supreme judge and general; but each of his brothers had, according to his seniority, the right of succession to the throne. The death of every elder brother brought the younger ones a step nearer to that goal. The order of advance was from Smolensk to Pereiaslavl, from Pereiaslavl to Tchernigov, from Tchernigov to Kiev. But none could attain to the highest dignity, save him whose father had held it before him. Sons of a father who had died before reaching the goal were excluded from Kiev and were confined to the possessions in their hands at the time of their father's death. The technical Russian term for those members of the Rurik family who were excluded from the highest dignity was Isgoi, and the attempts of the Isgoi to break through the law of exclusion have had no small share in the bloody and desolate history of Russia during the period upon which we now enter. But another factor contributed to the same end. The power of the grand prince was not so predominant as to enable him to enforce his will and put down disobedience. His position was based on the idea of patriarchal power, and was respected by the princes only when it was to their advantage. To maintain himself he had to resort to the expedient of making coalitions with some of the princes against the others, and the sword was the final arbiter between the grand prince and his nominal vassals.[c] Accordingly the whole of Russia was always divided in its support of the claims of this or that candidate. The civil wars which ensued were after all but family quarrels.[a]

CIVIL WARS

Iaroslav left five sons. To Iziaslav, the oldest, he gave Kiev; to Svia-toslav, Tchernigov; to Vsevolod, Pereiaslavl; to Viatcheslav, Smolensk; and to Igor, Vladimir in Volhinia. The order in which they are given here repre-sents the order of their respective dignities and their position in the line of succession. Two of the brothers did not long survive their father. In '1056 Viatcheslav died, and Igor, in accordance with the law of sucession, moved to Smolensk, where he too died in 1060.

About this time a new wave of migration set in from Asia towards the south-Russian steppe — the Turkish tribe of the Polovtsi. In 1055 Vsevolod of Pereiaslavl concluded peace with them by bribing them to retire into the steppe. In 1061 he suffered a defeat at their hands, but they did not follow up their success and again retired into the steppe. The civil wars, how-ever, which soon broke out, were to bring them back as an ever-menacing plague to the Russian population.

SVIATOSLAV

Among the minor princes, who were excluded from the succession, was Vseslav of Polotsk, a descend-ant of St. Vladimir. He had helped his uncles in a war against the Torks, a tribe kindred to the Po-lovtsi, and expected a reward in an accession of territory. Being dis-appointed, he determined to help himself. First he ravaged the ter-ritory of Pskov, but being unable to take that city, he invaded the territory of Novgorod, and it seems that for a while he was master of the city. His bold procedure compelled his uncles Iziaslav, Sviatoslav, and Vsevolod to unite against him; but, though beaten by their superior forces, he could not be expelled from the north. The uncles thereupon resorted to treachery. They proposed to him a friendly meeting under a guarantee of his personal security and liberty, which they confirmed by an oath upon the cross. But when he had reached the vicinity of Smo-lensk, beyond the Dnieper, he was surprised, captured, and brought to Kiev, where he was imprisoned. At this juncture the Polovtsi made another of their raids and defeated the united forces of the brothers, so that Sviatoslav was obliged to take refuge at Tchernigov, while Iziaslav and Vsevolod fled to Kiev. There they intended to await the nomad hordes behind the walls of the cities, sacrificing the open country to the invaders. But the citizens of Kiev thought differently. At a stormy meeting of the *vetche* it was decided to take up arms, and when Iziaslav refused to lead them against the enemy they liberated Vseslav from his confinement and made him their prince (1068). Iziaslav was obliged to flee to Poland, where he found a champion in Boleslav the Bold. Menaced in front by the Poles, and suspicious of his uncles in his rear, Vseslav thought himself obliged to flee to Polotsk, leaving the Kievans to the vengeance of Iziaslav (1069). The events of two generations previous, when Boleslav the Brave captured Kiev for Sviatopolk, were now to be repeated. The Poles demeaned themselves as masters and committed many excesses. The Kievans bore it for a year; then exasperated, fell upon the Poles, who were scattered in their various quarters, and compelled Boleslav to evacuate the city. After protracted fighting and negotiations, Polotsk was finally restored to Vseslav, and the old order seemed re-established, when the two brothers of Iziaslav became suspicious of his designs and suddenly appeared before Kiev. Iziaslav now fled for the second time, Sviatoslav became grand prince, while Vsevolod advanced to the principality of Tchernigov.

Iziaslav left nothing unattempted to regain his position. He had escaped with his treasure into Poland, but Boleslav was unwilling to renew his former adventure. The German king Henry IV, whom Iziaslav met at Mainz in January, 1075, was more favourably disposed and sent an embassy to Sviatoslav; but it accomplished nothing. Iziaslav also entered into negotiations with pope Gregory VII, to whom he sent his son Iaropolk. The pope hoped to be able to annex Russia to the western church, and even went so far as to grant it to Iaropolk as a fief from the holy see.

But meanwhile Sviatoslav died (1076) and Vsevolod, a man whose mild character did not exclude the possibility of a peaceful settlement, became grand prince. Boleslav now lent troops to Iziaslav (1077), and though Vsevolod marched against him with an army of his own, yet they soon came to terms. Iziaslav was to be reinstated grand prince for the third time, while Vsevolod was to retire to Tchernigov, in return for which he was secured in the succession. Thus Iaropolk's plans came to naught, and with them the hope of a reunited church.

However, Vseslav of Polotsk did not yet give up his ambitious designs. Foiled in his attempt on the throne of Kiev, he tried to create an empire for himself in the Russian north, and it required three campaigns of the south-Russian princes to annul his plans. It was during these wars that Vladimir Monomakh, son of Vsevolod and son-in-law of King Harold of England, first distinguished himself, though not in a glorious manner. He was the first Russian prince to engage in a domestic quarrel the Polovtsi, with whose aid he ravaged the city and principality of Polotsk. Vseslav died in 1101 as prince of Polotsk, and his memory lived long after him in the traditions of the people, by whom he was regarded as a sorcerer. The *Song of Igor* tells how he accomplished in one night a march from Kiev to Tmoutorakan, and how he could hear at Kiev the ringing of the church bells as Polotsk.

Russian dynastic conditions had now been restored to the legal order, and there seemed nothing left to disturb the tranquillity. But the cupidity of the grand prince soon brought on new dissensions among the members of the house of Rurik. Viatcheslav and Igor died at an early age, leaving minor sons whom their uncle refused to provide with appanages. They therefore tried to gain their right by force. Boris, a son of Viatcheslav, temporarily got hold of Tchernigov, but being unable to maintain himself in that city he fled to Tmoutorakan, the last refuge of all the discontented. There he was soon joined by his brother Gleb, who was expelled by Iziaslav from Novgorod, and by another brother from Volhinian Vladimir, both of whose appanages were divided among the sons of Iziaslav and Vsevolod. In the civil war which followed, the nephews at first had the advantage and captured Tchernigov; but they were defeated in a decisive battle fought near that city on the third of October, 1078. Both the grand prince Iziaslav and Boris fell, and Oleg was obliged to flee once more to Tmoutorakan.

## Vsevolod

Iziaslav was succeeded by Vsevolod, whose reign (1078-1093) was even more unfortunate than his brother's had been. He too favoured his own sons and those of Iziaslav at the expense of his other nephews and in consequence the sons of Sviatoslav and Igor and of his nephew Rostislav waged against him unremitting warfare with the aid of the Polovtsi and Chazars, who wasted the country. Vsevolod's attempt in 1084 to conquer Tmoutorakan, the breeding-place of revolts, failed miserably. Finally even Iaropolk, the son of Iziaslav, who had received so many favours from his uncle, revolted against him and was assassinated during the war. In those days of turmoil and confusion, even old Vseslav ventured forth once more from Polotsk and plundered Smolensk. The grand prince was ill most of the time at Kiev and the conduct of his affairs lay in the hands of his son Vladimir Monomakh.

## Sviatopolk

Vsevolod died April 13th, 1093, leaving two sons, Vladimir Monomakh, who held Tchernigov, and Rostislav, who held Pereiaslavl. He was succeeded

by Sviatopolk, the second son of Iziaslav, who was the rightful successor after the death of his brother Iaropolk, who, it will be remembered, was assassinated. Monomakh could easily have made himself grand prince, for he was the most popular of the princes and gained great fame in his campaigns against the Polovtsi, whom he defeated twelve times during the reign of his father; but he was anxious to avoid violating the law of succession and thus inviting civil war.

Sviatopolk's reign began with a violation of the law of nations by imprisoning ambassadors of the Polovtsi, who had come to negotiate a treaty with him. In retaliation the nomads invaded the country, and with so great a force that Vladimir and Rostislav, who had come to the aid of the grand prince, advised him to purchase peace from the enemy. He paid no heed to them, but the event soon justified the prudence of their counsel. In the battle of Tripole, fought on May 23rd, 1093, the Russians sustained a disastrous defeat.

SVIATOPOLK

Rostislav was drowned, while Sviatopolk and Vladimir saved themselves by flight. The next year's campaign against the Polovtsi was equally disastrous, and Sviatopolk returned to Kiev with but two companions. Tortchesk was compelled to capitulate, and the nomads returned to the steppe rich with booty and prisoners  Sviatopolk now bought peace and took to wife a daughter of the Polovtsian khan. They returned, however, the same year under the leadership of Oleg, son of Sviatoslav, who had stayed till now in Tmoutorakan and thought the moment opportune for enforcing his undoubted rights upon Tchernigov, which had been the original seat of his father as the second son of Iaroslav, and which was held by Monomakh, who was the son of Iaroslav's third son.

Oleg, was therefore, no Isgoi and would not be treated as such. When he appeared before Tchernigov, Monomakh had only a small band with him, and after a siege of eight days was compelled to evacuate the city and retire to Pereiaslavl, where he had to defend himself during the next three years against continual irruptions of the Polovtsi. The refusal of Oleg to join in a combined campaign of the princes against the Polovtsi, and the sudden capture of Smolensk by his brother David, gave the occasion for a general war that lasted two years and covered the whole territory of Russia, from Novgorod to Murom and thence to the steppe, and in course of which one son of Monomakh fell in battle, while two other sons suffered a decisive reverse at the hands of Oleg. Finally, a congress of princes was held at Lubetz, in the territory of Tchernigov, for the settlement of all existing disputes. The result of its deliberations was that the grand prince was to retain Kiev and Turov, while to Vladimir were assigned Pereiaslavl, Smolensk, and Rostov; Novgorod to his son Mstislav, and Tchernigov with all its dependencies to the sons of Sviatoslavl — Oleg, David, and Iaroslav. The latter thus gained possession of the greater part of Russia. There still remained to be satisfied the three Isgoi, Volodar, and Vassilko, sons of Rostislav, and David, son of Igor. Of the former two, Volodar received Peremishl, Vassilko received Terebovl, while Vladimir in Volhinia was given to David. Polotsk remained in the hands of Vseslav.

The congress of Lubetz (1097) brought a respite to the sorely tried Russian north, but the south was soon subjected to new calamities. Vassilko, son of Rostislav, was revolving in his mind extensive plans of conquest in Poland, among the Danubian Bulgarians, and finally against the Polovtsi. He had begun making extensive preparations, and had taken into his pay several nomad hordes. David of Volhinia, who was ignorant of Vassilko's plans, became alarmed at these warlike preparations, began to suspect a conspiracy between Monomakh and Vassilko, and succeeded in inoculating the grand prince with his own alarms and suspicions. Vassilko was allured to Kiev to attend a religious festival, and there he was captured, thrown into chains, dragged to Bielgorod, and blinded in an unspeakably cruel manner. The horror of the bloody deed resounded throughout Russia. Monomakh united his forces with those of his old enemies, the sons of Sviatoslav, and marched upon Kiev. The grand prince tried to clear himself of blame and throw the guilt upon David, and peace was arranged through the mediation of the metropolitan of Kiev and of Monomakh's mother.

The grand prince took upon himself the obligation to revenge the outrage on Vassilko, who was surrendered to Volodar; and David was obliged to flee to Poland (1099). The grand prince annexed David's territory, and then turned, most unjustifiably, against the sons of Rostislav. Defeated by Volodar, he formed an alliance with Koloman, king of Hungary. The alliances now assumed a most unexpected and distorted character. David united with the Rostislavitchi and with Buiak, khan of the Polovtsi; and at Peremishl defeated the grand prince and his allies. The war, the horrors of which were increased by repeated raids of the Polovtsi, seemed to draw out without end or aim, when finally Monomakh convoked a second congress of the princes, which met in August, 1100, at Uvetitchi, on Kievan territory. The result of its deliberations was that only a few towns of Volhinia were left to David, the greater part of the principality being transferred to Iaroslav, son of Sviatopolk; while the Rostislavitchi were to remain in the undiminished possession of their territories.

Thus order was restored for some time, but the direction of affairs really passed out of the hands of the grand prince into those of Monomakh. Under his leadership the Russian princes were now united against the Polovtsi, and there ensued a series of campaigns of which no clear account has come down to us. The Russians generally had the upper hand, but for a long time the balance wavered, and the enemy seemed so dangerous to the princes that, following the example of Sviatopolk, they entered into matrimonial alliances with him. Thus Monomakh, as well as the two sons of Sviatoslav, David and Oleg, took Polovtsian wives for their sons. But the year 1111 witnessed a decisive campaign, in which Monomakh is again seen at the head of the Russian princes. After crossing the Dnieper and the Vorskla, the Russians pressed on into the enemy's country as far as the Don. Two Polovtsian cities were taken, and one was reduced to ashes; the Don was crossed, and on March 24th and 26th a great battle was fought. The Russians were on the Sula, the last tributary of the Don before reaching the sea of Azov, in a most unfavourable position and surrounded from all sides by the Polovtsi. But the scales were turned when the drujinas of David and Monomakh, which had been kept all the time in the rear, made a terrific onset on the exhausted enemy, who fled in panic. According to tradition, angels preceded the Russians and smote the Polovtsi with blindness.

### Vladimir Monomakh (1113–1125 A.D.)

After a reign filled with civil war and misfortune Sviatopolk died (April 16th, 1113), and all eyes turned toward Monomakh. Legally, however, the throne belonged to his cousin Oleg, son of Sviatoslav, and Monomakh seemed at first resolved to recognise his superior right. But the Kievans were determined to accept no one but Monomakh, and an uprising of theirs, which was directed primarily against the Jews, whom Sviatopolk had employed for fiscal purposes, but which threatened to assume larger dimensions, induced him to yield to the universal demand. Thus the race of Sviatoslav — otherwise called the Olgovitchi — was excluded, and Monomakh succeeded in bringing a large part of Russia under his house. During his reign he continued the wars against the Polovtsi, as well as against the Finns in the north and east, and the Poles in the west. The steppe was cleared so thoroughly that tradition, with its customary exaggeration, says that he forced the Polovtsi back into the Caucasus.

His relations with the Byzantine Empire have not yet been sufficiently cleared up. He himself was the son of a Byzantine princess, and his daughter Maria was married to Leo, son of the unfortunate emperor Romanus Diogenes, who was blinded in 1071 and banished to an island. Leo then made an attempt at revolt against Alexius Comnenus, but was poisoned in 1116. Vladimir now espoused the cause of Leo's son Basil and sent an army to the Danube, which returned without accomplishing its purpose. According to a later tradition, which arose under the influence of Moscow, the emperor Alexius Comnenus, in order to put an end to the devastation of Thrace by the Russian troops, sent to Vladimir a diadem and other imperial insignia through Neophyte, metropolitan of Ephesus, who put the diadem on Vladimir's head and called him czar. But contemporary accounts tell us nothing of all this, and it is inherently improbable that Byzantium would bestow

[1122-1125 A.D.]

upon the Russian grand prince, who was no longer formidable, a title whose exclusive possession it so jealously guarded. On the other hand, it is known that in 1122, or six years after the supposed campaign to Thrace, a grand-daughter of Monomakh was married to a prince of the house of Romanus.

But the greater portion of Monomakh's military activity fell into the reigns of his two predecessors. He was in his sixty-first year when he became grand-prince, and he naturally avoided all fighting as far as it could be avoided, employing force only when requisite to maintain his position as overlord of Russia. As far as circumstances permitted, he was a prince of peace, and a number of most important legislative measures are attributed to him, especially the laws relating to usury and to the half-free *(zakupi)*. Russia had suffered very severely from the civil wars and the raids of the Polovtsi, and men of small property were reduced to extreme poverty. Being unable to maintain themselves on their wasted lands, they went to live in large numbers on the estates of the rich, who sought to reduce them to absolute slavery, or else they borrowed money at usurious rates and soon sank into a servile condition. To remedy this ruinous state of affairs, Monomakh reduced the rate of interest from 120 per cent. to 20 per cent., and decreed that one who had paid one year's interest according to the old rate, was thereby absolved from his debt. He also ordered the expulsion of the Jews from the whole of Russia.[1] But the problem of the *zakupi* could not be solved in this summary fashion. According to the regulations adopted they were to be regarded as free men who had become bound to the soil by contract, but who retained the right to acquire property and were not subject to the master's jurisdiction. A half-free man loses his freedom only when he attempts to escape from his master. It was also fixed what payments and services he was to render, and it was made impossible for the lord to reduce him to a condition of unrestricted serfdom.

Monomakh died in 1125, at the ripe age of seventy-three. He has left us a curious paper of instructions to his sons, which dates from 1117, and in which he gives them much sound advice, enforced by examples from his own life.[c]

## The "Instruction" of Vladimir Monomakh

The grand prince begins by saying that his grandfather Iaroslav gave him the Russian name of Vladimir and the Christian name of Vasili, and his father and mother that of Monomakh; either because Vladimir was really through his mother the grandson of the Greek emperor Constantine Monomachus, or because even in his tenderest youth he displayed remarkable warlike valour. "As I draw near to the grave," writes he, "I give thanks to the Most High for the increase of my days. His hand has led me to a venerable age. And you, my beloved children and whosoever reads this writing, observe the rules set forth in it. When your heart does not approve them, do not condemn my intentions, but only say: The old man's mind was already weakened." Having described in their chief features, and for the greater part in the words of the Psalmist, the beauty of the works and the goodness of the Creator, Vladimir continues:

"O my children! give praise to God and love also mankind. Neither fasting, nor soltitude, nor monastic life shall save you, but good deeds. Forget

[1 They were during the Middle Ages the representatives of the money-power throughout Europe — a foreign element in the "natural economy" of that time. Hence the universal hatred against them.]

not the poor, feed them; and remember that every possession is God's, and only confided to you for a time. Do not hide your riches in the bowels of the earth: this is against the law of Christianity. Be fathers to orphans; judge the widows yourselves: do not let the strong destroy the weak. Do not slay either the righteous or the guilty: the life and soul of the Christian are sacred. Do not call upon the name of God in vain; ratify your oath by kissing the cross, and do not transgress it. My brothers said to me: Let us drive out the sons of Rostislav and take their possessions, otherwise thou art no ally of ours! But I answered: I cannot forget that I kissed the cross. I turned to the Psalter and read with compunction: 'Why art thou so vexed, O my soul? O put thy trust in God, for I will yet thank him. Fret not thyself because of the ungodly: neither be thou envious against the evil doers.' Do not forsake the sick and do not fear to look upon the dead: for we shall all die; receive the blessing of the clergy lovingly; do not withdraw yourselves from them; do good unto them, for they shall pray to the Most High for you.

"Do not have any pride either in your mind or heart, and think: we are but mortal; to-day we live, to-morrow we are in the grave. Fear every lie, drunkenness and fornication, equally pernicious for the body and the soul. Esteem old people as fathers, love the young as brothers. In your household see carefully to everything yourselves, do not depend either on your pages or bailiffs, that your guests may not blame either your house or your dinner. Be active in war, serve as an example to your captains — it is no time then to think of feasting and luxury. When you have set the night watch, take your rest. Man perishes suddenly, therefore do not lay aside your arms where you may meet danger; and get to horse early. When you travel in your dominions, do not let the princely pages be a cause of offence to the inhabitants, but wherever you stop give your host food and drink. Above all, respect your guests and do them honour, both the distinguished and the supplicants, both merchant and ambassador; if you cannot give them presents, at any rate regale them with food and drink, for guests spread good and evil reports of us in foreign lands. Greet every man when he passes by. Love your wives, but do not let them have an authority over you. Everything good that you learn, you must remember; what you do not know, learn. My father, sitting at home, spoke five languages, for which those of other lands praised him. Idleness is the mother of vices; beware of it. A man should ever be occupied; when you are on the road, on horseback, without occupation, instead of indulging in idle thoughts repeat prayers by heart — or the shortest, but best prayer of all, 'Lord have mercy!' Never sleep without bowing yourself down to the earth; and if you feel unwell, bow down to the earth three times. Let not the sun find you in your bed! Go early to church to render morning praise to God: so did my father; so did all good men. When the sun shone on them, they praised God joyfully and said: 'Lighten mine eyes, Christ God, and give me Thy beauteous light.' Then take counsel with the droujina, or judge the people, or go to the chase; and at midday sleep, for God has ordained that not only man but also the beasts and birds should rest at midday.

"Thus lived your father. I myself did all that could be ordered to a page; at the chase and at war, day and night, in the heat of summer and the cold of winter I knew no rest. I did not put my trust in burgomasters or heralds, I did not let the strong give offence to the poor and widows, I myself supervised the church and the divine service, the domestic organisation, the stables, the chase, the hawks and the falcons." Enumerating his military exploits, Vladimir thus writes: "My campaigns were in all eighty-three; the other smaller ones I do not remember. I concluded nineteen treaties of peace with the Polovtsi, took prisoners more than a hundred of their chief princes and let them go free, and I had more than two hundred put to death and drowned in the rivers. Who has travelled faster than I? Starting early from Tchernigov, I was at Kiev with my parents before vespers. We loved the chase, and often trapped and caught beasts with your grandfather. How many times have I fallen from my horse! Twice I broke my head, injured my arms and legs, without caring for my life in youth or sparing my head. But the Lord preserved me. And you, my children, fear neither death nor combats, nor wild beasts, but show yourselves men in every circumstance sent from God. If providence decrees that a man shall die, neither his father nor his brothers can save him. God's protection is man's hope."

If it had not been for this wisely written testament, we should not have known all the beauty of Vladimir's soul; he did not lay waste other states, but was the glory, the defender, the consolation of his own, and none of the Russian princes has a greater right to the love of posterity, for he served his country jealously and virtuously. If once in his life Monomakh did not hesitate to infringe the law of nations and perfidiously slay the Polovtsian princes, we can but apply to him the words of Cicero, "The age excuses the man." Regarding the Polovtsi as the enemies of Christianity (they had burned the churches), the Russians thought that the destruction of them — no matter in what manner — was a work pleasing to God.[d]

### The Fall of Kiev and the Rise of Suzdal

In the forty-four years that followed the death of Vladimir Monomakh, the over-lordship passed eighteen times from one hand to another, the average duration of governments being only two years and a half, and the dignity attaching to the grand princedom declined in rapid progression until it sank to a complete nullity. With this constant change of rulers, the devastation and barbarisation of south Russia proceeded apace, so that it soon ceased to be the centre of political life. A rapid review of these evil years will suffice for an understanding of the causes that brought about this retrogression.

We have seen that Vladimir Monomakh reached the throne of the grand princedom in violation of the superior right of the Olgovitchi. He succeeded in bringing the greater part of Russia under his sons. Mstislav, the eldest, held Kiev and southern Russia, while his sons were in Novgorod, Kursk and Smolensk; Iaropolk held Pereiaslavl; Viatcheslav, Tourov; Iuri, Suzdal; and Andrew, Vladimir in Volhinia. On the other hand, the princes of Polotsk were independent; the descendants of Rostislav ruled in Red Russia or Galicia; and the descendants of Oleg, in Tchernigov, Murom, Riazan, erstwhile the land of the Viatitchi and Radimitchi, and in the extreme southeast, Tmoutorakan. With union among the descendants of Monomakh and with strong grand princes at Kiev, south Russia might have been able to maintain its ascendancy notwithstanding its unfavourable proximity to the steppe; but these conditions did not exist. Monomakh's first successor, Mstislav, did, indeed, maintain his position, and even annexed Polotsk, whose princes fled to Greece. But he soon died (1132), and his successor, the brave but wavering Iaropolk, sowed the seeds of discord in his family by bestowing Pereiaslavl upon the eldest son of Mstislav and naming him his successor. Therewith he offended his own younger brothers, one of whom, Iuri Dolgoruki (Longhand), sought to maintain his right by force. The prince of Pereiaslavl found support among the Olgovitchi, who were delighted at the sight of quarrels among the descendants of Monomakh. One of the Olgo-vitchi, Vsevolod by name, raised himself to the grand princedom by utilising these quarrels (1139–1146). But immediately after his death his brother was overthrown, and Iziaslav, son of Mstislav, became grand prince (1146–1154). Twice he was expelled by Iuri Dolgoruki, and only maintained himself by making one of his uncles the nominal ruler.

After his death the turbulence and confusion increased still further. His

A MORDIRNE WOMAN (ERGIAN TRIBE)

brother Rostislav of Smolensk was expelled after one week's reign by the prince of Tchernigov, who was expelled in his turn by Iuri Dolgoruki. The latter might have shared the same fate, for a confederation of the princes of Smolensk, Tchernigov, and Volhinia had already been formed against him, but for his timely death (1157). One of the confederates ruled for eight months, and then he had to make room for his successor, who ruled four months. In the eighty-three years that elapsed between the death of Iuri and the capture of Kiev by the Mongols, the government changed hands thirty times. How much the importance of Kiev and the dignity of the grand princedom had declined at this period, we can estimate from the refusal of Andrew of Suzdal, son of Iuri Dolgoruki, to take the throne, though he came next in the line of succession. He rightly comprehended that the future belonged to the Russian north, rather than to the south, and it was his constant endeavour to consolidate his power in that quarter; and when one of those powerless grand princes, Mstislav Iziaslavitch, attempted to strengthen himself by forming an alliance with Novgorod,

Andrew brought about a combination of eleven princes against him. After a three days' siege Kiev was taken by assault and plundered for two days (March, 1169), and Andrew's brother Gleb was then installed as grand prince of Kiev. The decay of the south is attributable chiefly to the following causes:

(1) Its geographical position exposed it to the constant inroads of the nomads of the steppe. This evil, it is true, existed from remotest times, but its seriousness was increased by the action of the Russian princes themselves, who employed the nomads in their civil wars. Many of these nomads, Torks, Berendians, and Petchenegs, settled on the Ros and Dnieper, meddled in Russian affairs, and contributed to the barbarising of the country. (2) Every new grand-prince brought with him into Kiev a new following from

his own principality. These foreign elements contributed ever anew to the unsettling of existing conditions, and prevented the growth of a landed aristocracy that had its roots in the soil, and of a burgher class. The establishment of a political tradition thus became impossible. (3) The trade with Greece had greatly declined owing to the increasing dangers of the journey to the sea, and more than once the princes were obliged to defend caravans to and from Byzantium with their entire army.

But while the south was decaying, a new centre was forming in the north that was destined to gather around itself the whole of Russia, the principality of Suzdal-Rostov. The city of Rostov, situated in the country of the Finnish Merians, was one of the oldest in Russia, and it is reported that Rurik had bestowed it on one of his warriors. Suzdal also arose at an early date, at the latest toward the end of the ninth century. The early history of the region is not known to us, but we know that Iaroslav founded the city of Iaroslavl, that it was temporaily united to Novgorod, and that after the death of Sviatoslav II (1076) it was merged in the principality of Pereiaslavl. Vladimir Monomakh founded Vladimir on the Kliasma, a tributary of the Oka, and built a church at Rostov. The congress of Lubetz assigned the entire territory to Monomakh's sons, and Iuri Dolgoruki became the first independent prince of Rostov. Although this prince always looked to the south, yet the colonisation of the north made rapid progress during his reign. We know that three cities were founded by him, and the chronicle also attributes to him the foundation of Moscow in 1147. Suzdal was his capital. When he became grand-prince of Kiev he bestowed this whole country upon his son Vassilko, while he gave Vishgorod, to the north of Kiev, to his eldest son Andrew.

But the latter had no liking for the south, and fled from Vishgorod with a miracle-working image of the Virgin, which he deposited in a church that he built at a place where he had a vision and which he called Bogolubvo (God's love). After the death of his father, in 1157, Rostov and Suzdal refused to obey his younger brothers and called in Andrew, who was also joined by those of his father's followers who had fled from Kiev. But it is most characteristic of the man and his far-sighted policy that he made no claims to the throne of Kiev, nor did he establish himself at Rostov or Suzdal but stayed at Vladimir, where there were no old families nor refractory citizens to deal with. His brothers, his nephews, the boyars of his father, he expelled from his dominions and made himself sole ruler. In 1169 he gave Kiev to his brother Gleb, but he took to himself the title of grand prince. To become the virtual master of the whole of Russia he only needed to subject Novgorod, and though the combination of princes that he formed against it was routed before its gates, yet he ultimately succeeded, by cutting off its supply of corn, in compelling it to acquiesce in his supremacy and to accept the prince that he chose for it.

This first would-be autocrat of Russia also comprehended the importance of making the clergy subservient to his will. He tried to make his capital Vladimir independent of Kiev in church affairs by establishing in it a metropolitan, and though he failed in his object, owing to the determined refusal of the patriarch of Constantinople, yet he succeeded in obtaining the important concession that in future the Russian metropolitan was to be appointed only with the assent of the grand prince.

His despotic and cruel rule finally made him hated by his nobles, and he was assassinated on June 29th, 1175, at Bogolubovo. After a period of confusion his second brother, Vsevolod, became grand prince. During this reign the influence of Suzdal was still further increased, and the entire north, and even the Olgovitchi of Tchernigov, recognised his supremacy. In the west and south, however, Roman Mstislavitch of Volhinia, who conquered Galicia and ruled temporarily at Kiev, offered a successful resistance. But after the death of the latter in battle with the Poles in 1205, Vsevolod conquered Riazan, and even deprived the Olgovitchi of Tchernigov, giving them Kiev in exchange. This prince, like his predecessor, attained his object by diplomacy rather than by the sword, and at his death in 1212 he was the most powerful prince in Russia.

His death was followed by a civil war between his two sons Constantine and Iuri. The latter, though the younger, was nominated by Vsevolod as his successor, but in 1217 he was beaten by Constantine and his allies — Novgorod amongst them — and compelled to resign the throne. But Constantine died in 1218 and Iuri reigned undisturbed till 1237. He fought with success against the Volga Bulgarians, and founded Nijni-Novgorod (1221). But his power never became as great as had been that of his father, and he exerted no influence in southern Russia, which was devastated by Petchenegs from the steppe and by Poles and Hungarians from the west. All south Russia now lay exhausted before the impending irruption of the Tatars.[c]

# CHAPTER III

## THE TIME OF TATAR DOMINATION

### [1235-1462 A.D.]

In the thirteenth century the steppes of central Asia sent forth a new conquering horde, constituting the last wave of that migration of peoples which had commenced in remote antiquity.[1] This Mongol-Tatar horde dominated Russia for 240 years and left enduring traces of its domination. It definitively broke the bond between western and eastern Russia, and thus contributed to the formation of the principality of Lithuania in the west; while in the east it promoted the rise of the principality of Moscow, which finally absorbed all the other Russian principalities, threw off their Tatar yoke, recoiled in its turn upon the steppe, and finally, by turning Russia into an empire, made forever impossible another invasion from the steppe.

The cradle of the Mongolian race was in all probability the country lying at the foot of the Altai Mountains. At the time of the appearance of Jenghiz Khan the Mongols were divided into numerous tribes, which were governed by their elders and lived in mutual enmity. An unpleasing description of the exterior and life of the Mongols is given by a Chinese writer, a contemporary of Jenghiz Khan, and also by Mussulman writers:

"Their faces are wide, flat, and square, with prominent cheek-bones, their eyes have no upper lashes, their beard and moustaches are of scanty growth, their general appearance is repulsive. But the present Tatar sovereign, Temuchin (Jenghiz Khan) is of enormous stature, with broad forehead and long beard, and distinguished for his valour. They reckon the year

[1] This is, of course, meant only in a limited sense. The migration of peoples still continues with unabated force, but its centre has moved from Asia to Europe. Thence it moves in a twofold direction : on the one hand, from western Europe to America and Australia ; and on the other hand, from eastern Europe to the remotest confines of Asia.]

according to the growth of grass. When one of them is asked for his age, he replies — so many grasses. ·When asked for the number of the month, they laugh and reply that they do not know. The Tatars are born in the saddle and grow up on horseback. They learn to fight almost by instinct, for they hunt the whole year round. They have no infantry, but only cavalry, of which they can raise several hundred thousand. They hardly ever resort to writing, but all, from the commander-in-chief to the commander of ten, give their orders in person. When they want to take a big town, they first attack the small places in the vicinity, take all the inhabitants prisoners, and drive them forward to the attack. For this purpose a command is issued that every man on horseback should capture ten prisoners, and when this number is completed they are compelled to collect a certain amount of grass or wood, earth or stones. The Tatars urge them on night and day, killing those who become exhausted. Having reached the town, they are compelled to dig trenches or fill up fosses. In a siege the Tatars reck not of the loss of tens of thousands: hence they are invariably successful. When they capture a city they kill all without sparing either young or old, the beautiful or the ugly, rich or poor, those who submit or those who resist. No person, however distinguished, escapes this unrevokable penalty of death. The spoil is divided in proportionate shares among high and low. This people have no need of baggage or provision wagons; their herds of sheep, cows, horses, and other animals follow them on their marches, and they eat meat and nothing else. Their horses do not know barley, but they tear up the ground with their hoofs and live on the roots. As to their faith, the Tatars worship the sun at the time of its rising. They do not regard anything as forbidden, and eat all animals, even dogs and pigs. Marriage is unknown to them, but many men come to a woman, and when a child is born it does not know its father."

Similar descriptions are met with in the narratives of Europeans who knew the Mongols in the days of their power.

### JENGHIZ KHAN; THE TATAR INVASION

It was among this rude nomad people that Jenghiz Khan was born in 1162. The son of the chief of a tribe dwelling at the mouths of the Onon and the Ingoda, affluents of the Amur, Jenghiz was far removed from the focus of central Asian political life, and his power was originally very small. The first forty years of his life were spent in struggles with the surrounding peoples; it is even said that for ten years he was in captivity with the Nyûché, or Chûrché (the Manchurian rulers of northern China known under the name of the dynasty of Kin), during which time he became acquainted with Chinese customs and manners, and also with the weakness of the rulers of China. Having conquered various Mongolian tribes, he proclaimed himself emperor at a general assembly of the princes, which was held at the sources of the river Onon (1206).

"By thus taking the imperial title," says V. P. Vasiliev, "he gave perfect expression to the purely Chinese conception that, as there is only one sun in the heavens, so there must be only one emperor on earth; and all others bearing this title, all states having any pretensions to independent existence thereby offend the will of heaven and invite chastisement." His successes in Mongolia are explained by his surpassing military talent, the system of purely military organisation adopted by him, and by the fact that he gave places in his service to all those who were gifted, of whatever race they might be.[1] Jenghiz Khan's conquests advanced rapidly; in 1206 he devastated the kingdom of Tangut (in southern Mongolia) and in 1210 he commenced a war with the Nyûché, ruling in northern China. The war dragged on, and meanwhile the shah of Khuarezm (Bokhara) gave offence to Jenghiz Khan by slaying the Mongolian ambassadors. Leaving his captains in China, the Mongolian khan marched to Bokhara (1219), whence, partly in pursuit of the shah and partly led on by the passion for pillage, the Mongolian troops directed their way to the west, doubled the southern shore of the Caspian Sea, crossed the Caucasus, and penetrated into the steppes of the Polovtsi.

The leaders of these troops were Chépé and Subutai Bahadar. The Polovtsi applied for help to the Russian prince Mstislav Mstislavitch, and he called together the princes of southern Russia, amongst whom the most important were Mstislav Romanovitch of Kiev and Mstislav Sviatoslavitch of Tchernigov. The armies of the princes moved to the help of the Polovtsi, and although the Tatars sent ambassadors saying, "God has permitted us to come on our steeds with our slaves against the accursed Polovtsi; come and make peace with us, for we have no quarrel with you," the princes decided upon a battle which took place by the river Kalka in the government of Iekaterinoslav. The Russian princes, who did not act in unison, were beaten (1223), and many were killed, amongst others Mstislav of Kiev. The Tatars did not penetrate far into Russia, but turned back and were soon forgotten.[2] Meanwhile the Tatar captains returned to Jenghiz Khan, who, having definitively subdued Tangut and northern China, died in 1227. He had during his lifetime divided his possessions amongst his four sons: to the descendants of Juji (then already dead) was allotted Kiptchak (that is the steppe extending from central Asia into southern Russia); to Jagatai, Turkestan; to Okkodai (Ogdai) China; to Tuli, the nomad camps adjoining the share of Okkodai. Over these princes was to be exalted the great khan, chosen in a solemn assembly of all the princes. In 1228 Okkodai was proclaimed great khan.

At first the question of succession, then the final consolidation of the empire in northern China, and then again the commencement of the war with the south kept the princes around the great khan, and it was only in 1235 that Okkodai sent his nephew Batu, son of Juji, together with Manku, son of Tuli, and his own son Kuiuk, to conquer the western lands; to their number was added Sabutai, famous for his Kiptchak campaign. First of all they conquered the Bulgarians on the Volga, and then came to the land of Riazan. Here they exacted from the princes a tribute of a tenth of all their possessions

[1 A modern army inevitably loses in numbers and its difficulties increase as it advances from its base of operations into the enemy's country. The very reverse was the situation of the Tatars. They needed no base of operations, for they took along with them their flocks, their tents, and all their belongings, and while their flocks fed upon the grassy steppes, they in turn fed upon their flocks. And the nomadic and predatory tribes whom they encountered on their march led the same kind of life as themselves, and were easily induced to join in the certain expectation of plunder. Thus the tide kept on ever increasing and gaining in force. In fact, the Tatars can hardly be styled an army, but a people in motion.[a]]

[2 At first the Russians had only very vague notions as to who this terrible enemy was. The old chronicler remarks briefly: "For our sins unknown people have appeared. No one knows who they are or whence they have come, or to what race and faith they belong. They are commonly called Tatars, but some call them Tauermen, and others Petchenegs. Who they really are is known only to God, and perhaps to wise men deeply read in books." Some of these " wise men deeply read in books " supposed them to be the idolatrous Moabites who had in Old Testament times harassed God's chosen people; whilst others thought that they must be the descendants of the men whom Gideon had driven out, of whom a reverent saint had prophesied that they would come in the latter days and conquer the whole earth, from the East even unto the Euphrates, and from the Tigris even unto the Black Sea.[c]]

both in lands and in men; the courageous resistance of the Riazan princes proved unsuccessful, chiefly because the princes of northern Russia did not unite, but decided on defending themselves separately. After the devastation of Riazan and the slaughter of her princes (1237), followed that of Suzdal. Having taken Moscow, the Tatars marched to Vladimir, where they slew the family of the grand prince, while he himself was defeated and killed on the banks of the Sit (1238). Thence they were apparently going to Novgorod, but returned — probably to avoid the marshes. On their way back, Kozelsk detained them for a long time, but it was finally taken and pillaged.

The tactics of the Tatars in this war consisted in first encompassing each region as hunters do, and then joining forces at one centre, thus devastating all. In the years 1239–1240 the Tatars ravaged southern Russia, and in 1240 they took and laid waste Kiev. All Europe trembled at the horrors of the Tatar invasion; the emperor Frederick II called for a general arming, but his calls were in vain. Meanwhile the Tatars advanced to Hungary (1241) and Poland, and defeated the Polish princes at Liegnitz in Silesia; and it was only the courageous defence of Olmütz in Moravia, by the Czech voyevode Iaroslav, and the gathering of armies under the command of the Czech king and the dukes of Austria and Carinthia, that finally caused the Tatars to turn back. They then founded their chief dwelling place on the Volga, where near the present town of Tsareva (government of Astrakhan) they established a wintering place for the horde — Sarai. There the Russian princes began to arrive with tribute. At first, however, they were obliged to go to the great khan in Mongolia; for the first khans, Okkodai, Kuiuk, and Mangku, were lawfully chosen by the princes, and maintained their authority over all the empire of Jenghiz Khan; and it was only from the time of Kublai (1260), who arbitrarily took possession of the throne and removed the seat of government to China, that the bond was definitively severed.

### INFLUENCES OF TATAR DOMINATION

The domination of the Tatars over Russia is regarded by historians from various points of view: some (such as Karamzin and especially N. I. Kostomarov) ascribe a decided influence to the Tatars in the development of Russian life. S. M. Soloviov, on the contrary, is of the opinion that the influence of the Tatars was not greater than that of the Polovtsi. Both these opinions are extreme: it is senseless to deny the influence of the Tatars, for the reason that Russia was long associated with them, and that, since in her intercourse with the east, Moscow employed Tatar services, much that was eastern entered into the administration, notably the financial system; traces of eastern custom may also be found in the military organisation. These are direct consequences; the indirect ones are hardly less important, because a considerable share in the interruption of civilisation and the roughening of the manners and customs of the people may be ascribed to the separation of eastern Russia from western. On the other hand, it is impossible to regard the corporal punishments as entirely Tatar, for they were known in Byzantium, and came to Russia in the manuals of church statutes; they were known also in the west, and are to be met with in places which were but little under Tatar domination, such as Pskov. The opinion that the autocratic power had its origin in the domination of the Tatars must, it would seem, be entirely rejected, especially when we call to mind the constant preaching of the clergy, and the fact that John the Terrible directly appeals to the authority of the Bible and the example of the Roman emperors.

Civilisation and letters were almost unknown to the Tatars. The writers in their chanceries were for the greater part taken from the nations they had conquered, as were also the artists who embellished the wintering places of their khans. Much luxury was to be met with amongst them, but neither elegance nor cleanliness: in this respect they kept to the very end the customs of the Mongolian steppes. Also in moral respects they showed themselves dwellers of the steppes even to the end of their career in history. Cruel and coarse though they were, they possessed, however, some good qualities. They were temperate in their lives, and their cupidity was not so great as that of other Asiatic nations; they were far less given to deceit in trade — in general, with them, violence predominated over deceit.[b]

Throughout all of their conquests in Russia, they obviously acted upon a principle which was well calculated to facilitate their own complete ascendency. At first they destroyed the walled places that stood in the way of their projects, and afforded a means of defence to the people; they destroyed the population wherever they went, in order that the remnant which survived should feel the more surely the weight of their power; and, at length, as their advance became the more safe and certain, they relaxed slightly in their cruelties, enrolling under their standard the slaves they captured, thus turning their conquests into armaments. But the climate of Russia rendered it an unsuitable place for their location. As they could not remain upon the soil which they had vanquished, they established themselves on the frontiers to watch over their new possessions, leaving nominal Russian princes to fight for them against the invading tribes that continually rushed in. Those very invasions served also to strengthen the Tatar yoke, by weakening the resisting power of the natives.[d]

In conquering Russia they had no wish to take possession of the soil, or to take into their own hands the local administration. What they wanted was not land, of which they had enough and to spare, but movable property which they might enjoy without giving up their pastoral, nomadic life. They applied, therefore, to Russia the same method of extracting supplies as they had used in other countries. As soon as their authority had been formally acknowledged they sent officials into the country to number the inhabitants and to collect an amount of tribute proportionate to the population. This was a severe burden for the people, not only on account of the sum demanded, but also on account of the manner in which it was raised. The exactions and cruelty of the tax-gatherers led to local insurrections, and the insurrectionists were of course always severely punished. But there was never any general military occupation nor any wholesale confiscations of land, and the existing political organisation was left undisturbed. The modern method of dealing with annexed provinces was wholly unknown to the Tatars. The khans never for a moment dreamed of attempting to Tatarise their Russian subjects. They demanded simply an oath of allegiance from the princes, and a certain sum of tribute from the people. The vanquished were allowed to retain their land, their religion, their language, their courts of justice, and all their other institutions.

The nature of the Tatar domination is well illustrated by the policy which the conquerors adopted towards the Russian church. For more than half a century after the conquest the religion of the Tatars was a mixture of Buddhism and paganism, with traces of sabaism or fire-worship. During this period Christianity was more than simply tolerated. The grand khan Kuiuk caused a Christian chapel to be erected near his domicile, and one of his successors, Khubilai, was in the habit of publicly taking part in the

Easter festivals.   In 1261 the khan of the Golden Horde allowed the Russians to found a bishopric in his capital, and several members of his family adopted Christianity.   One of them even founded a monastery, and became a saint of the Russian church!   The orthodox clergy were exempted from the poll tax, and in the charters granted to them it was expressly declared that if anyone committed blasphemy against the faith of the Russians he should be put to death.   Some time afterwards the Golden Horde was converted to Islam, but the khans did not on that account change their policy.

A FEMALE SAMOYED

They continued to favour the clergy, and their protection was long remembered.   Many generations later, when the property of the church was threatened by the autocratic power, refractory ecclesiastics contrasted the policy of the orthodox sovereign with that of the "godless Tatars," much to the advantage of the latter.

At first there was and could be very little mutual confidence between the conquerors and the conquered. The princes anxiously looked for an opportunity of throwing off the galling yoke, and the people chafed under the exactions and cruelty of the tribute collectors, whilst the khans took precautions to prevent insurrection, and threatened to devastate the country if their authority was not respected.   But in the course of time this mutual distrust and hostility greatly lessened.   The princes gradually perceived that all attempts at resistance would be fruitless, and became reconciled to their new position.   Instead of seeking to throw off the khan's authority, they sought to gain his favour, in the hope of thereby forwarding their personal interests.   For this purpose they paid frequent visits to the Tatar chief, made rich presents to his wives and courtiers, received from him charters confirming their authority, and sometimes even married members of his family.   Some of them used the favour thus acquired for extending their possessions at the expense of neighbouring princes of their own race, and did not hesitate to call in Tatar hordes to their assistance.   The khans, in their turn, placed greater confidence in their vassals, entrusted them with the task of collecting the tribute, recalled their own officials who were a constant eyesore to the people, and abstained from all interference in the internal affairs of the principalities so long as tribute was regularly paid.   The princes acted, in short, as the khan's lieutenants, and became to a certain extent Tartarised.   Some of them carried this policy so far that they were reproached by the people with "loving beyond measure the Tatars and their language, and giving them too freely land, and gold, and goods of every kind."c

## ALEXANDER NEVSKI

The recognition of Tatar sovereignty was complete in the homage and tribute they demanded and received. Every prince was forced to solicit his investiture from the khan of Kiptchak; and even when Iaroslav was established as grand prince over the rest, Batu cunningly allowed several rivals to put in their claims to that authority, and obliged them to wait so long for his decision that the order of succession remained unsettled. This state of suspense in which the feudal lords were kept, and a series of famines which followed the destructive march of the Tatars, plunged the country into a condition of abject wretchedness.

During this period of indecision on the one hand, and forlorn imbecility on the other, the Lithuanians succeeded in appropriating to themselves some portions of the northwestern division of Russia; and the Swedes, and Danes, and Livonian knights of the sword proceeded to make demonstrations of a descent upon Novgorod. Alexander, however, who had succeeded his father in that principality, finding that the grand prince was unable to render him any assistance towards the defence of the city, anticipated the advance of the intruders, and giving them battle on the banks of the Neva gained a decisive victory. He immediately built strong forts on the spot to repel any future attempts, and returned in triumph to Novgorod. So signal was the overthrow of the enemy that Alexander was honoured by the surname of Nevski, in commemoration of the achievement.

Flushed with a triumph as unexpected as it was important, Alexander Nevski desired to enlarge the bounds of his power at home. The army was warmly attached to him, for his personal intrepidity was no less remarkable than his sagacity — qualities which were rarely so strongly developed in so young a man. The Novgorodians, however, always jealous of their municipal privileges, and suspicious of the motives of their rulers, resisted the extension of Alexander's power, and, apprehensive that he would abuse his advantages, they remonstrated against his proceedings, and at last broke out into open rebellion. The proud spirit of the young prince was justly offended at the impetuous revolt of his subjects, and he retired at once from the city, going over to his father at Vladimir, to request the aid of a sufficient force to restore order. But Iaroslav, in the conviction of his own inadequacy, was unwilling to interfere with the wishes of the Novgorodians; and, conferring upon Alexander the inferior principality of Pereiaslavl, he sent another of his sons, at the request of the people, to reign over the disaffected province.

The Novgorodians, however, speedily discovered their error. The Danes, induced to speculate upon the absence of Alexander, a second time appeared within the boundary, and the new prince, an inexperienced young man, made choice of such measures as clearly proved him to be unfit for his office. The people became dissatisfied, and, being now convinced that Alexander was the only man who could relieve them in their difficulty, petitioned him to return; but he indignantly rejected the request. A second embassy, headed by the archbishop, was more fortunate, and Alexander Nevski once more placed himself at the head of the army, and obtained a second victory over the invaders. Resolved to profit by the obligations under which he laid his subjects by resuming, at their own instance, the reins of government, and by freeing them from the presence of a dangerous foe, he now pushed on to Livonia, and routed the combined forces of a triple alliance of Germans, Danes, and Tchuds, on the borders of Lake Peipus. This exploit, which the youthful hero achieved in the year 1245, not only obtained him the love and admiration of his own subjects, but speedily spread his name through every part of the empire, until it finally reached the court of the Golden Horde, where it elicited an unusual degree of curiosity and applause.

In the person of the prince of Novgorod, a new dawn of hope broke over Russia, and nothing but the disheartening feuds of the chiefs checked the growth of that incipient desire for liberty which the influence of his successes was calculated to create. Alexander was adapted to the occasion; and if the disunited sovereigns could now have consented to forego their low animosities, and to merge their personal differences in the common cause, Alexander was the instrument of all others the most fit to undertake the conduct of so gallant an enterprise. But it required an extraordinary combination of circumstances to awaken the Russian princes to a full sense of their degradation, and to inspire them with resolution to set about the rescue of their country from the chains of the spoiler. Alexander's example was useless. He could do no more than demonstrate the possibility of improvement within the reach of his own domain; but for all purposes of a national and extensive character, his exertions failed to procure any favourable results.

On the death of the grand prince Iaroslav, whose reign appears to have passed unmarked by any events of importance, the khan invited or rather summoned Alexander to the horde. A number of competitors or claimants for the grand princedom had already brought forward their petitions: some were lingering in person at the court; others were represented by ambassadors bearing rich tributes; and all were in a state of considerable anxiety pending the decision of the Tatar. Alexander alone was silent. The fame of his deeds had preceded him. He did not come to supplicate for an honour to which he felt that he possessed an unexceptionable claim, but he attended as a point of duty, without reference to a nomination that could hardly increase his popularity. His independent bearing, his manly figure, and the general candour and fearlessness of his manners gained him at once the confidence and admiration of the khan, who did not hesitate to assure him that, although he had heard much in his favour, report had fallen short of his distinguished merits.

Auspicious, however, as this reception was, it did not terminate in Alexander's appointment to the suspended sceptre of Vladimir. The policy of the Tatar was to keep the order of succession in periodical uncertainty, so that the Russians might the more distinctly see how much the destinies of the country depended on his supreme will. It was not until Alexander paid a second visit to the horde, in 1252, that he was raised to the dignity of grand prince. It was accorded to him in a very gracious spirit, and he entered upon his new office with more earnest zeal than had for a long time before been displayed by his predecessors.

The first act of the grand prince was an expedition against Sweden, undertaken with two objects: (1) to crush a formidable foe that occasionally harassed the frontier districts; and (2) to give employment and opportunity for pillage to his numerous army, which he had already taught to calculate upon the rewards of spoliation. The expedition terminated in victory. The triumphant army laid a part of the Swedish territory under contribution, succeeded in capturing a number of prisoners, and returned home laden with spoils.

These successes and the skilful policy of the grand prince made the most favourable impression on the mind of the khan, who now, whenever dissensions arose amongst the princes, either referred the adjustment of their differences to Alexander, or confiscated their dominions and annexed them to the grand princedom. Two instances of the latter description may be recorded as evidences of the cunning displayed by the Tatar in the protection of the Greek religion. While Alexander was at the height of his prosperity, the prince of Kiev, affected by some sudden admiration of the Roman Catholic ritual, signified his submission to the pope, acknowledging his holiness's supremacy over the churches of his principality. Another prince, his brother-in-law, adopted a similar measure, which was equally offensive to Tatars and Russians. The khan, irritated by proceedings so directly at variance with his will, deprived them of their authority, and transferred their territories to the grand prince, who, according to some writers, was even assisted by the Tatars in seizing upon them.

The tribute which had been originally imposed upon the Russians by their conquerors had always been levied by the princes, the khan being satisfied to receive it at their hands. As the power of Alexander increased, the khan gradually recalled this system of delegation, and adopted a more strict and jealous mode of collection. The first contribution was raised upon the princes, as tribute money, and they were left to procure it amongst their subjects as well as they could. But it now assumed the shape of a tax on persons and property. In order to ensure the regularity of its payment, and protect the khan against evasions, Tatar officers were appointed in every district to attend exclusively to the rigid collection of the revenue. From this tax, which was imposed without distinction upon every Russian, and rated according to his means, the clergy alone were exempt: and even they, in one instance, were attempted to be taxed in later times; but the khan who sought to enforce it was obliged to yield to the double argument of long-established usage and weighty presents from the wealthy monks.

The new burthen lay heavily upon the people, and the mode in which it was enforced through foreign collectors, of the nation of their oppressors enhanced its mortifications. Universal discontent followed the tax-gatherers. They were treated with unreserved displeasure. It was with great difficulty they could carry into effect the objects of their unpopular mission, and in some places, particularly the cities where the population was more compact, and the communication of opinion more rapid and complete, they were received with execration. This resistance on the one hand no doubt produced increased severity on the other; and as the levy advanced, the people became less cautious in the exhibition of their feelings, and the collectors more rigorous and despotic. Novgorod, which had always been the rallying point for the assertion of freedom in Russia, took the lead in this revolt against the khan's authority. The Novgorodians, to a man, refused to pay the tax, and even threatened to wreak their vengeance upon the officers who were appointed to collect it. The prince of Novgorod, one of Alexander's sons, urged to extremities by his republican advisers, sanctioned these declarations of independence, and openly signified his determination to prevent the exactions of so ignominious a tribute within the districts dependent upon his rule. Alexander, perceiving, in this dangerous obstinacy of his son, the source of serious calamity to the empire at large, and knowing well that neither the Novgorodians, nor any other fraction of the Russian people, were in a condition to resist the powerful armies of the khan, should he be provoked to compel compliance at the point of the sword, undertook in person to appease the growing tumult, and presenting himself in the city, rebuked the inhabitants for having perilled the safety of the country by their contumacy, severely punished rash advisers of his son, and finally arranged the payment of the tax to the satisfaction of the Tatar offices. Still the Novgorodians were not content.

They remonstrated against the unequal pressure of the tax, setting forth that it fell more grievously upon the poor than upon the rich, and that if they were obliged to submit to such a penalty, it should at all events be adjusted proportionately to the means of individuals. Even this difficulty Alexander was enabled to meet by assuming the responsibility of the payment himself, a vexatious and ungrateful duty, which, however, he willingly accepted, as it afforded him the means of quelling discontents that might have otherwise terminated in a sanguinary convulsion.[d]

### Death of Alexander Nevski; Appreciation of His Character

In 1262, disturbances arose in the country of Rostov, where the people became exasperated at the violence of the Tatar collectors of tribute; a council was called together and the collectors were driven out of Rostov, Vladimir, Suzdal, Pereiaslavl, and Iaroslavl; in the last mentioned town the enraged inhabitants killed the collector Izosim, who had embraced Mohammedanism to become a Tatar tax-gatherer, and persecuted his former fellow-citizens worse than the Tatars themselves. Naturally such an occurrence could not be calmly passed over by the horde, and Tatar regiments were already sent to take the Christians into captivity. In order to avert this calamity from the people, Alexander repaired a fourth time to the horde; he was evidently successful, possibly because of the Persian War which was then greatly occupying the khan Bergé. But it was his last work; he left the horde, where he had passed the whole winter, a sick man, and died on the way back to Vladimir on the 14th of November, 1263; "having laboured greatly for the Russian land, for Novgorod and Pskov, for all the grand princedom, and having given his life for the orthodox faith." By preserving Russia from calamities on the east, and by his famous exploits for faith and country in the west, Alexander gained for himself a glorious memory throughout Russia and became the most conspicuous historical personage in Russian history from Monomakh to Donskoi. A token of this remembrance and fame is to be found in the special narrative of his exploits that has come down to us. "The grand prince Alexander Iaroslavitch," says the author of the narrative, "conquered everywhere, but himself was nowhere conquered;" there came to Novgorod from the western countries a famous knight, who saw Alexander, and when he returned to his own land he said: "I have gone through many countries and nations, but nowhere have I seen such a one, no such king among kings and no such prince among princes;" and a similar honourable mention was made of him by the khan. When, after the death of his father, Alexander came to Vladimir, his coming was terrible, and the news of it flew even to the mouth of the Volga, and the Muscovite women began to frighten their children, saying: "Be quiet, the grand duke Alexander is coming!" It happened once that ambassadors were sent to him from great Rome by the pope, who had commanded them to speak to Alexander as follows: "We have heard of thee, O Prince, that thou art honourable and wonderful, and that thy country is great, therefore have we sent unto thee two of the wisest of our twelve cardinals, that thou mayest hearken to their teaching." Alexander, having taken counsel with his wise men, wrote down and described to the pope all that had taken place from the creation of the world to the seventh œcumenical council, and added: "All this is well known unto us, but we cannot accept your teachings." Following in the footsteps of his father, Alexander gave much gold and silver to the horde to ransom prisoners. The metropolitan Cyril was in

Vladimir when he heard of the death of Alexander, which he thus announced to the people: "My beloved children! learn that the sun of the land of Russia has set;" and all the people cried out in reply: "Then we perish!"[e]

"It was as vassal and agent of the khan," says Brueckner, "that Alexander broke the resistance of Novgorod and compelled it to pay tribute. On the one hand representing the interests of the khan and repressing the revolts of the Russians, on the other hand mollifying the anger of the khan and acting like a shrewd diplomat, Alexander represents a curious combination of egotism and patriotism. We are not in the possession of sufficient evidence to form a just estimate of the measure of his services or of his opportunistic policy, but he is certainly a most interesting character in that unfortunate and disgraceful period of Russian history."[i]

## The Grand Princedom

With the death of Alexander commenced afresh the hurtful contests of the princes for the grand princedom. The division of interests which had gradually grown up amongst the Tatars, greatly increased the internal disorders of Russia. Nogay, the Tatar chieftain, who had thrown off the rule of the khan of Kiptchak, asserted his sovereignty in the southern provinces, and contended against his rival of the horde, for the right of tribute in many districts which had hitherto acknowledged implicitly the government of the first conqueror. This strife between the ruling powers produced much treachery amongst the Russian princes, who generally allied themselves to the chief who happened at the moment to obtain the ascendency, and who thus played a false game to assist them in the accomplishment of their own individual objects. In this way they wasted their strength; for whenever a prince profited by the sale of his allegiance, he paid so dearly for the assistance which procured him the end he had in view, that the gain in such a case was usually discovered to be a severe loss. The grand princedom was the prize for which they all struggled; and in the contentions which marked the struggle, almost every inferior principality became more enfeebled than before.

Alexander Nevski was one of the few great men whose names stand apart from the tumultuous throng that crowd the early pages of Russian history. He was a wise statesman, and a brave soldier. His victories over the enemies of his country were not less remarkable for completeness and brilliancy, than his measures of domestic improvement were distinguished by prudence and foresight. The Danes, the Swedes, the Lithuanians, and the Teutonic knights severally gave way before him: he enlarged the bounds of his territory, inspired his army with a fresh spirit of activity, rebuilt several Russian cities that had been destroyed during the Tatar invasions, and founded others in well-chosen situations. Russia, under his sway, might have redeemed her fallen fortunes; but the unnatural hostility of the feudal princes to the grand princedom, their hatred to any chief whose virtues elevated him above them, and their ruinous conflicts amongst themselves upon insignificant grounds of quarrel, paralysed the efforts of Alexander, and deprived him of the power of rendering that service to his country which he was eminently qualified to confer. His fame was so universal, that his death gave opportunity to the display of a fresh burst of superstitious feelings. His approaching decease was said to have been notified to the metropolitan by a voice from heaven; and as the body lay in the coffin, the dead man was said to have opened one of his hands, as the prayer of absolution was spoken by the officiating clergyman. These miracles obtained Alexander a niche amongst the Russian saints; and, less in honour of his real merits than his attributed powers, he was duly canonised after death. Some centuries subsequently, a monastery was raised to his memory by Peter I, and his relics were removed to St. Petersburg with extraordinary ceremonies of devotion. An order of knighthood was afterwards instituted in his name, which ranks amongst its members some of the monarchs of Europe. These facts connected with the reputation of Alexander Nevski in Russia are memorable, as proofs of the veneration in which he was held.[d]

MUSCOVITE WOMAN

The khans committed a serious fault in preserving a grand prince; it was a still more striking one, and a consequence of the first, to place in his hands a sovereignty disproportioned to those by which he was surrounded, to select him for too long a time from the same branch, and to give him armies to establish himself, and the means of seducing even themselves by the most costly presents. The consequence of this was, that the appanaged princes dared not enter so readily into a contest with the grand princes, who were already more powerful than themselves, and were so formidably supported. Not daring to contend with them, they turned their arms against each other, and thus enhanced by their own weakness the strength of the grand princes.

Nevertheless, till 1324, that is, for a century posterior to the Tatar invasion, the power of the grand princes was doubtful; but then, amidst the crowd of pretenders to the grand princedom, two rival branches made themselves conspicuous, and the other princes of the blood resigned to them an arena, in which the scantiness of their own resources no longer permitted them to appear. One of these branches was that of the princes of Tver; the other that of the princes of Moscow.[g]

### THE GROWING ASCENDENCY OF MOSCOW

Moscow becomes a princely appanage at a rather late date, although it is mentioned in the chronicle as early as 1147. The place is also called Kutchkovo. With this appellation there is connected a tradition, which seems quite trustworthy, that Moscow had belonged to a certain Kutchka, and the chronicle also speaks of the Kutchkas as relatives of the wife of Andrew Bogoliubski and of his murderers. It seems that the first prince of Moscow was Michael Iaroslavitch, who died in 1248. Other princes are mentioned as having been at Moscow before that time, but it is difficult to decide whether they resided there temporarily or permanently. The true line of Moscow princes begins with Daniel Alexandrovitch [a son of Alexander

[1303–1313 A.D.]

Nevski], who died in 1303 and was succeeeded by his son Iuri, the famous rival of the Tver princes.[b]

Iuri married, in 1313, the sister of Usbek Khan. It was then that, after having excited the hatred of the Novgorodians, in persisting to subdue them by means of the Tatars, Michael of Tver drew down upon his head all the wrath of Usbek, by defeating Iuri, and taking prisoners his wife, who was the khan's sister, and Kavadgi, a Tatar general, who came to put the prince of Moscow in possession of the grand princedom.

For Usbek, after having preferred and supported the rights of Michael of Tver to the grand principality, had changed his mind in favour of Iuri of Moscow, who had become his brother-in-law. The enmity of Usbek, however, remained suspended, until his sister, the wife of Iuri, and the prisoner of Michael, expired at Tver. Iuri then hastened to the horde, and accused Michael of having poisoned the princess. The offended pride of Usbek lent itself to this base calumny; he entrusted the investigation of the affair to Kavadgi; appeared to the summons; the vanquished passed sentence on his vanquisher, whom he caused to be put to death; and the infamous Iuri of Moscow was appointed grand prince in the place of his murdered rival (1320). His triumph was short: being accused of withholding the tribute due to the khan, he journeyed to the horde, and was assassinated by the son of his victim, who was himself immediately executed by Usbek. This vengeance restored the grand principality to the branch of Tver, in the person of Prince Alexander Michael's second son. It remained in it for three years; but then, in 1328, this madman caused all the Tatars at Tver to be massacred. To the brother of Iuri, Ivan I, surnamed Kalita,[1] prince of Moscow, Usbek immediately gave Vladimir and Novgorod, the double possession of which always distinguished the grand princedom. This concession formed, in the hands of Ivan, a mass, the connection of which Tver, weakened as it was, did but little diminish. Consequently, with this power, and the troops that Usbek added to it, Ivan speedily compelled all the Russian princes to combine, under his orders, against the prince of Tver; who, after having undergone various misfortunes, was executed with his son at the horde.

Here begin the two hundred and seventy years of the reign of the branch of Moscow. This first union of the Russians, under Ivan I, denominated Kalita, constitutes an epoch; it exhibits the ascendancy of this second grand prince of Moscow over his subjects; an ascendancy the increase of which we shall witness under his successors; and for which, at the outset, this branch of the Ruriks was indebted to the support they received from the Tatars. For as a word from the khan decided the possession of the throne, that one of the two rival branches of Moscow and Tver was sure to triumph which displayed the most shrewd and consistent policy towards the horde. It was not that of the princes of Tver which thus acted. On the contrary they sometimes solicited the protection of the khans, and sometimes fought against them; we have even seen one of them ordering the massacre of the Tatars in his principality.

The princes of Moscow pursued a different system; they no doubt, detested the yoke of the khans as much as their rivals did; but they were aware that, before they could cope with the Tatars, the Russians must be united, and that is was impossible to subject and unite the latter without the assistance of the former. They therefore espoused the daughters of the khans, manifested the utmost submission to the horde, and appeared to be wholly devoted to its interests.

[1] Or the Purse.

Now this policy, which, at the commencement of the Mongol invasion, acquired for Alexander Nevski the empire of all Russia, gave it, seventy-four years later, still more completely to Ivan I: for the sway of the Tatars was then more recognised; the Russians were more docile to their yoke; and the cities, which composed the grand principality were more powerful in themselves, and also by comparison with the rest of Russia, which became daily more and more exhausted. The wealth of Ivan I was another cause of the extension of his power.

The complaints of the prince of Tver, in 1323, prove that Iuri I, grand prince of Moscow, when he undertook to execute the vengeance of his brother-in-law Usbek, against Tver, was also entrusted with the collecting of the tributes; which, however, he retained, instead of sending them to the horde. Ivan Kalita, his brother and successor, profited by this example. Thus it was, that by making themselves lieutenants of the khan, the Muscovite grand princes first became the collectors, and finally the possessors, of the taxes throughout the whole of Russia; and thus they succeeded to all the rights of conquest enjoyed by the Tatars, and to their despotism.

There can be no doubt that one of the most copious sources of power to those sovereigns was the periodical census and the perpetual imposts, so alien to feudalism, and especially to a feudalism of princes: these imposts and censuses nothing but the Tatar conquest could have established, and they were inherited by the grand princes. Already, in the first half of the fourteenth century, these taxes had rendered Ivan Kalita rich enough to purchase entire domains and appanages,[1] the protection of Usbek Khan, and the preference of the primate, who removed his residence from Vladimir to Moscow, by which means the latter city became the capital of the empire.

It was by virtue of his authority as collector for the Tatars that Ivan Kalita practised extortion upon his subjects. We see him requiring a double tribute from the Novgorodians, under pretext that such was the will of the khan. Armed against the Russians with the dread inspired by the Tatar name, and against the Tatars with the money of the Russians; intoxicating the khan and his courtiers with gold and adulation in his frequent journeys to the horde; he was enabled, as lord paramount, to bring about the first union of all the appanaged princes against his competitor, the prince of Tver, whom he drove from Pskov and from Russia, being aided by the primate with the thunder of the church, then heard in the empire for the first time. The nobility imitated the clergy. Impelled either by fear, or cupidity, several boyars of other princes rallied round this grand prince, preferring the fiefs of so rich and so potent a lord paramount to those of the petty princes whom they abandoned.

Ivan Kalita pushed forward with horrible vigour in his ambitious career. "Woe, woe to the princes of Rostov!" exclaims Nicon, "because their power was destroyed, and everything was concentrated in Moscow." In fact, from the Kremlin, which he fortified, Ivan proclaimed himself the arbiter of his kinsfolk; he reigned in their principalities by the medium of his boyars; he arrogated to himself the right of being the sole distributor of fiefs, judge, and legislator; and if the princes resisted, and dared to wage against him a war of the public good,[2] he hurried to the horde, with purse in hand, and denunciation

---

[1] In the governments of Novgorod, Vladimir, Kostroma, and Rostov, and the cities of Duglitch, Bielozersk, and Galitch. — [See Karamsin, and an act of Dmitri Donskoi.]

[2] From 1333 to 1339 the princes who held appanages espoused the cause of the prince of Tver against the grand prince of Moscow, whom they called a tyrant. In 1339 the grand prince of Moscow returned to the horde, and so terrified Usbek Khan by his denunciations

[1353 A.D.]

on his lips; and the short-sighted Usbek, deceived by this ambitious monitor, was impolitic enough to disembarrass him of the most dangerous of his competitors, whom he consigned to frightful torments. The prince of Tver and his son were the most remarkable victims of this atrocious policy.

Meanwhile, Lithuania, which, from the period of the first overwhelming of Russia by the Tatars, had emancipated itself from its yoke, had now become a conquering state. About 1320, Gedimin, its leader, seized on the Russian appanages of the south and west, which had long ceased to be dependent upon the grand principality of Vladimir. Kiev, Galitch, Volhinia, became sometimes Lithuanian, sometimes Polish or Hungarian: driven to despair, their inhabitants emigrated; they formed the two military republics of the Zaparogians and Cossacks of Don. Rallying around them the unfortunate of all countries, they were destined to become one day strong enough to make head against the Turks and Tatars, between whom they were situated; and thus to embarrass the communication between those two peoples, whom a common religion, origin, and interest conspired to unite.

The grand principality was, on the other hand, repeopled by unfortunate fugitives from the southern Russian provinces, who sought refuge at Moscow. The empire, it is true, lost in extension; but it was thus rendered more proportionate to the revived power of its grand prince, who had also fewer competitors in it: those who remained could not, in point of resources, be compared with the grand principality. After all, it was much better that the latter should one day have to recover some provinces from a foreign foe, than from its domestic enemies: it was suffering an external evil instead of an internal one, which is the worst of all.

Thus, the macchiavellism of Ivan prospered. It is true that, by the confidence with which he inspired the horde, and the terrible war which he waged against his kinsmen, he restored to Russia a tranquillity to which she had long been a stranger. A dawning of order and justice reappeared under a sceptre acquired and preserved by such horrible acts of injustice; the depredations to which Russia had been a prey were repressed; commerce again flourished; great marts and new fairs were established, in which were displayed the productions of the East, of Greece, and of Italy; and the treasury of the prince was swelled still further by the profit arising from the customs.[1]

Such were the rapid effects of the first steps which Ivan took to execute the system of concentration of power; this great political impulse was so vigorously given, that it was perpetuated in his son Simeon the Proud, to whom Ivan left wherewithal to purchase the grand princedom from the horde, and in whom he revived the direct succession. Accordingly, Simeon effected, against Novgorod, a second union of all the Russian princes. It is to be remarked, that he was obliged to cede one half of the taxes to his brothers; but, at the same time, he reserved to himself the whole authority, which soon gives to its possessor the mastery of the revenue.

Simeon having died without children, in 1353, after a reign of twelve years, Ivan II, his brother, purchased the sovereignty with the wealth of Kalita. After the six years' reign of Ivan II, this system and this order of succession were, indeed, transiently interrupted in the person of a prince, alien to the branch of Moscow; but we shall soon see the great Dmitri Donskoi

against the prince of Tver and other princes, that the khan immediately summoned them to the horde, in order to restrain, or get rid of them. — [See Karamsin.]

[1] See Kamenevitch (translated by Karamsin), describing the great mart of Mologa, where the commerce of Asia and of Europe met in the seventy inns of its Slavonian suburb; and where seven thousand two hundred pounds' weight of silver were collected for the treasury of the prince.

establish them as fixed principles; that prince did not neglect to increase the wealth[1] of his grandfather Ivan. The people had given to Ivan the surname of The Purse; as much, perhaps, with allusion to his treasures, as to the purse, filled with alms for the poor, which is said to have been always carried before him. At a later period, the constantly progressive riches of the grand princes of Moscow enabled them to enfeoff directly from the crown lands three hundred thousand boyar followers; and next, to keep up a body of regular troops, sufficiently strong to reduce their enemies and their subjects.[2]

This system of concentration of power which Ivan Kalita commenced, by means of his wealth, by the union of the sceptre with the tiara, and by restoring the direct order of succession; his horrible but skilful macchiavellism against the princes holding appanages; finally, the fifty years' repose which, thanks to his policy, and to their dissensions, the Tatars permitted Russia to enjoy; these are the circumstances which entitle Ivan to be considered as standing next after Alexander Nevski among the most remarkable grand princes of the third period. It was he who had the sagacity on this stubborn soil to open and to trace so deeply the path which led to monarchical unity, and to point out its direction so clearly to his successors that they had nothing to do but to persevere in it, as the only safe road which it was then possible for Russia to follow.

This concentration of power brought about great changes from 1320 to 1329; as, at that epoch, all the Russian princes in concert solicited from the horde the recall of the Tatar governors. It was then that, more firmly fixed, the throne of the grand princes became the rallying point of the Russians: along with the consciousness of their strength, it inspired them with a public spirit, which emboldened them. This good understanding was, in reality, an effect of the ascendency which a direct and sustained succession, in a single branch of the Ruriks, had already given to it over all the others.

### The Principle of Direct Succession

In fact, sometimes natural justice, sometimes oriental negligence and cupidity, often the fear of being disobeyed, and lastly, and especially, the power and riches of the princes of Moscow — whose presents always surpassed those of the other princes — all these motives had induced the khans to allow the succession to the grand principality to descend regularly from father to son in the branch of Moscow.[3] This natural order of succession Dmitri Donskoi, in 1359, established by a treaty, in which his kinsmen con-

---

[1] See the treaty of Dmitri Donskoi with Vladimir his uncle, who promised to pay to him the tribute of his appanage, which bore the name of the khan's tribute; and the second treaty with the same Vladimir, by which the latter prince engaged that his boyars should pay to Dmitri the same tax which the grand prince might think proper to impose on his own boyars.

[2] It was thus that, in France, in 1445, Charles VII took advantage of the exactions of the English, and of the terror which they inspired, to render perpetual the temporary taxes, and to keep up a permanent corps of twenty-five thousand men.

[3] Usbek, it is true, with macchiavellian policy, designated all the children of Ivan I as his successors; but, in 1340, he allowed Simeon, the oldest and ablest of them, to make himself sole master of the throne. Ianisbek Khan nominated Ivan II, the brother of Simeon, after his death and that of his children, to the exclusion of a prince of the branch of Tver or Nevski. A prince Dmitri, of the Nevski branch, who had been made grand prince by a whim of Naurus Khan, was deposed in 1362 by Murat Khan, who chose Dmitri Donskoi, grandson of Ivan I, and son of Ivan II. Taktamuisch also gave the throne to Vasili II, the eldest son of Donskoi (1389). Lastly, Ulu-Mahomet nominated Vasili III, son of Vasili II, and father of the great Ivan III, whom this long succession rendered so powerful that he completely crushed the horde.

sented to renounce the mode of succession from brother to brother. It was the most remarkable among them, Vladimir the Brave, who was the first to sign this act. In several other conventions, Vladimir acknowledged himself the vassal and lieutenant, not merely of Dmitri, but also of Vasili his son, and even of the son of Vasili, when he was only five years of age. This example, set by a prince who, of all the possessors of appanages, was the most renowned for his prudence and his valour, was followed by the others. Thus, like the Capets, kings of France, did Ivan I, and particularly Dmitri Donskoi, begin the monarchy by restoring the direct succession, in causing, while they lived, their eldest sons to be recognised as their successors. Afterwards we see Vasili, son of Dmitri, persevering in this practice, and Vasili the Blind, his grandson, raising up his tottering throne, and preparing the autocracy of the fourth Russian period, by associating with himself his next heir, the great Ivan III.

It is easy to conceive the infallible effect of this order of succession, and with what promptitude it must necessarily have extended and consolidated the power of the grand princes. In fact, the ideas of the father being transmitted to the son by education, their policy was more consistently followed up, and their ambition had a more direct object. The nobles could not fail to attach themselves more devotedly to a prince whose son and heir, growing up amongst them, would know only them, and would recompense their services in the persons of their children; for the necessary consequence of the succession of power in the same branch, was the succession of favours and dignities in the same families.

Even before Dmitri had established the principle, the boyars saw the advantages which this order of succession held out to them. Here, as elsewhere, the fact preceded the law. This was the reason of their restoring the direct line in the grandson of Ivan Kalita; it was they who made him grand prince at the age of twelve years, and who subjected the other princes to him. In like manner, about 1430, they maintained this order of succession in Vasili the Blind. Contemporary annalists declare that these ancient boyars of the grand principality detested the descent from brother to brother; for, in that system, each prince of the lateral branch arrived from his appanage with other boyars, whom he always preferred, and whom he could not satisfy and establish but at the expense of the old. On the other hand, the most important and transmissible places, the most valuable favours, an hereditary and more certain protection, and greater hopes, attracted a military nobility around the grand princes. In a very short time, their elevation to the level of the humbled petty princes flattered their vanity, and completed their junction with the principal authority. This circumstance explains the last words of Dmitri Donskoi to his boyars, when he recommended his son to their protection. "Under my reign," said he, "you were not boyars, but really Russian princes." In fact (to cite only some examples), we see that his armies were as often commanded by boyars as by princes, and that, from this epoch, it was no longer a prince of the blood, but a boyar of the grand prince, who was his lieutenant at Novgorod.

Nay, more, when the succession from father to son was once established, there were, at the very beginning, two minorities (those of Dmitri, and of Vasili, his grandson), during which the boyars composed the council of regency, governed the state, and were the equals, and even the superiors, of the princes who held appanages. This will explain why, in 1392, the boyars of Boris, the last prince of Suzdal, gave up him and his appanage to Vasili Dmitrievitch of Moscow. The motive is to be found only in their interest; as the grand prince of Moscow entrusted them with the government of the appanages, and thus substituted the nobles in the place of the princes.

A very remarkable circumstance, with respect to Dmitri Donskoi, is, on the one hand, the energy with which he subdued those princes, and, on the other, his circumspect treatment of his boyars. According to Karamsin, it is more especially to their pride and jealousy of the tyssiatchsky of Moscow (the boyar of the city, or of the commune, a sort of civil and military tribune, elected by the people), that we are to attribute the abolition of that office by Donskoi. During the preceding reign, another tyssiatchsky of Moscow, who claimed precedence of even the boyars of the grand prince, had been murdered by them.

DMITRI DONSKOI

When this hereditary protection afforded by the grand princes of the Moscow branch was once fairly established, the nobles of each appanage, who constituted its army, had thenceforth an asylum, and, as it were, a tribunal for redress, to which they could appeal whenever they were dissatisfied with their prince. It was this which made Tver fall before Ivan Kalita; for the sovereign prince of that first and last rival of Moscow having preferred to his boyars the people of Pskov, who had defended him, the former withdrew to Moscow.

The power of Ivan Kalita being once raised by the Tatars' aid, and by the re-establishment of the direct line of succession, and thoroughly developed by his son and grandson, Simeon the Proud and Dmitri Donskoi, it followed, as a natural consequence, that he who was most able to reward and to punish drew around him, and retained, the whole of the nobles. These constituted the sole strength of the appanaged princes; their defection, therefore, completed the subjugation of the princes. Dmitri Donskoi was, therefore, in reality sovereign, as is proved by his treaties with the princes who held appanages, all of whom he reduced to be his vassals. And, accordingly, notwithstanding the appanages which he gave to his sons, and the dissensions which arose out of that error — an error as yet, perhaps, unavoidable — the attachment of the nobles, for which we have just assigned a reason, always replaced the legitimate heir on the throne.

Already, so early as about 1366, the Russian princes could no longer venture to contend against their lord paramount by any other means than by denunciations to the horde; but to what khan could they be addressed? Discord had created several: what result was to be hoped from them? Divided among themselves, the Tatar armies had ceased to be an available force. The journeys to the Golden Horde, which had originally contributed to keep the Russian princes in awe, now served to afford them an insight into the weakness of their enemies. The grand princes returned from the horde with the confidence that they might usurp with impunity; and their competitors with envoys and letters, which even they themselves well knew would be of no avail. It was, then, obvious in Russia, that the only protecting power was at Moscow: to have recourse to its support was a matter of necessity. The petty princes could obtain it only by the sacrifice of their independence; and thus all of them became vassals to the grand prince Dmitri.

Never did a great man arise more opportunely than this Dmitri. It was a propitious circumstance, that the dissensions of the Tatars gave them full occupation during the eighteen years subsequent to the first three of his reign:[1] this, in the first place, allowed him time to extinguish the devastating fury of Olgerd the Lithuanian, son of Gedimin, father of Iagello, and conqueror of all Lithuania, Volhinia, Smolensk, Kiev, and even of Taurida; secondly, to unite several principalities with his throne; and lastly, to compel the other princes, and even the prince of Tver, to acknowledge his paramount authority.

The contest with the latter was terrible: four times did Dmitri overcome Michael, and four times did the prince of Tver, aided by his son-in-law, the great Olgerd, prince of Lithuania, rise again victorious. In this obstinate conflict, Moscow itself was twice besieged, and must have fallen, had it not been for its stone walls, the recent work of the first regency of the Muscovite boyars. But, at length, Olgerd died; and Dmitri, who, but three years before, could appear only on his knees at the horde, now dared to refuse the khan his tribute, and to put to death the insolent ambassador who had been sent to claim it.

We have seen that, fifty years earlier, a similar instance of temerity caused the branch of Tver to fall beneath that of Moscow; but times were changed. The triple alliance of the primate, the boyars, and the grand prince, had now restored to the Russians a confidence in their own strength: they had acquired boldness from a conviction of the power of their grand prince, and from the dissensions of the Tatars. Some bands of the latter, wandering in Muscovy in search of plunder, were defeated; at last the Tatars have fled before the Russians! they are become their slaves, the delusion of their invincibility is no more!

The burst of fury which the khan exhibited on learning the murder of his representative, accordingly served as a signal for the confederation of all the Russian princes against the prince of Tver. He was compelled to submit to the grand prince, and to join with him against the horde.

### The Battle of the Don or Kulikovo (1380 A.D.)

Russia now began to feel that there were three things which were indispensably necessary to her; the establishment of the direct succession, the concentration of the supreme power, and the union of all parties against the Tatars. The movement in this direction was taken very opportunely; for it happened simultaneously that the Mongolian chief, Mamai, was also disembarrassed of his civil wars (1380), and he hastened with all his forces into Russia to re-establish his slighted authority; but he found the grand prince Dmitri confronting him on the Don, at the head of the combined Russian princes and an army of two hundred thousand[2] men. Dmitri put it to the choice of his troops whether they would go to encounter the foe, who were encamped at no great distance on the opposite shore of the river, or remain on this side and wait the attack? With one voice they declared for going

[1] From 1362 to 1380.
[2] 150,000 in Soloviov and Rambaud.]

over to the assault. The grand prince immediately transported his battalions across the river, and then turned the vessels adrift, in order to cut off all hopes of escaping by retreat, and inspire his men with a more desperate valour against an enemy who was three times stronger in numbers. The fight began. The Russians defended themselves valiantly against the furious attacks of the Tatars; the hosts of combatants pressed in such numbers to the field of battle, that multitudes of them were trampled under foot by the tumult of men and horses. The Tatars, continually relieved by fresh bodies of soldiers as any part was fatigued by the conflict, seemed at length to have victory on their side. Nothing but the impossibility of getting over the river, and the firm persuasion that death would directly transport them from the hands of the infidel enemy into the mansions of bliss, restrained the Russians from a general flight. But all at once, at the very moment when everything seemed to be lost, a detachment of the grand prince's army, which he had stationed as a reserve, and which till now had remained inactive and unobserved, came up in full force, fell upon the rear of the Tatars, and threw them into such amazement and terror that they fled, and left the Russians masters of the field. This momentous victory, however, cost them dear; thousands lay dead upon the ground, and the whole army was occupied eight days in burying the bodies of the dead Russians: those of the Tatars were left uninterred upon the ground. It was in harmony of this achievement that Dmitri received his honourable surname of Donskoi. *g*

### Significance of Battle of Kulikovo

The chronicles say that such a battle as that of Kulikovo had never before been known in Russia; even Europe had not seen the like of it for a long time. Such bloody conflicts had taken place in the western half of Europe at the beginning of the so-called Middle Ages, at the time of the great migration of nations, in those terrible collisions between European and Asiatic armies; such was the battle of Châlons-sur-Marne, when the Roman general saved western Europe from the Huns; such too was the battle of Tours, where the Frankish leader saved western Europe from the Arabs (Saracens). Western Europe was saved from the Asiatics, but her eastern half remained long open to their attacks. Here, about the middle of the ninth century, was formed an empire which should have served Europe as a bulwark against Asia; in the thirteenth century this bulwark was seemingly destroyed, but the foundations of the European empire were saved in the distant northwest; thanks to the preservation of these foundations, in a hundred and fifty years the empire succeeded in becoming unified, consolidated — and the victory of Kulikovo served as a proof of its strength. It was an omen of the triumph of Europe over Asia, and has exactly the same signification in the history of eastern Europe as the victories of Châlons and Tours have in that of western Europe. It also bears a like character with them — that of a terrible, bloody slaughter, a desperate struggle between Europe and Asia, which was to decide the great question in the history of humanity: which of these two parts of the world was to triumph over the other.

But the victory of Kulikovo was one of those victories which closely border upon grievous defeats. When, says the tradition, the grand prince ordered a count to be made of those who were left alive after the battle, the boyar Michael Aleksandrovitch reported to him that there remained in all forty thousand men, while more than four hundred thousand had been in action. And although the historian is not obliged to accept the latter statement literally, yet the ratio here given between the living and the dead is of great importance to him. Four princes, thirteen boyars, and a monk of the monastery of Troitsa, were among the slain. It is for this reason that in the embellished narratives of the defeat of Mamai we see the event represented on one hand as a great triumph and on the other as a woeful and lamentable event. There was great joy in Russia, says the chronicler, but there was also great grief over those slain by Mamai at the Don; the land of Russia was bereft of all voyevods (captains) and men and all kinds of warriors, and therefore there was a great fear throughout all the land of Russia. It was this depopulation through loss of men that gave the Tatars a short-lived triumph over the victors of Kulikovo.[e]

## THE DESTRUCTION OF MOSCOW (1382 A.D.)

The immediate and inevitable consequence of the battle was a sensible reduction of the Russian army. The numbers that fell before the Tatars could not be easily or speedily supplied: nor were the means of a fresh levy accessible. Those districts from which the grand army was ordinarily recruited had already exhausted their population; all the remote principalities had contributed in nearly equal proportion, and the majority of the rest of the empire was composed of persons who were unaccustomed to the use of arms, having been exclusively occupied in tillage or commerce. These circumstances, which did not damp the joy of the victory, or diminish its real importance, presented to the implacable foe a new temptation for crossing the border. But it was not until two of the wandering hordes had formed a junction that the Tatars were able to undertake the enterprise. The preparations for it occupied them two years. In 1382, the hordes of the Don and the Volga united, and making a descent upon the frontier provinces with success, penetrated as far as Moscow. The city had been previously fortified by the boyars with strong ramparts and iron gates; and Dmitri, trusting with confidence to the invincibility of the fortifications, left the capital in the charge of one of his generals, while he imprudently went into the interior to recruit his army. His absence in the hour of danger spread consternation amongst the peaceable part of the inhabitants, particularly the clergy, who relied upon his energies on the most trying occasions. The metropolitan, accompanied by a great number of the citizens, left the city upon the approach of the Tatars. The small garrison that remained made an ineffectual show on the ramparts, and the Tatars, who might not otherwise have gained their object, prevailed upon the timidity of the Russians, who consented to capitulate upon a promise of pardon. The Tatars observed their pledge in this instance as they had done in every similar case — by availing themselves of the first opportunity to violate it. They no sooner entered Moscow than they gave it to the flames, and massacred every living person they met in the streets. Having glutted their revenge with a terrible scene of slaughter and conflagration, they returned home, satisfied with having reduced the grand princedom once more, after their own fashion, to subjection. They did not perceive that in this exercise of brutal rage they strengthened the moral power of Russia, by giving an increased motive to co-operation, and by rendering the abhorrence of their yoke still more bitter than before. All they desired was the physical and visible evidence of superiority; either not heeding, or not comprehending, the silent and unseen progress of that strength which combined opinion acquires under the pressure of blind tyranny.

Dmitri, thus reduced to submission, was compelled once more to perform the humiliating penance of begging his dignity at the hands of the khan. Empire had just been within his grasp; he had bound up the shattered parts of the great mass; he had effected a union of sentiment, and a bond of co-operation; but in the effort to establish this desirable end, he had exhausted the means by which alone it could be perpetuated. Had the Tatars suffered a short period more to have elapsed before they resumed the work of spoliation, it is not improbable but that a sufficient force could have been raised to repel them: but they appeared in considerable numbers, animated by the wildest passions, at a time when Dmitri was unable to make head against their approach. The result was unavoidable; and the grand prince, in suing to be reinstated on the throne from which he was virtually expelled, merely acquiesced in a necessity which he could not avert.

But the destruction of Moscow had no effect upon the great principle that was now in course of development all over the empire. The grand princedom was still the centre of all the Russian operations: the grand prince was still the acknowledged authority to which all the subordinate rulers deferred. While this paramount virtue of cohesion remained unimpaired, the incursions of the Tatars, however calamitous in their passing visitations, had no other influence upon the ultimate destiny of the country than that of stimulating the latent patriotism of the population, and of convincing the petty princes, if indeed any further evidence were wanted, of the disastrous impolicy of wasting their resources in private feuds.

### THE DEATH OF DMITRI DONSKOI; HIS PLACE IN HISTORY

The example of Dmitri Donskoi had clearly pointed out the course which it was the policy of the grand prince to follow; but, in order to place his own views beyond the reach of speculation, and to enforce them in as solemn a manner as he could upon his successors, that prince placed a last injunction upon his son, which he also addressed in his will to all future grand princes, to persevere in the lofty object of regeneration by maintaining and strengthening the domestic alliances of the sovereignty, and resisting the Tatars until they should be finally driven out of Russia. His reign of twenty-seven years, crowned with eventful circumstances, and subjected to many fluctuations, established two objects which were of the highest consequence to the ultimate completion of the great design. Amidst all the impediments that lay in his way, or that sprang up as he advanced, Dmitri continued his efforts to create an order of nobility — the boyars, who, scattered through every part of the empire, and surrounding his court on all occasions of political importance, held the keys of communication and control in their hands, by which the means of concentration were at all times facilitated. That was one object, involving in its fulfilment the gradual reduction of the power of the petty princes, and contributing mainly to the security of the second object, which was the chief agent of his designs against the Tatars. In proportion as he won over the boyars to his side, and gave them an interest in his prosperity, he increased the power of the grand princedom. These were the elements of his plan: the progressive concentration of the empire, and the elevation of the grand princedom to the supreme authority. The checks that he met in the prosecution of these purposes, of which the descent of the Tatar army upon Moscow was the principal, slightly retarded, but never obscured, his progress. The advances that he had made were evident. It did not require the attestation of his dying instructions to explain the aim of his life: it was visibly exemplified in the institutions he bequeathed to

[1389 A.D.]

his country; in the altered state of society; and in the general submission of the appanages to a throne which, at the period of his accession, was shaken to its centre by rebellion.[d]

In 1389 Dmitri died at the early age of thirty-nine. His grandfather, his uncle, and his father had quietly prepared ample means for an open decisive struggle. Dmitri's merit consisted in the fact that he understood how to take advantage of these means, understood how to develop the forces at his disposal and to impart to them the proper direction at the proper time. We do not intend to weigh the merits of Dmitri in comparison with those of his predecessors; we will only remark that the application of forces is usually more evident and more resounding than their preparation, and that the reign of Dmitri, crowded as it was from beginning to end with the events

LIVE-FISH MERCHANT

of a persistent and momentous struggle, easily eclipsed the reigns of his predecessors with their sparse incidents. Events like the battle of Kulikovo make a powerful impression upon the imagination of contemporaries and endure long in the remembrance of their descendants. It is therefore not surprising that the victor of Mamai should have been given beside Alexander Nevski so conspicuous a place amongst the princes of the new northeastern Russia. The best proof of the great importance attributed to Dmitri's deeds by contemporaries is to be found in the existence of a separate narrative of the exploits of this prince, a separate embellished biography. Dmitri's appearance is thus described: "He was strong and valiant, and great and broad in body, broad shouldered and very heavy, his beard and hair were black, and very wonderful was his gaze." In his biography the severity of his life is extolled, his aversion to pleasure, his piety, gentleness, his chastity both before and after marriage; among other things it is said: "Although he was not learned in books, yet he had spiritual books in his heart." The end of Dmitri is thus described: "He fell ill and was in great pain, then it abated, but he again fell into a great sickness and his groaning came to his heart, for it touched his inner parts and his soul already drew near to death."

The important consequences of Dmitri's activity are manifested in his will and testament, in which we meet with hitherto unheard-of dispositions. The Moscow prince blesses his eldest son Vasili and endows him with the grand principality of Vladimir, which he calls his paternal inheritance. Donskoi no longer fears any rivals to his son, either from Tver or Suzdal. Besides Vasili, Dmitri had five sons: Iuri, Andrew, Peter, John, and Constantine; but the two latter were under age, Constantine having been born only four days before his father's death, and the grand prince confides his paternal domain of Moscow to his four elder sons. In this domain, that is in the town of Moscow and the districts appertaining to it, Donskoi had ruled over two parts or shares, the share of his father Ivan and of his uncle Simeon, while the third share was under the rule of Vladimir Andreevitch, to whom it now remained. Of his two shares the grand prince left one half to his eldest son Vasili; the other half was divided in three parts among the remaining sons, and the other towns of the principality of Moscow were divided among the four sons; Kolomna went to Vasili, the eldest, Zvenigorod to Iuri, Mozhaisk to Andrew, Dmitrov to Peter.

### THE REIGN OF VASILI-DMITRIEVITCH (1389–1425 A.D.)

From the very commencement of his reign the young son of Donskoi showed that he would remain true to the traditions of his father and grandfather. A year after the khan's ambassador had placed him on the grand prince's throne at Vladimir, Vasili set out for the horde and there purchased a *iarlik* (letter-patent of the khans) for the principality of Nijni-Novgorod, which not long before, after many entreaties, had been obtained from the horde by Boris Constantinovitch. When the latter heard of Vasili's designs, Boris called together his boyars and said to them with tears in his eyes: "My lords and brothers, my boyars and friends! remember your oath on the cross, remember what you swore to me!" The senior among his boyars was Vasili Rumianietz, who replied to the prince: "Do not grieve, my lord prince! we are all faithful to thee and ready to lay down our heads and to shed our blood for thee." Thus he spoke to his prince, but meanwhile he sent to Vasili Dmitrievitch, promising to give up Boris Constantinovitch to him. On his way back from the horde, when he had reached Kolomna, Vasili sent from there to Nijni the ambassador of Toktamish and his own boyars. At first Boris would not let them enter the town, but Rumianietz said to him: "My lord prince, the khan's ambassador and the Muscovite boyars come here in order to confirm peace and establish everlasting love, but thou wishest to raise dissensions and war; let them come into the town; what can they do to thee? we are all with thee." But as soon as the ambassador and boyars had entered the town, they ordered the bells to be rung, assembled the people, and announced to them that Nijni already belonged to the prince of Moscow. When Boris heard this he sent for his boyars and said to them: "My lords and brothers, my beloved drujina! remember your oath on the cross, do not give me up to my enemies." But this same Rumianietz replied: "Lord prince! do not hope in us, we are no longer thine, we are not with thee, but against thee!" Boris was seized, and when somewhat later Vasili Dmitrievitch came to Nijni, he placed there his lieutenants; and Prince Boris, with his wife, children, and partisans, he ordered to be carried away in chains to various towns and kept in strict imprisonment.*e*

The princes of Suzdal, Boris' nephews, were banished, and Vasili also acquired Suzdal. Later on the princes of Suzdal made peace with the grand prince and received back from him their patrimonial estates, but from genera-tion to generation they remained dependants of Moscow and not independent rulers. In 1395 took place an event which raised the moral importance of Moscow: on account of an expected invasion of Timur (Tamerlane), which, however, never took place, Vasili Dmitrievitch ordered to be transported from Vladimir to Moscow that famous ikon which Andrew had formerly taken from Kiev to his beloved town of Vladimir; this ikon now served to consecrate the pre-eminence of Moscow over all other Russian towns.

Following in the steps of his predecessors, Vasili Dmitrievitch oppressed Novgorod, but did not however entirely attain to the goal of his designs. Twice he endeavoured to wrest her Dvinsk colonies from her, taking advan-tage of the fact that in the Dvinsk territories a party had been formed which preferred the rule of the Moscow grand prince to that of Grand Novgorod. The people of Novgorod were fortunate in defending their colonies, but they paid dearly for it: the grand prince laid waste the territory of Novgorod, and ordered some of the inhabitants who had killed a partisan of his at Torzhok to be strangled; but worse than all, Novgorod itself could not get on without the grand prince and was obliged to turn to him for help when another grand prince, namely the Lithuanian, attempted its conquest.

At that period the horde was so torn up with inward dissensions that Vasili had not for some years paid tribute to the khan and regarded himself as independent; but in 1408 an unexpected attack was made on Moscow by the Tatar prince Edigei, who like Mamai, without being khan himself, made those who bore the name of khan obey him. Vasili Dmitrievitch being off his guard and thinking that the horde had become weakened, did not take early measures against his wily adversary, who deceived him by his hypocrisy and pretended good-will. Like his father he escaped to Kostroma, but pro-vided better than his father for the defence of Moscow by confiding it to his brave uncle, Prince Vladimir Andreevitch. The inhabitants themselves burned their faubourg, and Edigei could not take the Kremlin, but the horde laid waste many Russian towns and villages. Moscow now learned that although the horde had no longer the power to hold Russia in servitude, yet it might still make itself terrible by its sudden incursions, devastations, and capture of the inhabitants. Shortly thereafter, in 1412, Vasili went to the horde to do homage to the new khan Djelalledin, brought him tribute, and made presents to the Tatar grandees, so that the khan confirmed the grand principality to the prince of Moscow, although he had previously intended to bestow it upon the exiled prince of Nijni-Novgorod. The power of the khans over Russia was now only held by a thread; but for some time yet the Moscow princes could take advantage of it in order to strengthen their own authority over Russia and to shelter their inclinations under the shadow of its ancient might. Meanwhile they took measures of defence against the Tatar invasions, which might be all the more annoying because they were directed from various sides and from various fragments of the crumbling horde. In the west the Lithuanian power, which had sprung up under Gedimin, and grown great under Olgerd, had attained to its utmost limits under Vitovt.

Strictly speaking, the supreme authority over Lithuania and the part of Russia in subjection to it belonged to Iagello, king of Poland; but Lithuania was governed independently in the quality of viceroy by his cousin Vitovt, the son of that Keistut who had been strangled by Iagello. Vitovt, following the example of his predecessors, aimed at extending the fron-tiers of Lithuania at the expense of the Russian territories, and gradually subjugated one after another of them. Vasili Dmitrievitch was married to the daughter of Vitovt, Sophia; throughout his reign, he had to keep up friendly relations with his kinsman, and yet be on his guard against the ambitious designs of his father-in-law. The Muscovite prince acted with great caution and prudence, giving way to his father-in-law as far as possible, but safeguarded himself and Russia from him. He did not hinder Vitovt from taking Smolensk, chiefly because the last prince of Smolensk, Iuri, was a villain in the full sense of the word, and the inhabitants themselves preferred to submit to Vitovt, rather than to their own prince. When however Vitovt showed too plainly his intentions of capturing Pskov and Novgorod, the grand prince of Moscow openly took up arms against his father-in-law and a war seemed imminent; but in 1407 the matter was settled between them, and a peace was concluded by which the river Ougra was made a boundary between the Muscovite and the Lithuanian possessions.

### VASILI VASILIEVITCH (AFTERWARDS CALLED "THE BLIND" OR "THE DARK")

Vasili Dmitrievitch died in 1425. His successor, Vasili Vasilievitch, was a man of limited gifts and of weak mind and will, but capable of every villainy and treachery. The members of the princely house had been held in utter subjection under Vasili Dmitrievitch, but at his death they raised their heads, and Iuri, the uncle of Vasili Vasilievitch, endeavoured to obtain the grand principality from the horde. But the artful and wily boyar, Ivan Dmitrievitch Vsevolozhsky, succeeded in 1432 in setting aside Iuri and assuring the grand principality to Vasili Vasilievitch. When Iuri pleaded his right of seniority as uncle, and in support of his claim cited precedents by which uncles had been preferred, as seniors in years and birth, to their nephews, Vsevolozhsky represented to the khan that Vasili had already received the principality by will of the khan and that this will should be held above all laws and customs. This appeal to the absolute will of the khan pleased the latter and Vasili Vasilievitch remained grand prince. Some years later this same boyar, angered at Vasili because the latter had first promised to marry his daughter and then married Marie Iaroslavna, the grand-daughter of Vladimir Andreevitch Serpukhovski, himself incited Iuri to wrest the principality from his nephew. Thus Russia again became the prey of civil wars, which were signalised by hideous crimes. Iuri, who had taken possession of Moscow, was again expelled and soon after died. The son of Iuri, Vasili Kossoi (the Squinting) concluded peace with Vasili, and then, having treacherously violated the treaty, attacked Vasili, but he was vanquished, captured, and blinded (1435). After a few years the following events took place at the Golden Horde: the khan Ulu Makhmet was deprived of his throne and sought the aid of the grand prince of Moscow. The grand prince not only refused him his aid, but also drove him out of the boundaries of the territory of Moscow. Ulu Makhmet and his partisans then established themselves on the banks of the Volga at Kazan, and there laid the foundations of a Tatar empire that during a whole century brought desolation on Russia. Ulu Makhmet, as ruler of Kazan, avenged himself on the Muscovite prince for the past, was victorious over him in battle, and took him prisoner. Vasili Vasilievitch only recovered his liberty by paying an enormous ransom. When he returned to his native land, he was against his will obliged to lay upon the people heavy taxes and to receive Tatars into his principality and give them estates. All this awakened dissatisfaction against him, of which the Galician prince Dmitri Shemiaka, the brother of Kossoi, hastened to take

[1447-1448 A.D.]

advantage, and joining himself to the princes of Tver and Mozhaisk, in 1446 he ordered Vasili to be treacherously seized at the monastery of Troitsa and blinded. Shemiaka took possession of the grand principality and kept the blind Vasili in confinement, but observing an agitation among the people, he yielded to the request of Jonas, bishop of Riazan, and gave Vasili his liberty, at the same time making him swear that he would not seek to regain the grand principality. Vasili did not keep his oath, and in 1447 the partisans of the blind prince again raised him to the throne.

It is remarkable that from this period the reign of Vasili Vasilievitch entirely changed in character. While he had his eyesight, Vasili was a most insignificant sovereign, but from the time that he lost his eyes, his reign becomes distinguished for its firmness, intelligence, and decision. It is evident that clever and active men must have ruled in the name of the blind prince. Such were the boyars: the princes Patrikeev, Riapolovski, Koshkin, Plesktcheev, Morozov, and the famous voyevods, Striga-Obolenski and Theodore Bassenok, but above all the metropolitan Jonas.

RUSSIAN WOMAN

### Jonas Becomes Metropolitan

Jonas was a native of Kostroma. When he was made bishop of Riazan he did not in any wise become a partisan of the local views, his sympathies inclined to Moscow because, in conformity with the conditions of that epoch, Jonas saw in Moscow alone the centre of Russian unification. In 1431, at the death of the metropolitan Photius, Jonas was elected metropolitan, but the patriarch of Constantinople had already named the Greek Isidore to that office. This Isidore had participated in the capacity of Russian metropolitan, in the Florentine council which had proclaimed the union of the Greek church with the Roman, the pope of Rome to be the head of the Universal church. Isidore, together with the patriarch of Constantinople and the Byzantine emperor had submitted to the pope; for Isidore was at heart a Greek: all his aims were directed to the salvation of his perishing country, and like many other Greeks he hoped through the pope to arouse Europe against the Turks. It was these hopes that had caused the Greeks of that time to sacrifice the independence of their church. In the eyes of Isidore Russia too was to serve as an instrument for Greek patriotic designs; but the union was rejected at Moscow, Isidore was driven out, and for some years the office of metropolitan of Moscow remained unoccupied. Kiev had its own metropolitans since the days of Vitovt, but Moscow did not wish to have anything to do with them. The bishop of Riazan, Jonas, having been already named metropolitan by the Russian clergy, enjoyed at Moscow a pre-eminent importance and influence, and finally, in 1448, this archbishop was raised to the rank of metropolitan by an assembly of the Russian bishops, without regard to the patriarch. This event was a decisive breach with the past, and from that time the eastern-Russian church ceased to depend upon the patriarch of Constantinople and acquired full independence. The centre of her supreme power was Moscow, and this circumstance definitively established that moral importance of Moscow, which had been aimed for by the metropolitan Peter, which had been held up by Alexis, and which had received greater brilliancy from the transfer of the ikon of the Blessed Virgin from Vladimir. From that time the Russian territories not yet subject to Moscow and aiming to preserve their independence from her — Tver, Riazan, Novgorod — were bound to her more closely by spiritual bonds.

When he had for the third time ascended the throne of Moscow, the grand prince designated as co-regent with himself his eldest son Ivan, who was thenceforth called grand prince like his father, as is shown by the treaties of that period. It was from that time that the political activity of Ivan commenced and gradually widened; and there is no doubt that when he attained his majority it was he, and not his blind father that directed the accomplishment of the events which led to the strengthening of Moscow. Prince Dmitri Shemiaka, who had been obliged to promise on his oath to desist from any further attempts upon the grand principality, did not cease to show his enmity against Vasili the Dark. The clergy wrote to Shemiaka a letter of admonishment, but he would not listen to their remonstrances, and the armies of Moscow marched with the blessing of Jonas and accompanied by the young prince, against Shemiaka in Galicia. Shemiaka was defeated and fled to Novgorod, where the inhabitants gave him a refuge, and Galicia with its dependencies was again joined to Moscow. Shemiaka continued to plot against Vasili, took Ustiug, and established himself there; but the young prince Ivan Vasilievitch drove him out, and Shemiaka again fled to Novgorod. The metropolitan Jonas issued an edict declaring Shemiaka excommunicated from the church, forbidding orthodox persons to eat and drink with him, and reproaching the people of Novgorod for having received him. It was then decided at Moscow to put an end to Shemiaka by secretly murdering him; the secretary Borodati, through Shemiaka's boyar Ivan Kotov, induced Shemiaka's cook to prepare and serve to him a poisoned fowl (1453).

Vasili the Dark died on the 5th of March, 1462, from an unsuccessful treatment of burns. He outlived his chief counsellor, the metropolitan Jonas, by a year, the latter having died on the 31st of March, 1461.[h]

A REVIEW OF THE INTERNAL DEVELOPMENT DURING THE TATAR PERIOD

The beginning of the fourteenth century was the commencement of a new epoch in the life of Russia; in its two halves two empires began to chrystallize: that of Moscow in the east and that of Lithuania in the west, and the scattered elements began to gather around the new centres. Such a centre for eastern Russia was Moscow, until then an insignificant town, rarely mentioned in the chronicles, being the share of the younger and therefore less powerful princes. Under Daniel Aleksandrovitch[1] the town of Moscow constituted the whole principality. With the acquisition of Pereiaslavl (1302), Mozhaisk (1303), and Kolomna (1308) this region became somewhat

[1] A son of Alexander Nevski.

[1462 A.D.]

more extended, but when it fell to the share of Ivan Danilovitch after the death of his brother Iuri, it was still very insignificant; and yet through its resources the princes of Moscow managed to become the first in eastern Russia and little by little to gather round them the whole of eastern Russia. The rise of the principality of Moscow is one of the most remarkable phenomena in the history of Russia. It is therefore not surprising that particular attention should have been directed towards it by historians, and by the light of their united investigations the phenomenon becomes sufficiently clear.

In the thirteenth century, under the domination of the Tatars in eastern Russia, there was a continual struggle amongst the princes for the title of grand prince, to which they also strove to unite the possession of Vladimir. We also observe another distinctive feature of the time, which was that the princes did not remain to live in Vladimir, but only strove to unite it to their own possessions, and thus augment them, and, if possible, secure them for their families. The struggle was for the preponderance of one family over another through the extension of its territorial possessions. In the Kievan period, whoever became prince of Kiev, removed to Kiev, and named someone of his own family as ruler in his own principality, so that if Kiev were lost and it should pass into another family, he would not lose his own patrimony.

During the Tatar period we note a new phenomenon: the princes did not merely separate themselves from their patrimonial lands, but even from their capitals; for instance: Iaroslav lived in Tver, Basil in Kostroma, Andrew in Gorodeza, Dmitri in Pereiaslavl, and so on. The power of a grand prince at that time was only a hegemony, a preponderance over other princes; as a testimony of their independence the other princes, the elders of their families (such as Riazan, Tver, etc.) began also to call themselves grand princes, and the preponderance of the grand prince of Vladimir little by little lost its significance. To all this there must yet be added another special circumstance, that in order for anyone to unite Vladimir and its territory to his possessions and thus obtain the predominance, a *iarlik* or letter of the khan was required; no rights were necessary and a wide field was open for every guest. Thus there appeared a new basis for the right of succession: the favour of the khan. To obtain this favour was the aim of all the princes, to keep it — a peculiar art. Whoever possessed this art would be the head over all eastern Russia, and whoever could maintain this position was bound to subordinate all the rest to himself. In consequence of this, the first condition for success at that time was a dexterous tactfulness, and whoever possessed this quality must come out victor. This dexterousness was a peculiar distinction of the Muscovite princes, and in it lay the chief cause of their success. They had neither power nor higher rights, and all their hopes were founded on their own skill and the favour of the khan. They had no riches, and their patrimonial lands, poor and secluded, away from the great rivers which were then the chief means of communication, did not yield them large means.

But to ensure success with the khan, his wife, and the princes of the horde, money was necessary; so they became saving and scraping, and all their capacities were directed to the acquisition of gain. Their qualities were neither brilliant nor attractive, but in their position it was only by these sober qualities that anything could be obtained. Alexander Iaroslavitch (Nevski) pointed out to his successors that their policy should be to give way when necessary and to wait when uncertain. He who followed this counsel was successful; whosoever hurried, like Alexander Mikhailovitch (of Tver), was a loser in the game.

But while taking advantage of every means of influence at the horde, the Muscovite princes did not lose sight of those means by which they could also act within Russia itself. Ivan Danilovitch managed to induce the metropolitan St. Peter to come to Moscow, and his successors continued to reside in that town. The alliance with the spiritual power, the only power that embraced the whole of Russia, was of extraordinary advantage to the Muscovite princes.

The metropolitan could exert his influence everywhere. Thus Theognost closed the churches at Pskov when that city offered an asylum to Alexander Mikhailovitch, and St. Sergius did likewise at Nijni-Novgorod when it accepted a prince to whom Moscow was opposed. This alliance was a most natural one: if the princes needed the authority of the church, the clergy — at that time the representatives of the most advanced ideas concerning the civil order — sought to realise that order of which it stood in need even for its purely economic interests. There is not the slightest doubt that one of the chief causes of the devotion of the clergy to the views and policies of the Muscovite princes, lay in its conviction that it was bound to derive material advantages from the concentration of all power in the hands of one prince. In fact, while the system of appanages prevailed, it was, on the one hand, extremely difficult for the clergy to enjoy its possessions and privileges in security, because the maintenance of this security depended not on one, but on many; while on the other hand, the princes of appanages infringed on clerical privileges more frequently than the grand prince. The dispersion of the monastic estates over several principalities still further contributed to the desire of the clergy for the abolition of the appanage system, which increased the difficulties of managing those estates. Especially in the case of war among the princes of appanages, the clergy of one appanage might easily be deprived of its possessions in another appange, because at such a time all means of injuring the enemy were considered permissible.

In the increase of power of the Muscovite princes a leading part also belongs to the Moscow boyars, whose activity was principally displayed during the youth or minority of the grand princes.[1]

Such were the principal causes of the strength of the Moscow princes; to them should be added (according to the historians N. V. Stankevitch and S. M. Soloviov) the central position of the principality of Moscow, both in the

[1] "The origin of the Russian aristocracy," says Turgeniev_f_, quoting from Karamzin, "is lost in the most remote antiquity. The dignity of boyar is perhaps even more ancient than that of prince; it distinguished the knights and the most notable citizens, who, in the Slav republics, commanded the armies and administrated the country. This dignity appears never to have been hereditary, but only personal. Although in the course of time it was sometimes conferred by the princes, each of the ancient towns had nevertheless its own boyars, who filled the principal elective offices; even the boyars created by the princes enjoyed a certain independence. Thus, in the treaties of the fourteenth and fifteenth centuries, we often see the contracting parties confirming to the boyars the right of quitting the service of one prince to enter the service of another. Dissatisfied at Tchernigov, the boyar went with his numerous following to Kiev, Galitch, or Vladimir, where he found new fiefs and tokens of general respect. But when southern Russia had become transformed into Lithuania, when Moscow began to grow larger at the expense of the neighbouring principalities, when the number of princes possessing appanages began to diminish, at the same time that the sovereign's power over the people was becoming more unlimited, then the dignity of boyar also lost its ancient importance. Popular power was favourable to that of the boyars, which acting through the prince on the people, could also act through these latter on the prince. This support at last failed them. Nothing remained to the boyars but to obey their prince, or to become traitors or rebels; there was no golden mean to take, and in the face of the sovereign, no legal means of opposition existed. In a word absolute power was developing itself."

[1462 A.D.]

sense that Moscow is near the sources of the chief rivers, and that an attack from without must first fall on the surrounding principalities. But these causes are evidently secondary and would have no significance without the others: Moscow is not so far from the other principalities that these advantages would belong to her alone. It was much more important that a wise policy, by preserving Moscow from the attacks of the Tatars, attracted thither an increased population and thus enriched the principality. A final important cause was the weakening of the Tatar horde and its dismemberment at the end of this period, of which the princes of Moscow did not fail to take advantage for their own ends.*b*

### THE INFLUENCE OF TATAR DOMINATION

Karamsin, in relating the history of the invasion of Russia by the Mongols, makes some reflections on the consequences of the domination of these barbarians for the Russian people. In spite of his devotion to autocratic power, he cannot prevent himself from keenly regretting the liberty which this power had superseded.

"There was a time," he says, "when Russia, shaped and elevated by the unity of the sovereign power, yielded neither in force nor civilisation to the foremost of the European powers founded by the peoples of Germany on the ruins of the Western Empire. Having the same character, the same laws, the same usages, the same political institutions, which were communicated to Russia by the Varangian or Norman princes, she took her place in the new political system of Europe with some real claims to a great importance, and with the remarkable advantage of being under the influence of Greece, the only one of all the powers which had not been overthrown by the barbarians. This happy time for Russia, is that of Iaroslav the Great. Strengthened by both Christianity and public order, she possessed a religious teaching, schools, laws, an important trade, a numerous army, a fleet, unity of power, and civil liberty. What was Europe at the beginning of the eleventh century? The theatre of feudal tyranny, of the weakness of sovereigns, of audacity amongst the barons, of slavery in the peoples, of superstition and of ignorance. The genius of Afred and Charlemagne shone through the darkness, but soon faded away; their memory only has survived, their beneficent institutions, their generous intentions, disappeared with them.

"The shadow of barbarism, by veiling the horizon of Russia, hid Europe from its sight at the very time at which enlightenment was beginning to spread there; when the people began to shake off slavery, and the towns to contract alliances for their mutual guarantee against oppression; when the invention of the compass extended navigation and commerce; the time which saw the foundation of universities, in which fine manners began to soften, etc. During this period Russia, oppressed and torn asunder by the Mongols, was collecting all her forces merely that she might not perish. There was then no question of civilisation for the Russians. The rigours of the climate did not permit the Mongols to establish themselves in Russia as they had done in China and India. The khans wished to reign over Russia only from afar. But the envoys of the horde, representing the person of the khan, did what they chose in Russia; the traders, even the Mongol vagabonds, treated Russians as vile slaves. What was the natural consequence? Moral degradation. Forgetting national pride Russians learnt base cunning — the ruses and bravado of the weak. They deceived the Tatars, and one another they deceived still more. While ransoming themselves at the price of gold from the oppressions of the barbarians, they became more greedy, and less sensitive to insults and to shame, exposed as they were to the violence of foreign tyrants. From the time of Vasili Iaroslavitch down to that of Ivan Kalita (that most unhappy period!) Russia resembled a black forest rather than a state; might appeared to be right; he who could pillage, pillaged, foreigners and natives alike; there was no safety, either on the roads or at home; robbery destroyed property everywhere. And when this terrible anarchy began to disappear, when the stupor and the terror had ceased, and law, which is the soul of society, could at least be re-established, it was then necessary to have recourse to a severity unknown to the ancient Russians. Light pecuniary fines had formerly sufficed for the repression of theft, but already in the fourteenth century, thieves were hanged. The Russian of Iaroslav's day knew no other blows than those he might receive in a private quarrel; under the yoke of the Mongols corporal punishment was introduced. It may be that the present character of the nation still offers traces which were impressed upon it by the barbarity of the conqueror. It must be remarked also that, together with other noble qualities, valour and military courage grew visibly weaker. Formerly the princes had struck with the sword; during this period they redressed their grievances by means only of baseness and complaints brought before the khans. If, after two centuries of such slavery, Russians have not lost all moral sense, all love for virtue, and all patriotism, let us thank the influence of religion; it is religion which has maintained them in the position of men and citizens, which has not allowed hearts to grow hard, and conscience to be silenced. Humiliated as Russians they again raised themselves under the name of Christians, and they loved their country as being a country of true believers.

The internal constitution of the state was changed; everything which was free, everything which was founded on ancient rights, civil or political, became extinct. After having humbly cringed to the horde, the princes returned to their homes as terrible masters, for they were commanding in the name of a supreme suzerain. That which could not be done either in the days of Iaroslav the Great or in those of Andrew and of Vsevolod III, was accomplished noiselessly and without difficulty in the time of the Mongols. At Vladimir and everywhere else, except Novgorod and Pskov, there was no longer heard the sound of the vetché bell, that manifestation of popular sovereignty; a manifestation which was often tumultuous, but dear to the descendants of Slavo-Russians. This right of the ancient towns was no longer known to the new towns, like Moscow and Tver, which became important during the Mongol dominion. Once only do the chronicles make mention of the vetché of Moscow and they speak of it as an extraordinary event — when the capital, threatened by the enemy, and abandoned by the sovereign, found itself thrown on its own resources. The towns had lost the right of electing their chiefs, who, by their importance and the splendour of their elective dignity, had given umbrage not only to the princely dignitaries but to the princes themselves."*

## Wallace's View

The Tatar domination did not by any means Tatarise the country. The Tatars never settled in Russia proper, and never amalgamated with the people. So long as they retained their semi-pagan, semi-Buddhistic religion, a certain number of their notables became Christians and were absorbed by the Russian noblesse; but as soon as the horde adopted Islam, this movement was arrested.

[1462 A.D.]

There was no blending of the two races such as has taken place — and is still taking place — between the Russian peasantry and the Finnish tribes of the north. The Russians remained Christians, and the Tatars remained Mahommedans; and this difference of religion raised an impassable barrier between the two nationalities.

It must, however, be admitted that the Tatar domination, though it had little influence on the life and habits of the people, had a very deep and lasting influence on the political development of the nation. At the time of the conquest Russia was composed of a large number of independent principalities, all governed by the descendants of Rurik. As these principalities were not geographical or ethnographical units, but mere artificial, arbitrarily defined districts, which were regularly subdivided or combined according to the hereditary rights of the princes, it is highly probable that they would in any case have been sooner or later united under one sceptre; but it is quite certain that the policy of the khans helped to accelerate this unification and to create the autocratic power which has since been wielded by the czars.[c]

## CHAPTER IV

## FROM IVAN THE GREAT TO IVAN THE TERRIBLE

[1462-1584 A.D.]

The great ruler who occupied the throne of Moscow at the end of the fifteenth century, was richly endowed with understanding ; to his contemporaries he appeared more lucky than active, but meanwhile it was his active mind that directed all the complicated and tangled threads of the foreign and domestic relations. If his contemporaries did not always do justice to the great unificator of the land of Russia, neither is posterity always just to him. We must allow that much had been prepared by his predecessors, and this was also recognised by contemporaries ; but it is nevertheless impossible not to acknowledge that Ivan towers far above his predecessors, both by his solution of ancient problems — the unification of Russia (which he had almost completed) and the throwing off of the Tatar yoke — and the raising of new ones. The ability to take advantage of circumstances places Ivan in the rank of great men. If we do not recognise his greatness, then we must apply the same judgment in part to Peter, who was largely only the more determined successor of his brother, father, and grandfather. — BESTUZHEV RIUMIN.[b]

### ACCESSION OF IVAN (III) VASILIEVITCH

THE dynasty of the Muscovite princes, which commenced in the person of Ivan Kalita, and was preserved unbroken in the lineal descent, was fortunately strengthened by the accident of the longevity of his successors. The reigns of Ivan, of Simeon the Proud, of Dmitri Donskoi, of Vasili, and of Vasili the Blind, embraced a period of 130 years. During that time the people had become habituated to a right which saved them from the contests of rival competitors. So many protracted reigns had stamped the legitimate authority with an unquestioned ascendency, and with this growth of time its powers inevitably increased. The manners of the Russians were now formed under a rule in which the succession was fixed and immutable, and under which a progressive system of legislation was gradually assuming a compact and tangible form. The chaos of antagonistic principles — of that misrule which is born of short-lived theories, of constant interruption, and unsettled governments — was rapidly dissolving; the light of defined administration and regulated power was rising upon the empire; and the people, who were now beginning to understand the benefits of constituted rights, were ready to support their maintenance.

Under these auspicious circumstances, Ivan III, or, as he is called by some historians, Ivan the Great, ascended the throne.

It was not to be expected that a liberal and enlightened government could at once spring from the materials which were accumulated in seasons of anarchy, relieved only by interstitial gleams of peace. The natural issue of a power purchased by enormous sacrifices, and reared up amidst difficulties, was unmitigated despotism. The grand princedom was erected in storms. Its power was built up by constant accessions won at the point of the sword, or procured by profligate bribery. It was not the growth of steady improvement, of public opinion, of the voluntary acquiescence of the people. It began by direct oppression, absolute tyranny, and open injustice. The acts of outrage which the grand princes committed in their efforts to sustain their authority were acts of necessity. They were placed in a situation of peril that exposed them equally to barbarian spoilers without, and insidious enemies within; and they were compelled to vindicate their authority by the force of arms and the arts of perfidy. Their whole career was a fluctuating war against a series of resistances. They conciliated less than they subdued, and the unity which was at last gained by perseverance in a mixed policy of violence and hypocrisy was more the bond of an interest in common, than the reasonable allegiance of a free people to a government of their own choice.

Throughout the struggle for the concentration of the supreme control in one head the church, as will already have been perceived, bore a prominent part. The authority of the clergy had gone on gradually assuming a more stern and arbitrary aspect, even while the political affairs of the country were undergoing daily vicissitudes. The evils that afflicted the state passed harmless over the church; and while the one was subjected to disasters that checked its progress towards prosperity, the other was constantly enlarging its powers, profiting by the misfortunes that surrounded it, and gleaning its share of the good fortune that occasionally improved the hopes of the people. In the early periods when Russia was merely the victim of her own dissensions, the church was freely admitted as a mediator, partly in virtue of her office as the dispenser of charity and peace, and partly from the veneration in which religion and its ordinances were held. When the Tatars invaded Russia, they perceived the mighty influence which the priests exercised over the passions of the people, and, fully persuaded of the wisdom of attaching to their cause an order of men who wielded so enormous a power, they increased their privileges, exonerated them from taxes, and placed such premiums of gain and protection upon the monkish habit, that the highest amongst the nobility, and many of the princes, embraced the clerical profession, and added their rich possessions to the revenues of the church. To such an extravagance was this estimation of the benefits of the cowl carried, that the majority of the grand princes took vows before their death, and died in the retired sanctuaries of the religious houses. The monks of the Greek religion, loaded with the spoils of friends and enemies, lived in fortified dwellings, like the nobles of other lands, and were defended by formidable retinues. The primate held a court superior in magnificence to that of the grand prince, and surrounded by boyars, guards, and all the luxuries of the east, he possessed almost unlimited power over life and death; he was the first person who was consulted on all questions of difficulty, and, as a means of exhibiting the supremacy of his station, he instituted public ceremonies, at which the princes assisted, holding the bridle of the ass on which he rode. This tendency of the church to outgrow the space wherein its roots were laid, was greatly forwarded by the fertilizing contributions which flowed in upon it from all quarters. Whenever a phenomenon in the physical world alarmed the superstitions of the people, the major part of the population bequeathed their wealth to the monasteries, with the hope of propitiating the favour of Heaven and securing happiness in the next world. The corruptions of the church of Rome had already crept into the administration of the Greek faith. The system of donations that prevailed in Papal Italy, where even the kingdoms of earth were bartered for the kingdom of heaven, had set an example of which the Russian clergy were not slow to avail themselves. It was, perhaps, a natural conclusion that the clemency of the Godhead could be purchased in a country where earthly justice and exemptions from punishments were sold for pecuniary considerations.

But the lenity and favour shown by the Tatars to the Greek clergy did not produce the effect upon which they calculated. The Tatars, accustomed to rule people of different religions, and possessing within themselves no ecclesiastical foundations, for their wandering mode of life prevented their priesthood from resolving itself into a corporation, viewed with comparative indifference the spreading institutions and growing strength of the church. They only contemplated in the honours and advantages they heaped upon it, the policy of gaining over to their side a powerful body of auxiliaries. But the indestructible spirit of Christianity shrunk from a union with the creed of the pagans; while the barbarous intolerance of the Tatars furnished a further motive to array the priests against the enemies of their religion and their country. They knew that in the grand princedom resided the sole power by which the Tatars were ultimately to be driven out of the land; they saw that to arm that power with sufficient means it was necessary to enrich its treasury, to enlarge its bounds, and to attract within the circle of its sway the allegiance of the whole of the Russian principalities; they perceived in the civil commotions that oppressed the empire a constant source of internal weakness, and they dedicated their energies and their influence to the one object of rendering the grand prince supreme. Mohammedanism assailed them on the one hand, and the papal church on the other: they wanted a rallying point of resistance against both; and they could only find it in the elevation of the throne to an imperial height. Hence, the clergy supported the principle of legitimacy, which by its consistency and perpetuity was calculated to promote the progressive ascension of the princely authority; and thus by degrees, and the inevitable progress of an active doctrine that survived through every obstacle, the church became blended with the state; and the policy of the priesthood, exercising its subtle influence governed and directed the motions of the civil jurisdiction.

### CHARACTER AND AIMS OF IVAN

Ivan the Great, favoured by such auspicious dispositions on the part of the clergy, and by the rapid coherence of the principalities, ascended the

[1462 A.D.]

throne in 1462, at the age of twenty-two. He was a man of great cunning and prudence, and was remarkable for indomitable perseverance, which carried him triumphantly to the conclusions of his designs in a spirit of utter indifference to the ruin or bad faith that tracked his progress. Such a man alone, who was prepared to sacrifice the scruples of honour and the demands of justice, was fit to meet the difficulties by which the grand princedom was surrounded. He saw them all clearly, resolved upon the course he should take; and throughout a long reign, in which the paramount ambition of rendering Russia independent and the throne supreme was the leading feature of his policy, he pursued his plans with undeviating consistency. But that policy was not to be accomplished by open and responsible acts. The whole character of Ivan was tinged with the duplicity of the churchmen who held so high a place in his councils. His proceedings were neither direct, nor at first apparently conducive to the interests of the empire; but the great cause was secretly advancing against all impediments. While he forbore to risk his advantages, he left an opportunity for disunion amongst his enemies, by which he was certain to gain in the end. He never committed himself to a position of the security of which he was not sure; and he carried this spirit of caution to such an extremity that many of the early years of his reign present a succession of timid and vacillating movements, that more nearly resemble the subterfuges of a coward than the crafty artifices of a despot.

The objects of which he never lost sight were, to free himself from enemies abroad, and to convert the princedom at home into an autocracy. So extensive a design could not have been effected by mere force of arms, for he had so many domestic and foreign foes to meet at once, and so many points of attack and defence to cover, that it was impossible to conduct so grand a project by military means alone. That which he could not effect, therefore, by the sword, he endeavoured to perform by diplomatic intrigue; and thus, between the occasional victories of his armies, and the still more powerful influence of his subtle policy, he reduced his foes, and raised himself to an eminence to which none of his most ambitious predecessors had aspired.

The powers against whom he had to wage this double war of arms and diplomacy were the Tatars and Lithuanians, beyond the frontier; and the independent republics of Novgorod, Viatka, and Pskov, and the princes of the yet unsettled appanages within. The means he had at his command were fully sufficient to have enabled him to subdue those princes of the blood who exhibited faint signs of discontent in their appanages, and who could have been easily reached through the widely diffused agency of the boyars; but the obstinate republics of the north were more difficult of access. They stood boldly upon their independence, and every attempt to reduce them was followed by as fierce a resistance, and by such a lavish outlay of the wealth which their commercial advantages had enabled them to amass, that the task was one of extraordinary difficulty. Kazan, too, the first and greatest of the Tatar cities, claimed a sovereignty over the republics, which Ivan was afraid to contest, lest that which was but a vague and empty claim might end in confirmed authority. It was better to permit the insolent republicans to maintain their entire freedom, than to hazard by indiscretion their transference to the hands of those Tatars who were loosened from the parent stock.

His first act, therefore, was to acknowledge, directly or indirectly, according to the nature of their different tenures, the rights of all his foes within and without. He appeared to admit the justice of things as he found them;

betrayed his foreign enemies into a confidential reliance upon his acquiescence in their exactions; and even yielded without a murmur to an abuse of those pretensions to which he affected to submit, but which he was secretly resolved to annihilate. This plausible conformity procured him time to prepare and mature his designs; and so insidiously did he pursue his purpose, that he extended that time by a servility which nearly forfeited the attachment of the people. The immediate object of consideration was obviously the Golden Horde, because all the princes and republics, and even the Poles and Lithuanians, were interested in any movement that was calculated to embarrass the common enemy. Ivan's policy was to unite as many of his enemies as he could against a single one, and finally to subdue them all by the aid of each other. Had he ventured upon any less certain course, he must have risked a similar combination against himself. He began by withholding the ordinary tribute from the khan, but without exhibiting any symptoms of inallegiance. He merely evaded the tax, while he acknowledged the right; and his dissimulation succeeded in blinding the Tatar, who still believed that he held the grand prince as a tributary, although he did not receive his tribute. The khan, completely deceived, not only permitted this recusancy to escape with impunity, but was further prevailed upon to withdraw the Tatar residents, and their retinues, and the Tatar merchants, who dwelt in Moscow, and who infested with the haughty bearing of masters even the avenues of the Kremlin.*g*

## IVAN VASILIEVITCH MARRIES THE GREEK PRINCESS SOPHIA (1472 A.D.)

By completing the work of his predecessors in destroying the independence of the townships and the appanaged princes, Ivan created the empire of Moscow. The form of government of this empire and all the outward surroundings of power were greatly influenced by the marriage of Ivan to Sophia, daughter of Thomas Palæologus, and niece of the last emperor of Byzantium, who brought to Moscow the customs and traditions of the Byzantine Empire. Ivan had lost his first wife in 1467, and two years later the question arose of his marriage with the Greek princess. Thomas Palæologus had retired with his family to Rome; the idea of finding a bridegroom for his daughter belongs to the Greek vissarion, one of the most zealous partisans of the union and at that time cardinal. The cardinal and pope had naturally in view the finding of a new champion against the then terrible Turks, and at the same time of bringing Russia into the union. The envoy sent to Moscow was a Greek by the name of Iuri, who said that Sophia had several suitors, whom she had refused because she did not wish to enter the Latin church. Ivan, after taking counsel with his mother and boyars, sent to Rome Karl Friazin (whose brother Ivan had been coiner of money at the court of Moscow) to see the bride and confer with the pope; the latter gave his consent and required that boyars should be sent from Moscow to fetch the bride; Friazin was sent for the bride and carried on the negotiations; finally in June, 1472, Sophia, accompanied by the papal legate, left Rome. She was met with honours at Pskov in November of the same year, and was afterwards greeted with like homage at Novgorod. When Sophia was drawing near Moscow, warm disputes arose in the grand prince's council as to whether it could be allowed that a Latin crucifix should be carried before the legate. The metropolitan declared that in the event of it being permitted, the pope's legate should enter by one gate and he at another: it is unbecoming to us to hear of such a thing, not to say witness it, for he who shows honour and love to another religion offends his own; finally the legate had to enter without the crucifix. On the day of the entry the marriage ceremony took place (November 12), after which the legate presented his credentials and entered into a controversy with the metropolitan Philip, who called to his aid the scribe Nikita Popovitch. The chronicler says that being in despair of getting the better of the Russian scribes, the legate gave up the controversy, saying that he had no books with him.[b]

The marriage of the sovereign of Moscow with the Greek princess was an event of great importance in Russian history. Properly speaking, an alliance with the Byzantine emperors was not a novelty, and such marriages, excepting the first of them — that of St. Vladimir — had no important consequences and changed nothing essential in Russian life. But the marriage of Ivan with Sophia was concluded under peculiar circumstances. In the first place, his bride did not come from Greece, but from Italy, and her marriage opened the way to intercourse between Muscovite Russia and the west. In the second place, the empire of Byzantium had ceased to exist, and the customs, political conceptions, the manners and ceremonies of court life, deprived of their original soil, sought a fresh field and found it in a country of a like faith — Russia. As long as Byzantium had existed, although Russia adopted her entire ecclesiastical system, yet in political respects she had always remained purely Russian, and the Greeks had no inclination to transform Russia into a Byzantium; now, however, that Byzantium no longer existed, the idea arose that Greece ought to re-incarnate herself in Russia and that the Russian monarchy ought to be a continuation by right of succession of Byzantium, in the same degree as the Russian Church was by order of succession bone of the bone and flesh of the flesh of the Greek church. It happened opportunely that eastern Russia had freed herself from the subjugation of the Tatars precisely at the time when Byzantium was enslaved by the Turks, and there arose the hope that the youthful Russian monarchy, strengthened and consolidated, would become the chief mover in the liberation of Greece.

The marriage of Sophia with the Russian grand prince thus acquired the signification of a transfer of the hereditary rights of the descendants of Palæologus to the ruling house of Russia. It is true that Sophia had brothers who had otherwise disposed of their hereditary rights; one of them, Manuel, had submitted to the Turkish sultan, another, Andrew, had twice visited Moscow, but had not stayed there long, and had gone to Italy and sold his hereditary rights, first to the French king Charles VIII, and afterwards to the Spanish Ferdinand the Catholic. But in the eyes of the orthodox a transfer of the rights of the Byzantine monarchs to Catholic kings could not be regarded as lawful; and such being the case a far greater right was represented by Sophia, who had remained faithful to orthodoxy, who was the wife of an orthodox sovereign, who must become and did become the mother and ancestress of his successors, and who during her lifetime earned the reproaches of the pope and his partisans, who had been greatly mistaken in counting on her mediation to bring Muscovite Russia into the Florentine union.

### THE GROWTH OF AUTOCRACY

The first visible and outward sign of the fact that Russia came to regard herself as a successor to Greece, was the adoption of the two-headed eagle, the arms of the eastern Roman Empire, which thenceforth became the arms of Russia. From that time much in Russia was changed and assumed a Byzantine likeness; the change was not effected suddenly, but proceeded during the entire reign of Ivan Vasilievitch and continued after his death. In the court household the high-sounding title of czar was introduced, and the custom of kissing the monarch's hand. Court ranks were established also: master of the stables, master of the horse, and chamberlains (the latter, however, appeared only at the end of Ivan's reign). The importance of the boyars as the highest class of society fell before an autocratic sovereign; all became equal, all alike were his slaves. The honourable appellation of boyar was bestowed by the grand prince as a reward for services; besides the boyars there was also created a somewhat lower rank — that of the Iokolnitchi [1] — the commencement of the Russian hierarchy of ranks. To the time of Ivan Vasilievitch may also be attributed the establishment of bureaus *(prikazi)* with their secretaries and clerks. But most important and essential of all was the change in the dignity attaching to the grand prince, strongly to be felt and clearly visible in the actions of the deliberate Ivan Vasilievitch; the grand prince had become an autocratic sovereign. Even in his predecessors do we notice an approximation to this, but the first autocrat in the full sense of the word was Ivan Vasilievitch, and he became so especially after his marriage to Sophia. From that time all his activity was consistently and unswervingly consecrated to the strengthening of monarchy and autocracy.[c]

### SUBJUGATION OF THE REPUBLICS

From the beginning of Ivan's reign there was no change in political policy; the old system of the gradual annihilation of the independent republican communities and appanaged princes continued, as well as the old waiting policy in regard to the Tatars, which was based on the exploitation of their internecine quarrels. Vasili had already prepared to deal the final blow to Novgorod, but had been prevented by the interference of Archbishop Jonas; and the inhabitants, remembering this, were in expectation of fresh action on the part of Moscow and sought support from other quarters. Such support could at that time be afforded them only by the grand prince of Lithuania, but it was difficult for the people of Novgorod to enter into relations with him, because such relations would have the signification of a betrayal of orthodoxy. This being well understood at Moscow, the rulers there hastened to forestall the danger: the grand prince wrote a letter to Archbishop Jonas, declaring to him that the Lithuanian metropolitan Gregory was a disciple of Isidore and a defender of the "unia," and that relations with him must not be entered into. In order to support the right on his side, the metropolitan of Moscow in the interests of Novgorod rejected the solicitations of the people of Pskov who wished to have a separate bishop; the grand prince himself left unheeded the insults shown to men of Moscow in Novgorod, and even the infringement of his ancient princely rights. Occupied in a war with Kazan, he only exchanged embassies with Novgorod.

Meanwhile the party in Novgorod which was hostile to Moscow became more and more rampant; the leaders of this party were the Boretski, the children of the dead burgomaster *(posadnick)*. They were incited by their mother Martha, who as an "honourable widow" enjoyed great esteem; the Boretski were wealthy and had great influence in the *vetché*. At their instigation Prince Michael Olelkovitch, brother of Simon, prince of Kiev, was invited to come from Lithuania to Novgorod. Previously the Lithuanian princes that had been called upon to serve Novgorod had lived together

---

[1] From *ókolo*, about, around — persons about the czar.

with the Muscovite lieutenants; now the question was already different and the Lithuanian party decided to go further.    At the end of 1470 Jonas died and the question was raised in the vetché of having the archbishop nominated in Lithuania; this time, however, the archbishop Theophilus was chosen and his partisans stood out for his consecration in Moscow and were successful, so that a consent to his passing through was obtained from the grand prince.    An ambassador coming from Pskov with the news that the grand prince called the men of Pskov upon Novgorod, and offering proposals of mediation, again gave preponderance to the Lithuanian party. The vetché assembled, and people in it began to cry out:  "We are free men of great Novgorod and the grand prince of Moscow does us many wrongs and much injustice; we are for the king of Poland;" with the help of the "wicked peasants of the vetché" they gained the victory, and an embassy was sent to Casimir, the result of which was a convention for the submission of Novgorod to him.    Olelkovitch soon left Novgorod, having wronged the provinces of Novgorod in various ways.    The grand prince still wished to try peaceful measures and sent his ambassador to Novgorod with an exhortation, and the metropolitan Philip sent a letter of admonishment.    After the failure of this embassy the grand prince assembled his council (douma) and proposed the question:   Shall we march on Novgorod now or wait until winter?   It was well known that a march to Novgorod in summer was very difficult, yet it was decided to go at once, and a declaration of war was sent. In July, 1471, the grand prince himself with troops from Moscow and Tver, and accompanied by his brothers, set out from Moscow; the men of Pskov joined the Moscow troops on the way.    A religious character was given to the expedition.    Before starting, the grand prince went to pray in the cathedral of Moscow, and chroniclers liken this expedition to that of Gideon against the Midianites and that of Dmitri against Mamai.

After the battle at Tskorost, Prince Kholmski, a voyevod of Ivan, decisively defeated the people of Novgorod at the river Shelon (July 14th, 1475?) and the same day the Moscow voyevod Obrazets defeated Prince Vasili Shuiski, who was in the service of Novgorod, at the river Shilenga, and subjugated all the Dvinsk territories; "everywhere the Lord God helped the grand prince to defend his rights."    Nothing remained for Novgorod but to submit, for Casimir, occupied with his own affairs, had not come to her defence. Ivan, coming after his armies, first had Boretski and three other prisoners put to death, then he relented, accepted the petition of Theophilus which was supported by a letter from the metropolitan, took a ransom of 15,500 roubles from Novgorod, and concluded a treaty by which the inhabitants were bound not to be subject to Lithuania and to have their archbishop nominated at Moscow.

In October, 1475, Ivan visited Novgorod and remained there until February, 1476.    Received with honours and gifts by great Novgorod and her dignitaries, the grand prince administered justice as of old; The Slavnovski and Nikitinski appeared with a complaint against the honourable burgomaster (posadnick), Vasili Annanin, and nineteen other boyars who had attacked and robbed them; a similar complaint was brought by the boyars Ponarin against other boyars who had made incursions into their lands and robbed them; for such incursions were of very frequent occurrence in Novgorod.    Ivan sent the guilty persons to be imprisoned in Moscow, observing in his judgment all the ancient forms, and requiring that with his commissaries there should also be sent commissaries from Novgorod; it was also then that he allowed the authorities of Novgorod to conclude, as in ancient times, a treaty with Sweden. In 1477 complainants from Novgorod came to Moscow; "Such a thing," says the chronicle, " had never happened before since the beginning of Novgorod and since it began to have grand princes from the house of Rurik." Their coming was quite comprehensible; the smaller folk were persuaded that it was only by appealing to the tribunal of the grand prince that they could obtain redress against the greater, and therefore they had recourse to him. Such a result having been attained, it only remained to await the first pretext in order to put an end to the independence of Novgorod. The occasion soon presented itself; in 1477 the envoys from the bishop and from all Novgorod, Nazar of Podvoiski and Zacharias, the secretary of the vetché, called Ivan and his son, young Ivan, *gospodá* and not lords,[1] as had always been previously done, and the grand prince sent ambassadors to Novgorod to demand the confirmation of this title. Tumults, brawls, and even murder took place in Novgorod, and the ambassador was sent away with an insulting message. Then Ivan assembled his troops to go against Novgorod; he called upon Tver and Pskov for aid, ordered his brothers to assemble, and sending before him the Tatar prince, Daniar Kasimovitch, he set out himself. The people of Novgorod began to negotiate while the grand prince was still on the way; they had even tried to do so before, but Ivan, properly calculating that a satisfactory result could only be obtained by a warlike demonstration, avoided negotiations. All December, 1477, and the beginning of January, 1478, passed in negotiations; finally Novgorod submitted when her defender, Prince Vasili Shuiski, bent his knee[2] before Ivan and refused to serve Novgorod any longer. Novgorod submitted to the "entire will" of Ivan; the vetché was abolished and its great bell taken to Moscow to ring with other bells; estates were taken from the monasteries, and allotted to the grand prince, the first example of secularisation: till then the princes had not possessed estates in Novgorod. When he left, Ivan took with him the boyars and Martha Boretski, who is said to have died at Staritza.

It is reported that in 1479 Novgorod again tried to enter into relations with Casimir, and taking advantage of threatening danger from the Golden Horde, re-established the ancient form of government, and that the grand prince came to the town, ordered the gates to be opened, frustrated the attempt at the very beginning, and took away many of the inhabitants with him. This account is confirmed by the fact that other chronicles speak of the arrival of the grand prince at Novgorod, and of the imprisonment of the archbishop Theophilus. The loss of their independence was a heavy blow to the people, and as a consolation legends were composed of the foolishness of the first bishop sent from Moscow, Sergius by name, and of the flame that came out of the tomb of St. Bartholomew of Khoutinski and burned the feet of the grand prince.

Viatka, whose inhabitants refused to help the Moscow troops in the war against Kazan in 1469, was definitively subdued in 1489. The policy of the transfer of the natives to the ancient provinces and of sending others to take their places, was also applied to Viatka.

Pskov remained submissive and thereby preserved a shadow of independence; but the grand prince kept a zealous watch over all that was done there and did not allow any aspirations to greater independence. Although consenting that the inhabitants might ask for any prince they wished, he did not approve of any wilful change of princes, and strongly took the part of Prince Iaroslav

[1] *Gospodá*, plural of *gospodin*.
[2] Literally " beat his forehead."

Obolenski, who had had a quarrel with Pskov and whom the people wished to get rid of; it was only the desire to have done with Novgorod that induced the grand prince to give way to Pskov and give them a new lieutenant — Prince Vasili Shuiski (1477). When, later, Ivan named his son Vasili grand prince of Novgorod and Pskov, the inhabitants sent an envoy begging that they might be separated, but the grand prince replied wrathfully that he would give the principality to whomsoever he liked; Pskov also endeavoured in vain to get its province separated from the rule of the bishop of Novgorod.

Towards the appanaged princes Ivan pursued the same policy as towards the townships. Vasili, prince of Riazan, had already been taken by Vasili the Dark to be educated in Moscow; in 1464 he was sent back to Riazan, returned to Moscow, married a sister of the grand prince and went back to Riazan. He died in 1483, leaving two sons: Ivan and Theodore. Ivan, as grand prince, concluded a treaty with Moscow by which he was placed on a level with the brother of the grand prince of Moscow, Andrew Vasilievitch. In 1496 a treaty was concluded betwen the brothers, by which the younger was bound, in case he were to die childless, to leave his share to his elder brother; but Prince Theodore survived his brother and bequeathed his share to the grand prince of Moscow. In the year 1500 Ivan, grand prince of Riazan, died, leaving a young son under the guardianship of his mother and grandmother, who were entirely subservient to the prince of Moscow.

Since 1461 the prince of Tver, Michael Borisovitch, was Ivan's brother-in-law. When he came to the throne Ivan concluded a treaty with him, but although Michael helped Ivan against Novgorod, yet in their mutual relations the signs that usually preceded the fall of a separate principality might be observed. In 1476 certain boyars of Tver went over to Moscow. In 1484 it became known in Moscow that the prince of Tver had concluded a treaty with Casimir and married his granddaughter. Ivan sent troops to lay waste the districts around Tver; Michael hastened to appease him and concluded a new treaty with him, by which the prince of Tver was placed on a level with the second brother of the Moscow grand prince and bound himself not to appeal to Lithuania without his consent. Meanwhile the departure of the boyars from Tver continued and Ivan encouraged them by his policy; in the event of frontier disputes, if the men of Tver were injured they could not obtain justice, but if those of Moscow were injured, Ivan rigourously demanded satisfaction. Michael entered into relations with Casimir, but the envoy was seized, and Ivan sent his troops to Tver; the town surrendered, and Michael fled to Lithuania. In 1463 the princes of Iaroslav ceded their domain to the Muscovite monarch, and in 1474 the princes of Rostov, who ruled over only half of Rostov, for the other half had already been acquired by Kalita, sold their half to the grand prince. Equally slowly and gradually did the grand prince also crush the appanaged princes of Moscow; all these princes were his brothers, with the exception of Michael Andreevitch Vereiski (the son of Andrew Dmitrievitch, brother of Ivan of Mozhaisk). With Michael Ivan concluded several treaties that gradually cut down his rights; finally by the treaty of 1482 Michael ceded, after his death, Belozero to the grand prince. There was no pretext for this annexation, but one was soon found; desiring to make a present to his daughter-in-law Helen [1] (upon the occasion of the birth of his grandson Dmitri) of the ornaments that had belonged to his first wife, Ivan learned that the grand princess Sophia had given away much to her niece, who was married to a son of Michael named Vasili; the

---

[1] Daughter of Stephen, Gospodin of Moldavia, married to Ivan's son Ivan.

irritated grand prince then ordered Vasili to be seized, but he fled to Lithuania; whereupon Ivan took Vereia from Michael and only returned it to him as a possession for life.   Michael Andreevitch died in 1485, leaving his domains by will to the grand prince.   The appanages of the brothers also little by little, for one reason or another, were joined to the grand principality; in 1472 Iuri Vasilievitch, of Dmitriev, died, without leaving any testamentary disposition of his territory; the grand prince took possession of it; the brothers were angered, but satisfying them with some provinces, the grand prince concluded a treaty with two of them, Andrew of Uglitch and Boris of Volotsk, by which they recognised the priority of their nephew Ivan the Younger and renounced the succession after their brother.

In 1480 the younger brothers again rose against the elder, and Prince Obolenski Liko went from Moscow to enter the service of Boris; Ivan, probably learning of his brother's relations with the people of Novgorod, ordered Prince Obolenski to be seized at the court of Boris.   The princes went to Rzhev, thence to the boundary of Lithuania, and entered into relations with Casimir, who however did not help them.   Until then they had rejected negotiations, but seeing Casimir's inaction, they asked for the intercession of their mother, but Ivan refused them; they also sought support in Pskov, but were unsuccessful.   The invasion of Ahmed induced Ivan to make peace with his brothers, and Andrew received a part of the appanage of Iuriev. Andrew the younger died in 1481, leaving his domain to the grand prince. In 1484 the mother of the grand prince, who had in some degree restrained the dissensions of the brothers, died, and in 1486 Ivan bound his brothers by a new treaty to renounce their rights of inheritance in regard to appanages. In 1491 Andrew was seized and thrown into prison, where he died in 1494; his sons were imprisoned with him.   Boris also died soon after, leaving his domains to his sons Theodore and Ivan: the latter, dying in 1504, left his part by will to the grand prince, whom he calls "gossudar"[1] (sovereign or sire).

### THE FINAL OVERTHROW OF THE TATARS

The most conspicuous event in the reign of Ivan — the casting off of the Tatar yoke — is connected by many with his marriage.   But it should be borne in mind that this was the ancient and sacred ideal of the Moscow princes, to the fulfilment of which all their desires had long been directed, and for which they had been gradually preparing the means.   Such an event cannot be explained by one merely accidental circumstance, although it is impossible not to agree that the dependence of her husband upon the Tatar khan must have been humiliating to the proud Sophia, and therefore it cannot be denied that there is some truth in the traditions relating to this subject.   But in any event the circumstance was a merely accessory one, for it is known that long before this the expression: " May the Lord cause the horde to perish," was to be met with in the wills of the Moscow princes; the same expression also occurs in the testament of Vasili the Dark.   The Moscow princes had prepared for this by taking into their service Tatar princes, in whom they saw the best means of fighting their enemies, the Tatars.   And in this work bequeathed to him by his forefathers, Ivan Vasilievitch remained true to the deliberate, persistent policy of his predecessors, never losing sight of his aim, but never hurrying too much in its attainment.

[1 A title borne by the Russian emperors.]

At the time when Ivan Vasilievitch began to reign, the Tatar horde no longer constituted an undivided kingdom; previously it had been sometimes divided and then again reunited, but at this period it was definitively divided into three chief hordes; the Golden, the Kazanese, and the Crimean, at the head of the last of which, during the reign of Vasili the Dark, was Azi Girai.

Ivan's policy consisted in exploiting one horde against the other and one pretender against the other. Of the principal Tatar hordes, the nearest and weakest was the Kazan horde, and it was the first which he attempted to bring under his influence. In 1467 the vassal Kasim, who was in the service of Ivan, was invited by some of the Tatar princes *(mourzas)* to come to Kazan, but the khan Ibrahim met him at the Volga and prevented him from crossing the river; after insignificant mutual devastations in 1469 a great army was sent against Kazan, composed of sons of the boyars and Moscow troops, under the leadership of Constantine Bezzubtiev. The troops marched right up to the town, but beyond ravaging its territory nothing was done. In the summer of the same year, two of the grand prince's brothers, Iuri and Andrew the Big, marched against Kazan, besieged the town, and Ibrahim hastened to conclude peace "at the entire will of the grand prince and his voyevods," and liberated the prisoners that had been taken during the preceding forty years. For eight years there was peace, but in 1479 the Kazanese army made a raid on Russian territory (at Ustiug and Viatka). To avenge this, troops were sent from Moscow under the leadership of the voyevod Vasili Obrazets, while from the other side came the men of Viatka and Ustiug and besieged Kazan. Ibrahim again concluded peace "according to the will of the grand prince." At the death of Ibrahim disturbances arose in Kazan; one of his sons Ali Khan or Alegam, from the younger wife, became khan, and Muhammed Amin, the son of the elder wife, came to Moscow and asked for help against his brother.

In 1487 troops were despatched from Moscow under the leadership of Daniel Kholmski, the town was taken, Alegam made prisoner, and Muhammed Amin established on the throne of Kazan; he was so entirely subject to Moscow that he asked the grand prince's permission to marry, and even paid a certain tribute to Moscow. In 1496 the people of Kazan, dissatisfied with Muhammed Amin, called in the Nogaians; the Moscow troops came to the aid of the khan, but hardly had they been dismissed before the Nogaian prince Mamuk came to Kazan, and the khan fled to Moscow. Mamuk, fearing treason, seized the very persons who had called for him, and in general began to act arbitrarily. When he went to attack the princes of Arsk, the inhabitants of Kazan shut the gates against him and sent to Moscow to ask for another khan, only not Muhammed Amin. Ivan sent them Muhammed's brother, Abdul Letiv, and gave to the former Koshira and Serpukhov as fiefs. In 1502, at the complaint of the people of Kazan, Abdul Letiv was deposed and banished to Belozero. Muhammed Amin again returned, but he was already dissatisfied with Moscow, and in this attitude he was supported by his wife, the widow of Alegam. In 1505, under the pretext that the grand prince had not satisfied his complaints, Muhammed Amin plundered some Russian merchants that had come to the fair and marched against Nijni-Novgorod; Ivan died soon after, before he was able to revenge himself.

The extension of the Russian possessions in the east was accomplished in another way; in 1472 the grand prince sent troops to the territory of Perm — which was numbered amongst the Novgorodian possessions — and its prince was taken prisoner; but until 1505 native princes were left to reign there, and it was only in that year that Prince Vasili Kover was sent to Perm as lieutenant. The continual incursions of the Voguls obliged Ivan to send troops to the Ugrian territory and Prince Kurbski even crossed the Ural. While leaving there native princes, Ivan nevertheless included the lands of Perm and Ugria in his title. With the Golden Horde Ivan did not begin war, although from the very beginning he did not pay tribute punctually. Ivan's enemy, the grand prince of Lithuania, incited the Tatars against Moscow, and in 1471 Casimir called upon Ahmud to rise against the grand prince of Moscow; Ahmud however took a whole year to assemble his troops, and meanwhile during the migration of the Tatars from Sarai, which took place every summer, the people of Viatka came and plundered it. In 1472 Ahmed at last assembled his troops and took Alexin, but on meeting the grand prince's brothers with a strong army at the river Oka, he decided not to go further.

After this, until 1480, the relations with the Golden Horde remained indefinite. Meanwhile intercourse was established with the Crimean horde. Azi Girai died in 1467, and his son Nordovlat succeeded him, but he was deposed by his brother Mengli Girai, and sought a refuge with Casimir. Ivan hastened to enter into relations with Mengli Girai through the intermediation of a Jew of Feodosia, named Kokos; Mengli Girai, without breaking with Casimir, hastened to affirm these relations, which, however, were not very profitable, on account of the disturbances in the Crimea: the overthrow of Mengli Girai, by Aidar, the taking of Feodosia by the Turks, and the consequent destruction of the power of the Genoese in the Crimea; the capture of Mengli Girai and his liberation on the condition of his becoming a Turkish tributary; the devastation of the Crimea by the son of Ahmed, and the rise of the czarevitch Zenebek to the supreme power. It was only in 1479 that Mengli Girai finally established himself in the Crimea and that his constant relations with Moscow commenced.[1]

In 1480 the khan of the Golden Horde, Ahmed, incited by Casimir of Lithuania, prepared to march against Russia. It is reported that about that time Ivan refused to pay tribute, and that Sophia persuaded Ivan not to go out to meet the Tatar envoys under the pretext of illness, and also by her cunning managed to destroy the hospice of the Tatars in the Kremlin; it is said that she wrote to the wife of the khan telling her that she had had a vision in which she had been commanded to build a church upon the very same site, and that the wife of the khan, who was bribed with presents, managed to arrange the matter, and when the envoys came there was no resting place to be found for them in Moscow. However this may be, it is certain that Ivan ceased to pay tribute. When he heard of Ahmed's coming Ivan took up his position on the banks of the Oka, where he remained encamped from July until September; Ahmed being informed that the passage was here occupied, passed through the territories of Lithuania and came to the Ugra, but here he also found the passages occupied. The two armies remained in this position until November, and in the camp of the grand prince councils were held as to what should be done, for two parties had arisen, the one proposing to offer a ransom, while the other was for fighting; the famous letter of Archbishop Vassain of Moscow was written in the latter spirit. The grand prince was sometimes at Kolomna and sometimes at Moscow to consult with the metropolitan. When the frosts set in, by which the Tatars greatly suffered, the grand prince commanded the Russians to fall back on Kremenets, and

[1] Mengli Girai's rivals : Adir, Nordovlat, and Zenebek, fled to Moscow and were detained by Ivan, who thus rendered Mengli Girai a service at the same time that he held out their liberation as a tacit menace.

meanwhile the Tatars fled.[1]   Soon after his return to Sarai, Ahmed was killed by Ivak, prince of the Nogaian Tatars; and Mengli Girai delivered Russia from the sons of Ahmed, with whom he was constantly at war.

The relations with the Crimea, which were of importance in the struggle against the Golden Horde, were also of importance in the conflict with Lithuania, and therefore Ivan constantly maintained them; but zealously looked after his own interests.   Of course many presents had to be given to the Tatars of the Crimea, although Ivan was economical to such a degree that when sheep were given to the envoys he required the skins to be returned; but he spent his wealth all the more willingly for this object, because Lithuania on her side also endeavoured to bribe the horde, and a regular auction went on in the Crimea.   The conquest of Feodosia by the Turks made it necessary for the Russians to enter into relations with them for commercial reasons.

## AFFAIRS OF LITHUANIA

The friendship of Mengli Girai, which had been of value to Ivan in his conflicts with the Tatars, was of still greater importance in his dealings with Lithuania: Casimir, occupied with matters in the west, principally the establishment of his son on the throne of Bohemia, had incited both the inhabitants of Novgorod and the Golden Horde against Ivan, while Ivan on his side had instigated Mengli Girai against Lithuania and carried on relations with Casimir's enemy, the king of Hungary, Matthias (I) Corvinus.   The quarrels of the border princes serving in the various armies, and their passing into the service of the Muscovite sovereign, served as the chief pretext for dissatisfaction.   The grand prince of Moscow, taking advantage of the fact that in the treaty concluded between Vasili Vasilievitch and Casimir, the subject of the princes had been treated very vaguely, began to receive those that passed into his service.   Thus he received together with their domains Prince I. M. Vorotinski, Prince I. V. Bielski, and Prince D. Th. Vorotinski.   The complaints at their desertions, the quarrels of the border princes, and in general, the frontier disagreements, were a continual subject of friction, which occasionally went as far as slight skirmishes.   In 1492 Casimir died, and Lithuania chose as king his son Alexander, while Poland took as king his other son John.   Ivan again roused Mengli Girai against Lithuania and sent detachments of his troops to lay waste the frontiers.   Propositions of peace were sent from Lithuania and negotiations for a marriage with one of the daughters of Ivan were entered upon.   In Moscow it was insisted that the negotiations for peace should precede those for marriage.   Meanwhile more princes passed into the Russian service: two more princes Vorotinski, Prince Mezetski and Prince Viazemski; the frontier incursions also continued.   Finally in 1494 Alexander sent his ambassadors to open negotiations both for peace and for the marriage.   The treaty concluded by them recognised the passing of the princes into Ivan's service, and what was of even greater importance, Ivan was therein called sovereign of all Russia. Ivan then gave his consent to the marriage of his daughter Helen with the grand prince of Lithuania, Alexander, stipulating however that a promise in writing should be given that Helen would not be constrained to change her religion.   When all this was concluded, in 1495 Ivan sent Helen to Lithuania, giving her detailed instructions.   At the celebration of the marriage

---

[1] Soloviov [h] decisively confutes the story that the cause of Ahmed's retreat was the destruction of Sarai by Nordovlat.

ceremony the Russian ambassadors insisted that the ceremony should also be celebrated by an orthodox priest.  But even from the very beginning it was manifest that seeds of discord lay hidden in this alliance.  Alexander refused to build an orthodox church at his court, the boyars from Moscow who were with Helen were soon sent back, and finally Alexander ceased to give Ivan the title of sovereign of all Russia.  The dissatisfaction grew, so that Ivan wrote to Mengli Girai: "If Alexander makes peace with you now, let us know if he does not, also let us know, and we are with you, our brother."  More princes passed into the service of the grand prince of Moscow, amongst them Prince Simon Bielski, who asserted that persecutions against orthodoxy had commenced in Lithuania, and accused the bishop of Smolensk, Joseph, of co-operating with the Latins; Prince Simon Ivanovitch (son of Ivan of Mozhaisk) with Tchernigov, and Prince Vasili Ivanovitch (a grandson of Shemiaka) with Novgorod Severski also came over (1499).  Ivan sent Alexander a declaration of war; which began with incursions of the vassal princes, and on the 14th of July, 1500, Prince Daniel Kholmski, who led the troops of Tver and Moscow, and the vassal Tatars and princes, met the Lithuanian hetman Prince Constantine, defeated him, and took him prisoner; on the other hand the grand prince's son, Prince Dmitri Ivanovitch, was unable to take Smolensk, and in general during four years warlike action proceeded very feebly.  Diplomatic intrigue was however carried on with great activity; Moscow incited Mengli Girai against Lithuania, who sent his sons to devastate Lithuania and Poland, in spite of tempting offers from Alexander.

Stephen of Moldavia, however, hearing of the disgrace and abandonment into which his daughter Helen (widow of Ivan's son) had fallen at the court of Moscow, made peace with Alexander; his enmity however did not express itself in any important act.  Far more important was the help given to Alexander by the Livonian grand master Plettenberg.  Notwithstanding the truce which had been concluded, the continual collisions between the Livonians and the inhabitants of Pskov did not cease.  To avenge one of these incursions, Ivan sent twenty thousand troops to Livonia who laid waste the land, captured towns, and carried away prisoners.  A fresh truce was concluded (1482) which was extended in 1493, but the Germans burned a certain Russian in Reval, and in answer to Russian complaints they replied that they would have burned the grand prince himself.  This, it is supposed, explains the order given in 1495 to expel the Hanseatic merchants and close their shops; but perhaps it is more probable that the true reason was the treaty concluded with the king of Denmark, the enemy of the Hansa, who had asked for help against the Swedes, promising in the event of success to cede a part of Finland to Russia.  Ivan sent an army against Sweden; but when the Danish king took possession of Sweden he gave nothing to Russia.  Such being the relations between Russia and Livonia, it was quite natural that the grand master Plettenberg should hasten to conclude an alliance with Lithuania (1501).  He defeated the Russians near Izborsk, but did not take the town and turned back, while the Russians continued to ravage Livonia.  Plettenberg again entered Russian territory, besieged Pskov, and a battle took place near Lake Smolin, but it was not decisive (1502).  Meanwhile Alexander began negotiations for peace, partly through his brothers John (after whose death in 1502 he occupied the throne of Poland) and Vladislav, and partly through embassies.  Finally, in 1503, a treaty was concluded by which Russia kept all her acquisitions and Ivan was granted the title of sovereign of all Russia.  A truce was then concluded with Livonia.

DEATH OF VASILI IVANOVITCH

*Painted especially for " The Historians' History of the World " by P. L. de Czernichowski*

Relations with the German Empire began under Ivan.   They commenced with the visit of the knight Poppel to Moscow;  his narratives revealed Russia to Germany and he came as ambassador in 1489.   Negotiations were opened for the marriage of one of the grand prince's daughters with Maximilian, the son of the emperor Frederick;  but nothing came of them.   The hope that it might be possible to incite the emperor against the Polish king was also frustrated, for Maximilian, who had pretensions to the throne of Hungary, made peace with Vladislav.

## LAST YEARS OF IVAN; INHERITANCE LEFT TO HIS SONS

The last years of Ivan's life were darkened by dissensions and intrigues in his family.   In 1490 died Ivan the Younger, whom Ivan had proclaimed as his co-ruler.   Two parties were then formed at the court;  the boyars wished to see Dmitri, the son of Ivan the Younger, and Helen of Moldavia recognised as heir;  and Sophia designed her son Vasili (born in 1479) to be heir.   A plot was laid against Dmitri;  the sovereign heard of it, ordered the conspirators to be executed, and was greatly angered with Sophia, because he had been told that she had called in sorcerers to her aid (1497).   Ivan then had his grandson crowned as his successor (1498);  but soon Sophia again triumphed: a conspiracy was discovered in which were involved the princes Patrikëiev and Riapolovski;  Prince Simon Riapolovski was beheaded and the Patrikëievs were forced to take holy orders.   It was supposed that the plot had been directed against Sophia.   From the first Ivan did not "rejoice in his grandson," and proclaimed Vasili grand prince of Novgorod and Pskov, and in 1502 he had Dmitri placed under arrest and declared Vasili his successor. The ambassadors to the various courts were given orders to explain these occurrences.

Ivan died on the 27th of October, 1505, leaving a will and testament by which he bequeathed sixty-six of the most important towns to Vasili, and only thirty to his remaining sons (Iuri, Dmitri, Simon, and Andrew);  Moscow was divided into parts, Vasili receiving two-thirds and the others one-third in all, but the elder was to have a share even in this third;  the younger brothers were commanded to esteem the elder as a father and to leave him their inheritance in the event of their dying childless.   Thus were changed the relations of the grand prince to the appanaged princes!   In the treaty concluded between the brothers Vasili and Iuri during the lifetime of Ivan, Iuri calls his brother "lord," and binds himself to hold his principality "honourably and strictly."

## APPRECIATIONS OF IVAN VASILIEVITCH

"He sits at home and sleeps, and his dominions augment, while I fight every day and yet can hardly defend my frontiers."   Such were the words, it is said, with which Stephen of Moldavia frequently characterised his daughter's father-in-law, the grand prince Ivan Vasilievitch.

The observation is a remarkable one, for it represents the first and most salient feature in the policy of the famous Russian monarch, who in himself concludes one period of Russian history and opens another.   Under him Russia passes out of its condition of exclusiveness;  the west learns that besides that Russia which is subject to Lithuania, there is already another Russia, independent, powerful, and self-sufficing;  it is even possible that at first this power was somewhat exaggerated, but it struck contemporaries because it had, so to say, grown imperceptibly. It would seem that all around it, as if submitting to some fatal influence, hastened to yield to this new-born power, while Russia herself did not hasten to announce herself, but only manifested herself at the last moment when everything was already prepared for this manifestation, and when it only remained to gather the fully ripened fruits.

S. M. Soloviov[h] compares Ivan to the fortunate heir of a long line of careful merchants who, having amassed a considerable capital, provided their heir with the means for carrying on vast enterprises. N. I. Kostomarov's[c] judgment is still more severe; he denies any merit in Ivan, judges his activity by the requirements of other times and circumstances, and does not recognise in him and his descendants anything beyond their own ambitious and self-interested motives. Such views were probably called forth as a contradiction to Karamzin, who on his part, carried away by his dislike of the violence which — according to him — characterised the reform of Peter, placed Ivan above Peter. The question "Lithuania or Moscow" was raised with entire firmness and determination by Ivan, for by the defence of Helen's orthodoxy and by receiving into his service the Lithuanian princes who expatriated themselves because of the persecution of orthodoxy, he became the protector of the Greek church in Lithuania and thus strove to gain influence in its internal affairs. The secular policy of Russia was thus marked out; it was also marked out by his insistence on the recognition of his title grand prince of all Russia and by his demand for the restoration of Kiev; intercourse with the west also begins with him.[b]

In war Ivan showed a caution which his enemies called cowardice. As behooved a prince, he conducted everything of importance himself. He exacted strict obedience, and was indefatigable in studying the thoughts and private circumstances of all important men in his kingdom, and even in foreign lands. The whole court and people trembled before his spirit and will; shy women are said to have fainted before his angry and fiery look; seldom, if ever, did a petitioner dare to approach his throne, and none of the nobles at the princely table ventured to say a word to another, or to leave his place, if the ruler, overcome by eating or drinking, happened to fall asleep and remained so for many hours. All the guests sat there dumb until Ivan awoke and gave them further orders, either to amuse or to leave him.

He was by no means prodigal of the life of his warriors; in fact, he expected to gain more from the mistakes of his enemies than others do from battles; and he knew how to incite his enemies into committing mistakes, as well as to make use of them. He had the enlargement of his kingdom as much at heart as his absolute power. He boldly projected many far-seeing plans, and sought with indefatigable zeal to realise them. After he had broken the pride of Novgorod he considered nothing impossible, and regarded his own will as the supreme command. We find no trace of his having been accessible to the petitions of his subjects, or of his granting public audience days for the hearing of their requests and complaints.

Arbitrary power over the common people became stronger and prevailed, and officials abused their power unpunished, for complainants and helpers were wanting. To enlighten the minds of his people through the study of science was not a part of his plans, perhaps because he may have thought that it is easier for the tyrant to rule over rude slaves than over a free-thinking and enlightened people. He must not be denied the merit of having raised great edifices at Moscow by means of foreign, especially Italian, architects; but vanity and love of show probably had more to do with this

than artistic sense and taste.   The wide and majestic walls of the venerable
Kremlin with its battlements and towers, secret underground passages, and
fortified gates, were to serve less as objects of beauty than as means of protection against domestic and foreign enemies.   Amongst the useful arts he
especially favoured those of the cannon founder and silversmith; with the former he desired to terrify his enemies, and with the latter to spread the renown
of his power and glory.   His greatest services to the Russian state include,
besides the regulation of the law code, the increase of the state revenues,
partly through the conquest of new provinces, and partly through a better
system of taxation, so that the government could collect a treasure for
unforeseen emergencies and would become less dependent upon chance.

Thus there can be no doubt that as a prince Ivan ranks high and belongs
to the number of those regents who decide the fate of their people and land
for many years, and are a blessed or a cursed remembrance to posterity: but
neither can it be denied that his greatness and fame lose much when we come
to consider him as a man, and see the harshness of his character, his unlimited pride, his contempt of all human rights, his wild and passionate nature,
and his greed of power.   That he was the founder of autocracy, as modern
writers assert, is not altogether his own exclusive merit, although it cannot
be denied that he contributed much towards it by his shrewdness and wise
moderation.   When in the early days of his youth he seized the reins of government, he found much that had been prepared towards the future greatness of Russia; but Russia was still in a chaotic condition, and its forces were
scattered and sunk as it were in a lethargy; they required an awakening and
regulating hand, and this was principally Ivan's work.   Owing to the unfortunate system of appanages, which had been the ruin of Russia for many
centuries, by destroying all unity in course of time, sowing the seeds of discord, and making the Russian state an easy prey to its enemies, the idea of a
common fatherland had quite disappeared; and the internal dissensions
among the princes, as well as the despotic pressure of the foreign barbarians,
had so deranged and disjointed it, that the praiseworthy attempts of individual grand princes could meet with no brilliant success, and it seemed as if
Russia were fated to play a deeply subordinate part in the hierarchy of states.

Nevertheless those attempts were not quite lost, and the prudent might
surmise that the time would yet come when they would bear fruit, once the
hydra of discord had been conquered and the scattered forces had been
reunited.   Ivan's proceedings in this respect were certainly of a macchiavellian nature.   We have seen that for twenty-three years he patiently
acknowledged the rights of other Russian princes and even their independence, and that by keeping his conquests to himself and not sharing them with
his brothers and the other princes, and by taking his brother's inheritance
and giving none to his other brothers, he first began to consider himself as
autocrat and ruler of all Russia, and thus gradually prepared the princes for
a recognition of his undivided sway and their own impotency and subordination.

We do not inquire as to whether the means he used for the attainment of
his end deserve our approval; we will only remark that great conquerors
and founders of new empires, or such as reorganise and rejuvenate old and
decaying states, cannot be judged with the same standard by which wise
regents are judged in regulated states.   The resort to violent measures is
often their highest duty, if they are to persist in their work and arrive at the
aim they have imposed on themselves.   From a political point of view, Ivan's
harsh proceedings therefore deserve some exculpation, all the more so when

we consider that he lived at a time when revolutions of every kind were taking place in the states and their institutions, in the modes of thinking and in the religion of men, in the arts and sciences, the new forms often seeking to supplant the old in a violent manner; and when this change also began in Russia, where intellectual enlightenment was so rare, we should not be surprised to see the forces of brutality often gaining the upper hand over the forces of reason.

We now find ourselves at one of the most important turning points of Russian political history, when by a regulated system of succession and by the incorporation of the independent principalities with the grand principality, the Russian monarchy began to establish itself firmly and to extend its bounds; when the hitherto terrible defiance of over-powerful nobles and of princes who claimed equal rank with the grand prince submits to the restraints of a common obedience; when no more dangers threaten Russia from the side of Novgorod and the Tatars; when a regulated system of taxation, a treasury and an organised army protect the throne; and finally when science and art, the administration of justice, personal safety on the roads and in the towns, besides other blessings of peace and order, also begin to attract attention, protection, and cultivation in Russia.*d*

### ACCESSION OF VASILI IVANOVITCH (1505 A.D.)

Vasili Ivanovitch succeeded his father, and continued his policy both in foreign and domestic affairs. He endeavoured to extend the frontiers of the Russian monarchy on the Lithuanian side, destroyed the independence of the last appanaged princes and the last republican township, Pskov, and strove to keep Kazan in subjection.

In his personal character Vasili resembled his father in his sterner aspect. He let his nephew, the unfortunate Dmitri, die "destitute" in prison; over his brothers he maintained a strict surveillance, not allowing his brother Andrew to marry until 1533, when he himself had already two children; with his boyars he was also stern, though there were but few executions and punishments during his reign. He preferred, in case of any suspected intention of departure on the part of a boyar, to take a written guarantee in which the security promised, in the event of departure, to pay a sum of money for those for whom he went bail. Vasili even forgave his brother Simon, who had the intention of going over to Lithuania, and only changed his counsellors. Stern on the occasion of his divorce from his first wife, Vasili was tender towards his second wife, and was very fond of his children. In general the characteristics of Vasili are most faithfully summed up by Karamzin in the following sentence: "He followed the path indicated by the wisdom of his father, without fear, without impulses of passion, moving forward with measured and prudent steps, and drew near to his aim, the aggrandisement of Russia, without leaving to his successor either the duty or the glory of repairing his faults." In the eyes of the historian this, of course, redeems the personally rather stern sides of his character, which were, however, quite comprehensible to contemporaries.[1]

### WARS WITH LITHUANIA

From the very commencement of his reign Vasili found himself confronted with two questions: that of Kazan — for Muhammed Amin had risen even

---

[1] Thus the courtiers regarded it as a matter of course that he should take away from his envoys the gifts made to them by the sovereigns to whom they had been accredited.

during the reign of Ivan and had to be subdued — and that of Lithuania. From the ambassadors whom Alexander had sent to Ivan he learned that a new sovereign was now reigning in Moscow. Having given information of this in Livonia, so that in any case the grand master might be prepared, Alexander despatched an embassy to Moscow demanding the cession of the towns that had been conquered by Ivan. The ambassadors received a firm reply from the new sovereign to the effect that he only reigned over his legitimate possessions, which he intended to retain.

Alexander saw the necessity of delay before taking a decisive line of action, of which course he informed the grand master. Meanwhile the ambassadors who had come from Moscow to announce Vasili's accession to the throne required that Alexander should not constrain his wife to change her religion. But Alexander died in 1506, and when Vasili heard of his death he wrote to his sister that she should endeavour to persuade the Polish lords and landed gentry to serve the Russian sovereign, promising at the same time to protect the Catholic faith. In answer to this first attempt on the part of Moscow to unite with Lithuania, Helen replied that Sigismund, the son of Casimir, was being chosen to the throne of Lithuania. Sigismund also sent ambassadors with the demand to return the conquered towns, and received the same reply demanding that Helen should not be constrained to adopt the Catholic faith. At this time Sigismund found an unexpected ally in the Crimean khan Mengli Girai, who having met with support in Lithuania before the death of Alexander and being dissatisfied with the Muscovite sovereign because of his expedition against Kazan, sent an embassy to Lithuania with proposals for an alliance. Sigismund promised him tribute, and Mengli Girai gave him a *yarlik* for the Russian territories of Novgorod, Pskov, and Riazan. Sigismund informed the grand master of Livonia of the relations with the Crimea and with Kazan and called upon him to go to war, and measures for the commencement of war were taken in the diet; but this time his allies were of but little assistance to Sigismund; Kazan submitted, while the Crimea and Livonia did not move. On the other hand, Vasili found an important ally in Lithuania itself in the person of Prince Michael Vasilievitch Glinski.

Prince Michael Glinski, the descendant of a Tatar prince that had left the horde during the reign of Vitovt and been baptised, had enjoyed great distinction and influence under Alexander. Glinski was a skilful general and a highly educated man for those times; he had spent twelve years abroad and had learned the art of war in the armies of Albrecht of Saxony during the war in Friesland and of the emperor Maximilian in Italy; he also visited Spain. In these expeditions and in his continual intercourse with western kings and princes, Glinski had adopted all the German customs and had become penetrated with the civilisation of the west. When he returned to Lithuania, Glinski gained the favour and confidence of King Alexander, who raised him to the dignity of court marshal and so increased his possessions that, according to the hyperbolical expression of a Polish historian, he owned almost half of the entire Lithuanian principality and stood at the head of the numerous Russian party amongst the Lithuanian lords. It was for this reason that at the death of Alexander the Lithuanian party hastened to choose Sigismund, for they feared that Glinski might obtain the throne of the grand principality and transfer the centre from Lithuania to Russia.

When Sigismund came to the throne he showed an offensive coldness to Glinski, and paying no attention to his complaints against the lords who were at enmity with him, at the head of whom was Zaberezhsky, he left for Poland. Glinski thereupon decided to obtain satisfaction on his own account; he made an incursion on the estates of Zaberezhsky, killed him, and raised a revolt against the king.   To this end he entered into relations with Mengli Girai, and Vasili Ivanovitch, on his side, sent one of his secretaries to propose to him to become the subject of Russia, and promising to leave him the lands which he might occupy.   Glinski however still wavered and tried to effect a reconciliation with the king; finally losing all hope of this, he joined the grand prince's voyevods, who had marched up to the frontiers of Lithuania. To Glinski and the foreign princes in the Russian service was confided the task of devastating Lithuania, but the voyevods did not move to their help, for in Moscow it was counted advantageous to let others do its work.   Meanwhile Sigismund sent an embassy, complaining of Glinski's reception by Vasili and of the opening of hostilities.   The letter was written in the name of Helen, and in his reply to her the grand prince directed her attention to the constraint put upon the orthodox in Lithuania and enjoined her to remain firm in her faith.   Sigismund received no aid from Mengli Girai, but nevertheless he began warlike operations, which however were limited to insignificant skirmishes.   Finally a treaty was concluded by which all Ivan's acquisitions remained to Russia, and all that had been taken by Glinski was given back (1508).   Glinski came to Moscow, where Medin and Maloiaroslavetz were given to him but he remained dissatisfied.

The peace of 1508 could not however put an end to the inimical relations between the two principalities: Glinski could not remain quiet until he was avenged on his enemies, and Lithuania could not be quiet so long as Glinski lived; while on his side Vasili Ivanovitch demanded better treatment for his sister Helen.   Thus the relations between the two neighbouring states were strained.   In 1509 Sigismund demanded the surrender or execution of Glinski, accusing him of the death of Alexander; in the same year he announced his connection with the Danish king; it can also be easily understood that each reciprocal embassy complained of frontier quarrels, as is always the case in such circumstances.   In 1512 Vasili informed Sigismund that it had come to his ears that the voyevods of Vilna and Trotski had seized Helen and held her captive — which does not appear at all improbable when the unruliness of the Lithuanian lords is borne in mind — Sigismund denied the fact.   That Helen officially received various rights, for instance that of a tribute or tax from the town of Bielsk, also does not prove that her position was a very advantageous one, for this was worth nothing more than other official favours. In 1513 Helen died and the metropolitan of Kiev was sent for to officiate at her funeral; thus this victim of political calculations left the scene.   Helen herself, as far as can be judged from her correspondence with her father and brother, was possessed of considerable tact and energy.

At last a reason for beginning war presented itself; it became known at Moscow that the incursions made by the Crimeans on the Russian frontier territories in 1512 were the result of a secret treaty that had been concluded between Sigismund and Mengli Girai, by which the king had promised to pay the khan a yearly sum of 15,000 ducats to attack his enemies.   Having sent Sigismund a declaration of war, Vasili began his warlike preparations.   The time was well chosen.   In 1511 Albrecht of Brandenburg had been chosen as Prussian grand master, and although he was a nephew of the Polish king he refused to acknowledge himself as his vassal, which he was obliged to do by the Treaty of Thorn; the emperor and the estates of the empire declared themselves for the grand master.   Advised by Glinski, Vasili had entered into relations with the emperor as early as 1508, but the treaty between them was only concluded in 1514.

Without waiting for the termination of these negotiations, the grand prince assembled an army and in December, 1512, took the field. He marched against Smolensk and having beseiged it unsuccessfully, returned in March, 1513. His second expedition, from June until November of the same year, was also unsuccessful, but in the third (June, 1514), Smolensk was at last captured. Vasili made a triumphal entry into the town, being received with an address of welcome by the bishop of Smolensk. He confirmed the rights that had been given to its inhabitants by the Lithuanian government; those in the Lithuanian service who did not desire to remain under him he sent back to Lithuania, and he appointed Prince V. V. Shuiski, governor of Smolensk. After the submission of Smolensk the prince of Mstislavl also submitted to the grand prince. Sigismund himself hastened to the deliverance of Smolensk. Glinski, probably dissatisfied because Smolensk had not been given to him, entered into secret intercourse with him. Learning of this treachery Vasili ordered Glinski to be brought in fetters to Moscow and sent a voyevod against the king; the king himself remained at Borissov and sent Constantine Ostrozhski to meet the Moscow troops.

The Russian voyevods, Tcheliadin and Prince Michael Golitza met Ostrozhski at Orsha on the Dnieper and sustained a terrible defeat. The fidelity of the boyars of Smolensk and of the bishop himself wavered and they entered into communication with Sigismund; but the burghers informed Shuiski of this treachery, and it was only the terribly energetic measures taken by him that preserved Smolensk for Russia: he ordered all the traitors except the bishop to be hanged on the walls of the city, the presents that had been given them by the sovereign to be suspended round the neck of each one. The assault on Smolensk was unsuccessful, and the war was afterward carried on feebly, which is explained by the exhaustion of Moscow after the battle of Orsha and the probable reluctance of the Lithuanian nobility to take an active part in it. After this Sigismund instigated the Tatars against Russia, in particular those of the Crimea, where in 1515 Mengli Girai had been succeeded by Muhammed Girai, who, notwithstanding his relations with Moscow, made in 1517 an attack on Tula and was repulsed. On his side Vasili strengthened his relations with Albrecht who kept his vassal, the grand master of Livonia, in check. However while Albrecht hesitated and demanded money, Vasili required that he should begin to act. The emperor, instead of beginning the war, as had been at first supposed he would do, offered his mediation, and it was with this aim in view that in 1517 the famous baron Sigismund Herberstein came to Moscow. Polish ambassadors also came; but with the news of their coming, Moscow also learned of the attack on Opochka by the Lithuanian troops and their repulse, and when Vasili heard of its failure he allowed the ambassadors access to him. The negotiations however came to nothing. The Moscow sovereign demanded Kiev and other towns, and the Lithuanian king refused to give up Smolensk. The death of Maximilian (1519) put an end to the imperial mediation; anyhow the emperor had not wished to give any real assistance: "It is not well" — he wrote to the grand master Albrecht — "to drive out the king, and make the czar of all Russia great."

In 1518 Albrecht again asked for money; the grand prince agreed, and at the former's request sent a notification of his alliance with him to the French king, Francis I — the first instance of intercourse between Russia and France. In answer to a fresh embassy from Albrecht bringing information of an invitation from the pope to join an alliance against the Turks, which Albrecht would not enter into without the grand prince's consent, an ambassador was sent to Koenigsberg from Moscow, who was received with the highest honours by the grand master. But Albrecht's help was not very efficacious; he was soon obliged to conclude a treaty with King Sigismund by which he acknowledged himself his vassal, in return for which he obtained Prussia as an hereditary possession, laid aside his title of grand master, and assumed a new title with his new faith, that of duke of Prussia.

The war at that time was limited to incursions, and Vasili Ivanovitch had even decided to seek peace; but the envoys that came would not make any concessions, only letting negotiations drag on in the hope of some event coming to their assistance; in this manner the war was prolonged until the Lent of 1521, when negotiations were to be again renewed; however they were not opened: in Kazan reigned Sahib Girai, the brother of Muhammed Girai, and they both threatened Moscow, indeed the former advanced as far as Moscow itself (1521). The devastations of the Tatars weakened Russia for a time and the negotiations with Lithuania were renewed; although a lasting peace was not concluded, a truce was continued for five years without the exchange of prisoners, and by this truce Smolensk remained to Russia. In 1526, through the medium of the emperor's envoys, negotiations for a definitive peace were again opened, but Smolensk was an obstacle, neither side consenting to give up the town which was regarded as the key to Kiev. Smolensk was treated in the same manner as the other territories annexed; the inhabitants were transferred to Moscow as had been done with the inhabitants of Pskov and Novgorod, and it was for this reason that Smolensk stood by Moscow in 1612.

## WARS WITH THE TATARS

Besides the relations with Lithuania, the relations with the Tatars constituted the chief problem of the reign of Vasili Ivanovitch. At his accession his first enterprise was to send against Kazan an army, amongst the leaders of which was his brother Dmitri; the siege of Kazan (1506) was unsuccessful, nevertheless in 1507 Muhammed Amin sent a letter to the grand prince with proposals of peace. Intercourse with the Crimea originally bore the same character as in the time of Ivan; a difference was however soon observable; the Crimea had no longer anything to fear from the remnants of the Golden Horde, and the Crimeans were therefore ready to make friends with whatever state would give them most. "Intercourse between the Crimea and the states of Moscow and Lithuania" — justly remarks Soloviov — "assumed the character of a bribery of robbers."

Such being the condition of affairs, it is not surprising that in spite of the confirmation of the treaty concluded between Ivan and Mengli Girai, the Tatars should have begun their attacks. In 1507 they were defeated at the Oka, and in consequence of this, envoys were sent demanding presents, the liberation of Abdul Letiv, former czar of Kazan and stepson of Mengli Girai, and asking for assistance against Astrakhan. Vasili Ivanovitch liberated Abdul Letiv, gave him the town of Iuriev, and by an oath of alliance obliged him to promise faithfully to serve the czar, not to have relations with his enemies, not to permit his servants to plunder on the roads or insult the churches, to live at peace with the other princes, not to wage war against Kazan without permission, and not to leave the confines of the state of Moscow. In 1515 Mengli Girai died, and his son Muhammed Girai, who succeeded him, demanded from Vasili Ivanovitch not only the cession to the Polish king of Smolensk, at the acquisition of which without his knowledge he was much incensed, but also of those towns which had been taken by Ivan. After long delays and much trouble, many insults and, of course, presents, an oath of alliance was obtained of Muhammed Girai in 1519, but meanwhile the attacks of the Crimeans continued. The son of Muhammed Girai, the czarevitch Bogatir, laid waste the borderland of Riazan; and in 1517 the Tatars — notwithstanding the Russian offer of Koshira, bordering on the steppes, to Ahmed Girai, brother of the khan — penetrated as far as Tula, where they were repulsed.

The grand prince then proposed to the council (*douma*) the question whether relations with the Crimea should be maintained, and it was decided that they must be maintained in order to prevent the rupture from becoming an open one. Meanwhile in 1518 Muhammed Amin of Kazan died, and Abdul Letiv, who had previously been czar, died a month after him; at the request of the inhabitants of Kazan a czar was named from Moscow in 1519 — Shig Alei, a prince of Astrakhan, and descendant of the czars of the Golden Horde. The Crimean khan was greatly dissatisfied at this choice of one whose family was at an eternal enmity with his own. Shig Alei remained in Kazan until 1521 when the inhabitants, dissatisfied with him, formed a conspiracy and invited Sahib Girai, brother of Muhammed Girai, to come and rule over them. Having established his brother on the throne of Kazan, Muhammed Girai advanced towards Moscow. The grand prince, warned too late by his well-wishers at Azov, could not take the necessary measures, and left Moscow, confiding the defence of the city to the boyars and baptised Tatar prince, Peter; they entered into negotiations with the enemy and paid him a ransom. The heroic defence of Pereiaslavl in Riazan by Khabar Simski somewhat softened the mournful impression of this calamity, which was augmented by the fact that Sahib Girai had at the same time devastated the territories of Nijni-Novgorod and Vladimir. The khan was preparing to repeat his expedition, and the grand prince himself took the field in expectation of his coming, but he never came.

Another undertaking then occupied Muhammed Girai: in 1523 he joined the Nogaians and conquered Astrakhan. There the Nogaians quarreled with him and killed him; his place was taken by Saidat Girai, who sent the grand prince the following conditions for an alliance: To give him 60,000 altines (an ancient coin of the value of three kopecks) and to make peace with Sahib Girai; but Vasili seeing the devastation of the Crimea both by the Nogaians and the Cossacks of Dashkevitch, who had hitherto acted in concert with the Crimeans, rejected these proposals. To avenge himself on Sahib Girai, who had massacred the Russians in Kazan where blood flowed like water, Vasili himself came to the land of Kazan (1523), devastated it, and made the inhabitants prisoners; on his return he built the town of Vasilsursk. When in 1524 a great army was sent from Moscow to Kazan, Sahib Girai fled to the Crimea, and the inhabitants of Kazan proclaimed his young nephew Sava Girai as czar; the expedition from Moscow was however unsuccessful, although the people of Kazan, who had lost their artillery engineer, sued for peace.

## THE GROWING POWER OF RUSSIA

Their dependence upon the grand prince was irksome to the inhabitants of Kazan; fresh disputes arose, Vasili brought on an intrigue, and Kazan soon asked for a new czar. Vasili named Shig Alei, who was at that time in Nijni, but when the people of Kazan entreated that his brother Jan Alei (Enalei), who then ruled over Kassimov, should be nominated in his stead,

Vasili consented.   Jan Alei was established at Kazan and Shig Alei was given Koshira, but as he did not keep the peace, and entered on negotiations with Kazan, he was exiled to Belozero.   Disturbances took place in the Crimea; Saidat Girai was overthrown by Sahib, but the relations between the Crimea and Moscow remained the same; the Tatars continued to make insignificant raids and obtained presents.   Nevertheless the Tatar messengers began to be less respectfully treated at Moscow: " Our messengers "—wrote Sahib Girai —"complain that thou dost not honour them as of old, and yet it is thy duty to honour them; whoever wishes to pay respect to the master, throws a bone to his dog."   Of other diplomatic relations those with Sweden and Denmark bore the character of frontier disputes; the intercourse with the pope was entered upon through the desire of the latter to convert Russia to Catholicism and incite her to war against Turkey.   The intercourse with the latter power had no particular results.   It is curious to observe that at this period relations were entered into with India; the sultan Babur sent ambassadors (1533) with proposals of mutual commercial dealings.*b*

Each day added to the importance of Russia in Europe.  Vasili exchanged ambassadors with the eastern courts and wrote to Francis I the great king of the Gauls.   He numbered among his correspondents Leo X, Clement VII, Maximilian, and Charles V; Gustavus Vasa, founder of a new dynasty; Sultan Selim, conqueror of Egypt and Soliman the Magnificent.   The grand mogul of the Indes, Baber, descendant of Timur, sought his friendship.   The autocracy affirmed itself each day more vigourously.   Vasili governed without consulting his council of boyars.  " *Moltchi, smerd!* " (Hold, clown!) said he to one of the nobles who dared to raise an objection.  This growing power manifested itself in the splendour of the court, the receptions of the ambassadors displaying a luxury hitherto unprecedented.   Strangers, though not in large numbers, continued to come to Moscow, of whom the most illustrious was a monk from Mount Athos, Maxine the Greek.*e*

## MAXINE THE GREEK

In the early days of his reign, when Vasili was examining the treasures left to him by his father, he perceived a large number of Greek church books which had been partly collected by former grand princes and partly brought to Moscow by Sophia, and which now lay covered with dust in utter neglect. The young sovereign manifested the desire of having a person who would be capable of looking them over and of translating the best of them into the Slavonic language.   Such a person was not to be found in Moscow, and letters were written to Constantinople.   The patriarch, being desirous of pleasing the grand prince, made search for such a philosopher in Bulgaria, in Macedonia and in Thessalonica; but the Ottoman yoke had there crushed all the remains of ancient learning and darkness and ignorance reigned in the sultan's realms.   Finally it was discovered that in the famous convent of the Annunciation on Mount Athos there were two monks, Sabba and Maxine, who were learned theologians and well versed in the Slavonic and Greek languages.   The former on account of his great age was unable to undertake so long a journey, but the latter consented to the desire of the patriarch and of the grand prince.

It would indeed have been impossible to find a person better fitted for the projected work.   Born in Greece, but educated in the enlightened west, Maxine had studied in Paris and Florence, had travelled much, was acquainted with various languages, and was possessed of unusual erudition, which he had acquired in the best universities and in conversation with men of enlightenment. Vasili received him with marked favour. When he saw the library, Maxine, in a transport of enthusiasm and astonishment, exclaimed: "Sire! all Greece does not now possess such treasures, neither does Italy, where Latin fanaticism has reduced to ashes many of the works of our theologians which my compatriots had saved from the Mohammedan barbarians." The grand prince listened to him with the liveliest pleasure and confided the library to his care. The zealous Greek made a catalogue of the books which had been until then unknown to the Slavonic people. By desire of the sovereign, and with the assistance of three Muscovites, Vasili, Dmitri and Michael Medovartzov, he translated the commentary of the psalter. Approved by the metropolitan Varlaam and all the ecclesiastical council, this important work made Maxine famous, and so endeared him to the grand prince that he could not part with him, and daily conversed with him on matters of religion. The wise Greek was not, however, dazzled by these honours, and though grateful to Vasili, he earnestly implored him to allow him to return to the quiet of his retreat at Mount Athos: "There," said he, "will I praise your name and tell my compatriots that in the world there still exists a Christian czar, mighty and great, who, if it pleases the Most High, may yet deliver us from the tyranny of the infidel." But Vasili only replied by fresh signs of favour and kept him nine years in Moscow; this time was spent by Maxine in the translation of various works, in correcting errors in the ancient translations, and in composing works of piety of which more than a hundred are known to us.

Having free access to the grand prince, he sometimes interceded for the noblemen who had fallen in disgrace and regained for them the sovereign's favour. This excited the dissatisfaction and envy of many persons, in particular of the clergy and of the worldly-minded monks of St. Joseph, who enjoyed the favour of Vasili. The humble-minded metropolitan Varlaam had cared little for earthly matters, but his successor, the proud Daniel, soon declared himself the enemy of the foreigner. It began to be asked: "Who is this man who dares to deface our sacred church books and restore to favour the disgraced boyars?" Some tried to prove that he was a heretic, others represented him to the grand prince as an ungrateful calumniator who censured the acts of the sovereign behind his back. It was at this time that Vasili was divorced from the unfortunate Solomonia, and it is said that this pious ecclesiastic did really disapprove of it; however we find amongst his works a discourse against those who repudiate their wives without lawful cause. Always disposed to take the part of the oppressed, he secretly received them in his cell and sometimes heard injurious speeches directed against the sovereign and the metropolitan. Thus the unfortunate boyar Ivan Beklemishef complained to him of the irascibility of Vasili, and said that formerly the venerable pastors of the church had restrained the sovereigns from indulging their passions and committing injustice, whereas now Moscow no longer had a metropolitan, for Daniel only bore the name and the mask of a pastor, without thinking that he ought to be the guide of consciences and the protector of the innocent; he also said that Maxine would never be allowed to leave Russia, because the grand prince and the metropolitan feared his indiscretions in other countries, where he might publish the tale of their faults and weaknesses. At last Maxine's enemies so irritated the grand prince against him, that he ordered him to be brought to judgment and Maxine was condemned to be confined in one of the monasteries of Iver, having been found guilty of falsely interpreting the Holy Scriptures and the dogmas of the church. According to the opinion of some contemporaries the charge was a calumny invented by Jonas, archimandrite of the Tchudov monastery, Vassian, bishop of Kolomna, and the metropolitan.*f*

### PRIVATE LIFE OF VASILI IVANOVITCH ; HIS DEATH

There is one event in the private life of Vasili Ivanovitch which has great importance on the subsequent course of history, and throws a clearer light on the relations of men and parties at this epoch. This event is his divorce and second marriage. Vasili Ivanovitch had first contracted a marriage in the year of his father's death with Solomonia Sabourov; but they had no children and Solomonia vainly resorted to sorcery in order to have children and keep the love of her husband. The grand prince no longer loved her and decided to divorce her. He consulted his boyars, laying stress on the fact that he had no heir and that his brothers did not understand how to govern their own appanages; it is said that the boyars replied "The unfruitful fig-tree is cut down and cast out of the vineyard." The sovereign then turned with the same question to the spiritual powers: the metropolitan Daniel gave his entire consent, but the monk Vassian, known in the world as Prince Vasili Patrikeiev, who, together with his father, had been forced to become a monk during the reign of Ivan because he belonged to the party of Helen, but who was now greatly esteemed by Vasili, was against the divorce and was therefore banished from the monastery of Simon to that of Joseph. Maxine the Greek and Prince Simon Kurbski were also against the divorce, and suffered for their opinion; and the boyar Beklemishev, who was on friendly terms with Maxine, was executed. Solomonia was made to take the veil at the convent of Suzdal and Vasili married Helen Vasilievna Glinski, the niece of Michael Glinski who had been liberated from prison (1526). From this marriage Vasili had two sons; Ivan (born 1530) and Iuri (born 1533). Vasili's love for his second wife was so great that according to Herberstein he had his beard cut off to please her. Towards the end of 1533 Vasili fell ill and died on December 3rd, leaving as his heir his infant son Ivan.*b*

### A FORECAST OF THE REIGN OF IVAN (IV) THE TERRIBLE

The rôle and the character of Ivan IV have been and still are very differently appreciated by Russian historians. Karamzin, who has never submitted his accounts and his documents to a sufficiently severe critic, sees in him a prince who, naturally vicious and cruel, gave, under restriction to two virtuous ministers, a few years of tranquillity to Russia; and who subsequently, abandoning himself to the fury of his passions, appalled Europe as well as the empire with what the historian designates "seven epochs of massacres." Kostomarov re-echoes the opinions of Karamzin.

Another school, represented by Soloviev and Zabielin, has manifested a greater defiance towards the prejudiced statements of Kurbski, chief of the oligarchical party; towards Guagnini, a courtier of the king of Poland; towards Tanbe and Kruse, traitors to the sovereign who had taken them into his service. Above all, they have taken into account the times and the society in whose midst Ivan the Terrible lived. They concern themselves less with his morals as an individual than with his rôle as instrument of the historical development of Russia. Did not the French historians during long years misinterpret the enormous services rendered by Louis XI in the great work of the unification of France and of the creation of the modern

[1533 A.D.]

state? His justification was at length achieved after a more minute examination into documents and circumstances.

At the time when Ivan succeeded his father the struggle of the central power against the forces of the past had changed character. The old Russian states, which had held so long in check the new power of Moscow; the principalities of Tver, Riazan, Suzdal, Novgorod-Seversk; the republics of Novgorod, Pskov, Viatka had lost their independence. Their possessions had served to aggrandise those of Moscow. All northern and eastern Russia was thus united under the sceptre of the grand prince. To the ceaseless struggles constantly breaking out against Tver, Riazan, Novgorod, was to succeed the great foreign strife — the holy war against Lithuania, the Tatars, the Swedes.

Precisely because the work of the unification of Great Russia was accomplished, the resistance in the interior against the prince's authority was to become more active. The descendants of reigning families dispossessed by force of bribery or arms, the servitors of those old royal houses, had entered the service of the masters of Moscow. His court was composed of crownless princes — the Chouiski, the Kurbski, the Vorotinski; descendants of ancient appanaged princes, proud of the blood of Rurik which coursed through their veins. Others were descended from the Lithuanian Gedimine, or from the baptised Tatar *Monzas*.

All these princes, as well as the powerful boyars of Tver, Riazan, Novgorod, were become the boyars of the grand prince. There was for all only one court at which they could serve — that of Moscow. When Russia had been divided into sovereign states, the discontented boyars had been at liberty to change masters — to pass from the service of Tchernigov into that of Kiev, from that of Suzdal into that of Novgorod. Now, whither could they go? Outside of Moscow, there were only foreign rulers, enemies of Russia. To make use of the ancient right to change masters was to go over to the enemy — it was treason. "To change" and "to betray" were become synonymous: the Russian word *izmiyanit* (third person singular of "to change") was become the word *izmiyanik* ("traitor").

The Russian boyar could take refuge neither with the Germans, the Swedes, nor the Tatars; he could go only to the sovereign of Lithuania — but this was the worst possible species of change, the most pernicious form of treason. The prince of Moscow knew well that the war with Lithuania — that state which Polish in the west, by its Russian provinces, in the east exercised a dangerous attraction over subjects of Moscow — was a struggle for existence. Lithuania was not only a foreign enemy — it was a domestic enemy, with intercourse and sympathies in the very heart of the Russian state, even in the palace of the czar; her formidable hand was felt in all intrigues, in all conspiracies. The foreign war against Lithuania, the domestic war against the Russian oligarchy are but two different phases of the same war — the heaviest and most perilous of all those undertaken by the grand prince of Moscow. The dispossessed princes, the boyars of the old independent states had given up the struggle against him on the field of battle; they continued to struggle against him in his own court.

It was no longer war between state and state; it was intestine strife — that of the oligarchy against autocratic power. Resigned to the loss of their sovereignty, the new prince-boyars of Moscow were not yet resigned to their position as mere subjects. The struggle was thus limited to a narrower field, and was therefore the more desperate. The court at Moscow was a tilt-yard, whence none could emerge without a change of masters — the Lithuanian for the Muscovite — without treason: hence the furious nature of the war of two principles under Ivan IV.*e*

### THE MINORITY OF IVAN IV

On the death of his father, Ivan was only three years of age. Helena, his mother, a woman unfit for the toils of government, impure in her conduct, and without judgment, assumed the office of regent, which she shared with a paramour, whose elevation to such a height caused universal disgust, particularly among the princes of the blood and the nobility. The measures which had of late years been adopted towards the boyars were not forgotten by that haughty class; and now that the infirm state of the throne gave them a fair pretext for complaint, they conspired against the regent, partly with a view to remove so unpopular and degraded a person from the imperial seat, but principally that they might take advantage of the minority of the czar, and seize upon the empire for their own ends. The circumstances in which the death of Vasili left the country were favourable to these designs. The licentiousness that prevailed at court, the absence of a strict and responsible head, and the confusion that generally took the place of the order that had previously prevailed, assisted the treacherous nobles in their treasonable projects. They had long panted for revenge and restitution, and the time seemed to be ripe for the execution of their plans.

IVAN THE TERRIBLE
(1530–1584)

Amongst the most prominent members of this patrician league, were the three paternal uncles of the young prince. They made no scruple of exhibiting their feelings; and they at last grew so clamourous, that the regent, on the ground that they entertained designs upon the throne, condemned them to loathsome dungeons, where they died in lingering torments. Their followers and abettors suffered by torture and the worst kinds of ignominious punishment. These examples spread such consternation amongst the rest of the conspirators, that they fled to Lithuania and the Crimea, where they endeavoured to inspire a sympathy in their misfortunes. But the regent, whose time appears to have been solely dedicated to the worst description of pleasures, being unable to preserve herself without despotism, succeeded in overcoming the enemies whom her own conduct was so mainly instrumental in creating.

The reign of lascivious folly and wanton rigour was not, however, destined to survive the wrath of the nobles. For five years, intestine jealousies and thickening plots plunged the country into anarchy; and, at last, the regent died suddenly, having, it is believed, fallen by poison administered through the agency of the revengeful boyars. The spectacle of one criminal executing summary justice upon another, is not destitute of some moral utility; and in this case it might have had its beneficial influence, were it not that the

[1533 A.D.]

principal conspirators had no sooner taken off the regent than they violently seized upon the guardianship of the throne.

The foremost persons in this drama were the Shuiski — a family that had long been treated with suspicion by the czars, their insolent bearing having always exposed them to distrust.    Prince Shuiski was appointed president of the council of the boyars, to whom the administration of affairs was confided, and although his malignant purposes were kept in check by the crowd of equally ambitious persons that surrounded him, he possessed sufficient opportunities to consummate a variety of wrongs upon the resources of the state and upon obnoxious individuals — thus revenging himself indiscriminately for the ancient injuries his race had suffered.    During this iniquitous rule, which exhibited the extraordinary features of a government composed of persons with different interests, pressing forward to the same end, and making a common prey of the trust that was reposed in their hands, Russia was despoiled in every quarter.    The Tatars, freed for a season from the watchful vigilance of the throne, roamed at large through the provinces, pillaging and slaying wherever they went; and this enormous guilt was crowned by the rapacious exactions and sanguinary proscriptions of the council.    The young Ivan was subjected to the most brutal insults: his education was designedly neglected; he was kept in total ignorance of public affairs, that he might be rendered unqualified to assume the hereditary power; and Prince Shuiski, in the midst of these base intrigues against the future czar, was often seen to treat him in a contemptuous and degrading manner. On one occasion he stretched forth his legs, and pressed the weight of his feet on the body of the boy.    Perhaps these unexampled provocations, and the privations to which he was condemned, produced the germs of a character which was afterwards developed in such terrible magnificence. The fiend that lived in the heart of Ivan might not have been born with him; it was probably generated by the cruelties and wrongs that were practised on his youth.

In vain the Belski, moderate and wise, and the primate, influenced by the purest motives, remonstrated against the ruinous proceedings of the council.    The voice of admonition was lost in the hideous orgies of the boyars, until a sudden invasion by the Tatars awakened them to a sense of their peril.    They rallied, order was restored, and Russia was preserved. But the danger was no sooner over than the Shuiski returned in all their former strength, seized upon Moscow in the dead of the night, penetrated to the couch of Ivan, and, dragging him out of his sleep, endeavoured to destroy his intellect by filling him with sudden terror.    The primate, whose mild representations had displeased them, was ill-treated and deposed: and the prince Belski, who could not be prevailed upon to link his fortunes with their desperate courses, was murdered in the height of their frenzy.    Even those members of their own body who, touched by some intermittent pity, ventured to expostulate, were beaten in the chamber of their deliberations, and cast out from amongst them.

Under such unpropitious auspices as these, the young Ivan, the inheritor of a consolidated empire, grew up to manhood.    His disposition, naturally fierce, headstrong, and vindictive, was most insidiously cultivated into ferocity by the artful counsellors that surrounded him.    His earliest amusements were the torture of wild animals, the ignoble feat of riding over old men and women, flinging stones from ambuscades upon the passers-by, and precipitating dogs and cats from the summit of his palace.    Such entertainments as these, the sport of boyhood, gave unfortunately too correct a prognostic of the fatal career that lay before him. By a curious retribution, the first exercise of this terrible temper in its application to humanity fell upon the Shuiski, who certainly, of all mankind, best merited its infliction. When Ivan was in his thirteenth year, he accompanied a hunting party at which Prince Gluiski — another factious lord — and the president of the council were present. Gluiski, himself a violent and remorseless man, envied the ascendency of Shuiski, and prompted the young prince to address him in words of great heat and insult. Shuiski, astonished at the youth's boldness, replied in anger. This was sufficient provocation. Ivan gave way to his rage, and, on a concerted signal, Shuiski was dragged out into the public streets, and worried alive by dogs in the open daylight. The wretch expiated a life of guilt by the most horrible agonies.

Thus freed from one tyranny, Ivan was destined for another, which, however, accepted him as its nominal head, urging him onward to acts of blood which were but too congenial to his taste. The Gluiski having got rid of their formidable competitor in the race of crime, now assumed the direction of affairs. Under their administration, the prince was led to the commission of the most extravagant atrocities; and the doctrine was inculcated upon his mind, that the only way to assert authority was by manifesting the extremity of its wrath. He was taught to believe that power consisted in oppression. They applauded each fresh instance of vengeance; and initiated him into a short method of relieving himself from every person who troubled or offended him, by sacrificing the victim on the spot.

## IVAN ASSUMES THE REINS OF GOVERNMENT

This terrible system continued for three years. The pupilage of the prince was an uninterrupted scene of horror; and he was crowned czar of all the Russias in his eighteenth year, after a minority of blood. The citizens, unsafe and trembling under a despotism which was so capricious in its enormities, were at length driven to desperation. They fired the city in several places one night, and Ivan awoke the next morning amidst flame and smoke, the tossing of brands, and the imprecations of the multitude. He had been accustomed to terrors, but this conflagration smote him to the heart. In the midst of the confusion, Sylvester, a monk belonging to that roving order of persons who then wandered through the country affecting to be inspired with a divine mission, suddenly appeared in the presence of the affrighted despot. With a Gospel in one hand, while the other was raised in an attitude of prophecy, he pointed to the ruins that surrounded him, and invoking the attention of the prince to the consequences of his infatuation, he dwelt upon certain appearances from heaven which prognosticated evil to the dynasty if these courses were not abandoned; and, working powerfully upon a mind already agonised with fear, he finally succeeded in gaining a complete ascendency over the czar. The effect was sudden and extraordinary. The virtuous Alexis Adaschev aided Sylvester in his efforts to reclaim Ivan; and these, assisted by the gentle persuasions of the beautiful Anastasia, Ivan's young consort whom he had but recently married, appeared to produce a strong impression upon his feelings.

The result was an entire change in the system of government. Able and upright men displaced the corrupt and audacious counsellors who had hitherto filled the empire with alarm; a new organisation of the army took place; a just assessment of the fiefs, the various services, and contingents, was established; proprietors of estates were obliged to contribute to the

[1533 A.D.]

maintenance of the military strength according to their means; and by a bonus in the pay of the soldiery, which was now adopted, the available force of the country was raised to the number of three hundred thousand men. Thus strengthened, with prudent ministers and a powerful army, Ivan set himself to the worthy task of subduing the rebellious Tatars. His ardour even appears to have carried him into extremes, for in the depth of winter he marched at the head of the soldiery to the siege of Kazan, although his followers did not hesitate to declare that no good commander would think of conducting his troops in so rigorous a season into the quarters of the enemy. But such ebullitions of discontent were punished with so much severity, that the troops soon learned to be content with the severities which procured such victories as Ivan was fortunate enough to gain. The first measure of great utility which he accomplished, was the erection of forts on the frontier to repel the aggressions of the enemy; but apprehending that even these were not sufficient to deter the marauders, he advanced upon Kazan, and captured it by springing a mine — a process in the art of war which was quite novel to the Russians, and filled them with astonishment and admiration. Having taken the city, he turned the mosques of the Tatars into Christian temples, and caused the khan to be baptised; which proofs of his religious zeal were admirably calculated to ingratiate him in the regards of the people.

In one of those ecstatic moods which sometimes assail the better judgment of the old chroniclers, the Russian historian informs us that Ivan, upon entering Kazan, wept at the sight of the dead bodies with which the streets were strewn. We certainly cannot put in any evidence in disproof of this apocryphal assertion, but the picture of Nero fiddling while Rome was burning is even more probable.

In addition to his successes at Kazan, Ivan was triumphant in the kingdom of Astrakhan, which he afterwards annexed to the Russian empire. This acquisition was very valuable, as in that district the vine, and other rich productions of the soil, grew in remarkable luxuriance. Fortune seemed on all hands to favour the interval of grace that visited the czar. While he was pursuing his course of victory in other places, eighty thousand Turks, who had been despatched by Selim II against Astrakhan, perished in the desolate steppes by which it was surrounded. The wars were thus terminated in glorious and important achievements, which laid the foundations of that expanded commerce which afterwards rendered illustrious the era of one of the greatest monarchs the world ever produced.

## THE DISCOVERY OF SIBERIA

But the most important event which distinguished this period of the reign of Ivan was the discovery of Siberia, an empire of extraordinary magnitude, producing the richest furs, and studded with inexhaustible mines of salt, copper and silver. The discovery was accidental, and caused at first so slight a degree of attention, that it was suffered to be forgotten until another accident, some years afterwards, recalled it to the consideration of the government. A body of men, who had been sent across the mountains of Ingermanland by the czar, penetrated as far as the banks of the Oley; but the discoveries they reported were either so imperfect, or so ill-described, that they were passed over in silence. It subsequently occurred, however, that a merchant of the name of Strogonov, who was the proprietor of some salt mines on the confines of Siberia, had his curiosity stimulated by several persons who traded with him, and whose strange costume and foreign manners excited in him a desire to become acquainted with the interior of the country from whence they came. Accordingly he commissioned a few of his people to return with them into Siberia, and to collect such information respecting it as their opportunities might enable them to acquire. These people, having explored the unknown districts, which they found to be inhabited by a race of Tatars, who possessed a capital called Sibir, returned to their employer charged with a history of wonders, and a quantity of costly furs, which promised to open a new source of gain to the diligent merchant. Strogonov, however, resolved not to keep the knowledge he had thus attained exclusively to himself, and immediately communicated all he knew to the court. In the mean time, Iermak, a Don Cossack adventurer, who, at the head of a gang of those lawless robbers, infested the roads, plundering the inhabitants and travellers in that part of Russia, happened to come, accidentally, to the merchant's dwelling, on his flight from some Russian troops that had been sent in search of him. While he remained there, he learned by chance, from Strogonov, of the newly discovered land; and he and his band, being persons who had nothing to lose, and who subsisted solely by desperate predatory practices, resolved to enter the strange country, and seek in its unknown retreats a source of safety and support. The resistance this adventurer experienced from the Siberians greatly thinned the ranks of his daring troops, but the forlorn character of the expedition inspired them with reckless valour; and, after many exhausting conflicts, they finally over-ran the country, and made themselves master of the capital. Iermak now bethought him of what he should do with his perilous conquest; and seeing that he possessed no means of accumulating sovereign power, or even of possessing by tribute, or otherwise, so vast a territory, he threw himself at the feet of the czar, tendered to him the territory he had won, and solicited in return a full pardon for all the delinquencies he and his followers had committed. Ivan readily granted the pardon, and took possession of his new acquisition. The work of annexation went rapidly forward. Several commodious towns were built, strong forts were constructed, the mines were garrisoned, and that great expanse of desert and mountains, which was afterwards destined to become the convict settlement of Russia, was formally and permanently consolidated in the dominions of the autocrat.

### THE RESTRAINING INFLUENCE OF ANASTASIA

The civil and social improvement of the empire kept pace with the armed progress. A number of celebrated artists were engaged from the dominions, and by the permission, of Charles V; the art of letterpress printing was introduced, and the first type that ever was seen in Russia was imported by Ivan; the northern parts were opened to a new mercantile intercourse; and Archangel was established. The laws were revised; and the fees of the governors of the provinces who administered justice, paying themselves by pecuniary mulcts on the suitors, were abolished, and in their place gratuitous justice was administered, and a general assessment levied, which was collected by officers appointed by government. The grasping demands of the clergy were restrained, their revenues placed upon a more equitable basis, and their morals improved by mild but decisive restrictions.

Such were the fruits of the influence of Anastasia, which procured a hearing for the wisdom of Alexis and Sylvester. While that amiable and enlightened lady lived, Ivan pursued a course of just and wise measures that reflected honour upon his name, and conferred extensive benefits upon his country. But the latent nature was not extinguished: it only slept, hushed into slumber by the sweet influences before which his savage dispositions were subdued. An old bishop, who had formerly been banished from the court on account of his crimes, and who was one day consulted by Ivan, replied to the czar in some memorable words which were ever afterwards cherished in his memory, and were not without their power over his subsequent life. "If you wish," exclaimed the bishop, "to be truly a sovereign, never seek a counsellor wiser than yourself; never receive advice from any man. Command, but never obey; and you will be a terror to the boyars. Remember that he who is permitted to begin advising, is certain to end by ruling, his sovereign. Ivan, kissing the old man's hand, is said to have answered, "My own father could not have spoken more wisely!" This remarkable advice — similar to that which is attributed to a celebrated cardinal of modern times, on his death-bed — seems to have governed the conduct of Ivan from the moment that the death of the princess Anastasia released him from the embarrassment of her counsels. She died in 1560.

## IVAN'S ATROCITIES

The incarnate fiend, relieved from the oppressive presence of virtue, resumed at once his original nature. If the narrative of his crimes could be spared from the page of history, it would rescue us from a series of details, the very relation of which must sicken the least susceptible mind. But there was a passion so unearthly in this paragon of monsters — he was so elevated in atrocity, and reached so sublime a height in the perpetration of cruelties — that his life, incredible and disgusting as it is, fills too great a space in the annals of despotism to be passed over lightly. One of his historians charitably supposes him to have been a lunatic.

The first act of Ivan was to banish his prudent advisers, the men who had hitherto preserved him from the worst calamities. Those persons were replaced by others, who studiously laboured to destroy their predecessors by false stories of their treachery to the czarina, whose death was unequivocally laid to their charge. That weakness, or superstition, which is an inherent quality in all savage natures, led Ivan to believe, or to fancy, that he believed those absurd accusations; and he acted with promptitude upon the miserable excuse which they afforded him. He hunted the partisans of the late ministers wherever they could be detected; some he put to the most disgraceful deaths, others he imprisoned or banished, varying the monotony of their solitary lives by the infliction of exquisite tortures. One prince, who refused to join in the lascivious pleasures of the court, was poinarded at prayers in the church; and another was stabbed to the heart by the czar's own hand, because he had the presumption to remonstrate with one of the new favourites. The prince Andrew Kurbski, a noble who, both in the cabinet and the field, had rendered the most important services to the government and the country, received intimation that a similar fate awaited him; and, indignant at the prospect of such an unworthy return for his devotion to the throne of the czars, he retired into Lithuania, and united himself with Sigismund, the king of Poland, and, at that time, one of the most formidable enemies of Russia. This revolt maddened Ivan beyond control; and his exasperation was increased by the receipt of a letter from the prince, in which he boldly charged the czar with all the miseries that were entailed upon their common country, with having shed the blood of Israel's elders in the temples of the Lord; and wound up by threatening him with the vengeance of that tribunal before which he must one day answer to the accusations of the spirits of the murdered.   The messenger who was daring enough to present this epistle to the czar suffered for his temerity.   Ivan, on learning from whnece he came, struck him across the legs with an iron rod which he usually carried in his hand; and while the blood flowed copiously from the wounds, leaned unconcernedly upon his rod to read the rebellious letter.   The correspondence that ensued upon this occasion, like all the correspondence of Ivan's which has come down to us, is remarkable for the most blasphemous presumption and arrogant hyperbole. He wrote all his letters with his own hand, and was proud of his literary attainments, which, had they been directed into worthier channels, might have rendered him a distinguished ornament of his age.

### THE POLISH INVASION

The consequence of the disaffection of Kurbski was the enrolment of a Polish army with a view to a descent upon Russia, and an invasion of the southern provinces by the Tatars at the instigation of Sigismund.   This demonstration increased the rage of the czar: he treated everybody around him as if they were the creatures of Kurbski: he distrusted everybody; and put numbers to the rack and to death on the bare suspicion of their guilt, and was overheard to lament that he could not find victims enough to satisfy his wrath.   He charged the boyars indiscriminately with harbouring secret designs against the welfare and happiness of the state; he dispossessed many of them of their private fortunes; and in a letter which is still extant, he urged against them as crimes, all the benefits which the sane portion of his rule had conferred upon Russia.   In this delirium of the fever of despotism, the clergy remonstrated with some firmness; and, in order to obtain a fresh excuse for making new victims, he adopted an expedient as unexpected as it was singular. He caused a report to be spread on a sudden, that he was about to leave Moscow; but the point of his destination, or the reason of his withdrawal were preserved as profound secrets.   The mystery of this announcement created a panic at Moscow.   The people knew not what was to come next, whether the tyrant was about to put some scheme of universal destruction into execution, or whether it was merely a prelude to some extravagant exhibition of superstitious credulity, which always assumed in their eyes the aspect of religious devotion.   Agreeably to this vague announcement of the czar's design, one morning in December, at an early hour, the great square of the Kremlin was filled with travelling sledges, some of which contained gold and silver, others clothes, and not a few crosses, images, and the relics of saints. These preparations attracted crowds of astonished gazers, who looked on in stupid wonder at the extraordinary sight.   In a few minutes the czar, followed by his family, was seen to descend from the palace, with the officers of his household, and a numerous retinue.   From the palace he passed on to the church of the Assumption; and, having ordered the metropolitan to celebrate mass, he prayed with great devotion, and received the blessing of Athanasius. Returning from the church, he held out his hand to the assembled multitudes, that they might satisfy themselves with a farewell kiss; and then, having in silence, and with unusual solemnity, walked through the groups that beset his path, he mounted his sledge, and drove off accompanied by a regiment of horse. The inhabitants of Moscow, astonished and terror-struck by the scene, were lost in conjecture.   The city was without a government.   Ivan had so dexterously contrived to impress them with an idea that he derived his sovereignty

[1560 A.D.]

from God, that he found no great difficulty ultimately in confounding to the imagination of an enslaved and uninstructed people the distinction between God and the sovereign; and in every crisis of disaster that occurred, the people fell back upon their fanaticism, and looked to the czar for that succour which could alone come from heaven. Deserted at this moment by Ivan, they began to believe that they were deserted by Omnipotence.

A month elapsed, and no tidings were received of the destination or proceedings of the czar. At length, at the end of that period, two letters were received from him; the one addressed to the metropolitan, the other to the people. The former epistle contained a recapitulation of the disorders that had prevailed during his minority, all of which he attributed to the clergy and the boyars; and he asserted that similar crimes against the majesty of the state were about to break out anew. He also complained that his attempts to secure the public tranquillity were constantly thwarted by the evil interference of Athanasius and the clergy; that, therefore, he had abandoned the helm of affairs, and had left Moscow to wander about the earth. In his letter to the people, he assured them of his good will, repeated that he had no cause of complaint against them, and concluded by bidding them farewell for ever. It appeared by his epistles that he had intrenched himself in Alexandrovski, a distant fortress that lay in the depths of a gloomy forest.

These communications spread dismay amongst the Muscovites. Ivan's severity towards the nobility and clergy had, even against the grain of reason, procured him no inconsiderable popularity with the bulk of the people; and on this occasion it broke forth in lamentations, which derived much of their force from the association of the ideas of the throne of the czar and the throne of heaven. Groups of disconsolate citizens assembled in the street to confer upon what was to be done; the shops were shut, the tribunals of justice and public offices were closed, and every kind of business was suspended. "The czar," they exclaimed, "has forsaken us, and we are lost. Who will now defend us against the enemy? what are sheep without the shepherd?" In this state of despair a deputation of the principal inhabitants waited upon the metropolitan, and besought of him to solicit Ivan to return to his faithful subjects. Frantic with desperate zeal, they cried, "Let him punish all those who deserve it; has he not the power of life and death? The state cannot remain without a head, and we will not acknowledge any other than the one God has given us." It was at last resolved that a numerous body of prelates and nobles should hasten to Alexandrovski, prostrate themselves in the dust before Ivan, and entreat of him to return to Moscow. This proceeding had the desired effect. They discovered Ivan in his retreat, struck the ground before him with their heads, and supplicated him for the sake of the souls of millions, which were now perishing in his absence as the head of the orthodox church, to resume his holy functions. This was what Ivan wanted: he affected to be much moved by their prayers, and with a show of reluctance consented to return, provided the clergy pledged themselves not to interfere whenever he found it necessary to punish those who engaged in conspiracies against the state, or against him or his family. This artful condition was immediately granted; and the magnanimity of a tyrant who thus entrapped the people into an admission of the necessity of his despotic proceedings, was extolled to the skies.

The restoration of the despot was received with acclamations; but the Muscovites were astonished by the great alteration which had taken place in his personal appearance during his absence. Only a month, say their historians, had elapsed, yet they hardly knew him again. His powerful and muscular body, his expanded chest, and robust limbs, had shrunk to a skeleton; his head, once covered with luxuriant locks, was now bald; his rich and flowing beard was reduced to a few ragged stumps; his eyes were dull; and his features, stamped with a ravenous ferocity, were now deformed by apparent thought and anguish. Yet these sad changes, — the fearful effects of the incessant tortures of a mind bewildered by its own fury — excited the sympathies of the infatuated citizens who beheld them.

After his entry into Moscow he addressed the people, again expatiating on the crimes of the boyars and the necessity for exercising the dominant sovereign sway in its extreme development. To this succeeded a pious exhortation on the vanities of the world — one of the arguments by which he endeavoured to reconcile his victims to their miserable fate — which he concluded by a proposal to institute a new body-guard, to be composed of one thousand men of noble birth, chosen from the general body of the army, and to be called the Opritshnina, or select legion. The people, blind to the danger of conceding so great a power to the sovereign, willingly acceded to this proposal, the execution of which was but a new instrument for destroying their liberties. The select legion, better known in subsequent years by the name of the Strelitz, was the foundation of a regular standing army in Russia; for until the formation of that corps the military force of the empire was raised upon occasions, each nobleman contributing according to his ability to meet the exigencies of the demand.[1]

### THE REIGN OF TERROR

This was the first step to the new reign of terror; and while the select legion was in course of formation, Ivan employed himself in the erection of a new palace outside the walls of the Kremlin; for it appears that his ambition or his fears produced in him a dislike for the ancient residence of the royal family. In order to build this unnecessary palace, he drove out all the inhabitants of the adjacent streets, and posted his satellites around the neighbourhood to keep it free from intrusion. Twelve thousand of the richest inhabitants were dispossessed of their estates to make room for his designs, and upon the creatures of his disgraceful bounty he bestowed the spoils of his plunder. The new palace was to all intents an impregnable fortress; yet such were the secret horrors engendered by his course of villanies, that Ivan, thinking that it was not sufficiently secure, retired again to Alexandrovski, which expanded from an humble village into a considerable town. It contained a celebrated church of our Lady, which was painted on the outside with the most gaudy colors, every brick containing the representation of a cross. Here the czar possessed a large palace surrounded by a ditch and ramparts: his civil and military functionaries had separate houses; and the legionaries and trades-people had distinct streets. One of the rules imposed by the tyrant was that no person should enter or leave the town without his express permission, and a patrol constantly occupied the neighbourhood to observe that this order was fulfilled. A new notion now possessed him. Buried in the forlorn solitudes of the deep forests, he converted his palace into a monastery, assumed the style and title of abbot, turned his favourites into monks, and called his body of select and depraved legionaries by the name of the Brothers. He provided them all with black vestments, under

[1 The Opritshnina, composed at first, or supposed to be composed, of men of noble birth, was really filled by persons of the lowest class, who acted as spies, informers and assassins.

which they wore splendid habits, embroidered with gold and fur; and he instituted a code of practice as austere as it was inconsistent. At three o'clock in the morning, the matin service began, which lasted until seven; at eight mass commenced again, and at ten the whole body, except Ivan, who stood reading aloud from some religious book, sat down to a sumptuous repast. The remnants of the table were afterwards distributed amongst the poor — for throughout the whole of Ivan's actions there was always an evident desire to win the favour of the multitude; the czar dined after the rest, and then descended to the dungeons to witness the infliction of tortures upon some of his victims, which gave him extraordinary delight. At eight o'clock vespers were read; and at ten Ivan retired to his chamber, where he was lulled to sleep by three blind men. To diversify this monotonous life, he sometimes visited the monasteries, or hunted wild beasts in the woods; but he was constantly employed in issuing his instructions upon public business, and even during prayers often gave his most cruel and sanguinary orders. Such was the life of the tyrant in his gloomy seclusion at Alexandrovski.

During this period, the select legion increased in number to six thuousand men, embracing in their body all the abandoned and infamous wretches who could be procured for hire. As types of their office, they were ordered to suspend from the saddle-bow a dog's head and a broom — the former to signify that they worried the enemies of the czar, and the latter to indicate that they swept them off the face of the earth. They went from street to street armed with long daggers and hatchets in search of victims, who amounted daily to a score. They soon became the objects of fear and execration. The first victims were the prince Shuiski and his son. At the place of execution, the younger offered himself first to the axe; but the feelings of nature were so strong in the heart of the parent, that he could not endure to witness the death of his son, and he insisted on receiving his death first. When his head rolled off, his son embraced it in a passion of tears; and while the lips of the living yet clung to the quivering and agonised features of the dead, the executioner's axe descended upon the son's neck. On the same day four other princes were beheaded, and a fifth impaled. Several boyars were exiled, others forced to embrace the monastic vows, and a still greater number were beggared by confiscation. These horrors increased every day. The streets and squares were filled with dead bodies; and such was the universal terror, that the survivors did not dare to appear to give the rites of burial to the dead. It would appear that the murder of individuals ceased at length to satisfy the insatiate appetite of the monster: he longed for massacre on a more extended scale; his eyes grew tired of the slow process of execution in detail. Accordingly he sought for excuses to lay whole towns in blood. A few of the inhabitants of Tortchesk happening one day to quarrel with some of the legionaries, Ivan declared them all to be rebels, and instantly caused them *en masse* to be either tortured to death or drowned. The inhabitants of Kolomna were similarly disposed of, merely because they were the dependents of a nobleman who had outgrown his favour. He spared neither sex nor age. Many ladies were exposed in the streets, and then shot in the public sight.

#### THE MARCH AGAINST NOVGOROD

These atrocities, unparalleled in the annals of the world, form but the prelude to the enormous crimes of this infamous prince. His march of devastation to Novgorod may be considered as the grand act of his career of blood. The provocation which led to the sanguinary punishment of that city was a falsehood invented by a profligate fellow who wanted to escape justice, and to take revenge upon the authorities, who had found him guilty of the commission of some offences. This criminal, knowing that Ivan rewarded all those who came before him with charges of disaffection, wrote a letter in the name of the archbishop and inhabitants of Novgorod to the king of Poland, offering to put the city under that monarch's protection. This letter he carefully concealed behind an image of the Virgin in the church of St. Sophia, and then laid before the czar at Moscow a private revelation of the conspiracy which he had himself invented. Ivan despatched a trusty messenger to Novgorod, who discovered the letter in the spot to which the informer had referred, and, upon this evidence, the city was denounced to the vengeance of the select legion. But as it was likely that the sight of this dreadful deed would be more exciting than any he had hitherto witnessed, Ivan put himself at the head of his guards, and in December 1569, accompanied by his son, departed from Alexandrovski on his mission of destruction.

On his way he passed through the town of Klin, and exterminated the whole of the population. When he arrived at the city of Tver, he took up his quarters at a monastery outside the gates, and sent his soldiers into the city to massacre and plunder the inhabitants at will. The horrors of the scene reminded the unfortunate people of the terrible cruelties inflicted upon their ancestors by the khan Usbak in 1327. At some of the feats of death, Ivan himself assisted: and his confidential minister Skuratov secretly entered the cell of a monastery where the virtuous and deposed metropolitan was confined, and strangled him.

Proceeding onwards from Tver, Ivan depopulated all the towns on his route to the banks of the Ilmen: and on the 2d of January his advanced guard entered the devoted and miserable city of Novgorod. The preparations made upon this occasion to ensure the complete carnage meditated by the tyrant, are memorable proofs of the coolness with which the demons of the Opritshnina executed the will of their savage leader. They ordered the churches and convents to be closed, and demanded a temporary levy from the monks of twenty roubles per head; and such unfortunate ecclesiastics as were unable to comply with this exorbitant exaction were deliberately flogged from morning till night. The houses of the inhabitants were placed under seizure, and guarded at the entrances, and the owners thrown into chains. This was merely preliminary to the arrival of the monarch.

In four days afterwards Ivan and the remainder arrived, and rested within two versts of the city. On the following morning all the monks who had failed to pay the redemption tax were taken out, beaten to death with clubs, and their bodies sent to their respective monasteries for interment. On the next day, accompanied as before by his son, Ivan made his solemn entrance at the head of his troops into the city. The archbishop, with the clergy, carrying the miraculous images, met him on the bridge, and attempted to utter the accustomed benediction: but Ivan, interrupting the ceremony, addressed them in a long harrangue, which consisted of an elaborate curse against their order. Having satisfied his rage by the delivery of this anathema, he ordered the crucifix and images to be borne into the church of St. Sophia, where he heard mass, praying with great fervour, and then retired to the episcopal palace, where he sat down to dinner surrounded by his boyars. Suddenly, in the midst of the feast, he started up and raised a terrible cry. The signal was scarcely given when his satellites, as if by magic, appeared in a body before him, and seized the archbishop, and the officers and servants.   The palace and the cloisters were then given up to plunder.   The czar's confessor, assisted in the sacrilege by the master of the ceremonies, burst into the cathedral and carried off its sacred treasures, the rich vestments, the images, and the bells. The churches and monasteries were all pillaged, and not a fragment of the precious accumulations of the temples and religious houses escaped the impious hands of the spoliators.

Next came the massacre of the inhabitants, which was conducted with the utmost patience and regularity.   Every day from five hundred to one thousand Novgorodians were brought before Ivan and his son, and immediately put to death either by torture or fire.   Some were tied to sledges and dragged into the Volkhov; others flung over the bridge into the river — wives with their husbands, mothers with their tender infants; while soldiers armed with long sharp spears sailed on the water to pierce and hew those who attempted to escape by swimming.   When the massacre had continued in this way for five weeks, Ivan drew off and visited the neighbouring monasteries, which he pillaged indiscriminately, levelling houses, destroying cattle, and burning the corn.   He then returned to Novgorod, and inspected in person the remaining work of destruction.   He passed through the streets while his myrmidons plundered the shops and houses, which were entered by the doors or windows indifferently: rich silks and furs were divided by the brutal soldiery, and all unavailable goods, such as hemp and wax and tallow, were either burnt or cast into the river.   Detachments were then sent into the adjacent domains to plunder and murder without any respect of persons.

Having exhausted all his arts of ruin, Ivan now relaxed, and issued a general pardon to the few wretched persons who survived, and to whom death would have been an act of mercy.   He summoned them to appear before him; and a ghastly assemblage of skeletons, motionless and in despair, stood in the presence of the murderer like ghosts invoked from the grave.   Untouched by the appalling sight, he addressed them in the mildest language, desired to have their prayers that he might have a long and happy reign, and took his leave of them in the most gracious words.   The miserable inhabitants were smote with delirium; they looked around them in vain for the friends that had been sacrificed, for the houses and the wealth that had been laid waste.   Sixty thousand victims were stretched dead in the streets of the once proud and opulent republic: and to complete its melancholy doom, pestilence and a famine succeeded, sweeping off nearly all those who had survived the extermination of the less merciful czar.   The city was now entirely depopulated, and presented the sepulchral aspect of a vast cemetery.

The monster passed on to the city of Pskov, where, however, he consented to forego his terrible schemes of destruction, satisfying himself with plundering the principal inhabitants.   He then returned home to Moscow, loaded with plunder, and carrying in his train the archbishop of Novgorod, and other distinguished victims, whom he reserved for a public execution.

### CARNAGE IN MOSCOW

He had no sooner arrived in Moscow than he caused several of his favourites to be arrested on the ground of suspicion, but really in order to increase the number of the wretches he designed to put to death; and thus, naming a day for a general execution of the whole, extensive preparations were made in the market place to carry his inhuman project into execution.   Eighteen gibbets were erected, numberless instruments of torture were exhibited, and a great fire was made in the centre, over which a huge copper cauldron was suspended. The inhabitants, seeing these dreadful preliminaries, believed that the czar's object was to set the city on fire, and consign the people to death; and, flying from the spot, they abandoned their shops and merchandise, leaving their property to the mercy of the select legion. In a few hours Moscow was utterly deserted, and not a living person was to be seen but a troop of the Opritshnina ranged in gloomy silence round the gibbets and blazing fire. Presently the beating of drums rose upon the air, and the czar was seen advancing on horseback, accompanied by his favourite son, and followed by his devoted guards. In the rear came the spectral troop of victims, in number about three hundred, wan and bloody, and hardly able to crawl upon the ground. On perceiving that the theatre of carnage was destitute of an audience, Ivan commanded his soldiers to collect the inhabitants; and, after a short pause, finding that they did not arrive with promptitude, he went in person to demand their presence at the treat he had prepared for them, assuring them at the same time of the good-will he entertained towards them. The wretched Muscovites dared not disobey him, and hurrying in terror from their hiding places, they crowded to the scene of execution, which was speedily filled with spectators even to the roofs of the houses. Then the dreadful rites began. The czar addressed the people with exclamations upon the righteousness of the punishments he was about to inflict, and the people, oppressed with horror, replied in terms of approbation. A crowd of one hundred and twenty victims, who were declared to be less guilty than the rest, were first separated from the others and pardoned. The condemned were called one by one, and some, after hearing the accusation in general terms from the lips of the czar, accompanied by occasional blows on the head from a whip which he held in his hand, were given over to the assassins, who hung them up by the feet, and then cut them to pieces, or plunged them half alive into the boiling cauldron. These executions, which are too horrible to be related in detail, lasted for about four hours; during which time nearly two hundred victims, innocent of the crimes with which they were charged, suffered deaths of the most exquisite and prolonged agony.

A despotism so sanguinary and so wanton was well calculated to endanger the safety of those institutions which the wisdom of others had established. Russia, distracted through all her provinces by the atrocities of Ivan, soon became a prey to those unwearied foes who never lost an opportunity of taking advantage of her domestic difficulties. The declaration of Ivan's supremacy to his unfortunate subjects was, "I am your god as God is mine; whose throne is surrounded by archangels, as is the throne of God." But this piece of blasphemy, which had the effect of making the Russians tremble, only increased the determination of his external enemies. Sweden had already wrested Esthonia from him; Kettler, the last grand-master of the Livonian knights, satisfied himself with Courland and Semigallia; while Battori of Poland, the successor of Sigismund Augustus, deprived him of Livonia, one of the most important points in his dominions. In 1566, Ivan laid before an assembly of the states-general, consisting of a convocation of ecclesiastics, nobles, citizens, and traders, a statement of his negotiations with Poland on the subject of Livonia; but as his real object was to assert his tyrannical power rather than to gain the political advantages he pointed out, the issue of the assembly was merely an admission from all the parties present that the will of the czar was indisputable, and that they had no right even to tender him their advice. The great advantage of recovering Livonia from Poland was obviously to secure it as an outlet upon the Baltic for Russian commerce, and as a means of opening a communication with Europe. To the ministry of Sylvester and Adaschev belongs the credit of this admirable project; but a design which they would have accomplished with comparative facility, was suffered by Ivan to be wasted in fruitless contentions.

Battori terrified Ivan in the midst of his tyrannies; and the monster who could visit his people with such an example of cruelties, crouched before the king of Poland. His fear of Battori carried him to extremes. He not only supplicated terms at his hands, but suffered him to offer personal insults to the officers who represented the czar at his court. The grovelling measures and cowardice of Ivan disgusted his adversary; and in reply to some fresh instance of dastardly submission, Battori charged him with the grossest crimes — with having falsified the articles of treaties, and applied inhuman tortures to his peoples. The letter containing these strong, but just, animadversions, closed with a challenge to single combat, which the poverty of the czar's spirit met by renewed protestations of the most abject character.

## THE STRUGGLE FOR LIVONIA

At length, urged by the clamour of his advisers, Ivan organised an army of three hundred thousand men; but, although he could instigate and assist at the most revolting punishments, he shrunk from a personal share in the numerous petty conflicts which took place between his forces and the Livonian knights. Instead of advancing boldly upon the enemy, who could not have maintained war against the superior numbers of the Russians, he suffered himself to be shielded by a jesuit, the pope's envoy, whose intercession with Battori he had procured by representing, with consummate audacity, that he hoped to be able to effect the conversion of the Russians to catholicism. Whenever he fell in with the Livonians, and the collision terminated in victory, he committed the wildest excesses: plundered the captives of their wealth, which he transmitted to his own private coffers, and then sentenced the prisoners to be flung into boiling cauldrons, spitted on lances, or roasted at fires which he amused himself by stirring — while the sacrificial murders were in progress. Wars so irregularly conducted, and terminating in such frightful revenge could not but entail calamities upon the empire. All that was gained by the long struggle for Livonia, was the occasional plunder which Ivan appropriated to himself.

To support the system of profligate expenditure to which the whole life of this extraordinary man inevitably led, he laid on the most exorbitant taxes, and lent himself to the most unjust monopolies. Nor was he satisfied with exceeding in this way the most arbitary examples that had preceded him; but, with a recklessness of human life, and a disregard of the common decencies and obligations of the worst condition of society, he proceeded to rifle his subjects of their private means, sometimes upon slight pretences, but oftener without any pretence whatever. It would almost appear that his appetite for sights of destruction had palled with ordinary gratification; and that he had jaded his invention to discover new modes of cruelty. Having exhausted in all its varieties the mere art of slaughter, he proceeded to make his objects violate before his eyes the sacred feelings of nature. He demanded fratricide and parricide at their hands: one man was forced to kill his father, another his brother: eight hundred women were drowned, and, bursting into the houses of his victims, he compelled the survivors to point out the places where the remnant of their wealth was concealed. His excesses carried him beyond all law, human and divine. He assumed the place, and even usurped the attributes of the Deity, and identified himself to a proverb with the Creator.   Not content with indulging his insane passions in the frenzy of an undisciplined mind, he trampled the usages of Russia under foot, and married seven wives — which was held by the tenets of the Greek religion to be a crime of great magnitude.*g*

## PROJECTS OF ALLIANCE WITH ENGLAND

The unfortunate issue of the war with Sweden did not however make Ivan the Terrible give up the idea of compensating himself for his losses; he continued to seek for alliances with European states.   With this object Theodore Pissemski was sent to England in 1582 with instructions to endeavour to bring about a close alliance with Elizabeth against his enemy the king of Poland, and at the same time to enter into matrimonial negotiations for the czar with the queen's relative, Maria Hastings.   The English would not entertain either project, but only sought to obtain an exemption from entry duties for their trade with Russia.   In 1583 Jeremiah Bowes was sent to Moscow from England with the delicate mission of attaining this object.   The negotiations dragged on a long time; first the czar sent away Bowes and then recalled him again, and in fact they had not come to an end before the death of Ivan the Terrible.*b*

## DEATH OF IVAN THE TERRIBLE

We have already seen what was the life of Ivan: we shall now see its ending — which was equally astonishing — desirable indeed for mankind, but terrifying to the imagination; for the tyrant died as he had lived, that is, exterminating men, although in contemporary narratives there is no mention of his last victims.[1]   Strong in bodily constitution, Ivan had hoped for a long life; but what bodily strength could withstand the furious rage of the passions that agitated the sombre existence of the tyrant?   The continued outbursts of wrath and fear, the racking of the unrepentant conscience, the odious transports of abominable sensuality, the torments of shame, the impotent fury at the reverses of his arms, finally the horrible remembrance of the murder of his own son, had exhausted the measure of Ivan's strength.   At times he experienced a painful languor, the precursory symptom of dissolution, but he struggled against it and did not noticeably weaken until the winter of the year 1584.   At that time a comet appeared in the sky between the churches of Ivan the Great and of the Annunciation, which had the form of a cross.   Curious to see it, Ivan went out on the red staircase, gazed at it long, grew pale, and said to those around him: "there is the portent of my death."   Pursued by this idea, it is said that he caused astrologers and pretended magicians to be sought for throughout Russia and Lapland, brought together about sixty of them, assigned to them a house in Moscow, and daily sent his favourite Belski, to confer with them concerning the comet.   Soon he fell dangerously ill.   It is said that the astrologers predicted his death on the 18th of March.   During February he was still able to occupy himself with affairs; but on the 10th of March a courier was despatched to delay the arrival of the Lithuanian ambassador who was on his way to Moscow, by reason of the illness of the czar.   Ivan himself had given the order; he had still hopes of recovery, nevertheless he called together the boyars and com-

---

[1] Oderborn says that a few days before his death Ivan had six noblemen executed.   In other narratives it is only said that he destroyed men up to the very end of his life.

manded that his will and testament should be written down. He declared the czarevitch Theodore heir to the throne and monarchy, and chose well-known men for councillors to watch over the prosperity of the state and lighten for Theodore (who was feeble both in mind and body) the burden of the cares of the state; these men were: Prince Ivan Petrovitch Shuiski (the famous defender of Pskov), Ivan Mstislavski, son of a niece of the grand prince Vasili, Nikita Romanovitch Iuriev (brother of Ivan's first wife, the virtuous Anastasia), Boris Godunov, and Belski. To the young Dmitri and his mother he assigned the town of Uglitch as appanage, the boy's education to be exclusively confided to Belski. He declared his gratitude to all his boyars and voyevods, calling them his friends and companions in arms in the conquest of unbelieving kingdoms, in the victories gained over the knights of the Livonian order, the khan, and the sultan. He exhorted Theodore to rule piously, lovingly and mercifully, advising him and the five chief dignitaries of the state to avoid war with Christian powers. He spoke of the disastrous consequences of the wars with Lithuania and Sweden, deplored the exhaustion of Russia, enjoined a reduction of the taxes and the liberation of all captives, even of the Lithuanian and German prisoners.

The strength of the sick man presently left him; his thoughts were beclouded; stretched in unconsciousness upon his bed, Ivan called loudly for his murdered son, imagined he saw him and spoke to him tenderly. On the 17th of March he felt better from the effects of a warm bath, so that he commanded the Lithuanian ambassador to come without delay from Mozhaisk to Moscow. The next day (if Horsey is to be believed) he said to Belski, "Go and tell those liars, the astrologers, that they shall die: according to their fables I am to die now, but I feel a great deal better." But, answered the astrologers, the day has not yet passed. A bath was again prepared for the czar in which he remained about three hours, then he lay down on his bed and rested. Soon he asked for a chessboard, and sitting up in bed in his dressing-gown, he himself set up the chessmen and wanted to play with Belski.[1] Suddenly he fell back and closed his eyes for all eternity. The doctors rubbed him with strengthening fluids, while the metropolitan — probably fulfilling the will of Ivan that had been long known to him — read the prayers for the taking of orders over the dying man, giving him the monastic names of Jona. During these moments a deep silence reigned throughout the palace and the capital; people waited in expectancy, but nobody dared to ask. Ivan lay already dead, yet he appeared still terrible to the surrounding courtiers, who for a long time could not believe their eyes and did not announce his death. On the third day magnificent obsequies took place in the church of St. Michael.

### KARAMZIN'S ESTIMATE OF IVAN

Amidst the various and heavy trials imposed by destiny on Russia, besides the miseries of the feudal or appanage system, besides the Mongolian yoke, Russia had also to bear the ferocity of the autocrat-tormentor: yet she preserved her love for autocracy, believing that plagues, earthquakes and tyrants are sent by God. Instead of breaking the iron sceptre in the hands of Ivan, she bore for twenty-four years with the destroyer, arming herself solely with prayer and patience in order that in happier times she might have a Peter the Great, a Catherine II (history does not like to name

---

[1] The historian Kostomarov relates that Ivan could not set the king in its place and fell back dead as he endeavoured to do so.

the living[1]). Magnanimously submissive, the martyrs died on the scaffold like the Greeks at Thermopylæ, for their country, their faith and fealty, without thought of rebellion or riot. In order to excuse Ivan's cruelties some foreign historians have spoken of plots and conspiracies against which they were directed; but such plots only existed in the troubled mind of the czar, as all our chronicles and state papers bear witness. The clergy, the boyars, the prominent citizens would not have called forth the wild beast from his lair of Alexandrovski, if they had had thoughts of the treachery imputed to them with as much absurdity as witchcraft. No, the tiger gorged himself with the blood of the lambs, and his victims, casting a last glance on the distressful earth, demanded from their contemporaries and from posterity both justice and compassionate remembrance.

In spite of all speculative explanations, the character of Ivan, a virtuous hero in his youth, and an insatiable, bloody tyrant in the years of his manhood and old age, remains an enigma, and we should doubt the truth of the most trustworthy narratives concerning him, if the history of other nations did not show us equally astonishing examples; if for instance Caligula, at first a model for sovereigns and afterwards a monster of cruelty — if Nero, the pupil of the wise Seneca, an object of love and an object of loathing, had not reigned at Rome.

Thus Ivan possessed a superior intellect, he was not uneducated, and his knowledge was united to an uncommon gift of speech, yet he was the shameless slave of the most abominable vices. He had an unusually fine memory, he knew the Bible by heart, he was also well acquainted with Greek and Roman history, besides the history of his own country, and only used his knowledge in order to give the most absurd interpretations in favour of tyranny. He boasted of his firmness and self control, because he could laugh loudly in the hour of fear and of inward uneasiness. He boasted of his clemency and generosity, because he enriched his favourites with the possessions of the boyars and citizens who had fallen into disgrace. He boasted of his justice, and punished with equal satisfaction the meritorious and the criminal. He boasted of his sovereign spirit and of knowing how to maintain the sovereign dignity, ordering that an elephant which had been sent to him from Persia should be cut to pieces because the animal would not kneel before him, and cruelly punishing the unfortunate courtiers who dared to play at cards or chess better than his majesty. Finally he prided himself on his deep statecraft in exterminating systematically, at certain fixed epochs, with cold blooded calculation, some of the most illustrious families under the pretext of their being dangerous to the royal power; raising to their rank new and mean families; touching with his destroying hand even the future, for like a swarm of famine-bringing insects, the band of informers, of calumniators, of "*opritchniki*"[2] that he had formed, left, as they disappeared, the seed of evil among the people, and if the yoke of Bati had lowered the spirit of the Russians, there is no doubt that the reign of Ivan did nothing to raise it.

But justice must be rendered even to a tyrant: even in the extremity of evil, Ivan at times seems the phantom, as it were, of a great monarch, zealous, unwearying, often showing proofs of great penetration in state matters. For valour he liked to compare himself to Alexander of Macedonia, although there was not a shadow of courage in his soul: yet he was a conqueror; in his outward policy he followed unswervingly the great schemes

[1 A compliment to Alexander I, the author's patron.]
2 The life guards of Ivan the Terrible.

of his grandfather. He wanted justice to be observed in the tribunals, and not frequently himself examined the lawsuits, listened to complaints, read every paper laid before him, and was prompt in his decisions. He punished the oppressors of the people, unscrupulous functionaries, and extortioners, both corporally and by putting them to shame (he had them

clothed in sumptuous attire, seated in carts and driven by the hangmen through the streets). He forbade all drunken excesses and only allowed the people to divert themselves in the public houses during the Easter holidays and at Christmastide; at every other time drunken people were sent to prison. Although he did not like daring reproaches, yet at times Ivan detested coarse flattery; of the latter we will give an instance: The voyevods, the princes Shtcherbati and Iri Boriatinski, who had been ransomed by the czar from captivity in Lithuania, were honoured with his favour, were given presents, and had the distinction of dining with him. He questioned them about Lithuania. Shtcherbati spoke the truth, but Boriatinski lied

CATHEDRAL OF ST. BASIL, MOSCOW

(Built by Ivan the Terrible, who considered it so beautiful that he had the architect's eyes put out that he might not build another)

shamelessly, averring that the king had neither troops nor fortresses and trembled at the name of Ivan. "Poor king!" said Ivan quietly, shaking his head: "how I pity thee!" and suddenly seizing his staff he broke it to splinters over Boriatinski's back, saying: "Take that, you shameless fellow, for your flagrant lying!"

Ivan was distinguished by a wise tolerance in matters of religion (excepting that of the Jews); but although he at first allowed the Lutherans and the Calvinists to have churches in Moscow, five years later he ordered their churches to be burned. It is possible, however, that he had heard of the people's dissatisfaction and was afraid of some scandal; in any case he did not hinder their meeting for worship in the houses of their pastors. He was fond of disputing with learned Germans upon matters of faith and was not angry at contradiction: thus in the year 1570 he had a solemn discussion in the palace of the Kremlin with the Lutheran theologian Rotsita, whom he accused of heresy: Rotsita was seated before him on a raised platform covered with rich carpets; he spoke boldly in defence of the dogmas of the Augsburg Confession, and was honoured with tokens of the czar's favour.

Ivan evinced esteem for the arts and sciences, showing marks of favour to educated foreigners. Although he did not found academies, yet he contributed to popular education by increasing the number of ecclesiastical schools where the laity also could study reading, writing, religion, and even history, and in particular prepare to become clerks in the chanceries; to the shame of the boyars, many of whom were not yet able to write. Finally Ivan is famous in Russian history as a lawgiver and organiser of the state.*f*

## IVAN THE TERRIBLE COMPARED WITH PETER THE GREAT

Deeply tragic were the life and destiny of Ivan the Terrible! As we penetrate into the full signification of his work, we are involuntarily drawn to the comparison which suggests itself between him and the hero czar of the eighteenth century. It was not without reason that, according to tradition, Peter looked upon Ivan as his precursor: they had both entertained the same projects. Even in the circumstances of their childhood and early youth there were points of resemblance; but Ivan had not a tender, loving mother at his side, and this difference was an essential one. There is also another very essential difference: by nature Ivan was a man of more abstract character, less capable of and less inclined to practical activity; for this reason he at times confided in others, then suddenly became suspicious, but never acted himself. It appeared to him that the duty of a czar was only to direct the activity of others. Although this is a true view in ordinary times, it may sometimes become a false one, and Peter served Russia as much with the carpenter's hatchet as he did with the sword of Pultowa. The practical Peter believed in his people, and if at times he overstrained the bow, yet it was as if he felt that matters would adjust themselves. Ivan lost faith in everything and everyone; it may also be added that Peter thought less of himself and in this respect he was larger minded than his terrible predecessor. The painful impression produced on the historian by Ivan's trying to secure a refuge in England, has no parallel in the life of Peter. Also, however terrible were the executions and punishments in the time of Peter, and although at times there may be observed in them signs of personal irritation, yet the impression produced by the narrative of the devastations in Novgorod is still more distressing. Practical statesmen never go to such lengths as abstract theorists: Peter never entered into theoretical controversies, which were foreign to his nature. For the same reason Peter, however well disposed he might be towards foreigners, always counted himself a Russian, while Ivan took pleasure in tracing the descent of his race from Cæsar Augustus. It was also for this reason that Peter could not entirely abase himself in sensual delights; he had too much work on his hands; his was a practical, not a contemplative nature. And this is one of the principal causes of Peter's success and Ivan's failure; another and more important reason lies in the fact that Russia was weaker in the time of the Terrible czar than in the time of Peter the Great.*b*

## CHAPTER V

## THE CENTURY AFTER IVAN THE TERRIBLE

### [1584–1682 A.D.]

Ivan left two sons, Feodor and Dmitri, the first of whom, at twenty-two years of age, succeeded him. The second, born in 1581, was sprung from a seventh marriage, contracted by Ivan in contempt of the canons of the Greek church, which recognises no union as legitimate after the fourth widowhood. Notwithstanding this circumstance, the right of Dmitri to the title of czarevitch was not disputed, and he was even regarded as the presumptive heir to the crown, as the feeble health of Feodor rendered it extremely probable that he would die without issue.

The character of the new czar contrasted strangely with that of his father. Gentle and timid as a child, and devout even to superstition, Feodor spent his days in prayer, or in listening to and commenting upon pious legends. He was constantly to be seen in the churches, and he frequently took delight in ringing the bells himself, to call the faithful to divine service. "He is a sacristan," said Ivan the Terrible, "not a czarevitch." When not engaged in devotional exercises, Feodor used to shut himself up with his buffoons; or else, from a balcony, he would watch his huntsmen combating with bears. To a mind so weak, the cares of government were insupportable; and he therefore lost no time in transferring them to one of his own favourites, the boyard Boris Godunov, his brother-in-law. He first bestowed upon him the office of master of the horse, and attached to that title many important duties and immense power. Shortly afterwards, by a public confession of his own incapacity, he appointed him *pravitel*, or regent of the empire.[b]

## CHARACTER OF BORIS GODUNOV

From that time on, for eighteen years, the destiny of the Russian monarchy and people was bound up with the personality of Boris Godunov. His family traced its origin from the Tatar prince (*mourza*) Tchet, who in the fourteenth century had been baptised in the horde by the metropolitan Peter and had settled in Russia under the name of Zacharias. The Ipatski monastery, erected by him near Kostroma, was a monument of the piety of the newly baptised Tatar; it became the holy place of his descendants, who provided for it by their offerings and were buried there. The grandson of Zacharias, Ivan Godum, was the forefather of that branch of the family of Prince Tchet which from the appellation of Godum received the name of Godunov. The posterity of Godum flourished remarkably; the Godunovs owned estates, but they did not play an important rôle in Russian history until the time when one of the great-grandsons of the first Godunov had the honour of becoming the father-in-law of the czarevitch Feodor Ivanovitch. Then there appeared at the court of Ivan the Terrible the brother of Feodor's wife, Boris, who was married to a daughter of the czar's favourite, Maluta Skuratov. Ivan liked him. The exaltation of persons and families through relationship with the czaritsas was a very ordinary occurrence in the history of Moscow, but such exaltation was often precarious. The relatives of Ivan's wives were destroyed as freely as the other victims of his bloodthirstiness. Boris himself, by his nearness to the czar, was in imminent peril, and it is reported that Ivan wounded him badly with his staff when Boris interceded for the czarevitch Ivan, murdered by his father. But the czar himself lamented his son and afterwards showed Boris even greater favour for his boldness, which nevertheless cost him some months' illness. But towards the end of his life Ivan, under the influence of other favourites, began to look askance at Boris, and perhaps things might have gone badly with Godunov had not Ivan died suddenly.

After Ivan's death Boris found himself in a position such as had never before been occupied by a subject in the empire of Moscow. The feeble-minded Feodor had become czar, and as he could not in any case have ruled himself, he was obliged to give up his power to that one among his immediate entourage who proved himself the most capable and crafty. Such a one in the court circles of that time was Boris. At the time of Ivan's death he was thirty-two years of age; of a handsome presence, distinguished for his remarkable gift of speech, intelligent, prudent, but egotistical to a high degree. All his activity was directed to the serving of his own interests, to his enrichment, to the increase of his power, to the exaltation of his family. He understood how to wait, to take advantage of propitious moments, to remain in the shade or advance to the front when either manœuvre seemed opportune, to put on the mask of piety and of every virtue, to show kindness and mercy, and where it was necessary severity and harshness. Ever deliberate, he never gave way to enthusiastic impulses and always acted with reflection. Like all such characters, he was ready to do good if good did not stand in the way of his personal interests; neither did he stop at any wickedness or crime if he considered it necessary for the furtherance of his personal advantages, and least of all when it was a question of personal safety.

There was nothing creative in his nature. He was incapable of becoming the propagator of any idea or the guide of men into new pathways; egotistical natures are not fitted for such tasks. As regent of the state he was not far-seeing, but only apprehended proximate circumstances, and could only take advantage of them for close and pre-eminently self-centered aims. The lack of a good education still further narrowed the horizon of his vision, although his strong common sense enabled him to understand the profitableness of acquaintance with the west for the furtherance of his power. All the good of which his mind was capable was frustrated by his narrow egotism and the extraordinary mendacity that penetrated his whole being and was reflected in all his actions. This last quality, however, had become a distinguishing characteristic of the people of Moscow at that period. The seeds of this vice had long existed, but they were in a very great measure fostered and developed by the reign of Ivan the Terrible, who was himself falsehood personified. By creating the *opritchniki* Ivan had armed the Russians against one another, and taught them to look for favour or safety in the ruin of their neighbours; by punishments and executions for imaginary crimes, he had taught them to give false information; and by perpetrating the most inhuman villanies for pure diversion, he had educated those around him in heartlessness and cruelty. Respect for right and morality vanished after the czar, who according to the national ideal should be the guardian of both, had organised before the eyes of his subjects such spectacles as the baiting of innocent persons by bears or the public torture of naked girls, while at the same time he observed the strictest rules of monastic piety. In moments of personal danger everyone naturally thinks only of himself; but when such moments were prolonged for Russians into decades, it is comprehensible that a generation of self-seeking and hard-hearted egotists must have arisen, whose whole thought and aspiration were directed to the preservation of their own safety — a generation for whom, in spite of the outward observance of the customary forms of piety, lawfulness, and morality, there remained no inward righteousness. He who was clever beyond the average, was bound to become a model of falsity; it was an epoch when the mind, rivetted in the narrow fetters of the self-interested motives inherent in the whole contemporary sphere of existence, could only show its activity in the attainment of its personal aims by means of deceit. Desperate diseases of human society, like physical illnesses, are not quickly cured when the general conditions of life contribute not to the cessation but rather to the prolongation of the unhealthy state; the terrible phenomena of the "troubled times" can be explained only as the outbreaking of the hidden corruptions accumulated during the awful period of the tyranny of Ivan the Terrible.

The mendacity which constituted a feature of the period is powerfully reflected in the contemporary Russian sources of information, and it would be easy to fall into error and inaccurate inferences if we were to trust to them and accept their guidance; fortunately the evident contradictions and absurdities into which they fall sufficiently testify to their untruthfulness.c

### WAR WITH SWEDEN

Russia boasted of her power, having in reality the largest army in Europe, yet a part of old Russia was in Sweden's power. The peace concluded with King John expired at the beginning of the year 1590. The second interview with the ambassadors on the borders of the Plusa was fruitless, the Swedes having refused to restore their conquests. Under such circumstances no understanding could be arrived at. Sweden proposed a mere exchange, giving up Koporie for Sumersk on the banks of the Neva. John complained that the Russians annoyed Finland by incursions, ravaging the land like tigers. Feodor reproached the voyevods for their brigandage in the Zaonega, Olonetz,

Ladoga, and Dvina countries. During the summer of 1589 they came from Caianie to pillage the lands belonging to the convents of Sklovetzk, Petchensk, Kola, Kereta, and Kovda, seizing as booty more than half a million of silver roubles in cash. In engaging the king to make concessions, the czar spoke to him of his great allies, the emperor and the shah. But John answered ironically: "I am delighted to see you now know your weakness and wait for help from others. We shall see what kind of aid our relation Rudolph will give you. As for ourselves, we do not need allies to finish you off." Notwithstanding this insolence, John asked for a third interview with the ambassadors. But Feodor declared to him that neither peace nor a truce was wanted unless the Swedes would yield, besides the lands belonging to Novgorod which they had invaded, Revel and all Esthonia. In short, Russia declared war.

ESTHONIAN GIRL

Up to that time, Godunov had only shone by his genius in interior and exterior politics. Always prudent and inclined to peace, not warlike nor aspiring to glory through arms, he yet wished to prove that his love of peace did not arise from cowardice on this occasion when, without being ashamed or failing in the sacred use of power, bloodshed could not be avoided. To fulfil this duty he employed every means necessary to ensure success. He put on the field (if one can credit official documents of the time) nearly three hundred thousand fighters, infantry and cavalry, with three hundred pieces of artillery. All the boyars, all the czarevitches (Muhammed, Koul of Siberia, Rouslanei son of Kaiboula, and Ouraze Magmet of the Kirghiz), the voyevods of countries near and far, towns and hamlets where they lived in quiet, were obliged to be at a certain time under the royal flag; for the pacific Feodor, having left — not without regret — his religious occupations, himself headed his army. This was just what Godunov needed to animate the troops and hinder senseless disputes among the principal dignitaries concerning ancient lineage and precedence.

Prince Feodor Mstislavski commanded the grand army; the advance guard was under Prince Dmitri Khvorostinin, a voyevod distinguished for talent and courage. Godunov and Feodor Romanov-Turiev (descended from the illustrious Philarete), the czar's second cousin, were combined with him under the title court voyevods. The czarina Irene followed her husband from Moscow as far as Novgorod, where the monarch assigned the destination of the troops. He ordered some to march to Flanders beyond the Neva; others to Esthonia as far as the coast; he himself at the head of the principal army set out on the 18th of January, 1590, against Narva. It was a hard campaign on account of the severe cold, but distinguished by the zeal of the troops. The Russians marched to retake what was theirs, and, on the 27th of January, seized Jama. Twenty thousand Swedes, as many cavalry as infantry, commanded by Gustav Banér, met Prince Dmitri Khvorostinin near Narva, but were defeated and driven back into the town, which was full of people but destitute of provisions. That was why Banér, having left the necessary number of soldiers in the fortress, fled during the night and went to Vesemberg, pursued by the Russian Asiatic cavalry, and left all his baggage and artillery. Among the prisoners were several Swedes of distinction.

On the 4th of February the Russians besieged Narva, and having managed by a vigourous bombardment to make three breaches demanded a submission. The commander, Charles Horn, called them on to the assault and valiantly repulsed the enemy. The voyevods Saburov and Prince Ivan Tokmakov, as well as certain boyar children, Strelitz, and Mordiren, and Tcherckess women and soldiers perished in the breach. Nevertheless, this affair, however brilliant for the Swedes, could not save the town: the cannonade did not cease; walls were tottering and the Russian troops prepared for a new assault on the 21st of February. Even at this epoch the Russians ravaged Esthonia without opposition as far as Revel, and in Finland as far as the Abo, for King John had more pride than forces. Then negotiations were opened. Russia demanded Narva and all Esthonia in return for peace from the Swedes; but the czar, "yielding to the Christian insistance of Godunov," as it is said in official documents, contented himself with re-establishing the former frontier.

On the 22nd of February Horn, in the king's name, concluded a peace for one year, yielding the czar Jama, Ivangorod, and Koporie, with all stores and war ammunition. It was agreed to fix the fate of Esthonia at a nearby meeting of Russians and Swedes, by promising to yield to Russia even Karelia, Narva, and other Esthonian towns. Russia gained in glory by her moderation. Feodor, after leaving the voyevods in the three fortresses taken, hastened to return to Novgorod and his wife, and go thence with her to Moscow to celebrate a victory over those same European powers with which his father, doubtful of his military skill, had warned him not to engage. The clergy, headed by the cross, came to meet the sovereign outside the town; and the metropolitan, Job, in a pompous discourse compared him to Constantine the Great and Vladimir, according him thanks in the name of country and church for having driven the infidels from the heart of Holy Russia, also for having re-established the altars of the true God in the town of Ivan III and in the old Slav possessions of Ilmen.

Soon Swedish perfidy gave new and important success to the arms of the pacific Feodor. King John, accusing Horn of cowardice, declared that the convention signed by him was incriminating. He reinforced his troops in Esthonia, and sent two seigneurs, lieutenants from Upsala and Vestergöt, to the mouths of the Plusa, there to have an interview with Prince Feodor Mstislavski and a member of the Pissemski council, not to give Esthonia to Russia, but to exact that Jama, Ivangorod, and Koporie should be returned. At this news not only Feodor's ambassadors but even the Swiss soldiers showed their discontent. Ranged on the other side of the Plusa they called on the Russians, but Russia desired no more slaughter, and they forced their plenipotentiaries to forego their pretentions, so that nothing but peace was sought and they ended by consenting to yield all Karelia to Russia. But she insisted on having Narva, and the ambassadors separated.

That same night the Swiss general, Joran Boyé, treacherously besieged Ivangorod whilst the terms of the Narva convention had not yet expired. But the intrepid voyevod Ivan Saburov completely defeated by a vigourous sortie not only General Boyé but the duke of Sudermania joined with him. The principal Moscow army was at Novgorod but was not in time to help. They found the fortress already delivered and saw only from a distance the enemy fleeing.[d]

SERFDOM

It was Boris Godunov, to whom his contemporaries give the title Lieutenant of the Empire, who in reality introduced into it the attachment of serfs to the soil. Up till then the peasants, using and abusing the faculty of passing from one estate to another, had changed masters on every occasion; and many were the inconveniences which resulted, notably this that they accustomed themselves to no given situation with its climate, men, and accessories, were not attached to the ground, and remained strangers to the locality they inhabited. Boris was besieged with the landowners' complaints on this subject, and saw, besides, that the cultivators themselves, frequently deceived in their hope of finding a better landlord, would then abandon themselves to discouragement; and this engendered poverty, increased the number of vagabonds and the lowest classes, and caused numerous habitations, well suited to shelter field-labourers, to be deserted, become dilapidated, and fall into ruin. Boris had favoured agriculture by releasing the peasants on the czar's estates, and perhaps those on his own, from the tax. His intentions were doubtless benevolent: his aim was to unite the labourers and the landlords as by a family tie, and to augment the well-being of both, by establishing between them an indissoluble community of interest to their mutual advantage. It was in this hope that he instituted the law of 1592 or 1593, by which the peasant's undisputed right to liberty of removal (vykhod) was suppressed.

We may, however, believe that Boris had still another motive. In a country of the extent of Russia and administered as she was, the government had some difficulty in keeping up direct relations with the peasants who were bound to pay it the tax and to provide for the recruiting of the army, which had recently been transformed like the rest. The government was then very glad to avail itself of the nobles as intermediaries and enlightened executors of its orders. Consequently it made them its delegates for the administration and police, an arrangement which simplified the machinery; and the nobles, acting in their own most apparent interests, must have afterwards pushed matters to extremes. However that may be, the peasants were now inscribed in review books and forbidden to go away from their commune except by the authority of their lord. In spite of the discontent which this measure produced, it was further strengthened by the ukase of the 21st of November, 1597, relative to fugitive peasants, of which there were a great number in consequence of these legal prescriptions, so evidently contrary to the temperament and genius of the nations. Those who had hired themselves out for a certain time were forbidden to redeem themselves from the effects of this new régime, even by reimbursing the sum stipulated as the price of hire. What was more, these peasants who had disposed of their persons by contract were not the only ones affected by these laws of oppression; they touched even the freemen who, without having signed any engagement, happened to be in the service of the landlords. If they had been there for more than three months, they were obliged to remain permanently, and where their time of service was not so long all they gained was the power of choosing between the last lord and another, but always renouncing the right of being their own masters. A new ukase ordained that all boyars, princes, nobles, the military and legal classes, etc., should present, on account of the individuals in their service, present or in the course of flight, their letters of serfdom, in order to have them inscribed in the registers of the chamber for the regulation of serfs.

The measure once taken, Godunov, who wished to be agreeable to the mass of the rural proprietors, gave it all the extension possible; still, at the same time he declared the emancipated to be free forever, as well as their wives and their children; this last, however, was a very feeble amelioration of an evidently iniquitous law, which did not fail to produce extreme indignation in the whole rural population. In various places the peasants protested by flight against the tyranny exercised over them by a power whose despotism had never gone so far. Want was doubtless not long in bringing the greater part back to their abandoned homes, or they were constrained to return by armed force; but St. George's day, the date when this law of enslavement was put into execution, was graven in their memories as a day of ill-omen; the people have never pardoned it for its disgrace and will perhaps continue to curse it, although the day of reparation is come at last. But the peasant was not the only one to suffer; the great number of men in flight gave occasion to a thousand ruinous suits between landowners; they accused each other of offering an asylum to the fugitives and of keeping them in concealment. The evil was so great, says the historian upon whose narratives ours is based, that Boris, though unwilling to abolish a law passed from good motives, decided at least to declare that it should be only temporary, and, by an ukase of the 21st of November, 1601, he authorised the peasants of boyars' children, and of other nobles of the secondary classes, to return, within a fixed period, from one proprietor to another of the same rank; not more than two at a time, however, and exception being made of the Moscow district. On the other hand, he ordered the peasants belonging to the boyars and other great nobles, and those of the crown, the bishoprics, and the convents, not to stir during this same year 1601, but to remain in their respective habitations. Karamzin adds that the sensation produced by all this was such that Boris was personally affected by it. It is asserted, he says, that the abolition of the old *régime* and the uncertainty of the new, a source of discontent to so many, exercised a great influence over the fate of the unfortunate Godunov. In the end he seems to have left the matter in suspense, and it was Prince Chuïski who, raised to the throne under the name of Vasili (V) Ivanovitch, consummated the social revolution we are speaking of, by his ukase of the 9th of March, 1607, confirming that of 1593 and, in addition, laying down the penalties to be inflicted on whoever should give asylum to the fugitives. The lot was cast — the peasant had lapsed into a serf attached to the soil.[e]

## DEATH OF DMITRI (1591 A.D.)

Boris desired above all things to be feared, but he did not disdain a certain amount of popularity for his family; and he left no means untried to render his sister Irene dear to the Russian people. All rigourous measures were executed in the name of the czar, and by order of the regent; but acts of clemency and favours of every kind were ascribed to the intercession of the czarina Irene, who, indeed, was always a docile instrument in the hands of her brother. She acted and thought only in obedience to his inspirations, blending with great simplicity of heart her respect and admiration of Boris with the passionate love which she felt for Feodor.

The intimidated boyars were reduced to silence. Dmitri, still a child, could cause no apprehension; but his mother, the czarina-dowager, Maria Féodorovna, and his three uncles, Michael, Gregory, and Andrew Nagoi, might perhaps attempt to avail themselves of their alliance with the reigning family. Boris therefore banished them to the town of Uglitch, which had been assigned as an appanage to young Dmitri by the will of Ivan; and, under the pretext of intrusting them with the education of the czarevitch, he kept them there in a kind of exile.

At Uglitch, in 1591, Dmitri, at ten years of age, had his little court — his *jiltsy* (children brought up with the young princes), and his great officers, among whom the regent had doubtless introduced many a spy. The pensions of the young prince and his family were paid and controlled by a *deak*, or secretary of chancery, named Michael Bitiagovski, a creature of Boris; and between this functionary and the Nagoi there naturally arose frequent discussions, which increased in bitterness from day to day. Strong in the authority with which the regent had invested him, the secretary delighted to cavil at all the pretensions of the family of the czarevitch. It seemed his constant aim, by the incessant renewal of petty vexations, to make them feel that their fortune had greatly declined since the death of Ivan the Terrible. To the complaints which they laid before the czar, Bitiagovski replied by denouncing any imprudent expressions that might have escaped from the Nagoi during their exile. If we may believe the report of the secretary of chancery, the czarevitch already exhibited the ferocious instincts and cruel tastes of his father. He took pleasure in nothing, it was said, but in seeing animals beaten, or else in mutilating them with a refinement of barbarity. It is related that, one winter's day, when playing with some children of his own age, he constructed several figures of men out of the snow in the courtyard of his palace. To each of these he gave the name of one of the great functionaries of the empire; and the largest of all he called Boris. Then seizing a wooden sabre, he knocked off either their arms or their heads. " When I am a man," said the child, " that is how I will treat them." These and similar anecdotes were carefully collected and commented upon at Moscow. Perhaps they may have been invented by the agents of Boris, in order to render the Nagoi odious to the Russian nobility; or perhaps, educated as he was by servants and courtiers in disgrace, the young prince repeated only too faithfully the lessons which he was taught.

The hopes and fears occasioned by his education were, however, speedily dissipated by the sudden death of Dmitri. His end was strange, and it is difficult to say whether it was the result of an accident or of a crime. On the 15th of May, 1591, the czarevitch, whom his mother had just left for a moment, was amusing himself with four children, his pages or *jiltsy*, in the courtyard of his palace — a spacious enclosure which contained several separate dwelling houses, built irregularly in various parts. He was still attended by Vasilissa Volokhov his governess, his nurse, and a chambermaid. It is probable that they may have lost sight of him for a moment. According to the unanimous testimony of the three women and of the pages, he was holding a knife, which he was amusing himself by sticking into the ground, or with which he was cutting a piece of wood. On a sudden, the nurse looked around, and saw him weltering in his blood. He had a large wound in his throat, and he expired without uttering a word. On hearing the cries of the nurse, the czarina ran up, and in the first transports of her despair exclaimed that her son had been assassinated. She flew upon the governess, whose duty it was to take care of him, and beat her furiously with a heavy stick, accusing her of having admitted the murderers who had just slain her son. At the same time, as her thoughts doubtless turned to her recent quarrels with Bitiagovski, she invoked upon that man the vengeance of her brothers and of the servants of her household.

Michael Nagoi now came up, having just left the dinner table, in a state of intoxication, according to the testimony of several witnesses; in his turn he began to beat the poor governess, and ordered that the alarm bell should be rung at the church of the Saviour, which stood near the palace. In an instant the courtyard was filled with inhabitants of Uglitch and domestics, who ran up with pitchforks and hatchets, beieving that the palace of the czarevitch was on fire. With them arrived Bitiagovski, accompanied by his son and by the gentlemen employed in his chancery. He endeavoured to speak, to appease the tumult, and cried out at once that the child had killed himself by falling on his knife in an epileptic fit, from which it was well known that he frequently suffered. "Behold the murderer!" exclaimed the czarina. A hundred arms were immediately raised to strike him. He fled into one of the houses in the enclosure, and barricaded the door; but it was soon burst open, and he was cut to pieces. His son was slain at the same time. Whoever raised his voice in his defence, whoever was known to be connected with him, was immediately struck down and put to death. The governess Vasilissa, covered with blood and half-killed by the blows she had received, lay on the ground near the czarina, bareheaded, and with dishevelled hair; for the servants of the Nagoi had taken off her cap — which was considered by the Russians, at this period, a more infamous outrage even than blows. One of her serfs, compassionating her disgrace, picked up her cap, and replaced it on her head; he was instantly massacred. The furious crowd, still pursuing and murdering those who were pointed out to its vengeance, carried the bleeding body of the czarevitch into the church. Thither they dragged Daniel Volokhov, the son of the governess, who was known to be intimate with Bitiagovski. This was enough to procure his condemnation as an accomplice in the crime; and he was immediately put to death before the eyes of his mother, in front of the body of the young prince. It was with great difficulty that the priests of the church of the Saviour rescued Vasilissa and the daughters of Bitiagovski from the hands of the multitude. All these women, however, were shut up in one of the buildings adjoining the cathedral; and guards were placed at all the approaches.[b]

Public opinion denounced Boris, and in order to quiet the people he ordered an investigation. His emissaries had the audacity to declare that the young prince, in an access of folly, had cut his own throat, and that the Nagoi and the people of Uglitch had killed, as murderers, men who were innocent. The result of this policy was the extermination of the Nagoi and the depopulation of Uglitch.

Seven years afterward the pious Feodor died: in the person of this pale and virtuous sovereign ended the violent and sanguinary race of men of prey who had made Russia. The dynasty, issue of André Bogoliubski, had accomplished its mission — it had founded a united Russia. The task of bringing into the heart of Europe this semi-Asiatic country was to devolve on another dynasty.[f]

## THE REIGN OF BORIS (1598–1605 A.D.)

In 1598 Boris Godunov, by the voice of the electors and through the intrigues of his friends, ascended the throne of Russia. A crown obtained by indirect and fraudulent measures could not be preserved without tyranny. Boris, conscious of the jealousies which his elevation engendered in the minds of the nobles, and especially in the family of the Romanovs, who were allied to the race of Rurik but not to the Moscow line, was constantly haunted by apprehensions, and sought to lose them in the revel, and to propitiate them by the sacrifice of all persons whom he suspected. Had he been a legitimate sovereign he would have conferred lasting benefits upon his country, because he was a wise and paternal ruler in all matters apart from his personal affairs. He bestowed considerable pains on many laudable measures of improvement; but these were so sullied by acts of merciless revenge, to which he was moved by the danger in which he was placed by his usurpation, that it is difficult to separate his merits from his crimes.

The Tatars of the Crimea, immediately after Boris was proclaimed czar, exhibited a disposition to renew their old hostilities; but Boris promptly turned his attention to that part of the empire, and, assembling a numerous army, availed himself of the opportunity of ingratiating himself with the troops. The descent of the Tatars was merely an idle threat; but the occasion was one which contributed considerably to enlarge the popularity of Boris. He exceeded all his predecessors in the splendour and hospitality of his entertainments, in the frequency of the amusements which he provided for the soldiery and the citizens, and the general amenity and condescension of his bearing in public. It seems to have been the policy of the tyrants of Russia to conciliate the lower orders, in order that they might, with the greater facility, crush the aristocracy, from whom they chiefly dreaded opposition; and Boris was eminently successful in his attempts to ensnare the affections of the multitude, although he had actually deprived them of the only fragment of liberty they possessed.

In the commencement of his reign he evinced a strong desire to cultivate the friendship of the different powers of Europe, from whom severally he received ambassadors at his court; to extend to all his subjects in common the means of procuring cheap and rapid justice, in the fulfilment of which he gave audiences for the purpose of receiving and redressing complaints; and to diffuse abroad a taste for European knowledge and instruction in those arts and sciences which had hitherto been neglected and despised. In some of these wise projects he met great resistance from the clergy, who, released from the presence of a sovereign who ruled them by a mission from heaven, began to exhibit uneasiness and impatience of control. Thus constantly thrown back upon the uncertain tenure of his power, and reminded that he was not a legitimate master, Boris was forced to exert arbitrary and unjust means to maintain his authority. The current of the official and privileged classes was running against him, and he was compelled to erect such defences as the necessities of the occasion required. But even out of this difficulty he contrived to extract some benefits for the country.

For three years a famine fell upon Russia, paralysing the efforts of industry, and spreading misery and distress over the whole empire. Throughout the whole of this calamitous period, Boris incessantly employed himself in devising modes of relief, and levying from the surplus funds of the rich a treasury of alms to alleviate the wants of the poor. Out of his own abundant coffers he daily distributed several thousand rubles, and he forced the nobility

BORIS GODUNOV, IN RETIREMENT AT THE MONASTERY, INTREATED TO
ACCEPT HIS ELECTION AS CZAR

(Painted for the HISTORIANS' HISTORY OF THE WORLD by Thure de Thulstrup)

and the clergy, who, with a grasping avariciousness, kept aloof from the miseries that surrounded them, to open their granaries, and to sell him their stores of corn at half price, that he might distribute it gratuitously amongst the impoverished people. These exactions depressed the wealthy, and won the gratitude of the needy; but still they were insufficient to meet the whole demand of poverty. Great numbers died, and Boris, unable to provide sustenance for them while living, caused them to be buried with respect, furnishing to each corpse a suit of linen grave-clothes.

These benevolent exertions of Boris were viewed with distrust and malice by the nobility, who clearly enough discerned the policy that lay at the bottom. Their murmurs arose in private, and gradually assumed a sterner expression in public. At the feasts, and even in the court itself, the signs and words of disaffection could not be misunderstood. The insecurity of his position urged Boris to protect himself by a machinery of terror. Into a small space of time he crowded a number of executions, and consigned several of the discontented grandees to imprisonment and exile. His alarm magnified his danger, and supplied him with expedients of cruelty. At his own banquets he did not hesitate to rise up and denounce particular individuals, who were immediately seized upon by his adherents, and either put to death or cast into dungeons, or banished, and their properties confiscated to the state. Despotism penetrated to all classes; the peasantry, bound to the soil, were further oppressed by penal laws.

Amongst other sanguinary provisions, it was enacted that all the individuals of a family were held to be involved in the punishment of a single member. It was also declared that every Russian who passed beyond the frontiers was a rebel to his country and a heretic. A father was invested with all the powers of a despot in his hut, and allowed to inflict summary punishment upon his wife and children, the latter of whom he was permitted to sell four times; and this regulation was annulled only by the bondage to the fief, which substituted a worse tyranny for the domestic slavery. The merciless rule of Boris may be regarded as the consequence of his situation, which exposed him to hazards from which he could not escape except by some such decisive and terrible measures. The iron sway pressed down the expiring spirit of licentious freedom. The wandering minstrels who had hitherto travelled through the country, perpetuating in their songs the historical glories of Russia, and inspiring the people with proud sentiments of national emulation, disappeared. The metrical chronicles perished in the general dismay. The immediate result of this struggle to preserve the object of his guilty ambition was an extensive emigration of the peasantry, who fled from the scene of misery to embrace the wild freedom of the Cossacks or seek protection from the king of Poland; and an atrocious *jacquerie* succeeded, which was, for a short time, triumphant.*g*

Never had the government of Boris met with fewer obstacles; never had the authority of a czar appeared more firmly established. At peace with foreign powers, and quietly watching the conflicts of his neighbours, he applied himself to the task of civilising his people, of encouraging commerce, and of establishing an exact system of police in all the provinces of his empire. Every one of his acts was received with submission and executed with alacrity; but, nevertheless, all minds were agitated by a secret disquietude. The czar could not conceal from himself the aversion with which he was regarded by the Russians; all classes, nobles and serfs, alike detested him. He saw all his intentions, all his decrees interpreted as violations of the laws of the country. At this period of benighted ignorance the Russians, even of the higher classes, regarded foreigners with a kind of superstitious horror. They made no difference between a foreigner and an infidel, and applied the name of "pagan" indiscriminately to the idolatrous Tcheremiss, the Mussulman Tatar, and the Lutheran or Catholic German. Love of their country, or, to speak more correctly, of their native soil, was confounded by them with their attachment to their national religion. They called themselves the "orthodox people," and their country Holy Russia. Elsewhere than in that privileged land it was impossible, they believed, to obtain salvation. The early troubles of the Reformation in Germany had brought into Russia a large number of poor adventurers, who had sought to turn their superior knowledge to account. The people were not slow to perceive the pre-eminence of these foreigners in the arts and industry, but they only detested them the more on this account. The Germans were continually charged by the vulgar herd with a desire to corrupt the national faith, and to appropriate to themselves the wealth of the country. Boris, indeed, flattered them and invited them into his dominions, feeling that he had need of them to guide his subjects towards a higher stage of civilisation. But the commercial privileges and facilities which he granted to Livonian and German merchants only served as a pretext to the most terrible accusation which could be brought against a sovereign — that of betraying his country and his religion. He sent eighteen young gentlemen to study in Germany, France, and England; their families lamented them as doomed victims. On either side of the frontier all contact with foreigners was deemed a pollution.[b]

A FEMALE OSTIAK

### The False Dmitri Appears

Suddenly, a surprising rumour was brought from the frontiers of Lithuania, and spread with incredible rapidity through all the provinces of the empire. The czarevitch Dmitri, who was believed to have been assassinated at Uglitch, was still living in Poland. Having been favourably received by a palatine, he had made himself known to the principal nobles of the republic, and was preparing to reclaim his hereditary throne. It was related that he had wandered for some time in Russia, concealed beneath the frock of a monk. The archimandrite of the convent of the Saviour at Novgorod Seversk had given him a lodging without recognising him. The prince had proceeded thence to Kiev, leaving in his cell a note, in which he declared that he was Dmitri, the son of Ivan the Terrible, and that he would one day recompense the hospitality of the archimandrite. On the other hand it was stated that the persons worthy of belief had seen the czarevitch among the Zaparogian Cossacks, taking part in their military expeditions and distinguishing himself by his courage and address in all warlike exercises. The name of the ataman under whose orders he had enrolled himself was also given. Other authorities declared that they had seen the same person at the same time studying Latin at Huszcza, a small town in Volhinia. Though reports were contradictory as to details, they all agreed on this one point — that Dmitri was still living, and that he intended to call the usurper to account for all his crimes.[b]

Who was the personage whom the Russian historians have called the "false Dmitri." Was he really the son of Ivan the Terrible, saved by the foresight of the Nogai from the assassins' knife and replaced in the coffin, as he related, by the son of a pope (Russian parish priest)? Was he, as the czar and the patriarch proclaimed him, a certain Gregori Otrepiev, a vagabond monk who was for a time secretary to the patriarch Job and was thus enabled to surprise state secrets — who in his nomadic life afterwards appeared amongst the Zaparogians, where he is said to have become an accomplished rider and an intrepid Cossack? To all these questions, in the present state of our information, no absolutely certain answer can be given. Kostomarov compared the handwriting of the pretender with that of the monk Otrepiev and affirms that they do not resemble each other. Captain Margeret knew people who conversed with Otrepiev after the pretender's death. Not to prejudge the solution we will give this last not the name of Dmitri but that of Demetrius, with which he signed his letters to the pope.

About the year 1603 a young man entered the service of the Polish *pan*, Adam Vichnevetski. He fell or feigned to fall ill, sent for a Catholic priest, and under the seal of professional secrecy revealed to him that he was the czarevitch Dmitri, who had escaped from the assassins of Uglitch. He showed, suspended from his neck, a cross enriched with precious stones, which he asserted that he had received from Prince Mstislavski, the godfather of Dmitri. The priest dared not keep such a secret to himself. Demetrius was recognised by his master Vichnevetski as the legitimate heir of Ivan the Terrible. Mniszek, palatine of Sandomir, promised him his help. Demetrius had already fallen in love with Marina, the eldest daughter of Mniszek, and swore to make her czarina of Moscow; the father and the young girl accepted the proposal of marriage.

Meantime the strange tidings of the resuscitation of Dmitri spread through the whole kingdom of Poland. Mniszek and Vichnevetski conducted Demetrius to Cracow and presented him to the king. The papal nuncio interested himself in his behalf; the Jesuits and Franciscans worked in concert for his conversion; in secret he abjured orthodoxy and promised to bring Moscow within the pale of the Roman church. He corresponded with Clement VIII whose least servant, *infimus cliens*, he declared himself to be. Thus he was recognised by the king, the nuncio, the Jesuits, and the pope. Did they really believe in his legitimacy? It is probable that they saw in him a formidable instrument of disturbance; the king flattered himself that he would be able to turn it against Russia and the Jesuits — that they might use it against orthodoxy. Sigismund dared not take upon himself to break the truce concluded with Boris and expose himself to Muscovite vengeance. He treated Demetrius as czarevitch, but only in private; he refused to place the royal troops at his disposal, but authorised the nobles who were touched by the misfortunes of the young prince to aid him as they might desire.

The pans had no need of a royal authorisation; many of them, with the light-heartedness and love of adventure which characterised the Polish nobility, took arms.

No revolution, be it the wisest and most necessary, is accomplished without setting in motion the dregs of society, without coming into collision with many interests and creating a multitude of outcasts. The transformation then being accomplished in Russia for the creation of the modern unitary state had awakened formidable elements of disorder. The peasant, whom the laws of Boris had just attached to the glebe, was everywhere covertly hostile. The petty nobility, to whose profit this innovation had been made, could only with great difficulty live by their estates: the czar's service had become ruinous; many were inclined to make up for the inadequacy of their revenues by brigandage. The boyars and the higher nobility were profoundly demoralised and were ready for any treason. The military republics of the Cossacks of the Don and Dnieper, the bands of serfs or fugitive peasants which infested the country districts, were only waiting an opportunity to devastate Moscow. The ignorance of the masses was profound, their minds greedy of marvels and of change: no nation has allowed itself to be so often captured by the same fable — the sudden reappearance of a prince believed to be dead. The archives of the secret chancery show us that there were in Russia, during the seventeenth and eighteenth centuries, hundreds of impostors, of false Dmitris, false Alexises, false Peters II, false Peters III. It might be thought that the Russian people, the most Asiatic of European peoples, had not renounced the oriental dogma of reincarnations and *avatars*.

So long as power was in the hands of the skilful and energetic Godunov, he succeeded in maintaining order, in restraining the fomenters of disturbance, and in discouraging Demetrius. The patriarch Job, and Vasili Shuiski, who had directed the inquiry at Uglitch, made proclamations to the people and affirmed that Dmitri was indeed dead and that the pretender was no other than Otrepiev. Messengers were despatched bearing the same affirmations to the king and the diet of Poland. Finally troops were set on foot and a cordon was established along the western frontier. But already the towns of Severia were agitated by the approach of the czarevitch; the boyars ventured to say publicly that it was "difficult to bear arms against a legitimate sovereign"; at Moscow the health of the czar Dmitri was drunk at festive gatherings. In October, 1604, Demetrius crossed the frontier with a host of Poles, and banished Russians, German mercenaries, and Zaparogians. Severia immediately broke out into insurrection, but Novgorod Seversk resisted. After Severia, the towns of Ukraine joined in defection. Prince Mstislavski tried to arrest Demetrius by giving battle; but his soldiers were seized with the idea that the man against whom they were fighting was the real Dmitri. "They had no arms to strike with," says Margeret. Twelve thousand Little-Russian Cossacks hastened to join the pretender's standard. Vasili Shuiski, the successor of Mstislavski, did his best to restore their *morale;* this time Demetrius was vanquished at Dobrinitchi. Boris fancied that the war was ended: it was only beginning. Four thousand Don Cossacks came to join the brigand. The inaction of the Muscovite voyevods announced that the spirit of treason was gaining the higher nobility.

In 1605 Boris died, after recommending his innocent son to Basmanov, the boyars, the patriarch, and the people of Moscow. All took the oath to Feodor Borissovitch. But Basmanov had no sooner taken command of the army of Severia than he was in a position to convince himself that neither the soldiers nor their leaders intended to fight for a Godunov. Rather than be the victim of an act of treason he preferred to be its perpetrator; the man in whom the dying Boris had placed all his confidence joined Galitzin and Soltikov, the secret partisans of Demetrius. He solemnly announced to the troops that the latter was indeed the son of Ivan the Terrible and the legitimate master of Russia; he was the first to throw himself at the feet of the pretender, who was immediately proclaimed by the troops. Demetrius marched on Moscow. At his approach his partisans rose: the son and the wife of Godunov were massacred. Such was the sanguinary end of the dynasty which Boris had thought to found in the blood of a czarevitch.

Let us bear in mind that in 1586 had appeared the narrative of Jean Sauvage, sailor and merchant of Dieppe, who had come to reconnoitre the harbours of the White Sea and prepare the way for French traffic. The same year the czar Feodor Ivanovitch sent to Henry III a Frenchman of Moscow, Pierre Ragon, to notify him of his accession; at Moscow appeared the first ambassador sent there by France, François de Carle. In 1587 a company of Parisian merchants obtained a commercial charter from the same czar. Henry IV was in correspondence with the czars Feodor Ivanovitch and Boris.

## CAREER AND MURDER OF DEMETRIUS (1606 A.D.)

What was now taking place in Russia is one of the most extraordinary events of which the annals of the world make mention. An unknown man was making his triumphal entry into Moscow and the Kremlin (June 20th–30th). All the people wept for joy, thinking they beheld the scion of so many princes. One man alone dared to affirm that he had seen Dmitri murdered and that the new czar was an impostor; this was Vasili Shuiski, one of those who had superintended the inquiry of Uglitch and who, at the battle of Dobrinitchi, had defeated the pretender. Denounced by Basmanov, he was condemned to death by an assembly of the three orders. His head was already on the block, when the czar sent an express bearing his pardon.

The son of the terrible czar was not recognisable in this act of mercy. Later on Demetrius was to repent of it. Job, the creature of Godunov, was replaced in the patriarchate by a creature of the new prince, the Greek Ignatius. The czar had an interview with his pretended mother, Marie Nagoi, the widow of Ivan IV: whether because she wished to complete the work of an avenger, or because she was glad to recover all her honours, Marie recognised Demetrius as her son and publicly embraced him. He heaped favours on the Nagoi as his maternal relatives: the Romanovs also were recalled from exile and Philaret was made metropolitan of Rostov.

The czar presided regularly at the douma; the boyars admired the correctness of his judgment and the variety of his knowledge. Demetrius was a man of learning, brave and skilful in all bodily exercises. He was fond of foreigners and spoke of sending the Russian nobles to study in the west. This taste for foreigners was not unaccompanied by a certain contempt for the national ignorance and rudeness. He offended the boyars by his mockeries; he alienated the people and the clergy by his contempt for Russian religious rites and usages. He ate veal, did not sleep after dinner, did not frequent the baths, borrowed money from the convents, turned the monks into ridicule, opposed the hunting with bears, paid familiar visits to foreign jewellers and artisans, took no heed of the strict etiquette of the palace, himself pointed cannon, organised sham fights between the national and foreign troops, took pleasure in seeing the Russians beaten by the Germans, surrounded himself with a European guard at the head of which were found men like Margeret, Knutzen, Van Dennen. A conflict having broken out between the clergy and the pope's legate on the occasion of his entry into Moscow, two bishops were exiled.　No one thanked him for resisting the pope and the king of Poland, refusing to the one to occupy himself in the cause of the reunion of the two churches, declaring to the other that he would not yield an inch of Russian territory.　The arrival of his wife, the Catholic Marina, with a suite of Polish noblemen, who affected insolence towards the Russians, completed the irritation of the Muscovites.　Less than a year after the entry of Demetrius [or as we may henceforth call him, Dmitri] into the Kremlin, men's minds were ripe for a revolution.*

## The False Dmitri; Marriage and Death

It is difficult to understand why, though as unscrupulous as most adventurers, Demetrius persisted in his determination to espouse a Catholic Pole, although he was well aware that such a union would be highly distasteful to his people.　When compelled to solicit the assistance of the palatines of Lithuania by all means in his power, it was not surprising that he eagerly sought to ally himself with Mniszek: but now that he was seated upon the throne of the czars, such an alliance could not be otherwise than prejudicial to his interests.　Yet he was the first to remember his promise, and as soon as he had been crowned at Moscow he sent to invite Marina to share his throne. When he signed the promise of marriage in Poland, he was, doubtless, under the influence of Marina's charms, but at Moscow we cannot ascribe his impatience to conclude the projected union to the eagerness of love.　For whilst Vlassiev, bearing magnificent presents for the bride and all her family, was on his way to Cracow to hasten their departure for Russia, the czar had an acknowledged mistress, who resided with him in the Kremlin, and this mistress was no other than the daughter of Boris.

"Xenia," writes a contemporary author, "was a girl of the greatest intelligence; her complexion was pink and white, and her black eyes sparkled with vivacity.　When grief caused her to shed tears, they shone with a still greater radiance.　Her eyebrows joined; her body was formed with perfect symmetry, and was so white that it seemed to have been moulded with cream. She was an accomplished person, speaking more elegantly than a book.　Her voice was melodious, and it was a real pleasure to hear her sing songs."

This beauty was fatal to Xenia.　After witnessing the death of her mother and brother, she took refuge first of all in a convent, or, according to some annalists, she found an asylum in the house of Prince Mstislavski.　Soon afterwards she entered the palace of the enemy of her family, and for some months she was the favourite mistress of the czar.　It was probably to her influence that several of the Godunovs were indebted for their lives, and even for some degree of favour.　Whether she yielded to seduction or to violence, as some modern authors have asserted, it is impossible to discover at the present day.　It is no less impossible to decide whether Dmitri allowed himself to be subdued by the charms of his captive, or whether, like a pitiless conqueror, he sacrificed her to his arrogant vanity, and desired, with a refinement of vengeance, to inflict the greatest dishonour on the enemy's family. At all events, it appears certain that for some time Xenia exercised such marked influence over him that Mniszek grew alarmed, and seriously remonstrated with the czar.　It was only when Marina was actually on her way to Moscow that Dmitri dismissed his captive.　He sent her into a monastery, according to the usage of the time.　She took the vows in the convent of St. Sergius, at Moscow, under the name of Olga, and died there in 1622.

These singular amours, this fidelity to his engagements in the midst of

RUSSIAN WEDDING FEAST OF THE SEVENTEENTH CENTURY

(From the painting by C. Makovski)

inconstancy and even of debauchery, this boldness in attempting a desperate enterprise, this imperturbable coolness in maintaining an audacious imposture, this gracefulness in acting the part of a legitimate monarch, so many brilliant qualities united with puerile vanity and the most imprudent levity — such are the contrasts presented by the character of Dmitri, which are perhaps explicable by his extreme youth and his adventurer's education. Nothing, however, is more rare than a character all the parts of which are in perfect harmony. Contradiction is the characteristic of most men, and there are very few whose lives correspond to the projects which they have formed or to the hopes to which they have given rise. Who can say that the pleasure of exhibiting himself in all the splendour of his high fortune before the eyes of those who had witnessed his poverty had not the greatest share in the resolutions of Dmitri? Mniszek and Marina were probably the first persons whose esteem appeared precious to him. To obtain the approbation of a few Polish palatines, he risked his crown; but does not every man believe that the world's opinion is that of the little circle in which he is accustomed to move? [b]

The security of the pretender was, however, but seeming. Vasili Shuiski, whom Dmitri had pardoned, presently organised a plot for his destruction. The czar's extreme confidence was his ruin. One night the boyars assailed the Kremlin where no guard was kept. Demetrius was flung from a window and slaughtered in the courtyard of the palace. Basmanov, who had tried to defend him, was killed at his side. The corpse of Demetrius was taken up, a fool's mask was placed on the face, and the body exposed in the place of executions between a bagpipe and a flute. The father-in-law and the widow of Dmitri, the envoys of the Polish king and the Poles who had come to attend the imperial nuptials were spared but retained as prisoners by the boyars. The corpse of the " sorcerer " was burned; a cannon, turned in the direction of Poland, was charged with the ashes and scattered them to the winds (May, 1606). [f]

### VASILI IVANOVITCH SHUISKI (1606–1610 A.D.)

Immediately after the death of Demetrius, the boyars concerted measures for convoking deputies from all the towns and proceeding to the election of a new sovereign; but they were not allowed to accomplish their design. The throne had been but four days vacant when Shuiski directed his partisans to proclaim himself. They led him forth into the public place, named him czar by acclamation, and immediately escorted him to the cathedral. There, in order to ingratiate himself with his new subjects and make them forget the illegality of his election, he took a solemn oath not to punish anyone without the advice and consent of the boyars; not to visit the offences of the fathers on the children; and that he would never revenge himself in any way on those who had offended him in the time of Boris. Since Novgorod lost its privileges, this was the first time that a sovereign of Russia had pledged himself to any convention with his subjects; but Shuiski's oath was no guarantee for its fulfilment.

Having good reason to dread the resentment of the Polish nation, Shuiski sent Prince Volkonski on an embassy to them, to represent the late czar as an impostor, who had deluded both Poland and Russia; but the ambassador was not even listened to. Sigismund and his subjects were resolved to be revenged on the Russians, and to profit by the disturbances which they foresaw would soon break out among them. Shuiski was not liked by the Russian nobles, many of whom might have competed with him for the throne had the choice of the nation been free; and his conduct after his elevation augmented the number of his enemies. In spite of his oath he could not forget any of his old grudges; and he ventured to indulge them just enough to exasperate their objects without depriving them of the power of retaliation. Moscow was the only city in the empire on the allegiance of which he could rely; but even there the people had imbibed from their late excesses an alarming propensity to disorder and mutiny. To meet all the dangers thickening round him Shuiski had neither an army nor money; for Dmitri's profusions and the pillage of the Kremlin had exhausted the imperial treasury. His chief strength lay in his renown for orthodoxy, which insured him the favour of the clergy. The more to strengthen his interests in that direction, he made it his first business to depose and send to a monastery the heretic patriarch Ignatius, who had been appointed by Dmitri, and to nominate in his stead Hermogenes, bishop of Kasan, an aged prelate whose simplicity rendered him a useful tool in the hands of the crafty czar.

Rumours began to be rife in the provinces, and even in Moscow, that Dmitri was not dead. Many of those who had seen his mangled body exposed denied its identity, and believed that one of the czar's officers had been massacred instead of him. Four swift horses were missing from the imperial stables; and it was surmised that by means of them Dmitri had escaped in the midst of the tumult. Three strangers in Russian costume, but speaking Polish, crossed the Oka in a boat, and one of them gave the ferryman six ducats, saying, "You have ferried the czar; when he comes back to Moscow with a Polish army he will not forget this service." The same party held similar language in a German inn a little farther on. It was afterwards known that one of them was Prince Shakhovskoi, who, immediately upon the death of Dmitri, had, with singular promptitude, conceived the idea of finding a new impostor to personate the dead one.

To put an end to the alarming rumours, Shuiski sent to Uglitch for the body of the real czarevitch, that with the help of the patriarch he might make a saint of him. When the grave was opened the body of the young prince was found in a perfect state of preservation, with the fresh hue of life upon it, and still holding in his hands some nuts as miraculously preserved as itself. It is curious that Shuiski should have forgotten that nothing was said of these nuts in the report of the inquest at Uglitch signed by himself. That document only stated that at the moment of his death the czarevitch was amusing himself with sticking his knife in the ground. Notwithstanding this oversight, the act of canonisation was good policy; for if the czarevitch became an object of veneration for the people, if it was notorious that his body worked miracles on earth, and consequently that his soul was in heaven, then anyone assuming his name could be nothing but an impostor. The czar took pains to make known far and wide what prodigies were effected by the relics of the blessed martyr. But the credit of the new saint was of short duration: Shuiski himself damaged it by a gross blunder in permitting the pompous removal to the monastery of Troitsa of the remains of Boris Godunov, whom but a few days before he had named as the murderer of the sainted Dmitri. No doubt he hoped in this way to conciliate the partisans of a still powerful family; but his enemies immediately accused him of blasphemous wickedness, alleging that he had substituted the body of a newly murdered boy for the decomposed corpse of the real Dmitri.

The public retractations of the dowager czaritza obtained no more credit than the miracles imputed to her son. In a letter signed by her, and immediately published by Vasili, she declared that the impostor Grishka Otrepiev had threatened her with death to herself and all her family if she did not recognise him as her son. But who could believe in her sincerity after so many contradictory avowals and disavowals? Her declaration that she had been compelled by fear to yield to the threats of a man whose aversion to cruelty was notorious, suggested to everybody the idea that she acted at that moment under the coercion of threats and fear.

Civil war began. Prince Shakhovskoi had raised the inhabitants of Putivle, and in a few days assembled a great number of Cossacks and peasants, who routed the forces sent against them. The insurrection spread rapidly; but still the prince, twice miraculously saved, did not make his expected appearance. Instead of him there came from Poland a general with a commission bearing the imperial seal of Dmitri. This was an adventurer named Ivan Bolotnikov, originally a serf to Prince Teliatevski. He had been a prisoner among the Turks, and having escaped to Venice had probably acquired some military experience in the service of the republic. His commission was recognised at Putivle; he took the command of the insurgents, defeated Shuiski's forces in two engagements, and pursued them to within seven versts of the capital. But the inexplicable absence of the prince for whom they fought damped the ardour of Bolotnikov's men; for they could not believe that if Dmitri was alive he would delay to put himself at their head. The ataman of the Cossacks, too, was mortified at being supplanted in the command by an adventurer, and suffered himself to be corrupted by Shuiski. Deserted by a part of his army, Bolotnikov was defeated by Skopin Shuiski, the czar's nephew, and forced to shelter himself in the fortress of Kaluga.

It is probable that all this while Shakhovskoi and the Poles were looking about for a fit person to play the part of Dmitri; but it required time to find him, and to put him through training. In this conjuncture the false Peter Feodorovitch, who had made a brief appearance in the former reign, repaired to Putivle, and offered himself to Shakhovskoi and the people as regent in the absence of his uncle. The rebel cause stood in need of the prestige of a royal name, and the czarevitch Peter was eagerly welcomed. Presently, the czar having marched against him in person, the impostor and Shakhovskoi shut themselves up in the strongly fortified town of Tula, where they were joined by Bolotnikov. Vasili laid siege to the town with an army of a hundred thousand men; but the besieged, who had no mercy to expect if taken, fought more earnestly for their own lives than did Shuiski's soldiers for the rights of a master to whom they were but little attached. Seeing the light progress he made, the czar began to doubt the success of an enterprise to fail in which would be ruin.

While he was in this anxious state, an obscure ecclesiastic, named Kravkov, presented himself before the czar and his council, and undertook, if his directions were followed, to drown all the people of Tula. They laughed at him at first as an idle braggart, but he reiterated his assertion with such confidence that the czar at last desired him to explain his plan. Tula is situated in a valley, and the little river Upa flows through the town. Kravkov proposed to dam the stream below the town, and engaged to answer for it with his head if in a few hours after the execution of that work the whole town was not laid under water. All the millers in the army, men accustomed to such operations, were immediately put under his orders, and the rest of the soldiers were employed in carrying sacks of earth to the spot chosen for the dam. The water soon rose in the town, inundated the streets, and destroyed a great number of houses; but the garrison still fought for several months with unabated courage, though decimated by famine, and afterwards by a terrible epidemic. All the efforts both of the besiegers and the besieged were concentrated about the dam, the former labouring to raise and maintain it, the latter to break it down. The inhabitants of Tula were persuaded that magic must have had some share in raising so prodigious a work with such rapidity, and magic was not neglected among the means by which they sought to destroy it. A monk, who boasted his proficiency in that art, offered to effect the desired object for a reward of a hundred roubles. His terms being accepted by Bolotnikov, he stripped, plunged into the river, and disappeared. An hour afterwards, when everyone had given him up for dead, he rose to the surface, with his body covered with scratches. "I have just had to do," he said, "with the twelve thousand devils at work on Shuiski's dam. I have settled six thousand of them, but the other six thousand are the worst of all, and will not give in."

For a long time the inhabitants of Tula continued to fight against men and devils, encouraged by letters they received in Dmitri's name, with promises of succour which never came. Shakhovskoi, the chief instigator of the rebellion, was the first to propose a capitulation, and was thrust into a dungeon by the Cossacks. At last, when the besieged had eaten their horses, dogs, and all other carrion, and had not so much as an oxhide left to gnaw, Bolotnikov and Peter offered to capitulate on condition of amnesty for their heroic garrison. They asked nothing for themselves, but declared that unless their soldiers obtained honourable conditions they were resolved to die with arms in their hands, and even to eat each other, rather than surrender at discretion. Vasili accepted these terms, and the gates were opened to him (October, 1607). Bolotnikov advanced before the czar with undaunted mien, and presenting his sword, with the edge laid against his neck, offered himself as a victim, saying, "I have kept the oath I swore to him who, rightfully or wrongfully, calls himself Dmitri. Deserted by him, I am in thy power. Cut off my head if thou wilt; or if thou wilt spare my life, I will serve thee as I served him." Shuiski, who did not pique himself on generosity, sent Bolotnikov to Kargopol, where he soon after had him drowned. The false Peter Feodorovitch was hanged; but Shakhovskoi, the most guilty of the three, was more fortunate. The victor found him in chains when he entered Tula, and Shakhovskoi made a merit of his sufferings at the hands of the obstinate rebels whom he had urged to submit to their sovereign. He obtained his liberty; but the first use he made of it was to rekindle the flames of insurrection.

Before Shuiski had terminated the siege of Tula, and whilst the issue of his conflict with one pretender was still dubious, another, assuming the name of Dmitri, appeared in the frontier town of Starodub, where he was hailed with enthusiasm. Bolotnikov sent an officer to him from Tula, to acquaint him with the desperate condition of the town. This envoy was a Polish adventurer, named Zarucki, who had become one of the atamans of the Don Cossacks, had fought bravely for the first Demetrius, and been distinguished by his favour. Although the first glance must have satisfied Zarucki that the new pretender was an imposter, he affected without the least hesitation to recognise him as his former master. Another false witness of this identity was the Pane Miechaviecki, a Pole, who was well known for the eminent position he had held at the court of the first Demetrius, and who was now the secret instructor of his successor in what we may call the histrionic details belonging to his assumed character.

The pupil profited but badly by the lessons he received; for in everything but profusion he was the reverse of his prototype, and the least attentive observer could see that he was a coarse, ignorant, vulgar knave, qualified only by his impudence for the part he had undertaken.  The Cossacks were not such fastidious critics as to be shocked by his uncourtly manners; but the Poles, whilst treating him as a sovereign for their own ends, were by no means the dupes of his gross imposture.  Baer states that he was originally a schoolmaster of Sokol, in White Russia; but, according to the Polish writers, who had better opportunities of learning the truth, he was a Lithuanian Jew, named Michael Moltchanov.

The adherents of Dmitri, as we may continue to call him, increased so rapidly in numbers that he was able to defeat a detachment of Vasili's army sent against him from Tula, and to make himself master of the town of Kozelsk on the road to the capital.  When the fall of Tula had left the czar at liberty to act against him with all his forces, Dmitri retreated to Novgorod Seversk. There he was joined by unexpected reinforcements led by Rozynckil Sapieha, Tiszkievicz, Lissovski, and others, the flower of the Polish and Lithuanian chivalry.  Prince Adam Viszinoviecki, the patron of the first false Dmitri, came in person to the aid of his successor at the head of two thousand horse. The Don Cossacks brought in chains to him another schemer, who had tried to put himself at their head.  All that is known of the man is that he called himself Feodor Feodorovitch, and pretended to be the son of the czar Feodor. His more prosperous rival in imposture condemned him to death.

Dmitri's army, commanded by the veteran prince Roman Rozinski, defeated that of the czar with great havoc near Volkhov, on the 24th of April 1608.  All the vanquished who escaped the lances of the Poles and Cossacks fled in disorder to Moscow, and had the victors pressed their advantage, the capital would have fallen into their hands.  Possibly the Polish leaders were in secret unwilling to let their *protégé* triumph too soon or too completely, or to give up Moscow to pillage, which is always more profitable to the soldier than to the general; but, whatever was the reason, they halted at the village of Tushino, twelve versts from Moscow, which the impostor made his head-quarters, and there he held his court for seventeen months.

With a view to prevail on Sigismund to recall the Polish volunteers in Dmitri's service, Vasili resolved to liberate the ambassadors, the palatine of Sendomir and his daughter, and the other Poles whom he had kept in captivity since the massacre of Moscow.  With their liberty he bestowed on them indemnifications for their losses, and only exacted from them a pledge that they would not bear arms against Russia, or in any way favour the new pretender.  Thus, after having made sport of the most solemn oaths, Vasili expected to find in men, so deeply provoked, scruples of conscience which he had never known himself.  He sent Mniszek and his daughter away under charge of an escort; but they were intercepted by a detachment of Poles, and carried to Dmitri's camp.

They had been prepared for this event by a letter previously received by the palatine from his pretended son-in-law, which contained this remarkable phrase: "Come both of you to me, instead of going to hide yourselves in Poland from the world's scorn."  He could hardly have dropped a hint more adapted to move a woman of Marina's character.  Rather than go back to encounter ridicule at Sendomir, she was willing to share the bed of a bandit who might bestow a crown upon her.  It is said, however, that in their first interview with Dmitri neither she nor her father testified all the emotion befitting so touching an occasion, nor could quite conceal their surprise at the sight of a man not at all like him whose name he bore.  But after a few days the scene of meeting was played over again with more success and the whole camp was witness of Marina's demonstrations of tenderness for her husband.

In apology for her previous coldness it was said that, having so long believed her Dmitri was dead, she durst not yield to the delight of seeing him alive again until she had received the most certain proofs that it was not a delusion. This clumsy excuse was admitted; Marina's recognition of the impostor brought over to him numbers who had doubted till then; and, the news being soon spread abroad, almost all Russia declared for him, except Moscow, Novgorod, and Smolensk.

This was the culminating point of his fortunes: their decline was rapid. The mutual jealousy of the Polish commanders rose to such a pitch that it became necessary to divide the army; and Sapieha quitted the camp of Tushino, with thirty thousand men and sixty cannon, to lay siege to the famous monastery of the Trinity, near Moscow, which was at the same time a powerful fortress and the most revered sanctuary of Russian orthodoxy. The support which Shuiski received from the monks was worth more to him than an army; for besides large subsidies he derived from them a moral force which still kept many of his subjects true to their allegiance. The loss of such auxiliaries would have consummated his ruin; therefore the capture of the monastery was of extreme importance to the impostor. But in spite of the most strenuous efforts, continued for six weeks, Sapieha was unable to obtain the least advantage over a garrison whose courage was exalted by religious enthusiasm; and meanwhile the Poles had to sustain a harassing and murderous guerilla warfare, waged against them by the plundered peasants, whom they had made desperate. These partisan bands were about to be supported by a more formidable army, led by Skopin Skuiski and by James de la Gardie, who brought five thousand Swedish auxiliaries to Vasili's aid.

Early in 1609 these two generals began a brilliant campaign in the north; the Poles and the partisans of the impostor were beaten in several encounters, and in a few months the whole aspect of the war was changed. Finally, Sapieha himself was defeated in an obstinate engagement, forced ignominiously to raise the siege of the monastery, and shut himself up with the remnant of his force in Dmitrov. Skopin entered Moscow in triumph; but Vasili's jealousy kept him there inactive for two months until he died suddenly, in his twenty-fourth year. Vasili, to whose cause the young hero's death was fatal, was accused by public rumour of having effected it by poison.

For some months before this time there had been a new champion in the field, whose appearance was equally to be dreaded by Shuiski and Dmitri. About the end of September, 1609, Sigismund, king of Poland, laid siege to Smolensk, with an army of twelve thousand men, and immediately summoned to his standard the Poles who served under Dmitri. The greater part of them complied, and the impostor fled to Kaluga. In the spring of 1610 Russia presented a most deplorable spectacle, being devastated by three great armies, all opposed to one another. In the west, Sigismund was pressing the siege of Smolensk; in the south, Dmitri was in possession of Kaluga, Tula, and some other towns. Some of the Poles who had quitted the impostor's service had established themselves on the banks of the Ugra, in a fertile country, which had not yet experienced the sufferings of war; and there, under the command of their new leader, John Sapieha, they offered their services simultaneously to Sigismund and the false Dmitri, being ready to join whichever of them bid highest. Nor was this all: one of the Russian princes, Procope Liapunov, took advantage of the general confusion to raise a new banner. He proclaimed himself the defender of the faith, and, at the head of a considerable force, waged a war of extermination against the Poles and the Russians who recognised either Dmitri or Vasili. A chronicler applies to him the phrase which had served to characterise Attila — "No grass grew where his horse's hoof had been. And, as if all these armies were not enough for the desolation of the land, the Tatars of the Crimea had crossed the Oka, under pretence of succouring Vasili, their ally, but in reality to plunder the villages, and make multitudes of captives, whom they carried off into slavery.

Such was the condition of Russia at the moment of Skopin's death. Vasili still derived some hope from the division of his enemies, and turned his whole attention against the most formidable among them. He despatched to the relief of Smolensk an army of nearly sixty thousand men, consisting partly of foreign mercenaries, under James de la Gardie; but he gave the chief command to his brother, Dmitri Shuiski, who was neither liked nor respected by the soldiers. Chiefly in consequence of this fatal appointment the whole army was defeated at Klushino, by a force of only three thousand horse and two hundred infantry, led by the veteran Zolkiewski, and was forced to lay down its arms. But for the enormous blunders subsequently committed by Sigismund, the battle of Kiushino might have determined forever the preponderance of Poland in the north.

A WOMAN OF TSCHUTSKI

The defeat of Klushino was immediately followed by an insurrection at Moscow. Vasili Shuiski was deposed, and forced to become a monk; and being soon after delivered up to Sigismund, he ended his days in a Polish prison. The same event was equally disastrous to the false Dmitri. Deserted by Sapieha and his Poles, he lost all hope of ascending the throne of Moscow; he lived as a robber in Kaluga, at the head of his ferocious gangs of Cossacks and Tatars, until he was murdered by the latter in December, 1610, in revenge for the death of one of their countrymen whom he had drowned. Marina was far advanced in pregnancy when she lost her second husband. She was delivered of a son, who received the name of Ivan, and to whom the little court of Kaluga swore fealty. Zarucki declared himself the protector of the mother and the child, and put himself at the head of the still numerous remnant of the faction that remained obstinately attached to the name of Dmitri. But the cause was hopeless; for Zarucki was neither a general nor a statesman — his talents were those only of a bold leader of Cossack marauders.

Russia was without a sovereign, and the capital was in the hands of the Polish marshal. Zolkiewski used his advantages with wise moderation, and easily prevailed on the weary and afflicted Muscovites to resign themselves to the foreign yoke, and agree to offer the throne to Wladislaw, the son of Sigismund. One word from the latter's lips might have reversed the subsequent fortunes of Russia and Poland; but in his selfish vanity he preferred the appearance of power to its reality, and claimed the crown of the czars, not for his son but for himself. Philaretes, bishop of Rostov, and other ambassadors, were sent to him at his camp before Smolensk, to make known the resolution of the Russians in favour of Wladislaw. Sigismund insisted that they should at once put him in possession of Smolensk, which he had been besieging for a year; and, this being refused, he seized the ambassadors, and afterwards carried them away to Poland, where they remained nine years in captivity.

Zolkiewski, foreseeing the consequences of his master's folly, against which he had remonstrated in vain, retired from the government of Moscow, leaving Gonsiewski as his successor. The Polish troops seized the principal towns, proclaimed Sigismund, and observed none of that discretion by which the great marshal had won the confidence and esteem of the vanquished. National feeling awoke again among the Russians; eagerly responding to the call of their revered patriarch, Hermogenes, they took up arms in all parts of the empire, and war was renewed with more fury than ever.

Smolensk fell after an obstinate resistance of eighteen months; but at the moment of the last assault the explosion of a powder magazine set fire to the city, and Sigismund found himself master only of a heap of ruins. The Poles in Moscow, assailed by the Russians, secured themselves in the Kremlin, after burning down the greater part of the city, and massacreing a hundred thousand of the inhabitants. They were besieged by an immense levy from the provinces, consisting of three armies; but these seemed more disposed to fight with each other than to force the Poles in their intrenchments. One of them consisted chiefly of vagabonds escaped from the camp at Tushino, and was commanded by Prince Trubetskoi. Zarucki led another in the name of Marina's son; the third army, and the only one, perhaps, whose commander sincerely desired the independence of his country, was that of Prince Procope Liapunov; but that brave leader was assassinated, and the besiegers, disheartened by his death, immediately dispersed. About the same time the patriarch Hermogenes, the soul of the national insurrection, died in his prison in the Kremlin, to which he had been consigned by the Poles.

Anarchy was rampant in Russia; every town usurped the right to act in the name of the whole empire, and set up chiefs whom they deposed a few days afterwards. Kazan and Viatka proclaimed the son of Marina; Novgorod, rather than open its gates to the Poles, called in the Swedes, and tendered the crown to Charles Philip, second son of the reigning king of Sweden, and brother of Gustavus Adolphus. Another imposter assumed the name of Dmitri, and kept his state for awhile at Pskov; but being at last identified as one Isidore, a fugitive monk, he was hanged. When all seemed lost in irretrievable disorder, the country was saved by an obscure citizen of Nijni-Novgorod. He was a butcher, named Kozma Minin, distinguished by nothing but the possession of a sound head and a brave, honest unselfish heart. Roused by his words and his example, his fellow-citizens took up arms, and resolved to devote all their wealth to the last fraction to the maintenance of an army for the deliverance of their country. From Nijni-Novgorod the same spirit spread to other towns, and Prince Pojarski who had been lieutenant to the brave Liapunov, was soon able to take the field at the head of a considerable force, whilst Minin, whom the popular voice styled the elect of the whole Russian Empire, ably seconded him in an administrative capacity.

Pojarski drove the Poles before him from town to town; and having at length arrived under the walls of the Kremlin, in August, 1612, he sustained for three days a hot contest against Chodkiewicz, the successor of Gonsiewski, defeated him, and put him to flight. Part of the Polish troops, under the command of Colonel Nicholas Struss, returned to the citadel and defended it for some weeks longer. At the end of that time, being pressed by famine, they capitulated; and on the 22nd of October, 1612, the princes Pojarski and Dmitri Trubetzkoi entered together into that inclosure which is the heart of the country, and sacred in the eyes of all true Russians. The assistance of Sigismund came too late to arrest the flight of the Poles.

Upon the first successes obtained by Prince Pojarski the phantom of Dmitri, and all the subaltern pretenders, disappeared as if by magic. Zarucki, feeling that an irrisistible power was about to overwhelm him, was anxious only to secure himself a refuge. Carrying Marina and her son with him, he made ineffectual efforts to raise the Don Cossacks. After suffering a defeat near Voroneje, he reached the Volga, and took possession of Astrakhan, with the intention of fortifying himself there; but the generals of Michael Romanov, the newly elected czar, did not allow him time. Driven from that city, and pursued by superior forces, he was preparing to reach the eastern shore of the Caspian, when he was surprised, in the beginning of July, 1614, on the banks of the Iaik, and delivered up to the Muscovite generals, along with Marina and the son of the second Dmitri. They were immediately taken to Moscow, where Zarucki was impaled; Ivan, who was but three years old, was hanged; and Marina was shut up in prison, where she ended her days.

## ACCESSION OF THE HOUSE OF ROMANOV (1613 A.D.)

The deliverance of Moscow had alone been awaited in order to fill the vacant throne by a free election. This could not properly take place except in that revered sanctuary of the imperial power, the Kremlin, where the sovereigns were crowned at their accession, and where their ashes reposed after their death. Delivered now from all foreign influence, the boyars of the council, in November, 1612, despatched letters or mandates to every town in the empire, commanding the clergy, nobility, and citizens to send deputies immediately to Moscow, endowed with full power to meet in the national council (zemskii soveth), and proceed to the election of a new czar. At the same time, to invoke the blessing of God upon this important act, a fast of three days was commanded. These orders were received with great enthusiasm throughout the whole country: the fast was so rigorously observed, according to contemporory records, that no person took the least nourishment during that interval, and mothers even refused the breast to their infants.

The election day came: it was in Lent, in the year 1613. The debates were long and stormy. The princes Mstislavski and Pojarski, it appears, refused the crown; the election of Prince Dmitri Trubetskoi failed, and the other candidates were set aside for various reasons. After much hesitation the name of Michael Romanov was put forward; a young man sixteen years of age, personally unknown, but recommended by the virtues of his father, Philaretes, and in whose behalf the boyars had been canvassed by the patriarch Hermogenes, the holy martyr to the national cause. The Romanovs were connected through the female branch with this ancient dynasty. The ancestors of Michael had filled the highest offices in the state. He fulfilled, moreover, the required conditions. "There were but three surviving members in his family," says Strahlenberg; "he had not been implicated in the preceding troubles; his father was an ecclesiastic, and in consequence naturally more disposed to secure peace and union than to mix himself up in turbulent projects."

The name of the new candidate, supported by the metropolitan of Moscow,[1] was hailed with acclamation, and after some discussion he was elected. The unanimous voice of the assembly raised Michael Feodorovitch to the throne. Before he ascended he was required to swear to the following conditions: that he would protect religion; that he would pardon and forget all that had been done to his father; that he would make no new laws, nor alter the old, unless circumstances imperatively required it; and that, in important causes, he would decide nothing by himself, but that the existing laws and the usual forms of trial should remain in force; that he would not at his own pleasure make either war or peace with his neighbours; and that, to avoid all suits with individuals, he would resign his estates to his family, or incorporate them with the crown domains. Strahlenberg adds that Alexis, on his accession, swore to observe the same conditions.

These forms, however futile they may have been, are remarkable: not because they render sacred a right which stands in no need of them, but because they recall it to mind; and also because they prove that, even on the soil most favourable to despotism, a charter which should give absolute power to a monarch would appear such a gross absurdity that we know not that an instance of the kind ever existed.

Nothing could be more critical than the state of the empire at the moment when its destinies were confided to a youth of seventeen. Disorder and anarchy everywhere prevailed. Ustrialov gives us the following picture: "The strongholds on the frontier which should have served to defend his dominions were in the hands of external or internal enemies. The Swedes possessed Kexholm, Oresheck, Koporie, and even Novgorod. The Poles ruled in Smolensk, Dorogobuje, Putivle, and Tchernigov; the country around Pskov was in the power of Lisovski; Raisin, Kashira, and Tula struggled feebly against the Tatars of the Crimea and the Nogai; Sarutzki (Zarucki) was established in Astrakhan; Kazan was in revolt. At home bands of Cossacks from the Don, and the Zaparogians, and whole divisions of Poles and Tatars ravaged the villages and the convents that were still entire, when there were hopes of finding booty. The country was wasted, soldiers were dying of hunger, the land-tax was no longer collected, and not a kopeck was in the treasury. The state jewels, crowns of great price, sceptres, precious stones, vases — all had been plundered and carried into Poland.

"The young prince was surrounded by courtiers belonging to twenty different factions. There were to be found the friends of Godunov, the defenders of Shuiski, the companions of Wladislaw, and even partisans of the brigand of Tushino — in a word, men professing the most various opinions and aims, but all equally ambitious, and incapable of yielding the smallest point as regarded precedence. The lower class, irritated by ten years of misery, had become habituated to anarchy, and it was not without difficulty and resistance on their part that they were reduced to obedience." Such, then, was the situation of the country; but Michael found means to redeem it.

Notwithstanding the desperate state of his finances, the insubordination of his troops, the ill-will of the diets, and the confederations continually springing up against him, Sigismund did not abandon his attempts upon Russia; but the negotiations which ensued in consequence, upon various occasions, produced no result. Wladislaw, at the head of an army, once more crossed the

---

[1] There was no patriarch at that time.

frontiers, and appeared for the second time, in 1617, under the walls of Moscow, which he assaulted and whence he was repulsed.   Deceived in the expectation which the intelligence he kept up with various chiefs had induced him to form, harassed by his troops, who were clamorous for pay, he consented to renounce the title of czar, which he had up to that period assumed, and concluded, on the 1st of December, 1618, an armistice for fourteen years.   The Peace of Stolbovna, January 26th, 1617, had terminated the preceding year the war with Sweden, and was purchased by the surrender of Ingria, Karelia, and the whole country between Ingria and Novgorod; besides the formal renunciation of Livonia and Esthonia, and the payment of a sum of money.

The captivity of Philarete had now lasted nine years; from Warsaw he had been removed to the castle of Marienburg, and it was from that place, as it is asserted, that he found means to communicate with the council of the boyars, and use his influence in the election of the czar, never dreaming that it would fall upon his son.   The cessation of hostilities restored him to freedom.   He returned to Moscow on the 14th of June, 1619, and was immediately elevated to the patriarchal chair, which had remained vacant from the death of Hermogenes, in 1613.   His son made him co-regent, and the ukases of that date are all headed "Michael Feodorovitch, sovereign, czar, and grand prince of all the Russias, and his father Philarete, mighty lord and most holy patriarch of all the Russias, order," etc.   There exist, moreover, ukases issued in the sole name of the patriarch, thus called out of his usual sphere of action, and placed in one in which absolute power was granted him.   He took part in all political affairs; all foreign ambassadors were presented to him, as well as to the czar: and at those solemn audiences, as well as at table, he occupied the right of the sovereign.   He held his own court, composed of stolnicks and other officers; in a word, he shared with his son all the prerogatives of supreme power.   From this period dates the splendour of the patriarchate, which at a later epoch excited the jealousy of the czar Peter the Great, who was induced to suppress it in 1721.

Philarete always gave wise advice to his son, and the influence he exercised over him was always happily directed.   A general census, of which he originated the idea, produced great improvement in the revenue; but, perhaps without intending it, he contributed by this measure to give fixity to the system of bondage to the soil.   In the performance of his duty as head pastor, he directed all his efforts to re-establish a press at Moscow,[1] which had been abandoned during the troubles of the interregnum; and he had the satisfaction of seeing, after 1624, many copies of the Liturgy issue from it.[h]

### THE COSSACKS

In the year 1627 the Cossacks of the Don, in one of their periodical uprisings, conquered Azov, which they offered to the czar, but which he did not accept.   As we shall meet the Cossacks again from time to time, it is worth while to interrupt our main narrative to make inquiry as to the antecedents of this peculiar people.[a]

Soloviev gives the following definition of the term "cossacks": "At the end of the first half of the fifteenth century we encounter for the first time the name of Cossack, principally the Cossacks of Riazan.   Our ancestors understood by this name, in general, men without homes, celibates obliged to earn their bread by working for others.   In this way the name "cossack" took the

[1] Established in 1560.   The first book printed in Moscow, *The Evangelist*, appeared in the month of March, 1564.

meaning of day-labourer. They formed a class altogether opposed to land owners; that is, the villagers. The steppes, so agreeable to live on, not lacking fertility, watered by rivers filled with fish, attracted in these countries the more hardy, namely the Cossacks; the people who could not stay in villages, those who were pursued for some crime, fugitive serfs, united with each other; it is this group of individuals who formed the population of the frontiers and were known under the name of Cossacks. The Cossacks were therefore of great importance; being an enterprising people they were the first to lead the way to the great solitudes which they peopled. It was not difficult for a Russian to become a Cossack; in going to the steppes he did not enter a strange country, nor did he cease to be a Russian; there among the Cossacks he felt at home. The Cossacks who remained near the frontier recognised the right of the Russian government over them in all things, but obeyed it only when it would prove useful to them. They depended somewhat on the government, while those who lived far away were more independent." [i]

Polish authors have acquainted western Europe with the name and the fact of the existence of the Cossacks. This name (in Russian *kazak*) has passed into other languages, by the writings of the seventeenth century, with the Polish pronunciation. The etymology of this word long exercised the sagacity of northern savants. Some derive it from the Slavonic *koza* "goat" —the Cossacks, they argued, wandered about like goats. Others believe it comes from *kossa*, which signifies "tress of hair," "scythe," "body of land projecting into a river." Justifications are not wanting for these different acceptations, since (1) the Cossacks were formerly in the habit of wearing long braids; (2) they used scythes to make hay, as well as in battle; (3) their first colonies were on the river banks, which abounded in promontories. In these days, when etymological study has made such great progress, the word cossack is generally accepted as derived from the Turkish. In that language *cazak* signifies marauder, plunderer, soldier of fortune. Such were in effect the first Cossacks established on the banks of the Dnieper and its tributaries, between the Polish, the Tatar, and the Muscovite territories. Their customs greatly resembled those of the inhabitants on the Border, or Scottish frontier; and the name of the country where they first appeared, Ukrania (Pokraina) signifies border, frontier, in the Slavonic dialects.

The Cossacks have never formed a distinct nationality, but their manners and institutions separate them from the rest of the Russian people. The *Cossackry* — to translate by a single word all that the Russians understand by *Kazatchestvo* — is the species of society, government, political organisation which the Russian peasant understands by instinct, so to speak, to which he conforms most easily and which he probably regards as the best. The different fractions of the Cossacks were designated as armies according to the provinces which they occupied. There was the army of the Dnieper, the army of the Don, that of the Iaïk (Ural), etc. Each of these armies was divided into small camps or villages, called *stanitsas*. The ground round the stanitsa, the flocks which grazed on its meadows, formed the undivided property of the commune. At regular intervals equal partitions took place for cultivation; but each gathered the fruit of his own labour and could increase his share in the common fund by his private industry. Every man was a soldier and bound to take up arms at the word of the chief whom the public suffrage had designated. There was one of these for each expedition and he bore the name of "errant captain," *ataman kotchévoï*, which was distinct from the *ataman* or political chief for life of the whole army. This captain had under his orders an adjutant or lieutenant, *iéssaoul*, then centurions, commanders of fifties, and commanders of tens.  During peace the administration of each stanitsa belonged to the elders, *startchini;* but every resolution of any importance had to be submitted to a discussion in which all the men of the community could take part and vote.  The political or administrative assembly was called the circle, *kroug.*  There were no written laws, the circle being the living law, preserving and adding to the traditions.  It left, moreover, complete liberty to the individual, so long as this was not harmful to the community.  As to the foreigner, anything, or almost anything, was permitted.  Such institutions find fanatics amongst men in appearance the most rebellious against all discipline.  The filibusters at the end of the seventeenth century had similar ones.

We are ignorant of the period of the first organisation of the Cossacks; it appears, however, very probable that it is contemporary with the Tatar conquest.  The little republic of the Zapa-rogians in the islands and on the banks of the Dnieper seems to be the model on which the other Cossack governments were formed; for their dialect, the Little Russian, has left traces amongst the Cossacks most remote from Ukraine.  There is no doubt that the first soldiers who established themselves in the islands of the Dnieper were animated by patriotic and religious sentiments.  Their first exploits against the Tatars and Turks were a protest of the conquered Christians against their Mussulman oppressors.  In consequence of having fought for their faith they loved war for its own sake and pillage became the principal object of their expeditions.  In default of Tatars their Russian or Polish neighbours were mercilessly despoiled.

MICHAEL ROMANOV

Formerly the Cossacks had been recruited by volunteers arriving on the borders of the Dnieper — some from Great Russia, others from Lithuania or Poland.  The association spread.  It colonised the banks of the Don and there instituted the rule of the stanitsas and the circle.  The czars of Muscovy, while they sometimes suffered from the violence of the newcomers, beheld, with pleasure the formation on their frontiers of an army which fought for them, cost them nothing, and founded cities of soldiers in desolate steppes.

From the Don the Cossacks carried colonies along the Volga, to the Terek, to the Ural; they conquered Siberia.  In 1865 descendants of these same men were encamped at the mouths of the Amur and fringed the Chinese frontier.  The Don Cossacks, conquerors of a country subdued by the Tatars, submitted to Russia in 1549, but they enjoyed a real independence.  It is true that in war-time they furnished a body of troops to the czar; but war was their trade and a means of acquiring fortune.  They appointed their own atamans, governed themselves according to their own customs, and scarcely permitted the Moscow government to interfere at all in their affairs.  They even claimed the right to make war without command of the czar, and in spite of his injunctions devoted themselves to piracy on the Black Sea and even on the Caspian Sea.  In 1593, when Boris Godunov instituted serfdom in Russia, by a ukase which forbade the peasants to change their lord or their domicile, the Cossacks received immense additions to their numbers. All those who wished to live in freedom took refuge in a stanitsa, where they were sure of finding an asylum. In their ideas of honour, the atamans considered it their first duty to protect fugitives. Consequently the most usual subject of disputes between the government of Moscow and the hordes of the Don was the restoration of serfs. At times exacted by the czars, when they had no foreign enemy to fear, it was evaded by the atamans; at times it was in some sort forgotten, whenever the services of the Cossacks became necessary. Practically it was considered impossible to get back a serf once he had procured his adoption into a stanitsa.

There were always two parties among the Cossacks, which might be called the aristocratic party and the democratic faction, although there was no nobility amongst them. The old-established Cossacks, possessing a fortune acquired either by raids or industry, did not look with a friendly eye on the newcomers, who were strangers to the country. The first preached in the circle respect of treaties and obedience to the czar; the others, on the contrary, declared themselves in favour of every violent course, supported those bold spirits who were meditating some hazardous expedition, and troubled themselves little concerning the danger of compromising the privileges of the army of the Don by abusing them. The old Cossacks in contempt called the newcomers *gole* (nakedness, trash), and this name, like that of *gueux* in Flanders, had ended by being borne proudly by the opposite faction.

The class of poor Cossacks, which was unceasingly recruited from fugitives, hated the Russian government and obtained the sympathy of the serfs who dared not break their chain. The condition of the latter was deplorable; at a time when the life of a freeman was held of small account, a slave was less than a beast of burden and certainly more miserable. The savagery of manners, the harshness of the masters, was equalled only by the ferocity of the laws. One example will be enough to show what the legislation of this epoch was like. The serf was responsible for his master's debts. If the lord did not pay his creditors the serf was put in prison and daily beaten before the courts of justice until the debtor had paid or the creditors had abandoned their claims. In their wretchedness the serfs were witnesses of the liberty of the Cossacks, who spoke the same language as themselves and who had the same origin. We need not be astonished if, in their despair, they were disposed to accept as their liberators the Cossacks who came to pillage their masters. A slave rarely dares to conceive the idea of conquering his liberty; but he is always ready to aid the freeman who declares himself his protector. Thus it is to be noted that all the great insurrections of serfs which broke out in Russia were organised by Cossacks. The False Dmitri, Stenka Radzin, and Pugatchev furnish the proof of this.[b]

## LAST YEARS OF MICHAEL

The peace with Poland being only for a stated term of years, Michael endeavoured, before its expiration, to have his troops placed in such a condition by foreign officers that he might be able to reconquer the countries ceded to the Poles. Nay, on the death of Sigismund, ere the armistice had expired, he began the attempt to recover these territories, under the idle pretext that he had concluded a peace with Sigismund and not with his successor. But the Russian commander, Michael Schein, the very same who had valiantly defended Smolensk with a small number of troops against the Poles, now lay two whole years indolently before that town, with an army of fifty thousand

[1645 A.D.]

men and provided with good artillery, and at length retreated on capitulation, a retreat for which he and his friends were brought to answer with their heads. The Russian nation were so dissatisfied with this campaign, and the king of Sweden, whom Michael wanted to engage in an alliance with him against the Poles, showed so little inclination to comply, that the czar was fain to return to the former amicable relation with Poland. Peace was therefore again agreed on, and matters remained as they were before.

During his reign, which continued till 1645, Michael had employment enough in endeavouring to heal the wounds which the spirit of faction had inflicted on his country; to compose the disorders that had arisen; to restore the administration which had been so often disjointed and relaxed; to give new vigour and activity to the laws, disobeyed and inefficient during the general confusions; and to communicate fresh life to expiring commerce. It redounds greatly to his honour that he proceeded in all these respects with prudence and moderation, and brought the disorganised machine of government again into play. More than this, the restoration of the old order of things, was not to be expected of him. Much that he was unable to effect was accomplished by his son and successor, Alexis.

## ALEXIS (1645-1676 A.D.)

The administration, however, of the boyar Boris Morosov, to whom Michael at his death committed the education of Alexis, then in his sixteenth year, well-nigh destroyed the tranquillity which had so lately been restored. Morosov trod in the footsteps of Boris Godunov, put himself, as that favourite of the czar had done, into the highest posts, and thus acquired the most extensive authority in the state, turned out all that stood in his way, distributed offices and dignities as they fell vacant among his friends and creatures, and even became, like Boris, a near relation of the czar Alexis, by marrying a sister of the czaritza. Like his prototype, indeed, Morosov effected much good, particularly by making the army a main object of his concern, by strengthening the frontiers against Poland and Sweden, erecting manufactories for arms, taking a number of foreigners into pay for the better disciplining of the army, and diligently exercising the troops himself.

But these important services to the state could not render the people insensible to the numerous acts of injustice and oppression which were practised with impunity by the party protected by this minion of the czar. The most flagrant enormities were committed, more particularly in the administration of justice. The sentence of the judge was warped to either side by presents; witnesses were to be bought; several of the magistrates, however incredible it may seem, kept a number of scoundrels in readiness to corroborate or to oppugn, for a sum of money, whatever they were required to confirm or to deny. Such profligates were particularly employed in order to get rich persons into custody on charges of any species of delinquency sworn against them by false witnesses, to condemn them to death, and then to seize upon their property, as the accumulation of wealth seemed to be the general object of all men in office. From the same corrupt fountain flowed a multitude of monopolies and excessive taxes on the prime necessaries of life. The consequence of all this was the oppression of the people by privileged extortioners and murmurs against injustice and the exorbitance of imposts. In addition to this, those grandees who had now the reins of government in their hands assumed a haughty, austere behaviour towards the subjects, whereas

Michael and his father had been friendly and indulgent, and their gentleness communicated itself to all who at that time took part in the administration.

From these several causes arose discontents in the nation; such great men as were neglected and disappointed contributed what they could to fan these discontents, and to bring them to overt act. Moscow, the seat of the principal magistrate, who, himself in the highest degree unjust, connived at the iniquities of his subordinate judges, was the place where the people first applied for redress. They began by presenting petitions to the czar, implored the removal of these disorders, and exposed to him in plain terms the abuses committed by the favourite and his adherents. But these petitions were of no avail, as none of the courtiers would venture to put them into the hand of the czar, for fear of Morosov's long arm. The populace therefore, once stopped the czar, as he was returning from church to his palace, calling aloud for righteous judges. Alexis promised them to make strict inquiry into their grievances, and to inflict punishment on the guilty; the people, however, had not patience to wait this tardy process, but proceeded to plunder the houses of such of the great as were most obnoxious to them. At length they were pacified only on condition that the authors of their oppressions should be brought to condign punishment. Not, however, till they had killed the principal magistrate, and other obnoxious persons, and forced from the czar the abolition of some of the new taxes and the death of another nefarious judge, could they be induced to spare the life of Morosov, though the czar himself entreated for him with tears. Thenceforth Morosov ceased to be the sole adviser of his sovereign, though he continued to enjoy his favour and affection.

TATAR GIRL OF THE TELEUT TRIBE

Some time after these events, disturbances not less violent occurred in Pleskov and Novgorod, and were not quelled until much mischief had been done. The pacification of Novgorod was mainly due to the wisdom and intrepidity of the celebrated Nicon, who was afterwards patriarch.

While the nation was in this restless and angry mood, another false Dmitri thought to avail himself of an opportunity apparently so favourable to gather a party. He was the son of a draper in the Ukraine, and was prompted to his imposture by a Polish nobleman, named Danilovski. One day, when the young man was bathing, marks were observed on his back which were thought to resemble letters of some unknown tongue. Danilovski, hearing of this freak of nature, determined to build a plot upon it. He sent for the young man, and had the marks examined by a Greek pope whom he had suborned. The pope cried out, "A miracle!" and declared that the letters were Russian, and formed distinctly these words: Dmitri, son of the czar Dmitri. The public murder of Marina's infant son was notorious; but that difficulty was met by the common device of an alleged change of children, and the Poles were invited to lend their aid to the true prince thus miraculously identified. They were willing enough to do so; but the trick was too stale to impose on the Russians. The impostor found no adherents among them; and after a wretched life of vagrancy and crime, he fell into the hands of Alexis, and was quartered alive.

Alexis soon had an opportunity to repay in a more substantial manner the ill will borne to him by the Poles, who had further offended him by rejecting him as a candidate for their throne, and electing John Casimir. The cruel oppressions exercised by the Poles upon the Cossacks of the Ukraine had roused the latter to revolt, and a furious war ensued, in which the enraged Cossacks avenged their wrongs in the most ruthless and indiscriminate manner. At last, after many vicissitudes, being deserted by their Tatar allies, the Cossacks appealed for aid to Alexis, offering to acknowledge him as their suzerain. With such auxiliaries the czar could now renew with better prospects the attempt made by his father to recover the territories wrested from Russia by her inveterate foe. He declared war against Poland; his conquests were rapid and numerous, and would probably have terminated in the complete subjugation of Poland, had he not been compelled to pause before the march of a still more successful invader of that country, Charles Gustavus, king of Sweden.

Incensed at seeing his prey thus snatched from him when he had nearly hunted it down, Alexis fell upon the king of Sweden's own dominions during his absence; but from this enterprise he reaped neither advantage nor credit; and he was glad to conclude, in 1658, a three years' truce with Sweden, and subsequently a peace, which was an exact renewal of the Treaty of Stolbova in 1617. The war in Poland ended more honourably for Russia. An armistice for thirteen years, agreed upon at Andnissov, in Lithuania, and afterwards prolonged from time to time, was the forerunner of a complete pacification, which was brought to effect in 1686, and restored to the empire Smolensk, Severia, Tchernigov, and Kiev, that primeval principality of the Russian sovereigns. The king of Poland likewise relinquished to the czar the supremacy he had till then asserted over the Cossacks of the Ukraine.

Russia had as much need as Poland of repose; for the empire was suffering under an accumulation of evils — an exhausted treasury, commercial distress, pestilence and famine, all aggravated by the unwise means adopted to relieve them. To supply the place of the silver money, which had disappeared, copper of the same nominal value was coined and put in circulation. At first these tokens were received with confidence, and no inconvenience was experienced; but ere long the court itself destroyed that confidence by its audacious efforts to secure to itself all the sterling money, and leave only the new coin for the use of commerce. The cupidity displayed in transactions of this kind, especially by Ilia Miloslavski, the czar's father-in-law, taught the public to dislike the copper coinage; it became immensely depreciated, and extreme general distress ensued. A rebellion broke out in consequence in Moscow (1662), and though it was speedily put down it was punished in the most atrocious manner in the persons of thousands of wretches whose misery had driven them to crime; whilst the authors of their woe escaped with impunity. The prisoners were hanged by hundreds, tortured, burned, mutilated, or thrown by night, with their hands bound, into the river. The number who suffered death in consequence of this arbitrary alteration of the currency was estimated at more than seven thousand; the tortured and maimed, at upwards of fifteen thousand.

The conduct of the Don Cossacks was soon such as to make it questionable whether the acquisition of these new subjects was not rather a loss than a gain to the empire. At the end of the campaign of 1665 the Cossacks were refused permission to disband as usual and to return to their homes. They mutinied; and several of them were punished with death. Among those who were executed was an officer, whose brother, Stenka Radzin, had no difficulty in rousing his countrymen to revenge this violation of their privileges, and at the same time to gratify their insatiable appetite for havoc and plunder.

He began his depredations on the Volga by seizing a fleet of boats belonging to the czar, which was on its way to Astrakhan, massacring part of the crews, and pressing all the rest into his service. Having devastated the whole country of the Volga, he descended into the Caspian, and having swept its shores, returned to the Volga laden with booty. For three years this flagitious ruffian continued his murderous career, repeatedly defeating the forces sent against him. At last, having lost a great number of men in his piratical incursions into Persia, he was hemmed in by the troops of the governor of Astrakhan, and forced to sue for pardon. The imperial commander thought it more prudent to accept Radzin's voluntary submission than to risk an engagement with desperate wretches whose numbers were still formidable. Radzin was taken to Astrakhan, and the voyevod went to Moscow, to learn the czar's pleasure respecting him. Alexis honourably confirmed the promise made by his general in his name, and accepted Radzin's oath of allegiance; but instead of dispersing the pardoned rebels over regions where they would have been useful to the empire, he had the imprudence to send them all back to the country of the Don, without despoiling them of their ill-gotten wealth, or taking any other security for their good behaviour.

The brigand was soon at his old work again on the Volga, murdering and torturing with more wanton ferocity than ever. To give to his enormities the colour of a war on behalf of an oppressed class, he proclaimed himself the enemy of the nobles and the restorer of the liberty of the people. As many of the Russians still adhered to the patriarch Nicon, who had been deposed and sent to a monastery, he spread it abroad that Nicon was with him; that the czar's second son (who had died at Moscow, January 16th, 1670) was not dead, but had put himself under his protection; and that he had even been requested by the czar himself to come to Moscow, and rid him of those unpatriotic grandees by whom he was unhappily surrounded.

These artifices, together with the unlimited license to plunder which Radzin granted to everyone who joined his standard, operated so strongly that the rebel found himself, at length, at the head of two hundred thousand men. The czar's soldiers murdered their officers, and went over to him; Astrakhan betrayed its governor, and received him; he was master of the whole country of the lower Volga; and on the upper course of the river, from Nijni-Novgorod to Kazan, the peasants rose to a man and murdered their lords. Had Stenka Radzin been anything better than a vulgar robber and cut-throat, he might have revolutionised Russia; but he was utterly without the qualities most requisite for success in such an enterprise. Disasters overtook him in the autumn of 1670: a division of his army was cut to pieces; twelve thousand of his followers were gibbeted on the highroad, and he himself was taken in the beginning of the following year, carried to Moscow, and executed.

The Turks had by this time made war on Poland, and Alexis was bound by the Treaty of Andnissov, as well as by regard for the safety of his own dominions, to support the latter power. In 1671 the Turks made themselves masters of the important town of Kaminitz, and the Cossacks of the Ukraine, ever averse to subjection, could not tell whether they belonged to Turkey,

THE ANSWER OF ZAPOROGIAN COSSACKS TO SULTAN MUHAMMED IV

(From the painting by Elias Repin)

Poland, or Russia. Sultan Muhammed IV, who had subdued and lately imposed a tribute on the Poles, insisted, with all the insolence of an Ottoman and of a conqueror, that the czar should evacute his several possessions in the Ukraine, but received as haughty a denial. The sultan in his letter treated the sovereign of the Russias only as a Christian *gospodin* (hospodar), and entitled himself Most Glorious Majesty, King of the World. The czar made answer that he was above submitting to a Mohammedan dog, but that his sabre was as good as the grand seignior's scimitar.

Alexis sent ambassadors to the pope, and to almost all the great sovereigns in Europe, except France, which was allied to the Turks, in order to establish a league against the Porte. His ambassadors had no other success at Rome than not being obliged to kiss the pope's toe; everywhere else they met with nothing but good wishes, the Christian princes being generally prevented by their quarrels and jarring interests from uniting against the common enemy of their religion. Alexis did not live to see the termination of the war with Turkey. His death happened in 1676, in his forty-eighth year, after a reign of thirty-one years.

### FEODOR (1676–1682 A.D)

Alexis was succeeded by his eldest son, Feodor, a youth in his nineteenth year, and of very feeble temperament. The most pressing task that devolved on him was the prosecution of the war with Turkey, which, as far as Russia was interested, had regard chiefly to the question whether the country of the Zaparogian Cossacks should be under the sovereignty of the czar or of the sultan. The contest was terminated, three years after Feodor's accession, by a treaty which established his right over the disputed territory. Only one other memorable event distinguished his brief reign.

Nothing could equal the care with which the noble families kept the books of their pedigrees, in which were set down not only every one of their ancestors but also the posts and offices which each had held at court, in the army, or in the civil department. Had these genealogies and registers of descent been confined to the purpose of determining the ancestry and relationship of families no objection could be alleged against them. But these books of record were carried to the most absurd abuse, attended with a host of pernicious consequences. If a nobleman were appointed to a post in the army, or at court, or to some civil station, and it appeared that the person to whom he was now subordinate numbered fewer ancestors than he, it was with the utmost difficulty that he could be brought to accept of the office to which he was called. Nay, this folly was carried to still greater lengths: a man would even refuse to take upon him an employ, if thereby he would be subordinate to one whose ancestors had formerly stood in that position towards his own.

It is easy to imagine that a prejudice of this kind must have been productive of the most disagreeable effects, and that discontents, murmurs at slights and trifling neglects, disputes, quarrels, and disorders in the service must have been its natural attendants. It was, therefore, become indispensably necessary that a particular office should be instituted at court in which exact copies of the genealogical tables and service-registers of the noble families were deposited; and this office was incessantly employed in settling the numberless disputes that arose from this inveterate prejudice. Feodor, observing the pernicious effects of this fond conceit — that the father's capacity must necessarily devolve on the son, and that consequently he ought to inherit his posts — wished to put a stop to it; and with the advice of his sagacious minister, Prince Vasili Galitzin, fell upon the following method. He caused it to be proclaimed that all the families should deliver into court faithful copies of their service-rolls, in order that they might be cleared of a number of errors that had crept into them. This delivery being made, he convoked the great men and the superior clergy before him. In the midst of these heads of the nobles, the patriarch concluded an animated harangue by inveighing against their prerogatives. "They are," said he, "a bitter source of every kind of evil; they render abortive the most useful enterprises, in like manner as the tares stifle the good grain; they have introduced, even into the heart of families, dissensions, confusion, and hatred; but the pontiff comprehends the grand design of his czar. God alone can have inspired it!"

At these words, and by anticipation, all the grandees blindly hastened to express their approval; and, suddenly, Feodor, whom this generous unanimity seemed to enrapture, arose and proclaimed, in a simulated burst of holy enthusiasm, the abolition of all their hereditary pretensions — "To extinguish even the recollection of them," said he, "let all the papers relative to those titles be instantly consumed!" And as the fire was ready, he ordered them to be thrown into the flames before the dismayed eyes of the nobles, who strove to conceal their anguish by dastardly acclamations. By way of conclusion to this singular ceremony, the patriarch pronounced an anathema against everyone who should presume to contravene this ordinance of the czar; and the justice of the sentence was ratified by the assembly in a general shout of "Amen!" It was by no means Feodor's intention to efface nobility; and, accordingly, he ordered new books to be made, in which the noble families were inscribed; but thus was abolished that extremly pernicious custom which made it a disgrace to be under the orders of another if his ancestry did not reach so high, or even — in case of equal pedigree — if a forefather of the commander had once been subordinate in the service to the progenitor of him who was now to acknowledge him for his superior. Feodor died in February, 1682, after a reign of five years and a half, leaving no issue.[h]

## CHAPTER VI

## PETER THE GREAT

### [1684–1725 A.D.]

> When, towards the beginning of the eighteenth century, Peter the Great laid the foundation of Petersburg or rather of his empire, no one predicted success. Had anyone at that time imagined that a sovereign of Russia could send victorious fleets to the Dardanelles, subjugate the Crimea, drive out the Turks from four great provinces, dominate the Black Sea, establish the most brilliant court of Europe, and make all the arts flourish in the midst of war — if anyone had said that he would merely have been taken for a visionary.—VOLTAIRE.[b]

THE question of the succession was now again thrown open to discussion, and the family feuds were revived. Ivan, the next in succession, was nearly blind, and, according to some historians, nearly dumb, and inferior in mind and body; and shortly before his death Feodor expressed his wish that his half-brother, Peter, then between nine and ten years of age, should be nominated to the throne; a nomination of which Ivan had just sense enough to approve. The imbecility of Ivan was so great that, had it not been for the influence of the family to which he belonged, and the bold and ambitious spirit of his sister Sophia, he must have been set aside at once, and Peter without further difficulty raised to the sovereignty. The Miloflavskoi, however, were resolved to preserve the right of succession in their own blood; and Sophia, a princess of singular beauty and high mental endowments, in the meridian of youth and possessed of indomitable courage, set the example of contesting the throne, first in the name of her idiot brother and next in her own name: for when her plans were ripe she did not scruple to declare that she aspired to the sceptre in the default of the rightful heir. But as all her machinations were carefully conducted with a colour of justice on behalf of Ivan, she escaped from the charge of interested motives, which, in the early part of the plot, would have defeated her grand object.

While Sophia was employed in devising her plans, the Narishkins urged with unabating activity the claims of Peter. Friends arose in different quarters for both parties, and the city was thrown into consternation. But the Miloflavskoi had the advantage of possession: the keys of power were in their hands: the officers of the state were in their immediate confidence, and the bands of the strelitz, the janissaries of Russia, were under their control. Sophia, availing herself of these fortunate circumstances, pleaded with her supplicating beauty in the name of her brother; besought the strelitz, by arts of fascination which were irresistible, to make common cause with her; and where her eyes failed to impress their sluggard hearts, she was bountiful in money and promises. A body so corrupt and slavish as the strelitz was easily won by bribes to any offices of depredation, and they accordingly declared for the beautiful and prodigal Sophia.

The accession of fourteen thousand soldiers to her side — men who were ready at any moment to deluge the capital in blood — determined the scales at once. It was necessary in the first instance to exterminate the Narishkins, the formidable supporters of Peter; and next, if it could be accomplished with safety, to make away with the life of the prince. A rumour was accordingly disseminated that the Narishkins had compassed the death of Feodor, in order to make room for the young Peter; that they had poisoned him through the agency of foreign physicians; and that they contemplated a similar act of treachery towards Ivan. The zeal of the Narishkins seemed to justify these charges; and the populace, who were universally in favour of the direct lineal succession, were brought to believe them; particularly as Galitzin, the favourite minister of Feodor, was the chief counsellor and friend of Sophia. Affairs were now ripe for revolt. The chiefs of the strelitz, having previously concerted their plans, broke out into open violence; and for three days in succession this band of legalised plunderers committed the most extravagant excesses in the streets of Moscow, secretly abetted by the encouraging patronage of Sophia. In their fury they murdered all those officers of the state whom they suspected to be inimical to the views of the princess; and bursting into the palace of the czars demanded the lives of the Narishkins. Two brothers of Natalia, the widow of Alexis, were sacrificed on the spot, and sixty of her immediate kindred were shortly after put to death in the most cruel manner.

The czarina herself was forced to flee for safety from the capital, accompanied, providentially for the destiny of Russia, by the young prince Peter. For sixty versts she fled in consternation, carrying the boy, it is reported, in her arms: but the ferocious strelitz had tracked her footsteps, and followed close upon her path. Her strength at last began to fail: her pursuers were rapidly gaining on her; she could hear the sound of their yells, and the tramp of their approaching feet: her heart trembled at the horrors of her situation, and in despair she rushed into the convent of the Trinity to seek for a last shelter in the sanctuary. The strelitz, uttering cries of savage triumph, followed on the moment: the despairing mother had just time to gain the foot of the altar, and place the child upon it, when two of the murderous band came up. One of them seized the prince, and, raising his sword, prepared to sever the head from the body, when a noise of approaching horsemen was heard without: the ruffian hesitated — his fellow murderers at the distant part of the church were struck with terror — dismayed by the apprehension of some sudden change in the fortune of the day, he abandoned his grasp of the prince and fled, and Peter the Great was preserved to Russia.

The immediate result of those violent efforts of the strelitz was the declaration of the sovereignty in the name of Ivan. That prince, however, trembled at the prospect of incurring the responsibility of a trust to which he felt himself to be unequal, and entreated his counsellors to permit his half-brother Peter to be associated with him in the government. This request, which was considered on all sides reasonable enough, could not be refused without increasing the difficulties of Sophia's party, and rendering such further measures necessary as might probably betray her motives too soon. It was therefore sanctioned by the nobles; and on the 6th of May, 1681, the coronation of Ivan and Peter were celebrated in due form; Sophia being nominated regent, on account of the imbecility of the one and the youth of the other. Thus far Sophia had carried her purpose. She was now in possession of the power to which her ambition tempted her to aspire; but she panted to have that power formally assigned and publicly acknowledged. In order the more effectually to exclude Peter from any future lien upon the throne, she brought about a marriage between Ivan and a young Soltikov; trusting to the issue for an insurmountable obstacle in the path of the prince, whose dawning genius, even at that early age, she appeared to dread.c

### THE CHILDHOOD AND YOUTH OF PETER

During Sophia's government Peter continued to reside with his mother in the village of Preobrazhenski. His education was entirely neglected; his teacher, Nikita Zotov, was taken away from him and not replaced by another; he spent his time in play, surrounded by companions of his own age and without any intelligent occupation: such an existence would certainly have spoiled and maimed a less gifted nature. Upon Peter it only had the effect, as he himself afterwards recognised, of making him feel in later years the want of that knowledge which is indispensable for a sound education. By reason of this neglect Peter had to study much when he reached maturity; besides this, the manner in which his boyhood was spent deprived him of that training of the character in intercourse with other people which is the mark of an educated man. From his youth Peter adopted the rough habits of those who surrounded him, an extreme want of self-restraint, and hideous debauchery.

But his unusually gifted nature could not be crushed by this absence of all intellectual interests. Peter had no early instruction, but the love of knowledge inherent in him could not be destroyed. He himself afterwards communicated the circumstances which directed him into the paths he elected to follow. When he was fourteen years of age, he heard from Prince Iakov Dolgoruki that he had possessed an instrument " by means of which it was possible to measure distances or extension without being on the spot." The young czar wished to see the instrument, but Dolgoruki replied that it had been stolen; so Peter commissioned the prince, who had gone to France as ambassador, to purchase there for him such an instrument. In 1688 Dolgoruki brought from France an astrolabe and case of mathematical instruments, but there was no one amongst the czar's entourage who had any understanding of what they were for. Peter applied to a German doctor, but neither did he know how to use the instruments; finally he found a Dutchman, Franz Timmerman, who explained to him the significance of the objects. The czar began to study arithmetic, geometry, and the science of fortification with him. The teacher was not a great authority in these matters, but he knew sufficient to give Peter indications, and the talented pupil worked out everything himself; but his education had been neglected to such an extent that when he was learning the four rules of arithmetic, at the age of sixteen, he could not write a single line correctly and did not even know how to divide one word from the other, joining two or three together with continual mistakes and omissions.

Some time later Peter was in the village of Izmailov, and strolling through the storehouses, he looked over a lot of old things that had belonged to the cousin of the czar Michael Feodorovitch — Nikita Ivanovitch Romanov, who had been distinguished in his time for his remarkable love of knowledge. Here he found a foreign-built vessel and questioned Franz Timmerman about it; the latter could tell him only that it was an English boat, which had the superiority over Russian boats as being able to sail not only with the wind but also against it. Peter inquired whether there was anyone who could mend the boat and show him how to sail it. Timmerman replied that there was and found for Peter the Dutchman, Christian Brandt (Karstein Brandt, as Peter called him). The czar Alexis Michailovitch had thought of building a ship and launching it at Astrakhan, and had therefore sent for shipwrights from Holland; but the ship that had been built and launched at Astrakhan was destroyed by Stenka Radzin, the shipwrights were dispersed, and one of them, the ship's carpenter, Karstein Brandt, lived in Moscow where he gained a living by doing carpenter's work.

PETER THE GREAT

(1672–1725)

By order of the czar Brandt mended the boat, put in a mast and sail, and in Peter's presence manœuvred it on the river Iauza. Peter was astonished at such art and himself repeated the experiment several times with Brandt, but not always successfully; it was difficult to turn the boat, which stuck to the shore because the channel was too narrow. Peter then ordered the boat to be taken to a pond in the village of Izmailov, but there also navigation was difficult. Then Peter learned that the lake near Pereiaslavl would be suitable for his purpose; it was thirty versts in circumference and had a depth of six sazhen.[1] Peter asked his mother's leave to go on a pilgrimage to the Troitsa monastery, came to Pereiaslavl, and examined the lake, which greatly pleased him. On his return to Moscow he entreated his mother to let him go again to Pereiaslavl in order to take the boat there. The czaritza could not refuse

[1] A verst is 3500 English feet and a sazhen 7 feet.

her beloved son, although she was much against such a project out of fear for his life. Together with Brandt, Peter built a wharf at the mouth of the river Troubezh, which falls into the lake of Pereiaslavl and thus he laid the foundation of his ship building.

At that period Peter's diversions with his companions began to lose their playful character. He enrolled amongst them volunteers of every condition and in 1687 he formed with them two regular regiments, called by the name of the two royal villages near Moscow — the Preobrazhenski and the Semenovski. Sophia and her partisans endeavoured to represent these diversions as foolish extravagances; Natalia Kirillovna, the mother of Peter, did not herself see anything more in them than the amusements of a spirited, impetuous youth, and thought to steady him by marriage. She found for him a bride in the person of Eudoxia Lapoukhin, a beautiful young girl; her father, an *okolnitchi*, or courtier of the second rank, called Sarion, had his name changed to Theodore, and the marriage took place on the 27th of January, 1689. Peter had no attachment or love for his wife and only married to please his mother; in fact, he married as the majority of men married at that period. His mother hoped that when the young man was married he would begin to lead the life that was considered fitting for exalted personages. But soon after the marriage, as soon as the ice began to break up in the rivers, Peter galloped away to Pereiaslavl and there occupied himself with the building of ships. His mother wished to draw him away and demanded his return to Moscow under the pretext of a requiem service for the czar Theodore: "You were pleased to summon me to Moscow," wrote the czar to his mother, "and I was ready to come, but verily there is business on hand." His mother insisted that he should come to the capital; Peter obeyed and came to Moscow, but after a month he was again back at the Pereiaslavl lake. He loved his mother and in his letters shared with her the satisfaction he experienced in the success of his work. "Thanks to your prayers," he wrote, "all is well, and the ships are a great success." But the czaritza Natalia did not understand her son's passion, and moreover feared Sophia's inimical designs; therefore she called him again to Moscow. His young wife also wearied for his presence and wrote to him, calling him "her joy, her light, her darling," and begging him either to come back or let her come to him. Peter, recalled by his mother's persistent demands, unwillingly returned that summer to Moscow.[d]

### PETER ASSERTS CONTROL

It is alleged, with what truth we know not, that at this period Sophia and her favourite, Prince Galitzin, engaged the new chief of the Strelitz to sacrifice the young czar to their ambition. It appears at least that six hundred of those soldiers were to seize on that prince's person, if not to murder him. Peter was once more obliged to take refuge in the monastery of the Trinity, the usual sanctuary of the court when menaced by the mutinous soldiery. There he convoked the boyars of his party, assembled a body of forces, treated with the captains of the strelitz, and sent for some Germans who had been long settled in Moscow, and were all attached to his person, from his already showing a regard to foreigners. Sophia protested her abhorrence of the plot, and sent the patriarch to her brother to assure him of her innocence; but he abandoned her cause on being shown proof that he himself was among those who had been marked out for assassination.

Peter's cause prevailed. All the conspirators were punished with great severity; the leaders were beheaded, others were knouted, or had their tongues cut out, and were sent into exile. Prince Galitzin escaped with his life, by the intercession of a relative, who was a favourite of the czar Peter, but he forfeited all his property, which was immense, and was banished to the neighbourhood of Archangel.

The scene concluded with shutting up the Princess Sophia in a convent near Moscow, where she remained in confinement until her death, which did not happen until fifteen years afterwards. From that period Peter was real sovereign. His brother Ivan had no other share in the government than that of lending his name to the public acts. He led a retired life, and died in 1696.

Nature had given Peter a colossal vigour of body and mind, capable of all extremes of good and evil. It is impossible to review his whole history without mingled feelings of admiration, horror, and disgust. That he was

Sophie Alexievna

(1658-1704)

not altogether a monster of wickedness was not the fault of Sophia and her minister, whose deliberate purpose it was to destroy in him every germ of good, that he might become odious and insupportable to the nation. They succeeded only in impairing the health, corrupting the morals, and hardening the heart of the youthful czar; it was no more in their power to deprive him of his lofty nature than to have given it to him. General Menesius, a learned Scotchman, to whom Alexis had intrusted his education, refused to betray him, and was, therefore, driven from his charge. The first impressions on the mind of Peter were allowed to be received from coarse and sordid amusements, and from foreigners, who were repulsed by the jealousy of the boyars, hated by the superstition of the people, and despised by the general ignorance. Thus it was hoped that he would at last be driven by public execration to quit the palace for a monk's cell; but the very means which were taken to ensure his disgrace served to lay the foundations of his greatness and glory.

Kept at a distance from the throne, Peter escaped the influence of that atmosphere of effeminacy and flattery by which it is environed; the hatred with which he was inspired against the destroyers of his family increased the energy of his character. He knew that he must conquer his place upon the throne, which was held by an able and ambitious sister, and encircled by a barbarous soldiery; thenceforth, his childhood had that which ripened age too often wants, it had an aim in view, of which his genius, already bold and persevering, had a thorough comprehension. Surrounded by adventurers of daring spirit, who had come from afar to try their fortune, his powers were rapidly unfolded. One of them, Lefort, who doubtless perceived in this young barbarian the traces of civilisation, which had perhaps been left there by his first tutor, gave him an idea of the sciences and arts of Europe, and particularly of the military art.

MILITARY REFORMS

Lefort, in whom Peter placed his whole confidence, did not understand much of the military service, neither was he a man of literature, having applied himself deeply to no one particular art or science; but he had seen a great deal, and was capable of forming a right judgment of what he saw. Like the czar, he was indebted for everything to his own genius: besides, he understood the German and Dutch languages, which Peter was learning at that time, in hopes that both those nations would facilitate his designs. Finding himself agreeable to Peter, Lefort attached himself to that prince's service: by administering to his pleasures he became his favourite, and comfirmed this intimacy by his abilities. The czar intrusted him with the most dangerous design a Russian sovereign could then possibly form — that of abolishing the seditious and barbarous body of the strelitz. The attempt to reform the janissaries had cost the great sultan Osman his life. Peter, young as he was, went to work in a much abler manner than Osman. He began with forming, at his country residence of Preobrajen, a company of fifty of his youngest domestics; and some of the sons of boyars were chosen for their officers. But in order to teach those young boyars a subordination with which they were wholly unacquainted, he made them pass through all the military degrees, setting them an example himself, and serving successively as private soldier, sergeant, and lieutenant of the company.

This company, which had been raised by Peter only, soon increased in numbers, and was afterwards the regiment of Preobrajenski guards. Another company, formed on the same plan, became in time the regiment of guards known by the name of Semenovski. The czar had now a regiment of five thousand men on foot, on whom he could depend, trained by General Gordon, a Scotchman, and composed almost entirely of foreigners. Lefort, who had seen very little service, yet was qualified for any commission, undertook to raise a regiment of twelve thousand men, and effected his design. Five colonels were appointed to serve under him; and suddenly he was made general of this little army, which had been raised as much to oppose the strelitz as the enemies of the state.

Peter was desirous of seeing one of those mock fights which had been lately introduced in times of peace. He caused a fort to be erected, which one part of his new troops was to defend and the other to attack. The difference on this occasion was that, instead of exhibiting a sham engagement, they fought a downright battle, in which there were several soldiers killed and a great many wounded. Lefort, who commanded the attack, received a considerable wound. These bloody sports were intended to inure the troops to martial discipline; but it was a long time before this could be effected, and not without a great deal of labour and difficulty. Amidst these military entertainments, the czar did not neglect the navy: and as he had made Lefort a general, notwithstanding this favourite had never borne any commission by land, so he raised him to the rank of admiral, though he had never before commanded at sea. But he knew him to be worthy of both commissions. True, he was an admiral without a fleet, and a general without any other troops than his regiment.

By degrees the czar began to reform the chief abuse in the army, viz., the independence of the boyars, who, in time of war, used to take the field with a multitude of their vassals and peasants. Such was the government of the Franks, Huns, Goths, and Vandals, who, indeed, subdued the Roman Empire in its state of decline, but would have been easily destroyed had they contended with the warlike legions of the ancient Romans, or with such armies as in our times are maintained in constant discipline all over Europe.

Admiral Lefort had soon more than an empty title. He employed both Dutch and Venetian carpenters to build some long-boats, and even two thirty-gun ships, at the mouth of the Voroneje, which discharges itself into the Don. These vessels were to fall down the river, and to awe the Crim Tatars. Turkey, too, seemed to invite the czar to essay his arms against her; at the same time disputes were pending with China respecting the limits between that empire and the possessions of Russia in the north of Asia. These, however, were settled by a treaty concluded in 1692, and Peter was left free to pursue his designs of conquest on the European side of his dominions.

### AZOV TAKEN FROM THE TURKS

It was not so easy to settle a peace with the Turks; this even seemed a proper time for the czar to raise himself on their ruin. The Venetians, whom they had long overpowered, began to retrieve their losses. Morosini, the same who surrendered Candia to the Turks, was dispossessing them of the Morea. Leopold, emperor of Germany, had gained some advantages over the Ottoman forces in Hungary; and the Poles were at least able to repel the incursions of the Crim Tatars.

Peter profited by these circumstances to discipline his troops, and to acquire, if possible, the empire of the Black Sea. General Gordon marched along the Don towards Azov, with his regiment of five thousand men; he was followed by General Lefort, with his regiment of twelve thousand; by a body of strelitz, under the command of Sheremetrev and Schein, officers of Prussian extraction; by a body of Cossacks, and a large train of artillery. In short everything was ready for this grand expedition (1694). The Russian army began its march under the command of Marshal Sheremetrev, in the beginning of the summer of 1695, in order to attack the town of Azov, situated at the mouth of the Don. The czar was with the troops, but appeared only as a volunteer, being desirous to learn before he would take upon him to command. During their march they stormed two forts which the Turks had erected on the banks of the river.

This was an arduous enterprise, Azov being very strong and defended by a numerous garrison. The czar had employed several Venetians in building long-boats like the Turkish saicks, which, together with two Dutch frigates, were to fall down the Voroneje; but not being ready in time, they could not get into the sea of Azov. All beginnings are difficult. The Russians, having never as yet made a regular siege, miscarried in this their first attempt.

A native of Dantzic, whose name was Jacob, had the direction of the artillery under the command of General Schein; for as yet they had none but foreign officers belonging to the train, and indeed none but foreign engineers and foreign pilots. This Jacob had been condemned to the rods by Schein, the Prussian general. It seemed as if these severities were necessary at that time in support of authority. The Russians submitted to such treatment, notwithstanding their disposition to mutiny; and after they had undergone that corporal punishment, they continued in the service as usual. This Dantziker was of another way of thinking, and determined to be revenged; whereupon he spiked the cannon, deserted to the enemy, turned Mohammedan, and defended the town with great success. The besiegers made a vain attempt to storm it, and after losing a great number of men, were obliged to raise the siege.

Perseverance in his undertakings was the characteristic of Peter the Great. In the spring of 1696 he marched a second time to attack the town of Azov with a more considerable army. The most agreeable part of the czar's success was that of his little fleet, which he had the pleasure to see completely equipped and properly commanded. It beat the Turkish saicks that had been sent from Constantinople, and took some of them. The siege was carried on regularly, though not entirely after the English manner. The trenches were three times deeper than the English, and the parapets were as high as ramparts. At length the garrison surrendered, the 28th of July, 1696, without obtaining any of the honours of war; they were likewise obliged to deliver up the traitor Jacob to the besiegers.

The czar immediately began to improve the fortifications of Azov. He likewise ordered a harbour to be dug, capable of holding large vessels, with a design to make himself master of the straits of Caffa, which open the passage into the Black Sea. He left two-and-thirty armed saicks before Azov, and made all the preparations for fitting out a strong fleet against the Turks, which was to consist of nine sixty-gun ships, and of one-and-forty carrying from thirty to fifty pieces of cannon. The principal nobility and the wealthiest merchants were obliged to contribute to the fitting out of this fleet; and, as he thought that the estates of the clergy ought to bear a proportion in the service of the common cause, orders were issued that the patriarch, the bishops, and the superior clergy should find money to forward this new expedition, in honour of their country, and for the general advantage of Christendom. He likewise obliged the Cossacks to build a number of light boats, such as they use themselves, with which they might easily infest the whole coast of the Crimea. The scheme was to drive the Tatars and Turks forever out of the Crimea, and afterwards to establish a free and easy commerce with Persia, through Georgia. This is the very branch of trade which the Greeks formerly carried on to Colchis, and to this peninsula of the Crimea, which the czar seemed likely to subdue.

Before Peter left the Crimea he repudiated his wife Eudoxia, and ordered her to be sent to a convent, where, before his return to Moscow, she became a nun, under the name of Helena. She had long made herself distasteful to her husband by her querulous jealousy, for which, indeed, she had ample cause, and by her aversion to his foreign favourites and the arts they introduced.

After his successful campaign against the Turks and Tatars, Peter wished to accustom his people to splendid shows, as well as to military toil. With this view, he made his army enter Moscow under triumphal arches, in the midst of fireworks and other tokens of rejoicing. The soldiers who had fought on board the Venetian saicks against the Turks led the procession. Marshal Sheremetrev, generals Gordon and Schein, Admiral Lefort, and the other general officers, took precedence of their sovereign, who pretended he had no rank in the army, being desirous to convince the nobility by his example that merit ought to be the only road to military preferment.

This triumphal entry seemed, in some measure, to resemble those of the ancient Romans, especially in that as the triumphers exposed the captives to public view in the streets of Rome, and sometimes put them to death, so the slaves taken in this expedition followed the army; and Jacob, who had betrayed them the year before, was carried in a cart, with the gibbet, to which he was fastened after he had been broken upon the wheel.

Upon this occasion was struck the first medal in Russia. The legend, which was in the language of that country is remarkable: "Peter I, the august emperor of Muscovy." On the reverse is Azov, with these words, "Victorious by fire and water."

## SCHEMES OF CONQUEST

The paramount idea of Peter's whole life displayed itself in the siege of Azov, his first military enterprise. He wished to civilise his people by beginning with the art of war by sea and land. That art would open the way for all the others into Russia, and protect them there. By it the czar was to conquer for his empire that element which, in his eyes, was the greatest civiliser of the world, because it is the most favourable to the intercourse of nations with each other.

But ignorant and savage Asia lay stretched along the Black Sea, between Russia and the south of Europe. It was not, therefore, through those waters that Peter could open himself a passage to European knowledge. But towards the northwest, another sea, the same whence, in the ninth century, came the first Russian founders of the empire, was within his reach. It alone could connect Muscovy with ancient Europe; it was especially through that inlet, and by the ports on the gulfs of Finland and of Riga, that Russia could aspire to civilisation. Those ports belonged, however, to a warlike land, thickly studded with strong fortresses. It mattered not; everything was to be tried to attain so important an object.

Peter, however, did not deem it proper to begin such an arduous enterprise until he should have made himself better acquainted with the nations which he wished to conciliate, or to conquer, and which were recommended to him as models. He was desirous, with his own eyes, of beholding civilisation in what he supposed to be its mature state, and to improve himself in the details of government, in the knowledge of naval affairs, and of the several arts which he wished to introduce among his countrymen.

## CONSPIRACY TO MURDER PETER

But he was not allowed to depart in peace. The announcement of his intention was received with deep disgust by his bigoted subjects. The strelitz in particular, who saw themselves supplanted by the regiments disciplined in the European manner, were actively hostile. The childhood and youth of Peter had several times escaped from their rage; and now, in the horror which was inspired by his approaching departure for profane Europe, they determined to sacrifice the impious czar who was ready to defile himself by the sacrilegious touch of foreigners whom they abhorred. They saw in the midst of them twelve thousand heretics, already organised, who would remain masters of their holy city; while they themselves, exiled to the army, were destined to fight at a distance on the frontier. Nor was this their only grievance, for Peter had given orders to construct a fleet of a hundred vessels; and of this sudden creation they complained, as being an insupportable tax in the midst of an already ruinous war, and as rendering it necessary to introduce into their sacred land a fresh supply of those schismatical artisans who were preferred to them. A few days before the departure of their sovereign, Tsikler and Sukanim, two of the strelitz leaders, plotted a nocturnal conflagration. They knew that Peter would be the first to hasten to it; and in the midst of the tumult and confusion common to such accidents, they meant to

[1697 A.D.]

murder him without mercy, and then to massacre all the foreigners who had been set over them as masters.

Such was the infamous scheme. The hour fixed for its accomplishment was at hand. The principal conspirators assembled at a banquet, and sought in intoxicating liquors the courage requisite for the dreadful work before them. But drunkenness produces various effects on different constitutions. Two of the villains lost in it their boldness, left the company under a specious pretext, promising their accomplices to return in time, and hurried to the czar to disclose the plot.

At midnight the blow was to have been struck; and Peter gave orders that, exactly at eleven, the haunt of the conspirators should be closely surrounded. Shortly after, thinking that the hour was come, he went thither alone, and entered boldly, not doubting that he should find them already fettered by his guards. But his impatience had anticipated the time, and he found himself, single and unarmed, in the midst of the ferocious gang at the instant when they were vociferating an oath that they would achieve his destruction.

At his unexpected appearance they all rose in confusion. Peter, at once comprehending the full extent of his danger, exasperated at the supposed disobedience of his guards, and furious at having thrown himself into peril, had yet the presence of mind to conceal his emotions. Having gone too far to recede, he unhesitatingly advanced among the throng of traitors, greeted them familiarly, and, in a calm and natural tone, said, that "as he was passing by their house he saw a light in it, and guessing that they were amusing themselves, he had entered in order to share their pleasures." He then seated himself, and drank to his assassins, who, standing up around him, could not avoid putting the glass about, and drinking his health.

But they soon began to exchange looks and signs. At last one of them leaned over to Sukanim, and said, in a low voice, "Brother, it is time!" The latter, for what reason is unknown, hesitated, and had scarcely replied, "Not yet," when Peter, who heard these words, and along with them the footsteps of his guards, started from his seat, knocked him down by a blow in the face, and exclaimed, "If it is not yet time for you, scoundrel, it is for me!" This blow, and the sight of the guards, threw the assassins into consternation; they fell on their knees and implored forgiveness. "Chain them!" replied the terrible czar. Then turning to the officer of the guards, he struck him, and reproached him with his want of punctuality; but the latter showed him his order; and the czar perceiving his mistake, clasped him in his arms, kissed him on the forehead, proclaimed his fidelity, and entrusted him with the custody of the traitors.

His vengeance was terrible; the punishment was more ferocious than the crime. First the rack, then the successive mutilation of each member; then death, when not enough of blood and life was left to allow of the sense of suffering. To close the whole, the heads were exposed on the summit of a column, the members being symmetrically arranged around them, as ornaments—a scene worthy of a government of masters and of slaves, brutifying each other, whose only god was fear.

## PETER TRAVELS TO ACQUIRE KNOWLEDGE

After this terrific execution, Peter began his journey in April, 1697, travelling incognito in the retinue of his three ambassadors, General Lefort, the boyar Alexis Golovin, and Vonitsin, *diak*, or secretary of state, who had been long employed in foreign courts. Their retinue consisted of two hundred persons. The czar, reserving to himself only a *valet de chambre*, a servant in livery, and a dwarf, was confounded in the crowd. It was a thing unparalleled in history, either ancient or modern, for a sovereign of five-and-twenty years of age to withdraw from his kingdoms, only in order to learn the art of government. His victory over the Turks and Tatars, the splendour of his triumphant entry into Moscow, the multitude of foreign troops attached to his interest, the death of his brother Ivan, the confinement of the princess Sophia to a cloister, and the fearful example he had just made of the conspirators might naturally encourage him to hope that the tranquillity of his dominions would not be disturbed during his absence. The regency he entrusted to the boyar Strecknev and Prince Romadonovski, who in matters of importance were to consult with the rest of the nobility.

The troops which had been trained by General Gordon continued at Moscow, with a view to awe the capital. The disaffected strelitz, who were likely to create a disturbance, were distributed on the frontiers of the Crimea, in order to preserve the conquest of Azov and check the incursions of the Tatars. Having thus provided against every contingency, he gave a free scope to his passion for travelling, and his desire of improvement. He had previously sent threescore young Russians of Lefort's regiment into Italy, most of them to Venice and the rest to Leghorn, in order to learn the art of navigation and the method of constructing galleys: forty more set out by his direction for Holland, to be instructed in the art of building and working large ships: others were ordered to Germany, to serve in the land forces and to learn the military discipline of that nation.

At that period, Mustapha II had been vanquished by the emperor Leopold; Sobieski was dead; and Poland was hesitating in its choice between the prince of Conti and Augustus of Saxony; William III reigned over England; Louis XIV was on the point of concluding the Treaty of Ryswick; the elector of Brandenburg was aspiring to the title of king; and Charles XII had ascended the throne.

Setting out from Novgorod, Peter first visited Livonia, where, at the risk of his liberty, he reconnoitred its capital, Riga, from which he was rudely repulsed by the Swedish governor. Thenceforth he could not rest till he had acquired that maritime province through which his empire was one day to be enriched and enlightened. In his progress he gained the friendship of Prussia, a power which, at a future time, might assist his efforts; Poland ought to be his ally, and already he declared himself the supporter of the Saxon prince who was about to rule it.

The czar had reached Amsterdam fifteen days before the ambassadors. He lodged at first in a house belonging to the East India Company, but chose afterwards a small apartment in the yards of the admiralty. He disguised himself in a Dutch skipper's habit, and went to the great shipbuilding village of Zaandam. Peter admired the multitude of workmen constantly employed; the order and exactness observed in their several departments; the prodigious despatch with which they built and fitted out ships; and the vast quantity of stores and machines for the greater ease and security of labour. He began with purchasing a boat, and made a mast for it himself. By degrees he executed every part of the construction of a ship, and led the same life all the time as the carpenters of Zaandam — clad and fed exactly like them; working hard at the forges, at the rope-yards, and at the several mills for sawing timber, extracting oil, manufacturing paper, and wire-drawing. He entered himself as a common carpenter, and was enrolled in the list of workmen by the name of Peter Michaelov. They commonly called him Master Peter, or Peter-bas; and though they were confounded at first to behold a sovereign as their companion, yet they gradually accustomed themselves to the sight.

Whilst Peter was handling the compass and axe at Zaandam, he received intelligence of the division in Poland, and of the double nomination of the elector Augustus and the prince of Conti. Immediately the carpenter of Zaandam promised King Augustus to assist him with thirty thousand men. From his shop he issued orders to his army in the Ukraine, which had been assembled against the Turks.

His troops obtained a victory over the Tatars, in the neighbourhood of Azov; and a few months after became masters of the town of Orkapi, or Perekop. For his part he persisted in making himself master of different arts. With this view he frequently went from Zaandam to Amsterdam, in order to hear the anatomical lectures of the celebrated Ruisch. Under this master he made such progress as to be able to perform some surgical operations, which, in case of necessity, might be of use, both to himself and to his officers. He likewise studied natural philosophy, under Vitsen, celebrated for his patriotic virtue and for the noble use he made of his immense fortune.[e]

### Peter in Holland, England, and Austria

Besides shipbuilding Peter also turned his attention to machinery, factories, and industry of every kind. Sometimes he was to be found sitting at the weaver's loom, sometimes handling the sledge-hammer, axe, and plane. He could truthfully write to the patriarch Adrian concerning himself: "We act obedient to the word of God to our first parent Adam and are working — not beceuse it is necessary, but in order that we may have a better insight into naval affairs and be the more able to go against the enemies of Jesus Christ's name and conquer by his grace."

On the 9th of September Peter, accompanied by Vitsen and Lefort, journeyed to Utrecht for a conference with the hereditary stadholder William of Orange, king of England. On his return he visited the whale-fishing fleet which had shortly before arrived, so as to become acquainted with everything concerning whale-fishing — that important branch of the seaman's activity.

Peter always took note of everything new and important that he saw. Vitsen had to take him everywhere — to the hospitals, the foundling asylums, and the prayer meetings of different religious sects. He found great pleasure in the anatomical cabinet of the celebrated Ruisch, who had greatly advanced the art of preserving corpses from decomposition by injections. It was with difficulty that the czar could be got out of the room. He stood there transfixed and as it were unconscious, and he could not pass before the body of a child, that seemed to smile as if it were alive, without kissing it. His taste for being present at surgical operations went so far that at his request a special door was made in the wall of the St. Peter Hospital, by which he could enter it with Ruisch from the embassy, unobserved and unmolested by the curious. It was this doctor who recommended to him the surgeons for the new Russian naval and military troops.

After a stay of two months the Russian embassy went to the Hague, where it had long been expected. The entry was even more magnificent than at Amsterdam. Peter wished to attend the formal audience of his embassy in strict incognito. Vitsen, accompanied by two gentlemen, fetched him in his carriage. The czar wished to take along his dwarf, and when told that space was lacking, he replied: "Very well, then, he will sit on my lap." At his command a drive was taken outside the town. At every one of the many mills that he passed, he asked what it was for; and on being told that one before which there were no stores was a grinding-mill, he jumped out of the carriage, but it was locked. On the road to Haarlem he observed a small water-mill for irrigating the land. It was in vain that they told him it was encompassed by water. "I must see it," was the reply. The czar satisfied his curiosity and returned with wet feet. Twilight was already setting in, and the Dutch escort of the czar were rejoicing that the sight-seeng was at an end. But alas! before entering the Hague, Peter felt the carriage give a sharp jolt. "What is it?" he inquired. He was told that the carriage had driven on to a ferry-boat. "I must see it," said he, and by lantern light the width, length, and depth of the ferry-boat had to be taken. Finally, at eleven at night, one of the best hotels in the Hague was reached. The czar was given a beautiful bedroom with a four-post bed. He preferred a garret. After midnight it occurred to him to spend the night at the hotel where his ambassadors were. Looking there for a place to sleep in, he found a Russian servant snoring on a bear skin. With a few kicks he awakened him. "Go away, go away, I am going to sleep here." At last he found a comfortable resting place.

On the day of the audience, Peter dressed himself as an ordinary nobleman in a blue garment not overladen with gold lace, a large blond wig, and a hat with white feathers. Vitsen led him to the anteroom of a hall where soon the members of the states general and many distinguished spectators assembled. As some time passed before the retinue of his embassy arrived, and meanwhile all eyes in the hall were turned towards the ante-chamber where the czar was, he became extremely restless. "It takes too long," he said and wanted to depart. But Vitsen represented to him that he would have to pass through the hall where the states general were already assembled. Thereupon he demanded that the lords should turn their backs to him as he passed through the room. Vitsen replied that he could command the lords nothing, as they were the representatives of the sovereignty of the land, but that he would ask them. The reply brought back was that the lords would stand up as the czar passed through the room, but would not turn their backs. Peter then drew his great wig before his face and ran at full speed through the assembly room and down the porch.

In the Hague also Peter had several informal meetings with the stadholder, King William; he became personally acquainted with the eminent statesmen Heinsius, Van Slingerland, Van Welde, Van Haven, and with the recorder of the states general, Franz Flagel. He besought the latter to find him someone who would know how to organise the Russian chancellery on the Dutch model. He also entered into connection with the celebrated engineer, General Coehorn, and on his recommendation took many Dutch engineering officers into the Russian service.

As Peter next undertook a journey to Leyden, the great scientist Leeuwenhoek had to come on board his yacht. He brought some of his most beautiful apparatus and a microscope with him. Peter conversed with him for two hours, and manifested much pleasure in the observation of the circulation of the blood in fishes. Boerhaave took him to the Botanical Gardens and to the anatomical lecture-room. On observing that one of his suite could not hide his aversion for a body which seemed to him particularly worthy of observation on account of its exposed sinews, he ordered him to tear out one of these sinews with his teeth.

From Leyden, Peter returned to Amsterdam. Here he often joined in the work on the galley which had been commenced at his request. In the name of the town Vitsen requested the czar to accept this ship as a present. Peter gave it the name *Amsterdam*, and in the following year, laden with wares bought by Peter himself, it started on its first journey to Archangel. From Amsterdam Peter often made excursions to Zaandam, ever keen and confident, although his Russian attendants trembled and quaked at the threatening dangers. On market days he was greatly entertained by the quacks and tooth drawers. He had one of the latter brought to him, and with great dexterity soon acquired the knack necessary for this profession. His servants had to provide him with opportunities for practising the newly acquired art.

Through Vitsen the Dutch Jews petitioned the czar to permit their nation, which had been banished by Ivan IV from Russia, to re-enter it, and they offered to prove their gratitude by a present of 100,000 gulden. "My good Vitsen," replied Peter, "you know my nation and that it is not yet the time to grant the Jews this request. Tell them in my name that I thank them for their offer, but that their condition would become pitiable if they settled in Russia, for although they have the reputation of swindling all the world in buying and selling, I am afraid they would be greatly the losers by my Russians."

During his sojourn in Amsterdam Peter received the joyful news of two successful engagements against the Tatars in July and August. To celebrate this victory he gave a brilliant fête to the authorities and merchants of the town. The brilliant victory of Prince Eugene at Zenta was yet more decisive for the issue of the war against the Turks.

On the 9th of November Peter, accompanied only by Lefort, returned to the Hague, where he informed King William III of his desire to see England. The king preceded him, and sent three men of war and a yacht under the command of Admiral Mitchel to conduct the czar. On the 18th of January, 1698, accompanied by Menshikov and fifteen other Russians of his suite, he set sail at Hellevoetsluis. Soon after the first days of his arrival in England, he exchanged the dwelling assigned to him in the royal castle of Somerset for the house of Mr. Evelyn at Deptford in the neighbourhood of the admiralty works, whence he could enter the royal construction yards unseen. There he learned from the master builders how to draw up the plan according to which a ship must be built. He found extreme pleasure in observing the cannon at the Tower, and also the mint, which then excelled all others in the art of stamping.

In his honour Admiral Carmarthen instituted a sham sea fight at Spithead on the 3rd of April which was conducted on a greater scale than a similar spectacle given for him in Holland. He often visited the great cathedrals and churches. He paid great attention to the ceremonial of English church worship; he also visited the meeting-houses of the Quakers and other sects. At Oxford he had the organisation and institutions of the university shown him. As in Holland, he preferred to pass most of his time with handicraftsmen and artists of every kind; from the watchmaker to the coffin maker, all had to show him their work, and he took models with him to Russia of all the best and newest. During his stay he always dressed either as an English gentleman or in a naval uniform.

In Holland the English merchants had presented the czar with a memorial through the Earl of Pembroke on the 3rd of November, in which they had petitioned for permission to import tobacco (which had been so strongly forbidden under the czars Michael and Alexis), and offered to pay a considerable sum of money for the privilege. The marquis of Carmarthen now again broached the subject, and on the 16th of April a treaty was signed with the Russian ambassador Golovin for three years, which authorised Carmarthen's agents to import into the Russian Empire in the first year three thousand hogsheads (of five hundred English pounds each), and in each of the following two years four thousand hogsheads, against a tax of 4 kopecks in the pound. Twelve thousand pounds were paid down in advance. This money placed the czar in a position to make still greater purchases, as well as to engage a greater number of foreigners in his service; amongst them the astronomer and professor of mathematics Fergsuon of Scotland, the engineer Captain Perry, and the shipbuilders John Dean and Joseph Ney.ƒ

King William made Peter a present of the *Royal Transport*, a very beautiful yacht, which he generally used for his passage over to Holland. Peter went on board this vessel, and got back to Holland in the end of May, 1698. He took with him three captains of men-of-war, five-and-twenty captains of merchant ships, forty lieutenants, thirty pilots, thirty surgeons, two hundred and fifty gunners, and upwards of three hundred artificers. This colony of ingenious men in the several arts and professions sailed from Holland to Archangel on board the *Royal Transport;* and were sent thence to the different places where their service was necessary. Those whom he engaged at Amsterdam took the route of Narva, at that time subject to Sweden.

While the czar was thus transporting the arts and manufactures from England and Holland to his own dominions, the officers whom he had sent to Rome and Italy succeeded so far as also to engage some artists in his service. General Sheremetrev, who was at the head of his embassy to Italy, made the tour of Rome, Naples, Venice, and Malta; while the czar proceeded to Vienna with the other ambassadors. All he had to do now was to observe the military discipline of the Germans, after seeing the English fleet and the dockyards in Holland. But it was not the desire of improvement alone that induced him to make this tour to Vienna, he had likewise a political view; for the emperor of Germany was the natural ally of the Russians against the Turks. Peter had a private audience of Leopold, and the two monarchs stood the whole time of the interview, to avoid the trouble of ceremony.

During his stay at Vienna, there happened nothing remarkable, except the celebration of the ancient feast of "landlord and landlady," which Leopold thought proper to revive upon the czar's account, after it had been disused during his whole reign. The manner of making this entertainment, to which the Germans gave the name of *Wirthschaft*, was as follows: The emperor was landlord, and the empress landlady; the king of the Romans, the archdukes, and the archduchesses were generally their assistants; they entertained people of all nations, dressed after the most ancient fashion of their respective countries. Those who were invited as guests drew lots for tickets; on each of which was written the name of the nation, and the character to be represented. One had a ticket for a Chinese mandarin, another for a Tatar mirza, another for a Persian satrap, or a Roman senator; a princess might happen to be allotted the part of a gardener's wife, or a milkwoman; and a prince might act the peasant or soldier. They had dances suited to these different characters; and the landlord and landlady with their family waited at table. On this occasion Peter assumed the habit of a Friesland boor, and in this character was addressed by everybody, at the same time that they talked to him of the great czar of Muscovy. "These indeed are trifles," says Vol-

EXECUTION OF THE STRELITZ BY COMMAND OF PETER THE GREAT

(Painted for THE HISTORIANS' HISTORY OF THE WORLD by Thure de Thulstrup)

taire, from whom the account is taken, "but whatever revives the memory of ancient customs is, in some measure, worthy of being recorded."

## THE INSURRECTION OF THE STRELITZ

Peter was preparing to continue his journey from Vienna to Venice and Rome when he was recalled to his own dominions by news of a general insurrection of the strelitz, who had quitted their posts on the frontiers, and marched on Moscow. Peter immediately left Vienna in secret, passed through Poland, where he had an interview with King Augustus, and arrived at Moscow in September, 1698, before anyone there knew of his having left Germany.*e*

When Peter I arrived from Vienna he found that his generals and the douma had acted with too great leniency. He cherished an old grudge against the strelitz; they had formed the army of Sophia which had been arrayed against that of the czar, and in his mind was still alive the memory of the invasion of the Kremlin, the murder of his maternal relatives, the terrors undergone by his mother in Troitsa, the plots that had well-nigh prevented his departure for the west, and the check placed by the mutineers on the plans he had matured for the good of his country during his journey through Europe. He resolved to seize the opportunity thus placed in his hands to crush all his enemies at one blow, and to inaugurate in old Russia a reign of terror that should recall the days of Ivan IV. The particular point of attack had been his taste for foreign fashions, for shaven chins, and abbreviated garments. These therefore should be the rallying-sign of the Russia of the future. Long beards had been the standard of revolt; long beards must fall. He ordered all the gentlemen of his realm to shave, and even performed that office with his own hand for some of the highest nobles of his court. On the same day the Red Square was covered with gibbets. The patriarch Adrian tried in vain to divert the anger of the czar. "My duty is to protect the people and to punish rebels," was the only answer he received.

On the 10th of October a first consignment of two hundred prisoners arrived in the Red Square, followed by their wives and children, who ran behind the carts chanting funeral dirges. The czar ordered several officers to assist the headsman in his work. Johann Korb, an Austrian who was an eye-witness of the scene, relates that the heads of "five rebels were struck off by the noblest hand in Russia." Seven more days were devoted to the executions, and in all about a thousand victims perished. Many were previously broken on the wheel or given up to other frightful tortures. The czar forbade the removal of any of the bodies, and for five months Moscow was given the spectacle of corpses hanging from the turrets of the Kremlin, or exposed in the public squares. Two of Sophia's female confidantes were buried alive, and Sophia herself and the repudiated czarina, Eudoxia Lapukhin, noted for her attachment to old customs, were confined in monasteries. After the revolt of the inhabitants of Astrakhan, who murdered their voyevod (1705), the militia was abolished and the way was clear for the establishment of a new army.*g*

## WAR WITH SWEDEN

The external relations as well as the domestic circumstances of the empire were at this juncture peculiarly favourable to the czar's grand design of opening a communication with the Baltic. He had just concluded a treaty of peace for thirty years with the Turks, and he found himself at the head of a numerous army, a portion, at least, of which was well disciplined, and eager for employment. The death of General Lefort, in 1699, at the early age of forty-six, slightly retarded the progress of his movements; but in the following year he prepared to avail himself of events that called other powers into action and afforded him a feasible excuse for taking the field.

Charles XII, then only eighteen years of age, had recently succeeded to the throne of Sweden. The occasion seemed to yield an auspicious opportunity to Poland and Denmark for the recovery of certain provinces that in the course of former wars had either been wrested from them by Sweden, or ceded by capitulation. Augustus, the elector of Saxony, called by choice to the throne of Poland, was the first to assert this doctrine of restitution, in which he was quickly followed by the Danish king. Livonia and Esthonia had been ceded by Poland to Charles XI, and the provinces of Holstein and Schleswig had been conquered from Denmark in the same reign, and annexed to the Swedish territories. The object of the allies was to recover those places. Sweden, thus assailed in two quarters, presented an apparently easy victory to the czar, whose purpose it was to possess himself of Ingria and Karelia, that lay between him and the sea. A confederacy was, therefore, entered into by the three powers for the specific view of recovering by war those provinces that had previously been lost by war. But Peter miscalculated his means. The arms of Sweden were crowned with triumphs, and her soldiery were experienced in the field. The Russian troops, on the contrary, were for the greater part but raw recruits, and, except against the Turks and Tatars, had as yet but little practice in military operations. The genius of Peter alone could have vanquished the difficulties of so unequal a contest.

The preparations that were thus in course of organisation awakened the energies of Charles. Without waiting for the signal of attack from the enemy, he sent a force of eight thousand men into Pomerania, and, embarking with a fleet of forty sail, he suddenly appeared before Copenhagen, compelled the king of Denmark within six weeks to sign a peace by which the possession of Holstein was confirmed to the reigning duke, and a full indemnity obtained for all the expenses of the war. He had no sooner overthrown the designs of the Danish monarch than he turned his arms against Poland. Augustus had laid siege to Riga, the capital of Livonia; but that city was defended with such obstinacy by Count Dalberg that the Polish general was glad to abandon the enterprise, upon the shallow pretext that he wished to spare the Dutch merchandise which was at that time stored in the port. Thus the confederation was dissolved, and the struggle was left single-handed between the Russians and the Swedes.

Peter, undismayed by the reverses of his allies, poured into Ingria an army of sixty thousand men. Of these troops there were but twelve thousand disciplined soldiers; the remainder consisted of serfs and fresh levies, gathered from all quarters, rudely clad, armed only with clubs and pikes, and unacquainted with the use of fire-arms. The Swedish army, on the other hand, was only eight thousand strong; but it was composed of experienced battalions, flushed by recent successes, and commanded by able generals. The advanced guards of the Russians were dispersed on their progress, in some skirmishes with the Swedes; but the main body penetrated to the interior, and intrenched itself before the walls of Narva, a fortified place on the banks of the Narova, a river that flowed from Lake Peipus into the Baltic Sea. For two months they lay before the town, when Peter, finding it necessary to hasten the movements of some regiments that were on their march from

Novogorod, as well as to confer with the king of Poland in consequence of his abandonment of the siege of Riga, left the camp, delegating the command to the duke of Croy, a Flemish officer, and prince Dolgoruki, the commissary-general.

His absence was fatal to this undertaking. Charles, during a violent snow-storm, that blew directly in the face of the Russians, attacked the enemy in their intrenchements. The besiegers were filled with consternation. The duke of Croy issued orders which the prince Dolgoruki refused to execute, and the utmost confusion prevailed amongst the troops. The Russian officers rose against the Germans and massacred the duke's secretary, Colonel Lyons, and several others. The presence of the sovereign was necessary to restore confidence and order, and, in the absence of a controlling mind the soldiers, flying from their posts and impeding each other in their attempts to escape, were slaughtered in detail by the Swedes. In this exigency, the duke of Croy, as much alarmed by the temper of the Russians as by the superiority of the enemy, together with almost all the German officers in the service, surrendered to the victorious Charles, who, affecting to despise his antagonist, contented himself with retaining a few general officers and some of the Saxon auxiliaries, as prisoners to grace his ovation at Stockholm, and suffered the vanquished troops to return home. Thus failed the first descent upon Ingria, which cost Russia, even on the statement of the czar himself, between five thousand and six thousand men. The loss of the Swedes is estimated by Peter at three thousand, but Voltaire reduces the number to twelve hundred, which, considering the relative positions of both armies, and the disadvantages of other kinds under which the Russians were placed, is more likely to be accurate.

This unpropitious event did not discourage Peter. "The Swedes," he observed, "will have the advantage of us for some time, but they will teach us, at last, how to beat them." If Charles, however, had followed up his success, and pushed his fortunes into the heart of Russia immediately after this victory, he might have decided the fate of the empire at the gates of Moscow. But, elated with his triumphs in Denmark, and tempted by the weakness of the Poles, he embraced the more facile and dazzling project of concentrating his whole power against Augustus, declaring that he would never withdraw his army from Poland until he had deprived the elector of his throne. The opportunity he thus afforded Peter of recruiting his shattered forces, and organising fresh means of aggression, was the most remarkable mistake in the whole career of that vain but heroic monarch.

### RALLYING FROM DEFEAT

While Charles was engaged in Poland, Peter gained time for the accomplishment of those measures which his situation suggested. Despatching a body of troops to protect the frontiers at Pskov, he repaired in person to Moscow, and occupied himself throughout the ensuing winter in raising and training six regiments of infantry, consisting of 1000 men each, and several regiments of dragoons. Having lost 145 pieces of cannon in the affair at Narva he ordered a certain proportion of the bells of the convents and churches to be cast into field pieces; and was prepared in the spring of the year 1701 to resume hostilities with increased strength, and an artillery of 100 pieces of cannon, 142 field pieces, 12 mortars, and 13 howitzers.

Nor did he confine his attention to the improvement of the army. Conscious of the importance of diffusing employment amongst his subjects, and increasing their domestic prosperity, he introduced into the country flocks of sheep from Saxony, and shepherds to attend to them, for the sake of the wool; established hospitals, and linen and paper manufactories; encouraged the art of printing; and invited from distant places a variety of artisans to impart to the lower classes a knowledge of useful crafts. These proceedings were treated with levity and contempt by Charles, who appears all throughout to have despised the Russians, and who, engrossed by his campaign in Courland and Lithuania, intended to turn back to Moscow at his leisure, after he should have dethroned Augustus, and ravaged the domains of Saxony.

Unfortunately the divisions that prevailed in the councils of Poland assisted to carry these projects rapidly into effect. Peter was anxious to enter into a new alliance with Augustus, but, in an interview he held with that prince at Birzen, he discovered the weakness of his position and the hopelessness of expecting any effectual succour at his hands. The Polish diet, equally jealous of the interference of the Saxon and Russian soldiery in their affairs, and afraid to incur the hostility of Charles, refused to sanction a league that threatened to involve them in serious difficulties. Hence, Augustus, left to his own resources, was easily deprived of a throne which he seemed to hold against the consent of the people, while Peter was forced to conduct the war alone. His measures were consequently taken with promptitude and decision. His army was no sooner prepared for action than he re-entered Ingria, animating the troops by his presence at the several points to which he directed their movements. In some accidental skirmishes with small bodies of the Swedes, he reaped a series of minor successes, that inspired the soldiers with confidence and improved their skill for the more important scenes that were to follow. Constantly in motion between Pskov, Moscow, and Archangel, at which last place he built a fortress called the New Dvina, he diffused a spirit of enthusiasm amongst the soldiers, who were now becoming inured to action.

An open battle at last took place in the neighbourhood of Dorpat, on the borders of Livonia, when General Sheremetrev fell in with the main body of the enemy on the 1st of January, 1702, and, after a severe conflict of four hours, compelled them to abandon their artillery and fly in disorder. On this occasion, the Swedes are said to have lost three thousand men, while there were but one thousand killed on the opposite side. General Sheremetrev was immediately created a field-marshal, and public thanks were offered up for the victory.

Following up this signal triumph, the czar equipped one fleet upon Lake Peipus to protect the territory of Novgorod, and manned another upon Lake Ladoga, to resist the Swedes in case they should attempt a landing. Thus guarded at the vulnerable points, he was enabled to prosecute his plans in the interior with greater certainty and effect.

Marshal Sheremetrev in the meantime marched upon Marienburg, a town on the confines of Livonia and Ingria, achieving on his progress another triumph over the enemy near the village of Humolova. The garrison at Marienburg, afraid to risk the consequences of a siege, capitulated at once, on condition that the inhabitants should be permitted a free passage, which was agreed to; but an intemperate officer having set fire to the powder magazine, to prevent the negotiation from being effected, by which a number of soldiers on both sides were killed, the Russians fell upon the inhabitants and destroyed the town.

### THE ANTECEDENTS OF AN EMPRESS

Amongst the prisoners of war was a young Livonian girl, called Martha, an orphan who resided in the household of the Lutheran minister of Marienburg.

She had been married the day before to a sergeant in the Swedish army; and when she appeared in the presence of the Russian general Bauer, she was bathed in tears, in consequence of the death of her husband, who was supposed to have perished in the melée. Struck with her appearance, and curious to learn the history of so interesting a person, the general took her to his house, and appointed her to the superintendence of his household affairs. Bauer was an unmarried man, and it was not surprising that his intercourse with Martha should have exposed her to the imputation of having become his mistress; nor, indeed, is there any reason, judging by the immediate circumstances as well as the subsequent life of that celebrated woman, to doubt the truth of the charge. Bauer is said to have denied the fact, which is sufficiently probable, as it was evidently to his interest to acquit the lady of such an accusation; but, however that may be, it is certain that Prince Menshikov, seeing her at the general's house, and fascinated by her manners, solicited the general to transfer her services to his domestic establishment; which was at once acceded to by the general, who was under too many obligations to the prince to leave him the option of a refusal.

Martha now became the avowed mistress of the libertine Menshikov, in which capacity she lived with him until the year 1704, when, at the early age of seventeen, she enslaved the czar as much by her talents as by her beauty, and exchanged the house of the prince for the palace of the sovereign. The extraordinary influence she subsequently exercised when, from having been the mistress she became the wife of the czar, and ultimately the empress Catherine, developing, throughout the vari-

CATHERINE I
(1679-1727)

ous turns of her fortune, a genius worthy of consort with that of Peter himself, opens a page in history not less wonderful than instructive. The marriage of the sovereign with a subject was common in Russia; but, as Voltaire remarks, the union of royalty with a poor stranger, captured amidst the ruins of a pillaged town, is an incident which the most marvellous combinations of fortune and merit never produced before or since in the annals of the world.

### MILITARY SUCCESS: FOUNDATION OF ST. PETERSBURG

The most important operations of the campaign in the year 1702 were now directed to the river Neva, the branches of which issue from the extremity of Lake Ladoga, and, subsequently reuniting, are discharged into the Baltic. Close to the point where the river flowed from the lake was an island, on which stood the strongly fortified town of Rottenburg. This place, maintaining a position that was of the utmost consequence to his future views, Peter resolved to reduce in the first instance; and, after laying siege to it for nearly a month, succeeded in carrying it by assault. A profusion of rewards and honours were on this occasion distributed amongst the army, and a triumphal procession was made to Moscow, in which the prisoners of war followed in the train of the conqueror. The name of Rottenburg was changed to that of Schlüsselburg, or city of the key, because that place was the key to Ingria and Finland. The solemnities and pomp by which these triumphs were celebrated were still treated with contempt by Charles, who, believing that he could at any moment reduce the Russians, continued to pursue his victories over Augustus. But Peter was rapidly acquiring power in the very direction which was most fatal to his opponent, and which was directly calculated to lead to the speedy accomplishment of his final purpose.

The complete occupation of the shores of the Neva was the first object to be achieved. The expulsion of the enemy from all the places lying immediately on its borders and the possession or destruction of all the posts which the Swedes held in Ingria and Karelia were essential to the plans of the czar. Already an important fortress lying close to the river was besieged and reduced, and two Swedish vessels were captured on the lake by the czar in person. Further successes over the Swedish gun-boats, that hovered near the mouth of the river, hastened his victorious progress; and when he had made himself master of the fortress of Kantzi, on the Karelian side, he paused to consider whether it would be advisable to strengthen that place, and make it the centre of future operations, or push onwards to some position nearer to the sea. The latter proposal was decided upon; and a marshy island, covered with brush-wood, inhabited by a few fishermen, and not very distant from the embouchure of the Neva, was chosen as the most favourable site for a new fortress. The place was, by a singular anomaly, called Lust Eland, or Pleasure Island, and was apparently ill adapted for the destinies that in after-times surrounded it with glory and splendour. On this pestilential spot, Peter laid the foundations of the fortress of St. Petersburg, which gradually expanded into a city and ultimately became the capital of the empire.

The country in the neighbourhood of this desolate island, or cluster of swamps, was one vast morass. It did not yield a particle of stone, and the materials with which the citadel was built were derived from the ruins of the works at Nianshantz. Nor were these the only difficulties against which Peter had to contend in the construction of the fortifications. The labourers were not furnished with the necessary tools, and were obliged to toil by such expedients as their own invention could devise. So poorly were they appointed for a work of such magnitude that they were obliged to carry the earth, which was very scarce, from a considerable distance in the skirts of their coats, or in bags made of shreds and matting. Yet the fortress was completed within five months, and before the expiration of a year St. Petersburg contained thirty thousand houses and huts of different descriptions.

So gigantic an undertaking was not accomplished without danger, as well as extreme labour. Peter, who could not be turned aside from his purposes by ordinary obstacles, collected a vast concourse of people from a variety of countries, including Russians, Tatars, Kalmucks, Cossacks, Ingrians, and Finlanders; and employed them, without intermission, and without shelter from an inclement climate of sixty degrees of latitude, in deepening the channels of the rivers and raising the general level of the islands which were in the winter seasons usually sunk in the floods. The severity of the labour, and the insufficiency of provisions, caused a great mortality amongst the workmen. A hundred thousand men are said to have perished in the first year. While this fort was in progress of erection, Peter despatched Menzikov to a little island lying nearer to the mouth of the river, to build another fortress for the protection of the entrance. The model of the fortress

[1702 A.D.]

was made by himself in wood. He gave it the name of Kronstadt, which, with the adjacent town and buildings, it still retains. Under the cannon of this impregnable fortress the largest fleet might float in shelter.

The establishment of a new city on so unfavorable a site, and the contemplated removal of the seat of government, received considerable opposition from the boyars and upper classes, as well as from the inferior grades, who regarded the place with terror, in consequence of the mortality it had already produced. The discontent of the lower orders broke out in loud complaints during Peter's temporary absence. No measures short of the most despotic could have compelled the inhabitants of Moscow to migrate to the bleak and dismal islands of the Neva, and Peter was not slow to carry such measures into effect.

If the people could have looked beyond the convenience of the moment into the future prospects of the empire, they must at once have perceived the wisdom of the change. The paramount object of Peter's policy was the internal improvement of Russia. The withdrawal of the nobility, the merchants, and the artisans from their rude capital in the interior, to an imperial seat on the gulf of Finland, by which they would be brought into closer intercourse with civilised Europe, and acquire increased facilities for commercial enterprise, was evidently calculated to promote that object, which was distinctly kept in view in the place upon which the city was built. Peter had not forgotten the practical lessons he had learned during his residence in Holland. That country, the inhabitants of which in Pliny's time were described to be amphibious, as if it were doubtful to which element, the land or the sea, they really belonged, had been redeemed from the ocean by the activity and skill of the people; and Peter, profiting by their experience, adopted Amsterdam as his model in securing the foundations of St. Petersburg. He employed several Dutch architects and masons; and the wharfs, canals, bridges, and rectilineal streets, planted with rows of trees, attest the accuracy with which the design was accomplished. To a neighbouring island, which he made a depot for timber, he gave the name of New Holland, as if he meant to leave to posterity an acknowledgement of the obligations he owed to that country.

The speculations of the czar were rapidly fulfilled in the commercial relations invited by the establishment of St. Petersburg. Five months had scarcely elapsed from the day of its foundation when a Dutch ship, freighted with merchandise, stood into the river. Before the expiration of a year, another vessel from Holland arrived; and the third vessel, within the year, that entered the new port was from England. These gratifying facts inspired confidence amongst those who had been disposed to look upon the project with such hasty distrust; and Peter, whose power was now rapidly growing up on all sides, was enabled to extend his operations in every direction over Ingria. The variety of affairs which, at this juncture, occupied his attention sufficiently proves the grasp of his capacity and the extraordinary energy of his mind. At nearly the same time that he founded a new capital he was employed in fortifying Pskov, Novgorod, Kiev, Smolensk, Azov, and Archangel; and in assisting the unfortunate Augustus with men and money. Cornelius van Bruyer, a Dutchman, who at that period was travelling in Holland, states that Peter informed him that, notwithstanding all these undertakings, he had 300,000 roubles remaining in his coffers, after providing for all the charges of the war.

The advances that the czar was thus making in strengthening and civilising the empire were regarded with such contempt by Charles that he is reported to have said that Peter might amuse himself as he thought fit in building a city, as he should soon find him to take it from him and set fire to his wooden houses. The Porte, however, did not look with indifference upon his movements, and sent an ambassador to him to complain of his preparations; but Peter replied that he was master of his own dominions, as the Porte was of his, and that his object was not to infringe the peace, but to render Russia "respectable" upon the Euxine.

RENEWED HOSTILITIES

The time was now approaching when the decision of the disputes in Poland enabled Charles to turn back upon Ingria, where Peter was making so successful a stand. On the 14th of February, 1704, the primate of Warsaw threw off his allegiance to Augustus, who was in due form deposed by the diet. The nomination of the new king was placed in the hands of Charles, who proposed Stanislaus Leszczynski, a young nobleman distinguished for his accomplishments, who was accordingly declared king of Poland and grand duke of Lithuania. But Lithuania had not as yet sent in her adherence to either side; and Peter, still taking a deep interest in the fortunes of Augustus, whose Saxon troops were every day suffering fresh discomfitures from the Swedish army, sent that monarch a reinforcement of twelve thousand men to support his claims in the undecided province. The military force of Russia had now become a formidable body, highly disciplined, and fully equipped; and Peter, without loss of time, in the spring of 1704, disposed the remainder of his army into two divisions, one of which he sent under the command of Field-Marshal Sheremetrev, to besiege Dorpat, while he took in person the conduct of the other against Narva, where he had formerly endured a signal defeat.

Dorpat, which is better known by this siege than by the university which Gustavus Adolphus had previously established there, was forced to capitulate by a *ruse de guerre*. It was necessary in the first instance to become master of Lake Peipus, for which purpose a Russian flotilla was placed at the entrance of the Embach. Upon the advance of a Swedish squadron a naval battle ensued, which ended in the capture or destruction of the whole of the enemy's fleet. Peter now sat down before Dorpat, but, finding that the commandant held out for six weeks, he adopted an ingenious device to procure entrance into the town. He disguised two regiments of infantry and one of cavalry in the uniforms of Swedish soldiers, giving them Swedish standards and flags. These pretended Swedes attacked the trenches, and the Russians feigned a fight. The garrison of the town, deceived by appearances, made a sortie, when the false attackers and the attacked reunited, fell upon the troops, and entered the town. A great slaughter ensued, and, to save the remainder of the garrison, the commandant surrendered.

At Narva Peter was equally successful. The siege was conducted under his own personal command. Sword in hand, he attacked three bastions that offered the strongest points of defence, carried them all, and burst into the town. The barbarities that ensued were of a nature to revolt even the czar himself. Pillage, slaughter, and lustful excesses were committed by the infuriated men; and Peter, shocked at the cruelties he witnessed, threw himself amongst the barbarians who refused to obey his orders and slew several of them in the public streets. A number of the unfortunate citizens had taken refuge in the hôtel de ville; and the czar, appearing in the midst of them, cast his bloody sword on the table, declaring that it was stained not

[1704 A.D.]

with the blood of the citizens but of his own soldiers, which he had shed to save their lives.

These victories were decisive of the position of Peter. He was now master of all Ingria, the government of which he conferred upon Menzikov, whom he created a prince of the empire and major-general in the army. The elevation of Menzikov, through the various grades of the service, from his humble situation as a pastrycook's boy to the highest dignities in the state, was a practical reproof to the indolent and ignorant nobility, who were now taught to feel that merit was the only recommendation to the favour of the czar. The old system of promotion was closed. The claims of birth and the pride of station ceased to possess any influence at court. The great body of the people, impressed with the justice that dictated this important change in the dispensation of honour and rewards, began for the first time to be inspired with a spirit of emulation and activity; and exactly in proportion as Peter forfeited the attachment of the few, whose power was daily on the decline, he drew around him the mixed wonder and allegiance of the many, whose power he was daily enlarging. Thus were laid the foundations of a mighty empire in the hearts of a scattered population, as various in habits and in language as it had always been discordant in interests and disunited in action.

Having acquired this valuable possession, and secured himself in St. Petersburg against the Swedes, it was the profound policy of Peter to keep up the war between Charles and Augustus, with a view to weaken by diversion the strength of the former. He accordingly made a great offer of assistance to the dethroned king, and despatched General Repuin with six thousand horse and six thousand foot to the borders of Lithuania; while he advanced in person into Courland at the head of a strong force. Here he received a severe check, having fallen in with the Swedish general Lewenhauft, who defeated the Russians after an obstinate battle, in which the czar's troops lost between five thousand and six thousand men, and the Swedes no more than two thousand. Peter, notwithstanding, penetrated into Courland, and laid siege to the capital, which surrendered by capitulation. On this occasion the Swedes degraded themselves by committing an extensive pillage in the palace and archives of the dukes of Courland, descending even into the mausoleums to rob the dead of their jewels. The Russians, however, before they would take charge of the vaults, made a Swedish colonel sign a certificate that their sacrilegious depredations were the acts of his own countrymen.

## POLISH AFFAIRS

The greatest part of Courland, as well as the whole of Ingria, had now been conquered in detail by Peter, and, as Charles was still engrossed by his operations in Poland and Saxony, he returned to Moscow to pass the winter; but intelligence of the approach of the Swedish king at the head of a powerful force towards Grodno, where the combined armies of Russia and Saxony were encamped, recalled him from his repose. Peter immediately hastened to the field, and found all the avenues occupied by Swedish troops. A battle ensued near Frauenstadt, in which the flower of the confederated battalions, under the command of General Schullemberg, to the number of eighteen thousand men, six thousand of whom were Russians, suffered a complete defeat. With an insignificant exception, they were nearly all slain. Some authorities attribute this disaster to the treachery of a French regiment, which had the care of the Saxon artillery; but it is certain that the most sanguinary atrocities were committed on both sides, in a contest upon the issues of which two crowns appeared to be dependent.

The consequences of this overthrow would have been immediately fatal to Augustus, but for the energy of the czar, who, rapidly organising an army of twenty thousand men, urged that wavering prince to take advantage of the absence of Charles in Saxony, and throw himself once more into Poland. A revolt in Astrakhan called Peter into that part of his territories; but he deputed General Patkul, a brave Livonian, who had formerly made his escape from the hands of Charles, and had passed from the service of Augustus into that of the czar, to explain the necessity of the measure. Augustus yielded to the advice of his ally, and marched into Poland; but he had no sooner made good his progress than, suddenly panic-struck by the increasing successes of Charles, he resolved to sue for peace upon any terms at which it could be procured. He accordingly invested two ambassadors with full powers to treat confidentially with Charles, and had the temerity to cast Patkul into prison. While the plenipotentiaries were negotiating this shameful treaty at the camp of Charles XII, Menshikov joined the forces of Augustus at Kalish with thirty thousand men. The consternation of Augustus at this unexpected reinforcement was indescribable; and his confusion amounted almost to despair upon the receipt of intelligence that ten thousand Swedes, under the command of General Meierfeldt, were on their march to give him battle.

WIFE OF A MERCHANT OF KALONGA

In this dilemma he transmitted a private message to General Meierfeldt to inform him of the negotiation he had opened with his master; but that general, naturally treating the whole affair as a mere pretext to gain time, made preparations for hostilities. The superior force of the Russians decided the fate of the day, and, after having defeated the Swedes with great slaughter, they entered Warsaw in triumph. Had Augustus relied upon the energy and friendship of his ally, he would now have been replaced upon his throne; but the timidity that tempted him to cast himself upon the mercy of Charles was prolific of misfortunes. He had scarcely entered Warsaw as a victor when he was met by his own plenipotentiaries, who placed before him the treaty they had just concluded, by which he had forfeited the crown of Poland forever. His humiliation was complete. Thus the weak and vacillating Augustus, fresh from a triumph that ought to have placed him upon the throne of Poland, was a vassal in its capital, while Charles was giving the law in Leipsic and reigning in his lost electorate.

His struggles to escape from the disgrace into which his folly and his fears had plunged him only drew down fresh contempt upon his head. He wrote to Charles a letter of explanation and apology, in which he begged pardon for having obtained a victory against his will, protesting that it was entirely the act of the Russians, whom it was his full intention to have abandoned, in conformity with the wishes of Charles; and assuring that monarch that he would do anything in his power to render him satisfaction for the great wrong he had committed in daring to beat his troops. Not content with this piece of humility, and fearing to remain at Warsaw, he proceeded to Saxony, and, in the heart of his own dominions, where the members of his family were fugitives, he surrendered in person to the victorious Swede. Charles was too conscious of his advantages not to avail himself of them to the full, and not only made the timid Augustus fulfil all the stipulations of the treaty, by which he renounced the crown of Poland, abandoned his alliance with the czar, surrendered the Swedish prisoners, and gave up all the deserters, including General Patkul, whom Augustus had arrested by a violation of good faith, but he forced him to write a letter to Stanislaus, congratulating him on his accession to the throne. The unfortunate Patkul was no sooner delivered into the hands of Charles than he condemned him to be broken on the wheel and quartered.

The timid and treacherous conduct of Augustus and the deliberate cruelty of Charles drew from Peter expressions of unbounded indignation. He laid a statement of the whole circumstances before the principal potentates of Europe, and declared his determination to use all the means in his power to drive Stanislaus from the throne of Poland. The first measure he adopted was the holding of a conference with several of the Polish grandees, whom he completely gained over to his side by the suavity of his manners. At a subsequent meeting it was agreed that the throne of Poland was in fact vacant, and that a diet should be summoned for the purpose of electing a king. When the diet assembled, Peter urged upon their attention the peculiar circumstances in which the country was placed, and the impossibility of effecting any substantial resistance against the ambitious intrigues of Charles, unless a new king were placed upon the throne. His views were confirmed by the voice of the assembly, who agreed to the public declaration of an interregnum, and to the investiture of the primate in the office of regent until the election should have taken place.

## CHARLES XII INVADES RUSSIA (1707 A.D.)

But while these proceedings were going forward at Lublin, King Stanislaus, who had been previously acknowledged by most of the sovereigns of Europe, was advancing into Poland at the head of sixteen Swedish regiments, and was received with regal honours in all the places through which he passed. Nor was this the only danger that threatened to arrest the course of the proposed arrangements for the settlement of the troubles of Poland. Charles, whose campaign in Saxony had considerably enriched his treasury, was now prepared to take the field with a well-disciplined army of forty-five thousand men, besides the force commanded by General Lewenhaupt; and he did not affect to conceal his intention to make Russia the theatre of war, in which purpose he was strengthened by an offer on the part of the Porte to enter into an offensive alliance with him against Peter, whose interference in the affairs of Poland excited great jealousy and alarm in Turkey. Charles calculated in some degree upon the support he might receive from the Russians themselves, who, he believed, would be easily induced to revolt against Peter, in consequence of the innovations he had introduced and the expenses that he would be likely to entail upon them by a protracted war.

But the people of Russia were well aware that mere personal ambition did not enter into the scheme of Peter, and that, although he had broken through many antiquated and revered customs, yet he had conferred so many permanent benefits upon the empire as entitled him to their lasting gratitude. Whatever prospects of success, therefore, Charles might have flattered himself upon deriving from the dissatisfaction of the great mass of the community were evidently vague and visionary. But the argument was sufficient for all his purposes in helping to inspire his soldiers with confidence. About this time the French envoy at the court of Saxony attempted to effect a reconciliation between Charles and the czar, when the former made his memorable reply that he would treat with Peter in Moscow; which answer being conveyed to Peter produced his equally memorable commentary — "My brother Charles wishes to play the part of Alexander, but he shall not find a Darius in me."

Rapid preparations were made on both sides for the war which had now become inevitable. In the autumn of 1707 Charles commenced his march from Altranstädt, paying a visit to Augustus at Dresden as he passed through that city, and hastening onwards through Poland, where his soldiers committed such devastations that the peasantry rose in arms against them. He finally fixed his winter quarters in Lithuania. During the time occupied by these movements Peter was wintering at Moscow, where, after an absence of two years, he had been received with universal demonstrations of affection. He was busily occupied in inspecting the new manufactories that had been established in the capital, when news reached him of the operations of the Swedish army. He immediately departed, and with six hundred of the guards established his headquarters in the city of Grodno. Charles no sooner heard of his arrival at that place than, with his usual impetuosity, he hastened forward with only eight hundred men to besiege the town.

By a mistake, the life of Peter was nearly sacrificed. A German officer, who commanded the gate towards which Charles approached, imagining that the whole Swedish army was advancing, fled from his post and left the passage open to the enemy. General consternation prevailed throughout the city as the rumour spread; and the victorious Charles, cutting in pieces the few Russians who ventured to contest his progress, made himself master of the town. The czar, impressed with the belief that the report was true, retreated behind the ramparts, and effected his escape through a gate at which Charles had placed a guard. Some Jesuits, whose house, being the best in the town, was taken for the use of Charles, contrived in the course of the night to inform Peter of the real circumstances; upon which the czar re-entered the city, forced the Swedish guard, and contended for possession in the streets. But the approach of the Swedish army compelled him at last to retire, and to leave Grodno in the hands of the conqueror.

The advance of the Swedes was now marked by a succession of triumphs; and Peter, finding that Charles was resolved to pursue him, and that the invader had but five hundred miles to traverse to the capital, an interval unprotected by any places of consequence, with the exception of Smolensk, conceived a masterly plan for drawing him into a part of the country where he could obtain neither magazines nor subsistence for his army, nor, in case of necessity, secure a safe retreat. With this design he withdrew to the right bank of the Dnieper,[1] where he established himself behind sheltered lines, from which he might attack the enemy at an advantage, preserving to himself a free communication with Smolensk, and abundant means of retreat over a country that yielded plentiful resources for his troops.

In order to render this measure the more certain, he despatched General Goltz at the head of fifteen thousand men to join a body of twelve thousand Cossacks, with strict orders to lay waste the whole province for a circle of thirty miles, and then to rejoin the czar at the position he had taken up on the bank of the Dnieper. This bold movement was executed as swiftly as it was planned; and the Swedes, reduced to immediate extremity for want of forage, were compelled to canton their army until the following May. Accustomed, however, to the reverses of war, they were not daunted by danger or fatigue, but it was no longer doubtful that both parties were on the eve of decisive events. They regarded the future, however, with very different hopes. Charles, heated with victories, and panting for further acquisitions, surveyed the vast empire, upon the borders of which he now hung like a cloud, as if it were already within his grasp; while Peter, more wary and self-possessed, conscious of the magnitude of the stake for which he fought, and aware of the great difficulties of his situation, occupied himself in making provision against the worst.[c]

### REVOLT OF THE COSSACKS OF THE DON; MAZEPPA

Meantime there were foes at home that had demanded the attention of the czar.[a] The strelitz were not the only military body belonging to old Russia whose existence had become incompatible with the requirements of a modern state. The undisciplined Cossack armies, which had hitherto formed a rampart for Russia against barbarian hordes, were also to undergo transformation. The empire had many causes of complaint against the Cossacks, particularly those of the Ukraine and the Don who had formerly sustained the usurper, Dmitri, and from whose ranks had issued the terrible Stenka Radzin.

In 1706 the Cossacks of the Don had revolted against the government of the czar because they were forbidden to give asylum in their camp to refugee peasants or taxpayers. The ataman Boulavine and his aids, Nekrassov, Frolov, and Dranyi, called them to arms. They murdered Prince George Dolgoruki, defeated the Russians on the Liskovata, took Tcherkask, and menaced Azov, all the while proclaiming their fidelity to the czar and accusing the voyevods of having acted without orders. They were in turn defeated by Vasili Dolgoruki, Bulavin was murdered by his own soldiers and Nekrassov with only two thousand men took refuge in the Kuban. After clearing out the rebel camps Dolgoruki wrote: "The chief traitors and mutineers have been hung, together with one out of ten of the others; and all the bodies have been placed on rafts and allowed to drift with the current that the Dontsi may be stricken with terror and moved to repent."

Since the disgrace of Samoilovitch, Mazeppa had been the hetman of the Little Russian Cossacks in Ukraine. Formerly a page of John Casimir, king of Poland, he had in his youth experienced the adventure made famous by

---

[1] The ancient Borysthenes.

the poem of Lord Byron and the pictures of Horace Vernet. Loosened from the back of the untamed horse that fled with him to the deserts of Ukraine, he at once took rank in the Cossack army, and rose by means of treachery, practised against all the chiefs in turn, to fill the highest posts in the military service. His good fortune created for him numerous enemies; but the czar, who admired him for his intelligence and had faith in his fidelity, invariably delivered over to him his detractors. He put to death the monk Solomon for revealing his intrigues with Sophia and the king of Poland, and later denunciators shared the same fate.

Ukraine, meanwhile, was being undermined by various factions. In the Cossack army there was always a Russian party, a party that wished to restore the Polish domination, and a party which designed to deliver over the country to the Turks. In 1693 Petrik, a Turkish chief, invaded Ukraine but failed in his attempts at subjugation. Moreover, profound dissent existed between the army and the sedentary populations of Ukraine. The hetman was constantly scheming to make himself independent, the officers of the army objected to rendering an account of their actions to others, and the soldiers wished to live at the country's expense without working or paying taxes. The farmers, who had founded the agricultural prosperity of the country, the citizens in towns who were not secure in the pursuit of their avocations, the whole peaceful and laborious population, in fact, longed to be free from this turbulent military oligarchy and called upon the czar at Moscow to liberate them.

Mazeppa represented the military element in Ukraine and knew that he was odious to the quiet classes. The czar showered proofs of confidence upon him, but Mazeppa had reason to fear the consolidation of the Russian state. The burdens that the empire imposed upon the vassal state were day by day becoming heavier, and the war against Charles XII served to increase them still more. There was everything to fear from the imperious humour and autocratic pretensions of the czar, and the imminent invasion of the Swedes was certain to precipitate a crisis; either Little Russia would become independent with the aid of strangers, or their defeat on her soil would deal the death-blow to her prosperity and hopes for the future. Knowing that the hour was approaching when he should be obliged to obey the white czar Mazeppa allowed himself to be drawn into communication with Stanislaus Leszczynski, the king of Poland elected by the Swedish party. The witty princess Dolskaia gave him an alphabet in cipher. Hitherto Mazeppa had given over to the czar all letters containing propositions of betrayal, just as the czar had surrendered to him his accusers. On receiving the letters of the princess he remarked with a smile: "Wicked woman, she wishes to draw me away from the czar."

When, however, the hand of the sister of Menshikov was refused to one of his cousins, when the Swedish war and the passage of Muscovite troops limited his authority and increased taxation in his territory, when the czar sent urgent injunctions for the equipment of troops after the European fashion, and he could feel the spirit of rebellion against Moscow constantly growing around him, he wrote to Leszczynski that though the Polish army was weak in numbers it had his entire good will. His confidant Orlik was in the secret of all these manœuvres, and several of his subordinates who had divined them undertook to denounce him to the czar. The denunciation was very precise and revealed all the secret negotiations with the emissaries of the king and of the princess Dolskaia; but it failed before the blind confidence of the czar. Palei, one of the denunciators, was exiled to Siberia; Iskra and

Kotchonbei, the remaining two, were forced by torture to avow themselves calumniators, and were then delivered over to the hetman and beheaded Mazeppa realised that good fortune such as his could not long endure, and the malcontents urged upon him the consideration of the common safety. At this juncture Charles XII arrived in the neighbourhood of Little Russia. "It is the devil who brings him here!" cried Mazeppa, and placed between his two powerful enemies he exerted all his craft to preserve the independence of his little state without giving himself into the hands of either Charles XII or Peter the Great. When the latter invited him to join the army he feigned illness; but Menshikov approaching simultaneously with Charles XII, it was necessary to make a choice. Mazeppa left his bed, rallied his most devoted Cossacks about him, and crossed the Desna for the purpose of effecting a junction with the Polish army. At this the czar issued a proclamation denouncing the treason of Mazeppa, his alliance with the heretics, his plots to bring Ukraine once more under vassalage to Poland and to restore the temples of God and the holy monasteries to the uniates. Mazeppa's capital, Baturin, was taken by Menshikov and rased to the ground, his accomplices perished on the wheel or the scaffold.*g*

## MAZEPPA JOINS CHARLES XII ; PULTOWA

Mazeppa with his army passed over the Desna; his followers, however, believed they were being led against Charles, and deserted their hetman as soon as his views were known, because they had more to fear from Peter than to hope from Charles. The hetman joined the Swedes with only seven thousand men, but Charles prosecuted his march and despised every warning. He passed the Desna; the country on the farther side became more and more desolate, and appearances more melancholy, for the winter was one of the most severe; hundreds of brave Swedes were frozen to death because Charles insisted upon pursuing his march even in December and January. The civil war in Poland in the mean time raged more violently than ever, and Peter sent divisions of his Russians to harass and persecute the partisans of Stanislaus. The three men who stood in most immediate relation to the Swedish king, Piper, Rehnskold, and Levenhaupt, belonged, indeed, among the greatest men of their century; but they were sometimes disunited in their opinions, and sometimes incensed and harassed by the obstinacy of the king.

Mazeppa fell a sacrifice to his connection with Charles, his residence (Baturin) was destroyed by Menshikov, and his faithful Cossacks, upon Peter's demand, were obliged to choose another hetman (November, 1708). Neither Piper nor Mazeppa could move the obstinate king to relinquish his march towards the ill-fortified city of Pultowa. Mazeppa represented to him in vain that, by an attack upon Pultowa he would excite the Cossacks of the Falls (Zaparogians) against him; and Piper entreated him, to no purpose, to draw nearer to the Poles, who were favourable to his cause, and to march towards the Dnieper; he continued, however, to sacrifice his men by his march, till, in February (1709), a thaw set in.

He was successful in gaining the favour of the Zaparogians through their hetman, Horodenski; but fortune had altogether forsaken the Swedes since January. In that month they were in possession of Moprik; in February, the battles at Goronodek and Rashevka were decided in favour of the Russians; in March, Sheremetrev took Gaditch, which was occupied by the Swedes, and thereby gave a position to the Russian army which could not but prove destructive to the Swedes, who were obliged to besiege Pultowa without the necessary means, because their intractable king insisted upon the siege. In April and May, the Swedes exerted themselves in vain in throwing up trenches before the miserable fortifications of Pultowa, whilst the Russians were enclosing them in a net. One part of the Russians had already passed the Vorskla in May, and Peter had no sooner arrived, in the middle of June, than the whole army passed the river, in order to offer a decisive engagement to the invaders.

Rehnskold acted as commander-in-chief at the battle of Pultowa; for Charles had received a dangerous wound in his foot ten days before, and was unable to mount his horse. The Swedes on this day performed miracles of bravery, but everything was against them, for the Russians fought this time at least for their country, and had at length gained experience in the field. The defeat of the Swedes is easily explained, when it is known that they were in want of all the munitions of war, even powder and lead, that they were obliged to storm the enemy's fortifications in opposition to an overwhelming numerical force, and that Levenhaupt and Rehnskold were so much disunited in opinion that the former, in his report of the engagement at Pultowa, makes the bitterest complaints against the commander-in-chief, which have since that time been usually adopted by all historians. Of the whole Swedish army, only fourteen or fifteen thousand under Levenhaupt and Kreuz succeeded in erecting an ill-fortified camp on the Dnieper, where they were shut up by the Russians and the river.

This small force might possibly have succeeded in fighting its way into Poland, and Charles had at first adopted this determination; he was, however, with great trouble, induced to pass the Dnieper, and accompanied by a small guard, to take refuge in Turkey. His plan was to reach the Bug over the pasture lands which then belonged to the Tatars on the Black Sea, and, aided by the Turks and the Tatars, to make his way first to Otchakov and then to Bender, whence he hoped to persuade the Turks to take part in the Polish affairs. As soon as the king had escaped (July 10th, 1709), Levenhaupt, mourning over the sacrifice which the wilfulness of Charles had brought upon his Swedes, concluded a capitulation, in virtue of which all the baggage and artillery were surrendered to the Russians, together with the remnant of the Swedish army, which, calculating those who had been taken prisoners in the battle, amounted in all to about eighteen thousand men.

Charles' flight to Bender, and his long residence of five years in Turkey, were the most favourable events which could have occurred for the accomplishment of Peter's great plans. He was now master in Poland. In the Swedish, German, and French adventurers who had been in Charles' army, he received the very best instructors of his people. Among those who entered into his service, there were experienced officers, artillerymen, architects, and engineers.

The Swedes, who for thirteen long years were neither set at liberty nor accorded by their impoverished country the usual support of prisoners of war, were distributed over the whole of Russia, and sent far into Siberia. They founded schools and institutions, in order to get a livelihood, and used their knowledge and experience against their will for the promotion of Peter's designs. This was the more important, as there was not a man among those many thousand prisoners who was not in a condition to teach the Russians to whom he came something of immediate utility, drawn from his experience in his native land. Many never returned to their homes, because they had raised up institutions and commenced undertakings which were as advantageous to themselves as to the Russian Empire.[e]

## PETER AND THE POWERS

A treaty was entered into by Poland, Prussia, and Denmark, which restored to those states the conquests of Gustavus Adolphus, and to Russia her sovereignty over her ancient possessions of Livonia, Ingria, and a part of Finland. When these preliminaries were settled, Peter went in person to make a defensive treaty with the elector of Brandenburg, the first king of Prussia; a mode of negotiation unusual amongst sovereigns, but which was perfectly consistent with the individual character and promptitude of the czar. Having concluded these important plans, he proceeded to reduce some Swedish fortresses, and to bombard the town of Riga, the capital of Livonia, where he lost between nine and ten thousand men by a pestilence that was then raging in that place. The garrison, struck down by two enemies — the plague and the Russians, and scarcely able to decide which was the more fatal — speedily capitulated; and Livonia was once more rendered tributary to Muscovy.

In the meanwhile Charles was employing all his interest at Constantinople to prevail upon the sultan to undertake a war against Russia, which the sultan was easily induced to embrace, in consequence of the ravages committed by the Muscovite troops on the frontiers of Turkey, and the rapidly extending power of the czar on the sea of Azov and the Black Sea. The khan of the Crimean Tatars naturally regarded with apprehension the Russian establishment at Azov, which the Turks had been forced to surrender a few years before; and he, therefore, strengthened the arguments that were submitted to the Divan to persuade them into a declaration of hostilities against the common enemy. A statement setting forth the formidable advances that Russia was making in her navy on the Don and in the harbour of Taganrog, and of the spirit of acquisition she was constantly exhibiting in her encroachments upon the border lands, was laid before the council by Poniatowski, the active friend of the Swedish king, and was immediately assented to by the mufti. In order to render the views of the sultan still more impressive, Count Tolstoi, the czar's ambassador at Constantinople, was arrested in the public streets, and committed to the castle of the Seven Towers.

The indignity offered to Peter in the person of his minister was scarcely necessary to inflame his irritable temper. Within a short space of time his plenipotentiary in Saxony was broken on the wheel, and his ambassador in London imprisoned for debt; but these events had taken place before the battle of Pultowa, which suddenly elevated him to the highest consideration amongst contemporary sovereigns. The insult, therefore, which the sultan cast upon him by the arrest of Count Tolstoi was the more acutely felt, as it appeared to treat him with contempt in the very hour of victory. He soon made the necessary arrangements for the approaching war, sending one division of his army to Moldavia, another to Livonia; and fleets to Azov, the Baltic, and the Black Sea. It was necessary, however, to return to Moscow to make provision for the government during his absence, and while he was there he issued a conscription for the purpose of recruiting his army.

## CATHERINE ACKNOWLEDGED AS PETER'S WIFE (1711 A.D.)

The time was now arrived for acknowledging before his subjects his marriage with Catherine, which had taken place privately in 1707; and accordingly, on the 6th of March, 1711, the czarina Catherine Alexievna was solemnly declared to be his legitimate wife. The ascendency which Catherine had acquired over him was not more extraordinary than it was propitious. Peter's disposition was naturally impatient and cruel, and when he was excited to acts of severity he could not be restrained by any appeal to his reason or his humanity. The only influence that possessed any permanent power over him was that of female society; and the remarkably sweet temper of Catherine, who was never known to be out of humour, invariably tranquillised him, even in his most angry moods, so complete was the fascination she exercised over his mind that the agony of those spasmodic fits to which he was subject yielded to her soothing presence. Without forgetting the low condition from which she sprang, she maintained the pomp of majesty with irreproachable propriety, and united an air of ease and authority that excited the admiration of those by whom she was surrounded. She was not distinguished by that lofty beauty which would seem to sympathise with these august qualities; nor was she either very brilliant in conversation or of a very quick imagination, but she was graceful and animated; her features were pretty and expressive, and a tone of good sense and kindness always pervaded her actions. She was admirably formed for the sphere she embellished, and, above all, for the peculiar necessities of the era that called her to the throne. Her devotion to Peter was boundless. She constantly attended him, even upon occasions of the utmost danger, and especially upon this eventful expedition, when she accompanied him upon his campaign into Turkey.

## WAR WITH TURKEY

The whole body of troops which the precautions of the czar had enabled him to collect amounted to 130,000 men; but, being distributed in different quarters, and failing to join the czar on the Pruth, as he expected, he was obliged to proceed with an army that fell short of 40,000 men. The perils of the enterprise were so apparent that Peter issued orders requiring the women who followed in the train of the army to return; but Catherine, who insisted upon remaining with the czar, prevailed upon him to retract his determination. This slight circumstance eventually proved to be the salvation of the czar and his empire.

From Sorokat the army proceeded to Jassy, where Peter was led to expect supplies from the prince of Wallachia, with whom he had entered into a secret negotiation; but the sultan, warned of the prince's intended revolt, suddenly deposed him, and appointed Cantemir in his place. But Cantemir, who was a Christian prince, was no less inclined to assist the czar, and proffered him such aid as he could command; admitting very candidly, however, that his subjects were attached to the Porte,[1] and firm in their allegiance. In this extremity Peter found himself at the head of a very inadequate force in the heart of a wild and rugged country, where the herbage was destroyed by swarms of locusts, and where it was impossible to procure provisions for the troops. The dangers of his situation, however, offered a valuable test of the fidelity and endurance of the soldiers, who, although they suffered the most severe privation, never uttered a single complaint.

In this state of things, intelligence was received that the Turkish army had crossed the Danube, and was marching along the Pruth. Peter called a council of war, and declared his intention of advancing at once to meet the enemy; in which measure all the generals, except one, expressed their con-

[1] Porte is the name given to the chief office of the Ottoman government, so called from the gate of the palace at which justice was administered. The name is applied also to the Ottoman court—the government of the Turkish Empire.]

currence. The dissentient officer reminded the czar of the misfortunes of the king of Sweden in the Ukraine, and suggested to him the possibility that Cantemir might disappoint him; but Peter was resolved, and, after a fatiguing march for three nights over a desert heath, the troops arrived on the 18th of June at the river Pruth. Here they were joined by Prince Cantemir, with a few followers, and they continued their march until the 27th, when they discovered the enemy, to the number of 200,000 men, already crossing the river. There was no alternative left but to form the lines of battle; and Peter, perceiving that the enemy was endeavouring to surround him with cavalry, extended his lines a considerable way along the right bank.

The situation of the army at this juncture was extremely unfortunate. The great body of the Turkish soldiers were before the Russians on one side of the river, and on the other the hostile Tatars of the Crimea. The czar was thus completely surrounded, his means of escape by the river were cut off, and the great numbers of the Turks rendered a flight in the opposite direction impossible. He was placed in more critical circumstances than Charles at Pultowa, and he had been misled, like that unfortunate prince, by an ally who did not possess the power of fulfilling his promise. But his presence of mind and indomitable courage never forsook him. He formed his army, which consisted in detail of 31,554 infantry, and only 6,692 cavalry, into a hollow square, placing the women in the centre, and prepared to receive the disorderly but furious onslaught of the Turks. It is evident that, if the forces of the sultan had been commanded by skilful officers, the contest must have been speedily terminated. But the superior discipline of the Russians was shown in the steadiness with which they met the charge, and maintained themselves against such great odds. The Turks injudiciously confined their attack to one side of the square, by which, although the loss sustained by the Russians was immense, the czar was enabled constantly to relieve the troops, and supply the front with fresh men. The fight continued for three days. Their ammunition was at last exhausted, and there remained no choice between surrendering and making a desperate attempt to cut their way through the enemy. This latter proposition is said to have been entertained by Peter, who proposed to force a passage in the night, accompanied by his officers and a few select men; but it is extremely unlikely that he should have contemplated a step that must inevitably have sacrificed the czarina and the remnant of his brave army.

### Catherine's Heroism; the Peace of Pruth

It is not improbable, however, that Peter may have conceived some heroic design for forcing a passage; but the certainty of failure must have overruled such an intention almost as soon as it was formed. After the agitation of that eventful day, he surrendered himself to the anxiety by which he was oppressed, and, retiring to his tent on the third night, gave strict orders that he should be left undisturbed. It was on this occasion that the genius and influence of the czarina preserved the empire, her consort, and the army. She who had accompanied him through so many dangers, who had shared in the toils of the field without murmuring, and partaken in the fatigues consequent upon his reforms and improvements, had a right to be heard at a moment of such critical importance. In despite, therefore, of his prohibition she entered his tent, and representing to him the perils by which they were on all sides environed, urged upon him the necessity of seeking to negotiate a peace. She not only suggested this measure, which was probably the very last that might have occurred to Peter, but she undertook to carry it into effect herself. It is the immemorial custom in the East to approach all sovereigns, or their representatives, with presents, and Catherine, aware of that usage, collected all her own jewels and trinkets, and those of the women who had accompanied the expedition, giving a receipt for their value to be discharged on their return to Moscow, and dispatched the vice chancellor, accompanied by an officer, with a letter from Marshal Sheremetrev to the grand vizir, proposing negotiations for a treaty of peace.[1]

Some hours elapsed, and no answer was returned. It was supposed that the bearers of the letter were put to death, or placed under arrest, when a second officer was despatched with a duplicate of the letter, and it was determined in a council of war, that, should the vizir refuse to accept the proffered terms, an attempt should be made to break through the enemy's ranks. With this view an intrenchment was rapidly formed, and the Russians advanced within a hundred paces of the Turkish lines. A suspension of arms, however, was immediately proclaimed by the enemy, and negotiations were opened for a treaty.

It would appear strange that the vizir should have consented to a cessation of hostilities under such circumstances, when the Russians were completely at his mercy; but he was aware that the Russian troops in Moldavia had advanced to the Danube after reducing the town of Brabilow, and that another division of the general army was on its march from the frontiers of Poland. He, therefore, considered it advisable to avail himself of that opportunity to dictate to Peter the terms upon which he wished to terminate the campaign, knowing that if he postponed the treaty he would be compelled to renew the war against the whole force of the empire. The conditions he proposed were sufficiently humiliating. He demanded the restitution of Azov, the demolition of the harbour of Taganrog, the renouncement of all further interference in the affairs of Poland and the Cossacks, a free passage for Charles back to his own country, and the withdrawal from the sea of Azov and the Black Sea. Peter subscribed to all these conditions, but refused to deliver up Prince Cantemir to the sultan, declaring that he would rather cede to the Turks the whole country as far as Kursk than violate his word.

This treaty, however, did not satisfy the expectations of Charles; and, indeed, obtained for him scarcely any advantage. The only passage it contained which directly related to him was that which bound Peter to give him a safe return home, and to conclude a peace with him, if the terms could be agreed upon. He never ceased to importune the sultan to dismiss the vizir and make war upon Russia, until the Porte, wearied by his ungrateful and frantic complaints, at last recalled the pension allowed him, and sent him an order to leave the Turkish dominions. The sequel of that monarch's career presents a series of acts that abundantly justify the suspicion that his mind was shattered by the reverses of fortune he had undergone; for, after remaining five years in Turkey, and venturing with a band of grooms and valets, secretaries and cooks to make a stand against an army of janissaries, spahis, and Tatars he fled in the disguise of a courier to his own kingdom, where he

---

[1] Bruce, who was in the battle of the Pruth, asserts his belief that this negotiation was conducted without Peter's knowledge; and the *Journal de Pierre le Grand* alludes to the transmission of the letter, but is silent as to the share Catherine took in the affair. There is no doubt, however, that the details of her interference are correct, and Peter afterwards appears to have confirmed them by his declaration at the coronation of the empress in 1723, that she "had been of great assistance to the empire in all times of danger, but particularly at the battle of the Pruth."

had not been seen during that long interval and where his death had for some time been currently believed in.

The battle of the Pruth, so fatal in its results to Peter, was a very destructive engagement. If the statements of the czar be correct, his army, on the first day of the engagement, consisted of 31,554 infantry, and 6,692 cavalry, and was reduced on the last day to 22,000 men, which would make his loss amount to 16,246. The loss sustained by the Turks was still greater in consequence of their irregular and scattered method of attack. But numerical details cannot always be relied upon, since they are frequently modified to suit the views of one party or the other. There can be no doubt, however, that the czar fought at an extraordinary disadvantage, and that the losses on both sides were dreadful.

When the treaty was concluded, Peter returned into Russia, causing the fortresses of Samara and Kamenka to be demolished ; but, as some unavoidable delay occurred in the surrender of Azov and Taganrog, the sultan became dissatisfied, and Peter entered into a fresh treaty, by which he pledged himself to evacuate Poland within three months; stipulating, however, that Charles, who was still intriguing with the Divan, should be required immediately to withdraw from Turkey. The fatigues of the campaign required repose; and Peter, who had suffered considerably by ill health, rested for some time at Carlsbad for the benefit of the waters.

When Peter returned to St. Petersburg, he again solemnised his wedding with the czarina, and held a festival in that city which was remarkable for its pomp and the expression it drew forth of the popular confidence. But this was only the prelude to fresh labours. He renewed his plans for the improvement of the country, laid down a number of new roads, cut several canals, enlarged his navy, and encouraged the erection of more substantial dwellings in the new city. His ultimate design of establishing St. Petersburg as the capital of the empire now gradually developed itself; and the first open measure he adopted towards the accomplishment of that object was the removal of the senate from Moscow. The commercial advantages the people had already gained through their communication with the Baltic had reconciled them to the change, and the opposition with which the return had been originally received was now considerably relaxed. But much remained yet to be done before the prosperity of the new capital could be secured. Resistance from without was more to be apprehended than remonstrances at home; and Peter was not slow to act upon the necessity of circumstances.

## WAR WITH SWEDEN (1714 A.D.)

The possession of Pomerania, the most northerly of the German provinces, was necessary to the projects of the czar, who desired as much to humiliate the king of Sweden as to secure the safety of his establishment on the embouchure of the Neva. Pomerania, which lies north and south between the Baltic and Mecklenburg, had passed through the hands of several masters, and had at last been ceded to Gustavus Adolphus in the Thirty Years' War. In order to render his design more certain, Peter entered into a league with the electors of Brandenburg and Hanover, and the king of Denmark, drawing up the articles himself, and the details of the necessary operations. Stralsund was first blockaded, and the allied forces proceeded along the Wismar road, followed at a distance by the Swedish troops under the command of Count Stenbock, who, coming up with the Danish and Saxon divisions before the

Russians had time to join them, completely routed them in a few hours. This slight check to their progress was soon repaired by a victory obtained by Peter over Stenbock (whose march was signalised by disgraceful excesses), in the little town of Altona, close to Hamburg, which he reduced to ashes.

The Russian army went into quarters for the winter, and the campaign was again renewed with vigour in the following year, when Stenbock was compelled to abandon the town of Tenningen, into which he had obtained entrance by the intrigues of Baron Görtz, one of the most crafty and unprincipled diplomatists of his age. Stenbock and eleven thousand Swedes surrendered themselves prisoners of war, and although the ransom demanded for the liberation of that general was only 8,000 imperial crowns, he was suffered to linger in the dungeons of Copenhagen until the day of his death. Nearly the whole of Pomerania was overrun and partitioned amongst the allies, scarcely a place remaining in the possession of Sweden except Stralsund, the siege of which Peter confided to Menshikov, while he returned to St. Petersburg to make preparations for a descent upon Helsingfors in the gulf of Finland. His operations along the whole line of that coast were equally successful. He soon mastered Bergo and Abo, the capital; and, transferring to St. Petersburg from the latter town a magnificent library, he raised a building for its reception, which still remains a witness to his enterprise and the spirit of improvement which seemed to preside over all his actions.

## A Naval Victory; Peter's Triumph

But the Swedes, viewing the encroachments of the czar in Finland with terror, and resolving to spare no means to arrest his progress, fitted out a considerable squadron to cruise in the gulf. The czar, however, was ready to meet them; and, setting sail from Kronstadt, fell in with them close to the island of Åland, where, after a severe engagement, he destroyed several of their ships, and took the admiral prisoner. The consternation which the news of this victory spread over Sweden was so great that even Stockholm trembled for its safety.

His return to St. Petersburg on this occasion was an ovation of more than ordinary magnificence. The czarina had just given birth to a daughter; and, upon his triumphal entry, Peter instituted the order of St. Catherine to commemorate his sense of her devotion and magnanimity. The galleys of the conquerors and the conquered sailed up the Neva in procession, and the czar, in his capacity of rear-admiral, presented to the senate a report of the battle, and was immediately created vice-admiral, amidst the rejoicings of the people. It was not the least remarkable feature in the character of this great man that he set the example, in his own person, of ascending through the different grades of the service by the force of his individual claims. At Pultowa he served as major-general, and in the action in the gulf of Finland he acted as rear-admiral, under the command of Admiral Apraxin. This precedent could not fail to have due weight with a people who had been so long accustomed to oppression and the right of the strong hand. It had more effect in generating a spirit of emulation, and in eradicating the prejudices and vices of feudal slavery, than a code of the wisest laws could have accomplished.

St. Petersburg presented a scene of festivity such as had never been known in Russia before. The intercourse of the people with other nations had in a few years changed the whole character of society. Balls and entertainments, upon a large scale, diffused amongst the inhabitants a taste for pleasures that had been hitherto unknown to them. Public dinners were given in the palace of the czar, to which all classes of persons were invited, and at which the different ranks were appropriately divided at separate tables, the czar passing from table to table, freely conversing with his subjects on matters connected with their particular trade or occupations. Civilisation was thus promoted in detail, and insinuated in the most agreeable shape into the domestic usages of the citizens.

### PETER AT THE HEIGHT OF POWER

But while amusements occupied a part of the czar's time, he was not forgetful of the more important affairs that demanded consideration. The necessity of establishing a naval force had always been apparent, and his recent victories over the Swedes sufficiently testified the facility with which it might be rendered available for the ulterior projects which the extension and security of the empire required. He accordingly devoted much care to the subject, and in an incredibly short period was master of so large a fleet that he contemplated a descent upon Sweden, and even calculated upon the possibility of entering Stockholm. Besides a variety of galleys and other vessels, he built fifty ships of war, which were all ready for sea within a twelve-month.

The discovery of some large peculations amongst the ministers and several favourites of the court just at this juncture directed the czar's proceedings, for a short time, into an unexpected channel. It appeared that Menshikov, Apraxin, and others who held high offices of trust and responsibility had, either by themselves or through their servants, embezzled a part of the finances of the empire; that the revenues were consequently in a state of confusion, that trade was greatly deranged, and that the payments to the army had been made very irregularly. The ministers, availing themselves of the new outlet for commerce, had monopolised its chief advantages; and the Dutch merchants complained bitterly of a system by which they were deprived of the greater part of their profits. Peter at once established an inquisition into the facts, and proceeded to act with the utmost rigour. He felt that the prosperity of his new capital depended mainly upon the justice with which its affairs were administered, and that its geographical position, which afforded it so complete a command of maritime resources, must cease to attract a foreign trade unless its fiscal officers possessed the confidence of the merchants. Menshikov and the rest pleaded that they had been engaged abroad in the service of the country, and could not be aware of the malpractices of their servants. The czar admitted that their plea was in some measure founded in justice; but, resolved to make an example, he confiscated the greater part of the property of those whose agents were proved to be guilty. The estates of the remainder were wholly forfeited; some individuals were sentenced to the knout, and others were banished to Siberia. This measure was loudly called for by the necessities of the case, and the inflexible honesty of the sovereign was never exercised with a more beneficial result.

The unhappy wife of Alexis, who had been treated by her husband with the most cruel neglect, expired in a few days after having given birth to a son, whose fortunes she committed to the guardianship of the czar. The court was plunged into deep affliction by this melancholy circumstance, and the czar in particular exhibited profound grief. But the birth of a prince to the czarina converted their mourning into congratulations, and the most extravagant festivities were held in honour of the event.

St. Petersburg had now gradually become the capital of Russia. Foreign merchandise imported at Archangel was prohibited from being sent to Moscow, and was consequently transmitted to St. Petersburg, which was the residence of the court, of the principal nobility, and of all the ambassadors from other powers, including at this period two from the East. The rapidity with which its prosperity advanced was unparalleled. Its manufactures increased with its external trade, and it soon assumed a rank equal to that of some of the most important cities in Europe. The fame and power of Peter were attaining their utmost height. Livonia, Esthonia, Karelia, Ingria, and nearly the whole of Finland were now annexed to the Russian Empire. He had established outlets to the sea by which he could communicate in security with civilised Europe; and within his own territories he had created new establishments adapted to the various departments of industry, to the army, the navy, and the laws. Prince Galitzin occupied Finland with a disciplined army; generals Bruce and Bauer had the command of thirty thousand Russians, who were scattered through Poland; Marshal Sheremétrev lay in Pomerania with a large force; Weimar had surrendered by capitulation, and all the sovereigns of the north were either his allies or his instruments. The dream of Russian aggrandisement appeared now to be realised almost in full by the sleepless activity and fertile genius of the czar. It was not surprising, therefore, that the people of Stockholm daily expected that he would appear before their gates, and, taking advantage of the disasters of their fugitive monarch, reduce Sweden to subjection, as he had previously laid waste the provinces that separated him from the coast of the Baltic Sea on the one side, and the Black Sea on the other. He was master of both shores of the gulf of Finland, and the possession of Sweden would have given him the entire command of the Baltic and the gulf of Bothnia, over which, even as it was, his flag ranged in freedom. But Peter was too politic to attempt at this juncture so enormous an extension of power. He was aware of the jealousies which such a disposition must have excited in Germany and Poland, and he wisely contented himself with the acquisitions he had already secured; suffering the headstrong Charles to bring his kingdom into greater jeopardy, in the hope, probably, that it might ultimately fall to pieces by its own weakness.

At this crisis of affairs the unprincipled Görtz endeavoured to effect a union between the two monarchs; and negotiations, having that object in view, were actually commenced, and might have been carried to a more decisive conclusion but for events which diverted the attention of both sovereigns into other channels. Görtz has been blamed for projecting this treaty of reconciliation, and accused of desiring to accomplish through its means a variety of results, such as the restoration of Pomerania to Sweden and the crown of Poland to Stanislaus, the dethronement of the king of England, and, by a conspiracy against the duke of Orleans, the reduction of France under a Spanish regency. It is very probable that the subtle minister might have contemplated some of these projects, that he might have anticipated from the combined armies of the two northern heroes the rescue of Spain and the advancement of Alberoni, and that he might have even calculated upon the cession of Pomerania and the recognition of Stanislaus. But, as the adviser of Charles XII, he was justified in seeking an alliance which must in any case have greatly benefited his master and protected his country against those imminent dangers that appeared to be impending over it at the moment; and if he looked beyond immediate advantages, to remote contingencies, the design was not, on that account, the less worthy of applause. As it was, it had the effect of openly confirming the dispositions of Peter towards Sweden, the czar declaring that he did not enter into war for the sake of glory, but for the good of the empire, and that he had no desire to exhibit any feelings of animosity against an enemy whom he had deprived of the power of doing mischief. Whatever faults may be charged upon Görtz — and there is no doubt that they were numerous enough — history must pronounce his conduct upon this occasion to have been guided by a sagacious policy.

## PETER'S SECOND EUROPEAN TOUR (1717 A.D.)

Satisfied with the circumstances of the empire, and anxious to improve his knowledge of other nations, Peter now resolved to undertake a second tour through Europe. His first tour had been limited to practical inquiries into the useful arts; but his second was mainly addressed to an examination of the political systems of the European cabinets. When he first left his own country to acquire information abroad, he was young, ardent, uninstructed, and undistinguished; but now he had achieved a name that was famous all over the world, and he was regarded, with justice, as one of the most extraordinary persons of the age. During the nineteen years that had elapsed, in the interval, he had strengthened and enlarged his dominions, had traversed and subjugated many provinces, had succeeded in accomplishing the great purposes of his wise ambition, and had experienced amidst the splendid triumphs of his career some serious reverses, from which such a mind as his could not fail to extract useful admonitions. He went forth, followed by the gratitude of Russia, to improve his knowledge of the means by which he could contribute still more largely to her prosperity. The czarina accompanied him upon this journey, but being in her third pregnancy she rested for a short time at Schwerin, whence she soon afterwards set out to rejoin her husband at Holland. On her way, however, she was again taken ill, and delivered at Wesel of a prince, who died on the following day. This event, it appears, did not delay her intention of meeting her husband in Holland, as we find that in ten days afterwards she arrived in Amsterdam.

In the meantime Peter had visited Stralsund, Mecklenburg, Hamburg, and Pyrmont, and subsequently proceeded to Copenhagen, where he was received with great distinction by the king of Denmark. On this occasion, a squadron of British ships, under the command of Sir John Norris, and a squadron of Dutch ships, commanded by Rear-Admiral Grave, arrived at Copenhagen; and, it being understood that a Swedish fleet was out at sea, the four armaments, Russian, Danish, Dutch, and English, united under the standard of the czar, and put out to sea. Not falling in with the Swedes, who had secured their safety in Karlskrona, the fleets separated, and Peter, taking leave of the court of Denmark, proceeded to Hamburg. This incident was always referred to by Peter as one of the most gratifying circumstances of his life, and even his proudest victories appeared to afford him less pleasure than the recollection of the moment when he raised his flag as commander-in-chief of the united fleets.

From Hamburg he continued his route to Lubeck, and had a private interview with the king of Prussia at Havelberg, whence he returned by the Elbe to Hamburg. The anecdotes of his journey that have been preserved in a variety of personal memoirs are all calculated to show the simplicity of his manners and his natural aversion to parade and ceremony. At Nimeguen, where he arrived late at night in a common postchaise, accompanied by only two attendants, he is said to have supped upon poached eggs and a little bread and cheese, for which the landlord charged 100 ducats the next morning. Peter remonstrated against the demand, and inquired if eggs were so very scarce in that place. "No," replied the landlord, "but emperors are." Peter paid the bill, and was well satisfied to have purchased such a hint of European tactics at so small a rate.

At Amsterdam he was received with a feeling of delight almost approaching idolatry. The people regarded him as their pupil in the arts of commerce and ship-building; and shared in the glories of the victor of Pultowa, as if he were one of themselves. Nor did Peter hesitate in putting them as much at their ease in his presence as he had done when he had formerly lived amongst them, working like themselves and participating in their hard labour and rude fare. The cottage in which he had resided when he was learning the art of ship-building he now found just as he had left it, but distinguished by the name of the Prince's House, and preserved in order by the affectionate people with unabated interest. Upon entering this humble scene, he was deeply affected, and desired to be left alone. The recollections that pressed upon him at that moment were not amongst the least impressive of his busy life.

His residence in Holland, where he remained for three months, exhibited a succession of trivial incidents connected with his former associates, all of whom were recognised by the czar with the greatest cordiality; but while he was thus engaged in revisiting the dockyards, in examining models, and receiving small tokens of popular attachment, he was not indifferent to matters of higher importance. The Hague, from the time of the Peace of Nimeguen, had acquired the reputation of being the centre of the negotiations of Europe, and was crowded with travellers and foreign ministers. The foundations of a European revolution were then being laid in the diplomatic circles of that place; and the czar prolonged his stay in the Netherlands, with a view to assure himself more clearly of the state of parties in the south and in the north, and to prepare for the side which, in the course of time, it might become advisable for him to take.

Keeping himself aloof from the intrigues by which he was surrounded, and availing himself of all the opportunities within his reach of improving his information respecting the state of Europe, he proceeded to fulfil his intention of visiting France, after he had satisfied his curiosity in Holland. Vast preparations, worthy of the occasion, were made in France for his reception; but Peter, with his accustomed contempt of splendour, desired to avoid the display as much as possible. Accompanied by four gentlemen, he outstripped the escorts, and entered Paris without ostentation. His journey was a succession of fêtes; wherever he appeared he was treated with magnificence. His fame had penetrated the haunts of art and science, as well as the halls of palaces; portraits of himself and the czarina, medals with flattering inscriptions, and the most ingenious devices, representing some of the events of his life, started up before him in places where he least expected to meet such evidences of his greatness. He stepped in the midst of triumphs, and renewed, in his ovation at the French capital, the whole history of his glories as a hero and a legislator. But he could not be flattered out of his simplicity. Declining the offers of the court, he retired to a private hotel in a remote quarter of the town, in order that he might employ his time agreeably to his own wishes, instead of being trammelled by the fatiguing and idle ceremonies of the Louvre.

He left Catherine behind him in Holland on this occasion, apprehending that the witty court of France, with its sarcasms and its ceremonials, might possibly wound by neglect the delicacy of a woman whose greatness of soul elevated her above the conventions of the palace. The marriage of Louis XIV with Madame de Maintenon bore some resemblance, it is true, to his own union with Catherine; but Madame de Maintenon was an accomplished person, and Catherine's merits were of a different order. Catherine was a heroine, Madame de Maintenon a fascinating woman. Catherine had perilled life by the side of her husband, from the Pruth to the Baltic, upon land and sea; Madame de Maintenon, retreating from political display, was content to attest her devotion, and preserve her supremacy, in retirement. Catherine was of obscure origin, Madame de Maintenon was of noble birth; and while the czarina was publicly acknowledged by Peter, Madame de Maintenon became the wife of Louis XIV in private. Yet, although Peter determined not to risk the feelings of the czarina in the French court, especially as the death of Louis XIV had removed Madame de Maintenon from the position which she had previously held, the last wish he expressed on leaving Paris was to see that celebrated woman, the widow of the king.

Peter was not only a practical artist, but was well acquainted with those sciences upon which the practical arts are based. He possessed a mathematical mind and a skilful hand. The rapidity with which he accumulated knowledge could be paralleled only by the tenacity with which he retained it, and the facility with which he could employ it as the occasion served. At the Academy of Sciences they placed before him, amongst other curiosities, a map of Russia, which he instantly discovered to be full of errors, and pointed out to the exhibitors the mistakes they had made in the geography of his dominions, and of the tracts on the borders of the Caspian Sea. He afterwards accepted at their hands the honour of being admitted as a member of their body. He visited the manufactories and mercantile depots, and carried away all the information he could glean from them; had several private conferences with the French ministers in relation to the subsisting peace between the northern powers; and drew up the minutes of a treaty of commerce, which he caused to be shaped into regular form, and negotiated on his return to St. Petersburg.

Every moment was filled with business. He visited the tapestry of the Gobelins, the carpets of the Savonnerie, the residences of the goldsmiths, painters, sculptors, and mathematical instrument makers; and so far overcame his scruples against appearing in public that he went to see the French parliament, and attended public worship on two occasions in state. Amongst the objects that extracted unbounded admiration from him was the tomb of Cardinal Richelieu, one of the richest specimens of sculpture in Paris. But it was not on account of the glories of the chisel that it occupied his attention. He is said to have exclaimed, upon seeing it, "Great man! I would have given half of my empire to learn of thee how to govern the other half!"

Having satisfied his curiosity in France, he took his leave of that country, carrying with him several artisans for the purpose of establishing their different crafts in Russia. During the period of his short residence in the French capital he inspired a universal sentiment of respect. Although he did not hesitate to protest against the luxurious extravagance of the court, and even carried the expression of his opinions so far as to say that he "grieved for France and its infant king, and believed that the latter was on the point of losing his kingdom through luxury and superfluities"; yet the witty and satirical courtiers, who observed him closely, were compelled to bear testimony to the magnanimity of his nature. Contemporary criticism is of so much value in the attempt to determine historical character that the opinions which were pronounced concerning him at this period cannot be excluded from the estimate which posterity will make of his faults and merits. Louville,[l] who was attached to the court, describes him thus:

"His deportment is full of dignity and confidence, as becomes an absolute master. He has large and bright eyes, with a penetrating and occasionally stern glance. His motions, which are abrupt and hasty, betray the violence of his passions and the impetuosity of his disposition; his orders succeed each other rapidly and imperiously; he dismisses with a word, with a sign, without allowing himself to be thwarted by time, place, or circumstance, now and then forgetting even the rules of decorum; yet with the regent and the young king he maintains his state, and regulates all his movements according to the points of a strict and proud etiquette. For the rest, the court discovered in him more great qualities than bad ones; it considered his faults to be merely trivial and superficial. It remarked that he was usually sober, and that he gave way only now and then to excessive intemperance; that, regular in his habits of living, he always went to bed at nine o'clock, rose at four, and was never for a moment unemployed; and, accordingly, that he was well-informed, and seemed to have a better knowledge of naval affairs and fortification than any man in France." The writers of that period, who possessed the best opportunities of becoming acquainted with his movements, speak in terms of admiration of the experienced glance and skilful hand with which he selected the objects most worthy of admiration, and of the avidity with which he examined the studios of the artists, the manufactories, and the museums. The searching questions which he put to learned men afforded sufficient proof, they observe, of the sagacity of a capacious mind, which was as prompt to acquire knowledge as it was eager to learn.

The journey of the czar through France, to rejoin the czarina at Amsterdam, was distinguished by the same insatiable love of inquiry. Sometimes he used to alight from his carriage, and wander into the fields to converse with the husbandmen, taking notes of their observations, which he treasured up for future use. The improvement of his empire was always present to his thoughts, and he never suffered an occasion to pass away, however trivial, from which he could extract a practical hint, without turning it to account. His activity appeared to be incapable of fatigue. From Amsterdam, accompanied by Catherine, he passed on to Prussia. Upon his arrival at Berlin he went at once to a private lodging; but the king sending his master of the ceremonies to attend upon him, the czar informed that officer that he would wait upon his majesty the next day at noon. Two hours before the time, a magnificent cortege of royal carriages appeared before the door of the czar's lodging; but when noon arrived, they were informed that the czar was already with the king. He had gone out by a private way, to avoid the magnificence which he regarded as an impediment to action.

The character of Frederick of Prussia was distinguished by the same blunt, persevering, military qualities which belonged to that of Peter. He lived plainly, dressed like a common soldier, was extremely abstemious, and exhibited in his habits even a needless severity of discipline. The meeting, therefore, between sovereigns who so closely resembled each other in their tastes, who were equally self-devoted to the good of their people, and equally uncorrupted by the pomp and temptations of power, was a spectacle such as history rarely presents. The czarina was worthy of entering into the scene, for she was the only female sovereign in Europe who could share, without shrinking, the toils and difficulties of their career. Voltaire remarks that if Charles XII had been admitted to the group, four crowned heads would have been seen together, surrounded by less luxury than a German bishop or a Roman cardinal.

But, while Peter, Catherine, and Frederick entertained an utter contempt for ostentatious display, the fashion of the court, which was probably directed by the queen, rendered it necessary that the illustrious visitors should be treated with a show of grandeur and parade which they despised. They were entertained in a costly style at the palace; and their manners did not fail to excite the sarcasms and gossip of the courtiers, who were incapable of comprehending the real dignity of their character, and who were disappointed to find in the czar and czarina of Russia a couple of plain, rough, and, agreeably to their notions, vulgar persons. The particulars of this visit to the court of Prussia are minutely commemorated in the loose and satirical memoirs of the day; while the visits to Paris, Amsterdam, and London are recorded, without a single exception, in a spirit of grave admiration, that exhibits a curious contrast to the flippant tracasseries of Berlin.

Amongst the most pert and lively writers who chronicled the visit and caricatured the czar and his simple train of followers, is the markgräfin von Bayreuth. She gives a very amusing account in her memoirs of the reception at court; and says that when Peter approached to embrace the queen, her majesty looked as if she would rather be excused. Their majesties were attended, she informs us, by a whole train of what were called ladies, as part of their suite, consisting chiefly of young German women, who performed the part of ladies' maids, chamber-maids, cook-maids, and washerwomen; almost every one of whom had a richly clothed child in her arms. The queen, it is added, refused to salute these creatures. At table the czar was seized with one of his convulsive fits, at a moment when he happened to have a knife in his hand, and the queen was so frightened that she attempted to leave the table; but Peter told her not to be uneasy, assuring her that he would do her no harm. On another occasion, he caught her by the hand with such force that she was obliged to desire him to be more respectful; on which he burst out into a loud fit of laughter, and said that she was much more delicate than his Catherine. But the most entertaining part of the whole is a sketch of the personal appearance of the uncultivated sovereigns. "The czarina," says the markgräfin, "is short and lusty, remarkably coarse, and without grace or animation. One needs only see her to be satisfied of her low birth. At the first blush one would take her for a German actress. Her clothes looked as if bought at a doll-shop, everything was so old-fashioned and so bedecked with silver and tinsel. She was decorated with a dozen orders, portraits of saints, and relics, which occasioned such a clatter that when she walked one would suppose an ass with bells was approaching. The czar, on the contrary, is tall and well made. His countenance is handsome; but there is something in it so rude that it inspires one with dread. He was dressed like a seaman, in a frock, without lace or ornament." The spirit of the tiring-woman shines through the whole of this saucy and superficial description. The markgräfin took the measure of the illustrious visitors as she would of her lady's robe — colour, spangles, and shape. It never occurred to her that, in the little coarse woman who looked so like a German actress, she saw the heroine of the Pruth; and that the rude seaman who frightened the queen was the man who, amidst ignorant wonder and superstitious resistance, laid the foundations of the most gigantic empire that the world has ever seen! But the circumstances under which the markgräfin obtained her impressions were unfavourable to the formation of a just opinion, or, indeed, of any opinion at all. She was only eight years of age when she saw Peter and Catherine, although she had arrived at a mature age when she wrote her memoirs.  She retained no more than the silly whispers and jests of the ante-chamber.  She noted down what she heard rather than what she thought; but it serves to show very clearly the sort of atmosphere in which the eccentric Frederick moved, and the courtly weaknesses against which, in his own person, he must have been compelled to sustain a continual warfare.

On Peter's return through Holland, he purchased a variety of pictures of the Dutch and Flemish schools, several zoölogical, entomological, and anatomical cabinets, and a large collection of books.  With the treasures thus accumulated he laid the foundation of the imperial Academy of Sciences, the plan of which he drew up himself.  He would probably have lingered longer in those countries, but for the intelligence which he received concerning the conduct of his son Alexis, which induced him to hasten to St. Petersburg under the agitation of bitter feelings, in which the natural dispositions of the father were drawn into direct collision with the duty of the sovereign.[c]

### THE CZAREVITCH ALEXIS DISINHERITED (1718 A.D.)

The czar arrived at St. Petersburg from his foreign tour on the 21st of October, 1717.  Twenty years before he had signalised his return from a first visit to civilised countries by the inhuman butchery of the strelitz, and now he was about to give still more appalling evidence of the deep depravity of his heart.

Peter's early aversion to Eudoxia had a most deplorable influence on Alexis, the son she bore him in 1690.  The dissensions between the father and the mother speedily diminished the father's affection for Alexis.  Moreover, as Peter's vast labours prevented him from paying much attention to the education of his son, Alexis at first grew up under female tuition, and then fell into the hands of some of the clergy, under whose guidance he daily conceived a greater abhorrence for his father.  This being observed by Peter, he put an end to the spiritual education, and appointed Menshikov superintendent of the prince's preceptors.

Menshikov was no friend to Alexis, and the latter had been early inspired by his mother with contempt and aversion for the favourite of his father. The tutors who were now placed about the prince were not able to eradicate the prejudices impressed on his mind from his infancy, and now grown inveterate; besides, he had an unconquerable dislike to them as foreigners.  The future sovereign of so vast an empire that was now reformed in all its parts, and by prosperous wars still further enlarged; the heir of a throne whose possessor ruled over many millions of people, had been brought up from his birth as if designed for a Russian bishop; theology continued to be his favourite study.  With a capacity for those sciences which are useful in government, he discovered no inclination to them.  Moreover, he addicted himself early in life to drunkenness and other excesses.  There were not wanting such as flattered his perverse dispositions, by representing to him that the Russian nation was dissatisfied with his father, that it was impossible for him to be suffered long in his career of innovation, that even his life was not likely to hold out against so many fatigues, with many other things of a like nature.

The conduct of Alexis, particularly his indolence and sloth, were highly displeasing to Peter.  Menshikov, from political motives, to preserve himself and Catherine, was constantly employed in fanning the czar's resentment, while the adherents of Alexis, on the other hand, seized every opportunity to increase the aversion of the prince, who, from his very cradle, had never known what it was to love, and had only dreaded his father. Alexis at times even gave plain intimations that he would hereafter undo all that his father was so sedulously bringing about. Nay, when the latter, in 1711, appointed the prince regent during his absence, in the campaign of the Pruth, Alexis made it his first business to alter many things in behalf of the clergy, so as clearly to evince in what school he had been brought up.

The czar was in hopes of reforming his son by uniting him with a worthy consort; but even this attempt proved fruitless. The princess of Brunswick-Wolfenbüttel, who was selected for his bride, and to whom Alexis was married at Torgau, in 1711, notwithstanding all her eminent qualities of mind and heart and her great beauty, could make no impression on him, and sank under the load of grief brought on by this unhappy connection, soon after giving birth to a prince, who was called by the name of his grandfather, Peter (1715). By a continuance in his dissolute mode of life, by his bad behaviour towards his spouse, and his intercourse with persons who were notorious for their hatred of Peter and his reforms, Alexis seemed bent upon augmenting his father's displeasure.

After the death of the princess, Peter wrote his son a letter, the conclusion of which ran thus: "I will still wait awhile, to see if you will amend; if not, know that I will deprive you of the succession, as a useless limb is cut off. Do not imagine I am only frightening you; nor would I have you rely on the title of being my eldest son; for since I do not spare my own life for the good of my country and the prosperity of my people, why should I spare yours? I shall rather commit them to a stranger deserving such a trust than to my own undeserving offspring."

At this very juncture the empress Catherine was delivered of a prince, who died in 1719. Whether the above letter disheartened Alexis, or whether it was imprudence or bad advice, he wrote to his father that he renounced the crown, and all hopes of reigning. "God is my witness," said he, "and I swear upon my soul, that I will never claim the succession; I commit my children into your hands, and for myself desire only a subsistence during life."

His father wrote to him a second time. "I observe," says he, "that all you speak of in the letter is the succession, as if I stood in need of your consent. I have represented to you what grief your behaviour has given me for so many years, and not a word do you say of it; the exhortations of a father make no impression on you. I have brought myself to write to you once more; but for the last time. If you despise my counsels now I am living, what regard will be paid to them after my death? Though you may now mean not to violate your promises, yet those bushy beards will be able to wind you as they please, and force you to break your word. It is you those people rely on. You have no gratitude to him who gave you life. Since you have been of proper age, did you ever assist him in his labours? Do you not find fault with, do you not detest everything I do for the good of my people? I have all the reason in the world to believe that, if you survive me, you will overthrow all that I have been doing. Amend, make yourself worthy of the succession, or turn monk. Let me have your answer either in writing, or personally, or I will deal with you as a malefactor."

Though this letter was harsh, the prince might easily have answered that he would alter his behaviour; but he only acquainted his father, in a few lines, that he would turn monk. This assurance did not appear natural; and it is something strange that the czar, going to travel, should leave behind him a son so obstinate, but this very journey proves that the czar was in no manner of apprehension of a conspiracy from his son. He went to see him before he set out for Germany and France; the prince being ill, or feigning to be so, received him in bed, and confirmed to him, by the most solemn oaths, that he would retire into a convent. The czar gave him six months for deliberation, and set out with his consort.

He had scarcely reached Copenhagen when he received advice (which was no more than he might well expect) that Alexis admitted into his presence only evil-minded persons, who humoured his discontent; on this the czar wrote to him that he must choose the convent or the throne, and, if he valued the succession, to come to him at Copenhagen.

The prince's confidants instilled into him a suspicion that it would be dangerous for him to put himself into the hands of a provoked father and a mother-in-law, without so much as one friend to advise with. He therefore feigned that he was going to wait on his father at Copenhagen, but took the road to Vienna, and threw himself on the protection of the emperor Charles VI, his brother-in-law, intending to continue at his court till the czar's death.

This was an adventure something like that of Louis XI, who, whilst he was dauphin, withdrew from the court of Charles VII, his father, to the duke of Burgundy. Louis was, indeed, much more culpable than the czarevitch, by marrying in direct opposition to his father, raising troops, and seeking refuge with a prince, his father's natural enemy, and never returning to court, not even at the king's repeated entreaties.

Alexis, on the contrary, had married purely in obedience to the czar's order, and had not revolted nor raised troops; neither, indeed, had he withdrawn to a prince in anywise his father's enemy; and, on the first letter he received from his father, he went and threw himself at his feet. For Peter, on receiving advice that his son had been at Vienna, and had removed thence to Naples, then belonging to the emperor Charles VI, sent Romanzov, a captain of the guards, and Tolstoi, a privy-councellor, with a letter in his own hand, dated from Spa, the 21st of July, N.S. 1717. They found the prince at Naples, in the castle of St. Elmo, and delivered him the letter, which was as follows:

"I now write to you, and for the last time, to let you know that you had best comply with my will, which Tolstoi and Romanzov will make known to you. On your obedience, I assure you, and promise before God, that I will not punish you; so far from it, that if you return I will love you better than ever. But if you do not, by virtue of the power I have received from God as your father, I pronounce against you my eternal curse; and as your sovereign, I assure you I shall find ways to punish you; in which I hope, as my cause is just, God will take it in hand, and assist me in revenging it. Remember further that I never used compulsion with you. Was I under any obligation to leave you to your own option? Had I been for forcing you, was not the power in my hand? At a word, I should have been obeyed."

Relying on the faith thus solemnly given by a father and a sovereign, Alexis returned to Russia. On the 11th of February, 1717, N.S., he reached Moscow, where the czar then was, and had a long conference in private with his father. A report immediately was spread through the city that a reconciliation had taken place between the father and son, and that everything was forgotten; but the very next day the regiments of guards were ordered under arms, and the great bell of Moscow tolled. The boyars and privy-councillors were summoned to the castle; the bishops, the archimandrites, and two monks of the order of St. Basil, professors of divinity, met in the cathedral. Alexis was carried into the castle before his father without a sword, and as a prisoner; he immediately prostrated himself, and with a flood of tears delivered to his father a writing, in which he acknowledged his crimes, declared himself unworthy of the succession, and asked only his life. The czar, raising him up, led him to a closet, where he put several questions to him, declaring, that if he concealed anything relating to his escape, his head should answer for it. Afterwards the prince was brought back into the council-chamber, where the czar's declaration, which had been drawn up beforehand, was publicly read.

The father in this piece reproached his son with his manifold vices, his remissness in improving himself, his intimacy with the sticklers for ancient customs, his misbehaviour towards his consort: "He has," says he, "violated conjugal faith, taking up with a low-born wench whilst his wife was living." Alexis might fairly have pleaded that in this kind of debauchery he came immeasurably short of his father's example. He afterwards reproaches him with going to Vienna, and putting himself under the emperor's protection. He says that Alexis had slandered his father, intimating to the emperor Charles VI that he was persecuted; and that a longer stay in Muscovy was dangerous, unless he renounced the succession; nay, that he went so far as to desire the emperor openly to defend him by force of arms.[e]

## Death of the Czarevitch Alexis

The proceedings against the czarevitch and his friends lasted for about half a year: they were begun in Moscow and continued in St. Petersburg; the cells of the fortress of the latter place were filled with prisoners, amongst whom were two members of the royal family — the czarevitch and Marie Alexievna; fresh persons were continually added to their number, denounced under the pressure of unbearable tortures. One of the differences between the legal proceedings of that period and the present consists in the fact that, when we now have the evidence of a crime before us, we endeavour to discover the persons guilty of it, whereas then they sought to find out whether someone had not done something criminal.

In May a "declaration" or manifesto was issued setting forth the czarevitch's crimes. His whole life was related in the manifesto; mention was made of his idleness in studying, his disobedience to his father's will, his ill treatment of his wife, and finally his flight and his apparent solicitation of the help of the German emperor and "the protection of an armed hand," — which was not at all clearly proved by the evidence. There was, however, no mention in the manifesto of the fact that he had been promised an unconditional pardon and the permission to live at a distance with his beloved Euphrosyne. For all these offences, for his disobedience to his father, his treachery and dissimulation, the czarevitch and his "accomplices" were delivered up for judgment to the tribunal; but this tribunal was not an ordinary one: it was a special one, composed of persons named by Peter himself. Why was such a departure made from the usual order of things? In matters of peculiar importance, when it happened that persons in proximity to the throne were to be judged, it was not unfrequent in western Europe that special, so-called supreme tribunals were named. But this custom always gave reason to suppose that the members of those supreme tribunals were only chosen from amongst those who would be ready to fulfil the will of him who had named them.

The committee appointed to judge the czarevitch consisted of 127 members of the clergy and laity; in the instructions given by the czar to the first it was enjoined that they should act "without any hypocrisy or partiality"; in the instructions given to the laity the following was signified: "I ask you in order that this matter may be truthfully accomplished, without seeking to flatter me; without any respect for persons, to act righteously, and not to destroy your souls and mine, so that our consciences may be pure at the terrible day of judgment, and our country secure." Such were the words that the czar addressed to the tribunal; they were fine in themselves, but their signification could not have been great, because the judges were not independent. The conceptions of the present time require that judges should not be afraid of being dismissed from their functions, of being deprived of the salaries accompanying these functions, and so on — then only can a judge be entirely impartial; but were the judges of the czarevitch and in general all the judges of that time in such a position? They were all persons in the government service and entirely dependent on their chiefs; in the present case whom was it they risked displeasing? The czar himself! It was natural that they should try and read the czar's will in the eyes of Menshikov, Tolstoi, and others of his intimates.

On the 24th of June, 1718, the sentence of the supreme tribunal was pronounced. The clergy refused to pronounce sentence, but the laity unanimously decreed the penalty of death against the czarevitch. Execution, however, did not follow, but something far more terrible than a public death on the scaffold did — the czarevitch was tortured on the rack. In fact, during the last days of the sitting of the tribunal, he had been several times subjected to it and, he was even tortured after sentence had been passed upon him! All this was more than the feeble organism of the czarevitch could bear, and on the 26th of June he died in a cell of the Petersburg fortress. Amongst the number of his friends and sharers in his flight many were executed, others banished to distant places, to monasteries and fortresses; amongst the latter was also the czarevna Marie Alexievna, who was sent to Schlüsselburg.

Such is one of the darkest episodes of the reign of Peter. The czarevitch Alexis could not have continued the work commenced by his father; he could not have succeeded him; he might have been judged, even condemned, if the tribunal (but an impartial tribunal) had found him guilty, and his head might have fallen at the hands of the public executioner like that of a criminal. But he was promised pardon if he would return, and having returned he was delivered up to the tribunal, he was judged by persons in whose impartiality it is impossible to believe; finally he was tortured after sentence was pronounced, when everywhere, even to the most insignificant of men and the greatest of criminals, time is given to prepare for death. For these things history cannot forgive the czar. Upon contemporaries the judgment and death of the czarevitch produced a deep impression. There were persons who admired the czar's decision to sacrifice his son to the welfare of the country and his great plans; they compared him to Brutus. But there were but few such persons and they for the greater part were foreigners and not Russians. The greatness of Brutus and civic virtues in general did not powerfully move the hearts of our forefathers; but each of them felt that it was unnatural for a father to take away his son's life!

Terrible rumours as to the details of the czarevitch's death began to be current amongst the people; some said that he had been secretly poisoned,

MEETING OF CATHERINE II OF RUSSIA AND JOSEPH II OF AUSTRIA

(Painted for THE HISTORIANS' HISTORY OF THE WORLD by Thure de Thulstrup)

others that he had been strangled, and yet others that the czar himself had cut off his head in the cell. All these were fables, but fables which, however, may even now be met with in the works of many foreign authors and which also prove how powerfully the imagination of contemporaries was affected by this event and how much it was talked of. That noble quality of human nature — sympathy with sufferings even when they are deserved — made the czarevitch dearer still to his numerous partisans. The idea that Peter had indeed been "changed" became stronger. The common people, the merchants, the clergy, even distinguished persons, when they were not afraid of being overheard, said: "Would such a thing have been possible if he were the rightful czar — would he have killed his son and made the czarevna take the veil?" In some more fanatical minds the idea became confirmed that the czarevitch was alive and the name of the unfortunate young man became, as did in previous times the name of the czarevitch Dmitri, an ensign for impostors and pretenders.[h]

## DOMESTIC AFFAIRS

The appalling episode we have just related was so far from engrossing the thoughts of the czar that it hardly interrupted the course of his ordinary occupations. Nay, as if to darken still more the tragic horrors of the year 1718, by mingling with them the coarsest and most disgusting buffoonery, it was in that very year he instituted the crapulous burlesque of the Conclave. The occasion of it was this: During the czar's visit to Paris, the doctors of the Sorbonne addressed him with the view of effecting a union between the Russo-Greek church and that of Rome, and they presented to him a memorial full of learned arguments against the schismatical tenets of his co-religionists. This memorial only gave great offence to the court of Rome, without pleasing either the emperor or the church of Russia.

"In this plan of reunion," says Voltaire, "there were some political matters which they did not understand, and some points of controversy which they said they understood and which each party explained according to its humour. There was a question about the Holy Ghost, who, according to the Latins, proceeds from the Father and the Son; and according to the Greeks, at present, proceeds from the Father, through the Son, after having, for a long time, proceeded from the Father only. They quoted St. Epiphanius, who says that 'the Holy Ghost is not the Son's brother, nor the Father's grandson.' But the czar, at leaving Paris, had other business than to explain passages from St. Epiphanius; however, he received the Sorbonne's memorial with great affability. They also wrote to some Russian bishops, who returned a polite answer; but the greater number received the overture with indignation." It was to dissipate the apprehensions of this reunion that, after expelling the Jesuits from his dominions, he instituted the mock conclave, as he had previously set on foot other burlesque exhibitions, for the purpose of turning the office of patriarch into ridicule.

There was at his court an old man named Sotov, an enormous drunkard, and a court-fool of long standing; he had taught the czar to write, and by this service imagined that he deserved the highest dignities. Peter promised to confer on him one of the most eminent in the known world: he created him *kniaz papa*, that is to say, prince-pope, with a salary of 2,000 roubles, and a palace at St. Petersburg, in the Tatar ward. Sotov was enthroned by buffoons; four fellows, who stammered, were appointed to harangue him on his exaltation; his mock holiness created a number of cardinals, and rode in procession at the head of them, sitting astride on a cask of brandy, which was laid on a sledge drawn by four oxen. They were followed by other sledges loaded with food and drink; and the march was accompanied by the rough music of drums, trumpets, horns, hautboys, and fiddles, all playing out of tune; and the clattering of pots and pans, brandished by a troop of cooks and scullions. The train was swelled by a number of men dressed as monks of various Romish orders, and each carrying a bottle and glass. The czar and his courtiers brought up the rear, the former in the garb of a Dutch skipper, the latter in various comic disguises.

When the procession arrived at the place where the conclave was to be held the cardinals were led into a long gallery, part of which had been boarded off into a range of closets in each of which a cardinal was shut up with plenty of food and intoxicating liquors. To every one of their eminences were attached two conclavists — cunning young fellows, whose business it was to ply their principals well with drink, carry real or pretended messages to and fro between the members of the sacred college, and provoke them to bawl out all sorts of abuse of each other and of their respective families. The czar listened eagerly to all this ribaldry, not forgetting in the midst of his glee to note down on his tablets any hints of which it might be possible for him to make a vindictive use. The cardinals were not released from confinement until they were all agreed upon a number of farcical questions submitted to them by the *kniaz papa.*

The orgie lasted three days and three nights. The doors of the conclave were at last thrown open in the middle of the day, and the pope and his cardinals were carried home dead drunk on sledges — that is to say, such of them as survived; for some had actually died during the debauch, and others never recovered from its effects. This stupid farce was repeated three times; and on the last occasion especially it was accompanied with other abominations, which admit of no description. Peter himself had his death accelerated by his excesses in the last conclave.

From 1714 to 1717 Peter published ninety-two ordinances or regulations; in 1718 alone, in that year of crime, thirty-six ukases, or regulations, were promulgated, and twenty-seven in 1719. The majority of them related directly to his new establishments. The council of mines dates in its origin from that period, as do also the uniformity of weights and measures, the institution of schools for teaching arithmetic in all the towns of the empire; that of orphan-houses and foundling-hospitals, of workshops for the poor, and of manufactories of tapestry, silks, linens, and cloths for soldiers' clothing; the founding of the city of Ladoga; the canal of the same name, which he began with his own hands; that of Kronstadt; the plan of another, which now unites the Baltic to the Caspian by the intermedium of the Volga; besides numerous measures of detail, including the police, the health of towns, lighting and cleansing, founded upon what he had remarked during the previous year in the great cities of Europe.

At this sanguinary epoch it was that, by this multitude of establishments for the promotion of all kinds of industry, he gave the most rapid impulse to the knowledge, commerce, and civilisation to which he sacrificed his son; as though, by thus redoubling his activity, he had sought to escape from himself, or to palliate, by the importance of the result, the horror of the sacrifice. In several of these ordinances it is remarkable that, either from the inconsistency which is inherent in our nature or from the pride of a despot, which believes itself to be detached from and above everything, he required respect to be paid to religion, at the very moment when, with such cruelty, he was paying no respect to the sanctity of his own oath; and yet the importance of keeping sworn faith must have been well known to a prince who one day said, "The irreligious cannot be tolerated because, by sapping religion, they turn into ridicule the sacredness of an oath, which is the foundation of all society."

It is true that, on this occasion, pushing right into wrong, as he too often did, he mutilated and banished to Siberia a miserable creature who, when drunk, had been guilty of blasphemy. So intolerant was he against intolerance. The raskolniks were, and still are, the blind and uncompromising enemies of all innovation. One of them, at that period, even believed that he might avenge heaven by an assassination. Under the guise of a suppliant, this fanatic had easily penetrated into the chamber of the prince; he was already within reach of him, and, while he feigned to implore him, his hand was seeking for the dagger under his clothes, when, fortunately, it dropped and betrayed the assassin, by falling at the feet of the czar.

This abortive crime had made the persecution rage with redoubled fury when, all at once, a frightful report was spread; it was soon confirmed that several hundred of these wretched beings had taken refuge in a church, and, rather than abjure their superstitions, had set fire to their asylum, leaving nothing but their ashes to their persecutor. A horrible sacrifice, which, however, was not useless. Peter saw his error; his intolerance was only political — it was enlightened by these flames, which religious intolerance witnessed with such atrocious joy.

Yet, unable to forgive these sectaries an obstinacy which was victorious over his own, he once more tried against them the weapon of ridicule. He ordered that they should wear a bit of yellow stuff on their backs, to distinguish them from his other subjects. This mark of humiliation, however, they considered as a distinction. Some malignant advisers endeavoured to rouse his anger again, but he replied, "No; I have learned that they are men of pure morals; they are the most upright merchants in the empire; and neither honour nor the welfare of the country will allow of their being martyred for their errors. Besides, that which a degrading badge and force of reason have been unable to effect will never be accomplished by punishment; let them, therefore, live in peace."

These were remarkable words, and worthy the pupil of Holland and England, worthy of a prince to whom superstition was a most inveterate enemy. In reality, he was a believer, but not credulous; and even while he knelt on the field of victory, he gave thanks to God alone for the reward of so many toils, and could separate the cause of heaven from that of the priests; it was his wish that they should be citizens. We have seen that he subjected them to the same taxes as his other subjects; and because the monks eluded them he diminished their numbers. He unmasked the superstitious impostures of the priests, who all sought to close up every cranny by which the light might have a chance of reaching them.

For this reason, they held St. Petersburg in abhorrence. According to their description of it, this half-built city, by which Russia already aspired to civilisation, was one of the mouths of hell. It was they who obtained from the unfortunate Alexis a promise that it should be destroyed. Their prophecies repeatedly fixed the epoch at which it would be overthrown by the wrath of heaven. The labours upon it were then suspended, for so great was the fear thus inspired that the orders of the terrible czar were issued almost in vain.

On one occasion, these lying priests were for some days particularly active; they displayed one of their sacred images, from which the tears flowed miraculously; it wept the fate which impended over those who dwelt in this new city. "Its hour is at hand," said they, "and it will be swallowed up, with all its inhabitants, by a tremendous inundation." On hearing of this miracle of the tears, the treacherous construction which was put upon it, and the perturbation which it occasioned, Peter thought it necessary to hasten to the spot. There, in the midst of the people, who were petrified with terror, and of his tongue-tied court, he seized the miraculous image, and discovered its mechanism; the multitude were stupefied with a pious horror, but he opened their eyes by showing them, in those of the idol, the congealed oil, which was melted by the flame of tapers inside, and then flowed drop by drop through openings artfully provided for the purpose.

At a later period he did still more; the horrible execution of a young Russian by the priests was the cause. This unfortunate man had brought back from Germany a highly valuable knowledge of medicine, and had left there some superstitious prejudices. For this reason all his motions were watched by the priests; and they at last caught up some thoughtless words against their sacred images. They immediately arrested the regenerated young Russian, sentenced him without mercy, and put him to a torturing death. But this individual evil produced a general good. Indignant at their cruelty, Peter deprived the clergy of the right of condemning to death. The priests lost a jurisdiction which they alleged they had possessed for seven centuries, from the time of Vladimir the Great, and thus the source of their power was forever annihilated by this execrable abuse of it.

It was particularly in that sanguinary year, so fatal to the last hope which the old Russians placed in his successor, that Peter seemed in haste to sever them from their ancient customs, by giving an entirely new form to the administration of his empire. As far back as 1711, he had already replaced the old supreme court of the boyars by a senate, a sovereign council, into which merit and services might obtain admission, independent of noble origin. Subsequently, and every year, other changes had been effected. Thus, in 1717, he brought from France, along with a commercial treaty, the institution of a general police. But, in 1718, instead of the old prikaz, he substituted, at one stroke, colleges for foreign affairs, naval affairs, finance, justice, and commerce, and fixed, by a general regulation, and with the utmost minuteness, the functions and privileges of each of them.

At the same time, when capable Russians were not to be found, he appointed his Swedish prisoners, and the most eminent of the foreigners, to fill these administrative and judicial situations. He was careful to give the highest offices to natives, and the second to foreigners, that the native officers might support, against the pride and jealousy of their countrymen, these foreigners who served them as instructors and guides. For the purpose of forming his young nobles for the service of the state, he adjoined a considerable number of them to each college; and there merit alone could raise them from the lowest stations to the first rank.

### RENEWED HOSTILITIES WITH SWEDEN (1719-1721 A.D.)

The death of Charles XII was immediately followed by a revolution in Sweden. His sister Ulrica Eleonora, who was married to the crown prince of Hesse-Cassel, succeeded him on the throne; but the constitution was changed, the despotic authority of the crown was reduced to a mere shadow, and the queen and her husband became the tools of an oligarchy who usurped all the powers of the state. The czar and the new queen mutually protested their desire for peace; but Peter at the same time announced to the Swedish plenipotentiaries that, if the propositions he had made were not accepted within two months, he would march forty thousand men into Sweden to expedite the negotiations.

A project for the pacification of the north, the very opposite from that conceived by Görtz, was formed by the diet of Brunswick. The concocters of this scheme started from the principle that the German possessions of Sweden were more onerous than profitable to that power, as the occasions of interminable wars. It was resolved, therefore, that they should be abandoned to the powers that had conquered them; but as it was reasonable that the new possessors should purchase the ratification of their titles by some services to the common cause, they were required to aid Sweden in recovering possession of Finland and of Livonia, the granary of that kingdom. Of all the czar's conquests nothing was to be left to him but St. Petersburg, Kronstadt, and Narva; and, if he refused to assent to this arrangement, all the contracting powers were to unite their forces and compel him to submit. This was one of those brilliant and chimerical schemes with which diplomatists sometimes allow their minds to be so dazzled as not to be convinced of their impracticability until after a lavish waste of blood.

Whilst the allies were in imagination depriving Peter of his conquests, Siniavin, his admiral, took from the Swedes two ships of the line and a brigantine, which were carrying corn to Stockholm. The queen of Sweden, however, encouraged by the promises made her by Lord Carteret, the ambassador of George I, intimated to the czar that she would break off the conferences at Åland if he did not consent to restore all the provinces he had conquered. By way of reply, Peter went in June, 1719, with a fleet of 30 ships, 150 galleys, and 300 barges, carrying in all 40,000 men, to Åland, took up his station for a while under the cliffs of the island of Lämeland, and sent Apraxin to ravage the wastes on the right of Stockholm, whilst Lessy destroyed everything on the left of the city. North and south Telge, Nyköping, Norköping, Osthammer, and Oregrund, together with two small towns, were burned, besides 150 noble mansions, 43 mills, 1,360 villages, 21 copper, iron, and tile works — among the iron works one was worth 300,000 dollars; 100,000 cattle were slaughtered, and 80,000 bars of iron thrown into the sea. The mines were blown up and the woods set on fire, and Stockholm itself was seriously threatened. Meanwhile, the English fleet under Admiral Norris again entered the Baltic. Peter sent a message to the English admiral asking peremptorily whether he came only as a friend to Sweden or as an enemy to Russia. The admiral's answer was that as yet he had no positive orders. This equivocal reply did not hinder Peter from keeping the sea, and incessantly harrassing the Swedes before the eyes of their naval allies.

The Swedish oligarchs and their mock king[1] had reckoned in vain upon the intercession of the English ambassador, and the aid of the admiral and his fleet. Carteret was not even listened to by Peter, and Admiral Norris did not venture to attack the Russians, because he knew that the English nation was dissatisfied with the politics of their king and of his ministers, who favoured his Hanoverian plans. The Swedes were at length obliged to acquiesce in the Russian demands; negotiations for peace were again commenced in Nystad at the end of the year 1720, but their conclusion was only brought about at the close of the following year by the exercise of some further cruelties on the part of the Russians. The Swedes had demanded a

---

[1] Ulrica had ceded the crown to her husband.

cessation of hostilities during the whole time in which the negotiations were pending, but Peter only granted it till May, 1721, in order to compel the council of state to come to a resolution by that time; and as they still procrastinated, the whole coast of Sweden was again plundered and devastated in the month of June.

The Russian incendiaries landed in sight of the English, whose fleet under Admiral Norris, still continued in the Baltic, but did not venture to lend any assistance to the Swedes. The whole coast, from Gefle as far as Umea, was ravaged; four small towns, nineteen villages, eighty nobles' and five hundred peasants' houses burned; twelve iron-works and eight saw-mills destroyed; six galleys and other ships carried away. Peter's plenipotentiaries at last prevailed — for he so jocularly called his soldiers and sailors who were committing such horrible destruction in Sweden. Negotiations were again opened in Nystad, a small town in Finland, and the war of twenty-one years was closed by a peace dictated by the conquering czar.

The provinces ceded to Russia by the Peace of Nystad (September 10th, 1721) were Livonia, Esthonia, and Karelia, together with Viborg, Kexholm, and the island of Ösel; on the other hand, Peter restored Finland, with the exception of Viborg and Kexholm, and promised to pay two millions of dollars, but in the first years of the peace scarcely paid off half a million.

From this time forward, the despotic sway and military oppression of Russia became the dread of all neighbouring countries and people. All contributed to the external greatness and splendour of the ruler of a barbarous but powerful race of slaves, whom he constrained to adopt the vestments of civilisation. The czar commanded in Poland and Scandinavia, where weak or wicked governments were constantly in dread from the discontent of the people. He also gained an influence in Germany, which ultimately caused no small anxiety to the emperor and the empire. The Russian minister Bestuzhev played the chief part in Sweden in all political affairs, sometimes by counsel and sometimes by threats, sometimes by mediation and sometimes by commands. Bestuzhev was powerful in the Swedish council, and at the same time, in compliance with the wishes of his master, allured artists, artisans, workmen, and all those who had been deprived of occupation or ruined by the late inroads of the Russians, to remove with their tools, manufactures, and trades to Russia. Peter employed these people in all parts of his empire to raise up manufactories, to originate trades, and to set mines and iron-works in action.

The Russian minister spoke in a no less commanding tone in Copenhagen than in Sweden, for Denmark was also frightened by Peter's threats to adopt and second the cause of the duke of Holstein. The duke was detained in Russia by repeated promises, of whose fulfilment there was little prospect. The Poles, through Russian mediation, were at length reconciled to their king, and the Russians not only kept firm possession of Courland, but remained in Poland itself, under the pretence of preserving the peace of the country. Peter, nevertheless, in his negotiations with Görtz and Charles XII, had showed himself well inclined to sacrifice King Augustus to his plans; but this scheme was frustrated by the death of Charles.

## PETER AS ADMINISTRATOR

Peter had now achieved a prodigious amount of external and internal power; yet the original nucleus of it all was nothing more than fifty young companions in debauchery, whom he transformed into soldiers, and the remains of a sailing-boat, which had been left forgotten in a magazine. In twenty-five years this seed, nursed by a skilful and vigorous hand, had, on the one part, produced two hundred thousand men, divided into fifty-five regiments, and cantoned, with three hundred field pieces, in permanent quarters; a body of engineers, and, particularly, of formidable artillery-men; and fourteen thousand pieces of cannon, deposited in a great central establishment, in the fortresses, and three military magazines on the frontiers of the three chief national enemies, the Turks, the Poles, and the Swedes. On the other hand, from the relics of the sailing boat had arisen thirty ships of the line, a proportionate number of frigates and smaller vessels of war, two hundred galleys with sails and oars, and a multitude of experienced mariners.

But with what treasures did Peter undertake the moral and physical transformation of such an extensive empire? We behold an entire land metamorphosed, cities containing a hundred thousand souls, ports, canals, and establishments of all kinds, created; thousands of skilful Europeans attracted, maintained and rewarded; several fleets built, and others purchased; a permanent army of a hundred and twenty thousand men, trained, equipped, provided with every species of arms and ammunition, and several times renewed; subsidies of men and money given to Poland; and four wars undertaken. One of these wars spread over half of Europe and when it lasted twenty-one years the treasury from which it was fed still remained full. And Peter, whose revenues on his accession did not exceed a few hundred thousand pounds, declared to Munich that he could have carried on the war for twenty-one years longer without contracting any debt.

Will order and economy be sufficient to account for these phenomena? We must, doubtless, admire them in the czar, who refused himself every superfluity at the same time that he spared nothing for the improvement of his empire. Much must have been gained when, after having wrested the indirect taxes from the boyars, who were at once civil, military, and financial managers, and from those to whom the boyars sold in portions the collecting of them, Peter, in imitation of Holland, entrusted the finances to committees composed of select merchants. We may also feel less surprised at the increase of his revenue, after we have seen him subjecting to taxation the clergy as well as the laity; suppressing a number of monasteries, by forbidding monastic vows to be taken before the age of fifty; and uniting their estates to the domains of the crown, which were swelled by confiscations, by the reversion of his brother Ivan's appanage, and by his conquests from the Swedes.

We must remark, at the same time, that he had opened his states to foreign commerce and to the treasures of Europe, which were carried thither to be exchanged for the many raw materials which had hitherto remained valueless; we must consider the augmentation of revenue which necessarily ensued, and the possibility of requiring to be paid in money a multitude of taxes which had previously been paid in kind. Thus, in place of quotas of provisions, which were brought from great distances and were highly oppressive to the people, he substituted a tax; and the sum raised was applied to the payment of contractors. It is true that even under this new system the state was shamefully robbed; for the nobles contrived in secret to get the contracts into their own hands, in order to fatten upon the blood of the people; but Peter at length perceived them; the evil betrayed itself by its own enormity. The czar then created commissions of inquiry, passed whole days in them, and, during several years, keeping these great peculators always in sight, made them disgorge by fines and confiscations, and punished them by the knout, the halter, and the axe.

To this superintendence by the head of the state, which, subsequently to 1715, the contraction of the war within a narrower circle allowed him to exert, let us add the increase of salary to the collectors, which deprived them of all pretext for misconduct. Nor must it be forgotten that most of the stipends were paid in kind; and that, for several years, the war, being carried on out of the empire, supplied its own wants. It must be observed, too, that the cities and provinces in which the troops were afterwards quartered furnished their pay on the spot, by which the charge of discount was saved; and that the measures which they adopted for their subsistence appear to have been municipal, and consequently as little oppressive as possible. Finally, we must remark, in 1721, the substitution, in place of the Tatar house-tax, of a poll-tax, which was a real impost on land, assessed according to a census repeated every twenty years, the payment of which the agriculturists regulated among themselves, in proportion to the value of their produce.

At the same time, the reformer refused to foreigners the privilege of trading with each other in Russia; he even gave to his subjects exclusively the right of conveying to the frontiers of the empire the merchandise which foreigners had bought from them in the interior. Thus he ensured to his own people the profit of carriage. In 1716 he chose rather to give up an advantageous alliance with the English than to relinquish this right in their favour.

But all the causes we have enumerated will not yet account for the possibility of so many gigantic undertakings and such immense results, with a fixed revenue in specie which, in 1715, was estimated by an attentive observer at only some millions of roubles. But in the fiscal expedients of a despotic empire it is to fluctuating revenue, illegal resources, and arbitrary measures that we must direct our attention; astonishment then ceases, and then begins pity for one party, indignation against another, and surprise excited by the ignorance with respect to commercial affairs which is displayed by the high and mighty geniuses of despotism, in comparison with the unerring instinct which is manifested by the humblest community of men who are free.

It is the genius of Russian despotism, therefore, that we must question as to the means by which it produced such gigantic results; but however far it may be disposed to push its frightful candour, will it point out to us its army recruited by men whom the villages sent tied together in pairs, and at their own expense — soldiers at a penny a day, payable every four months, and often marching without pay; slaves whom it was thought quite enough to feed, and who were contented with some handfuls of rye or of oats made into gruel or into ill-baked bread; unfortunate wretches who, in spite of the blunders of their generals, were compelled to be victorious, under pain of being decimated! Or will this despotism confess that, while it gave nothing to these serfs, who were enlisted for life, it required everything from them; that, after twenty-one years of war, it compelled them to dig canals, like miserable bond-slaves? "For they ought to serve their country," said Peter, "either by defending or enriching it; that is what they are made for."

Could this autocrat pride himself on the perennial fulness of an exchequer which violated its engagements in such a manner that most of the foreigners who were in his service were anxious to quit it? What answer could he make to that hollow and lengthened groan which, even yet, seems to rise from every house in Taganrog, and in St. Petersburg, and from his forts, built by the most deadly kind of statute-labour, and peopled by requisitions? One half of the inhabitants of the villages were sent to construct them, and were relieved by the other half every six months; and the weakest and the most industrious of them never more saw their homes!

These unfortunate beings, whatever might be their calling, from the common delver to the watchmaker and jeweller, were torn without mercy from their families, their ploughs, their workshops, and their counting-houses. They travelled to their protracted torture at their own expense; they worked without any pay. Some were compelled to fill up swamps, and build houses on them; others, to remove thither suddenly, and establish their trade there; and all these hapless men, one part of whom were bent to the earth with toil, and the other part in a manner lost in a new world, were so badly fed and sheltered, or breathed such a pestilential air, that the Russians of that period used to say that St. Petersburg was built upon a bed of human skeletons.

Listen to the complaints of the nobles and the richest merchants: after the gift of a hundred vessels had been required from them, they were forced to unite in this slough to build stone houses, and were also constrained to live there at a much greater expense than they would have incurred in their own homes. And when even the clergy remonstrated against the excessive taxes laid upon the priests (who were able to indemnify themselves out of their flocks) who can be astonished at the possibility of so many creations, and at the plenitude of a treasury which opened so widely to receive and so scantily to disburse?

Personal services, taxes in kind, taxes in money — these were the three main sources of the power of the czar. We have just seen what estimate we ought to form as to the manner in which the first of these was employed. As to the taxes in kind and in money, how could the insulated cries of such a multitude of tax-payers, who were scattered over so wide a space, have reached the present age, if the excess of a simultaneous and universal evil had not blended them into one vast clamour, stronger than time and space? It is from this we learn the names of the throng of taxes which were laid upon everything, and at every opportunity, for the war, the admiralty, the recruiting-service, for the horses used in the public works, for the brick and lime-kilns required in the building of St. Petersburg, for the post-office, the government offices, the extraordinary expenses, for the contributions in kind, for the requisitions of men and their pay and subsistence, and for the salaries of those who were in place; to which must be added innumerable other duties on mills, ponds, baths, beehives, meadows, gardens, and, in the towns, on every square fathom of land which bore the name of black, or non-free. And all this was aggravated by other exorbitant and grinding burdens, and by fleecing the artisans in proportion to their industry and their assumed wealth — the result of which was that they concealed both; the most laborious of them buried their earnings that they might hide them from the nobles; and the nobles intrusted their riches to foreign banks, that they might hide them from the czar.

To this we have yet to add the secondary oppressions; collectors, whose annual pay was, for a long time, only six roubles; and who, nevertheless, accumulated fortunes in four years, for they converted to their own use two thirds of the sums which they extorted; executing by torture whoever was unable to pay, they made the most horrible misuse of the unlimited powers which according to the practice of absolute governments, were necessarily entrusted to them — despotism being unable to act otherwise than by delegation.

These men had the right of levying taxes on all the markets of the country, of laying whatever duties they pleased upon commodities, and of breaking into houses, for the purpose of preventing or discovering infractions of their orders, so that the unfortunate people, finding that they had nought which they could call their own, and that everything, even to their industry, belonged to the czar, ceased to exert themselves for more than a mere subsistence, and lost that spirit which only a man's personal interest can inspire. Accordingly, the forests were peopled with men driven to desperation, and those who at first remained in the villages, finding that they were obliged to pay the taxes of the fugitives as well as their own, speedily joined their companions.

What can bear witness more strongly to the disordered state of those times than the facts themselves? They show us grandees, who were possessed of the highest credit, repeatedly convicted of embezzling the public money; others hanged or beheaded! and a vice-chancellor himself daring, without any authority, to give places and pensions, and, in so poor a country, contriving to purloin nearly a hundred and fifty thousand pounds. It was not, therefore, the czar alone whom the people accused of their sufferings. But such is the tenure of despotism that, in depriving the people of their will, it takes upon itself the whole responsibility. All, however, agree that, about 1715, they beheld their czar astounded at the aspect of such numerous evils; they acknowledge the efforts which he had made, and that all of them had not been fruitless.

But, at the same time, to account for the inexhaustible abundance of the autocrat's treasury, they represent him to us as monopolising everything for his own benefit, giving to the current coin of his empire the value which suited his purpose, and receiving it from foreigners at no more than its intrinsic worth. They accuse him of having engrossed the purchase or sale of numberless native and foreign productions, either by suddenly taxing various kinds of merchandise or by assuming the right of being the exclusive purchaser, at his own price, to sell again at an exorbitant price when he had become the sole possessor. They say also that, forestalling everything, their czar made himself the sole merchant trading from European Russia to China and Siberia, as well as the sole mint-master, the sole trader in tobacco, soap, talc, pitch, and tar; that having also declared himself the only public-house keeper in an empire where drunkenness held sovereign sway, this monopoly annually brought back into his coffers all the pay that had been disbursed from them.

When, in 1716, he wished to defray the expenses of his second journey to Holland, and at the same time avoid being a loser by the rate of exchange, what was the plan which he adopted? He laid hands on all the leather intended for exportation, which he paid for at a maximum fixed by himself, and then exported it on his own account, the proceeds being made payable in Holland, where it was purchased by foreigners.

It is thus that many of his contemporaries explain the riches of a prince who was the principal manufacturer and merchant of a great empire — the creator, the superintendent of its arts. In his eyes, his subjects were nothing more than workmen, whose labours he prompted, estimated, and rewarded according to his own pleasure; he reserved to himself the sale of the produce of their industry, and the immense profits which he thus gained he employed in doubling that produce.

What a singular founder of commerce in his empire was a monarch who drew it all within his own sphere and absorbed it in himself! We may, however, be allowed to believe that he sometimes became a merchant and manufacturer, as he became a soldier and a sailor, for the sake of example, and that the obstinate repugnance of his ignorant subjects to many branches of industry and commerce long compelled him to retain the monopoly of them, whether he would or not. It is curious to remark how his despotism recoiled upon himself when he interfered with matters so impatient of arbitrary power as trade and credit. Soloviev is an example of this. Assisted by the privileges which Peter had granted to him, that merchant succeeded in establishing at Amsterdam the first commercial Russian factory that had ever been worthy of notice; but in 1717, when the czar visited Holland for the second time, his greedy courtiers irritated him against their fellow countryman. Soloviev had not chosen to ransom himself from the envy which his riches inspired. They therefore slandered him to their sovereign; he was arrested and sent back to Russia; his correspondents lost their advances; confidence was ruined, and the autocrat, by confiscating this source of riches, destroyed his work with his own hand. Yet he had a glimpse of something like free-trade principles. He would never impose any higher penalty on smuggling than confiscation. "Commerce," he said, "is like a timid maiden, who is scared by rough usage, and must be won by gentle means. Smuggle who will, and welcome. The merchant who exposes himself to the chance of having his goods confiscated runs a greater risk than my treasury. If he cheats me nine times and I catch him the tenth, I shall be no loser by the game."

### The Church and the Aristocracy

Peter had never been at any pains to conceal his indifference or contempt for the national church; but it was not until that culminating point in his history at which we are now arrived that he ventured to accomplish his design of abolishing the office of patriarch. He had left it unfilled for one-and-twenty years, and he formally suppressed it after the conclusion of the Peace of Nystad; when heaven had declared in his favour, as it seemed to the multitude, who always believe the Deity to be on the strongest side. In the following year, however, the synod, in spite of Theophanes, its president, whom we may consider as his minister for religious affairs, dared to desire that a patriarch might be appointed. But bursting into a sudden passion Peter started up, struck his breast violently with his hand and the table with his cutlass, and exclaimed, "Here, here is your patriarch!" He then hastily quitted the room, casting, as he departed, a stern look upon the panic-struck prelates.

Of the two conquests which Peter consummated about the same time — that over Sweden and that by which he annihilated the independence of the Russian clergy — it is hard to say which was the more gratifying to his pride. Someone having communicated to him the substance of a paper in the English *Spectator*, in which a comparison was made between himself and Louis XIV, entirely to his own advantage, he disclaimed the superiority accorded to him by the essayist, save in one particular: "Louis XIV," said he, "was greater than I, except that I have been able to reduce my clergy to obedience, while he allowed his clergy to rule him."

Soon after the abolition of the patriarchate, Peter celebrated the marriage of Buturlin, the second *kniaz papa* of his creation, with the widow of Sotov, his predecessor in that mock dignity. The bridegroom was in his eighty-fifth year, and the bride nearly of the same age. The messengers who invited the wedding guests were four stutterers; some decrepit old men attended the bride; the running footmen were four of the most corpulent fellows that could be found; the orchestra was placed on a sledge drawn by bears, which being goaded with iron spikes made with their horrid roarings an accompaniment suitable to the tunes played on the sledge. The nuptial benediction was given in the cathedral by a blind and deaf priest with spectacles on. The procession, the marriage, the wedding feast, the undressing of the bride and bridegroom, the ceremony of putting them to bed were all in the same style of repulsive buffoonery. Among the coarse-minded courtiers this passed for an ingenious derision of the clergy.

The nobles were another order in the state whose resistance, though more passive than that of the clergy, was equally insufferable to the czar. His hand had always been heavy against that stiff-necked race. He had no mercy upon their indolence and superstition, no toleration for their pride of birth or wealth. As landed proprietors he regarded them merely as the possessors of fiefs, who held them by the tenure of being serviceable to the state. Such was the spirit of the law of 1715 relative to inheritances, which till then had been equally divided; but from that date the real estate was to descend to one of the males, the choice of whom was left to the father, while only the personal property was to pass to the other children. In this respect the law was favourable to paternal authority and aristocracy; but its real purpose was rendered obvious by other clauses. It decreed that the inheritors of personal property should not be permitted to convert it into real estate until after seven years of military service, ten years of civil service, or fifteen years' profession of some kind of art or of commerce. Nay, more, if we may rely on the authority of Perry, every heir of property to the amount of five hundred roubles, who had not learned the rudiments of his native language or of some ancient or foreign language, was to forfeit his inheritance.

The great nobles had ere this been shorn of their train of boyar followers, or noble domestics, by whom they were perpetually attended, and these were transformed into soldiers, disciplined in the European manner. At the same time several thousand cavalry were formed out of the sons of the priests, who were free men, but not less ignorant and superstitious than their fathers. Against the inertness of the nobles, too, Peter made war even in the sanctuary of their families. Every one of them between the ages of ten and thirty, who evaded an enlistment which was termed voluntary, was to have his property confiscated to the use of the person by whom he was denounced. The sons of the nobles were arbitrarily wrested from them; some were placed in military schools; others were sent to unlearn their barbarian manners and acquire new habits and knowledge among polished nations; many of them were obliged to keep up a correspondence with the czar on the subject of what they were learning; on their return, he himself questioned them, and if they were found not to have benefited by their travels, disgrace and ridicule were their punishment. Given up to the czar's buffoon, they became the laughing-stocks of the court, and were compelled to perform the most degrading offices in the palace. These were the tyrannical punishments of a reformer who imagined that he might succeed in doing violence to nature by beginning education at an age when it ought to be completed, and by subjecting grown-up men to chastisements which would scarcely be bearable for children.

It is with reason that Mannstein reproaches Peter with having expected to transform, by travels in polished countries, men who were already confirmed in their habits, and who were steeped to the core in ignorance, sloth, and barbarism. "The greatest part of them," he says, "acquired nothing but vices." This it was which drew upon Peter a lesson from his sage; for such was the appellation which he gave to Dolgoruki. That senator having pertinaciously, and without assigning any reason, maintained that the travels of the Russian youth would be useless, made no other reply to an impatient and passionate contradiction from the despot than to fold the ukase in silence, run his nail forcibly along it, and then desire the autocrat to try whether, with all his power, he could ever obliterate the crease that was made in the paper.

At last, by his ukase of January 24th, 1722, Peter annihilated the privileges of the old Russian aristocracy, and under the specious pretext of making merit the only source of social distinction, he created a new order of nobility, divided into eight military and as many civil grades, all immediately and absolutely dependent on the czar. The only favour allowed to the old landed aristocracy was that they were not deprived of the right of appearing at court; but none of them could obtain the rank and appointments of an officer, nor, in any company, the respect and distinctions exclusively belonging to that rank, until they had risen to it by actual service. Such was the fundamental principle of that notorious system called the *tchin;* [1] and plausible as it may appear upon a superficial view, it has been fruitful of nothing but hideous tyranny, corruption, chicanery, and malversation. The modern nobility of Russia is in fact but a vile bureaucracy. The only thing truly commendable in the ukase of 1722 is that it degrades to the level of the rabble every nobleman convicted of crime and sentenced to a punishment that ought to entail infamy. Previously, as the reader has already seen, a nobleman might appear unabashed in public, and claim all the privileges of his birth, with his back still smarting from the executioner's lash.

### Commerce with the East

Peter had always encountered great difficulty in attracting to St. Petersburg the commerce of central Russia, which the merchants obstinately persisted in throwing away upon Archangel. Yet at St. Petersburg they enjoyed several privileges, and a milder climate allowed of two freights a year, while at Archangel the ice would admit of only one. To this must be added the advantage of a calmer sea, a better port, lower duties, a much shorter distance, and a much larger concourse of purchasers; but no persuasion could make the Russians abandon the old routine, until at last Peter treated them like ignorant and stubborn children, to whom he would do good in spite of themselves. In 1722 he expressly prohibited the carrying of any goods to Archangel but such as belonged to the district of that government. This ordinance at first raised a great outcry among the traders, both native and foreign, and caused several bankruptcies; but the merchants, accustoming themselves by degrees to come to St. Petersburg, at last found themselves gainers by the change.

The trade with the Mongols and Chinese had been jeopardised by the extortions of Prince Gagarin, the governor of Siberia, and by acts of violence committed by the Russians in Peking and in the capital of Contaish, the prince pontiff of a sect of dissenters from Lamaism. To check the growth of this evil, Peter sent Ismailov, a captain in the guards, to Peking, with presents to the emperor, among which were several pieces of turnery, the work of his own hands. The negotiation was successful; but the Russians soon lost the fruits of it by fresh acts of indiscretion, and were expelled from China by order of Kam-hi. The Russian court alone retained the right of sending a caravan every three years to Peking; but that right again was subsequently lost in

---

[1] The men who have no *tchin*, the *tchornii narod*, that is, the black people, or blackguards.

consequence of new quarrels. The court finally renounced its exclusive privilege, and granted the subjects leave to trade freely on the Kiakhta.

## WAR WITH PERSIA (1722–1724 A.D.)

Peter's attention had long been directed to the Caspian Sea with a view to making it more extensively subservient to the trade of Russia with Persia and central Asia, which as yet had been carried on at Astrakhan alone, through the medium of Armenian factors. Soon after the Peace of Nystad had left the czar free to carry his arms towards the East, a pretext and an opportunity were afforded him for making conquests on the Caspian shores. The Persian Empire was falling to pieces under the hand of the enervated and imbecile Husain Shah. The Lesghiians, one of the tributary nations that had rebelled against him, made an inroad into the province of Shirvan, sacked the city of Shemakha, put the inhabitants to the sword, including three hundred Russian traders, and plundered Russian property to the amount of 4,000,000 roubles. Peter demanded satisfaction; the shah was willing to grant it, but pleaded his helpless condition, and entreated the czar to aid him in subduing his rebellious subjects.

This invitation was promptly accepted. Peter set out for Persia on the 15th of May, 1722, his consort also accompanying him on this remote expedition. He fell down the Volga as far as the city of Astrakhan, and occupied himself in examining the works for the canals that were to join the Caspian, Baltic, and White seas, whilst he awaited the arrival of his forces and material of war. His army consisted of twenty-two thousand foot, nine thousand dragoons, and fifteen thousand Cossacks, besides three thousand sailors on board the several vessels, who, in making a descent, could do the duty of soldiers. The cavalry marched by land through deserts, which are frequently without water; and beyond those deserts, they were to pass the mountains of Caucasus, where three hundred men might keep a whole army at bay; but Persia was in such anarchy that anything might be attempted.

The czar sailed above a hundred leagues southward from Astrakhan, as far as the small fortified town of Andreeva, which was easily taken. Thence the Russian army advanced by land into the province of Daghestan; and manifestoes in the Persian and Russian language were everywhere dispersed. It was necessary to avoid giving any offence to the Ottoman Porte, which besides its subjects, the Circassians and Georgians, bordering on this country, had in these parts some considerable vassals, who had lately put themselves under its protection. Among them, one of the principal was Mahmud D'-Utmich, who styled himself sultan, and had the presumption to attack the troops of the emperor of Russia. He was totally defeated, and the public account says "his country was made a bonfire."

In the middle of September, Peter reached Derbent, by the Persians and Turks called Demir-kapu, i.e. Iron Gate, because it had formerly such a gate towards the south; it is a long narrow town, backed against a steep spur of the Caucasus; and its walls, at the other end, are washed by the sea, which, in stormy weather, is often known to break over them. These walls may be justly accounted one of the wonders of antiquity; they were forty feet high and six broad; flanked with square towers at intervals of fifty feet. The whole work seemed one single piece, being built of a kind of brown free-stone, and a mortar of pounded shells, the whole forming a mass harder than marble itself; it was accessible by sea, but, on the land side, seemed impregnable. Near it were the ruins of an old wall, like that of China, unquestionably built in times of the earliest antiquity; it was carried from the Caspian to the Black Sea, and probably was a rampart thrown up by the ancient kings of Persia against the numerous barbarian hordes dwelling between those two seas. There were formerly three or four other Caspian gates at different passages, and all apparently built for the same end; the nations west, east, and north of this sea having ever been formidable barbarians; and from these parts principally issued those swarms of conquerors which subdued Asia and Europe.

On the approach of the Russian army, the governor of Derbent, instead of standing a siege, laid the keys of the city at the emperor's feet — whether it was that he thought the place not tenable against such a force, or that he preferred the protection of the emperor Peter to that of the Afghan rebel Mahmud. Thus the army quietly took possession of Derbent, and encamped along the sea-shore. The usurper Mahmud, who had already made himself master of a great part of Persia, had neglected nothing to be beforehand with the czar and hinder him from getting into Derbent; he raised the neighbouring Tatars, and hastened thither himself; but Derbent was already in the czar's hands.

Peter was unable to extend his conquests further, for the vessels with provisions, stores, horses, and recruits had been wrecked near Astrakhan; and as the unfavourable season had now set in he returned to Moscow and entered it in triumph (January 5th, 1723), though he had no great reason to boast of the success of his ill-planned expedition.

Persia was still divided between Husain and the usurper Mahmud; the former sought the support of the emperor of Russia; the latter feared him as an avenger who would wrest from him all the fruits of his rebellion. Mahmud used every endeavour to stir up the Ottoman Porte against Peter. With this view, he sent an embassy to Constantinople; and the Daghestan princes, under the sultan's protection, having been dispossessed of their dominions by the arms of Russia, solicited revenge. The Divan were also under apprehensions for Georgia, which the Turks considered part of their dominions. The sultan was on the point of declaring war, when the courts of Vienna and Paris diverted him from that measure. The emperor of Germany made a declaration that if the Turks attacked Russia he should be obliged to join in its defence; and the marquis de Bonac, ambassador from France at Constantinople, seconded the German menaces; he convinced the Porte that their own interest required them not to suffer the usurper of Persia to set an example of dethroning sovereigns, and that the Russian Empire had done no more than the sultan should have done.

During these critical negotiations, the rebel Mahmud had advanced to the gates of Derbent, and laid waste all the neighbouring countries, in order to distress the Russians. That part of ancient Hyrcania, now known by the name of Ghilan, was not spared, which so irritated the people that they voluntarily put themselves under the protection of the Russians. Herein they followed the example of the shah himself, who had sent to implore the assistance of Peter the Great; but the ambassador was scarcely on the road ere the rebel Mahmud seized on Ispahan, and the person of his sovereign. Thamaseb, son of the captive shah, escaped, and getting together some troops fought a battle with the usurper. He was not less eager than his father in urging Peter the Great to protect him, and sent to the ambassador a renewal of the instructions which the shah Husain had given.

Though this Persian ambassador, named Ismail Beg, was not yet arrived, his negotiation had succeeded. On his landing at Astrakhan, he heard that

General Matufkin was on his march with fresh troops to reinforce the Daghestan army. The town of Baku, from which the Persians called the Caspian Sea, the sea of Baku, was not yet taken. He gave the Russian general a letter to the inhabitants, exhorting them, in his master's name, to submit to the emperor of Russia; the ambassador continued his journey to St. Petersburg, and General Matufkin went and sat down before the city of Baku. The Persian ambassador reached the czar's court at the same time as the news of the surrender of that city (August, 1723).

Baku is situated near Shemakha, where the Russian factors were massacred; and although in wealth and number of people inferior to it, is very famous for its naphtha, with which it supplies all Persia. Never was treaty sooner concluded than that of Ismail Beg. The emperor Peter, desirous of revenging the death of his subjects, engaged to march an army into Persia, in order to assist Thamaseb against the usurper; and the new shah ceded to him, besides the cities of Baku and Derbent, the provinces of Ghilan, Mazandaran, and Astarabath.

Ghilan, as we have already noticed, is the southern Hyrcania; Mazandaran, which is contiguous to it, is the country of the Mardi; Astarabath borders on Mazandaran; and these were the three principal provinces of the ancient kings of the Medes. Thus Peter by his arms and treaties came to be master of Cyrus' first monarchy; but this proved to be but a barren conquest, and the empress Anna was glad to surrender it thirteen years afterwards in exchange for some commercial advantages.

So calamitous was the state of Persia that the unhappy sophy Thamaseb wandering about his kingdom, pursued by the rebel Mahmud, the murderer of his father and brothers, was reduced to supplicate both Russia and Turkey at the same time, that they would take one part of his dominions to preserve the other for him. At last it was agreed between the emperor Peter, the sultan Achmet III, and the sophy Thamaseb, that Russia should hold the three provinces above mentioned, and that the Porte should have Kasbin, Tauris, and Erivan, besides what it should take from the usurper.

### LAST YEARS AND DEATH OF PETER

Peter, at his return from his Persian expedition, was more than ever the arbiter of the north. He openly took into his protection the family of Charles XII, after having been eighteen years his declared enemy. He invited to his court the duke of Holstein, that monarch's nephew, to whom he betrothed his eldest daughter, and from that time prepared to assert his rights on the duchy of Schleswig-Holstein, and even bound himself to it in a treaty which he concluded with Sweden (February, 1724). He also obtained from that power the title of royal highness for his son-in-law, which was a recognition of his right to the throne, should King Frederick die without issue. Meanwhile he held Copenhagen in awe of his fleet, and ruled there through fear, as he did in Stockholm and Warsaw.

The state of Peter's health now warned him that his end was near; yet still he delayed to exercise the right of naming a successor, which he had arrogated to himself in 1722. The only step he took which might be interpreted as an indication of his wishes in that respect was the act of publicly crowning his consort Catherine. The ceremony was performed at Moscow (May 18th, 1724) in the presence of the czar's niece, Anna, duchess of Courland, and of the duke of Holstein, his intended son-in-law. The manifesto published by Peter on this occasion deserves notice; after stating that it was customary with Christian monarchs to crown their consorts, and instancing among the orthodox Greek emperors Basilides, Justinian, Heraclius, and Leo the Philosopher, he goes on to say:

"It is also known how far we have exposed our own person, and faced the greatest dangers in our country's cause, during the whole course of the last war, twenty-one years successively, and which, by God's assistance, we have terminated with such honour and advantage, that Russia never saw a like peace, nor gained that glory which has accrued to it by this war. The empress Catherine, our dearly beloved consort, was of great help to us in all these dangers, not only in the said war but likewise in other expeditions, in which, notwithstanding the natural weakness of her sex, she voluntarily accompanied us, and greatly assisted us with her advice, particularly at the battle of the river Pruth against the Turks, where our army was reduced to 22,000 men, and that of the Turks consisted of 270,000. It was in this desperate exigency that she especially signalised a zeal and fortitude above her sex; and to this all the army and the whole empire can bear witness. For these causes, and in virtue of the power which God hath given us, we have resolved, in acknowledgment of all her fatigues and good offices, to honour our consort with the imperial crown, which, by God's permission, shall be accomplished this winter at Moscow; and of this resolution we hereby give notice to all our faithful subjects, our imperial affection towards whom is unalterable."

In this manifesto nothing was said of the empress' succeeding to the throne; but the nation were in some degree prepared for that event by the ceremony itself, which was not customary in Russia, and which was performed with sumptuous splendour. A circumstance which might further cause Catherine to be looked upon as the presumptive successor was that the czar himself, on the coronation day, walked before her on foot, as first knight of the order of St. Catherine, which he had instituted in 1714 in honour of his consort. In the cathedral he placed the crown on her head with his own hand. Catherine would then have fallen on her knees, but he raised her up, and when she came out of the cathedral the globe and sceptre were carried before her.

It was not long before Peter was with difficulty restrained from sending to the block the head on which he had but lately placed the crown. We have already mentioned that the enmity of his first wife is said to have sprung from her jealousy of Anne de Moens, who was for awhile the czar's mistress, and whom, as Villebois tells us, he had serious thoughts of raising to the throne. But she submitted to his passion only through fear, and Peter, disgusted with her coldness towards him, left her to follow her inclinations in marrying a less illustrious lover. Five-and-twenty years afterwards Eudoxia was avenged through the brother of her rival. Anne de Moens, then the widow of General Balk, was about the person of Catherine, and the handsome and graceful young Moens de la Croix was her chamberlain. A closer intimacy soon arose between them, and so unguarded were they that Villebois, who saw them together only in public during a very crowded reception at court, says that their conduct was such as left no doubt on his mind that the empress was guilty. The czar's suspicions were roused, and he set spies upon Catherine.

The court was then at Peterhof; Prince Repnin, president of the war department, slept not far from the czar; it was two o'clock in the morning; all at once the marshal's door was violently thrown open, and he was startled by abrupt and hasty footsteps: he looked round in astonishment; it was Peter the Great; the monarch was standing by the bedside; his eyes sparkled with rage, and all his features were distorted with convulsive fury. Repnin tells us that at the sight of that terrible aspect he was appalled, gave himself up for lost, and remained motionless; but his master, with a broken and panting voice, exclaimed to him, " Get up! speak to me! there's no need to dress yourself"; and the trembling marshal obeyed.

He then learned that, but the instant before, guided by too faithful a report, the czar had suddenly entered Catherine's apartment; that the crime was revealed, the ingratitude proved; that at daybreak the empress should lose her head — that the emperor was resolved!

The marshal, gradually recovering his voice, agreed that such a monstrous act of treachery was horrible; but he reminded his master of the fact that the crime was as yet known to no one, and of the impolicy of making it public; then, growing bolder, he dared to call to recollection the massacre of the strelitz, and that every subsequent year had been ensanguined by executions; that, in fine, after the imprisonment of his sister, the condemning of his son to death, and the scourging and imprisonment of his first wife, if he should likewise cut off the head of his second, Europe would no longer look upon him in any other light than that of a ferocious prince, who thirsted for the blood of his subjects and even of those who were a part of himself. Besides, he added, the czar might have satisfaction by giving up Moens to the sword of the law upon other charges; and as to the empress, he could find means to rid himself of her without any prejudice to his glory.

While Repnin was thus advising, the czar, who stood motionless before him, gazed upon him intently and wildly, and kept a gloomy silence. But in a short time, as was the case when he was labouring under strong emotions, his head was twisted to the left side, and his swollen features became convulsively contracted — signs of the terrible struggle by which he was tortured. And yet the excessive working of his mind held his body in a state of frightful immovability. At length, he rushed precipitately out of the chamber into the adjoining room. For two whole hours he hastily paced it; then suddenly entering again like a man who had made up his mind, he said to Repnin, "Moens shall die immediately! I will watch the empress so closely that her first slip shall cost her life!"

Moens and his sister were at once arrested. They were both confined in the winter palace, in an apartment to which none had admission except the emperor himself, who carried them their food. At the same time a report was spread that the brother and the sister had been bribed by the enemies of the country, in hopes of bringing the empress to act upon the mind of the czar prejudicially to the interests of Russia. Moens was interrogated by the monarch in presence of General Uschakov; and after having confessed whatever they pleased, he lost his head on the block (November 27th). At the same time his sister, who was an accomplice in the crime and a favourite of Catherine, received the knout, and was banished to Siberia; her property was confiscated; her two sons were degraded and were sent to a great distance, on the Persian frontier, as private soldiers.

Moens walked to meet his fate with manly firmness. He always wore a diamond bracelet, on which was a miniature of Catherine; but, as it was not perceived at the time of his being seized, he found means to conceal it under his garter; and when he was on the scaffold he confided this secret to the Lutheran pastor who accompanied him, and under cover of his cloak slipped the bracelet into his hand to restore it to the empress.

The czar was a spectator of the punishment of Moens from one of the windows of the senate. The execution being over, he got upon the scaffold, took the head of Moens by the hair, and expressed with brutal energy how delighted he was with the vengeance he had taken. The same day Peter had the cruelty to conduct Catherine in an open carriage round the stake on which was fixed the head of her unfortunate lover. He watched her countenance attentively, but fortunately she had self-command enough not to betray her grief. Repnin adds that, from that dreadful night till his death, Peter never more spoke to the empress except in public, and that, in his dwelling, he always remained separate from her.[e]

Peter the Great lived only to his fifty-third year. In spite of frequent attacks of illness and of his calling himself an old man, the emperor might have hoped to live yet a long while and to be able to dispose of his great inheritance in accordance with the interests of the state. But his days were already numbered. When Peter came to St. Petersburg in March, 1723, on his return from Persia, he appeared in much better health than before the campaign; in the summer of 1724 he became very weak, but in the second half of September he grew visibly better, walked at times in his gardens, and sailed on the Neva. On the 22nd of September he had a very severe attack; it is said that he fell into such a state of irritation that he struck the doctors and called them asses; afterwards he again became better, and on the 29th of September he was present at the launching of a frigate, although he told the Dutch minister Wild that he still felt rather weak. In spite of this he set off in the beginning of October to inspect the Ladoga canal, against the advice of his doctor Blumentrost; then he went to the Olonetz iron works and hammered out with his own hands a bar of iron of the weight of three pouds;[1] from there he went to Starya Rusa to inspect the salt works, and in the beginning of November he went by water to St. Petersburg. But there, at a place called Lakta, he saw that a boat coming from Kronstadt with soldiers had run aground; he allowed no one to restrain him, but went himself to their assistance and helped to float the boat and save the people, standing up to his waist in the water. The attacks were speedily renewed; Peter arrived at St. Petersburg ill and could not regain his health; the affair of Mons also aggravated his condition. He occupied himself but little with affairs, although he showed himself as usual in public. On the 17th of January, 1725, the malady increased; Peter ordered that a movable church should be constructed near his sleeping room and on the 22nd he made his confession and received the sacrament; his strength began to leave him, he no longer cried out as before from the violence of the pain but only groaned. On the 27th all criminals were pardoned who had been condemned to death or to the galleys according to the articles of war, excepting those guilty of the first two offences against the law — murder and repeated robbery; the noblemen who had not appeared at the military reviews at the appointed time were also pardoned. On that day, at the expiration of the second hour, Peter asked for paper and tried to write, but the pen fell out of his hand; of that which he had written only the words "give up everything" could be deciphered; he then ordered his daughter Anna Petrovna to be called so that she might write under his dictation, but he could not pronounce the words. The following day, the 28th of January, at the beginning of the sixth hour after midnight, Peter the Great was no more. Catherine was almost unceasingly with him, and it was she who closed his eyes.

In terrible physical sufferings, in full recognition of the weakness of humanity, asking for the comfort afforded by religion, died the greatest of historical workers. We have already spoken in the proper place of how the work of

---

[1] A poud contains forty Russian pounds, or about thirty-six pounds avoirdupois.

Peter was prepared by all preceding history; how it necessarily proceeded from the same; how it was required by the people, who by means of a tremendous revolution in their existence and customs, by means of an extraordinary effort of strength, had to be brought forth from their hopeless condition into a new way, a new life. But this in nowise diminishes the greatness of the man who in the accomplishment of so difficult an exploit lent his mighty hand to a great nation, and by the extraordinary power of his will strained all her forces and gave direction to the movement.

### SOLOVIEV'S ESTIMATE OF PETER'S WORK

Revolutionary epochs constitute a critical time for the life of nations, and such was the epoch of the reformation of Peter. Complaints of the great burdens were to be heard from all sides — and not without cause. The Russian knew no rest from recruiting: recruiting for painful, ceaseless military service in the infantry, and for the newly created naval service; recruiting of workmen for new and difficult labour in distant and unattractive places; recruiting of scholars for the schools, and of young men to be sent to study abroad. For the army and for the fleet, for the great works and undertakings, for the schools and the hospitals, for the maintenance of diplomats and diplomatic bribery, money was necessary. But there was no money in the impoverished state, and heavy taxes in money and in kind had to be levied upon all; in necessary cases they were deducted from the salaries; well-to-do people were ruined by the construction of houses in St. Petersburg; everything that could be taken was taken, or farmed out; the poor people had one object of luxury — oak coffins; but these were confiscated by the fiscus and sold at a high price; *raskolniki* (dissenters) had to pay double taxes; the bearded had to pay for the privilege of wearing their beards.

A BASHKIRIAN WOMAN

Orders upon orders were issued; men were to seek for ores and minerals, and for dye-stuffs; they were to tend their sheep not as they had previously done, to dress the skins differently, to build boats in a new way, to dare weave no narrow pieces of cloth, to take their goods to the west instead of to the north.[1] New government centres were created, new courts established, the people did not know where to turn, the members of these new institutions and courts did not know how to go about their novel duties, and official papers were sent from one place to another.

The standing army pressed heavily on the unarmed population. People tried to escape from the hard service and hide themselves, but all were not

[1 That is, to St. Petersburg instead of to Archangel.]

successful, and cruel punishments threatened the disobedient. Illiterate nobles were forbidden to marry. Meanwhile beneath the new French frocks and wigs there was the old coarseness of manners; the same want of respect for human dignity in oneself and in others; the same hideous drunkenness and noisy brawling with which every festivity was terminated. Woman was brought into the society of men, but she was not surrounded with the respect due to her sex and obligations; pregnant women were made to drink to excess. The members of the highest institutions quarrelled and abused each other in the coarsest manner; bribery was as bad as before; the weak were subjected to every violence from the strong, and, as formerly, the noble was permitted to oppress the *moujik* (peasant), the well-born the base-born.

But this is only one side: there is another. The people were passing through a hard school — the stern teacher was not sparing in punishments for the idle and those who violated the regulations; but the matter was not limited to threats and punishments alone. The people were really learning, learning not only figures and geometry, not only in Russian and foreign schools; the people were learning the duties of citizens, the work of citizens. At the emission of every important regulation, at the inauguration of every great reform, the lawgiver explains why he acts thus, why the new is better than the old. The Russians then received such instruction for the first time; what now seems to us so simple and within the reach of all was first learned by these people from the edicts and manifestoes of Peter the Great.

For the first time the mind of the Russian was awakened, his attention directed to the great questions of political and social organisation; whether he turned sympathisingly or unsympathisingly to the words and deeds of the czar was a matter of indifference — he was obliged to think over these words and deeds, and they were continually there to arouse him. That which might have ruined a decrepit society, a people incapable of development — the shocks of the epoch of reforms, the utter restlessness — developed the forces of a vigorous young nation which had been long asleep and required a violent shock to awaken it. And there was much to be learned. Above was the governing senate, the synod; everywhere was collegiate organisation, the advantages of which were set forth in the church statutes. Everywhere the principle of election was introduced. The trade guilds were withdrawn from the jurisdiction of the local governors and given their own independent administration. Peter's whole system of government was directed against the chief evils from which ancient Russia had suffered: the immaturity of forces, the want of a public spirit, the lack of independence of action, the absence of initiative capacity. The former council of the czar *(douma)* had suffered from all the deficiencies enumerated. Peter established the senate, to which fidelity had to be sworn and the ukases of which had to be obeyed as the ukases of the czar himself. Peter was not jealous of the power created

A PEASANT OF LITTLE RUSSIA

by him: he did not limit it; but on the contrary he continually and without ceremony required that it should profit by its importance, that it should really be a governing body.   Peter's reproaches and rebukes to the senate were directed against its slowness, its languor, its want of management, and its inability to carry its decrees into immediate effect.   The Russian of former times who had received a commission from the government went about in leading strings.   He was not trusted, his smallest movement was feared, he was swathed like a child in long detailed instructions, and upon every fresh occasion that presented itself and was not defined in the instructions, the grown up child required teaching.   This habit of asking for orders greatly angered Peter: "Act according to your own consideration, how can I tell you from such a distance!" he wrote to those who asked him for instructions. He employed the collegiate system — whether he had met with it in the west or whether it had been advised by Leibnitz is a matter of indifference; he employed it everywhere as the most powerful method of training the Russian people to unrestrained public activity.   Instead of separate individuals, institutions came to the front, and over all rose the state, the real significance of which the people of Russia now learned for the first time when they had to take the oath.

Having set forth the importance of the state, and demanding that heavy sacrifices should be made, to this new divinity, himself giving the example, he nevertheless took measures that the individual should not be crushed, but should receive the requisite, balancing development.   The first place must here naturally be given to the civilisation introduced by Peter, to the acquaintance with other nations in advance of Russia.   We know that before the time of Peter the bond of the family was powerfully maintained in Russia; its prolonged existence is easily explained by the condition of society, which was unable to safeguard its members, and who were therefore obliged to seek security in private associations, chief among which was the natural blood relationship between members of the same family or clan. The elder protected the younger, and had power over them because they had to answer to the government for them.   It was thus in every sphere of society; the independent Russian never presented himself alone, but always accompanied by his brothers and nephews; to be without clan and family was equivalent to being in the utmost poverty.   It is easy to understand that the clan association hindered the development of personality; the state could not give to personal merit power over clan rights; jealous to the last degree of any insult to the honour of his clan, the ancient Russian was indifferent to his own personal honour.   But by the end of the seventeenth century the demands of the state had so increased that the unity of the clan could not withstand them, and the destruction of precedence (*mest-nitchestov*) struck a blow to the clan bond in the highest class of society, among those in the service of the czar.   The reform of Peter struck a final blow by its decided, exclusive attention to personal merit, by raising persons "above their old parents" (that is, their kinsfolk), by bringing into the service a large number of foreigners; it became advantageous for new men to appear to have no clan relations, and many of them began willingly to trace their origin from foreign countries.

As to the lower ranks of the population, the blow to the clan bond was brought about by the poll-tax; the former expression, "such a one with his brothers and nephews," began to disappear, for the brothers and nephews had to pay separately each for himself, and appeared as separate, independent individuals.   And not only did the former clan relations disappear, but even within the family itself, while requiring the deepest respect from children to their parents,[1] Peter recognised the right of the individual, and enjoined that marriages should be celebrated by the agreement of the children, and not by the will of their parents; the right of the person was also recognised in the bond-servant, for the landowner had to swear that he would not compel his peasants to marry against their will. We have heard the dispassionate declaration of a contemporary Russian as to the corruption of persons in the service of the czars in the seventeenth and the beginning of the eighteenth centuries, of their indifference to honour, so that amongst them the shameful saying was current: "Flight may be dishonourable, but it is salutary." Under Peter this saying was extirpated, and he himself testified that in the second half of the Northern War flight from the field of battle had ceased. Finally the personality of woman was recognised in consequence of her liberation from the *terem*.[2]

Thus were the people of Russia trained in the stern school of reform. The terrible labour and privations they endured were not in vain. A vast and comprehensive programme was traced out for many future years, not on paper but on the earth which must open up its riches to the Russian, who through science had acquired the full right of disposing of it; on the sea, where the Russian fleet had now appeared; on the rivers, united by canals; it was traced out in the state by the new institutions and regulations; it was traced out in the people by the new civilisation, by the enlarging of its mental sphere, by the rich stores of mental food furnished by the west, now disclosed to his view, and by the new world created within Russia herself. The greater part of all this was only in its beginnings; the rest in rough outline — for much only the materials were prepared, only indications made; and therefore we have called the work of the epoch of reform a programme, which Russia is fulfilling until now, and will continue to fulfil, and any deviation from which has always been accompanied by grievous consequences.

Clearly recognising that the Russian people must pass through a hard school, Peter did not hesitate to subject it to the painful, humiliating position of a pupil; but at the same time he succeeded in balancing the disadvantages of such a position by glory and greatness: in converting it into an active one, he succeeded both in creating the political importance of Russia and the means for its maintenance. A difficult problem presented itself to Peter; for the education of the Russian people it was necessary to call in foreign instructors, directors who naturally endeavoured to subject their pupils to their influence, to set themselves above them; but this humiliated the pupils, of whom Peter wished to make masters as soon as possible. He did not give way to the temptation, did not accept proposals to carry the work to a speedy success with the aid of learned foreigners; he desired that his own Russian subjects should pass through an active, practical school, even though it might occasion great losses and be accompanied by great discomforts. We have seen how he hastened to rid himself of a foreign field-marshal, how he put Russians in all the highest positions and foreigners only in secondary ones; and we have also seen how he was rewarded for his faith in his people and his devotion to it.

It was with the same uncommon caution, with the skill required for remaining within due bounds that Peter solved the difficult problem of church

---

[1] Peter's own words were as follows: "Those who do not respect them that have given them life are most ungrateful creatures, and ingratitude is the most abominable of all vices." — GOLIKOV.[m]

[2] The separate female apartments, corresponding to the Attic γυναικών.]

reform.  He destroyed unipersonal government and replaced it by the collegiate or council system, which fully corresponded with the spirit of the eastern church; we have seen that one of Peter's chief cares was to raise the Russian clergy by means of education; in spite of his strong and comprehensible aversion to monasticism he did not abolish this institution as did Henry VIII of England — he only tried to give it a greater activity corresponding to its character.

From whatever point of view we study the epoch of reforms, we must fall into wonderment both at the mental and physical powers of Peter.  Powers are developed by their exercise, and we do not know of any historical worker whose sphere of activity was so vast.  Born with an unusually wide-awake intellect, Peter cultivated this quickness of perception to the highest degree. From his youth he listened and looked to everything himself, was not guided or restricted by anyone, but was excited and aroused by the state of society, already then on the threshold of changes and hesitating between two directions, agitated by the question of of the old and new, when by the side of ancient Moscow the advance guard of the west, the German suburb, was already in view.  Peter's nature was cast in the old Russian heroic mould; he loved breadth and scope; this explains the fact that besides his conscious attraction for the sea he had also an unconscious attraction for it: the heroes of ancient Russia yearned for the wide steppes — the new hero yearned after the broad ocean; places shut in by mountains were displeasing and wearisome to him.  Thus he complained to his wife of the situation of Karslbad: "This place is so merry that it might almost be called an honorable prison, for it is so squeezed in between mountains that the sun can hardly be seen."  In another letter he calls Karlsbad a hole in the ground.

To the powers of a hero of ancient times corresponded passions not moderated by any regular, skilful education.  We are aware to what lengths the unbridled passions of a vigorous man could be carried in ancient Russian society, unrestrained as it was by due bounds: how then could such a society put a check upon the passions of a man who stood at the very summit of power?  But an observant contemporary woman has very justly declared with regard to Peter that he was both a very good and a very bad man. Without denying or diminishing the dark side of Peter the Great's character, let us not forget the brighter side, which outweighed the dark and was able to attach people so strongly to him.  If his wrath burst forth at times so terribly against those whom he regarded as the enemies of the country and of the general welfare, yet he attached to himself strongly, and was strongly attached to persons of opposite tendencies.

An unusual greatness, joined to the recognition of the insignificance of mere human intellect, a stern insistence on the fulfilment of duties, a stern demand for truth, the capacity of listening to the harshest objections, an extraordinary simplicity, sociability, and kind heartedness — all these qualities powerfully attached to Peter the best of the men who had occasion to come in contact with him; and it is therefore easy to understand the impression produced upon them by the news of the death of the great emperor. Nepluev writes as follows: "In the month of February, of the year 1725, I received the lamentable news that the father of the country, the emperor Peter I had departed this life.  I watered this paper with my tears, both out of duty to my sovereign and in remembrance of his many kindnesses and favours to me; verily I do not lie when I say that I was unconscious for more than twenty-four hours, for it would have been sinful for me to have been otherwise.  This monarch brought our country into equality with others;

[1725 A.D.]

he taught us to know that we, too, are men; in a word, whatever you look upon in Russia was all begun by him, and whatever will be done in future will be drawn from the same source; as to me personally, above what I have already written, the sovereign was a good and merciful father. May the Lord grant to his soul, which laboured so greatly for the common good, rest with the righteous!"

Another person who was in close contact with Peter (Nartov) says: "If it should ever happen to a philosopher to look through the archives of Peter's secret acts, he would shudder with horror at what was done against the monarch. We who were the servants of that great sovereign sigh and shed tears, when we sometimes hear reproaches against the hard-heartedness and cruelty which were not in reality to be met with in him. If many knew what he endured and by what sorrows he was cut to the heart, if they knew how indulgent he was to the weaknesses of humanity and how he forgave crimes that did not deserve mercy they would be amazed. And although Peter the Great is no longer with us, yet his spirit lives in our souls, and we, who had the felicity of being near this monarch, shall die faithful to him, and the ardent love we had for our earthly god will be buried together with us. We are not afraid to proclaim the deeds of our father, in order that a noble fearlessness and truth shall be learned from them." *i*

A KABARDINIAN

### KOSTOMAROV'S ESTIMATE OF PETER

As an historical character Peter presents an original phenomenon, not only in the history of Russia but in the history of all humanity, of all ages and all nations. The immortal Shakespeare by his artistic genius created in Hamlet an inimitable type of a man in whom reflection takes the ascendancy over his will and does not permit him to give substance or effect to his desires and intentions. In Peter not the genius of the artist, understanding the meaning of human nature, but nature herself created the opposite type — that of a man with an irresistible, indefatigable will in whom every thought was at once transformed into action. "I will it, because I count it good, and what I will must infallibly be" — such was the device of the whole life and work of this man.

He was distinguished by an aptitude and enterprise unattainable for ordinary mortals. Not having received any regular education, he wished to know everything and was obliged to study a great deal; however, the Russian czar was gifted with such a wealth of capacities that even with his short preparation he astounded persons who had spent their lives over what Peter only studied by the way. All that he learned he endeavoured to apply in Russia in order to transform her into a mighty European state. This was the thought that he cherished sincerely and wholly during the continuation of his entire life. Peter lived at a time when it was impossible for Russia to remain in the same beaten track, but must necessarily enter upon the path of renovation. Being gifted with mental clearsightedness, he recognised this necessity of his fatherland and set about the task with all the force of his gigantic will.

Peter's autocracy, inherited from his forefathers, helped him more than anything. He created the army and the fleet, although for this was required an innumerable multitude of human sacrifices and the fruits of many years of national labour. All was offered by the people for this object, although the people itself did not clearly understand it and therefore did not desire it; but everything was given because the czar wished it. Incredible taxes were imposed, hundreds of thousands of the healthy young generation were sent to the war or to hard and painful labour never to return again. The people were ruined and impoverished in order that Russia might gain the sea, that she might extend her frontiers and organise an army capable of being measured against its neighbours. The Russians had grown attached to their ancient manners and customs, they hated everything foreign; immersed in outward forms of piety, they showed an aversion to the sciences. The autocratic czar compelled them to adopt foreign dress, to study foreign sciences, to disdain the customs of their forefathers, and to forswear their most sacred traditions. And the Russians mastered themselves; they were obedient because it was the wish of their autocratic sovereign.

During the whole of his reign Peter struggled against the prejudices and evil nature of his subjects and dependants; he prosecuted embezzlers of the public funds, takers of bribes, imposters, and lamented that things were not done in Russia as he could have wished. His partisans sought and even now seek to find in all this the cause of the obdurate vices and defects of the ancient Russian. But looking into the matter dispassionately, it follows that much must be ascribed to the character of Peter's action. It is impossible to make a man happy against his own will or to force his nature. History shows us that, in a despotically ruled society, the vices that chiefly hinder the fulfilment of the most laudable and salutary preconceived designs of the power are most frequently and saliently manifested. What were the measures that Peter employed for bringing his great reforms to fulfilment? The tortures of the Preobrajenski Edict and the secret chancery, sentences of a painful death, prisons, the galleys, the knout, the tearing of the nostrils, espionage, the encouragement by rewards of informers. It is comprehensible that by such means Peter could inoculate neither civil courage, nor the feeling of duty, nor that love for one's neighbour which is above all material or intellectual forces and more powerful than knowledge itself; in a word, although he established a multitude of institutions and created a new political organisation for Russia, yet Peter was not able to create a living, new Russia.

Possessed by the abstract idea of the state and sacrificing to this idea the temporary prosperity of the people, Peter did not act sincerely by the people. For him they only existed as the ciphers in a total — as the material good for the construction of the edifice of the state. He valued the Russian people as far as they were necessary to him in creating soldiers, masons, excavators, sailors; or, by their laboriously earned kopeck, in furnishing him with means for the maintenance of the state mechanism. Peter himself by his personality might serve as a model for the people he ruled over and transformed only in his boundless, untiring love of work; but in nowise by the moral qualities of his character. He did not even endeavour to restrain his passions, which not unfrequently led him to furious outbursts and bloody actions, although he severely punished like actions in those he ruled over. Peter allowed drunkenness and double dealing in himself, yet he prosecuted these same vices in his subjects. Many shocking actions that he committed have been justified by the sophisms of political necessity. To what an extent his ferocity and bloodthirstiness were carried is shown by the fact that he was not afraid to lower his royal dignity by taking upon himself the office of hangman during the time of the savage execution of the strelitz. Throughout his reign a bloody vapour arose from those who were tortured and put to death in accordance with the Preobrajenski Edict and contaminated the air of Russia, but it evidently did not trouble the slumbers of her sovereign.

Peter himself justified his cruel punishments by the requirements of justice, but facts prove that he was not equally inflexible in his justice to all and did not set an example to others in the indulgence he showed to his favourite, Menshikov, at whose hands such iniquities were committed as would have cost others their lives. His own outward political actions were not distinguished by irreproachable integrity and rectitude; the Northern War can never be justified from the point of view of justice. It is also impossible to call honourable the expedient Peter made use of with the English king George when, in spite of the clearest evidence, he assured him of his devotion and non-participation in the pretender's designs. How far Peter respected the rights of neighbouring foreign nations when he had no reason to fear them is shown by his savage behaviour to the uniat monks of Polosk — an action for which he himself would have probably punished by death any one of his subjects who had thus dared to take the law into his own hands in a foreign land.

All the dark sides of Peter's character may of course be easily excused by the features of the age in which he lived; it may justly be pointed out to us that for the greater part such traits are also to be found in the characters of his contemporaries. It remains indubitable that Peter surpassed the sovereigns contemporary with him by the vastness of his intellect and by his untiring love of work; but in moral respects he was not better than many of them; and it was for this reason that the society which he wished to re-create did not rise superior to those societies which were governed by Peter's contemporaries. Until Peter's reign Russia was plunged in ignorance; and, boasting of her bigoted, ceremonial piety, glorified herself with the name of the New Israel, whilst in reality she was by no means a "new Israel." By his despotic measures Peter created out of her a monarchy that was a terror to foreigners by her army and fleet; he communicated to the upper class of her people the outward marks of European civilisation; yet Russia after Peter did not in reality become the "new Israel" that she had desired to be before his time.

All Peter's pupils, the men of new Russia who outlived him, were entangled in their own snares; following their own egotistical aims, they perished on the scaffold or in exile, and the Russian public man adopted in his conscience the rule that he might do anything he found profitable, although it might be immoral, justifying himself by the fact that other nations did the same. Yet, in spite of all this, as a historical royal worker Peter has preserved for us in his personality such an exalted moral trait that it involuntarily draws our heart to him; this trait is his devotion to the ideal to which he wholly consecrated his soul during all his lifetime. He loved Russia, loved the Russian people, loved it in the sense of the mass of Russian men who were his contemporaries and subjects in the sense of that ideal to which he desired to bring his people; and this love constitutes in him that great quality which incites us, beyond our own will, to love his personality, setting aside both his bloody tribunal and all his demoralising despotism reflecting a baneful influence even on posterity. Because of Peter's love for the ideal of the Russian people, the

Russians will love Peter until he himself loses the national ideal, and for the sake of this love they will forgive him all that a heavy burden has laid upon his memory.[d]

### HAXTAUSEN'S ESTIMATE OF PETER'S INFLUENCE

From the sixteenth to the seventeenth centuries a national spirit dominated entirely. Moreover, Russian sovereigns had, for many years, perceived that the people were behind other nations who had sprung into being as late as themselves or who were inferior either in origin or in physical or intellectual faculties. To remedy this tardy growth they conceived it necessary to put themselves into direct contact with the west in order to borrow its light and imitate its progress. The best way of accomplishing this was, they thought, to get as many foreigners as possible into the country to train the young; to give the state new institutions, and remodel the old on western principles. Ivan Vasilievitch had already drawn a crowd of foreigners, and particularly Germans; had even tried to put his army on a European footing. The successors of the Romanov branch followed zealously in this path, but no prince felt more strongly than Peter I the necessity of letting Russia take a foremost place in Europe. His quick impetuous nature detested slow and incomplete measures. To him, to sow without reaping, or prune without tasting the fruits, was labour provoking all his repugnance.

The impetus he gave Russia is that in which she still continues. Everywhere in the public and social life of this people is to be noticed the impulse he gave. It is an accomplished fact that no human power can annul; so all inquiry to find out if this impetus was necessary and favourable to Russia would be inopportune and sterile. There is, however, no doubt that in Peter's haste in his work of reform he did not sufficiently consider national things both great and good; that he introduced a crowd of foreign innovations, some mediocre, some positively bad, without pausing to think whether they were suitable to the climate, the established order of things, or if they would fit in harmoniously with Russian nationality.[j]

## CHAPTER VII

## CATHERINE I TO PETER III

[1725–1762 A.D.]

### CATHERINE I (1725–1727 A.D.)

At the death of Peter the Great two powerful parties were arrayed against each other, one supporting his youthful grandson Alexievitch, and the other advancing the claims of Catherine, the Livonian. The Galitzins, the Dolgoruki, Repnins, and all Old Russia wished to crown Peter's son, Alexis; but those who owed their elevation to Peter I, or had been involved in the suit against his son, as well as the members of the tribunal that had condemned the czarevitch, felt that their only hope of safety lay in raising Catherine to the throne. This party, counting among its numbers the most capable and enlightened men, still held the highest authority in the administration and in the army, and its adversaries felt that a compromise was the most that they could expect. Dmitri Galitzin proposed to proclaim Peter II, but only under the guardianship of the widowed empress.

Tolstoi combated this proposition by showing that it was the surest method of arming parties against each other, of furnishing hostile factions a pretext for inc ting the people to rebellion against the regent. He demonstrated that in the absence of the testamentary disposition she had the best right to succeed Peter I; furthermore, she had been solemnly crowned, had received the oath of allegiance from her subjects, had been initiated into all the state secrets, and had learned from her husband the art of reigning. The officers and regiments of the guards declared energetically in favour of the heroine of Pruth, and it was finally decided that she should reign alone, with an authority as absolute as that of her dead husband. This was a greater novelty in Russia than the regency of Sophia; Catherine was not only a woman, but a foreigner, a captive, and a second wife, scarcely to be considered as a wife at all. Many were the protests against a decision which excluded from the throne the grandson of Peter the Great, and certain of the *raskolniks* submitted to the torture rather than swear allegiance to a woman.

Menshikov, one of Catherine's earlier lovers, now became all-powerful. He stopped the suit for mal-administration that the late czar had commenced against him, and obtained for himself Baturin, the former capital of Mazeppa, which was equivalent to the principality of Ukraine. His despotic and evil character rendered him odious to his companions and discord everywhere broke out among the "eaglets" of Peter the Great. Iagushinski publicly lamented on the tomb of the czar, and Tolstoi was later exiled to Siberia. Catherine, however, restrained the ambition of her favourite and refused to sacrifice her other councillors to him.

Catherine's rule, which was a continuation of that of Peter the Great, gave the lie to the pessimistic predictions that had announced the abandonment of St. Petersburg and the fleet, and the return to Moscow. The greater part of the plans for reform entertained by the czar were put in execution. The Academy of Sciences was inaugurated in 1726, the publication of the *Gazette* was carefully supervised, the order of Alexander Nevski, originated by Peter, was founded, the Danish captain Béhring was placed at the head of the Kamchatka scientific expedition, Chasirov, recalled from exile, was commanded to write the history of Peter the Great, and Anna Petrovna was solemnly married to the duke of Holstein, to whom she had been affianced by her father. On the other hand the senate and the holy synod lost their title of Directors, and the affairs of state were given into the hands of the secret high council which sat under the presidency of the empress and was composed of Menshikov, the admiral Apraxin, the chancellor Golovkin, Tolstoi, Dmitri Galitzin, and the vice-chancellor Ostermann.

On her deathbed Catherine designated as her successor Peter Alexievitch, the grandson of her husband, and in default of Peter her two daughters Anna of Holstein and Elizabeth. Pending the majority of the youthful emperor the regency was to be conducted by a council composed of Anna and Elizabeth, the duke of Holstein, Menshikov, Apraxin, Golovkin, Ostermann, and others; but Menshikov after the first sitting took the duties of regent upon himself.

### PETER II (1727–1730 A.D.)

The empress died on the 17th of May, 1727, and on the following day the nobility and clergy assembled in the palace to be present at the reading of the will by which Peter was made emperor of all the Russias. Menshikov had taken measures to retain his high position and even to increase his power under the new reign. With the design of removing all those who might be detrimental to him he banished Apraxin from court, sent Iagushinski to Ukraine and despatched Makarov on a mission to the mines of Siberia. Menshikov had further obtained Catherine's consent to the betrothal of his daughter to the young prince. He gave his own palace as a residence for the emperor and surrounded him with men on whose devotion he could count. He assumed the title of generalissimo and signed his letters to his sovereign "your father." He caused the members of his own family to be inscribed in the almanac beside those of the imperial house, and had his daughters mentioned in the public prayers; he also planned to obtain the hand of Peter's sister, Natalia Alexievna, for his son in addition to marrying his daughter to the emperor.

Peter II soon began to chafe under the rule of the generalissimo. Menshikov had appointed Ostermann to be his tutor, but the young prince hated study and preferred to spend his days hunting with his favourite, Ivan Dolgoruki. The adroit Ostermann excused himself to the prince for the disagreeable nature of his pedagogic duties, and contrived to cast all the blame on Menshikov. The emperor one day sent a present of 9,000 ducats to his sister Natalia, and Menshikov insolently confiscated them with the remark that the "emperor was too young to know the proper use of money." Peter

II rebelled at this and it was with difficulty that the prince appeased him. The generalissimo had another enemy in the person of Elizabeth, daughter of Peter the Great and aunt of Peter II. She was seventeen years old at the time, gay, careless, and lively, with a bright complexion and blue eyes; her laughter drove the insupportable tutor from his office.

An illness which overtook Menshikov and kept him absent for a time from court prepared his downfall; Peter II accustomed himself to the idea of getting rid of him. When the prince returned and began again to oppose the young ruler's wishes the latter left Menshikov's house, caused all the crown furniture to be removed from it to the imperial palace, treated his affianced wife with marked coldness, and finally gave orders to the guards that they were to obey no commands save those given by their colonels. This was the prelude to an overwhelming disgrace; in September, 1727, Menshikov was arrested, stripped of all his dignities and decorations, and banished to his own lands.

The Dolgorukis profited by the revolution they had caused. They fell, however, into Menshikov's error and oppressed the prince with the same officious care. Like Menshikov they banished all who gave them offence, even Ostermann for whom Peter began to feel affection, and the old czarina, Eudoxia Lapukhin, who had been liberated from the prison in Ladoga. Advancing as a pretext certain placards in which the services of Menshikov were extolled, they exiled the latter to Berezov, in Siberia, where he died in 1729. Taking no lesson by his example they imposed on the prince a new bride, Catherine Dolgoruki, sister of his favourite, Ivan. Their administration bore all the character of a reaction against the reforms instituted by Peter the Great.

In 1728, when the young emperor went to Moscow for his coronation, he was warmly received by the people. Ostermann, however, and all the other faithful servants of the "giant czar" were chagrined at the return of the court to Moscow and its indifference to European affairs in general. In order to gain more complete possession of their master the Dolgoruki encouraged his taste for dissipation and took him away on hunting expeditions that lasted weeks at a time. Peter would certainly have grown as weary of them as he had of Menshikov: and to the complaints of his aunt Elizabeth that she was left without money he had already replied: "It is not my fault: they do not execute my orders; but I shall find means to break my chains." The crisis came about in a different manner from what had been expected; the young emperor caught cold while attending the ceremony of the benediction of the waters, and died of small-pox at the age of fourteen years and four months. The two reigns of Catherine and Peter II, which lasted in all about five years, were peaceful.

In 1726 Russia had concluded an alliance with the court of Vienna and in 1727 it became involved in the war of the Quadruple Alliance. Despite the efforts of Campredon and Kurakin the failure of the project of marriage between Louis XV and Elizabeth had brought about coolness between France and Russia. The most remarkable episode of the foreign relations was the attempt of Maurice of Saxony, illegitimate son of King Augustus, to obtain possession of the duchy of Courland. The offer of his hand had been accepted by the widowed Anna Ivanovna, and he had been elected at Mittau by the deputies of the nobility. Disregarding the protestations of Prussia, Russia, and the Polish diet, he levied a body of troops with the money raised by the sale of the jewels belonging to an abbess of Quedlinburg, a certain French actress, his mother Aurora of Königsmark, and Adrienne Lecouvreur, and set about putting his duchy in a state of defence. His father disavowed him and Cardinal Fleury did not venture to support him even indirectly. Menshikov, restored to greater liberty since the death of Catherine I, himself laid claims to the duchy. He despatched Lacy at the head of eight thousand men to drive out the Saxon adventurer. The future victor of Fontenoy could get together no more than 247, and was obliged to swim across an arm of the sea in his retreat. His election was annulled, his father publicly reviled him as a *galopin*, or rascal, and Courland came once more under Russian influence.

During the reign of Peter II a treaty was signed with Prussia by virtue of which the two powers pledged themselves to sustain, on the death of Augustus II, the candidate they might choose for Poland. The emperor Charles VI and the "sergeant king" sounded Russia as to the eventual dismemberment of the Polish Republic. This was not the first time that the question of partition was brought forward. In Asia, Iagushinski concluded on the Bura a treaty of commerce with the Celestial Empire in the name of Peter II, by the terms of which Russian caravans could journey to Pekin every three years and could carry on their trade toll-free. Russia was also to have the privilege of keeping four priests and six young men in Pekin to learn Chinese. Kiakhta on the Russian territory and Maimatchin on the Chinese were to be the authorised depots.*f*

PRINCE ALEXANDER MENSHIKOV

The death of Peter II was universally regretted in Russia. During his reign, the empire enjoyed tranquillity at home and peace abroad; and he discovered such excellent qualities for government that the people looked forward to enjoying under his rule a period of freedom and prosperity such as they had never before experienced. There is no doubt, however, that if he had survived his own good intentions would have been perverted by those advisers who had obtained so strong a hold upon his mind. His predilection for Moscow had already produced serious injury to the maritime affairs of St. Petersburg: the fleet and the army suffered severely by his continued absence from the capital; and had he lived to complete the change by which he meditated Russia must have ultimately lost, by the neglect of her great station on the Neva, the national consequence she had maintained amongst the states of Europe during the two previous reigns. It was evident, also, that he would gradually have discouraged the residence of foreigners in his dominions; and that the old families were acquiring such power at court that they would finally have succeeded in restoring those national usages which had been set aside by Peter the Great. If the people, therefore, were deprived on the one hand of the temporary advantages of a tranquil reign, Russia on the other was preserved from the risk of permanent evils.

Disappointed in their expectations of an alliance with the emperor, the Dalgoruki did not wholly relinquish their hopes of securing some advantage by their position. The young Dalgoruki, impatient of delay, forged a testament in the name of Peter II, in which Catherine Dalgoruki was named as the successor to the throne. With this instrument in one hand and a drawn sword in the other he rushed into the hall, where the senators were assembled in deliberation, and cried aloud, "Long live the empress Dalgoruki!" But no voice seconding him in this wild and shallow trick, he sheathed his sword, and suppressed the fraudulent testament.

The question of the succession was now to be considered; and the only authentic document by which the proceedings of the council could be regulated was the will of Catherine I, which devised the succession to the princess Anna and her posterity, or, in failure, the princess Elizabeth. But Anna had died two years before, and her husband the duke of Holstein had retired into Germany. It was true that there was a young prince, the issue of this marriage; but the council were so averse to the introduction of foreigners into the state that they decided at once against any claim that might be set up in that quarter.

The princess Elizabeth, second in the order of nomination, exhibited no desire to avail herself of the testament of her mother, although she was strongly urged to do so by Lestocq, her physician, preferring to enjoy the ease of a life unburdened by the cares of the state. In these circumstances the council, the senate, and the great officers of state assembled to consult upon the election of a successor to Peter II. Although the male line of the Romanovs was extinct in that sovereign, yet the female line was preserved in the three daughters of Ivan, the stepbrother of Peter the Great, and for some time a partner with him in the government. The eldest was separated from her husband, the duke of Mecklenburg; the second, Anna, duchess of Courland, was a widow living at Mittau; and the third was still unmarried, residing at St. Petersburg. The objection that was entertained against foreign alliances determined the senate to reject the claims of the first, and the choice consequently fell upon Anna Ivanovna.

## ANNA IVANOVNA (1730–1740 A.D.)

From the time of the death of Catherine I the prejudice against foreigners had insensibly acquired weight amongst those influential persons who surrounded the throne. The Dolgoruki were the most active agents of this sentiment, through which they hoped at last to reap the largest share of profit themselves. Taking advantage of the jealousy in which the old aristocracy held their privileges, and apprehensive that the new sovereign might act upon the system of her immediate predecessors, they struck upon an expedient by which they hoped to deprive her of the power of exercising her own judgment, and to place her under the control of that irresponsible council which had been instituted by Catherine I. "The welfare of the nation," said Galitzin, in an address to the assembly, "demands that the supreme authority and the unlimited power of the sovereign, by which Russia has suffered so much and which has been sustained chiefly by the influx of foreigners, should be circumscribed, and that the crown should be conferred upon the new sovereign under certain conditions." This proposal was received with universal approbation, and the following conditions were unanimously agreed to:

That the empress should govern solely by the resolves of the high privy council; that she was not, of her own motion, either to wage war or make peace; that she could not, of herself, impose any new tax upon the people; that she could not dispose of any important office, nor inflict capital punishment on any nobleman, nor confiscate his estate, unless he had been previously convicted of the crime laid to his charge; that she should not alienate any lands belonging to the crown; and that she could not marry, or nominate an heir, without obtaining, in the first instance, the consent of the council. A strange article was added to these conditions — that her chamberlain, von Biren, should not accompany the empress into Russia.

These conditions, which were apparently intended to curb the tyranny of the throne, aimed at nothing more than the abolition of one description of despotism, for the purpose of substituting a worse in its stead. If it abrogated the supreme and unlimited power of the sovereign, it transferred that power to the secret council, which was thus elevated above the sovereignty and the senate and invested with a complete control over the administration of the public affairs. The proposed change was from an unlimited monarchy to an irresponsible oligarchy.

The drift of this capitulation was speedily detected by those whose interests it affected — the aristocracy. They saw that it concentrated the power of the state in the hands of seven persons; that the Dolgoruki had already possessed themselves of the voice of the council; and that the issue would be the sacrifice of the empire to a family contract. The capitulation, therefore, was scarcely passed when a powerful opposition was raised up against it; and the people, accustomed to the despotism of an unlimited sovereignty, from which, amidst all its severities, they had derived many valuable safeguards and benefits, declared that they preferred rendering obedience to one master instead of seven. This feeling rapidly spread amongst the guards, who had good reasons for objecting to a clause which would throw the patronage of the army into the hands of a few persons, who, instead of promoting the meritorious, would, as a matter of course, provide for their own friends and relatives.

ANNA IVANOVNA
(1693–1740)

Nor was the princess Anna insensible to the wrong which she suffered from this novel procedure; and, when the deputation from the council waited upon her to inform her of her election, and the conditions which were annexed to it, she would have refused to subscribe to the capitulation, had she not been already prepared by the advice of General Iagushinski as to the course she ought to pursue. That officer had previously recommended her to accept the conditions, but to revoke them immediately after she should be acknowledged as empress, assuring her, at the same time, that she would be powerfully supported in the proper quarter. She accordingly agreed to the demands of the deputation, and was crowned in the usual forms.

The empress Anna was no sooner established upon the throne, than her friends gave her an opportunity of carrying the advice of General Iagushinski into effect. A petition signed by several hundred noblemen was presented to her, in which she was entreated to abrogate the restrictions which the council had placed upon her authority, and to assume the unlimited power that had hitherto been exercised by her predecessors. Fortified by this requisition, the empress presented herself before the council and the senate, and, reading the terms of the capitulation, demanded whether such was the will of the nation. Being answered in the negative by the majority of those who were present, she exclaimed, "Then there is no further need of this paper," and tore the capitulation in pieces. This act was ratified and published in a manifesto which declared that the empress ascended the throne not by election but by hereditary right, and which exacted from the people an oath of allegiance, not to the sovereign and the country, as had formerly been the case, but to the empress alone, as unlimited sovereign, including not only the rights of sovereignty already existing but those that might be asserted hereafter.

Anna was now empress without conditions, and her chamberlain, von Biren, was raised to that place in her councils which Menshikov filled during the reign of Catherine I. The first exercise she made of her power was to abolish the council of seven and to restore to the senate the privileges it enjoyed under Peter the Great. She appointed, however, a cabinet of three persons, with Ostermann at its head, whose duty it was to superintend the affairs of the most pressing importance, leaving to the senate the management of less momentous matters. When these arrangements were completed, the urgent attention of the empress was directed to the foreign relations of the empire, which, at this crisis, demanded serious consideration.

The struggle for the throne in Poland had entailed jealousies which threatened not only to involve the peace of Russia but to draw France and Sweden into the quarrel. The cause of Augustus, the elector of Saxony, which had originally been espoused by Peter I, was still maintained by the Russian cabinet; and, although France made strenuous exertions to reinstate Stanislaus, the father-in-law of Louis XV, yet, by the determined interference of his northern ally, Augustus was proclaimed king of Poland, and Stanislaus was compelled to fly. The mortification which France endured under these circumstances excited in her a strong feeling of hostility against Russia; but there existed still more cogent reasons why she should make an attempt to restrain the advances of that power.

It had long been a favourite point in the policy of France to secure upon the throne of Poland a monarch who should be devoted to her will, and although she had been hitherto defeated in that object, she did not relinquish the hope of its ultimate accomplishment. She saw also rising in the north a gigantic empire, which had already acquired extraordinary power in Europe, and which threatened at last to overshadow and destroy the influence which she had been accustomed to exercise in that part of the globe. Urged by these considerations, and knowing how important it was to Russia to be at peace with Sweden, she left no means untried to engage the court at Stockholm on her side. Her diplomacy succeeded even better than she expected and Russia was once more compelled to watch with vigilance the movements of a dangerous neighbour, who was still suffering under the disastrous effects of a war from which Russia had reaped all the benefits and she the misfortunes.

But affairs pressed with still greater energy in a more remote quarter. It was found by experience that the territories which Peter had acquired in Persia by the treaty entered into between him, the sultan, and the shah were exceedingly burdensome to the country. In his desire for the enlargement of his dominions, Peter overlooked the necessity of ascertaining whether the new provinces were likely to be productive of advantages, either in the way of revenue or as adding strength to the frontiers. In order to preserve the possession of those provinces, it was necessary to maintain a considerable garrison in the interior, even in time of peace; they were also frequently exposed to scenes of warfare and devastation; and the climate was so injurious to the health of the Russians that in the course of a few years no less than 130,000 men perished there.

The great cost of these dependencies, and their uselessness in a territorial point of view, determined Anna to relinquish them upon the best terms she could procure from the shah. She accordingly proposed to that prince the restoration of the conquered provinces, upon condition that he would grant to the Russian merchants certain commercial privileges in the trade with Persia. To these terms the shah acceded, and in 1735 Russia made a formal surrender of her Persian possessions. This negotiation was connected with another of still greater importance — a defensive treaty between Persia and Russia, which was concluded at the same time. The motives which induced Anna to enter into this alliance require a brief recapitulation of preceding events.

The unfortunate situation in which Peter I was placed upon the banks of the Pruth compelled him to submit to the terms dictated by the Porte, by which he surrendered many important advantages which he had previously obtained by conquest. The principal sacrifices he had made upon that occasion were the evacuation of Azov and the destruction of the fortifications at Taganrog which had the immediate effect of shutting him out from the trade on the Euxine. The annoyances also to which the empire was subjected by the frequent incursions of the Crimean and other Tatars into the border lands, where they committed the most frightful excesses, and the haughty refusal of the Porte to acknowledge the imperial title which the people had conferred upon him, led Peter to meditate a new war against the Turks. He made ample preparations for the fulfilment of this design by fortifying the frontiers in the neighbourhood of Turkey; but his death arrested the execution of the project, which was entirely laid aside by Catherine I and Peter II.

Anna, however, relying upon the assistance of thirty thousand auxiliaries from Germany, considered this a favourable opportunity for reviving a stroke of policy which promised such signal advantages to the country, particularly as the Turk was at this period employed in hostilities against Persia. She did not long want an excuse for opening the war. The Tatars had of late made several predatory inroads upon the Russian territories, and laying waste the districts through which they passed carried off men and cattle on their return. These Tatars being under the protection of the Porte, the empress remonstrated upon the subject, and demanded satisfaction; but the sultan, in his reply, excused himself from interfering in the matter, upon the pretext that it was impossible to keep those roving bands under proper restraint. This evasive reply was precisely what Anna anticipated, and as the sultan declined to render her any atonement, she undertook to obtain retribution for herself. A force was immediately despatched into the country of the Tatars, which they overran, spreading ruin in their path, and destroying the marauders in great numbers. The expedition failed, however, in consequence of the incautious advance of the troops too far into the interior, where, not being prepared with a sufficient stock of provisions, they underwent severe privations, and sustained a loss of ten thousand men.

But this discomfiture did not divert the empress from her grand design; and in the year 1736 Count Munich, at the head of a sufficient force, was sent into the Ukraine, with a free commission to retaliate upon the Tatars. After a victorious course through that region, he passed into the peninsula of the

Crimea; the Tatars, unequal to contending with him in the open field, flying before him until they reached their lines, extending from the sea of Azov to the Euxine, behind the intrenchments of which they considered themselves secure. The lines were established with a view to protecting the Crimea from any attack on the land side; and, having been built with incredible toil, and being strongly fortified with cannon, the Tatars deemed them impregnable. They did not long, however, withstand the vigorous assault of the Russians, who speedily scaled them, and, driving the tumultuous hordes before them, soon possessed themselves of the greater part of the Crimea. But the same inconveniences were felt on this as on the former expedition. The Tatars on their flight laid the country in ashes, and it was impossible to provide sustenance for the troops without keeping up a constant communication with the Ukraine, where provisions at least were to be had, but which was attended with great difficulty. In this exigency, Count Munich was obliged to return to the Ukraine, to take up his winter quarters.

### War with Turkey

While Munich was thus engaged against the Tatars, a much more important movement, in which the real object of the Russian government was directly exhibited, was taking place elsewhere. General Lacy had laid siege to Azov, and reduced it to submission on the 1st of July, in the same year. This bold and decisive step forced the reluctant Divan to take into consideration the means by which the progress of the Russians could be most effectually stayed. The sultan was unwilling to commit himself in a war with Russia, content with the possession of the advantages he had gained by the Treaty of the Pruth; and even now that Russia had regained one of the ceded forts, and was manifestly prepared to follow up the victory, he preferred to attempt the negotiation of peace through the mediation of Austria, for the sake of avoiding hostilities as long as he could. Russia, however, would not agree to any accommodation; and, instead of being moved from her purpose by the representations of Austria, she demanded of that power the fulfilment of the treaty subsisting between them, by which, in case of need, she was bound to furnish thirty thousand auxiliaries. This demand placed the subject in a new light before the German cabinet. The required assistance would obviously have the effect of enabling Russia to extend her conquests without producing any benefits whatever to Austria; whereas, if Austria united herself with Russia in the war, she might derive some advantages from an alliance against which it appeared highly improbable that the Turks could make a successful stand. She decided, therefore, upon throwing the whole weight of her power into the scale, greatly to the consternation of the Turks, who had, in the first instance, solicited her friendly interference. The sultan, however, felt that, doubtful as must be the issue of a contest against such formidable enemies, it would be wiser to risk it than, yielding to intimidation, to make such sacrifices as would be inconsistent with the security and honour of the country. He accordingly lost no time in preparing for the campaign. He recruited the garrisons and forts, raised new levies, put his army into proper condition, and equipped a fleet for the protection of the Euxine; on the other hand, the combined forces rapidly prepared to act in concert.

The operations of the year 1737 were not followed by any important results. The Russian army, strengthened by forty thousand recruits, was separated into two divisions; one of which, under the command of Count Munich, proceeded to Otchakov on the Euxine, while General Lacy, with the other, entered the Crimea. The objects proposed to be attained by these expeditions were not adequate to the expenditure that attended them. Otchakov submitted, and was garrisoned by the conquerors; and the Crimea was again desolated. This was all Russia gained by the sacrifice of about fifty thousand of her veteran troops. The blame of these barren and expensive victories was to be attributed to that very union of forces which ought to have been productive of increased strength. The most unfortunate jealousies existed, not only amongst the Austrian officers, but between Count Munich and the Austrians. To so extravagant a length was this dangerous feeling carried that, with the exception of the affair at Otchakov, Munich remained inactive throughout the campaign, from an obstinate determination not to act upon the same plan that was pursued by the Austrians.

Nor was this the only evil that these feuds produced. The Turks, taking advantage of the dissension, poured in with greater force upon the German ranks, which they broke through on several occasions, gaining frequent petty advantages, which, at all events, had the effect of rendering their movements in a great measure abortive. Constant complaints were now made alternately by the courts of Vienna and St. Petersburg, respecting the conduct of the officers at both sides; and, although Munich was especially accused of thwarting the efforts of the allies, he always had the address to escape from reprehension, by throwing the censure on his accusers.

These circumstances inspired the Turks with fresh courage. A congress had been appointed to be held at Nemirov, in Poland, but they withdrew their ambassador; signifying, however, that if Russia would evacuate Azov and Otchakov, and the rest of her conquests, they might be induced to entertain a treaty of peace. This insolent proposition was at once rejected by Russia, and the war was resumed. In the campaign of the following year, Munich appeared to be anxious to make amends for his former inactivity; but, although he made some vigorous marches and vindicated the character of the soldiery, he effected nothing of substantial importance. A similar fortune attended General Lacy in the Crimea, from which, after a disastrous progress through a desolated country, and after a great mortality amongst his troops, occasioned partly by fatigue and partly by the deficiency of provisions, he was ultimately obliged to withdraw.

The opening of the year 1739 promised to make amends for these successive failures. General Munich, whose ability in the field was admitted on all hands, collected a numerous army at Kiev, and, crossing the Bug, met the Turks in a pitched battle, near Stavutshan, in which he obtained a signal victory. Pursuing his success with vigour, he advanced and, passing the Pruth, he possessed himself of Jassi, the capital of Moldavia, the whole of which territory he subjugated in an incredibly short space of time. Retracing his march, after having achieved this important conquest, he made preparations for a descent upon Bender. These brilliant triumphs, accomplished with such rapidity that the couriers were kept constantly occupied in the transmission of despatches to the court of St. Petersburg, encouraged, for a brief season the flattering prospects of complete restitution which the unpropitious commencement of the war had almost annihilated.

But unfortunately the same evil spirit which had frustrated the former campaigns broke out just at the moment when Turkey was so discomfited that Russia, had she pushed her successes a little further, might have dictated a settlement upon her own terms. Envy at the progress of the Russian army was again exhibited in the ranks of the Austrians, who were suffering under a contagious disease that helped in a still greater degree to paralyse their activity. Unfortunately, too, the emperor Charles VI was afflicted with a dangerous illness; and his daughter, shrinking from the apprehensions of the future, was extremely desirous by any means to bring about a peace with Turkey. This disposition on the part of Austria was gladly seized upon by the sultan; and, before there was time to reconcile the unhappy differences that existed amongst the allies, a treaty of peace was drawn up and signed between Austria and Turkey, on the 1st of September, 1739. By this inglorious treaty, Austria escaped from all further responsibility in the war; but she purchased the peace at so enormous a price that it is difficult to comprehend the tortuous policy which led her to adopt so extraordinary a measure. The war, in which she had embarked in the hope of securing territorial advantages, had cost her a considerable expenditure in troops and treasure; and she not only did not obtain an indemnity for this outlay, nor acquire a single rood of ground by her participation in the campaigns, but by the conditions of the treaty she was compelled to relinquish Belgrade, her Hungarian rampart against the Turks, and all those conquests which she had formerly obtained under the victorious flag of Prince Eugene.

This peace produced great dissatisfaction at St. Petersburg; for, although Austria reserved to herself the right of fulfilling her treaty with Russia by succouring her in the field, it was not deemed prudent to prosecute a war single handed, which had been commenced with such a formidable display of power. The Turks, relieved from one antagonist, were now the better enabled to resist the other; and the empress conceived that the wisest course she could pursue was to negotiate her differences with the sultan, to which proposal he was not unwilling to accede. A peace was consequently entered into between the belligerents with such promptitude that it was concluded as early as the 18th of September. The conditions of this treaty involved compromises on both sides. It was agreed that Azov and its surrounding territory should be evacuated and remain uncultivated, as a neutral boundary between the two empires; a similar arrangement was guaranteed respecting Kabarda, both governments agreeing to retain in their hands a certain number of hostages from that province, for better security against an abuse of the stipulation. It was also settled that Russia should be at liberty to erect a fortress on the Don, and that the Porte should construct another in the Kuban. Some minor conquests of the Russians were surrendered: Russian fleets were not to be allowed to be kept in the sea of Azov or the Euxine; and in the latter sea the commerce of Russia was to be conducted only in Turkish bottoms.

## Internal Administration

The empress Anna, in thus suddenly concluding a peace with Turkey, was actuated by a still stronger motive than that which was supplied by the desertion of Austria. She justly apprehended that Sweden, influenced by the intrigues of France, who had now attained a decided ascendency in the councils of Stockholm, would endeavour to distract Russia in the north, while the main body of her army was occupied with the Porte on the south. Secret negotiations, carried on between the three powers, appeared to confirm this suspicion. It was true that, at the conclusion of the last war, Russia and Sweden had entered into an amnesty for twelve years, which was renewed for a similar period, on its expiration in the year 1736. But this amnesty served only as a thin disguise for the rankling and bitter hostility which the Swedes entertained towards Russia. They had not forgotten the protracted and ruinous struggle between Charles XII and Peter I, which convulsed the whole kingdom and exhausted its resources; nor the sacrifices which they were compelled to make at the Peace of Nystad. These feelings were assiduously cultivated by the French court, which found easy means of securing a strong party in the national council, which in fact was paramount in Sweden, the king being completely under its control. The empress, warned of this increasing desire for a rupture on the part of Sweden, was the more anxious to come to terms with Turkey, that she might be free to act in Finland and that neighbourhood, should it become necessary.

Anna was evidently guided in the whole course of her policy by the example of Peter I, whom she adopted as her model. Fortunate in the choice of at least two of her advisers — Ostermann in the council of state, and Munich at the head of the army — she persevered in her attempts to complete those projects of improvement which her great predecessor had left unfinished. The canal connected with the Lake of Ladoga, which was designed to facilitate the transport of provisions to St. Petersburg, was brought to a close by her in the year 1738. She also fitted out an expedition to sail from Kamchatka towards the north, for the purpose of determining whether Siberia was connected with North America.

The manufacture and commerce of Russia, too, commanded a large share of her attention. She instructed her ambassadors at foreign courts to make vigilant inquiries after the most skilful persons engaged in those trades in which Russia was most deficient; and by this means she was enabled to draw into her dominions a great number of artisans, particularly those who were experienced in the production of such fabrics as silks and woollen stuffs. In furtherance of these views she entered into a treaty of commerce with Great Britain, from which the industry of her people derived a fresh and invigorating stimulus. It may be observed, also, that she increased the numerical population by the return of the Zaparogian Cossacks to their allegiance, shortly after the opening of the campaign in the Crimea, which they had forfeited by the rebellion of Mazeppa; and that she enlarged her territories by the acquisition of the province inhabited by the Kirghiz, a nomad tribe, on the Chinese borders. This latter accession was of great importance, from the protection it afforded to the frontiers against the incursions to which they had hitherto been continually exposed: while it not only created a new trade with the Kirghiz themselves, but gave greater freedom to the commercial intercourse with China, which had been constantly interrupted by these hostilities.

### Biron the Favourite

Throughout her life Anna placed unreserved confidence in a favourite who, rising from a humble station in society to the first place in the councils of his sovereign, at last aspired to the illicit possession of her affections. John Ernest Biron, the son of a gamekeeper in Courland, happening to attract the attention of the duchess, was appointed her private secretary. From this post he was elevated to the more important office of chamberlain; and even then it was rumoured that he stood higher in her grace's favour than was consistent with the position which he nominally occupied. When the council elected his mistress to the imperial throne, it was stipulated that Biron should not be suffered to accompany her into Russia; and one of the conditions of the capitulation restricted her from marrying, or choosing an heir, without the consent of the council and senate. The empress, accepting the sovereignty under these limitations, left Biron at Mittau, when she came to St.

Petersburg; but she had no sooner abrogated the stipulations within which her power was restrained, than Biron appeared at court, was created a Russian count, appointed first lord of the bedchamber, and raised at once to the same eminence which he had occupied before. Some years previously he had succeeded in prevailing on the nobility of Courland to confer upon him the title of duke; and when the Kettler family became extinct by the death of the duke of Courland, he procured that dignity from the hands of the electors for himself and his heirs in perpetuity.

Thus glittering with honours, which at best were but surreptitiously obtained, he took upon himself at once in St. Petersburg the character of one who wielded an absolute authority. He was careful, however, not to offend Ostermann or Munich, because, possessing no abilities for government himself, he was obliged to rely upon them as the instruments of his power. It was supposed that the Turkish war was undertaken at the instigation of this daring man, for the purpose of keeping Munich at a distance from the capital — that officer having attained in a high degree the confidence of the empress. By the most adroit measures Biron contrived to remove from a familiar intercourse at court everybody who might be likely to interfere with his ambitious designs. Apprehensive that the empress, freed from the control of the council, might entertain thoughts of marriage, he assiduously limited all opportunities that could lead to such a result; and even attempted to prevent a union between the princess Anna and Ulrich duke of Brunswick, the object of which had reference to the succession. In this scheme, however, the machinations of Biron were defeated,

RUSSIAN PEASANT WOMAN

and the marriage was celebrated in the month of July, 1739. This event seriously interfered with the projects of the favourite; but his ingenuity was not exerted in vain in the attempt to derive profit from circumstances which at first seemed so discouraging.

### Death of Anna (1740 A.D.); the Succession

In the August following, the duchess of Brunswick became the mother of a prince, who was immediately taken by the empress under her own guardianship and nominated to be her successor. This proceeding, apparently founded upon some show of justice, was in reality the result of a deep-laid conspiracy. The empress was in a declining state of health, and it was felt that she could not long continue to exercise the sovereignty. In this state of things, it became necessary to provide a successor by an authentic act that could not afterwards be called into question. Biron aimed at the concentration of the imperial power in his own hands; but as an open declaration to that effect would have provoked animosities dangerous to his safety, it was arranged that the young prince, then but a few weeks old, should be nominated to the throne, and that Biron should be appointed regent during the minority of Ivan. Ostermann and Munich, relying upon the future gratitude of Biron, favoured this crafty design. Biron coquetted for a time with the dignities which he was solicited to accept; and pretended at last that, in undertaking the toils of the regency, he yielded to the importunities of others at the sacrifice of his own private wishes.

The extent of the power thus delegated to him was specified in the provisions of the will of the empress, which ordained that he should be the administrator of government until the emperor Ivan had attained his seventeenth year; and that, should Ivan die before that time, Biron should continue guardian to Ivan's brethren, born after him, who should succeed him on the throne; but that, should neither Ivan nor any of his brethren survive, then Biron, with the concurrence of the state, should elect and confirm a new emperor as unlimited monarch. This was the final injunction of the czarina, who died in 1740.[b]

## A Russian Estimate of Anna and of Biron

Contemporaneous writers are unanimous in asserting that, during her entire reign, Anna Ivanovna was not only under the influence, but, so to say, under the domination of her favourite. On the basis of such authorities it therefore became customary to ascribe to Biron and the Germans who were grouped around him all the cruelties and coarseness that characterised her reign. But if we subject this question to a dispassionate and severe criticism it would appear that such an accusation of Biron — and in general of the Germans who governed with him — has no firm foundation. It is impossible to ascribe all the character of the reign to a German clique, because those Germans who were at the head of the government did not constitute a united corporation, but each of them followed his own personal interests; they were envious of one another and at enmity each with the rest.

Biron was a somewhat narrow-minded egotist, incapable of attracting any circle around him; his power rested exclusively on the personal favour of the empress; and therefore, as soon as Anna Ivanovna's eyes were closed forever, her former favourite had no sure ground to go upon, and although his deceased mistress had made his position secure yet he was not able to maintain it a month without her. There is no contemporary indication that the cruelties which signalised the reign of Anna emanated from Biron or that they were accomplished at his initiative.

Moreover, the cruelties and in general the harsh measures which signalised the reign of Anna Ivanovna were not an exclusive characteristic of that epoch; they did not begin to make their appearance in Russia with her and did not cease with her. The administration of Peter the Great was signalised by persecutions even more cruel and harsh of everything opposed to the supreme power. The actions of Prince Romodanovski in accordance with the Preobrajenski edict were in no wise milder or more humane than those of Andrew Ivanovitch Uskakov in the secret chancery. On the other hand, similar features of cruelty and contempt for human dignity are to be met with after Anna Ivanovna under Elizabeth Petrovna. Therefore we do not hesitate to say that all that disturbs us in the reign of Anna should not be ascribed to the empress herself, nor to her favourite, the duke of Courland, but to the whole age in which such occurrences took place. On the contrary, if we separate from that which belongs to the age what we may justly ascribe to the empress herself and the statesmen of her time, we come to a conclusion which is more to the advantage and credit of the government of the epoch than to its condemnation. Many dispositions of the government of that time in matters of interior policy were accomplished in the spirit of Peter the Great and it was not in vain that Anna Ivanovna confided the affairs of the state to the wise and gifted "fledgelings" of Peter. Thanks to them, in many respects the reign of Anna may be called a continuation of the glorious reign of her great uncle: in general the life of Russia moved forward and was not stagnant. The people of Russia suffered from bad harvests during the reign, besides other various accidental calamities, as for instance fires and robbers; for all such evils, of course, the governments of the period cannot be blamed, and there is no doubt that measures were taken to alleviate the distress of the people.[c]

## THE NOMINAL REIGN OF IVAN VI (1740–1741 A.D.)

For a short time after the death of Anna (1740) Biron maintained an autocratic rule, assuming the title of His Highness, Regent of the Russian Empire. But finally the people, jealous of seeing the administration of the imperial rule confided to the hands of a foreigner — and one too who, instead of exhibiting a sympathy in their interests, treated them with the most flagrant tyranny — betrayed universal discontent at the new order of things. It was held to be a direct act of injustice to debar the duke of Brunswick from the guardianship of his son; and a formidable party now rapidly sprang up, prepared to espouse the rights of that prince. The popular disaffection increased on all sides; but Biron had established his spies in every direction, and was unsparing in the punishments which he inflicted upon all those persons whom he had reason to believe inimical to his government. The streets groaned with the cries of the victims of the knout; the people fled before him, or, in an agony of fear, prostrated themselves upon the earth as he advanced; and the dungeons were filled with the unhappy objects of his suspicions. It was calculated that, throughout the period of his authority, including the reign of the empress Anna, no less than twenty thousand persons were exiled to Siberia.

At length the smothered flame broke out, and the demands in favour of Duke Ulrich took an affirmative shape. Count Munich, disappointed in his expectations by the hypocritical Biron, warmly embarked on the other side; and, by still affecting to be the friend of the regent, he was enabled to render essential service in the revolution which was now swiftly encircling the walls of the palace. The confidence which the military placed in Munich gave increased importance to his services; and, as he found that he had nothing to expect from the regent, he attached himself zealously to Duke Ulrich in the anticipation that he would ultimately be rewarded with the chief command of the army, which was the station he had long eagerly desired to obtain.

The revolution which was thus organised was promptly accomplished. The regent was arrested in the middle of the night, in his house, by a detachment of the guards; and the principal senators assembled in the palace before daybreak, and acknowledged the princess Anna as grand duchess of Russia, and guardian of her son the infant emperor. This proceeding was the work of a few hours. Biron was at first confined in the castle of Schlüsselburg, whence he was removed as a prisoner and brought to trial for obtaining the regency by improper means, for squandering the imperial treasures, for treating with contumely the parents of the emperor, and for violating the statutes and ordinances so as to throw the empire into confusion. For these capital offences he was condemned to death; but his sentence was mitigated to perpetual banishment to the deserts of Siberia, where, in addition to the ordinary miseries of that forlorn region, he was compelled to associate in the labours of the numerous wretches whom he had himself condemned to the same fate. [He was, however, set at liberty by Peter III, and Catherine II ultimately restored to him the duchy of Courland.]

### Anna of Brunswick Assumes the Regency (1740 A.D.)

The regency of the princess Anna was slightly perplexed at its opening, by the importunate demands of Munich to be placed at the head of the army — a post which Duke Ulrich appropriated to himself, and peremptorily refused to relinquish. As a compensation, however, to Munich, he removed Ostermann, and appointed his rival in his place as first minister of the government. Munich did not long hold this office: failing to accomplish a course of policy which he urged upon the regent, he tendered his resignation, which was unexpectedly accepted. Frustrated in his hopes, he lingered in St. Petersburg, anticipating that he would be recalled; but the period of his utility was past, and his anticipations were disappointed. The ground of his retirement involved a serious change in the foreign policy of the empire. Frederick II had just ascended the throne of Prussia, and, regarding with jealousy the alliance that had been formed between the courts of St. Petersburg and Vienna, endeavoured to accomplish a union with Russia through the agency of Munich, whose antipathy to Austria was notorious. Frederick did not find it very difficult to work upon the vanity and prejudices of the minister, who was easily brought to prevail upon the regent to enter into a defensive treaty with the cabinet of Berlin; both parties mutually binding themselves to furnish assistance, as occasion might require, to the extent of twelve thousand men. In consenting to this treaty, the regent mentally resolved to fulfil the stipulation it enjoined, only so long as Prussia should be at peace with Austria. An occasion soon offered which obliged her to act upon this secret resolution, Frederick having signified his intention of taking possession of Silesia as a part of the inheritance of Maria Theresa. In consequence of this proceeding, a new alliance was formed with Austria at the commencement of the year 1741, by which a fresh engagement to furnish auxiliaries was entered into. Munich in vain remonstrated against this measure; and at last, finding his influence at an end, he solicited permission to resign, which was granted to him at once. Notwithstanding the disposition thus manifested on the part of Russia, she did not take any part in the war between Prussia and Austria; particularly as the king of Poland and the elector of Saxony, who also raised pretensions to the patrimony of Theresa, protested against the progress of the Russian troops through Poland; Sweden at the same time threatening the empire on the borders of Finland.

### Sweden Renews the War

The Swedes had long looked anxiously for an excuse to make war against Russia; and now that the government of that empire was, to a certain degree, unpopular, and likely from that circumstance to undergo an alteration, a favourable opportunity appeared to present itself for executing a project so gratifying to the whole nation. The ambassador of France at the court of Stockholm encouraged the council to prosecute this war; while the French minister at St. Petersburg demonstrated its facility by representing in strong colours the weakness and instability of the new administration. The Swedes, flattered by the hopes in which they were led to indulge, already calculated with certainty upon the results of the campaign; and the diet at Stockholm were so sanguine of success that they actually drew up no less than three sets of articles containing the conditions which they intended to dictate at the conclusion of the war, when they were assured Russia would be compelled to submit to any terms they might propose. By these articles, they made provision for the resumption of all the provinces that had been ceded to Russia by the Treaty of Nystad; and prepared arrangements, in the event of these not being quite so successful as they expected, by which certain terms, less humiliating but exceedingly extravagant, were to be forced upon their adversary. It was decided, at all events, that, in any case, Russia should surrender Karelia, Ingermanland, and Livonia; that she should not be permitted to keep a single ship on the Livonia or Esthonian coasts; and that she should be compelled to grant the free exportation of corn.

These plans of aggrandisement were deliberately settled by the diet, before any preparations were made for their execution. The Swedes were zealous enough in their desire to wrest from Russia her conquered territories; but they were lamentably deficient in the means by which that desire was to be accomplished. Their fleet was not seaworthy; and the army, brave to a proverb, was insufficiently furnished with provisions, and so destitute of skilful commanders that if it had achieved a victory it must have been by some miracle of good fortune, and not by its own prowess. The generals Levenhaupt and Buddenbrock were the most strenuous advocates of the war; yet, although its conduct was committed to their own hands, the sequel proved that the enterprise was as rashly conceived as it was badly conducted.

Russia was the first in the field; and General Lacy, advancing on the Swedes in August, 1741, before they had time to organise their forces, obtained a signal victory over them near Vilmanstrand. This fortress immediately surrendered to the Russians; but the Swedes collected in such superior numbers that no further progress was made by Lacy throughout the rest of the campaign.

When Sweden entered upon this ill-advised war, she acted under a conviction that serious discontents prevailed in Russia against the regency of the duchess of Brunswick. The sudden changes, succeeding each other with marvellous rapidity, that had taken place in the imperial government, justified, in some measure, the supposition that the present regency was as much exposed to revolution as the preceding administrations. The question of the succession had been treated so vaguely, and had been subjected to such fluctuating decisions, that it was believed some new theory would be set up to annul the last election, as others had been annulled before. There was no doubt that the division of parties in Russia afforded a reasonable ground for anticipating a convulsion. The supreme power had latterly become the prize for which base and ambitious men, without hereditary pretensions and destitute of personal merit, had struggled with various degrees of success. There was evidently no settled principle of inheritance; and even the dangerous principle sanctioned by the example of Peter the Great, which gave to one unlimited sovereign the right of choosing another to succeed him, was acted upon capriciously, and appealed to or over-ruled as it happened to suit the exigency of the occasion.

The brief reigns of Catherine, of Peter, and of Anna, remarkable as they were for the confusion to which they led in the attempts to settle the crown, for the vicissitudes which they drew down upon persons who had previously enjoyed uninterrupted prosperity, and for the factious views which they extracted and condensed into conspiracies, might be referred to as furnishing the probabilities of the future, and confirming the hopes of those who desired, above all things, to see Russia once more broken up by civil commotions. The antipathy which existed against foreigners, and the objections of the old aristocracy to those European reforms that had been from time to time forced upon the people, were well known to the courts of Stockholm and Paris. The vulnerable point in the domestic concerns of the empire was laid bare; and Sweden, who anticipated a revolution from some cause or other, without being able to predicate from what precise ground of discontent it would spring, resolved, at all events, to expose to the Russians the permanent evil of their condition, leaving it to work its effects as it might. With this view she issued a manifesto, containing the following artful reasons, which were designed to draw with her the sympathies of the Russian population.

"The sole intention on the part of Sweden," observed the manifesto, "is to defend herself by arms against the oppressions exercised against her by the arrogant foreigners, the ministers of the Russian court; and at the same time to deliver the Russian nation from the yoke which these ministers have imposed on it, by assisting the Russians to regain their right of electing for themselves a lawful ruler." The foreigners particularly pointed at in this manifesto were Munich and Ostermann. The allusion, towards the close, of the design of Sweden to deliver Russia from the yoke of those ministers and to assist her in her right of electing a lawful ruler, touched upon topics which were well calculated to disturb the minds of the people, and to suggest to them notions of independence which they had been hitherto prevented by coercive institutions from entertaining. But there was either a stolid apathy on the part of the Russians, an indifference to or ignorance of the nature of liberty, or a national jealousy at the interference of other countries in their affairs, which rendered this ingenious and inflammatory document perfectly harmless. It was disseminated and forgotten; but, although Sweden could not create a revolution in Russia, there were elements of discord within which rendered revolution inevitable.

The assertion of the right of the sovereign to nominate his successor was productive of inconvenience in a variety of ways: (1) as it constantly brought the new monarch into collision with the authorities, who were thus deprived of the privilege of election; (2) as it was almost certain to dissatisfy some party, and to produce continual feuds; (3) as it led to dissensions and attempts to vindicate the ancient principle, whenever the sovereign, as we have seen, happened to die intestate; and (4) as it was calculated to perpetuate in particular families the inheritance of the patronage and the power of government. But the chief danger arose from the fatal precedent of its interruption, which was seized upon with avidity as a justification, on all future changes, of those revolutions which so frequently originated within the walls of the palace. Alterations had now followed each other so quickly in the persons to whom the administration of the government was committed, and they were conceived so rapidly, and executed with such suddenness and decision, that it was no longer surprising to find the imperial authority vested in the morning in different hands from those which exercised it the night before.

These bold transactions were, of course, founded upon some plausible pretext — the unpopularity of the late ruler, the more authentic claims of the new, the support of the army, or, perhaps, the rare argument of the national will, which it would be mockery to designate public opinion. The overthrow of Biron was effected by a combination of circumstances: the hatred in which he was universally held, his cruelty and rapacity, the obscurity of his origin, and the fact that he was an alien by birth. But the last of these objections lay with almost equal force against the young emperor Ivan, and might be employed with still greater truth against his father, the duke of Brunswick, who, as husband of the regent, exercised considerable influence at court. A stronger motive than this was not required to inflame the prejudices of a powerful section of the nobility, and to yield a satisfactory apology for removing the regent and her son, who was not considered a true Russian, from power. The project was not slow in arriving at maturity; and the term of authority permitted to the guardian of Ivan was, all circumstances considered, of little more duration than that extended to Biron, who held his perilous elevation only two-and-twenty days.

## Successful Conspiracy against the Regent

These designs against the throne were greatly facilitated by the strange conduct of the princess Anna and her husband. Since they had attained their wishes in the government, their behaviour towards each other had undergone a most remarkable change. Harmony and confidence seemed to have ceased between them; and, no longer acting in concert, but, on the contrary, opposing each other by conflicting views, the affairs of the state unavoidably fell into perplexity and confusion. The rivalry that had been produced between Ostermann and Munich in consequence of the favour shown, in the first instance, by the duke to the latter, contributed to increase that disagreement in action which was imperceptibly dividing the government into two parties. Ostermann, finding himself displaced to make way for Munich, attached himself still more closely to the duke, for the purpose of supplanting his rival upon the first opportunity; while Munich, on the other hand, smarting under the mortification he endured by the duke's repeated refusal of the office he solicited, sought to ingratiate himself in the good opinion of the regent. The consequence of this spirit of opposition, fed by the jealousies of those able ministers, was the daily counteraction by one party of the measures projected by the other.

The regent was a woman of serene temper and lenient disposition; she regarded severity with aversion, and always resorted to the prerogative of mercy where it was possible she could do so consistently with justice: but her desires were so completely thwarted by Ostermann that the public results of the administration bore a very different character from that by which they would have been distinguished had her own opinions been allowed their proper weight. Perhaps it was to this undercurrent of resistance that the indifference concerning the government into which she fell ought to be attributed. But, to whatever cause it might be referred, she gradually neglected the duties of her station, and suffered them to be discharged at hazard by the advisers of the duke. Totally estranging herself from her husband, she retired for weeks together from public affairs, and shut herself up with a Countess Mengden, who obtained so great an ascendency over her mind as to withdraw her attention almost wholly from the responsibility of her position. This circumstance produced considerable dissatisfaction, and heightened the antipathy with which the people regarded the German party that was now growing up at court. The aversion entertained towards foreigners now broke out with more violence than ever. It seemed as if the administration of affairs had completely passed out of the hands of the Russians. The convention that had been formed on the demise of Peter II, by which the supreme authority was vested in the council, which was composed almost exclusively of members of native families, would have had indirectly the effect of excluding strangers from the government; but the evils with which it was pregnant, and its immediate interference with the privileges of the empress, led to its abrogation. The ascendency of foreigners was then resumed with greater force than ever. Biron the insolent guardian, Ostermann the experienced politician, and Munich the able commander rose to the summit and swayed the destinies of the empire.

Nor did Ivan himself possess a much better claim to be considered as a Russian. He was but a remote descendant of the house of Romanov; his father was a German prince, his mother the daughter of a German prince; and the only member of the imperial house to whom he could refer his lineal descent was his grandfather Ivan, stepbrother to Peter I. The family, therefore, that occupied the throne, was almost exclusively of German blood, which was rendered still more repugnant to the people by the fact that all the most important offices under government were filled by foreigners. There was in these circumstances, and in the desire to arrest finally the influence of strangers — which appeared to progress with increasing certainty in each successive reign — a sufficient ground for protest; and the extraordinary indolence of the regent, her utter neglect of state affairs, her discouragement of Russian customs, and her lavish patronage of her immediate adherents, who were all obnoxious to the people, furnished the ready pretext upon which a plot was formed to expel her from the throne.

The princess Elizabeth, daughter of Peter I, residing at St. Petersburg, was the person in favour of whose claims this conspiracy was got up. By birth, she was closer to the throne than either the young emperor or the regent; and the habits of her life were much more congenial to the feelings of the country. She might have preferred her pretensions on the death of Peter II, when there was a strong probability that they would have commanded the suffrages of the council; but at that time she expressed no desire to enter upon the cares of sovereignty, choosing rather to cultivate the repose of a retired and tranquil life. Throughout the reign of the empress Anna she observed the same quiet course, kept aloof from politics, and avoiding, as much as possible, all intercourse with the great men or distinguished families at court. Her conduct was so entirely free from suspicion that she enjoyed the closest intimacy with the empress, who, believing that the princess was averse to the toils of power, bestowed her full confidence upon her; and even Biron, who distrusted almost everyone about him, never contemplated any measure to her prejudice. She enjoyed the immunities of a private person; never made any display of her rank in public; and was in truth, as she was in appearance, without a party in the country. The only exception to the privacy of her life was the attachment she showed for the soldiery, particularly the guards; which she did not hesitate to exhibit by frequently standing sponsor for their children.

Yet, although her conduct was so exempt from reproach, the Dolgoruki were accused of an intention of placing her upon the throne — an intention which they might have entertained without her knowledge or sanction; for there was sometimes as much violence committed in forcing the dignity upon unwilling shoulders as in deposing the possessor. That aspiring family fell under the displeasure of Biron, and its members were put to the torture towards the close of the year 1739; when they confessed that they had planned an insurrection, the purpose of which was to carry off the empress, the princess Anna, and her husband, to expel the Germans from Russia, to proclaim Elizabeth empress, and to bring about a marriage between her and one of the Nariskins. This confession might be true, or it might have been wrung from the accused by torture, which, in those times, was too often persuasively employed to make its victims confess more than the truth; but it was satisfactory for the ends of Biron, who, proceeding to capital punishment at once, broke one of the victims on the wheel, decapitated three others, and sentenced two more to a dungeon for life.

There is no reason to believe that Elizabeth contemplated any designs upon the throne during the reign of the empress Anna, or that the simplicity of her general conduct was assumed as a disguise for secret intrigues. The project seems to have occurred to her for the first time, when she saw an infant emperor consigned to the regency of a foreigner; it was probably strengthened afterwards, when the guardianship of the child was transferred to its parents, one of whom was a German by birth, and the other by descent; and it reached its maturity when she heard it reported currently that the regent intended to have herself declared empress on her birthday in the following December, 1741, and to establish the succession in the line of her daughters. This intelligence, which every day obtained fresh credit at court, imparted a new aspect to the question. It was no longer to be considered a choice between lineal and indirect descendants of the house of Romanov, but between a sovereign who should be chosen by the electors and one who was resolved to usurp by force what she could not legitimately obtain.

The discontent of the people, the inconsistent bearing of the regent, and the favourable disposition for a change which began to be developed in influential quarters, seemed to sanction the act of revolution, and to invoke Elizabeth from her retirement to fulfil its ends. Personally, she stood alone; she had never drawn around her any powerful friends; she had never mixed in the court feuds; and her whole reliance was upon the temper and accidents of the time. But it was not forgotten in her calculations that the individual who is the representative of a principle acquires at once all the power which the cause he espouses can confer, and that he is sure to be sustained by a party for the promotion of their own objects, although he might be destitute of support in the attempt to advance his own.

Lestocq, the physician and favourite of the princess, was the mainspring of the plot. It was by his advice that the enterprise was undertaken, and it was almost solely by his perseverance that it was prosecuted. He first addressed himself to the guards, who were individually devoted to the princess. The earliest confidants of his schemes were Grünstein, a broken merchant, who was then a corporal in the Preobrajenski guards, and Schwartz, a trumpeter. Through the agency of these persons, to whom he promised large rewards, Lestocq succeeded in gaining over to his views a strong party of the soldiery. M. de la Chetardie, the French ambassador resident at St. Petersburg, readily engaged in the conspiracy, acting, no doubt, under the sanction of his court, whose policy it was to convulse the Russian government by any means in its power, in the hope of ultimately effecting a disunion between that cabinet and the Austrian emperor. From that minister Lestocq procured the sums of money that were necessary to carry forward his plans, which now proceeded with rapidity.

But Elizabeth, who had entered into the project with reluctance, regarded its progress with fear, and was as anxious to postpone the catastrophe as Lestocq was eager for its accomplishment. This produced delays which were nearly fatal. The soldiers, entrusted with a secret of too much magnitude for persons in their condition, could not long preserve the confidence that was reposed in them; and at last the design began to be rumoured abroad. It even reached the ears of the regent, who, possessed by some unaccountable infatuation, treated it with the utmost carelessness. She either did not believe in its truth, or lulled herself into security by depending upon the fidelity of her friends. Unmoved by the danger that threatened her, she concealed from her husband the information she had received; for which, when it was too late to retrace her steps, he afterwards severely censured her. Ostermann, who was early made aware of the proceedings of the conspirators, warned the regent of her danger, and entreated her to take some decisive measures to avert it: and the British ambassador, detecting, probably, the insidious hand of France, predicted her destruction in vain. Her facile nature still lingered inactive, until at last she received an anonymous letter, in which she was strongly admonished of the perils by which she was surrounded. A more energetic mind would have acted unhesitatingly upon these repeated proofs of the approaching insurrection; but Anna, still clinging to the side of mercy, instead of seizing upon the ringleaders, who were known to her, and quieting at once the apprehensions of her advisers, read the whole contents of the letter in open court in the presence of Elizabeth, and stated the nature of the reports that had reached her. Elizabeth, of course, protested her ignorance of the whole business, burst into a flood of tears, and asserted her innocence with such a show of sincerity that the regent was perfectly satisfied, and took no further notice of the matter.

This occurred on the 4th of December, 1741. Lestocq had previously appointed the day of the consecration of the waters, the 6th of January, 1742, for Elizabeth to make her public appearance at the head of the guards, to issue declarations setting forth her claims upon the throne, and to cause herself to be proclaimed. But the proceedings that had taken place in the court determined him to hasten his plans. Now that the vigilance of the court was awakened, he knew that his motions would be watched, and that the affair did not admit of any further delay. He applied himself, accordingly, with redoubled vigilance, to the business of collecting and organising the partisans of the princess; continued to bribe them with French gold; and, when everything was prepared, he again impressed upon his mistress the urgent necessity of decision. He pointed out to her that the guards, upon whose assistance she chiefly relied, were under orders to march for Sweden, and that in a short time all would be lost. She was still, however, timid and doubtful of the result, when the artful Lestocq drew a card from his pocket, which represented her on one side in the habit of a nun, and on the other with a crown upon her head — asking her which fate she preferred; adding that the choice depended upon herself, and upon the promptitude with which she employed the passing moment. This argument succeeded; she consented to place herself in his hands; and, remembering the success that had attended the midnight revolution that consigned Biron to banishment, he appointed the following night, the 5th of December, for the execution of his plan — undertaking the principal part himself, in the hope of the honours that were to be heaped upon him in the event of success.

When the hour arrived Elizabeth again betrayed irresolution, but Lestocq overcame her fears; and after having made a solemn vow before the crucifix

[1741 A.D.]

that no blood should be shed in the attempt, she put on the order of St. Catherine, and placing herself in a sledge, attended by Lestocq and her chamberlain, she drove to the barracks of the Preobrajenski guards. When she arrived at this point, she advanced towards the soldiers on foot, holding the cross in her hand; and, addressing them in a speech of some length, justified the grounds on which she advanced her claims to the throne; reminded them that she was the daughter of Peter the Great; that she had been illegally deprived of the succession; that a foreign child wielded the imperial sceptre; and that foreigners were advanced, to the exclusion of native Russians, to the highest offices in the state. A considerable number of the guards had been previously prepared for this proceeding by bribes and promises, and inflammatory liquors were distributed amongst them to heighten their zeal. With the exception of a few, who would not violate their duty and who were, in consequence, manacled by the remainder, the whole body responded to the address with enthusiasm.

They now proceeded to the palace of the emperor and his parents, pressing into their train everybody they met on the way, to prevent their object from being betrayed; and, forcing the sentries at the gates, obtained easy admittance to the sleeping apartments of the regent and the duke, whom they dragged, unceremoniously, and without affording them time to dress, out of their beds, and conveyed to the palace of Elizabeth, where they confined them under a strong guard. The infant Ivan, unconscious of the misery that awaited him, was enjoying a gentle slumber during this scene of violence; and when he awoke he was carried, in a similar manner, to the place where his unhappy parents were immured. On the same night the principal persons connected with the government were seized in the same way, and thrown into prison. Amongst them were Lewis Ernest of Brunswick, the brother of the duke, Ostermann, and Munich.

This revolution was as rapid and complete as that which deprived Biron of the regency, and was effected by a similar stealthy proceeding in the silence of the night. Early on the following morning, the inhabitants were called upon to take the oath of fealty to Elizabeth. But they were accustomed to these sudden movements in the palace; and before the day was concluded the shouts of the intoxicated soldiery announced that the people had confirmed, by the usual attestation of allegiance, the authority of the empress.[1] A manifesto was immediately issued, which contained the following statement:

The empress Anna having nominated the grandson of her sister, a child born into the world only a few weeks before the empress's death, as successor to the throne; during the minority of whom various persons had conducted the administration of the empire in a manner highly iniquitous, whence disturbances had arisen both within the country and out of it, and probably in time still greater might arise; therefore all the faithful subjects of Elizabeth, both in spiritual and temporal stations, particularly the regiments of the lifeguards, had unanimously invited her, for the prevention of all the mischievous consequences to be apprehended, to take possession of the throne of her father as nearest by right of birth; and that she had accordingly resolved to yield to this universal request of her faithful subjects, by taking possession of her inheritance derived from her parents, the emperor Peter I and the empress Catherine.

[1] It is said that when the infant Ivan heard the shouts of the soldiers in front of the palace, he endeavoured to imitate their vociferations, when Elizabeth exclaimed, "Poor babe! thou knowest not that thou art joining in the noise that is raised at thy undoing."

Shortly after this another manifesto appeared, in which Elizabeth grounded her legitimacy on the will of Catherine I. As the statements in this document respecting the right of inheritance are singular in themselves, and as they illustrate in a very remarkable degree the irregularity with which the question of the succession was suffered to be treated, the passage touching upon those points appears to be worthy of preservation. It will be seen, upon reference to previous facts, that these statements are highly coloured to suit the demands of the occasion. After some preliminaries, the manifesto proceeds to observe, that on the demise of Peter II, whom she (Elizabeth) ought to have succeeded, Anna was elected through the machinations of Ostermann; and afterwards, when the sovereign was attacked by a mortal distemper, the same Ostermann appointed as successor the son of Prince Antony Ulrich of Brunswick and the princess of Mecklenburg, a child only two months old, who had not the slightest claim by inheritance to the Russian throne; and, not content with this, he added, to the prejudice of Elizabeth, that after Ivan's death the princes afterwards born of the said prince of Brunswick and the princess of Mecklenburg should succeed to the Russian throne; whereas even the parents themselves had not the slightest right to that throne. That Ivan was, therefore, by the machinations of Ostermann and Munich, confirmed emperor in October, 1740; and because the several regiments of guards, as well as the marching regiments, were under the command of Munich and the father of Ivan, and consequently the whole force of the empire was in the hands of those two persons, the subjects were compelled to take the oath of allegiance to Ivan. That Antony Ulrich and his spouse had afterwards broken this ordinance, to which they themselves had sworn; had forcibly seized upon the administration of the empire; and Anna had resolved, even in the lifetime of her son Ivan, to place herself upon the throne as empress. That, in order, then, to prevent all dangerous consequences from these proceedings, Elizabeth had ascended the throne, and of her own imperial grace had ordered the princess with her son and daughter to set out for their native country.

Such were the arguments upon which Elizabeth attempted to justify her seizure of the throne. With what sincerity she fulfilled the act of grace towards the regent and her family, expressed in the last sentence, will be seen hereafter.

### ELIZABETH PETROVNA (1741–1762 A.D.)

The revolution which elevated Elizabeth to the throne and the circumstances which preceded that elevation were in every respect remarkable. She had no claim to the dignity, either by birth or by the regulation in regard to the succession introduced by the innovating Peter. Elizabeth was the younger daughter of Peter: Anna, who had been married to the duke of Holstein, was the elder; and though this princess was dead, she left a son, the representative of her rights, who, as we shall hereafter perceive, did ultimately reign as Peter III. The right of primogeniture, indeed, had, in the regulation to which we have alluded, been set aside, and the choice, pure and simple, of the reigning potentate substituted; but the infant Peter had the additional claim of being expressly indicated in the will of Catherine I. These claims, however, had been utterly disregarded when Anna, duchess of Courland and daughter of Ivan, brother of Peter I, had been raised by a faction to the throne. On the death of this empress without issue, Peter, as we have seen, was again overlooked, through the ambition rather of an individual than of a faction — the bloodthirsty Biron.

[1741 A.D.]

Ivan, the son of Anna, had been preferred to his mother, who had been married to Prince Antony Ulrich of Brunswick; and no doubt could be entertained that the object of Biron, in prevailing on the empress to nominate the child, was to retain the supreme power in his own hands as regent. We have seen by what means his ruin was effected; what circumstances accompanied the regency of the duchess Anna, mother of the youthful emperor; and how, by a similar revolution, Anna herself was replaced by the princess Elizabeth.

That Ivan had no other right to the throne than that conferred by the will of the empress Anna, was one of the pretexts which Elizabeth employed to prove the validity of her own title. That will, in the manifesto published three days after the revolution, was insinuated — probably with great truth — to have been irregularly obtained; but in either case it was of no validity, since the right of Elizabeth was asserted to be superior even to that of the former empress. But the instrument was a tissue of sophistry. Though she had been placed on the throne by about three hundred soldiers, she did not hesitate to affirm that the revolution had been effected at the demand of all her subjects. In ostentatiously displaying her clemency, in proclaiming that she had sent back the parents of Ivan to their own country, with all the honours due to their station, she was equally insincere. Both passed their lives in captivity, and were transferred from one fortress to another, according to her caprice or jealousy. Until his eighth year Ivan was permitted to remain with them; but, apprehensive lest his mind should be taught ambition, he was consigned to solitary confinement first in the fortress of Oranienburg, next in that of Schlüsselburg. In one respect his fate was worse than that of his parents: they died in the course of nature[1]; he, as we shall hereafter perceive, perished by violence.

ELIZABETH PETROVNA
(1709-1762)

One of Elizabeth's first cares was to punish the men who had, during the former reigns, kept her from the throne — those especially who had assisted the regent Anna in overturning the power of Biron, and had instigated her afterwards to seize the throne. All were condemned to death; but the new empress was not a woman of blood, and the sentence was commuted into perpetual banishment. Ostermann, Munich, Golovkin, Mengden, Lövenwold, driven from a power scarcely less than supreme and from riches almost inexhaustible, were forced to earn their own subsistence in the wilds of Siberia. Munich opened a school. The hand which had conquered the Turks, which had given a king to Poland, was employed in tracing mathematical figures for children.

If Elizabeth could punish, she could also reward. The surgeon, Lestocq, was made head physician of the court, president of the college of the faculty, and privy councillor, with a magnificent income. The company of grenadiers who had raised her to the throne were all declared noble; and the common

---

[1] The mother died in childbed, 1746; the father survived until 1780.

soldiers ranked in future as lieutenants. But under a despotic government there is little security for the great, least of all for those whom capricious favour has exalted. Presuming on his services, the ambition of Lestocq urged him to demand higher preferment, and he had the mortification to be refused. Nor was this all: by his arrogance he offended the most powerful favourites of Elizabeth, especially the grand chancellor Bestuzhev, who had been the minister of Anna; and, in seven years after the revolution, he was exiled to a fortress in the government of Archangel. Exile, in short, was perpetual in this reign. The empress vowed that no culprit should suffer death; but death would often have been preferable to the punishments which were inflicted. Torture, the knout, slitting of the tongue, and other chastisements — so cruel that the sufferer frequently died in consequence — were not spared even females.

Soon after her accession a conspiracy was discovered, the object of which was the restoration of young Ivan. The conspirators, who were encouraged by a foreign minister, were seized, severely chastised, and sent into exile. Among them was a court beauty, whose charms had long given umbrage to the czarina, and we may easily conceive that the revenge was doubly sweet which could at once destroy the rebel and the rival. But the number of these victims was small, compared with that which was consigned to unknown dungeons, and doomed to pass the rest of life in hopeless despondency. With all her humanity, Elizabeth suffered that most inquisitorial court, the secret chancery, to subsist; and the denunciations which were laid before it were received as implicitly as the clearest evidence in other tribunals.

### Foreign Affairs (1743-1757 A.D.)

In her foreign policy this empress seems scarcely to have had an object. Averse to business, and fond of pleasure, she allowed her ministers, especially Bestuzhev, to direct the operations of the wars in which she was engaged, and to conduct at will the diplomacy of the empire. Her first enemy was Sweden. That power demanded the restitution of Finland, and was refused; hostilities which, indeed, had commenced at the instigation of France during the last reign, were resumed, but they were prosecuted with little vigour by the Swedes. The valour of the nation appeared to have died with their hero, Charles XII. So unfortunate were their arms that, by the Treaty of Nystad, in 1721, and that of Åbo, in 1743, Livonia, Esthonia, Karelia, Ingermanland, Viborg, and Kexholm passed under the domination of Russia.

Still worse than the loss of their possessions was the influence thenceforward exercised over the court of Stockholm by that of St. Petersburg. In vain did Sweden endeavour to moderate the exactions of the empress by electing the duke of Holstein, her nephew, successor to the throne of the Goths: the Treaty of Åbo was not the less severe. It is, indeed, true that the intelligence of this election did not reach St. Petersburg until Elizabeth herself, who was resolved never to marry,[1] had already nominated Duke Peter as her own successor; but she ought to have received in a better spirit a step designed as an act of homage to herself.

Had Elizabeth known her own interests, she would never have engaged in the celebrated war which during so many years shook all Europe to its centre. But, in the first place, she affected much commiseration for the Polish king, whose Saxon dominions were invaded by the Prussians, and whom she called

---

[1] She is said to have been privately married to a singer; but this is doubtful. What is certain is that her lovers were as numerous after as before the alleged union.

[1757 A.D.]

her ally. In the second, she was evidently actuated by a personal antipathy to Frederick, and whoever were his enemies were sure to be her allies. It would, however, be wrong to suppose that personal feeling alone was her sole motive for interfering in a foreign war. There can be no doubt that even at this early period, and indeed long before this period, the ministers of Russia had cast a longing eye on the possessions of Poland.

Courland and Semigallia, though nominally dependent on the Polish crown, were in reality provinces of Russia. They had been lost to Poland through the marriage of Anna, niece of Peter I, to Kettler, sovereign of the duchy. Though she had no issue; though Ferdinand, the successor of Kettler, was also childless; though the Polish diet contended, with justice, that the fief was revertible to the republic, Anna was resolved that its future destiny should be changed. Under the pretext of certain pecuniary claims, the Russian troops overran the territory; and the states were compelled to elect Biron, the parent of the empress, to the vacant dignity. After the fall of that unprincipled adventurer, the states, disgusted with Russian preponderance, had ventured to unite their suffrages in favour of Charles, son of Frederick Augustus III king of Poland; but Frederick durst not sanction the election until he had obtained the permission of the empress Elizabeth. She could, for once, well afford to be generous; and Duke Charles was suffered to take possession of the dignity. And, while on this subject, we may so far anticipate events as to add that Peter III, successor of Elizabeth, refused to admit the rights of Charles, whom he expelled from the duchy; and that Catherine II incorporated it with her dominions. That Elizabeth herself had the ambitious views of her father, in reference not only to Courland but to other provinces, is certain; and, as we have already observed, one of her motives for engaging in the great European contest was the prospect of ulterior advantages. The pretext of succouring an ally was sufficient to justify, in the eyes of Europe, the march of her armies. In this respect, her policy was macchiavellian enough. But to her the war was an imprudent one; whatever her views, the time was not yet arrived when they could be fully executed. Nor were the events always honourable to the military glory of the empire. The reason is generally and, perhaps, justly assigned to the partiality of the grand duke Peter, the heir presumptive, for the Prussian monarch — a partiality so great as to be inexplicable. The Russian generals, however anxious to win the favour of their sovereign, still more the honours of successful warfare, were yet loth to incur the dislike of Peter: hence the operations were indecisive; and success, when gained, was not pursued.

## Antecedents of the Future Peter III

Charles Peter Ulrich, duke of Holstein Gottorp, whom Elizabeth had nominated her successor, who had embraced the Greek religion, and who, at his baptism, had received the name of Peter Fedorovitch, had arrived at St. Petersburg immediately after her accession. He was then in his fourteenth year. The education of this unfortunate prince was neglected; and the cause must be attributed alike to his own aversion to study and to the indifference of the empress. Military exercises were the only occupation for which he had any relish, and in them he was indulged. At the palace of Oranienbaum, with which his aunt had presented him, he passed the months of his absence from court — a period of freedom for which he always sighed. As his recollections were German, so also were his affections. He had little respect for those over whom he was one day to reign: instead of native, he surrounded himself with young German officers. His addiction to such exercises became a passion, and was doubtless one of the causes that so strongly indisposed him to more serious and more important pursuits.

But it was not the only cause. In his native province he had probably learned to admire another propensity, common enough in his time — that of hard drinking; and it was not likely to be much impaired in such a country as Russia. His potations, which were frequent and long, were encouraged by his companions; and, in a few years, he became a complete bacchanalian. If we add that both he and they indulged in gratifications still more criminal — in licentious amours — we shall not hesitate to believe the charge of profligacy with which he has been assailed. Whether the empress was for some time privy to his excesses has been disputed; but probability affirms that she was, and that, by conniving at these ignoble pursuits, her policy was to keep him at a distance from the affairs of state. In this base purpose she was, from motives sufficiently obvious, zealously assisted by her ministers, especially by Bestuzhev. Profligate as was the grand duke, he was displeased with this state of restraint; and he sometimes complained of it with a bitterness that was sure to be exaggerated by the spies whom they had placed near him.

### The Future Catherine II Appears

The empress paid little attention to the reports concerning him. Her purpose was to disqualify him for governing, to render him too contemptible to be dreaded; nor was she much offended with his murmurs. That purpose was gained; for Peter had the reputation of being at once ignorant, vicious, and contemptible. In a country so fertile in revolutions, where unprincipled adventurers were ever ready to encourage the discontent of anyone likely to disturb the existing order of things, this reputation was one of the surest safeguards of Elizabeth's throne. She no longer feared that he would be made the tool of the designing, and she secretly exulted in the success of a policy which Macchiavelli himself would have admired. Nor did she prove herself unworthy of that great master in the refined hypocrisy which made her represent her nephew as a prince of hopeful talents. But even she blushed at some of his irregularities; and, in the view of justifying him, had furnished him with a wife. Her choice was unfortunate; it was Sophia Augusta, daughter of the prince of Anhalt-Zerbst, who, on her conversion to the Greek faith — a necessary preliminary to her marriage — had received the baptismal name of Catherine.

This union was entitled to the more attention as in its consequences it powerfully affected not only the whole of Russia but the whole of Europe. Shortly before its completion Peter was seized with the smallpox, which left hideous traces on his countenance. The sight of him is said so far to have so affected Catherine that she fainted away. But, though she was only in her sixteenth year, ambition had already over her more influence than the tender passion, and she smothered her repugnance. Unfortunately, the personal qualities of the husband were not of a kind to remove the ill impression; if he bore her any affection, which appears doubtful, his manners were rude, even vulgar; and she blushed for him whenever they met in general society. What was still worse, she soon learned to despise his understanding; and it required little penetration to foresee that, whatever might be his title after Elizabeth's death, the power must rest with Catherine. Hence the courtiers in general were more assiduous in their attentions to her than to him — a circumstance which did not much dispose him for the better. Finding no charms in his new domestic circle, he naturally turned to his boon companions; his orgies became frequent, and Catherine was completely neglected. Hence her indifference was exchanged into absolute dislike.

The contrast between their characters exhibited itself in their conduct. While he was thus earning contempt for himself, she was assiduously strengthening her party. She had the advantage — we should rather say the curse — of being directed by a wily mother, who had accompanied her into Russia, and whose political intrigues were so notorious that at length she was ordered by the empress to return into Germany. The grand duchess, however, had been too well tutored to suffer much by her mother's departure; and she prosecuted her purpose with an ardour that would have done honour to a better cause.

So long as the German princess remained at court, the conduct of Catherine was outwardly decorous; but now less restraint was observable in her behaviour. She was little deterred by the fear of worldly censure, in a court where the empress herself was anything but a model of chastity; and her marital fidelity soon came to be more than doubtful.

### Court Intrigues; the Death of Elizabeth (1762 A.D.)

That, in concert with several Russian nobles, of whom Bestuzhev was the chief, Catherine meditated the exclusion of her husband from the throne and the elevation of herself as regent during the minority of her son Paul, is a fact that can no longer be disputed. Hence the criminal condescension of the chancellor to the views of Catherine; hence his efforts to prevail on the empress to nominate the infant Paul as her successor. The indiscretion of the grand duke, who was no favourite with anybody; his frequent complaints of the tutelage in which he was held; his bursts of indignation at his exclusion from the councils of the empire — were carefully related to his aunt, with such exaggeration as were most likely to destroy the last traces of the lingering regard she bore him. All, indeed, who had been the friends of Catherine, all who had shared in the confidence of the minister, might well contemplate with alarm the succession of one that had vowed revenge against the partisans of both. Besides, the contempt which Peter felt, and which he seldom hesitated to express, for the Russian people, rendered his succession far from agreeable to them.

Thus, when, in 1757, Apraxin, field marshal of the Russian forces, invaded Prussia, took Memel, and, near Jägerndorf, obtained a brilliant victory over the troops of Frederick, yet, as if defeated, instantly fell back upon Courland, the cause was something more than the fear of offending Peter. This retrograde movement surprising, as well it might, both the empress and her people, Apraxin was placed under arrest, and the command of the army bestowed on another general. He was tried for the crime, but absolved — a result still more surprising to men who regarded merely the surface of things. The reason was that the grand-chancellor, Bestuzhev, had secretly ordered the marshal to retreat, and was, of course, his protector in the trial. It was not to please the heir-presumptive of the crown, whose blind adoration of the Prussian king was so well known, that Bestuzhev despatched the secret order for Apraxin to retreat: it was that the chiefs of the army, of whom many were his creatures, might be ready to join in effecting the revolution which was meditated. But the ambitious minister, presuming on the distaste which his imperial mistress generally showed for affairs, and still more on her bodily indisposition, which at this time placed her life in danger, proceeded too rapidly. His intrigues were discovered; his letter to the marshal was produced; he was deprived of all his power; and Peter had the joy of seeing him exiled.

The general who succeeded Apraxin obtained advantages over the Russian monarch, which had never been contemplated by his predecessor. But though he took Königsberg, placed most of Prussia under contribution, and defeated the Prussian army in a decisive engagement, he, too, was unwilling to irritate beyond forgiveness the heir of the empire, especially as the reports which daily reached him of Elizabeth's health convinced him that the succession was not far distant. Under the pretext of illness, he demanded leave to retire. His successor, Soltikov (not, we may be sure, the favourite of that name), was still more successful. Frederick was defeated in one of the best contested battles of this famous war; Berlin was taken, and Kolberg reduced after a vigorous siege. The news of this last success reached the empress, but she was no longer capable of deriving satisfaction from it. Much to her honour, she withstood all the solicitations of the intriguers who wished to exclude her nephew and to place Paul on the throne, under the regency of his mother. She died on the 5th day of January, 1762.[b]

## Spread of Art, Literature, and Education under Elizabeth

The empress Elizabeth had a passion for building; Peter the Great's summer palace and even the empress Anna's winter palace appeared to her small and confined. Upon the site of the latter she began to build the present edifices; during her reign was also built the vast, elegant, and beautiful palace at Tsarskoi Selo; the palace of Oranienbaum was reconstructed, and the fine churches of the Smolni convent, of Vladimirskaia and of Nicholas Morskoi (in St. Petersburg) were also erected. Some handsome private houses were built by Elizabeth's noblemen, and in general St. Petersburg, which had not long before been a desert place, consisting chiefly of wooden houses, became greatly embellished; the palace quay, as may be seen from drawings and engravings of the time, already showed a continuous row of huge stone edifices.

Of course all these buildings cost enormous sums which led private persons into debt and the government into superfluous expenditure, but it is impossible not to observe that there was to be seen in this luxury an artistic quality which had never before existed. The finest edifices of that period form a special style, which after temporary neglect is now beginning to be imitated; the creator of this style in Russia was Count Rastrelli — a foreigner, of whom, however, Russia has the right to speak. The palaces and churches built by Rastrelli merit description, and although painting at that time did not represent a very high standard, yet the ceilings painted in accordance with the fashion of the day, with bouquets of flowers and mythological goddesses, even now attract the attention of artists. The grandees gave high prices for pictures by foreign masters; their houses became distinguished not only for their handsome façades but also for the comfort of their interior arrangements; it would hardly be possible, for instance, to imagine anything more nobly elegant than the house of the chancellor Vorontzov (now the corps des Pages).

All these beautiful architectural productions, and likewise those of music and painting, were for the greater part the work of foreign artists — visitors to Russia; but under their influence Russian artists were formed and taste developed. The church of Nicholas Morskoi was built by a pupil of Rastrelli.

The almost daily theatrical representations produced at court gave rise to the idea of organising similar representations at the *corps des Cadets*. The empress took a lively interest in them; she often assisted at them and lent her diamonds for the women's costumes. In their turn these representations could not but assist the development of a taste for the stage, for dramatic art and literature in general and from amongst the number of cadet actors not a few became well-known writers, as for instance Beketov, Kheraskov, and Sumarokov.

We must dwell for a few moments on Sumarokov — a man who in his time enjoyed an extensive literary reputation and secured for himself the appellation of Father of the Russian Stage. The love of literature, and especially of the stage, was already developed in Sumarokov when he was in the corps des Cadets; when he was afterwards made aide-de-camp to Razumovski, he could almost daily assist at operas and ballets. At that period he read with avidity the dramatic authors then in fashion: Corneille, Racine, Voltaire, and Molière became his idols; he decided to try to imitate them in his own native language, then very undeveloped, and in 1747 he wrote a tragedy, the *Chorists*.

It was not the merits of this work, which were very insignificant, but the unwontedness of the appearance of an original Russian tragedy, and besides that the fact of its being in verse, that so astounded and enraptured his contemporaries that they proclaimed Sumarokov the "Russian Racine"; encouraged by such a success he wrote a second and yet, a third tragedy; he took up comedy (for which he had hardly any more vocation) and in fact wrote a whole repertory; there were, however, no actors; because neither in St. Petersburg nor in Moscow did there any longer exist such companies and such theatres as were begun in the time of Peter.

Meanwhile, far away from both capitals, in Iaroslav there was formed, almost of itself without any commands or even any encouragement being given, a Russian dramatic company which is indissolubly bound up with the name of Volkov. Theodore Volkov was the son of a merchant and had been educated in the Iaroslav seminary, where, following the example of the Academy of Kiev, and others, representations of a spiritual or religious character were given. They produced a great impression upon the young merchant; when later on he managed to get to St. Petersburg and saw on the stage of the corps des Cadets a dramatic representation given with scenery, lighting, and mechanical contrivances, Volkov was stupefied with rapture and astonishment. Being to the highest degree sensitive to every artistic impression, being a painter, a musician, and a sculptor — all self-taught — Volkov was also endued with that constancy and patience without which even gifted natures do not attain to any results. Volkov studied the material side of scenic art to the smallest details — that is, the arrangement of the machinery, of the scenes, etc.; when he returned to Iaroslav he asked his parents, with whom he lived, to let him have an empty tanner's shed; there he arranged a pit and a stage, and making up a company of young merchants like himself, sons of citizens and clerks, gave representations which aroused the enthusiasm of all the spectators. The intelligent and practical Volkov, seeing how the population of Iaroslav flocked to his representations, named a price for them — a five kopeck piece for the first rows — and thus little by little he amassed a sum with which in 1752 he was able to build a general public theatre with room for one thousand spectators.

The taste for the stage had meanwhile greatly spread in St. Petersburg; in various private houses dramatic representations were given at evening parties; it was therefore not surprising that the Iaroslav theatre soon began to be talked of. The empress invited Volkov to come to St. Petersburg with his company, as she wished to see his representations given on the stage of the court theatre. She was remarkably pleased with them, and four years later issued an ukase for the establishment of a public theatre. The first director of this theatre and almost the only dramatic writer was Sumarokov; according to the testimony of contemporaries Volkov was one of its most talented actors and his friend and fellow worker Dmitrievski a great artist.

We must here speak of another still more remarkable Russian native genius — Lomonosov. It is well known how, when he was a youth of sixteen, devoured by a thirst for knowledge, he secretly left the paternal roof and made his way on foot from Kholmogori to Moscow. How unattractive must life and learning have appeared to him in those early days! "Having only one altyn (a three-kopeck piece) a day for salary, it was impossible for him to spend more on food than a halfpenny a day for bread and a halfpenny worth of *kvass* (a kind of beer or mead); the rest had to go for paper, books, and other necessities." Thus he described his life in the Zaikonospaskvi Ecclesiastical Academy to Ivan Shuvalov and concluded with the following words: "I lived thus for five years and did not abandon science!" Theodore Prokopovitch, when he was already an old man, visited the Moscow academy a few years before his death; he noticed Lomonosov there and praised him for his laboriousness and learning. In 1737 Lomonosov was sent abroad to perfect himself and placed himself under the surveillance of the then famous scholar, Wolff, who, while despising him for his disorderly life, spoke with respect of his capacities and success in study. Lomonosov followed the lectures of the German professors and amused himself with the German students. The news of Minikh's great victories and the taking of Khotin reached him; his patriotic feelings were aroused, and he wrote an ode. When the verses were received in St. Petersburg everyone was struck with their harmony; and when Lomonosov returned from Germany in the beginning of Elizabeth's reign his reputation as a poet had already preceded him — the more he wrote the greater his fame became. Poetry, however, was not Lomonosov's strongest point, and verses do not occupy a quarter of his entire works. His mind worked even more than his imagination, and his scholarly writings are striking in their variety. He composed a grammar of the Russian language from which several generations have learned; he laid down rules of versification, the foundation of which are even now recognised by everyone; he wrote on chemistry, physics, astronomy, metallurgy, geology; he composed a Russian history, wrote a hypothesis concerning the great learned expeditions and memoranda bearing on questions of the state (as for instance measures for increasing and maintaining the population in Russia): in fact, Lomonosov's extraordinary intellect seemed to touch upon every branch of mental activity. He was made a member of the St. Petersburg Academy of Sciences, but there the German element reigned supreme and Lomonosov was one of those who, while venerating the work of Peter the Great and the European learning introduced by him, yet was oppressed by foreign tutorage and took offence when the Germans put forward their own countrymen to the detriment of meritorious Russians. Continual disputes and quarrels arose between Lomonosov and his fellow members; nor, being of a very impetuous and obstinate nature, was Lomonosov always in the right. His rough and sharp measures frequently led him into quarrels even outside the academy, for instance with his literary brethren, Frediakovski and Sumarokov. All this might greatly have injured Lomonosov, but fortunately for him he possessed powerful protectors in the persons of Count Worontzov and Count Razumovski, who liked to show favour to the first Russian scholar and poet.

But the strongest, truest, and most constant of his protectors was Ivan Shuvalov. Shuvalov had many defects — his character was weak, lazy, and careless; but he nevertheless represented one of the most consolatory types of his epoch: strong, energetic types were not uncommon in the first half of the eighteenth century, but gentle, benevolent, indulgent natures were rarely to be met with. Shuvalov was not captivated by clamorous deeds, like the men of Peter's time, but by the peaceful progress of science and art. Therefore if the weakness of his character made him an instrument for the ambitious designs of his cousin, his heartfelt sympathies drew him towards Lomonosov, of whom he naturally learned much and — what is of more importance — with whom he devised means for the spread of education in Russia. The result of these deliberations was a vast plan for the establishment of schools throughout the governments, and finally of a university in Moscow. The establishment of a university seemed of the first necessity, as it was to furnish Russia with teachers; this had been Peter's intention with regard to the academy, but it had not been fulfilled. In his report to the senate upon this subject, Shuvalov wrote that it would be desirable to appoint a "sufficient number of worthy men of the Russian nationality, acquainted with the sciences, to spread education in distant parts among the common people, so that thus superstition, dissent, and other like heresies proceeding from ignorance might be destroyed." The senate approved Shuvalov's proposition and in 1755 the University of Moscow was founded.

We have given as just and complete a picture of the period of the empress Elizabeth as is possible in view of the scarcity of information obtainable concerning many circumstances of that time. Elizabeth left behind her if not a great memory yet, broadly speaking, a good one. Her administration may be reproached with much: in its foreign policy it was not sufficiently independent; it was not sufficiently watchful in interior affairs, where oversights occasioned special evils; moreover examples of unlawful enrichment attained huge dimensions. But her reign may be said to have led Russia out of bondage to the Germans, while the level of education was not in the smallest degree lowered, but on the contrary considerably raised. Much that brought forth such brilliant fruits under Catherine II was sown under Elizabeth.[d]

### Estimates of Elizabeth

Bain[g] finds it a peculiar glory of Elizabeth Petrovna that she followed always in the footsteps of her illustrious father. Noting that Russia was the creation of Peter (before him there having been only Muscovy), he notes also that this new principality was many times in danger during the fifteen years following his death. And he sees in Elizabeth the power that sustained the empire. "Beneath her beneficent sceptre," he declares, "Russia may be said to have possessed itself again." He credits her with possessing her father's sovereign gift of choosing and using able councillors; and with having "an infinite good nature, radiant affability, and patriarchal simplicity, which so endeared her to her subjects as to make her, most deservedly, the most popular of Russian monarchs." In common with other critics, he feels that she laid the foundation upon which Catherine II was to build. He declares that all the great captains who were to serve Catherine with such effect—men like Rumiantsev, Suvarov, Riephin, Besborodko, the Panins and the Galitzins—were brought up in the school of Elizabeth.

Much of this is beyond controversy, but it is necessary to add that the private character of the sovereign was not such as to be spoken of with enthusiasm. Bell[b] defines its chief feature as voluptuousness. He notes with approval a certain sympathetic trait that led her to the abolition of capital punishment, but he declares that she was, on the whole, "no less feeble in mind than she was vicious in conduct." "Her superstition," he adds, "was equal to her lust; the sight of a person in mourning affected her more than a whole street of starving families; and her conscience reproached her more for violating a fast than for outraging the most sacred of moral virtues. While she encouraged a system of espionage destructive of all domestic freedom and happiness; while she punished with inexcusable rigour the crime of eating an egg on a day of abstinence, she was in no degree offended with the spread of the most baleful vices." But such contradictions as are here suggested between the public efficiency and the private character of a Russian sovereign are no novelty, as we shall have occasion to see in the succeeding pages. Moreover, it should not be forgotten that gossip is likely to exaggerate the frailties of a monarch situated as was Elizabeth. Circumstances that might have passed unnoticed in the history of an ordinary individual were sure to attain the widest publicity, and to be distorted with all the elements of exaggeration that characterise rumours of a disagreeable character. Making due allowance for this, however, there still seems little reason to doubt that Elizabeth's personal views of morality were curiously distorted. Still, in judging her, we may recall Bain's declaration that she had "passed through the bitter but salutary school of adversity." If she had "learnt the necessity of circumspection, deliberation, self-control," she had learnt also to hold in contempt certain of the elementary virtues. Meantime, her outlook upon the political world was wide and clear, and the tactfulness with which she approached her subjects and dealt with those with whom she came into personal contact, was of so subtle an order that her personal popularity was well earned. Her energy and firmness considerably facilitated the task of Catherine II.[a]

## PETER III (1762 A.D.)

As Elizabeth, on her death-bed, had confirmed the rights of Peter III; and as the conspirators, deprived of Bestuzhev their guide, were unable to act with energy, the new emperor encountered no opposition. On the contrary, he was immediately recognised by the military; and the archbishop of Novgorod, in the sermon preached on the occasion, thanked heaven that a prince so likely to imitate his illustrious grandfather was vouchsafed to Russia. Catherine was present. She wore a peculiar dress to conceal her pregnancy, and her countenance exhibited some indication of the anxious feeling which she was obliged to repress. Compelled to defer the execution of her ambitious purposes, and uncertain what vengeance the czar might exert for her numerous infidelities, she might well be apprehensive.

But she had no real foundation for the fear. Of all the sovereigns of that or any age, Peter was among the most clement. Whether he thought that clemency might bind to his interests one whose talents he had learned to respect, or that her adherents were too numerous and powerful to allow of her being punished — whether, in short, he had some return of affection for her, or his own conscience told him that she had nearly as much to forgive as he could have, we will not decide. One thing only is certain — that, in about three months after his accession, he invested her with the domains held by the

[1762 A.D.]

late empress. Certainly his was a mind incapable of long continued resentment. His heart was better than his head. Resolved to signalise his elevation by making others happy, he recalled all whom his predecessor had exiled, except Bestuzhev. Many he restored to their former honours and possessions. Thus the aged Munich was made governor-general of Siberia, restored to his military command; while Biron, who certainly deserved no favour, was reinvested with the duchy of Courland. He did more: he restored the prisoners made by the generals of Elizabeth, and gave them money to defray their passage home. And, as Frederick had always been the object of his idolatry, the world expected the armistice which he published, and which was preparatory to a peace between the two countries.

That declaration was an extraordinary document. In it the emperor declares that, his first duty being the welfare of his people, that welfare could not be consulted so long as hostilities were continued; that the war, which had raged six years, had produced no advantage to either party, but done incredible harm to both; that he would no longer sanction the wanton destruction of his species; that, in conformity with the divine injunction relative to the preservation of the people committed to his charge, he would put an end to the unnatural, impious strife; and that he was resolved to restore the conquests made by his troops. In this case he had been praised, and with great justice, for his moderation. We fear, however, he does not merit so high a degree of praise of humanity as many writers have asserted. At this moment, while proclaiming so loudly his repugnance to war, he was sending troops into his native principality of Holstein, with the intention of wresting from the king of Denmark the duchy of Schleswig, which he considered the rightful inheritance of his family. He even declared that he would never rest until he had sent that prince to Malabar.

PETER III
(1728–1762)

Nor must we omit to add that from the enemy he became the ally of Frederick; that his troops joined with the Prussians to expel the Austrians from the kingdom. His humanity only changed sides; if it spared the blood of Prussians, it had little respect for that of Austrians. We may add, too, that there was something like madness in his enthusiastic regard for Frederick. He corresponded with that monarch, whom he proclaimed his master, whose uniform he wore, and in whose armies he obtained the rank of major-general. Had he been capable of improvement, his intercourse with that far-sighted prince might have benefited him. Frederick advised him to celebrate at Moscow his coronation — a rite of superstitious importance in the eyes of the multitude. He was advised, too, not to engage in the Danish war, not to leave the empire. But advice was lost on him.

In some other respects, Peter deserves more credit than the admirers of Catherine are willing to allow him. (1) Not only did he pardon his personal enemies — not only did the emperor forget the wrongs of the grand duke — but on several he bestowed the most signal favours. He suppressed that abominable inquisitorial court, the secret chancery, which had consigned so many victims to everlasting bondage, which had received delations from the most obscure and vicious of men, which had made every respectable master of a family tremble lest his very domestics should render him amenable to that terrible tribunal. Had this been the only benefit of his reign, well would he have been entitled to the gratitude of Russia. (2) He emancipated the nobles from the slavish dependence on the crown, so characteristic of that barbarous people. Previous to his reign, no boyar could enter on any profession, or forsake it when it when once embraced, or retire from public to private life, or dispose of his property, or travel into any foreign country, without the permission of the czar. By breaking their chains at one blow, he began the career of social emancipation. (3) The military discipline of the nation loudly demanded reform, and he obeyed the call. He rescued the officers from the degrading punishments previously inflicted; he introduced a better system of tactics; and he gave more independence to the profession. He did not, however, exempt the common soldier from the corporal punishment which at any moment his superior officers might inflict. (4) He instituted a useful court to take cognisance of all offences committed against the public peace, and to chastise the delinquencies of the men entrusted with the general police of the empire. (5) He encouraged commerce, by lessening the duties on certain imports, and by abolishing them on certain exports. (6) In all his measures, all his steps, he proved himself the protector of the poor. In fact, one reason for the dislike with which he was regarded by the nobles arose from the preference which he always gave to the low over the high.

### Impolitic Acts of Peter III

But if impartial history must thus eulogise many of this monarch's acts, the same authority must condemn more. He exhibited everywhere great contempt for the people whom he was called to govern. He had no indulgence for their prejudices, however indifferent, however inveterate. Thus, in commanding that the secular clergy should no longer wear long beards, and should wear the same garb as the clergy of other countries, he offended his subjects to a degree almost inconceivable to us. In ordering the images to be removed from the churches — he was still a Lutheran, if anything — he did not lessen the odium which his other acts had produced. The archbishop of Novgorod flatly refused to obey him, and was in consequence exiled; but the murmurs of the populace compelled the czar to recall him. Still more censurable were his efforts to render the church wholly dependent on the state — to destroy everything like independence in its ministers; to make religion a mere engine in the hands of arbitrary power for the attainment of any object. His purpose, in fact, was to seize all the demesnes of the church — its extensive estates, its numerous serfs — and to pension the clergy like other functionaries.

In the ukase published on this occasion, he expressed a desire to relieve ecclesiastics of the temporal cares so prejudicial to their ghostly utility; to see that they indeed renounced the world, and free from the burden of perishing treasures, applied their whole attention to the welfare of souls. He therefore decreed that the property of the church should in future be managed by imperial officers; and that the clergy should receive, from the fund thus accumulated, certain annual pensions, corresponding to their stations. Thus the archbishops of Novgorod, Moscow, and St. Petersburg were to have each

2,500 rubles; and the same sum was to be allowed for the support of their households, of their capitular clergy, and for the sustentation of the sacred edifices. But the twenty-three other archbishops and bishops were to have only 3,000 rubles for both purposes. The salaries of the other ecclesiastics were carefully graduated. The inferior were divided into three classes — individuals of the first to receive 500, of the second 300, of the third 150 rubles per annum. The surplus funds were to be applied to the foundation of hospitals, to the endowment of colleges, and to the general purposes of the state.

Peter attempted these and other innovations in virtue of the two-fold character which, from the time of his grandfather, the czars had been anxious to assume, as supreme heads alike of religion and of the state. Not even the grand lama of Thibet ever arrogated a higher degree of theocractic authority. Indeed, our only surprise is that in addition to their other functions they did not assume that of bishops; that they did not array themselves in pontificals, and celebrate mass at the altar. But they certainly laid something like a claim to the sacerdotal character. Thus, on the death of the patriarch, Peter I opposed the election of another supreme head of the church; and when he found that the synod durst not venture on so far irritating the people as to dispense with the dignity, he insisted on being elected himself. If the sultan of Constantinople combined with himself the two-fold character, why should it be refused to him? The reign of Peter was too short to permit his designs of spoliation to be carried into effect; but, by confirming the dangerous precedent of his grandfather, he had done enough, and his successor Catherine was enabled to complete the robbery which he commenced.

But the most impolitic measure of Peter — that which rendered those who might have defended him indifferent to his fate — was his conduct towards the imperial guards. Two regiments he ordered to be in readiness for the Danish war. This was contrary to custom. In the faith of remaining near the court, most of the soldiers had embraced the military life; and they were as indignant as they were surprised when told that they must exchange the dissipations of a metropolis for the fatigues and privations attending a distant campaign. They were offended, too, with the introduction of the Prussian discipline, which they found by experience to be far more rigid than that to which they had hitherto been subject; and they patriotically condemned the innovation as prejudicial to the military fame of the empire. Still more irritating was the preference which he everywhere gave to the German over the native troops. His most intimate friends were Germans; the officers around his person were of the same nation; Germans directed the manœuvres not only of his household but of all his regiments; and a German — Prince George of Holstein, his uncle — was placed at the head of all the imperial armies.

Couple these acts of imprudence with others of which he was hourly guilty. In his palace of Oranienbaum he constructed a Lutheran chapel; and though he appears to have been indifferent to every form of religion, he held this in much more respect than the Greek form, which in fact, he delighted to ridicule. If churchmen became his enemies, the people in general were not likely to become his friends when they heard of a boast — probably a true one — that in the last war he had acquainted the Prussian monarch with the secrets of the imperial cabinet. Lastly, he insulted men of honour by making them the jest of his buffoons.

Circumstances much less numerous and much less cogent than these would have sufficed so ambitious, able, and unprincipled a woman as Catherine to organise a powerful conspiracy against the czar. But he was accused of many other things of which he was perfectly innocent. In fact, no effort seems to have been spared to invent and propagate stories to his disadvantage. In some instances, it is scarcely possible to separate the true from the false. Whether, for example, he, from the day of his accession, resolved to divorce his wife, to marry his mistress, to set aside Paul from succession, and to adopt Ivan, still confined in the fortress of Schlüsselburg, can never be known with certainty. That he secretly visited that unhappy prince seems undoubted; but we have little evidence for the existence of the design attributed to him. If, in fact, he sincerely contemplated raising the daughter of Count Vorontzov to the imperial throne, he would scarcely have adopted Ivan, unless he felt assured that no issue would arise from the second marriage. He could not, however, entertain any regard for a consort who had so grievously injured him, and little for a boy whom he knew was not his own. And, as there is generally some foundation for every report, there seems to be no doubt that Peter had promised to marry his mistress if she survived his wife. The report was enough for Catherine: on it she built her own story that her life was in danger; and that if her son were not designed for a similar fate, he would at least have that of Ivan.

## Catherine Plots against the Czar

The anxiety of the empress to secure adherents was continually active; and as her husband passed so much time in drunkenness, her motions were not so closely scrutinised as they should have been. Gregory Orlov, her criminal favourite, was the man in whom she placed the most reliance. Gregory had four brothers — all men of enterprise, of courage, of desperation; and none of them restricted by the least moral principle. Potemkin, afterwards so celebrated, was the sixth. This man was, perhaps, the most useful of the conspirators, as by means of his acquaintance with the priests of the metropolis he was able to enlist that formidable body in the cause. They were not slow to proclaim the impiety of the czar, his contempt of the orthodox faith, his resolution "to banish the fear of the Lord" from the Russian court, to convert churches into hospitals and barracks, to seize on all revenues of the church, and to end by compelling the most orthodox of countries to embrace the errors of Luther. The archimandrites received these reports from the parish priests, the bishops from the archimendrites; nor was there much difficulty in obtaining an entrance for them into the recesses of the neighbouring monasteries. The hetman of the Cossacks, an officer of great authority and of great riches, was next gained. Not less effectual than he was the princess Dashkov, who, though the sister of Peter's mistress, was the most ardent of the conspirators: perhaps the threatened exaltation of that sister, by rendering her jealous, only strengthened her attachment to the czarina. Through the instrumentality of this woman, Count Panin, the foreign minister and the governor of the grand duke Paul, was gained over. Whether the argument employed was, as one writer asserts, the sacrifice of her sister, or whether, as another affirms, she was the daughter of the count, who notoriously intrigued with her mother, is of no moment. What is certain is, that the count was exceedingly fond of her; and one authority expressly asserts that he became acquainted with the details of the conspiracy before her, and admitted her into the plot. This, however, is less probable than the relation we have given; for the princess had long been the friend of Catherine.

Her activity was unceasing. A Piedmontese adventurer, Odart by name, being forced to leave his native country for some crime, and having tried in

[1762 A.D.]

vain to obtain a subsistence in the neighbouring capitals, wisely resolved to try his fortune in St. Petersburg — a city where guilt might reside with impunity, and where it had only to be successful to win the applause of mankind. As he had a considerable knowledge of the fine arts, especially of music and painting, he had little difficulty in obtaining an introduction to the princess Dashkov. She, who had a shrewd insight into human character, soon perceived that this supple, crafty, active, sober, intriguing, unprincipled foreigner was just the man that was required to act as spy and confidential agent. He was introduced to Catherine, whose opinion confirmed that of her favourite  No choice could, indeed, have been better. Little cared he in what service he was employed. If a partisan were to be gained, no man could be more insinuating: if an enemy were to be removed, he had his pistols and his dirk, without which he never appeared in the street. His penetration soon enabled him to secure the aid of two other bravoes — the one, Possik, a lieutenant in the guards; the other, Globov, a lawyer in the employment of the senate. Of the character of these men, some notion may be formed from the fact that Possik offered to stab the emperor in the midst of the court. He knew how to ally duplicity with desperation; he was at once the hypocritical intriguer and the remorseless bravo.

Through the same Princess Dashkov, Volkonski, major-general of the guards, was won; and by Potemkin, or his ghostly allies, the archbishop of Novgorod was soon in the secret. The hetman of the Cossacks went further. Great as was the danger of entrusting that secret to many, he assembled the officers who served under him, assured them that he had heard of a conspiracy to dethrone the emperor, too irresistible to be appeased; and exhorted them to seize the favourable moment of propitiating the favour of the czarina, rather than, by remaining hostile or inactive, to bring down vengeance on their own heads. His advice had all the success that he could desire.

While these most vicious and in every way most worthless of men were thus employed in her behalf, Catherine was no less active. She knew that Count Panin espoused the cause of her son — less, perhaps, from affection to his charge, than from the hope of exercising more power under an infant emperor than under one of the mother's enterprising character. Her promise, that his influence should be second only to her own, made him her willing instrument. His defection constrained the rest of the conspirators: there was no more heard of a regency; and Catherine was to be proclaimed autocratrix of all the Russias.

Without increasing unnecessarily the number of the initiated, she yet prepared the minds of many for some impending change, and rendered them eager for its arrival by her artful and seasonable insinuations. If an officer of the guards stood near her, she whispered in his ear that the emperor had resolved on disbanding the present force, and exiling its chiefs; if an ecclesiastic, she bewailed the fate of the pure orthodox church; if a less interested person, she lamented her own misfortunes and those of her son — both doomed to immediate imprisonment, and she, at least, to an ultimate death. If a senator were near, she deplored the meditated destruction of the venerable and patriotic body to which he belonged; the transformation of the debauchees, perpetually around the emperor, into judges; and the substitution of the *Code Frédéric* for the ancient law of Russia.

By these means she prepared the minds of the people for the revolution: her affability, in fact, was the theme of their praise. But she did not trust merely to their good-will. She knew that, unless two or three regiments were secured, the insurrection might not find immediate supporters, and that the critical moment might be lost. Without money this object could not be obtained; and though both she and her confidential agents voluntarily disbursed all that they could command, and converted their most valuable effects into coin, the amount was alarmingly inadequate. In this emergency she applied to the French ambassador for a loan; and when he showed less readiness to accommodate her than she expected, she addressed herself, we are told, to the ambassador from England, and with more success. But this statement is untrue: it was not the English ambassador, but an English merchant, who furnished her with the sum she demanded. With this aid, she prevailed on the greater part of three regiments to await the signal for joining her.

Though the conspirators were, in point of numbers, formidable, their attempt was one of danger. Peter was about to leave Russia for Holstein, to prosecute the war against the Danish king; and of the troops whom he had assembled, though the greater part were on their march, some were now with him, and might be induced to defend him. Besides, the two great divisions of his fleet were at Kronstadt and Revel, and nobody could foresee how they would act. The conspirators agreed that he should be taken by surprise; that midnight should see him transferred from the throne to a dungeon. The festival of St. Peter and St. Paul — one of high importance in the Greek church — was approaching: the following day the emperor had resolved to depart. It was to be celebrated at Peterhov; there it was resolved to arrest him.

But accident hastened the execution of the plot. Until the arrival of the festival, Peter left St. Petersburg for Oranienbaum, to pass in riot and debauchery the intervening time. Accompanied by the most dissolute of his favourites, and by many of the court ladies, he anticipated the excesses which awaited his arrival. That he had received some hints of a plot, though he was unacquainted alike with its object and authors, is exceedingly probable. His royal ally of Prussia is said to have advised him to be on his guard, and several notes are supposed to have been addressed to him by his own subjects. If such information was received, it made no impression on him; and indeed its vagueness might well render him indifferent to it. But on the eve of his departure, when the superior officer of Passik, who had accidentally learned that danger attended the steps of the emperor, denounced the lieutenant, and the culprit was arrested, he had an opportunity of ascertaining all the details of the conspiracy. He treated the denunciation with contempt; affirmed that Passik belonged to the dregs of the people, and was not to be dreaded; and proceeded to Oranienbaum. The culprit, though narrowly watched, had time to write a line to the hetman, whom he exhorted to instant action, if they wished to save their lives. The note fell into the hands of the princess Dashkov, who immediately assembled the conspirators.

Not a moment was to be lost: the presence of Catherine was indispensable; and, though it was midnight and she was at Peterhov, seven leagues distant from St. Petersburg, one of the Orlovs went to bring her. He arrived at the fortress, entered a private door, and by a secret staircase ascended to the apartments occupied by the empress. It was now two o'clock in the morning: the empress was asleep; and her surprise was not unmixed with terror, when she was awakened by a soldier. In a moment she comprehended her situation: she arose, called one of her women, and both, being hastily clad in a strange habit, descended with the soldier to one of the gates, passed the sentinel without being recognised, and stepped into the carriage which was waiting for her. Orlov was the driver, and he urged the horses with so much severity that before they had proceeded half way from Peterhov to St. Petersburg, they fell down from exhaustion.   The situation of the empress was critical: she might at any moment be overtaken; and she was certain that with the dawn of day Peter would acquire some more definite intelligence of the plot.   In a state bordering on distraction, she took refuge in the first house that she approached: it was a tavern, and here she burned the letters which had passed between her and the conspirators.   Again she recommenced her journey on foot: by good fortune she met a countryman with a cart; Orlov seized the vehicle, the peasant ran away; Catherine ascended it, and, in this undignified manner, she, her woman, and Orlov entered St. Petersburg about seven o'clock on the morning of July the 9th.

### Catherine Usurps the Crown

No sooner was Catherine in the capital than she was joined by the hetman; and, accompanied by him, she hastened to the barracks of the troops which he commanded.   Four companies immediately declared for her;   their example constrained the rest of the regiment; three other regiments, hearing the acclamation, and seeing the people hurry to the spot, joined in the cry; all St. Petersburg was in motion; a report was spread that she and her son had just escaped assassination by order of the czar; her adherents rapidly multiplied; and, accompanied by about two thousand soldiers, with five times that number of citizens, who loudly proclaimed her sovereign of Russia, she went to the church of Our Lady of Kazan.   Here everything was prepared for her reception: the archbishop of Novgorod, with a host of ecclesiastics, awaited her at the altar; she swore to observe the laws and religion of the empire; the crown was solemnly placed on her head; she was proclaimed sole monarch of Russia, and the grand duke Paul her successor; and *Te Deum* concluded the eventful ceremony.

From the church she proceeded to the palace occupied by the late empress; the mob crowded to see her, and to take the oath of allegiance; while the more respectable portion of the citizens were awed into submission, or at least into silence, by a report that Peter had just been killed by falling from his horse.   To gratify the populace, the taverns were abandoned to them: the same fate visited the houses of all who were obnoxious to the conspirators; intoxication was general; robbery was exercised with impunity; the palace, to which Catherine had hastened, was strengthened; a numerous guard was stationed in its defence; a manifesto was proclaimed; a notification was delivered into the hands of each foreign minister, and the revolution was complete.

One object of the conspirators had been to close every avenue of egress from the capital, that Peter might not be acquainted with the revolution until it was too powerful to be repressed.   All the troops in the vicinity were called within the walls; but there was one regiment about sixteen hundred strong, which lay between the city and Peterhov, the conduct of which was doubtful. Without the slightest knowledge of what had taken place, the colonel arrived in the city, and was soon persuaded not only to declare for the new sovereign but to prevail on the regiment to follow his example.   He was successful; and, with the whole body, he returned in triumph to the capital.   On this very day Peter had promised to dine with Catherine: on reaching Peterhov he was surprised to hear of her flight.   Vorontzov, the father of his mistress, the father also of the princess Dashkov, who had witnessed without repugnance the dishonour alike of his wife and daughter, proposed to the emperor to visit

St. Petersburg to ascertain the cause of her departure; and, if any insurrection were meditated, to suppress it. He arrived in the presence of the empress, was induced to swear allegiance to her, and was ordered to retire into his own house.

But Peter had already been informed of the revolution; and he traversed with hasty steps the gardens of Peterhov, indecisive and terrified. Yet he was not wholly deserted. The brave Munich, whose locks were ripened by age, and whose wisdom equalled his valour, advised him instantly to place himself at the head of his Holstein troops, march on the capital, and thereby enable all who were yet loyal to join him. Whether the result would have been such as the veteran anticipated, *viz.* a counter-revolution, may well be doubted; but there can be no doubt that a considerable number of soldiers would have joined him, and that he would have been able to enter into negotiations with the hostile party. He was too timid to adopt the suggestion: nothing, in fact, could urge him to decisive action. When informed that Catherine was making towards Peterhov, at the head of ten thousand men, all that he could resolve to do was to send messengers to her with proposals. His first was that the supreme power should be divided between them; the second, when no reply was deigned to his letter, that he should be allowed to leave Russia, with his mistress and a favourite, and pass the rest of his days in Holstein. She detained his messenger, and still advanced.

Munich now advised him to embark for Kronstadt, and join his fleet, which was still faithful; but unfortunately he delayed so long that one of Catherine's emissaries had time to corrupt the garrison of the fort: on arriving, he was prohibited from disembarking, and told that if he did not immediately retire his vessel would be sunk by the cannon of the place. Still he had a fleet at Revel; and if it were disloyal he might escape into Prussia, Sweden, or Holstein. With the fatality, however, which characterised all his measures on this eventful day, he returned to Oranienbaum, where he disembarked at four o'clock in the morning of July the 10th. Here he was soon visited by the emissaries of Catherine; was persuaded to sign an act of abdication; was conducted to Peterhov; was divested of all his imperial orders; was clad in a mean dress, and consigned, first to one of the country houses of the hetman, and soon afterwards to the fortress of Ropscha, about twenty miles distant from Peterhov. He was not allowed to see the empress; and his mistress and attendants were separated from him.[b]

### Death of Peter III (1762 A.D.)

What was to be done with Peter? At the deliberations on this question Catherine calmly listened to arguments as to the necessity of measures being taken in order that the former emperor should not injure her rule by disturbing weak minds; she clearly realised all the dangers that might be created for her, if not by Peter himself at any rate by his partisans. They were not numerous, yet they did exist and they might multiply in the future. It was necessary that Peter should be definitively made harmless, but how was it to be done? During the deliberations on the means to be taken, no restraint was imposed by Catherine's presence. The empress was not an Elizabeth Petrovna: she at once understood the uselessness of imprisonment at Schlüsselburg or any other place; she was not likely to fall into a fainting fit at any proposition made. The examples of Ivan the Terrible and Peter the Great did not disturb her. Nevertheless, not one of those present, not even the persons nearest to her, reading in her eyes the secret desire decisively to finish once for all with this unbearable question, would have dared even to hint at an unnatural death — they knew Catherine, they might read her thought, but not aloud.

When the persons who surrounded Catherine were definitively convinced that Peter's removal was recognised by her as indispensable, they decided to devise a means for it without her knowledge and to accomplish it without her consent. In this were interested all the personal partisans of Catherine, those "chosen sons of the people," who had stirred up the empress to put herself at the head of the movement. They were far more interested in the matter than Catherine herself: the change had been brought about by all classes of society, by the whole nation, not by her; no one could even think of the detested Peter ascending the throne a second time — it was not on Catherine that the malcontents would revenge themselves, that is if there were or would be any, but on the "chosen of the people." Peter did not prevent a change being brought about; still, he might hinder not Catherine but many of the "chosen ones" from reaping the fruits of their labours. The Orlov brothers were above all interested in the matter; all of them, and especially Gregory, occupied important posts, which gave them the right to dream of great things; the realisation of these dreams could, it seemed to them, be prevented only by Peter's perpetual imprisonment. As long as Peter lived, Catherine was not free: it was now observed by everyone that in the manifesto of the 28th of June Peter was not once called the consort, the husband of Catherine; but such bonds imposed by the church are not broken either by manifestoes or imprisonment: Peter living, by the one fact of his being alive, prevented the Orlovs from attaining the final results of their efforts, their sacrifices. No matter by what means, somehow the Orlovs must guard not merely what was as yet only possible and cherished in their dreams, but the good fortune that had already been attained to; and, for this, haste must be made. The favour shown to them, especially to Gregory, was visible to every eye. At the court there were already snares laid for them, intrigues began to be carried on against them, endeavours were made to overthrow Gregory; if Gregory fell his brothers would fall with him. Haste must be made.

On Wednesday, the 3rd of July, on the fourth day after the appearance of the attacks of Peter's illness, in the evening the doctor, Leyders, came to Ropscha from St. Petersburg. On Thursday, the 4th of July, the former emperor probably grew worse: at any rate a second doctor came that day from St. Petersburg — the regimental surgeon Paulsen. The doctors did not observe any change for the worse, and according to the expressions of the language of contemporaries, the condition of the patient left nothing to be desired. Friday passed quietly. On Saturday, the 6th of July, in the morning while the prisoner was still asleep, the valet who attended on Peter went out into the garden, "to breathe the fresh air." An officer who was in the garden ordered him to be seized and the valet was put into a carriage which stood in readiness and removed from Ropscha. In the evening, at six o'clock, a messenger who had ridden from Ropscha gave to Catherine a packet from Alexis Orlov. On a sheet of soiled gray paper, in the ignorant handwriting of Alexis Orlov and by his own drunken hand was traced the following:

Merciful sovereign mother![1]
How can I explain, how describe what has happened; you will not believe your faithful servant; but before God I speak the truth. Matushka! I am ready to go to my death; but I myself do not know, how this calamity happened. We are lost, if you do not have mercy. Matushka, he is no more on earth. But no one had thought of this, and how could we have

[1 The exact expression in Russian is *Matushka* (little mother), a title of endearment given by the people to the sovereign.]

thought to raise our hands against the sovereign! But, your majesty, the calamity is accomplished. At table he began to dispute with Prince Theodore ; [1] we were unable to separate them and he was already no more ; we do not ourselves remember what we did ; but we are all equally guilty and deserving of punishment. Have mercy upon me, if it is only for my brother's sake. I have brought you my confession and seek for nothing. Forgive or command that it may be quickly finished. The world is not kind ; we have angered you and destroyed our souls forever.

The news of death is a great matter. It is impossible either to prepare for it or grow accustomed to it. In the present case the death of Peter, doing away with many perplexities, and giving a free hand to many persons, appeared as the only possible and most desirable issue to the political drama which was agitating the people of Russia. Nevertheless the news of this death struck some, disturbed others, and puzzled all as an unexpected sudden phenomenon. On Catherine it produced the strongest impression, and (justice must be rendered to her) she was the first to control herself, to examine into the mass of new conditions, created by the death of Peter, and to master the various feelings which made their invasion together with the news of the catastrophe of Ropscha.

"*Que je suis affectée: même terrassée par cette mort*" (How affected and even overwhelmed I am by this death), said Catherine to Princess Dashkov. She was touched by it as a woman; she was struck by it as empress. Catherine clearly recognised her position: the death of Peter, a death that was so sudden, would at such a time awaken rumours, throw a shadow on her intentions, lay a spot on the memory of those until then clear, bright ten days; yet she did not hide from herself that it was only by death that the great undertaking "begun by us" could be entirely consummated. The tragedy of Catherine's position was still further increased by the circumstance of Alexis Orlov's having taken an active part in the catastrophe of Ropscha: she was under great obligations to the Orlovs as empress, while as a woman she was bound by the ties of affection to Gregory Orlov; she loathed the crime, but she could not give up the criminal. "One must be firm in one's resolutions," said Catherine, "only weak-minded people are undecided." Even she herself, she must conceal the crime and protect the criminal, taking upon herself all the moral responsibility and political burden of the catastrophe. Catherine then for the first time showed a healthy political understanding of the widest diapason and played the rôle she had taken upon herself with the talent of a virtuoso.

The letter of Alexis Orlov, which entirely exculpated her from all suspicion was hidden in a cupboard, where it lay for thirty-four years, until the very death of the empress. With the exception of two or three persons in the immediate entourage of Catherine, who were near her at the moment when the letter was received besides Nikita Panin and the hetman Razumovski, no one ever read it, no one knew of it while the empress lived. Having decided upon the fate of the letter, she herself marked out the programme of her actions clearly and shortly: "*Il faut marcher droit; je ne dois pas être suspecte.*" (I must walk uprightly; I must not be suspected.)

The programme was exactly fulfilled. The letter of Alexis Orlov did not communicate the trifling details of the catastrophe, but the general signification of the narrative did not leave any doubts as to its chief features, and therefore Catherine considered it first of all necessary to certify whether poison had been employed; the postmortem examination, made by order of the empress, did not show the least trace of poison. Neither the medical

---

[1] Prince Theodore Sergeivitch Bariatinski.

certificate as to the cause of death nor the act of death has been preserved; we can only guess that these certificates directed the composition of the following "mourning" manifesto:

On the seventh day after our acceptation of the throne of all the Russias, we received the news that the former emperor Peter III, by an attack of hemorrhage which was common and previously frequent to him, had fallen into a most dangerous condition. In order therefore not to neglect our Christian duty and the sacred command, by which we are obliged to preserve the life of our neighbour, we immediately ordered that everything necessary should be sent to him in order to avert consequences that might be dangerous to his health through this mischance, and tend to assist to his speedy recovery. But to our extreme grief and trouble of heart, we yesterday evening received news that, by the will of God, he had departed this life. We have therefore commanded that his body should be taken to the Nevski monastery to, be there interred; meanwhile we incite and exhort all our true and faithful subjects by our imperial and maternal word that, without evil remembrance of all that is past, they should raise to God their heartfelt prayers that forgiveness and salvation of his soul may be granted to the deceased; this unexpected decree by God of his death we accept as a manifestation of the divine providence through which God in his inscrutable judgment lays the path, known to his holy will alone, to our throne and to the entire fatherland. Given at St. Petersburg on the 7th day of July, 1762. CATHERINE.

The Russian made the sign of the cross as he read this manifesto. Yes, the judgments of God are indeed inscrutable! The former emperor had experienced in his last days so many sorrows, so many reverses — no wonder his feeble, sickly nature, which had already suffered from attacks of hemorrhage, would not withstand these shocks; in the matter of death nobody is free: he had fallen ill and died. To the common people his death appeared natural; even the upper classes, although they might hear even if they did not know something, did not admit any thoughts of Catherine's having had any share in his death. The empress "must not be suspected" and she remained unsuspected. On the night between Sunday, the 7th of July, and Monday, the 8th, the body was brought straight to St. Petersburg, directly to the present monastery of St. Alexander Nevski to the same place where the body of the princess Anna of Brunswick was exposed for reverence, and later on the body of the princess Anna Petrovna, Catherine's daughter.[e]

## CHAPTER VIII

## THE AGE OF CATHERINE THE GREAT

### [1762-1796 A.D.]

> We must acknowledge that in many respects Catherine was far from
> irreproachable; her very accession to the throne casts a dark shadow
> on her moral image.  But the reproaches that must be made to her
> on this account cannot but be counteracted by the thirty-four years
> of greatness and prosperity which Russia enjoyed under her and to
> which the popular voice has given the appellation of the Age of
> Catherine. — SHEHEBALSKI.[b]

THERE are few names so popular in Russia and so dear to her as that of
Catherine II.  The generation of men who belonged to her time spoke of her
with the most profound emotion.  Memoirs and reminiscences of her contemporaries breathe almost without exception the same ardent devotion — a
sort of worship of her.  In opposition to these feelings, foreign reports of her
represent her as cruel, heartless, and unscrupulous to the last degree.  Some
authors represent her as a sort of monster.  However strange such contradictions may appear, they can readily be accounted for.  Foreigners view Catherine II more from the side of her external policy, which was certainly often
unsparing and unscrupulous in the means employed; they refer caustically
to her private life, which was certainly not irreproachable.  Russians, on the
other hand, felt above all the influence of her interior administraton, which
onctrasted sharply from that of her predecessors by its mildness, and which
was full of useful and liberal reforms.  The Russians of her day could not
remain indifferent to the glory with which Catherine surrounded Russia.  And
thus to the descendants of Catherine, acquainted as they are with the reports

[1762 A.D.]

given of her both by Russians and foreigners, she appears as the two-faced god of antiquity; her visage when turned to the neighbouring powers is stern and unwelcoming; that, on the contrary, which is turned toward Russia is full of majesty and mildness.

The state of affairs was very much entangled when Catherine ascended the throne, both in the interior of the empire and in respect to exterior policy. One of the first acts of the new empress was the conclusion of peace with all those who had taken part in the Seven Years' War. Not seeing any advantage to Russia in helping the king of Prussia in his war against the German emperor and his allies, Catherine did not consider it necessary to assist the latter. " I am of tolerably martial tastes," said she, in the first days after her accession to the throne, to one of the ambassadors to the Russian court, " but I will never begin war without a cause; if I begin war, it will not be as the empress Elizabeth did — to please others, but only when I find it favourable for myself." These words are characteristic of all Catherine's further foreign policy; to listen to them was not without profit for foreign courts, which, during the preceding reigns, had certainly been over-spoiled by the complaisance of the Russians.

The next circumstance must have enlightened them still further as to how little Catherine had the intention of allowing herself to be restrained by considerations which did not tend to the furtherance of the glory and prosperity of her dominions. We have already seen by what persistency — sometimes even to the sacrifice of their dignity — the preceding governments had succeeded in obtaining the recognition of their right to the imperial title. France had recognised it only under Elizabeth, and that under the condition that at all foreign courts the Russian ambassador must, as previously, yield the precedence to the French ambassador; the late empress Elizabeth herself engaged that this should be done. When Catherine came to the throne, it was proposed to her to renew this engagement; she, however, very decidedly refused to do so, and commanded that it should be declared that she would break off all relations with those courts that did not recognise her in the quality of empress — a title, she added, which, however, was in no degree more exalted than that of the czars. Such were the first acts of the new empress in regard to foreign governments: they were bold, firm, and determined.[b]

### CATHERINE'S OWN VIEWS ON RUSSIA

The interior condition of Russia and the position at that time occupied by Catherine are best described by herself, in her own words. In the very beginning of the year 1764 the procurator-general, A. I. Glebov, was removed from his functions. As his successor in this weighty and responsible office the empress named Prince A. A. Viasemski. The procurator-general had to superintend the finances of the empire, to direct the senate, and to govern all the interior affairs of the nation, thus uniting in himself the powers of minister of finance, of justice, and of home affairs. He was subordinate to none except the law, the good of the country, and the will of the empress. He was the right hand of the empress: " In cases where you may be in doubt," said Catherine to him, " consult with me, and put your trust entirely in God and in me; and I, seeing how gratifying your conduct is to me, will not forsake you." Prince Viasemski was still a young man — he was not yet thirty-seven years of age. A pupil of the land-forces cadet corps, he had taken part in the Prussian War — not, however, in the character of a brave soldier, but as the executor of " secret orders." At the accession of Catherine to the throne he was already quartermaster-general. In 1763 he was entrusted with the pacification of the peasants in the eastern provinces of Russia. He was well educated, industrious, and was recognised by everyone as an absolutely honest man. It was this last circumstance that determined Catherine's choice. Having selected for herself her " closest helper," with whom she would have to be in constant relations, the empress considered it necessary once for all to have a clear explanation with him, and with her own hand wrote him "instructions" in which she expressed her own views on Russia, on the chief branches of the administration, and on herself personally, drawing her portrait for him as empress:

" The Russian Empire," wrote Catherine, " is so vast in its extent that any other form of government excepting that of an autocratic sovereign would be prejudicial to it; for any other would be slow of accomplishment and would include in itself a multitude of diverse interests and passions which tend to the weakening of the administrative power. No, there must be one sovereign, invested with authority to destroy evil, and who esteems the public welfare as his own. Other rulers are, in the words of the Gospel, hirelings."

The first institution in the empire is the senate. Catherine thus describes it to the young procurator-general: " In the senate you will find two parties, but in my opinion a wise policy does not require that much regard should be paid to them, lest too much firmness should thus be given them: in this manner they will disappear the sooner; I have only kept a watchful eye over them and have used men according to their capabilities for one object or another. Both parties will now try to catch you for their side. In one you will find men of upright character, although not of far-seeing intellects; in the other I think their views are wider, but it is not clear whether they are always advantageous. Some think that because they have been in one or another country for a long time, everything must be arranged in politics for the good of their beloved land, and everything else without exception meets with their criticism, in spite of the fact that all interior administration is founded on the law of the rights of nations. You must not regard either one party or the other, but be courteous and dispassionate in your behaviour to both, listening to everything, having only the good of the country and justice in view, and walking in firm steps to the shortest road to truth."

The senate " by its want of attention to the deeds of certain of my forefathers left its fundamental principles, and oppressed other courts through which the lower tribunals fell greatly into decline. The servility and meanness of persons in these tribunals is indescribable and no good can be expected until this evil is done away with. Only the forms of bureaucracy are fulfilled, and people do not dare to act uprightly although the interests of the state thus suffer. The senate having once passed its proper bounds, it is now difficult to accustom it to the necessary order in which it should stand. Perhaps for the ambition of some members, the former measures have some charm, but at any rate while I live, it will remain my duty to command."

The "servility" of the members of the government offices was ascribed to the senate, but the senate was not to repair the evil it had occasioned. By a ukase of the 19th of December, 1763, Catherine required that the " government offices should be filled by worthy and honest men." The motive of this ukase is explained in the above cited instructions to Prince Viasemski. In these instructions Catherine draws his attention to the great burdensomeness for the people of the duties on salt and wine, but she confides to his particular care the question of silver or copper money, which had long interested her, as well as the position of trade and commerce. "This very delicate matter," she says, "of which many persons find it unpleasant to hear must however be looked into and examined by you." Catherine did not conceal from herself that the laws required amending. "Lack of time alone," she says, "has prevented the introduction of reforms."

Catherine did not forget to tell the young procurator-general what her views were on the frontier country of Russia: "Little Russia, Livonia, and Finland are provinces that must be governed in conformity with their privileges; to violate them by revoking them all suddenly would be quite unseemly, to call them foreign countries, however, and treat them on such a basis would be more than an error—it might rightly be called stupidity. These provinces, as also that of Smolensk, must by the lightest possible means be gradually russianised so that they shall cease to be looked upon as wolves in the forest. The attainment of such an object is quite easy if sensible persons are chosen for the governors of these provinces. When there is no longer a hetman in Little Russia, we must endeavour to abolish even the appellation of hetman."

Having initiated Prince Viasemski into the most secret matters, having reminded him that a procurator-general in the exercise of his functions is obliged to oppose the most powerful personages and that therefore the sovereign power is his only support, Catherine in the following passage expressed her views on her own sovereign power:

"You ought to know with whom you have to do. Occasions will arise daily which will lead you to seek my counsel. You will find that I have no other aims than the highest welfare

AN OLD MORDVINIAN WOMAN

and glory of the fatherland and desire nothing but the happiness of my subjects of whatever condition they may be. My only aspiration is that both within and without my dominions tranquillity, contentment, and peace should be preserved. I love truth above all things, and you may speak it, fearing nothing; I shall encourage discussion, if good can be accomplished by it. I hear that all esteem you as an honest man; I hope to show you by experience that persons with such qualities can live happily at court. I will add that I require no flattery from you, but solely frankness and sincerity in your dealings, and firmness in the affairs of state." Such an administration programme and such political principles gave Catherine full right to look calmly towards the future.c

## THE POLISH SUCCESSION; THE POLICY OF THE NATIONS

A subject of deep gravity soon claimed her attention — the approaching death of the king of Poland and the consequent opening of the succession. Two parties were contending for power in Warsaw — the court party with minister Brühl and his son-in-law Mniszek at its head, and the party which looked to Russia for support and had for chiefs the Czartoriski. The first-named faction wished to assure the succession to the prince of Saxony, an aim in which France and Austria shared, and the second, planning to elect a *piast* or native noble who should belong to their party, chose as candidate a nephew of the Czartoriski, Stanislaus Poniatovski. Thus France, which in 1733 had waged war in the cause of a piast against the Saxon candidate, now came to support the Saxon against Poniatovski. The face of affairs had completely changed, and the Polish monarchy, growing weaker day by day, arrived at the point where it could no longer stand erect save by the aid of Saxony, a German state. Frederick II had as much reason to dread an increase of power for Saxony as for Poland, since Saxony was an inveterate enemy of Prussia in the empire, as was Poland in the regions of the Vistula. Russia, which had formerly fought against Stanislaus Leszczynski, father-in-law of Louis XV, was now to oppose the candidate favoured by France and Austria; it was eager also to prevent the accession to the throne of any Polish noble wielding too much power of his own. The choice, therefore, of Stanislaus Poniatovski, a simple gentleman without personal following or influence, met fully the desires of Frederick II, the interests of the Russian Empire, and the private feelings of Catherine II, who was happy to bestow a crown upon one of her former lovers.

When Augustus III finally died, the diets of convocation and of election stirred up great agitation all over the country. The two rival parties waged fiercer strife than ever; at last the Czartoriski called upon the Russian army to help drive out their enemies, and it was under the protection of foreign bayonets that Poniatovski inaugurated that fatal reign during which Poland was to be three times dismembered and in the end wiped completely from the list of nations. Three principal causes were to bring about the ruin of the ancient royal republic:

(1) The national movement in Russia, which aimed to complete its territory on the west and recover, so said its historians, the provinces which had formerly been part of the domain of St. Vladimir, or White Russia, Black Russia, and Little Russia. With the national question was mingled another which had already led, under Alexander Mikhaïlovitch, to a first dismemberment of the Polish states. Complaints against the operations of the uniates had multiplied in Lithuania, and Russia had frequently attempted to intervene. Peter the Great protested to Augustus II against the treatment accorded to his co-religionists in Poland, and Augustus had issued an edict assuring free exercise of the orthodox religion; but this never went into effect owing to the inability of the monarchy to repress the zeal of the clergy and the Jesuits. In 1723 Peter begged the intervention of the pope, but his petition was refused and the abuses continued.

(2) The covetousness of Prussia. Poland being in possession of western Prussia, that is the lower Vistula including Thorn and Dantzic, eastern Prussia was completely cut off from the rest of the Brandenburg monarchy, which was thus made a divided state. The government of Warsaw committed, moreover, the serious error of confounding Protestant and orthodox dissenters and harassing them alike.

(3) The inevitable enkindling of Poland in its turn by the spirit of reform that spread abroad during the eighteenth century. Poniatovski and the most enlightened of his countrymen had long perceived the contrast presented by national anarchy as it prevailed at home and the order that was being established in neighbouring states. Nevertheless, while Prussia, Russia, and Austria were exerting every effort to re-form themselves into strictly modern states, Poland still clung obstinately to the traditions of the feudal ages, and allowed the other European monarchies to get so far ahead that when at last the impulse to reform did come it hastened the dissolution of the country.

From a social point of view Poland was a nation of agricultural serfs, above which had been superimposed a numerous petty nobility that was itself in bondage to a few great families, against whom even the king was powerless. There existed no third estate unless we can designate by that name a few thousand Catholic bourgeois and a million Jews, who had no interest in maintaining a condition of things that condemned them to everlasting opprobrium. From an economical point of view the country had only a limited agriculture carried on by serfs after the most primitive methods; but little commerce, no industries, and no public finances. From a political standpoint the "legal" nation was composed exclusively of gentleman — rivalry between the great families, anarchy in the diets, the *liberum veto*, and the inveterate habit of invoking foreign intervention having destroyed in Poland all idea of law or even of state. From a military point of view Poland was still in the feudal stage of undisciplined militia; it had scarcely any organised troops outside the cavalry formed of nobles, no infantry, but little artillery, and no fortresses worthy the name on frontiers that were thus left open to the enemy. What means of defence had a nation divided against itself, guilty of having received gold from the enemy, against the three powerful monarchies which beset it on all sides, and whose ambassadors had more power than its own king in his diets?

Catherine and Frederick were agreed on two essential points: to vindicate the rights of dissenters and prevent any reform in the anarchial constitution which made Poland their easy prey. By affecting to espouse the cause of tolerance they could blind Europe to their real designs against the integrity of the country, and Poland's own noisy fanaticism would further enable them to conceal their object.

In 1765 Koninski, an orthodox bishop of White Russia, presented a memoir to the king of Poland in which were recounted all the vexations which the followers of the Greek religion had been made to suffer in his kingdom. "The missionary fathers," said the memoir, "were particularly remarkable for their zeal; upheld by the secular authorities they were in the habit of summoning all the Greco-Russian inhabitants of the villages and banding them together like a flock of sheep six weeks at a time, forcing them to confess, and displaying thorny rods and stakes to intimidate the rebellious, separating children from their parents and wives from husbands. In case of stubborn resistance the recalcitrant ones were severely beaten, their hands were burned, or they were confined in prison for several months."

Russia supported the dissenters in the Polish diet and Stanislaus promised to sustain them. To do this it was necessary to assure to the people the free exercise of their religion, and to the nobles the political rights of which they had been despoiled under preceding legislators. The diet of 1766 violently opposed this proposition, and the deputy Gourovski who had tried to speak in favour of the dissenters narrowly escaped assassination.

Repnin, Catherine's ambassador, urged the dissenters to resort to the legal method of confederation. Those of the orthodox faith united at Sluth, the Protestants, under the patronage of the Prussian ambassador, at Thorn; even at Radom there was a confederation of Catholics and of all those who feared a reform in the constitution or the abolition of the *liberum veto*. Russia, which with Prussia had guaranteed the support of this absurd constitution, took these also under its protection. Such were the auspices under which was opened the diet of 1767; the Poles seemed insensible to the attack made on their independence and exerted themselves solely to maintain intolerance. Soltik, bishop of Cracow, Zaluski, bishop of Kiev, and two other of the pope's ambassadors were the most ardent in opposing the project of reform. Repnin had them seized and carried to Russia, and so persistently had Poland shown herself in the wrong that Europe applauded an act, in itself a violation of the rights of men, which seemed to assure liberty of conscience. The diet yielded and consented to the dissenting nobles being granted equal rights with the Catholics; in any case the state religion was to remain that of Rome.

### POLAND IS DISMEMBERED

In 1768 a treaty was drawn up between Poland and Russia by the terms of which no modification could be made in the constitution without the consent of the latter power. This was equivalent to legalising foreign intervention, from the abuse of which Poland was to perish. The Russian troops evacuated Warsaw, and the confederates sent deputies to render thanks to the empress.

The Radom Confederation, the most considerable of the three, which had taken up arms solely to prevent reforms in the constitution, not to support the dissenters, was gravely dissatisfied with the result. On its dissolution another and still more numerous confederation was formed, that of Bar in Podolia, which had for object the maintenance of the *liberum veto* and the securing of exclusive privileges to Catholics. It sent deputies to the courts of Dresden, Vienna, and Versailles to awaken interest in its cause. In the west opinions differed; on which side were right, the Polish nation, the brightest promise for the future? Were they at Warsaw with the king, the senate, and all those who had striven for the enfranchisement of the dissenters and the reconstruction of Poland, or were they at Bar with the turbulent nobles who, guided by fanatical priests, had revolted in the name of the *liberum veto* and religious intolerance? Voltaire and most of the French philosophers declared for the king; but the minister of Louis XV, Monsieur de Choiseul, favoured the confederates, without taking into consideration that in weakening the power of the Polish king he was weakening Poland itself. The royal army consisting of only nine thousand men, the government committed the grievous blunder of calling upon Russia for aid, and the result was that the Muscovite troops succeeded in recapturing from the confederates Bar, Berdichev, and Cracow. The Cossacks of the Ukraine, the Zaporogians and the laïdamaks or brigands were called to arms and a savage war, at once national, religious, and social, ensued, desolating the provinces of the Dnieper. The massacre of Ouman, a town belonging to Count Potocki, horrified the inhabitants of the Ukraine.

The confederates obtained the support of the Viennese court and established a council at Teschen, and their headquarters at Eperies, in Hungary. They were still in possession of three strongholds in Poland. Choiseul sent them money and commissioned successively De Taules, Dumouriez, and the baron de Viomesnil to assist in their organisation. From the memoirs of Dumouriez we learn that the forces of the confederation, distributed about over all Poland, consisted of sixteen thousand cavalry divided into five or six separate bands, each commanded by an independent chief. Dumouriez with his undisciplined troops was defeated at Landskron (1771); but Viomesnil, Dussaillans, and Choisy became masters of the château of Cracow (1772), which was finally recovered by Suvarov. An attempt made by certain confederates on the 3rd of November, 1771, to obtain possession of the person of the king, excited noisy but insincere indignation at the three northern courts, and increased Voltaire's aversion to the confederates.d

By the treaty of St. Petersburg (signed August 5th, 1772), the palatinates of Malborg, Pomerania, Warmia, Culm (except Dantzic and Thorn), and part of Great Poland was ceded to Prussia. Austria had Galicia, Sandomir, Cracow, and part of Podolia. Russia had Polotsk, Vitepsk, Mikislav, and Polish Livonia. The next point was to execute the treaty. A pretext could not long be wanting for the armed interference of all the three powers: each had been expressly invited by some one of the parties which divided that unhappy country, which were perpetually engaged in civil war. The three bandit chiefs despatched armies into Poland, and Europe waited with much anxiety the issue of this step. Its suspense was not of long continuance: the Treaty of St. Petersburg was presented to the Polish king and senate; and manifestoes, stating the pretensions of each power, were published.

Never were documents so insulting laid before rational men. King and senate could oppose little resistance to demands so powerfully supported; but their consent alone could not sanction the dismemberment of the republic. Hence the diet was convoked. That eight or ten members only should resist the destruction of their country, that all the rest should tamely sanction it, might appear incredible if it were not a matter of history. In this monstrous robbery the lion's share fell to Russia. She acquired an extent of territory estimated at 3,440 square leagues, with one million and a half of inhabitants: Austria had 2,700 leagues, but a greater population, viz. two millions and a half: Prussia had scarcely 1,000 square leagues, and less than a million of people.

As the three co-robbers were so courageous as to set at defiance both justice and public opinion, so magnanimous as to show themselves in their real character to all posterity, it may appear matter of surprise that they did not seize on the whole of the kingdom. But though they had resolved to seize the remainder, they were cautious enough to await the course of events — to take advantage of any favourable circumstance that might arise. The French Revolution furnished them with it. That event had many admirers in Poland, many who wished to imitate it at home. It was easy for the three neighbouring powers to take umbrage at the progress of republican opinions; to assert, as indeed truth authorised them to assert, that the Poles were in communication with the heads of the movement in Paris. In reality, in the year 1791 a new constitution was proclaimed, exceedingly like a republic. The reduction of Dantzic and Thorn, the two most important possessions in the north of Europe, convinced the Poles that they had been duped. Catherine was not a woman to let others derive the sole advantage where anything was to be gained. Preparatory to active operations, she declared war against Poland. The diet resolved to resist; but, as usual, the Poles were divided among themselves. One party declared for Russia; and though the greater number declared for independence, they could not be brought to combine. Success after success was obtained by the Russian general; the empress negotiated the details of another partition with Prussia; and the king and the diet were, as before, compelled to sanction it. By it the Russian frontier was extended to the centre of Lithuania and Volhinia; while the remainder of Great and a part of Little Poland were ceded to Frederick William. Much to the honour of Austria, she had no hand in this second iniquity.

The territory of the republic was now reduced to about 4,000 square miles; and her army, by command of the czarina, was in future not to exceed fifteen thousand men. The Poles were never deficient in bravery; and they were, on this occasion, sensitive to the national shame. They felt that the narrow limits still allowed them would soon be passed, and that their remaining provinces were intended soon to be incorporated with the neighbouring states. A general insurrection was organised; an army voluntarily arose, and Kosciuszko placed himself at its head. For a time wonders were wrought by the patriots; though opposed by two great enemies — Russia and Prussia — they expelled the enemy from most of the fortresses; and even when Austria acceded to the coalition and took Cracow they were not desponding. To effect impossibilities, however, was an absurd attempt: the majority felt it to be so, and they sullenly received the foreign law. Kosciuszko was made prisoner; the last outworks of the last fortress were reduced; Warsaw capitulated; Stanislaus was deposed; and a third partition ended the existence of the Polish Republic. By it Austria had Cracow, with the country between the Pilitza, the Vistula, and the Bug. Prussia had Warsaw, with the territory to the banks of the Niemen. The rest, which, as usual, was the lion's share, fell to Russia.

### War with Turkey (1769–1774 A.D.)

The wars with this power occupied a considerable portion of Catherine's reign; yet they were not originally sought by her. The Porte, at the suggestion of the French ambassador, whose master was anxious to divert her from her meditated encroachments on Poland, was, unfortunately for itself, induced to declare war against her. The Grand Seignior, indeed, was the ally of the republic; and he was one of the parties to guarantee its independence. But his dominions were not tranquil; the discipline of his armies was impaired, while that of the Russians was improving every day. Perhaps, however, he was ignorant of the disadvantages which must attend the prosecution of the war: certainly his pride was flattered by the insinuation that he held in his hands the balance of power in eastern and northern Europe. In 1769 hostilities commenced by the invasion of the Crimea, the khan of which was the vassal of the Porte. Azov and Taganrog were soon taken; Moldavia was entered; Servia was cleared of the Tatar allies. Before Kotzim, however, Prince Galitzin received a check, and was forced to repass the Dniester. A second attempt on that important fortress was equally unsuccessful. But the Turks, who pursued too far, were vanquished in some isolated engagement; and the campaign of 1769 ended by the acquisition of Kotzim.

The operations of the following year were much more decisive. Galitzin, disgusted by the arrogance of the favourite Orlov, resigned the command into abler hands than even his own — those of Count Romanzov. The reduction of Jassy and Brailov was preparatory to two great victories, which rendered the name of Romanzov forever memorable in the annals of his country. The first was on the banks of the Pruth. The Turks, in number eighty thousand, under the khan of the Crimea, were intrenched on a hill, in a position too strong to be assailed. But after three weeks, they became wearied of their inactivity; and believing, from a feint of the Russian general, that he was about to retire, twenty thousand of them rushed down the hill. They were repulsed with terrible loss; the remainder carried dismay into the camp; and the Russians, taking advantage of the circumstances, ascended, forced the intrenchments, killed many, compelled the rest to flee, and seized considerable booty, with thirty-eight pieces of cannon. Retreating towards the Danube, the Turks effected a junction with the grand vizir, whose army was thereby increased to 150,000.

Unaware of its extent, Romanzov pursued with ardour, and was suddenly in the presence of his formidable competitor. His position was a critical one. The vizir was intrenched; and the khan, resolved to efface the shame of his recent defeat, wheeled round his left flank, and encamped behind him. Hence he could not move backwards or forwards. On the following day the vizir gave the signal of battle; and the contest raged for some hours with desperate fury. Annoyed at the perpetual discharges of the enemy's artillery, which alarmingly thinned his ranks, the count ordered his men to fix their bayonets and rush on the intrenchments. Here the struggle was more deadly than before; but in the end numbers yielded to discipline and valour. The Turks fled, the vizir with them, leaving immense stores (among which were 143 pieces of cannon) in the power of the victors, and nearly one-third of their number on the field. Romanzov now crossed the Dniester; one of his generals, Repnin, reduced Ismailov; the other, Panin, took the most important fortress, Bender, after a siege of three months; while a detachment from the main army seized the capital of Bessarabia.

Nor were these the only successes of the year. Not satisfied with warfare on land, Catherine resolved to try her fortunes on the deep; and to do what none of her predecessors had ever dreamed — to send a powerful fleet into the Mediterranean, for the purpose of assailing her enemy in Greece. Many new ships were built; many English naval officers persuaded to command them, and to teach her seamen the arts by which the superiority of England had been so long maintained. The Greeks were impatient for the arrival of their co-religionists; the czarina's gold had gained over the chiefs, and a general insurrection of the people was meditated. Her designs were truly gigantic — no less than to drive the Mohammedans from Europe. The fleet sailed, arrived in the Archipelago, disembarked both on the islands and the continent; and while the Turkish possessions were assailed on the Danube, they were equally perilled in these southern latitudes.

A terrible warfare now commenced — the Greeks everywhere butchering the Mohammedans, the latter retaliating. A naval battle was inevitable; the hostile fleets met between Scio and Natolia: the engagement continued until night, to the manifest advantage of the Russians. That very night the Turkish admiral was so foolish as to run his ships into a narrow bay, in which he was instantly blockaded. Some fire-ships, sent by Vice-Admiral Elphinstone, a Scotchman in the service of the empress, set all of them on fire; and at sunrise the following morning not a flag was to be seen. This blow sensibly affected the Turks, especially as the appearance of the Russians in the Mediterranean had encouraged Tripoli, Egypt, and Syria to rebel against the Porte. Ali Bey, the governor of Egypt, an able, ambitious, and enterprising insurgent, was ready to assist his allies with all his might; but the incapacity yet egregious haughtiness of the Russian admiral, Alexis Orlov, prevented them from deriving much advantage from the union. The year, however, was one of brilliant success; and Catherine was so elated that she built a magnificent palace, which she called after the bay in which the last victory was gained.

In the spring of 1771, Orlov again resorted to the Mediterranean, where the Russian fleet still lay, with the intention of forcing the Dardanelles; while the armies on the Danube renewed their operations. The position of Turkey was, indeed, critical: not only was one-half of the empire in revolt, but the plague had alarmingly thinned the population. Fortunately, however, for this power, the same scourge found its way into the heart of Russia: its ravages were as fatal at Moscow as at Constantinople; and it no more spared the Christians on the Danube than it did the Mohammedans. This calamity slackened, but did not suspend operations. If the Russians were sometimes repulsed, the balance of success was decidedly in their favour. The famous lines of Perekop, from the Euxine to the sea of Azov, were forced by Prince Dolgoruki, though they were defended by fifty thousand Tatars; the whole of the Crimea, one fortress excepted, was subdued; and the surname of Krimski, or Conqueror of the Crimea, was given to the victor. The country, however, was not incorporated with the empire: on the contrary, while it was declared independent of the Porte, it was proclaimed as merely under the protection of Russia. The khan, Selim Girai, being thus expelled, proceeded to Constantinople, where he died. The exertions of the fleet, however, did not correspond with those of the land forces: all that Orlov effected was to destroy the Turkish commerce on the Levant.

During the year 1772 no hostilities were committed, and negotiations for peace were undertaken. Though the two contracting parties, which sent their representatives to Bucharest, could not agree on the conditions, both were anxious to recruit their strength, after the heavy losses they had sustained both by the sword and the plague. Catherine too had another motive for temporary inaction; she was busily effecting the first partition of Poland. With the return of the following spring, however, the banks of the Danube were again the theatre of war; but this campaign was not destined to be so glorious as the one of 1771. Its opening was unfavourable for the Russians: while a body of fourteen thousand, under Prince Repnin, were crossing that river, they were surprised by one of the Turkish generals; many perished; about six hundred, with the prince himself, were made prisoners and sent to Constantinople. Shortly afterwards, Romanzov who had passed that river and was marching on Silistria, was compelled to retrace his steps. At Roskana a considerable body of his troops was defeated by the vizir. This harassing warfare—for the Turks carefully avoided a general action—thinned the ranks and, what is worse, depressed the spirits of the invaders. Romanzov was no less averse to such a risk. Nor did the fleet in the Mediterranean effect anything to counterbalance their indecisive yet destructive operations. What little advantage there was belonged to the Turks.

The campaign of 1774 promised to be more important than the preceding; and the Porte, from the rebellion of Pugatchev, was confident of success. Several actions on the Danube, which, however bravely contested, led to no result, were yet considered as indicative of a severe if not a decisive struggle. But the anticipation was groundless. Though several bodies of Tatars, who were to effect a diversion in favour of Pugatchev, were defeated; though the Danube was crossed; though twenty-five thousand of the Turks were repulsed by Soltikov, and another body still stronger by Suvarov, though the vizir himself was blockaded in Shumla—Europe was disappointed in its expectations; for negotiations were opened for a peace which was soon concluded.

*The Treaty of Kutchuk-Kainardji (1774 A.D.)*

By the Treaty of Kutchuk-Kainardji (July, 1774) Russia obtained the free navigation of the Black Sea, the right of passage through the Danube, a large tract of land between the Bug and the Dnieper, with the strong fortresses of Azov, Taganrog, Kertch, and Kinburn. The rest of the Crimea was ceded — not, indeed, to the Turks, but to its own khan, who, though declared independent, must of necessity be the creature of the empress, in whose hands those fortresses remained. They were the keys to his dominions, and even to the command of the Black Sea. A sum of money sufficient to defray the expenses of the war was also stipulated; but it was never paid. The advantages which Russia derived from the other articles were ample enough: among them, not the least, was the commerce of the Levant and of the Black Sea.*e*

### THE MIGRATION OF THE KALMUCKS

It seemed as if Catherine's reign was destined to be marked by the most extraordinary events, and one of them was this simultaneous departure of [a horde variously estimated at from three hundred thousand] to six hundred thousand Tatars, an example at the end of the eighteenth century of one of those great migratory movements which history never expected again to record. Catherine was humiliated with having to furnish the example; it was in too striking contrast with that happiness which her philosophic friends said the human race enjoyed in her empire; and the peaceful migration of an indignant and angry people gave the formal lie to all the praises loud shouted by philanthropy. Our readers will not regret to find here were details of this unexpected event which suddenly made in the Russian Empire an empty spot, more than fifteen hundred versts in length, between Tzaritsin and Astrakhan. These Tatars, known under the name of Kalmucks, were originally included in three principal tribes. At first subject to China, they had been frequently at war either with it or with themselves. One of their khans, Amusanan, defeated and pursued by the Chinese, had taken refuge at Tobolsk in Siberia, where he died about 1757. These troubles, whose origin dated back more than sixty years, had in 1696 caused a great number of Kalmucks of the three tribes to reunite, quit a country devastated by constant war, and seek new homes at the eastern extremity of the Russian Empire.

They settled or located themselves in a vast stretch of territory close to the Caspian Sea, between the Ural and the Volga. The Chinese claimed that according to some ancient treaties Russia had to return all fugitive subjects, but received no reply except that there was nothing to prevent a wandering people from settling in waste places, a reply which seventy-five years later the Chinese made use of on their own part with advantage. Russia received these fugitive hordes and did not delay in getting service out of them. Another Tatar nation composed principally of Lesghians, who lived beyond Kisliar and were greedy for pillage, made frequent incursions into the empire and depopulated the border by the quantity of slaves they brought back with them. The new Kalmucks were charged with keeping them out and performed the duty if not with constant success, at least with a fidelity which did them great credit. The government felt that this permanent defence was more advantageous to it than a contribution necessarily small and hard to collect would be; and consequently, guided a long time by this wise principle, it contented itself with taking annually from the Kalmucks a certain number of men and horses for the light cavalry; but when once it deviated from a rule which it should never have broken, troubles began and the cupidity of its agents multiplied particular iniquities under pretext of collecting for the public funds. The Russian governors and even the minor officials were confirmed in the belief that everything was permitted them because they were sure that everything would be ignored.

Several of the Kalmuck chiefs were treated with indignity. It was established as a state maxim that they had no right to complain against injustice; all protest was regarded as a crime. Finally the khan Ubashi, alive to his people's misfortunes and wretched himself through the pride and rapacity of his oppressors who had taken his only son from him, dared to draw a picture of his sad position and wished to present it at St. Petersburg. But all means of getting there were closed to him. This attempt only aggravated his fate and vengeance was now added to oppression. Here is exhibited a truly interesting spectacle. This numerous people who, by joining the Lesghians, could, especially in the condition that Russia then was, give it the greatest alarm and mete out terrible retaliation, had no thought of using force. They had come to seek peace and had been deprived of it, so they withdrew. They withdrew without making use of arms, at least none but what they were forced to by the necessity of defending themselves and of procuring what they stood in need of for themselves and their large herds in occupying a front about one hundred leagues wide over a route nearly twelve hundred leagues in length.

A KALMUCK WOMAN

The preparations for this journey were made with a secrecy which concealed them from Russia's knowledge. A nomadic people travels with no other equipment than its herds, which furnish its drink and a portion of its nourishment. Obliged often to change locality in order to obtain grazing grounds, it might without arousing suspicion creep nearer and nearer the frontiers and even cross them without being stopped by detachments sent in pursuit. This is what happened. The preparations were furthered by the Ural Cossacks, who had experienced the same troubles with Russian officials and who were shortly to rise in open rebellion under Pugatchev. Furthermore the migration was carried out like all those of northeastern peoples — with this difference, however: the others came to Europe to invade realms and destroy and replace the inhabitants; while this one was returning to its ancestral home to reunite itself to the empire it had left at the end of the preceding century. In fact, while all known migrations have taken place

[1774 A.D.]

from the northeast and east to the west and south, this is the single exception which retrograded from west to east.

It divided itself into several columns in order to have sufficient stretch of territory to pasture the herds, and the first column left the Volga on the 16th of December, 1770. This prodigious assemblage of men, women, and children, formed of more than eighty thousand families and taking with it an immense number of cattle, was after a few days on the march vainly attacked by the Russians, continued its journey, was sometimes obliged to use force in making its way, and on the 9th of August appeared in the Elenth country on the borders of China near the river Obi. Its progress may be calculated at about five leagues per day, a rate that seems almost incredible when one thinks of all that composed the body. They also had with them as prisoners a hundred Russian soldiers as well as an officer named Dudun who had commanded them, who is believed to have been French. It was indeed a strange destiny for this officer to be brought to China as the slave of a Kalmuck!

### The Kalmucks Reach China

Ubashi, shortly after leaving the Volga, had informed the Chinese of the migration; and precautions were taken in advance that the arrival of such an enormous crowd should occasion no disorder. The emperor of China erected forts and redoubts in the most important places to watch the passing carefully and collect the necessary provisions. The Kalmucks, received like old subjects, found on arriving provision for clothing, food, and shelter. They were worn out by fatigue and in an extremely ragged condition. They had made their way north of the Caspian Sea, one division skirted the borders of Siberia to gain the fertile banks of the Irtish, the other kept farther south near the Usben country in order to reach that of the Elenths without crossing the Kobi desert, where no sustenance would have been found.

They lost on the way more than a third of their number by fatigue, by sickness, and in the battles they were frequently obliged to wage, especially against the wandering Tatars. They were but four hundred thousand on arriving. To each family was assigned a piece of ground suitable as much for pasturage as for agriculture, to which the government desired that they should devote themselves — an efficient means of fixing a people and attaching it to the soil which it cultivates. Ubashi appeared at court and was received with honour. Twenty thousand other Tatar families who had accompanied Amusanan in his flight or were dispersed along the Siberian frontiers followed the example of the Tatars of the Volga, and returned to their old homes. The Chinese government seemed truly paternal in greeting these children whose long misfortunes finally brought them back to their ancestral homes.

Catherine on learning of their departure became justly indignant against the Russian officials who by force of bad treatment had pushed the Kalmucks to this extremity; but the wrong was done, and it was impossible to right it. As soon as she knew what route they had taken she took measures to have the Peking government send them back. The emperor replied that these people were returning to their old homes, that he could not refuse them an asylum, and for the rest if she wished to know the reason of their flight she had only to ask those who had overwhelmed these people, their chiefs, and even their khan with outrages and injustices. Catherine, despairing of bringing them back, was obliged to make use of several bodies of light troops to protect the frontiers the Kalmucks had recently left.*f*

### INSURRECTIONS AND PRETENDERS

A riot in Moscow having clearly revealed the depths of barbarism in which were still plunged the lower classes of the capital — the domestic serfs, lackeys, and factory-workers; the insurrection headed by Pugatchev will show what elements of disorder were still fermenting in the most remote provinces of the empire. The peasants upon whom fell the whole burden of state charges, as well as the exactions of proprietors and functionaries, dreamed in their ignorance of all sorts of impossible changes, and were always ready to follow impostors; many were the false Peters and Ivans and Pauls who started up with worthless claims to trade on the credulity of these simple minds, deeply imbued as they were with the distrust of "women on the throne." The raskolniks, made savage and fanatical by previous persecutions, remained in their forests on the Volga, irreconcilable enemies of this second Roman empire that was stained with the blood of so many martyrs. The Cossacks of the Don and the Zaparogians of the Dnieper chafed under a yoke to which they were unused, and the pagan, Mussulman, or orthodox tribes of the Volga were but awaiting an opportunity to regain their former liberty and retake the lands occupied by the Russians.

A BOKHARIAN OF SIBERIA

How little these various ungovernable elements could accomodate themselves to the conditions of a modern state has been shown, when, in 1770, three hundred thousand of the Kalmuck-Turguts abandoned their encampments. Add to these malcontents a crowd of vagabonds of all sorts, ruined nobles, unfrocked monks, fugitive serfs, and pirates of the Volga, and it will be seen that Russia contained in its eastern portion all the materials necessary for an immense *jacquerie,* such as had before been unchained by the false Dmitri, or Stenka Radzin.

It was the Cossacks of the Jaïk, cruelly repressed after their insurrection in 1766, who were to provide the rebel serfs with a leader in the person of Emilian Pugatchev, a raskolnik who had escaped from prison to Siberia. Passing himself off as Peter III, who had been rescued from the hands of the executioner, he raised the banner of the Holsteins and declared his intention of marching on St. Petersburg to punish his wife and place his son on the throne. With a following of but three hundred men he laid siege to the little fortress of Jaïk. All the troops that were sent against him passed over to his side. He caused all the officers to be hanged, and put to death all the nobles in the towns through which he passed, capturing by means of such terrorisation several small fortresses on the steppes. By his intimates who knew the secret of his origin, he was treated in private as a simple Cossack, but the

[1775 A.D.]

populations were deceived and received him with the ringing of bells. Certain Polish confederates who were captives in these regions organised for him a body of artillery. For nearly a year he kept Kazan and Orenburg in a state of terror, defeating all the generals that were sent against him. Peasants began to rise against the nobles, Tatars and other tribes against the Russians, until the bitterest of social wars was unchained in the whole Volga basin. Moscow with its one hundred thousand serfs was thrown into agitation; among the lower classes there was talk of liberty and extermination of the masters. Catherine II charged Alexander Bibikov to check the progress of sedition.

Bibikov was aghast, on arriving at Kazan, to see the extent of the demoralisation. He set about reassuring the nobles and soothing the lower classes, but in letters to his wife he wrote: " Conditions are frightful, I fear all will go ill! " Without great confidence in his own troops he decided to attack the impostor, whom he recognised as merely an instrument in the hands of the Cossacks. He defeated Pugatchev twice, once at Tatistchev and once at Kargula, dispersing his army and seizing his cannon. Bibikov died in the full flush of victory, but his lieutenants, Michelson, Collongues, and Galitzin, continued to pursue the vanquished pretender. Hunted to the lower Volga, Pugatchev suddenly ascended the river and pillaged and burned Kazan, but was afterwards defeated on the Kazanka. Descending the river he entered Saransk, Samara, and Tsaritsin, and though hotly pursued by his enemies took time to establish there new municipalities. Meanwhile the populations on the route to Moscow were awaiting his coming, and to meet this expectation innumerable Peter III's and Pugatchevs arose, who at the head of furious bands went about assassinating proprietors and burning châteaux. It was high time that Pugatchev should be brought to justice. Tracked down between the Volga and the Jaik by Michelson and the indefatigable Suvarov, he was taken to Moscow, where the people were given the spectacle of his execution.

These troubles had been a warning to Catherine II, and she still bore them in mind when she destroyed the Zaparogian Republic in 1775. The valiant tribes of the Dnieper, expulsed under Peter the Great and recalled under Anna Ivanovna, no longer recognised their former territory of Ukraine. Southern Russia, freed from the incursions of the Tatars, was rapidly being colonised; cities were springing up on all sides and the vast herb-covered steppes were becoming transformed into cultivated fields. The Zaparogians were highly displeased at the transformation, and wished to have their lands restored to them in their former condition. They protected the *haïdamaks* who were constantly harassing the colonists, until Potemkin, the actual creator of "new" Russia, wearied of such uncomfortable neighbours, occupied on the empress' order the *sitcha* and destroyed it. The malcontents fled for refuge to the lands of the sultan; the rest were organised into the Cossacks of the Black Sea, and in 1792 the island of Phanagoria and the southern shore of the sea of Azov were assigned to them as residence. Such was the end of the great Cossack uprising which is heard of to-day only in the songs of the *kobzars.ᵈ*

### FAVOURITISM UNDER CATHERINE II

During the reign of Catherine favouritism attained a very wide development. In her *Mémoirsᵍ* we meet with the following characteristic passage which is not devoid of interest: " I was endowed by nature with great sensitiveness, and an exterior which if not beautiful was, nevertheless, attractive:

I pleased from the first moment and did not require to employ for this purpose artifice or embellishments. By nature my soul was of such a sociable character that always when anyone had spent a quarter of an hour with me, he felt perfectly at ease and could converse with me as if he had known me for a long time. By my natural indulgence I inspired confidence in those that had to do with me; because everyone was aware that nothing was pleasanter to me than to act benevolently and with the strictest honesty. I may venture to say (if I may be allowed thus to speak of myself) that I was like a knight of liberty and lawfulness; I had rather the soul of a man than that of a woman; but there was nothing repellent in this, for to the intellect and character of a man was united in me the charm of a most amiable woman. I trust I may be pardoned these words and expressions of my self-love: I use them counting them as true, and not desiring to screen myself by any false modesty.

"I have said that I pleased; consequently half of the temptation that arises is already included in that fact itself; the other half in such cases naturally follows from the very essence of human nature, because to be subjected to temptation and to yield to it are very near to each other. Although the very highest principles of morality may be impressed on the mind, yet they soon become involved, and feelings appear which lead one immeasurably further than one thinks. For my part even until now I do not know how they can be averted. People perhaps may say that there is one means — flight; but there are cases, positions, circumstances where flight is impossible; in fact where can one flee to, where seek a refuge, where turn aside amidst a court that makes a talk over the smallest action? And thus if you cannot flee, then in my opinion there is nothing more difficult than to shun that which is essentially pleasing to you. Believe me, all that may be said to you against this is hypocrisy and founded on a want of knowledge of the human heart. A man is not master over his own heart; he cannot at his will squeeze it in his fist and then set it free again."

Both contemporaries and posterity have not without foundation harshly judged favouritism under Catherine. One-sidedness and harshness of judgment in this respect have however deprived both contemporaries and immediate posterity of the possibility of dispassionately estimating the personality of the empress in general. Taking into consideration Catherine's unusual capacities, the circumstances in which she was placed, and her temperament, it is impossible not to acknowledge that in accusing her we must not lose sight of the age in general and of the morals at the court in particular. Favouritism was no new apparition under Catherine. Almost the same state of things had arisen during the reign of Elizabeth Petrovna. A particularly unpleasant impression, however, is made by frequent changes of favourites. One after another in turn there were "in favour": Gregory Orlov, Vasiltchikov, Potemkin, Zavadovski, Zoritch, Korsakov, Lanskoi, Ermolov, Mamonov and Zubov. Both Russians and foreigners have harshly censured Catherine for the rapidity of these changes, which were unexpected and sometimes without any visible cause. On the other hand, even writers who are unfavourable to Catherine have praised her for the fact that not one of the favourites banished from the court was ever persecuted or punished, while history presents a multitude of examples of cruelty and extreme arbitrariness on the part of crowned women in parallel cases.

It must be acknowledged, however, that favouritism, given the unbounded cupidity of Catherine's favourites and of their relations, friends, and acquaintances, cost the treasury and the nation very dear.[h]

[1775 A.D.]

Under the influence of new favourites and other confidants, the second half of Catherine's reign assumed an essentially different character as regards her actuating motives, although in the outward course of events a certain resemblance to the first half was preserved. When Catherine began to reign she had in mind a policy of peaceful splendour, advised also by Panin; she would willingly have secured the sovereignty of Poland by pacific means. It was only the force of circumstances which drew her into an undesired war.

Now her ambition assumed a different direction; we behold her recklessly bent on high-handed conquests, taking the initiative and deliberately making plans to bring about new wars. And, as this has often proved the case when government is vested in a woman, the change was caused by the most intimate personal circumstances. It would be out of place here to relate in detail the paltriness of all the court intrigues. It will suffice to recall the fact that Catherine, weary of the brutal tyranny of Gregory Orlov, tried to shake off his yoke and only succeeded with difficulty in wrenching herself free. She sent him at the time of the plague to Moscow, much against his will, and his numerous enemies hardly concealed their hope that he might never return. The empress endeavoured to keep him at a distance when he returned, but he struggled to remain master of the field and to stand his ground, although he saw himself supplanted in her personal favour by an insignificant young officer of the guards called Vasiltchikov.

### The Rise of Potemkin

When Catherine began after a time to feel ashamed of the insignificance of this young man, the much discussed General Gregory Alexandrovitch Potemkin, known to the empress in the days of her quarrels with her husband, knew how to take advantage of this favourable moment to force himself almost by violence into the long coveted position of her acknowledged and honoured favourite. The Orlovs tried for some time to wrest from him his sway over Catherine and over Russia, but they were obliged finally to give way, and retired to the ancient capital of the empire — which had remained the national capital, the capital of ancient Muscovy and the refuge of all who had reasons for avoiding the court.

There is much in this strife that is characteristic of time and place. When Gregory Orlov was forced to start on his dangerous journey to Moscow, many hoped, as already pointed out, that he would never return. When he reappeared safe and sound and in excellent health, and it was feared that he might regain his lost position in the favour of the empress, many a shrewd man was unable to conceal his vexation. The distinguished German doctor, Tode, to whom may be ascribed practically all the expedient measures taken in Moscow against the plague, remained not only unrewarded, but was unable for a long time to obtain compensation for the loss of his wardrobe. When he finally expressed his astonishment thereat, one of the senators is said to have solved the riddle with the dry remark: "Well, why did you bring the count back alive?" Then when Gregory Orlov got married in Moscow it was quite seriously proposed in the senate that the marriage should be dissolved as sinful, and that the fallen favourite and his wife should be shut up in penitential monasteries because they had married within the prohibited degrees. The empress, who had bestowed upon her former friend the title of prince as a consolation and a farewell, was angered by this decree and caused it to be revoked. However, in spite of the protection afforded him, Gregory Orlov came to a tragic end a few years later (1783). He died insane — as tradition will have it, a violent death, one of the mysterious occurrences that will never be cleared up.

But the empress Catherine, generally so acute, was singularly deceived concerning Potemkin, the Prince of Darkness, as he was afterwards called from a play on his name. He was the son of an insignificant nobleman of Smolensk, a retired major, and bore a name till then unknown in Russian history; a man of doubtful capabilities, ignorant, and in fact distinguished by nothing but a boundless and unscrupulous egotism, by an immense craving for coarse, extravagant pleasures, and by the nefarious energy with which he pursued his selfish desires. The first condition for his enjoyment of life was the power to exercise a boundless autocracy and to be able to tread under foot not only those who bowed before him but also those who attempted to resist him.

The empress, however, as a woman and conscious of her unauthorised position, feeling the need of energetic support, saw in the man, whose almost gigantic frame seemed to betoken a titanic nature, something really extraordinary, and believed him destined to accomplish great deeds. Thus Potemkin retained his ascendancy even after he had withdrawn from her most intimate favours under the pretence of long-continued ill-health, and had thrust forward all sorts of handsome insignificant young men who were one after the other loaded with riches. Potemkin understood how to increase the distrust which the empress felt for her son, and to keep it constantly awake. He made her believe that she was continually surrounded by dangers; that he was the only one who would protect her, and more especially that he was the only one who would wish to so under all circumstances. On the other hand he flattered her vanity still more than her ambition by plans on an adventurously large scale, by fantastic pictures of fame and greatness which he suggested to her imagination. Thus, he pointed to the conquest of Constantinople, the expulsion of the Turks from Europe, the foundation of a Greek empire on the Bosporus, not as triumphs which one might hope to see realised in the future but as deeds which might and should be accomplished within the next few years.

The general idea was not originated by Potemkin. Field-Marshal Munich had already pointed out to the empress that Constantinople was the necessary goal of Russian aspirations. But formerly an object so remote in time and place aroused but little interest. Now everything seemed to have advanced within grasp; the empress was to wear the crown of the new Greek empire during her lifetime; now the idea aroused in her the wildest enthusiasm. The very fact that no cautious statesman would consider these plans only made Potemkin appear all the greater in her eyes; his assurance raised him far above the everyday mediocrity of the others.

The eldest grandson of the empress received the name of Alexander, the second the no less significant name of Constantine. The former was in due time to inherit the Greek crown from his grandmother. They took care in a manner which bordered on exaggeration to make prophesies, or to announce to the whole world the vast schemes with which they deluded themselves. The young prince was not christened according to the Russo-Greek but the somewhat different oriental-Greek ritual, as it was practised in the churches of his future empire. They tried to procure a Greek nurse for him, but as that did not succeed they at least chose one called Helen. Greek playfellows were found for him, and he learned modern Greek as if it were his mother tongue.

The fascination which Potemkin exercised over Catherine may be attributed to her feeling of insecurity, to the support Potemkin promised her, and to the vast prospects he opened out for her ambition. There is one thing calculated to astonish us and that is that neither the empress nor Potemkin was able to realise how insufficient was the actual might of Russia at that time to carry out these gigantic schemes. It was scarcely surprising that Potemkin should be unable to judge of this, for he was an ignorant man, who was wanting in the most elementary political foresight and was besides no thinker. But how came it that Catherine should be so deceived, who had studied earnestly and had by that time accumulated a varied experience? How could it escape her that the comparatively limited financial resources of the empire, more especially, would prove quite inadequate, particularly as they were anything but well husbanded? They gave themselves up light-

heartedly to the magic of the bank-note press and thus brought down untold calamities upon Russia, as has been the case also in other countries. But this calamity did not stand alone; it is in fact not to be regarded as an independent manifestation, but rather as one of a whole series of necessary consequences of a premature effort of Russia to lay claim to a world-power of such magnitude and importance, before her might was fully established at home or had attained sufficient maturity.

The fact that the forces of the empire must from that time be almost entirely devoted to the support of a foreign policy; that little, if anything, could be done for the development of culture and industry (and that only as a matter of secondary importance), that no consideration could be given to the most necessary reforms — none of these circumstances worked Russia

GENERAL SUVAROV
(1729–1800)

such visible and tangible harm as the flooding of the country with unconsolidated paper money doomed in advance to depreciation; as matters stood, this was probably a greater evil. When Russia entered upon the grasping policy of Potemkin she began to lay out her future in advance, so to speak, and that on a scale utterly out of proportion to the actual gain which might be or which was in fact attained. The evils which resulted have continued to work themselves out down to the present day. As in this way the germs of a future power were constantly being sacrificed in order to conjure up power in the present by overdrawing the resources in hand, the real advancement of the empire was paralysed, and even the actual might in which they gloried remained partly a sham which certainly did not correspond with the reality. When later it became necessary for Russia to participate in the momentous struggles which involved the destiny of Europe, her power was not matured, concentrated, or husbanded at the decisive moment — as for instance the power of Prussia by Frederick William I; her future prospects were encumbered by a heavy burden and by manifold obligations, the inner development was behind the times, and her financial position was shaken. It became necessary continually to make fresh, feverish efforts, which always overreached the possibilities of the present and which hindered the inner development afresh, involved the future deeper and deeper, and exhausted its resources.*i*

## The Official Status of the Favourite

It may be deemed necessary in this place to explain what were the duties expected from and the distinguished honours paid to the favourites of Catherine. When her majesty had made choice of a new favourite, she created him her general aide-de-camp, in order that he might accompany her wherever she went, without incurring public censure. From that period the favourite occupied in the palace an apartment under that of his royal mistress, with which it communicated by a private staircase. The first day of his installation he received a present of 100,000 rubles, and every month he found 12,000 placed on his dressing-table. The marshal of the court was ordered to provide him a table of twenty-four covers, and to defray all his household expenses. The favourite was required to attend the empress wherever she went, and was not permitted to leave the palace without asking her consent. He was forbidden to converse familiarly with other women; and if he went to dine with any of his friends, the absence of the mistress of the house was always required.

Whenever the empress cast her eyes on one of her subjects, with the design of raising him to the post of favourite, he was invited to dinner by some one of her female confidants, on whom she called as if it were by chance. There she would draw the new candidate into discourse, and judge how far he was worthy of her destined favour. When the opinion she had formed was favourable, a significant look apprised the confidant, who, in her turn, made it known to the object of her royal mistress' pleasure. The next day he was examined as to the state of his health by the court physician, and as to some other particulars by Mademoiselle Protasov, one of the empress' ladies, after which he accompanied her majesty to the Hermitage, and took possession of the apartment that had been prepared for his reception. These formalities began upon the choice of Potemkin, and were thenceforth constantly observed.

When a favourite had lost the art of pleasing, there was also a particular manner of dismissing him. He received orders to travel, and from that moment all access to her majesty was denied him; but he was sure of finding at the place of his retirement such splendid rewards as were worthy of the munificent pride of Catherine. It was a very remarkable feature in her character that none of her favourites incurred her hatred or vengeance, though several of them offended her, and their quitting office did not always depend on herself.

## Potemkin's Schemes of Conquest

Potemkin's rule commenced at the very time in which the Peace of Kutchuk-Kainardji was concluded (July, 1774). The disputes with Poland and the rebellion of Pugatchev were no sooner ended than he immediately violated every condition of that treaty, well knowing that the empress would approve of everything he might do. Dowlet Gerai, who was elected khan by the now independent Tatars, still remained much more favourably disposed to the Turks than to the Russians: the latter, therefore, by means of money and intrigues, raised up a pretender against him; and then, under pretence of an armed mediation, a Russian army occupied a part of the Crimea, and seemed disposed to make the khan a prisoner, and to seize the whole province. Dowlet Gerai took refuge with the Turks in April, 1775, and Sahim Gerai, who was a mere creature of Russia, was elected in his stead, to the great satisfaction of the Russians, who foresaw that the majority of the Tatars would oppose the new khan, and thus furnish them with another pretext for a renewal of hostilities. A war with the Porte appeared unavoidable, and Romanzov received commands to collect a considerable army on the Dnieper, whilst Repnin in Constantinople was endeavouring to deceive the sultan, and Potemkin betrayed the unfortunate Sahim Gerai.

By this time Potemkin had ceased to be the personal favourite of the empress; but he himself recommended his successors in that post to her notice. Potemkin was indispensable to Catherine in consequence of those colossal undertakings which procured her the name of Great; and because the fear with which he inspired all her enemies secured to her the possession of the throne, which she withheld from her son Paul. Zavadovski had become the occupant of the apartments of the royal palace in November, 1776, and been created a major-general; as soon, however, as he fell under Potemkin's suspicion, the latter authoritatively insisted upon his dismissal. Zavadovski had turned against his patron, and was an eager favourer of the Orlovs and Field-Marshal Romanzov. For this reason Potemkin succeeded in obtaining leave of absence for the favourite in July, 1777, in order to provide during his temporary retirement a substitute who should eventually displace him. Potemkin had long before selected a Major Zoritch for his adjutant, who was politically insignificant, but very attractive in his hussar uniform, with a view to present him to the empress. Zavadovski had no sooner left the palace than he carried his design into effect, and the empress made Zoritch a colonel adjutant-general and her companion. At the expiration of nine months, he too fell under Potemkin's displeasure, and was obliged to retire, for the empress was completely under the control of her minister. Next came Korsakov, a handsome sergeant in the guards, who was suddenly raised to the rank of aide-de-camp general. He too was indignant at Potemkin's unbounded pride and avarice, but attempted in vain to open the eyes of the empress; he was obliged to yield to the influence of the indispensable tyrant after he had enjoyed the favour of the empress for fifteen months.

The circumstances of the year 1778 were peculiarly favourable to the accomplishment of Potemkin's plans of conquest, for war had broken out in the spring between France and England, and both powers were so fully occupied in the west that they had no leisure to attend to the concerns of the east. Potemkin, therefore, sent an army, commanded by Suvarov, against the Kuban and Bedjiak Tatars, whilst other Russians penetrated into the Crimea and were guilty of the most cruel devastations. This led to the seizure of some Russian ships in the straits of the Dardanelles on the part of the sultan, who was, however, unable to commence a war without the aid and co-operation of France. But that power, unwilling to break with Russia, insisted on mediating, and the sultan was forced to acquiesce. The result was that the Russian ships were restored, and the sultan formally recognised Sahim Gerai as the rightful ruler of the Crimea.

Catherine was so pleased with the conduct of France on this occasion that she embraced with alacrity the plan of the armed neutrality, which was devised by the French minister Vergennes; and in 1780 she put herself at the head of that league which was joined by almost all the powers of Europe except Great Britain. It was formed for the purpose of resisting the right asserted by the English navy to make prize of an enemy's goods, or of goods shipped for an enemy's port, wherever found, and even though covered by a neutral flag. The leading principle of the league was that free ships make free goods. Great Britain would not admit this; but at that time she did no more than expostulate with her good friend and ally the empress of Russia. It was not until the reign of Paul that she waged war for the maintenance of the opposite principle, which she later repudiated during the Crimean War.

From this time forward, as we have seen, Potemkin, Voltaire, and a host of flatterers amused the empress with dreams of the restoration of a Byzantine empire, and the erection of a new capital on the Black Sea. Sahim Gerai prized the slavish title of a lieutenant-colonel in the guards of a foreign empress more than that of prince of a nation to which the Russian czars for many years had been vassals, and he renounced the national costume of his people in order to glitter in a Russian uniform and wear the decorations of the order of St. Anne. Potemkin contrived every month to alienate him more and more from his people, till at last this miserable man was induced to lay down his khanate, from which he derived a revenue of three or four millions of rubles, in order, as he thought, to revel peacefully in the enjoyment of some hundred thousand rubles, which Potemkin was to pay him as the newly appointed Russian governor-general of Tauris, as the country was now to be called. Potemkin was too much accustomed to receive and not to give, and to contract debts without thinking of paying them, to give himself much concern about the payment of the promised salary, although the empress was led to believe that the yearly sum always charged to her was in reality regularly paid to the khan.

The shamelessness of the Russian government on this occasion fully equalled the audacity of their manifestoes respecting the partition of Poland, or that of the state-papers of a Genz and a Talleyrand. In the Russian manifestoes published in April, 1783, it was made as clear as the sun to the Tatars that the empress and Potemkin were really proposing to confer upon them the most signal benefits. It was stated that the Tatars, as Russian subjects, were in future to be delivered from all the evils of their internal disputes, and by the incorporation of the Crimea, the Kuban, and the eastern Nogaians an end was to be put to those oppressions from which they had hitherto suffered from the Turks and the Russians alternately. What the correspondence was between these promises and the subsequent reality may be learned from all the works of travellers who visited these districts, and gave accounts of the Crimea and the Tatars a generation or two later. That numerous, free, and rich race of people, clothed in silks and of noble appearance, had then dwindled into a crowd of starving beggars; their magnificent tented cities had become gipsy encampments, and their houses and palaces exhibited mere masses of ruin and decay.

These manifestoes, indeed, as is usually the case, were not intended for those to whom they were addressed, but merely to conceal in a cloud of words, from the eyes of those at a distance, the cruelties and bloodshed with which they were accompanied. The Tatars made an effort to defend their liberties, and their magnates made no secret of their dissatisfaction; Potemkin, therefore, had recourse to one of those heroic means which usually find defenders enough when they are applied for the support of the true faith and of autocratic government, and are only reviled and execrated in the hands of a Danton and a Robespierre. He proposed by a single massacre summarily to annihilate the malcontents, and to awe the rest into submission by the dread of a similar fate. Posorovski received express orders to make himself master of the malcontents, their families, and adherents, and put them all to the sword; he, however, possessed moral courage enough to decline the business of an executioner. Potemkin's cousin was not so scrupulous. According to the accounts, whose unanimous testimony we are obliged to follow, even when it appears to us incredible, Paul Potemkin caused above thirty thousand Tatars, of every age and sex, to be massacred in cold blood, and in this way procured for his cousin the easily won title of the Taurian, and the place of grand-admiral of the Black Sea and governor-general of the new province of Tauris.

The massacre in Tauris took place in April, 1783, and the Turks were unable to render any assistance to the Tatars without foreign support. Among the European powers, however, England was at that time fully occupied with the disturbances which in the following year brought Pitt to the helm of affairs; France was glad to see an end to the American war; Joseph II was bound by the Treaty of Tzarskoi Selo; Frederick II hoped to become master of Thorn and Dantzic, if Russia was well-disposed towards him; and Gustavus III of Sweden was the only monarch who could have rendered any aid. In the very same year, however, Gustavus suffered himself to be induced to go to Friedrichsham, where he sold himself to the empress; nothing, therefore, was now left to the Turks but to yield to their destiny. The sultan did what had been done by the king of Poland a few years before; by his consent he changed that into a righteous and legal possession which, being seized in the midst of peace, was previously a robbery. The whole territory of the Tatars, the Crimea, the island of Taman, and a great part of the Kuban were ceded to Russia, and a treaty of commerce was forced upon the Turks, by virtue of which the Russian consuls in the various ports of Turkey were erected into a power wholly independent of the government of the country. This treaty of commerce had been drawn up by Panin before he had been obliged to yield to the superior influence of Potemkin and withdraw from public affairs; and it was now concluded on the 10th of June, 1783. By virtue of this treaty the Turks were obliged to submit the decision of all mixed civil cases in which a Russian and a Turk were the respective parties, not to the local tribunals, nor to the higher authorities, nor to a court of arbitration, but to the Russian consul; and in all pecuniary transactions the claims of a Russian against a Turk were urged with much greater strictness than in those cases in which the Turk was the claimant and the Russian the debtor.

In the eyes of the world, which regards only externals, Potemkin was now a great and admired statesman; and so absolute was his sway over the empress herself, that she not only tolerated his insolence, his total neglect of all pecuniary obligations, his tyranny over all classes, and his imperial expenditure and magnificence, but allowed him to help himself to an unlimited extent out of the coffers of the state. Potemkin on the one hand did homage to the empress as if she were a goddess, and on the other he suffered himself to treat her with the most insolent familiarity and rudeness. He would even saunter from his own apartments into hers in his dressing-gown and slippers, with his stockings hanging down and his legs bare. He went so far as to extort from those who enjoyed the empress' favour a part of the money which they received from her, and yet he allowed poor Sahim Gerai to starve. He never paid him the assigned pension of 100,000 rubles which was yearly debited to the empress' account, and even the displeasure of Catherine could not induce him to bestow upon this Russian *protégé* the simplest means of life.

The founding of a new Russo-Grecian capital, with which Potemkin now busied himself, was a magnificent piece of flattery for the empress, but for which she was unhappily obliged to pay too dear. Catherine indulged with Voltaire in those visionary schemes of a utopian Greece, of a civilisation of which she and not the people was to be the source, of an enlightenment, industry, and trade to be carried into these conquered deserts by ukases and courtiers; Potemkin acted according to this fancy. He first erected a city with buildings of every description, and then sought for inhabitants, or forcibly drove them for a time from all quarters, when he wished to make a court-spectacle of this theatrical city and to enchant the empress. It was of no consequence to him that his city fell to pieces and its inhabitants disappeared as soon as he turned away his eyes. The new city was called Kherson, a name long since obscured by that of Odessa; the empress granted 18,000,000 rubles, most of which, however, Potemkin diverted to his own private use. The situation was badly chosen, and yet this shadow of a capital was for a length of time charmed into existence by innumerable arts of fraud and open violence; and the deserts of which it was to be the metropolis were erected into a province, to which Potemkin gave the name of Catherine's Glory (*Slava Ekatharina*). Another province, somewhat farther to the north, near the celebrated falls of the Kaidak, was also honoured with the name of the empress, and called Iekatarinoslav.

## GENERAL SUVAROV

The general to whom Potemkin at this time assigned the congenial task of havoc and destruction in the country of the Nogaian Tatars and in Kuban was Suvarov, a man who from that period till the end of the century had the misfortune to be continually employed as the instrument of a murderous military despotism. In Poland he executed three times those orders of annihilation which were issued from St. Petersburg. He destroyed the Turks and sacrificed the Russians by thousands at the will of Potemkin. He subsequently shared Paul's hatred against the French and every thought of civil freedom, and performed the same kind of heroic deeds for that madman's pleasure as he had previously done at the bidding of Potemkin. He was undoubtedly one of the greatest generals of modern times, but wholly destitute of humanity, for he sacrificed thousands without hesitation in order to secure a victory or storm a fortress, when either was calculated to produce a splendid effect though but for the moment. He not only flattered the empress, but even the common soldiers and their superstitions. Though he was a man of various knowledge, and had made himself master of all the arts of life as practised in the highest society, he assumed at court the character of a sort of court-fool, and acted often as if he were mad, merely in order to carry out some surprising piece of flattery. In the company of the common soldiers he affected the manners of the semi-barbarous Russian, lived as they did themselves, submitted to every privation which they might be called upon to endure, and knelt and prayed before every wayside image, often when the roads were deep with mud.

## THE FAVOURITES LANSKOI AND IËRMOLOV

At the time when a high-flown sentimentality was the fashion in Germany, and the empress was past fifty, she indulged in a fit of romantic love for the insipid and spiritless Lanskoi. This turn in her affections was very agreeable to Potemkin, for Lanskoi neither took up the cause of the destitute khan, nor yielded to the allurements of the king of Prussia, the emperor Joseph II, or the English, when they were desirous of engaging him in affairs of state. Potemkin freely permitted the empress to indulge her visionary love for the wonderfully handsome and youthful face which captivated her affections, and did not grudge her, among the many gross and degrading scenes of her life, the enjoyment of one romantic passion, after the manner of Werther and Siegwart, from the year 1780 till July, 1784. Catherine's love for Lanskoi had been romantic in his life, and her sorrow at his death was not less extravagant; but notwithstanding all this ideality, she had been also careful to show him substantial proofs of her affection at the cost of the country. She bestowed upon him not only all possible titles, orders, and decorations — diamonds, plate, and collections of every kind, but he left behind him in cash a property of 7,000,000 rubles.

The fantastic mourning for Lanskoi was no sooner evaporated than the empress allowed Potemkin, who presented candidates for every office, to supply her with a substitute for her departed lover. In order to exclude all other pretenders, Potemkin on every such occasion was prepared to fill the vacancy; and with this view he had for some time made Lieutenant Iermolov one of his adjutants. In 1785 this man became the declared favourite of the empress, and soon ventured to pursue a course which Lanskoi would never have thought of. He directed Catherine's attention to the tyranny of Potemkin, and gave her some hints respecting his behaviour towards Sahim Gerai. The empress expressed her displeasure without naming the person who had made her acquainted with the unhappy fate of the khan; Potemkin, however easily guessed that no man in the empire would dare to speak ill of him to the empress except Iermolov. He therefore threateningly replied, "That must have been said by the White Moor," as he was accustomed to call Iermolov on account of his fair countenance and flat nose.

Catherine did not hesitate severely to reproach Potemkin for his harsh and unjust conduct towards the khan, and she even wavered for some months between her favourite and this son of the Titans, whom she regarded as her protector and the creator of her glory and her greatness. At the end of June, 1786, a fresh scene occurred, by which the empress was compelled to declare either for the one or the other. Iermolov had made a new attempt to alienate the empress from Potemkin; the latter, therefore, haughtily insisted that either Iermolov or he must retire from her service; Catherine felt herself constrained to adhere to Potemkin, and Iermolov went upon his travels. During the course of the year he had been loaded with riches, and on his departure he was furnished with 100,000 rubles and imperial recommendations to the Russian ambassadors at all the European courts. On the day after his departure Momonov, another adjutant of Potemkin, occupied his place.

JOSEPH II VISITS CATHERINE; A SPECTACULAR TOUR

About this period Potemkin repeatedly travelled from St. Petersburg to Tauris and back with all the expedition of a courier, whilst he was engaged in the building of Kherson, in order to prepare a splendid triumph for the empress. The neglected Sahim Gerai hastened thither to meet him and make him acquainted with the urgency of his wants; but Potemkin, instead of rendering him any assistance, banished him to Kaluga, where he fell into a state of the deepest poverty. He then conceived that he might find some relief from his fellow believers, and fled to Turkey, but the sultan caused him to be arrested as a traitor and renegade at Khotin, to be conveyed to Rhodes, and there despatched by the bow-string (1787). The plan contemplated by Potemkin and the empress was to raise the grand duke Constantine, second grandson of the empress, to the dignity of emperor of Byzantium, at the expense of the Turks, and at the same time to incorporate the kingdom of Poland with Russia. The new city of Kherson was no sooner ready for this grand theatrical representation than the empress was to travel thither to receive the homage of her new subjects, and to deceive the world by an ostentatious display of magnificence and pomp.

Joseph II was invited to meet the empress in Kherson, in order to consult with her upon a partition of the Turkish Empire; but Constantine himself was in the first instance left at home. The luxury and extravagance exhibited by Potemkin during the empress' journey and the fêtes prepared for her reception and entertainment at Kherson were worthy of the heaven-storming characters of the pair. They remind us of the extravagance of the Abassides and the descendants of Timur, with this difference — that civilisation and the arts were strangers to the people of the caliphs and of the Great Mogul. Never perhaps was there seen in monarchical Europe, where such things are not rare, such a gross abuse of the wealth and well-being of the people, and such insult cast on public opinion by a contemptible comedy, as on the occasion of this imperial progress.

It began in January, 1787, and was continued night and day. To facilitate the journey by night, Potemkin had caused great piles of wood to be erected at every fifty perches, which were kindled at night-fall, and imparted to the whole district almost the brightness of day. On the sixth day the cortège reached Smolensk, and fourteen days afterwards Kiev, where the degraded Polish magnates, who made a trade of their nation, their honour, and their friendship, were assembled to offer their homage to the empress and join in the revelry of her court. Potemkin himself had gone forward in advance in order to arrange the side-scenes of the theatre which he erected from St. Petersburg to Kherson. Deserts were peopled for the occasion; and palaces were raised in the trackless wild. The nakedness of the plains was disguised by villages built for the purpose of a day, and enlivened by fire-works. Chains of mountains were illuminated. Fine roads were opened by the army. Howling wildernesses were transformed into blooming gardens; and immense flocks and herds were driven to the sides of the road in order to delight the eyes of the empress in her hasty transit. The rocks in the Dnieper were sprung, that the empress might descend the stream as conveniently as she had travelled thither in the chamber of her sledge. At the beginning of May the whole party embarked on the river in fifteen splendid galleys at Krementshuk, and on the following day Stanislaus of Poland presented himself at Kaniev, in order, as it were, by his insipid and pitful character to serve as a foil to the monarchial splendour of a woman. He accepted an alms of 100,000 rubles for the expenses of his journey, was very graciously received by Potemkin, treated with coldness and indifference by the empress, and as if his royal Polish income was simply a Russian pension he begged for an augmentation. He was not ashamed to acknowledge to all the courts whose ambassadors accompanied the empress that he regarded his kingdom as a Russian province, for he besought the empress to grant the succession to his nephew and to his nation the free navigation of the Dnieper. As is customary in such cases, there was no lack of promises; but none of his petitions were really granted, for it was impossible either to value or respect him, and in his situation he was incapable of inspiring fear.

[1787 A.D.]

The emperor Joseph, who had anticipated the arrival of his ally in Kherson, travelled to meet her as far as Kaidak, and returned with her. He soon perceived that she was shamefully deluded by the appearance of prosperity, civilisation, and population, and that soon as she had passed through all was again to become empty and deserted. Like the villages, flocks, and men by the wayside, the new buildings in which the distinguished travellers passed their nights and the houses and shops in Kherson all vanished again when they had served their temporary purpose. It will not be regarded as incredible that 7,000,000 rubles were expended on the journey, when it is known that the throne itself, which was erected for the empress in what was called the admiralty at Kherson, cost 14,000. Catherine made a magnificent entry into the new city, passing under a triumphal arch, on which was inscribed in the Greek tongue, "The way to Byzantium."

## OUTBREAK OF THE AUSTRO-RUSSIAN WAR WITH TURKEY

After the meeting at Kherson the two imperial allies prepared to direct their forces against the whole extent of the Turkish frontier, from the Adriatic to the Black Sea. Care was taken, however, to furnish an excuse for the participation of Austria, by inciting the Turks to make the first attack; for only in such a case was Austria bound to furnish auxiliaries to the Russians. To this end Bulgakov, Catherine's ambassador at Constantinople, was ordered by every means to excite commotions among the Greeks, Bulgarians, Wallachians, and Slavonians, as well as in Egypt and in Asia Minor. The Turks, justly incensed at these intrigues, insisted upon a distinct declaration of their views on the part of the Russians; and when they received for answer only the usual diplomatic subterfuge that the ambassador must wait for instructions from St. Petersburg, they immediately declared war, sent Bulgakov to the state prison of the Seven Towers, and nothing but the threatening interference of the English minister could have prevented them from inflicting summary vengeance upon him, to show their righteous displeasure at the conduct of his government. Catherine and Joseph had now gained their wishes. The Turks were the first to declare war, and a pretence was thus afforded to the Russians to call upon the Austrians for that aid which they were bound by treaty to render in case of an attack on the part of the Turks.

Catherine published a manifesto, in which after a long enumeration of the pretended wrongs ascribed to the Porte, she added that, provoked by a conduct, in itself so offensive, she had, very unwillingly, been obliged to have recourse to arms, as the only means left her for the support of those rights which she had acquired at the price of so much blood, and to avenge her wounded dignity, suffering from the violence that had been used towards her minister at Constantinople; that entirely innocent of all the calamities inevitably engendered by war, she relied with confidence, not only on the Almighty protection and the assistance of her allies, but on the prayers of the Christian world, for triumph in a cause so just as that which she was obliged to defend. This manifesto was soon followed up by a second, which declared that the Porte had arrogantly presumed to insist on a categorical answer to its absurd demands; and that the empress, forced to repel the aggression of the enemy of the Christian name, armed herself with confidence, under the protection of that just God who had so long and so powerfully shielded the Russian Empire.

Had Potemkin been as great a general as he was capable of devising magnificent plans and playing the Russian tyrant, great things would have been accomplished in 1787, for all the preparations for the war had been made long beforehand. Field-Marshal Romanzov was to share the command of the army with Potemkin; that is to say, he was to do all the work, and the other was to engross all the merit. Romanzov declined this thankless office, and Potemkin stood alone at the head of the army; but he did not succeed in deceiving posterity, for no one has ever ascribed to him what was effected by the officers under his command — by Repnin, Paul Potemkin, Suvarov, Kamenskoi, Galitzin, and Kutusov, all of whom became more or less renowned in later wars. Potemkin found in Suvarov precisely such an instrument as he needed; for to that general the will of the empress or her favourite was in all cases a law paramount to all moral obligations, or any feelings of humanity. He was sent to Kinburn, the chief object of the campaign being apparently the siege of Otchakov, by the main body under Potemkin, whilst other divisions were despatched to observe the movements of the Tatars in the Kuban.

Kinburn was a small fortress occupied by the Russians, and situated upon a promontory directly opposite to Otchakov, in and around which the Turkish army was stationed. The object of Suvarov's mission was to frustrate the efforts of the Turkish fleet to land a division on the promontory of Kinburn; and he executed the task in a masterly manner. At first he remained perfectly quiet in the fortress, after having erected a battery at the extremity of the promontory, in order to cannonade the Turkish ships from the land, at the same moment in which they might be attacked by the Russian fleet. He allowed the Turks to proceed without molestation till they had disembarked from six thousand to seven thousand men; he then sent a few regiments of Cossacks against them, and at the same time charged them at the head of two battalions of infantry with fixed bayonets, and exterminated them all. Immediately afterwards he employed his battery against the Turkish fleet. The prince of Nassau-Siegen, who had the command of the Russian gunboats of Niolaiev, attacked the Turkish ships at the very entrance of what is called the Liman, and within range of Suvarov's guns, to whose well-directed fire he was indebted for a great share of the advantages which he gained.

The whole remaining part of the year 1787, as well as the spring and a great part of the summer of 1788, elapsed without anything important having been undertaken; the whole of the Russian land-forces were, however, directed towards the Bug, in order to push forward with the greatest expedition to the Danube. The Turks had already suffered defeats at sea and in the Caucasus. The Russian fleet in the Black Sea, which was almost wholly commanded by foreigners, nearly annihilated the Turkish navy; generals Tallitzin and Tekeli massacred the Tatars of the Kuban, and Tamara reduced Georgia and Lesghistan. In August, Potemkin at length marched against Otchakov, but very wisely left the whole conduct of the military operations to Suvarov, the victor of Kinburn. The Russian operations were delayed in expectation of an Austrian army, which, in connection with a Russian force under Soltikov, was to make an incursion into Moldavia. This delay was protracted till King Gustavus began to exhibit symptoms of making an attack on the provinces contiguous to Sweden, which were now deprived of means of defence. He had to revenge on Russia a long series of wrongs, crowned by the intolerable conduct of Catherine's ambassador Razumovski, whom she had sent to form conspiracies against him, and to persecute and insult him in his own capital.

### THE SWEDISH WAR (1788–1790 A.D.)

Gustavus III would also willingly have induced Denmark to take part in the movement against Russia; in this, however, he was unsuccessful, although supported by England and Prussia.   Razumovski, the Russian ambassador, was ordered to leave Stockholm on the 23rd of June, and went to the army in Finland.   The king appeared as if he designed immediately to march against St. Petersburg, which excited no small concern in the minds of the government, because, in confident reliance on the king's misunderstanding with the Swedish nobles, the whole of their good troops had been despatched to the frontiers of Turkey.

The king of Sweden was acquainted with the feelings of his nobles, consequently with those of the generals and officers of his army; he therefore endeavoured to deprive the malcontents of the apparently legal point of a refusal to serve, by changing the offensive war which he contemplated into a defensive one, and for this purpose had recourse to a very childish subterfuge. There had been a long-existing dispute between the two countries respecting the bridge over the small river Kimmene, the boundary between the two states, whether it should be painted in Swedish or Russian colours; he provoked the Russians to maintain this disputed right by force of arms, and then proclaimed that he had been attacked by them, and was therefore justified in carrying on a defensive war without consulting the estates.   We leave it undecided whether he took possession of the bridge by force, and thereby compelled the Russians to resist force by force; or whether, as the best accounts allege, he caused some Swedes to be clothed in Russian uniforms in order to attack his own soldiers, and in this way to justify an offensive war.

The distance from the river Kimmene to St. Petersburg is less than 150 miles. There would have been no difficulty in storming the small fortresses of Viborg and Friedrichsham, which lay upon the route, and an unexpected attack from the sea might probably have led to the surprise and capture of Kronstadt and Kronslot, the former of which is less than twenty miles from the open waters, and the latter is situated on a sand-bank in the sea.[1]   The favourable moment, however, for an attack by sea had been already allowed to pass by the king's brother Charles, duke of Södermanland, who commanded the Swedish fleet, and by land the king was precipitate when he ought to have delayed, and hesitated when everything depended on rapidity.

On the 22nd of June Duke Charles, with fifteen ships of the line and five frigates, had fallen in with three sail of Russian ships, to the north of the island of Gothland, which he ought to have captured, but was restrained by a feeling of reluctance to begin the war (which was then actually commenced), and immediately a superior Russian fleet appeared.   Admiral Greig, an Englishman, commanded it; his fleet outnumbered the Swedish by two ships of the line and two frigates, and therefore the issue of the engagement between the two fleets which took place on the 17th of July was the less inglorious for the Swedes.   They fell in with the Russians off the island of Hogland, and fought with great skill and courage; they lost, it is true, one of their line-of-battle ships, but took one of the Russian fleet in its stead; at length, however, they were compelled to seek for safety in the harbour of Sveaborg, where they were kept in a state of blockade by the Russians during the whole of the campaign.

---

[1] The Swedes were not aware of the fortuitous advantage then offered them by a singular incident.   Just before the Russian admiral received orders to weigh, the empress had given the command of a ship to the famous Paul Jones.   As soon as the British officers in the Russian service heard of this appointment, they repaired in a body to the admiralty, and announced their determination to quit the squadron to which that pirate had been attached.   By this act on their part seven or eight ships were left without officers, until the empress, smothering her resentment, withdrew Paul Jones from the squadron, under pretence of sending him to the Black Sea; but, fearing a repetition of so unpleasant a scene, she contrived to get rid of the daring adventurer altogether.

The secretary of the king's embassy in St. Petersburg delivered such an extremely absurd ultimatum that no other answer was given than an order from the commandant to take his departure from the capital. Gustavus commanded armaments to be prepared and a commissariat to be provided, but left the whole superintendence to others, who neglected everything, and instead of preparing means to oppose entered into secret correspondence with the Russians. All this immediately appeared when the king at length resolved to storm the fortress of Friedrichsham. He found himself destitute of heavy artillery and other materials of war, which he supposed were all in readiness, and whilst the artillery was being slowly brought up by land, the nobles were devising the most shameful treason.

It was arranged that Friedrichsham should be at once attacked both by sea and by land; and Siegeroth had actually landed his troops and commenced operations when he suddenly received counter orders, because the troops which were with the king refused obedience. In these circumstances, Gustavus had no other alternative than to return to Stockholm, in order there to recover his royal dignity and power which he had lost at Friedrichsham. He entered Stockholm in September, and thenceforth occupied himself in preparing a *coup d' état*, which he accomplished on the 17th of February in the following year. Meanwhile, his traitorous nobles had concluded a truce with Russia, which was so far advantageous to Gustavus that it liberated his fleet from its captivity in the bay of Sveaborg. He was now dictator and autocrat; he had at command the means of prosecuting the war with Russia: but the favourable moment was past, and the Russians had already completed all their preparations by land and sea for the defence of their provinces bordering upon Sweden. Gustavus' project of burning the Russian fleet in the harbour of Copenhagen was discovered beforehand, and brought him nothing but disgrace. When he again joined the army in Finland, his Swedes gave evidence of their attachment and courage; but he himself again contrived to injure the success of the war by his interference in its conduct. In the murderous fights which ensued from the middle of June till the end of July, both the Russians and Swedes lost great numbers of men, without any other gain on either side than military renown. The Swedes in the meantime were unfortunate at sea, and could not have profited by their success had they been victorious by land.

Admiral Ehrenswerd commanded the Swedish flotilla of flat-bottomed boats, constructed for navigating the rocky shallows of the coast, whilst the similar Russian fleet was under the orders of the prince of Nassau-Siegen, who had shortly before been commander of the Russian fleet in the Black Sea, and had fallen into disputes with Potemkin, which led to his being sent to the Baltic. The Russian ships of the line were under the command of Admiral Tchitchakov, and had on board a considerable number of British naval officers of experience. This fleet had on the 26th of June fallen in with that of the Swedes, which was so injured in an engagement between Bornholm and Gothland as to be obliged to return to Karlskrona. The unfortunate issue of the battle was generally ascribed to disloyalty on the part of some of the naval officers.

The king still persisted in his determination of opening up a way for himself to St. Petersburg, and therefore of storming Friedrichsham. He himself directed the execution of the project, although he was, properly speaking, merely a volunteer with his army. By his interference he exposed the Swedish army to considerable loss, on the same day (August 24th) on which the Russian flotilla gained an important victory over the Swedes at Rogensalm.

Friedrichsham, according to the king's command, was to be stormed by the three generals, Siegroth, Kaulbart, and Platen; the assault, however, failed of success, and the Swedes were obliged to retire: their flotilla was twice beaten. The first victory of the Russians at Rogensalm was attributed to the prince of Nassau-Siegen, who, however, was accompanied by three or four persons who rendered him the same service which the British officers did to Admiral Tchitchakov. On the 1st of September the Swedish flotilla experienced a defeat at Högfors, and the land army, commanded by the king, was there also compelled to retreat. The loss in human life was indeed great, but the real injury small, for the Swedish army continued till the beginning of winter to occupy its quarters on the frontiers of Russia.

### The Campaign of 1790; the Treaty of Varela

During the winter, Gustavus withdrew from his army, but he resumed his duties as commander in March, 1790, and was now careful to supply all the deficiencies of the two previous years. On the 15th of April, in Finland, he reduced the two important posts of Kärnakoski and Pardakovski near Vilmanstrand; his Swedes were victorious at Valkiala; and on the 30th repulsed the Russians in their attempt to recover the two posts just mentioned. On the 4th and 5th of May the Swedes were afterwards beaten at Aberfors by the Russian general Numsen, and lost twelve pieces of cannon. The king having again taken Pardakovski, the key of Savolax, immediately caused a portion of his land forces to embark in the flotilla, of which he himself assumed the command, and ordered the remainder of the army to press forward by the shore towards St. Petersburg, relying on the assistance of the fleet, which was to receive them on board in case of a defeat. The fleet consisted of nineteen large ships, twenty-seven galleys, and a number of gunboats, which in all mounted about two thousand guns. It was absolutely necessary to the execution of this adventurous undertaking that Friedrichsham should in all haste be reduced by storm. The king, having been successful on the 15th in a naval engagement, made his third attempt at storming the fortress on the 17th and 18th of May, and notwithstanding a great loss in men failed in effecting his object. Although the way by land thus remained barred, he nevertheless persisted in his design of terrifying the empress in her capital.

Gustavus, having now embarked a greater number of Swedish troops than before, reached Viborg, and on the 2nd of June, 1790, disembarked a division of his army at Blörke, about forty miles from St. Petersburg. The whole success of this rash enterprise depended on his remaining master of the sea. In order to maintain this superiority, Duke Charles was to prevent the junction of the two Russian fleets, one of which was lying in Kronstadt and the other in Revel, and on the 3rd of June he was ordered to engage the division of the fleet in the former harbour. The Swedish fleet was no sooner thus withdrawn from its position than an opportunity was afforded to the Russians to form a junction between their two fleets, which actually took place on the day the duke entered the sound of Viborg (June 6th). The Swedish fleet was blockaded by the Russian squadrons, consisting, when united, of thirty ships of the line and eighteen frigates; the former, however, continued to keep up its connection with the flotilla. It appears that both the Swedish fleets would have been entirely lost had the two Russian admirals been qualified for such a command. Captain Pélissier, who had served in Holland, is said to have given Admiral Tchitchakov advice which he ought to have followed, had he not been too obstinately attached to his own opinions; Pélissier even pointed out to generals Suchtelen and Soltikov the places where they ought to have erected their batteries in order effectually to bar the egress of the Swedish fleet from the bay; no attention, however, was paid to his advice. The prince of Nassau-Siegen proved himself to be in no respect superior as a commander to Tchitchakov. On the other hand, if the advice of Duke Charles had been adopted, the Russians would have been victorious without a battle; King Gustavus and Stedingk, however, rescued the honour of the Swedish name.

The Swedes had now been closely shut up in the bay of Viborg for three weeks, and at the end of June were reduced to extremities; in the beginning of July a grand council of war was held. Duke Charles and many other members of the council recommended a capitulation, but the king and Stedingk were in favour of making a desperate effort to force their way through the enemy's line. The attempt was accordingly made on the 3rd of July, and through Tchitchakov's neglect it was so far successful, as it enabled the Swedish fleet to bring the blockading squadron to an engagement. But the Swedes lost in it not only seven ships of the line, three frigates, and more than thirty galleys and gunboats, but almost the whole of the royal guards, the queen's regiment, and that of Upland, amounting to six thousand or seven thousand men, which had been put on board the fleet. Whilst the larger Swedish ships thus endeavoured to gain the open sea, the flotilla had withdrawn for safety into an arm of the gulf, which runs parallel to the shore and stretches towards Friedrichsham. This inlet, called the sound of Suenske, is extremely difficult of access on the side towards Friedrichsham, in consequence of a group of rocky islands at its mouth, but it may be safely reached through the open harbour of Asph. By this way the prince of Nassau-Siegen determined to pass into the sound with the Russian flotilla, and attack the Swedes in their place of refuge.

The latter were well protected from the attack of the Russian fleet by rocks, and when the prince gave orders for the assault, on the 9th, the sailors were so exhausted and his orders for battle were so unskilful that the king of Sweden gained a splendid victory on that and the following day. The loss of the Russians was so great as to have surpassed any which they had suffered since the Seven Years' War. Fifty-five vessels were captured, a number of others destroyed, and fourteen thousand Russians either taken prisoners or slain. In spite of this signal victory, the king of Sweden now awoke from his dream of humbling the pride and glory of Russia; already he began to cast his eyes towards France, and in the following year he dreamed his monarchical dream in favour of the French émigrés. The idea of becoming the Godefroy de Bouillon of the aristocratic and monarchical crusade, which Burke at that time proclaimed in the English parliament and in his work on the French Revolution, had been awakened in his mind in 1790, and the empress of Russia found means of confirming him in his visionary projects. Moreover his means were exhausted, and he therefore lent a favourable ear to the proposal of Galvez, the Spanish ambassador, who began to mediate for a peace between Sweden and Russia.

This peace, concluded at Varela on the Kimmene on the 14th of August, 1790, served to show how empty all Gustavus' splendour was, and how unreal and inefficient were all the efforts he had made. It was now seen that all the blood had been shed to no purpose, and all the treasures of his very poor kingdom mischievously squandered, for everything remained on the footing on which it had been in the spring of 1788.

### PROGRESS OF THE AUSTRO-RUSSIAN WAR WITH TURKEY

We now return to the war in which Austria and Russia were jointly engaged against Turkey. The whole Austrian army was ready to take the field at the end of the year 1787: it formed an immense cordon stretching from the mountains on the coast of the Adriatic Sea to the Carpathians, and consisted of a main body and five divisions. Unhappily, the emperor Joseph was desirous of commanding the main army in person, under the unskilful direction of Lacy, his military Mentor, who, like his pupil Mack, was a good drill-sergeant, but no general. The main body consisted of 25,000 infantry and 22,000 horse, and the whole of the troops together amounted to 86,000 cavalry and 245,000 foot, accompanied by 898 pieces of artillery.

In February, 1788, Russia and Austria had simultaneously declared war against the Turks; but in August of that year England and Prussia entered into an alliance, the main object of which was to place Prussia in a situation to prevent the aggrandisement of Austria, if necessary, by force of arms. This, however, was superfluous in 1788, because the diversion effected by the king of Sweden prevented the Russians from proceeding with their usual rapidity, and the emperor Joseph by his presence with the army frustrated the effect of his immense armaments. The dissatisfaction with the whole conduct of the war became so general that Joseph was at length obliged earnestly to entreat Laudon, who had been the popular hero of the Austrians since the time of the Seven Years' War, and whom the emperor had hitherto neither employed nor consulted, to assume the command of the army in Croatia.

### Successes of Laudon (1788 A.D.)

Laudon, having made an express stipulation that the emperor was not to interfere with his plans marched against the Turks, defeated them under the walls of Dubitza the very day after he joined the army, and reduced that fortress; then, pushing into the heart of Bosnia, he compelled Novi to surrender, whilst the emperor himself was obliged to hasten to the aid of the army in the Bannat, which was very hard pressed by the Turks. The division under Wartensleben, which should have supported it, had been driven back by the Turks, who succeeded, in consequence of an incomprehensible neglect on the part of the Austrians, in getting complete possession of the rocky bed through which the Danube has forced a passage at a distance of six-and-twenty miles above New Orsova. The pass, which is not more than a pistol-shot in width, is commanded by a fortified cleft in the rock, called Veterani's Hole, and this post the Austrians should and could have maintained when the main body of the Turks appeared at Old Orsova on the 7th of August; this, however, they neglected to do. The Austrian general suffered himself to be defeated and lost thirteen pieces of cannon, and as his communications with the main army were cut off, he was obliged to retreat so far that the garrison of this important post was left to its fate. The Turks sacrificed great numbers of men in order to seize this fastness, by the possession of which they immediately became masters of the whole navigation of the Danube as far down as Belgrade. As soon as the Danube was lost, the imperial army found itself threatened in the rear.

Nothing but disaster attended the operations of Joseph and Wartensleben. The army under the prince of Coburg was somewhat less unfortunate. Khotin, which the Russians had captured in the last war without firing a shot, was reduced by it after a most heroic resistance of three months; and this was the last exploit of a campaign in which thirty thousand Austrians fell in desultory skirmishes, and forty thousand were swept off by pestilence — losses but poorly compensated by the capture of Szabatch, Khotin, Dubitza, and Novi. Circumstances, however, afterwards proved more favourable. Jassy was taken; in October, the Russians were in possession of five districts of Moldavia and of several passes in Wallachia, and the main army was again able to extend the limits of its operations. Wartensleben sat down with a part of the army before Mahadia; and the emperor kept possession of the country from Pantchova to Semlin.

### Victories of Suvarov (1788–1789 A.D.)

After the massacre perpetrated by Suvarov upon the Turks on the promontory of Kinburn, the Russians had remained for a long time quiet; but by their possession of the coasts they effectually prevented the Turks from landing any troops, and by the capture of the island of Beresam wholly excluded them from the mouth of the Dnieper. It was not till late in the year 1788 that Potemkin summoned Suvarov from Kinburn to conduct the siege of Otchakov, where, however, he was wounded, and after his return to Kinburn the siege made very little progress. The avarice of Potemkin deprived the soldiers of the necessary supplies; and the dreadful cold and disease proved far more injurious to them than the attacks of their enemies.

At length the frost became so intense that the men were obliged to excavate pits for dwellings, but the same frost also opened up a means of attacking the fortress and reducing it after the Russian fashion, that is, without regard to the sacrifice of thousands of men, a few weeks earlier than they could otherwise have done. The city is completely protected on the side towards the Black Sea by a marshy lake called Liman; and now that the lake was frozen, Potemkin issued orders to storm the fortress from the sea side, where it was weakest. The Russians were cruelly sacrificed: one regiment was no sooner mowed down than another was compelled to advance, and above four thousand men were slain before the storming of Otchakov was effected (December 16th), an exploit which was afterwards extolled to heaven. The Russians, having at length borne down all resistance and forced their way into the city, were compensated for their losses and sufferings during the siege by three days' murder and pillage; they put citizens and soldiers, men, women, and children to the sword without mercy or distinction. It is said that twenty thousand Turks perished in this massacre; but this piece of Russian heroism, which was not performed by Potemkin himself but by others at his command, was also rewarded after the Russian fashion. Every soldier who had taken part in the siege received a medal of honour, whilst Potemkin, who had contributed nothing to its success, derived the only real advantage. The empress had previously deprived Razumovski of the office of hetman, which she now conferred upon Potemkin, who received in addition a present of 100,000 rubles, besides what he had appropriated to himself out of the moneys destined for the besieging army, and what he had seized out of the rich booty which fell into his hands after the capture of the city.

The death of the sultan Abd-el-Habed in April, 1789, made no change in the relations between the Turks and Russians. His successor, Selim, continued to prosecute the war, and Suvarov having recovered from the effects of his wound again joined Potemkin's army, and was put at the head of the division which was to co-operate with the Austrians. Laudon had now the command of the whole Austrian army; the prince of Coburg, however, retained that of the division which was to keep open the communications with the Russians; and again he gave such numerous proofs of his incapacity to conduct any great undertakings, or even to help himself out of trifling difficulties, that the history of the campaign of 1789 alone ought to have prevented the emperor Leopold from entrusting him with the command against the French, who possessed generals and soldiers of a very different kind from those of the Turks. Selim III had succeeded in getting on foot a very considerable force which was destined to operate on the extreme point of Moldavia, where that country touches upon Transylvania, and is separated from Wallachia by a small river, which also divides the little town of Fokshani into two parts, one belonging to Moldavia, and the other to Wallachia. Coburg was advancing thither slowly and methodically, when the Turkish army encamped in the neighbourhood of the town turned suddenly upon him, and filled him with such apprehensions of being completely shut in that, instead of boldly doing what Suvarov afterwards did, he anxiously besought that general's speedy assistance.

Suvarov's army was lying at Belat in Moldavia; when the news reached him he at once began a march of between forty and fifty miles in a direct line over mountains, across ravines and pathless wilds, and in less than thirty-six hours reached the Austrians on the 30th of July, at five o'clock in the evening. At eleven that night he sent the plan of the attack upon the Turks, which was to commence at two in the morning, to the astonished prince, who had never heard of such rapidity of movement, or seen it equalled even on parade. The bewildered prince went three times to Suvarov's quarters without having seen him; in the battle he made no claim to the supreme command, which should have belonged to him as the eldest general, but submitted as a subordinate to Suvarov's orders. The Turks, to the number of between fifty and sixty thousand men, were in position at Fokshani when the Russians and Austrians with forty thousand men passed the river Purna and stormed their fortified camp, mounting the ramparts and driving them in at the point of the bayonet, as if they were assaulting ordinary field-works. The camp was taken in an hour, with the loss of about eight hundred men; the whole body of the Turkish infantry fell into disorder, their cavalry galloped off, were scattered in all directions, and pursued for some miles with the greatest impetuosity and vehement zeal. The whole of the baggage and artillery, all the stores collected in Fokshani, a hundred standards and seventy pieces of cannon, fell into the hands of the victors; the Austrians exhibited the same zeal, perseverance, and courage as the Russians, and had they possessed such a commander as Suvarov, they would have reaped immense fruits from the victory, but they became sensible, as early as August, that they were in want of a proper leader.

Suvarov returned to Moldavia; Coburg looked quietly on whilst the Turks were collecting a new army, and suffered the grand vizir to advance without obstruction in Wallachia. The Turks directed Hassan Pasha, who lay in Ismail, to make an expedition against Repnin, whilst the grand vizir was to march against Prince Coburg, who had taken up a position at Martinesti, on the river Rimnik. The news of this fresh attack no sooner reached the Austrian camp than Coburg, instead of attempting to help himself, again had recourse to Suvarov, who had already drawn nearer to Coburg from Belat. The grand vizir's army, which had been estimated at one hundred thousand men, pushed forward rapidly by Braila (Ibrahil), and compelled the advanced posts of the prince to retire into their camp. Suvarov received the prince's letter on the 16th of September, immediately gave orders to march, and two days afterwards succeeded in forming a junction with the Austrians, at the very moment in which they were to have been attacked by the Turks.

### Austrian and Russian Valour; Austria's Withdrawal (1789–1790 A.D.)

The Austrians then proved anew that they were not to be surpassed when not commanded as usual by princes and privileged persons, who become generals whilst they sleep. Coburg, as he had previously done at Fokshani, totally relinquished the command at Martinesti to Suvarov, who immediately availed himself of the oversight of the Turks in not fortifying their camp before they offered battle, and attacked them by storm in their unfinished trenches. The issue was as glorious as it had been on the 31st of July at Fokshani; the contest, however, was more obstinately maintained. On this occasion the Russians formed the left wing, whilst the centre and right were occupied by the Austrians, whose admirably served artillery scattered the Turkish cavalry, which had made an attempt to surround and cut off the small body of the Russians. The victory in this dangerous and hard-fought battle was gained not merely by the courage, activity, and bayonets of the Austrian and Russian infantry, but especially by the great military skill of the commander. His orders to avoid the village of Bochsa, and first to drive the Turks out of the woods by which they were covered before commencing the main attack, have been greatly admired, and above all his prudence in not sacrificing the infantry in a blind storm, which was the more remarkable in a general accustomed to bring everything to a rapid determination.

The victory was splendid, the booty immense, the Turkish army a second time utterly dispersed — a necessary consequence of the nature of its composition — and the number of killed and wounded much greater than at Fokshani. Prince Coburg, on account of this victory, in which he was entitled to little share, was created a field-marshal; Suvarov received the dignity of a count of the empire from the emperor Joseph, and the empress of Russia for once gave an honourable surname to a man who had really earned it by his personal services; she raised him to a level with her Tchesmian Orlov and her Taurian Potemkin, and called him Rimnikski, from the name of the river on the banks of which he had been victorious.

The victory of Rimnik and the capture of Belgrade by Laudon on the 9th of October were the harbingers of greater success. Hassan Pasha, the Turkish high-admiral and celebrated conqueror of Egypt, whose confidence in his good fortune had encouraged him to assume the command of an army, was totally defeated at Tobak, in Bessarabia, by Prince Potemkin, and his discomfiture was followed by the surrender of Bender, Akerman, Kilia Nova, and Isatza, and by the investment of Ismail. At the same time the prince of Coburg took Bucharest and Hohenlohe, forcing the passes which lead into Wallachia, made himself master of Rimnik and Krajova. Laudon also reduced Semendria and Kladova, and blockaded Orsova, which, being situated in an island of the Danube, was inaccessible to regular attacks. By these conquests the allies became masters of the whole line of fortresses which covered the Turkish frontier; the three grand armies, originally separated by a vast extent of country, were rapidly converging to the same point, and threatened, by their united force, to overbear all opposition, and in another campaign to complete the subversion of the Ottoman empire in Europe.

But in the midst of this successful career, the increasing ferment in the hereditary states of Austria, the rebellion in the Netherlands, and, still more,

AUSTRIANS ENTERING BELGRADE

(From the painting by Karl von Blaas in the Ruhmeshalle of the Arsenal in Vienna)

the interposition of the maritime powers and Prussia, checked the hopes of Joseph at the very moment when his projects of aggrandisement seemed hastening to their completion. Justly alarmed at the successes of the two imperial courts, the three combined powers incited Poland to throw off the yoke of Russia, delivered the king of Sweden from Danish invasion, and laid the foundation of a general alliance for reducing the overgrown power of Austria and Russia. The king of Prussia even encouraged the rising discontents in Hungary, fomented the troubles which the impolitic innovations of Joseph had excited in the Netherlands, and, in the beginning of 1790, opened a negotiation with the Porte for the conclusion of an offensive alliance, intended not only to effect the restoration of the dominions conquered during the existing war, but even of the Crimea, and the territories dismembered by the two imperial courts from Poland.

The only power to which Joseph might have turned as a counterpoise to this combination was France, from whose recent change of system he had flattered himself with hopes of a cordial support, and from which he had even received private largesses to a considerable amount. But now France was in the throes of her great revolution, and Joseph was left without a resource. Worn down by innumerable calamities and disease, he died in February, 1790; and his successor, Leopold, was fortunate enough to conclude a separate peace with the Porte.

### Russia Prosecutes the War; the Storm of Ismail (1790 A.D.)

Russia continued to prosecute the war against the Turks without the aid of Austria. Ismail still held out, and Potemkin, who had been besieging it for seven months, began to grow impatient. Living in his camp like one of those satraps whom he even surpassed in luxury, he was surrounded by a crowd of courtiers and ladies, who exerted every effort to amuse him. One of these ladies, pretending to read the decrees of fate in the arrangement of a pack of cards, predicted that he would take the town at the end of three weeks. Potemkin answered, with a smile, that he had a method of divination far more infallible. He instantly sent orders to Suvarov to come from Galatz and take Ismail in three days. Suvarov arrived and took such measures as would seem to indicate that he designed a renewal of the regular siege; he drew together the scattered divisions of the troops, formed them into a large besieging army of about forty thousand men, and ordered the small Russian fleet to come into the neighbourhood of the city; but his real design was to follow the course he had successfully pursued before Otchakov, take advantage of the frost, and reduce the fortress by storm.

Had not Ismail, according to ancient usage, been built without advanced works, even a general like Suvarov would scarcely have ventured on such an attack, which in the actual condition of the defences was attended by such murderous consequences. On the 21st of September the city was twice summoned, and on both occasions the garrison and inhabitants were threatened with the fate of Otchakov. The Turks, however, did not suffer themselves to be terrified into submission, and the fearful storm was commenced on the 22nd, at four o'clock in the morning. The wall was not mounted till eight o'clock, after an unexampled slaughter; but still the hottest part of the struggle took place in the city itself. Every street was converted into a fortress, every house became a redoubt, and it was twelve o'clock before the Russians, advancing through scenes of carnage and desperate resistance, reached the market-place, where the Tatars of the Crimea were collected.

The Tatars fought for two hours with all the energy of despair, and after they had been all cut to pieces the struggle was still carried on by the Turks in the streets.  Suvarov at length opened a passage for his cavalry through the gates into the devoted city; they charged through the streets, and continued to cut down and massacre the people till four o'clock in the afternoon.  At the conclusion of this dreadful butchery the Russians received the reward which had been promised them when they were led to the storm and to certain death, — the city was given up for three days to the mercy of the victorious troops.

Suvarov himself, in his official report of this murderous enterprise, states that in the course of four days 33,000 Turks were either slain or mortally wounded, and 10,000 taken prisoners.  He rates the loss of the Russians at 2000 killed and 2500 wounded: a number which seems to us as improbably small as the usual accounts, which assign 15,000 as the Russian loss, seem exaggerated.  There were two French émigrés present at this storm, one of whom afterwards became celebrated as a Russian governor-general and French minister, and the other as a Russian general in the war against his countrymen.  The first was the duke de Richelieu, or as he was then called de Fronsac, and the second the count de Langeron.  Kutusov also served in this affair under Suvarov and led the sixth line of attack.

### European Intervention; the Treaty of Jassy (1792 A.D.)

About this time the whole diplomacy and aristocracy of Europe were busily employed in endeavouring to rescue the Turks, in order to check the dangerously rapid progress of the French and Polish revolutionists.  There speedily grew up such a general desire as the English wished to promote — of two evils to choose the least —.to secure and uphold the empire of the Turks and to let the nationality of Poland perish.  Russia, however, declined the proffered mediation of England in the war with the Turks, as she had resolved for this time to give up her conquests in Turkey in order to indemnify herself in Poland: she accepted merely the intervention of the friendly Danes.

Potemkin and the empress were not unthankful for Suvarov's servility, since he threw himself and all his services at their feet, and ascribed everything to them alone.  Repnin, whom Potemkin left at the head of the army when he went to St. Petersburg in October, 1790, pursued a very different course, doing more in two months than Potemkin had done in three years.  He crossed the Danube with his army, pushed forward into Bulgaria, and caused the whole Turkish army to be attacked and beaten near Badadagh by Kutusov, after Gudovitch, the brother of him who had been the faithful aide-de-camp of Peter III, had completely put down the Tatars in the Kuban in January, 1791.  At the head of forty thousand Russians, Repnin then advanced against one hundred thousand Turks, under the command of the same vizir, Yussuf, who had fought with such success against the emperor Joseph in the Bannat.

Potemkin eager to appropriate the impending victory, started with great expeditiousness from St. Petersburg when both armies were ready for battle (July, 1791).  He took it for granted that Repnin would certainly await his arrival at the army; but he did no such thing.  He offered battle before the arrival of Potemkin, whose custom it was to enjoy the fruits in the gathering of which he had no share.  The victory which Repnin gained over the great Turkish army in July at Matchin led to a violent altercation between him and Potemkin, who came too late to have any participation in the honours

[1792 A.D.]

of the day; Repnin, however, still remained in command of the army. Potemkin afterwards did everything in his power to prevent the peace for which Repnin was to negotiate, although he clearly saw that the course of events required the Russians to give up this wholesale conquest of Turkish provinces. Happily, his death left Repnin's hands free, and a treaty was concluded at Jassy on the 9th of January, 1792, between Russia and the Porte, by which the former acquired nothing more than the fortress of Otchakov, the surrounding territory from the Dniester to the Bug, and the protectorate of Georgia.

## THE DEATH OF POTEMKIN (1792 A.D.); SÉGUR'S CHARACTERISATION

Not long after Potemkin's arrival at Jassy, where his headquarters or, to speak more properly, his capital and his court were established, he was seized with a malignant fever, and presumed to treat it with the same haughty contempt with which he had long been used to treat his fellow men: he laughed at his physicians, and ate salt meat and raw turnips. His disease growing worse, he desired to be conveyed to Otchakov, his beloved conquest, but had not travelled more than a few miles before the air of his carriage seemed to stifle him. His cloak was spread by the road-side; he was laid on it, and there expired in the arms of his favourite niece Branicka. Catherine fainted three times when she heard of his death: it was necessary to bleed her; she was thought to be dying. She expressed almost as much grief as at the death of Lanskoi; but it was not the lover she regretted: it was the friend whose genius assimilated with her own, whom she considered as the support of her throne and the executor of her vast projects. Catherine, holding her usurped sceptre, was a woman and timid: she was accustomed to behold in Potemkin a protector whose fortune and glory were intimately connected with her own. The character of this Russian vizir has been thus sketched by Count Ségur, who, as ambassador to St. Petersburg, lived long in habits of intimacy with him:

"Prince Gregory Alexandrovitch Potemkin was one of the most extraordinary men of his times; but in order to have played so conspicuous a part, he must have been born in Russia and have lived in the reign of Catherine II. In any other country, in any other time, with any sovereign, he would have been misplaced; and it was a singular stroke of chance that created this man for the period that tallied with him, and brought together and combined all the circumstances with which he could tally.

"In his person were collected the most opposite defects and advantages of every kind. He was avaricious and ostentatious, despotic and popular, inflexible and beneficent, haughty and obliging, politic and confiding, licentious and superstitious, bold and timid, ambitious and indiscreet. Lavish of his bounties to his relations, his mistresses, and his favourites, yet frequently paying neither his household nor his creditors. His consequence always depended on a woman, and he was always unfaithful to her. Nothing could equal the activity of his mind or the indolence of his body. No dangers could appal his courage; no difficulties force him to abandon his projects. But the success of an enterprise always brought with it disgust. He wearied the empire by the number of his posts and the extent of his power. He was himself fatigued with the burden of his existence; envious of all that he did not do, and sick of all that he did. Rest was not grateful to him, nor occupation pleasing. Everything with him was desultory — business, pleasure, temper, carriage. In every company he had an embarrassed air, and his presence was a restraint on every company. He was morose to all that stood in awe of him, and caressed all such as accosted him with familiarity.

"Ever promising, seldom keeping his word, and never forgetting anything, none had read less than he — few people were better informed. He had talked with the skilful in all professions, in all the sciences, in every art. None better knew how to draw forth and appropriate to himself the knowledge of others. In conversation he would have astonished a scholar, an artist, an artisan, or a divine. His information was not deep, but it was very extensive. He never dived into a subject, but he spoke well on all subjects.

"The inequality of his temper was productive of an inconceivable oddity in his desires, his conduct, and his manner of life. One while he formed the project of becoming duke of Courland; at another he thought of bestowing on himself the crown of Poland. He frequently gave intimations of an intention to make himself a bishop or even a simple monk. He built a superb palace, and wanted to sell it before it was finished. One day he would dream of nothing but war; and only officers, Tatars, and Cossacks were admitted to him: the next day he was busied only with politics; he would partition the Ottoman Empire, and put in agitation all the cabinets of Europe. At other times, with nothing in his head but the court, dressed in a magnificent suit, covered with ribbons presented to him by every potentate, displaying diamonds of extraordinary magnitude and brilliance, he was giving superb entertainments without any cause.

"He was sometimes known for a month, and in the face of all the town, to pass whole evenings at the apartments of a young woman, seeming to have alike forgotten all business and all decorum. Sometimes also, for several weeks successively, shut up in his room with his nieces and several men whom he honoured with his intimacy, he would lounge on a sofa, without speaking, playing at chess, or at cards, with his legs bare, his shirt collar unbuttoned, in a morning gown, with a thoughtful front, his eyebrows knit, and presenting to the view of strangers, who came to see him, the figure of a rough and squalid Cossack. These singularities often put the empress out of humour, but rendered him more interesting to her. In his youth he had pleased her by the ardour of his passion, his valour, and his masculine beauty. Being arrived at maturity, he charmed her still by flattering her pride, calming her apprehensions, confirming her power, and caressing her fancies of oriental empire, the expulsion of the barbarians, and the restoration of the Grecian republics.

"Potemkin began everything, completed nothing, disordered the finances, disorganised the army, depopulated his country, and enriched it with other deserts. The fame of the empress was increased by his conquests. The admiration they excited was for her; and the hatred they raised, for her minister. Posterity, more equitable, will perhaps divide between them both the glory of the successes and the severity of the reproaches. It will not bestow on Potemkin the title of a great man; but it will mention him as an extraordinary person; and, to draw his picture with accuracy, he might be represented as the real emblem, as the living image of the Russian Empire. For, in fact, he was colossal like Russia. In his mind, as in that country, were cultivated districts and desert plains. It also partook of the Asiatic, the European, the Tatar, and the Cossack; the rudeness of the eleventh century, and the corruption of the eighteenth; the surface of the arts, and the ignorance of the cloisters; an outside of civilisation, and many traces of barbarism."*i*

## THE QUESTION OF THE IMPERIAL SUCCESSION

Some time before the death of Potemkin, Catherine had begun proceedings intended to bar the czarevitch Paul from the imperial succession.*a* She was by no means the cruel, heartless mother that many writers are inclined to represent; but she knew her son thoroughly well, and foreseeing how destructive of all good his reign would be she could not think without fear of how the empire, which under her rule had made such rapid strides in the path of prosperity, glory, and civilisation, would after her remain without any guarantee for the stability and durability of its existence. With the intention of preserving the country from such a misfortune, Catherine wished to make over the throne to the grand duke Alexander Pavlovitch and therefore the setting aside of the czarevitch appeared in her eyes a state necessity. Meanwhile it is sufficiently well known that Catherine had long been accustomed to place the interests of the state above everything and to sacrifice to them all other considerations and feelings; therefore the difficulties with which so daring an administrative step was doubtless accompanied could not stop the creator of the changes of the year 1762. "Obstacles are created in this world," Catherine once wrote, "in order that persons of merit may set them aside and thus add to their reputation; that is the meaning of obstacles." Circumstances were also favourable to this new change contemplated by Catherine, for at that time no law existed that exactly established the order of succession to the throne. The statute of Peter the Great of the year 1722 was still maintained in full power, and by this statute the reigning Russian sovereigns had the right of naming anyone they liked as their successors to the throne according to their own judgment, without being restrained by any ancient right of primogeniture; and in cases where the heir already designated showed himself incapable, he could be removed from the throne.

The diary of Krapovitski can serve as a proof that in the year 1787, after Catherine's return from her travels in the south of Russia, the question as to the necessity of changing the succession to the throne had already matured in the mind of the empress; she entered upon the historical study of the matter and read "the right of will of monarchs." On the 20th of August, in connection with this same question, Catherine discussed with her secretary the extent to which the misfortunes of the czarevitch Paul Petrovitch had been caused by the false opinion that as eldest son the throne must belong to him. Further, on the 25th of August, Krapovitski writes: "Ukases as to the heirs to the throne, named since the time of Catherine I, have been asked for, and in the explanations a sort of displeasure was manifested." To what conclusions the historical study of the measures taken by Peter the Great led Catherine may be seen from the context of the following remarks, written by the empress' own hand:

"It must be acknowledged that the parent is unhappy who sees himself obliged for the safeguard of the public good to remove his offspring. This is a condition which accompanies or is joined to the autocratic and parental power. And thus I esteem that the most wise monarch Peter I had doubtlessly the strongest reasons for the removal of his ungrateful, disobedient, and incapable son, who was filled with hatred, malice, and viperous envy against him. He sought to find some particle of evil in his father's deeds and actions which were conceived in the spirit of good, he listened to flatterers, shut his ears to the truth, and nothing was so pleasing to him as to hear his most glorious father defamed and spoken evil of. He himself was a sluggard, a coward, double-faced, unstable, gloomy, timid, drunken, passionate, obstinate, bigoted, ignorant man, of most mediocre intelligence and of weak health."

Independent of these remarks, Catherine's ideas are even more clearly expressed in other rough draughts concerning the Greek project and written in her own hand. She writes as follows: "Should the successes of the war give Russia the means and occasion to drive out completely the enemies of the name of Christ from the European frontiers, then Russia, in return for such an entirely Christian service rendered to the human race, would reserve to herself the restoration on the ruins of the barbaric power, of the ancient Greek Empire. Russia would promise to leave such an empire incomplete independence, to entrust and give it up to the young Russian grand duke Constantine Pavlovitch, who must then give his promise not to make in any case any hereditary or other pretensions to the succession of all the Russias, as equally his brother must do in regard to the Greek succession." All these writings clearly testify that at the time of the second Turkish war the empress Catherine had definitively come to the conclusion that the welfare of the state required the setting aside from the succession of the czarevitch Paul Petrovitch and his replacement by the grand duke Alexander Pavlovitch.

Meanwhile the czarevitch on his part did all that was possible to justify in the eyes of Russia Catherine's intentions to exclude him from the throne. A contemporary who was in close relations with him, T. V. Rostopschin writes as follows: "It is impossible to see without shuddering and pity what the grand duke's father does; it is as if he sought for every means of inspiring hatred and disgust. He has taken it into his head that disrespect and neglect are shown to him; therefore for this reason, he catches and cavils at everything and punishes without distinction. Every day one only hears of violence, of quarrels about trifles of which any private individual would be ashamed. He sees a revolution everywhere; he sees Jacobite in everything."

Catherine's correspondence shows that already in the year 1791 the plan of excluding the czarevitch Paul from the throne was no secret to those who were in her intimacy. On the 1st of September, 1791, the empress in a letter to Grimm expresses herself quite definitely on the matter; in relating her supposition as to the consequences of the French Revolution, she writes: "But this will not be in my time and, I hope, not in the time of Alexander." Finally on the 14th of August, 1792, Catherine communicates to Grimm considerations which allow the nomination of Alexander as heir to be regarded as a matter settled. "Why should the coronation be hurried on?" writes she; "in the words of Solomon there is a time for everything. First we will marry Alexander, and then we will crown him with all possible ceremonies, solemnities, and popular festivities. Oh, how happy he will be himself, and how happy others will be with him!" The following letter addressed by Catherine to Count V. P. Mussin-Pushkin on the 14th of September, 1792, written by the empress' own hand, is characteristic of the relations which subsisted at that time between the czarevitch Paul Petrovitch and his mother:

COUNT VALENTINE PLATONOVITCH:

I herewith enclose a copy of Kushilev's letter to the governor of this town in which he says that the czarevitch has been pleased to order that more than half of the Alexandrovski square, as the plan sent by him to the governor indicates, should be given up to a certain merchant. The order itself is a mad one and of the greatest insolence. Tell Kushilev to come to you and tell him in my name that if he again dares to send such letters anywhere I will send him where the ravens will not have to seek for his bones; and tell the grand duke that in future he is not to send any orders by you at anyone's request.

September 17th, 1793.                                      CATHERINE.

Find out beforehand if this was certainly written by the grand duke.

In the year 1794 the empress had recourse to decisive measures for the accomplishment of the projected change and notified to the council her intention of setting aside her son Paul as her successor giving as reasons his character and his incapacity. The entire council was ready to submit to this decision, but was stopped by Count V. P. Mussin-Pushkin, who said that the character and instincts of the heir might change when he became emperor; these remarks put a stop to Catherine's intention of declaring her grandson Alexander as her successor, and for a time the matter rested there. But the opposition that Catherine met with in the council naturally did not stop her in the pursuit of the aim she had in view. As has already been observed, obstacles, in her opinion, are only created in order that they may be set aside by persons of merit; guided by such principles, the empress remained true to herself and to the matter that was so close to her heart and continued to seek for fresh ways of carrying through her intentions.[k] Nevertheless all her efforts failed in the end, and, as we shall see, Catherine's son succeeded her in due course.[a]

## THE LAST OF THE FAVOURITES

Plato Zubov, the twelfth and last of Catherine's avowed favourites, succeeded in some degree to the position which Potemkin had held as a sort of vice-emperor. Zubov had superseded Momonov, who, soon wearying of the faded charms of a mistress of sixty, became enamoured of the young princess Sherbatov, and had the courage to avow it and ask permission to marry her. Catherine had pride and generosity enough to grant his request without any reproaches. She saw him married at court to the object of his affection, and sent him to Moscow loaded with presents. But it was currently reported that Momonov was so imprudent as to mention to his wife some particulars of his interviews with the empress, and that she divulged them with a levity which Catherine could not forgive. One night, when the husband and wife were gone to rest, the master of the police at Moscow entered their chamber; and, after showing them an order from her majesty, left them in the hands of six women, and retired to an adjoining room. Then the six women, or rather the six men dressed as women, seized the babbling lady, and having completely stripped her, flogged her with rods in the presence of Momonov, whom they forced to kneel down during the ceremony. When the chastisement was over, the police-master re-entered the room and said: "This is the way the empress punishes a first indiscretion. For the second, people are sent to Siberia."

It was in the spring of 1789, when the empress was at Tsarsko Selo, that Momonov was married and dismissed. Lieutenant Zubov commanded the detachment of horse-guards in attendance, and being the only young officer in sight he owed his preferment to that fortunate circumstance. Nicholas Soltikov, to whom he was distantly related, and who was at that time in high credit, took pains to promote his interest, hoping to find in him a protector against Potemkin, whom he heartily disliked. After some secret conferences in presence of the Mentor, Zubov was approved, and sent for more ample information to Mademoiselle Protasov and the empress' physician. The account they gave must have been favourable, for he was named aide-de-camp to the empress, received a present of a hundred thousand roubles (£10,000) to furnish him with linen, and was installed in the apartment of the favourites with all the customary advantages.

The next day this young man was seen familiarly offering his arm to his sovereign, equipped in his new uniform, with a large hat and feather on his head, attended by his patron and the great men of the empire, who walked behind him with their hats off, though the day before he had danced attendance in their ante-chambers. His own were now filled with aged generals and ministers of long service, all of whom bent the knee before him. He was a genius discerned by the piercing eye of Catherine; the treasures of the empire were lavished on him, and the conduct of the empress was sanctioned by the meanness and the shameful assiduities of her courtiers.

### Debaucheries at Catherine's Court

The new favourite was not quite five-and-twenty years old, the empress was upwards of sixty. Yet even at this advanced period of her life she revived the orgies and lupercalia which she had formerly celebrated with the brothers Orlov. Valerian, a younger brother of Zubov, and Peter Soltikov, their friend, were associated in office with the favourite. With these three young libertines did the aged Catherine spend her days, while her armies were slaughtering the Turks, fighting the Swedes, and ravaging Poland; while her people were groaning in wretchedness and famine, and devoured by extortioners and tyrants.

It was at this time she formed a more intimate society, composed of her favourites and most trusty ladies and courtiers. This society met two or three times a week, under the name of the Little Hermitage. The parties were frequently masqued, and the greatest privacy prevailed. They danced, played at forfeits, joked, romped and engaged in all sorts of frolics and gambols. Leov Narishkin acted the same part there as Roquelaure at the court of Louis XIV; and a fool by title, Matrona Danilovna, seconded him. This was an old gossip, whose wit consisted only in uttering the most absurd vulgarities; and as she was allowed the common right of fools, that of saying anything, she was loaded with presents by the lower order of courtiers. Such foreign ministers as enjoyed the favour of the empress were sometimes admitted to the Little Hermitage. Ségur, Cobenzl, Stedingk, and Nassau chiefly enjoyed this distinction; but Catherine afterwards formed another assembly, more confined and more mysterious, which was called the Little Society. The three favourites of whom we have just been speaking, Branicka, Protasov, and some confidential women and valets-de-chambre, were its only members. In this the Cybele of the north celebrated her most secret mysteries. The particulars of these amusements are not fit to be repeated.

Catherine survived Potemkin but four years. The last ten years of her reign carried her power, her glory, and her political crimes to their highest pitch. When the great Frederick, dictator of the kings of Europe, died, she remained the eldest of the crowned heads of the continent; and if we except Joseph, all those heads together were unequal to her own. If Frederick was the dictator of these kings, Catherine became their tyrant. The immense empire which she had subjected to her sway; the inexhaustible resources she derived from a country and a people as yet in a state of infancy; the extreme luxury of her court, the barbarous pomp of her nobility, the wealth and princely grandeur of her favourites, the glorious exploits of her armies, and the gigantic views of her ambition threw Europe into a sort of fascination; and those monarchs who had been too proud to pay each other even the slightest deference felt no abasement in making a woman the arbiter of their interests, the ruling power of all their measures.

### THE SUBJUGATION AND FINAL PARTITION OF POLAND (1796 A.D.)

The annihilation of Poland, long meditated, was now resolved on. The empress could never forgive that nation either for the act of the diet in 1788, which abrogated the constitution dictated by violence in 1775, or the alliance of Prussia accepted in contempt of her own, or, above all, the constitution decreed at Warsaw on the 3rd of May, 1791. Big with these ideas of revenge, she gave orders to Bulgakov, her minister at Warsaw, to declare war against Poland.

The diet being assembled received this declaration with a majestic calmness, which was rapidly succeeded by the generous enthusiasm of a nation roused to self-defence. The king himself pretended to share the feelings that animated his people; and the Poles had the weakness to believe that, having abandoned his former servility to Russia and his customary indolence, he was becoming the defender of their freedom. An army was collected in haste, and the command of it given to the king's nephew, Joseph Poniatowski, an inexperienced young man, all of whose efforts were obstructed or misdirected by his traitorous uncle.

The Poles could have opposed the designs of Catherine with an army of fifty thousand men; but they never yet could be brought to unite their forces; and their different corps were soon after pressed between an army of eighty thousand Russians, who fell back from Bessarabia upon the territory which extends along the Bug, another of ten thousand collected in the environs of Kiev, and a third of thirty thousand, which had penetrated into Lithuania.

We shall not here attempt to draw the picture of the various battles that drenched the plains of Poland with blood, and which, notwithstanding some advantages obtained by the Poles, consumed the greater part of their troops. It was then that the illustrious Kosciuszko, who as yet was nothing more than one of the lieutenants of young Joseph Poniatowski, displayed qualities that justly obtained him the confidence of the nation, the hatred of the Russians, and the esteem of Europe.

During all this time Catherine, not trusting alone to the power of her own arms, had been negotiating with unremitted assiduity. She proposed the definitive partition of Poland to Frederick William, who was undoubtedly no less desirous of it than herself. She secretly won over to her views the two brothers Kassakovski, the hetman Branicki, Rejevuski, and particularly Felix Potocki, who, while flattering himself perhaps with the hopes of mounting the throne of Poland, became only the slave of Russia. She even insisted that Stanislaus Augustus should make a public declaration that it was necessary to yield to the superiority of the Russian arms. He submitted to this indignity; but was not on that account treated by the empress with greater indulgence.

In 1793 the confederation of the partisans of Russia assembled at Grodno, where the Russian general proudly seated himself under the canopy of the throne he was about to overturn. The Russian minister Sievers, at the same time, published a manifesto (April 9th) in which he declared that his sovereign would incorporate with her dominions all the territory of Poland which her arms had conquered. The king of Prussia, in concert with Catherine, had already marched an army into Poland.

The Russians, dispersed about the provinces of that kingdom, committed depredations and ravages of which history furnishes but few examples. Warsaw became likewise the theatre of their excesses. The Russian general Igelström, who governed that city, connived at the disorders of his soldiers, and made the wretched inhabitants feel the whole weight of his arrogance and barbarity. The defenders of Poland had been obliged to disperse. Their property was confiscated; their families were reduced to servitude. Goaded by so many calamities, they once more took the resolution to free their country of the Russians. Some of them assembled, and sent an invitation to Kosciuszko to come and put himself at their head. That general had retired to Leipsic, with Hugh Kolonti, Zajonchek, and Ignatius Potocki, a man of great knowledge and cagacity, a sincere friend to his country, and in all respects the opposite of his cousin Felix. These four Poles joined eagerly in the resolution adopted by their honest countrymen: but they were sensible that, in order to succeed, they must begin by giving liberty to the peasants, who till then had been treated in Poland like beasts of burden.

Kosciuszko and Zajonchek repaired, with all expedition, to the frontiers of Poland. The latter proceeded to Warsaw, where he had conferences with the chiefs of the conspirators. A banker named Kapustas, a bold and artful man, made himself responsible for the inhabitants of the capital. He saw likewise several officers, who declared their detestation of the Russian yoke. All, in short, was ripe for an insurrection, when the Russian commanders, to whom Kosciuszko's presence on the frontiers had given umbrage, forced him to postpone it for a time. To throw the Russians off their guard, Kosciuszko went into Italy, and Zajonchek to Dresden, whither Ignatius Potocki and Kolonti had retired, but all at once Zajonchek appeared again at Warsaw. The king himself impeached him to the Russian general Igelström, who had a conference with him, and ordered him to quit the Polish territory. No alternative now remained for him but to proceed immediately to action, or to abandon the enterprise altogether. Zajonchek resolved on the former.

In 1794 Kosciuszko was recalled from Italy, and arrived at Cracow, where the Poles received him as their deliverer. In spite of the orders of the Russians, Colonel Madalinski pertinaciously refused to disband his regiment. Some other officers had joined him. Kosciuszko was proclaimed general of his little army, amounting to three thousand foot and twelve hundred horse; and the act of insurrection was almost immediately published on the 24th of March. Three hundred peasants, armed with scythes, ranged themselves under the standard of Kosciuszko. That general soon found himself faced by seven thousand Russians, who were put to flight after a vigourous resistance.

On hearing at Warsaw of the success of Kosciuszko, the Russian general Igelström caused all those to be arrested whom he suspected to have any concern in the insurrection; but these measures served only the more to irritate the conspirators. The insurrection broke out on the 18th of April. Two thousand Russians were put to the sword. Their general, being besieged in his house, requested permission to capitulate; and profiting by the delay that was granted him, he escaped to the Prussian camp, which lay at a little distance from Warsaw. Vilna, the capital of Lithuania, followed the example of Warsaw; but the triumph of the insurgents was there less terrible. Colonel Iazinski, who was at their head, conducted himself with so much skill, that he took all the Russians prisoners, without shedding a drop of blood. The inhabitants of the cantons of Chelm and of Lublin declared themselves also in a state of insurrection, and were imitated by three Polish regiments who were employed in the service of the Russians. Some of the principal partisans of Russia, the hetman Kassakovski, the bishop his brother, Zabiello, Ozarovski, and Ankvitch were sentenced to be hanged, the first at Vilna, and the others at Warsaw.

Kosciuszko exerted himself to the utmost to augment his army.  He got recruits among the peasants; and to inspire them with more emulation he wore their dress, ate with them, and distributed encouragements among them; but those men too long degraded in Poland were not yet deserving of the liberty that was offered them.  They distrusted the intentions of the nobles, who, on their side, for the most part lamented the loss of their absurd prerogatives.  Stanislaus Augustus and his partisans augmented still further the ill-will of the nobles, by representing to them the intentions of Kosciuszko as disastrous to their order, and by caballing continually in favour of Russia.

In the mean time, the empress, not satisfied with augmenting the number of her troops in Poland, had sent her best generals thither.  After several battles, in one of which Frederick William, who had advanced to support the Russians, fought at the head of his troops against Kosciuszko, who was striving to prevent the junction of the Russian generals, Suvarov and Fersen, the Polish commander was attacked by the latter at Macziewice on the 4th of October.  His talents, his valour, and his desperation were unable to prevent the Poles from yielding to numbers.  Almost the whole of his army were cut to pieces or obliged to lay down their arms.  He himself, covered with wounds, was taken prisoner, ejaculating, "*Finis Poloniæ!*"

All who were able to escape from the conquerors went and shut themselves up in Praga, the eastern suburb of Warsaw, where 26,000 Poles and 104 heavy cannon and mortars defended the bridges over the Vistula and the approach to the capital.  Suvarov was soon before the gates with an effective force of but 22,000 men and 86 field pieces; but even with such odds against him he resolved to do as he had done at Ismail, and carry the Polish lines at the point of the bayonet.  After cannonading the defences for two days he gave the order for the assault at daybreak on the 4th of November.  The trenches were carried after a desperate fight of five hours; the Russians swept into the town, murdering all before them, old men, women, and children; the wooden houses were speedily on fire; the bridges were broken down, so that the helpless crowds who attempted to escape into the city were remorselessly driven into the Vistula.  Besides 10,000 Polish soldiers, 12,000 citizens of every age and sex perished in this wanton butchery.

Warsaw itself capitulated on the 5th of November, and was delivered up to the Russians on the 6th.  Poland was now annihilated.  One division of its troops after another was disarmed, and all the generals and officers who could be seized were carried off.  The king, however, who could be induced to do anything if his comforts were spared, was used as an instrument to give to power the impress of right.  He was again set nominally at the head of the kingdom till the robbers had agreed upon the division of the spoil, and had no longer need of him.  Suvarov held a splendid military court for a year in Warsaw, far eclipsing the king, till at length the city was given up to the Prussians.

The whole of the year 1795 was spent in negotiations with Prussia, and the last treaty for the partition of Poland was not signed till the 24th of October, 1795.  In December, Suvarov travelled from Warsaw to St. Petersburg, where the empress appropriated the Taurian palace for his residence, and nominated a special household for his service.  On the 1st of January, 1796, Warsaw was first given up to the Prussians, and negotiations were carried on till the 21st of October, 1796, respecting the boundaries of the palatinates of Warsaw and Cracow.  By virtue of this partition, first finally arranged in October, 1796, Austria obtained the chief parts of the waiwodeship of Cracow, the palatinates of Sendomir and Lublin, together with a portion of the district of Chelm and portions of the waiwodeships of Brzesc, Podalachia, and Massovia, which lie along the left bank of the Bug. All these districts contain about 834 German square miles. Prussia received those portions of Massovia and Podalachia which touch upon the right bank of that river, in Lithuania those parts of the palatinates of Troki and Samogitia which lie to the left of the Niemen, and, finally, a district in Little Poland which belonged to the waiwodeship of Cracow, making in all about one thousand German square miles. Russia received the whole of what had hitherto been Polish Lithuania as far as the Niemen, and to the frontiers of the waiwodeships of Brzesc and Novogrodek, and thence to the Bug, together with the greater part of Samogitia. In Little Poland she obtained that part of Chelm which lies on the right bank of the Bug and the remainder of Volhinia, in all about two thousand German square miles. During the negotiations for the partition, Russia caused Stanislaus Augustus to lay down the crown. The three partitioning powers ensured him a yearly income of 200,000 ducats, and promised to pay his debts.

### THE ANNEXATION OF COURLAND (1795 A.D.)

Catherine had now conquered, either by her arms or by her intrigues, almost one-half of Poland, the Crimea, the Kuban, and a part of the frontiers of Turkey. But she had no need of armaments and battles for usurping another rich and well-peopled country. Courland and Semigallia, where still reigned Duke Peter, the feeble son of the famous Biren, had long been prepared for that annexation, which was now effected almost without an effort. The flattering reception given to the Courish nobles in St. Petersburg by the empress, distinctions, honours, posts, and pleasures, rendering their abode in the imperial residence far preferable to continuing in Mittau, and made them desirous of being under the sway of the sovereign of a vast empire, rather than live in obedience to a duke the obscurity of whose origin they could not forget, and whom they regarded as their inferior. To bring the people to the same way of thinking as the nobles, Catherine artfully embroiled them with their neighbours, and created for them reasons of alarm.

She began by instigating the inhabitants of Livonia to insist upon the fulfilment of an ancient convention, by which the Courlanders were obliged to bring all their merchandises to Riga: certainly a very strange and hard condition, by which a nation, that had on its coasts excellent harbours happily situated, should be obliged to go, at a great expense, to embark the products of its soil in a foreign city. The quarrel between the Livonians and the Courlanders was not yet terminated, when the empress sent engineers into Courland, to mark out a canal, to facilitate the transport of the merchandises of that country into Livonia. The Courlanders seeing this, and fearing lest they should be soon forced to make use of this canal, thought it better for them to be protected than oppressed by the empress, and to be her subjects rather than her neighbours.

Catherine, being informed of these dispositions, called the duke of Courland to her, under the pretence of conferring with him on matters of importance. No sooner was that prince at the foot of the throne of the autocratrix of the north, than the states of Courland held an assembly, wherein it was proposed to put the country under the supremacy of Russia. The principal members of the grand council faintly opposed this motion, observing, that before they proceeded to a resolution it would be expedient to wait the return of the duke. The oberburgraf Hoven rose up, and spoke a long time

[1795 A.D.]

in favour of Russia. Some councillors expressed themselves of his opinion; others reproached him with treason. The dispute grew warm on both sides; challenges were reciprocally given and swords were about to be drawn, when the Russian general Pahlen appeared in the assembly. His presence restored tranquillity. No one presumed to raise his voice against Russia; and the proposal of the nobles was adopted.

The next day, March 18th, 1795, the act was drawn up, by which Courland, Semigallia, and the circle of Pilten made a formal surrender of themselves to the empress of Russia; and it was carried to St. Petersburg, where the duke of Courland learned, from the mouth of his own subjects, that they themselves had deprived him of his dominions. The empress immediately sent a governor thither. Some discontent, however, remained in Courland; discontent brought on proscription, and the possessions of the proscribed were given to the courtiers of Catherine. The favourite, Plato Zubov, and his brother Valerian obtained a great part of those rich and shameful spoils.*j*

CATHERINE II
(1729-1796)

### LAST YEARS AND DEATH OF CATHERINE

Before the breaking out of the French Revolution the governments of Louis XVI and Catherine II had entered into active negotiations for the formation of a quadruple alliance that should include Austria, Russia, and the two houses of Bourbon, and should have for its object the checking of England's maritime pretensions and the encroachments of Prussia. After the taking of the Bastille Catherine realised that she could no longer count upon the support of France, since that country was exclusively occupied with its own interior transformation. She kept anxious watch, however, upon the course of events in Paris, and manifested the liveliest antipathy to the new principles, falling ill at the news of the king's execution on the 21st of January. Led by fear into a violent reaction, the correspondent of Voltaire and Diderot set a close watch upon all Russians suspected of liberalism. She destroyed a tragedy of Kniaznin and exiled to Siberia Radichtchev, the author of a curious book entitled *Journey from St. Petersburg to Moscow*, in which were many sharp reflections on serfdom; Novikov was confined at Schlüsselburg, his printing houses were closed and all his enterprises ruined. She dismissed Genêt, the French ambassador, refused to recognise either the constitution of 1791 or the French Republic, issued an ukase announcing the rupture of diplomatic relations with France, refused to the tri-colour admission to Russian parts, expelled all French subjects who refused to swear allegiance to the monarchical principle, extended a warm welcome to French refugees, and lost no time in acknowledging Louis XVIII.

In 1792 she published her famous note on the restoration of royal power and aristocratic privileges in France, asserting that only ten thousand men would be necessary to effect a counter-revolution. She encouraged Gustavus III, who was assassinated by his nobles at a masked ball (March 16th, 1792), to place himself at the head of a crusade against democracy. She further urged England to assist the count d'Artois in a descent he had planned upon the French coast, and stimulated the zeal of Austria and Prussia. Notwithstanding this, though she had repeatedly negotiated treaties for subsidies and promised troops, she took care never to become involved in a war with the west. "My position is taken," she said, "my part assigned; I shall watch the movements of Turkey, Poland, and Sweden."

The latter country became reconciled to France after the death of Gustavus III. The punishment of the Jacobins of Warsaw and Turkey was an easier and more lucrative piece of work. We should also take into account an admission that she made to her vice-chancellor Ostermann in 1791: "Am I wrong? I cannot avow all to the courts of Berlin and Vienna, but I wish to keep them engaged in these affairs so that I may have freedom to carry on my unfinished enterprises." She excused herself for not taking part in the anti-revolutionary crusade by alleging the war with Turkey; then when in consequence of the revolution of the 3rd of May she was obliged to hasten the Peace of Jassy, she made the Polish war her excuse; and when this was ended she affected to excite Suvarov and his soldiers against the atheists of the west, but in reality thought only of gaining her own ends in the east. Muhammed, the new king of Persia, had recently invaded Georgia and burned Tiflis, the capital of Heraclius, a protégé of the empress. Catherine summoned to her court an exiled brother of Muhammed's and charged Valerian Zubov with the conquest of Persia. [His armies were actually under way when the death of Catherine led to the abandonment of the enterprise.]

Without being aware of it Catherine II really performed greater service to France than to the coalition. By her intervention in Poland and her projects against the east she had excited the jealousy and suspicion of Prussia and Austria. She took care to pit them against each other; made the second partition with Frederick William in spite of Austria, and effected the third with Francis II to the extreme dissatisfaction of Prussia. She contributed indirectly to weaken and dissolve the coalition, being herself prevented from joining it by the Polish insurrection that received so much encouragement from France. She died on the 17th of November, 1796, at the age of sixty-seven. Since Ivan the Terrible no monarch had extended the limits of the empire by such vast conquests. Catherine made the Niemen, the Dniester, and the Black Sea the boundaries of Russia.*d*

## A RUSSIAN ESTIMATE OF CATHERINE

The personality of the empress was as though created for a throne. We do not meet in history with any other woman so fitted to rule. On all and each she produced a profound impression. No one has spoken more harshly and disadvantageously of the empress' qualities than Masson, yet this pamphleteer-writer observes that during the space of ten years, having had occasion to see Catherine once or twice a week, he was always struck by her unusually attractive personality, by the dignity with which she held herself, and by the amiability of her behaviour to everyone.

In her *Memoirs* Catherine herself has left a detailed narrative of the course of her development, of her aspirations after power, and of her unscrupulousness in the means she used to attain her aims. The empress' frankness in this respect amounts almost to cynicism. In maturity she at last became an autocratic sovereign. After the terrible humiliations, the bitter trials she had endured in her youth, her delight when she found herself in the enjoyment of unbounded power was all the greater. The fact that the fundamental change in her surroundings, the rapid passage from entire dependency to entire potency, did not in any wise awaken in her any despotic inclinations testifies to the goodness inherent in her nature; when her son was subjected in his turn to a like change in outward circumstances his despotism knew no bounds.

We have see that the unfavourable circumstances in which Catherine found herself until the year 1762 exercised a baneful influence upon her character; whereas the power and preponderance which she later acquired had an ennobling effect upon her nature. Until then she had been necessarily obliged often to have resource to mean and trifling measures to better her position and to revenge herself on her opponents; when she was able to exert full power, to enjoy the advantages of her position, the respect of her contemporaries, the adoration of the persons that surrounded her, she no longer needed to employ those means which are generally made use of by the weak in their struggle against the strong. At the time when a sharp watch was kept over her, when she was not trusted by either Elizabeth or Peter, she understood how to dissemble, to play the hypocrite, to feign humility and modesty, whilst in her soul she was filled with arrogance and contempt for mankind. Now that she had surrounded herself entirely with persons devoted to her she could act openly and nobly. The grand duchess in her isolation had been remarkable for her coldness, her mistrust of mankind, her suspiciousness; the empress on the contrary gave full scope to the development of feelings of benevolence, condescension, indulgence, and sincere attention to the interests of the persons that surrounded her. It was not without reason that Peter and Elizabeth had mistrusted Catherine and been suspicious of her character; it was not without reason, either, that in after times many people highly esteemed Catherine's kindheartedness.

The history of the court under Peter I, under the empress Anna, and under Elizabeth is full of examples of tyranny, cruelty, and arbitrariness; all Catherine's contemporaries were astonished at the mildness of her behaviour to those around her and rejoiced at the absence of stiff formalities and hard measures in her intercourse with her subordinates. In spite of her quick temper and impulsiveness, Catherine had complete control over herself, and in her intercourse with her fellow creatures she was governed by principles of humanity. "I like to praise and reward loudly, to blame quietly," she once justly remarked in conversation with Ségur; she sought to avoid occasions of offending anyone, and was particularly careful in her intercourse with servants; "I will live to make myself not feared," she once said, observing that the stove-heater, who had deserved reproof for some neglect, avoided meeting her. Often when Catherine had given an order she would make excuses for the trouble and labour it occasioned. Krapovitski gives instances of such solicitude on her part; more than once the empress, when impatient or irritated, having expressed herself somewhat sharply, afterwards acknowledged her hastiness and endeavoured to repair her fault.

It is said that Catherine, who awoke early and usually rose at six in the morning, so valued the tranquillity of her servants that without requiring assistance she dressed herself, lit the fire, and without disturbing anyone sat down to her books and papers. Various anecdotes are to be found in the narratives of contemporaries testifying to her indulgence to her servants and her want of sufficient severity in her intercourse with them. When she was in a passion she turned up her sleeves, walked about the room, drank a glass of water, and deferred judgment. Her capacity for removing any misunderstanding that might have arisen between herself and others was particularly remarkable. In her letters to various great lords we meet with frequent exhortations not to give way to despair but to take courage, to believe in their own capacities, and to hope for success. In moments of danger she knew how to raise the spirits of those around her, inspiring them with firmness and courage.

The distinguishing features of Catherine's character were gaiety, humour, and an inclination for fun and amusements. She once remarked: "As to the gaiety of character of Frederick the Great, it must be observed that it proceeded from his superiority: was there ever a great man who was not distinguished by his gaiety and who did not possess in himself an inexhaustible store of it." She took the greatest pleasure in going to masquerades and, while preserving the strictest incognito, talking to various people; she herself related in detail how she had once gone to a masquerade in male attire and had made a declaration of love to a young girl who never suspected that it was the empress talking to her. It must not be regarded as a matter of chance or an act of complaisance that such a multitude of anecdotes testifying to the magnanimity of Catherine have been preserved; many contemporaries who do not unconditionally praise her maintain however that she was capable of listening to unpleasing truths, of recognising her faults and deficiencies, and of restraining her anger. Such assertions are to be met with in Razumovski, Derjavin, Mussin-Pushkin, and Teplov.

Of course traits are not wanting which show her obstinacy, self-will, and arrogance. Derjavin cites several circumstances to prove that in her actions Catherine was often governed by personal considerations and desires rather than the real good of the state and strict justice. It is also not without reason that she is reproached with the fact that, while protesting against the use of tortures and corporal punishment, she allowed full scope to the cruelties of Sheshkovski who frequently with his own hand tortured accused persons in the most atrocious manner; we cannot however determine how far the empress was cognisant of his barbarous treatment. Referring to some instances of arbitrariness and infringement of the law, Prince Scherbatov remarks that the empress held herself above the law and that she thus herself set a pernicious example to the great noblemen and dignitaries who imitated her in this respect.

As to Catherine's piety, Frederick II plainly accused her of hypocrisy and bigotry. We bear in mind that it was not easy for her to adopt the orthodox faith, but that when she had adopted it she used outward piety as a means of strengthening her position in Russia. By strictly observing the rules of the church, and conscientiously fulfilling her religious duties, she endeavoured to produce a certain impression on her subjects. At the same time she remained true to the principles of toleration preached in the literature of enlightenment. When Voltaire reproached her, saying that she humiliated herself by kissing the priest's hand, she justified herself by replying that it was only an outward observance which would little by little become obsolete. There is no doubt that Catherine's piety did not spring from any deep feeling. In her letters to Grimm, sallies against Luther and the Lutherans are to be met with more than once; she despised Lutherans for their intolerance and several times praised the orthodox faith as the best in the world; she compared it to an oak tree with deep roots.

Side by side with such remarks we meet with bold sallies both from the lips and in the letters of the empress against excessive piety and fanaticism; such are certain caustic remarks referring to Maria Theresa and the queen of Portugal. In certain *jeux d'esprit* which she allowed herself in connection with questions of the church and religion in her letters to Grimm, the same rationalism is to be observed as that which distinguished the votaries of French literature of the time. Catherine praised the works of Nicholas Sebaldus Nothanker, especially, because hypocrisy was condemned in them. Deep religious and philosophical questions she did not like; her chief characteristic was a certain worldliness. Her point of view was optimistic and her principal rule of earthly wisdom, gaiety. She did not like to meditate on sad events, to give way to grief, to dwell upon gloomy subjects; and this partly explains her esteem for Voltaire, whom she called the "god of gaiety." This playfulness and vivacity, this freshness and gaiety she preserved to the end of her life.[h]

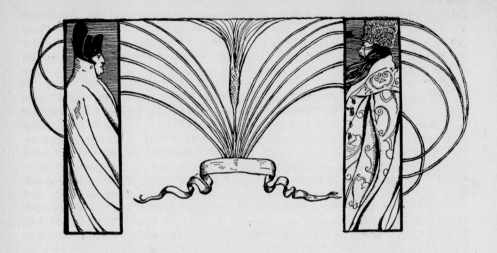

## CHAPTER IX

## RUSSIA IN THE NAPOLEONIC EPOCH

[1796-1815 A.D.]

Perhaps no sovereign since the days of the Antonines ever was called to higher destinies, or more worthily filled an important place in the theatre of the world, than the emperor Alexander I. Placed at the head of the most powerful and rising empire in existence, stationed midway between ancient civilization and barbaric vigour, he was called to take the lead in the great struggle for European freedom; to combat with the energy and enthusiasm of the desert the superiority of advanced information, and meet the condensed military force of a revolution, which had beaten down all the strength of continental power, with the dauntless resolution and enduring fortitude which arise in the earlier ages of social existence. Well and nobly he fulfilled his destiny. Repeatedly defeated, never subdued, he took counsel, like his great predecessor Peter, from misfortune, and prepared in silence those invincible bands which, in the day of trial, hurled back the most terrible array which ambition had ever marshalled against the liberties of mankind. — ALISON.*

### EARLY MEASURES OF THE REIGN OF PAUL I

THE emperor Paul I, Catherine's successor, had been long known for his singularities, his great dislike of the French, and to everything which Catherine had done. He appeared desirous of proceeding directly on the very opposite course to that which she had followed. She had chiefly directed her attention to foreign relations and affairs, whilst he appeared to occupy his mind solely with the internal state of his dominions. His very first act was a proof that he was quite ready to go in opposition to all the ordinary rules of political prudence, and when under the influence of his humour to follow his views, reckless of consequences. He caused splendid funeral honours and services to be performed for his murdered father, and forced the audacious and godless, though clever criminals, who had helped to place his mother on the throne, to be publicly exposed to the gaze of the people. Notwithstanding this, he suffered them to remain in possession of their honours and estates, whilst he designated them as murderers, and reminded the people that his mother had taken part in the murder of his father. The body of Peter III, which had been deposited in the convent of Alexander Nevski, was by his orders placed beside that of his wife; and it was notified by an inscription in the Russian language that, though separated in life, in death they were united.

Alexis Orlov and Prince Baratinski, two of the murderous band, were compelled to come to St. Petersburg to accompany the funeral procession on foot, but they were not so treated as to prevent them afterwards from doing further mischief. Alexis obtained permission to travel in foreign countries. Baratinski was ordered never again to show himself at court; which, under existing circumstances, could not to him be otherwise than an agreeable command. Single proofs of tender feeling, of a noble heart, and touching goodness, nay even the emperor's magnanimous conduct towards Kosciuszko and his brethren in arms, combined with his sympathy with the fate of Poland, could not reconcile a court, such as that of Russia under Catherine II had become, and a city like that of St. Petersburg, to the change of the court into a guard-room, and to the daily varying humours of a man of eccentric and half-deranged mind. Even the improvements in the financial affairs of the country were regarded as ruinous innovations by those who in times past had profited by the confusion. The whole of Russia, and even the imperial family, were alarmed and terrified; a complete flood of decrees, often contradictory, and mutually abrogatory, followed one another in quick succession; and the mad schemes of the emperor, who was, nevertheless, by no means wicked or insensible to what was good and true, reminded all observers of the most unhappy times of declining Rome.*b*

## Imperial Eccentricities

The guards, that dangerous body of men who had overturned the throne of the father, and who had long considered the accession of the son as the term of their military existence, were rendered incapable of injuring him by a bold and vigourous step, and treated without the least deference from the first day. Paul incorporated in the different regiments of guards his battalions that arrived from Gatshina, the officers of which de distributed among the various companies, promoting them at the same time two or three steps; so that simple lieutenants or captains in the army found themselves at once captains in the guards, a place so important and hitherto so honoured, and which gave the rank of colonel, or even of brigadier. Some of the old captains of the first families in the kingdom found themselves under the command of officers of no birth, who but a few years before had left their companies, as sergeants or corporals, to enter into the battalions of the grand duke. This bold and hasty change, which at any other time would have been fatal to its author, had only the effect of inducing a few hundreds of officers, subalterns and others, to retire.

Paul, alarmed and enraged at this general desertion, went to the barracks, flattered the soldiers, appeased the officers, and endeavoured to retain them by excluding from all employ, civil and military, those who should retire in future. He afterwards issued an order that every officer or subaltern who had resigned, or should give in his resignation, should quit the capital within four-and-twenty hours, and return to his own home. It did not enter into the head of the person who drew up the ukase that it contained an absurdity; for several of the officers were natives of St. Petersburg, and had families residing in the city. Accordingly, some of them retired to their homes without quitting the capital, not obeying the first part of the order, lest they should be found guilty of disobedience to the second. Arkarov, who was to see it put in force, having informed the emperor of this contradiction, directed that the injunction to quit St. Petersburg should alone be obeyed. A number of young men were consequently taken out of their houses as criminals, put out of the city, with orders not to re-enter it, and left in the road without shelter, and without any furred garments, in very severe weather. Those who belonged to very remote provinces, for the most part wanting money to carry them thither, wandered about the neighbourhood of St. Petersburg, where several perished from cold and want.

The finances of the empire, exhausted by the prodigalities and still more by the waste of Catherine's reign, required a prompt remedy; and to this

PAUL I
(1754–1801)

Paul seemed at first to turn his thoughts. Partly from hope, partly from fear, the paper money of the crown rose a little in value. It was to be supposed that the grand duke of all the Russias, who for thirty years had been obliged to live on an income of a hundred thousand rubles (£10,000) per annum, would at least have learned economy per force; but he was soon seen to rush into the most unmeasured sumptuosity, heap wealth upon some, and lavish favours upon others, with as much profusion as his mother, and with still less discernment. The spoils of Poland continued to add to the riches of men already too wealthy. All he could do towards restoring a sort of equilibrium between his receipts and disbursements was to lay an exorbitant tax on all the classes of his slaves. The poll-tax of the wretched serfs was doubled, and a new tax was imposed upon the nobles, which, however, the serfs would ultimately have to pay. After the first impressions which his accession caused in the heart of Paul, punishments and disgraces succeeded with the same rapidity and profusion with which he had lavished his favours. Several experienced the two extremes in a few days. It is true that most of these punishments at first appeared just; but then it must be allowed that Paul could scarcely strike any but the guilty, so corrupt had been all who were about the throne.

A whim which caused no little surprise was the imperial prohibition of wearing round hats, or rather the sudden order to take them away or tear them to pieces on the heads of those who appeared in them. This occasioned some disgraceful scenes in the streets, and particularly near the palace. The Cossacks and soldiers of the police fell on the passengers to uncover their heads, and beat those who, not knowing the reason, attempted to defend themselves. An English merchant, going through the street in a sledge, was thus stopped, and his hat snatched off. Supposing it to be a robbery, he leaped out of his sledge, knocked down the soldier, and called the guard. Instead of the guard, arrived an officer, who overpowered and bound him; but as they were carrying him before the police, he was fortunate enough to meet the coach of the English minister, who was going to court, and claimed his protection.   Sir Charles Whitworth made his complaint to the emperor; who, conjecturing that a round hat might be the national dress of the English as it was of the Swedes, said that his order had been misconceived, and he would explain himself more fully to Arkarov.   The next day it was published in the streets and houses that strangers who were not in the emperor's service, or naturalised, were not comprised in the prohibition.   Round hats were now no longer pulled off; but those who were met with this unlucky head-dress were conducted to the police to ascertain their country.   If they were found to be Russians, they were sent for soldiers; and woe to a Frenchman who had been met with in this dress, for he would have been condemned as a Jacobin.

A regulation equally incomprehensible was the sudden prohibition of harnessing horses after the Russian mode.   A fortnight was allowed for procuring harness in the German fashion; after the expiration of which, the police were ordered to cut the traces of every carriage the horses of which were harnessed in the ancient manner.   As soon as this regulation was made public, several persons dared not venture abroad, still less appear in their carriages near the palace, for fear of being insulted.   The harness-markers availed themselves of the occasion to charge exorbitant prices.   To dress the *ishvoshtshki*, or Russian coachmen, in the German fashion, was attended with another inconvenience.   Most of them would neither part with their long beards, their kaftans, nor their round hats; still less would they tie a false tail to their short hair, which produced the most ridiculous scenes and figures in the world.   At length the emperor had the vexation to be obliged to change his rigorous order into a simple invitation to his subjects gradually to adopt the German fashion of dress, if they wished to merit his favour.   Another reform with respect to carriages: the great number of splendid equipages that swarmed in the streets of St. Petersburg disappeared in an instant.   The officers, even the generals, came to the parade on foot, or in little sledges, which also was not without its dangers.

It was anciently a point of etiquette for every person who met a Russian autocrat, his wife, or son, to stop his horse or coach, alight, and prostrate himself in the snow or in the mud.   This barbarous homage, difficult to be paid in a large city where carriages pass in great numbers, and always on the gallop, had been completely abolished under the reign of the polished Catherine.   One of the first cares of Paul was to re-establish it in all its rigour.   A general officer, who passed on without his coachmen's observing the emperor riding by on horseback, was stopped, and immediately put under arrest.   The same unpleasant circumstance occurred to several others, so that nothing was so much dreaded, either on foot or in a carriage, as the meeting of the emperor.

The ceremony established within the palace became equally strict, and equally dreaded.   Woe betide him who, when permitted to kiss the hand of Paul, did not make the floor resound by striking it with his knee as loud as a soldier with the butt-end of his firelock.   It was requisite, too, that the salute of the lips on his hand should be heard, to certify the reality of the kiss, as well as of the genuflection.   Prince George Galitzin, the chamberlain, was put under arrest on the spot by his majesty himself, for having made the bow and kissed the hand too negligently.

If this new reign was fatal to the army and to the poor gentry, it was still more so to the unhappy peasantry.   A report being spread that Paul was about to restrict the power of masters over their slaves, and give the peasants of the lords the same advantages as those of the crown, the people of the capital were much pleased with the hopes of this change. At this juncture an officer set off for his regiment, which lay at Orenberg. On the road he was asked about the new emperor, and what new regulations he was making. He related what he had seen, and what he had heard; among the rest, mentioning the ukase which was soon to appear in favour of the peasants. At this news, those of Tver and Novgorod indulged in some tumultuous actions, which were considered as symptoms of rebellion. Their masters were violently enraged with them; and the cause that had led them into error was discovered  Marshal Repnin was immediately despatched at the head of some troops against the insurgents; and the officer who had unwittingly given rise to this false hope, by retailing the news of the city on his road, was soon brought back in confinement. The senate of St. Petersburg judged him deserving of death, and condemned him to be broken, to undergo the punishment of the knout, and if he survived this, to labour in the mines. The emperor confirmed the sentence. This was the first criminal trial that was laid before the public; and assuredly it justified but too well those remains of shame which had before kept secret similar outrages.

The most prominent of Paul's eccentricities was that mania which, from his childhood, he displayed for the military dress and exercise. This passion in a prince no more indicates the general or the hero than a girl's fondness for dressing and undressing her doll foretokens that she will be a good mother. Frederick the Great, the most accomplished soldier of his time, is well known to have had from his boyhood the most insuperable repugnance to all those minutiæ of a corporal to which his father would have subjected him; this was even the first source of that disagreement which ever subsisted between the father and the son. Frederick, however, became a hero; his father was never anything more than a corporal. Peter III pushed his soldato-mania to a ridiculous point, fancying he made Frederick his model. He loved soldiers and arms, as a man loves horses and dogs. He knew nothing but how to exercise a regiment, and never went abroad but in a captain's uniform.

Paul, in his mode of life when grand duke, and his conduct after his accession, so strongly resembled his father that, changing names and dates, the history of the one might be taken for that of the other. Both were educated in a perfect ignorance of business, and resided at a distance from court, where they were treated as prisoners of state rather than heirs to the crown; and whenever they presented themselves appeared as aliens and strangers, having no concern with the royal family. The aunt of the father (Elizabeth) acted precisely as did the mother of the son. The endeavours of each were directed to prolong the infancy of their heirs, and to perpetuate the feebleness of their minds. The young princes were both distinguished by personal vivacity and mental insensibility, by an activity which, untrained and neglected, degenerated into turbulence; the father was sunk in debauchery, the son lost in the most insignificant trifles. An unconquerable aversion to study and reflection gave to both that infatuated taste for military parade, which would probably have displayed itself less forcibly in Paul had he been a witness of the ridicule they attached to Peter. The education of Paul, however, was much more attended to than that of his father. He was surrounded in infancy by persons of merit, and his youth promised a capacity of no ordinary kind. It must also be allowed that he was exempt from many of the vices which disgraced Peter; temperance and regularity of manners were prominent features of his character — features the more commendable, as before his mother and himself they were rarely to be found in a Russian autocrat. To the same cause, education, and his knowledge of the language and character of the nation, it was owing that the differed from his father in other valuable qualities.

The similarity which, in some instances, marked their conduct towards their wives, is still more striking; and in their amours, a singular coincidence of taste is observable. Catherine and Marie were the most beautiful women of the court, yet both failed to gain the affections of their husbands. Catherine had an ambitious soul, a cultivated mind, and the most amiable and polished manners. In a man, however, whose attachments were confined to soldiers, to the pleasures of the bottle, and the fumes of tobacco, she excited no other sentiment than disgust and aversion. He was smitten with an object less respectable, and less difficult to please. The countess Vorontzov, fat, ugly in her person and vulgar in her manners, was more suitable to his depraved military taste, and she became his mistress. In like manner, the regular beauty of Marie, the unalterable sweetness of her disposition, her unwearied complaisance, her docility as a wife, and her tenderness as a mother were not sufficient to prevent Paul from attaching himself to Mademoiselle Nelidov, whose disposition and qualities better accorded with his own, and afterwards to a young lady of the name of Lopukhin, who, it is believed, rejected his suit. To the honour of Paul it is related that he submitted to that mortifying repulse with the most chivalric patience and generosity. Nelidov was ugly and diminutive, but seemed desirous, by her wit and address, to compensate for the disadvantages of her person; for a woman to be in love with Paul it was necessary she should resemble him.

On their accession to the throne, neither the father nor the son were favourites with the court or the nation, yet both acquired immediate popularity and favour. The first steps of Paul appeared to be directed, but improved, by those of Peter. The liberation of Kosciuszko and other prisoners brought to public recollection the recall of Biron, Munich, and Lestocq, with this difference — that Peter III did not disgrace these acts of clemency and justice by ridiculous violences, or by odious and groundless persecutions. Both issued ukases extremely favourable to the nobility, but from motives essentially different, and little to the honour of the son. The father granted to the Russian gentry those natural rights which every man ought to enjoy; while the son attempted the folly of creating a heraldic nobility in Russia, where that Gothic institution had never been known. In the conduct which he observed towards the clergy, Paul, however, showed himself a superior politician. Instead of insulting the priests, and obliging them to shave their beards, he bestowed the orders of the empire on the bishops, to put them on a footing with the nobility, and flattered the populace and the priesthood by founding churches, in obedience to pretended inspiration.

In his military operations, however, his policy appears to have abandoned him, because here he gave the reins to his ruling passion. The quick and total change of discipline he introduced in his armies created him nearly as many enemies as there were officers and soldiers. In the distrust and suspicions which incessantly haunted him, his inferiority to his father is also evident. One of the first acts of Peter III was to abolish the political inquisition established by Elizabeth; whereas Paul prosecuted no scheme with greater alacrity than that of establishing a system of spies, and devising means for the encouragement of informers. The blind confidence of the father was his ruin, but it flowed from a humanity of disposition always worthy of respect. The distrust of the son did not save him; it was the offspring of a timourous mind, which by its suspicions was more apt to provoke than to elude treason.*k*

## Paul's Foreign Policy

In regard to foreign matters Paul's initial policy was one of peace. He put a stop to the levying of recruits after the manner adopted by his mother — that is, in the proportion of three men to every five hundred souls — recalled his army from Persia, and left Georgia to take care of itself. He showed compassion for the Poles, recalled the prisoners from Siberia, transferred King Stanislaus from Grodno to St. Petersburg, visited Kosciuszko at Schlüsselburg and released him in company with the other prisoners. He bade Kolitchev, envoy extraordinary at Berlin, inform the king that he, Paul, wished neither conquest nor aggrandisement. He dictated to Ostermann a circular directed to the foreign powers, in which he declared that of all the countries of the world Russia alone had been constantly engaged in war since 1756; that forty years of warfare had reduced the population; that the emperor's humanity would not allow him to withhold from his beloved subjects the peace for which they longed; that though on account of these considerations Russia could take no active part in the struggle against France, the emperor would "nevertheless remain closely united with his allies, and would use every means to oppose the rise of the mad French Republic which threatened all Europe with upheaval by the destruction of its laws, privileges, property, religion, and customs." He refused all armed assistance to Austria, which was alarmed at Napoleon's victories in Italy, and recalled the fleet that Catherine had adjoined to the English fleet for the purpose of blockading the coasts of France and Holland. He even received overtures made by Caillard, the French envoy to Prussia, and caused him to be informed that the emperor "did not consider himself at war with the French, that he had never done anything to harm them, but was rather disposed to keep peace with them, and would induce his allies to hasten the conclusion of war, to which end he offered the mediation of Russia."

It was not long, however, before relations again became strained between France and Russia. By the Treaty of Campo Formio the Ionian Isles had been given to the French, who thus acquired a threatening position in the East and increased power over the Divan. The Directory authorised Dombrowski to organise Polish legions in Italy. Panin, at Berlin, intercepted a letter from the Directory to the French envoy, which spoke of a restoration of Poland under a prince of Brandenburg. Paul, on his side, took into his pay the troops of the prince of Condé, and established ten thousand émigrés in Volhinia and Podolia. He offered an asylum to Louis XVIII after his flight from Brunswick, and installed him in the ducal palace at Mitau with a pension of 200,000 rubles. The news that a French expedition was being secretly organised at Toulon made him fear for the security of the coasts of the Black Sea, which were immediately put in a state of defence. The abduction of Zagurski, the Russian consul at Corfu, the capture of Malta by Napoleon, the arrival at St. Petersburg of the banished knights who offered Paul the protectorate of their order and the title of grand master, the invasion of Helvetian territory by the Directory, the expulsion of the pope and the proclamation of the Roman Republic — all were events that precipitated the rupture.

Paul concluded an alliance with Turkey which had been disturbed by an Egyptian invasion, also with England, Austria, and the kingdom of Naples. Thus, by the double aggression of Bonaparte against Malta and Egypt, Russia and Turkey were led, contrary to all traditions, to make common cause. Paul pledged himself to unite his fleet with the Turkish and English squadron, and to furnish one body of troops for a descent on Holland, another for the conquest of the Ionian Isles, and a grand auxiliary army for the campaigns in Italy and Switzerland.

In the autumn of 1798 a Turkish-Russian fleet captured the French garrisons in the Ionian Isles. The king of Naples invaded the territory of the Roman Republic, but Championnet brought the Neapolitan troops back on to their own ground, and after making a triumphal entry into Naples proclaimed the Parthenopean Republic.

## THE CAMPAIGNS OF KORSAKOV AND SUVAROV (1798–1799)

The Russian army in Switzerland was placed under the command of Rimski-Korsakov, that of Holland under the orders of Hermann; while Austria, at the suggestion of England, requested that the victor of Fokshani and of the Rimnik should receive the command of the Austro-Russian army. Flattered by this mark of deference, Paul I recalled Suvarov from exile in his village. "Suvarov has no need of laurels," wrote the czar, "but the country has need of Suvarov."c

A few days after the battle of Magnano, Suvarov arrived on the Mincio with the first division of his forces, twenty thousand strong, and took the command of all the allied troops in Italy. The jealousy of the Austrian generals was naturally excited and they called a council of war, in order to examine his plans. The members of the council, beginning at the youngest, proposed their several schemes. Suvarov quietly heard them all, and when they had done, took a slate, drew two lines, and said, "Here, gentleman, are the French, and here the Russians; the latter will march against the former and beat them." So saying, he rubbed out the French line, and added, "This is all my plan; the council is concluded."

Suvarov kept his word, and in less than three months swept the French entirely out of Lombardy and Piedmont. Thrusting himself between the three French armies of Switzerland, northern Italy, and the Parthenopean Republic, it was his purpose, in concert with the archduke Charles of Austria, to penetrate into France on its most defenceless side, by the Vosges and the Jura, the same quarter on which the great invasion of 1814 was afterwards effected. The campaign opened on the 25th of April, on the steep banks of the Adda, behind which Moreau had posted his diminished force of twenty-eight thousand men in three divisions. The passage was forced with immense loss to the French, who were compelled to abandon Milan, which Suvarov entered in triumph on the 29th.

After a week's delay, during which all the principal places of Lombardy surrendered to the allies, Suvarov followed Moreau's retreat, and endeavoured to dislodge him from his advantageous position on the Po. Not succeeding in this attempt as rapidly as suited his impetuous habits, the Russian general suddenly changed his purpose, and advanced against Turin, whilst Moreau at the same moment had resolved to retire to Turin and the crests of the Apennines, in order to preserve his communications with France. On the 27th of May, Vukassovitch, who commanded the advance guard of the Russians, surprised Turin, and forced the French to take refuge in the citadel, leaving in the hands of the victors nearly three hundred pieces of artillery, sixty thousand muskets, and an enormous quantity of ammunition and military stores. Moreau's army, thus deprived of all its resources, was saved from destruction only by the extraordinary ability of its commander, who led it safely towards Genoa by a mountain path, which was rendered practicable for artillery, in four days. With the exception of a few fortresses, nothing now remained to the French of all Napoleon's conquests in northern Italy; they had been lost in less time than it had taken to make them.

Exulting in the brilliant success of his arms, Paul bestowed another surname, Italienski, or the Italian, on his victorious general, and ordered by an express ukase that Suvarov should be universally regarded as the greatest commander that had ever appeared. Meanwhile the results of his skill and vigour were neutralised by the selfish policy of the Austrian court, which had become by the Treaty of Campo Formio, and the acquisition of Venice, in some degree an actual accomplice with the aggressors against whom it was in arms. Suvarov was compelled to submit to the dictation of the emperor Francis I, and deeply disgusted he declared that he was no longer of any use in Italy, and that he desired nothing so ardently as to be recalled.

The disasters of the French in upper Italy were fatal to their ascendancy in the south, and Macdonald received orders to abandon the Parthenopean Republic, and unite his forces with those of Moreau. His retreat was exposed to great dangers by the universal insurrection of the peasants; but he accomplished it with great rapidity and skill. The two French commanders then concerted measures to dislodge the allies from their conquests — a project which seemed not unlikely to be fufilled, so obstinately had the Aulic council adhered to the old system of dispersing the troops all over the territory which they occupied. Though the allies had above a hundred thousand men in the field, they could hardly assemble thirty thousand at any one point; and Macdonald might easily have destroyed them in detail could he have fallen upon them at once; but the time he spent in reorganising his army in Tuscany, and in concerting measures with Moreau, was well employed by Suvarov in promptly concentrating his forces. Macdonald advanced against him with an army of thirty-seven thousand men, taking Modena on his way, and driving Hohenzollern out of it after a bloody engagement. The two armies met on the Trebbia, where a first and indecisive action took place on the 17th of June; it was renewed on each of the two following days, and victory finally remained with the Russians. In this terrible battle of three days, the most obstinately contested and bloody that had occurred since the beginning of the war, the loss on both sides was excessive; that of the French was above twelve thousand in killed and wounded, and that of the allies not much less. But nearly equal losses told with very unequal severity on the respective combatants; those of the allies would speedily be retrieved by large reinforcements, but the republicans had expended their last resources, were cut off from Moreau, and had no second army to fall back upon. Macdonald with infinite difficulty regained the positions he had occupied before the advance to the Trebbia, after losing an immense number of prisoners.

The fall of the citadel of Turin on the 20th of June was of great importance to the allies; for besides disengaging their besieging force it put into their hands one of the strongest fortresses in Piedmont, and an immense quantity of artillery and ammunition. This event, and Suvarov's victory on the Trebbia, checked the successful operations of Moreau, and compelled him to fall back to his former defensive position on the Apennines. Again, contrary to Suvarov's wishes, the allied forces were divided for the purpose of reducing Mantua and Alexandria, and occupying Tuscany. After the fall of those two fortresses, Suvarov laid siege to Tortona, when Joubert, who had meanwhile superseded Moreau, marched against him at the head of the combined forces of the French. On the 15th of August, another desperate battle was fought at Novi, in which Joubert was killed, but from which neither side derived any particular advantage. The French returned to their former positions, and the Italian campaign was ended.

Suvarov now received orders to join his forces with those under Korsakov, who was on the Upper Rhine with thirty thousand men. The archduke Charles might, even without this fresh reinforcement, have already annihilated Massena had he not remained for three months, from June to August, in complete inactivity; at the very moment of Suvarov's expected arrival, he allowed the important passes of the St. Gotthard to be again carried by a coup-de-main by the French, under General Lecourbe, who drove the Austrians from the Simplon, the Furka, the Grimsel, and the Devil's Bridge. The archduke, after an unsuccessful attempt to push across the Aar at Dettingen, suddenly quitted the scene of war and advanced down the Rhine for the purpose of supporting the English expedition under the duke of York against Holland. This unexpected turn in affairs proceeded from Vienna. The Viennese cabinet was jealous of Russia. Suvarov played the master in Italy, favoured Sardinia at the expense of the house of Habsburg, and deprived the Austrians of the laurels and the advantages they had won. The archduke, accordingly, received orders to remain inactive, to abandon the Russians, and finally to withdraw to the north; by this movement Suvarov's triumphant progress was checked, he was compelled to cross the Alps to the aid of Korsakov, and to involve himself in a mountain warfare ill-suited to the habits of his soldiery.

Korsakov, whom Bavaria had been bribed with Russian gold to furnish with a corps one thousand strong, was supported solely by Kray and Hotze with twenty thousand men. Massena, taking advantage of the departure of the archduke and the non-arrival of Suvarov, crossed the Limmat at Dietikon and shut Korsakov, who had imprudently stationed himself with his whole army in Zurich, so closely in that, after an engagement that lasted two days, from the 15th to the 17th of September, the Russian general was compelled to abandon his artillery and to force his way through the enemy. Ten thousand men were all that escaped. Hotze, who had advanced from the Grisons to Schwyz to Suvarov's rencontre, was, at the same time, defeated and killed at Schanis. Suvarov, although aware that the road across the St. Gotthard was blocked by the Lake of Lucerne, on which there were no boats, had the temerity to attempt the passage. In Airolo, he was obstinately opposed by the French under Lecourbe, and, although Shveikovski contrived to turn this strong position by scaling the pathless rocks, numbers of the men were, owing to Suvarov's impatience, sacrificed before it.

On the 24th of September, 1799, he at length climbed the St. Gotthard, and a bloody engagement, in which the French were worsted, took place on the Oberalpsee. Lecourbe blew up the Devil's Bridge, but, leaving the Urnerloch open, the Russians pushed through that rocky gorge, and, dashing through the foaming Reuss, scaled the opposite rocks and drove the French from their position behind the Devil's Bridge. Altorf on the lake was reached in safety by the Russian general, who was compelled, owing to the want of boats, to seek his way through the valleys of Schächen and Muotta, across the almost impassable rocks, to Schwyz. The heavy rains rendered the undertaking still more arduous; the Russians, owing to the badness of the road, were speedily barefoot; the provisions were also exhausted. In this wretched state they reached Muotta on the 29th of September and learned the discouraging news of Korsakov's defeat. Massena had already set off in the hope of cutting off Suvarov, but had missed his way. He reached Altorr, where he joined Lecourbe on the 29th, when Suvarov was already at Muotta, whence Massena found on his arrival that he had again retired across the Bragelburg, through the Klönthal. He was opposed on the lake of Klönthal by Molitor, who was, however, forced to retire by Auffenberg, who had joined Suvarov at Altorf and formed his advanced guard, Rosen, at the same time, beating off Massena with the rear-guard, taking five cannon and one thousand of his men prisoners. On the 1st of October, Suvarov entered Glarus, where he rested until the 4th, when he crossed the Panixer Mountains through snow two feet deep to the valley of the Rhine, which he reached on the 10th, after losing the whole of his beasts of burden and two hundred of his men down the precipices; and here ended his extraordinary march, which had cost him the whole of his artillery, almost all his horses, and a third of his men.

The archduke had, meanwhile, tarried on the Rhine, where he had taken Philippsburg and Mannheim, but had been unable to prevent the defeat of the English expedition under the duke of York by General Brune at Bergen, on the 19th of September. The archduke now, for the first time, made a retrograde movement, and approached Korsakov and Suvarov. The different leaders, however, did nothing but find fault with each other, and the czar, perceiving his project frustrated, suddenly recalled his troops, and the campaign came to a close.

Paul's anger fell without measure or reason on his armies and their chiefs. All the officers who were missing, that is to say who were prisoners in France, were broken as deserters, and Suvarov, instead of being well received with well merited honours, was deprived of his command and not suffered to see the emperor's face. This unjust severity broke the veteran's heart. He died soon after his return to St. Petersburg; and no Russian courtier, nor any member of the diplomatic body except the English ambassador, followed his remains to the grave.

### PAUL RECONCILED WITH FRANCE (1800 A.D.)

Frustrated in the objects for which he had engaged in war, Paul was now in a mood easily to be moved to turn his arms against the allies who had deceived his hopes. He had fought for the re-establishment of monarchy in France, and of the old *status quo* in Europe; and the only result had been the aggrandisement of Austria, his own immediate neighbour, of whom he had much more reason to be jealous than of the remote power of France. The rapid steps, too, which Bonaparte was taking for the restoration of monarchical forms in that country were especially calculated to conciliate Paul's good-will towards the first consul. The latter and his able ministers availed themselves of this favourable disposition through the connections they had made in St. Petersburg. Fouché had such confidential correspondence even with ladies in the Russian capital, that he afterwards received the earliest and most correct intelligence of the emperor's murder. Two persons at the court of St. Petersburg were next gained over to France, or rather to Bonaparte's rising empire; these were the minister Rostoptchin, and the emperor's favourite, the Turk Kutaisov, who had risen with unusual rapidity from the situation of the emperor's barber to the rank of one of the first Russian nobles. He was also nearly connected by relationship with Rostoptchin.

Rostoptchin first found means to send away General Dumourier from St. Petersburg, whither he had come for the purpose of carrying on his intrigues in favour of the Bourbons. He next sought to bring Louis Cobenzl also into discredit with the emperor, and he succeeded in this, shortly before the opening of the campaign in Italy in 1800, when the cabinet of Vienna was called upon to give a plain and direct answer to the questions peremptorily put by the emperor of Russia. Paul required that the cabinet should answer, without if or but, without circumlocution or reserve, whether or not Austria would, according to the terms of the treaty, restore the pope and the king to their dominions and sovereignty. Cobenzl was obliged to reply that if Austria were to give back Piedmont to the king of Sardinia it must still retain Tortona and Alessandria; and that it never would restore the three legations and Ancona. The measure of the emperor's indignation was now full; he forbade Count Cobenzl the court, and at a later period not only ordered him to leave the country, but would not even allow an embassy or chargé-d'affaires to remain.

The emperor proceeded more deliberately with regard to the English. At first he acted as if he had no desire to break with them; and he even allowed the Russians, whom they had hired for the expedition against Holland, to remain in Guernsey under Viomesnil's command, in order to assist their employers in an expedition against Brittany. The English government, however, at length provoked him to extremities. They refused to redeem the Russians who had been made prisoners in their service, by giving in exchange for them an equal number of French, of whom their prisons were full; they refused to listen to any arrangements respecting the grand mastership of the knights of Malta, or even as to the protectorate of the order, and gave the clearest intimations that they meant to keep the island for themselves. Bonaparte seized upon this favourable moment for flattering the emperor, by acting as if he had really more respect for Paul than the two powers for whom he had made such magnanimous sacrifices. Whilst the English refused to redeem the Russians made prisoners in their service by exchange, Bonaparte set them free without either exchange or ransom.

The emperor of Germany had broken his word, and neither restored the pope nor the king of Sardinia, whilst Bonaparte voluntarily offered to restore the one and give compensation to the other. He assailed the emperor in a masterly manner on his weak side, causing the six or seven thousand Russians, whom the English refused to exchange, to be provided with new clothing and arms, and he wrote a letter to Panin, the Russian minister, in which he said that he was unwilling to suffer such brave soldiers as these Russians were to remain longer away from their native land on account of the English. In the same letter he paid another compliment to the emperor, and threw an apple of mortal strife between him and England. Knowing as he did that his garrison in Malta could not hold out much longer, he offered to place the island in the hands of the emperor Paul, as a third party. This was precisely what the emperor desired; and Sprengporten, who was sent to France to bring away the Russians, and to thank the first consul, was to occupy Malta with them. The Russians were either to be conveyed thither by Nelson, who up to this time had kept the island closely blockaded, and was daily expecting its surrender, or at least he was to be ordered to let them pass; but both he and the English haughtily rejected the Russian mediation.

Paul now came to a complete breach with England. First of all he recalled his Russian troops from Guernsey, but on this occasion he was again baffled. It was of great importance to the English cabinet that Bonaparte should not immediately hear of the decided breach which had taken place between them and the emperor, and they therefore prevailed upon Viomesnil, an émigré, who had the command of the Russians in Guernsey, to remain some weeks longer, in opposition to the emperor's will. Paul was vehemently indignant at this conduct; Viomesnil, however, entered the English service, and was provided for by the English government in Portugal.

Lord Whitworth was next obliged to leave Russia, as Count Cobenzl had previously been. Paul recalled his ambassadors from the courts of Vienna and London, and forthwith sent Count Kalitchev to Paris to enter into friendly negotiations with Bonaparte. In the meantime, the English had recourse to some new subterfuges, and promised, that in case Malta capitulated, they would consent to allow the island to be administered, till the conclusion of a peace, by commissioners appointed by Russia, England, and Naples. Paul had already named Bailli de la Ferrette for this purpose; but the English refused to acknowledge his nominee, and even to receive the Neapolitans in Malta. Before this took place, however, the emperor had come to issue with England on a totally different question.

The idea of a union among the neutral powers, in opposition to the right alleged by England, when at war with any power whatsoever, to subject the ships of all neutral powers to search, had been relinquished by the empress Catherine in 1781, to please the English ambassador at her court; Paul now resumed the idea. Bonaparte intimated his concurrence, and Paul followed up the matter with great energy and zeal, as in this way he had an opportunity of exhibiting himself in the character of an imperial protector of the weak, a defender of justice and right, and as the head of a general alliance of the European powers. Prussia also now appeared to do homage to him, for the weak king was made to believe, that by a close alliance between Russia and France, he might be helped to an extension of territory and an increase of subjects, without danger or cost to himself, or without war, which he abhorred beyond everything else. The first foundation, therefore, for an alliance between Russia and France, was laid in Berlin, where Beurnonville, the French ambassador, was commissioned to enter into negotiations with the Russian minister Von Krüderer. Beurnonville promised, in Bonaparte's name, that the Russian mediation in favour of Naples and Sardinia would be accepted, and that, in the question of compensations for the German princes particular regard would be had to the cases of Baden and Würtemberg.

### THE ARMED NEUTRALITY (1800 A.D.)

As to the armed neutrality by sea against England, Prussia could easily consent to join this alliance, because she had in fact no navy; but it was much more difficult for Sweden and Denmark, whose merchant ships were always accompanied by frigates. In case, therefore, the neutral powers came to an understanding that no merchant vessels which were accompanied by a ship of war should be compelled to submit to a search, this might at any time involve them in hostilities with England. In addition to Denmark, Sweden, and Prussia, which, under Paul's protectorate, were to conclude an alliance for the protection of trading vessels belonging to neutral powers against the arrogant claims of England, Bonaparte endeavoured to prevail upon the North Americans to join the alliance. They were the only parties who, by a specific treaty in 1794, had acknowledged as a positive right what the others only submitted to as an unfounded pretension on the part of England. On that occasion the Americans had broken with the French Republic on the subject of his treaty, and Barras and Talleyrand had been shameless enough to propose that the Americans should pay a gratuity, in order to effect a renewal of their old friendship with France, which proposal, however, the Americans treated with contempt.

On the 30th of September, 1800, their ambassadors concluded an agreement at Bonaparte's country seat of Morfontaine, which referred especially to the resistance which all the neutral powers under the protectorate of the emperor of Russia were desirous of making to the pretensions and claims of England. The Americans first of all declared that neutral flags should make a neutral cargo, except in cases where the ship was actually laden with goods contraband of war. It was afterwards precisely defined what were to be considered goods contraband of war. By the fourth article it was determined that neutral ships must submit to be detained, but that the ships of war so detaining a merchantman with a view to search should remain at least at the distance of a cannon-shot, and only be allowed to send a boat with three men to examine the ship's papers and cargo; and that in all cases in which a merchantman should be under convoy of a ship of war, no right of search should exist, because the presence of the convoy should be regarded as a sufficient guarantee against contraband. Inasmuch as England and Denmark were at open issue concerning this last point, the Americans would have been inevitably involved in the dispute had they immediately ratified the treaty of Morfontaine: they were, however, far too cunning to fall into this difficulty; and they did not therefore ratify the treaty till the Russian confederation had been dissolved.

Sweden and Denmark had come to issue with England concerning the right of search in 1798 and 1799, when four frigates, two Swedish and two Danish, were captured and brought into English ports. True, they were afterwards given up, but without any satisfaction, for the English still insisted upon the right of search. The dispute became most vehement in the case of the Danish frigate *Freya*, which, together with the merchantmen under her convoy, were brought into an English port, after a sharp engagement on the 25th of July, 1800; and the English, aware of the hostile negotiations which were going on in the north, at once despatched an expedition against Denmark.

Sixteen English ships of war suddenly appeared before Copenhagen, and most unexpectedly threatened the harbour and city with a destructive bombardment, if Denmark did not at once acknowledge England's right of search at sea. Had this acknowledgment been made, Bonaparte's and the emperor's plan would have been frustrated in its very origin; but Denmark had the good fortune to possess, in its minister Bernstorff, the greatest diplomatist of the whole revolutionary era, who contrived for that time to save Copenhagen without the surrender of any rights. It was quite impossible to resist by force, but he refused to enter upon the question of right or wrong; and in the agreement which he signed with Lord Whitworth on the 25th of August, 1800, he consented that in the meantime all occasion for dispute should be avoided, and thus the difficulty be postponed or removed. Denmark bound herself no longer to send her merchantmen under convoy — whereupon the *Freya*, and the vessels by which she was accompanied, were set at liberty. On this occasion the emperor Paul offered himself as arbitrator; and when Lord Whitworth rejected his interference or arbitration, he immediately laid an embargo on all the English ships in Russian ports.

The news of the agreement entered into at Copenhagen, however, no sooner reached St. Petersburg, than this first embargo was removed, and the dispute carried on merely in a diplomatic manner. At last the emperor Paul put an end to this paper war, when Vaubois, who had defended Malta since July, 1798, against the English, Russians, Neapolitans, and sometimes also the Portuguese, at length capitulated, on the 5th of September, 1800. The island was taken military possession of by the English without any reference whatever to the order, to Naples, to the promise which they had made to the emperor, or to Bailli de la Ferrette, whom Paul had named as the representative of the order.  As soon as this news reached St. Petersburg, Paul's rage and indignation knew no bounds.  On the 7th of November, he not only laid an embargo upon three hundred English ships then in his ports, but sent the whole of their crews into the interior of Russia, and allowed them only a few kopecks a day for their support.

Lord Carysfort, the English ambassador in Berlin, was unable for six weeks to obtain any answer from the Prussian government with respect to its connection with the northern confederation, although he insisted strongly upon it; and yet Stedingk, the Swedish minister, and Rosenkranz, the Danish minister, had signed the agreement for an armed neutrality in the form of that of 1780 as early as the 17th of December, 1800, in St. Petersburg, and the Prussian minister, Von Luft, in the name of his king, had signified his acceptance of the alliance on the 18th.  When Lord Carysfort at length obtained an answer on the 12th of February to his demands, so long and repeatedly urged in vain, Haugwitz had drawn it up equivocally both in form and contents.  The emperor of Russia was so indignant at the ambiguity that he not only expressed his feelings on the subject warmly, but also took some hostile measures against Prussia.

On the other hand, the emperor invited Gustavus IV to St. Petersburg where he was received with the greatest splendour.  He arrived at St. Petersburg at Christmas, 1800, and immediately, as if to insult the English, a grand meeting of the order of Malta was held; the king himself was loaded with marks of honour of every possible description, and at the end of December he signed a new agreement, by which the objects of that of the 16th of the same month were greatly enlarged.  In the former alliance defensive operations alone were contemplated; but now offensive measures were also agreed upon, with the reservation, indeed, if they should become necessary.  Paul took measures to refit his fleet, and an army was equipped which was to be placed under the commands of Soltikov, Pahlen, and Kutusov; the Danish fleet was in good condition; the Russian minister in Paris appeared to regard the circumstances as very favourable for gaining Hanover to his master without danger or risk; and Pitt himself considered the state of affairs so unfavourable, that he seriously contemplated the propriety of retiring and making way for a new ministry, in order to render a peace possible.  This close confederacy against England was, however, dissolved at the very moment in which the first consul appeared to be disposed to favour Naples and Sardinia, in order to gratify the wishes of the emperor of Russia.


### ASSASSINATION OF PAUL (1801 A.D.)

The catastrophe in St. Petersburg is easily explained by the continually changing humours of the emperor, by his mental derangement, which had been constantly on the increase for several months previous to his murder, by the acts of violence and injustice which he suffered himself to commit, and by the dreadful apprehension which prevailed among all classes of society, from the empress and the grand duke down to the very lowest citizen.  The emperor's sober and rational intervals became progressively rarer, so that no man was sure for an instant either of his place or his life; thousands of persons completely innocent were sent to Siberia, and yet goodness and mildness alternated with cruel severity.  The emperor one while exhibited the most striking magnanimity, at another the meanest vindictiveness.

The beautiful and virtuous empress had patiently submitted to her husband's preference for the plain Nelidov, who at least treated her with honour and respect; but she was obliged also to submit to his attachment to Lopukhin, who continually provoked strife. She endured these things patiently, lived on good terms with the emperor, slept immediately under his chambers, and yet neither she nor her sons, Alexander and Constantine, were able to escape the suspicions of his morbid mind. It was whispered, by persons in the confidence of the court, that the emperor had said he would send the empress to Kalamagan, in the government of Astrakhan, Alexander to Shlüsselburg, and Constantine to the citadel of St. Petersburg. It is not worth while to inquire what truth there may have been in these reports; everyone felt that the time had arrived to have recourse to the only means which can be employed in despotic kingdoms for effecting a complete change in the measures of government. This means is the murder of the despot, which in such circumstances was usually effected in the Roman Empire by the Pretorians, in Constantinople by the Janizaries, or by a clamorous and infuriated mob, in St. Petersburg by a number of confederated nobles; and in all these cases was regarded as a sort of necessary appendage to the existing constitution.

Rostoptchin, the minister, who had long possessed the emperor's confidence, was dismissed and in disgrace; and Count Pahlen, who was at the head of the emperor's dreadful police, was suddenly and excessively favoured. He, too, observed, when he had reached the highest pinnacle, that he began to be suspected. The count was an Esthonian by birth, a man of a cold, deep, and faithless disposition, and the instrument of all the cruelties and severities which had been exercised by the emperor. He was also commander-in-chief of all the troops in the capital, and since the 10th of March had become a member of the ministry for foreign affairs. Up to this period he had been successful in discovering and frustrating all the real or pretended attempts at dethroning the emperor, but he now formed a conspiracy against him, because he knew that Paul had called to his aid two formidable assistants, to use them against himself in case of necessity. The emperor had previously sent away from St. Petersburg and now recalled Lindner and Araktcheiev, two of his most dreadful instruments of violence, the latter of whom played a fearful part in Russia even during the reign of the mild and clement emperor Alexander. Pahlen had previously taken his measures in such a manner that a number of those to whom the murder of an emperor was no novelty were at that time collected in St. Petersburg, and only waited for a hint, either with or without Pahlen, to fall upon the emperor, who had personally given them mortal offence.

Valerian, Nicholas, and Plato Zubov had first been publicly affronted by the emperor like the Orlovs, and afterwards dismissed; they remained under compulsory absence in Germany till they found a medium for securing the favour of the only person who had any influence over the emperor. This medium was the French actress, Chevalier, who ruled the Turk Kutaisov (formerly a *valet de chambre*, but now adorned with all possible titles, honours, and orders, with the broad ribbon and stars of Europe), and through him ruled the emperor. Chevalier obtained permission for the Zubovs to return to the court, and Plato held Kutaisov bound by his expressed intention of marrying the Turk's daughter. Plato had been previously commander-in-chief of the army, and could, in case of need, reckon upon it with the greater certainty, as it had been made discontented by the gross and ridiculous treatment of the generals of the whole army, and even of such a man as Suvarov.

Participators in a plan for setting aside the emperor were easily found among the nobles, as soon as it became certain that there was nothing to fear. It was necessary, however, to obtain the consent of the two eldest grand dukes; but not a word was said of the murder, but merely of the removal of their father from the government. Alexander was not easily prevailed upon to acquiesce in the deposition of his father, as, however numerous Alexander's failings in other respects may have been, both he and his mother were persons of gentle hearts. Pahlen undertook the business of persuading the prince, for which he was by far the best fitted, inasmuch as he knew all the secrets of the court, and combined all power in himself; he therefore succeeded in convincing the imperial family of the dangers with which they themselves were threatened, and of the necessity of deposing the emperor. He appears to have prevailed with Alexander by showing that he could only guard against a greater evil by consenting to his father's dethronement. Certain it is at least, that Alexander signed the proclamation, announcing his own assumption of the reins of government, two hours before the execution of the deed by the conspirators.

The emperor with his family lived in the Mikhailov palace; the 23rd of March, 1801, was chosen for the accomplishment of the deed, for on that day the Semenovski battalion of guards was on duty at the palace. The most distinguished men among the conspirators were the Zubov, General Count Benningsen, a Hanoverian, who had distinguished himself in the Polish wars under Catherine, Tchitchakov, Tartarinov, Tolstoi, Iashvel, Iesselovitch, and Uvarov, together with Count Pahlen himself, who did not accompany the others into the emperor's bed-chamber, but had taken his measures so skilfully that, if the enterprise failed, he might appear as his deliverer. Very shortly before the execution of the deed, Pahlen communicated the design to General Talitzin, colonel of the regiment of Preobrajénski guards, to General Deporade-vitch, colonel of the Semonovski guards, together with some fifty other officers whom he entertained on the night on which the murder was committed.

On the evening before his death Paul received, when sitting at supper with his mistress, a note from Prince Mechereki, warning him of his danger, and revealing the names of the conspirators. He handed it unopened to Kutaisov, saying he would read it on the morrow. Kutaisov put it in his pocket, and left it there when he changed his dress next day to dine with the emperor. He turned to get it, but Paul growing impatient sent for him in a hurry, and the trembling courtier came back without the letter on which so much depended. On the night of the 3rd Paul went early to bed; soon afterwards the conspirators repaired to his apartment, the outer door of which was opened to them in compliance with the demand of Argamakov, an aide-de-camp, who pretended that he was come to make his report to the emperor. A Cossack who guarded the door of the bedroom offered resistance and was cut down. The conspirators rushed in and found the bed empty. "He has escaped us," cried some of them. "That he has not," said Benningsen. "No weakness, or I will put you all to death." Putting his hand on the bed-clothes and feeling them warm, he observed that the emperor could not be far off, and presently he discovered him crouching behind a screen. The conspirators required him to sign his abdication. He refused, a conflict ensued; a sash was passed round his neck, and he was strangled after a desperate resistance.

Alexander was seized with the most passionate grief when he learned at what a price he had acquired the crown. He had supped with his father at nine o'clock, and at eleven he took possession of the empire, by a document which had been drawn up and signed two hours and a half previously. The most dreadful thing of all, however, was that he was obliged not only to suffer the two chief conspirators, Zubov and Pahlen, to remain about his person, but to allow them to share the administration of the empire between them. It was a piece of good fortune that those two thoroughly wicked men were of very different views, by which means he was first enabled to remove Pahlen, and afterwards Zubov also. Their associates, however, remained, and at a later period we shall find Count Benningsen at the head of the army which was to deliver Prussia after the battle of Jena.

Paul was twice married: by his first wife, Nathalie Alexeievna, princess of Hesse Darmstadt, who died in 1776, he had no family; by his second, Marie Feodorovna, princess of Würtemberg, who died in 1828, he had ten children, the eldest of whom, Alexander by name, now succeeded to the imperial throne.

## THE ACCESSION OF ALEXANDER I (1801 A.D.); HIS EARLY REFORMS

The accession of Alexander was hailed with sincere and universal delight, not only as an escape from the wretched and extravagant reign of Paul, but as the opening fulfilment of the expectations which had long been anxiously fixed on his heir. The new monarch was twenty-five years of age, of majestic figure and noble countenance, though his features were not perfectly regular. He possessed an acute mind, a generous heart, and a most winning grace of manner. "Still," says M. Thiers, "there might be discerned in him traces of hereditary infirmity. His mind, lively, changeable, and susceptible, was continually impressed with the most contrary ideas. But this remarkable prince was not always led away by such momentary impulses; he united with his extensive and versatile comprehension a profound secretiveness which baffled the closest observation. He was well-meaning, and a dissembler at the same time." Napoleon said of him at St. Helena, "The emperor of Russia possesses abilities, grace, and information; he is fascinating, but one cannot trust him; he is a true Greek of the Lower Empire; he is, or pretends to be, a metaphysician; his faults are those of his education, or of his preceptor. What discussions have I not had with him! He maintained that hereditary right was an abuse, and I had to expend all my eloquence and logic during a full hour to prove that hereditary right maintains the repose and happiness of nations. Perhaps he wished to mystify me; for he is cunning, false, and skilful."

In the beginning of Alexander's reign reform succeeded reform, and all Europe applauded. He quickly put a stop to the system of terror and to the absurd vexations which Paul had introduced. He disgraced the instruments who had worked out the will of that poor maniac; he repaired the crying injustice which had been committed; he once more abolished the terrible secret inquisition, but, as we already said, it was again established by his successor. He instituted a permanent council, and contemplated the complete reorganisation of the administration of the interior. He relaxed the rigour of the censorship of the press, and granted permission to introduce foreign works. He reduced the taxes and the expenditure of the court; and in the first year of his reign he abstained from exacting the recruits for his army, an exaction odious to those whom it affects, and therefore often accompanied with fearful violences.

He applied himself most diligently to affairs, and laboured almost as much as his grandmother, who had devoted three hours to the concerns of the state when her ministers came to confer with her. He required detailed reports from all the higher officers of state; and having examined them, caused them to be published, a thing never before heard of in Russia. He abolished punishment by torture; forbade the confiscation of hereditary property; solemnly declared that he would not endure the habit of making grants of peasants, a practice till then common with the autocrats, and forbade the announcement in public journals of sales of human beings. He applied himself to the reform of the tribunals; established pecuniary fines for magistrates convicted of evading or violating their duties; constituted the senate a high court of justice, and divided it into seven departments in order to provide against the slowness of law proceedings; and re-established the commission which had been appointed by Catherine for the compilation of a code. He applied himself to the protection of commerce; made regulations for the benefit of navigation, and extended and improved the communication in the interior of his empire. He did much to promote general education, and established several new universities with large numbers of subsidiary schools. He permitted every subject of his empire to choose his own avocation in life, regardless of restraints formerly imposed with respect to rank, and removed the prohibition on foreign travel which had been enacted in the last reign. He permitted his nobles to sell to their serfs, along with their personal freedom, portions of land which should thus become the *bona fide* property of the serf purchaser — a measure by which he fondly hoped to lay the basis of a class of free cultivators. It was under his auspices that his mother, Marie Feodorovna, founded many hospitals and educational institutes, both for nobles and burghers, which will immortalise her name.

One of the first acts of Alexander's reign was to give orders that the British sailors who had been taken from the ships laid under sequestration, and marched into the interior, should be set at liberty and carefully conducted at the public expense to the ports from which they had been severally taken. At the same time all prohibitions against the export of corn were removed — a measure of no small importance to the famishing population of the British Isles, and hardly less material to the gorged proprietors of Russian produce. The young emperor shortly after wrote a letter with his own hand to the king of England, expressing in the warmest terms his desire to re-establish the amicable relations of the two empires; a declaration which was received with no less joy in London than in St. Petersburg. The British cabinet immediately sent Lord St. Helens to the Russian capital, and on the 17th of June a treaty was concluded, which limited and defined the right of search, and which Napoleon denounced as "an ignominious treaty, equivalent to an admission of the sovereignty of the seas in the British parliament, and the slavery of all other states." In the same year (October 4–8) Alexander also concluded treaties of peace with France and Spain; for between Russia and the former power there had previously existed only a cessation of hostilities, without any written convention.

### THE INCORPORATION OF GEORGIA

The incorporation of Georgia with the empire, an event long prepared by the insidious means habitually employed by Russia, was consummated in this year. The people of Georgia have always had a high reputation for valour, but at the end of the seventeenth century they suffered immensely from the Tatars and the Lesghians. Russia supported Georgia, not sufficiently indeed to prevent the enemy from destroying Tiflis, but quite enough to prove to the country that, once under the Russian rule, it would be safe from the Mussulmans. Alexander's manifesto of the 12th of September, 1801, says that he accepts the weight of the Georgian throne, not for the sake of extending the empire, already so large, but only from humanity! Even in Russia very few

[1803 A.D.]

could believe that the Georgians surrendered themselves to the czar from a spontaneous acknowledgment of the superiority of the Russian rule, and of its ability to make the people happy; to disabuse themselves of any such notion, they had but to look at the queen of Georgia, Maria, who was detained at St. Petersburg, in the Tauric palace — a name that might well remind her of the treacherous acquisition of another kingdom.  She rode through the streets in one of the court carriages, and her features expressed great affliction. The covering which she wore on her head, as usual in Georgia, prevented the people from seeing the scars of the sabre wounds she had received before she quitted the country.  Her consort, George XIII, had bequeathed the kingdom to the Russians, but she protested against the act; and when the Russian colonel Lazarev came to carry her away to St. Petersburg, she refused to go with him.  He was about to use violence, but the queen took out a poniard from her bosom and stabbed him.  The interpreter drew his sabre and gave her several cuts on the head, so that she fell down insensible.

ALEXANDER I
(1777–1825)

### RUSSIA JOINS THE THIRD COALITION

Concurrently with his domestic reforms, Alexander occupied himself in an extensive series of negotiations, having for their object the general settlement of Europe upon such new bases as the results of the last war had rendered necessary.  In particular, he was engaged as joint arbiter with Bonaparte in the matter of the indemnifications to be made to those princes who had lost a part or the whole of their possessions by the cession of the left bank of the Rhine. Alexander was secretly dissatisfied with the part he was made to play in these transactions, for the authority which he shared in appearance with Bonaparte, was in reality monopolised by the latter.  He abstained, however, from remonstrating, contenting himself for the present with the outward show of respect paid to his empire, and with a precedent which, added to that of Teschen, established in future the right of Russia to mix itself up in the affairs of Germany.  The Peace of Amiens between France and England was broken, and a war was declared on the 18th of May, 1803, between the two powers, which was ultimately to involve the whole of Europe.  Meanwhile, many cases were arising to increase Alexander's displeasure against Bonaparte.

The relations between Russia and France were at this time of such a nature that the Russian chancellor, Vorontzov, said plainly, in a note of the 18th of July, that if the war were to be prolonged between France and England, Russia would be compelled finally to take part in it.  Before this declaration on the part of Russia, Bonaparte had a scene with Markov, which alone might well have caused a rupture.  He addressed the Russian ambassador, in a public audience, so rudely and violently that even Bignon, who is disposed to worship Bonaparte as a demi-god, is obliged to confess that his hero entirely lost his dignity, and forgot his position.

When Markov withdrew in November, he left his secretary of legation, D'Oubril, as acting ambassador in his place. Everyone, however, foresaw a breach at no very distant period; and Russia had already, in the autumn of 1803, when nothing was to be done with Prussia, entered into a closer connection with England. Negotiations were also commenced with Austria, and a union with Sweden and Denmark, for the purpose of liberating Hanover, was spoken of. This was the state of affairs at the beginning of 1804: the murder of the duke d'Enghien brought matters to a crisis. The mother of the Russian emperor had been all along hostile to everything proceeding from Bonaparte; and the mild and gentle spirit of the emperor, like that of all persons of good feeling in Europe, was deeply wounded by the fate of the duke. From the beginning of 1804, he had no further political reasons for keeping up a friendly relation with France; he therefore gave himself up entirely to his natural feelings on hearing of the catastrophe at Vincennes.

By the declarations interchanged between the courts of St. Petersburg and Berlin (May 3rd and 24th, 1805), it was agreed that they should not allow the French troops in Germany to go beyond the frontier of Hanover; and that should this happen, each of the two powers should employ 40,000 men to repel such an attempt. A convention was also signed between Russia and Austria before the end of the year, and they agreed to set on foot an army of 350,000 men. England, under the administration of William Pitt, added her strength to these combinations, and united the several powers in a third coalition for the purpose of wresting from France the countries subdued by it since 1792, reducing that kingdom within its ancient limits, and finally introducing into Europe a general system of public right. The plan was the same as that which ten years afterwards was executed by the Grand Alliance; it failed in 1805, because the participation of Prussia, on which the allies had reckoned, was, from the most ignoble motives withheld.

The negotiations of the several treaties connected with the coalition, occupied the greater part of the year 1805. By the Treaty of St. Petersburg (August 11th), between Great Britain and Russia, it was agreed that Alexander should make another attempt for arranging matters with Bonaparte, so as to prevent the war. The Russian minister Novosiltzov was sent to Paris by way of Berlin, where he received the passports procured for him from the French cabinet by that of Prussia; but at the same time, orders reached him from St. Petersburg, countermanding his journey. The annexation of the Ligurian Republic to France, at the moment when the allies were making conciliatory overtures to Napoleon, appeared to the emperor too serious an outrage to allow of his prosecuting further negotiations. War was consequently resolved on.

### THE CAMPAIGN OF AUSTERLITZ (1805 A.D.)

Napoleon seemed to be wholly intent on his design of invading England. Part of his troops had already embarked (August 27th), when on a sudden the camp of Boulogne was broken up, and the army put in march towards the Rhine, which river it passed within a month after. Austria had set on foot three armies. The archduke Charles commanded that of Italy; his brother John was stationed with the second army on the Tyrol; and the third was commanded nominally by the archduke Frederick, the emperor's cousin, but in reality by General Mack. The first Russian army under Kutusov had arrived in Galicia, and was continuing its march in all haste. It was followed by another under Michelson. The Russian troops in Dalmatia were to attempt a landing in Italy.

Mack having crossed the Inn (September 8th), and entered Swabia, Napoleon's plan was to cut him off from the army of Kutusov, which was marching through Austria. In this he succeeded by a violation of the Prussian territory. Marmont, who had marched by way of Mainz, and Bernadotte, who had conducted an army into Franconia, where they were joined by the Bavarians, traversed the country of Anspach, and thus came on the rear of the Austrian army (October 6th). From that date, scarcely a day passed without a battle favourable to the French. Several Austrian divisions were forced to lay down their arms. Mack, who had thrown himself into Ulm, lost all resolution, and capitulated with 25,000 men (October 19th). Mack's army was thus totally dissipated, except 6000 cavalry, with which the archduke Ferdinand had opened himself a passage through Franconia, and 20,000 men, with whom Kienmayer had retired to Braunau, where he was met by the vanguard of Kutusov. The two generals continued their retreat. The Russians repassed the Danube near Grein (November 9th), and directed their march towards Moravia. A few days after (November 13th), Vienna fell into the hands of the French. The Austrians had renounced the design of defending their capital, but decided that the passage of the river should be disputed.

Vienna is situated at some distance from the Danube, which flows to the right of the city between wooded islands. The Austrians had placed explosive materials under the floorings of the wooden bridge which crosses the several arms of the river, and were ready to blow it up the moment the French should show themselves. They kept themselves in readiness on the left bank, with their artillery pointed, and a corps of 7000 or 8000 men, commanded by Count Auersberg. The French, nevertheless, got possession of the bridge by stratagem. Murat, Lannes, Belliard, and their staff, leaving their troops behind them, crossed the bridge, told the Austrians that an armistice was agreed on, and asked to see their general. He was sent for. Meanwhile, the French officers kept the Austrian gunners in conversation, and gave time for a column of French grenadiers to come up unseen, under cover of the woods, seize the cannon, and disarm the artillerymen. The Austrian commander who had come to the spot just at the critical moment, fell completely into the trap. He himself led the French column over the bridge, and ordered the Austrian troops to be drawn up on parade to receive them as friends. The possession of the bridge afforded the French troops the means of reaching Znaim sooner than Kutusov, and thus preventing his junction with Buxhövden.

Meanwhile, Alexander had gone to Berlin, to exert his personal influence over the timorous king, and prevail on him to abandon his wretched neutral policy, in which there was neither honour, honesty, nor safety. Alexander was warmly seconded by the beautiful queen of Prussia, and by the archduke Anthony, who arrived at the same time on a special mission from Vienna. French influence rapidly declined in Berlin; Duroc left it on the 2nd of November, without having been able to obtain an audience, for some days previously, either from the king or the emperor; and on the following day a secret convention was signed between the two monarchs for the regulation of the affairs of Europe, and the erection of a barrier against the ambition of the French emperor.

The Prussian minister Haugwitz, who had signed this convention only to gain time, and with a secret determination to elude its provisions, was to be entrusted with the notification of it to Napoleon, with authority, in case of its acceptance, to offer a renewal of the former friendship and alliance of the

Prussian nation; but in case of refusal, to declare war, with an intimation that hostilities would begin on the 15th of December — when they would be too late. Before that day came, Prussia relapsed into her old temporising habits; her armies made no forward movement towards the Danube, and Napoleon was permitted to continue without interruption his advance to Vienna, while 80,000 disciplined veterans remained inactive in Silesia; a force amply sufficient to have thrown him back with disgrace and disaster to the Rhine.

A characteristic scene took place at Potsdam during Alexander's visit. The king, the queen, and the emperor went one night by torchlight into the vault where lay the coffin of Frederick the Great. They knelt before it. Alexander's face was bathed in tears; he pressed his friend's hands, he clasped him in his arms, and together they swore eternal amity: never would they separate their cause or their fortunes. Tilsit soon showed what was the value of this oath, which probably was sincere for the moment when it was taken.

During the retreat of the Austrians and Russians under Kienmayer and Kutusov from Passau to Krems, the imprudence of Mortier, who had crossed to the left bank of the Danube at Linz, gave occasion to engagements at Stein and Dirnstein, in which the French lost more men than they ever acknowledged. Mortier's army of 30,000 men consisted of three divisions, under Generals Gazan, Dupont, and Dumonceau. This army had positive orders to keep always near to the main body, which was pursuing its march along the right bank, and never to advance beyond it. Kutusov had long retreated on the right bank; but on the 9th of November he crossed to the left at Grein, as before mentioned, and lay in the neighbourhood of Krems, when Mortier's troops advanced. The French divisions maintained the distance of a whole day's march one from another, because they thought they were following a fleeing army; but between Dirnstein and Stein they fell in with the whole Russian army, 20,000 strong, at a place where the French were obliged to pass through a frightful ravine. On the 11th of November, Mortier ventured to make an attack with Gazan's division alone; but near Dirnstein (twenty hours from Vienna), he got into a narrow way, enclosed on both sides by a line of lofty walls, and there suffered a dreadful loss. When the French, about noon, at length supposed themselves to have gained some advantage, the Russians received reinforcements, outflanked the French, cut them off, and would have annihilated the whole division, had not Dupont's come up at the decisive moment. The latter division had also suffered severely on the same day. Whilst Kutusov was sharply engaged with Mortier, whose numbers were being rapidly diminished, and his cannon taken, the Austrian general Schmidt attacked Dupont at Stein, where the contest was as murderous as at Dirnstein, till Schmidt fell, and the French forced their way out.

Kutusov, on his march to Znaim, was overtaken by the van of the French, under Belliard, near Hollabrunn; and everything depended on detaining the latter so long as might enable Kutusov to gain time for getting in advance. For this purpose, Bagration, with about six thousand men, took up a position in the rear of the main body. Nostitz served under Bagration, and had some thousand Austrians and a number of Russians under his immediate command. He occupied the village of Schöngraben, in the rear of the Russians, and in the very centre of their line of march. Belliard ought to have attacked him first; but as his corps was not superior in number to that of Bagration, he had again recourse to the expedient which he had already tried, with such signal success, at the bridge of Vienna. He entered into a parley; declared that peace with Austria was already concluded, or as good as concluded;

assured them that hostilities henceforth affected the Russians alone; and by such means induced Nostitz to be guilty of a piece of treachery unparalleled in war. Nostitz, with his Austrians, forsook the Russians, even those whom he had under his own command; and they being unable to maintain the village of Schöngraben, it was taken possession of without a shot; and Bagration and Kutusov seemed lost, for Murat's whole army was advancing upon them.

In the meantime the Russians at Hollabrunn extricated themselves from their difficulty; for they were not so stupidly credulous as the Austrians, but knew how to deceive the Gascons, by whom they were pursued, as Belliard had deceived the Austrians. For this purpose, they availed themselves of the presence in Kutusov's camp of Count von Winzingerode, the adjutant-general of the emperor of Russia, who had been employed in all the last diplomatic military negotiations in Berlin. Murat having sent his adjutant to call upon Kutusov, whose line of march had come into the power of the enemy, in consequence of Nostitz's treachery in capitulating, the Russian general assumed the appearance of being desirous to negotiate, and Winzingerode betook himself to the French camp. Belliard and Murat, without taking the trouble to inquire what powers the count and Kutusov had to conclude a treaty which should be generally binding, came to an agreement with Winzingerode, by virtue of which all the Russians, within a certain number of days, were to evacuate every part of the Austrian territory. This capitulation was to be sent to the emperor Napoleon, at Schönbrunn, for confirmation; and to this condition there was necessarily attached another, for the sake of which Kutusov had commenced the whole affair. There was to be a suspension of hostilities till the arrival of Napoleon's answer; and it was agreed that in the meantime both parties should remain in their then positions.

Bagration, with seven or eight thousand Russians, complied with this condition, and remained in his position at Hollabrunn, because he could be observed by the French; but Kutusov, with all the rest of the army, which lay at a greater distance, quietly continued his route to Znaim; and this, with a full knowledge of the danger of Bagration being afterwards overwhelmed by a superior force. On being made acquainted with the capitulation, Napoleon was enraged, for he immediately perceived how grievously his brother-in-law had suffered himself to be deceived; and he ordered an immediate attack. This was indeed made; but eighteen hours had been irreparably lost, and Kutusov gained two marches on Murat; the whole French army, above thirty thousand strong, therefore fell upon Bagration.

Bagration, who had still with him the Austrian regiment of hussars of the crown-prince of Homburg, commanded by Baron von Mohr, offered a vigorous resistance to the whole French army with his seven or eight thousand men. The Russian bombs set fire to the village in which was stationed the corps which was to fall upon Bagration's flank; the consequence was, that this corps was thrown into confusion, and the Russians opened up a way for themselves at the point of the bayonet. The Russian general, it is true, was obliged to leave his cannon in the hands of his enemy, and lost the half of his force; it must, however, always be regarded as one of the most glorious deeds of the whole campaign, that, after three days' continued fighting, he succeeded in joining the main body under Kutusov, at his headquarters at Wischau, between Brünn and Olmütz, and, to the astonishment of all, with one-half of his little army. Even the French admit that the Russians behaved nobly, that they themselves lost a great number of men, and that, among others, Oudinot was severely wounded.

On the same day on which Bagration arrived in Wischau, a junction had been formed by Buxhövden's army, with which the emperor Alexander was present, with the troops under Kutusov, who thenceforward assumed the chief command of the whole.   Napoleon himself came to Brünn, and collected his whole army around him, well knowing that nothing but a decisive engagement could bring him safely out of the situation in which he then was, and which was the more dangerous the more splendid and victorious it outwardly appeared to be.   It is beyond a doubt that the precipitation and haughtiness of the Russians, who were eager for a decisive engagement, combined with the miserable policy of the Prussian cabinet and the cowardice of the king, as well as the fears and irresolution of the poor emperor Francis, and the want of spirit among his advisers, contributed more to the success of Napoleon's plans respecting Prussia, Germany, and Italy, than his victories in the field.

A glance at the situation of affairs at the time of the battle of Austerlitz will show at once how easily he might have been stopped in his career.   There was nothing Napoleon feared more than that the Russians should march either to Hungary or to Upper Silesia, and avoid a decisive engagement; he therefore took means to ascertain the characters and views of the personal attendants and advisers of the emperor Alexander; and when he had learned that young men of foolhardy dispositions had the preponderance in his councils, he formed his plans accordingly.   He first advanced from Brünn to Wischau, and afterwards retired again into the neighbourhood of Brünn, as if afraid to venture upon an attack.   The emperor of Germany, as well as Napoleon, appeared seriously desirous of a peace; but the former was obliged to propose conditions which the latter could not possibly accept; and Napoleon wished first completely to set the emperor Francis free from the Russians, his allies, and from Prussia, before he came to an agreement with him.   As Count Stadion, who came to the headquarters of the French on the 27th of November, with Giulay, as ambassadors to treat for peace, was a sworn enemy of Napoleon, and remained so till 1813, and had, moreover, been very instrumental in founding the whole coalition, and in maturing their plans, his appearance on this occasion was of itself no good omen for the favourable issue of the mission.

The proposals made as the basis of a peace were the same as had been contemplated in the event of a victory on the part of the allies — the French were to evacuate Germany and Italy.   When Napoleon sent Savary (afterwards duke of Rovigo), the head of his gendarmerie police, under pretence of complimenting the emperor Alexander, it was indisputably a great part of this envoy's object, as appears from the 30th bulletin, to make himself thoroughly acquainted with the prevailing opinions and the leading characters during the three days of his sojourn in the emperor's camp.   Savary was very well received, and sent away with every courtly attention by Alexander; but it was intimated that it was intended to make common cause with Prussia, and that it was expected that Novosiltzov, whom the emperor Alexander wished to send to Napoleon, would meet Haugwitz in Brünn.   The hint was sufficient to induce Savary to decline the company of Novosiltzov.

When Savary informed the emperor of the illusion of the Russian generals, and of their belief that fears were entertained of the Russians, and that on this account embassies were sent to seek for peace — Napoleon very cunningly took care to strengthen the fools in their folly.   Savary was sent again to the enemy's camp to propose an interview between Napoleon and the emperor of Russia.   The interview was declined; but Prince Dolgoruki was sent to propose conditions to Napoleon.   The latter did not allow him to come into his camp, but received him at the outposts.

If it be asked why the Russians, with whom there were only some twenty thousand Austrians, did not wait for their third army, under Bennigsen, or reduce Bonaparte to the greatest perplexity, by taking up a strong position in Hungary or Upper Silesia, or remaining quietly upon the heights of Pratzen, the reply is, that the whole system of supplies was bad, and that want had reached so great a pitch, that it would have been impossible for them to remain. Certain it is that they suffered themselves to be drawn down from the heights, and away from Austerlitz, near Brünn, where the talents of their generals were unable to devise any plan of battle which Napoleon could not immediately oversee; it would have been otherwise in the mountains. The French allege, that Napoleon had long before fixed upon the very place in which the Russians offered him battle at Austerlitz, on the 2nd of December, as his battle-field, and laid all his plans accordingly. The possession of the heights of Pratzen was regarded by those skilled in strategy as the key of this battle-field. The Russians were in full possession of these heights, with all their force, on the 1st of December; on the 2nd they descended from them, when Bonaparte drew back one of the wings of his army. He had long calculated on gaining the victory by the possession of these heights, and thus rendering the retreat of the Russians impossible. He did not, therefore, fail, in the very opening of the battle, to seize upon them.

A column of the third Russian army, under Bennigsen, commanded by Michelson, just arrived at the decisive moment when Napoleon had also called to his aid Bernadotte's corps, and when the Bavarians were on their march from Budweis to Moravia; but none of their leaders could lay any claim to the reputation of a commander of genius. Napoleon's proclamation to his army shows his full confidence in his own superiority, as well as in that of his generals and soldiers; and this confidence was fully realised on the bloody field of Austerlitz on the 2nd of December.

### THE CAMPAIGN OF EYLAU AND FRIEDLAND (1806–1807 A.D.)

After the defeat at Austerlitz the emperor made an attempt, whether sincere or not is uncertain, for a reconciliation with Napoleon. He sent D'Oubril to Paris, who, after a negotiation of ten days, concluded a treaty with the French plenipotentiary, General Clarke (July 20th, 1806). But Alexander refused to ratify the treaty, upon the very questionable allegation that his ambassador had exceeded his powers.

Prussia now suffered the just consequences of her policy. Disappointed in her hopes of acquiring Hanover, the reward for which she crouched to Napoleon, she imprudently provoked him to war without waiting for the arrival of the aid due to her by Russia. The campaign was decided in one day by the two terrific defeats of Jena and Auerstadt (October 14th, 1806). Prussia was hopelessly ruined before the Russian armies, ninety thousand strong, under Bennigsen and Buxhövden, could arrive to save her. The Russians entered Prussia in November, and on the 26th of December the battle of Pultusk was fought with great obstinacy and loss of blood on both sides. The French spent the whole of a December night without covering; rain and snow fell incessantly; they waded up to their knees in marshes, spent twelve hours in making an advance of eight miles, and were obliged to pay dearly for their passage over the Narev. During the battle, Marshal Lannes and other generals were several times obliged to put themselves at the head of single regiments and battalions, and yet no decisive advantage was gained. The French, indeed, boasted of the victory; because the Russians, after having maintained their ground on a part of the field, retreated the next day.

If the victory at Pultusk, of which Bennigsen boasted, and on account of which he was afterwards rewarded by his emperor, and appointed commander-in-chief, was very doubtful, on the other hand, Prince Galitzin completely defeated the French at Golymin, on the very day on which they were to attack Buxhövden, at Ostrolenka. This victory, too, was the more glorious, inasmuch as the Russians were less numerous than their opponents. The French, however, had not been able to bring up their artillery; and the superiority of the Russians in this particular decided the event. The weather and the time of the year rendered active operations impossible for some weeks. Bennigsen retired to Ostrolenka, and afterwards still farther; whilst the French, under Ney and Bernadotte, were scattered in the country on the farther side of the Vistula, in which Ney at length pushed forward as far as Heilsberg.

In January, 1807, Bennigsen and Napoleon came, almost simultaneously, upon the idea of changing the seat of war from the extreme east to the west. In the east, the struggle was afterwards carried on by two particular corps — a Russian, under Essen, and a French, first under Lannes, and then under Savary. This bloody struggle, however, had no influence on the issue of the war. Bennigsen no sooner learned that Ney had scattered his troops widely over the country on the farther side of the Vistula, than he broke up his quarters, and resolved to attack him, before Bernadotte, who was near, could come to his relief; but he was too late. Ney had already retreated when Bennigsen arrived; whether it was as the French allege, because Napoleon, who had seen the danger with which he was threatened, sent him orders to retreat, which arrived on the very day on which he was to be attacked by the Russians, or that General Markov was at first too eager, and Bennigsen afterwards too irresolute. Ney luckily marched from Heilsberg, nearer to the Vistula, and Bennigsen followed him hesitatingly, so that Bernadotte was able to keep him employed for some days till Napoleon came up. On receiving news of Bennigsen's march, the French emperor had sent orders to all his corps to renew the campaign on the 27th, and he had so taken his measures, that before the Russians had any suspicion of an attack, the main army of the French would fall upon their left flank, whilst they were on their march. For this purpose, Bernadotte was to allure Bennigsen quite to the Vistula; and then to advance again as soon as Napoleon had outflanked the left of the Russians.

The despatch containing these orders for Bernadotte fell into the hands of the Russians, through the inexperience of the officer entrusted with it, who failed to destroy the document at the right time. Thus warned of the impending danger, and finding themselves pressed on all sides, they allowed their stores and heavy baggage, at various places, to fall into the hands of the enemy, and thereby escaped being surrounded. After considerable sacrifices, they succeeded, on the 6th of February, in reaching the Prussian town of Eylau, which is only nine hours' distance from Königsberg. Soult attacked their rear, on the low hills behind the town, on the 7th, and drove them in; on the following day a general engagement took place. The honour of the victory is probably due to the Russians, as even Savary admits, who shared in the battle. It is not less certain, however, that the whole advantage accrued to the French, who, indeed, admit that the battle was one of the most dreadful recorded in history. The French accuse Bernadotte of having, by his delay, prevented the victory from being complete; whilst the Russians are just enough to admit that Lestocq, with his Prussians, saved their wing from utter defeat. The number of deaths in the battle, and on the day preceding it, was immense. Great numbers fell, not by the sword, but by cold, want, and excessive exertion. Whole battalions and regiments of the French — as, for example, that of Colonel Sémelé — were literally annihilated. Few prisoners were made, because the whole battle was fought with the bayonet.

The royal family of Prussia was placed in a very melancholy position by the issue of the battle, for they were obliged, in the middle of winter, to flee to Menel, where they found themselves among Russians, of whom their own emperor alleged, that, notwithstanding his despotic power, he was not able to restrain their barbarity, or to put a stop to their rapacity. Here, in the farthest corner of Prussia, they received news every month of the fall of one fortress after another, or of forced contributions levied upon their people.

The French army also retired after the battle of Eylau as well as the Russians. Bennigsen marched towards Königsberg, and although Berthier, on the morning of the 7th, wrote to the empress that they would be in Königsberg with their army on the following day, the French, nevertheless, drew off nearer to the Vistula. Nothing important was undertaken by either party for some months, but vigorous preparations were made for a new struggle; whilst new means were tried to prevent Prussia from taking any energetic measures — that is, from forming a close union with England and Russia. The king hesitated between the bold advice of Hardenberg and his friends, and the unconditional submission to the will of Napoleon, which was recommended by von Zastrov. The Russians were thoroughly dissatisfied with the English, and complained of being very badly supported by them; they suffered want of all kinds, were worse treated in many places in Prussia than the French, and even borrowed 660,000 dollars in coin from the king of Prussia.

Hardenberg, who accompanied his master to Tilsit, succeeded in having a new treaty entered into at Bartenstein between Russia and Prussia. Its principle was the same as that of the agreement made on the 12th of October, of the preceding year, at Grodno, by virtue of which the emperor bound himself to support the cause of the king with all his forces. In this treaty, it was not only promised, just as if they were before Paris, that Prussia should receive back all that had been lost, but it was formally determined what was to be done with the conquests wrested from France, and how even the left bank of the Rhine was to be partitioned among the allies.

About this time Bennigsen was appointed commander-in-chief of the Russian armies; but he is generally accused of incapacity, and fearful descriptions are given of the disorders, fraud, and embezzlement which prevailed, and of the plunder and barbarity which they practised against unfortunate Prussia. The emperor Alexander, as soon as he arrived at the army, did everything in his power to restore order; he was able, however, only to remedy single abuses; even Nicholas, who manifested a degree of severity from which Alexander shrank back, was not able to reach the source of the evil. Towards the end of May, Bennigsen thought his troops already sufficiently reinforced to make an attack upon the French, and drive them across the Vistula; whilst the combined army of English, Swedes, and Prussians, were to make an attack from Pomerania. The French army, lying from Dantzic to the Narev, was brought, before the beginning of June, when the campaign commenced, to 150,000 men, whose pay and sustenance were drawn from the requisitions and contributions imposed on Prussia. In April, 1807, the French senate passed a decree levying 80,000 conscripts, 60,000 of whom were to be immediately sent to the army; and the Poles, too, deceived by the hope of the restoration of their nationality, raised a body of between 25,000 and 30,000 men, among whom were whole regiments recruited by the Polish nobility, or formed exclusively of nobles who volunteered their service, although Napoleon limited all the expectations of the Poles to the country on this side of the Vistula.

As soon as Bennigsen, in the beginning of June, made a serious movement in advance towards the Vistula, a series of murderous engagements began, similar to those which preceded the battle of Eylau; on the 9th, the main body of both armies came in sight of each other at Heilsberg, and on the 10th the French made an attempt to drive the Russians from their position. The united corps of Soult and Lannes, supported by the cavalry under Murat, made repeated attempts to force the Russians to give way; they, however, kept their ground.

Bennigsen afterwards heard, at Wehlau, that the French had separated into two divisions, and he resolved on the 13th, instead of continuing his route on the farther side of the Alle, to wheel about before Wehlau, and attack the French. By this step, as all writers admit, he gave himself into the hands of his great opponent, who never suffered his enemy to commit a fault with impunity. The position taken up by Bennigsen was such as to leave him no alternative between victory and destruction, for he had the Alle in his rear, and a marsh on one flank. Napoleon took advantage of this mistake, as usual; and the orders which he issued before the battle prove that he was sure of the victory. About five o'clock in the evening of the 14th of June, a battery of twenty guns gave the signal for the fight; it was bravely maintained on both sides, and both armies suffered great loss. The French accounts exaggerate the number of the Russians who were led into the battle of Friedland, as well as the number of prisoners: certain it is, however, that seventeen thousand Russians were either killed or wounded.

After the battle of Friedland, there was no longer any account to be taken of the Prussians; and it was a piece of great good fortune that such a sovereign as Alexander reigned in Russia, otherwise Prussia would have been wholly lost. Lestocq, with his Prussians, was obliged hastily to cross the Haff to Memel; and their magazines, considerable stores of powder and ammunition, together with one hundred thousand muskets, which the English had sent by sea to Königsberg, fell, with the town, into the hands of the French. Bennigsen was not very closely pursued on the other side of the Alle; he passed the Niemen on the 19th, and burned down the bridge behind him; immediately afterwards, Bonaparte arrived in Tilsit. Of all the Prussian fortresses, Colberg alone might have been able to maintain itself for some weeks, and Graudenz was saved merely by the peace. The treaty with England, which the Prussian minister signed in London on the 17th of June, and by which £1,000,000 sterling was promised in subsidies, came too late.

Schladen informs us that all those who were about the king of Prussia had so completely lost courage, that Von Hardenberg, Von Stein, Von Schladen himself, and many others who recommended perseverance, found none upon whom they could reckon. With respect to the Russians, he informs us that there was a party who assumed a threatening aspect — that the army was dissatisfied with the war — that the grand duke Constantine behaved often very rudely towards the Prussians, and allowed himself to be used as an instrument for working on the fears of his brother Alexander. On the 7th of June, the emperor manifested a disposition altogether contrary to the agreements and partition-projects of the convention of Bartenstein. He was dissatisfied with England, and perceived that the Austrians had no other object than to fish in troubled water, and he was, therefore, desirous, as much as possible, to withdraw from the whole affair. He proposed a truce for himself, with a clause that the Prussians also should obtain a cessation of hostilities; but the Russians and Prussians were to negotiate each for themselves respecting the conditions. Napoleon having entertained the proposal, Russia agreed, that during the continuance of the truce, the French should retain possession of the whole of Poland, except the circle of Bielostok. The agreement was signed on the 21st, and a four weeks' notice of the renewal of hostilities was reserved. By the terms of the truce granted to Prussia, the French remained in possession of the whole kingdom; and the few fortresses which were not yet reduced were not to be supplied either with new works, ammunition, or provisions. Blücher, who commanded the Prussian auxiliary forces in Pomerania, was to leave the king of Sweden to his fate. The peace was to be negotiated at Tilsit, and for that purpose one half of the town was to be declared neutral.[k]

### Meeting of Alexander and Napoleon at Tilsit (1807 A.D.)

Napoleon desired, as far as means and powers would allow, to give all possible pomp and solemnity to the interview with his mighty adversary. With this object, in the middle of the Niemen, opposite Tilsit, a raft was constructed, on which were two pavilions, covered in white cloth. The one which was destined for the two monarchs was of vaster dimensions and was adorned with all possible luxury; the other and smaller one was for their suites. On the frontals of the pavilions were painted in green, on the Russian side, an enormous A, and on the side turned towards Tilsit an N of equal size. To the annoyance of the Prussians, the monogram of Frederick William III was absent from the decorations of the Niemen raft. The French guards were ranged in lines, fronting the river. "All this army," writes an eye-witness, "awaited the appearance of their invincible leader, their thunder-bearing semi-divinity, in order to greet him at the moment of his swift passage to the wharf." Thousands of the inhabitants of Tilsit and French soldiers covered the high left bank of the Niemen.

The emperors got into the boats simultaneously. When both boats put off, the grandeur of the spectacle, the expectation of an event of world-wide importance took the ascendency over all other feelings. Universal attention was concentrated upon the boat that carried that wonderful man, that leader of armies, the like of whom had never been seen or heard of since the times of Alexander the Great and Julius Cæsar. Napoleon stood on the boat in front of his suite, solitary and silent, his arms folded on his breast as he is represented in pictures. He wore the uniform of the Old Guard and the ribbon of the Legion of Honour across his shoulder, and on his head that little historical hat, the form of which has become famous throughout the world. Reaching the raft somewhat sooner than Alexander, Napoleon rapidly got onto it, and hastened to meet the emperor. The rivals embraced and silently entered the pavilion, accompanied by the joyful acclamations of the troops and the inhabitants, who were witnesses of a world-wide event — the reconciliation of Russia and France. At that moment a large boat put off from the left bank of the Niemen, having on it about twenty armed soldiers — and remained between the raft and the Russian shore. Evidently Napoleon did not hesitate to take open measures of safeguarding against any possible unforeseen occurrences.

That day the king of Prussia did not assist at the interview: Napoleon did not wish to see him, and Frederick William remained on the right bank of the Niemen. "In that fateful hour, whilst the destiny of his monarchy was being decided, his gaze was constantly fixed and his ear directed towards the raft, as though he desired to listen to the conversation between the two emperors. Once he went down to the edge of the river and only stopped when the water was up to his horse's middle." The first interview between Alexander and Napoleon lasted an hour and fifteen minutes. "I detest the English no less than you do," were the first words of the emperor Alexander, "and I am ready to support you in everything that you undertake against them." "If such is the case," answered Napoleon, "then everything can be arranged and peace secured."

Taking advantage of Alexander's inimical disposition towards Great Britain, Napoleon entered upon a terrible philippic against the perfidy of Albion, representing it as a greedy, extortionate nation ever ready to sacrifice everyone, even its most faithful allies, for its own profit. In further conversation Napoleon strove to instil into Alexander that he was victimised by his allies, that he was mistaken in protecting the Germans, those ungrateful and envious neighbours, and in supporting the interests of a set of greedy merchants who showed themselves to be the representatives of England; all this was occasioned, according to him, by a feeling of generosity carried to excess, and by doubts which arose from the incapacity or corruption of ministers. After this Napoleon began to praise the valour and bravery of the Russian troops, with which he had been much struck at Austerlitz, Eylau, and Friedland; he considered that the soldiers on both sides had fought like veritable Titans and was of the opinion that the united armies of Russia and France might dominate the world, and give to it prosperity and tranquillity. Up till now Russia had squandered her forces, without having any recompense in view; by an alliance with France she would acquire glory, and in any case reap substantial advantages. Of course Russia was bound by certain obligations to Prussia, and in that respect it was indispensable that the honour of the emperor Alexander should be carefully guarded. In conclusion Napoleon expressed his intention of restoring to Prussia sufficient territory honourably to rid the emperor of his ally; after that, he affirmed, the Russian cabinet would be in a position to pursue a fresh line of policy similar in everything to that of the great Catherine. Only such a policy, in Napoleon's opinion, could be possible and advantageous for Russia.

Having flattered Alexander as emperor, Napoleon in order to complete the charm proceeded to flatter him as a man. "We shall come to an agreement sooner," said he, "if we enter upon negotiations without intermediaries, setting aside ministers, who frequently deceive or do not understand us; we two together shall advance matters more in a single hour than our intermediaries in several days. Nobody must come between you and me; I will be your secretary and you shall be mine," added Napoleon. Upon this basis he proposed to the emperor Alexander for convenience's sake to transfer the negotiations to Tilsit, declaring the position of the town to be a central one. The emperor gladly accepted Napoleon's invitation, and it was settled that negotiations should at once be entered upon in order to come to a definitive agreement[1] on the matter.g

### RUSSIA DECLARES WAR AGAINST ENGLAND (1807 A.D.)

The English government, alleging that in the secret articles of the treaty of Tilsit, of which they had possessed themselves, they had proof of Napoleon's

[1 For the terms of the treaty, see volume XII.]

design to seize the Danish fleet, fitted out an expedition against Denmark with extraordinary celerity. Copenhagen was bombarded for three days, and a great part of the city destroyed. The Danes then capitulated (September 7), and surrendered their fleet to the English, with all their naval stores in their arsenals and dockyards.

The expedition against Copenhagen was soon followed by a declaration of war on the part of Russia against England. In the manifesto published on this occasion (September 16th), Alexander complained bitterly of the bad faith of England, as manifested especially in the little aid she had afforded to the allies who had taken up arms in a cause in which she was more directly interested than any other power, and in the robber-like act of aggression she had committed against Denmark. He annulled all former conventions between Russia and England, especially that of 1801; proclaimed anew the principle of the armed neutrality; and declared that there should be no communication between the two powers until Denmark had received just compensation, and peace was concluded between France and England. In consequence of this declaration, an embargo was laid on all the English vessels in Russian ports, and Prussia was compelled to follow this example.

## THE CONQUEST OF FINLAND (1807 A.D.)

It was not till the 6th of October that a formal demand was made upon Sweden to close the ports of the Baltic against English ships and trade. The king persevered in his alliance with England; and finally, because the emperor of Russia had conferred upon Napoleon the order of St. Andrew, he sent back his insignia; whereupon Alexander not only returned his Swedish order, but quietly adopted measures to take possession of Finland, whilst the Danes were preparing, in concert with the French, to invade the western provinces of Sweden. Although in the months of November and December, Gustavus repeatedly declined the proposals of the Russians for a union against England, everything went on in Sweden as in times of the most profound peace; and even when the Russian forces were collected on the very frontiers of Finland, the unfortunate king adopted no measures of defence whatever. On the 21st of January he was, for the last time, called upon to declare war against England; he replied by concluding a new alliance with her on the 8th of February. On the 21st, the Russians invaded Finland, without any specific declaration of war, and on the 14th of March, 1808, Denmark declared war against Sweden. The whole of Finland as far as Vasa, the island of Åland, and even the islands of Gotland, Åbo, Sveaborg, and all the fortresses, were taken possession of by the Russians even before the Swedish army and fleet were prepared. It was not till the end of April and beginning of May that a Swedish army under Klingspor and Aldercreutz, supported by a Swedish fleet, appeared in the field, and fought with various success.

We have lately seen Alexander take military possession of the Danubian provinces as a "material guarantee," whilst affecting not to be at war with Turkey. This was in exact conformity with Russian precedents. Finland, as we have said, was occupied without a declaration of war; but manifestoes were issued by General Buxhövden, one of which contained the following passage: "Good neighbours, it is with the greatest regret that my most gracious master, the emperor of all the Russias, sees himself forced to send into your country the troops under my orders. But his majesty the king of Sweden, whilst withdrawing more and more from the happy alliance of the two greatest empires in the world, draws closer his connections with the common enemy, whose oppressive system and unparalleled conduct towards the most intimate allies of Russia and of Sweden herself cannot be coolly endured by his imperial majesty. These motives, as well as the regard which his imperial majesty owes to the safety of his own states, oblige him to place your country under his protection, and to take possession of it in order to procure by these means a sufficient guarantee in case his Swedish majesty should persevere in the resolution not to accept the equitable conditions of peace that have been proposed to him, etc."

When the Russians took possession of Finland, the king gave them a pretence for incorporating it with their empire, which, however, they would no doubt have done in any case. He caused Alopeus, the Russian ambassador, to be arrested. This took place on the 3rd of March, and on the 25th a declaration was published on the part of the emperor of Russia, announcing to all the powers that "from that moment he regards the part of Finland hitherto reputed Swedish, and which his troops had only been able to occupy after divers battles, as a province conquered by his arms, and that he unites it forever to his empire."

It was easy to anticipate that the superior force of the Russians must in the end prevail; although the Russian garrison in Gotland, and that in the island of Åland, were at first taken prisoners, the island occupied, and the Russians beaten by land at Vasa on the 26th of July, and by sea at Roggerwick on the 26th of August. The Swedes lost all the advantages they had thus gained by the bloody battle fought at Ormais on the 14th of September, and by the defeat at Lokalar on the 18th. The Russian generals, probably in order to give courage to the malcontents, who were very numerous in Sweden, issued orders not to receive any letters or any flags of truce which were sent in the king's name, and carried on negotiations with the Swedish generals alone, for a suspension of arms, which was concluded for an indefinite time, on the 20th of September, but only continued till the 27th of October, when the Russians resumed hostilities, and the Swedes were driven to the north, across the Kemistrom. On the 20th of November a new truce was agreed upon between the Swedish general Adlercreutz and the Russian general Kamenskoi, with the reserve of fourteen days' notice before renewal of operations. By the conditions of this agreement the Swedes were to evacute the whole of Uleåborg, and to retire completely behind the Kemistrom, with all their artillery, arms, and stores.

On the 13th of March in the following year a revolution was effected in Sweden, by which Gustavus was deposed; his uncle, the duke of Södermanland, became regent, and was afterwards proclaimed king (June 5, 1809) under the title of Charles XIII. At Stockholm the people flattered themselves that the dethronement of Gustavus would speedily bring peace to Sweden; but it was not so. Alexander refused to treat with a government so insecure as a regency, and hostilities continued. General Knorring who had passed the Gulf of Bothnia on the ice with twenty-five thousand Russians, took possession of the Åland islands, and granted the Swedes a cessation of hostilities, to allow them time to make overtures of peace. Apprised of this arrangement, Barclay de Tolly, who had crossed the gulf with another body of Russians towards Vasa, and taken possession of Umeå, evacuated west Bothnia, and returned to Finland. A third Russian army, under Shuvalov, penetrated into west Bothnia by the Torneå route, and compelled the Swedish army of the north under Gripenberg to lay down their arms (March 25th). This sanguinary affair occurred entirely through ignorance; because in that country, lying under the 66th degree of north latitude, they were not aware of the armistice granted by

Knorring. On the expiry of the truce, hostilities began again in May, and the Russians took possession of the part of west Bothnia lying north of Umeå.

The peace between Russia and Sweden was signed at Frederikshamm on the 17th of September. The latter power adhered to the continental system, reserving to herself the importation of salt and such colonial produce as she could not do without. She surrendered Finland, with the whole of east Bothnia, and a part of west Bothnia lying eastward of the river Torneå. The cession of these provinces, which formed the granary of Sweden and contained a population of 900,000 souls, was an irreparable loss to that kingdom which had only 2,344,000 inhabitants left. In the following year Bernadotte, prince of Ponte Corvo, was elected crown prince of Sweden, and eventual successor to the throne, under the name of Charles John.

The loss of Finland had been but slightly retarded by some advantages gained over the Russian fleet by the combined squadrons of England and Sweden. The Russian vessels remained blockaded on the coast of Esthonia, but in an unassailable position, from which they were at last delivered by the weather and the exigencies of navigation in those dangerous seas. Another Russian fleet under Admiral Siniavin, which sailed to Portugal to co-operate with the French against the English, was obliged to surrender to Admiral Cotton after the convention of Cintra. It was afterwards restored to Russia. The war declared by that power against England in 1807, was little more than nominal, and was marked by no events of importance.

### WAR WITH PERSIA AND WITH TURKEY

The annexation of Georgia to Russia, effected as we have seen, in the beginning of Alexander's reign, drew him into a war with Persia, which did not terminate until 1813. The principal events of that war were the defeat of the Persians at Etchmiadzin by Prince Zitzianov (June 20, 1804): the conquest of the province of Shirvan by the same commander (January, 1806); the taking of Derbent by the Russians (July 3rd); and the defeat of the Persians by Paulucci, at Alkolwalaki (September 1st, 1810).

About 1805 the condition of the Ottoman Empire, badly organised and worse governed, was such that everything presaged its approaching dissolution. Everywhere the sultan's authority was disregarded. Paswan Oglu, pasha of Widdin, was in open revolt. Ali Pasha of Janina was obedient only when it suited his convenience. Djezzar, the pasha of Syria, without declaring himself an enemy to the Porte, enjoyed an absolute independence. The sect of the Wahhabees was in possession of Arabia. After the departure of the English from Egypt, first the beys, and afterwards Muhammed Ali reigned over that country, and only paid their yearly tribute to the sultan when they pleased. In Servia, Czerni George was making himself independent prince of the Slavonians of the Danube. Ipsilanti and Morusi, both Greeks, by the permission, or rather by the command of Russia, were appointed hospodars of Moldavia and Wallachia, for seven years at least, and were therefore rather subjects of the Russians than of the Turks. Selim III, who had reigned since 1789, convinced that the Porte could never re-establish its authority except by better organising the army, had endeavoured to model it on the European system. This attempt afterwards cost him his throne.

The English and Russian ambassadors ruled either alternately or together in Constantinople. But for their interference the old friendship between France and the Porte would most likely have been restored in July, 1802. At the time of the foundation of the empire in France, the sultan hesitated long whether he would lean upon the English and Russian, or upon the French influence, for he felt a great want of confidence in Napoleon, since he had been informed by the English of the language which fell from the emperor in conversation with Lord Whitworth. He was reported to have taken the partition of Turkey for granted — as a thing unavoidable; and that on such partition the province of Egypt ought necessarily to fall to the share of France. This conversation was printed, in 1803, among the documents connected with the renewal of the war between England and France, and was communicated to the sultan. The French, indeed, in their official journals, contradicted the allegation; but who ever put any faith in their official journals?

On this ground we must explain the fact that the Turks favoured the Russians in the war which they were carrying on with the Persians; suffered them to sail up the Rion (ancient Phasis), and even to build a fort at its mouth. They were even desirous of renewing the friendly alliance formed with Russia in 1798, which renewal, indeed, the emperor of Russia was afterwards unwilling to confirm, because the English had taken care to have the inviolability of the Turkish Empire incorporated in the treaty of 1798. Had, therefore, the emperor of Russia ratified the alliance, he would have guaranteed to the Turks the actual condition of their empire in Europe, which he did not wish to do. This excited the suspicion of the Turks, who inclined more and more towards the French, and did not suffer themselves to be frightened by the threats of the English and Russians. Immediately after the Peace of Presburg, the Turks, who had previously acknowledged Napoleon's empire, sent a new ambassador to Paris. In return, Napoleon sent engineers, officers, artillerymen, workmen, and materials, in order to enable the sultan to improve his army, artillery, and the bulwarks of his empire; whilst, on the other hand, the Russian ambassador, Italinski, and the English ambassador, Arbuthnot, threatened war if the alliance with the French was not relinquished; and Italinski's threats fell with a double weight because a corps of Russians were ready for action on the Bug.

About the time at which Napoleon adopted the resolution of attacking Prussia also, and therefore foresaw a war with Russia, a Turkish army was assembled to take the field against the Russians on the Turkish frontiers, and Napoleon clearly saw how advantageous to him a war between the Russians and the Turks would be. He therefore sent General Sébastiani as ambassador extraordinary to Constantinople. Sébastiani arrived there in August, 1806; and soon gained so great an influence that for some time the Divan was entirely under his direction. At his instance it refused to renew the treaty of alliance with England, which was on the point of expiring; and it dismissed Ipsilanti and Morusi, as creatures of Russia, from their offices. In consequence of the threatening language held by Arbuthnot, the English ambassador, they were reinstated; but when this took place hostilities had already begun. The emperor Alexander had ordered General Michelson to enter Moldavia and Wallachia. The Porte then declared war against Russia (December 30th); but deviating for the first time from a barbarous custom, it allowed Italinski, the Russian minister, to depart unmolested.

A few days afterwards, Arbuthnot quitted Constantinople, after having repeatedly demanded the renewal of the alliance and the expulsion of Sébastiani. On the 19th of February, 1807, an English fleet, commanded by Vice-Admiral Duckworth, forced the passage of the Dardanelles, and appeared before Constantinople. Duckworth demanded of the Divan that the forts of the Dardanelles and the Turkish fleet should be surrended to him; that the Porte should cede Moldavia and Wallachia to Russia, and break off alliance with Napoleon. But instead of profiting by the sudden panic which his appearance had excited, he allowed the Turks time to put themselves in a posture of defence. Encouraged and instructed by Sébastiani, they made their preparations with such energy and success that in the course of eight days the English vice-admiral found that he could not do better than weigh anchor and repass the Dardanelles.

Shortly afterwards Admiral Siniavin appeared in the Archipelago, and incited the Greek islanders to throw off the Turkish yoke; whilst Duckworth sailed to Egypt upon a fruitless expedition in favour of the mameluke beys against Muhammed Ali. Siniavin defeated the Turkish fleet on the 4th of April, captured several ships, and took possession of some islands. The bad condition of his ships, however, compelled him to give up the blockade of the Dardanelles, and to retire, in order to refit, after having another time defeated the Turkish fleet. Meanwhile, Selim had been deposed. His successor, Mustapha IV, declared that he would continue to prosecute the war with England and Russia. But Siniavin, before he retired to refit, met the Turkish fleet off Lemnos, on the 1st of July: the Turks were beaten, lost several ships, and a great many men.

The campaign of the Russians on the Danube, in 1807, was not productive of any decisive result, as General Michelson received orders to detach the third army corps to oppose the French in Poland. Czerni George, the leader of the revolted Servians, took Belgrade, Shabatz, and Nish, penetrated into Bulgaria, where he was reinforced by some Russian troops, and gained divers signal advantages. The war was conducted with more success on the frontiers of the two empires in Asia. The seraskier of Erzerum was entirely defeated by General Gudovitch (June 18); and that victory was the more important, as it prevented the Persians from making a bold diversion in favour of the Turks.

The emperor Alexander had agreed by the public articles of the Treaty of Tilsit (July, 1807) to evacuate Moldavia and Wallachia; but this was only a collusion between the two contracting parties. The Russians not only aimed at the permanent possession of the two provinces, but regarded all the Slavonians of the Danube as allies or subjects of the czar. When the Turks, on the 14th of July, concluded a peace with Czerni George, whereby Servia became in some measure independent — and Czerni George afterwards called himself prince of Servia — a Russian general guaranteed the treaty by his signature, as one of the parties to the agreement. In the following year Radovinikin, a Russian envoy, repaired to Belgrade to establish the new principality; called an assembly of the nobles; drew up a sketch of a constitution for Servia, and tried to organise the administration.

The French general, Guilleminot, was sent to the Turkish camp to negotiate a truce on the terms ostensibly laid down in the Treaty of Tilsit: namely, that the Russians should evacute Moldavia and Wallachia, but that the Turks should not occupy the two provinces until after the conclusion of a definitive peace. But Guilleminot's instructions contained a direct command to use the whole weight of the French influence in favour of the Russians and against the Turks; even one of Napoleon's greatest admirers, although owning occasional republican scruples, admits that their tone was very equivocal. In fact, it very soon became obvious that the whole mission of the general was a mere piece of diplomatic imposture and treachery. A congress was held at Slobozia, in the neighbourhood of Giurgevo, on the 24th of August, 1807, and a truce was signed, which, it was said, was to continue till the 30th of April, 1808. The Russians were to withdraw; the fortresses of Ismail, Braila, and Giurgevo to be given up to the Turks, whose troops, however, were to evacuate Moldavia and Wallachia in thirty-five days. Everything, however, which afterwards took place in consultation between the French and Russians, in reference to Turkey, bore upon a scheme of partition.

The Russians at length, on the 7th of August, had left Cattaro and the other strong places in Dalmatia to the French; their emperor, on the 9th, had ceded all his rights as protector of the republic of the seven united islands to Napoleon, and the latter was busy making preparations thence to extend his operations and his dominion further to the east. Marmont, who administered the province of Dalmatia, received orders to fortify Ragusa more strongly, and to make a report on the best plan to be adopted in case it should be desirable to send an army quickly from Corfu, through Albania, Macedonia, and Thrace. The Russians continued to be quiet observers of all this, and in the mean time made firm their footing in the provinces on the Danube. They made a pretence of the conduct of the Turks on the occupation of Galatz, and their ill-treatment of the inhabitants of Moldavia, for not fulfilling the agreement entered into at Slobozia. The Russian troops, who, according to the terms of the treaty, were already retiring, received contrary orders; and the Turks, again driven out of the two provinces, occupied Galatz anew.

The conduct of the negotiation respecting the division of the Turkish booty, was committed to the chief of Napoleon's secret police, who had been actively engaged in the murder of the duke d'Enghien. He now held a princely rank as the duke of Rovigo, and was sent to St. Petersburg with this and similar commissions. In the Russian capital the emperor Alexander and the duke acted as rivals in the art of dissimulation; the emperor loaded him with civilities of all kinds, as some compensation for the coolness and contempt with which he was at first treated, to a surprising extent, by the empress-mother and the Russian nobility. He was, indeed, soon consoled, for the slaves of the czar were as zealous in showing respect in the presence of their master, as they were gross in their insolence when not under his observation. The accounts which Savary gives us of the political principles of the pious emperor and his chancellor, and their complete agreement with Napoleon's morality and his own, would be quite incredible to us, did he not literally quote their words. Savary's secret report to the emperor Napoleon, partly written in the form of a dialogue, is to be found among the fragments of Napoleon's unprinted correspondence. A contempt for public agreements, and the plunder of Sweden, even before the declaration of war, astonish us less than Romanzov's audacious contempt of the opinion of all Europe; he thought it not worth a moment's consideration; and this was quite in accordance with the language held by his master in speaking on the subject of Turkey. Thibaudeau has given so correct an opinion of both the emperors — of the nature of their consultations — of Savary and Romanzov that we cannot do better than refer the reader to the words of that writer.

Turkey would at that time undoubtedly have been partitioned, had Austria been willing to follow the numerous gentle hints to join the alliance of the emperors, who imagined themselves able to make their will the right and law of all nations; or if Napoleon had not found it inconsistent with his plans to bring on at an unfavourable moment a new war with Austria, which he clearly foresaw in 1808. The Russians, in the mean time, remained, throughout the whole of the year 1808, in quiet possession of the provinces which had been previously evacuated by them, and ruled not only in them, but extended their dominion as far as Belgrade, for the new prince of Servia was likewise under Russian protection. The army under the command of the grand vizir, which lay at Adrianople during the winter of 1807-1808, dwindled, during the continuance of the truce of Slobozia, to a few thousand men, because, according to ancient custom, the janissaries returned to their homes in winter; it again increased, however, in the beginning of summer. Bairaktar's army, which was organised on the new European principle, was computed at from twenty to thirty thousand men; it remained on the Danube till its leader, at length, resolved to put an end to the anarchy prevailing in Constantinople. He deposed Mustapha IV, who supported the faction of the janissaries, and placed his brother, Mahmud, on the throne. Bairaktar perished, however, in an insurrection (November 14th), and Mahmud, too, would have been murdered, had he not been the last scion of the imperial family. But he was compelled entirely to change his ministry, and to resign the government into the hands of those who enjoyed the favour of the ulemas and the janissaries.

During the disturbances in the internal affairs of the Turkish Empire, the foreign relations continued the same as they were in the year 1807, immediately after the truce of Slobozia. When Napoleon's plan of removing the negotiations respecting a peace between the Russians and the Turks to Paris failed of success, he found it advisable, in consequence of an impending war with Austria, to give the Turks into the hands of the Russians. One of the chief causes of the war between France and Austria in 1809 was the close union between the latter power and England in reference to Turkish affairs, which appeared in the co-operation of Lord Paget and Baron von Stürmer, the English and Austrian ambassadors in Constantinople. It was the Austrians who mediated the peace between England and the Porte of the 5th of January, 1809, after the conclusion of which the Turks refused to cede Moldavia and Wallachia to the Russians, at the congress of Jassy, as they had formerly done at Bucharest. This led to a new war, of which we shall have to speak hereafter.

### CONGRESS OF ERFURT (1808 A.D.)

In consequence of the complete stoppage of trade which followed the declaration of war in 1807, Russia suffered much more severely than England, and the Russian magnates, supported by the aversion of the emperor's mother to Napoleon, were very far from showing that good-will to the French which their emperor manifested for Napoleon and his representatives. This was soon experienced by Savary, duke of Rovigo, who, though overloaded with marks of politeness by the emperor, in reality proved unable to make any way at the court of St. Petersburg. Caulaincourt, duke of Vicenza, was afterwards deceived for some years by appearances, and by Alexander's masterly art of dissimulation; but Napoleon soon came to experience in Spain that the personal proofs of friendship exhibited by the emperor were by no means always in accordance with the Russian policy. The emperor Alexander himself, for example, on the urgent request of Caulaincourt, acknowledged Joseph Bonaparte as king of Spain; whilst Strogonov, the Russian ambassador in Madrid, alleged that he had no instructions to that effect, and corresponded with the insurgents. In the same way, Admiral Siniavin, who, on the breaking out of war with England, had taken refuge in Lisbon with nine ships of the line and a frigate, not only refused to render any assistance to Marshal Junot, who was threatened in that city by the English, but even to make a demonstration as if he were prepared to assist him. The manner in which he afterwards capitulated, on the 3rd of September, 1808, to Admiral Cotton, who caused his ships to be taken to England, might indicate a very different disposition, especially as the ten ships were afterwards given back.

There was, indeed, no want of interchange of civilities between the two emperors. Whoever compares the attentions and marks of regard which have been recorded as shown by the one to the other with the secret intrigues which they were at the same moment weaving against each other in Turkey and Spain, and with the open enmity which was shown as early as 1811, will learn from such a comparison what is the real worth of diplomatic and princely friendships. The emperor of Russia made presents to his imperial brother of vessels and ornaments of malachite and other precious stones, which the latter exhibited in the Salon du Prix in the Tuileries, in order to be able to boast of the friendship of the emperor of Russia in presence of the circles of the faubourg St. Germain. Busts of Alexander were manufactured in the imperial porcelain manufactory at Sèvres, and were everywhere to be seen in the palace and rooms of the imperial family. All who had access to the court, or wished to make themselves agreeable to the emperor, found it necessary to purchase these ornaments, and place them conspicuously in their houses. The friendship was so intimate that one of the emperor of Russia's adjutants accompanied the emperor of the French when he went to Bayonne to set aside the whole reigning family of Spain. This adjutant, however, was the same Tchernitchev who was engaged in constantly travelling backwards and forwards between St. Petersburg and Paris, who surrounded Napoleon, in spite of all his police, with a net of Russian espionage, and bribed all the employés who were venal in order to obtain papers. He intrigued with ladies to elicit secrets from them; and finally, in 1812, he even purchased a copy of the plan of operations for the war, when it was too late to change it.

Napoleon knew that Austria was thinking of taking advantage of the general discontent and the secret associations in Germany to frustrate the plans of France and Russia with respect to Poland and Turkey; he was, therefore, very desirous of assuring himself once more of the Russian emperor before his journey to Spain. This design was a cause of great anxiety to the very numerous partisans of the English and Prussian policy at the Russian court, when the question was raised of a conference between the two emperors in Erfurt. Von Schladen, the friend of the minister von Stein, therefore presented a memorial to the emperor of Russia, shortly before his departure to Erfurt on the 7th of September, 1808, in which Alexander was forewarned of all that would take place there. From this it may be seen that the emperor of Russia was continually receiving secret counsel and warning from the enemies of the French, and that he played his part in Erfurt more ably than Napoleon, from whom he separated, as even the French writers report, with all the outward signs of indescribable friendship and esteem, but inwardly full of distrust. Von Schladen says very freely to the emperor, that he had given him the advice laid down in his memorial, "in order that he might see through the sophisms, falsehoods, and deceptions which were prepared for him by Napoleon, and awaited him in Erfurt."

On his way to the congress, the emperor visited the king and queen of Prussia in Königsberg, and arrived on the 26th of September in Weimar, where his brother Constantine had been staying since the 24th. On the 27th Napoleon entered Erfurt, and at one o'clock drove out a distance of several miles from the town to meet the emperor of Russia, who was coming from Weimar. Our modest object does not permit us to incorporate in our prose the poetry of the subsequent festivities, nor in glowing language to extol the skill displayed by the masters of the ceremonies. That splendour enough was exhibited in Erfurt may be sufficiently gathered from the fact that the four vassal-kings of the confederation of the Rhine, thirty-four princes, twenty-four ministers of state, and thirty generals, were by express command to summon up for the occasion everything which imagination could suggest in the way of courtly splendour and extravagance. Talma and the Parisian company of actors had been sent to Erfurt, to act, as Napoleon said, before a pit of kings. Two armchairs were placed for the two emperors, whilst the other rulers sat behind them on common chairs. We know not what truth there was in the story, which was at that time in every mouth, and related in all the French works written for effect, that the emperor Alexander, whilst Talma was being applauded on the stage, played his own part with Napoleon in the pit in quite as masterly a manner. The latter, amidst applause, pronounced the following line:

> The friendship of a great man is a favour of the gods.

when the emperor seized Napoleon's hand, made a profound bow, and feelingly exclaimed: "That I have never more truly felt than at the present moment." The festivities continued from the 27th of September till the 14th of October, and furnished to the Germans the most melancholy spectacle of their princes and nobles conducting themselves publicly, not only as slaves of Napoleon, but even as servants and flatterers of all his generals and courtiers.

In order to flatter the emperor of Russia, Napoleon acted as if he had been influenced by Alexander's application in favour of Prussia; but, in reality, oppressed the king and his subjects afterwards just as before. He profited by Alexander's admiration and friendship to make a show of his pretended willingness to conclude a peace with England. Though he had written three times directly to the king of England, and had always been referred to the minister, he nevertheless prevailed upon Alexander to unite with him in signing another letter addressed to King George. The result was such as might have been foreseen; the object, however, was attained: the letters and answers were printed, and officially commented upon in the journals.

The negotiations were carried on personally in Erfurt between the two emperors themselves, and much was agreed upon which neither the one nor the other intended to observe. A written treaty of alliance was besides concluded by Romanzov and Champagny, which was calculated with a view to a new war with Austria. The substance of the agreement consists in a closer alliance of the two powers against England, and the cession of Moldavia and Wallachia to Russia. Hitherto Napoleon had only been willing to concede this last point on conditions which referred to Silesia. In the fifth article of the Treaty of Erfurt, which was kept strictly secret, the two emperors agreed to conclude a peace with England on condition only that that country should acknowledge Moldavia and Wallachia as a part of the Russian Empire. Then follow several articles on the cession of those Turkish provinces. In the eleventh article it is stated, that further negotiations were to be carried on respecting a further partition. It was agreed, too, that the treaty was to be kept secret for ten years. Buturlin boasts, with reason, that the emperor Alexander in Erfurt, by his Greco-Slavonian arts of deception, gained a victory over the Italo-Gallic talents of Napoleon; and, in fact, the very highest triumph is to outwit the deceiver.

Even as early as this Napoleon is said to have thrown out the idea of a marriage with Catherine Pavlovna, Alexander's sister, which inferred, of course, a previous separation from the empress Josephine. Alexander, on his part, is said to have raised difficulties on the question of religion, and to have referred the matter to his mother, who very speedily had the princess betrothed to Duke Peter of Oldenburg. Moreover, the reception of the duke of Oldenburg into the confederation of the Rhine was one of the results of the meeting in Erfurt.

The war which broke out in April, 1809, between France and Austria, put the sincerity of the Russo-French alliance to a practical test. Russia complied with the letter of her engagements to the one belligerent power by declaring war against the other; but Prince Galitzin, who was to have made a powerful diversion in Galicia, came so late into the field and his movements were so dilatory that it was evident he had no desire to contribute to the success of his sovereign's ally. There was no longer any show of cordiality in the diplomatic intercourse between France and Russia; but both parties found it convenient for the present to dissemble their mutual alienation. By the Treaty of Schönbrunn, signed by vanquished Austria (October 14th, 1809), that power ceded, partly to France and partly to the confederation of the Rhine, several towns in Germany and Italy, with their dependencies; she was despoiled, in favour of the duchy of Warsaw, of all western Galicia and the city of Cracow; and surrendered to Russia a territory whose population was estimated at 400,000 souls. The emperor of Austria, moreover, recognised the rights which Napoleon arrogated over the monarchies of the south of Europe, adhered to his continental system, and renounced all the countries comprised under the name of the Illyrian Provinces. But the house of Habsburg, true to the adage, *Tu, felix Austria, nube*, retrieved its fortunes at the expense of its pride, by bestowing a daughter in marriage on the conqueror.

### RENEWED WAR WITH TURKEY (1810 A.D.)

Immediately after Alexander's return from Erfurt orders were given to open negotiations with the Turks. The conference took place at Jassy; but it was immediately broken off after the Russian plenipotentiaries had demanded, as preliminary conditions, the cession of Moldavia and Wallachia, and the expulsion of the British minister from Constantinople. Hostilities were then resumed. The Russians were commanded by Prince Prosorovski, and after his death by Prince Bagration. With the exception of Giurgevo, all the fortresses attacked by them fell into their hands, until they encountered the army of the grand vizir, near Silistria, and being defeated with a loss of ten thousand men (September 26th), were compelled to evacuate Bulgaria. The grand vizir, without taking advantage of his victory, retired to winter quarters.

In May, 1810, the Russian main army, under Kamenskoi, again crossed the Danube at Hirsova, passed through the Dobrudja, and marched straight against the Turkish main army to Shumla and Varna. At the same time, the corps of Generals Langeron and Sacken proceeded to blockade Silistria and Rustchuk. The Turks could nowhere keep the field. At Kavarna they were routed; at the storming of Bazardjik they lost ten thousand men; at the storming of Rasgrad three thousand. Silistria was reduced in seven days by Langeron. So far everything was favourable for the Russians. If they had added to their advantages the conquest of Rustchuk, the passes of Tirnova and of Sophia towards Adrianople would have been open, the fortress of Shumla would have been avoided, and the main army of the enemy would have been manœuvred out of it. The taking of Rustchuk, and above all the sparing of the troops, was consequently the next problem for General Kamenskoi. Instead of doing this, the Russians attempted to storm almost simultaneously the fortifications of Varna, Shumla, and Rustchuk, were repulsed from these three places, the defence of which was conducted by English officers, and suffered so enormously, that the Turks felt themselves strong enough to come out from behind their intrenchments, and attack the Russian camp before Shumla. They failed, however, in their attempt to storm it.

To relieve Rustchuk, the grand vizir sent Mukhtar Pasha with picked troops, by way of Tirnova, to the Danube. But if the Turks with their united forces were too weak to force the Russians to abandon the intrenchments before Shumla, they could certainly not expect with a part of their army to rout the enemy near Rustchuk, where he stood with his united forces between their separate wings. Only in case Mukhtar Pasha, who had increased his forces to forty thousand men, entered Wallachia at Turna, and marched against Giurgevo, could the offensive have a meaning, or any influence, upon the siege of Rustchuk, because here it met with the weak point of the enemy. But to enter upon the offensive with an army in Wallachia, whilst the Russians stood before the fortresses of the Danube in Bulgaria, never came into the heads of the Turks. Mukhtar Pasha intrenched himself at the mouth of the Yantra to cover the passes of Tirnova and Sophia. On the 7th of September he was attacked in front, flank, and rear, held out with his best troops till the next morning, and then surrendered with five thousand men, and all his artillery. After this Sistovo and Cladova capitulated, and on the 27th of September Rustchuk and Giurgevo surrendered.

The road to Adrianople was now open for the Russians, but their enormous losses, caused by their own folly, would have prevented their assuming the offensive beyond the Balkan for this year, even if the season had not been so far advanced. Reinforcements for the next year could not be expected, as Napoleon was preparing to attack Russia, and therefore they began to negotiate. Another insurrection of the janissaries interrupted these negotiations, but did not induce the grand vizir to profit by this opportunity, and fall with his whole force upon the Russians, who, at this time, were scattered over the country from Widdin to Sophia and thence as far as Varna. Not until Czerni George, in February, 1811, had placed the principality of Servia under the protection of Russia, did the grand vizir awake from his apathy in Thrace, and cross the Balkan, with only fifteen thousand men. He, however, proceeded so slowly that Kamenskoi had time enough to assemble sufficient forces.

They met at Lofteh on the Osma; the Turks were defeated, and lost three thousand men. Achmed Pasha, however, a violent and sturdy soldier, without any higher military education, led fifty thousand fresh troops to Shumla, and insisted upon their taking the offensive. The Russians had received no reinforcements, but Kutusov had taken the command. Without any considerable losses, he concentrated his small army at Silistria and Rustchuk, and abandoned Bulgaria as far as the latter place, after having rased the fortresses. In the battle before Rustchuk, on the 4th of July, the Turks were driven back, but on the 7th, they forced the twenty thousand Russians who stood on the right bank of the Danube to give up Rustchuk also, though not until its works had been rased.

Instead of crossing the river from the Dobrudja, and operating with a superior force upon the Russian lines of communication, the grand vizir allowed himself to be induced, by the retreat of Kutusov, to cross the Danube at Rustchuk, without a fortress in his rear. Arrived on the left bank with his main army, a Russian flotilla barred his retreat, while Russian corps recrossed the Danube above and below Rustchuk, and took possession of the town (no longer fortified) and of the Turkish camp (September 7th). The grand vizir fled, but his main army, still consisting of 25,000 men and 56 pieces of artillery, was forced to surrender in the vicinity of Giurgevo. A few days afterwards Count St. Priest took Shirtov, with the whole of the Turkish flotilla on the Danube. Nicopoli and Widdin next surrendered, so that by the end of the campaign the Russians were masters of the whole right bank of the Danube. The Servians, also, aided by a body of Russians, had wrested from the Turks the last fortresses they held in the principality.

The grand vizir asked for a suspension of arms, with a view to negotiating a peace; but the terms now demanded by the victorious Russians were such as the Porte would not accede to. The war was continued in 1811, but always to the disadvanatge of the Turks. Resolved on a last desperate effort, they assembled a formidable army whilst the conference at Bucharest was still pending. At last, the rupture between France and Russia changed the aspect of affairs, and compelled the latter power to abandon the long-coveted prey when it was already in its grasp. The Russian minister, Italinski, contented himself with requiring that the Pruth should for the future form the boundary between the two empires. The sultan regarded even this concession as disgraceful; but the Russians carried their point by bribery, and the Treaty of Bucharest was concluded. Its chief provisions were these:

Article 4. The Pruth, from the point where it enters Moldavia to its confluence with the Danube, and thence the left bank of the latter to its embouchure on the Black Sea at Kilia, shall be the boundary between the two empires. Thus the Porte surrendered to Russia a third of Moldavia, with the fortresses of Khoczim and Bender, and all Bessarabia, with Ismail and Kilia. By the same article, the navigation of the Danube is common to the subjects of Russia and Turkey. The islands enclosed between the several arms of the river below Ismail are to remain waste. The rest of Moldavia and Wallachia are to be restored to the Turks in their actual condition. Article 6. The Asiatic frontier remains the same as it was before the war. Article 8 relates to the Servians, to whom the Porte grants an amnesty and some privileges, the interpretation of which offers a wide field for the exercise of diplomatic subtlety. Article 13. Russia accepts the mediation of the Porte for the conclusion of a peace with Persia, where hostilities had begun anew, at the instigation of the English ambassador.

## WAR WITH NAPOLEON

Notwithstanding all the demonstrations to the contrary made since the Peace of Tilsit, England, Russia, Prussia, and also Austria partially, always continued to maintain a certain mutual understanding, which was, however, kept very secret, and somewhat resembled a conspiracy. The most distinguished statesmen both in Russia and Prussia felt how unnatural was an alliance between Napoleon, Alexander, and Frederick William III, and directed attention to the subject. This was also done on the part of England, and it is certain that the emperor Alexander, as early as the meeting in Erfurt in 1808, expressed his doubts respecting the duration of his alliance with France. The conduct of Russia in the campaign against Austria, in 1809, first shook Napoleon's confidence in his ally. Mutual complaints and recriminations ensued; but neither party thought it advisable to give any prominence to their disunion, and Napoleon, even when he had entered, through Thugut, upon the subject of an Austrian marriage, still continued to carry on negotiations for an alliance with a Russian princess.

The enlargement of the territory of the duchy of Warsaw, extorted by

Napoleon at the Peace of Schönbrunn, at length led to an exchange of diplomatic notes, which tended strongly to a war. The Poles naturally expected from Napoleon and his advisers that he would in some way give new life and currency to the name of Poland; against this the emperor of Russia earnestly protested. The whole of the diplomatic correspondence between Russia and France in the years 1810 and 1811 turns upon the use of the words Poles and Polish, although Russia had again obtained by the Peace of Schönbrunn a portion of Austrian Poland, as it had previously obtained a part of Prussian Poland by the Peace of Tilsit. Seeing that the whole of western Galicia, Zamoisk, and Cracow had been united to the duchy of Warsaw by the Peace of Schönbrunn, Russia called upon the emperor of the French to bind himself expressly by treaty not to revive the names of Pole and kingdom of Poland.

Before the end of 1809 many notes were exchanged concerning this point, apparently so insignificant, but in reality so important for the peace and safety of the Russian Empire. Napoleon agreed to give the assurance so earnestly desired by Alexander, and Caulaincourt, the French ambassador in St. Petersburg, signed a regular concession of the Russian demand in January, 1810. By the first two articles of this agreement it was laid down that the word Poland, or Polish, was not to be used when any reference was made to the enlargement of the duchy of Warsaw. By the third article the two emperors bound themselves not to revive or renew any of the old Polish orders. In the fifth, the emperor of the French agreed not further to enlarge the duchy of Warsaw by the addition of provinces or cities belonging to the former state of Poland.

This agreement, signed by Caulaincourt, still required the confirmation of the emperor of the French: and Napoleon had given instructions to his ambassador only to agree to such an arrangement on condition that the agreement was drawn up in the usual diplomatic manner: that is to say, in employing words and phrases so chosen as to be capable of any subsequent interpretation which may best suit the parties. This was not done. The articles were very brief, the language so clear and definite as to be incapable of mistake or misrepresentation. Without directly refusing his sanction to the treaty, Napoleon required that it should be couched in different language, and caused a new draft of it to be presented in St. Petersburg. The Russians saw at once through his purpose, and Alexander expressed his displeasure in terms which plainly indicated to the French ambassador his belief that Napoleon was really meditating some hostile measures against him, and was only seeking to gain time by the treaty.

This occurred in February, 1810; in the following months both Romanzov and Caulaincourt took the greatest possible pains to bring the question to a favourable issue, and negotiations continued to be carried on respecting this subject till September. They could not agree; and after September there was no more talk of the treaty, much less of its alteration. The relation between the two emperors had undergone a complete change in the course of the year.

The cupidity of Russia, far from being glutted by the possession of Finland, great part of Prussian and Austrian Poland, Moldavia, and Bessarabia, still craved for more. Napoleon was, however, little inclined to concede Constantinople and the Mediterranean to his Russian ally (to whose empire he assigned the Danube as a boundary), or to put it in possession of the duchy of Warsaw. The Austrian marriage, which was effected in 1809, naturally led Russia to conclude that she would no longer be permitted to aggrandise herself at the expense of Austria, and Alexander, seeing that nothing more was to be gained by complaisance to France, consequently assumed a threatening posture, and condescended to listen to the complaints of his agricultural and mercantile subjects. No Russian vessel durst venture out to sea, and a Russian fleet had been seized by the British in the harbours of Lisbon. At Riga lay immense stores of grain in want of a foreign market. On the 31st of December, 1810, Alexander published a fresh tariff permitting the importation of colonial products under a neutral flag (several hundred English ships arrived under the American flag), and prohibiting the importation of French manufactured goods. Not many weeks previously, on the 13th of December, Napoleon had annexed Oldenberg to France. The duke, Peter, was nearly related to the emperor of Russia, and Napoleon, notwithstanding his declared readiness to grant a compensation, refused to allow it to consist of the grand-duchy of Warsaw, and proposed a duchy of Erfurt, as yet uncreated, which Russia scornfully rejected.

The alliance between Russia, Sweden, and England was now speedily concluded. Sweden, which had vainly demanded from Napoleon the possession of Norway and a large supply of money, assumed a tone of indignation, threw open her harbours to the British merchantmen, and so openly carried on a contraband trade in Pomerania, that Napoleon, in order to maintain the continental system, was constrained to garrison Swedish Pomerania and Rügen and to disarm the Swedish inhabitants. Bernadotte, upon this, ranged himself entirely on the side of his opponents, without, however, coming to an open rupture, for which he awaited a declaration on the part of Russia. The expressions made use of by Napoleon on the birth of the king of Rome at length filled up the measure of provocation. Intoxicated with success, he boasted, in an address to the mercantile classes, that he would, in despite of Russia, maintain the continental system, for he was lord over the whole of continental Europe; and that if Alexander had not concluded a treaty with him at Tilsit, he would have compelled him to do so at St. Petersburg. The pride of the haughty Russian was deeply wounded, and a rupture was nigh at hand.

Russia had, meanwhile, anticipated Napoleon in making preparations for war. As early as 1811, a great Russian army stood ready for the invasion of Poland, and might, as there were at that time but few French troops in Germany, easily have advanced as far as the Elbe. It remained, however, in a state of inactivity. Napoleon instantly prepared for war and fortified Dantzic. His continual proposals of peace, ever unsatisfactory to the ambition of the czar, remaining at length unanswered, he declared war.[k]

But, to get within reach of Russia, it was necessary for Napoleon to pass beyond Austria, to cross Prussia, and to conciliate Sweden and Turkey; an offensive alliance with these four powers was therefore indispensable. Austria was subject to the ascendency of Napoleon, and Prussia to his arms: to them, therefore, he had only to declare his intentions; Austria voluntarily and eagerly entered into his plans, and Prussia he easily prevailed on to join him.

Austria, however, did not act blindly. Situated between the two giant powers of the north and the west, she was not displeased to see them at war: she looked to their mutually weakening each other, and to the increase of her own strength by their exhaustion. On the 14th of March, 1812, she promised France thirty thousand men, but she prepared prudent secret instructions for them. She obtained a vague promise of an increase of territory as an indemnity for her share of the expenses of the war, and the possession of Galicia was guaranteed to her. She admitted, however, the future possibility of a cession of part of that province to the kingdom of Poland, but in exchange for that she would have received the Illyrian Provinces. The sixth article of the secret treaty establishes this fact.

The success of the war, therefore, in no degree depended on the cession of Galicia, or the difficulties arising from the Austrian jealousy respecting that possession. Napoleon consequently might, on his entrance into Vilna, have publicly proclaimed the liberation of the whole of Poland, instead of betraying the expectations of her people, confounding and rendering them indifferent by expressions of doubtful import. This was one of those decisive issues which occur in politics as well as in war, and which determine the future. No consideration ought to have made Napoleon swerve from his purpose. But whether it was that he reckoned too much on the ascendency of his genius, or the strength of his army and the weakness of Alexander; or that, considering what he left behind him, he felt it too dangerous to carry on so distant a war slowly and methodically; or whether, as we shall presently be told by himself, he had doubts of the success of his undertaking, certain it is that he either neglected or could not yet venture to proclaim the liberation of that country whose freedom he had come to restore. Yet he had sent an ambassador to her diet; and when this inconsistency was remarked to him he replied that that nomination was an act of war, which only bound him during the war, while by his words he would be bound both in war and peace. Thus it was that he made no other answer to the enthusiasm of the Lithuanians than evasive expressions, at the very time he was following up his attack on Alexander to the very capital of his empire.

He even neglected to clear the southern Polish provinces of the feeble hostile armies which kept the patriotism of their inhabitants in check, and to secure, by strongly organising their insurrection, a solid basis of operation. Accustomed to short methods and to rapid attacks, he wished to do as he had done before, in spite of the difference of places and circumstances; for such is the weakness of man that he is always led by imitation, either of others or of himself, which in the latter case is habit, for habit is nothing more than the imitation of one's self. Accordingly, it is by their strongest side that great men are often undone![h]

### Napoleon Invades Russia (1812 A.D.)

On the 24th of June, 1812, Napoleon crossed the Niemen, the Russian frontier, not far from Kovno. The season was already too far advanced. It may be that, deceived by the mildness of the winter of 1806 to 1807, he imagined it possible to protract the campaign without peril to himself until the winter months. No enemy appeared to oppose his progress. Barclay de Tolly, the Russian commander-in-chief, pursued the system followed by the Scythians against Dairus, and perpetually retiring before the enemy gradually drew him deep into the dreary and deserted steppes. This plan originated with Scharnhorst, by whom General Lieven was advised not to hazard an engagement until the winter, and to turn a deaf ear to every proposal of peace. General Lieven, on reaching Barclay's headquarters, took into his confidence Colonel Toll, a German, Barclay's right hand, and Lieutenant-Colonel Clausewitz, also a German, afterwards noted for his strategical works.

General Pfül, another German, at that time high in the emperor's confidence, and almost all the Russian generals opposed Scharnhorst's plan, and continued to advance with a view of giving battle: but on Napoleon's appearance at the head of an army greatly their superior in number, before the Russians had been able to concentrate their forces, they were naturally compelled to retire before him; and, on the prevention, for some weeks, of the junction of a newly levied Russian army under Prince Bagration with the forces under Barclay, owing to the rapidity of Napoleon's advance, Scharnhorst's plan was adopted as the only one feasible.

Whilst the French were advancing, a warm and tedious discussion was carried on so long in the imperial Russian council of war at Vilna, whether to defend that city, or adopt the plan of Barclay de Tolly, the minister of war and commander-in-chief, that they were at length obliged to march precipitately to the Dvina with the sacrifice of considerable stores, and to take possession of a fortified camp which had been established at Drissa. As late as the 27th the emperor Alexander and the whole of his splendid staff and court were assembled at a ball, at the castle of Zacrest, near Vilna, belonging to General Bennigsen, so that the French found everything on the 28th just as it had been prepared for the reception of the emperor of Russia. They plundered the castle, and carried off the furniture as booty; the Russians were even obliged to leave behind them considerable quantities of ammunition and provisions.

In this way the line of the Russian defences was broken through; and even a portion of their army under Platov and Bagration would have been cut off, had the king of Westphalia obeyed the commands of his brother with the necessary rapidity. The difficulties of carrying on war in such an inhospitable country as Lithuania and Russia became apparent even at Vilna; the carriages and wagons fell behind, the cannon were obliged to be left, discipline became relaxed, above ten thousand horses had already fallen, and their carcases poisoned the air. General Balakov could scarcely be considered serious in the proposals which he then made for peace in the name of the emperor of Russia, because the Russians required as a preliminary to all negotiation that the French army should first retire behind the Niemen. The mission of a general, who had been minister of police, and had therefore had great experience in obtaining information, had no doubt a very different object in view from that of making peace at such a moment.

Napoleon, in the hope of overtaking the Russians, and of compelling them to give battle, pushed onwards by forced marches; the supplies were unable to follow, and numbers of the men and horses sank from exhaustion, owing to over-fatigue, heat, and hunger. On the arrival of Napoleon in Witepsk, of Schwarzenberg in Volhinia, of the Prussians before Riga, the army might have halted, reconquered Poland, have been organised, the men put into winter quarters, the army have again taken the field early in the spring, and the conquest of Russia have been slowly but surely completed. But Napoleon had resolved upon terminating the war in one rapid campaign, upon defeating the Russians, seizing their metropolis, and dictating terms of peace. He incessantly pursued his retreating opponent, whose footsteps were marked by the flames of the cities and villages and by the devastated country to their rear. The first serious opposition was made at Smolensk, whence the Russians, however, speedily retreated after setting the city on fire. On the same day, the Bavarians, who had diverged to one side during their advance, had a furious encounter at Polotsk with a body of Russian troops under Wittgenstein. The Bavarians remained stationary in this part of the country for the purpose of watching the movements of that general, whilst Napoleon, careless of the peril with which he was threatened by the approach of winter and by the multitude of enemies gathered to his rear, advanced with the main body of the grand army from Smolensk across the wasted country upon Moscow, the ancient metropolis of the Russian empire.

Russia, at that time engaged in a war with Turkey, whose frontiers were watched by an immense army under Kutusov, used her utmost efforts, in which she was aided by England, to conciliate the Porte in order to turn the whole of her forces against Napoleon. By a master-stroke of political intrigue, the Porte was made to conclude a disadvantageous peace at Bucharest on the 28th of May, as we have already related. A Russian army under Tchitchakov was now enabled to drive the Austrians out of Volhinia, whilst a considerable force under Kutusov joined Barclay. Buturlin, the Russian historian of the war, states that the national troops opposed to the invaders numbered 217,000 in the first line, and 35,000 in the second. Chambray, whose details are very minute, after deducting the men in hospital, gives the number of those present under arms as 235,000 of the regular army, without reckoning the garrisons of Riga, etc. This computation exceeds that of Buturlin, under the same circumstances, by 17,000. M. de Fezensac allows 230,000 for the total of the two armies of Barclay de Tolly and Bagration, but adds the army of Tormassov on their extreme left, 68,000, and that defending Courland, on the extreme right, 34,000, to make up the Russian total of 330,000 men.

Had the Russians at this time hazarded an engagement, their defeat was certain. Moscow could not have been saved. Barclay consequently resolved not to come to an engagement, but to husband his forces and to attack the French during the winter. The intended surrender of Moscow without a blow was, nevertheless, deeply resented as a national disgrace; the army and the people raised a clamour. Kutuzov, though immeasurably inferior to Barclay, was nominated commander-in-chief, took up a position on the little river Moskva near Borodino, about two days' journey from Moscow. A bloody engagement took place there on the 7th of September, in which Napoleon, in order to spare his guards, neglected to follow up his advantage with his usual energy, and allowed the defeated Russians, whom he might have totally annihilated, to escape. Napoleon triumphed; but at what a price! — after a fearful struggle, in which he lost forty thousand men in killed and wounded, the latter of whom perished, almost to a man, owing to want and neglect.[k]

## The Abandonment of Moscow

On his birthday, which was the 30th of August (11th of September of the Russian calendar), the emperor Alexander received a report from Prince Kontonzov of the battle that had taken place at Borodino on the 26th of August, and which as the commander-in-chief wrote, "had terminated by the enemy not gaining a single step of territory in spite of their superior forces." To this Kutuzov added that after having spent the night on the field of battle, he had, in view of the enormous losses sustained by the army, retreated to Mozhaisk. The losses on either side amounted to forty thousand men. As Ermolov very justly expressed it, "the French army was dashed to pieces against the Russian." Although the emperor Alexander was not led into any error as to the real signification of the battle of Borodino, yet wishing to maintain the hopes of the nation as to the successful termination of the struggle with Napoleon and their confidence in Kutuzov, he accepted the report of the conflict of the 26th of August as the announcement of a victory. Prince Kutuzov was created general field-marshal and granted a sum of 100,000 rubles. Barclay de Tolly was rewarded with the order of St. George of the second class, and the mortally wounded Prince Bagration with a sum of 50,000 rubles. Fourteen generals received the order of St. George of the third class, and all the privates who had taken part in the battle were given five rubles each.

Prince Kutuzov's despatch of the 27th of August to the emperor Alexander was read by Prince Gortchakov at the Nevski monastery before a thanksgiving service which took place in the presence of their majesties, and was printed in the *Northern Post*  But the following lines were omitted from the report: "Your imperial majesty will deign to agree that after a most sanguinary battle, which lasted fifteen hours, our army and that of the enemy could not fail to be in disorder. Moreover, through the losses sustained this day the position has naturally become incompatible with the depleted number of our troops — therefore, all our aims being directed to the destruction of the French army, I have come to the decision to fall back six versts, that is, beyond Mozhaisk."

A moment of anxious expectation approached in St. Petersburg. Meanwhile Kutuzov, retreating step by step, led the army to Moscow, and on the 1st of September he assembled a council of war at the village of Filiakh. There was decided the fate of the first capital of the empire. After prolonged debates Kutuzov concluded the conference by saying: "I know that I shall have to pay the damage, but I sacrifice myself for the good of my country. I give the order to retreat."

It was already towards nightfall when Rostoptchin received the following letter from Kutuzov: "The fact that the enemy has divided his columns upon Zvenigorod and Borovsk, together with the disadvantageous position now occupied by our troops, oblige me to my sorrow to abandon Moscow. The army is marching on the route to Riazan." It was thus that Rostoptchin received the first definite information of Kutuzov's intention to leave Moscow a few hours before the French were in sight of the capital; under these circumstances the Moscow commander-in-chief did all that was possible on his side and took all measures for setting the town on fire at the approach of the army. Rostoptchin departed unhindered in a droshky by the back gates.

When on the 2nd of September Napoleon reached the Dragomilovski barriers, he expected to find there a deputation, begging that the city might be spared; but instead of that he received the news that Moscow had been abandoned by its inhabitants. "Moscow deserted! What an improbable event! We must make sure of it. Go and bring the boyars to me," said he to Count Darn, whom he sent into the town. Instead of the boyars a few foreigners were collected who confirmed the news that Moscow had been abandoned by nearly all its inhabitants. Having passed the night on the outskirts of the city, on the morning of the 3rd of September Napoleon transferred his headquarters to the Kremlin. But here a still more unexpected occurrence awaited him. The fires, which had already commenced the eve, had not ceased burning; and on the night between the 3rd and the 4th of September the flames, driven along by a strong wind, had enveloped the greater part of the town. At midday the flames reached the Kremlin, and Napoleon was forced to seek a refuge in the Petrovski palace, where he remained until the 6th of September, when the fire began to abate.[1] Nine tenths of the city became the prey of the flames, and pillage completed the calamities that overtook the inhabitants who had remained in it.

It was only on the 7th of September that the emperor Alexander received through Iaroslav a short despatch from Count Rostoptchin to the effect that Kutuzov had decided to abandon Moscow. The next day, the 8th of Septem-

---

[1] Gazing from the Kremlin on Moscow in flames, Napoleon said, "This forebodes the greatest calamity for us." *Journal du Maréchal Castellane*, Paris, 1895.

ber, the fatal news of Napoleon's occupation of the capital of the empire was confirmed by a despatch from the field-marshal dated the 4th of September and brought in by Colonel Michaud. Kutuzov wrote from the village of Jilin (on the march to the Borovsk bridge) as follows:

"After the battle of the 26th of August, which in spite of so much bloodshed resulted in a victory for our side, I was obliged to abandon the position near Borodino for reasons of which I had the honour to inform your imperial majesty. The army was completely exhausted after the combat. In this condition we drew nearer to Moscow, having daily greatly to do with the advance guard of the enemy; besides this there was no near prospect of a position presenting itself from which I could successfully engage the enemy. The troops which we had hoped to join could not yet come; the enemy had set two fresh columns, one upon the Borovsk route and the other on the Zvenigorod route, striving to act upon my rear from Moscow: therefore I could not venture to risk a battle, the disadvantages of which might have as consequences not only the destruction of the army but the most sanguinary losses and the conversion of Moscow itself to ashes.

"In this most uncertain position, after taking counsel with our first generals, of whom some were of contrary opinion, I was forced to decide to allow the enemy to enter Moscow, whence all the treasures, the arsenal, and nearly all property belonging to the state or private individuals had been removed, and in which hardly a single inhabitant remained. I venture most humbly to submit to your most gracious majesty that the entry of the enemy into Moscow is not the subjection of Russia. On the contrary, I am now moving with the army on the route to Tula, which will place me in a position to avail myself of the help abundantly prepared in our governments. Although I do not deny that the occupation of the capital is a most painful wound, yet I could not waver in my decision.

"I am now entering upon operations with all the strength of the line, by means of which, beginning with the Tula and Kaluga routes, my detachments will cut off the whole line of the enemy, stretching from Smolensk to Moscow, and thus avert any assistance which the enemy's army might possibly receive from its rear; by turning the attention of the enemy upon us, I hope to force him to leave Moscow and change the whole line of his operations. I have enjoined General Winzengerode to hold himself on the Tver route, having meanwhile a regiment of Cossacks on the Iaroslav route in order to protect the inhabitants against attacks from the enemy's detachments. Having now assembled my forces at no great distance from Moscow I can await the enemy with a firm front, and as long as the army of your imperial majesty is whole and animated by its known bravery and our zeal, the yet retrievable loss of Moscow cannot be regarded as the loss of the fatherland. Besides this, your imperial majesty will graciously deign to agree that these consequences are indivisibly connected with the loss of Smolensk and with the condition of complete disorder in which I found the troops."

This despatch from Prince Kutuzov was printed in the *Northern Post* of the 18th of September, with the exception of the concluding words of the report: "and with the condition of complete disorder in which I found the troops." The sorrowful news brought by Colonel Michaud did not, however, shake the emperor Alexander in his decision to continue the war and not to enter into negotiations with the enemy. When he had finished listening to Michaud's report, he turned to him with the following memorable words: "Go back to the army, and tell our brave soldiers, tell all my faithful subjects, wherever you pass by, that even if I have not one soldier left, I will put myself at the head of my dear nobles, of my good peasants, and will thus employ the last resources of my empire; it offers more to me than my enemies think for, but if ever it were written in the decrees of divine providence that my dynasty should cease to reign upon the throne of my ancestors, then, after having exhausted every means in my power, I would let my beard grow and go to eat potatoes with the last of my peasants, rather than sign the shame of my country and of my beloved people whose sacrifices I know how to prize. Napoleon or I — I or he; for he and I can no longer reign together. I have learned to know him; he will no longer deceive me."

"The loss of Moscow," wrote Alexander to the crown prince of Sweden on the 19th of September, "gives me at least the opportunity of presenting to the whole of Europe the greatest proof I can offer of my perseverance in continuing the struggle against her oppressor, for after such a wound all the rest are but scratches. Now more than ever I and the nation at the head of which I have the honour to be, are decided to persevere. We should rather be buried beneath the ruins of the empire than make terms with the modern Attila."

The letter that Napoleon addressed to the emperor from Moscow, dated the 8th of September, in which he disclaimed the responsibility of the burning of the capital, was left unanswered. In informing the crown prince of it, the emperor Alexander added: "It contains, however, nothing but bragging."

## The Retreat of the Grand Army

At length the sorrowful days which the emperor Alexander had lived through passed by, and the hope of better things in the future manifested itself. On the 15th of October Colonel Michaud arrived in St. Petersburg from the army, for the second time; but on this occasion he was the bearer of the joyful intelligence of the victory of Tarontin, which had taken place on the 6th of October. The envoy also informed the emperor of the army's desire that he should take the command of it in person. The emperor replied as follows:

"All men are ambitious, and I frankly acknowledge that I am no less ambitious than others; were I to listen to this feeling alone, I should get into a carriage with you and set off to the army. Taking into consideration the disadvantageous position into which we have induced the enemy, the excellent spirit by which the army is animated, the inexhaustible resources of the empire, the numerous troops in reserve, which I have lying in readiness, and the orders that I have despatched to the army of Moldavia — I feel undoubtingly sure that the victory must be inalienably ours, and that it only remains for us, as you say, to gather the laurels. I know that if I were with the army all the glory would be attributed to me, and that I should occupy a place in history; but when I think how little experience I have in the art of war in comparison with my adversary, and that in spite of my good will I might make a mistake, through which the precious blood of my children might be shed, then setting aside my ambition, I am ready willingly to sacrifice my glory for the good of the army. Let those gather the laurels who are worthier of them than I; go back to headquarters, congratulate Prince Michael Larionovitch with his victory, and tell him to drive the enemy out of Russia and then I will come to meet him and will lead him triumphantly into the capital."

At that time the fate of the *grande armée* was already definitively decided. Having lost all hope of the peace he so desired, Napoleon began to prepare

RETREAT OF NAPOLEON FROM THE BURNING CITY OF MOSCOW

(Painted for The Historians' History of the World by Thure de Thulstrup)

for retreat. The defeat of his vanguard at Tarontin on the 6th of October hastened the departure of the French from Moscow; it began in the evening of the same day. Napoleon's intention was first to move along the old Kaluga road, to join Murat's vanguard, and then go on to the new Kaluga road; the emperor thus hoped to go round the Russian army and open a free access for himself to Kaluga. But the partisan Seslavin, who had boldly made his way through on to the Borovsk route discovered Napoleon's movements. Standing behind a tree in the road, he saw the carriage in which was the emperor himself, surrounded by his marshals and his guards. Not satisfied with this exploit, Seslavin besides caught a non-commissioned officer of the Old Guard, who had got separated from the others in the thickness of the wood, bound him, and throwing him across his saddle, galloped off with him.

The intelligence obtained by Seslavin had for consequences the immediate move of Dokhtorov's corps to Malo-Iaroslavetz; at the same time Kutuzov decided to follow from Tarontin with the whole army, and these arrangements led, on the 12th of October, to the battle near Malo-Iaroslavetz. The town passed from the hands of one side to the other eight times, and although after a conflict of eighteen hours it was finally given up to the French, yet Kutuzov succeeded in opportunely concentrating the whole army to the south of it, at a distance of two and one-half versts.

Here, as Ségur justly remarks, was stopped the conquest of the universe, here vanished the fruits of twenty years of victory and began the destruction of all that Napoleon had hoped to create. The author of this success, Seslavin, writes: "The enemy was forestalled at Malo-Iaroslavetz; the French were exterminated, Russia was saved, Europe set free, and universal peace established: such are the consequences of this great discovery."

The field-marshal had now to decide the question whether a general battle should be attempted for the annihilation of the French army, or whether endeavours should be made to attain this object by more cautious means. The leader stopped at the latter decision. "It will all fall through without me," said Kutuzov, in reply to the impatient partisans of decisive action. He expressed his idea more definitely on this occasion to the English general Wilson, who was then at the Russian headquarters: "I prefer to build a 'golden bridge,' as you call it, for my adversary, than to put myself in such a position that I might receive a 'blow on the neck' from him. Besides this, I again repeat to you what I have already several times told you — I am not at all sure that the complete annihilation of the emperor Napoleon and his army would be such a great benefit to the universe. His inheritance would give the continent not to Russia or any other power, but to that power which now already rules the seas; and then her predominance would be unbearable." Wilson replied: "Do what you ought, come what may." The Russian army began to depart on the night between the 13th and 14th of October for Detchina.*g*

### Napoleon on the Road to Smolensk

When, on the 14th of October, Kutuzov and his army approached Detchina, Napoleon turned again from Gorodni in the direction of Malo-Iaroslavetz. Half-way there, a report was brought to him which announced that the Russian out-posts had quitted this latter town. Napoleon stopped, and, seating himself near a fire which had been lighted in the open: "What design," he said, "had Kutuzov in abandoning Malo-Iaroslavetz?" He was silent for a moment and then added: "He wants to stop our road to the south." And, determined as he was not to fight, Napoleon ordered the army to return along the Smolensk road, preferring to contend with want of provisions rather than find himself on the other track, under the necessity of using force in order to pursue the direction he had intended to take when he quitted Moscow. Thus the whole plan of campaign was thwarted and the fortune of Napoleon compromised. From Malo-Iaroslavetz to Waterloo Napoleon's career presents nothing but a series of defeats, rarely interrupted by a few victories. It was in profound silence and with dejection painted on every visage that the French army, as though under the presentiment of its fatal destiny, retraced the way to Smolensk. Napoleon marched pensive in the midst of his downcast regiments, reckoning with Marshal Berthier the enormous distances to be traversed and the time it must take him to reach Smolensk and Minsk, the only towns on the Vilna road where food and ammunition had been prepared.

Kutuzov, learning on the 14th of October that Napoleon had left Malo-Iaroslavetz, immediately advanced his army on the Miadin road in the direction of some linen factories, and detached Platov with fifteen Cossack regiments and some flying squadrons, that they might inform him of Napoleon's movements. The next day he received from these squadrons the assurance that the latter was indeed effecting his retreat by the Smolensk route. Thus the manœuvres of Kutuzov were crowned with complete success. Thus it happened that just two months after the 17th of August, the day on which he had assumed command of the armies, the conqueror's eagles were flying with all speed towards the place whence they had taken flight. The movement carried out on the enemy's left flank as far as Malo-Iaroslavetz, and thence to the linen factories, disconcerted all Napoleon's plans, closed to him the road to Kaluga and Iukhnov, and forced him to follow a route which two months before had been ruined from end to end, and which led across deserts that Napoleon seemed to have prepared for himself. The enemy's army, which still amounted to one hundred thousand men, continued to bear a threatening aspect, but the want of provisions and the attacks it had to repulse must diminish its forces and hasten its disorganisation. Hunger, like a gnawing worm, was exhausting the enemy, while Russian steel completed his destruction. The nearest French magazines were at Smolensk, eight hundred versts away. To cross this distance with the little food he possessed, to suffer an immense loss, and, in addition, to be continually exposed to attacks — such were the exploits now before Napoleon and such was the position in which Kutuzov had placed him.

The question was: How is Napoleon to be pursued? What direction shall the army take in order to derive all the advantage possible from the retreat of the French? To follow the enemy's steps in columns was impossible without exposing the army to the pangs of hunger. "I think," said Kutuzov, "that I shall do Napoleon most harm by marching parallel with him and acting on the way according to the movements he may execute." This happy idea seemed to be a basis for the manœuvres which Kutuzov subsequently effected. He gave orders to the army to march on Viazmabi Kussov, Suleïka, Dubrova, and Bikov; to Miloradovitch to direct his way, with two corps of infantry and two of cavalry, between the army and the route to Smolensk, and to approach this route in the neighbourhood of Gzhatsk, and then, proceeding in the direction of Viazma, along the same road, to take advantage of every favourable opportunity of attacking the enemy; to Platov, who had been reinforced by Paskevitch's division, to follow the French in the rear; and finally to the guerilla corps to fall on the enemy's columns in front and in flank. In ordering these dispositions Kutuzov addressed the following order of the day to the army: " Napoleon, who thought only of ardently pursuing a war which has become national, without foreseeing that it might in one moment annihilate his whole army, now finding in every inhabitant a soldier ready to repulse his perfidious seductions, and seeing the firm resolution of the whole population to present, if need be, their breasts to the sword directed against their beloved country — Napoleon, in fine, after having attained the object of his vain and foolhardy thoughts, namely that of shaking all Russia by rendering himself master of Moscow, has suddenly made up his mind to beat a retreat. We are at this moment in pursuit of him, whilst other Russian armies occupy Lithuania anew and are ready to act in concert with us to complete the ruin of the enemy who has ventured to menace Russia. In his flight he abandons his caissons, blows up his projectiles, and covers the ground with the treasures carried off from our churches. Already Napoleon hears murmurs raised by all ranks of his army; already hunger is making itself felt, while desertion and disorder of every kind are manifested amongst the soldiers. Already the voice of our august monarch rings out, crying to us, ' Extinguish the fire of Moscow in the blood of the enemy. Warriors, let us accomplish that task, and Russia will be content with us — a solid peace will be again established within the circle of her immense frontiers! Brave soldiers of Russia, God will aid us in so righteous an achievement!"

Immediately, as Kutuzov had ordered, a general movement of the army began in the enemy's rear. The French left on the road sick, wounded — all this might delay the march of the retiring troops. The cavalry began no longer to show themselves in the rearguard. For lack of food and shoeing the horses became so enfeebled that the cavalry were outdistanced by the infantry, who continued to hasten their retreat. Speed was the enemy's only means of escaping from the deserts in which no nourishment could be procured, and of reaching the Dnieper, where the French counted on finding some corn magazines, and forming a junction with the corps of Victor and St. Cyr and the battalions on the march, the various columns which were there at the moment, the dépôts, and a great number of soldiers who had fallen off from the army and were following it. Convinced of the necessity of hurrying their steps, all, from the marshals down to the meanest soldiers, went forward at full speed.

But the temperature grew daily more rigorous. The cold wind of autumn rendered bivouacs insupportable to the enemy, and drove him thence in the morning long before daybreak. He struck camp in the darkness, and lighted his way along the road by means of lanterns. Each corps tried to pass the other. The passage of the rivers, on rafts or bridges, was made in the greatest disorder, and the baggage accumulated so as to arrest the movements of the army. The provisions which the soldiers had laid in at Moscow, and which they carried on their backs, were quickly consumed, and they began to eat horseflesh. The prices of food and of warm clothes and footgear became exorbitant. To stray from the road for the purpose of procuring food was an impossibility, for the Cossacks who were prowling right and left killed or made prisoners all who fell into their hands. The peasants from the villages bordering on the route, dressed in cloaks, shakos, plumed helmets, and steel cuirasses which they had taken from the French, often joined the Don Cossacks or Miloradovitch's advance guard. Some were armed with scythes, others with thick, iron-shod staves, or halberds, and a few carried firearms. They came out of the forests in which they had taken refuge with their families, greeted the Russian army on its appearance, congratulated it on the flight of the enemy, and by way of farewells to the latter took a just vengeance upon it. With the enemy the fear of falling into the hands of the Cossacks and peasants triumphed over the sense of hunger and deterred them from plundering. The French began to throw away their arms. The first to set the example were the regiments of light cavalry, to whom infantry muskets had been distributed at Moscow. The regiments being mixed together, they shook off all discipline. The disarmed men were at first few in number, and as they trailed along in the wake of the army they agglomerated them like snowballs.

The sick and those overcome by fatigue were abandoned on the road without the least pity. In fear of losing their flags the leaders of regiments removed them from their staves and gave them in keeping to the strongest and most tried soldiers, who hid them in their haversacks or under their uniforms, or wrapped them round their bodies. When Napoleon had passed Gzhatsk, he no longer rode on horseback in the midst of his troops, but drove in a carriage, wrappped himself in a green velvet cloak lined with sable furs, and put on warm boots and a fur cap.

### The Battle of Viazma; Smolensk is Found Evacuated

The retreat was performed so rapidly, that Miloradovitch could not begin the pursuit of the enemy till he had arrived at Viazma. On the 22nd of October, he attacked the French near this town and beat them. Three guns and two flags were taken from them and two thousand of them were made prisoners. When Viazma had been passed, Kutuzov ordered Miloradovitch to follow in the enemy's track and to press him as much as possible, and Platov to get ahead of his right, and attack it in front, as Orlov Denissov was to do on his left; the guerillas had orders to march quickly on Smolensk. He exhorted the whole army to harass the French day and night. Kutuzov with the main body proceeded on the left, on a level with Miloradovitch, to be able to reach Orscha by the shortest road, in case Napoleon should effect his retreat on that town; but, if he took the direction of Mohilev, to stop his way and cover the district whence the Russian army drew its provisions. Kutuzov was inflexible in the resolution he had taken to keep Napoleon on the Smolensk road, which was so completely wasted, and to force him to die of hunger there rather than allow him to penetrate into the southern governments, where he might have obtained provisions. Anxious to know if Napoleon would not bear to the left towards Ielna and Mstislavl, and thence to Mohilev, Kutuzov did not confine himself to insisting on personally directing his army on the road, whence he could prevent this movement, but he ordered the Kaluga militia, reinfored by Cossacks and some regular cavalry regiments, to advance rapidly from Kaluga and Roslavl on Ielna; that of Tula to march on Roslavl, that of Smolensk on Ielna, and that of Little Russia to do its utmost promptly to occupy Mohilev.

Such were, in outline, the directions which Kutuzov gave to the army after the battle of Viazma, when the enemy found itself under the stern necessity of struggling with a new calamity which it had not yet experienced —namely, severe cold. The winds raged and thick snow fell for five days; it blinded the soldiers and lay so thick as to arrest their march. The French horses, not being rough-shod, fell under the guns, under the carts, and under their riders; men were lying on the route, dead or dying, dragging themselves along like reptiles, in villages reduced to ashes and round overturned wagons and caissons which the powder had blown to pieces. Many among them were seized with madness. It was in this state that, on the 31st of October, Napoleon led his army back to Smolensk, which he hastened to reach as the promised land, never doubting that he would be able to halt there. The thought of wintering in Smolensk supported soldiers exhausted by fatigue and warmed those overcome by the cold; each one collected his remaining strength to reach the town where their misfortunes were to end. On catching sight of the distant summits of Smolensk, the enemy rejoiced and forgot hunger and thirst. Arrived at the town they rushed into it by thousands, stifling and killing each other in its narrow gates, ran for the provisions they believed themselves sure of finding, and seeking for warm habitations; but it was in vain; for soon like a thunderclap the news was echoed that there was in Smolensk neither food nor refuge; that it was impossible to stay there; that they must go on. Twenty degrees of cold came to crown their misfortunes, but this suddenly ceased — the next day it thawed; otherwise the sudden extinction of the enemy would have been inevitable.

Smolensk presented a horrible spectacle. From the Moscow gate to the line of the Dnieper, the ground was strewn with corpses and dead horses. Fire had turned the Moscow suburb into a desert; in it and on the snow which covered the ice on the Dnieper were to be seen wagons, caissons of ammunition, ambulances, cannon, pontoons, muskets, pistols, bayonets, drums, cuirasses, shakos, bearskins, musical instruments, ramrods, swords, and sabres. Amongst the corpses on the banks appeared a long file of wagons, not yet unharnessed but whose horses had fallen down and whose drivers lay half dead in their seats. In other places horses were lying with the entrails protruding from their bodies. Their bellies were split open, for the soldiers had tried to warm their frozen limbs there, or to appease their hunger. Where the river banks ended, along the road which skirted the walls of the town, were seen five versts away six or more ranks of caissons of ammunition and projectiles, calashes from Moscow, carriages, droshkies, travelling forges. The French, frozen with cold, ran hither and thither, wrapped in priests' cassocks, in surplices, in women's cloaks, with straw wound about their legs, and hoods, Jews' caps, or mats on their heads; nearly all cursed Napoleon, emitted volleys of blasphemies, and, calling upon Death in their despair, bared their breasts and fell under his inexorable scythe.

### Kutuzov's Policy

Kutuzov, who had reduced Napoleon to this horrible situation, and who, by means of his flying squadrons, was kept aware of his every step, had succeeded in hiding all his own movements. Napoleon believed, as we see by the orders he gave his marshals, that Kutuzov was not marching parallel with the French army, but behind it; and yet Kutuzov continued his side movement round Smolensk, daily receiving reports of defeats of the enemy.

Already, between Moscow and Smolensk, one hundred pieces of cannon had been taken from the French and 10,000 men made prisoners. In congratulating the army on its successes, Kutuzov said in an order of the day: "After the brilliant success which we obtain every day and everywhere over the enemy, it only remains for us to pursue him speedily, and perhaps the soil of that Russia which he sought to subjugate will enclose all his bones within her breast; let us then pursue him without pause. Winter declares itself, the frost increases, the snow is blinding. Is it for you, children of the North, to fear all these harsh inclemencies? Your iron breasts resist them as they resist the rage of enemies. They are the ramparts, the hope of our country, against which everything is broken. If momentary privations should make themselves felt, you will know how to support them. True soldiers are distinguished by patience and courage. The old will set an example to the young. Let all remember Suvarov; he taught us to endure hunger and cold where victory and the honour of the Russian people were concerned. Forward, march! God is with us! The beaten enemy precedes us; may calm and tranquillity be restored behind us." *i*

Kutuzov did not allow himself to be tempted by the disastrous position of his adversary and remained faithful to the cautious policy he had adopted, sparing as far as possible the troops entrusted to him. He never once altered his ruling idea, and remained true to it until the very end of the campaign. To those who were in favour of more energetic measures he replied: "Our young folks are angry with me for restraining their outbursts. They should take into consideration that circumstances will do far more for us by themselves than our arms." Kutuzov's indecision at Viazma and Krasnoi, Tchitchagov's mistakes, and Count Wittgenstein's caution, however, gave Napoleon's genius the possibility of triumphing with fresh brilliancy over the unprecedented misfortunes that pursued him: on the 14th of November began the passage of the French across the Beresina at Stondianka, and then the pitiful remains of the *grande armée*, amounting to nine thousand men, hurriedly moved, or it would be more correct to say fled to Vilna, closely pursued by the Russian forces. The frost, which had reached thirty degrees, completed the destruction of the enemy; the whole route was strewn with the bodies of those who had perished from cold and hunger. Seeing the destruction of his troops and the necessity of creating a fresh army in order to continue the struggle, Napoleon wrote from Molodechno on the 21st of November his twenty-ninth bulletin, by which he informed Europe of the lamentable issue of the war, begun six months previously, and after transferring the command of the army to the king of Naples, Murat, he left Smorgoni for Paris on the 23rd of November.

As the remains of Napoleon's army approached the frontiers of Russia, the complicated question presented itself to the emperor Alexander as to whether the Russian forces should stop at the Vistula and complete the triumph of Russia by a glorious peace or continue the struggle with Napoleon in order to re-establish the political independence of Germany and the exaltation of Austria. The emperor inclined to the latter decision — that is, to the prolongation of the war; such an intention was in complete accordance with the conviction he had previously expressed: "Napoleon or I — I or he; but together we cannot reign." At the end of the year 1812 the final object of the war was already marked out by the emperor Alexander. This is evident from his conversation with Mademoiselle Sturdza not long before his departure for Vilna, in which the sovereign shared with her his feelings of joy at the happy results of the war. Alexander referred in their colloquy to the extraordinary man who, blinded by fortune, had occasioned so many calamities to mankind. Speaking of the enigmatical character of Napoleon, he called to mind how he had studied him during the negotiations at Tilsit; in reference to this the emperor said: "The present time reminds me of all that I heard from that extraordinary man at Tilsit. Then we talked a long while together, for he liked to show me his superiority and lavishly displayed before me all the brilliancy of his imagination. 'War,' said he to me once, 'is not at all such a difficult art as people think, and to speak frankly it is sometimes hard to explain exactly how one has succeeded in winning a battle. In reality it would seem that he is vanquished who is afraid of his adversary and that the whole secret lies in that. There is no leader who does not dread the issue of a battle; the whole thing is to hide this fear for the longest time possible. It is only thus that he can frighten his opponent, and then there is no doubt of ultimate success.' I listened," continued the emperor, "with the deepest attention to all that he was pleased to communicate to me on the subject, firmly resolving to profit by it when the occasion presented itself, and in fact I hope that I have since acquired some experience in order to solve the question as to what there remains for us to do." "Surely, Sire, we are forever secure against such an invasion?" replied Mademoiselle Sturdza. "Would the enemy dare again to cross our frontiers?" "It is possible," answered Alexander, "but if a lasting and solid peace is desired it must be signed in Paris; of that I am firmly convinced."

Kutuzov was of an entirely opposite opinion; he considered that Napoleon was no longer dangerous to Russia, and that he must be spared on account of the English, who would endeavour to seize upon his inheritance to the detriment of Russia and other continental powers. All the thoughts of the field-marshal were directed to the salvation of the fatherland, and not that of Europe, as those English and German patriots would have desired, who were already accustomed to look upon Russia as a convenient tool for the attainment and consolidation of their political aims. Kutuzov's opinions, as might have been expected, were strongly censured by those around Alexander and in general by persons who judged of military movements from the depths of their studies.

The frame of mind of such persons is best described in the correspondence of Baron Ampheldt, who devoted the following witty lines to this burning question: "Our affairs might even go still better if Kutuzov had not taken upon himself the form of a tortoise, and Tchitchagov that of a weather-cock, which does not follow any plan: the latter sins by a superfluity of intellect and a want of experience, the former by excessive caution. I suppose, however, that after his passage across the Niemen Bonaparte has not a very large company left; cold, hunger, and Cossack spears must have occasioned him some difficulties. Meanwhile, as long as the man lives, we shall never be in a condition to count on any rest; and therefore war to the death is necessary. Our good emperor shares these views, in spite of the opinion of those contemptible creatures who would have wished to stop at the Vistula. But this is not the desire of the people, who, however, alone bear the burden of the war and in whom are to be found more healthy good sense and feeling than in powdered heads ornamented with orders and embroideries."

On the 28th of November the Russian forces occupied Vilna, after having taken 140 guns, more than 14,000 prisoners, and vast quantities of stores. Prince Kutuzov arrived on the 30th of November; he came to a place with which he was already well acquainted, having formerly filled the position of Lithuanian military governor. The population, forgetting Napoleon and their vanished dreams of the re-establishment of the kingdom of Poland, welcomed the triumphant leader with odes and speeches, and on the stage of the theatre Kutuzov's image was represented with the inscription: "The saviour of the country."

After the evacuation of Vilna the enemy fled, without stopping to Kovno; but on the 2nd of December Platov's Cossacks made their appearance in the town, which was quickly cleared of the French. The piteous remainder of that once brilliant army crossed the Niemen; only 1,000 men with nine guns and about 20,000 unarmed men were left of it. "God punished the foolish," wrote the emperor Nicholas twenty-seven years later in his order of the day to the troops, on the occasion of the unveiling of the Borodino monument; "the bones of the audacious foreigners were scattered from Moscow to the Niemen — and we entered Paris." *g*

## CAMPAIGNS OF THE GRAND ALLIANCE (1813–1814 A.D.)

Rallying with amazing promptitude from the tremendous blow he had suffered in Russia, Napoleon raised a fresh army of 300,000 men in the beginning of 1813, in order to crush the insurrection in which all northern Germany had joined, with the exception of Saxony, after Prussia had openly adhered to the Russian alliance. By the Treaty of Kalish, which established that alliance, Alexander engaged not to lay down his arms until Prussia had recovered the territory it possessed before the war of 1800. Great efforts were now made by the cabinets of St. Petersburg and Berlin to detach Austria from France; and so strongly were the national feelings declared in favour of that policy, that Metternich had the utmost difficulty in withstanding the torrent, and evading the hazard of committing his government prematurely. Temporising with consummate art, he offered the mediation of his government between the hostile parties, and at the same time prosecuted his military preparations on such a scale as would enable Austria to act no subordinate part on the one side or the other in the coming struggle. Meanwhile, hostilities began; the Russians and Prussians were defeated by Napoleon at Lützen and at Bautzen, where Alexander commanded the allied armies in person; and they were fortunate in concluding an armistice with him at Pleisswitz on the 4th of June, 1813. They availed themselves of this truce to reinforce their armies, and more than sixty thousand fresh troops reached the seat of war from the south and the middle of Russia.

On the 27th, Austria signed a treaty at Reichenbach, in Silesia, with Russia and Prussia, by which she bound herself to declare war with France, in case Napoleon had not, before the termination of the armistice, accepted the terms of peace about to be proposed to him. A pretended congress for the arrangement of the treaty was again agreed to by both sides; but Napoleon delayed to grant full powers to his envoy, and the allies, who had meanwhile heard of Wellington's victory at Vittoria and the expulsion of the French from Spain, gladly seized this pretext to break off the negotiations. Meanwhile, Metternich, whose voice was virtually to decide Napoleon's fate, met him at Dresden with an offer of peace, on condition of the surrender of the French conquests in Germany. Napoleon, with an infatuation only equalled by his attempts to negotiate at Moscow, spurned the proposal, and even went the length of charging Count Metternich with taking bribes from England. The conference, which was conducted on Napoleon's part in so insulting a manner, and at times in tones of passion so violent as to be overheard by the attendants, lasted till near midnight on the 10th of August, the day with which the armistice was to expire. The fatal hour passed by, and that night Count Metternich drew up the declaration of war, on the part of his government, against France. Austria coalesced with Russia and Prussia, and the Austrian general, Prince Schwarzenberg, was appointed generalissimo of the whole of the allied armies.

The plan of the allies was to advance with the main body under Schwarzenberg, 190,000 strong, through the Hartz mountains to Napoleon's rear. Blücher, with 95,000 men, was meanwhile to cover Silesia, or in case of an attack by Napoleon's main body to retire before it and draw it further eastward.   Bernadotte, crown prince of Sweden, was to cover Berlin with 90,000 men, and in case of a victory was to form a junction, rearward of Napoleon, with the main body of the allied army.   A mixed division under Wallmoden, 30,000 strong, was destined to watch Davout in Hamburg, whilst the Bavarian and Italian frontiers were respectively guarded by 25,000 Austrians under Prince Reuss, and 40,000 Austrians under Hiller.   Napoleon's main body, consisting of 250,000 men, was concentrated in and around Dresden.

The campaign opened with the march of a French force under Oudinot against Berlin.   This attack having completely failed, Napoleon marched in person against Blücher, who cautiously retired before him.   Dresden being thus left uncovered, the allies changed their plan of operations, and marched straight upon the Saxon capital.   But they arrived too late, Napoleon having already returned thither, after despatching Vandamme's corps to Bohemia, to seize the passes and cut off Schwarzenberg's retreat.   The allies attempted to storm Dresden, on the 26th of August, but were repulsed after suffering a frightful loss.   On the following day Napoleon assumed the offensive, cut off the left wing of the allies, and made an immense number of prissoners, chiefly Austrians.   The main body fled in all directions; part of the troops disbanded, and the whole must have been annihilated but for the misfortune of Vandamme, who was taken prisoner, with his whole corps, on the 29th.   It was at the battle of Dresden that Moreau, who had come from his exile in America to aid the allies against his old rival Napoleon, was killed by a cannon ball whilst he as speaking to the emperor Alexander.

At the same time (August 26th) a splendid victory was gained by Blücher, on the Katzbach, over Macdonald, who reached Dresden almost alone, to say to Napoleon, "Your army of the Bober is no longer in existence."   This disaster to the French arms was followed by the defeat of Ney at Dennewitz by the Prussians and Swedes on the 6th of September.   Napoleon's generals were thrown back in every quarter, with immense loss, on Dresden, towards which the allies now advanced again, threatening to enclose it on every side. Napoleon manœuvred until the beginning of October, with the view of executing a *coup de main* against Schwarzenberg and Blücher, but their caution foiled him, and at length he found himself compelled to retreat, lest he should be cut off from the Rhine, for Blücher had crossed the Elbe, joined Bernadotte, and approached the head of the main army under Schwarzenberg.   Moreover, the Bavarian army under Wrede declared against the French on the 8th of October, and was sent to the Main to cut off their retreat.   Marching to Leipsic, the emperor there encountered the allies on the 16th of October, and fought an indecisive action, which, however, was in his case equivalent to a defeat.   He strove to negotiate a separate peace with the emperor of Austria, as he had before done with regard to the emperor of Russia, but no answer was returned to his proposals.   After some partial engagements on the 17th, the main battle was renewed on the 18th; it raged with prodigious violence all day, and ended in the defeat of Napoleon; Leipsic was stormed on the following day, and the French emperor narrowly escaped being taken prisoner.   He had lost 60,000 men in the four days' battle; with the remainder of his troops he made a hasty and disorderly retreat, and after losing many more in his disastrous flight, he crossed the Rhine on the 20th of October with 70,000 men.   The garrisons he had left behind gradually surrendered, and by November all Germany, as far as the Rhine, was freed from the presence of the French.

In the following month the allies simultaneously invaded France in three directions: Bülow from Holland, Blücher from Coblentz, and Schwarzenberg, with the allied sovereigns, by Switzerland and the Jura; whilst Wellington also was advancing from the Pyrenees, at the head of the army which had liberated the peninsula. In twenty-five days after their passage of the Rhine the allied armies had succeeded, almost without firing a shot, in wresting a third of France from the grasp of Napoleon. Their united forces stretched diagonally across France in a line three hundred miles long, from the frontiers of Flanders to the banks of the Rhone. On the other hand, the French emperor, though his force was little more than a third of that which was at the command of the allies, had the advantage of an incomparably more concentrated position, his troops being all stationed within the limits of a narrow triangle, of which Paris, Laon, and Troyes formed the angles. Besides this, there was no perfect unanimity among his enemies. Austria, leaning on the matrimonial alliance, was reluctant to push matters to extremities, if it could possibly be avoided; Russia and Prussia were resolute to overthrow Napoleon's dynasty; whilst the councils of England, which in this diversity held the balance, were as yet divided as to the final issue. There was a prospect, therefore, that the want of concert between the allies would afford profitable opportunities to the military genius of the French emperor.

On the 29th of January, 1814, Napoleon made an unexpected attack on Blücher's corps at Brienne, in which the Prussian marshal narrowly escaped being made prisoner. But not being pursued with sufficient vigour, and having procured reinforcements, Blücher had his revenge at La Rothière, where he attacked Napoleon with superior forces and routed him. Still Schwarzenberg delayed his advance and divided his troops, whilst Blücher, pushing rapidly forward on Paris, was again unexpectedly attacked by the main body of the French army, and all his corps, as they severally advanced, were defeated with terrible loss, between the 10th and 14th of February. On the 17th, Napoleon routed the advanced guard of the main army at Nangis, and again on the 18th he inflicted a heavy defeat on them at Montereau. Augereau, meanwhile, with an army levied in the south of France, had driven the Austrians under Bubna into Switzerland, and had posted himself at Geneva, in the rear of the allies, who became so alarmed as to resolve on a general retreat, and proposed an armistice. Negotiations for peace had been in progress for several weeks at Châtillon, and the allies were now more than ever desirous that the terms they offered should be accepted. But so confident was Napoleon in the returning good fortune of his arms, that he would not even consent to a suspension of hostilities while the conferences for an armistice were going on. As for the conference at Châtillon, he used it only as a means to gain time, fully resolved not to purchase peace by the reduction of his empire within the ancient limits of the French monarchy.

Blücher became furious on being informed of the intention to retreat, and with the approval of the emperor Alexander, he resolved to separate from the main army, and push on for Paris. Being reinforced on the Marne by Winzingerode and Bülow, he encountered Napoleon at Craon on the 7th of March. The battle was one of the most obstinately contested of the whole revolutionary war; the loss on both sides was enormous, but neither could claim a victory. Two days afterwards the emperor was defeated at Laon; but Blücher's army was reduced to inactivity by fatigue and want of food.

Napoleon now turned upon the grand army, which he encountered at Arcis-sur-Aube; but after an indecisive action, he deliberately retreated, not towards Paris but in the direction of the Rhine. His plan was to occupy the fortresses in the rear of the allies, form a junction with Augereau, who was then defending Lyons, and, with the aid of a general rising of the peasantry

[1814 A.D.]

in Alsace and Lorraine, surround and cut off the invaders, or, at least, compel them to retreat to the Rhine. But this plan being made known to the allies by an intercepted letter from Napoleon to the empress, they frustrated it by at once marching with flying banners upon Paris, leaving behind only ten thousand men, under Winzingerode, to amuse Napoleon and mask their movement. After repulsing Mortier and Marmont, and capturing the forces under Pacthod and Amey, the allies defiled within sight of Paris on the 29th. On the 30th they met with a spirited resistance on the heights of Belleville and Montmartre; but the city, in order to escape bombardment, capitulated during the night; and on the 31st, the sovereigns of Russia and Prussia made a peaceful entry. The emperor of Austria had remained at Lyons.[k]

### ALEXANDER I AT THE CAPITULATION OF PARIS (1814 A.D.)

The success at Paris was dearly bought; on the day of the battle the allies lost 8,400 men, of whom 6,000 were Russians. The magnitude of the losses is explained by the absence of unity in the operations of the allies and the consequent want of simultaneousness in the attacks from all parts of the allied army. However, the success of the day dealt a direct and decisive blow at the very strongest part of the enemy's position. While negotiations were being carried on with the French marshals for the surrender of Paris, the emperor Alexander made the tour of the troops, which were disposed near Belleville and Chaumont, and congratulated them on the victory; he then raised Count Barclay de Tolly to the rank of field-marshal. After that he returned to Bondy.

Meanwhile negotiations for the capitulation of Paris were being carried on in a house occupied by Marshal Marmont. There a large company had assembled anxiously awaiting the decision of the fate of Paris. At the head of those present was Talleyrand. An agreement between the French and the representatives of the allied armies was at last arrived at, and at the third hour after midnight the capitulation of Paris, composed by M. F. Orlov, was signed; the victors, however, had to give up their original stipulation that the French troops which had defended Paris should retire by the Brittany route. In the concluding 8th article of the capitulation, specially referring to the approaching occupation of Paris by the allies, it was said that the town of Paris was recommended to the generosity of the allied powers.

Orlov told Marshal Marmont that the representatives of the town of Paris could unrestrainedly express their desires in person to the emperor Alexander. A deputation from the town was therefore assembled which should proceed without delay to the headquarters of the allies; it consisted of the prefect of police Pasquier, the prefect of the Seine Chabrolles, and a few members of the municipal council and representatives of the garde nationale. At dawn the deputies set off in carriages for Bondy accompanied by Colonel Orlov, who led them through the Russian bivouacs.

On their arrival at headquarters the French were taken into a large room in the castle. Orlov ordered that his arrival should be announced to Count Nesselrode, who went to meet the deputies, whilst Orlov went straight to the emperor, who received him lying in bed. "What news do you bring?" asked the emperor. "Your majesty, here is the capitulation of Paris," answered Orlov. Alexander took the capitulation, read it, folded the paper, and putting it under his pillow, said, "I congratulate you; your name is linked with a great event."

At the time when the above described events were taking place before

Paris, Napoleon had made the following arrangements. When Winzinge-rode's division reached Saint-Dizier Napoleon moved from Doulevant to Bar-sur-Aube. In order to ascertain the real intentions of the allies he ordered increased reconnoitering, which led to the combat at Saint-Dizier, and Winzingerode was thrown back on Bar-le-Duc. From the questions addressed to prisoners Napoleon was convinced that only the cavalry division was left against him and that the chief forces of the allies were directed towards Paris. "This is a fine chess move! I should never have thought that a general of the coalition would have been capable of it!" exclaimed Napoleon. Without delaying, on the 27th of March, Napoleon directed the forces he had at his disposal towards Paris by a circuitous route through Troyes and Fontainebleau. On the 30th of March, at daybreak, when the allies were already before Paris and were preparing to attack the capital, Napoleon and his vanguard had hardly reached Troyes (150 versts from Paris). In the hope that at least by his presence he might amend matters in Paris, the emperor left the troops behind and galloped off to Fontainebleau; arriving there at night, he continued his journey without stopping to Paris. But it was already late, and on the night of the 31st of March, at twenty versts from Paris, Napoleon met the fore ranks of the already departing French troops, from whom he learned of the capitulation concluded by Mar-mont. At six in the morning Napoleon returned to Fontainebleau.

It was about the same time, on the morning of the 31st of March, that the deputation from Paris was received by the emperor Alexander at Bondy. Count Nesselrode presented the members by name to the emperor; after which Alexander addressed to them a discourse which Pasquier has repro-duced in his Mémoires in the following manner: "I have but one enemy in France, and that enemy is the man who has deceived me in the most shame-less manner, who has abused my trust, who has broken every vow to me, and who has carried into my dominions the most iniquitous and odious of wars. All reconciliation between him and me is henceforth impossible, but I repeat I have no other enemy in France. All other Frenchmen are favourably regarded by me. I esteem France and the French, and I trust that they will enable me to help them. I honour the courage and glory of all the brave men against who I have been fighting for two years and whom I have learned to respect in every position in which they have found themselves. I shall always be ready to render to them the justice and the honour which are their due. Say then, gentlemen, to the Parisians, that I do not enter their walls as an enemy, and that it only depends on them to have me for a friend, but say also that I have one sole enemy in France, and that with him I am irreconcil-able." Pasquier adds that this thought was repeated in twenty different tones and always with the expression of the utmost vehemence, the emperor meanwhile pacing up and down the room.

### THE RUSSIAN OCCUPATION OF PARIS

Then entering into details as to the occupation of Paris, the emperor Alex-ander consented to leave the preservation of tranquillity in the capital to the national guard, and gave his word that he would require nothing from the inhabitants, beyond provisions for the army; it was decided that the troops should be bivouacked. Having dismissed the deputation, the emperor Alex-ander ordered Count Nesselrode to set off immediately for Paris to Talley-rand and concert with him as to the measures to be taken in the commence-ment; the count entered the town accompanied by a single Cossack.

[1814 A.D.]

"The boulevards were covered with well-dressed crowds of people," writes Count Nesselrode in his Mémoires. "It seemed as if the people had assembled for a holiday rather than to assist at the entry of the enemy's troops. Talleyrand was at his toilet; his hair only half-done; he rushed to meet me, threw himself into my arms and bestrewed me with powder. When he was somewhat tranquillised he ordered certain persons with whom he was conspiring to be called. They were the duke of Dalberg, the abbe de Pradt, and Baron Louis. I transmitted the desires of the emperor Alexander to my companions, telling them that he remained firmly determined upon one point — not to leave Napoleon on the throne of France; that later on the question as to what order of things must from henceforth reign would be decided by his majesty, not otherwise than after consultation with the prominent personages with whom he would be brought into relations."[1]

The emperor Alexander had intended to stop at the Élysée palace (Élysée Bourbon), but, having received information that mines had been laid under the palace, he sent the communication on to Count Nesselrode; when Talleyrand heard of it he would not believe the truth of the information, but, from excess of caution, he proposed that the emperor should stay with him until the necessary investigations should be made. In all probability the alarm raised had been prepared by the dexterity of Prince Bénévent himself, who thus made sure of the presence of the head of the coalition in his house.

After Count Nesselrode's departure for Paris, Colencourt made his appearance at Bondy, being sent to the emperor Alexander by Napoleon with proposals for the conclusion of immediate peace on conditions similar to those exacted by the allied powers at Châtillon. The emperor told the duke of Vicenza that he considered himself bound to secure the tranquillity of Europe, and that therefore neither he nor his allies intended to carry on negotiations with Napoleon. It was in vain that Colencourt endeavoured to shake Alexander's decision, representing to him that the allied monarchs, by deposing from the throne a sovereign whom they had all acknowledged, would show themselves upholders of the destructive ideas of the revolution. "The allied monarchs do not desire the overthrow of thrones," replied Alexander, "they will support not any particular party of those dissatisfied with the present government but the general voice of the most estimable men of France. We have decided to continue the struggle to the end, in order that it may not have to be renewed under less favourable circumstances, and we shall combat until we attain a solid and durable peace, which it is impossible to look for from the man who has devastated Europe from Moscow to Cadiz." In conclusion Alexander promised to receive Colencourt at any time in Paris.

"The subjection of Paris has shown itself to be an indispensable inheritance for our chroniclers. Russians could not open the glorious book of their history without shame if after the page on which Napoleon is represented standing amidst Moscow in flames did not follow that where Alexander appears in the midst of Paris."

As he left Bondy, Napoleon's envoy saw the horse prepared for Alexander to ride on his approaching entry into Paris; it was a light-grey horse called Eclipse which had formerly been presented to the emperor when Colencourt was ambassador in St. Petersburg. About eight o'clock in the morning Alexander left Bondy. "All were prepared to meet a day unexampled in history," writes an eye-witness.

After he had ridden about a verst, the emperor met the king of Prussia

[1] From the Russian State Archives.

and the guards; letting the Russian guard and his own guard's light cavalry pass in front, as they were to head the troops entering Paris, Alexander followed after them with the king of Prussia and Prince Schwarzenberg, accompanied by a suite of more than a thousand generals and officers of various nationalities. After them came the Austrian grenadiers, the Russian grenadier corps, the foot-guards, and three divisions of cuirassiers with artillery. The most superb weather favoured the triumph of this memorable day.

What were the feelings which then filled the soul of Alexander? Of what was the sovereign thinking that had lived through the painful experiences of Austerlitz, the glitter of Tilsit, changing to the defeat of Friedland and the burning of Moscow? In entire humility he was prepared to repay the evil and mortification he had endured by a magnanimity unheard of in history. Actually there appeared in the midst of Paris a victor who sought for no other triumph but the happiness of the vanquished. Even at Vilna, in December, 1812, the emperor Alexander had said: "Napoleon might have given peace to Europe. He might have — but he did not! Now the enchantment has vanished. Let us see which is best: to make oneself feared or beloved." In Paris a noble field awaited the emperor for changing into action these generous thoughts and aspirations after the ideal.

The streets were crowded with people, and even the roofs of the houses were covered with curious spectators. White draperies hung from the windows and the women at the windows and on the balconies waved white handkerchiefs. Henri Houssaye has very justly defined the frame of mind of the Parisian population on the day of the 31st of March: "They did not reason, they breathed." Answering graciously to the greetings of the populace, the emperor said in a loud voice: "I do not come as an enemy. I come to bring you peace and commerce." The emperor's words called forth acclamations and exclamations of "Vive la paix!" A Frenchman who had managed to push his way right up to the emperor said: "We have been waiting for you a long time." "It is the fault of the bravery of your troops if I have not come sooner," answered Alexander. "How handsome the emperor Alexander is, how graciously he bows. He must stay in Paris or give us a sovereign like himself," said the French to each other.

The allied troops were met with joyful exclamations of "Long live Alexander! Long live the Russians! Long live the allies!" As the allies approached the Champs-Elysées, the enthusiasm grew and began to assume the character of a demonstration against the government of Napoleon; white cockades made their appearance on hats and the exclamations resounded: "Long live the Bourbons! Down with the tyrant!" All these manifestations did not, however, arouse the least sympathy among the people for the Bourbons, who were unknown to it; the movement was purely superficial and partly artificial. The French, seeing the white bands on the Russian uniforms, imagined that Europe had taken up arms for the Bourbons, and in their turn showed the colour for which in their hearts they had no sympathy.

### ALEXANDER I AND THE CONGRESS OF VIENNA (1815 A.D.)

The restoration of the French Empire hastened the settlement of the disputed points at the congress of Vienna. On the 3rd of May, 1815, treaties were signed between Russia, Austria, and Prussia which determined the fate of the duchy of Warsaw; it was forever united to the Russian Empire, with the exception of Posen, Bromberg, and Thorn, which were given to Prussia; Cracow was declared a free town, and the salt mines of Weliczka were returned to Austria, together with the province of Tarnopol, which had belonged to Russia since 1809. Alexander took the title King of Poland and reserved to himself the right of giving to this kingdom, which was destined to have a social government, that "interior extension" which he judged right. In general it was proposed to give to the Russian as well as the Austrian and Prussian subjects the right of national representation and national government institutions in conformity with the form of political states which each government would consider most advantageous and most fitted to the sphere of its possessions. On the same day a treaty was concluded between the plenipotentiaries of Prussia and Saxony, according to the conditions of which the king of Saxony ceded to Prussia almost all Lusatia and a part of Saxony. Finally, more than a month later, on the 8th of June, 1815, the act of the German alliance was signed, and on the following day, the 9th of June, the chief act of the congress of Vienna.

Upon the basis of the conditions of the treaty of 1815, Russia increased her territory to the extent of about 2,100 square miles with a population of more than three millions; Austria acquired 2,300 square miles with three million inhabitants, and Prussia 2,217 square miles with 5,362,000 inhabitants. Thus Russia, who had borne all the three years' war with Napoleon, and made the greatest sacrifices for the triumph of the interests of Europe, received the smallest reward.

A few days before the signing of the treaties that determined the fate of the duchy of Warsaw, which had so long remained in an indefinite position, the emperor Alexander informed the president of the Polish senate, Count Ostrovski, of the approaching union of the kingdom of Poland to the Russian empire. In this letter, amongst other things, it was said: "If in the great interest of general tranquillity it could not be permitted that all the Poles should become united under one sceptre, I have at least endeavoured as far as possible to soften the hardships of their separation and to obtain for them everywhere all possible enjoyment of their nationality." Following upon this came the manifesto to the inhabitants of the kingdom of Poland granting them a constitution, self-government, an army of their own, and freedom of the press.

On the 21st of May, 1815, the solemnity of the restoration of the kingdom of Poland was celebrated in Warsaw. In his letter to the emperor Alexander, Prince Adam Czartoriski expressed the conviction that the remembrance of that day would be for the generous heart of the sovereign a reward for his labours for the good of humanity. All the functionaries of the state assembled in the Catholic cathedral church, where, after divine service had been celebrated, were read the act of renunciation of the king of Saxony, the manifesto of the emperor of all the Russias, king of Poland, and the basis of the future constitution. The council of the empire, the senate, the officials, and the inhabitants then took the oath of allegiance to the sovereign and the constitution. Then the Polish standard with the white eagle was raised over the royal castle and on all government buildings, whilst in all the churches thanksgiving services were celebrated, accompanied by the pealing of bells and firing of cannon. After this all the state dignitaries set off to wait on the czarevitch, Constantine Pavlovitch. The troops were assembled in the plain near Wola, where an altar had been erected; there, in the presence of the august commander-in-chief of the Polish army, the soldiers took the oath in battalions. The cannonades and salvoes of artillery which concluded the solemnity were interrupted by the loud exclamations of the people: "Long live our king Alexander!"

Prince Adam Czartoriski, who had been sent by the emperor from Vienna, occupied a place in the council. On the 25th of May Alexander wrote to him as follows: "You have had occasion to become acquainted with my intentions as to the institutions that I wish to establish in Poland, and the improvements that I desire to carry on in that country. You will endeavour never to lose sight of them during the deliberations of the council and to direct the attention of your colleagues to them in order that the course of government and the reforms, which are confided to them to bring into execution, may be in accordance with my views." A committee was formed for the framing of a constitution, composed of Polish dignitaries under the presidency of Count Ostrovski.

But this benign condition of affairs in the newly created kingdom was not of long duration, and on the 29th of July, 1815, Prince Czartoriski had to complain to the emperor of the czarevitch, and expressed his conviction that no enemy could occasion greater injuries to Alexander. It was, he said, as though he wished to bring matters to a rupture. "No zeal, no submission can soften him," wrote Prince Adam to the emperor. "Neither the army, nor the nation, nor private individuals can find favour in his sight. The constitution in particular gives him occasion for ceaseless, bitter derision; everything of rule, form, or law is made the object of mockery and laughter, and unfortunately deeds have already followed upon words. The grand duke does not even observe the military laws which he himself has established. He absolutely wishes to bring in corporal punishments and gave orders yesterday that they should be brought into force, in spite of the unanimous representations of the committee. Desertion, which is already now considerable, will become general; in September most of the officers will ask for their discharge. In fact, it is as if a plan were laid to oppose the views of your majesty, in order to render the benefits you have conferred void, in order to frustrate from the very beginning the success of your enterprise. His imperial highness in such a case would be, without himself knowing it, the blind instrument of this destructive design, of which the first effect would be to exasperate equally both Russians and Poles and to take away all power from your majesty's most solemn declarations. What would I not give for it to be possible to here satisfy the grand duke and fulfil the desires of your majesty in this respect! But this is decidedly impossible, and if he remains here I on the contrary foresee the most lamentable consequences!"

Indeed, as we look more closely into the state of affairs in Warsaw in the year 1815, it remains an unsolved enigma how the emperor Alexander, knowing as he did the indomitable character of his brother, could resolve to confide the destiny of the kingdom he had newly created to the wilful, arbitrary hands of the czarevitch, whose personality as the probable heir to the throne of Russia had disturbed the Poles since the time of the termination of the war of 1812. Prince Czartoriski's letter did not alter Alexander's determination: the czarevitch remained in Warsaw, and continued his impolitic course of action, the lamentable results of which were revealed by subsequent events.

On the 21st of May in Vienna the emperor signed the manifesto calling upon all the powers who observed the laws of truth and piety to take up arms against the usurper of the French throne. In the same manifesto the annexation to Russia of the greater part of the former duchy of Warsaw was announced: "Security is thus given to our frontiers, a firm defence is raised, calumnies and inimical attempts are repulsed, and the ties of brother-

[1815 A.D.]

hood renewed between races mutually united by a common origin. We have therefore considered it advantageous to assure the destiny of this country by basing its interior administration upon special regulations, peculiar to the speech and customs of the inhabitants and adapted to their local position. Following the teaching of the Christian law, whose dominion embraces so vast a number of people of various races, but at the same time preserves their distinctive qualities and customs unchanged, we have desired in creating the happiness of our new subjects, to plant in their hearts the feeling of devotion to our throne and thus for ever efface the traces of former misfortunes arising from pernicious discord and protracted struggles." Without waiting for the termination of the congress the emperor Alexander left Vienna on the 25th of May; he desired to be nearer the Rhine until the arrival of the Russian troops and in closer proximity to the seat of the approaching military action.[g] The Russians, however, who were to have formed the army of the middle Rhine, were unable, though making forced marches, to arrive in time to take part in the brief campaign which terminated Napoleon's reign of the hundred days.[k]

### ALEXANDER'S RELIGIOUS MYSTICISM; BARONESS KRÜDENER

When he had left Vienna, the emperor Alexander stopped for a short time at Munich and Stuttgart, and on the 4th of June he arrived at Heilbronn, which had been chosen for the Russian headquarters. Here took place his first meeting with Baroness Juliane Krüdener.

Baroness Krüdener (born Vietinghov), the author of the famous novel *Valérie*, had already long since been converted from a vain woman of the world, and had entered upon the path of mystical pietism. Her acquaintance with the Moravian brethren and in particular with Johann Jung had definitely confirmed her ideas in a pious philanthropic direction. With the exaltation that was natural to her she became more and more persuaded that a great work lay before her, that God himself had entrusted her with a lofty mission, to turn the unbelieving to the path of truth. As her biographer observes, she was ready to affirm in imitation of Louis XIV that "*Le ciel c'est moi*" (Heaven is I). In 1814 Baroness Krüdener became intimate with the maid of honour Mlle. R. S. Sturdza, and through her penetrated to the empress Elizabeth Alexievna.

But, according to her own words, an inward voice told her that the matter was not to end there; the final aim of her aspiration was a friendship with the emperor Alexander, whose spiritual condition at that time was fully known to her from her conversations with Mademoiselle Sturdza as well as after the emperor's interviews with Johann Jung which took place during his majesty's stay at Bronchsaal. During the congress of Vienna Juliane Krüdener kept up an active correspondence with Mademoiselle Sturdza; in it she referred to the emperor Alexander and the great and beautiful qualities of his soul. "I have already known for some time that the Lord will grant me the joy of seeing him," wrote Baroness Krüdener; "if I live till then, it will be one of the happiest moments of my life. I have a multitude of things to tell him, for I have investigated much on his behalf: the Lord alone can prepare his heart to receive them; I am not uneasy about it; my business is to be without fear and reproach; his, to bow down before Christ, the truth." With these spiritual effusions were artfully mixed mysterious prophecies, such as: "The storm draws nigh, the lilies have appeared only to vanish."

Mademoiselle Sturdza was struck by these mysterious prognostications and showed the letter to the emperor Alexander; he commissioned her to write to Baroness Krüdener that he would esteem it a happiness to meet her. The correspondence was further prolonged in the same spirit and finally the "prince of darkness" appeared on the scene, preventing her conversing with Alexander, that instrument of mercy, of heavenly things. "But the Almighty will be stronger than he," wrote Baroness Krüdener; "God, who loves to make use of those who in the eyes of the world serve as objects of humiliation and mockery, has prepared my heart for that submission which does not seek the approval of men. I am only a nonentity. He is everything, and earthly kings tremble before Him." The emperor Alexander's first religious transport, in the mystical sense, had manifested itself in the year 1812, when heavy trials fell upon Russia and filled his soul with alarm. His religious aspirations could not be satisfied with the usual forms and ceremonies of the church; in the matter of religion he sought for something different. Having separated himself, under the influence of fatal events, from those humanitarian ideals which to a certain degree had animated him in his youth he had adopted religious conventions; but here, also, by the nature of his character, he was governed by aspirations after the ideal, without, however, departing from the sentimental romanticism that was peculiar to him. Under such conditions Alexander must necessarily have been impressionable to the influence of pietists and mystics.

When he came to Heilbronn he was overwhelmed with weariness and sadness after the pompous receptions at the courts of Munich and Würtemberg, and his soul thirsted for solitude. During the first interview Baroness Krüdener lifted the veil of the past before the eyes of Alexander and represented to him his life with all its errors of ambition and vain pride; she proved to her listener that the momentary awakening of conscience, the acknowledgment of weaknesses, and temporary repentance do not constitute a full expiation of sins, and do not yet lead to spiritual regeneration. "No, your majesty," said she to him, "you have not yet drawn near to the god man, as a criminal begging for mercy. You have not yet received forgiveness from him, who alone has the power to absolve sins upon earth. You are still in your sins. You have not yet humbled yourself before Jesus, you have not yet said, like the publican, from the depths of your heart: 'God, I am a great sinner; have mercy upon me!' And that is why you do not find spiritual peace. Listen to the words of a woman, who has also been a great sinner, but who has found pardon of all her sins at the foot of the cross of Christ." Baroness Krüdener talked to Alexander in this strain for nearly three hours. Alexander could only say a few broken words, and bowing his head on his hands, he shed abundant tears. All the words he heard, were, as the Scripture expresses it, like a two-edged sword, piercing to the very depths of the soul and spirit, and trying the feelings and thoughts of his heart. Finally, Baroness Krüdener, alarmed by the agitated state into which her words had thrown Alexander, said to him: "Sire, I beg you to pardon the tone in which I have spoken. Believe that in all sincerity of heart and before God I have said to you truths which have never before been said to you. I have only fulfilled a sacred duty to you." "Do not be afraid," answered Alexander, "all your words have found a place in my heart: you have helped me to discover in myself what I had never before observed; I thank God for it, but I must often have such conversations, and I ask you not to go away."

From that day such conversations became a spiritual necessity to the emperor Alexander and a moral support in the pathway upon which he from thenceforth stood. According to the opinion of Prince Galitzin, Alexander's conversations with Baroness Krüdener were of a spiritual tendency, and perhaps only in part touched upon contemporary events. "There is no doubt," says Prince Galitzin, "that Baroness Krüdener, who lived by faith, strengthened the development of faith in the emperor by her disinterested and experienced counsels; she certainly directed the will of Alexander to still greater self-sacrifice and prayer, and perhaps at the same time revealed to him the secret of that spiritual, prayerful communion which, although designed by God as an inheritance for all mortals, is unfortunately the portion of a very few chosen ones." From that time it only remained for Prince Galitzin to experience a lively feeling of satisfaction as he observed, "with what giant strides the emperor advanced in the pathway of religion."

If the moral sphere in which Alexander began to move awakened the entire sympathy of Prince Galitzin, others looked upon the matter from another point of view.

In accordance with the course he had adopted during the campaigns of 1813 and 1814, the emperor desired to remain at the centre of military operations. This intention was not to the taste of the Austrians, and from their headquarters at Heidelberg they sent a notification that it was difficult to find suitable premises in such a small place and that his majesty would be far more tranquil if he prolonged his stay at Heilbronn. The emperor ordered an answer to be sent to the effect that he requested that only one or two houses should be allotted for his occupation in Heidelberg, and that his headquarters should be established in the neighbouring villages. After this, on the 6th of June, Alexander removed to Heidelberg and finally took up his abode outside the town, upon the banks of the Necker, in the house of an Englishman, named Pickford, and here remained until the 10th of June, awaiting the approach of his army to the Rhine. The Baroness Krüdener also did not delay removing to Heidelberg; she settled not far from the house occupied by the emperor. He spent most of his evenings with her and, listening to her instructions, in confidential intercourse he told her of the griefs and passions which had darkened his sorrowful life. In these conversations, the fellow traveller and collaborator of Baroness Krüdener, Empaitaz, also took part. Baroness Krüdener did not flatter Alexander, she possessed the gift of speaking the truth without giving offence. According to the opinion of her admirers she might have become a beneficent genius for Russia, but this was hindered by the hypocrisy of various unworthy persons, who took advantage of this new frame of mind of the emperor, using it as a means for the attainment of aims which were not at all in accordance with Alexander's lofty sentiments and intentions.

Becoming more and more convinced of the power of repentance and prayer, the emperor once said to Empaitaz: "I can assure you that when I find myself in awkward situations I always come out of them through prayer. I will tell you something which would greatly astonish everyone if it were known: when I am in counsel, with ministers, who are far from sharing my principles, and they show themselves of opposite opinions, instead of disputing, I lift up an inward prayer, and little by little they come round to principles of humanity and justice."

Alexander had adopted the habit of daily reading the Holy Scriptures and began to seek in them immediate answers to his doubts. "On the 7th of June," relates Empaitaz, "he read the 35th psalm; in the evening he told us that this psalm had dispersed all remaining anxiety in his soul as to the success of the war; thenceforth he was convinced that he was acting in accordance with the will of God."

ALEXANDER'S HOLY ALLIANCE (1815 A.D.)

The conclusion of the Holy Alliance belongs to this period (1815). In conceiving the idea of it, the emperor Alexander intended, independently of ordinary political negotiations, to strengthen the common bond between monarchies by an act based on the immutable truths of the divine teaching, to create an alliance which should bind together monarchies and nations by ties of brotherhood, consecrated by religion, and should be for them, like the Gospel, obligatory by conscience, feeling and duty. The emperor Alexander said one day to Baroness Krüdener: "I am leaving France, but before my departure I want by a public act to give due praise to God the Father, the Son, and the Holy Ghost, for the protection he has shown us, and to call upon the nations to stand in obedience to the Gospel. I have brought you the project of this act and ask you to look over it attentively, and if you do not approve any of the expressions used to indicate them to me. I desire that the emperor of Austria and the king of Prussia should unite with me in this act of adoration, in order that people may see that we, like the eastern magi, confess the supreme power of God the Saviour. You will unite with me in prayer to God that my allies may be disposed to sign it."

Alexander wrote out the draft of the Act of the Holy Alliance with his own hand, and Mademoiselle Sturdza and Count Vapadistria took part in the wording of it. The latter ventured to observe that no such act was to be met with in the annals of diplomacy and that his majesty might express the ruling idea of the act in a declaration or manifesto. Alexander replied that his decision was unchangeable, that he took it upon himself to obtain the signature to it of his allies, the emperor of Austria and the king of Prussia. As to France, England, and other courts — "that," said the emperor to him, "will already be your concern."

The treaty of the Christian brotherly alliance, imagined by Alexander and called the Holy Alliance, consisted of three articles according to which the allies bound themselves: (1) to remain united by the indissoluble ties of brotherly friendship, to show each other help and co-operation, to govern their subjects in the same spirit of fraternity in order to maintain truth and peace; (2) to esteem themselves members of one Christian people, placed by providence to rule over three branches of one and the same family; and (3) to invite all the powers to acknowledge these rules and to enter the Holy Alliance. The sovereigns who signed the treaty were bound, "both in ruling over their own subjects and in political relations with other governments, to be guided by the precepts of the holy Gospel, which, not being limited in their application to private life alone, should immediately govern the wills of monarchs and their actions."

King Frederick William willingly declared his consent to become a member of the Holy Alliance, conceived in the same spirit as the scene that had once taken place at night at the tomb of Frederick the Great in the garrison church at Potsdam, and appearing to be the realisation of the thought expressed by the sovereigns after the battle of Bautzen: "If the Lord blesses our undertakings," said they, "then will we give praise to him before the face of the whole world."

The emperor Francis, however, received with greater reserve the proposal to join the Holy Alliance; he was in general incapable of letting himself be carried away by fantastic ideas and romanticism or of being subject to enthusiastic impulses of any kind. He consented to sign the treaty only after Metternich had tranquillised him with the assurance that the project should only

[1815 A.D.]

be regarded as inoffensive chatter. But although in his narrative of the formation of the Holy Alliance Metternich contemptuously calls it "this empty, sonorous monument," he passes over one point in silence: by joining this treaty Austria obtained a valuable instrument for placing Russia at the head of the reactionary movement in Europe, and Metternich did not hesitate to take advantage of this circumstance with inimitable art in order to attain the political aims he had traced out. Only two sovereigns did not receive invitations to join the Holy Alliance: the pope and the sultan. The prince regent limited himself to a letter in which he expressed his approval of the context of the treaty, but on account of parliamentary considerations the English government did not join the alliance.

The Act of the Holy Alliance concluded in Paris with the emperor of Austria and the king of Prussia remained secret for some time, as the emperor Alexander did not desire to make it generally known. Christmas Day (December 25th, 1815) (January 6th, 1816) was the occasion chosen for the publication of the treaty. In the manifesto issued, it is said: "Having learned from experiences and consequences calamitous to the whole world that the course of former political relations between the European powers was not based on those principles of truth through which the wisdom of God, made known in his revelation, assures the peace and prosperity of nations, we have, conjointly with their majesties, the Austrian emperor Francis I and the king of Prussia, Frederick William, entered upon the establishment of an alliance between ourselves (inviting other Christian powers to take part in the same), by which we are mutually bound, both between ourselves and in relation to our subjects, to take for the sole means of attaining our ends the rule drawn from the words and teaching of our Saviour Jesus Christ, enjoining men to live as brothers, not in enmity and malice, but in peace and love. We desire and pray to the most High that he may send down his grace upon us, that he may confirm this Holy Alliance between all the powers, to their common welfare, and may no one venture to hinder unanimity by falseness to our compact. Therefore, adding to this a transcript of the alliance, we command that it shall be made public and read in all churches."

The most holy synod, in its turn, ordered that the treaty of the Holy Alliance should be printed and placed on the walls of churches or affixed to boards, and also that ideas should be borrowed from it for preaching. And thus, from the year 1816 Russia entered upon a new political path — an apocalyptic one; from thenceforth in diplomatic documents relating to the epoch, instead of clearly defined and political aims, we meet with obscure commentaries concerning the spirit of evil, vanquished by Providence, the word of the Most High, the word of life.[1] The ideal of the government administrators of that period, who stood at the head of affairs, became a sort of vague theological, patriarchal monarchy. Over Europe was lowered the dark veil of continuous and close reaction.*g*

The real significance of European history during the next period is best understood by studying the development of the alliances formed against the power of Napoleon, like the one under consideration, and which endured being renewed from time to time as occasion demanded. At first these were directed towards a definite object, but they gradually assumed wider scope, and in a spirit quite foreign to the "Holy Alliance," endeavoured to arrest

[1] The letter written by Emperor Alexander on the 18th of March, 1816, to Count Sieven, Ambassador in London, upon the occasion of the publication of the treaty of the Holy Alliance and preserved in the Russian State Archives, affords a clear instance of the direction of politics at that time.

and stem the aspirations of the period, whether legitimate or degenerate. The partly stationary, partly retrograde attitude of all, or most, of the European governments, which afterward became general, had its inception at this time. The spirit of absolutism, in short, found expression in the Holy Alliance. That this mystic Alliance was not suitable for any practical purpose was proved on the spot.[1]

It was quite apparent and recognised by all that France could not be left to herself, for it had been determined to leave an allied army of 150,000 men under the Duke of Wellington in possession of the French fortresses. For what purpose and under what conditions this was to take place, naturally had to be decided by some explicit treaty. On the same day on which peace with France was signed — 20th November — the four powers which had signed the Treaty of Chaumont, England, Russia, Austria, and Prussia concluded among themselves a new Alliance of real and far-reaching significance. The new treaty confirmed the compacts made at Chaumont, and on the 25th of March, of the current year 1815, the allies expressed their conviction that the peace of Europe depended upon the consolidation of the restored order of things in France, on the maintenance of the royal authority and of the constitutional charter; they pledged themselves to reinforce the garrison troops in France, if necessary by 60,000 men from each of the four Powers, or if required by their combined army, in order to exclude Bonaparte and his family for ever from the French throne, but to support the sovereignty of the Bourbons and the Constitution. They further agreed, after the time fixed for the investment of France by the allied troops had elapsed, to adopt measures for the maintenance of the existing order of things in France and of the peace of Europe. In order to facilitate the execution of these duties and to consolidate the friendly relations of the four powers, it was arranged that from time to time, at certain fixed intervals, meetings of the sovereigns in person or of their ministers — congresses in fact — should take place, to consult concerning the great and common interests of the allies, and the measures that might be considered necessary at the time to promote the welfare and peace of the nations and of Europe.

It was this treaty which founded and introduced the Congress policy of the next decade, and it is well to note that France although a member of the Holy Alliance was excluded from this league, as was to be expected, and that England which had remained outside the Holy Alliance, here stood at the head of affairs. The true position and significance of things are thereby made clear.[j]

[1 Skrine[l] says, however: "For nearly half a century the Holy Alliance was the keystone of the edifice erected at Vienna, the hidden chain which linked Russia with the other military powers."]

# CHAPTER X

## ALEXANDER I, MYSTIC AND HUMANITARIAN

### [1801–1825 A.D.]

> Heaven grant that we may one day attain our aim of making Rus-
> sia free and of preserving her from despotism and tyranny. This is
> my unique desire, and I willingly sacrifice all my labours and my life
> to the aim that is so dear to me.—ALEXANDER I.

#### THE COMPLEX CHARACTER OF ALEXANDER I

In the preceding chapter, we followed the history of the external affairs
of Russia during fourteen years of the reign of Alexander I. Now we shall
witness the incidents of that monarch's later years, and, in particular, shall
consider the internal condition of Russia during the reign of one of the most
interesting of sovereigns. Clearly to appreciate the complex character of
the reigns, we may follow Shilder, partly by way of recapitulation, in dividing it into three periods, each of which seems to represent a phase of the
mental evolution of Alexander.[a]

The first period embraces the time between the years 1801 and 1810,
and is usually designated as the epoch of reforms, but as we penetrate more
deeply into the spirit of that period, we come to the conclusion that it might
more justly be termed the epoch of vacillations. Actually, at this time,
that is from 1801 to 1810, ceaseless vacillations took place in the governmental life of Russia, both in regard to the outward as well as the inward
policy of the empire; throughout every branch of the administration of the
state an entire instability of views and brusque changes from one political
system to another were to be observed. All these manifestations were conditional exclusively on the personality of the emperor Alexander, who pos-

sessed the characteristic of not unfrequently vacillating at short intervals between two entirely opposed frames of mind, without reference to the direction he had elected to follow.

The second period is continued from 1810 to 1816 and in its inner signification is entirely concentrated in the struggle with France. This period in contrast to the preceding, is distinguished by the pursuit of one ruling idea, carried out with remarkable consecutiveness to the end, an instance which is almost unique in the whole reign of Alexander. Unexpectedly to all, to the astonishment of the whole world, in 1812, he showed himself immovable and decided to be or not to be. Meanwhile Napoleon, preparing himself for the invasion of Russia, had based his political and military calculations upon the imaginary weakness of Alexander's character, and in this respect the conqueror's hidden thoughts corresponded with the secret calculations of his allies, Metternich and Hardenburg. All these three enemies of Russia were however destined to experience complete disenchantment. The ruling idea of Alexander, which he then steadfastly followed, consisted in the overthrow of Napoleon. [These two periods we have covered in the preceding chapter, but we shall have occasion to revert to certain phases and incidents of their development.]

The third period, beginning from the year 1816, finishes with the death of the emperor Alexander in 1825. Historians usually call it the period of congresses and of the preservation of order in Europe established by them. It would be more exact and nearer to the truth to call this last decade the period of reaction.

After the overthrow of Napoleon the emperor Alexander appears as a weary martyr, wavering between the growing influence of Araktcheiev and his own personal convictions which he had adopted in the days of his youth. Amongst the reactionary measures which commenced in 1816 there can still be traced bright gleams of the enthusiasms and dreams of his youth. The speech pronounced in 1818 by the emperor at the opening of the Polish diet testifies to this. But from the year 1820 a complete vanishing of all the previous ideals to the realisation of which he had once aspired with sincere enthusiasm, is to be observed. To this moral condition was also united an incurable weariness of life, the signs of which had already been observed in the emperor Alexander by Metternich at the congress of Verona in 1822.

As we enter upon a closer analysis of the three periods into which we have divided this reign, we remark another curious feature in the development of Alexander. Metternich calls this phenomenon that of the periodic evolutions of the emperor's mind *(les évolutions périodiques de son esprit).* The phenomenon was repeated with striking regularity about every five years of his reign. Assimilating to himself any idea with which he was inspired, Alexander gave himself up to it, unhesitatingly and with full enthusiasm. The incubation required about two years, during which the idea acquired for him the importance of a system; the third year he remained faithful to the system chosen, he became more and more attached to it, he listened with real enthusiasm to its upholders and at such a time was inaccessible to any influence that might shake the justness of the views he had adopted. The fourth year he grew disturbed at the consequences which might possibly arise; the fifth year there became observable a medley of the old and vanishing system with some new idea which was beginning to take birth in his mind. This idea was usually diametrically opposed to the one that had left his horizon. After that, when he had assimilated the new convictions, he did not preserve any remembrance of the ideas he had abandoned, beyond the obligations which bound him to the various representatives of the former views. [b]

From 1806 to 1812 the preponderating influence over Alexander I was that of Speranski. Son of a village priest, educated in a seminary, and afterwards professor of mathematics and philosophy in the seminary of Alexander Nevski, Speranski became preceptor to the children of Alexis Kurakin, thanks to whom he quitted the ecclesiastical for a civil career, and became secretary to Trochtchinski, who was then chancellor of the imperial council. Later, after he had become director of the department of the interior under Prince Kotchubei, Speranski rose to the position of secretary of state and gained the complete confidence of the emperor. The favourites of the preceeding period had all been imbued with English ideas; Speranski, on the contrary, loved France and manifested a particular admiration for Napoleon. These French sympathies, shared at the time by Alexander I, formed a new bond between the prince and the minister which was not severed until the rupture with Napoleon. "We know," said Monsieur Bogdanovitch, "Alexander's fondness for representative forms and a constitutional government, but this taste resembles that of a dilettante who goes into ecstacies over a fine painting. Alexander early convinced himself that neither Russia's vast extent nor the constitution of civil society would permit the realisation of his dream. From day to day he deferred the execution of his utopian ideas, but delighted to discourse with his intimates upon the projected constitution and the disadvantages of absolutism. To please the emperor, Speranski ardently defended the principles of liberty, and by so doing exposed himself to accusations of anarchy and of having conceived projects dangerous to institutions that had received the consecration of time and custom." Painstaking, learned, and profoundly patriotic and humane, he was the man best able to realise all that was practicable in the ideas of Alexander.

Speranski presented to the sovereign a systematic plan of reform. The imperial council received an extension of privileges. Composed as it was of the chief dignitaries of the state, it became in a measure the legislative power, and had the duty of examining new laws, extraordinary measures, and ministerial reports; it was in reality a sketch of a representative government. After the interview at Erfurt, during which Napoleon had showed him marked attention, Speranski entered into relations with the French legal writers, Locré, Legras, Dupont de Nemours, and made them correspondents of the legislative commission of the imperial council. The Code Napoleon was not adapted to any but a homogeneous nation emancipated from personal and feudal servitude, with a population whose members all enjoyed a certain equality before the law. Thus to Speranski the emancipation of the serfs was the corner-stone of regeneration. He dreamed of instituting a third estate, of limiting the number of privileged classes, and of forming the great aristocratic families into a peerage similar to that of England. He encouraged Count Stroinovski to publish his pamphlet, *Rules to be Observed between Proprietors and Serfs*. As early as 1809 he had decided that the holders of university degrees should have the advantage over all others in attaining the degrees of the *tchin*. Thus a doctor would at once enter the eighth rank, a master of arts the ninth, a candidate the tenth, and a bachelor the twelfth.

Like Turgot, the minister of Louis XVIII, and the Prussian reformer, Stein, Speranski had aroused the hostility of everyone. The nobility of court and antechamber, and all the young officials who wished to rise by favour alone were exasperated by the ukase of 1809; proprietors were alarmed at Speranski's project for the emancipation of the serfs; the senators were irritated by his plans for reorganisation which would reduce the first governing body of the empire to the position of a supreme court of justice; and the high aristocracy was incensed at the boldness of a man of low condition, the son of a village priest. The people themselves complained at the increase in taxation, all those whose interests had been set aside united against the upstart; he was accused of despising the time-honoured institutions of Moscow and of having presented as a model to the Russians the Code Napoleon when the country was on the eve of war with France. The ministers Balachev, Armfelt, Guriev, Count Rostoptchin, Araktcheiev, and the grand duchess Catherine Pavlovna, sister of the emperor, influenced Alexander against him. Karamzin, the historian, addressed to the emperor an impassioned memoir on *New and Old Russia*, in which he stepped forth as the champion of serfdom, of the old laws, and of autocracy. Speranski's enemy even went to the length of denouncing him as a traitor and an accomplice of France. In March, 1812, he was suddenly sent from the capital to Nijni-Novgorod and afterwards deported to a distant post where he was subjected to close surveillance. He was recalled in 1819, when passions had somewhat cooled, and was appointed governor of Siberia. In 1821 he returned to St. Petersburg, but did not recover his former position.

A new epoch now set in. The adversaries of Speranski, Armfelt, Schichkov, and Rostoptchin attained high positions, but the acknowledged favourite was Araktcheiev, the rough "corporal of Gachina," born enemy to progress and reform and apostle of absolute dominion and passive obedience. He gained the confidence of Alexander, first by his devotion to the memory of Paul, next by his punctuality, his unquestioning obedience, his disinterestedness and habits of industry, and lastly by his ingenuous admiration for the "genius of the emperor." He was the most trustworthy of servitors, the most imperious of superiors, and the most perfect instrument for a reaction. His influence was not at once exclusive. After having conquered Napoleon, Alexander looked upon himself as the liberator of nations. He had set Germany free; he dealt leniently with France and obtained for it a charter; he granted a constitution to Poland, with the intention of extending its benefit to Russia. Though the censorship of the press had recently forbidden the *Viestnik slovesnosti* to criticise, "the servants of his majesty," Alexander had not entirely renounced his utopian ideas. English Protestant influence succeeded to the influence of France; French theatres were closed and Bible societies opened.

Nevertheless, this first period of favour for Araktcheiev soon became an epoch of sterility; though reaction had not yet set in there had at least come a decided pause. The reforms interrupted by the war of 1812 were not to be again resumed. The code of Speranski had come to an end and all efforts to compile one better suited to Russian traditions were of no avail.*

### EDUCATIONAL ADVANCES; THE LYCÉE AND THE LIBRARY

On the 23rd of January of the year 1811 was promulgated the statute of the lycée of Tsarskoi Selo, which had been definitely worked out by secretary of state Speranski. The aim of the establishment of the lycée was the education of young men, and chiefly of those who were destined to fill the most important posts of the government service. The following circumstance was the primary cause of the foundation of this higher educational establishment: although the emperor did not interfere in the matter of the education of his younger brothers, the grand dukes Nicholas and Michael Pavlovitch, which was entirely left to the empress, Marie Feodorovna, a case soon presented itself where the emperor recognised the necessity of departing from the rule he had established. The widowed empress desired to send her sons to the university of Leipsic for the completion of their studies; this was, however, firmly opposed by the emperor, and instead he had the idea of establishing a lycée at Tsarskoi Selo, where his younger brothers could assist at the public lectures. A wing of the palace, connected by a gallery with the chief building, was adapted to this purpose, and the solemn opening of the Tsarskoi Selo lycée took place on the 31st of October, 1811, in the presence of the emperor Alexander. It commenced with a thanksgiving service in the court chapel of Tsarskoi Selo, after which those present accompanied the clergy who made the tour of the edifice, sprinkling it with holy water. At the conclusion of the ecclesiastical ceremony, the imperial charter given to the lycée was read in the hall of the building, and the speeches began. Amongst them that of the adjunct professor Kunitzin earned the special approbation of the emperor for the art with which it avoided generalisations and dwelt on the beneficence of the founder. In conclusion, Alexander inspected the premises allotted to the students, and was present at their dinner table.

TOWER OF IVAN VELIKA, MOSCOW

The year 1811 was also signalised by the completion of the building of the Kazan cathedral, the first stone of which had been laid by the emperor Alexander on the 8th of September, 1801. The constructor of the cathedral was the Russian architect Andrew Nikivorovitch Voroniknin. The building committee was under the direction of the president of the Academy of Arts, Count Alexander Stroganov. The building of the cathedral took ten years, and on the 27th of September, 1811, on the anniversary of the emperor's coronation, the solemn consecration of the new cathedral took place in the presence of the emperor. Count Stroganov was that day elevated to the dignity of actual privy councillor of the first rank. He was not destined to enjoy for long the completion of his work: ten days later he died.

In the very thick of the preparations for war, and amidst such agitating political circumstances as had been unknown till then, the emperor Alexander continued to labour for the enlightenment of his subjects. Notable among his acts at this time was the foundation of a public library. Catherine II's idea of founding in the capital a library for general use, and of rendering it accessible to all, was only brought to fulfilment by Alexander. A special edifice was built with this object; its construction had been already commenced during Catherine's reign. By 1812 all the preliminary work in the building of this library was completed, and on the 14th of January the emperor honoured the newly constructed library with a visit, and examined in detail all its curiosities. Following on this the "draft of detailed rules for the administration of the Imperial Public Library" was ratified by his majesty on the 7th of March.

The events of 1812, however, deferred the actual opening of the library: soon measures had to be thought of to save its treasures. The opening ceremony took place, therefore, two years later, in 1814, on the 14th of January, the anniversary of the day on which the emperor Alexander made his gracious visit to the library, on the memorable occasion of its founding.

A great many festivities took place at the Russian court upon the occasion of the marriage of the grand duke Nicholas Pavlovitch with the princess Charlotte of Prussia (July 13th, 1817). About the same time (July 31st, 1817), a modest festival was celebrated at Tsarskoi Selo — the first distribution of prizes to students of the lycée. On that day the emperor Alexander, accompanied by Prince A. N. Galitzin, was present in the conference hall of the institution he had founded; he himself distributed the prizes and certificates to the pupils, and after having announced the awards to be given to them and their teachers he left, bidding a fatherly farewell to all. The poet Pushkin was amongst the students who took part in the festival.

### EXPULSION OF THE JESUITS FROM ST. PETERSBURG

The year 1815, which had been filled with a series of unexpected events, terminated with an important administrative measure which no one had foreseen. On the 18th of January, 1817, an imperial ukase was issued ordering the immediate expulsion of all the monks of the order of Jesuits from St. Petersburg, and at the same time forbidding their entry into either of the two capitals. In the middle of the night they were provided with fur cloaks, and warm boots, and despatched in carts to the residence of their brethren at Polotsk.[1] It was enjoined in this ukase that the Catholic church in St. Petersburg should be "placed on the same footing that had been established during the reign of the empress Catherine II and which had endured up to the year 1800." This expulsion put an end to the pedagogical activity of the Jesuits in St. Petersburg. The words of N. J. Turgeniev, spoken in the year 1812 and addressed to his successor Gruber, the Berezovski Jesuit, were, in fact, realised for the order in the most unpleasant way. He said: "This is the beginning of the end; you will now do so much that you will be sent away." The government was compelled to have recourse to decisive measures in view of cases of conversion to Catholicism amongst the orthodox pupils of the Jesuit school in St. Petersburg; besides which the influence of Jesuit propaganda was spreading in a remarkable way amongst the ladies of the high society of St. Petersburg.

This measure, however, did not put a limit to the misfortunes that descended upon the Jesuits during the reign of Alexander. A few years later (on the 25th of March, 1820) the order was given that the Jesuits should be expelled finally from Russia, adding that they were not under any aspect or

---

[1] In the year 1812 Alexander had granted a charter to the Jesuit College of Polotsk, raising it to the rank of an "academy" and giving it rights and privileges equal to those of the university; he was then probably governed by political considerations concerning Poland, and in the charter he refers to the college as "affording great advantages for the education of youth" and trusts that the "Jesuits will labour in Poland *dans le bon sens*" (along the right lines.)

denomination to be allowed to return; and at the same time the Polotsk academy was suppressed, as well as all the schools depending on it.

## LIBERATION OF THE PEASANTS OF THE BALTIC PROVINCES (1816–1818 A.D.)

The nobility of Esthonia had in 1811 announced their desire of giving up their rights of servitude over their peasants. In the year 1816 this intention led to the confirmation of the establishment of the Esthonian peasants upon a new footing, according to which the individual right of servitude was abolished. The nobility kept the land as their property, and the relations between the peasants and the landowners were from thenceforth based upon mutual agreement by free will contracts conformable with rules determining essential conditions; a period of transition was appointed for bringing in the new order of things. After the first trial, the individual, landless liberation of the peasants spread throughout the Baltic provinces and in other governments — namely, in Courland in 1817 and in Livonia in 1819. The introduction of the new order of things was everywhere accomplished without any particular difficulty.

In expressing to the Livonian nobility his satisfaction upon the occasion of the reform effected, the emperor Alexander said: "I rejoice that the Livonian nobility has justified my expectations. Your example deserves imitation. You have acted in accordance with the spirit of the times and have understood that liberal principles alone can serve as a basis for the happiness of nations." From these words it is evident that the emperor entertained, according to Shishkov's expression, an unfortunate prejudice against the right of servitude in Russia, and it appeared to many that in other parts of the empire words would be followed by deeds.[1]

From the year 1816, the peasant question began to occupy society. The aide-de-camp of his majesty, Kisselev, even presented a memoir to the emperor which bore the title *Of the Gradual Abolition of Slavery in Russia*. The memoir began with the words: "Civic liberty is the foundation of national prosperity. This truth is so undoubted that I consider it superfluous here to explain how desirable it is that the lawful independence of which serfs and agriculturists are unjustly deprived, should be established for them throughout the empire. I consider this measure the more needful now that the progress of enlightenment and our closer contact with Europe, which hourly increases the fermentation of minds, indicate to the government the necessity of averting the consequences which may follow, and whose menace it would be already difficult or impossible to deny. The blood in which the French Revolution was steeped bears witness to this." In what manner the emperor Alexander regarded the memoir presented by his aide-de-camp, and what fate overtook this production of his pen have remained unknown.

P. D. Kisselev was not the only nobleman who recognised the urgent necessity of the government's occupying itself with the peasant question. The following circumstance serves as a proof of this: in this same year, 1816, many of the richest landowners of the government of St. Petersburg, knowing the emperor's moral aspirations to better the lot of the peasant serfs, decided to turn them into obligatory settlers upon the basis of the then existing regu-

---

[1] Much earlier, in 1807, the emperor had expressed himself to General Savari upon this question in the following words: "I want to bring the country out of the state of barbarism in which this traffic in men leaves it. I will say more — if civilisation were more advanced, I would abolish this slavery even if it were to cost me my head."

lations. The act was drawn up and signed by sixty-five landowners; it only remained to take it to be ratified by the emperor, and for this purpose the general aide-de-camp J. V. Vasiltchikov was chosen. Those who had taken part in the signature of the act supposed that the emperor knew nothing of the meetings that had taken place on the occasion and were convinced that he would receive graciously a proposition, which was in accordance with his manner of thinking. But the emperor Alexander was aware of the determination of the nobles and hardly had Vasiltchikov, after requesting permission to present himself to his majesty, begun to speak of the matter, when Alexander, interrupting him, inquired: "To whom, in your opinion, does the legislative power belong in Russia?" And when Vasiltchikov replied: "Without doubt to your imperial majesty as an autocratic emperor," Alexander, raising his voice, said, "Then leave it to me to promulgate such laws as I consider most beneficial to my subjects."

The emperor's reply gave little hope of a favourable solution of this important question. In the then existing state of affairs, the matter could not avoid passing through the hands of Araktcheiev. This indeed actually happened. In February, 1818, before the departure of the emperor Alexander from Moscow for Warsaw to open the first Polish diet, Count Araktcheiev announced that his majesty had deigned to issue an edict for the liberation of landowners' peasants from the condition of serfdom, with the stipulation that the edict should not in any of its measures be oppressive to the landowners, and especially that it should not present anything of a violent character in its accomplishment on the part of the government: but, on the contrary, that it should be accompanied by advantages for the landowners and awaken in them a desire to co-operate with the government in the abolition of the conditions of serfdom in Russia, an abolition corresponding to the spirit of the times and the progress of education, and indispensable for the future tranquillity of the possessors of serfs.

### THE EMPEROR AND THE QUAKERS

In 1814, at the time of the emperor Alexander's stay in London, the famous philanthropist Quakers, De Grelle de Mobillier,[1] and Allen, had been inspired with the idea of taking advantage of a favourable occasion, and instilling into the minds of the allied sovereigns the conviction that the kingdom of Christ is a kingdom of justice and truth. With this object they first set off to visit the king of Prussia, who received them and praised the Quakers living in his dominions, but expressed his conviction that war is indispensable for the attainment of peace. The emperor Alexander showed them more sympathy; he visited a Quaker meeting and received a deputation. The emperor assured the Quakers that he was in agreement with the greater part of their opinions, and that although on account of his exceptional position his mode of action must be other than theirs, yet he was in union with them in the spiritual worship of Christ. In taking leave of the Quakers, Alexander invited them to come to see him in Russia and said: "I bid you farewell as a friend and brother."

Grelle and Allen arrived in St. Petersburg in November, 1818, during the

---

[1] Étienne de Grelle Mobillier was born in France in 1760 and was brought up in the Roman Catholic faith. At the beginning of the French Revolution he went to America and there entered the society of Friends or Quakers. He subsequently repeatedly visited Europe with various philanthropic aims, mainly in order to strengthen the principles of a morally religious life amongst mankind.

emperor's absence.  They went to Prince A. N. Galitzin, of whom Grelle wrote: "He is a man penetrated by a truly Christian spirit."  Galitzin received the Quakers with an open heart and informed them that the emperor had sent him a letter telling him of their coming to Russia and requesting that they might be received as his friends.  After various questions upon religious matters the Quakers, together with Prince Galitzin, gave themselves up to silent, inward meditation, and this method, writes Grelle, "did not appear at all unknown to the prince.  Inspired by the love of Christ, we felt in ourselves, after silent, heartfelt prayer, the beneficent moving of grace. In taking leave of the prince, he offered us free access to all that could interest us — to the prisons, to reformatory institutions, and to refuges for the poor."

Their visit to the St. Petersburg prisons deeply agitated the pious Quakers; according to Grelle's observations, some of them were very dirty and overrun with vermin; the odour was unbearable and the air contaminated to such a degree that it affected the heads and lungs of the visitors.  The Quakers also inspected a few refuges and schools.

On a subsequent evening the emperor Alexander received the Quakers alone.  He called them his old friends, made them sit beside him on the sofa, and called to mind with inward emotion their interview in London in 1814, saying that it had given him the spirit of courage and firmness amidst all the difficult circumstances in which he was then placed.  "The emperor then," writes Grelle, "suggested to us some questions upon religious matters, thus showing his sincere desire to progress in the saving knowledge of truth.  He further questioned us as to what we had seen and done in Russia.  We took advantage of the opportunity to relate to him the distressing condition of the prisons; and in particular we directed his attention to the wretched state of the prison in Åbo, and told him about an unfortunate man who had been kept in irons there for nineteen years.  The emperor was touched by our narrative and said, 'This ought not to be; it shall not occur again.'  The Quakers also informed the emperor how deeply grieved they had been to see, upon inspecting one of the schools, that the pupils were given books to read that were pernicious to their morals; after which they showed him a specimen of extracts they had made from the Holy Scriptures for the use of schools.  The emperor remained wrapped in thought for a moment, and then turning to his companions, he observed:  "You have done precisely what I much desired. I have often thought that schools might serve as a powerful instrument for the furtherance of the kingdom of Christ, by leading the people to the knowledge of the Saviour and the principles of true piety.  Send me as soon as possible all that you have succeeded in preparing."

The conversation then touched on Daniel Villers, also a Quaker, whom the emperor had called to St. Petersburg to drain the marshes; Alexander said that he regarded his presence in Russia as a blessing to the people.  "It was not the draining of the marshes," added the emperor, "nor any other material necessity that was the cause of my inviting some of your 'friends' to come here; no, I was guided by the wish that their true piety, their probity, and other virtues might serve as an example for my people to imitate."

In conclusion the emperor said, "Before we separate, let us try to spend some time in common prayer."  "We willingly consented," writes Grelle in regard to this matter, "feeling that the Lord with His beneficent power was near us.  Some time passed in silent, inward contemplation; our souls were humbled, and a little later I felt within me the heavenly breathing of the spirit of prayer and compunction; enfolded by the spirit, I bent my knees before the greatness of God; the emperor knelt beside me.  Amidst the inward outpourings of the soul we felt that the Lord had consented to hear our prayers. After that we spent a little while longer in silence and then withdrew. In bidding us farewell the emperor expressed the desire to see us again before we left. We spent two hours with him."

After this remarkable audience, which so graphically expresses the religious-idealistic frame of mind of the emperor Alexander, the Quakers visited under the patronage of the widowed empress the female educational establishments, the young pupils of which aroused much sympathy in them.

RUSSIAN PRIEST

Grelle found that some of them had hearts open for receiving evangelical inspiration. These visits were followed by the reception of the Quakers by the empress Marie Feodorovna. They told the empress that they were much pleased at the condition of the institutions under her patronage, but at the same time they could not be otherwise than grieved to see how little attention was paid in St. Petersburg, and in general throughout Russia, to the education of children of the lower classes; they also spoke to the empress of the unsatisfactoriness of the then existing prison accommodations for women, and indicated how advantageous it would be if the prisons were visited by women capable of instructing and consoling the unfortunate prisoners. The empress entirely agreed with these ideas.

Soon the emperor again invited the Quakers to come and see him. "He again received us in his private apartments," writes Grelle, "to which we were taken by a secret way, avoiding the guard and the court servants. Nobody seemed surprised to see us keeping our heads covered. The emperor, as before, received us with sincere affability. He began by informing us that the chains in which we had seen the prisoners at Åbo had been taken off, that the unfortunate man of whom we had told him had been set at liberty, and that orders had been given that the other prisoners were to be better treated. He then asked us to relate to him openly all that we had noticed in the prisons during our stay in Russia. The governor-general (Count Miloradovitch) had informed him of the changes and improvements which he considered it advantageous to carry out in the gaols, and the emperor entirely approved of the changes that had already been made. He further told us that the widowed empress had spoken to him with pleasure of our visit to her; that she had taken to heart what we had said of the extreme neglect of the education of children of the poorer classes, and that she was occupying herself in searching for the most effectual measures of remedying this defect as soon as possible. The emperor added that he had named a certain sum of money to be used for

[1818 A.D.]

the establishment of six schools for poor children in the capital, and that the children were to receive there a religious and moral education. He further told us that he had attentively perused the books we had prepared and was delighted with them; that if we had only come to Russia to do this, we had already accomplished a very important work, and that he intended to bring our books into use throughout all the schools of his empire."

Before their departure for Moscow the emperor received his old friends a third time, and on this occasion he related to them various details of how he had himself been educated under the supervision of his grandmother, the empress Catherine. "The persons attached to me," said he, "had some good qualities, but they were not believing Christians and therefore my primary education was not united with any profound moral impressions; in accordance with the customs of our church, I was taught formally to repeat morning and evening certain prayers I had learned; but this habit, which did not in any wise satisfy the inward requirements of my religious feelings, soon wearied me. Meanwhile it happened more than once that, when I lay down to rest, I had a lively feeling in my soul of my sins, and of the various moral deficiencies of my mode of life; thus penetrated by heartfelt repentance I was moved by a desire to rise from my bed and in the silence of the night to throw myself upon my knees and with tears ask God for forgiveness and for strength to preserve greater watchfulness over myself in future. This contrition of heart continued for some time; but little by little, in the absence of moral support on the part of the persons who surrounded me, I began to feel more seldom and more feebly these salutary movings of grace. Sin, together with worldly distractions, began to reign more and more within my soul. Finally, in 1812, the Lord in His love and mercy, again called to me, and the former movings of grace were renewed with fresh strength in my heart. At that period a certain pious person[1] advised me to take to reading the Holy Scriptures and gave me a Bible, a book which until then I had never had in my hands. I devoured the Bible finding that its words shed a new and never previously experienced peace in my heart, and satisfied the thirst of my soul. The Lord in His goodness granted me his Spirit to understand what I read; and to this inward instruction and enlightenment I owe all the spiritual good that I acquired by the reading of the divine Word; this is why I look upon inward enlightenment or instruction from the Holy Ghost as the firmest support in the soul — saving knowledge of God."

The emperor then related to his companions how deeply his soul was penetrated with the desire to abolish forever wars and bloodshed upon earth. "He said," writes Grelle, "that he had passed many nights without sleep in strained and intense deliberation as to how this sacred desire could be realised, and in deep grief at the thought of the innumerable calamities and misfortunes that are occasioned by war. At that time when his soul was thus bowed down in ardent prayer to the Saviour the idea arose in him of inviting the crowned heads to unite in one holy alliance, before the tribunal of which all future disagreements that should arise should be settled, instead of having recourse to the sword and to bloodshed. This idea took such possession of him that he got up from his bed, expounded his feelings and aspirations in writing with such liveliness and ardour that his intentions were subjected on the part of many to unmerited suspicion and misinterpretation — 'Although,' added he with a sigh, 'ardent love for God and mankind was

[1 Prince A. N. Galitzin.]

the sole motive that governed me.' Thoughts of the formation of the Holy Alliance again arose in him during his stay in Paris. After we had spent some time in conversing on this important subject, the emperor said to us: 'And thus we part, in this world, but I firmly trust that we, being separated by space, will however remain by the goodness of the spirit of God forever united through inward spiritual fellowship, for in the kingdom of God there are no limitations of space. Now, before we part, I have one request to make to you: let us join in silent prayer and see if the Lord will not consent to manifest His gracious presence to us, as He did the last time.'

"We gladly consented to fulfil his desire. A solemn silence followed during which we felt that the Lord was amongst us; our souls were reverently opened before Him and He himself was working within us through His grace. Somewhat later, I felt, through the breathing of the love of Christ, the lively desire of saying a few words of approbation to our beloved emperor in order to encourage him to walk with firm steps in the Lord's way and to put his whole trust, unto the end of his earthly journeyings, in the efficaciousness of the divine grace; in general I felt the necessity of guarding him from evil and strengthening him in his good intention of ever following the path of truth and righteousness. The words that I said produced a profound impression upon the emperor and he shed burning tears. Then our dear Allen, kneeling, raised a fervent prayer to God for the emperor and his people. The emperor himself fell on his knees beside him and remained a long while with us in spiritual outpourings before the Lord. Finally we solemnly and touchingly took leave of each other."

A VALDAI WOMAN

### SECRET SOCIETIES UNDER ALEXANDER I

After the year 1815, when the emperor Alexander already appeared as a weary martyr, immersed in mystic contemplation and wavering between the evergrowing influence of Count Araktcheiev and the convictions he had himself formed in the days of his youth, the events of 1812 were reflected in a totally different manner upon the movement of social ideas in Russia. The war of the fatherland was accompanied in Russia by an unusual rising of the spirit of the nation and a remarkable awakening of the public conscience. The continuation of the struggle with Napoleon beyond the frontiers of Russia had led Alexander's troops to Paris. This enforced military exploit widened the horizon of the Russian people; they became acquainted with European manners and customs, were in closer

[1818 A.D.]

contact with the current of European thought, and felt drawn towards political judgment. It was quite natural that the Russian people should begin to compare the order of things in their own country with political and public organisation abroad. An unrestrainable impulse to criticise and compare was awakened; thenceforth it was difficult to become reconciled to the former status of Russian life and the traditional order of things.

It will be asked what abuses presented themselves to the gaze of the Russian conquerors, who had liberated Europe, upon their return to their country. An entire absence of respect for the rights of the individual was patent; the forcible introduction of monstrous military settlements, the exploits of Magnitski and others of his kind in the department of public instruction were crying shames; and, finally, the cruelties of serfdom were in full activity. The subtile exactions which then prevailed in service at the front completed the development of general dissatisfaction amongst military circles. There is, therefore, nothing astonishing in the fact that the misfortunes which then weighed upon the Russian people should have found an answering call in the hearts of men who were at that time in the grip of a violent patriotic revival.

The natural consequence of this joyless condition of affairs in Russia was a hidden protest, which led to the formation of secret societies. Under the then existing conditions there was no possibility of carrying on reformatory deliberations with the cognisance of the government. Thus a remarkable phenomenon was accomplished; on the one hand Russian public thought was seeking for itself an issue and solution of the questions that oppressed it; while on the other the emperor Alexander, disenchanted with his former political ideals and standing at the head of the European reaction, had become the unexpected champion of aspirations which had nothing in common with the ideas of which he had been the representative during the best period of his life. This circumstance made a break in the interior life of Russia, which imperceptibly prepared the ground for events until then unprecedented in Russian history. "What has become of liberalism?" is a question that one of the contemporaries of that epoch sets himself. "It seems to have vanished, to have disappeared from the face of the earth; everything is silent. And yet it is just at this instant that its hidden forces have begun to grow dangerous." The time had come when secret societies were in full bloom. The masonic lodges, which had been allowed by the government, had long since accustomed the Russian nobility to the form of secret societies. Officers' circles, in which conversations were carried on about the wounds of Russia, the obduracy of the people, the distressing position of the soldier, the indifference of society to the affairs of the country, imperceptibly changed into organised secret societies.

It happened that yet another time the emperor Alexander expressed the conviction that the interior administration of Russia ought to be thought of, that it was necessary that means should be taken for remedying the evil; but the sovereign did not pass from words to deeds. In reference to this, the ideas expressed by Alexander to the governor of Penza, T. P. Lubianovski, on the occasion of his visit to that town in 1824 are worthy of attention. The emperor had inspected the second infantry corps there assembled; the manœuvres had deserved particular praise. Observing signs of weariness on the emperor's face, Lubianovski ventured to remark that the empire had reason to complain of his majesty.

"Why?" "You will not take care of yourself." "You mean to say that I am tired?" replied the emperor. "It is impossible to look at the troops without satisfaction; the men are good, faithful and excellently trained; we have gained no little glory through them. Russia has enough glory; she does not require more; it would be a mistake to require more. But when I think how little has been as yet done in the interior of the empire, then the thought lies on my heart like a ten-pound weight. That is what makes me tired.'

The profoundly true thought that fell from the lips of the sovereign in his conversation with Lubianovski was not, however, put into application. At that period it was impossible to count upon the amendment of the state edifice through the administrations of the government. The dim figure of Araktcheiev had definitively succeeded in screening Russia from the gaze of Alexander, and his evil influence was felt at every step. Therefore in the main everything led to the sorrowful result that the emperor, as Viguel expressed it, was like a gentleman who, having grown tired of administering his own estate, had given it over entirely into the hands of a stern steward, being thus sure that the peasants would not become spoiled under him.

A few words remain to be said of the fate that overtook the secret societies after the closing of the Alliance of the Public Good. Benkendorf's[1] supposition that a new and more secret society would be formed after this, which would act under the veil of greater security, was actually justified. The more zealous members of the alliance only joined together more closely, and from its ruins arose two fresh alliances — the Northern and the Southern.

The leaders of the Northern Alliance in the beginning were Muraviev and Turgeniev. Later on, in 1823, Kondratz Bileiev entered the society, of which he became the leader. The aspirations of the Northern Alliance were of a constitutional-monarchic character. In the Southern Alliance, chiefly composed of members of the second army, the principal leader was the commander of the Viatka infantry regiment, Colonel Paul Pestel, son of the former governor-general of Siberia. Thanks to Pestel's influence the Southern Alliance acquired a preponderating republican tendency; he occupied himself with the composition of a work which he called *Russian Truth*, in which he expounded his ideas on the reconstruction of Russia. Many members of this society inclined to the conviction that the death of the emperor Alexander and even the extermination of the entire imperial family were indispensable to the successful realisation of their proposed undertakings; at any rate there is no doubt that conversations to this effect were carried on amongst the members of the secret societies. Soon the active propaganda of the members of the Southern Society called another society into existence — the Slavonic Alliance or the United Slavonians. In it was chiefly concentrated the radical element from the midst of the future Dekabrists. The members of this society proposed insane and violent projects and insisted chiefly on the speedy commencement of decisive action, giving only a secondary importance to deliberations on the constitutional form of government. Sergei Nuraviev Apostol called them mad dogs chained.

There yet remained a better means for strengthening the designs of the secret societies — this was to enter into relations with the Polish secret societies. Negotiations with the representative of the Polish patriotic alliance, Prince Tablonovski, were personally carried on by Pestel; but the details of this agreement are even now little known. Such was the dangerous and fruitless path into which many of the best representatives of thinking Russia were drawn: each year the crisis became more and more inevitable; and

[1] General-adjutant, chief of the guards staff.

[1818 A.D.]

meanwhile the government became more decisively confirmed than ever in the pathway of reaction, thus indirectly giving greater power to secret revolutionary propaganda.

### Closing of the Masonic Lodges

In August, 1822, a rescript was issued in the name of the minister of the interior, ordering the closing of all secret societies, under whatever name they might exist — masonic lodges or others — and forbidding their establishment in future. All members of these societies had to pledge themselves not to form any masonic lodges or other secret societies in the future; and a declaration was required from all ranks of the army and from the civil service that neither soldiers nor officials should thenceforth belong to such organisations: "If any person refuses to make such a pledge, he shall no longer remain in the service."

All the measures drawn up by the rescript of August were, however, put into effect only with regard to the closing of the masonic lodges. As to the secret societies, which had undoubtedly a political aim, they continued to develop in all tranquillity. "At that time," writes a contemporary, "there was a triple police in St. Petersburg — namely, the governor general, the minister of the interior, and Count Araktcheiev; but that it did not bring forth any advantages is proved by the events of 1825."

According to the remarks of the same contemporary, card-playing had then spread in St. Petersburg society to an incredible degree. "Certainly in ninety houses out of a hundred they play," writes Danilevski, "and although the circle of my acquaintances has become very vast this year and I go out a great deal yet I never see people doing anything else than playing at cards. If one is invited to an evening party, it means cards, and I have hardly made my bow to the hostess before I find the cards in my hand. When one is asked out to dinner one sits down to whist before the meal is served. Card-playing occupies not only elderly people but young ones also. I think this has arisen partly from a defect in education which is in general observable in Russia — for when education finishes at seventeen, what store of ideas and knowledge, what passion for science can one expect to find in adults? This condition is further exaggerated by the fact that all political matters are banished from conversation: the government is suspicious, and spies are not unfrequently to be met with in society. The greater part of them are, however, known; some belong to old noble families, are decorated with orders, and wear chamberlains' keys."

The closing of the masonic lodges called forth the following deliberations from Danilevski: "As far as I know, masonry had no other object in Russia beyond benevolence and providing an agreeable way of passing time. The closing of the lodges deprived us of the only places where we assembled for anything else besides card-playing, for we have no society where cards do not constitute the principal or rather the only occupation. We are as yet so unversed in political matters that it is absurd for the government to fear that such subjects would furnish conversation at the masonic lodges. With us, notable persons have rarely been masons; at least none such have visited our lodge, which is usually full of people of the middle class, officers, civil-service employees, artists, a very few merchants, and a large percentage of literary men."[b]

These of course are the words of a partisan and must be taken with a certain allowance. The same remark applies with full force to the testimony of the historian Turgeniev, whose association with the secret unions has already been mentioned, and whose comments on the subject, despite a certain bias, are full of interest. Turgeniev is speaking of the period just following that in which the government had taken action against the societies.[a]

## Turgeniev's Comment on the Secret Societies.

The government contributed much [he declares] by its suspicions and precautions, to strengthen the reports which were afloat concerning secret societies: to them all was suspect. A species of insurrection having broken out in a regiment of the guards, of which the emperor was head, the government thought they could trace it to the action of some society, whereas it was caused by the brutal and ridiculous conduct of a new colonel they had placed in command. That such was their conviction there was no doubt, because two of the officers of the insurrectionary companies were traduced before a council of war, and condemned, not only without any proof but with no specification of the crime or fault with which they were charged, whereas in reality neither the one nor the other officer had ever belonged to a secret society.

A rash Englishman took it into his head to go round the world and publish an account of his travels. He arrived at St. Petersburg, went over Russia, and thence to Siberia. There he was taken for a spy, and soon an order came from St. Petersburg to conduct him to the frontier. Even pious Protestant missionaries, propagating with their accustomed zeal Christian morals among savage peoples, were suspected by the government. They were hindered in the holy warfare they desired to carry on in the farthest and least civilised regions of the empire. The powers only saw in them emissaries of European liberalism.

The public for their part did not fail to take appearances for reality. That is the common propensity of the crowd in every country. How many times, before and after this epoch, might not men have been seen addressing themselves to those who were supposed to be at the head of such societies, and insistantly asking to be admitted. In the army subalterns thus addressed their chiefs, and old generals sought their young subordinates to obtain the same favour. It might have been said with equal truth to both parties that no secret societies existed. Men's minds, however, were all on the strain for political events. It was thought that some great change was to come soon, and everyone wanted to get an inkling of it. Restless curiosity was not the worst of the inconveniences caused to such associations. Doubtless, the evil was less due to societies than to persons who judged them after their deceitful appearances. Perhaps it was the fault of the political order which made secret societies necessary or, at any rate, inevitable; but it was nevertheless a serious matter which only publicity could remedy. The strong energy of a free man would advantageously replace the trickery and restlessness of a slave.

However, at the epoch of which we now speak, individuals were able to agitate in various ways, but without the least result. But if such a thing as an organised secret society did exist, how is it I did not know of it — I who knew many of those called liberals? I will give convincing proof of what I here maintain; I quote the words of Pestel, a man sent to the scaffold by the government not because he had committed some political crime but because he was considered as the most influential of those who were supposed to belong to secret associations. Pestel was in St. Petersburg just as my depar-

[1818 A.D.]

ture was decided on. He came to see me and spoke with regret of the dissolution of the Bien Public Society. "As for us"(the 2nd army), he said, "we have not observed the dissolution. It would be too disheartening. We are believed to be strong and numerous; I encourage the delusion. What would be said were it known that we are but five or six who form the association?" He ended by advising me to renounce my journey, or, at any rate to return as soon as possible and take up the abandoned work again. "I see quite well," he said, "there is absolutely nothing left here of the old society, but at your house and a few others one can always believe in the existence of the society. Your departure will weaken this belief."

I explained that my health forced me to leave my affairs, and that, furthermore, I had little faith in the efficacy of secret societies. He seemed impressed by my reasoning and even agreed that I might be right on this last point.

A TATAR WOMAN

His attention was much occupied with certain social theories that he and some of his friends had formulated. They thought to find in me one proselyte more. But they were disappointed, and Pestel was much surprised and disconcerted. These theories, which so many ardent imaginations had adopted, were no doubt excellent in intention, but they hardly promised great results. The genius, or something akin to it, in a Fourier, the zeal of an Owen, the utopianism of many others, might make proselytes and excite admiration; but the dreams of such men remained but dreams although they sometimes touched on the sublime. Only, in default of possible realisation, these theories might help humanity by directing the attention and effort of serious men towards certain things of which they had sufficiently appreciated the importance and utility. But to ensure that result more imagination was required. One of the fundamental points in the theory of Pestel and his friends was a universal distribution of territory, its cultivation to be determined by a supreme authority. At least they wanted to divide vast crown lands among those who had no property. What Elizabeth had guaranteed to all Englishmen — the right of being supported by the poor rates in default of other means of subsistance — they wanted to guarantee by means of the possession or at least the enjoyment of a certain quantity of land free for cultivation.

I tried to the best of my power to refute their arguments. It was not easy. The refutation of certain theories is difficult, and there are some whose very absurdity makes them unassailable. At last I came to think that Pestel and his friends were far more discontented with my opposition to their social theories than with my opinions on secret societies.*d*

## LITERARY ACTIVITY OF THE PERIOD

The awakening of the Russian spirit was not manifested in political conspiracies alone. In science, in letters, and in art the reign of Alexander was an epoch of magnificent achievement. The intellectual like the liberal movement no longer bore the exotic and superficial character that had been apparent during the reign of Catherine; it penetrated to the deepest layers of society, gained constantly in power and extent, carried away the middle classes, and was propagated in the remotest provinces. The movement started in 1801 had not yet ceased, although the government failed to support the efforts it had itself aroused, and Alexander, embittered and disillusioned, had come to mistrust all intellectual manifestations. The increased severity of the censorship had not availed to prevent the formation of learned societies; literary journals and reviews continued to multiply.

During this period the Besieda, a literary club representing the classical tendencies, was formed, and the romanticists, Jukovski, Dachkov, Ouvarov, Pushkin, Bludov, and Prince Viazemski founded the Arzamas. At St. Petersburg appeared the *Northern Post*, the *St. Petersburg Messenger*, the *Northern Messenger*, the *Northern Mercury*, the *Messenger of Zion*, the *Beehive*, and the *Democrat*, in which latter Kropotkov inveighed against French customs and ideas, and in the *Funeral Orison of my Dog Balabas* congratulated the worthy animal on never having studied in a university, or read Voltaire.

Literary activity was, as usual, greatest at Moscow, where Karamzine was editing the *European Messenger*, Makarov the *Moscow Mercury*, and Glinka the *Russian Messenger*. In his journal Glinka endeavoured to excite a national feeling by first putting the people on their guard against all foreign influence, but more particularly that of France, and then arming them against Napoleon, teaching them the doctrine of self-immolation, and letting loose the furies of the "patriotic war." When the *Russian Messenger* went out of existence after the completion of its task, the *Son of the Soil*, edited by de Gretch, took up the same work and carried the war against Napoleon beyond the frontiers. "Taste in advance," it cried to the conqueror, "the immortality that you deserve; learn now the curses that posterity will shower on your name! You sit on your throne in the midst of thunder and flame as Satan sits in hell surrounded by death, devastation, and fire!" The *Russian Invalide* was founded in 1813 for the benefit of wounded and infirm soldiers. Even after the war-fever had somewhat subsided, and considerations less hostile to France were occupying the public mind, the literary movement still continued.

Almost all the writers of the day took part in the crusade against Gallomania and the belief in Napoleon's omnipotence. Some had fought in the war against France and their writings were deeply tinged with patriotic feeling. Krilov, whose fables rank him not far below La Fontaine, wrote comedies also. In the *School for Young Ladies* and the *Milliner's Shop* he ridiculed the exaggerated taste for everything French. Besides his classical tragedies Ozerov wrote *Dmitri Donskoi*, in which he recalled the struggles of Russia against the Tatars, and in a measure foretold the approaching conflict with a new invader. In the tragedy named after Pojarski, the hero of 1812, Kriukovski made allusions of the same order. The poet Jukovski put in verse the exploits of the Russians against Napoleon in 1806 and 1812, and Rostoptchin did not await the great crisis before opening out on the French the vials of his wrath.

[1818 A.D.]

Viewed in general, the literature of Alexander's period marked the passage from the imitation of ancient writers and French classicists to the imitation of French and English masterpieces.   The Besieda and the Arzamas were the headquarters of two rival armies which carried on in Russia a war similar to that waged in Paris by romantic and classical schools.   Schiller, Goethe, Byron, and Shakespeare were as much the fashion in Russia as in France, and created there as close an approach to a literary scandal.   While Ozerov, Batiuchkov, and Derjavine upheld the traditions of the old school, Jukovski gave to Russia a translation of Schiller's *Joan of Arc* and of Byron's *Prisoner of Chillon;* and Pushkin published *Ruslan and Liudmilla, the Prisoner of the Caucasus, Eugene Oniegin,* the poem *Poltava,* and the tragedy *Boris Godunov.*

As in France the romantic movement had been accompanied by a brilliant revival of historical studies, so in Russia a fresh impulse was given to letters, and dramatists and novelists were inspired with a taste for national subjects by Karamzin's *History of the Russian Empire,* a work remarkable for eloquence and charm [as our various extracts testify] though deficient in critical insight.   Schlötzer had recently edited Nestor, the old annalist of Kiev and father of Russian history.*f*

## *Alexander I as a Patron of Literature*

Protection and encouragement were shown to literature by Alexander I. Storck*i* writes as follows: "Rarely has any ruler shown such encouragement to literature as Alexander I.   The remarkable literary merits of persons in the government service are rewarded by rises in the official ranks, by orders and pensions, whilst writers who are not in the government service and whose literary productions come to the knowledge of the emperor not unfrequently receive presents of considerable value.   Under the existing conditions of the book trade, Russian authors cannot always count on a fitting recompense for large scientific works, and in such cases the emperor, having regard to these circumstances, sometimes grants the authors large sums for the publication of their works.   Many writers send their manuscripts to the emperor, and if only they have a useful tendency he orders them to be printed at the expense of the cabinet and then usually gives the whole edition to the author."

In view of the desire manifested by Karamzin to devote his labours to the composition of a full history of the Russian Empire, the emperor by a ukase of the 31st of October, 1803, bestowed upon him the title of historiographer and a yearly pension of 2,000 rubles.

During the reign of the emperor Paul, Alexander, in a letter to Laharpe dated September 27th, 1797, expressed his conviction of the necessity of translating useful books into the Russian language, in order "to lay a foundation by spreading knowledge and enlightenment in the minds of the people."   When he came to the throne, Alexander did not delay in accomplishing the intention he had already formed when he was czarevitch, and actually during the epoch of reforms a multitude of translations of works appeared, which had the evident object of inspiring interest in social, economic, and political questions and of communicating to Russian society the latest word of western science upon such questions.

In the establishment of the ministries the question of censorship was not overlooked; it was transferred to the ministry of public instruction.   In consequence of this arrangement a special statute was issued (July 9th, 1804), "not in order to place any restraint," as is stated in the minister's report, "upon the freedom of thought and of writing, but solely so as to take requisite measures against the abuse of such freedom." The entire statute contained forty-seven paragraphs — a circumstance worthy of attention if we take into consideration the fact that the censorship statute presented in the year 1826 by A. S. Shishkov had grown to 230 paragraphs. According to the statute of Alexander I the censorship was designed chiefly to "furnish society with books and works contributing to the true enlightenment of minds and to the formation of moral qualities, and to remove books and works of contrary tendencies." The censorship was entrusted to the university, constituting in its general jurisdiction the then newly organised department of the ministry of public instruction, which had the chief direction of schools. The basis of the functions of the censorship thus constituted was found in the three provisions following:

(1) Watchfulness that in the books and periodicals published, and in the pieces represented on the stage "there shall be nothing against religion, the government, morality, or the personal honour of any citizen." (2) Care that in the prohibition of the publication or issue of books and works the committee shall be "guided by a wise indulgence, setting aside all biased interpretation of the works or of any part of them which might seem to merit prohibition; and wisdom to remember that when such parts seem subject to any doubt or have a double meaning, it is better to interpret them in the manner most favourable to the author than to prosecute him." (3) A discreet and wise investigation of truths concerning faith, mankind, the position of the citizen, the law, and all branches of the administration, are to be treated by the censorship not only in the most lenient manner, but should enjoy entire liberty of publication, as contributing to the progress of enlightenment."

Such was the aspect of the censorship and statute which remained unchanged for more than twenty years, that is during the whole reign of the emperor Alexander. It was only from the year 1817, from the establishment of the ministry of public worship and of public instruction, that the censorship acquired a particularly irksome tendency which was in opposition to the liberal spirit of the statute: the most complete intolerance, fanaticism, and captiousness, which had been absent at the commencement of Alexander's reign, then made their appearance.

In January, 1818 the emperor Alexander came for a short time to St. Petersburg, and Karamzin took advantage of his stay in order to present to him the eight volumes of the *History of the Russian Empire* which he had just published. "He received me in his private apartments, and I had the happiness of dining with him," wrote Karamzin to his friend I. I. Dmitriev. "On the 1st of February my *History of the Russian Empire* was on sale; the edition was of three thousand copies, and in spite of the high price at which the work was sold (55 rubles, paper money, per copy), a month later not a copy was left at the booksellers."[b]

### FAILURE OF THE POLISH EXPERIMENT

The constitution granted to Poland in 1815, based the government on a tripartite division of power; the three estates of the realm being the king, a senate, and a house of representatives — the latter two being comprehended under the name of a diet. The executive was vested in the king, and in functionaries by him appointed. The crown was hereditary; it was the prerogative of the king to declare war, convoke, prorogue, or dissolve the diet. He was empowered to appoint a viceroy, who, unless a member of the royal family, was to be a Pole.   The king or viceroy was assisted by a council of state and five responsible ministers, their several departments being instruction, justice, interior and police, war, finance.   These five ministers were subordinate to the president of the council.   Considering the exhaustion, humiliation, and misery to which Poland had been reduced, such a constitution was apparently a great boon, for it guaranteed civil, political, and religious freedom; but by the very nature of things it was foredoomed to destruction.

The first Polish diet assembled at Warsaw on the 27th of March, 1818. The grand duke Constantine, commander-in-chief of the Polish army, was elected a deputy by the faubourg of Praga, and during the session was obliged to renounce his privilege as a senator, because, by the terms of the constitution, no person could sit in both houses.   He was elected by a major-

HOUSE OF THE ROMANOV CZARS

ity of 103 votes to 6, an evident proof that the new reign had excited the liveliest hopes.   The emperor arrived at Warsaw on the 13th of March; he devoted himself laboriously to the examination of state affairs, and on the 27th he opened the diet in person with a speech in the French language.   He said, "the organisation which existed in vigorous maturity in your country permitted the instant establishment of what I have given you, by putting into operation the principles of those liberal institutions which have never ceased to be the object of my solicitude, and whose salutary influence I hope by the aid of God to disseminate through all the countries which He has confided to my care.   Thus you have afforded me the means of showing my country what I had long since prepared for her, and what she shall obtain when the elements of a work so important shall have attained their necessary development."

There is no reason to doubt that Alexander cherished these intentions in his own sanguine but impractical way.   The enfranchisement of the serfs of Esthonia, undertaken in 1802 and completed in 1816, and that of the serfs of Courland in 1817, exhibit the same principles.   And when in 1819 the deputies of the Livonian nobility submitted to the approbation of the emperor a plan to pursue the same course with the serfs of their province, the following was his remarkable reply: "I am delighted to see that the nobility of Livonia have fulfilled my expectations. You have set an example that ought to be imitated. You have acted in the spirit of our age, and have felt that liberal principles alone can form the basis of the people's happiness."

"Such," says Schnitzler, "was constantly, during nearly twenty years, the language of Alexander. He deeply mourned the entire absence of all guarantees for the social well-being of the empire. His regret was marked in his reply to Madame de Staël, when she complimented him on the happiness of his people, who, without a constitution, were blessed with such a sovereign: 'I am but a lucky accident.'" After 1815 he was no longer even that.

A year had hardly elapsed from the time when Alexander had addressed the words we have quoted to the diet at Warsaw, ere the Poles began to complain that the constitution was not observed in its essential provisions; that their viceroy Zaionczek had but the semblance of authority, whilst all the real power was in the hands of the grand duke Constantine, and of Novosiltzov the Russian commissioner. The bitterness of their discontent was in proportion to the ardour of their short-lived joy. Russian despotism reverted to its essential conditions; the liberty of the press was suspended; and in 1819 the national army was dissolved. On the other hand, the spirit of opposition became so strong in the diet, that in 1820, a measure relating to criminal procedure, which was pressed forward with all the force of government influence, was rejected by a majority of 120 to 3. Thenceforth there was nothing but mutual distrust between Poland and Russia.

## CONSTITUTIONAL PROJECTS

The institutions which Alexander had given to Poland worked no happy results, and those which he designed for Russia would have been little better. He failed to accomplish even the good which he might have effected without organic changes. But he felt himself arrested by innumerable difficulties. He often wanted instruments to carry out his will, oftener still the firmness to support them against court cabals. The immense distances to be traversed, which, according to Custine, the emperor Nicholas feels to be one of the plagues of his empire, presented the same obstacle to Alexander. Again, his desire to exercise European influence distracted his attention from his proper work at home, and the empire sank back into its old routine. Discouraged at last, and awakening as he grew older from some of the illusions of his youth, he gave way to indolence more and more. He saw himself alone, standing opposed to an immense festering corruption; in despair he ceased to struggle against it; and in the latter portion of his reign he grievously neglected the care of his government.

The helm thus deserted by the pilot passed into the hands of General Araktcheiev, a shrewd, active man, devoted to business, perhaps also well-intentioned, but a Russian of the old school, without the necessary enlightenment, without political probity — arbitrary, imperious, and enthralled by qualities and notions inimical to progress; governed, moreover, by unworthy connections of a particular kind. Under the rule of Araktcheiev the censorship became more severe than ever. Foreign books were admitted with difficulty, and were subject to tyrannical restrictions; many professors of the new university of St. Petersburg were subjected to a despotic and galling inquisition; others were required most rigidly to base their course of instructions upon a programme printed and issued by the supreme authority. Freemasonry was suppressed. Foreign travellers were surrounded with trouble-some and vexatious formalities. Many rigorous regulations, which had been long disused and almost forgotten, were revived. In short, Araktcheiev exercised with intolerable severity a power which he derived from a master who carried gentleness to an extreme of weakness — who loved to discuss the rights of humanity, and whose heart bled for its sufferings.

### THE MILITARY COLONIES (1819 A.D.)

It was by the advice of Araktcheiev that military colonies were established in Russia in 1819. The system was not new, for Austria had already adopted it on some of her frontiers; but its introduction into Russia was a novelty from which great results were expected, and which neighbouring states regarded with much uneasiness. The plan was to quarter the soldiers upon the crown-peasants, build military villages according to a fixed plan, appor-tion a certain quantity of field to every house, and form a statute-book, according to which these new colonies should be governed. The plan at once received the approbation of the czar. It was the intention of Araktcheiev, by means of these colonies, to reduce the expense entailed by the subsistence of the army, and to compel the soldier to contribute to his own maintenance by cultivating the soil; to strengthen the ranks by a reserve picked from among the crown-peasants, equal in number to the colony of soldiers; to fur-nish the soldier with a home, in which his wife and children might continue to dwell when the exigencies of war called him away; and to increase the population, and with it the cultivation of the soil, in a land where hands only are wanting to change many a steppe into a garden, many a scattered village into a thriving town.

Russian colonies were thus established in the governments of Novgorod, Mohilev, Kharkov, Kiev, Podolia, and Kherson; that is to say, in the neigh-bourhood of Poland, Austria, and Turkey. Political and military considera-tions had combined to fix the choice of localities for these colonies. In consequence of the vast dimensions of the Russian Empire, troops raised in the north and west can only reach the southern provinces after long intervals; and if, on any emergency, Russia should wish to concentrate a large part of her forces in the neighbourhood of the southern and western frontiers, such a concentration, it was thought, would be greatly facilitated by the fact of military colonies, with a large population, being already on the spot. The vil-lages destined for the reception of military colonies were all to be inhabited by crown-peasants; these people were now relieved from the duties they had been accustomed to pay to the government, in consideration of their quartering men in their houses. All peasants more than fifty years of age were selected to be so-called head colonists, or master-colonists. Every master-colonist received forty acres of land, for which he had to main-tain a soldier and his family, and to find fodder for a horse, if a corps of cav-alry happened to be quartered in the village. The soldier, on his part, was bound to assist the colonist in the cultivation of his field and the farm labours generally, whenever his military duties did not occupy the whole day. The soldier, who in this way became domiciliated in the family, received the name "military peasant." The officers had the power of choosing the soldiers who were to be quartered upon the master-colonists. If the colonist had several sons, the oldest became his adjunct; the second was enrolled among the reserve; the third might become a military peasant; the others were enrolled as colonists or pupils. Thus, in the new arrangements, two entirely different elements were fused together, and one population was, so to speak, engrafted upon another.

The labour of these agricultural soldiers is of course dependent upon the will of the officers, for they can only attend to agricultural work when freed from military duty. The man himself continues half peasant, half soldier, until he has served for five-and-twenty years, if he be a Russian, or twenty years if he be a Pole. At the expiration of this time he is at liberty to quit the service, and his place is filled up from the reserve. Beside the house of each master-colonist stands another dwelling constructed in exactly the same manner, and occupied by the reserve-man, who may be regarded as a double of the soldier. He is selected by the colonel of the regiment from among the peasants, and is generally a son or relation of the master-colonist. The reserve-man is instructed in all the duties appertaining to the soldier's profession, and is educated in every particular, so that he may be an efficient substitute. If the agricultural soldier dies, or falls in battle, his reserve-man immediately takes his place. The colonist now takes the place of the reserve-man, who in his turn is succeeded by the pupil. The master-colonist, peasant-soldier, and reserve-man, may all choose their wives at pleasure, and they are encouraged to marry. The women, on the other hand, are allowed to marry within the limits of their colony, but not beyond it. The sons of the master-colonists, soldiers, or reserve-men, between the ages of thirteen and seventeen, are called "cantonists." They are drilled like soldiers, and occasionally attend schools. The children between the ages of eight and thirteen visit the school of the village in which their parents dwell, and are exercised in the use of arms on alternate days. Like the cantonists, they wear uniforms, and are looked upon as future soldiers. All male children are sent to school, where, by the method of reciprocal education, they are taught to read, write, and cipher, alternately with their military studies. They are taught to recite a kind of catechism, setting forth the duties of the soldier; they learn the use of the sabre; are practised in riding, and, when they have attained the age of seventeen years, are mustered in the head-quarters of the regiment, and divided into corps, those who distinguish themselves by attention and diligence being appointed officers. The several component parts of a colony are as follows:

1. The head colonist — the master of the house and possessor of the estate. 2. His assistant, who joins him in the cultivation of his farm. 3. The military peasant, who likewise takes part in agricultural labour. 4. The reserve-man, who supplies the place of the soldier in case of need. 5. The cantonist, between the ages of thirteen and seventeen. 6. The boys, from eight to thirteen years old. 7. Male children under the age of eight years. 8. The female population. 9. The invalids.

The colonies in the south of Russia comprise 380 villages in the provinces of Kherson, Kharkov, and Iekaterainoslav. The crown has here 30,000 peasants. Every village contains two or three squadrons, according to its size; thus they contain altogether 80,000 men. These military districts, as the regions are called in which the colonies occur, are so strictly divided from the remaining portions of the provinces, that no man can enter them without a special passport, granted by the military authorities. Their constitution is entirely military, even the postal service being executed by soldiers. At every station a subaltern receives the order for post-horses and inspects it; another soldier harnesses the horses; a third greases the wheels; and a fourth mounts the box as coachman. As soon as the military coat appears in sight, every

[1819 A.D.]

peasant on the high-road stops, plants his hands stiffly against his sides, and stands in a military attitude of "attention."

The laws are administered in the first instance by a detachment from every squadron, one of the officers acting as president. From the decision of this tribunal an appeal can be made to the regimental council, which is composed of the colonel, two captains, and six deputies from among the colonists. The judgments of this court are laid before the commandant-in-chief of the colonies, against whose decision neither soldiers nor colonists may protest, officers alone having the privilege of appealing to the emperor. In the headquarters of every regiment a copy of the code of laws is kept, and in most military villages churches are to be found, where a priest, who belonged to the church before the village was transformed into a military colony, performs the service.

The success of the military colonies in Russia fell far short of the expectations of their founders. To the unfortunate crown serfs they brought an intolerable aggravation of their wretchedness, by making them feel their slavery even in their homes and their domestic affections. The consequence was seen in the madness of their revenge on several occasions when they broke out into rebellion, as for instance at Novgorod, in 1832. "Nothing," says Dr. Lee, "could be sold without the knowledge of the officers in these military colonies. It is said that when a hen lays an egg, it is necessary to make an entry of the fact in a register kept for this and other equally important purposes. I was told that when a priest was speaking to some of these peasants about the punishments of hell, they answered they dreaded them not, because a worse hell than that in which they were doomed to pass their whole lives here, could not possibly exist.

"The military colonies," Lee continues, "please one at first sight from the order and cleanliness everywhere prevailing in them; but their population is said to be wretched in the highest degree. When the emperor Alexander was here, some years ago, he went round visiting every house; and on every table he found a dinner prepared, one of the principal articles of which consisted of a young pig roasted. The prince Volkhonski suspected there was some trick, and cut off the tail of the pig and put in his pocket. On entering the next house the pig was presented, but without the tail, upon which Prince Volkhonski said to the emperor, 'I think this is an old friend.' The emperor demanded his meaning, when he took out the tail from his pocket and applied it to the part from which it had been removed. The emperor did not relish the jest, and it was supposed this piece of pleasantry led to his disgrace. A more effectual, though bold and dangerous method of exposing to the emperor the deceptions carried on throughout the military colonies under Count Araktcheiev could not have been adopted than that which Prince Volkhonski had recourse to on this occasion. From that time Count Araktcheiev became his bitter enemy."

## ALEXANDER AND THE GREEK UPRISING

We have now touched upon all that is worthy of note in Alexander's home policy during the last ten years of his reign. That portion of his life was spent in perpetual motion and perpetual agitation to little or no good purpose, whilst his proper functions were delegated to Count Araktcheiev, whose name was a word of terror to everyone in Russia. Absorbed by affairs foreign to the interests of his empire, Alexander was consistent or persevering in nothing but his efforts to enforce the dark, stagnant policy of Austria, which had become that of the Holy Alliance. He was present at the congresses of Aix-la-Chapelle, Troppau, Laibach, and Verona, and zealously participated in all the repressive measures concerted there. He was the soul of the deliberations held at the latter place in 1822, and whilst he refused aid to the Greeks in their rebellion against their "legitimate sovereign," the sultan, he was all but inclined to use constraint to his ally, France, to compel her, in spite of the opposition of England, to take upon herself the execution of the violent measures resolved on in behalf of the execrable Ferdinand of Spain. A speech made at this congress to Châteaubriand, the French plenipotentiary, has been praised by some of the emperor's biographers for its "noble sentiments." To us it seems well worthy of record for its unconscious sophistry and signal display of self-delusion.

"I am very happy," said the emperor to Châteaubriand, "that you came to Verona, because you may now bear witness to the truth. Would you have believed, as our enemies are so fond of asserting, that the alliance is only a word intended to cover ambition? That might have received a colour of truth under the old order of things, but now all private interests disappear when the civilisation of the world is imperilled. Henceforward there can be no English, French, Russian, Prussian, or Austrian policy; there can only be a general policy, involving the salvation of all, admitted in common by kings and peoples. It is for me, the first of all, to declare my appreciation of the principles on which I founded the Holy Alliance. An opportunity presents itself; it is the Greek insurrection. Certainly no event appeared more adapted to my personal interests, to those of my subjects, and to the feelings and prejudices of the Russians, than a religious war against Turkey; but in the troubles of the Peloponnesus I saw revolutionary symptoms, and from that moment I held aloof. What has not been done to dissolve the alliance? Attempts have been made by turns to excite my cupidity, or to wound my self-love; I have been openly outraged; the world understood me very badly if it supposes that my principles could be shaken by vanities, or could give way before resentment. No, no; I will never separate myself from the monarchs with whom I am united. It should be permitted to kings to form public alliances, to protect themselves against secret associations. What temptations can be offered to me? What need have I to extend my empire? Providence has not placed under my command eight hundred thousand soldiers to satisfy my ambition, and to conserve those principles of order on which society must repose."

This was not the language of "noble sentiment," but of an intellect narrowed by sinister influences, perverted to the views of a most sordid policy, and flattering itself on its own debasement with the maudlin cant of philanthropy.

We may well conceive that it was not without inward pain and self-reproach that the benevolent Alexander stifled in his heart the voice that rose in favour of the Greeks, and resisted the wishes of his people, who were animated by a lively sympathy for their co-religionists. That sympathy was manifested as strongly as it could be under this despotic government, where every outward demonstration is interdicted, unless when specially commanded or permitted by authority. They could not see without surprise the head of the so-styled orthodox church enduring the outrages of the infidels, and looking on unmoved whilst one of her chief pastors was hung at the porch of his church, and multitudes of her children were massacred. These Greeks had of late been regarded as under the protection of Russia; she was their old ally — nay, more, their accomplice, who had more than once instigated

[1824 A.D.]

them to break their chains. The supineness of the emperor under such circumstances mortified the nobility, shocked the clergy, and was a subject of sincere affliction to the people, for whom, in their debased condition, religious sentiments held the place of political emotions.

High and low obeyed, however; murmurs were suppressed; but the Russians failed not to attribute to the wrath of God the misfortunes which befel Alexander, amongst which was the malady with which he was afflicted in 1824. It began with erysipelas in the leg, which soon spread upwards, and was accompanied with fever and delirium. For a time his life was in danger, and the people, who sincerely loved him, believed that they saw in this a punishment from on high because he had abandoned an orthodox nation.

## THE GREAT INUNDATION OF 1824

Another misfortune was a frightful calamity which befel St. Petersburg in 1824. The mouth of the Neva, opening westward into the gulf of Finland, is exposed to the violent storms that often accompany the autumnal equinox. They suddenly drive the waters of the gulf into the bed of the river, which then casts forth its accumulated floods upon the low quarters on both its banks. It may be conceived how terrible is the destruction which the unchained waters make in a city built upon a drained marsh, on the eve of a northern winter of seven months' duration. There were terrific inundations in 1728, 1729, 1735, 1740, 1742, and in 1777, a few days before the birth of Alexander; but the worst of all was that which occurred on the 19th of November, 1824, a year before his death. A storm blowing from the west and southwest with extreme violence, forced back the waters of the Neva, and drove those of the gulf into it.[e]

At eight o'clock in the morning the waters began to rise rapidly and had soon submerged all the lower parts of the town. On the Nevski Prospect the water had reached the Troitski Perenlok, and by twelve three parts of the town were submerged, owing to a southwesterly wind which rose to a violent tempest. At a quarter to three the waters began suddenly to subside. The emperor was profoundly moved by the awful calamity which took place before his eyes, and in the gloomy frame of mind that had possession of him he regarded it as a punishment for his sins. As soon as the water had so far subsided as to make it possible to drive through the streets he set off for the Galernaia (in the lower part of the town). There a terrible picture of destruction was unfolded before him. Visibly affected he stopped and got out of the carriage; he stood for a few moments without speaking, the tears flowing down his cheeks: the people, sobbing and weeping, surrounded him: "God is punishing us for our sins," said someone in the crowd. "No, for mine," answered the emperor sorrowfully, and he himself began to give orders about arranging temporary refuge and affording assistance to the sufferers. On the next day, the 8th (20th) of November, Count Araktcheiev, Alexander's favourite, wrote the following letter to the emperor:

"I could not sleep all night, knowing what your state of mind must be, for I am convinced how much your majesty must be now suffering from the calamity of yesterday. But God certainly sometimes sends such misfortunes in order that His chosen ones may show in an unusual degree their compassionate care for the unfortunate. Your majesty will of course do so in the present case. For this money is necessary and money without delay, in order to give assistance, not to the well-to-do but to the poorest. Your subjects must help you, and therefore I venture to submit my idea to you.

"The wise dispositions that you made, *batushka*,[1] with regard to my insignificant labours have constituted a tolerably considerable capital. In my position I have not required to use any of this capital even as table money, and now I ask as a reward that a million may be separated from the capital and employed in assisting the poor people. God will certainly give his help in this matter to the benefit of the country and the glory of your majesty, and bring about a still better means for its accomplishment. Batushka, order that a committee may be formed of compassionate people, in order that they may without delay occupy themselves with the relief of the poorest. They will glorify your name, and I, hearing it, shall thus enjoy the greatest pleasure on earth."

The emperor answered Count Araktcheiev the same day in a few gracious lines, full of heartfelt gratitude: "We are in complete agreement in our ideas, dear Alexis Andreivitch. Your letter has comforted me inexpressibly, for it is impossible that I should not be deeply grieved at the calamity of yesterday, and especially at the thought of those who have perished or who mourn for relatives. Come to me to-morrow so that we may arrange everything. Ever your sincerely affectionate Alexander."

TVERSKI GATE, MOSCOW

The emperor sent a note of the following content to Adjutant-General Diebitsch: "In order to afford effectual relief to the sufferers from the inundation of the 7th of November, and on account of the destruction of the bridges and the difficulties of communication between the various parts of the town, the following military governors are temporarily appointed under the direction of the military governor-general, Count Miloradovitch: for Vasili Oetroo, Adjutant-General Benkendorv; for the St. Petersburg side, Adjutant-General Komarovski; and for the Viboz side, Adjutant-General Depreradovitch."

On the 8th of November the emperor sent for the newly appointed military governors and declared his will to them — that the most speedy and effectual assistance should be given to the unfortunate sufferers from the awful catastrophe. Count Komarovski, in describing the reception given to him and the other military governors, says that tears were observed in the emperor's eyes. "I am sure that you share my feelings of compassion," continued Alexander; "here are your instructions, which have been hastily drawn up — your hearts will complete them. Go from here straight to the minister of finance who has orders to give each of you 100,000 rubles to begin with." According to Komarovski the emperor spoke with such feeling and eloquence that all the assembled governors were deeply touched.

At the time of the inundation in a space of five hours about 5,000 persons

[1 Little father," a title sometimes given to the Russian sovereigns by their subjects.]

[1824 A.D.]

perished and 3,609 domestic animals; 324 houses were destroyed or carried away, and 3,581 damaged; besides this pavements, foot ways, quays, bridges, etc. were either destroyed or damaged.  Considerable destruction and damage was also occasioned in the environs of the capital, on the Petershov road, in old Petershov, Oranienbaum, and Kronstadt, along the northern shore. More than 100 persons perished in these places, while 114 buildings were destroyed and 187 damaged.

On the 22nd of November the emperor assisted at a requiem service in the Kazan cathedral for those who had perished during the inundation.  The historian Karamzin writes that the people as they listened to the requiem wept and gazed at the czar.[b]

## THE CLOSE OF ALEXANDER'S REIGN

The czar, deeply affected by the sad spectacles he had witnessed, never recovered from the shock.  This increased his disgust of life and the heavy melancholy that had of late being growing upon him.  The whole aspect of Europe gave fearful tokens that the policy of the Holy Alliance was false and untenable; it was everywhere the subject of execration, and its destruction was the aim of an almost universal conspiracy, extending even into Alexander's own dominions.  Poland inspired him with deep alarm, and his native country, notwithstanding her habits of immobility, seemed ripe for convulsions.  Thus his public life was filled with disappointment and care, and his private life was deeply clouded with horrors.

The diet of Warsaw had become so refractory, that in 1820 Alexander had found it necessary to suspend it, in violation of the constitution given by himself; and though he opened a new diet in 1824, he did so under such restrictions, that the Poles rightly considered it a mere mockery of representative forms.

Russia herself was by no means tranquil.  In the year 1824 insurrections of the peasants occurred in several governments, and especially in that of Novgovod, in dangerous vicinity to the first-founded of the military colonies. The latter themselves shared the general discontent, and threatened to become a fearful focus of rebellion, as was actually the case in 1832.  There existed also in Russia other centres of disaffection, the existence of which might have been long before known to Alexander, but for his culpable habit of allowing petitions to collect in heaps in his cabinet without even breaking their seals. He, however, learned the fact on his last journey into Poland in June, 1825, or immediately after his return. [1]  He then received the first intimation of the conspiracy which had for many years been plotting against himself and against the existing order of things in Russia — a conspiracy which, as many believe, involved the perpetration of regicide.  It is a curious fact, but one by no means unparalleled, that in a country where the police is so active, such a plot should have remained for years undetected.  In 1816, several young Russians who had served in the European campaigns of the three preceding years, and who had directed their attention to the secret associations which had so greatly contributed to the liberation of Germany, conceived the idea of establishing similar associations in Russia; and this was the origin of that abortive insurrection which broke out in St. Petersburg on the day when the troops were required to take the oath of allegiance to Alexander's successor. These details would be sufficient of themselves to account for the melan-

[1] The informer was an inferior officer of lancers.  His name was Sherwood, and he was of English origin.

choly that haunted Alexander in the later years of his reign, and which was painfully manifest in his countenance. But he had to undergo other sufferings.

He was not more than sixteen years of age when his grandmother, Catherine II, had married him to the amiable and beautiful princess Maria of Baden, then scarcely fifteen.[1] The match was better assorted than is usually the case in the highest conditions of life, but it was not a happy one. It might have been so if it had been delayed until the young couple were of more mature years, and had not the empress unwisely restricted their freedom after marriage, and spoiled her grandson as a husband by attempting to make him a good one in obedience to her orders. Moreover, the tie of offspring was wanting which might have drawn the parents' hearts together, for two daughters, born in the first two years of their union, died early. Alexander formed other attachments, one of which with the countess Narishkin, lasted eleven years, until it was dissolved by her inconstancy. She had borne him three children; only one was left, a girl as beautiful as her mother, who was now the sole joy of her father's sad heart. But the health of Sophia Narishkin was delicate, and he was compelled to part with her, that she might be removed to a milder climate. She returned too soon, and died on the eve of her marriage, in her eighteenth year. The news was communicated to Alexander one morning when he was reviewing his guard. "I receive the reward of my deeds," were the first words that escaped from his agonised heart.

Elizabeth, whose love had survived long years of neglect, had tears to shed for the daughter of her rival, and none sympathised more deeply than she with the suffering father. He began to see in her what his people had long seen, an angel of goodness and resignation; his affection for her revived, and he strove to wean her from the bitter recollections of the past by his constant and devoted attention. But long-continued sorrows had undermined Elizabeth's health, and her physicians ordered that she should be removed to her native air. She refused, however, to comply with this advice, declaring that the wife of the emperor of Russia should die nowhere else than in his dominions. It was then proposed to try the southern provinces of the empire, and Alexander selected for her residence the little town of Taganrog, on the sea of Azov, resolving himself to make all the arrangements for her reception in that remote and little frequented spot. A journey of 1800 versts, after the many other journeys he had already made since the opening of the year, was a fatigue too great for him to sustain without injury, suffering as he still was from erysipelas; but he was accustomed to listen to no advice on the subject of his movements, and two or three thousand versts were nothing in his estimation; besides, on this occasion, in the very fatigue of travelling he sought his repose: he would fulfil a duty which was to appease his conscience. He quitted St. Petersburg in the beginning of September, 1825, preceding the empress by several days. His principal travelling companions were Prince Volkhonski, one of the friends of his youth of whom we have already heard; his aide-de-camp general, Baron Diebitsch, a distinguished military man who had been made over to him by the king of Prussia; and his physician, Sir James Wylie, who had been about his person for thirty years, and was at the head of the army medical department.

The journey was prosperous, and was accomplished with Alexander's usual rapidity in twelve days, the travellers passing over 150 versts a day; but his mind was oppressed with gloomy forebodings, and these were strengthened by the sight of a comet; for though brought up by a philosophic grand-

---

[1] She took the name of **Elizabeth Alexievna**.

mother, and by a free-thinking tutor, he was by no means exempt from superstition. "Ilia," he called out to his old and faithful coachmen, "have you seen the new star? Do you know that a comet always presages misfortune? But God's will be done!" A very favourable change having taken place in the empress's health in Taganrog, Alexander ventured to leave her early in October, for a short excursion through the Crimea. On the 26th of that month Dr. Robert Lee, family physician to Count Vorontzov was one of the emperor's guests at Alupka. He relates that at dinner Alexander repeatedly expressed how much he was pleased with Orianda, where he had been that day, and stated that it was his determination to have a palace built there as expeditiously as possible. "To my amazement," says Dr. Lee, "he said after a pause, 'When I give in my demission, I shall return and fix myself at Orianda, and wear the costume of the Taurida.' Not a word was uttered when this extraordinary resolution was announced, and I thought that I must have misunderstood the emperor; but this could not have been, for in a short time, when Count Vorontzov proposed that the large open flat space of ground to the westward of Orianda should be converted into pleasure-grounds for his majesty, he replied: 'I wish this to be purchased for General Diebitsch, as it is right that the chief of my état-major and I should be neighbours.'"

During the latter part of his tour in the Crimea, Alexander had some threatenings of illness, but peremptorily refused all medical treatment. He returned to Taganrog on the 17th of November, with evident symptoms of a severe attack of the bilious remittent fever of the Crimea. He persisted in rejecting medical aid until it was too late, and died on the 1st of December. For a long time the belief prevailed throughout Europe that he had been assassinated; but it is now established beyond question that his death was a natural one. The empress survived him but five months.

Alexander's last days were embittered by fresh disclosures brought to him by General Count de Witt, respecting the conspiracy by which, if the official report is to be believed, he was doomed to assassination. From that time he declared himself disgusted with life. Once when Sir James Wylie was pressing him to take some medicine, "My friend," said Alexander, "it is the state of my nerves to which you must attend; they are in frightful disorder." — "Alas!" rejoined the physician, "that happens more frequently to kings than to ordinary men." — "Yes," said the emperor, with animation, "but with me in particular there are many special reasons, and at the present hour more so than ever." Some days afterwards, when his brain was almost delirious, the czar gazed intently on the doctor, his whole countenance manifesting intense fear. "Oh, my friend," he exclaimed, "what an act, what a horrible act! The monsters! the ungrateful monsters! I designed nothing but their happiness." *e*

"It is difficult to represent the condition of St. Petersburg during the last years of the reign of the emperor Alexander," writes a contemporary. "It was as though enveloped in a moral fog; Alexander's gloomy views, more sad than stern, were reflected in its inhabitants. Many people said: What does he want more? He stands at the zenith of power. Each one explained after his own fashion the inconsolable grief of the emperor. For a man who must live to all eternity, who was famed as the friend of liberty, and who had out of necessity become her oppressor, it was grievous to think that he must renounce the love of his contemporaries and the praise of posterity. Many other circumstances and some family ones also weighed on his soul. The last years of Alexander's life," writes in conclusion the eye-witness of these sorrowful days, "may be termed a prolonged eclipse."

### The Death of Alexander I

On the 1st of December, 1825, a truly great misfortune fell upon Russia: the best of European sovereigns had ceased to exist. When he vanished from the political arena, only the finer side of his life came into view; the remainder was given over to oblivion. A contemporary who was at the same time a poet writes: "You see arising before you that beautiful spirit that was welcomed with such joy in 1801; you see that glorious czar to whom Russia owes the years 1813 and 1814; you see the comforter of the people after last year's inundation; you see that gracious, benevolent man who was so amiable in personal intercourse," and who, in the words of Speranski, will ever remain a true charmer. There was much that was ideally beautiful in his soul, he sincerely loved and desired good, and attained to it. There was indeed cause for grief, particularly in view of the uncertainty of the future that awaited Russia, which, according to the picturesque expression of a Russian writer after the death of Alexander, had, as it were, to enter a cold, uninviting passage to a long dark tunnel. This was a feeling that was shared by many contemporaries.

Independently of the grief which fell upon all Russia, for the persons who had surrounded the deceased monarch at his death a truly tragic moment had approached. Far from the capital and from all the members of the imperial family, in an isolated town (Taganrog) of the Russian empire, at two thousand versts from the centre of government the terrible question arose: Who would now be emperor, to whom was the oath of allegiance to be taken, and by whom in future would orders issue? Moreover, it was amidst the ramifications of a vast conspiracy and a universal fermentation that these questions presented themselves.

"The sphinx, undivined even to the grave," as the poet justly called Alexander, had not revealed his royal will, and even in view of the inevitable end he had not considered it necessary to refer by a single word or hint to the question that was of such crucial interest to the welfare of Russia. On the contrary, during the last days of his life Alexander had as though consciously set aside all earthly matters and died like a private individual who has closed his accounts with the world. Therefore it is not surprising that he failed to indicate the successor he had chosen; being satisfied with the dispositions he had previously made in secret, he seemed to think: "After my death they will open my will and testament and will learn to whom Russia belongs."

During the life of Alexander no one knew of the existence of the act naming the grand duke Nicholas Pavlovitch heir to the throne except three state dignitaries: Count Araktcheiev, Prince A. N. Galitzin, and the archbishop of Moscow, Philaret. By a fatal concurrence of circumstances, not one of them was present at the decease of the emperor at Taganrog. Of the three persons of confidence who were with Alexander, Adjutant-general Prince Volkonski, Baron Diebitsch, and Tchernichev, not one was aware that the elder brother's right to the succession of the throne had been transferred to the second. Adjutant-general Diebitsch afterwards said to Danilevski: "The emperor, who had confided many secrets to me, never, however, told me a word of this. Once we were together at the settlement, and he, directing the conversation to the grand duke Nicholas Pavlovitch, said, "You must support him." I concluded from these words only that, judging from the age of the grand duke, he might be expected to outlive the emperor and the czarevitch, in which case he would naturally be their successor."

Such were the limits of the knowledge that Diebitsch had at his disposal

in Taganrog as the question of the succession.   Nor did Prince Volkonski
know anything about the matter.   Even the empress Elizabeth Alexievna
was in the same ignorance regarding the rejection of the grand duke Constantine Pavlovitch.

"When the illness of Alexander at Taganrog no longer gave any hopes of
recovery," relates Diebitsch, "Prince Volkonski advised me to ask the
empress to whom, in case of the emperor's death, I as chief of his majesty's
general staff must address myself, for my position was one of very great difficulty; I was left chief of the army at a time when instances of a conspiracy
were being disclosed.   I could not decide upon personally proposing such a
question to the empress, fearing to distress her, besides which, although I
enjoyed her favour, yet it was not to such a degree as Prince Volkonski,
who was the friend of the imperial family; therefore I urgently requested him
to take upon himself this explanation with the empress.   He only consented
under the condition that I should be present.   We went together into the
room where the emperor was lying unconscious, and Prince Volkonski,
going up to Elizabeth Alexievna said to her that I, as chief of the staff, requested her to say to whom, in case of misfortune, I was to address myself?
'Is the emperor then so ill that there is no hope?' asked the empress.   'God
alone can help and save the emperor: only the tranquillity and security of
Russia demand that the traditional forms should be observed,' answered the
prince Volkonski.

"'Of course in case of an unhappy event the grand duke Constantine Pavlovitch must be referred to,' said the empress.   The words plainly proved
the empress' ignorance as to who was named heir to the throne.   Prince
Volkonski and I supposed that the late emperor Alexander had made a will,
for he had an envelope with a paper in it always with him, which never left
him.   When we opened it after his death we found that it contained some
written-out prayers."

Such being the position of affairs it only remained for Adjutant-general
Diebitsch to inform the czarevitch Constantine Pavlovitch in Warsaw of the
melancholy event, as the person who, according to the law of succession, had
become emperor of all the Russias.   It was then that Diebitsch wrote a letter
to the empress Marie Feodorovna in which he said in conclusion: "I humbly
await the commands of our new lawful sovereign, the emperor Constantine
Pavlovitch."   The act of the decease of the emperor Alexander was drawn up
in Taganrog, annexed to the report of Baron Diebitsch, dated December 1st,
1825, and sent to the emperor Constantine.[b]

### ALISON'S ESTIMATE OF ALEXANDER I

Majestic in figure, a benevolent expression of countenance, gave Alexander
I that sway over the multitude which ever belongs to physical advantages
in youthful princes; while the qualities of his understanding and the feelings
of his heart secured the admiration of all whose talents fitted them to judge
of the affairs of nations.   Misunderstood by those who formed their opinion
only from the ease and occasional levity of his manner, he was early formed
to great determinations, and evinced in the most trying circumstances, during
the French invasion and the congress of Vienna, a solidity of judgment
equalled only by the strength of his resolution.   He had formed, early in life,
an intimacy with the Polish prince, Czartorinski, and another attachment,
of a more tender nature, to a lady of the same nation; and in consequence he
considered the Poles so dear to him, that many of the best informed patriots

in that country hailed his accession to the throne as the first step towards the restoration of its nationality. A disposition naturally generous and philanthropic, moulded by precepts of Laharpe, had strongly imbued his mind with liberal principles, which shone forth in full and perhaps dangerous lustre when he was called on to act as the pacificator of the world after the fall of Paris. But subsequent experience convinced him of the extreme danger of prematurely transplanting the institutions of one country into another in a different stage of civilisation; and his later years were chiefly directed to objects of practical improvement, and the preparation of his subjects, by the extension of knowledge and the firmness of government, for those privileges which, if suddenly conferred, would have involved in equal ruin his empire and himself.*g*

### SKRINE'S ESTIMATE OF ALEXANDER I

Of Alexander I it may be truly said that no monarch ever wielded unlimited power with a loftier resolve to promote the happiness of his people. And not theirs alone; for he sympathised with all the myriads doomed to suffering by false ideals and effete institutions. In him men saw the long-expected Messiah who was to give peace to a distracted world. But his nature had an alloy of feminine weakness, unfitting him to bear the reformer's cross. He was too sensitive of impressions derived from without; too easily led by counsellors who gained his confidence but were not always worthy of it. In youth he was swayed by noble infatuations and enamoured of the most diverse ideas in turn. But when he stood confronted with a crisis in his country's fortunes he rose superior to vacillation and kept a great design steadily in view. The will-power thus developed, and the resources at his command, made him for a brief period the leading figure in the civilised world. Despondency came with the inevitable reaction which followed the effort. He was drawn into the mazes of German illuminism, which lessened his capacity for persistent resolve. Its effect was heightened by his failure to pierce the dense phalanxes of ignorance around him, and by the unvarying ingratitude which requited his efforts for the public weal. Increasing physical weakness hastened the death of his generous illusions. An excessive devotion to duty exhausted his flagging powers and he became unequal to the task of governing all the Russias. As a dying tree is strangled by parasitical growths, so was Alexander in his decadence attacked by the enemies of human progress. When Metternich and Araktcheiev gained the mastery, all hope of domestic reform and consistent foreign policy disappeared. But despite the shadows which darkened his declining years, Alexander I of Russia will stand out in history as one of the few men born in the purple who rightly appraised the accident of birth and the externals of imperial rank; who held opinions far in advance of his age, and never wittingly abused his limitless powers; who displayed equal firmness in danger and magnanimity in the hour of triumph.*h*

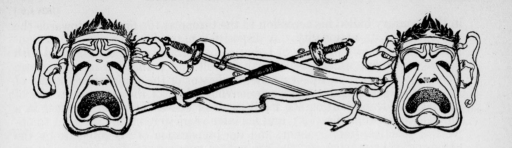

## CHAPTER XI

## THE REIGN OF NICHOLAS I

### [1825–1855 A.D.]

Nicholas Pavlovitch triumphed over two military revolts; then, as if the twelve days' interregnum had not existed, he dated his reign from the 1st of December, 1825, the day of Alexander's death. During the first ten or twelve years of his reign embarrassments of every kind, followed hard upon one another. These embarrassments were foreign war, first with Persia, and next with Turkey; the enmity of Austria whilst this latter struggle was going on; the abandonment of the Russian alliance by France, in consequence of the revolution of July, 1830; the insurrection of Poland; the epidemic of Asiatic cholera in 1831 and the popular riots to which this scourge gave rise, especially in St. Petersburg; a revolt in the heart of the military colonies; a famine which desolated the southern provinces during the years 1834 and 1835; the fires at Åbo, Tula, Kazan, and at last (December, 1837) at the emperor's own residence, the Winter Palace. But all these cruel trials did not daunt the courage of the new autocrat; they served only to bring out the firmness of his mind and the strong cast of his character.—SCHNITZLER.[c]

### THE INTERREGNUM

AFTER the 24th of November, 1825, Adjutant-general Diebitsch had begun to send information to Warsaw of the illness of the emperor Alexander, by means of letters addressed to General Kuruta. The first courier, bearing this alarming news, arrived at Warsaw on the 1st of December in the evening of the very day of the emperor Alexander's death.

The czarevitch Constantine Pavlovitch did not conceal the painful presentiment that took possession of him, and wrote to Baron Diebitsch the same day in the following terms: "In spite of all the consolations expressed in your letter, I cannot rid myself of the painful impression it has produced on me. I tell you frankly that if I were to obey the dictates of my heart I should set off and come to you. But unfortunately my duties and my position do not permit me to give way to these natural sentiments."

The grand duke Michael Pavlovitch was at that time at Warsaw, and the czarevitch hid even from him and Princess Lovitch the alarming letters that he received from Taganrog. "I do not speak to you of the condition of mind in which I now find myself," wrote the czarevitch to Adjutant-general Diebitsch on the 5th of December, "for you know only too well of my devotion and sincere attachment to the best of brothers and monarchs to doubt them.

My position is rendered all the more painful from the fact that, the emperor's illness is only known to me and my old friend Kuruta and my doctor; the news has not yet reached here, so that in society I have to appear calm, although there is no such calmness in my soul. My wife and brother do not suspect anything, so that I had to invent an explanation for the arrival of your first messenger, which I shall have to do again to-day. If I were to obey only the suggestions of my heart of course I should have been with you long ago, but you will naturally understand what hinders me."

Meanwhile couriers continued to follow upon each others' heels and finally on December 7th, at seven in the evening, the czarevitch received the fatal intelligence of the death of his brother. The report of Adjutant-general Diebitsch did not shake the czarevitch's decision as to the question of the succession to the throne, and he then said to the grand duke Michael Pavlovitch, "Now the solemn moment has come to show that my previous mode of action was not a mask, and to terminate the matter with the same firmness with which it was commenced. My intentions and my determinations have not changed one iota, and my will to renounce the throne is more unchangeable than ever."

Summoning the persons of his entourage and informing them of the loss that had overtaken Russia, the czarevitch read them his correspondence with the emperor Alexander in 1822 and ordered that letters to the empress Marie Feodorovna, and to the grand duke Nicholas Pavlovitch, should be prepared, stating that he ceded his rights to the succession to the throne to his younger brother, by virtue of the rescript of the emperor Alexander of the 14th of February, 1822. The czarevitch here used the expression "cede the throne to the grand duke Nicholas Pavlovitch," because he knew nothing of the existence of the state act which as long ago as 1824 had invested this cession with the power of a law. Such were the misapprehensions with which was accompanied Alexander's secret and evasive manner of action in regard to the question of the succession.

Meanwhile what was taking place in St. Petersburg? The news of the death of the emperor Alexander was received in the capital only on December 9th, during prayers which were being said for the recovery of the emperor in the church of the Winter Palace. The circumstances are thus narrated by the empress Elizabeth Alexievna herself:

On the 9th inst. at the termination of the liturgy, when prayers for the health of the emperor had already commenced, his highness was called out from the sacristy by Count Miloradovitch and informed by him that all was over. His imperial highness became faint, but recovering himself he returned with Doctor Rule to the sacristy. The empress was on her knees and being already prepared by the grand duke's prolonged absence, and guessing her lot from his face she grew faint; meanwhile the priest presented the cross to her, and as she kissed it she lost consciousness.

His imperial highness, turning to his wife, said to her "Take care of our mother, and I will go and do my duty." With these words he entered the church, ordered that a reading desk should be brought in, and took the oath of allegiance to his beloved brother and emperor, Constantine, which he ratified by his signature; some others who happened to be there also subscribed to the same: they were the minister of war Tatistchev, General Kutusov, the general in waiting Potapov, and all the others who were present.

Then he presented himself before the Preobrajenski regiment that was on guard in the palace (the company of his majesty's grenadiers), and informed them of the emperor's death and proclaimed Constantine emperor. The grenadiers received the announcement with tears, and immediately took the oath of allegiance. After this his imperial highness commissioned the general in waiting, Potapov, to inform the chief and all the other guards of what had taken place and to bring them from their posts to take the oath, which was done without delay and with sorrow and zeal; meanwhile General Neitgart was sent to the Nevski monastery, where were all the general officers of the guards' corps, with the proposal to General Voinov to do the same throughout all the regiments of the guards. Finally similar announcements and instructions were sent to all the regiments and detachments in both the city and its environs.

Meanwhile the council of the state had assembled and opened its sitting by the proposal to break the seals of the envelope which contained the will of the late emperor. Some discussion arose, and finally it was decided to unseal the packet, in order to learn the last will of the czar.

NICHOLAS I
(1796–1855)

In the act was drawn up the renunciation of the throne by the czarevitch and the nomination of the grand duke Nicholas as the emperor's heir. Some discussion again arose upon this question, but it was cut short by the suggestion that his highness should be invited into the presence of the council. Count Miloradovitch replied that his highness had already taken the oath and that in any case he considered it unfitting that his highness should be called, or should come to the council, but offered to bring all this to his knowledge and to ask that they might be allowed to come to him in order to report all that had taken place; this was done and the grand duke replied that he could not hinder their coming.

When the members of the council presented themselves before the grand duke he informed them that the contents of the act had long been known to him, namely since July 25th, 1819, but that in no case would he dare to occupy the place of his elder brother, from whose supreme will his lot depended, and that holding it as a sacred obligation most humbly to obey him in all things, he had therefore taken the oath and felt entirely certain that the council, having in view the welfare of the state, would follow his example.

The council followed his highness into the church and at his request took the oath before him; they were then introduced by him into the presence of the empress mother, who was pleased to inform them that the act and its content were known to her, and were made with her maternal consent, but that she also was enthusiastic over her son's conduct. Confirming all his actions she requested the council by their united endeavours to preserve the tranquillity of the empire.

In accordance with the measures taken, by three o'clock in the afternoon the troops as well as all grades of officials in the government service had taken the oath confirming the accession to the throne of the emperor Constantine. During the whole time tranquillity and order were preserved. It is easy to imagine the astonishment and vexation of the czarevitch when, instead of receiving the expected commands of the new emperor, he was informed that all Russia had taken the oath of allegiance to him as lawful sovereign, and that the will of the late emperor had not been fulfilled.

Meanwhile early in the morning of December 15th the grand duke Michael Pavlovitch arrived in St. Petersburg with letters from the czarevitch. To the amazement of the court and the inhabitants, the grand duke did not follow the general example of swearing fidelity to the emperor Constantine. He did not conceal his regret at what had taken place in St. Petersburg, nor the apprehension with which the necessity of a new oath filled him. He dwelt on the difficulty of explaining to the public why the place of the elder brother to whom allegiance had already been sworn should suddenly be taken by the younger. The grand duke Nicholas in answer to his brother repeated what he had already said, that he could not have acted otherwise in such a position as that in which he was placed by his ignorance of the sacred acts of the late emperor, and that neither his conscience nor his reason reproached him. "Everything, however," added he, "might yet be amended and take a more favourable turn if the czarevitch himself were to come to St. Petersburg; his obstinacy in remaining at Warsaw may occasion disasters, the possibility of which I do not deny, but of which in all probability I shall myself be the first victim."

After long deliberation the grand duke Nicholas decided to write a fresh persuasive letter to the emperor Constantine, in which he asked him to decide finally what his fate was to be; and in conclusion he wrote, "In God's name, come." The empress Marie Feodorovna added her persuasions to those of her son, and not satisfied with these measures it was decided a few days later to despatch the grand duke Michael to Warsaw to convince the czarevitch of the necessity of his presence in St. Petersburg.

An answer from the czarevitch to the grand duke Nicholas' letter dated the 14th of December was brought to St. Petersburg by Lazarev, aid-de-camp to Nicholas: "Your aide-de-camp, dear Nicholas, on his arrival here, confided your letter to me with all exactitude. I read it with the deepest grief and sorrow. My decision is unalterable and consecrated by my late benefactor the emperor and sovereign. Your invitation to come quickly cannot be accepted by me, and I must tell you that I shall remove myself yet further away, if all is not arranged in accordance with the will of our late emperor. Your faithful and sincere friend and brother for life." But even this letter did not decide the matter; the return of Belussov from Warsaw with the answer to the grand duke Nicholas' letter of December 15th had yet to be awaited.

A new complication remained to be added to all these difficulties. On December 24th there came to St. Petersburg and presented himself to the grand duke Nicholas, Colonel Baron Fredericks of the Izmailovski Life Guards, who had fulfilled the functions of commandant in Taganrog. He brought to the grand duke a packet from Baron Diebitsch addressed to his imperial majesty, to be given into his own hands. To the question as to whether he knew of the contents of the packet, Fredericks replied in the negative, but added that as the place of residence of the emperor was unknown in Taganrog, exactly the same paper had been sent also to Warsaw.

Nothing therefore remained for Nicholas to do but to open the mysterious packet and "at the first rapid glance over its contents," writes Baron Korv, "an inexpressible horror took possession of him." It was on reading the report contained in this packet that the grand duke first learned of the existence of secret societies formed with the object of destroying to the very roots the tranquillity of the empire. The existence of these societies had been carefully hidden from him by the late emperor Alexander.

Almost immediately thereafter the courier Belussov returned from Warsaw with the czarevitch's decisive answer, which put an end to the interregnum. Nicholas Pavlovitch was emperor. At nine o'clock in the evening the emperor sent the following postscript to Adjutant-general Diebitsch:

The decisive courier has returned ; by the morning of the day after to-morrow I shall be emperor or else dead. I sacrifice myself for my brother ; happy if as a subject I fulfil his will. But how will it be with Russia ? What about the army ? General Tolle is here and I shall send him to Mohilev to bear the news to Count Saken. I am looking out for a trustworthy person for the same commission to Tultchin and to Ermolov. In a word, I hope to be worthy of my calling, not in fear and mistrustfulness, but in the hope that even as I fulfil my duty so will others fulfil their duty to me. But if anywhere anything is brewing and you hear of it, I authorise you to go at once where your presence is necessary. I rely entirely upon you and give you leave beforehand to take all the measures you deem necessary. The day after to-morrow if I am alive I will send you, I do not know by whom, information as to how matters have passed off ; on your part do not leave me without news of how everything is going on around you, especially with Ermolov. I again repeat that here until now everything is incomprehensibly quiet, but calm often precedes a storm. Enough of this, God's will be done ! In me there must only be seen the vicar and executor of the late emperor's will and therefore I am ready for everything. I shall ever be your sincere well wisher, NICHOLAS.

## THE ACCESSION OF NICHOLAS

The czarevitch's decisive answer was brought by Belussov, not through Riga, but by the Brest-Lithuani road; and therefore the grand duke Michael Pavlovitch was still in ignorance of the events at Nennal. The emperor Nicholas immediately sent an express after him commanding him to hasten to St. Petersburg. The return of the grand duke to the capital where his presence was of urgent necessity was thus by chance delayed.

Nicholas had now to occupy himself with the composition of his manifesto; the inexplicable had to be explained and it presented a task of no little difficulty: Karamzin and Speranski were set to work upon it. The emperor Nicholas signed the manfesto on the 25th of December, but dated it the 24th, as the day on which the question of his accession had been definitely settled by the czarevitch. It was proposed to keep the manifesto secret until the arrival of the grand duke Michael, but it was decided that the troops should take the oath of allegiance on the 26th of December; meanwhile notifications were sent to the members of the council of state, calling upon them to assemble on Sunday, December 25th, at eight in the evening, for a general secret meeting.

When the council of state had assembled at the hour designated, Prince Sopukhin announced that the grand duke Michael would be present at the sitting. The hours passed in anxious expectation; midnight approached and the expected arrival of the grand duke did not take place. Then Nicholas decided to be present at the sitting alone. Taking the place of the president, Nicholas himself began to read the manifesto announcing his acceptance of the imperial dignity in consequence of the persisted rejection of it by the czarevitch Constantine Pavlovitch. Then the emperor ordered that the czarevitch's rescript, addressed to Prince Sopukhin, president of the council, should be read. The 26th of December, 1825, had come. Commands had been issued that on that day all persons having access to the court should assemble at the Winter Palace for a *Te Deum;* eleven o'clock was the hour first named, but this was afterwards changed to two. Circumstances arose, however, which postponed the *Te Deum* to a still later hour. The members of the secret society decided to take advantage of the end of the interregnum and the approach of the new oath of allegiance in order to incite the troops to rebellion and to overthrow the existing order of things in Russia. The secrecy in which the negotiations with Russia had been enveloped had given occasion for various rumours and suppositions, and for the spread of false reports which occasioned alarm in society and especially in the barracks: all this favoured the undertakings and designs of the conspirators.

The only issue from the position that had been created by Nicholas in a moment of chivalrous enthusiasm "undoubtedly noble, but perhaps not entirely wise," would have been the arrival of the grand duke Constantine in the capital with the object of publicly and solemnly proclaiming his renunciation of the throne. But the czarevitch flatly refused to employ this means of extricating his brother from the difficult position in which he placed himself; Constantine considered that it was not for him to suffer from the consequences of an imprudence which was not his, and the danger of which might have been averted if matters had not been hurried on, and if he had been previously applied to for advice and instructions. Thus led into error, some of the lower ranks of the guards' regiments refused to take the oath of allegiance to Nicholas Pavlovitch, and assembled at the Petrovski square, before the senate buildings, appearing as though they were the defenders of the lawful rights of the czarevitch Constantine to the throne.

Meanwhile distinguished persons of both sexes began to drive up to the Winter Palace. Amidst the general stir and movement going on in the palace, there sat isolated and immoveable three magnates, "like three monuments," writes Karamzin: Prince Lopukhin, Count Araktcheiev, and Prince A. B. Kurakin. At the time when the military men had already gone out on the square, Count Araktcheiev, as might have been expected, preferred to remain in the palace. "It was pitiful to look at him," writes V. R. Martchenko in his *Mémoires*.

The rioters were stubborn for a long time and would not yield to exhortation; Count Miloradovitch fell mortally wounded. It began to grow dusk; Then the emperor Nicholas, at last convinced of the impossibility of pacifying the rioters without bloodshed, gave orders with a breaking heart for the artillery to fire. A few grape-shot decided the fate of the day; the rioters were dispersed, and tranquillity at once reigned in the capital.

The *Te Deum* announced could take place only at half past six. The troops bivouacked round the palace. "Dear, dear Constantine," wrote the emperor the same evening to the czarevitch, "your will is fulfilled: I am emperor, but at what price, my God! — at the price of the blood of my subjects." Arrests were made during that night and investigations pursued to discover the leaders of the revolt. And thus in the troubles of the 26th of December, the 1st of December, 1825, was terribly recalled. "The day was one of misfortune for Russia," writes Prince Viasenski, "and the epoch which it signalised in such a bloody manner was an awful judgment for deeds, opinions, and ideas, rooted in the past and governing the present." According to the words of Karamzin, on that day Russia was saved from a calamity "which, if it had not destroyed her, would certainly have torn her to pieces." "If I am emperor even for an hour, I will show that I was worthy of it"; thus spoke Nicholas on the morning of December 26th to the commanders of the guard regiments assembled at the Winter Palace; and on that awful day he triumphantly justified his first and impressive words.

## TRIAL OF THE CONSPIRATORS (1826 A.D.)

The emperor Nicholas gave all possible publicity to the proceedings against the secret societies, the Southern, Northern, the United Slavonians, and the Polish; then the whole matter was transferred to the supreme criminal court, which had to pronounce sentence on the principal participators in the conspiracy. Of the accused, Rileeks, Muraviev-Alostob, Bestuzhev-Riumin, Pesteb, and Kakhovski were condemned to death, and the remaining members of the secret societies brought before the court were exiled to Siberia or other places of incarceration.

No one had expected such a termination to the affair. During the whole of Alexander's reign there had not been one case of capital punishment, and it was looked upon as entirely abolished. "It is impossible to describe in words the horror and despair which have taken possession of all," writes a contemporary and eye witness of the events of 1826 in Moscow. This frame of mind was reflected in the coronation ceremonies. The emperor Nicholas appeared extremely gloomy; the future seemed more sad and fuller of anxiety than ever; all was in sharp contrast to the enthusiasm and hopes that had accompanied the coronation of Alexander in 1801.

## THE CORONATION OF NICHOLAS (1826 A.D.)

Immediately after the termination of the trial of the Dekabrists, the court proceeded to Moscow for the approaching coronation, which took place on the 3rd of September  Previously the emperor was rejoiced at the unexpected arrival of the grand duke Constantine Pavlovitch. According to Benkendorf "the czarevitch's appearance was a brilliant public testimony of his submission to the new emperor and of his conscientious renunciation of the throne; it was at the same time a precious pledge of the harmony which bound together all the members of the reigning family, a harmony conducive to the peace of the empire. The public was delighted and the *corps diplomatique* completely astounded. The people expressed their satisfaction to the czarevitch by unanimous acclamations; whilst the dignitaries of the state surrounded him with marks of respectful veneration."

The day of the coronation was signalised by an important reform in the administration of the court; the ministry of the imperial court was created, and confided to Prince P. M. Volkonski. Thus the old and tried companion of the emperor Alexander I again occupied the post of a trusty dignitary by the side of his successor. Prince Volkonski remained minister of the court until his decease, which took place in 1852. Amongst the favours and the mitigations of punishments which were granted on the 3rd of September, the state criminals who had lately been condemned were not forgotten; by special ukases the sentences of all those sent to the galleys, to penal settlements, and hard labour were mitigated. Those who had been sent to the Siberian, Orenburg, and Caucasian garrisons, both with and without deprivation of the rights of nobility, were enrolled in the regiments of the Caucasian corps.

During the emperor's stay in Moscow, the poet Pushkin, who had been banished to the village of Mikhailovski, was recalled. From that moment he regained his lost liberty, besides which the emperor Nicholas said to him: "In future you are to send me all you write — henceforth I will be **your** censor."

## CHANGES IN INTERNAL ADMINISTRATION

On the 18th of October, 1826, the emperor Nicholas returned to St. Petersburg; although his accession to the throne did not constitute the opening of a new era for Russia, yet certain changes were made in the system of administration which had prevailed during the last decade of the reign of Alexander I. After Count Araktcheiev had been relieved of the management of the general affairs of the state, it was to be foreseen that he would not remain long at the head of the direction of the military settlements. And thus it turned out. In the spring of 1826 Count Araktcheiev, on account of illness, was given leave to go abroad. In the report presented by him on this occasion to the emperor he announced to him economies of more than 32,000,000 rubles made on the military settlements, and concluded his epistle by observing, "Those impartial judges — posterity and the future — will pronounce a just sentence on all things."

On the return of Count Araktcheiev in the autumn from his travels abroad he did not again take up his duties. In accordance with a ukase which then followed, the staff office of the military settlements was united to the general staff of his imperial majesty, under the jurisdiction of its adjutant-general Baron Diebitsch. At the same time the Novgorod military settlement passed under the entire direction of General Prince Schahovski, who was nominated commander of the grenadier corps; the Kherson and Iekaterinoslav settlements were put under the supervision of their chief, Count Vitt (who was also commander of a separate corps), while the settlements in the villages of the Ukraine and Mohilev governments remained under the jurisdiction of their former chiefs, who bore the rank of commanders of divisions. Count Araktcheiev, when he had finally bidden adieu to his administrative career, settled on his Georgian estates, where he died in 1834.

Having delivered Russia from the administrative guardianship of Count Araktcheiev, the emperor Nicholas, in addition, delivered Russian instruction from the influence of Michael Leontievitch Magnitzki. On the 18th of May, 1826, a ukase was issued in which it was stated that "the curator of the University of Kazan and of its educational district, the actual councillor of state Magnitzki, is by our command relieved of his functions and of his position as member of the administration of schools." But the matter was not limited to this ukase. Magnitzki continued to live in Kazan and in accordance with his character he continued to intrigue as usual and indirectly to influence the university he had left. General Jeltukhin, who had been commissioned to make a detailed revision of the Kazan University, brought this fact to the emperor's knowledge. Nicholas' reply was rapid and decisive; a courier was sent with orders to the governor to arrest Magnitzki and send him to Revel under the surveillance of the commandant. Magnitzki lived there six years, having given his promise not to absent himself.

An equally sad fate overtook the champion and imitator of Magnitzki, Dmitri Pavlovitch Runitch, who had filled the office of curator of the St. Petersburg educational district. By a ukase of the 7th of July, 1826, Runitch was deprived of his functions and of the position of member of the chief administration of schools, for his incompetence in the matter of the direction of the St. Petersburg educational district. The requital experienced by Runitch for his educational labours was a terrible one; he languished beneath the consequences for sixteen years and died in 1860 in the conviction that he had formerly saved Russia, and was suffering for the good work he had accomplished in the University of St. Petersburg.

### Reforms in the Administration of Justice

The lamentable condition of the administration of justice in Russia was one of the first subjects to which the careful attention of the emperor Nicholas was directed. In a speech pronounced by the sovereign many years later, in 1833, before the council of state, Nicholas Pavlovitch thus expressed himself:

"From my very accession to the throne I was obliged to turn my attention to various administrative matters, of which I had scarcely any notion. The chief subject that occupied me was naturally legislation. Even from my early youth I had constantly heard of our deficiencies in this respect, of chicanery, of extortion, of the insufficiency of the existing laws or of their admixture through the extraordinary number of ukases which were not infrequently in contradiction to one another. This incited me from the very first days of my reign to examine into the state of the commission appointed for the constitution of the laws. To my regret, the information presented to me proved to me that its labours had remained almost fruitless. It was not difficult to discover the cause of this: the deficient results proceeded chiefly from the fact that the commission always directed its attention to the formation of new laws, when in reality the old ones should have been established on a firm foundation. This inspired me above all with a desire to establish a definite aim towards which the government must direct its actions in the matter of legislation; from the methods proposed to me I selected

MARRIED WOMAN OF VALDAI

one in entire opposition to the former methods of reform. Instead of drawing up new laws, I commanded that first those which already existed should be collected and set in order, whilst I took the matter itself, on account of its great importance, under my own immediate direction and closed the previous commission."

With this object was formed and opened on the 6th of May, 1826, the "second section of his imperial majesty's own chancery." M. A. Balongianski was appointed chief of the second section, but in reality the work itself was confided to Speranski. The emperor's choice rested on the latter, out of necessity, as he did not find anyone more capable around him. When Balongianski was appointed chief of the second section, the emperor, in conversing with his former tutor, said to him, speaking of Speranski: "See that he does not play any pranks, as in 1810." Nevertheless, in proportion to Speranski's successful accomplishment of the work confided to him, the emperor Nicholas' prejudices against him gradually softened and finally gave way to sincere favour and full confidence. All the accusations and calumnies directed against Speranski were, in accordance with the emperor's own expression," "scattered like dust."

Thus the emperor Nicholas in his almost involuntary choice was favoured by a peculiarly fortunate chance and could hardly have found a person better fitted for the accomplishment of the work he had planned. The results of Speranski's fresh efforts, under completely different circumstances from those against which he had formerly contended, were the "complete collection of laws," and a systematic code.

A WOMAN (SAILOR) OF THE NOGAI TRIBE

Even before the termination of the trial of the Dekabrists, the emperor Nicholas took another important measure, which left an imprint on all the succeeding years of his reign and is directly connected with the events of the 26th of December.

On the 15th of July, 1826, a supreme edict was issued in the name of the minister of the interior Lanskoi, by which the private chancery of that ministry was abolished and transformed into the third section of his imperial majesty's own chancery. In fulfilment of this ukase, it was prescribed that the governors of provinces, in matters which entered within the sphere of the former division, should no longer present their reports to the ministry of the interior, but should submit them directly to his majesty.

Some days before, on the emperor Nicholas' birthday, the 6th of July, a supreme order appeared naming the chief of the first cuirassier division, Adjutant-general Benkendorf, chief of the gendarmerie and commandant of the emperor's headquarters; to him was confided the direction of the third section. Adjutant-general Benkendorf explains in his memoirs in the following manner the reasons for establishing the institution confided to his direction: "The emperor Nicholas aimed at the extirpation of the abuses that had crept into many branches of the administration, and was convinced by the sudden discovery of the conspiracy which had stained the first moments of the new reign with blood, of the necessity of a universal and more diligent surveillance. The emperor chose me to organise a higher police, which should protect the oppressed and guard the nation against conspiracies and conspirators. Never having thought of preparing myself for this sort of service, I had hardly the most superficial understanding of it; but the noble and beneficent motives which inspired the sovereign in his creation of this institution and the desire to be of use to him, forbade me to evade the duty to which his high confidence had called me. I set to work without delay and God helped me to fulfil my new duties to the satisfaction of the emperor and without setting general opinion against me. I succeeded in showing favours to many, in discovering many conspiracies, and averting much evil." With the creation of the new third section, the committee of the 13th of January,

1807, established by the emperor Alexander, became superfluous; and on the 29th of January a ukase was issued closing it.

The disturbances of the year 1825 did not pass without leaving traces on the peasant population; a momentary confusion ensued, freedom was talked of, and disorders arose in some provinces — a phenomenon often seen in previous times. The movement amongst the peasants incited the emperor Nicholas to publish, on the 24th of May, 1826, a manifesto in which it was declared that all "talk of exempting the villagers in the state settlements from paying taxes and of freeing landowner's peasants and menials from subjection to their landowners are false rumours, imagined and spread by evil intentioned persons out of mere cupidity with the object of enriching themselves through these rumours at the expense of the peasants, by taking advantage of their simplicity." It was further said in the manifesto that all classes throughout the empire must absolutely submit to the authorities placed over them, and that disturbers of the public tranquillity would be prosecuted and punished in accordance with the full severity of the laws. It was commanded that the manifesto should be read in all the churches and at the markets and fairs during a space of six months; the governors of provinces were sternly admonished to be watchful in anticipating disorders.

If, however, the emperor Nicholas was forced by circumstances to promulgate this punitive manifesto, he also issued two rescripts in the name of the minister of the interior, enjoining upon the nobility behaviour towards their peasants, which should be in accordance with the laws of Christianity, thus clearly expressing his desire to protect the peasant against the arbitrariness and tyranny of the landowners. "In all cases," wrote the emperor: "I find it, and shall ever find it, better to prevent evil, than to pursue it by punishment when it has already arisen."

Finally the solicitude of the emperor Nicholas for the peasant classes manifested itself by yet another action. On the 18th of December, 1826, a special secret committee was formed to which was confided the inspection of the entire state organisation and administration, with the order to represent the conclusions it arrived at as to the changes deemed necessary; the labours of the committee were to be directed also to the consideration of the peasant question. Besides this the emperor did not leave without attention what had been said by the Dekabrists, during the time of their examination before a committee of inquiry, in regard to the internal conditions of the state in the reign of Alexander I. The emperor ordered a separate memorandum of these opinions to be drawn up for him and often perused this curious document, from which he extracted much that was pertinent.[b]

## WAR WITH PERSIA (1826–1828 A.D.)

The shah of Persia thought he saw in the change of rulers and the troubles by which it was accompanied circumstances favourable to the recovery of the provinces ceded to Russia by the Treaty of Gulistan. In August, 1826, he ordered his troops to move forward. The solemnity of his coronation, which was then being celebrated and whose splendour was enhanced by the presence of the czarevitch, did not prevent Nicholas from promptly organising the defence of the empire. A few weeks afterwards General Paskevitch defeated the Persians at Ielisavetpol, and in the following year, transferring the theatre of war to the enemy's territory, he seized the celebrated convent of Etchmiadzine, the seat of the Armenian patriarch, and Erivan, one of the great towns of Armenia; he moreover penetrated as far as Tauris, capital of the Azerbaijan and residence of the prince royal, Abbas Mirza. Then the shah asked for peace. It was signed at Turkmantchaï, the 22nd of February, 1828, and advanced Russia as far as the line of the Araxes, by giving up to her the provinces of Erivan and Nakhitchevan.

WAR WITH TURKEY (1828-1829 A.D.)

This treaty was concluded, to the great regret of Persia, when the war with Turkey broke out. This war had been threatening for years; for, deeply affected by the violences to which the Greeks in the Ottoman Empire had been exposed ever since the hetaerist insurrection of 1821, and by the martydom which the Greek patriarch had been made to suffer, Alexander left the sword in its sheath only out of deference to the members of the Holy Alliance. His successor was thoroughly determined no longer to subordinate the direction of his cabinet's policy to the interested views of these princes and to their fears, though it is true that the latter were well founded. The Divan, by signing the Treaty of Akerman (October 6th, 1826), had momentarily averted the storm which was ready to burst; but still more irritating disputes had afterwards arisen. The conclusion of the Treaty of London of the 6th of July, 1827, in virtue of which France, England, and Russia gave existence to a Christian kingdom of Greece placed under their common protection, was shortly followed by the naval battle of Navarino, fought on the 20th of October of the same year by the combined fleets of the three powers, against Ibrahim Pasha, commander-in-chief of the Egyptian forces in the Morea; and in this memorable conflict, expected by no one, but a subject of joy to some whilst judged untoward by others, the whole of the navy which the Porte still had at its disposal was destroyed. Very soon Mahmud II, yielding to the national desire, let it be understood that he had never had any intention of lending himself to the execution of a treaty in virtue of which Moldavia, Wallachia, and Servia were almost as much the czar's vassals as his own. This was the beginning of a rupture, and Nicholas answered it by a declaration of war, which appeared June 4th, 1828, when his army had already crossed the Pruth.

The campaign of 1828, which accomplished nothing more than the taking of Braïla and Varna, did not give a high idea of the strength of Russia; and when the emperor made up his mind to take part in it in person, his presence wrought no change in the feebleness of the results. But it was not the same with the campaign which followed. Not only did the Russians again pass the Danube, but after having beaten the grand vizir, Reschid Pasha, at Koul-evtcha, on the 11th of June, Diebitsch marched them across the Balkans for the first time, a feat which won him the name of *Sabalkanski*, and proceeded straight to Adrianople, where he was scarcely more than two hundred kilometres (about 125 miles) from the Ottoman capital. At the same time Paskevitch took Erzerum in Asia, and the two generals would doubtless have joined hands in Constantinople but for the efforts of diplomacy and the fear of a general conflagration. For Russia was already too powerful; she had been allowed more than was compatible with the policy of the system of balance, no doubt from the fear of incurring a grave responsibilty by troubling the peace of Europe. But a prospect like that of the occupation by Russia of Constantinople and the Straits silenced this fear.

Austria was ready to send her troops to the help of the Turks, and the English also seemed likely to declare for the vanquished. It was therefore necessary to come to a halt. Russia reflected that, after all, "the sultan was

[1829 A.D.]

the least costly governor-general she could have at Constantinople,' and lent an ear to moderate conditions of peace. Nevertheless, if the Treaty of Adrianople, signed September 14th, 1829, delivered nothing to her in Europe save the mouths of the Danube, in itself a very important point, it enlarged her territories in Asia by a part of the pashalik of Akhalzikh, with the fortress of that name, besides abandoning to her those of Anapa and Pothi on the Black Sea; it considerably strengthened Muscovite influence in the principalities, and still further weakened Turkey, not only morally but also materially by the great pecuniary sacrifices to which she had to subscribe. That power, once so formidable, was henceforth at the mercy of her northern neighbour, the principal instrument of her decay.

### THE POLISH INSURRECTION (1830–1831 A.D.)

But Russia was in her turn rudely shaken by the insurrection in Poland, always her mortal enemy after she had ceased to be her rival.[c]

It was in Moscow that the emperor Nicholas received news of the further progress of the Belgian revolution, in consequence of which the king of the Netherlands found himself obliged to ask for the assistance of his allies by virtue of the existing treaties. The emperor at once despatched orders to Count Tchernishev, Field-marshal Saken, and the czarevitch to place the army on a war footing. The czarevitch was not pleased at the martial turn given to the diplomatic negotiations; still more dissatisfied was the Polish Society of that time, which sympathised with the revolution of July; neither was the army in sympathy with the approaching campaign, which would bring it into armed collision with France in the name of the principles of the Holy Alliance. Although tranquillity apparently reigned in Warsaw, yet the secret societies continued to carry on their destructive work with success.

COUNT DIEBITSCH-SABALKANSKI
(1785–1831)

Various ominous signs of the approaching catastrophe were not, however, wanting; but the czarevitch continued to lull himself with impossible hopes that all was peaceful and tranquil and would remain so. As to the European powers allied to Russia, they did not enter into the matter with such decided zeal. In the present case it was the Russian autocrat alone who was ready with entire disinterestedness to take up the defence of the infringed lawful order. The other powers found it incomparably more expedient to have recourse to the co-operation of diplomatic remedies; the result was that, instead of an armed intervention, a general European conference for the settlement of the Belgian question by peaceful means took place in London.

Count Diebitsch was still in Berlin awaiting the termination of the negotiations confided to him, when they were suddenly broken off by an event upon which the field-marshal had not in the least calculated at the given moment. On the 3rd of December, 1830, Diebitsch received from the Prussian minister, Count Berastorf, news of the revolution which had taken place in Warsaw on the 29th of November: the Polish army, forming a prepared coalition, had taken up arms against Russia. There remained but one thing for Diebitsch to do and that was to hasten to St. Petersburg as quickly as possible. Meanwhile in St. Petersburg the emperor Nicholas had received only the report of the czarevitch concerning the rising of the troops and of inhabitants of Warsaw on the evening of the 7th of December, 1830.

On the next day a parade of the Preobrajenski regiment was appointed to take place, and as usual the emperor came to the riding school. At first everything proceeded in the usual manner; there were even no traces of inward agitation manifest upon the handsome face with its regular, classic profile, which preserved its habitual expression of majestic nobility. At the termination of the parade the emperor rode into the middle of the riding school, called the officers around him, and personally communicated to them the intelligence of the Warsaw rebellion: "I have already made arrangements that the troops designated by me should move on Warsaw, and if necessary you too shall go, to punish the traitors and re-establish order and the offended honour of Russia. I know that under every circumstance I can rely upon you," said the emperor. A unanimous outburst of indignation momentarily seized upon all present and then enthusiastic cries resounded: "Lead us against the rebels: we will revenge the offended honour of Russia." They kissed the emperor's hands and feet and the hem of his garment with shouts and cheers. The outburst of indignation was so violent that Nicholas considered it necessary to moderate it, and with the majesty that was natural to him he reminded the officers surrounding him that not all the Poles had broken their oath; that the ringleaders of the insurrection must be punished, but that vengeance must not be taken on the people: that the repentant must be pardoned and hatred not allowed.

From the subsequent reports of the grand duke the emperor learned that the czarevitch had permitted the portion of the Polish army that remained with him to return to Warsaw; in exchange for this the deputies who came to the czarevitch promised him and the Russian detachment a free passage to the frontiers of the empire. It was decided that a sufficient number of troops should be concentrated in the Polish frontier to allow of decisive measures being taken against the insurgents. Count Diebitsch was appointed commander-in-chief of the acting army, whilst the office of chief of the staff was filled by Count Tolle.

When the czarevitch reached the Russian frontier he wrote as follows to the emperor Nicholas: "And now the work of sixteen years is completely destroyed by a set of ensign-bearers, young officers, and students. I will not further enlarge on the matter, but duty commands me to bear witness to you that the landed proprietors, the rural population, and in general all holders of property of any kind are up in despair over this. The officers and generals as well as the soldiers are unable to keep from joining the general movement, being carried away by the young people and ensign-bearers who led everyone astray. In a word, the position of affairs is extremely bad, and I really do not know what will come of it. All my measures of surveillance have led to nothing, in spite of the fact that everything was beginning to be discovered. Here are we Russians at the frontier, but, great God, in what a condition! — almost barefoot, for we all came out as if at the sound of an alarm, in the hopes of returning to barracks, whilst instead awful marches have had to be made. The officers have been deprived of everything and have almost nothing with which to clothe themselves. I am broken hearted; at the age of fifty-one and a half years I never thought to finish my career in this lamentable manner after thirty-five and a half years of service. I pray to God that the army to which I have devoted sixteen years of my life may be brought to reason, and return to the path of duty and honour, acknowledging its previous errors, before coercive measures have to be taken. But this is too much to expect from the age in which we live, and I greatly doubt the realisation of my desires."

Any agreement with Poland became daily more impossible and both sides prepared for war. On the 17th of December the emperor Nicholas' proclamation to the Polish army and nation was issued, and on the 24th a manifesto was published offering means of reconciliation to all those who returned to their duty. Meanwhile General Chlopicki was installed as dictator in Warsaw, but he was unable to save Poland from a rupture with Russia. Two deputies were sent to St. Petersburg to enter into negotiations with the emperor Nicholas; they were the minister of finance, Prince Lubetzki and a member of the diet, Count Ezerski. But neither could these negotiations avert the bloody events of the year 1831. "It is hard to foresee the future," wrote the emperor to the czarevitch; "but weighing the relative probabilities of success, it is difficult to suppose that the new year will show itself more distressing for us than the year 1830; God grant that I may not be mistaken. I should like to see you peacefully settled in your Belvedere and order re-established throughout; but how much there yet remains to be accomplished before we are in a condition to attain to this! Which of the two must perish — for it appears inevitable that one must perish, Russia or Poland? Decide for yourself. I have exhausted all possible means in order to avert such a calamity — all means compatible with honour and my conscience — but they are exhausted. What remains for me to do?"

Soon the diet assembled in Warsaw took a decision which completed the rupture between Poland and Russia. On the 25th of January, 1831, the diet declared the Romanov dynasty to be deprived of the throne of Poland. The Poles themselves thus unbound the hands of the emperor, and the duel between Russia and Poland became inevitable. The emperor replied to the challenge by a manifesto in accordance with which the Russian troops crossed the Polish frontier, and on the 25th of February a decisive battle took place before Prague at Grokhov, by which the Polish army was obliged to retreat to Warsaw with a loss of twelve thousand men.

But Count Diebitsch did not recognise the possibility of taking advantage of the victory gained, and which would have been inevitably completed by the occupation of the Polish capital; and Sabalkanski was not fated to become prince of Warsaw. The Polish troops retreated unhindered across the only bridge to Warsaw; the new Polish commander-in-chief Skrjinetzski set out to reorganise the army, the rising spread even to the Russian governments, and the campaign, against all expectations, dragged on for six months. Meanwhile it was a war upon which depended, according to the expression used by the emperor, "the political existence of Russia."

On the 26th of May Diebitsch gained a second victory over the Polish army, which also terminated by the favourable retreat of the latter; and on the 13th of June, the emperor found occasion to write to his field-marshal: "Act at length so that I can understand you." The letter was however not read by Count Diebitsch, for on the 10th of June the field-marshal suddenly died of cholera in the village of Kleshov near Pultiusk.

He was replaced by Field-marshal Count Paskevitch-Erivanski, who was as early as April, 1831, called by the emperor from Tiflis to St. Petersburg. It was decided to cross the lower Vis-Suta and move towards Warsaw. The czarevitch Constantine outlived Count Diebitsch only by a few days. He also died suddenly of cholera at Vitebsk, in the night between the 26th and 27th of June of the year 1831.

The Polish insurrection from that time daily grew nearer to its definitive conclusion; it was determined by the two days' storming of Warsaw, which took place on the 7th and 8th of September. Finally Field-marshal Paskevitch was able to communicate to the emperor the news that "Warsaw is at the feet of your imperial majesty." Prince Suvorov, aide-de-camp of the emperor, was the bearer of this intelligence to Tsarskoi-Selo on the 16th of September.

FIELD-MARSHAL PASKEVITCH
(1782–1856)

Nicholas wrote as follows to his victorious field-marshal: "With the help of the all-merciful God, you have again raised the splendour and glory of our arms, you have punished the disloyal traitors, you have avenged Russia, you have subdued Warsaw — from henceforth you are the most serene prince of Warsaw. Let posterity remember that the honour and glory of the Russian army are inseparable from your name, and may your name preserve for everyone the memory of the day on which the name of Russia was again made glorious. This is the sincere expression of the grateful heart of your sovereign, your friend, and your old subordinate."

After the fall of Warsaw the war still continued for a while, but not for long. The chief forces of the Polish army, which had retired to Novogeorgievsk, finished by passing into Prussian territory at the end of September, and on the 21st of October the last fortress surrendered. The Polish insurrection was at an end. But the peace, attained by such heavy sacrifice, was accompanied by a new evil for Russia; in Europe appeared the Polish emigration, carrying with it hatred and vociferations against Russia and preparing the inimical conditions of public opinion in the west against the Russian government.

### THE OUTBREAK OF CHOLERA AND THE RIOTS OCCASIONED BY IT (1830 A.D.)

The emperor had hardly returned to St. Petersburg from opening the diet in Warsaw, when suddenly a new care occupied the attention of the government. The cholera made its appearance in the empire. This terrible illness, until then known to Russia only by name and by narratives describing its devastations, brought with it still greater fear, because no one knew or could indicate either medical or police measures to be taken against it. General opinion inclined, however, towards the advantages to be derived from quarantine and isolation, such as had been employed against the plague, and the government immediately took necessary measures in this direction with the activity that the emperor's strong will managed to instil into all his dispositions. Troops were without delay stationed at various points and cordons formed from them and the local inhabitants, in order to save the governments in the interior and the two capitals from the calamity.

In spite of all precautions, however, a fresh source of grief was added to all the cares and anxieties that pressed upon the emperor at that period. Since the 26th of June the cholera had appeared in St. Petersburg and in a few days had attained menacing dimensions. This awful illness threw all classes of the population into a state of the greatest terror, particularly the common people by whom all the measures taken for the preservation of the public health — such as increased police surveillance, the surrounding of the towns with troops, and even the removal of those stricken with cholera to hospitals— were at first regarded as persecutions. Mobs began to assemble, strangers were stopped in the streets and searched for the poison they were supposed to carry on them, while doctors were publicly accused of poisoning the people. Finally, on the 4th of July, the mob, excited by rumours and suspicions, gathered together at the Hay Market and attacked the house in which a temporary cholera hospital had been established. They broke the windows, threw the furniture out into the street, wounded and cast out the sick, thrashed the hospital servants, and killed several of the doctors. The police were powerless to restore order and even the final appearance of the military governor-general Count Essen did not attain the necessary result. A battalion of the Semenov regiment forced the people to disperse from the square into the side streets, but was far from putting a stop to the disturbance.

The next day the emperor Nicholas went on a steamer from St. Petersburg to Elagium Island. When he had heard the reports of various persons as to the state of the town he got into a carriage with Adjutant-general Prince Menshikov and drove to the Preobrajenski parade-ground in the town, where a battalion of the Preobrajenski regiment was encamped. When he had thanked the troops, the emperor continued his way along the carriage road were he threatened with his displeasure some crowds and shopkeepers; from there he drove to the Hay Market where about five thousand people had assembled. Standing up in his carriage and turning to the mob, the emperor spoke as follows: "Misdeeds were committed yesterday, public order was disturbed; shame on the Russian people for forgetting the faith of their fathers and imitating the turbulence of the French and Poles! They have taught you this: seize them and take those suspected to the authorities; but wickedness has been committed here, here we have offended and angered God — let us turn to the church, down on your knees, and beg the forgiveness of the Almighty!"

The people fell on their knees and crossed themselves in contrition; the emperor prostrated himself also, and exclamations of "We have sinned, accursed ones that we are!" resounded throughout the air. Continuing his speech to the people, the emperor again admonished the crowd: "I have sworn before God to preserve the prosperity of the people entrusted to me by providence; I am answerable before God for these disorders: and therefore I will not allow them. Woe be to the disobedient!"

At this moment some men in the crowd raised their voices. The emperor then replied: "What do you want — whom do you want? Is it I? I am not afraid of anything — here I am!" and with these words he pointed to his breast. Cries of enthusiasm ensued. After this the emperor, probably as a sign of reconciliation, embraced an old man in the crowd and returned, first to Elagium and afterwards to Peterhov. The day afterwards the emperor again visited the capital. Order was re-established, but the cholera continued to rage. Six hundred persons died daily, and it was only from the middle of July that the mortality began to diminish.

Far more dangerous in its consequences was the revolt that arose in the Novgorod military settlements. Here the cholera and rumours of poisoning only served as a pretext for rebellion; the seed of general dissatisfaction among the population belonging to this creation of Count Araktcheiev continued to exist in spite of all the changes introduced by the emperor Nicholas into the administration of the military settlements. A spark was sufficient to produce in the settlements an explosion of hitherto unprecedented fury, and the cholera served as the spark. Order was however finally re-established in the settlements and then the emperor Nicholas set off for them quite alone and presented himself before the assembled battalions, which had stained themselves with the blood of their officers and stood awaiting, trembling and in silence the judgment of their sovereign.[b]

### THE WAR IN THE CAUCASUS (1829–1840 A.D.)

The possession of the Caucasus is a question vitally affecting the interests of Russia in her provinces beyond that range of mountains, and her ulterior projects with regard to the regions of Persia and Central Asia. Here are the terms in which this subject is handled in a report printed at St. Petersburg, and addressed to the emperor after the expedition of General Emmaneul to Elbruz in 1829:

"The Circassians (Tsherkessians) bar out Russia from the south, and may at their pleasure open or close the passage to the nations of Asia. At present their intestine dissensions, fostered by Russia, hinder them from uniting under one leader; but it must not be forgotten that, according to traditions religiously preserved amongst them, the sway of their ancestors extended as far as to the Black Sea. They believe that a mighty people, descended from their ancestors, and whose existence is verified by the ruins of Madjar, has once already overrun the fine plains adjacent to the Danube, and finally settled in Panonia. Add to this consideration their superiority in arms. Perfect horsemen, extremely well armed, inured to war by the continual freebooting they exercise against their neighbours, courageous, and disdaining the advantages of our civilisation, the imagination is appalled at the consequences which their union under one leader might have for Russia, which has no other bulwark against their ravages than a military line, too extensive to be very strong."

For the better understanding of the war which Russia has been so long waging with the mountaineers, let us glance at the topography of the Caucasus, and the respective positions of the belligerents.

The chain of the Caucasus exhibits a peculiar conformation, altogether different from that of any of the European chains. The Alps, the Pyrenees, and the Carpathians are accessible only by the valleys, and in these the inhabitants of the country find their subsistence, and agriculture developes its wealth. The contrary is the case in the Caucasus. From the fortress of Anapa on the Black Sea, all along to the Caspian, the northern slope presents only immense inclined plains, rising in terraces to a height of 3,000 or 4,000 yards above the sea level. These plains, rent on all directions by deep and narrow valleys and vertical clefts, often form real steppes, and possess on their loftiest heights rich pastures, where the inhabitants, secure from all attack, find fresh grass for their cattle in the sultriest days of summer. The valleys on the other hand are frightful abysses, the steep sides of which are clothed with brambles, while the bottoms are filled with rapid torrents foaming over beds of rocks and stones. Such is the singular spectacle generally presented by the northern slope of the Caucasus. This brief description may give an idea of the difficulties to be encountered by an invading army. Obliged to occupy the heights, it is incessantly checked in its march by impassable ravines, which do not allow of the employment of cavalry, and for the most part prevent the passage of artillery. The ordinary tactics of the mountaineers is to fall back before the enemy, until the nature of the ground or the want of supplies obliges the latter to begin a retrograde movement. Then it is that they attack the invaders, and, intrenched in their forests behind impregnable rocks, they inflict the most terrible carnage on them with little danger to themselves.

On the south the character of the Caucasian chain is different. From Anapa to Gagri, along the shores of the Black Sea, we observe a secondary chain composed of schistous mountains, seldom exceeding 1000 yards in height. But the nature of their soil, and of their rocks, would be enough to render them almost impracticable for European armies, even were they not covered with impenetrable forests. The inhabitants of this region, who are called Circassians, are entirely independent, and constitute one of the most warlike peoples of the Caucasus.

The great chain begins in reality at Gagri, but the mountains recede from the shore, and nothing is to be seen along the coast as far as Mingrelia but secondary hills, commanded by immense crags, that completely cut off all approach to the central part of the Caucasus. This region, so feebly defended by its topographical conformation, is Abkhasia, the inhabitants of which have been forced to submit to Russia. To the north and on the northern slope, westward of the military road from Mozdok to Tiflis, dwell a considerable number of tribes, some of them ruled by a sort of feudal system, others constituted into little republics. Those of the west, dependent on Circassia and Abadja, are in continual war with the empire, whilst the Nogaians, who inhabit the plains on the left bank of the Kuma, and the tribes of the great Kabarda, own the sovereignty of the czar; but their wavering and dubious submission cannot be relied on. In the centre, at the foot of the Elbruz, dwell the Suanetians, an unsubdued people, and near them, occupying both sides of the pass of Dariel, are the Ingutches and Ossetans, exceptional tribes, essentially different from the aboriginal peoples. Finally we have, eastward of the great Tiflis road, near the Terek, little Kabarda, and the country of the Kumicks, for the present subjugated; and then those indomitable tribes, the Lesghians and Tchetchens, of whom Schamyl is the Ab del Kadir, and who extended over the two slopes of the Caucasus to the vicinity of the Caspian.

In reality, the Kuban and the Terek, that rise from the central chain, and fall, the one into the Black Sea, the other into the Caspian, may be considered as the northern political limits of independent Caucasus. It is along those two rivers that Russia has formed her armed line, defended by Cossacks, and detachments from the regular army. The Russians have, indeed, penetrated those northern frontiers at sundry points, and have planted some forts within the country of the Lesghians and Tchetchens. But those lonely posts, in which a few unhappy garrisons are surrounded on all sides, and generally without a chance of escape, cannot be regarded as a real occupation of the soil on which they stand. They are, in fact, only so many pickets, whose business is only to watch more closely the movements of the mountaineers. In the south, from Anapa to Gagri, along the Black Sea, the imperial possessions never extended beyond a few detached forts, completely isolated, and deprived of all means of communication by land. A rigorous blockade was established on this coast; but the Circassians, as intrepid in their frail barks as among their mountains, often passed by night through the Russian line of vessels, and reached Trebizond and Constantinople. Elsewhere, from Mingrelia to the Caspian, the frontiers are less precisely defined, and generally run parallel with the great chain of the Caucasus.

Thus limited, the Caucasus, including the territory occupied by the subject tribes, presents a surface of scarcely 5000 leagues; and it is in this narrow region that a virgin and chivalric nation, amounting at most to 2,000,000 of souls, proudly upholds its independence against the might of the Russian empire, and has for upwards of twenty years sustained one of the most obstinate struggles known to modern history.

The Russian line of the Kuban, which is exactly similar to that of the Terek, is defended by the Cossacks of the Black Sea, the poor remains of the famous Zaparogians, whom Catherine II subdued with so much difficulty, and whom she colonised at the foot of the Caucasus, as a bulwark against the incursions of the mountaineers. The line consists of small forts and watch stations; the latter are merely a kind of sentry-box raised on four posts, about fifty feet from the ground. Two Cossacks keep watch in them day and night. On the least movement of the enemy in the vast plain of reeds that fringe both banks of the river, a beacon fire is kindled on the top of the watch box. If the danger becomes more pressing, an enormous torch of straw and tar is set fire to. The signal is repeated from post to post, the whole line springs to arms, and 500 or 600 men are instantly assembled on the point threatened. These posts, composed generally of a dozen men, are very close to each other, particularly in the most dangerous places. Small forts have been erected at intervals with earthworks, and a few pieces of cannon; they contain each from 150 to 200 men.

But notwithstanding all the vigilance of the Cossacks, often aided by the troops of the line, the mountaineers not unfrequently cross the frontier and carry their incursions, which are always marked with massacre and pillage, into the adjacent provinces. There are bloody but justifiable reprisals. In 1835 a body of fifty horsemen entered the country of the Cossacks, and proceeded to a distance of 120 leagues, to plunder the German colony of Madjar and the important village of Vladimirovka, on the Kuma, and what is most remarkable they got back to their mountains without being interrupted. The same year Kisliar, on the Caspian, was sacked by the Lesghians. These daring expeditions prove of themselves how insufficient is the armed line of the Caucasus, and to what dangers that part of southern Russia is exposed.

The line of forts until lately existing along the Black Sea was quite as weak, and the Circassians there were quite as daring. They used to carry off the Russian soldiers from beneath the fire of their redoubts, and come up to the very foot of their walls to insult the garrison. Hommaire de Hell relates that, at the time he was exploring the mouths of the Kuban, a hostile chief had the audacity to appear one day before the gates of Anapa. He did all he could to irritate the Russians, and abusing them as cowards and woman-hearted, he defied them to single combat. Exasperated by his invectives, the commandant ordered that he should be fired on with grape. The horse of the mountaineer reared and threw off his rider, who, without letting go the bridle, instantly mounted again, and, advancing still nearer to the walls, discharged his pistol almost at point-blank distance at the soldiers, and galloped off to the mountains.

As for the blockade by sea, the imperial squadron has not been expert enough to render it really effectual. It was only a few armed boats, manned by Cossacks, that gave the Circassians any serious uneasiness. These Cossacks like those of the Black Sea, are descended from the Zaparogians. Previously to the last war with Turkey they were settled on the right bank of the Danube, where their ancestors had taken refuge after the destruction of their Setcha. During the campaigns of 1828–29, pains were taken to revive their national feelings, they were brought again by fair means or by force under the imperial sway, and were then settled in the forts along the Caucasian shore, the keeping of which was committed to their charge. Courageous, enterprising, and worthy rivals of their foes, they waged a most active war against the skiffs of the mountaineers in their boats, which carry crews of fifty or sixty men.

The treaty of Adrianople was in a manner the opening of a new era in the relations of Russia with the mountaineers; for it was by virtue of that treaty that the czar, already master of Anapa and Sudjuk Kaleh, pretended to the sovereignty of Circassia and of the whole seaboard of the Black Sea. True to the invariable principles of its foreign policy, the government at first employed means of corruption, and strove to seduce the various chiefs of the country by pensions, decorations, and military appointments. But the mountaineers, who had the example of the Persian provinces before their eyes, sternly rejected all the overtures of Russia, and repudiated the clauses of the convention of Adrianople; the political and commercial independence of their country became their rallying cry, and they would not treat on any other condition. All such ideas were totally at variance with Nicholas' schemes of absolute dominion; therefore he had recourse to arms to obtain by force what he had been unable to accomplish by other means.

Abkhasia, situated on the eastern coast of the Black Sea, and easily accessible, was the first invaded. A Russian force occupied the country in 1839, under the ordinary pretence of supporting one of its princes, and putting an end to anarchy. In the same year General Paskevitch, then governor-general of the Caucasus, for the first time made an armed exploration of the country of the Circassians beyond the Kuban; but he effected absolutely nothing, and his expedition only resulted in great loss of men and stores. In the following year war broke out in Daghestan with the Lesghians and the Tchetchens. The celebrated Kadi Mulah, giving himself out for a prophet, gathered together a considerable number of partisans; but unfortunately for him there was no unanimity among the tribes, and the princes were continually counteracting each other. Kadi Mulah never was able to bring more than 3,000 or 4,000 men together; nevertheless, he maintained the struggle with a courage worthy of a better fate, and Russia knows what it cost her to put down the revolt of Daghestan. As for any real progress in that part of the Caucasus, the Russians made none; they did no more than replace things on the old footing. Daghestan soon became again more hostile than ever, and the Tchetchens and Lesghians continued in separate detachments to plunder and ravage the adjacent provinces up to the time when the ascendancy of the celebrated Schamyl, the worthy successor of Kadi Mulah, gave a fresh impulse to the warlike tribes of the mountain, and rendered them more formidable than ever.

After taking possession of Anapa and Sudjuk Kaleh, the Russians thought of seizing the whole seaboard of Circassia, and especially the various points suitable for the establishment of military posts. They made themselves masters of Guelendchik and the important position of Gagri, which commands the pass between Circassia and Abkhasia. The Circassians heroically defended their territory; but how could they have withstood the guns of the ships of war that mowed them down whilst the soldiers were landing and constructing their redoubts? The blockade of the coasts was declared in 1838, and all foreign communication with the Caucasus ostensibly intercepted. During the four following years Russia suffered heavy losses; and all her successes were limited to the establishment of some small isolated forts on the sea-coast. She then increased her army, laid down the military road from the Kuban to Guelendchik, across the last western offshoot of the Caucasus, set on foot an exploration of the enemy's whole coast, and prepared to push the war with renewed vigour.

In 1837 the emperor Nicholas visited the Caucasus. He would see for himself the theatre of a war so disastrous to his arms, and try what impression his imperial presence could make on the mountaineers. The chiefs of the country were invited to various conferences, to which they boldly repaired on the faith of the Russian parole; but instead of conciliating them by words of peace and moderation, the emperor only exasperated them by his threatening and haughty language. "Do you know," said he to them, "that I have powder enough to blow up all your mountains?"

During the three following years there was an incessant succession of expeditions. Golovin, on the frontiers of Georgia, Grabe on the north, and Racivski on the Circassian seaboard, left nothing untried to accomplish their master's orders. The sacrifices incurred by Russia were enormous; the greater part of her fleet was destroyed by a storm, but all efforts failed against the intrepidity and tactics of the mountaineers. Some new forts erected under cover of the ships, were all that resulted from these disastrous campaigns. "I was in the Caucasus in 1839," says Hommaire de Hell, "when Grabe returned from his famous expedition against Shamyl. When the army marched it had numbered 6000 men, 1,000 of whom, and 120 officers, were cut off in three months. But as the general had advanced further into the country than any of his predecessors, Russia sang pæans, and Grabe became the hero of the day, although the imperial troops had been forced to retreat and entirely evacuate the country they had invaded. All the other expeditions were similar to this one, and achieved in reality nothing but the burning and destruction of a few villages. It is true the mountaineers are far from being victorious in all their encounters with the Russians, whose artillery they cannot easily withstand; but if they are obliged to give way to numbers, or to engineering, nevertheless they remain in the end masters of the ground, and annul all the momentary advantages gained by their enemies."

The year 1840 was still more fatal to the arms of Nicholas. Almost all the new forts on the seaboard were taken by the Circassians, who bravely attacked and carried the best fortified posts without artillery. The military road from the Kuban to Guelendchik was intercepted, Fort St. Nicholas, which commanded it, was stormed and the garrison massacred. Never yet had Russia endured such heavy blows. The disasters were such that the official journals themselves, after many months' silence, were at last obliged to speak of them; but the most serious losses, the destruction of the new road from the Kuban, the taking of Fort St. Nicholas, and that of several other forts, were entirely forgotten in the official statement.

On the eastern side of the mountain the war was fully as disastrous for the invaders. The imperial army lost four hundred petty officers and soldiers, and twenty-nine officers in the battle of Valrik against the Tchetchens. The military colonies of the Terek were attacked and plundered, and when General Golovin retired to his winter quarters at the end of the campaign, he had lost more than three-fourths of his men.

[1839 A.D.]

The great Kabarda did not remain an indifferent spectator of the offensive league formed by the tribes of the Caucasus; and when Russia, suspecting with reason the unfriendly disposition of some tribes, made an armed exploration on the banks of the Laba in order to construct redoubts, and thus cut off the subjugated tribes from the others, the general found the country, wherever he advanced, but a desert. All the inhabitants had already retired to the other side of the Laba to join their warlike neighbours.[d]

### THE EMPEROR'S CONSERVATIVE PATRIOTISM

However, in spite of all these disastrous campaigns, Nicholas had not lost sight of his most important task — that of consolidating internal order by reforms. His attention had been directed above all to the administration, from the heart of which he had sought especially to exterminate corruption with a severity and courage proportioned to the immensity of the evil. Then he had announced his firm desire to perfect the laws, and had charged Count Speranski to work at them under his personal direction. The digest (svod) promulgated in 1833 was the first fruit of these efforts and was followed by various special codes. Finally, turning his attention to public instruction, he had assigned to it as a basis the national traditions and religion and charged Uvarov, president of the Imperial Academy of Sciences, a man of learning and talent, to animate it with this spirit, so hostile to the ideas of the west, but — let us say it at once — better suited to the real needs of the country.

Nicholas, allowing himself to be ruled by this spirit, plunged further and further into a system which, though contrary to that of Peter the Great, we do not pretend absolutely to condemn on that account, and which the marquis de Custine[e] has highly extolled in his celebrated book, La Russie en 1839. "The emperor Nicholas," he said, "thought that the day of mere seeming was past for Russia, and that the whole structure of civilisation was to remake in that country. He has relaid the foundations of society. Peter, called the Great, would have overturned it a second time in order to rebuild it: Nicholas is more skilful. I am struck with admiration for this man who is secretly struggling, with all the strength of his will, against the work of Peter the Great's genius. He is restoring individuality to a nation which has strayed for more than a century in the paths of imitation."

Without ceasing to borrow diligently from Europe her inventions and arts, her progress in industry, in administration, in the conduct of land and sea armies — in a word, all the material improvements which she devises and realises, he endeavoured to close Russia to her ideas on philosophy, politics, and religion. He condemned exotic tendencies as pernicious to his states, and, without depriving himself of the services of the Germans, the principal depositaries of superior enlightenment in that country, as yet only imperfectly moulded to civilisation, he relied by preference on the party of the old Russians, which included the clergy, whom he treated with respect in spite of the inferiority of their position. Nationality, autocracy, orthodoxy — these three words, taken as the national watchword, sum up the ideas to which he subordinated his internal policy. The expression, Holy Russia, which has been the object of such profound astonishment to the Latin world, reflects also this spirit.

He surrounded with great solemnity those acts which he performed in his quality of head of the church in his own country, and posed as the protector of all his co-religionists in Moldavia, Wallachia, Servia, Montenegro, and other countries. Like his ancestors of preceding dynasties, he adorned himself on solemn occasions with a gold cross which he wore diagonally on his breast. This bias was summed up in the new word *cæsaropapism*. He regarded with special enthusiasm that one act on account of which, the accusation of religious intolerance was fixed upon him — an accusation justified by many of his deeds. In consequence of the decisions of the council of Florence, and up till 1839, there were in Russia 1,500,000 United Greeks, subjected to the papal obedience. At their head was the archbishop, sometimes the metropolitan, of White Russia, and the bishop, or archbishop, of Lithuania. In 1839 these two prelates, having met in conjunction with a third, at Polotsk, the seat of the first of these eparchies, had signed a document in which they expressed the wish to unite, they and their church, with the national and primitive church, and prayed the emperor to sanction this union. Nicholas referred the matter to the holy synod, and, the latter having with great eagerness signified its approval of the act, he sanctioned it in his turn, adding these words beneath his signature: "I thank God and I authorize it." It is well known to what complaints on the part of the pope this suppression of the uniate Greek church soon afterward gave rise.[c]

### UNVEILING OF THE MONUMENT AT BORODINO

The emperor Nicholas was fond of great gatherings of the troops, and an occasion for such was afforded in 1839 by the unveiling of the monument erected on the battlefield of Borodino. The thought of this muster of the troops had already occupied the emperor's mind since 1838, but at that time he had in view not merely the participation of the troops in manœuvres and exercises, but the immortalisation of the tradition of the valorous exploits of the Russian army in the defence of the fatherland against the invasion of Napoleon. On the day of the unveiling of the Borodino monument, August 26th, 120,000 men were gathered around it. The emperor invited to take part in the solemnities all the surviving comrades of Kutuzov and many foreign guests.

On the anniversary of the battle of Borodino a great review of all the troops assembled on this historic spot took place. In the morning, before the review began, the following order of his imperial majesty, written by the emperor's hand, was read to the troops:

"Children. Before you stands the monument which bears witness to the glorious deeds of your comrades. Here, on this same spot, 27 years ago, the arrogant enemy dreamed of conquering the Russian army which fought in defence of the faith, the czar and the fatherland. God punished the foolish: the bones of the insolent invaders were scattered from Moscow to the Niemen — and .we entered Paris. The time has now come to render glory to a great exploit. And thus, may the eternal memory of the emperor Alexander I be immortal to us: for by his firm will Russia was saved; may the glory of your comrades who fell as heroes be also everlasting, and may their exploits serve as an example to us and our further posterity. You will ever be the hope and support of your sovereign and our common mother Russia."

This order aroused the greatest enthusiasm amongst the troops, but it was highly displeasing to the foreigners; it appeared to them strange and almost offensive, they considered that "in reality it was nothing but high sounding phrases."

Three days later the emperor Nicholas had the battle of Borodino reproduced. After the unveiling of the Borodino monument the laying of the first stone of the cathedral of Christ the Saviour took place in Moscow. This solemnity brought to a close the commemoration of the year 1812 which had delivered Russia from a foreign invasion and was the dawn of the liberation of Europe.

The year 1839 was remarkable for yet another important event: the reunion of the Uniates.[1]

## DEATH OR RETIREMENT OF THE OLD MINISTERS

Little by little the workers in the political arena of Alexander's reign had disappeared. Count V. P. Kotchulzi, who had been president of the senate since 1827 and afterwards chancellor of the interior, died in 1834 and had been replaced by N. N. Novseltsev as president of the senate. After his death the emperor Nicholas appointed to that office Count I. V. Vasiltchikov, who remained at his post until his death, which took place in 1847.

The emperor was above all grieved at the death of Speranski in the year 1837. He recognised this loss as irreparable, and in speaking of him said: "Not everyone understood Speranski or knew how to value him sufficiently; at first I myself was in this respect perhaps more in fault than anyone. I was told much of his liberal ideas; calumny even touched him in reference to the history of December 26th. But afterwards all these accusations were scattered like dust, and I found in him the most faithful, devoted and zealous servant, with vast knowledge and vast experience. Everyone now knows how great are my obligations and those of Russia to him — and the calumniators are silenced. The only reproach I could make him was his feeling against my late brother; but that too is over " . . . . . The emperor stopped without finishing his thought, which probably contained a secret, involuntary justification of Speranski.

In 1844 died another statesman who was still nearer and dearer to the emperor Nicholas; this was Count Benkendorv of whom the emperor said: "He never set me at variance with anyone, but reconciled me with many." His successor in the direction of the third section was Count A. F. Orlov; he remained at this post during all the succeeding years of the emperor Nicholas' reign.

In that same year Count E. F. Kankrin who had been minister of finance even under Alexander I was obliged on account of ill health to leave the ministry of which he had been head during twenty-two years. As his biographer justly observes Kankrin left Russia as an heritage: "Well organised finances, a firm metal currency, and a rate of exchange corresponding with the requirements of the country. Russia was in financial respects a mighty power whose credit it was impossible to injure. And all this was attained without any considerable loans, and without great increase in taxes, by the determination, the thrift and the genius of one man, who placed the welfare of the nation above all considerations and understood how to serve it."

But at the same time it must not be forgotten that all these brilliant results were attainable only because behind Count Kankrin stood the emperor Nicholas. The enemies of the minister and of his monetary reforms were many; but the snares they laid were destroyed before the all powerful will of a person who never wavered. This time that inflexible will was directed in the

[1 The Uniate is a part of the Greek church which has submitted to the supremacy of the pope.]

right path, and the results showed unprecedented financial progress, in spite of the three wars which it had been impossible for Russia to avoid, despite the ideally peace-loving disposition of her ruler; and to these calamities must be added also the cholera and bad harvests. Kankrin's resignation was accompanied by important consequences; he was replaced by the incapable Vrontchenko, while Nicholas took the finances of the empire into his own hands, as he had previously acted regarding the other branches of the administration of the state.

Among the old-time servitors of Alexander I, Prince P. M. Volkonski remained longest in office. He lived until he attained the rank of field-marshal and died in 1852, having filled the office of minister of the court during twenty-five years.

One of the younger workers of the Alexandrine period, P. D. Kisselev, former chief of the staff of the second army, attained to unusual eminence in the reign of the emperor Nicholas. In 1825 his star nearly set forever, but soon it shone again with renewed brilliancy and on his return from the Danubian provinces, which he had administered since 1829, Kisselev was created minister and count. "You will be my chief of the staff for the peasant department," said the emperor to him, and with this object, on the 13th of January, 1838 there was established the ministry of state domains, formed from the department which had until that time been attached to the ministry of finance.

### GREAT FIRE IN THE WINTER PALACE

A disastrous fire at the Winter Palace began on the evening of the 29th of December, 1837, and no human means were able to stay the flames; only the Hermitage with its collection of ancient and priceless treasures was saved. The ruins of the palace continued to burn during three days and nights. The emperor and the imperial family took up their abode in the Anitchkov palace.

The rebuilding of the Winter Palace upon its previous plan was begun immediately; the palace was consecrated on the 6th of April, 1839 and the emperor and his family were installed there as previously. As a token of gratitude to all those who had taken part in the rebuilding of the palace a medal was struck with the inscription: "I thank you." — "Work overcomes everything."

On the last day of the Easter holidays the emperor Nicholas resolved to allow visitors access to all the state rooms, galleries, etc.; and in that one day as many as 200,000 persons visited the palace between the hours of six in the evening and two in the morning.

Twice the emperor and his family passed in all directions through the palace that was thronged with the public. An eye-witness writes that "the public by prolonging their visitation for seven hours so filled the palace with damp, steamy, suffocating air that the walls, the columns, and carvings on the lower windows sweated, and streams of damp poured down on to the parquet flooring and spoiled everything, while the marble changed to a dull yellowish hue." 35,000 paper rubles were required to repair the damage. But the matter did not terminate with this; during one night that summer, fortunately while the imperial family were staying at Peterhov, the ceiling in the saloon of St. George fell down with the seventeen massive lustres depending from it.

### THE 25TH ANNIVERSARY OF THE CORONATION OF NICHOLAS I (1851 A.D.)

In August 1851, upon the occasion of the twenty-fifth anniversary of his coronation the emperor Nicholas left St. Petersburg for Moscow, accompanied by his family. For the first time the journey was accomplished by the newly completed Moscow railway, constructed in accordance with the will of the emperor, and in opposition to the desires of many of his enlightened contemporaries. The opening of the railway to the public followed only on the 13th of November. In Moscow the emperor was met by Field-marshal Paskevitch, prince of Warsaw. On the eve of the festivities in honour of the anniversary of the coronation Nicholas visited the field-marshal, and addressed the following memorable words to him:

"To-morrow will complete twenty-five years of my reign — a reign which you, Ivan Feodorovitch, have made illustrious by your valiant service to Russia. It was under sorrowful prognostications that I ascended the throne of Russia and my reign had to begin with punishments and banishments. I did not find around the throne persons who could guide the czar — I was obliged to create men; I had none devoted to me. Affairs in the east required the appointment there of a man of your intellect, of your military capacity, of your will. My choice rested on you. Providence itself directed me to you. You had enemies: in spite of all that was said against you, I held fast to you, Ivan Feodorovitch. You proved, commander, that I was right. Hardly had affairs in the east quieted down when my empire was overtaken by a public calamity — the cholera. The people ascribes every misfortune to the person who governs. God knows how much suffering this national affliction cost me. The war with Poland was another grievous trial. Russian blood was shed because of our errors or because of chastisement sent from above. Our affairs were in a bad way. And again I had resource to you, Ivan Feodorovitch, as the only means of salvation for Russia; and again you did not betray my trust, again you exalted my empire. By your twenty years' administration of the Polish land you have laid the foundation for the happiness of two kindred yet hostile elements. I hope that the Russian and the Pole will constitute one Russian Empire — the Slavonic Empire; and that your name will be preserved in history beside the name of Nicholas. It is not so long ago — when western Europe was agitated by aspirations after wild, unbridled freedom; when the people overthrew lawful authority and thrones; when I decided to give a helping hand to my brother and ally, the monarch of Austria — that you, commander, led my soldiers to a new warfare: you tamed the hydra of rebellion. In six weeks you had finished the war in Hungary, you supported and strengthened the tottering throne of Austria, Ivan Feodorovitch. You are the glory of my twenty-five years' reign. You are the history of the reign of Nicholas I."

### THE EMPEROR NICHOLAS' VIEWS ON LOUIS NAPOLEON

When Prince Louis Napoleon had accomplished his *coup d'état* of the 2nd of December, 1851, and the restoration of the second empire was to be expected, the emperor Nicholas, judging by a letter which he had received from Frederick William IV, said: "Before the end of next year Louis Napoleon will become our colleague. Let him become what he likes, even the great mufti, if it pleases him, but to the title of Emperor or King I do not think he will be so imprudent as to aspire." According to the emperor's opinion, as soon as Louis Napoleon desired to make himself emperor he would become a usurper, because he did not possess the divine right — he would be emperor in fact but never by right; in a word, "a second Louis Philippe, less the odious character of that scoundrel."

When the French diplomatic representatives in St. Petersburg and Warsaw evidenced an intention to celebrate the 15th of August, the emperor Nicholas drew up the following resolution: "A public church service for Napoleon cannot be allowed, because he ceased to be emperor, being banished and confined to the island of St. Helena. There is no propriety in celebrating the birthday of the late Napoleon in our country, whence he was despatched with befitting honour." The Napoleonic empire had already transcended the limits which the emperor Nicholas would at one time have allowed; it was in direct contradiction to the stipulations of the congress of Vienna, which formed the basis of the national law of Europe. The emperor's allies, however, looked on the matter somewhat differently. Austria and Prussia recognised Napoleon III; it therefore only remained to the emperor Nicholas, against his will, to follow their example; but still he departed from the usually accepted diplomatic forms, and in his letter to Napoleon III he did not call him brother, but "*le bon ami*" (good friend). Soon on the political horizon appeared the Eastern question, artfully put forward with a secret motive by Napoleon III; his cunning calculations were justified without delay; the Russian troops crossed the Pruth in 1853, and occupied the principality, as a guarantee, until the demands presented to the Ottoman Porte by the emperor Nicholas were complied with. Austrian ingratitude opened a safe path for the snares of Anglo-French diplomacy. The Eastern War began, at first upon Turkish territory and afterwards concentrated itself in the Crimean peninsula around Sebastopol; France, England, and afterwards, in 1855, little Sardinia, in alliance with Turkey, took up arms against Russia; on the side of the allies lay the sympathy of all neutral Europe, which already dreamed of wresting Russia's conquests from her.[b]

### EVENTS LEADING UP TO THE CRIMEAN WAR

The revolution of July, 1830, by threatening Europe with the ideas then triumphing in France, had tightened the bonds, previously a little relaxed, between the czar and the two great German powers, Austria and Prussia. Independently of diplomatic conferences, the three monarchs had frequent interviews for the purpose of adopting measures to oppose the invasion of the revolutionary principle. Even whilst affecting to abandon the west to the dissolution towards which he felt it was marching, and to regard it as afflicted with approaching senility, Nicholas by no means lost sight of its development. But the East, then in combustion, remained the true mark of Russian policy. A movement was on foot for the overthrow of the declining Ottoman power, and its substitution by an Arab power, inaugurated by Muhammed Ali, the pasha of Egypt. France regarded this movement with no unfriendly eye, but Russia entered a protest. By giving the most colossal proportions to this Eastern Question, which extended as far as the countries of central Asia, the situation created grave embarrassments for the British government. For, to begin with, when, in 1833, Ibrahim Pasha, at the head of the Egyptian army, was ready to cross the Taurus and march on Constantinople, within two months the northern power (summoned to aid by that very sultan whom Russia had hitherto so greatly humiliated) landed on the Asiatic coast of the Bosporus a body of fifteen thousand men in readiness to protect that

[1853 A.D.]

capital; then the secret treaty of Unkiar-Skelessi (July 8th, 1833) granted her, as the price of an offensive and defensive alliance with the Porte, the withdrawal in her exclusive favour of the prohibition forbidding armed vessels of foreign nations to enter the waters of Constantinople; finally, by the conclusion of the Treaty of London July 15th, 1840, which left France, still obstinately attached to the cause of Muhammed Ali, outside the European concert, she had the joy of causing the rupture of the *entente cordiale* between that country and Great Britain — but only momentarily, for a new treaty, concluded the 13th of July, 1841, likewise in London, readmitted the French government to the concert.

The events of the year 1848, by bringing back the Russians into Moldavia and Wallachia, afforded Europe new apprehensions relative to the preservation, growing daily more difficult, of the Ottoman Empire and the political balance, the latter of which was seriously threatened if not destroyed by the colossus of the north, with its population now increased to as much as sixty-five million souls. But Germany was absorbed by the serious situation of her own affairs, to which the czar was far from remaining a stranger; and the latter linked himself by new ties to Austria, in whose favour he had already renounced his share in the protectorate over the republic of Cracow, when at the request of the Vienna cabinet he marched against insurgent Hungary (June, 1849) an army which beat the insurrectionary forces, compelled them to submission, and thus closed the abyss in which one of the oldest monarchies of Christendom was about to be engulfed. Then, in 1850, chosen as arbiter between Austria and Prussia, who were on the point of a rupture, the czar turned the scale in favour of Austria, and kept Prussia in check by threats.

"Austria will soon astonish the world by her immense ingratitude": this famous prophetic saying of Prince Felix of Schwarzenberg, prime minister of the young emperor Francis Joseph, was not slow of accomplishment. The ingratitude was a necessity which the history of Austria explains; for in her case, as for the rest of Europe, the continued and immoderate aggrandisement of Russia was the greatest of dangers. This leads us, in finishing this general glance over the history of the period, to say a word on the complications which, at the moment of the empire's attaining its apogee, commenced for it a new phase.

We have elsewhere explained the final cause of the decay of Turkey. That decay was consummated in favour of the northern neighbour who followed with attentive gaze the progress of what she called the death struggle. Certain words pronounced by the autocrat on this subject, and consigned to diplomatic despatches, had, not long ago, a great circulation. But the influence of Russia was counterbalanced by that of France and that of Great Britain. The cabinets of Paris and Vienna obtained important concessions, we might say diplomatic triumphs, from Constantinople — the one in relation to the Holy Places, the other on the subject of Montenegro. Russian jealousy immediately awoke. According to the czar, Turkey had a choice between two things only: she must regard Prussia as either her greatest friend or her greatest enemy. To remind her of this, and to neutralise the embassy of the prince of Linanges on behalf of Austria, Nicholas sent Prince Menshikov, one of his ministers and confidants, to Constantinople. Arriving February 28th, 1853, Menshikov exhibited a haughty and irritable demeanour; and, after astonishing the Divan by his noisy opposition, put forward pretensions relative to the Holy Places which were only designed to lull the vigilance of England, but were soon followed by others more serious and exorbitant; for they amounted to nothing less than the restoration to the czar of the pro-

tectorate over all the sultan's subjects professing the Græco-Russian worship
— that is to say the great majority of the inhabitants of Turkey in Europe.

### OUTBREAK OF THE CRIMEAN WAR (1853 A.D.)

In vain the Divan protested; in vain the friendly powers interceded.
Unable to obtain the satisfaction he was demanding with the extreme of violence, the Russian ambassador extraordinary quitted the Bosporous with
menace on his lips. And, in effect, on the 2nd of July, the czar's troops crossed
the Pruth to occupy, contrary to all treaty stipulations, the two Danubian principalities. Nicholas was not prepared for war and did not expect to be obliged
to have recourse to that last appeal; he hoped to triumph over the Divan by
audacity. Moreover, he did not think the western powers were in a position to
come to an understanding and to act in common. He was mistaken: Turkey's
death struggle did not prevent her from making a supreme effort to sell her
life dearly, if it were impossible for her to save it; and on the 26th of September the sultan declared war on the aggressor. Hostilities began in the course
of the month of October, first on the Danube and afterwards in Asia, where a
surprise made the Turks masters of the little maritime fort of St. Nicholas or
Chefketil. The Porte was not long abandoned to its own resources, for the
time of political torpor in regard to the territorial aggrandisement of the
Muscovite colossus had gone by; the eyes of all were at last opened and a
European crisis was inevitable. At that moment, the fleets of France and
England were already at the entrance of the Dardanelles; and even before
the end of October these fine naval armies passed the straits under the
authority of a firman, and approached Constantinople. In consequence of
the position taken up by these two states, the autocrat broke off relations
with them in the beginning of February, 1854. On the 21st of the same
month he informed his subjects of the fact in a manifesto, recalling to some
extent, by its tone, by its biblical references, and its exalted language, the
Treaty of the Holy Alliance. It may be worth while to reproduce here the
following passage:

"Against Russia fighting for orthodoxy England and France enter the
lists as champions of the enemies of Christianity. But Russia will not fail in
her sacred vocation; if the frontier is invaded by the enemy we are ready to
resist him with the energy of which our ancestors have bequeathed us the
example. Are we not to-day still the same people whose valour was attested
by the memorable displays of the year 1812? May the Most High aid us to
prove it by our deeds. In this hope, and fighting for our oppressed brothers
who confess the faith of Christ, Russia will have but one heart and voice to
cry: 'God, our Saviour! whom have we to fear? Let Christ arise and let his
enemies be scattered!'"

### FRANCE, ENGLAND, AND TURKEY IN ALLIANCE

Thus, by an almost miraculous concourse of circumstances, an alliance
was formed between France and England, those two ancient and ardent
rivals. Preceded by a formal alliance with the Porte (March 12th), it was
signed in London, April 10th, 1854. This was not all: this memorable document was immediately submitted to the governments of Austria and Prussia
and sanctioned by a protocol signed at Vienna by the four powers, by which
the justice of the cause sustained by those of the west was solemnly proclaimed.

Austria and Prussia laid down the conditions of their eventual participation in the war in another treaty, that of Berlin, of the 20th of April, 1854, to which the Germanic Confederation on its side gave its adhesion. Finally at Baïadji-Keui, on the 14th of June, 1854, the great Danubian power also concluded a treaty with the Ottoman Porte, in virtue of which she was authorised to enter into military occupation of the principalities, whether she should have previously expelled the Russian army or whether the latter should of its own will have decided to evacuate them. Russia was in the most complete isolation; the Scandinavian states, who had hitherto been her allies, declared themselves neutral; an insurrection in her favour, which was preparing in Servia, was prevented; that of the Greeks, openly favoured by King Otto, was stifled. The Turks, thus effectively protected, were able to turn all their forces on the frontiers, and to prove by heroic acts that they had not lost all the bravery of their ancestors. In return for Europe's efforts in favour of the integrity of his empire, and in order to ward off the reproach they might incur by supporting the cause of the crescent against a Christian state, the sultan as early as the 6th of June, 1854, publshed an edict or *irade*, by which he improved in a notable manner the condition of the rayas, and prepared for their civil freedom, as well as for a complete remodelling of the laws which, governing up to that day the internal government of the Ottoman Empire, seemed to render its preservation almost impossible.

Thus that movement of expansion to which Russia had been impelled during four centuries, and which by conquest after conquest, due either to diplomacy or the sword, had made Russian power the bugbear of Europe, finds itself suddenly arrested. "Republican or Cossack," was the famous prognostic of Napoleon.[c]

The immense superiority of the marines belonging to the allies made it possible to attack Russia on every sea. They bombarded the military port of Odessa on the Black Sea (April 22nd, 1854), but respected the city and the commercial port; the Russian establishments in the Caucasus had been burned by the Russians themselves. They blockaded Kronstadt on the Baltic, landed on the islands of Åland, and took the fortress of Bomarsund (August 16th, 1854).[f]

### THE TAKING OF BOMARSUND

This fight had lasted from four in the morning until four in the evening, when the allies saw a white flag over the tower battlements. The commander asked an armistice of two hours, which was granted. He recommenced firing before the interval was over. The French batteries overthrew the armaments, whilst the Vincennes *chasseurs* acting as free-shooters attacked the cannoneers. Resistance ceased towards evening and the tower yielded at three o'clock in the morning. One officer and thirty men were made prisoners. On Monday no notice was taken of provocation from the fortress, but preparations were made for the morrow.

On the morning of August 15th the English attacked the north tower. In six hours three of their large cannon had been able to pierce the granite and make a breach of twenty feet. The north tower was not long in surrendering; four English and two French vessels directed their fire on the large fortress. A white flag was hoisted on the rampart nearest the sea. Two officers of the fleet were sent to the governor, who said, "I yield to the marine." This officer had only a few dead and seventy wounded, but smoke poured in through the badly constructed windows, bombs burst in the middle of the fortress, without mentioning the carbine fire of the free-shooters. A longer resistance was useless.*g*

In 1855 the Russians bombarded Sveaborg. The allies attacked the fortified monastery of Solovetski, in the White Sea, and in the sea of Okhotsk they blockaded the Siberian ports, destroyed the arsenals of Petropavlovsk, and disturbed the tranquillity of the Russians on the river Amur.

Menaced by the Austrian concentration in Transylvania, and by the landing of English and French troops at Gallipoli and Varna, the Russians made a last and vain attempt to gain possession of Silistria, which they had held in a state of siege from April to July at the cost of a great number of men. In the Dobrudja an expedition directed by the French was without result from a military point of view, the soldiers being thinned out by cholera and paludal fevers. The Russians decided to evacuate the principalities, which were at once occupied by the Austrians in accord with Europe and the sultan. The war on the Danube was at an end.

### THE SEAT OF WAR TRANSFERRED TO THE CRIMEA (1854 A.D.)

The war in the Crimea was just about to commence.*j* Siege-trains were ordered from England and France, transports were prepared, and other preparations were gradually made. But the cholera attacked both the armies and the fleets, which for two months lay prostrate under this dreadful scourge.

In the Black Sea, meantime, the preparations for the Crimean expedition were pressed forward with greater energy in proportion as the cholera abated. But many successive delays occurred. Originally the invading force was to have sailed on the 15th of August; then the 20th was the day; then the 22nd; then the 26th; then the 1st of September (by which time the French siege-train would have arrived at Varna); then the 2nd of September. At length all was ready; and 58,000, out of 75,000 men, cavalry, infantry, and artillery, were embarked at Baltjik on the 7th. The French numbered 25,000, the English the same; and there was a picked corps of about 8,000 Turks. In a flotilla of between two and three hundred vessels, this first and much larger part of the united army were transported up the coast to Fidonisi, or the Island of Serpents; from which point to Cape Tarkhan, in the Crimea, they would make both the shortest and the most sheltered passage. Being reviewed and found all ready at Fidonisi, the armada took its second departure on the 11th, and reached without accident the destined shore on the 14th. On that day the troops were landed prosperously at "Old Fort," some twenty miles beyond Eupatoria, or Koslov, within four or five easy days' march from Sebastopol. Upon this great fortress the columns were at once directed; while the transports returned in haste to fetch the reserves, amounting to about 15,000 men.

Contrary to the expectation of the allies, Prince Menshikov, who commanded in the Crimea, had resolved not to oppose their landing, but to await them on the left, or southern, bank of the river Alma. The nature of his position may be gathered from Lord Raglan's despatch. He says:

"In order that the gallantry exhibited by her majesty's troops, and the difficulties they had to meet, may be fairly estimated, I deem it right, even at the risk of being considered tedious, to endeavour to make you acquainted with the position the Russians had taken up.

"It crossed the great road about two miles and a half from the sea, and is very strong by nature. The bold and almost precipitous range of heights, of from 350 to 400 feet, that from the sea closely border the left bank of the river, here ceases and formed their left, and turning thence round a great amphitheatre or wide valley, terminates at a salient pinnacle where their right rested, and whence the descent to the plain was more gradual. The front was about two miles in extent. Across the mouth of this great opening is a lower ridge at different heights, varying from 60 to 150 feet, parallel to the river, and at distances from it of from 600 to 800 yards. The river itself is generally fordable for troops, but its banks are extremely rugged, and in most parts steep; the willows along it had been cut down, in order to prevent them from affording cover to the attacking party, and in fact everything had been done to deprive an assailant of any species of shelter. In front of the position on the right bank, at about 200 yards from the Alma, is the village of Burliuk, and near it a timber bridge, which had been partly destroyed by the enemy. The high pinnacle and ridge before alluded to was the key of the position, and consequently, there the greatest preparations had been made for defence. Half-way down the height and across its front was a trench of the extent of some hundred yards, to afford cover against an advance up the even steep slope of the hill. On the right, and a little retired, was a powerful covered battery, armed with heavy guns, which flanked the whole of the right of the position. Artillery, at the same time, was posted at the points that best commanded the passage of the river and its approaches generally. On the slopes of these hills (forming a sort of table land) were placed dense masses of the enemy's infantry, whilst on the height above was his great reserve, the whole amounting, it is supposed, to between 45,000 and 50,000 men."

It was against this fortress — for it was little less — the British, French, and Turkish forces were led, having broken up their camp at Kimishi on the 19th of September. The way led along continual steppes, affording no shelter from the burning heat of the sun, nor water to assuage the intolerable thirst suffered by all. The only relief was afforded by the muddy stream of Bulganak, which the men drank with avidity. That day an insignificant skirmish took place between a body of Cossacks and the light division. On passing over the brow of a hill, the former were discovered drawn up in order. A slight fire was opened, which wounded three or four of the allies, but a gun drove up and threw a shell with such wonderful precision in the midst of the enemy that above a dozen were knocked over by this one projectile, and the Cossacks speedily disappeared.[d]

### THE BATTLE OF THE ALMA (1854 A.D.)

The allies' plan of aggression was quite as simple as the Russian plan of defence. It consisted in turning the enemy's two wings and then overwhelming them by a front attack. On the extreme right General Bosquet, in advance of the rest of the army, was to approach rapidly the Alma, cross it at a point not far from its mouth, ascend the slopes at all costs, then fall suddenly on the Russians' left, surround them, and throw them back on the centre. This movement carried out, Canrobert's and Prince Napoleon's divisions, supported by a portion of the English army, would cross the river, climb the heights between Almatamak and Burliuk, and make the grand attack. At the same moment the English army at the left of the French lines would endeavour to turn the enemy's right, and thus secure the day. Forey's division would remain in reserve ready to help either the weaker columns or those in immediate danger, as the case might be. On the evening of the 19th of September Field-Marshal Saint-Arnaud had sent to each division a tracing of the proposed order of battle. The plan was so simple that the soldiers had already anticipated and guessed it. At nightfall they gathered round the camp fires and discussed the chances of the plan with gleeful excitement. They pointed out to each other the Russian camp fires, scintillating dots of light shining out on the hill sides, and tried to reckon up the enemy's number by the number of lights. A good deal of imagination mingled with their calculations, but the results did not frighten them, they were convinced that the following day they would rest victorious on the plateau.

At the first sounds of the reveille the troops of Bosquet's division were a-foot and ready to start, very proud of the place assigned them by the confidence of the commander-in-chief. The fog having somewhat lifted, at seven o'clock they left the banks of the Bulganak and marched off in quick time towards the Alma. They were not more than two kilometres distant from it when one of the field-marshal's aides-de-camp arrived hot-foot with orders to halt, as the English were not ready. Obedience was yielded with some degree of unwillingness, which grew to impatience as the halt was prolonged. It was already half-past eleven when the march was resumed. The division was formed into two columns; Autemarre's brigade marched towards Almatamak, where the French scouts had just discovered a ford; the other brigade, under Bouat, turned towards the sea, so as to cross the river near its mouth by a sand bank shown them by a steam pinnace. From their dominating positions the Russians could see this manœuvre, but they paid no attention to it, judging that nature had provided sufficient defence for them on that side. They looked upon the whole of this movement as merely a diversion, and concentrated all their watchfulness on the main body of the army, which had hitherto remained motionless three kilometres to the rear of the Alma.

In the mean time Autemarre's brigade, close on Almatamak and hitherto hidden from the enemy by the escarpments of the neighbouring cliff, began to cross the Alma. The 3rd zouaves were the first over the ford, and began with amazing "go" to climb the plateau. This ascent, which the Russians, heavily equipped and accustomed to the level, believed impossible, was relatively easy for men accustomed time out of mind to the foot-tracks of African mountains. It was wonderful to see these strong, agile soldiers springing up the slopes, giving a helping hand to one another, clinging to tufts of grass and scrub, and profiting by the smallest foothold. The Algerian sharp-shooters followed, then the 50th foot. The most difficult matter was to get the artillery over, and the boldest faltered before such a task. By a sheer miracle of stout-heartedness and energy they managed to hoist several pieces the whole length of the escarpments. Suddenly the zouaves appeared at the top of the hill, before the very eyes of the astonished Russians, and by a brisk fire drove off the enemy's vedettes. In another moment Algerian sharp-shooters and men of the 50th foot climbed the last slopes in their turn; then the field guns, dragged up to the heights, were placed in line. At this identical moment Bouat's brigade, which had been delayed in crossing the bar, appeared on the extreme right and began to scale the cliffs nearest the sea. Only the second battalion of the Minsk infantry occupied this position, which had hitherto been held impregnable. Debouching from the little village of Aklese they ran forward; but confused by the fantastic aspect of this unexpected enemy, flurried by the gaps made in their ranks by the French long-range guns, they wasted no time over doubling back. Soon, running away altogether, they threw themselves on the Russian reserves, followed by the shots of French artillery and by the missiles thrown on to the plateau by the fleet at anchor near the shore.

Saint-Arnaud, from his position in the rear of the Alma, had watched the zouaves climb the hill. When they had disappeared over the crest, he had listened anxiously for the sharp-shooters to open fire. Soon the roar of cannon was heard, but it was difficult to believe that the artillery was already engaged. "Are they French guns or Russian guns?" asked the staff-officers grouped round the commander-in-chief. But the field-marshal joyfully cried: "I assure you it is Bosquet's cannon; he has reached the heights." Then searching the distance with his glasses: "I can see red trousers. Ah! there I recognise my African veteran Bosquet!" Summoning his generals, Saint-Arnaud gave then the final instructions. The sound of the guns had revived his failing strength; his voice was as strong as in his palmiest days, and his face was lighted up with confidence, a last and touching reflection of his warrior spirit. By a gesture he indicated to his officers the course of the river and the hills which shut in the horizon: "Gentlemen," he said, "this battle will be known as the battle of the Alma."

It being now one o'clock in the afternoon, the front attack was immediately begun. The first division, under command of General Canrobert, held the right; to the left was drawn up the 3rd division commanded by Prince Napoleon. Following the common plan, the latter was to attach itself to the English right, but it did so only imperfectly, on account of the slowness of the allies. Set in motion simultaneously, the two French divisions marched towards the Alma. This time the Russians had anticipated the attack and were ready to repulse it. Sheltered by clumps of trees, enclosing walls, and the gardens bordering the river, innumerable sharp-shooters directed a well-sustained fire against the enemy, and, in addition, a battery established on the edge of the plateau covered the plain with missiles. Overwhelmed by this murderous fire the French troops halted. But the artillery of the 1st and 3rd divisions shelled the ravines, compelling the Russian sharp-shooters to retreat against a high bank on the left, and by thus diverting their attention enabled the rest of the French army to advance as far as the Alma. Laying down their knapsacks the soldiers themselves sounded the river with branches of trees and boldly crossed wherever it appeared practicable. Towards two in the afternoon the 3rd division effected a crossing not far from Burluk. As to Canrobert's division, it had, almost entirely, already found a footing on the left bank a little above Almatamak. His first battalions had already reached the heights and slanted off to the right so as to join hands with Bosquet's division.

It was quite time. When Prince Menshikov was informed of the appearance of Bosquet on the heights near the mouth of the Alma, he at first refused to believe the news and only the roar of the cannon had convinced him. Realising the greatness of the danger, the Russian commander-in-chief immediately hurried to reinforce his left flank, which in his excess of confidence he had left almost uncovered. As the brigades of Autemarre and Bouat took up a position, fresh Russian troops debouched on the western side of the plateau. First a battery of light artillery, which arrived before the infantry it was summoned to support, lost half its number in a few moments; then four battalions of the Moscow infantry regiment supported by another battery. Shortly after this occurred, Prince Menshikov, having himself visited the scene of action, decided to make a fresh attempt. By his orders three battalions of the Minsk regiment, four squadrons of hussars and two batteries of Cossacks were drawn from the reserve to afford active support to the troops already engaged. Happily for the French these troops arrived only in driblets, so that their impact was weakened by being broken up. Even so their little main body, launched on the plateau with no retreat possible, found itself in a position almost as critical as it was glorious. If it continued to penetrate into the Russian flank victory was assured, but if it faltered it had no other prospect than to be brought to bay on one escarpment after another and routed in the valley, beyond hope of salvation. The Russian troops were not more numerous than the French, but the twelve guns of the latter could scarcely hope to hold out against the forty pieces which the Russians had brought into this part of the field. On receiving overnight the commander-in-chief's instructions, General Bosquet had replied: "You can count on me, but remember I cannot hold out for more than two hours."

ALEXANDER SERGEVITCH MENSHIKOV
(1787-1869)

The general weariness was great and moreover the ammunition was giving out. With growing anguish Bosquet turned his gaze towards the plain, waiting for the general attack which was to lighten his task. His joy may be imagined when he heard on the left, above Almatamak, the sharp crack of the zouaves' rifles, and saw appearing over the edge of the plateau General Canrobert's first battalions.

Help was at hand, and with help the almost certainty of victory. At that very moment a happy inspiration of Saint-Arnaud's rendered assurance sure. Judging that the moment had arrived for calling on his reserves, he sent orders to General Forey to bring up one of his brigades to succour Bosquet, and with the other to support General Canrobert. From that moment the tide of battle set steadily against the Russians. Surrounded on their left wing, outflanked in their centre, threatened by the French reserves, they yielded step by step, no doubt with fearful reprisals, but finally they retired. It was in vain that the Minsk and Moscow regiments, retreating obliquely, tried to resist both Bosquet's and Canrobert's divisions; these brave endeavours only prolonged the resistance without affecting the result. After losing the greater number of their leaders they were compelled to retreat behind the heights and to retire to a tower for telegraphic communication which marked the enemy's centre. There a final bloody engagement took place. At last the flags of the 3rd zouaves and the 39th foot were hoisted on the top of the tower, signal of the victory which the Russians thenceforward never disputed.[h]

The part taken by the British troops in the final assault is thus described by the special correspondent of the *Times*:

"The British line was struggling through the river and up the heights in masses, firm, indeed, but mowed down by the murderous fire of the batteries and by grape, round shot, shell, canister, case shot, and musketry, from some of the guns of the central battery, and from an immense and compact mass of Russian infantry. Then commenced one of the most bloody and determined struggles in the annals of war. The 2nd division, led by Sir De

L. Evans in the most dashing manner, crossed the stream on the right. The 7th Fusiliers, led by Colonel Yea, were swept down by fifties. The 55th, 30th, and 95th, led by Brigadier Pennefather, who was in the thickest of the fight, cheering on his men, again and again were checked indeed, but never drew back in their onward progress, which was marked by a fierce roll of Minié musketry; and Brigadier Adams, with the 41st, 47th, and 49th, bravely charged up the hill, and aided them in the battle. Sir George Brown, conspicuous on a grey horse, rode in front of his light division, urging them with voice and gesture. Gallant fellows! they were worthy of such a gallant chief. The 7th, diminished by one-half, fell back to re-form their columns lost for the time; the 23rd, with eight officers dead and four wounded, were still rushing to the front, aided by the 19th, 33rd, 77th, and 88th. Down went Sir George in a cloud of dust in front of the battery. He was soon up and shouted, '23rd, I'm all right. Be sure I'll remember this day,' and led them on again, but in the shock produced by the fall of their chief the gallant regiment suffered terribly while paralysed for a moment. Meantime the Guards, on the right of the light division, and the brigade of Highlanders were storming the heights on the left. Their line was almost as regular as though they were in Hyde Park. Suddenly a tornado of round and grape rushed through from the terrible battery, and a roar of musketry from behind thinned their front ranks by dozens. It was evident that we were just able to contend against the Russians, favoured as they were by a great position. At this very time an immense mass of Russian infantry were seen moving down towards the battery. They halted. It was the crisis of the day. Sharp, angular, and solid, they looked as if they were cut out of the solid rock. It was beyond all doubt that if our infantry, harassed and thinned as they were, got into the battery they would have to encounter again a formidable fire, which they were but ill calculated to bear. Lord Raglan saw the difficulties of the situation. He asked if it would be possible to get a couple of guns to bear on these masses. The reply was, 'Yes,' and an artillery officer (Colonel Dixon) brought up two guns to fire on the Russian squares. The first shot missed, but the next, and the next, and the next cut through the ranks so cleanly, and so keenly, that a clear lane could be seen for a moment through the square. After a few rounds the square became broken, wavered to and fro, broke, and fled over the brow of the hill, leaving behind it six or seven distinct lines of dead, lying as close as possible to each other, marking the passage of the fatal messengers. This act relieved our infantry of a deadly incubus, and they continued their magnificent and fearful progress up the hill. The duke encouraged his men by voice and example, and proved himself worthy of his proud command and of the royal race from which he comes. 'Highlanders,' said Sir C. Campbell, ere they came to the charge, 'don't pull a trigger till you're within a yard of the Russians!' They charged, and well they obeyed their chieftain's wish; Sir Colin had his horse shot under him, but his men took the battery at a bound. The Russians rushed out, and left multitudes of dead behind them. The Guards had stormed the right of the battery ere the Highlanders got into the left, and it is said the Scots Fusilier Guards were the first to enter. The second and light division crowned the heights. The French turned the guns on the hill against the flying masses, which the cavalry in vain tried to cover. A few faint struggles from the scattered infantry, a few rounds of cannon and musketry and the enemy fled to the south-east, leaving three generals, three guns, 700 prisoners, and 4,000 wounded behind them. The battle of the Alma was won. It is won with a loss of nearly 3,000 killed and wounded on our side. The Russians' retreat was covered by their cavalry, but if we had had an adequate force we could have captured many guns and multitudes of prisoners."

It appears from papers found in Prince Menshikov's carriage, that he had counted on holding his position on the Alma for at least three weeks. He had erected scaffolds from which his ladies might view the military exploits during the period of obstruction he had provided for the invading force, but he was hurried away in the midst of a flying army, in a little more than three hours.

### THE SEIZURE OF BALAKLAVA (1854 A.D.)

Without sufficient cavalry, and having exhausted the ammunition of the artillery, the allies did not pursue the defeated foe; but rested for a couple of days, to recruit the able-bodied, succour the wounded, and bury the dead. Then they went forward towards Sebastopol. A change now took place, as remarkable an incident as any in the campaign. Learning that the enemy had established a work of some force on the Belbek, and that this river could not readily be rendered a means of communication with the fleet, and calculating that preparations would be made for the defence of Sebastopol chiefly on the north side, the commanders resolved to change the line of operations, to turn the whole position of Sebastopol, and establish themselves at Balaklava. After resting for a couple of days, they started on the march, turned to the left after the first night's bivouac, and struck across a woody country, in which the troops had to steer their way by compass; regained an open road from Bagtcheserai to Balaklava; encountered there at Khutor Mackenzia (Mackenzie's Farm) a part of the Russian army, which fled in consternation at the unexpected meeting; and were in possession of Balaklava on the 26th — within four days after leaving the heights above the Alma. Thus an important post was occupied without a blow.

Balaklava is a close port, naturally cut by the waters in the living rock; so deep that the bowsprit of a ship at anchor can almost be touched on shore, so strong that the force possessing it could retain communication with the sea in spite of any enemy. It is a proof of Menshikov's want of foresight, or of his extreme weakness after the battle of the 20th, that Balaklava was left without effectual defence. The change of operations reminds one of Nelson's manœuvre at the Nile, in attacking the enemy on the shore side, where the ships were logged with lumber and unprepared for action.

By this date, however, the allies were destined to sustain a grave loss, in the departure of Marshal Saint-Arnaud. The French commander-in-chief had succeeded in three achievements, each one of which would be sufficient to mark the great soldier. He had thrown his forces into the battle on the Alma with all the ardour of which his countrymen are capable, but with that perfect command which the great general alone retains. He had succeeded in exciting the soldierly fire of the French, and yet in preserving the friendliest feelings towards their rivals and allies, the English. He had succeeded in retaining his place on horseback, notwithstanding mortal agonies that would have subdued the courage, or at least the physical endurance, of any other man. Many can meet death, numbers can sustain torture; but the power of holding out in action against the depressing and despairing misgivings of internal maladies, is a kind of resolution which nature confers upon very few indeed, and amongst those very few Marshal Saint-Arnaud will be ranked as one of the most distinguished. He was succeeded in the command of the French army by General Canrobert, and died at sea on the 29th. By this event Lord Raglan became commander-in-chief of the allied forces in the Crimea.

## THE ADVANCE ON SEBASTOPOL

Had Marshal Saint-Arnaud lived, it is hardly to be doubted that he would have attempted to take Sebastopol by the summary process of breaching and storming instead of the slower one of a regular siege. The former plan might have been successful, for it is now known, upon the authority of the Russians themselves, that when the allies first broke ground before the fortress its preparations for resistance were very incomplete. On the other hand, events have too painfully demonstrated that the force with which the siege was undertaken was totally inadequate, both in numbers and weight of metal. It was not sufficient to invest the place on every side, or to hinder the garrison of one of the strongest fortresses in the world from receiving unlimited reinforcements and supplies of all kinds. Hence, to use General Peyronnet Thompson's homely but very apt illustration, the operations before Sebastopol have hitherto been like the work of drawing a badger out of one end of a box, with an interminable series of badgers entering at the other.

The position occupied by the English before Sebastopol was to the right of the French, at a distance of six miles from their ships. They held the summit of a ridge, whence at long range, they could fire with some effect on the Russian outworks; but as they descended the slope, their force was broken in two or three parts, while they were exposed to a fire like that which destroyed so many brave men at the Alma. The French, on the left, rested on Cape Chersonesus, and were within three miles of their ships, in a position where, though they might suffer from the fire of the garrison, they were protected from the attacks of the Russian army in the field. The attack on the place by the land batteries and by the ships began on the 17th of October. The Russians had closed the entrance to the harbour by sinking two ships of the line and two frigates (they subsequently sank all the rest of their fleet), and the fire of the allied ships at long range produced so very little effect, whilst the casualties sustained by them were so disproportionate to the damage they inflicted, that the experiment was not repeated.

Eight days afterwards the Russians in turn became the assailants. A large reinforcement having been received under Liprandi, that general was detached to the Tchernaia with some 30,000 troops to attack our rear. The peculiarity of the position of the allied army facilitated its efforts. It has already been explained that Balaklava is at some distance from the lines of the besiegers. The road connecting the two runs through a gorge in the heights which constitute the rear of the British position, and which overlook the small grassy plain that lies to the north of the inlet of Balaklava. The possession of the port and the connecting road are essential to the success of the siege. To defend them, Lord Raglan had placed a body of marines and sailors with some heavy guns on the heights above the village and landing place of Balaklava; beneath the heights he had stationed the 93rd Highlanders, under Sir Colin Campbell, who barred the road down to the village. The plain running northward towards the Tchernaia is intersected by a low, irregular ridge, about two miles and a half from the village, and running nearly at right angles to the rear of the heights on the north-western slopes of which lay the British army. This ridge in the plain was defended by four redoubts, intervening between the Tchernaia and the British cavalry encamped on the southern part of the plain; and the rising ground in their rear was held by the zouaves, who had entrenched themselves at right angles with the redoubts. The extreme right of our position was on the road to Kamara; the centre about

Kadakoi, with the Turkish redoubts in front; the left on the eastern slopes of the high lands running up to the Inkerman ravine.

## THE BATTLE OF BALAKLAVA

The object of the Russians was to turn the right and seize Balaklava, burn the shipping in the port, and, cutting off our communication with the sea, establish themselves in our rear. To accomplish this, General Liprandi gathered up his troops behind the defiles at Tchorgun on the Tchernaia. Here, having previously reconnoitred our position, he divided his forces on the morning of the 25th of October, directing one body by the great military road, the other by Kamara, and debouching upon the plain near the Turkish redoubts. The redoubts were armed with two or three heavy ship-guns, and each manned by about 250 Turks. The Russians coming on with the dawn, some 12,000 strong, with from thirty to forty field-guns, attacked the redoubts with horse artillery, and carried them in succession; the Turks firing a few shots, and then flying in disorder under a fire of artillery and the swords of the Cossacks. Sir Colin Campbell, aroused by the firing, instantly drew up the 93rd in front of the village of Kadakoi; and the affrighted Turks rallied for a moment on the flanks of that "living wall of brass," to use the language of a French writer, presented by the Highlanders. But the redoubts being taken, the enemy's artillery advanced and opened fire; and the cavalry came rapidly up. As the 93rd was within range, Sir Colin Campbell drew them a little backward behind the crest of the hill. The British cavalry lay to the left of the Highlanders, and a large body of Russian cavalry menaced both. The larger section went towards the encampment of the British cavalry, and were met at once by the heavy brigade, under General Scarlett. A brief but brilliant encounter followed: for a moment the Greys and Enniskillens in the first line seemed swallowed up, in another they reappeared victorious. The long, dense line of the Russian horse had lapped over their flanks; but the second British line, consisting of the 4th and 5th Dragoons, charging, the Russians were broken and rapidly made off. While this was proceeding, a body of some 400 cavalry rode at the Highlanders, who, not deigning to form square, mounted the crest of the hill, behind which they had taken shelter, fired in line two deep, and sent the enemy flying.

But the fighting was not yet over. Seven guns taken in the redoubts yet remained in the possession of the enemy; and Lord Raglan sent an order to Lord Lucan to prevent the enemy from carrying off the guns, if possible. The order was wrongly interpreted as a peremptory order to *charge*, and in that sense it was repeated by Lord Lucan to Lord Cardigan, who obeyed it and charged into the very centre of the enemy's position, with a desperate sacrifice of men, but not without inflicting severe blows upon the enemy. Nor was the loss of life entirely a waste. To the Russians the incident proved the unmeasured daring of the foe they had to face; to the British troops it showed the lengths to which discipline and fidelity can be carried. The light cavalry brigade mustered 607 sabres that morning; in the twenty minutes occupied by the charge and the return, they lost 335 horses, and had nearly as many officers and men killed or wounded. The heavy dragoons and the Chasseurs d'Afrique covered the retreat of the bleeding remnant of this daring band. It was now nearly noon: the fourth division, under Sir George Cathcart, and the first division, under the Duke of Cambridge, had come up; and the Russians abandoned all the redoubts, except the furthest one to the right. Nothing more was done that day. Looking to the extent of the position previously occupied, Lord Raglan determined to contract his line of defence to the immediate vicinity of Balaklava and the steeps in the right rear of the British army.

Next day the enemy sallied forth from Sebastopol, 7000 or 8000 strong, and attacked the right flank of the British army; but, steadily met by the second division under Sir De Lacy Evans, supported by the brigade of Guards, a regiment of Rifles, two guns from the light division, and two French battalions, the Russians were gallantly repelled, and then chased down to the slope, with a loss of some 600 killed and wounded, and 80 prisoners.

### THE BATTLE OF INKERMAN (NOVEMBER 5TH, 1854)

Another fierce engagement, the most important of all in which the belligerents have yet been engaged, took place on the 5th of November. For some days previously, the Russians, who already possessed a large force in the prolonged fortifications, and others to the rear of the allies in the neighbourhood of Balaklava, had been observed to receive large reinforcements, which, added to Liprandi's corps on the Russian left, of 30,000 or more, and the garrison, would probably justify Lord Raglan's estimate of 60,000 men arrayed against the allies on the memorable 5th of November. To augment the weight of the force brought down to crush the besiegers, the now useless army of the Danube had been withdrawn from Moldavia, leaving Bessarabia still defended by its special army, but not, it is supposed, entirely exhausting the reinforcements to be brought from the interior. The effort of Menshikov to throw his strength into a succession of powerful and, if possible, decisive blows, is shown by the advance of Dannenberg's army in the very lightest order, augmenting the numbers about Sebastopol without much regard either to their equipment or provision. The aim was to bear down by accumulated pressure; and it was with such a view that the batteries resumed the bombardment of the allies in their besieged camp, a strong force from the garrison moved out to act with Dannenberg's army, and Liprandi made a feint, that might have been, had it succeeded, a penetrating attack towards the rear; and as it was, it did busy a portion of the British and French forces. Thus the allies were to be occupied all round, while the weak, unintrenched, and unfortified point in their position towards the valley of the Inkerman was to be penetrated by a force of great weight and momentum.[d]

The English encampments were established between Karabelnaia and the valley of the Tchernaia, on a plateau called Inkerman, which two ravines narrowed at the south in a way which made it a kind of isthmus. Two strong Russian columns, consisting together of thirty-six thousand men, converged in this direction. The first came out from Karabelnaia; the second descended from the heights on the opposite bank of the Tchernaia and crossed that river near its mouth in the bay.

They had to join in order to turn the English camp and take it from the back. Their movements were badly planned; each acted on its own initiative instead of joining. However, the English were in extreme danger. The Karabelnaia column surprised one of their divisions and nearly overwhelmed it by force of numbers. With a small reinforcement the English disputed every inch of ground with desperation and the struggle was prolonged through rain and fog, till the Russian general Soimonov was mortally wounded; fear struck his battalions: they ceased to advance, then retreated, not receiving any orders, and did not return to the combat.

The column which came from the opposite side of the Tchernaia, and which General Pavlov commanded, had in the meantime commenced its attack on the other part of the English camp. Here were furious shocks and long alternations of success and defeat. Although the English right had been joined by their left, having got rid of the Karabelnaia column, the inequality of numbers was still great. The English had driven back the advance guard of Pavlov's column to the valley of the Tchernaia; but the greater part of this column, supported by an immense artillery (nearly one hundred guns) pushed forward its closely serried battalions with such violence that in the end they were masters of an earthwork, which protected the right side of the English camp (a battery of sand bags).

Had the Russians remained in this position, the allies would have lost the day. Till then the English had made it their pride to keep up the struggle without the help of the French. There was not a moment to lose; two of their generals were killed, several no longer able to fight; the soldiers were exhausted. Lord Raglan called the French, who were awaiting the signal.

General Bosquet, who commanded the corps nearest the English, sent out the first two battalions he had at hand. It would have been too late if the enemy had passed the fortification they had seized and had extended beyond the isthmus. The Russians had been less active than brave. The French foot soldiers renewed the marvellous charge of the English cavalry at Balaklava. In their vehemence, they drove the greater number of the Russians far behind the battery of sand bags; they were repulsed in their turn by the mass of the enemy; but the movement of the latter had nevertheless been checked. The Russian leaders were not able to manœuvre promptly enough to place themselves, as they might have done, between the English and the new reinforcements of French.

The French battalions arrived in double quick time with that agility already shown at Alma by the soldier trained in African wars. The Russians repulsed a second attack; they succumbed under a third made with more reinforcements. One of their regiments was precipitated by the French zouaves and turcos from the summit of the rocks into a deep ravine where it was shattered. The rest of the Russian troops made a slow and painful retreat under the terrible fire of the French artillery.

This sanguinary day cost the Russians twelve thousand men, killed, wounded, or missing. The English lost about twenty-six hundred men, the French seventeen to eighteen hundred. Beside their decisive intervention on the plateau of Inkerman, the French troops had repulsed a sortie of the garrison at Sebastopol.

According to military historians, the check of the Russians was due, to a great extent, to their want of mobility and their incapacity for manœuvring; the pedantic and circumstantial tactics imposed on them by Nicholas only served to hinder them in presence of the enemy.

The allies, victorious, but suffering after such a victory, suspended the assault and decided to keep on the defensive until the arrival of new forces. They completed the circumvallation which protected the plateau of Chersonesus, from Inkerman to Balaklava; the Russians had retired completely; the French protected themselves on the town side by a line of contravallation.[i]

While the allies were occupied in digging trenches, laying mines, and increasing the number of their batteries, the Russians, directed by the able Todtleben, strengthened those defences of the city that were already in existence and under the fire of the enemy erected new ones. The allies, in spite of the sufferings incident to a severe winter, established themselves more and more securely, and on a strip of sandy coast prepared to defy all the forces of the empire of the czar.

On the 26th of December, 1825, Nicholas had been consecrated by the blood of conspirators as the armed apostle of the principle of authority, the destroying angel of counter-revolution. This was a part that he played not without glory for thirty years, having put down the Polish, Hungarian, and Rumanian revolutions and prevented Prussia from yielding to the seductions of the German revolution. He had obstructed if not destroyed the French Revolution in all its legal manifestations, the monarchy of July, the republic, and the empire. He had saved the Austrian Empire and prevented the creation of a democratic German empire. Like Don Quixote he was chivalrous, generous, disinterested, but represented a superannuated principle that was out of place in the modern world. Day by day his character as chief of a chimerical alliance became more of an anachronism; particularly since 1848 aspirations of the people had been in direct contradiction to his theories of patriarchal despotism. In Europe this contradiction had diminished the glory of the czar, but in Russia his authority remained unimpaired owing to his successes in Turkey, Persia, Caucasus, Poland, and Hungary. All complaints against the police were forgotten as well as the restrictions laid on the press, and all efforts to control the government in matters of diplomacy, wars, and administration were reliquished; it was believed that the laborious monarch would foresee everything and bring all affairs of state to a fortunate conclusion. Indeed the success of this policy was sufficient to silence the opposition offered by a few timid souls, and to furnish justification for blind confidence in the existing government.

The disasters in the East were a terrible awakening; invincible as the Russian fleet had hitherto been considered, it was obliged to take refuge in its own ports or to be sunk in the harbour of Sebastopol. The army had been conquered at Alma by the allies and at Silistria by the despised Turks; a body of western troops fifty thousand strong was insolently established before Sebastopol, and of the two former allies Prussia was neutral and Austria had turned traitor. The enforced silence of the press for the last thirty years had favoured the committal of dishonest acts by employes, the organisation of the army had been destroyed by administrative corruption. Everything had been expected of the government, and now the Crimean War intervened and threatened complete bankruptcy to autocracy; absolute patriarchal monarchy was obliged to retreat before the Anglo-French invasion. The higher the hopes entertained for the conquest of Constantinople, the deliverance of Jerusalem and the extension of the Slavonic empire, the more cruel the disappointment. At this moment a prodigious activity manifested itself throughout Russia, tongues were unloosed, and a great manuscript literature was passed secretly from hand to hand, bringing audacious accusations against the government and all the hierarchy of officials:

"Awake, O Russia!" exhorted one of these anonymous pamphlets; "awake from your deep sleep of ignorance and apathy. Long enough we have been in bondage to the successors of the Tatar khans; rise to your full height before the throne of the despot and demand of him a reckoning for the national disaster. Tell him plainly that his throne is not God's altar and that God has not condemned our race to eternal slavery. Russia, O czar, had given into your hands the supreme power, and how have you exerted it? Blinded by ignorance and passion, you have sought power for its own sake and have forgotten the interests of the country. You have consumed your life in reviewing troops, in altering uniforms, and in signing your name to the legislative projects of ignorant charlatans.  You have created the detestable institution of press-censorship that you might enjoy peace and remain in ignorance of the needs and complaints of your people.  You have buried Truth and rolled a great stone to the door of her sepulchre, and in the vanity of your heart you have exclaimed, 'For her there shall be no resurrection!'  Notwithstanding, Truth rose on the third day and left the ranks of the dead.  Czar, appear before the tribunal of history and of God!  You have trodden truth under foot, and refused to others liberty while you were yourself a slave to passion. By your obstinacy and pride you have exhausted Russia and armed the rest of the world against her.  Bow your haughty head to the dust and implore forgiveness, ask advice.  Throw yourself upon the mercy of your people; with them lies your only hope of safety!" *i*

## DEATH OF THE EMPEROR NICHOLAS I

The chivalrous soul of the Emperor Nicholas could not reconcile itself to the complete wreck of all its political and spiritual ideals.  Nicholas fell a sacrifice to his persistent pursuit of traditions bequeathed to him by the Alexandrine policy of the last decade.

On the 2nd of March, 1855, Russia, and all European nations, were dismayed by the unexpected news of the sudden death of the emperor Nicholas. *b* "Serve Russia!" were his last words to his son and heir.  "I wished to overcome all national afflictions, to leave you a peaceful, well-organized and happy empire. . .  Providence has ordained otherwise!" *i*

## ESTIMATES OF NICHOLAS

Skrine,*k* reviewing the life of Nicholas in the light of the evolutionary philosophy of our own time, declares that the autocrat failed because in a progressive century he had become an anachronism.  He believes, however, that Nicholas I died as grandly as he had lived, in the firm assurance that he had done his duty.  While he ruled his subjects with a rod of iron, he was ever ready to serve them with an unselfishness which has no parallel in history.

Sweeping assertions such as these are usually to be taken with some measure of allowance.  In the present case we may quote, by way of antidote, the estimate of Nicholas that appeared in the London *Times* of March 3rd, 1855: "In the long array of history, and among those figures dimly seen along the ages of the past which bear imperishable traces of their guilt and their doom, none stands a more visible mark of retributive justice than he who has abruptly passed from the scene of human affairs. Nicholas ascended the throne in the prime of life, and he won his crown by his own daring composure in the face of great dangers.  The conduct of the Emperor Nicholas during those eventful and perilous years, from 1848 to 1851, raised him higher than he had ever stood before; he was regarded as one of the wisest, as well as one of the most powerful, sovereigns of Europe, and those even who detested his despotic government could not deny that he had shown moderation, temper, and a strong desire for peace.  No sovereign ever succeeded in inspiring his own subjects of the Muscovite race with a more fanatical attachment to his person, and it is perfectly true that wherever the lofty stature and imperial port of the czar was seen throughout his dominions, he was hailed as a demigod rather than as a man.  His pride rose with his station and his power, and at times he seemed possessed with hallucinations acting upon a mystical and excitable nature, as if he indeed transcended the appointed limits of all human greatness.

"By what marvellous fatality, by what infatuation could it then happen that a ruler of men already past the illusions of youth, versed in the affairs of Europe, and professedly solicitous to maintain the constituted order of things, suddenly descended from his exalted position, committed acts of astonishing imprudence and injustice, destroyed his own influence throughout the world, and died at last without a friend? He was warned early, frequently, and emphatically, that if he failed to control that indomitable pride which gave a pernicious import to his smallest actions, he would fall under the ban of Europe; and it is impossible to doubt that the agonising sense of humiliation and remorse at the loss of all he had reason to prize has terminated his life. It is one of the most solemn and forcible examples of the tie which links human greatness to human frailty; and throughout all future time the reign of Nicholas of Russia will be remembered as an instance of the miserable ending of a career which has been sacrificed to bad and destructive passions, when it might have been prolonged in peace, good fame, and honour."[a]

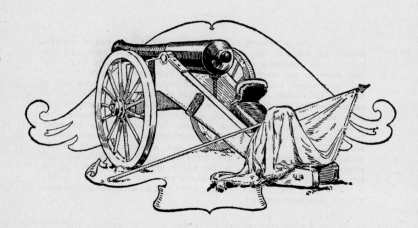

# CHAPTER XII

## ALEXANDER II, THE CZAR LIBERATOR

### [1855–1881 A.D.]

In recalling to memory all that the Russian nation passed through during the reign of the emperor Alexander II, and comparing the position and condition of Russia at the end of the reign with what they were in the beginning, it is impossible not to marvel at the beneficent change which took place throughout all the branches of national life during that short space of time. The liberation of the peasants from the dependence of serfdom, which had weighed on them for some centuries, and the organisation of their existence, the abolition of shameful and cruel corporal punishments, the introduction of provincial and territorial institutions, of the self-government of towns, the new tribunals and general military service, without mentioning other less important reforms, innovations and improvements accomplished by the will of the Czar Liberator, had an immeasurable influence upon the intellectual and moral regeneration of the people, and, it may be said, gave to Russia a complete inward revival. — SCHUMACHER.[d]

BORN in 1818, Alexander came to power at the age of thirty-seven under circumstances of the greatest difficulty both at home and abroad. "Your burden will be a heavy one," his father had said to him when dying. Alexander's first care was to terminate under honourable conditions the war that was exhausting Russia. At the news of the death of Nicholas the value of stocks and bonds rose in every exchange in Europe; and the general peaceful mood was not disturbed by the new emperor's proclamation that he would "endeavour to carry out the views of his illustrious predecessors, Peter, Catherine, the beloved Alexander, and our father of imperishable memory." A new conference took place at Vienna between the representatives of Austria, Russia, and the two western powers. France demanded the neutralisation of

[1855 A.D.]

the Black Sea, or the limitation of the naval powers that the czar might place there. "Before limiting our forces," replied Gortchakov and Titov, the representatives of Russia, "take from us Sebastopol!"

The siege continued. Sardinia in its turn sent 20,000 men to the East. Austria agreed to defend the principalities against Russia, and Prussia agreed to support Austria. On the 16th of May Pélissier succeeded Canrobert as general-in-chief of the French forces. During the night of the 22nd of May the Russians made two sorties, which were repulsed; all the allied forces occupied the left bank of the Tchernaia, and an expedition was sent out which destroyed the military posts of Kertch and Jenikale, occupied the Sea of Azov, and bombarded Taganrog, leaving the Russians no route by which to receive supplies save that of Perekop. The Turks occupied Anapa and incited the Circassians to revolt.

Pélissier had announced that he would gain possession of Sebastopol, and on the 7th of June he took by storm the Mamelon Vert (Green Hillock) and the Ouvrages Blancs (White Works), on the 18th he sent the French to attack Malakov and the English to lay siege to the great Redan, but both expeditions were repulsed with a loss of 3,000 men. On the 16th of August the Italian contingent distinguished itself in the battle of Traktir on the Tchernaia. The last day of Sebastopol had arrived. Eight hundred and seventy-four cannon directed their thunder against the bastions and the city; and the Russians, who displayed a stoical intrepidity that nothing could shake, lost 18,000 men from the effects of the bombardment alone. A million and a half of projectiles were thrown upon the city. The French had dug 80 kilometres of trenches and sunk 1,251 metres of mines before the Mast bastion alone, and their parallels had been extended to within thirty metres of Malakov. Under a terrible fire, the noise of which could be heard at a distance of a hundred kilometres, the Russian bastions crumbled away, and their artillerists and reserve soldiers fell by thousands. Korinlov, Istomin, and Nakhimov succumbed. The besieged had not even time to substitute good cannon for those that had been damaged, and could scarcely accomplish the burial of their dead. The very eve of the crisis that was to end all had arrived.[b]

During the protracted siege of Sebastopol death had claimed Marshal Saint-Arnaud; the French commander general Canrobert succeeded him, and he was now superseded by General Pélissier. Lord Raglan had fallen a victim to cholera, and General Simpson was now in command of the English army.

In these weary months of waiting there had been many sanguinary encounters both by day and by night, and repeated bombardments. But it was not until September the 8th, 1855, that the grand assault was made.[a]

## THE FALL OF SEBASTOPOL

At half-past eleven in the morning (September 8) all the trenches before the Karabel faubourg were occupied by the attacking force. Pélissier, surrounded by his staff, was installed on the Green Mamelon. In the sixth parallel was Bosquet, attentive to everything and influencing everyone around him by his calm energy. The troops, excited, eager, with their clothes loosened so as to fight the better, filled beforehand with the rage of battle (for the long siege had tried their patience), impatiently awaited the signal. From time to time bayonets showed above the parapets. "Down with the bayonets," shouted Bosquet, who feared to reveal to the enemy the position of the French: then he added more gently: "Have patience! the time will come." It had as a fact almost come, being now on the stroke of noon. "Forward!" cried Bosquet, and immediately his colours as commandant were planted on the parallel. The order flew from mouth to mouth; drums beat, trumpets sounded; the officers with naked swords led their troops out of the trenches.

The Malakov garrison at that time was composed of 500 artillery, certain militiamen or workmen, and 1400 infantry belonging to the Modlin, Praga and Zamosc regiments. After being prepared for an attack at daybreak the garrison was no longer upon the alert. Only the gunners remained by their guns, with a few riflemen along the ramparts. All the rest were hidden in their bomb-proof shelters and were about finishing their dinner. Having become accustomed to alarms, they were resting at comparative ease, and, yielding to that lassitude which often overtakes the mind and will after a night of anxious watching. They did not move except to salute the commandant of the fort, General Bessau, who was making an examination of the casemates and bestowing the cross of St. George on the most deserving. Suddenly, on the stroke of noon, the sharp crack of the French rifles rent the air, and the zouaves in their brilliantly coloured uniforms were seen bounding up the Malakov slopes. "The French are upon us! We are attacked!" cried the guard. Before the defenders of the bastion had even had time to pick up their arms, the zouaves had thrown themselves on the work. They cleared the fosse, and without waiting for ladders scaled the escarp and precipitated themselves through the embrasures. The Russian gunners stood to their guns, defending themselves with stones, pickaxes, and sponges. Meantime the men of the Modlin regiment rushed from their shelters and massed themselves towards the front of the fort. There took place one of those hand-to-hand fights, so rare in the history of battles, a desperate, merciless fight, full of terrible episodes. But the Russians were hampered by their long cloaks; the assailants, more active than they, dodged the blows of their enemies, surrounded them, closed with them, and little by little gained ground. The number of assailants momentarily increased. Immediately following the zouaves, almost side by side with them, appeared a battalion of the 7th line regiment, supporting the African troops with energy and bravery. General Bessau fell, mortally wounded, nearly all the other Russian leading officers were killed. Pressed and outflanked on every side the besieged fell back, surrendering the terre-plein, and retiring beyond the first traverses, and the colours of the 1st zouaves were hoisted on the captured redoubt. The battle had lasted only half an hour.

During this same space of time Dulac's division had invaded the Little Redan and driven back the riflemen as far as the second enceinte; whilst La Motterouge's division took possession of the curtain between the Malakov and the Little Redan. From this post of observation the commander-in-chief had seen the French eagle planted on the Malakov; he had also witnessed the triumphant passage of Dulac's and La Motterouge's divisions. Immediately he hoisted the queen's colours on the Green Mamelon. This was the signal for which the English were waiting.

At the sight of it they poured out of their trenches; with the intrepid coolness characteristic of their temperament and their country. First came their rifles, next the men with scaling ladders, then the attacking columns composed of the light division and the 2nd division. In making their attack our allies were at a double disadvantage; in the first place the Russians were on the alert throughout the length of their line of defence, and, secondly, a distance of 200 yards lay between them and the Great Redan. A murderous

XVII.  AFTER THE STORMING OF MALAKOFF: THE DEAD COLOUR-BEARER

(*From the painting by Moreau de Tours*)

[1855 A.D.]

fire greeted them, and before they could reach the work the ground was strewn with their red coats. They continued to advance notwithstanding, doubled to the fosse, scaled it, drew up their ladders, reached the now almost demolished salient-angle and routed the battalions of the Vladimir regiment. Before them stretched a great space, open and exposed; beyond it were the bomb-proof shelters from which the Russians kept up their hottest and best directed fire. Vainly the attacking party strove to push their undertaking further: vainly even did they strain every nerve to maintain the ground they had gained. After an hour and a half of futile attempts they fell back on their trenches.

Whilst the English were being foiled at the Great Redan, Levaillant's division approached the central bastion at about two o'clock and met with no better fate. At first Couston's brigade succeeded in getting possession of the Schwartz redoubt, to the left of the bastion; it even fought a battle in the gully known as the Town Gully. But the commanding officer was wounded, reinforcements arrived for the enemy, and it was brought back to the foremost parallels. To the right of the bastion Trocher's brigade had invaded the Bielkine lunette and gained the bastion itself, but could no longer maintain its advantage. Like General Couston, General Trocher was wounded, and the Russian reprisals shattered his unhappy regiments. A second attempt was not more happy, and orders came from the commander-in-chief forbidding a continuance of such bloody efforts.

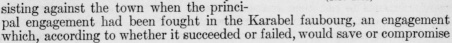

ALEXANDER II
(1818–1881)

And indeed where was the use of persisting against the town when the principal engagement had been fought in the Karabel faubourg, an engagement which, according to whether it succeeded or failed, would save or compromise everything else?

At the Little Redan fortune had made the French columns pay dearly for their early success. Barely mistress of the bastion, Dulac's division had been assailed by a heavy fire from the batteries of the *Maison-en-Croix* and of the three vessels moored in the roads. Moreover the Russians had brought up a large number of field-pieces to all the more favourable points, whilst a considerable number of reserve troops debouched from the Uchakov gully. Outnumbered, crushed by showers of missiles, and finally compelled to evacuate a redoubt filled with their dead, our troops had retired to their place-of-arms. At the curtain La Motterouge's division had itself given way before the attacks of the enemy. New columns were formed from the débris of Saint-Pol's brigade, which had already lost its general, de Marolles' brigade, and the guards division. A little later arrived at full gallop two batteries of the Lancaster artillery which, by the hotness of their fire, strove to work havoc in the enemy's columns, and, above all, to disperse the fog. The Little Redan was taken, lost, retaken, abandoned. The bloodshed was terrific. General de Marolles was killed, Generals Bourbaki, Bisson, Mellinet and de Pontevès wounded, the latter mortally; the trenches were so heaped with dead that it was almost impossible to move in them. Atop of all this General Bosquet was wounded in the right side by the bursting of a shell. He was obliged to relinquish his command, and a rumour even got about that he was dying. Shortly after a loud report was heard from the direction of the curtain. A powder-magazine had exploded, claiming fresh victims; General de la Motterouge was among the wounded. So many casualties, the loss of so many officers, the difficulty of fighting in a narrow space choked up with dead and dying, even extreme exhaustion, all combined to dissuade from a renewed attack on the Little Redan. Only a portion of La Motterouge's division partially held its own on the ramparts.

It was now three o'clock. Judging only by the results as a whole the allies had to count more disappointments than successes. The English had been beaten back at the Great Redan. The central bastion withstood all attacks. And finally, in the Karabel faubourg the Little Redan, already carried, had just slipped from our grasp. But, notwithstanding, there was more joy than depression amongst those surrounding the commander-in-chief. All eyes were turned obstinately towards the Malakov. Were the Malakov safely held, not only would the other checks be made good but the advantage of the day would rest with the allied army; for the occupation of this dominant position would render all further resistance impossible. Now, according to all accounts, MacMahon was keeping safe hold of his prize and stengthening himself there.

He had maintained his position, God only knows at what cost of valour. We have related how the terre-plein fell into the hands of the allies, and how this brilliant success had determined the great attack. But inside the work, fortified and improved with so much care during the long days of siege, the Russians had thrown up a multitude of traverses beneath which were their bomb-proof shelters, which formed all over the fort so many trenches easy of defence. The salient-angle once occupied, it would be necessary to carry one by one these traverses behind which were drawn up what remained of the Modlin regiment and the Praga and Zamosc battalions. Happily General MacMahon had recalled the 2nd, Vinoy's, division. Thanks to these reinforcements he had been enabled to force back the enemy, dislodge them from their positions and drive them towards the gorge of the redoubt.

There an engagement had taken place more terrible than any throughout the day. Driven to bay at the extremity of the work, the Russians had, by a series of heroic rushes, attempted to retake the fort, the veritable palladium of their city. Whilst MacMahon hastily ordered up Wimpfen's brigade, and the zouaves of the guard, in short all the reserves, the Muscovite officers sacrificed themselves one after the other in their efforts to avert a total defeat. First it was General Lisenko with a few remnants of the Warsaw, Briansk and Ieletz regiments; then General Krulov with four battalions of the Ladoga regiment; lastly General Iuverov with the same men newly led on to battle. Lisenko was mortally wounded, Krulov dangerously so, Iuverov killed. In the end the Malakov gorge was ours. The engineers began at once to put it in a state of defence: the capitulation of the little garrison of the tower, isolated in the midst of the fort, completed the victory. A supreme effort made a little later by General de Martinau with the Azov and Odessa regiments only served to demonstrate the powerlessness of our enemies to wrest the magnificent prize from us.

And magnificent it certainly was. The corpses heaped around the fortress showed plainly enough the Russians' obstinate intention to defend or re-capture it. Notwithstanding the fact that our triumph was complete the fusilade had not ceased. There were still certain volunteers risking their lives around the Mamelon, meditating some desperate stroke. "Give us cartridges," they cried: "Let someone lead us again to battle." But nearly all their officers were either dead or in the ambulances, and the remainder scarcely troubled to answer them. Not that they were indifferent to so crushing a defeat, but after such desperate fighting an immense weariness had overtaken them, and, having done all they could to avert their fate they now submitted to it impassively.

Towards four o'clock Prince Gortchakov arrived on these scenes of confusion and woe. On receiving the first intelligence of the assault he had crossed the roads and had been able to follow all the varying chances of the fight. For a long time he surveyed the Karabelnaia, as if to gauge the defensive strength of the faubourg; for a yet longer time he contemplated the Malakov, so lately the pride of the Russians and now lost to them. Neither the still hot firing which killed one of his officers at his side, nor the time which pressed availed to cut short this searching examination.

At last, judging that the town was no longer tenable he decided on consummating the sacrifice. The moment seemed to him a favourable one, for two reasons: the success gained at the Great and Little Redans and at the safeguarded central bastion, had established the honour of the Muscovite arms; whereas the extreme weariness of the allies guaranteed that the remainder of the day and the ensuing night would be allowed by them to pass without further offensive action. The Russian commander-in-chief therefore resolved to evacuate Sebastopol and to make all his troops cross over to the northern bank. The idea once conceived he hurried to the Nicholas battery to secure the immediate execution of his orders.

At his post of observation on the Green Mamelon, Pélissier had learnt of MacMahon's signal success, and this great advantage, somewhat counterbalanced it is true by the checks received in other engagements, filled all hearts with hope. Nevertheless, by reason of this multitude of engagements, victory appeared to be, though probable, still uncertain. Would MacMahon be able to maintain his position at the Malakov? Might not some exploding mine change the triumph into a catastrophe? Would not the defeated Russians defend themselves from behind their second enceinte, in their streets, in their houses even? And would not the battle of September 8 have a yet more bloody morrow? No answer was forthcoming to these questions, and faces that had begun to brighten grew troubled.

Things were at this stage when, towards the end of the day, General Martimprey turning his glasses towards the town thought he detected an unaccustomed movement on the great bridge spanning the roads. Glasses were passed from hand to hand and, despite the first shades of evening, long processions of soldiers, waggons, carriages, guns, could be distinctly seen wending their way towards the northern bank. The bridge gave under the weight, and shaken by a high wind swayed it beneath the swell which from time to time submerged and almost swamped it. In spite of this hindrance the march continued, whilst ferry-boats filled with people crossed to the northern bank, and then returned empty to fetch other passengers. The rapidly falling darkness prevented further observation, but the spectators felt no doubt that they were watching the retreat of the Russians.

They had not all retreated, however. At this supreme moment Gortchakov bethought himself of Moscow. Several volunteer corps and several detachments of sappers and marines were left behind, not to give battle to an already victorious enemy, but to level to the dust the city it was no longer possible to defend. As night fell the work of devastation was begun. Powder-magazines were blown up. The cannon and siege trains that could not be removed were sunk in the bay. All that remained of the North Sea squadron was sunk; even the *Empress Marie* was not spared, that splendid vessel which was commanded by the glorious Nahkimov at the battle of Sinope. Only the war steamers were saved and taken across to the northern bank. The blowing up of the Paul battery completed the work of destruction. When all was finished the great bridge was broken up. Then the executors of those savage orders departed in boats for the further shore. With them went the generals who up to that moment had remained at Sebastopol to guard the retreat. Of this number was Count Osten-Sacken, governor of the town, who was one of the last to leave, as a captain abandons his burning ship only when all the hands have left.

PRINCE A. M. GORTCHAKOV

(1798–1883)

The explosions of that terrible night had kept the allies on the alert in their camp, and had triumphed over their immense fatigue. At daybreak on the 9th of September, Sebastopol, already nearly deserted, appeared to them as an immense heap of ruins from which shot up tongues of flame kindled by the incendiaries. For a long time French and English contemplated with a mixture of joy and horror those ruins which attested the greatness of their triumph and also the tenacity of their enemies. Beyond the roadstead, on the northern heights, appeared the Russians, vanquished but still menacing.

On the morrow, September 10th, 1855 — after 332 days of siege, three set battles, and three assaults more bloody even than the battles — Pélissier, as marshal of France, in the name of the emperor, planted his country's flag among the smoking ruins.[e]

With the fall of Sebastopol the war was practically at an end. Hostilities continued for some time longer, but neither side won any material advantage. The allies were not in complete accord on the question of the continuance of the war, England being inclined to push matters to a complete overthrow of Russia, while France was ready to talk about terms of peace. Lord Palmerston himself was a strenuous opponent of peace, and declared that Russia had not been sufficiently humbled. At this juncture Prince A. M. Gortchakov, the Russian ambassador at Vienna, taking advantage of the divided councils of the allies, urged Austria to act as peacemaker. The emperor Francis Joseph thereupon took the occasion to press upon Russia an acceptance of the four conditions on which Turkey was prepared to make peace, backing the communication with an implied threat of war in case of denial. On January 16th, 1856, the czar, much against his will, signified his acceptance of Austrian intervention. The preliminaries of peace were signed on February 1st and on the 25th of the same month representatives of the great powers assembled at Paris to settle the details of the peace. Negotiations proceeded for over a month, France and Russia drawing together and Austria insisting upon the maximum of Russian cessions.[a]

Under the Treaty of Paris, March 30th, 1856, the powers bound themselves not to intervene singly in the administration of Turkey, to respect her independence and territorial status, and to treat disputes between any of them and the Porte as matters of general interest. A Hatti-sherif, or ordinance, had been obtained by England from the sultan before the congress opened, which guaranteed equal religious privileges to all his subjects. This was set forth as an article in the treaty. Russia renounced her claims to a protectorate over Turkish Christians. She abandoned similar pretensions with regard to the Danubian principalities, which were in future to be governed by hospodars elected under European control. She surrendered to Moldavia the southern portion of Bessarabia, which had been ceded under the Treaty of Bucharest, retaining however the principal trade-routes southwards and the fortress of Khotin. The navigation of the Danube was declared free to all nations, and placed under an European commission.

A clause, through which Russia drew her pen as soon as an opportunity presented itself, declared the Black Sea neutral and closed it to men-of-war of all nations. Russia surrendered Kars to Turkey, but regained the portion of the Crimea in the allies' occupation. By a separate act she undertook not to fortify the Åland Isles or to make them a naval station. Thanks to the astuteness of her diplomacy, she scored a decided success against England in securing the insertion of articles which limited the scope of naval warfare. The Treaty of Paris abolished privateering, and provided that a neutral flag should protect the enemy's goods, while neutral property, even under a hostile flag, was exempted from capture. "Contraband of war" was indeed excepted, but no attempt was made to define the meaning of this ambiguous phrase. The recognition of a blockade by neutrals was to be conditional on its effectiveness.[g]

### AMELIORATION IN THE CONDITION OF THE SOLDIER

On the 26th of August, 1856, the emperor Alexander Nikolaivitch placed on his head, in the cathedral of the Assumption at Moscow, the imperial crown and received the sacrament of anointing with the Holy Chrism. The sacred day of the coronation was one of rejoicing and hitherto unprecedented favours and therefore left the most joyful remembrance in the hearts of the people.

When he had taken upon himself the imperial crown, the emperor Alexander II immediately set about the preparation of those great administrative reforms, which were so full of humanity and justice, which made his reign illustrious and which immortalised his name.

Solicitous for the welfare of his people, the emperor first of all directed his attention to the improvement of the condition of the soldier and entered upon a series of reforms in the organisation and administration of that army, which was so dear to his heart, with the object of raising the moral spirit of the troops, of arousing the lower ranks to the consciousness of their dignity and in general of placing the military profession upon its proper elevated footing.

As the preserver of order in the state during times of peace and the defender of the country in time of war, the soldier is justly proud of his profession; he should not be given cause for mortification by finding beside him in the service men condemned to the ranks as punishment for vicious behaviour. Yet in previous times men were frequently made soldiers by way of punishment for some crime instead of being banished to the settlements: fugitives, vagabonds, horse stealers, thieves, swindlers, and such vicious persons found a place in the ranks of the army.

The emperor Alexander II put an end to this shameful state of things: by the imperial manifesto of 1860 the enrolment of soldiers as a punishment for crimes and offences, an abuse which had attained vast dimensions, was abolished and replaced by other forms of punishment. But the czar's chief care was to bring to fulfilment his most sacred idea, one which he cherished day and night: to give liberty to the peasants who were dependent as serfs upon the landowners; to abolish the law of serfdom. Amongst the great administrative reforms accomplished during the reign of the emperor Alexander II, the liberation of the peasants occupies incontestably the first place and served as the chief foundation for all the reforms that followed. All further changes were directly or indirectly called forth by the abolition of the law of serfdom. This glorious accomplishment which gave new life to Russia, which breathed a new soul into the millions of Russian peasantry, was the most important of all the great deeds of the emperor Alexander II, and the brightest jewel in the crown of his glory.

A Peasant Costume

### THE EMANCIPATION OF THE SERFS
#### (1861 A.D.)

The predecessors of Alexander II had already felt all the evils of the law of serfdom and had not unfrequently aimed, if not directly at its abolition, at least at the amelioration of the position of the peasant serfs and their gradual preservation against the arbitrariness of the landowners' authority. But all these beneficent measures were insufficient for the abolition of the firmly established order; they only limited the rights of serfdom, put a certain restraint upon it, but did not abolish the right of the possession of serfs The glory of the complete emancipation of the peasants from the dependency of serfdom, the great and difficult initiative of the entire abolition of the law of serfdom in Russia belongs wholly to the emperor Alexander II.

The question of the abolition of the law of serfdom constituted the chief care of the emperor Alexander II during the first years of his reign; all the course of the work in connection with the matter of the peasants testified to what firmness of will, immovable convictions and persistency were brought by the emperor himself into this matter which he regarded as "sacred and most vital" for Russia.

The emperor spoke many times in public on the peasant question during the time when the measure was under discussion. The sovereign's speeches all displayed his firm, inflexible intention of bringing the work he had conceived to a successful termination; they had kept up the courage of those labouring for the peasantry reforms, attracted the wavering, kept opponents in check, and thus had an enormous influence both on public opinion and on the course of local and general work in the matter of peasant reforms.

The solution of the peasant question, which was of such vital importance to Russia, presented many difficulties. Of course it would have been far easier to master the problem if the emperor had desired to solve it as it had already been solved in some kingdoms of western Europe, where the peasants had been at one time in the same position as the Russian serfs; there the peasants had only been declared individually free, the land remained the property of the landowner. But such was not the will of the emperor Alexander II. He desired that the interests of the landlords should be as far as possible guarded, and also that the emancipated peasants should be endowed with a fixed quantity of land; not converted into homeless, landless labourers.

Much labour had to be expended over this great problem before an issue was found for its successful solution. The chief executor of the emperor's preconceived plans in the matter of the peasant question was Adjutant-General J. T. Rostovtsev, in whom Alexander found an enlightened and boundlessly devoted assistant. In his turn Rostovtsev found a most zealous and talented collaborator in the person of N. A. Milutin, who warmly took up the cause of the emancipation of the peasants and who, after the death of Rostovtsev in 1860, became the chief director of all the work upon this question. The emperor attentively followed the course of the preparatory labours on the peasant reforms and without giving any serious heed to the wiles and opposition of the obstinate partisans of the law of serfdom, he firmly and unwaveringly directed these labours to the object marked out.

But of course it was impossible to accomplish so vast a work at once. Four years passed in the indispensable preparatory work. The thoughts of the sovereign were full of this administrative measure; his heart must have been frequently overwhelmed with anxieties and fears in regard to the successful solution of the peasant question. But the czar's will never weakened, his love for his people was never exhausted, and the great, holy work of the emancipation of the rural population of Russia from the bondage of serfdom, and the organisation of this population into a new form of existence was at last brought to a successful conclusion.

On the 19th of February, 1861, in the sixth year of the reign of the emperor Alexander II, all doubts were resolved. On that memorable day, which can never be forgotten in Russia, was accomplished the greatest event in the destinies of the Russian people: the emperor Alexander II, after having fervently prayed in solitude, signed the imperial manifesto for the abolition of the right of serfdom over the peasants living on the landlords' estates and for granting to these peasants the rights of a free agricultural status. Through the initiative and persistent efforts of their czar more than twenty-two million Russian peasants were liberated from the burden of serfdom, which had weighed on them and their forebears for nearly three centuries. They obtained their freedom and together with it the possibility of enjoying the fruits of their free labour, that is, of working for themselves, for their own profit and advantage and of governing themselves and their actions according to their own will and discernment. Freedom was given to the Russian peasant by the emperor Alexander II himself; it was not given under him, but by him; he personally maintained the right of his people to freedom, personally broke the chains of serfdom; the initiative of this great work, its direction and its execution belong wholly to the emperor. We repeat, the laws of serfdom crumbled away at his royal word alone. Together with the imperial manifesto of the 19th of February, 1861, were promulgated in both capitals and afterwards throughout all Russia, laws for the organization of the liberated peasants into the social order, entitled "General regulations concerning the peasants issuing from the dependence of serfdom." Upon the basis of these laws and in particular by virtue of the reforms that followed, the liberated peasants were thus granted personal, social, and individual rights which placed them almost on a footing of equality with the other classes of the state.

### Laws and Social Rights Granted to the Peasants

In conferring upon the liberated peasants the individual rights, common to all citizens of the empire, the czar was solicitous for the establishment of laws actually conducive to the security and amelioration of their condition, indissolubly bound up as it had been with the use and enjoyment of the land. With this object in view it was established that the peasant should have a share in the perpetual enjoyment of the farm settlements and arable land, in accordance with the qualities of the land of each locality and with local requirements. But as the peasants had not means to give the landowner at once all the value due for their share of the land, and on the other hand as the prospect of receiving the sum allotted, in small proportions during a period of thirty to forty years, was not an alluring one for the landowner, the state took upon itself the office of intermediary between the landowners and the liberated peasants and paid the landowner in redeemable paper all the sums due to him and inscribed them as long term debts against the peasants, who were under the obligation of paying them off by yearly instalments.

Together with the reservation of individual and property rights to the emancipated peasants, a special peasant government was established for them. The peasants received the right of disposing independently of their agricultural and public work, and of choosing from amongst themselves the wisest and most reliable persons for conducting their affairs under the direction of peasant assemblies. And as in the life of the Russian peasants many ancient customs and rules are preserved which are esteemed and observed as sacred, being the product of the experience of their forefathers, the emperor granted them also their own district peasant tribunals which decide upon purely local questions and arbitrate according to the conscience and traditions of these communities.

The imperial manifesto was, as has already been said, signed on the 19th of February, 1861, but it was universally proclaimed only on the 5th of March of the same year; the news of the emancipation evoked an indescribable enthusiasm, a touching gratitude in the people towards their liberator throughout the whole length of the Russian land, beginning with the capital and finishing with the last poor little hamlet.[d]

Having thus summarised the results achieved by this remarkable manifesto, we give below a literal translation of the full text of the document itself.[a]

*Text of the Imperial Proclamation*

Manifesto of the Emancipation of the Serfs:
By the Grace of God
We, Alexander the Second,
Emperor and Autocrat
Of All the Russias,
King of Poland, Grand Duke of Finland,
et cætera, et cætera, et cætera,
Make known to all Our faithful subjects.

Having been called by God's Providence and the sacred law of succession to the throne of our forefathers and All the Russias, We have in accordance with this calling vowed to comprehend in Our royal love and care all Our faithful subjects of every calling and condition, from him who nobly wields the sword in the defence of the fatherland to the modest worker with the tools of the artisan, from him who serves in the highest service of the state to him who draws the furrow over the field with the plough.

A Street Vender

Upon examining into the position of the various callings and conditions of the state structure, We have observed that the legislation of the state, while organising actively and well the higher and middle classes by determining their duties, rights and privileges, has not attained to an equal activity in regard to the people bound to the soil and called serfs because they, partly through ancient laws, partly from custom, are hereditarily settled under the authority of the landowners, upon whom at the same time the obligation lies to provide for their welfare. The rights of the landowners have been until now extensive and not defined with any exactitude by the law, the place of which has been taken instead by tradition, custom and the good will of the landowner. In the most favourable cases there have proceeded from this state of things kind, patriarchal relations of sincere and true guardianship and beneficence on the part of the landlord, and good tempered obedience on the part of the peasant. But with the increasing complexity of manners and customs, with the increasing diversity of relations, the lessening of direct intercourse between the landowners and peasants, the occasional falling of the landowner's rights into the hands of persons who only seek their own profit, these good relations have weakened, and a path has been opened for an arbitrariness which is burdensome to the peasants and unfavourable to their welfare, and to which the peasants have responded by insensibility to improvement in their own existence.

These matters were observed also by Our ever to be remembered predecessors and they took measures to effect a change for the better in the position of the peasants; but these measures were indecisive. In many cases they depended on the co-operation of the landowners; in others they concerned only particular localities and were instituted to meet special requirements or else as experiments. Thus the emperor Alexander I issued a regulation concerning the freedom of agriculturists, and Our deceased parent Nicholas I, who rests in God, a regulation as to the obligations of peasants. In the western governments inventory rules have defined the distribution of the peasants by the land and their obligations. But the regulations concerning the freedom of agriculturists and the obligations of peasants have been carried out only to a very limited extent.

Thus, We have become convinced that the amelioration of the condition of the serfs or people bound to the soil, is for us a testament of Our predecessors and a lot appointed to Us, through the course of circumstances, by the hand of Providence.

We have entered upon this work by an act showing Our confidence in the Russian nobility, Our confidence in their devotion to the throne, which has been proved by great trials, and in their readiness to make large sacrifices for the good of the country. We left the nobility, at its own request, responsible for the new legislation in behalf of the peasantry. It thus became the duty of the nobles to limit their rights over the peasants and to take up the difficulties of the reformation; and this involved a sacrifice of their own interests. But Our confidence has been justified. In the government committees, invested with the confidence of the nobility of each government, the nobility has voluntarily renounced its rights over the persons of the serfs. In these committees when the necessary information had been collected, propositions were drawn up for the new code regulating the conditions of persons bound to the soil, and their relations to the landowners.

These propositions, which, as might have been expected from the nature of the matter, were very various, have been compared, brought into harmony, arranged in a regular form, amended and completed in the higher commission appointed for this matter; and the new propositions thus constituted in the interests of landowners, peasants, and menials have been examined in the council of state.

Calling upon God to assist us, We have decided to bring this work to its accomplishment.

In virtue of the new regulations, the serfs will receive at the proper time the full rights of free villagers.

The landowners while preserving the rights of property over all the land belonging to them, will leave the peasants, in return for the dues established, in perpetual enjoyment of their farm settlements; Moreover, in order to ensure the security of their existence and the fulfilment of their obligations before the Government, the quantity of arable land and other necessaries allotted will be determined by regulation.

Thus profiting by a share of the land, the peasants are in return obliged to pay in to the landowner certain dues determined by the regulations. In this condition which is transitory the peasants are denominated as temporarily bound to work for the landlords.

Together with this they are given the right to buy their farm settlements,

[1861 A.D.]

and with the consent of the landlords they can acquire as property the arable land and other appendages, allotted for their perpetual enjoyment. By such acquisitions of certain determined quantities of land, the peasants are freed from any obligations to the landowners on the land purchased and enter into the position of free peasant-proprietors.

By special regulation in regard to menials or domestic servants, a transitory position is determined for them adapted to their occupations and requirements; after the expiration of a space of two years from the day of the issue of this regulation, they will receive full emancipation and exemption from taxes.

These are the chief principles by which are determined the future organisation of the peasants and the menials. They indicate in detail the rights granted to the peasants and menials and the duties laid upon them in respect to the government and the landlords.

Although these regulations, general, local and special as well as supplementary rules for certain particular localities, for the estates of small landed proprietors, and for peasants working in their landlords' manufactories are as far as possible adapted to the economic requirements, yet in order to preserve the usual order, We leave to the landlords the option of making a voluntary agreement with the peasants regarding land and dues.

As the new system, on account of the inevitable multitude of changes it involves, cannot be at once introduced, but requires time for adjustment, therefore in order to avoid disturbance in public and private affairs, the order existing until now shall be preserved for two years, when, after the completion of the necessary preparations, the new laws shall go into force.

For the lawful attainment of this, We have considered it well to command that:

A WOMAN OF KAMCHATKA

1. In every government a government council on peasant affairs shall be opened, having the supreme direction of the affairs of the peasant societies installed on the landowners' territories.

2. Arbiters of peace are to be nominated in the districts, and district assemblies formed from them in order to investigate on the spot into any misunderstandings and disputes which may arise in the fulfilment of the regulations.

3. Besides this, communal councils are to be established on the landowners' estates, in order that, while leaving the village communities in their present formation, *Volost*[1] councils should be opened in the principal villages, uniting the smaller village communities under one *Volost* administration.

4. A charter shall be drawn up in each village specifying, on the basis of the local regulations, the quantity of land appointed for the perpetual enjoyment of the peasants, and the dues to be paid the landowner.

5. These charters shall be executive, and brought into operation within a space of two years from the day of the issue of this manifesto.

6. Until the expiration of this term, the peasants and menials are to remain

[1 A district containing several villages.]

in their previous condition of subjection to the landlords and indisputably to fulfil their former obligations.

7. The landowners are to see that order is maintained on their estates, and preserve the right of the dispensation of justice until the formation and opening of the *Volost* tribunals.

In contemplating the inevitable difficulties of the reform, We first of all lay Our trust in God's most gracious Providence, which protects Russia.

After this We rely on the valiant zeal of the Honourable body of the Nobility, to whom We cannot but testify the gratitude it has earned from Us and from the whole country for its disinterested action in the realisation of Our preconceived plans. Russia will not forget that it has voluntarily, incited only by respect for the dignity of man and Christian love for its neighbour, renounced serfdom and laid the foundation of the new agricultural future of the peasant. We believe unquestioningly that it will continue its good work by ensuring the orderly accomplishment of the new regulations, in the spirit of peace and benevolence; and that each landowner will complete within, the limits of his own estate, the great civic movement of the whole body, by organising the existence of the peasants settled on his lands, and that of his domestic servants, upon conditions advantageous to both sides, thus setting the rural population a good example, and encouraging it in the exact and conscientious fulfilment of the state regulations.

The examples that We have in view of the generous solicitude of the landlords for the welfare of the peasants, and the gratitude of the peasants for the beneficent solicitude of the landlords, confirm in Us the hope that mutual, spontaneous agreement will solve the greater number of difficulties; difficulties which are inevitable in the adaptation of general rules to the diversity of conditions existent in separate estates; and that by this means the transition from the old order to the new will be facilitated, and that for the future, mutual confidence, good understanding and unanimous striving for the common welfare will be consolidated.

For the more convenient accomplishment of those agreements between the landlords and peasants, by which the latter will acquire property, together with the farms and agricultural appendages, assistance will also be afforded by the government, on the basis of special rules, by the payment of loans, and the transfer of debts lying on the estates.

We rely upon the good sense of Our people. When the government's idea of the abolition of serfdom became spread amongst the peasants who were unprepared for it, it aroused partial misunderstandings. Some thought of liberty and forgot all about obligations. But the mass of the people did not waver in the conviction, that by natural reasoning, a society that freely enjoyed benefits must mutually minister to the welfare of society by the fulfilment of certain obligations, and that in accordance with the Christian law, *every soul* must be *subject unto the higher powers* (Rom. xiii, 1), must *render therefore to all their dues*, and especially to whom are due *tribute, custom, fear, honour* (v. 7); that the lawfully acquired rights of the landowners cannot be taken from them without fitting recompense for their voluntary concession; and that it would be opposed to all justice to avail oneself of the land belonging to the landlord without rendering certain obligations in return for it.

And now we hopefully expect that the serfs, in view of the new future opening for them, will understand and gratefully receive the great sacrifice made by the honourable nobility for the improvement of their condition.

They will understand, that having received a firmer foundation of property and greater freedom in the disposition of their agricultural labours, they have

[1861 A.D.]

become bound, before society and themselves to complete the beneficence of the new law by a faithful, well-intentioned and diligent use of the rights conferred by it upon them.  The most beneficent law cannot make people happy and prosperous, if they do not themselves labour to establish their felicity under the protection of the law.  Competence and ease are not acquired and increased otherwise than by unremitting labour, a wise use of powers and means, strict thrift and an honest, God-fearing life.

The executors of this new system will see that it is accomplished in an orderly and tranquil manner, so that the attention of the agriculturists may not be drawn off from their necessary agricultural occupations.  May they carefully cultivate the earth, and gather its fruits in order that afterwards from well-filled granaries the seed may be taken for sowing the land that is for their perpetual enjoyment, or that will be acquired by them as their own property.

Sign yourselves with the sign of the cross, orthodox people, and call upon God with Us for His blessing on your free labour, on your homes and on the public welfare.

Given in St. Petersburg, on the nineteenth day of February in the year one thousand eight hundred and sixty-one from the birth of Christ, and the seventh of Our reign.

ALEXANDER.*f*

### EFFECTS OF THE NEW CONDITIONS

Let us now turn our attention to the epoch in which this law was published. As regards the effect of the new law on the mind of the population, it was soon evidenced, that the cultivated classes, burdened as they were with sacrifices for the work of reform, expressed their joy and satisfaction at this great acquisition, far more readily than the peasants, whom it immediately concerned.  The disaffected portion of the Russian nobility was and remained decidedly in the minority, especially under the first impression of the great and decided step that had been taken, and no one ventured to manifest disapproval.  Public opinion had declared itself too decidedly in favour of the government for any one to venture on opposition.  On the contrary, the number was by no means unimportant, of those among the nobles and officials, who exceeded even the demands of the government, and who could not suppress their vexation, that their desire that the lands possessed by the community should be gratuitously transferred into their property, had been disregarded.  Although these voices were not distinctly audible until a later period, still from the first they had influence, because they could reckon on the sympathies of the freed portion of the population.  Moreover a great part of the nobles, at that time, looked for a rich compensation for the sacrifice they had made; they hoped to be able to excite public opinion in favour of the embryo demand for the restoration of a constitution, and by its assistance to reach the desired goal.  Thus the disaffected feelings of the hitherto ruling classes were veiled, and maintained in one balance, by hopes of the future; at the most a small band of stubborn adherents to the system of Nicholas grumbled at the liberalism come into fashion, could not conceal their vexation at the loss of their revenues, and used every effort to recover their lost influence in the court circles.

The Russian peasant received the important tidings of the breaking of his fetters with profound silence; and some time elapsed before he had made up his mind what position to assume with regard to it.  Partly, the habitual want of freedom had become too inveterate, and was too deeply rooted, to be at once cast aside; and partly, the attention of the people was too eagerly directed to the still pending agricultural arrangements with the proprietors, for the publication of the emancipation edict to make at once any evident impression. The effect of the emancipation act was felt most strongly and evidently in the two capitals of the empire; here there were thousands of serfs living (as merchants, second-hand dealers, artisans, drivers, servants, etc.) who had been obliged to purchase with high obroc-payments the right of seeking their gain, and were always in danger of being recalled by the will of their masters and constrained to return to the old position of dependence. To these, the advantages of the newly established arrangement of things were manifest, and the fruits of it could at once be enjoyed; the emancipation law limited the duration of their dependence to merely two years, and fixed an unimportant obroc-sum for this transition period. From these town-serfs, therefore, proceeded the first exhibitions of thankfulness and joy, the first ovations to the "liberating czar." But here also the weak, womanish character of the Slavonic race, did not belie itself; there was no idea of passionate outbursts. The St. Petersburg descriptions of those momentous February days tell most characteristically of intoxicated bands of bearded cab-drivers and artisans, who reeled through the streets, humming as they went "Volyushka, Volyushka," (literally, "beloved freedom"). Truly effective, however, was the shout of rejoicing, with which the masses of the people received the emperor when he quitted the winter-palace, on the 19th of February, in order to be present at the reading of the emancipation-ukase in the Kazan church; and subsequently, the addresses sent to the emperor by the drivers and lower class of citizens in the two capitals, who had been freed from serfdom.

Although this law had been published throughout the whole empire on the same day in all churches, and the peace-mediators (mirovuye-Posredniki) had at once proceeded to regulate the agricultural questions; the first more important manifestations in the country did not occur until two months later, in the end of April, 1861. These were manifestations of dissatisfaction and disappointment, which appeared east of the Volga, and had the districts of Kazan and Nijni-Novgorod for their principal centre. In all probability they were revolutionary agitators from the higher and more cultivated classes who first scattered the seeds of discontent. The people were persuaded that the true emancipation-ukase of the czar had been craftily intercepted by the nobles and officials; that the will of the czar was to consign to the peasants, without compensation or hindrance, the land they had hitherto cultivated. These doctrines fell on a soil all the more ready, as the services yielded to the masters were in the eyes of the people of a purely personal nature, and were no equivalents for the lands conceded to the communities. "We belong to the proprietors, but the common land belongs to us," was the creed of the peasant; hence the feeling was, that the abolition of personal servitude was synonymous with the establishment of free property. In the Kazan district, matters soon reached a pitch of open refusal to obedience; and when the magistrates interfered, they amounted to attempts at resistance. Popular discontent assumed at once a genuinely national stamp; it found a leader in a new Pugatchev, the peasant Anton Petrov, who personated the czar (who had fled from St. Petersburg, pursued by the boyars); and within a short time he had gathered round him 10,000 men. After vain attempts to bring back the infatuated men by gentle means to obedience, military power was obliged to be employed. Some battalions, led by Count Apraxin, marched through the insurgent country, and took the ringleader prisoner; and after Petrov had fallen into their hands, and had been immediately shot, order was again so completely established, that in May nothing further was thought of this episode. The peasants returned to their obedience, and everywhere the arrangements of the peace-arbitrator were complied with. Yet the idea of the perfect freedom hoped for, was not yet wholly forgotten; the Volga districts remained for some time longer the scene of revolutionary experiments, which excited the people with the hope of a "new freedom" still to be expected and held fast to the old idea of a gratuitous division of the soil. Under the title *Zemliyä i Volyä* (Land and Freedom), there appeared from time to time secretly published pamphlets, which endeavoured to give the agrarian question a revolutionary colouring, and which were numerously circulated, in the eastern districts especially. These manifestations of a propaganda, secretly inflaming the public mind, we shall meet with again in other places, and under other forms.

In general, the completion of the arrangement between peasant and lord was unexpectedly quick, and favourable in its course. Little as it can be asserted, that the Russian peasant subsequently made a just use of his newborn liberty, or that agricultural progress exhibited any favourable influence from it; still it is evident, that the peasant population manifested in the arrangement good-will, a just insight into the state of affairs, and great tractableness; and that this matter was justly conceived and handled by those entrusted with it. The execution of the law of the 19th of February, 1861, was not placed in the hands of ordinary magistrates, but was consigned to officials, who were selected *ad hoc* from the number of landed proprietors, and were furnished with extensive authority. It was a happy idea, and one of decided and lasting importance, that these peace mediators, or arbitrators, as they were called, were not reckoned in the service of the state, and were not fettered to the orders of the bureaucratic hierarchy. For the first time in Russia, men of the most different calling, and social position, stood side by side with equal right to join hands for the execution of a patriotic work, which promised neither title, rank, nor advancement. Generals in command, and mere lieutenants, councillors of the state, and simple titular councillors, once the choice of their fellow-citizens and class-equals fell on them, demanded leave of absence from service, in order to undertake, according to the law, the demarcation between the estates of the nobles and the lands of the community within definite districts, and to induce both parties to agree; it was only where this result could not be attained, that the strict orders of the regulations were enforced, and the co-operation of higher authority was appealed to.[h]

## ABOLITION OF CORPORAL PUNISHMENT (1863 A.D.)

The first reform that followed on the abolition of the law of serfdom, which had been an unsurmountable obstacle to any improvement and reform in the political organisation of the state, was the abolition of the cruel and shameful corporal punishments which were formerly allotted for crimes.

In the beginning of the reign of Alexander II attention had been directed to the fact that corporal punishment as a punitive measure did not accomplish the reformation amendment of the criminal, but only dishonoured the personality of the man, lowered his feeling of honour and destroyed in him the sense of his manhood.

The emperor began by diminishing the number of offences amenable to corporal punishment; the new position which had been given to the peasants by the abolition of serfdom, soon led to the almost total suppression of corporal punishment for them.

On the 29th of April, 1863, an imperial ukase followed, by which corporal punishment was entirely abolished as a punitive measure, determined by the sentence of the public tribunals. By this memorable ukase, which will ever remain a glorious monument in the legislation of Russia, were abolished by the will of the czar-liberator, the last traces of slavery in Russia; the running of the gauntlet, the spur, the lash, the cat, the branding of the human body, all passed away into eternal oblivion; the punishment of the rod, to which persons belonging to the class not exempt from corporal punishment had hitherto been subjected, was replaced for them by arrest or confinement in prison, and was preserved only in two or three cases and then in the most moderate measure.

### REFORMS IN THE COURTS OF JUSTICE

Almost simultaneously with the establishment of the provincial and territorial institutions, the emperor Alexander II recognised it as indispensable for the welfare of his people, to reform the existing judiciary system and law proceedings, to render all his subjects equal before the legal authorities, and to afford them all the same protection of the tribunals and the law.

Ancient Russian tribunals, as is well known, were far from being distinguished either by their uprightness or the rapidity of their procedure. It is hardly necessary to remind readers that justice was administered in secret, behind closed doors, besides which not merely outsiders were refused admittance to the courts, but even the persons implicated and interested in the affair. Such chancery secrecy resulted in great lack of truth and justice in the tribunals. Taking advantage of the secrecy of the proceedings, the judges allowed themselves to commit every possible abuse: they extorted money from the suitors, behaved unfairly and against their own consciences, distorted facts and afterwards decided the affair in accordance with their own views and pleasure, that is, as was most advantageous and convenient to them. Another great defect in the ancient Russian tribunals was due to the fact that the entire procedure was carried on in them exclusively on paper, upon the foundation of notes alone; verbal explanations were not permitted in the tribunals. This complicated form of written procedure led to litigations of incredible length; the most trivial lawsuit sometimes dragged on for years, requiring enormous expenditure and often in the end ruining the litigants. In a like manner, the accused, not infrequently innocent people, and only suspected of some crime or offence, had to languish for years in prison, awaiting the termination of their affairs before the courts.

The emperor Alexander II was well aware of all these defects and imperfections in the ancient courts of justice, and as a true friend of humanity could not remain indifferent to such an order of things. He therefore desired that there should be established in Russia a system of justice that would be "speedy, righteous, merciful, and equitable." The reign of truth and mercy in the tribunals could be attained only by a complete reorganisation of the ancient tribunals, in consequence of which, by command of the czar, new legal statutes were composed, and received the imperial confirmation towards the end of November, 1864.

The enormous superiority of the new tribunals over the old ones was at once evident. The new courts, carrying on their business in public, punished crimes without respect of persons; all Russian subjects were recognised as equal before the law and the courts. The appearance of justices of the peace had a particular importance for the people newly liberated from the dependence of serfdom; they afforded the hitherto poor and almost defenceless lower classes a possibility of protecting themselves against every kind of offence, violence and oppression, and of claiming their legal rights almost without trouble or expense.

### THE POLISH INSURRECTION OF 1863

In spite of his ardent reformatory activity in the interior of the empire, the emperor Alexander II did not neglect foreign policy. Although, at the conclusion of the Crimean war, the emperor had recognised the necessity of a prolonged peace for Russia, and therefore continually endeavoured to avoid becoming entangled in the affairs of nations, nevertheless in all cases where the interests of Russia were affected, he firmly and calmly declared his requirements, and by means of peaceful persuasions maintained the honour and interests of his country.

The suppression of the Polish rebellion of 1863 is particularly remarkable in this respect: The amelioration of conditions in Poland had occupied Alexander II immediately after his accession to the throne, and he had at once eliminated inequalities of legislation between his Russian and Polish subjects: all that was granted to Russia was granted also to the kingdom of Poland.

All these favours aroused a feeling of gratitude in the more moderate and wiser portion of the population. But they were not received in the same spirit by those Poles who dreamed of the re-establishment of the ancient Poland with its former frontiers, and of giving entire self-government to the kingdom by means of its separation from Russia, and the formation of a separate state. These persons looked with hostility upon all the actions of the Rus-

A MESTCHER COSTUME

sian government and, with the design of entering into an open conflict with Russia, secretly began to incite the people of Poland to revolt.

In January, 1863, a fresh insurrection burst forth in Poland. But the revolutionaries were unsuccessful, and the Russian troops defeated them at every point, taking 300 prisoners and a considerable number of guns. Being desirous of again trying mild measures, and in the hope of at last bringing the Poles to reason, the emperor declared that pardon would be granted to all who laid down their arms by the 13th of May. But the term allotted expired without good sense having triumphed. Then Count Birg was appointed viceroy in Warsaw, and Adjutant-General Muraviev, governor-general of the northwest border. Under the direction of these two men, the conflict took a more decided character and the suppression of the rebellion was made effective.

Meanwhile, when the insurrection was already almost put down by the Russian troops, three great western European powers — England, France and Austria — expressed their sympathy with the Polish movement and at the same time gave the Poles hopes of assistance.   Having concerted together, and being besides supported by Turkey, these powers simultaneously sent the Russian government threatening exactions for concessions to Poland.   Naturally, these pretensions on the part of the powers were offensive to Russian national honour.   A feeling of profound indignation and wounded dignity took possession of the Russian nation, and readiness was expressed to sacrifice everything to the defence of the fatherland.   Prince A. M. Gortchakov showed himself a worthy champion of Alexander II in the resistance shown to the European powers.

Meeting with such decided opposition to their interference, the powers became convinced that the entire Russian nation stood behind the czar, and they were obliged to withdraw their exactions.   The final suppression of the Polish insurrection became thenceforth a matter of internal policy.   Complete tranquillity was restored in Poland in the year 1864.

Following on these events a series of measures was undertaken tending to the gradual union of the kingdom of Poland with the Russian empire.   The most beneficial of all these measures was the ukase of the 2nd of March, 1864, for the reorganisation of the peasantry in the kingdom of Poland.

Strictly speaking, the law of serfdom had been abolished in Poland as early as the beginning of the nineteenth century, but the freedom the peasants had then received was no better than servitude; they were individually free, but had no share in the possession of land.   By virtue of the ukase of the 2nd of March, 1864, the land of which the peasants had the use became their property, and the compensation to the landowners was defrayed by the state.

Upon this important measure followed a series of other measures, contributing to the development of the general welfare of Poland; and finally in 1869 it was declared by the imperial will that measures should be taken for the complete union of the kingdom of Poland with the other parts of the empire, by which the definitive pacification of Poland was completed.


THE SUBJECTION OF THE CAUCASUS (1864 A.D.)

The subjection of the Caucasus took place in the year after the suppression of the Polish insurrection.

Of all the nations that populated the Caucasus, only the Georgians and Armenians had succeeded, some centuries before the birth of Christ, in establishing independent kingdoms.   But being surrounded by powerful and warlike mountaineers and bounded on the south by the dominions of Persia and Turkey, the kingdoms of Georgia and Armenia had gradually fallen into decay, and therefore Georgia itself turned to Russia, as professing the same religion, with the request to be received into the empire.   Yielding to the urgent request of the unfortunate country, the emperor Paul I, who was then reigning in Russia, annexed Georgia in 1800 A.D.

After the annexation of Georgia to Russia, the mountain people made their appearance from the north and south amongst Russian possessions, but by continuing their previous plundering and incursions into Russian territory, they hindered relations between the Caucasus and the empire.   Thus, in order to secure the tranquil possession of Georgia nothing remained but to subject to Russian domination those wild tribes of the Mohammedan faith which lived in the mountains separating Russia from the Caucasus. Therefore during the first years of the nineteenth century there commenced an almost continuously persistent and truly heroic struggle of the Russian army against the Caucasian tribes, which was prolonged for more than sixty years until that definitive subjection of the Caucasus which took place during the reign of Alexander II.

## The Taking of Schamyl

The struggle against the Caucasian mountaineers was rendered peculiarly difficult at that time by the appearance of Schamyl as their leader, uniting as he did all the qualities of a brave and experienced soldier to his spiritual calling. The possessor of an iron will and an astonishing skill in ruling over the wild mountain tribes, Schamyl converted them into an organ of war which he directed against the Russians. Added to this he fortified the almost impregnable mountains, constructed excellent fortresses and established powderworks, foundries, etc. Seeing all this the Russians began to carry on a regular warfare against the mountaineers. The commander-in-chief in the Caucasus, who also exercised the functions of Caucasian viceroy, was Adjutant-general Prince Bariatinski, with whose nomination the war took a decisive turn.

Prince Bariatinski directed his efforts first of all against the eastern group of the Caucasian mountains. The general aggressive movement of the Russian army, which was accomplished after mature reflection, soon placed Schamyl in an embarrassing position which put an end to the fascination he had exercised over the mountaineers, who had hitherto been blindly devoted to him. One tribe after another fell away from Schamyl and declared its submission to Russia. Defeated and pressed on every side, Schamyl fled to Daghestan, the extreme eastern province of the Caucasus, on the shores of the Caspian Sea and took refuge with his family and a little band of adherents in the village of Gunib situated on the heights of an inaccessible mountain, where he decided to defend himself to the last. Meanwhile, the Russian troops, which had indefatigably pursued Schamyl, finally besieged him at Gunib and surrounded the village itself with a thick chain of soldiers. Upon the proposal of the commander-in-chief to put an end to the useless defence, and to spare the village the horrors of an assault, Schamyl, hitherto deemed invincible, saw his hopeless position, left his refuge, and surrendered himself as prisoner on the 6th of September, 1859, throwing himself upon the mercy of the czar. The taking of Schamyl produced an impression of astonishment on all the mountain tribes: the whole Caucasus trembled with desire for peace. After the taking of Gunib, and the captivity of Schamyl the whole eastern portion of the Caucasus submitted to the Russian domination.

After this all the efforts of the Russian troops were immediately directed towards the western Caucasus, adjoining the eastern shore of the Black Sea; but the definitive subjection of this part of the Caucasus required yet four years of uninterrupted and unrelaxed conflicts. Meanwhile, at the beginning of the year 1863, Field-marshal Prince Bariatinski was on account of impaired health replaced by a new Caucasian viceroy in the person of the emperor's youngest brother, the grand duke Michael Nikolaivitch, after which the aggressive movements of the Russian troops proceeded with such rapidity, that the entire conquest of the western portion of the Caucasus was accomplished in the spring of the year 1864. Thus ended the costly and bloody Caucasian war, and since then all the Caucasus has belonged to Russia.

## WARS WITH KHOKAND AND BOKHARA

Following on the subjection of the Caucasus, Russia began to settle accounts with three small neighbouring Mohammedan khanates, those of Khokand, Bokhara, and Khiva. These khanates were situated amidst the arid, sandy steppes of central Asia and were populated by half savage robber tribes who continually made audacious incursions upon Russian central Asian frontier possessions, attacking Russian mercantile caravans, and plundering the merchants, either killing or carrying them into captivity and selling them as slaves. All this greatly hindered Russian trade with Asia, it destroyed the tranquillity of Russian frontier possessions and therefore had long been a source of preoccupation and disquietude on the part of the Russian government.

Therefore, in 1864, two small detachments of Russian troops, under the command of Colonel Tchernaiev and General Verevkine, were despatched from two sides for the punishment of the hostile tribes and the preservation of the Russian eastern frontier from their plundering incursions. Colonel Tchernaiev, by storm, took the Khokand fortress of Auliet, while General Verevkine seized the Khokand town of Turkestan. In the following year, 1865, General Tchernaiev took by assault one of the most important towns of the Khokand khanate — Tashkend — after which the khan of Khokand ceased hostilities and declared his submission to the Russian czar.

Then, however, one of the khanates neighbouring upon that of Khokand — Bokhara — began to disturb peace on the Russian frontiers and it became necessary to quiet it. A detachment of Russian troops under the command of General Romanovski was sent against Bokhara.

The war with Bokhara was as successful as that with Khokand. In the year 1866 the chief forces of the emir of Bokhara were utterly defeated and the Russians took some towns and fortresses. But it was only after the Russian troops had taken the ancient, famous, and wealthy town of Samarkand, that the emir finally submitted, being bound by a special treaty to allow the Russian merchants entire liberty to trade in the Bokharan possessions, and to abolish slavery throughout his dominions. This greatly raised the prestige of the czar in Asia.

The newly conquered territories in central Asia (in Khokand and Bokhara) were joined to the Russian possessions, and from them was formed (in 1867) the special government general of Turkestan, with Tashkend for its chief town.[d]

## A GLANCE AT THE PAST HISTORY OF BOKHARA

It may be of interest to recall in a few words the past history of the somewhat important territory thus acquired by Russia. We have already become acquainted with Bokhara in ancient history under the name of Sogdiana; afterwards in Persian history it appears as Transoxania, or by the Arabic name of Mawarra an-nahr. The country was conquered by the Arabs in the early part of the eighth century, and towards the end of the ninth it was conquered by Ismail, the founder of the Samanids dynasty, who became emir of Bokhara and Kharezm (Khiva) in 893. Towards the end of the eleventh century the celebrated Seljuk sultan Malik Shah conquered the country beyond the Oxus, and in 1216 it came for a short time under the power of the Kharezmian prince, Muhammed Kutbuddin. In about 1220 the land was subdued by Jenghiz Khan and incorporated into the khanate of

Jagatai. Bokhara remained under the successors of Jenghiz until the whole country was overrun and conquered by Timur (Tamerlane), who selected Samarkand as his capital and raised it to a high stage of prosperity. The descendants of Timur ruled in the country until about the year 1500, when they were overthrown by the Usbeg Tatars under Muhammed Shaibani, a descendant of Shaiban, the fifth son of Juji. Muhammed ruled over Transoxania, Ferghana, Khwarizm and Hissar, but in 1510 he was defeated and killed by Shah Ismail, the founder of the Persian dynasty of Sufi.

The Shaibani dynasty ruled for nearly a century when it was replaced by the dynasty of Astrakhan, a house related to the Shaibanis by marriage. Under two rulers of this family — Iman Kuli Khan and Subhankuli Khan — Bokhara recovered somewhat of its former glory, and Subhankuli ruled over Khiva also for a time. In 1740 Bokhara had been so reduced under weak rulers that it offered its submission to Nadir Shah of Persia, and after his death the Astrakhan dynasty was overthrown by the house of Mangit (1784), which is the dynasty at present ruling in the country. Under the first sovereign of this family, Mir Maasum, Bokhara enjoyed a certain degree of prosperity, although the ruler was a cruel tyrant and a bigoted ascetic. He led a curious life of pretended piety, living in filth and misery although surrounded by wealth. He conquered and almost exterminated the city of Merv and invaded and devastated Khorassan. At his death in 1802 he was succeeded by his son Saïd, a weak ruler who lived until 1826. He was succeeded by one of the worst tyrants who ever occupied a throne — the emir Nasrullah Bahuder; he was cruel, lustful, treacherous, hypocritical, ungrateful to friends, whom he rewarded for service by putting them to death — in short, he appears to have had all the vices it is possible for a human being to have. It was during his reign that England and Russia tried to acquire influence in Bokhara. Two English envoys, Colonel Stoddart and Captain Conolly, were executed in 1842 after several years' imprisonment in a loathsome dungeon. The Russian envoy did indeed come away alive from the court of the tyrant but he succeeded in gaining no concessions for his country. Nasrullah died in 1860, his last act being to have his wife killed and her head brought to his bedside. He was succeeded by his son Mozaffer-eddin, during whose reign the Russian conquest took place.[a]

## THE CONQUEST OF KHIVA (1873 A.D.)

After Khokand and Bokhara came the turn of Khiva. In the early spring of 1873 three detachments of Russian troops marched on Khiva from different sides under the command of the governor-general of Turkestan, Adjutant-general V. P. von Kaufmann. Incredible privations and difficulties had to be borne and overcome by the Russian troops during this march across the steppes. First they endured frosts and snowstorms, and then under the sun's burning rays they courageously accomplished in the space of one month a thousand versts march across a desert, and finally reached the borders of the khanate of Khiva in the beginning of May. In three weeks' time the entire khanate was subjugated; some of the towns were taken after a combat, others surrendered without resistance, and on the 10th of June the capital of the khanate — Khiva — fell. The Russian troops entered the town in triumph, covered with fresh glory.

After the taking of Khiva by the Russians, the khan of Khiva fled to the steppes, but he afterwards returned and declared his submission, in consequence of which he was reinstated on his throne. But in spite of this a portion of the Khivan possessions fell to Russia. Besides this, the khan had to acknowledge a partial dependence upon Russia, he was obliged to reimburse her by a considerable sum of money for the expenses incurred in the campaign, and to allow the Russian merchants to trade freely in his dominions; he was pledged to discountenance plundering, to set at liberty all prisoners and slaves, and to abolish throughout his possessions forever all traffic in slaves. Thus, through the medium of the Czar Liberator, freedom was brought into central Asia — the land of slavery and of arbitrary rule. The complete pacification of a great country was accomplished.

### THE RUSSO-TURKISH WAR (1877–1878 A.D.)

Besides the wars already enumerated, Russia had, under the reign of the Czar Liberator, to carry on another war, which entailed innumerable sacrifices.

In the summer of 1875, the Slavonians of the two Turkish dependencies of Bosnia and Herzegovina, inhabited by Servian races, rose against their oppressors, the Turks, and decided to take up arms in defence of their faith, freedom, and property, and the honour of their wives and daughters, and to endeavour to obtain equal rights with the Mussulman subjects of Turkey.

In the summer of 1876 the neighbouring Slavonian principalities of Montenegro and Servia came to the aid of the Bosnians and Herzegovinians, and declared war against Turkey. The Montenegrins were under the leadership of their Prince Nicholas, and the Servian troops under the command of the Russian General Tchernaiev, the hero of Tashkend, who volunteered his services to the Slavonians.

Although Montenegro, which was small in the number of its sons, but mighty by their bravery and their love of freedom, had more than once defeated the Turkish army, Servia with her few troops could not stand against the Turkish troops, which definitively overcame the Servian forces and were about to invade the frontiers of Servia. Russia, however, did not allow this invasion to take place, and in October, 1876, the emperor Alexander II required from the Turkish sultan the immediate cessation of further hostilities against the Servians, and in order to support these demands he ordered that a portion of the Russian army should be placed on a war footing. The decisive action of the czar towards the Turkish government at once stopped the invasion of the Turkish hordes into Servia, and a two months' armistice was concluded between Servia and Turkey.

But in spite of this, the Turks continued their cruelties amongst the Christians of the Balkans; defenceless Bulgaria in particular suffered from the fury of the Turks. They traversed the country with fire and sword, striving to stifle the movement taking place there by the savage slaughter of thousands of the inhabitants, without distinction of sex or age.

For a long while Russia endeavoured to avert the situation, without having recourse to arms, in order — as Alexander II expressed it — "to avoid shedding the precious blood of the sons of Russia." But all his efforts were unsuccessful, all means of arbitration were exhausted and also the patience of that most peace-loving of monarchs, the emperor Alexander II. He found himself obliged to declare war against Turkey and to advance his troops towards the Turkish frontier. On the 19th of April, 1877, the emperor joined his army at Kishinev, where it had been commanded to assemble, and on the 24th of the same month, after public prayers, he informed the troops of their approaching entry upon the frontiers of Turkey. Thus commenced the Russo-

Turkish war, which was carried on simultaneously in two parts of the world — in Europe and in Asia.

The commander-in-chief of the Russian troops upon the Asiatic theatre of the war was the grand-duke Michael Nikolaivitch, governor of the Caucasus. A few days after the issue of the manifesto declaring war, the Russian troops had occupied the Turkish fortress of Bajazet without a struggle (April 30th), and had proceeded to besiege the first class fortress of Kars, justly regarded as one of the chief points of support of the Turkish army in Asia Minor, after which at the beginning of May they took by assault another sufficiently important Turkish fortress — that of Ardahan.

As to the Danubian army, of which the grand-duke Nicholas Nikolaivitch was appointed commander-in-chief, on the very day of the declaration of war it entered into the principality of Roumania, which was subject to Turkey, and directed its march towards the Danube. At the passage of the Danube, the problem consisted in diverting the attention of the Turks from the spot where the chief forces of the Russian army were to cross. This was accomplished with entire success; complete secrecy was maintained, and during the night between the 26th and 27th of June the Russian troops crossed the Danube with the assistance of pontoons and rafts, at a point where the Turks least expected it, namely from Zimnitzi (between the fortresses of Rustchuk and Nikopol) to Sistova; the Russian losses in this great undertaking did not exceed 1,000 men fallen from the ranks. Having thus crossed the Danube and disembarked on the enemy's shores, the Russian troops, without giving their adversaries time to recover, began to move into the heart of Bulgaria, and took town after town and fortress after fortress from the Turks.

But in Asia as well as in Europe the first brilliant successes of the Russians were followed by some serious reverses, which like the victories were first manifested upon the Asiatic seat of the war. The most serious reverse of the Russians in Asia was the unsuccessful attack (June 25th) upon the Turkish stronghold near Zeven, after which the Russian troops were obliged to raise for a time even the siege of Kars, and to retire within their own frontiers. But the temporary reverses of the Russian troops on the European theatre of the war were far more important. The most serious reverse during the entire period of the Eastern war was the attack of the Russian troops upon Plevna. Plevna was an insignificant Bulgarian town. The Russian troops hoped easily to overcome it, and on the 20th of July a small detachment of them attacked Plevna. But it turned out that the Turks had already managed to concentrate considerable forces within the little town, under the command of the best of their leaders, the gifted and resolute Osman-Pasha, added to which the most talented European engineers had constructed round Plevna, in the space of a few days, a network of fortifications, rendering Plevna an impregnable position. In consequence of this the first attack of the Russian troops on Plevna was repulsed by the Turks; the losses of the Russians amounted to three thousand killed.

Ten days later (on the 30th of July) the Russian troops made a second attack against Plevna. But this time again the attack resulted in a like defeat; the enemy's forces, which far exceeded those of the Russians, repelled all the assaults of the Russian troops, added to which this second attack on Plevna cost the Russians 7,500 men. Following upon this, with the arrival of fresh reinforcements for the army encamped before Plevna, a third and final heroic effort was made to take this fortified position by storm. The chief part in the attack was taken by the brave young general Skobelev and his detachment. But in spite of his brilliant action, in spite of the heroism

and self-sacrifice displayed by his soldiers, this assault also was unsuccessful.
On the 12th of September, Skobelev repulsed five furious attacks by the whole
mass of Turks, but not receiving assistance, he was obliged to retreat.  This
last reverse cost the Russians as many as 3,000 killed and nearly 10,000
wounded.  But following on these reverses came a rapidly successive series
of victories of the Russian troops over the Turkish, both in Asia and in
Europe.

The crowning success of the Russian troops in Asia was the fall on the
18th of November of the terrible stronghold of Kars, which was taken by
General Loris-Melikov, after a heroic assault by night.  All Europe recognised the taking of Kars as one of the greatest and most difficult of military
exploits ever achieved.  At the same time, on the European theatre of the
war, on the southern slope of the Balkans a great Turkish body of troops was
concentrated under the command of the talented leader Suleiman Pasha, with
the object of retaking at any cost the Shipka pass, which was occupied by a
small Russian detachment.  During the space of seven days (from the 21st
to the 28th of August) the Turks endeavoured to wrest from the Russians the
Shipka pass, and a series of furious attacks was made with this object.  On
the first two days a handful of heroes, who defended the heights of Shipka,
repulsed all the desperate efforts of Suleiman Pasha's entire army!  The echo
of the incessant artillery fire became one endless roll of thunder.  The Russian ranks dwindled and were exhausted from wounds and fatigue.  It was
at that time that the Russian gunners, under the command of General Radetzki came to their assistance, and by the 24th of August fresh reinforcements
arrived.  The Turks' insane attacks still continued during the 25th, 26th
and 27th, but on the evening of the 27th of August all was suddenly quiet;
the Turks had become convinced that they could not overcome the steadfast-
ness and bravery of the Russian troops defending the Shipka pass, and had
retired.

Meanwhile, after the third attempt on Plevna, it was decided not to renew
any more such dearly bought attacks, but to limit operations to encircling
the Turkish positions in order to cut off communication between Plevna and
the surrounding places, and thus to starve the Turks into surrender.

At the end of October General Gurko's division, amongst which were the
guards, took Gorni Dubinak, Telisch and a series of other Turkish strongholds, situated to the southwest of Plevna and protecting the Sophia road,
along which reinforcements and stores had hitherto been brought into Plevna,
and thus to cut off entirely all communications between that town and the
outside.  After less than a month's time all the provisions that the Turks
had in Plevna were definitively exhausted.  On the morning of the 10th of
December, Osman Pasha, being desirous of penetrating through the Russian
lines to the Danube, made a violent attempt to get out of Plevna.  He cut
his way through, but after some hours of desperate fighting — during which
he was wounded in the leg — he was thrown back and compelled to surrender,
with all his army to the number of more than 40,000 men.  This heated action
cost the Russians 600 men killed, and double that amount wounded.

Taking deeply to heart the successes of his valiant army and the holy
work for which it was fighting, the emperor Alexander II had at the end of
May, 1877, at the very commencement, that is, of the war, arrived in Bulgaria, and in spite of the weak state of his health had remained all the while
amongst the acting army of the Danube, sharing all reverses and privations
of military life on the march.

"I go as a brother of mercy," said the czar when he set off for the active army. And actually, leaving to others all the martial glory of victory over the enemy, the emperor concentrated his attention upon the sick and wounded soldiers to whom he showed himself not a brother, but a very father of mercy. Zealously visiting the sick and wounded soldiers in the hospitals and ambulances, the emperor showed them heartfelt sympathy, comforted, encouraged, and sustained the sufferers, listened to their tales with fatherly love, and with his own hand rewarded those who had distinguished themselves by their services in battle.

The wounded and their families were the object of the emperor Alexander's unwearied care. He was rejoiced when the provisions sent out for the use of the wounded by the empress Marie Alexandrovna arrived from St. Petersburg. Alexander unfailingly distributed them himself, carefully inquiring of each soldier what he wanted, what he liked, and strove to satisfy each sufferer: to the musicians he gave accordions, to the readers books, to the smokers tobacco pouches, to the non-smokers tea, dainties, etc. Both soldiers and officers were as pleased as children at receiving presents from the hand of the royal "brother of mercy," and listening to his cordial, gracious words. The soldiers' love for the emperor, their joy and rapture at seeing him acted like living water on the wounded; everyone that could move strove to rise, to stand up, to take courage; they stretched out their hands to the czar, kissed his raiment and blessed his name. It was only after the fall of Plevna when the war clearly inclined to the advantage of the Russians, and further success was entirely secured that the emperor, bidding farewell to his troops, left the active army and in the beginning of December, 1877, returned to Russia.

Immediately after the taking of Plevna it was decided that, without losing time, the Balkans should be crossed. Meanwhile a severe winter had already set in and the Turks did not even admit the possibility of the Russian troops crossing the Balkans at such a time. But here again all the valour of the Russian army was displayed. To take a whole army across the Balkans in winter was a work of the very greatest difficulty and danger; but to cross the Trievna pass had never yet been attempted by any army in the world. Strictly speaking, the chief part of the Russian army crossed the Balkans at two other points, but it was part of the Russian strategy to carry an insignificant portion of the troops across by the Trievna pass in order that the attention of the Turks should be diverted from the chief army, and the passage of the latter thus be facilitated. The accomplishment of this terribly difficult and almost impossible feat was entrusted to General Kartzov's division. On the night between the 3rd and 4th of January the division moved on its road. After having reached by incredible efforts the very summit of the pass, where a short time was spent, on the 7th of January General Kartzov's division stormed the Turkish redoubt, forced their way into it and drove out the Turks. After this the Russians had to descend to the so-called Valley of Roses on the southern slope of the Balkans, which was even much steeper than the northern. As soon as the Russians had come down from Trievna, the Turks abandoned their positions at the feet of the Great Balkans, and General Kartzov's division entered into communication on one side with General Gurko's division, and on the other with the Shipka division of General Radetzki.

After descending the Balkans to the Valley of Roses, General Radetzki, together with General Skobelev, who had come to his assistance after the fall of Plevna, attacked on the 9th of January an army of 40,000 Turks at Kezanlik, who after a stubborn resistance were defeated and taken prisoners. After having devastated and scattered the Turkish army of Shipka and accomplished the feat unexampled in history of the passage of the Balkans, the Russian army continued its victorious advance; Adrianople, the second capital of the Turkish empire, was taken without a struggle and the troops drew near to Constantinople itself. Then, on the 3rd of March, 1878, at a little place called San Stefano, at ten versts from Constantinople, Turkey signed the conditions of peace offered her by Russia.

Meanwhile the great European powers required that three conditions of peace should be submitted to their consideration, and thus the treaty of San Stefano showed itself to be only a preliminary one; the great European powers ratified it only after considerable changes. These altered conditions of peace were signed in 1878 by the plenipotentiaries of all the great powers at the Congress of Berlin; after which on the 8th of February, 1879, a final treaty of peace, based on these same conditions, was signed at Constantinople between Russia and Turkey.

The emperor Alexander might certainly with full right have insisted on the ratification of the treaty of peace of San Stefano without any alterations; but then Russia would have incurred a fresh war with Europe, while the emperor deeply felt the necessity of peace. It was time to give the Russian people rest after they had made such sacrifices in the struggle for their Slavonian brethren! Pitying his people, the emperor decided — however painful it might be to him — not to insist on all that had been gained at the price of Russian blood and confirmed by the treaty of San Stefano with Turkey, but consented in Berlin to great concessions which did not, however, in any way interfere with the liberation of the Christian population of Turkey.

By the treaties of San Stefano and Berlin, that part of Bessarabia was returned to Russia which, by the Peace of Paris in 1856, had been ceded to her by Turkey after the Crimean campaign. Thanks to this, Russia again reached the mouths of the river Danube; in Asia she acquired a portion of the Turkish possessions, with the port of Batum and the fortress of Kars, which guaranteed her security and future development. Finally, in compensating for the military expenditure incurred by Russia, Turkey was bound to pay her an indemnity of 300 million rubles.

Thus terminated the Russo-Turkish War of 1877-1878 — that decisive struggle for the liberation of the Slavonians of the Balkan peninsula, and although in consequence of the interference of Europe Russia was far from attaining what she had a right to expect after the enormous sacrifices she had made, and the glorious victories she had gained, nevertheless the great and sacred object of the war was attained; on the memorable day of the emancipation of the peasants in Russia, also the Slavonian nations of the Balkan peninsula were liberated, by the help of Russia and her great monarch, from the Turkish yoke which had oppressed them for ages. To the emperor Alexander II, who gave freedom to many millions of his own subjects, was allotted also the glorious rôle of liberator of the Balkan Christians, by whom he was a second time named the Czar Liberator!

### SPREAD OF EDUCATION AND CIVILISATION

The new order of things established in Russia, thanks to the great reforms of Emperor Alexander II, called forth a particular want of educated, enlightened men. They were necessary to the wise interpretation and execution of the luminous ideas of the czar-liberator.

Recognising that the spread of education amongst the people is an indispensable condition of its prosperity, the emperor Alexander II, who had

[1878 A.D.]

become convinced by a personal survey of Russia, that one of the chief obstacles to her progress lay in the ignorance of the people, wished to give to his subjects the means for the highest degree of enlightenment. This solicitude was expressed in a radical reform of all the educational establishments of the empire, beginning with the university and finishing with the national schools. Properly speaking, it may be asserted that the primary national schools and village schools were created during the reign of Alexander II, for until his reign the primary education of the people was in a sad condition, and amongst them an almost total ignorance prevailed.

His legislation for the education of the masses should justly be numbered amongst the most important works of the Czar Liberator. But many were the other reforms accomplished by him that also had a great and beneficent signification for the Russian people. During the reign of the emperor Alexander II the country which had until then but few means of intercommunication, became covered with a network of railways. In conjunction with the extraordinarily rapid development of railway communication, the postal service was perfected, the telegraph made its appearance, while commerce and trade acquired wide development. Finally, essential changes and improvements were introduced into the financial administration of the empire; the police was reorganised and certain modifications were granted to the press, in consequence of which there was a powerful awakening in the intellectual life of the people.

A WINTER COSTUME

## THE DEATH OF ALEXANDER II

In studying the wars which took place during the reign of Alexander II, it is impossible not to remark that they were all entered upon and carried on, not under the influence of ambition, not with the thirst for conquest, but exclusively out of a feeling of humanity, in order to preserve those living on the frontiers of the Russian empire from the plundering incursions of half savage Asiatic tribes (as was the case in the subjection of the Caucasus, of Khokand, Bokhara, and Khiva), or for the deliverance of the oppressed coreligionists of Russia (as, for example, the deliverance of the Slavonians of the Balkans).

The emperor Alexander II was actively solicitous for the welfare of his subjects during the twenty-six years of his glorious reign, never losing sight of the exaltation of the country and the consolidation of the prosperity of the nation. But in spite of the indefatigable labours and fatherly care of the emperor Alexander II, in spite of the enormous services he rendered to the country, of his boundless goodness of heart, his great clemency and unusual humanity — amongst the Russian people were to be found those who had

more than once tried by violence to shake the existing state and social organisation of Russia and who did not stop at any crime for the attainment of
their ends. Their boundless audacity finally reached the last limits, and
they dared more than once to make attempts on the life of the Czar-Liberator.

On the 2nd of March, 1880, the 25th year of the reign of the emperor
Alexander II was accomplished, and this memorable day was celebrated with
heartfelt enthusiasm in both capitals and throughout the whole Russian
Empire. But amongst the millions of joyous Russian hearts, for one man
alone in Russia the festivity was not a festivity. That man was the czar
himself, the creator of the happiness of many millions of Russians and the
cause of the rejoicings. The emperor did not doubt the sincere affection of
the people towards him; he knew and felt that Russia loved her czar with
all her soul; but at the same time he knew and felt, that in spite of all the
glory of his reign, in spite of the great measures he had accomplished, the
Russian land bore a handful of malcontents, whose designs it was beyond
the power of anyone to arrest.

The fatal 13th of March, 1881, came. About one o'clock in the afternoon
the emperor drove in a carriage from the Winter Palace in St. Petersburg,
accompanied by his usual escort, to the Michael riding school to assist at a
grand military parade, appointed to take place that day. Coming out of
the riding school at the end of the parade, at about a quarter to three, and
learning that the grand duke Michael Nikolaivitch, who was present at the
parade intended to visit the grand duchess Catherine Mikhailovna at the
Mikhailovski palace, the emperor proposed to his brother that they should
go together. After spending about half an hour at the Mikhailovski palace
the emperor came out alone, without the grand duke and told the coachman
to "drive home by the same way." The carriage set off along the Catherine
canal, in the direction of the Theatre bridge.

At three o'clock in the afternoon, at a distance of about 350 feet from
the corner of the Engineer street, the emperor's carriage as it drove along the
side of the canal, past the garden of the Mikhailovski palace, came alongside
a young man at the foot-path of the canal; he afterwards turned out to be
the citizen Nicholas Ivanovitch Rissakov. When he came on a line with the
imperial carriage, Rissakov turned his face towards it, and before the escort
could notice anything, quickly threw beneath the feet of the horses harnessed
to the carriage something white like snow, which afterwards turned out to be
an explosive instrument wrapped up in a handkerchief. At the same instant
a deafening crash, like a salvo of artillery, resounded; two Cossacks riding
behind the czar's equipage fell from their horses wounded, and a fourteen
year old peasant boy, mortally wounded, lay groaning on the pavement; a
thick cloud of snow and splinters filled the air. The emperor's carriage
appeared much damaged by the explosion, all the four windows and the little
glass behind were broken, the frame of the door was splintered at the side
and back, the side of the carriage was broken and the bottom seriously
injured. When he had thrown the explosive instrument under the carriage,
Rissakov began to run off in the direction of the Nevski Prospect, but at a
few yards from the spot where the explosion had taken place, he slipped,
fell, and was seized by some soldiers who came up. The emperor himself
was entirely uninjured. He ordered the coachman to stop the horses, opened
the left door, got out of the carriage, and went to the spot where Rissakov
was already surrounded by a crowd of people.

Then, when the emperor, desiring to examine the spot where the explosion
had taken place, had left Rissakov, and had made a few steps along the path-

[1881 A.D.]

way of the canal, another man — who turned out to be a Pole named Grine-vetzki — waiting till the emperor was at a distance of two yards from him, raised his arms and threw something on the footpath at the very feet of the emperor. At the same moment, not more than four or five minutes after the first explosion, another deafening explosion was heard, after which a mass of smoke, snow and scraps of clothing enveloped everything for some moments. When the column of smoke dispersed, to the stricken gaze of the spectators a truly awful sight was presented: about twenty men more or less severely wounded by the two explosions lay on the pavement, and amongst them was the emperor. Leaning his back against the railing of the canal, without his cap or riding cloak, half sitting on the footpath, was the monarch; he was covered with blood and breathing with difficulty; the bare legs of the august martyr were both broken, the blood flowed copiously from them, and his face was covered with blood. The cap and cloak that had fallen from the emperor's head and shoulders, and of which there remained but blood-stained and burnt fragments, lay beside him.

At the sight of such an unexpected, such an incredible disaster, not only the uninjured, but also the sufferers from the explosion rushed to the emperor's help. Raising the wounded emperor, who was already losing consciousness, the persons who surrounded him, with the grand duke Michael, who had arrived on the spot, carried him to the sledge of Colonel Dvorginski, who had been following the emperor's equipage. Leaning over the emperor's shoulder, the grand duke inquired if he heard, to which the emperor replied, "I hear," and then in answer to the question of how he felt the emperor said: "Quicker . . . to the palace," and then as if answering the proposal to take him to the nearest house to get help, the emperor said, "Take me to the palace to die . . . there." These were the last words of the dying monarch, heard by an eye-witness of the awful crime of the 13th of March. After this the emperor was placed in Colonel Dvorginzki's sledge and transported to the Winter Palace. When the palace was reached the emperor was already unconscious, and at 25 minutes of 4 o'clock Alexander II was no more.

The emperor Alexander II was great not only as the czar of a nation of many millions, but by a life devoted to the welfare of his subjects; he was great as the incarnation of goodness, love and clemency. The autocratic monarch of one of the vastest empires of the world, this czar was governed in all his actions by the dictates of his loving heart. Showing himself a great example of self-sacrificing human love, he lived only in order to exalt the land of Russia, to alleviate the necessities and consolidate the welfare of his people.[d]

# CHAPTER XIII

## REACTION, EXPANSION, AND THE WAR WITH JAPAN

### [1881–1904 A.D.]

In the history of Russia the period extending from 1882 to 1902 was much less eventful than the thirty years immediately preceding. The reign of Alexander II had been a time of important administrative reforms and of great economic, social, and intellectual changes in the life of the nation. Serfage had been abolished, the emancipated peasantry had been made communal proprietors of the soil, a democratic system of rural and municipal self-government for local affairs had been introduced, the tribunals of all degrees had been radically reorganised, means had been taken for developing more energetically the vast natural resources of the country, public instruction had received an unprecedented impetus, a considerable amount of liberty had been accorded to the press, a liberal spirit had been suddenly evoked and had spread rapidly among all sections of the educated classes, a new imaginative and critical literature dealing largely with economic, philosophical, and social questions had sprung into existence, and for a time the young generation fondly imagined that Russia, awakening from her traditional lethargy, was about to overtake, and soon to surpass, on the paths of national progress, the more advanced nations of western Europe.

These sanguine expectations were not fully realised. The economic and moral condition of the peasantry was not much improved, and in many districts there were signs of positive impoverishment and demoralisation. Local self-government, after a short period of feverish and not always well-directed activity, showed symptoms of organic exhaustion. The reformed tribunals, though incomparably better than their predecessors, did not give universal satisfaction. In the imperial administration the corruption and long-established abuses which had momentarily vanished began to reappear. Industrial enterprises did not always succeed. Education produced many unforeseen and undesirable practical results. The liberty of the press not unfrequently degenerated into license. The liberal spirit, which had at first confined itself to demanding feasible reforms, soon soared into the region of socialistic dreaming and revolutionary projects.

In short, it became only too evident that there was no royal road to national prosperity, and that Russia, like other nations, must be content to advance slowly and laboriously along the rough path of painful experience. In these circumstances sanguine enthusiasm naturally gave way to despondency, and the reforming zeal of the government was replaced by tendencies of a decidedly reactionary kind. Already in the last years of the reign of Alexander II, these tendencies had found expression in ukases and ministerial circulars, and zealous liberalism was more and more discountenanced in the official world. Partly from a feeling of despondency, and partly from a conviction that the country required rest in order to judge the practical results of the reforms already accomplished, the czar refrained from initiating any new legislation of an important kind, and the government gave it to be understood that the period of radical reforms was closed.

In the younger ranks of the educated classes this state of things had produced much dissatisfaction, which soon found expression in revolutionary agitation. At first the agitation was of an academic character, and was dealt with by the press censure, but it gradually took the form of secret associations, and the police had to interfere. There were no great, well-organised secret societies, but there were many small groups, composed chiefly of male and female students of the universities and technical schools, which worked independently for a common purpose. That purpose was the overthrow of the existing régime and the reorganisation of society on collectivist principles. Finding that the walls of autocracy could not be overturned by blasts of revolutionary trumpets, the young enthusiasts determined to seek the support of the masses, or, as they termed it, "to go in among the people" (*idti v narod*). Under the guise of doctors, midwives, teachers, governesses, factory hands, or common labourers, they sought to make proselytes among the peasantry and the workmen in the industrial centres by revolutionary pamphlets and oral explanations.

For a time the propaganda had very little success, because the uneducated peasants and factory workers could not easily understand the phraseology and principles of scientific socialism; but when the propagandists descended to a lower platform and spread rumours that the czar had given all the land to the peasants, and that the proprietors were preventing his benevolent intentions from being carried into effect, there was a serious danger of agrarian disturbances, and energetic measures were adopted by the authorities. Wholesale arrests were made by the police, and many of the accused were imprisoned or exiled to distant provinces, some by the regular judicial procedure, and others by so-called "administrative procedure," without trial. The activity of the police and the sufferings of the victims naturally produced intense excitement and bitterness among those who escaped, and a secret body calling itself the executive committee announced in its clandestinely printed organs that those who distinguished themselves by endeavouring to suppress the propaganda would be removed. A number of officials had been condemned to death by this secret terrorist tribunal, and in some cases its sentences were carried out. As these terrorist measures had quite the opposite of the desired effect, repeated attempts had been made on the life of the emperor. At last, on the 13th of March, 1881, the carefully-laid plans of the conspirators, [as related in the last chapter], were successful.

## THE REACTIONARY POLICY UNDER ALEXANDER III

Finding repressive police measures insufficient to suppress the revolutionary movement, Alexander II had entertained the idea of giving a certain satisfaction to moderate liberal opinion without restricting his autocratic power. With this object in view he had appointed General Loris-Melikov, who was credited with liberal views, minister of the interior, and on the morning of his death he had signed a ukase creating several commissions, composed of high official personages and eminent private individuals, who should prepare reforms in various branches of the administration.

His son and successor Alexander III (1881–94), who had never shown much sympathy with liberalism in any form, entered frankly on a reactionary policy, which was pursued consistently during the whole of his reign. He could not, of course, undo the great reforms of his predecessor, but he amended them in such a way as to counteract what he considered the exaggerations of liberalism.   Local self-government in the village communes, the

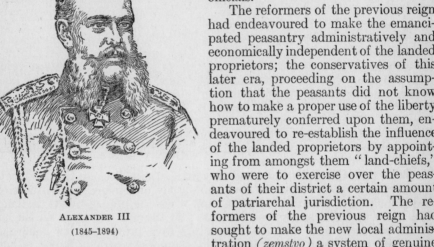

rural districts, and the towns was carefully restricted, and placed to a greater extent under the control of the regular officials.

The reformers of the previous reign had endeavoured to make the emancipated peasantry administratively and economically independent of the landed proprietors; the conservatives of this later era, proceeding on the assumption that the peasants did not know how to make a proper use of the liberty prematurely conferred upon them, endeavoured to re-establish the influence of the landed proprietors by appointing from amongst them "land-chiefs," who were to exercise over the peasants of their district a certain amount of patriarchal jurisdiction.   The reformers of the previous reign had sought to make the new local administration (*zemstvo*) a system of genuine

ALEXANDER III
(1845–1894)

rural self-government and a basis for future parliamentary institutions; these later conservatives transformed it into a mere branch of the ordinary state administration, and took precautions against its ever assuming a political character.   Even municipal institutions, which had never shown much vitality, were subjected to similar restrictions.   In short, the various forms of local self-government, which were intended to raise the nation gradually to the higher political level of western Europe, were condemned as unsuited to the national character and traditions, and as productive of disorder and demoralisation.   They were accordingly replaced in great measure by the old autocratic methods of administration, and much of the administrative corruption which had been cured, or at least repressed, by the reform enthusiasm again flourished luxuriantly.

In a small but influential section of the educated classes there was a conviction that the revolutionary tendencies, which culminated in nihilism and anarchism, proceeded from the adoption of cosmopolitan rather than national principles in all spheres of educational and administrative activity, and that the best remedy for the evils from which the country was suffering was to be found in a return to the three great principles of nationality, orthodoxy, and autocracy.   This doctrine, which had been invented by the Slavophils of a previous generation, was early instilled into the mind of Alexander III by Pobiedonostsev, who was one of his teachers, and later his most trusted adviser, and its influence can be traced in all the more important acts of the government during that monarch's reign. His determination to maintain autocracy was officially proclaimed a few days after his accession. Nationality and eastern orthodoxy, which are so closely connected as to be almost blended together in the Russian mind, received not less attention.

## THE RUSSIFICATION OF THE PROVINCES

Even in European Russia the regions near the frontier contain a great variety of nationalities, languages, and religions. In Finland the population is composed of Finnish-speaking and Swedish-speaking Protestants; the Baltic provinces are inhabited by German-speaking, Lett-speaking, and Esth-speaking Lutherans; the inhabitants of the southwestern provinces are chiefly Polish-speaking Roman Catholics and Yiddish-speaking Jews; in the Crimea and on the middle Volga there are a considerable number of Tatar-speaking Mohammedans; and in the Caucasus there is a conglomeration of races and languages such as is to be found on no other portion of the earth's surface. Until recent times these various nationalities were allowed to retain unmolested the language, religion, and peculiar local administration of their ancestors, but when the new nationality doctrine came into fashion attempts were made to spread among them the language, religion, and administrative institutions of the dominant race. In the reigns of Nicholas I and Alexander II these attempts were merely occasional and intermittent; under Alexander III they were made systematically and with very little consideration for the feelings, wishes, and interests of the people concerned. The local institutions were assimilated to those of the purely Russian provinces; the use of the Russian language was made obligatory in the administration, in the tribunals, and to some extent in the schools; the spread of eastern orthodoxy was encouraged by the authorities, whilst the other confessions were placed under severe restrictions; foreigners were prohibited from possessing landed property, and in some provinces administrative measures were taken for making the land pass into the hands of orthodox Russians. In this process some of the local officials displayed probably an amount of zeal beyond the intentions of the government, but any attempt to oppose the movement was rigorously punished.

Of all the various races the Jews were the most severely treated. The great majority of them had long been confined to the western and southwestern provinces. In the rest of the country they had not been allowed to reside in the villages, because their habits of keeping vodka-shops and lending money at usurious interest were found to demoralise the peasantry, and even in the towns their number and occupations had been restricted by the authorities. But, partly from the usual laxity of the administration and partly from the readiness of the Jews to conciliate the needy officials, the rules had been by no means strictly applied. As soon as this fact became known to Alexander III he ordered the rules to be strictly carried out, without considering what an enormous amount of hardship and suffering such an order entailed. He also caused new rules to be enacted by which his Jewish subjects were heavily handicapped in education and professional advancement. In short, complete russification of all non-Russian populations and institutions was the chief aim of the government in home affairs.

FOREIGN POLICY; THE FRENCH ALLIANCE

In the foreign policy of the empire Alexander III likewise introduced considerable changes. During his father's reign its main objects were: in the west, the maintenance of the alliance with Germany; in south-eastern Europe, the recovery of what had been lost by the Crimean war, the gradual weakening of the sultan's authority, and the increase of Russian influence among the minor slav nationalities; in Asia, the gradual but cautious expansion of Russian domination. In the reign of Alexander III the first of these objects was abandoned. Already, before his accession, the bonds of friendship which united Russia to Germany had been weakened by the action of Bismarck in giving to the cabinet of St. Petersburg at the Berlin congress less diplomatic support than was expected, and by the Austro-German treaty of alliance (October, 1879), concluded avowedly for the purpose of opposing Russian aggression; but the old relations were partly re-established by secret negotiations in 1880, by a meeting of the young czar and the old emperor at Dantzic in 1881, and by the meeting of the three emperors at Skiernewice in 1884, by which the Three Emperors' League was reconstituted for a term of three years.

Gradually, however, a great change took place in the czar's views with regard to the German alliance. He suspected Bismarck of harbouring hostile designs against Russia, and he came to recognise that the permanent weakening of France was not in accordance with Russian political interests. He determined, therefore, to oppose any further disturbance of the balance of power in favour of Germany, and when the treaty of Skiernewice expired in 1887, he declined to renew it. From that time Russia gravitated slowly towards an alliance with France, and sought to create a counterpoise against the Triple Alliance of Germany, Austria, and Italy. The czar was reluctant to bind himself by a formal treaty, because the French government did not offer the requisite guarantees of stability, and because he feared that it might be induced, by the prospects of Russian support, to assume an aggressive attitude towards Germany. He recognised, however, that in the event of a great European war the two nations would in all probability be found fighting on the same side, and that if they made no preparations for concerted military action they would be placed at a grave disadvantage in comparison with their opponents of the Triple Alliance, who were believed to have already worked out an elaborate plan of campaign. In view of this contingency the Russian and French military authorities studied the military questions in common, and the result of their labours was the preparation of a military convention, which was finally ratified in 1894. During this period the relations between the two governments and the two countries became much more cordial. In the summer of 1891 the visit to Kronstad of a French squadron under Admiral Gervais was made the occasion for an enthusiastic demonstration in favour of a Franco-Russian alliance; and two years later (October, 1893) a still more enthusiastic reception was given to the Russian admiral Avelan and his officers when they visited Toulon and Paris. But it was not till after the death of Alexander III that the word "alliance" was used publicly by official personages. In 1895 the term was first publicly employed by Ribot, then president of the council, in the chamber of deputies, but the expressions he used were so vague that they did not entirely remove the prevailing doubts as to the existence of a formal treaty. Two years later (August, 1897), during the official visit of President Félix Faure to St. Petersburg, a little more light was thrown on the subject. In the complimentary speeches delivered by the president of the French Republic and the czar, France and Russia were referred to as allies, and the term *nations alliées* was afterwards repeatedly used on occasions of a similar kind.

In south-eastern Europe Alexander III adopted an attitude of reserve and expectancy. He greatly increased and strengthened his Black Sea fleet, so as to be ready for any emergency that might arise, and in June, 1886, contrary to the declaration made in the Treaty of Berlin (Article 59), he ordered Batum to be transformed into a fortified naval port, but in the Balkan Peninsula he persistently refrained, under a good deal of provocation, from any intervention that might lead to a European war. The Bulgarian government, first under Prince Alexander and afterwards under the direction of Stambolov, pursued systematically an anti-Russian policy, but the cabinet of St. Petersburg confined itself officially to breaking off diplomatic relations and making diplomatic protests, and unofficially to giving tacit encouragement to revolutionary agitation. In Asia, during the reign of Alexander III, the expansion of Russian domination made considerable progress.[b]

### THE CONQUEST OF THE TEKKE-TURCOMANS (1877-1881 A.D.)

Transcaspia is the official name given to the territory east of the Caspian which was annexed by Russia in 1881 shortly after the accession of Alexander III. The country was inhabited by the Turcomans — a branch of the Turkish race — who have been identified with the old Parthians. They were a brave but wild and lawless people, bands of whom would frequently sweep down upon a peaceful village, kill the men, and carry off the women and children to be sold as slaves in Bokhara and Khiva. Whole villages were sometimes wiped out in this way. The maurauding raids of the Turcomans were a constant menace to the northern frontier of Persia and we frequently find the Persians engaged in war with them. The great Nadir Shah was himself a Turcoman. In 1861 the Persians had made a final attack on the Turcomans or Tekkes, as they are commonly called, and defeated them.

The Russian conquest of the Central Asian khanates, however, materially altered the situation of these nomadic robbers; they could no longer sell slaves in Bokhara, as the Russian laws forbade slavery, neither could they carry on their depredations in lands guarded by the Russians, hence they turned to Persia and offered her their allegiance in return for her support against these civilised intruders. But they were now a serious obstacle in the way of these same Russians. Caravans from Bokhara and the East, to reach the Caspian, had to cross the Turcoman desert or else make a long detour to the north, and these plundering tribes seriously interfered with commerce.

In 1877 General Lomakin was sent against the Tekkes, but the Russo-Turkish war intervened before he had accomplished anything. In 1878 Lomakin attacked Dengil Teppe, was defeated by the Tekkes, and forced to retreat. The natives were greatly encouraged by this victory, their raids increased, and they tried to stir up the Bokharans and Khivans to revolt. The Russians now undertook more vigorous measures. General Skobelev was put in charge of the campaign, a portable railway was started from the shores of the Caspian towards the Amu Daria, a large force of artillery was conveyed to the front, and a water distillery — of the greatest service in this waterless region — was established at Krasnovodsk. Colonel Kuropatkin, who had been on Skobelev's staff in the Russo-Turkish war, came by forced marches to assist his former chief.

The Turcomans were intrenched in three camps — Yangi Kala, Dangil Teppe, and Geok Teppe. The Russians began the main attack on January 1st, 1881, charging first upon Yangi Kala. The Tekkes fought with the greatest bravery, but the Russian artillery forced them to evacuate. The Turcoman sorties were made usually a little after sunset and the attacks were exceedingly fierce. The Tekkes had their wives and children in camp with them, huddled in their felt tents, and their sufferings under the continual artillery fire must have been terrible. Finally upon January 24th, after three weeks of fighting, the Russians were successful, the Tekkes were routed

CATHEDRAL OF THE ARCHANGEL MICHAEL

with great loss to both Russians and Turcomans. There are different estimates given as the total number killed.

Beverdidge's [c] figures, given below, cannot be far from right. He uses this siege to illustrate the Russian method of conquest. Their method, he says, "is to wage war while war exists and to employ the methods of peace only when war is over. Skobelev at Geok Teppe refused to accept the surrender of the heroic Tekkes who had terrorised Central Asia for centuries, and he slaughtered more than twenty thousand men, women and children in twenty days. It seemed quite terrible and was as terrible as it seemed; but it is hard to see that it is much worse to destroy 20,000 men, women, and children and secure peace for all time than it is to kill that number during twenty years and in the process increase the irritation, the disorder, and the feud. For from the red day of Geok Teppe to this hour, order, law, safety to travellers, security of commerce and all other things which help to make up civilisation have existed in Central Asia, as firmly guarded as they are in the United States. War is bad under any circumstances, but if it must be it should be thorough, that it may be brief and not fruitless."

After calling attention to the efficacy of this method in Manchuria during the Boxer movement, the author continues: "It is worth the attention of all men that when Russia has once inflicted her punishment there has seldom been any recurrence of insurrection. Where Russian law and order and system have been established they have remained, upheld not by the bayonets of the soldiers who established them, but by the hands of the very people among whom and against whose resistance they were planted. Among all the defects of Russian civilisation, its virtues are striking and elemental, and one of the chief of them is stability."

The country of the Turcomans thus conquered was annexed to the Russian Empire, the final annexation of Merv taking place in 1884.[a] Alexander III then allowed the military authorities to push forward in the direction of Afghanistan, until in March, 1885, an engagement took place between Russian and Afghan forces at Penjdeh. Thereupon the British government, which had been for some time carrying on negotiations with the cabinet of St. Petersburg for a delimitation of the Russo-Afghan frontier, intervened energetically and prepared for war; but a compromise was effected, and after more than two years of negotiation a delimitation convention was signed at St. Petersburg on July 20th, 1887. The forward movement of Russia was thus stopped in the direction of Herat, but it continued with great activity farther east in the region of the Pamir, until another Anglo-Russian convention was signed in 1895. During the whole reign of Alexander III the increase of territory in central Asia is calculated by Russian authorities at 429,895 square kilometres.

## ACCESSION OF NICHOLAS II (1894 A.D.)

On November 1st, 1894, Alexander III died, and was succeeded by his son, Nicholas II, who, partly from similarity of character and partly from veneration for his father's memory, continued the existing lines of policy in home and foreign affairs. The expectation entertained in many quarters that great legislative changes would at once be made in a liberal sense was not realised. When an influential deputation from the province of Tver, which had long enjoyed a reputation for liberalism, ventured to hint in a loyal address that the time had come for changes in the existing autocratic régime they received a reply which showed that the emperor had no intention of making any such changes. Private suggestions in the same sense, offered directly and respectfully, were no better received and no important changes were made in the legislation of the preceding reign. But a great alteration took place noiselessly in the manner of carrying out the laws and ministerial circulars.

Though resembling his father in the main points of his character, the young czar was of a more humane disposition, and he was much less of a doctrinaire. With his father's aspiration of making holy Russia a homogeneous empire he thoroughly sympathised in principle, but he disliked the systematic persecution of Jews, heretics, and schismatics to which it gave rise, and he let it be understood, without any formal order or proclamation, that the severe measures hitherto employed would not meet with his approval. The officials were not slow to take the hint, and their undue zeal at once disappeared. Nicholas II showed, however, that his father's policy of russification was neither to be reversed nor to be abandoned.   When an influential deputation was sent from Finland to St. Petersburg to represent to him respectfully that the officials were infringing the local rights and privileges solemnly accorded at the time of the annexation, it was refused an audience, and the leaders of the movement were informed indirectly that local interests must be subordinated to the general welfare of the empire.   In accordance with this declaration, the policy of russification in Finland was steadily maintained and caused much disappointment, not only to the Finlanders, but also to the other nationalities who desired the preservation of their ancient rights.

COUNT LYEFF TOLSTOI
(1828—)

In foreign affairs Nicholas II likewise continued the policy of his predecessor, with certain modifications suggested by the change of circumstances. He strengthened the cordial understanding with France by a formal agreement, the terms of which were not divulged, but he never encouraged the French government in any aggressive designs, and he maintained friendly relations with Germany.   In the Balkan Peninsula a slight change of attitude took place.   Alexander III, indignant at what he considered the ingratitude of the Slav nationalities, remained coldly aloof, as far as possible, from all intervention in their affairs. About three months after his death, De Giers, who thoroughly approved of this attitude, died (January 26th, 1895), and his successor, Prince Lobanov, minister of foreign affairs from March 19th, 1895, to August 30th, 1896, endeavoured to recover what he considered Russia's legitimate influence in the Slav world.

For this purpose Russian diplomacy became more active in south-eastern Europe.   The result was perceived first in Montenegro and Servia, and then in Bulgaria.   Prince Ferdinand of Bulgaria had long been anxious to legalise his position by a reconciliation, and as soon as he got rid of Stambulov he made advances to the Russian government.   They were well received, and a reconciliation was effected on certain conditions, the first of which was that Prince Ferdinand's eldest son and heir should become a member of the Eastern orthodox church.   As another means of opposing Western influence in south-eastern Europe, Prince Lobanov inclined to the policy of protecting rather than weakening the Ottoman empire.   When the British government seemed disposed to use coercive measures for the protection of the Armenians, he gave it clearly to be understood that any such proceeding would be opposed by Russia.

After Prince Lobanov's death and the appointment of Count Muraviev as his successor in January, 1897, this tendency of Russian policy became less marked. In April, 1897, it is true, when the Greeks provoked a war with Turkey, they received no support from St. Petersburg, but at the close of the war the czar showed himself more friendly to them; and afterwards, when it proved extremely difficult to find a suitable person as governor-general of Crete he recommended the appointment of his cousin, Prince George of Greece — a selection which was pretty sure to accelerate the union of the island with the Hellenic kingdom. How far the recommendation was due to personal feeling, as opposed to political considerations, it is impossible to say.

In. Asia, after the accession of Nicholas II the expansion of Russia, following the line of least resistance and stimulated by the construction of the Siberian railway, was effected at the expense of China. As a necessary basis for a strong foreign policy the army was systematically strengthened. At one moment the schemes for military reorganisation involved such an enormous expenditure that the czar conceived the idea of an agreement among the great powers to arrest the increase of national armaments. The idea was communicated to the powers somewhat abruptly by Count Muraviev, Prince Lobanov's successor in the direction of foreign affairs, and an international conference was held at the Hague to discuss the subject; but it had very little practical result, and certainly did not attain the primary object in view. [Its final act is given in the appendix to this volume.]

A sketch of the recent history of Russia, however brief, would be incomplete without some mention of the remarkable industrial progress made during the period under consideration. Protected by high tariffs and fostered by the introduction of foreign capital, Russian manufacturing industry made enormous strides. By way of illustration a few figures may be cited. In the space of ten years (1887–1897) the number of workers employed in the various branches of industrial enterprise rose from 1,318,048 to 2,098,262. The consumption of cotton for spinning purposes, which was only 117 million kilograms in 1886, was 257 millions in 1898, and the number of spindles, according to the weekly journal *Russia* of August 2nd, 1902, was estimated at that date at 6,970,000. Thanks chiefly to this growth of the cotton industry, the town of Lódz, which was little more than a big village in 1875, has now a population of over 300,000. The iron, steel, and petroleum industries have likewise made enormous progress. Between 1892 and 1900 the estimated value of metallic articles manufactured in the country rose from 142 millions to 276 millions of rubles. As is generally the case in such circumstances, protection led to temporary over-production, which brought about a financial and economic crisis; but if we may accept certain figures given by Henry Norman, [d] the crisis could not have been very severe, for he states that "no fewer than 580 companies declared a dividend during the first nine months of 1901, their total nominal capital being £105,000,000, and the average dividend no less than 10.1 per cent." Much of this progress is due to the intelligence and energy of M. Witte, minister of finance. [b]

### KUROPATKIN ON THE RUSSIAN POLICY OF EXPANSION

In connection with the Russian advance in Asia with its climax in the war with Japan, it may be interesting to notice an address made by General Kuropatkin to a party of English tourists at Askabad in November, 1897.

Its protestations of peaceful intent will come as a surprise to many who have seen in the Russian advance only an insatiable land-hunger. General Kuropatkin, whose fortune it was seven years later to command the Russian army in the war with Japan, said in part, as quoted in a recent work: [a]

"The policy of our government in Central Asia, since the accession of the late czar, has been eminently one of peace; and recourse has never been had to arms until every other means of gaining a given object had failed. The principles which govern the policy of Russia are very simple. They are the maintenance of peace, of order, and of prosperity in all classes of the population. The means employed to compass these ends are equally free from complexity. Those who fill responsible positions are expressly informed by our government that the assumption of sovereignty over alien nationalities must not be attempted without very serious deliberation, inasmuch as such become, on annexation, Russian subjects, children of the czar, and invested with every privilege enjoyed by citizens of the empire. His majesty has enjoined on his representatives, as their first duty, a fatherly care of his Asiatic subjects. In order to prevent the possibility of internal discord, we have disarmed the natives, and no pains have been spared to induce them to adopt peaceful pursuits.

A RUSSIAN CHILD

The fruits of this action are already visible. A solitary traveller can now cross central Asia, from the Caspian to the Siberian frontier, without incurring the smallest risk of attack.

"We may boast with perfect truth that the thirty-five years during which central Asia has enjoyed the blessings of a firm and civilised rule, have been years of sustained progress, of daily-increasing strength in bonds of attachment and goodwill, which unite these subject peoples to the inhabitants of other Russian provinces. Between 1885 and 1888 we established a stable and logical frontier with the aid of Great Britain; and in the twelve years which have since elapsed there have been no expeditions throughout its length of 600 miles bordering on Persia, and 400 on Afghanistan. The latter country contains much inflammable material, but we have taken every means in our power to ensure that the internal disorders of that state shall not react on our frontier. So scrupulous is our regard for the *status quo*, that whole tribes have cast themselves on our protection in vain.

"Piruzkuhis, Khezaris, and Jamshidis have crossed our borders in troops of as many as 1,000 families, but we have always repatriated such refugees. There have been similar cases in our dealings with Persian subjects. Turkestan proper has been free from war since the occupation of Farghana — twenty-one years ago. The Bokhara frontier has remained intact since the capture of Samarkand in 1868. The last complication on the Persian border dates from 1829 — nearly 70 years ago. Throughout our frontier conterminous with China we have had no disturbance for more than a century. I am led to mention these significant facts in order to show that our policy in Asia is essentially a peaceful one, and that we are perfectly satisfied with our present boundaries. And I may claim to speak with authority, apart from my official position, for I have been personally concerned in all our important military and political movements in Central Asia since 1868, when, only twenty, I took part in storming Samarkand."[e]

### RUSSIA IN MANCHURIA

Russian advance in the Far East has been going on so steadily and so quietly that few realise to what an extent north-eastern Asia is becoming russianised. Russian ships are seen in Chinese and Japanese harbours, Russian banks are found on Chinese territory, Russian railways are connecting those remote parts of the world with Europe, and, most important of all, Russian peasants are being landed in the Far East. The russification movement is especially active in Manchuria, which province has become prominent in the last few years. Although on a map of Asia Manchuria does not look very large, it covers nearly as much space as France and Germany together. Beveridge[c] recently said of it: "It is an empire more favourably situated as to its climatic conditions than any part of Asia. It is in the same latitude as southern Canada and the northern portion of the United States. Its northern limits are about the same as the northern limits of Quebec. Its southern limits are about the same as the southern limits of Maryland. It is bounded on the north by the richest portions of Siberia, which not many years ago was itself a part of the dominion of the Manchus; for several hundred miles on the east by the grain-fields of the Ussuri district of Russian Siberia, also until recently a part of the Chinese Empire; on the east and south by Korea, over which the world's next great war will probably be fought, and soon; on the west by Mongolia, and on the south by Korea, China, and the gulfs and extensions of the Yellow Sea, which touches or commands much of that empire. On these gulfs are two of the finest military and commercial ports of Asia, or the world — Port Arthur and Talienwan, or, as the Russians call it, Dalny."

Russian designs upon Manchuria first became prominent after the Chino-Japanese war when Russia objected to Japan's acquiring any territory in that quarter. During the Boxer uprising in 1900 Russian troops overran Manchuria and in a convention concluded between Russia and China at the end of the movement, the civil and military administration of the province was placed practically under the control of Russia. Owing to objections on the part of the other powers, however, Russia withdrew this convention and another was signed in place of it on April 8th, 1902. According to this Manchuria was to remain "an integral portion of the Chinese Empire"; China pledged herself to protect the railway and all Russian subjects and their enterprises in Manchuria, while Russia for her part agreed to withdraw her troops gradually. This agreement on the part of Russia remained a promise only. In the meanwhile Manchuria was rapidly becoming russianised. The important cities along the railway such as New-Chwang, Mukden, Liauyang and Kirin became centres of Russian forces, Russian immigrants built and inhabited whole towns laid out like European cities with all modern improvements. Harbin, which in 1897 was a collection of mud huts, became a Russian city and a centre of Manchurian trade.

### THE WAR WITH JAPAN

Russia's policy in the Far East was the cause of friction with England and the United States, and especially with Japan; relations with the latter becoming more and more strained until they finally led to a war which broke out in February, 1904. In April of the preceding year Russia's representative at Peking presented certain demands to the Chinese government which virtually excluded all foreigners — except Russians — from Manchuria, and were a plain violation of the principle of the "open door" which Russia had pledged herself to maintain in that province. Owing to the opposition of the United States and Japan, however, most of these demands were withdrawn and permission was granted to open two Manchurian ports, although this was not carried out. In Korea also Russia opposed Japan, refusing to allow her to open the port of Wi-ju to foreign trade, and objecting to a Japanese telegraph from Seul to Fusan, although Russia herself laid a telegraph line on Korean territory.

In August, 1903, Russia took the important step of establishing a special vice-royalty in the Amur provinces which had been leased to her in the Liaotung peninsula. Vice-admiral Alexiev was appointed as first Russian viceroy of the Far East, and was invested with civil and military authority which made him to a great extent independent of St. Petersburg.

In September the Russian ambassador at Peking had announced that New-Chwang and Mukden would be evacuated on October 8th, but that date passed and Russian troops were still there, while Russia continued to strengthen her army and navy in the Far East. Japan demanded that Russia should evacuate Manchuria in agreement with her promises and that she should discontinue her aggressive attitude in Korea.

Russia's answers to Japan's repeated demands were evasive, and on January 8th, 1904, Japan sent a final note to Russia and, receiving no reply, withdrew her minister and legation from St. Petersburg on February 6th, 1904. On February 7th both governments issued statements announcing the severance of diplomatic relations. On February 8th the main Japanese fleet, under Vice-admiral Togo, opened the war by surprising the Russian fleet at Port Arthur in a state of unpreparedness, and inflicting much damage.

The attack was repeated on the following day with a repetition of the result of the first day's assault. On the same day Admiral Uriu and a small Japanese squadron attacked and destroyed two Russian cruisers in the harbour of Chemulpo. Thus at the very outset the Japanese had secured a decided advantage over their opponents on the sea. At once the cry arose in Russia that Japan, by not giving official notice of the proposed attack had violated international law, but neutral nations generally saw in Russia's complaint only an attempt to excuse her defeats, and held that the severing of diplomatic relations was warning enough. Still that the Russians were not entirely crippled was shown by the fact that within a fortnight their squadron of four cruisers at Vladivostok cut its way out of the ice, which was supposed to hold it captive, and harried the Japanese coast.  But this danger did not hinder the transportation of Japanese troops to Korea, which began on February 18th.  The following month saw a continuation of Japanese successes and of Russian losses.  Several times Admiral Togo attacked Port Arthur, at one time or another almost all of the Russian ships of war sustaining more or less serious damage.  Vladivostok was bombarded, and a succession of minor engagements took place between the outposts of the two opposing armies advancing toward one another from opposite sides of the Yalu river. On February 24th Admiral Togo made an unsuccessful attempt to "bottle up" the Russian fleet in the harbour of Port Arthur by sinking five old steamships in the channel.  Early in March, General Kuropatkin, the Russian minister of war, was appointed by the czar to the supreme command of the Russian armies in Manchuria to succeed Viceroy Alexiev and Admiral Makarov was at the same time appointed to the command of the fleet.  By the end of the month the Japanese had, on the Manchurian border, in Korea, with which country they had concluded a close alliance, a force estimated at eighty thousand, with a base at Ping Yang.  This was faced by a Russian force, slightly smaller, but increased daily by reinforcements which kept arriving in a continuous stream over the Trans-Siberian and Manchurian railways. The Japanese successes appeared well nigh to stupefy Russia, and the demoralisation of the czar's official advisers seemed complete.  Beside the loss of General Kuropatkin, who was succeeded as minister of war by General Sakarov, both Count Lamsdorf, minister of foreign affairs, and M. Witte, the finance minister, retired from the cabinet.  On April 13th, the Russian battleship *Petropavlovsk* struck a mine or floating torpedo near the entrance to Port Arthur harbour and sank with all on board, including Admiral Makarov and the war artist Verestchagin.

During the succeeding month war operations of importance or interest were confined to the land.  By the first of May the principal points in the Japanese military programme had unfolded themselves.  The absolute command of the sea and coast, thus assuring ease and safety in the transportation of troops and munitions of war, had been secured, and an efficient and formidable army had been landed on the Asiatic mainland.  Korea too had been thoroughly occupied.  The Japanese army, in the last days of April, began its forward movement under General Kuroki, the purpose being to cross the Yalu at several points and drive the Russians back into Manchuria.

On May 1st, after a six days fight on the Yalu near Wi-ju, the Japanese won their first land victory, and secured a firm footing on the Manchurian side of the Yalu.  During the month of May Kuroki continued his advance into the interior, but his progress was slow owing to the difficulty in maintaining communication with the coast and constant skirmishing with the Cossacks who opposed his advance guard.  Kuropatkin meanwhile proceeded to concentrate his forces at Liauyang on the Manchurian Railway south of Harbin, with the apparent intention of leaving Port Arthur to its fate.

It was about the latter place that the activity now centred and against it a second Japanese army under General Oku advanced.  On May 25th Oku landed a force of some forty thousand men near Kin-chau on the narrowest point of the Liao-tung peninsula.  At this point the Nanshan hills extending from Kin-chau, on the western side of the isthmus toward Dalny on the east afforded the Russians an excellent opportunity for defence and here they had constructed a strong line of fortifications, mounted a large number of guns and manned them with the flower of the Port Arthur army. After a series of tentative attacks, Oku made a grand assault under cover of fire from warships in the harbour of Kin-chau. In the charge up the heights he lost over 4,000 men, but drove out the Russians, who lost 2,000 men and 78 cannon. Two days later the Japanese occupied Russia's great commercial port, Dalny, finding the docks, piers, and railway yards uninjured. It was thenceforward the Japanese base.

Port Arthur was now left to its fate, save for the single effort of General Stakelberg who was detached with 40,000 men to make a dash southward, but was defeated by Oku at Telissu (Vofangow), eighty miles north of Port Arthur (June 14–16), and by Kuroki. He made his escape, having lost some 10,000 men on his vain foray.

Kuropatkin's tactics were Fabian and his eventual reliance was the reinforcements which the Siberian railway poured in as fast as possible. The Japanese forced the attack. Marshal Oyama was in charge of the armies opposed to Kuropatkin, his subordinates being Nodzu and the brilliant Kuroki. General Oku also joined Oyama, the Port Arthur siege being placed in the command of General Nogi. June 26–27 the Japanese took the well-nigh impregnable position at Fen-shiu-ling pass. Shortly after Kuroki took the important pass of Motien-ling. On July 17 General Count Keller made a desperate effort to recapture it, but was repulsed with heavy loss. July 24 Oku took Tashichiao and forced the Russians back to the walled city of Hai-cheng. July 29 Kuroki took the Yangtse pass, in whose defence General Keller was killed. Oku having turned his right flank, Kuropatkin was forced to evacuate Hai-cheng and retreat to his base at Liauyang. He was also compelled to give up the important city of New-Chwang.

The capture of Liauyang was a great problem. The Japanese were not ready to open battle till August 24, when they began a twelve days' combat which takes a permanent place as one of the largest and fiercest battles in history. The Russians were estimated at 200,000; the Japanese at 240,000. The Japanese confessed a loss of 25,000; the Russian loss was perhaps still greater, as they were defeated and escaped capture or annihilation only by Kuropatkin's ingenuity in retreat.

The Russians retired to Mukden. October 2nd Kuropatkin felt strong enough to take the offensive, and assailed Oyama on the river Shakhe or the Sha-ho. A series of battles followed, lasting till October 18, when the Russians fell back again to Mukden, after a loss of 45,000 men killed and wounded, according to a Russian staff report. Oyama claimed to have found 13,300 Russians dead on the field, and admitted a loss of 15,800 on his own side.

Meanwhile Port Arthur was undergoing one of the most important sieges in history. The siege began on May 26th, when Nan-shan hill was taken and Dalny occupied, though on August 12th the last of the outlying defences was taken and the Japanese sat down before the permanent works. They combined a patient and scientific process of sapping, trenching and tunnelling, with a series of six grand assaults. The collaboration of such skill with such reckless heroism had its inevitable result. The garrison under General Stoessel held out with splendid courage against an army totalling perhaps 100,000, but the gradual exhaustion of ammunition, food, and strength, together with the appearance of scurvy, compelled a surrender. January 3rd, 1905, the Japanese took possession, finding 878 officers, 23,491 men, besides several thousand non-combatants.

The fleet which had made several efforts to escape had been reduced by loss after loss, and finally, on the capture of 203 Metre Hill, had been subjected to the fire of the land artillery and completely destroyed.

During the leaguer of Port Arthur and the gradual beating back of Kuropatkin, other Russian activities kept diplomacy busy. The seizure of neutral ships in the Red Sea by two vessels that passed the Dardanelles as merchantmen and then equipped as cruisers, provoked such indignation in England and Germany that the seizures were discontinued. The Vladivostok squadron made daring raids upon Japanese and neutral vessels, but after a long pursuit was caught by Admiral Kamimura, who sank the Ruric and crippled the other two cruisers.

About the middle of October, after innumerable delays, the powerful Baltic fleet, under command of Admiral Rojestvensky, set out with the avowed purpose of aiding Port Arthur. On the night of the 21st, while in the North Sea off the Dogger Banks, a part of the fleet mistook some English fishing trawlers for Japanese torpedo boats, fired upon them, and sank one boat and killed two fishermen. The indignation of the English people was intense; war for a time seemed imminent; but the matter was ultimately referred to a board of arbitration, which, in the following February, found that the action of the fleet had been unjustifiable. In March, 1905, Russia paid the sum of £65,000 in damages.

## DISORDERS AT HOME

The internal condition of Russia was rendered critical by the war, and by profound commercial distress. June 15th the Governor-General over Finland, Bobrikov, was assassinated by an opponent of the russification policy. On July 29th the Czar's minister of the interior, Von Plehve, was slain by a bomb thrown at his carriage. Rightly or wrongly, Von Plehve was considered the special author and adviser of the increasing vigour and tyranny of the czar's internal administration. Jews abhorred him as the man responsible for the Kishinev massacres, and the Finns looked upon him as the destroyer of their national institutions. He was succeeded by Prince Peter Sviatopolk-Mirsky, a man of comparatively liberal and progressive views.

This gave some encouragement to the zemstvos, the farthest step toward representative government yet taken in Russia. They date only from the czar's ukase of January, 1864. Each of the districts in which Russia is divided is represented by an assembly, elected by the three estates, communes, municipalities, and land-owners. Each district assembly in a province sends delegates to a general provincial assembly or zemstvo, which body controls the roads, primary schools, etc. Alexander II meant that these zemstvos should acquire large power, but after his death they fell under the sway of provincial governors. November 21st, 1904, the zemstvos lifted their heads again, and their presidents met in a congress which, by a majority of 105 to 3, voted to beg the czar to grant Russia a constitution and a genuine representative government.

The czar, with some asperity of tone, refused a constitution, and while promising certain reforms, rebuked the zemstvos and forbade their further discussion of such unsettling topics. Prince Sviatopolk-Mirsky now resigned, declaring that Russia was on the brink of a great revolution, and that the bureaucracy must be supplanted by "the freely elected representatives of the people." In January, 1905, Sergius de Witte succeeded to the office of minister of the interior. One of the most prominent European statesmen, a liberal, and an enemy of Von Plehve, his first statements were nevertheless disappointing to believers in radical reforms.

Opposition to the war and hostility to bureaucracy and autocracy, discontent among the working classes, and general disaffection now resulted in an important outbreak. On the 18th of January, the workmen employed at the Putiloff, Neva Shipbuilding, and other works in St. Petersburg went on strike, and at the same time drafted a petition demanding legislation dealing with poverty and the oppression of labour by capital, guarantees of personal security, freedom of speech and worship, compulsory education, equality before the law, responsibility of ministers, a representative assembly, and other reforms. On the 22d a delegation led by an unfrocked priest, Father Gapon, marched towards the Winter Palace in order to present these demands to the czar. Their way was blocked by the military, and upon their persisting in their attempt they were shot down by hundreds. On the 24th General Trepoff, a man much hated because of his harsh methods, was appointed governor-general of the city with plenary powers, and every outbreak was put down in the most merciless manner. Many leading revolutionists, among them Maxim Gorky, the celebrated novelist, were arrested, but some of them were afterwards released. Lesser disturbances also broke out at Moscow, Reval, Riga, Odessa, Warsaw, Lodz, and elsewhere, but were likewise put down. As usual the revolutionists resorted to the use of dynamite and to assassination. On the 17th of February the Grand Duke Sergius, one of the most hated of the supporters of the bureaucracy, was blown to pieces at Moscow by a bomb. On the 3d of March the czar denounced in a manifesto "the evil-minded leaders of the revolutionary movement" for rendering assistance to the enemies of Russia, by attempting to set up a system of government not "suitable for our fatherland." On the evening of the same day, however, he issued a rescript in which he promised "to convene the worthiest men possessing the confidence of the people and elected by them to participate in the elaboration and consideration of legislative measures." This rather vague concession did not allay the public discontent; serious agrarian troubles and peasant riots took place soon after, and during the months of April and May more than one hundred attempts at assassination were made, of which more than forty are said to have succeeded.

### MUKDEN, THE SEA OF JAPAN, AND THE PEACE OF PORTSMOUTH

Meanwhile events at the seat of war had continued to be extremely disastrous for Russia. Late in January an offensive movement was undertaken by the Russian second army under General Grippenberg against the Japanese left, but the movement was repulsed with great loss, and Grippenberg, claiming that he had not been properly supported by General Kuropatkin, resigned his command. About the same time General Oyama's army was heavily reinforced by General Nogi with the veteran army which had overcome Port Arthur. On the 19th of February the Japanese began a stupendous offensive movement. After more than two weeks of terrible fighting, General Kuropatkin was forced to retreat from Mukden, and to retire beyond Tie Pass, after suffering one of the heaviest losses experienced by any modern army. Soon after this disastrous defeat General Kuropatkin was relieved from command, and General Linevitch undertook the task of reorganising the demoralized army.

The sole remaining hope of Russia now lay in her navy. On the 8th of April Admiral Rojestvensky with the Baltic fleet passed Singapore, and on May 5th was joined off the coast of French Indo-China by another squadron under Admiral Nebogatoff. After some days spent in refitting, the combined fleet sailed northward to meet the enemy. But the voyage which had been so inauspiciously begun was to have a disastrous ending. On the 27th and 28th of May, in a battle which is more fully described under Japan, the ill-manned Russian fleet was practically annihilated by Admiral Togo.

Nothing now remained but to make peace. By invitation of President Roosevelt, envoys representing the two belligerent powers held a conference at Portsmouth, New Hampshire, and there on the 29th of August they arrived at a preliminary agreement, which was later elaborated into a formal treaty. This treaty, the terms of which are given under Japan, was more favourable to Russia than had been generally expected; but nevertheless it marked the complete defeat of the policy which had caused the war.

### FURTHER ATTEMPTS AT REVOLUTION

In the meantime disorders in Russia had increased rather than diminished. Riots and outbreaks occurred in Poland, the Caucasus, and elsewhere. Towards the end of June, the crews of the *Kniaz Potemkin* and *Georgei Pobiedonosetz* of the Black Sea fleet mutinied, murdered those of their officers who resisted, and proceeded to Odessa, where thousands of strikers and revolutionists made common cause with them. After much loss of life and destruction of property, however, the revolt was put down; the crew of the *Georgei Pobiedonosetz* surrendered and many of them were shot; and the mutineers on the *Kniaz Potemkin* surrendered the vessel on the 9th of July to the authorities of Rumania on condition that they should be allowed to escape.

On the 19th of August, the czar, influenced by these events and by representations and warnings from deputations from the zemstvos and dumas and from the marshals of the nobility, issued a manifesto in which he said: "The time is come to summon elected representatives from the whole of Russia to take a constant and active part in the elaboration of laws, attaching for this purpose to the higher state institutions a special consultative body entrusted with the preliminary elaboration and discussion of measures and with the examination of the state budget." This national assembly, or duma, as it was called, was to meet not later than January, 1906, but the date was subsequently postponed. The concession involved in calling it was much more apparent than real, for no guarantees were made of popular rights and liberties; its powers were to be only consultative; and the middle and lower classes were practically excluded from taking part in choosing its members. The scheme was far from satisfactory to the revolutionists and reformers; and riots and disturbances of various kinds continued, especially in Finland and at Baku, where many hundreds of persons were killed.

On the 25th of September, a congress of about three hundred delegates representing the zemstvos and municipalities of the empire met in Moscow to consider the situation. After a heated debate a resolution was carried to the effect that while the proposed duma would not be a truly representative body, it might "serve as a rallying point and support for the general movement for the attainment of political freedom," and that therefore "Russian citizens, who are united on the political programme formulated by the zemstvo congresses of the preceding and present years, should seek to enter the duma in as large numbers as possible for the purpose of forming there a united group with the object of obtaining guarantees for personal liberty and equality." The congress further declared that the suffrage should be placed on a national and not a class basis.

## PROMULGATION OF A CONSTITUTION

On October 21st an organized strike for the furtherance of political objects began on all the railways, and the railway employees were soon joined by workers in other occupations, until probably a million men were engaged in the movement. Moscow and St. Petersburg were cut off from communication with the rest of the empire; famine became imminent in many cities; business everywhere was at a standstill. The whole object of the movement was to force the government to adopt reforms, and in part this object was realized. On the 30th of October the czar signed what has been called by some people the "Magna Charta of Russian Liberties," and on the same day appointed Count Witte, who had gained greatly enhanced prestige by his success as one of the Russian peace envoys, head of a responsible ministry. In substance the manifesto promised to the people inviolability of person, freedom of conscience, speech, and association, further extension of the right to vote for representatives to the duma, the establishment of the principle that no law can be enacted without the approval of the duma. Four days later as a result of the situation in Finland, the czar repealed many harsh ordinances which applied to that country, admitted the responsibility of the secretary of state to the Finnish diet rather than to the monarch, and called a special session of the diet to discuss laws granting freedom of speech, of the press, of public meeting, of association, and for the establishment of a national assembly based on universal suffrage.

But the revolutionists still remained unsatisfied. They demanded "the immediate convocation of a constituent assembly elected by the universal, equal, and direct suffrages of all adult citizens, without distinction of sex, creed, or nationality, and the provision of all guarantees of civic freedom." Anarchy reigned over practically the whole country. At Odessa more than five thousand persons are reported to have been killed or wounded, while terrible riots occurred at Kazan, Warsaw, Tiflis, and elsewhere. At Kieff, Kishineff, Kherson, Rostoff, and other towns, horrible massacres of Jews took place; these massacres were practically unchecked by the governmental authorities, and were perhaps even instigated by them for reactionary purposes. On the 9th of November, a mutiny broke out among the sailors at Kronstadt, and a few days later another among both soldiers and sailors at Vladivostok, but both were ultimately suppressed. Disturbances created by the independence party in Poland led to the proclamation, on the 13th, of martial law in that country. As a protest against the government's action at Kronstadt and in Poland a new general strike was called, but on the 20th it was ended by order of the Central Labour Committee. The workingmen were, however, at the same time urged to further the revolutionary propaganda, and to prepare themselves for "the last general encounter of all Russia with bloody monarchy now living in its last days." On the 23d a zemstvo congress which was sitting at Moscow passed a resolution demanding universal direct suffrage and the calling of a constituent assembly. The congress also passed resolutions which are tantamount to a vote of no confidence in the government.

## THE GOVERNMENT REGAINS CONTROL

The revolt now entered upon its most acute phase. On the 24th of November a combined strike and mutiny broke out at Sevastopol. The revolutionists captured the city, wounded Admiral Pisarevsky, and for several days controlled affairs almost completely. The government, however, dispatched overwhelming forces to the seat of the trouble; the rebel trenches were stormed; the ships were retaken; and many of the rebels were executed. Less important outbreaks occurred at Kronstadt, Vladivostok, and other places. In December, Lithuania and other regions around the Baltic were in open revolt; uprisings occurred in the Caucasus, at Irkutsk, and elsewhere; a new general strike began on the 21st; assassinations and attempted assassinations were everywhere common; the peasants were rising against their lords; the whole Russian state seemed to be falling to pieces. One of the bloodiest struggles took place in Moscow, the old capital. For several days the rebels controlled a large part of the city; but the troops generally remained loyal; and after frightful street fighting in which hundreds of men, women, and children lost their lives, order was again restored. Elsewhere, also, the government gradually regained its authority. The most violent part of the storm of revolution was past.

With the triumph of the government it was freely prophesied that a policy of thoroughgoing reaction would set in, and that, temporarily at least, the concessions already given would be ignored. But on the 26th of December a more liberal electoral law was issued, which granted the suffrage to many classes which had hitherto been excluded, while it was announced that the ultimate decision upon the subject of universal suffrage would be left to the duma. Early in January registration for the election of this body began. Charges were made that the minister of the interior, Durnovo, was seeking to control the election in the interests of reaction by arresting popular leaders; for this and other reasons the revolutionary socialists refused to register, but later changed their attitude. To allow a full registration, the time originally granted for this purpose was extended. On the 26th of February, a ukase officially fixed May 10th as the date for the meeting of the duma. On March 5th it was announced that no law would hereafter be valid without the consent of the duma and of the council of the empire. This latter body was to consist of an equal number of appointed and elected members taken from the clergy, nobility, zemstvos, academy of science, universities, trade, and industry. The annual sessions were to be convoked and closed by imperial ukase, and the sittings were to be public. Either house was to have the power to interpellate ministers and to initiate legislation; but neither was to be allowed to meddle with "the fundamental laws of the empire."

## THE FIRST DUMA

For a considerable time it seemed as if the duma would never be convened. But at last, on May 10, 1906, the first Russian parliament was opened in solemn pomp by Czar Nicholas II in the Tavrida Palace. There the so-called "best men" of Russia, the Scythian and the Celt, the Lithuanian and the Pole, the Catholic priest and the Jewish rabbi, had come together to deliberate upon the country's welfare. Professor Muromtsev was unanimously elected president. But the first Russian parliament was a frail infant destined to a premature end. War, famine, economic distress, had assisted at its birth, and opposition, secret or open hostility, was watching over its infancy. It could not thrive under such circumstances.

But, although a speedy dissolution of the first duma as soon as it had been opened by Czar Nicholas in solemn state had been predicted, the ukase dissolving the first Russian parliament came somewhat as a surprise to the European world. And yet this issue was the only logical one. The government of the czar soon perceived the impossibility of working with a duma whose members were speaking only for the gallery of the country. A decisive step had to be taken in order to avoid a disgraceful compromise on the part of the government. At this juncture, whilst the Premier Goremykin, who had succeeded Count Witte early in May, was officially representing the government, the Star Chamber was busily engaged in finding a solution of the perplexing problem. Three parties, representing three distinct currents of opinion, were formed at court, and each endeavoured to persuade Nicholas II to adopt and carry out the plan it had worked out for the welfare of the nation.

The three parties were headed respectively by Trepov, by Count Ignatev, and by Goutshkov and Stolypin. Strange and almost incredible as it will sound, Trepov advised liberal concessions. The man who had arranged pogroms, the *policier* who had knouted, sent to mines and to Siberia, who had incarcerated in the prison cells of Sts. Peter and Paul and in the fortress of Schlusselburg thousands of revolutionaries, advised the czar to hold out the olive branch to the cadets.

Trepov was neither more nor less than a faithful Yanitshar, a faithful bull-dog, whose qualities we cannot praise, but whose fidelity may perhaps elicit some admiration. When he found out that it became of paramount importance to the interests of his imperial master to grant concessions, all the arguments of the reactionary party became as nought with him, and the implacable enemy of revolutionaries, the stage manager of pogroms and of riots, the terror of nihilists and of students, suddenly appeared as liberal as the cadets themselves, without in the least having changed his views. It was for this reason, too, that shortly before death put an end to his zeal, Trepov was not a *persona grata* in court circles. His programme had been as follows: "The cadets," he said, "are strong, influential, and above all, ambitious. They are thirsting for power. The view of portfolios and ministerial benches is dazzling them. Let us stretch out a hand to the cadets, let us grant them concessions, and, with united effort, build the bridge over the gulf which is dividing new and old Russia."

Trepov advised the czar to form a mixed cabinet, consisting of himself, perhaps, as minister of war, of liberal bureaucrats like Yermolov, former minister of agriculture, and of three or four prominent members from among the cadets. He thus hoped to satisfy the ambition of the latter, and, by granting them concessions, at the same time persuade them to abandon at least the idea of the compulsory expropriation of landowners, which he considered too dangerous a measure. But two other parties claimed the attention of the czar, and both equally strongly condemned the Trepov programme. Count Ignatev—who has since been assassinated—urged the czar to crush the hydra-head of opposition. Ignatev represented that powerful class, the rich landowners, which is the mainstay of autocracy. He could see no possibility of concession. There was no necessity either, for Ignatev disbelieved in the danger of the revolution. It was only a bluff, he said, of Count Witte, whose ambition it was to be the president of the first Russian republic. The *ancien régime* must maintain its prerogatives; prisons, exile, and Siberia would soon

[1906 A.D.]

teach the few unwise dreamers that autocracy was as firm as ever, and meant to remain so for the future. The famous framer of the May laws advised a policy of oppression,—openly and unhesitatingly.

## The Programme of Stolypin and the Dissolution of the Duma

Standing between these two programmes, the liberal of Trepov and the reactionary of Ignatev, was that of Stolypin and Goutshkov, which ultimately gained favour with the czar. Goutshkov's programme was briefly this: To dissolve the duma, to promise the nation to convene another duma within a few months, and in the meantime to take the necessary steps so as to be sure of a government majority in the next assembly. Goutshkov maintained that he had carefully studied the causes of revolutions in western Europe and the course they had taken. He had arrived at the conclusion that revolution was a malady, a fever which will occasionally break out in the normal social body, but was not dangerous in itself, if properly attended to. The best remedies for this disease were patience and perseverance. Had the western European governments at various periods and in various countries been armed with a sufficient dose of these antidotes, had they not lost courage, and in a frenzy of despair either made concessions or adopted extreme measures, but simply tried to gain time, the revolutionary fever would gradually have abated, and the social pulse regained its normal state. Russia should now be wise and try to benefit by the experience gained from the study of western Europe. No extreme measures, but also no concessions. The programme, therefore, which Goutshkov, in conjunction with Stolypin, elaborated, was as follows: The duma must be dissolved by an imperial ukase; at the same time, however, hope must be held out to the country in the shape of a promise to convene a new assembly within a few months. In the meantime a strong endeavour should be made to organise all the conservative forces, who would rally round the party of the Octobrists and form the government party in the new duma.

Nicholas II, as might have been expected from a man of his undecided character, listened neither to the liberal plan of his friend Trepov, nor to the advice of the reactionary Ignatev, but adopted the programme elaborated by Goutshkov and Stolypin. He decided to dissolve the duma and to issue a ukase convening a new one in a few months, in which care should be taken that the government and conservative elements should form the preponderating majority. And thus the struggle between the three parties in the Star Chamber ended in the victory of Goutshkov-Stolypin, and the result was the ukase of July 21, 1906, dissolving the duma—a ukase which startled Europe at the very moment when the English premier was welcoming the delegates of the Inter-parliamentary Conference in London. The cadets and the labour party assembled at Viborg and drafted a manifesto to the nation. It was, however, of no avail. Although the cadets were not arrested, the nation was too frightened to respond to their appeal for support against the government.

## Autocracy Triumphs

And thus Nicholas II, in uttering his famous words, "My autocracy is as famous as ever," sent home the representatives of the nation, some of them to prison and death. Many fell as glorious martyrs in the battle for liberty. A shot fired at Terioki, by an assassin hired by the reactionaries, caused the untimely death of one of the most intelligent and useful ex-members of the duma, M. J. Herzenstein.

And although Trepov had in the meantime died, his spirit was still hovering round the imperial palaces of Peterhof and Tsarskoe Selo. There began a period of oppression. Inspired undoubtedly by the example of the *tribunaux révolutionnaires* of 1789, the Russian courts of justice were replaced by courts-martial. In the course of a few weeks more than 150 persons were either hanged or shot. Thousands were sent at the expense of the government to the mines or to the Siberian snowfields, where they could find leisure to cool their burning revolutionary brows.

Even the optimists had to admit that things looked grave. M. Milyoukov, the eminent leader, urged at the Congress of Helsingfors the necessity of abandoning the idea of a passive resistance and of refusing to furnish recruits and to pay taxes. The idea of a general strike had to be abandoned, the armed local revolts were speedily suppressed, the much talked-of agrarian rising came to nothing. The struggle for liberty was gradually being crushed. Thousands of brave men were court-martialled, piteously murdered, slaughtered, tortured and imprisoned, sent to fortresses and to mines. Autocracy triumphed.

Events which followed the dissolution of the duma thus tended to prove the soundness and the advantage of the Goutshkov-Stolypin programme. The revolutionary fever, as Goutshkov had called it, broke out; the crisis was reached, but it did not turn out to be fatal. The country did not rise. The plans of revolutionaries to get into their power the whole district round Tsarskoe Selo and to arrest the czar were frustrated. The mutinies of Svyborg and Kronstadt were premature, remained unsupported, and were easily and speedily crushed. The great peasant mass remained passive. A new duma had been promised and the country decided to wait. The cadets, on the other hand, committed a blunder with the Viborg manifesto, and thus furnished the government with a pretext to prosecute them as revolutionaries; the party suffered considerably; its clubs were closed, its pamphlets confiscated, and its organs suspended.

## THE SECOND DUMA

In the meantime preparations for the election of members for the new duma were carried on. Goutshkov proceeded to work out his plans in arranging the electoral campaign. Neither money nor trouble was spared in the endeavour to secure a governmént majority for the new duma. Dozens of journals were started by the Octobrists in the provinces, hundreds of orators were sent out to enlighten the people, millions of proclamations were distributed among the peasants, fighting bands were organised and provided with sticks for the purpose of beating Jews, students, and the wives and children of the intellectuals. A great number of guns and revolvers from the arsenals were distributed among the Black-hundreds. Clergymen were commanded by their ecclesiastical superiors to preach from their pulpits in the interest of the government, and to brand the first duma as a *Jewish Kahal*. All the parties that were ever so little more radical than that of the Octobrists were accused of being revolutionary and their existence declared to be illegal; their bureaus were closed, their newspapers suspended, and their books and pamphlets confiscated and burned. Many suspected of radicalism were arrested, taken away from their families and sent to prison or to Siberia. In order to frighten the Jews a pogrom was arranged in Sedlice. The government further found the senate a willing instrument in its hands for the business of interpreting the electoral laws. In order to eliminate the radical elements and to invalidate them as electors, the senate interpreted the election laws in such a manner as to suit the government.

In spite, however, of all the endeavours made by the government—in spite of terrorism, hooliganism, police and clergy—the opposition was clearly in a majority in the new duma. It held its first session on March 5th. Feodor Golovin, a Constitutional Democrat, was elected president. On March 18th M. Stolypin, in reading the ministerial declaration, announced that the "country must be transformed into a constitutional state" and laid before the body bills for determining the civic status of the inhabitants, for ameliorating the condition of the peasants, for securing liberty of conscience and inviolability of person, for improving the system of education, etc. He announced, however, that in legislating upon the subject of toleration the government was determined to lay down the principle of a Christian state in which the orthodox religion should be privileged. Later he opposed a bill for making field courts-martial illegal. Either from inclination or from policy, the new duma showed itself more moderate than its predecessor and endeavoured to avoid giving a pretext for its dissolution; but late in May it rejected resolutions condemning terrorism and on June 8th began to discuss the reform of rural justice. At a secret sitting on June 14th the premier presented charges of treason against practically all the members of the Social Democratic party and demanded the immediate arrest of sixteen and authority for the indictment of fifty-five members. By an overwhelming majority the subject was referred to a committee. On June 16th the Czar issued a ukase dissolving the duma and fixing November 14th as the date for the meeting of a new one. At the same time, in direct defiance of one of the essential guaranties of the constitution, he promulgated a new election law, reducing the peasant electorate, diminishing by half the number of deputies from Siberia, Poland and the Caucasus, and instituting in the larger cities direct elections with a higher property test, thereby placing four-fifths of the electoral power in the hands of about 130,000 landowners, the majority of whom are reactionary.

### THE THIRD DUMA

The country received this *coup d'état* quietly, and the new elections, which took place in the fall, attracted comparatively little interest. The result, as was natural, was a strong conservative majority. The first session was held on November 14th.

In August a convention with Japan stipulating for the territorial integrity of the Chinese Empire and for the principle of the "open door" was published. On September 23rd a convention with Great Britain for the purpose of settling by mutual consent the various questions affecting their interests in Asia was ratified.[a]

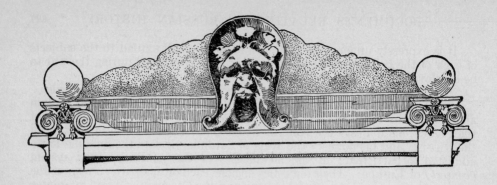

# APPENDIX

## DOCUMENTS RELATING TO RUSSIAN HISTORY

### I

### TREATY OF PARIS

GENERAL TREATY BETWEEN THE QUEEN OF THE UNITED KINGDOM OF GREAT BRITAIN AND IRELAND, THE EMPEROR OF AUSTRIA, THE EMPEROR OF THE FRENCH, THE KING OF PRUSSIA, THE EMPEROR OF RUSSIA, THE KING OF SARDINIA, AND THE SULTAN

*Signed at Paris, March 30th, 1856. Ratifications exchanged at Paris, April 27th*

Art. 1. From the day of the exchange of the ratifications of the present treaty there shall be peace and friendship between her majesty the Queen of the United Kingdom of Great Britain and Ireland, his majesty the Emperor of the French, his majesty the King of Sardinia, his imperial majesty the Sultan, on the one part, and his majesty the Emperor of all the Russias, on the other part, as well as between their heirs and successors, their respective dominions and subjects in perpetuity.

Art. 2. Peace being happily re-established between their said majesties, the territories conquered or occupied by their armies during the war shall be reciprocally evacuated.

Special arrangements shall regulate the mode of the evacuation, which shall be as prompt as possible.

Art. 3. His majesty the Emperor of all the Russias engages to restore to his majesty the Sultan the town and citadel of Kars, as well as the other parts of the Ottoman territory of which the Russian troops are in possession.

Art. 4. Their majesties the Queen of the United Kingdom of Great Britain and Ireland, the Emperor of the French, the King of Sardinia, and the Sultan, engage to restore to his majesty the Emperor of all the Russias the towns and ports of Sebastopol, Balaklava, Kamiesch, Eupatoria, Kertch, Yenikale, Kinburn, as well as all other territories occupied by the allied troops.

Art. 5. Their majesties the Queen of the United Kingdom of Great Britain and Ireland, the Emperor of the French, the Emperor of all the Russias, the King of Sardinia, and the Sultan, grant a full and entire amnesty to those of their subjects who may have been compromised by any participation whatsoever in the events of the war in favour of the cause of the enemy.

626

It is expressly understood that such amnesty shall extend to the subjects of each of the belligerent parties who may have continued during the war to be employed in the service of one of the other belligerents.

Art. 6. Prisoners of war shall be immediately given up on either side.

Art. 7. Her majesty the Queen of the United Kingdom of Great Britain and Ireland, his majesty the Emperor of Austria, his majesty the Emperor of the French, his majesty the King of Prussia, his majesty the Emperor of all the Russias, and his majesty the King of Sardinia, declare the Sublime Porte admitted to participate in the advantages of the public law and system (concert) of Europe. Their majesties engage, each on his part, to respect the independence and the territorial integrity of the Ottoman empire; guarantee in common the strict observance of that engagement; and will, in consequence, consider any act tending to its violation as a question of general interest.

Art. 8. If there should arise between the Sublime Porte and one or more of the other signing powers any misunderstanding which might endanger the maintenance of their relations, the Sublime Porte and each of such powers, before having recourse to the use of force, shall afford the other contracting parties the opportunity of preventing such an extremity by means of their mediation.

Art. 9. His imperial majesty the Sultan having, in his constant solicitude for the welfare of his subjects, issued a *firman* which, while ameliorating their condition without distinction of religion or of race, records his generous intentions towards the Christian population of his empire, and wishing to give a further proof of his sentiments in that respect, has resolved to communicate to the contracting parties the said firman, emanating spontaneously from his sovereign will.

The contracting powers recognise the high value of this communication. It is clearly understood that it cannot, in any case, give to the said powers the right to interfere, either collectively or separately, in the relations of his majesty the Sultan with his subjects, nor in the internal administration of his empire.

Art. 10. The convention of the 13th of July, 1841, which maintains the ancient rule of the Ottoman empire relative to the closing of the straits of the Bosporus and of the Dardanelles, has been revised by common consent.

The act concluded for that purpose, and in conformity with that principle, between the high contracting parties, is and remains annexed to the present treaty, and shall have the same force and validity as if it formed an integral part thereof.

Art. 11. The Black Sea is neutralised; its waters and its ports, thrown open to the mercantile marine of every nation, are formally and in perpetuity interdicted to the flag of war, either of the powers possessing its coasts or of any other power, with the exceptions mentioned in Articles 14 and 19 of the present treaty.

Art. 12. Free from any impediment, the commerce in the ports and waters of the Black Sea shall be subject only to regulations of health, customs, and police, framed in a spirit favourable to the development of commercial transactions.

In order to afford to the commercial and maritime interests of every nation the security which is desired, Russia and the Sublime Porte will admit consuls into their ports situated upon the coast of the Black Sea, in conformity with the principles of international law.

Art. 13. The Black Sea being neutralised according to the terms of Art.

11, the maintenance or establishment upon its coast of military-maritime arsenals becomes alike unnecessary and purposeless; in consequence, his majesty the Emperor of all the Russias and his imperial majesty the Sultan engage not to establish or to maintain upon that coast any military-maritime arsenal.

Art. 14. Their majesties the Emperor of all the Russias and the Sultan having concluded a convention for the purpose of settling the force and the number of light vessels necessary for the service of their coasts, which they reserve to themselves to maintain in the Black Sea, that convention is annexed to the present treaty, and shall have the same force and validity, as if it formed an integral part thereof. It cannot be either annulled or modified without the assent of the powers signing the present treaty.

Art. 15. The act of the Congress of Vienna having established the principles intended to regulate the navigation of rivers which separate or traverse different states, the contracting powers stipulate among themselves that those principles shall in future be equally applied to the Danube and its mouths. They declare that this arrangement henceforth forms a part of the public law of Europe, and take it under their guarantee.

The navigation of the Danube cannot be subjected to any impediment or charge not expressly provided for by the stipulations contained in the following articles; in consequence, there shall not be levied any toll founded solely upon the fact of the navigation of the river, nor any duty upon the goods which may be on board of vessels. The regulations of police and of quarantine to be established for the safety of the states separated or traversed by that river shall be so framed as to facilitate, as much as possible, the passage of vessels. With the exception of such regulations, no obstacle whatever shall be opposed to free navigation.

Art. 16. Establishing a temporary international commission for the control of navigation on the Danube.

Arts. 17–19. Establishing a permanent commission for the improvement and control of navigation on the Danube.

Art. 20. In exchange for the towns, ports, and territories enumerated in Art. 4 of the present treaty, and in order more fully to secure the freedom of the navigation of the Danube, his majesty the Emperor of all the Russias consents to the rectification of his frontier in Bessarabia.

Art. 21. The territory ceded by Russia shall be annexed to the principality of Moldavia under the suzerainty of the Sublime Porte. The inhabitants of that territory shall enjoy the rights and privileges secured to the principalities; and during the space of three years they shall be permitted to transfer their domicile elsewhere, disposing freely of their property.

Art. 22. The principalities of Wallachia and Moldavia shall continue to enjoy, under the suzerainty of the Porte and under the guarantee of the contracting powers, the privileges and immunities of which they are in possession. No exclusive protection shall be exercised over them by any of the guaranteeing powers. There shall be no separate right of interference in their internal affairs.

Arts. 23–27. Concerning the government, administration, preservation of order in, and defence of the principalities of Wallachia and Moldavia.

Art. 28. The principality of Servia shall continue to hold the Sublime Porte, in conformity with the imperial *hats* which fix and determine its rights and immunities, placed henceforward under the collective guarantee of the contracting powers. In consequence the said principality shall preserve its independent and national administration, as well as full liberty of worship, of legislation, of commerce, and of navigation.

Art. 29. The right of garrison of the Sublime Porte, as stipulated by anterior regulations, is maintained. No armed intervention can take place in Servia without previous agreement between the high contracting powers.

Art. 30. His majesty the Emperor of all the Russias and his majesty the Sultan maintain in its integrity the state of their possessions in Asia, such as it legally existed before the rupture. A mixed commission for the verification or rectification of the frontiers is provided for.

Art. 31. The territories occupied during the war by the troops of their majesties the Queen of the United Kingdom of Great Britain and Ireland, the Emperor of Austria, the Emperor of the French, and the King of Sardinia, according to the terms of the conventions signed at Constantinople on the 12th of March, 1854, between Great Britain, France, and the Sublime Porte; on the 14th of June, of the same year, between Austria and the Sublime Porte; and on the 15th of March, 1855, between Sardinia and the Sublime Porte, shall be evacuated as soon as possible after the exchange of the ratifications of the present treaty. The periods and the means of execution shall form the object of an arrangement between the Sublime Porte and the powers whose troops have occupied its territory.

Art. 32. Until the treaties or conventions which existed before the war between the belligerent powers have been either renewed or replaced by new acts, commerce of importation or of exportation shall take place reciprocally on the footing of the regulations in force before the war; and in all other matters their subjects shall be respectively treated upon the footing of the most favoured nation.

Art. 33. The convention concluded this day between their majesties the Queen of the United Kingdom of Great Britain and Ireland, the Emperor of the French, on the one part, and his majesty the Emperor of all the Russias on the other part respecting the Åland Islands, is and remains annexed to the present treaty, and shall have the same force and validity as if it formed a part thereof.

### CONVENTIONS ANNEXED TO THE PRECEDING TREATY

1. *Convention between the Queen of the United Kingdom of Great Britain and Ireland, the Emperor of Austria, the Emperor of the French, the King of Prussia, the Emperor of Russia, and the King of Sardinia, on the one part, and the Sultan on the other part, respecting the Straits of the Dardanelles and of the Bosporus.*

Art. 1. His majesty the Sultan, on the one part, declares that he is firmly resolved to maintain for the future the principle invariably established as the ancient rule of his empire, and in virtue of which it has at all times been prohibited for the ships of war of foreign powers to enter the Straits of the Dardanelles and of the Bosporus, and that, so long as the Porte is at peace, his majesty will admit no foreign ship of war into the said Straits.

And their majesties the Queen of the United Kingdom of Great Britain and Ireland, the Emperor of Austria, the Emperor of the French, the King of Prussia, the Emperor of all the Russias, and the King of Sardinia, on the other part, engage to respect this determination of the Sultan's, and to conform themselves to the principle above declared.

Art. 2. The Sultan reserves to himself, as in past times, to deliver firmans of passage for light vessels under flag of war, which shall be employed, as is usual, in the service of the missions of foreign powers.

Art. 3. The same exception applies to the light vessels under flag of war, which each of the contracting powers is authorised to station at the mouths of the Danube, in order to secure the execution of the regulations relative to the liberty of that river, and the number of which is not to exceed two for each power.

2. *Convention between the Emperor of Russia and the Sultan, limiting their naval force in the Black Sea.*

Art. 1. The high contracting parties mutually engage not to have in the Black Sea any other vessels of war than those of which the number, the force, and the dimensions are hereinafter stipulated.

Art. 2. The high contracting parties reserve to themselves each to maintain in that sea six steam-vessels of fifty metres in length at the line of floatation, of a tonnage of 800 tons at the *maximum,* and four light steam or sailing vessels, of a tonnage which shall not exceed 200 tons each.

3. *Convention between her Majesty the Queen of the United Kingdom of Great Britain and Ireland, the Emperor of the French, and the Emperor of Russia, respecting the Åland Islands.*

Art. 1. His majesty the Emperor of all the Russias, in order to respond to the desire which has been expressed to him by their majesties the Queen of the United Kingdom of Great Britain and Ireland and the Emperor of the French, declares that the Åland Islands shall not be fortified, and that no military or naval establishment shall be maintained or created there.

*Declaration respecting maritime law, signed by the plenipotentiaries of Great Britian, Austria, France, Prussia, Russia, Sardinia, and Turkey, assembled in congress at Paris, April 16th, 1856.*

The plenipotentiaries who signed the treaty of Paris, of the 30th of March, 1856, being duly authorised, and having come to an agreement, have adopted the following solemn declaration:—

1. Privateering is, and remains, abolished.
2. The neutral flag covers enemy's goods, with the exception of contraband of war.
3. Neutral goods, with the exception of contraband of war, are not liable to capture under enemy's flag.
4. Blockades, in order to be binding, must be effective — that is to say maintained by force sufficient really to prevent access to the coast of the enemy.

The governments of the undersigned plenipotentiaries engage to bring the present declaration to the knowledge of the states which have taken part in the congress of Paris, and to invite them to accede to it.

Convinced that the maxims which they now proclaim cannot but be received with gratitude by the whole world, the under-signed plenipotentiaries doubt not that the efforts of their governments to obtain the general adoption thereof will be crowned with full success.

The present declaration is not and shall not be binding, except between those powers who have acceded, or shall accede, to it.

Done at Paris, the 16th of April, 1856.

[Here follow the names of the plenipotentiaries of the signatory powers.]

## II

## TREATY OF BERLIN, 1878

Her Majesty the Queen of the United Kingdom of Great Britain and Ireland, Empress of India, His Majesty the Emperor of Germany, King of Prussia, His Majesty the Emperor of Austria, King of Bohemia, etc., and King Apostolic of Hungary, the President of the French Republic, His Majesty the King of Italy, His Majesty the Emperor of All the Russias and His Majesty the Emperor of the Ottomans, being desirous to regulate with a view to European order, conformably to the stipulations of the Treaty of Paris of 30th March, 1856, the questions raised in the East by the events of late years and by the war terminated by the Preliminary Treaty of San Stefano, have been unanimously of opinion that the meeting of a Congress would offer the best means of facilitating an understanding.

[Here follow the names of the ambassadors.]

Who, in accordance with the proposal of the Court of Austria-Hungary, and on the invitation of the Court of Germany, have met at Berlin furnished with full powers, which have been found in good and due form.

An understanding having been happily established between them, they have agreed to the following stipulations:

Art. 1. Bulgaria is constituted an autonomous and tributary Principality under the suzerainty of His Imperial Majesty the Sultan; it will have a Christian government and a national militia.

Art. 2. The Principality of Bulgaria will include the following territories:

[Here follows a detailed account of boundaries. These having mainly a technical interest are omitted here and in other articles of the treaty of the same nature. Those articles likewise whose importance is purely local are given in abbreviated form.]

This delimitation shall be fixed on the spot by the European Commission, on which the Signatory Powers shall be represented. It is understood: 1. That this Commission will take into consideration the necessity for His Imperial Majesty the Sultan to be able to defend the Balkan frontier of Eastern Rumelia. 2. That no fortifications may be erected within a radius of 10 kilommetres from Samakov.

Art 3. The Prince of Bulgaria shall be freely elected by the population and confirmed by the Sublime Porte, with the assent of the Powers. No member of the Reigning Dynasties of the Great European Powers may be elected Prince of Bulgaria. In case of a vacancy in the princely dignity the election of a new Prince shall take place under the same conditions and with the same forms.

Art. 4. An Assembly of Notables of Bulgaria convoked at Tirnovo, shall, before the election of the Prince, draw up the Organic Law of the Principality. In the districts where Bulgarians are intermixed with Turkish, Rumanian, Greek or other populations, the rights and intents of these populations shall be taken into consideration as regards the elections and the drawing up of the Organic Law.

Art. 5. Differences of religious creed not to be a bar to office holding in Bulgaria. Complete freedom of worship assured.

Art. 6. The provisional administration of Bulgaria.

Art. 7. The provisional *régime* shall not be prolonged beyond a period of nine months from the exchange of the ratifications of the present

Treaty    When the Organic Law is completed the election of the Prince of Bulgaria shall be proceeded with immediately.    As soon as the Prince shall have been installed, the new organisation shall be put into force, and the Principality shall enter into the full enjoyment of its autonomy.

Art. 8. The treaties of commerce and navigation as well as all conventions and arrangements concluded between Foreign Powers and the Porte, and now in force are maintained in the Principality of Bulgaria, and no change shall be made in them with regard to any Power without its previous consent.    No transit duties shall be levied in Bulgaria on goods passing through that principality.    The subjects and citizens of commerce of all the powers shall be treated in the principality on a footing of strict equality.    The immunities and privileges of foreigners, as well as the rights of consular jurisdiction and protection as established by the capitulations and usages, shall remain in full force so long as they shall not have been modified with the consent of the parties concerned.

Art. 9. Tribute to be paid by Bulgaria to suzerain court, etc.

Art. 10. Railway questions in Bulgaria.

Art. 11. Evacuation and demolition of Bulgarian fortresses.

Art. 12. Land rights of non-resident Moslems and others.    Commission to settle questions of state property.    Bulgarians travelling in Turkey subject to Ottoman laws.

Art. 13. A province is formed south of the Balkans which will take the name of " Eastern Rumelia," and will remain under the direct political and military authority of His Imperial Majesty, the Sultan, under conditions of administrative autonomy.    It shall have a Christian Governor-General.

Art. 14. Boundaries of Eastern Rumelia.

Art. 15. His Majesty, the Sultan, shall have the right of providing for the defence of the land and sea frontiers of the province by erecting fortifications on those frontiers and maintaining troops there.    Internal order is maintained in Eastern Rumelia by a native gendarmerie assisted by a local militia. In forming these corps, the officers of which are nominated by the Sultan, regard shall be paid in the different localities to the religion of the inhabitants.

His Imperial Majesty, the Sultan, undertakes not to employ irregular troops, such as Bashi-Bazouks and Circassians, in the garrisons of the frontiers.    The regular troops detailed for this service must not in any case be billeted on the inhabitants.    When they pass through the province they shall not make a stay there.

Art. 16. The governor-general shall have the right of summoning the Ottoman troops in the event of the internal or external security of the province being threatened.    In such an eventuality the Sublime Porte shall inform the representatives of the Powers at Constantinople of such a decision, as well as of the exigencies which justify it.

Art. 17. The governor-general of Eastern Rumelia shall be nominated by the Sublime Porte, with the assent of the Powers for a term of five years.

Arts. 18 and 19. Creating a European commission for the organisation of Eastern Rumelia.

Arts. 20 and 21. Concerning foreign relations, religious liberty and railway administration of Eastern Rumelia.

Art. 22. Regulations concerning Russian occupation of Bulgaria and Eastern Rumelia.    Evacuation of Rumania.

Art. 23. The Sublime Porte undertakes scrupulously to apply, in the Island of Crete the Organic Law of 1868 with such modifications as may be considered equitable.    Similar laws adapted to local requirements, excepting as regards the exemption from taxation granted to Crete shall also be introduced into the other parts of Turkey in Europe, for which no such organisation has been provided by the present Treaty. The Sublime Porte shall depute special Commissions, in which the native element shall be largely represented, to settle the details of the new laws in each province. The schemes of organisation resulting from these labours shall be submitted for examination to the Sublime Porte, which, before promulgating the Acts for putting them into force, shall consult the European Commission instituted for Eastern Rumelia.

Art. 24. In the event of the Sublime Porte and Greece being unable to agree upon the rectification of frontiers suggested in the 13th protocol of the Congress of Berlin, Germany, Austria-Hungary, France, Great Britain, Italy, and Russia reserve to themselves to offer their mediation to the two parties to facilitate negotiations.

Art. 25. The provinces of Bosnia and Herzegovina shall be occupied and administered by Austria-Hungary. The government of Austria-Hungary, not desiring to undertake the administration of the Sandjak of Novibazar, which extends between Servia and Montenegro in a south-easterly direction to the other side of Mitrovitz, the Ottoman administration shall continue to exercise its functions there. Nevertheless, in order to assure the maintenance of the new political state of affairs, as well as the freedom and security of communications, Austria-Hungary reserves the right of keeping garrisons and having military and commercial roads in the whole of this part of the ancient Vilayet of Bosnia.

Arts. 26–33. Recognition of the independence of Montenegro and regulations as to its boundaries, freedom of worship, debt, commerce and defence.

Art. 34. The High Contracting Parties recognise the independence of Servia, subject to the conditions set forth in the following Article.

Art. 35. Differences of religious creed to be no bar to officeholding in Servia; freedom of worship assured.

Art. 36. Boundaries of Servia.

Arts. 37–42. Concerning commercial relations and consular jurisdiction in Servia; railway administration and property rights.

Art. 43. The High Contracting Parties recognise the independence of Rumania, subject to the conditions set forth in the two following Articles.

Art. 44. Differences in religious creed to be no bar to officeholding in Rumania: freedom of worship assured.

Arts. 45–46. Concerning the cession of Bessarabian territory by Rumania to Russia and the addition of the Danubian Delta, etc., to Rumania.

Arts. 47–49. Concerning fisheries, transit dues and rights of foreign consuls in Rumania.

Art. 50. Reciprocity of consular rights between Turkey and Rumania. Transfer of public works in ceded territory.

Art. 52. In order to increase the guarantees which assure the freedom of navigation on the Danube, which is recognised as of European interest, the High Contracting Parties determine that all the fortresses and fortifications existing on the course of the river from the Iron Gates to its mouths shall be rased, and no new ones erected. No vessel of war shall navigate the Danube, below the Iron Gates, with the exception of vessels of light tonnage in the service of the river police and customs. The "stationnaires" of the Powers at the mouths of the Danube may, however, ascend the river as far as Galatz.

Arts. 53–56. Concerning the rights and duties of the European Commission of the Danube.

Art. 57. Rights of Austria-Hungary on the Danube.

Art. 58. The Sublime Porte cedes to the Russian Empire in Asia, the territories of Ardahan, Kars, and Batum, together with the latter port, as well as all the territories comprised between the former Russo-Turkish frontier and the following line:

[Here follows new boundary line between Russia and Turkey.]

Art. 59. His Majesty the Emperor of Russia declares that it is his intention to constitute Batum a free port, essentially commercial.

Art. 60. Restoration of Alaschkerd to Turkey: cession of Khotour to Persia.

Art. 61. The Sublime Porte undertakes to carry out, without further delay, the improvements and reforms demanded by local requirements in the provinces inhabited by the Armenians, and to guarantee their security against the Circassians and Kurds.

Art. 62. Pledge of Turkey to maintain the principle of religious liberty.

Art. 63. The Treaty of Paris, of March 30th, 1856, as well as the Treaty of London, of March 13th, 1871, are maintained in all such of their provisions as are not abrogated or modified by the preceding stipulations.

Art. 64. The present treaty shall be ratified, and the ratifications exchanged at Berlin, within three weeks, or sooner if possible.

In faith whereof the respective Plenipotentiaries have signed it, and affixed to it the seal of their arms. Done at Berlin, the thirteenth day of the month of July, one thousand eight hundred and seventy-eight.

[Signatures.]

## III

## THE FIRST HAGUE PEACE CONFERENCE

[An international conference of representatives of the principal powers of the world assembled at The Hague, May 18th, 1899, in response to a call issued by the Czar of Russia with a view to concerted action in regard to an amelioration of the hardships of war, the furtherance of the principle of the arbitration of international disputes, the maintenance of a general peace and the possible reduction of the world's military and naval armaments. The states represented were Germany, Austria-Hungary, Belgium, China. Japan, France, Mexico, the United States, Great Britain, Sweden and Norway, Denmark, Russia, Spain, Italy, Servia, Siam, the Netherlands, Rumania, Turkey, Bulgaria, Greece, Switzerland, Luxembourg, Persia and Portugal. Sessions continued until July 29th, when the delegates embodied the conclusions reached in a final act for submission to the several states represented. This final act consisted of three conventions, three formal declarations and a series of six resolutions. The resolutions embodied an expression of the desire that certain unsettled points in regard to neutrals, contraband and so forth might be passed upon by an international tribunal at an early date. The conventions were (1) For the pacific settlement of international conflicts; (2) Regarding the laws and customs of war by land; (3) For the adaptation to maritime warfare of the principles of the Geneva Convention, August 22nd, 1864. The declarations had to do with (1) The prohibition of launching explosives and projectiles from balloons; (2) The prohibition of the use of projectiles diffusing poisonous gases; (3) The prohibition of the use of expanding or flattening bullets. The Conventions were signed at once by 16 powers, Germany, Great Britain, Austria-Hungary, Japan, Italy, and several minor powers, withholding their assent temporarily but finally accepting them.]

## A. CONVENTION FOR THE PACIFIC SETTLEMENT OF INTERNATIONAL DISPUTES

### Title I — On the Maintenance of the General Peace

Art. 1. Agreement of powers to use best efforts to ensure peaceful settlement of international disputes.

### Title II — On Good Offices and Mediation

Arts. 2-4. Recommendation of the principle of mediation, the exercise of which is never to be considered an unfriendly act.

Art. 5. The functions of the mediator are at an end when once it is declared, either by one of the parties to the dispute, or by the mediator himself, that the means of reconciliation proposed by him are not accepted.

Art. 6. Good offices and mediation, either at the request of the parties at variance, or on the initiative of powers strangers to the dispute, have exclusively the character of advice, and never have binding force.

Art. 7. The acceptance of mediation not to hinder preparations for, or interfere with the prosecution of war.

Art. 8. Concerning special mediation.

### Title III — On International Commissions of Inquiry

Arts. 9-13. Appointment and procedure of the Commissions of Inquiry.

Art. 14. The report of the International Commission of Inquiry is limited to a statement of facts, and is in no way the character of an arbitral award.

### Title IV — On International Arbitration

#### CHAPTER I — ON THE SYSTEM OF ARBITRATION

Arts. 15-19. Recognition of the efficacy of arbitration conventions, and the implied engagement of loyal submission to the award.

#### CHAPTER II — ON THE PERMANENT COURT OF ARBITRATION

Art. 20. Undertaking of the signatory powers to organise a permanent court.

Art. 21. The permanent court shall be competent for all arbitration cases, unless the parties agree to institute a special tribunal.

Art. 22. An international bureau, established at The Hague, serves as record office for the court, and the channel for communications relative to the meetings of the court. It has the custody of the archives and conducts all the administrative business.

Art. 23. Selection of members of the court.

Art. 24. Arbitrators are to be chosen from the general list of members of the court. Alternative provisions in case of failure of direct agreement.

Art. 25. Seat of the tribunal to be ordinarily at The Hague.

Art. 26. The jurisdiction of the permanent court may within the conditions laid down in the regulations, be extended to disputes between non-signatory powers, or between signatory powers and non-signatory powers if the parties are agreed on recourse to this tribunal.

Art. 27. Reminding powers of the existence of the court not to be considered an unfriendly act.

Art. 28. Institution and duties of a permanent administrative council to be composed of the diplomatic representatives of the signatory powers accredited to The Hague and of the Netherland minister for foreign affairs, who will act as president.

Art. 29. The expenses of the bureau.

### Chapter III — On Arbitral Procedure

Arts. 30-31. Regarding agreement to submit to arbitration.

Art. 32. Failing the constitution of the tribunal by direct agreement between the parties, the following course shall be pursued: Each party appoints two arbitrators and these latter together choose an umpire. In case of equal voting the choice of the umpire is entrusted to a third power, selected by the parties by common accord. If no agreement is arrived at on this subject, each party selects a different power, and the choice of the umpire is made in concert by the powers thus selected.

Arts. 33-38. Concerning umpires, seat of tribunal, counsel, and language.

Art. 39. As a general rule the arbitral procedure comprises two distinct phases; preliminary examination of documents, manuscripts and briefs and oral discussion of the agreements of the parties.

Arts. 40-51. Concerning procedure as to documents and arguments.

Art. 52. The award, given by a majority of votes, is accompanied by a statement of reasons. It is drawn up in writing and signed by each member of the tribunal. Those members who are in the minority may record their dissent when signing.

Art. 53. Publication of the award.

Art. 54. The award puts an end to the dispute definitively, and without appeal.

Art. 55. Concerning demand for a revision of the award on account of the discovery of new evidence.

Art. 56. The award binding only on parties who submitted to arbitration. Right to intervene of other nations parties to a convention interpreted.

Art. 57. Parties to arbitration to share expenses equally.

### General Provisions

Arts. 58-60. Ratification and notification of ratification and the adherence of non-signatory powers.

Art. 61. In the event of one of the high contracting parties denouncing the present Convention, this denunciation would not take effect until a year after its notification made in writing to the Netherland government, and by it communicated at once to all the other contracting powers. This denunciation shall only affect the notifying power.

### B. CONVENTION WITH RESPECT TO THE LAWS AND CUSTOMS OF WAR ON LAND

[Here follow the names of the signatory powers and a statement of the reasons for and the necessities which have led to the following convention.]

Art 1. Contracting powers to accept "Regulations" adopted by the present conference.

Art. 2. Regulations to be binding only in case of war between two contracting powers, and cease to be binding when a non-contracting power joins one of the belligerents.

Arts. 3–5. Concerning ratification by contracting powers, the adherence of non-contracting powers, and denunciation by a contracting power.

### ANNEX TO THE CONVENTION

Regulations Respecting the Laws and Customs of War on Land.

### Section I — On Belligerents

#### CHAPTER I — ON THE QUALIFICATIONS OF BELLIGERENTS

Art. 1. The laws, rights, and duties of war apply not only to the armies, but also to militia and volunteer corps, fulfilling the following conditions: I. To be commanded by a person responsible for his subordinates; II. To have a fixed distinctive emblem recognisable at a distance; III. To carry arms openly; and IV. To conduct their operations in accordance with the laws and customs of war. In countries where militia or volunteer corps constitute the "army," or form part of it, they are included under the term.

Art. 2. The population of a territory which has not been occupied who, on the enemy's approach, spontaneously take up arms to resist the invading troops without having time to organise themselves in accordance with Article I, shall be regarded a belligerent, if they respect the laws and customs of war.

Art. 3. The armed forces of the belligerent parties may consist of combatants and non-combatants. In case of capture by the enemy both have a right to be treated as prisoners of war.

#### CHAPTER II — ON PRISONERS OF WAR

Arts. 4–12. Prisoners of war; their personal property, their imprisonment, utilisation of their labor, maintenance, recapture of escaped prisoners and parole.

Art. 13. Individuals who follow an army without directly belonging to it, such as newspaper correspondents and reporters, sutlers, contractors, who fall into the enemy's hands, and whom the latter think fit to detain, have a right to be treated as prisoners of war, provided they can produce a certificate from the military authorities of the army they were accompanying.

Art. 14. A bureau for information relative to prisoners of war to be instituted, on the commencement of hostilities, in each of the belligerent states, to answer all inquiries about prisoners of war, to keep an individual return for each prisoner of war.

Arts. 15–16. Concerning rights and privileges of relief societies and information bureaus.

Art. 17. Officers taken prisoners may receive, if necessary, the full pay allowed them in this position by their country's regulations, the amount to be repaid by their government.

Arts. 18–20. Right of prisoners to freedom of worship; wills; repatriation.

## CHAPTER III—ON THE SICK AND WOUNDED

Art. 21. The obligations of belligerents with regard to the sick and wounded are governed by the Geneva Convention of the 22nd of August, 1864, subject to any modifications which may be introduced into it.

### Section II—On Hostilities

## CHAPTER 1—ON MEANS OF INJURING THE ENEMY, SIEGES, AND BOMBARDMENTS

Art. 22. The right of belligerents to adopt means of injuring the enemy is not unlimited.

Art. 23. Besides the prohibitions provided by special conventions, it is especially prohibited: (a) To employ poison or poisoned arms; (b) To kill or wound treacherously individuals belonging to the hostile nation or army; (c) To kill or wound an enemy who, having laid down arms, or having no longer means of defence, has surrendered at discretion; (d) To declare that no quarter will be given; (e) To employ arms, projectiles, or material of a nature to cause superfluous injury; (f) To make improper use of a flag of truce, the national flag, or military ensigns and the enemy's uniform, as well as the distinctive badges of the Geneva Convention; (g) To destroy or seize the enemy's property, unless such destruction or seizure be imperatively demanded by the necessities of war.

Art. 24. Ruses of war and the employment of methods necessary to obtain information about the enemy and the country, are considered allowable.

Art. 25. Attack or bombardment of undefended towns prohibited.

Art. 26. Providing for warning before bombardment.

Art. 27. In sieges and bombardments all necessary steps should be taken to spare as far as possible edifices devoted to religion, art, science, and charity, hospitals and places where the sick and wounded are collected, provided they are not used at the same time for military purposes. The besieged should indicate these buildings or places by some particular and visible signs, which should previously be notified to the assailants.

Art. 28. Pillage of a town even when taken by assault prohibited.

[Chapters II–V, containing Arts. 29–41, are concerned with Spies, Flags of Truce, Capitulations, and Armistices.]

### Section III—On Military Authority over Hostile Territory

Art. 42. Territory is considered occupied when it is actually placed under the authority of the hostile army. The occupation applies only to the territory where such authority is established, and in a position to assert itself.

Art. 43. The authority of the legitimate power having actually passed into the hands of the occupant, the latter shall take all steps in her power to re-establish and ensure, as far as possible, public order and safety, while representing, unless absolutely prevented, the laws in force in the country.

Arts. 44–45. Any compulsion of the population of occupied territory to take part in military operations against its own country or oath to the hostile powers is prohibited.

Art. 46. Family honours and rights, individual lives and private property, as well as religious convictions and liberty, must be respected.    Private property cannot be confiscated.

Art.. 47.  Pillage is formally prohibited.

Arts. 48–49.  Right of hostile power to levy taxes, dues, and tolls in occupied territory for the administration of such territory.

Art. 50.  No general penalty, pecuniary or otherwise, can be inflicted on the population on account of the acts of individuals for which it cannot be regarded as collectively responsible.

Art. 51.  No tax shall be collected except under a written order on the responsibility of a commander-in-chief.  For every payment a receipt shall be given to the taxpayer.

Art. 52.  Neither requisitions in kind, nor services can be demanded from communes or inhabitants except for the necessities of the army of occupation. They must be in proportion to the resources of the country, and of such a nature as not to involve the population in the obligation of taking part in military operations against their country.  These requisitions and services shall only be demanded on the authority of the commander in the locality occupied.  The contributions in kind shall as far as possible, be paid for in ready money; if not, their receipt shall be acknowledged.

Art. 53.  An army of occupation can only take possession of the cash, funds, and property liable to requisition belonging strictly to the state, depots of arms, means of transport, stores and supplies, and generally all movable property of the state which may be used for military operations. Railway plants, land telegraphs, telephones, steamers, and other ships, apart from cases governed by maritime law, as well as depots of arms and, generally, all kinds of war material, even though belonging to companies or to private persons, are likewise material which may serve for military operations, but they must be restored at the conclusion of peace, and indemnities paid.

Art. 54.  The plant of railways coming from neutral states whether the property of those states, or of companies or of private persons, shall be sent back to them as soon as possible.

Art. 55.  The occupying state shall only be regarded as administrator and usufructuary of the public buildings, real property, forests, and agricultural works belonging to the hostile state, and situated in the occupied country.

Art. 56.  The property of the communes, that of religious, charitable, and educational institutions, and those of arts and science, even when state property, shall be treated as private property.  All seizure of, and destruction, or intentional damage done to such institutions, to historical monuments, works of art or science, is prohibited.

*Section IV—On the Internment of Belligerents and the Care of the Wounded in Neutral Countries.*

Arts. 57–60.  Concerning the internment, detention and maintenance of belligerents, and of the sick and wounded of a belligerent in a neutral country.  Application of the Geneva Convention.

### DECLARATIONS

(I) The contracting powers agree to prohibit, for a term of five years, the launching of projectiles and explosives from balloons, or by other new methods of a similar nature.

(II) The contracting parties agree to abstain from the use of bullets which expand or flatten easily in the human body, such as bullets with a hard envelope which does not entirely cover the core, or is pierced with incisions.

(III) The contracting powers agree to abstain from the use of projectiles the object of which is the diffusion of asphyxiating or deleterious gases.

The above declarations are only binding on the contracting powers in the case of a war between two or more of them. They shall cease to be binding from the time when in a war between the contracting powers, one of the belligerents shall be joined by a non-contracting power.

The non-signatory powers can adhere to the above declarations.

In the event of one of the high contracting parties denouncing the declarations, such denunciation shall not take effect until a year after the notification made in writing to the government of the Netherlands, and forthwith communicated by it to all the other contracting powers. This denunciation shall only affect the notifying power.

### D. CONVENTION FOR THE ADAPTATION TO MARITIME WARFARE OF THE PRINCIPLES OF THE GENEVA CONVENTION OF AUGUST 22ND, 1854

Arts. 1–5. Military hospital-ships owned either by a state or a private individual or society not to be considered belligerent.

Art. 6. Neutral merchantmen, yachts, or vessels, having or taking on board, sick, wounded, or the shipwrecked of the belligerents, cannot be captured for so doing, but they are liable to capture, for any violation of neutrality.

Art. 7. Concerning the inviolability of the religious, medical, or hospital staff of any captured ship.

Art. 8. Sailors and soldiers who are taken on board when sick or wounded, to whatever nation they belong, shall be protected by the captors.

Art. 9. The shipwrecked, wounded, or sick of one of the belligerents who fall into the hands of the other, are prisoners of war.

Art. 10. Concerning the treatment of the shipwrecked, wounded, or sick, landed at a neutral port with the consent of the local authorities.

Art. 11. Concerning limitation, ratification, acceptance by a non-signatory power and denunciation of the above articles.

# BRIEF REFERENCE-LIST OF AUTHORITIES BY CHAPTERS

[The letter *a* is reserved for Editorial Matter.]

### CHAPTER I.  LAND AND PEOPLE AND EARLY HISTORY ( to 1054 A.D.)

*b* A. LEROY-BEAULIEU, *L'Empire des Tsars et les Russes.* — *c* M. KOVALEVSKI, *Russian Political Institutions.* — *d* PROCOPIUS, *Gothica seu Bellum Gothicum.* — *e* MAURICIUS, *Stategicum.* — *f* LEO, *Tacita seu de re militari.* — *g* T. SCHIEMANN, *Russland, Polen und Livland.* — *h* NESTOR, *Chronicle.* — *i* W. K. KELLY, *History of Russia.* — *j* A. RAMBAUD, *Histoire de la Russie.* — *k* ROBERT BELL, *History of Russia.*

### CHAPTER II.  THE PERIOD OF THE PRINCIPALITIES (1054–1224 A.D.)

*b* A. RAMBAUD, *Histoire de la Russie.* — *c* T. SCHIEMANN, *Russland, Polen und Livland.* — *d* N. M. KARAMZIN, *History of the Russian Empire.*

### CHAPTER III.  THE TIME OF TATAR DOMINATION (1235–1462 A.D.)

*b* R. N. BESTUZHEV-RIUMIN, *Russian History.* — *c* D. M. WALLACE, *Russia.* — *d* R. BELL, *A History of Russia.* — *e* S. M. SOLOVIOV, *History of Russia from the Earliest Times.* — *f* N. TURGENIEV, *La Russie et les Russes.* — *g* W. K. KELLY, *History of Russia.* — *h* N. I. KOSTOMAROV, *Russian History.* — *i* A. BRÜCKNER, *Geschichte Russlands.*

### CHAPTER IV.  FROM IVAN THE GREAT TO IVAN THE TERRIBLE (1462–1584 A.D.)

*b* R. N. BESTUZHEV-RIUMIN, *Russian History.* — *c* N. I. KOSTOMAROV, *Russian History.* — *d* P. STRAHL and E. HERMANN, *Geschichte des Russischen Staates.* — *e* A. RAMBAUD, *Histoire de la Russie.* — *f* N. KARAMZIN, *History of the Russian Empire.* — *g* R. BELL, *History of Russia.* — *h* S. M. SOLOVIOV, *History of Russia from the Earliest Times.*

### CHAPTER V.  THE CENTURY AFTER IVAN THE TERRIBLE (1584–1682 A.D.)

*b* PROSPER MÉRIMÉE, *Demetrius the Impostor.* — *c* N. I. KOSTOMAROV, *Russian History.* — *d* N. KARAMZIN, *History of the Russian Empire.* — *e* JEAN HENRI SCHNITZLER, *L'Empire des Tsars au point actuél de la science.* — *f* A. RAMBAUD, *Histoire de la Russie.* — *g* R. BELL, *History of Russia.* — *h* W. K. KELLY, *History of Russia.* — *i* S. M. SOLOVIOV, *History of Russia from the Earliest Times.*

### CHAPTER VI.  PETER THE GREAT (1682–1725 A.D.)

*b* VOLTAIRE, *Histoire de Russie.* — *c* R. BELL, *History of Russia.* — *d* N. I. KOSTOMAROV, *Russian History.* — *e* W. K. KELLY, *History of Russia.* — *f* P. STRAHL and E. HERMANN, *Geschichte des Russischen Staates.* — *g* A. RAMBAUD, *Histoire de la Russie.* — *h* P. SHTCHEBALSKI, *Readings from Russian History.* — *i* S. M. SOLOVIOV, *History of Russia from the Earliest Times.* — *j* AUGUSTE DE HAXTHAUSEN, *The Russian Empire, its People, Institutions and Resourses.* — *k* CLAUDE CARLOMAN DE RULHIÈRE, *Révolution de Pologne.* — *l* C. A. DE LOUVILLE, *Mémoires.* — *m* IVAN GOLIKOV, *The Acts of Peter the Great.*

### CHAPTER VII.  CATHERINE I TO PETER III (1725–1796 A.D.)

*b* R. BELL, *History of Russia.* — *c* N. I. KOSTOMAROV, *Russian History.* — *d* P. SHTCHEBALSKI, *Readings from Russian History.* — *e* V. A. BILBASSOV, *History of Catherine II.* — *f* A. RAMBAUD, *Historie de la Russie.* — *g* R. NISBET BAIN, *The Daughter of Peter the Great.*

### Chapter VIII. The Age of Catherine II (1769-1796 a.d.)

[b] P. Shtchebalski, *Readings from Russian History.* — [c] V. A. Bilbassov, *History of Catherine II.* — [d] A. Rambaud, *Histoire de la Russie.* — [e] R. Bell, *History of Russia.* — [f] Antoine de Ferrand, *Les trois démembrements de la Pologne.* — [g] Catherine II, *Mémoirs* — [h] A. Brückner, *History of Catherine II.* — [i] Theodor von Bernhardi, *Geschichte Russlands und der europäischen Politik in den Jahren 1814-1831* — [j] W. K. Kelly, *History of Russia.* — [k] N. K. Shilder, *The Emperor Alexander I.*

### Chapter IX. Russia in the Napoleonic Epoch (1796-1815 a.d.)

[b] F. C. Schlosser, *Geschichte des 18. und 19. Jahrhunderts.* — [c] A. Rambaud, *Histoire de la Russie.* — [d] R. Bell, *History of Russia.* — [e] R. Gossip, *History of Russia.* — [f] A. Alison, *History of Europe.* — [g] N. K. Shilder, *The Emperor Alexander I.* — [h] P. de Ségur, *History of the Expedition to Russia.* — [i] A. Mikhailovski-Danilevski, *Vie du Feld-Maréchal Koutouzoff.* — [j] T. von Bernhardi, *Geschichte Russlands und der europäischen Politik in den Jahren 1814-1831.* — [k] W. K. Kelly, *History of Russia.* — [l] F. H. Skrine, *The Expansion of Russia, 1815-1900.*

### Chapter X. Alexander I, Mystic and Humanitarian (1801-1825 a.d.)

[b] N. K. Shilder, *The Emperor Alexander I.* — [d] N. Turgeniev, *La Russie et les Russes.* — [e] W .K. Kelly, *History of Russia.* — [f] A. Rambaud, *Histoire de la Russie.* — [g] A. Alison, *History of Europe.* — [h] F. H. Skrine, *The Expansion of Russia 1815-1900.* — [i] Storck, *Russland unter Alexander dem Ersten.*

### Chapter XI. The Reign of Nicholas I (1825-1854 a.d.)

[b] N. K. Shilder, *The Reign of the Emperor Nicholas I.* — [c] J. H. Schnitzler, *La Russie, Ancienne et Moderne.* — [d] W. K. Kelly, *History of Russia.* — [e] A. P. de Custine, *La Russie en 1839.* — [f] A. Rambaud, *Histoire de la Russie.* — [g] T. Delord, *Histoire du second Empire.* — [h] P. De la Gorce, *Histoire du second Empire.* — [i] H. Martin, *Histoire de la France depuis 1789 jusqu'à nos jours.* — [j] A. A. Shumakr, *The Czar Liberator.* — [k] F. H. Skrine, *The Expansion of Russia 1815-1900.*

### Chapter XII. Alexander II, The Czar Liberator (1855-1881 a.d.)

[b] A. Rambaud, *Histoire de la Russie.* — [c] D. M. Wallace, *Russia.* — [d] A. A. Shumakr, *The Czar Liberator.* — [e] P. De la Gorce, *Histoire du second Empire.* — [f] Alexander II, *Manifesto or Proclamation.* — [g] F. H. Skrine, *The Expansion of Russia 1815-1900.* — [h] Julius Eckhardt, *Modern Russia.*

### Chapter XIII. Reaction, Expansion, and the War with Japan (1881-1904 a.d.)

[b] D. M. Wallace, article on Russian history in the *New Volumes* of the *Encyclopædia Britannica.* — [c] Albert J. Beveridge, *The Russian Advance.* — [d] Henry Norman, *All the Russias.* — [e] A. N. Kuropatkin, quoted in F. H. Skrine and E. D. Ross's *The Heart of Asia.*

### Appendix. Documents Relating to Russian History

These documents, given in a somewhat condensed form, are from the following sources : The Treaty of Paris, from H. Tyrrell's *History of the War with Russia;* The Treaty of Berlin and The Hague Peace Conference, from Sir Edward Hertslet's *State Papers,* Vol. CX.

# A GENERAL BIBLIOGRAPHY OF RUSSIAN HISTORY

BASED ON THE WORKS QUOTED, CITED, OR CONSULTED IN THE PREPARATION OF
THE PRESENT HISTORY; WITH CRITICAL AND BIOGRAPHICAL NOTES

**Anon.,** La guerre d'Orient en 1877-1878, par un tacticien, Paris, 1880; Tainy nashei gosudarstvennoi politiki v Polshye. Sbornik sekretnykh dokumentov (The secrets of our governmental policy in Poland. A collection of secret documents), London, 1899; Secret Memoirs of the Court of St. Petersburg, particularly towards the end of the reign of Catherine II and the commencement of that of Paul I (translated from the French), London, 1895; The Persecution of the Jews in Russia, published by the Russo-Jewish Committee, London, 1890; Russia, Its Industries and Trade (Official report prepared for the Glasgow Exhibition), Glasgow, 1901; Erinnerungen eines Dorfgeistlichen. Ein Beitrag zur Geschichte der Leibeigenschaft und ihrer Aufhebung. Aus dem russischen übertragen von M. Oettingen, Stuttgart, 1894 (Bibliothek russischer Denkwürdigkeiten. Edited by Th. Schiemann, vol. 5); An early newssheet. The Russian Invasion of Poland in 1563. An exact facsimile of a contemporary account in Latin, published at Douay. Together with an introduction and historical notes, and a full translation into English, London, 1874; The French bulletins relating to the war in Russia, London, 1813; Russia's March Towards India, by an Indian officer, London, 1893, 2 vols.; Russia Before and After the War. By the author of "Society in St. Petersburg," etc. Translated from the German, with later additions by the author, by E. F. Taylor, London and New York, 1880; Von Nicolaus I zu Alexander III: St. Petersburger Beiträge zur neuesten russischen Geschichte, Leipsic, 1881; Russisch-Baltische Blaetter, Beiträge zur Kenntniss Russlands und seiner Grenzmarken, 4 vol., Leipzig, 1886-1888; Russland vor und nach dem Kriege; auch "Aus der petersburger Gesellschaft, Leipsic, 1879; Russland am Scheidewege: Beiträge zur Kenntniss des Slawophilenthums, Berlin, 1888; Lose Blätter aus dem Geheim-Archive der russischen Regierung; Ein aktenmässiger Beitrag zur neuesten Geschichte der russischen Verwaltung und Beamten-Korruption, Leipsic, 1882. — **Abaza,** V. A. Istorya Rossii (History of Russia), St. Petersburg, 1893. — **Abbott,** J., Narrative of a Journey from Herat to Khiva, Moscow and St. Petersburg, during the late Russian invasion of Khiva, London, 1856, 2 vols. — **Adam,** Mme., Le général Skobélef, Paris, 1886. — **Adelung,** F. von, Kritisch-literarische Übersicht der Reisenden in Russland bis 1700, St. Petersburg, 1846, 2 vols. — **Alexander II,** Manifesto (The proclamation of emancipation) printed by the Senate, St. Petersburg, 1861. — **Alison,** A., History of Europe, London and New York, 1849-1850, 14 vols. — **Arnaud,** C. A. de, The New Era in Russia, Washington, 1890. — **Arnheim,** F., Der ausserordentliche Finländische Landtag, Leipsic, 1900. — **Avril,** A. d', Négociations relatives au traité de Berlin et aux arrangements qui ont suivi, Paris, 1886.

**Bain,** R. N., Charles XII and the Collapse of the Swedish empire (Heroes of the Nations series) New York, 1895; The Pupils of Peter the Great. A History of the Russian Court and Empire from 1697 to 1740, Westminster, 1897; The Daughter of Peter the Great. A History of Russian Diplomacy and of the Russian Court under the Empress Elizabeth Petrovna (1741-1762), Westminster, 1899. — **Bakunin,** A., M. **Herzen,** and others, Sozial-politischer Briefwechsel.    Mit einer biographischen Einleitung von M. Dragomanov.    Autorisirte Übersetzung aus dem russischen von B. Minzer, Stuttgart, 1895.    (Bibliothek russischer Denkwürdigkeiten, vol. 6).— **Bantysh-Kamenski,** D. N. Istorya maloi Rossii (History of Little Russia) Moscow, 1842.

*Bantysh-Kamenski* was born in Moscow in 1788.    Between 1825 and 1828 he was governor of Tobolsk, and from 1836 to 1838, governor of Vilna.    After that he was engaged in the ministry of the interior.    He died at St. Petersburg in 1850.    Besides his "History of Little Russia," which is to this day the only complete history in this department, he also wrote a biographical dictionary and the lives of a number of Russian statesmen and commanders.

**Bantysh-Kamenski,** N., Diplomatitcheskoe sobranie dyel mezhdu Rossiiskim i Kitaiskim gosudarstvom s 1619 po 1792 god (a collection of diplomatic papers between the Russian and Chinese empires from 1619 to 1792) Kazan, 1882; Obzor vnyeshnikh snoshenyi Rossii po 1800 g (a review of the foreign relations of Russia up to the year 1800, Courland, Livonia, Esthonia, Poland, and Portugal), Moscow, 1897. — **Bell,** R., Russia (Cabinet Cyclopædia series), London, 1836, 3 vol. — **Bernhardi,** T. von, Geschichte Russlands und der europäischen Politik in den Jahren 1814-1831, Leipsic, 1868-1878, 3 vols. — **Bestuzhev-Riumin,** K. N., Russkaya istorya (Russian history) St. Petersburg, 1872, 2 vol.

*Konstantin Nikelaievitch Bestuzhev-Riumin* was born in 1829.    From 1865 to 1882 he was a professor at the university of St. Petersburg.    Besides the History, he has been the author of a number of monographs.    His method is thorough, painstaking, and minute.    He insists on a many-sided study of the national life, and of the exclusion of all philosophical or general theories, and devotes much more space to internal than to external history, paying special attention to forms of family life, political organisation, law, religion, and literature.    The introductory chapters give a valuable account of the source and authorities of Russian history.    At his death, in 1897, he left his History a torso.    It was translated into German by Dr. Schiemann (Mitau, 1873-1875).

**Beveridge,** A. J., The Russian Advance, New York, 1903. — **Bigelow,** P., The German Emperor and his Eastern Neighbors, New York, 1892. — **Bilbassov,** V. A., Istorya Ekateriny II (History of Catherine II), London, 1895, 2 vols. — **Bilbassov,** B., Katherina II, Kaiserin von Russland, im Urtheile der Weltlitteratur.    Ubersetzt aus dem russischen mit einem Vorwort von T. Schiemann, Berlin, 1897, 2 vols; Geschichte Katharina II. Ubersetzt aus dem russischen von M. von Petzold, Berlin, 1893, 2 vols. — **Bodenstedt,** F. von, Die Völker des Kaukasus und ihre Freiheitskämpfe gegen die Russen, Berlin, 1855, 2 vols. — **Bogdanovitch,** M. I., Istorya tsarstvovanya imperatora Alexandra I i Rossii v yevo vremya (History of the reign of Alexander I and of Russia during his time) St. Petersburg, 1869-1871, 6 vols. — **Bond,** E. A., Russia at the Close of the 16th Century; comprising the treatise "Of the Russ Commonwealth," by G. Fletcher, and the travels of Sir J. Horsey (Hakluyt Society Publications, vol. 20), London, 1856. — **Bookwalter,** J. W., Siberia and Central Asia, New York, 1899. — **Boulger,** D. C., England and Russia in Central Asia, London, 1873, 5 vols. — **Brodhead,** J. M. N., Slav and Moslem: historical sketches, Charleston, S. C., 1894. — **Brooks,** C. W. S., Russians of the South, London, 1854. — **Browning,** O., Charles XII of Sweden, London, 1899. — **Brueckner,** A. Finanzgeschichtliche Studien: Kupfergeldkrisen, St. Petersburg, 1867; Kulturhistorische Studien: die Russen im Ausland: die Ausländer in Russland im 17. Jahrhundert, Riga, 1878 ; Ivan Possoschkow : Ideen und Zustände in Russland zur Zeit Peters des Grossen, Leipsic, 1878; Peter der Grosse, in Oncken's Allgemeine Geschichte in Einzeldarstellungen, Berlin, 1879; Der Zarewitsch Alexei, Heidelberg, 1880 ; Katharina II, in Oncken's Weltgeschichte in Einzeldarstellungen, Berlin, 1883; Istorya Yekateriny II (History of Catherine II), St. Petersburg, 1885, 3 vols; Bilder aus Russlands Vergangenheit, Leipsic, 1887;    Beiträge zur Kulturgeschichte Russlands im 17. Jahrhundert, Leipsic, 1887; Die Europäisierung Russlands, Gotha, 1888; Geschichte Russlands: Überblick der Entwicklung bis zum Tode Peters des Grossen, in Geschichte der europäischen Staaten, Gotha, 1896.

*Alexander Brueckner* was born August 5, 1834, at St. Petersburg.    After engaging for six years in business, he turned his attention to the study of history, which he pursued at Heidelberg, Jena, and Berlin.    After returning to St. Petersburg he became professor of history at the Imperial School of law, in 1867 professor at the university of Odessa, and in 1872 at Dorpat.    Owing to his German origin, he was removed in 1891 from Dorpat and transferred to the university of Kazan, but at his request he was permitted to settle at Jena.    Brueckner is, like Schiemann and Eckhardt, a German-Russian, and as such has a special qualification for the presentation of Russian history to a West-European audience.    He has written numerous works both in Russian and in German, and takes rank with the foremost historians of Russia.

**Brueggen,** E. von der, Polens Auflösung, Leipsic, 1878 ; Wie Russland europäisch wurde, Leipsic, 1885. — **Bunge,** F. G. von, Geschichtliche Entwicklung der Standesverhältnisse in Livonia, Esthonia, und Kurland bis 1561, Dorpat, 1838 ; der Orden der Schwertbrüder, Leipsic, 1875. — **Burtsev,** V., and S. M. **Kravtchinski,** Za sto lyet (1800-1896). Sbornik po istorii politicheskikh i obshtchestvennikh dvizhenyi v Rossii (One hundred years.    Documents Relating to the History of Political and Social Movements in Russia), London, 1897. — **Buturlin,** Knyaz D. P., Histoire militaire de la campagne de Russia en 1812, Paris, 1824, 2 vols.

**Cary,** C., The Trans-Siberian Route, New York, 1902. — **Catherine II,** empress of Russia, Memoirs of the Empress Catherine II, written by herself, with a preface by A. Herzen, translated from the French, New York, 1859. — **Celestin,** Fr. J., Russland seit Aufhebung der Leibeigenschaft, Laibach, 1875. — **Choiseul-Gouffier,** (Tisenhaus), comtesse de, Historical Memoirs of the Emperor Alexander I and the Court of Russia. Translated by M. B. Patterson, Chicago, 1901. — **Colquhoun,** A. R., Russia against India : The Struggle for Asia, New York, 1900. — **Coxe,** W., An Account of the Russian Discoveries between Asia and America : added, The Conquest of Siberia, and the history of the transactions and commerce between Russia and China, London, 1803. — **Crusenstolpe,** M. I. von, Der russische Hof von Peter I bis auf Nikolaus I, Hamburg, 1855–1859.—**Curzon,** G. N., Russia in Central Asia in 1889 and the Anglo-Russian Question, London, 1889 ; Persia and the Persian Question, London, 1892 ; Problems of the Far-East : Japan, Corea, China, London, 1894 ; The Pamirs and the Source of the Oxus, London, 1896. — **Custine,** le marquis de, La Russie en 1839, Paris, 1844, 4 vols.

**Danilevski,** N. Y., Rossiya i Evropa : Vzgliad na kulturnyia i polititcheskyia otnoshenya slavianskavo mira k germano-romanskomu (Russia and Europe : a glance at the cultural and political relations of the Slav world to the German-Romance world), St. Petersburg, 1895. — **Day,** W. A., The Russian Government in Poland. With a narrative of the Polish insurrection in 1863, London, 1867. — **De la Gorce,** P., Histoire du second Empire, Paris, 1894, 4 vols. — **Delord,** T., Histoire du second Empire, Paris, 1868–1875, 6 vols. — **Deutsch,** L. G., Sixteen Years in Siberia, New York, 1903. — **De Windt,** H., Finland as It Is, London, 1901. —**Drage,** G., Russian Affairs, New York, 1904. — **Dubrovin,** N. F., Pugatchev i yevo soobshtchniki (Pugatchev and his accomplices), St. Petersburg, 1884, 3 vols ; Prisoedinenie Krima k Rossii (The annexation of the Crimea to Russia), St. Petersburg, 1885–1889, 4 vols. — **Duggan,** S. P. H., The Eastern Question : A Study in Diplomacy (Columbia studies in history, economics, and public law), New York, 1902.

**Eckardt,** J., Jungrussisch und Altlivländisch. Politische und culturgeschichtliche Aufsätze, Leipsic, 1871 ; Distinguished persons in Russian society (translated from the Author's Aus der Petersburger Gesellschaft), London, 1873 ; Aus der Petersburger Gesellschaft, 5th edition, Leipsic, 1880 ; Neue Folge, Leipsic, 1881 ; Von Nikolaus I zu Alexander III, Leipsic, 1881 ; Russische Wandlungen. Neue Beiträge zur russischen Geschichte von Nikolaus I zu Alexander III, Leipsic, 1882.
*Julius von Eckhardt* was born August 1, 1836, at Wolmar in Livonia. From 1860 to 1867 he was the secretary of the Evangelical-Lutheran Consistory at Riga, one of the editors of the Riga *Zeitung,* and an active member of the Liberal-German party in the Baltic provinces of Russia. After the leaders of this party had been removed from their offices on account of their Germanising tendencies, Eckardt emigrated to Germany, where he was active first as a journalist, then as secretary of the Hamburg senate, and finally as German consul at Tunis, Marseilles and Stockholm. Eckardt was the author of numerous works and pamphlets, many of which were published anonymously, on Russian, Baltic, and German affairs. He was less an historian than a publicist and politician ; but he had an intimate knowledge of the Russia of his own day, the Russia of Alexander II and Alexander III, and his works are indispensable for an understanding of Russian parties and the vacillations of Russian public opinion. His own point of view is that of a conservative liberal.
**Edwards,** H. D., Russian Projects against India, London, 1885. — **Engelmann,** J., Peter der Grosse, seine Jugend und seine Reformen, Dorpat, 1872 ; Die Leibeigenschaft in Russland, Leipsic, 1884 ; Das Staatsrecht Russlands, in Marquardsen's Handbuch des öffentlichen Rechts, vol. 4, Freiburg, 1888. — **Engels,** F., Die auswärtige Politik des russischen Zarenthums, in *Neue Zeit,* Stuttgart, 1890.

**Favre,** L., Histoire de la guerre entre la Russie et la Turquie, Niort, 1879. — **Fenton,** F. de, La Russie dans l'Asie-Mineure; ou, Campagnes du Maréchal Paskewitch en 1828 et 1829, Paris, 1840. — **Ferrand,** A. de, Histoire des trois démembrements de la Pologne, Paris, 1865. 3 vols. — **Fischer,** I. E., Sibirskaya istorya s samavo otkrytya (A history of Siberia from its discovery), St. Petersburg, 1774. — **Fisher,** J. R., Finland and the Tsars, London, 1899. — **Flerovski,** N., Tri polititcheskya sistemy : Nikolai I, Alexander II, Alexander III, (Three political systems : Nicholas I, Alexander II. Alexander III), Geneva, 1897, (German translation, Berlin, 1898). — **Foster-Fraser,** J., The Real Siberia, London, 1902. — **Foulke,** W, D., Slav or Saxon : A Study of the Growth and Tendencies of Russian Civilisation, New York, 1887. — **Fowler,** G., History of the War between Turkey and Russia to the End of 1854, London, 1855. — **Fraehn,** C. M., Ibn Fosslans und anderer Araber Berichte über die Russen älterer Zeit, St. Petersburg, 1823. — **Fraser,** J. F., The Real Siberia ; with an account of a dash through Manchuria, New York, 1902. — **Frederica,** Sophia Wilhelmina, Princess Royal of Russia, Memoirs, London, 1812, 2 vols.

**Galakhov,** A. D., Istorya russkoi slovesnosti (History of Russian literature), Moscow, 1894, 2 vols. — **Galitsyne,** A., Le faux Pierre III, trad. de Pouchkine, Paris, 1858. — **George,** H. B., Napoleon's Invasion of Russia, New York, 1899. — **Gerebtzov,** N. de, Essai sur

l'histoire de la civilisation en Russie, Paris, 1858, 2 vols. — **Gerrare**, W., The Story of Moscow
(Mediæval Towns series), London, 1900; Greater Russia, London, 1903. — **Gogol**, N. V.,
Home Life in Russia, by a Russian noble; revised by the editor of "Revelations in Siberia,"
London, 1854, 2 vols. — **Golovin**, Knyas I, Russia under the Autocrat Nicholas I, London,
1846, 2 vols. — **Gossip**, R., History of Russia, London, 1800. — **Grigorev**, V. V., Rossya i
Azya, Sbornik izslyedovanyi i statey po istorii, etnografii i geografii (Russia and Asia.
Researches in history, ethnography, and geography), St. Petersburg, 1876. — **Grodekov**, N. G.,
A Ride from Samarcand to Herat, translated by C. Marvin, London, 1885. — **Gurowski, A.**,
Russia As It Is, New York, 1854.

**Hagemeister**, I. A., Rozyskanya o finansakh drevney Rossii (Investigations concerning the
finances of ancient Russia), St. Petersburg, 1833. — **Hakluyt**, R., Discovery of Muscovy
(Cassel's Nat. Lib.) — **Hamley**, E. R., The Story of the Campaign : a complete narrative of the
war in southern Russia. Written in a tent in the Crimea, Boston, 1855. — **Hanna**, H. B.,
Indian Problems, Westminster, 1895-1896, 3 vols. — **Hare**, A. J. C., Studies in Russia, London,
1885. — **Haumant**, E., La guerre du Nord (1655-1660), Paris, 1893. — **Haxthausen**, A. von,
Studien über die inneren Zustände, das Volksleben, und insbesondere die ländlichen Einricht-
ungen Russlands, Hanover, 1847-1852, 3 vols.; Die Kriegsmacht Russlands, Berlin, 1852 ;
Transcaucasia : sketches of the nations and races between the Black Sea and the Caspian,
translated by J. E. Taylor, London, 1854 ; Tribes of the Caucasus : with an account of
Schamyl and the Murids, translated by J. E. Taylor, London, 1855 ; Transkaukasia, Leipsic,
1856, 2 vols ; The Russian Empire, Its People, Institutions and Resources, translated by R.
Farie, London, 1856, 2 vols ; Die ländliche Verfassung Russlands, Leipsic, 1866.

*Baron August von Haxthausen* was born on his father's estate near Paderborn in Westphalia, February 3, 1792. He studied in a mining school and took part in the War of Liberation, 1813-1815. His life was mainly devoted to the study of agrarian conditions in eastern
Prussia and in Russia. His researches in the latter country were undertaken at the request
of Nicholas I, and he is generally regarded as the discoverer of the *mir* or Russian village
community. He died at Hanover, January 1, 1867.

**Hedin**, Sven, Through Asia, New York, 1899, 2 vols. — **Hehn**, V., De moribus Ruthenorum.
Zur Charakteristik der russischen Volksseele. Edited by Th. Schiemann, Stuttgart, 1892. —
**Hellwald**, F. A. H. von, The Russians in Central Asia, translated from the German by
Theo. Wirgman, London, 1874. — **Herzen**, A. I., Die russische Verschwörung und der Aufstand
vom 14. Dezember 1825, Hamburg, 1858 ; Russlands soziale Zustände. Aus dem russischen,
Hamburg, 1854 ; Du développement des idées révolutionnaires en Russie, par A. Iscander
(pseud), Paris, 1851 ; Le monde russe et la révolution ; mémoires, 1812-1835, traduits par H.
Delaveau, Paris, 1860-1862, 3 vols.— **Himmelstjerna**, S. H. von, Russland unter Alexander III.,
Leipsic, 1891, English translation, Russia under Alexander III., and in the preceding period,
New York, 1893 ; Verlumpung der Bauern und des Adels in Russland, nach G. I. Uspensky
und A. N. Terpigoriew, Leipsic, 1892. — **Historischer Atlas von Russland, Polen, etc.**, vom
Jahre 1155 bis zum Jahre 1816, Leipsic, 1817. — **Holland**, Th. E., A Lecture on the Treaty
Relations of Russia and Turkey from 1774 to 1853, London, 1877. — **Hourwich**, I. A., The
Economics of the Russian Village (Columbia studies in history, economics, and public law),
New York, 1892. — **Howard**, B., Prisoners of Russia : a personal study of convict life in
Sakhalin and Siberia, New York, 1902. — **Howorth**, H. H., History of the Mongols from the
Ninth to the Ninetenth Century, London, 1876-1880, 4 vols.

**Ignatovitch**, I., Pomyeshtchitchi krestyane nakanune osvobozhdenya (Proprietor's peasants on the eve of emancipation), in "Russkoe Bogatstvo," 1900. — **Ilovaiski**, D. I., Istorya
Rossii (History of Russia), Moscow, 1876-1890, 3 vols.; Smutnoe vremya moskocskavo gosudarstva (The Troublous Period in the Muscovite Empire), Moscow, 1894. — **Ivanin**, M. L., O
voyennom iskustvye i zavoevanyakh Mongolo-Tatar i srednyeazyatskikh narodov pri Tchingis
Khanye i Tammerlanye, (The Art of War and the Conquests of the Mongol-Tatars and Central-
Asian peoples under Jenghiz Khan and Tamerlane), St. Petersburg, 1875.

**Jauffret**, P. E., Catherine II., et son regne, Paris, 1860.

**Kapnist**, J., Code d'organisation judiciaire russe, Paris, 1893. — **Karamzin**, N. M., Istorya
gosudarstva rossiiskavo (History of the Russian Empire), St. Petersburg, 1818-1829, 12
vols.

*Nikolai Mikhailovitch Karamzin* was born December 12, 1765, at the village of Mik-
hailovka, in the government of Orenburg, and died June 3, 1826, at Tsarskoi Selo. His first
literary efforts consisted of translations of essays and poems from foreign languages. In 1789 he
undertook a journey to Germany, France, Switzerland and England, the literary result of which
was his *Letters of a Russian Traveller*, elegant, poetical and sentimental. These letters were
first published in the *Moscow Journal*, of which he was the founder, and which he edited in
1791-1792. In the same periodical also appeared some of his original stories, one of which
treats of the fall of Novgorod. From 1794 to 1799 he published a number of miscellanies,
*Aglaia, The Aonides*, and the *Pantheon*, containing original as well as translated matter. In

**1802-1803** Karamzin edited the *European Messenger*, destined to become one of the most important Russian reviews, and of which he was the founder. He then turned to the work of his life, the great *History of the Russian Empire*, which was to occupy him till his death. In this last enterprise he was aided and encouraged by the emperor Alexander I, who contributed 60,000 rubles to the cost of publication. The history terminates at the accession of Michael Romanov in 1613. Karamzin's work is the first great Russian history. Its style is elegant and flowing, its erudition large and solid, and it abounds in curious information. It is owing to these qualities that the book still maintains its place, although much of it has by this time become obsolete. The book is especially strong in description of battles and analysis of character. Its spirit is frankly reactionary. The barbarism of early Russia is glossed over by a glittering veil of romanticism, the material, intellectual and moral condition of the Russian people is almost entirely ignored, and the book has been styled the "epic of despotism." A French translation appeared at Paris in 1819-1820, and a German one at Leipsic in 1820-1833.

**Kelly,** W. K., History of Russia, London, 1854, 2 vols. — **Kennan,** G., Tent Life in Siberia, and Adventures Among the Koraks and Other Tribes in Kamtchatka and Northern Asia, New York, 1870 ; Siberia and the Exile System, New York, 1891, 2 vols. — **Kinglake,** A. W., The Invasion of the Crimea, London, 1863-1887, 8 vols. — **Klaczko,** J., Études de diplomatie contemporaine (1861-1864), Paris, 1866 ; Deux chanceliers (Gortchakov and Bismarck), Paris, 1877. — **Kleinschmidt,** A., Drei Jahrhunderte russischer Geschichte (1598-1898), Berlin, 1898. — **Knorr,** E., Die polnischen Aufstände seit 1830, Berlin, 1880. — **Kohl,** J. G., Russia: Travels, London, 1842. — **Kostomarov,** N. I., Istoritcheskya monografii i izslyedovanya (Historical Monographs and Researches), St. Petersburg, 1863-1867, 3 vols. ; Russkaya istorya v zhiznye opisanyakh yeya glavnyeishikh dyeiyatelyei (Russian History in the Biographies of its Chief Actors), St. Petersburg, 1892-1896, 4 vols. ; Smutnoe vremya moskovskavo gosudarstva v natchalye XVII. stolyetya (The Troublous Period in the Muscovite Empire at the Beginning of the Seventeenth Century), St. Petersburg, 1868 ; Poslyednie gody ryetchi-pospolitoi (The Last Years of the Polish Republic), St. Petersburg, 1870 ; Predanya pervonatchalnoi russkoi lyetopisi (The Traditions of the Earliest Russian Chronicles), St. Petersburg, 1881 ; Bogdan Khmelnitski: istoritcheskaya monografia (Bogdan Khmelnitsky: an Historical Monograph), St. Petersburg, 1884, 3 vols.; Syevernorusskie narodopravstva vo vremya udyelno-vyetchevovo uklada (Popular Rights in Northern Russia During the Period of Appanages and Republics. The History of Novgorod, Pskov, and Vyatka), St. Petersburg, 1886, 2 vols.; Otcherk domashney zhizni i nravov velikorusskavo Naroda v 16. i 17. stolyetii i starinnye zemskie sbory (A Sketch of the Domestic Life and Manners of the Great-Russians in the Sixteenth and Seventeenth Centuries; and the Ancient Provincial Assemblies), St. Petersburg, 1887 ; Otcherk torgovli moskovskavo gosudarstva v 16. i 17. stolyetyakh (A Sketch of the Commerce of the Muscovite Empire During the Sixteenth and Seventeenth Centuries), St. Petersburg, 1889.

*Nikolai Ivanovitch Kostomarov* was born May 4th, 1817, at Ostrogosh, in the government of Voronezh. In 1846 he was appointed to a professorship of history in the university of Kiev. Owing to his activity for the reviving of Little Russian literature he was accused of harbouring separatist tendencies, arrested, imprisoned for a whole year, and then banished to Saratov and forbidden to teach or publish his writings. On the accession of Alexander II he was pardoned, and in 1859 he was appointed professor of history at the university of St. Petersburg. But in 1862, when the university was closed in consequence of students' disorders, he resigned his post, and henceforth devoted himself exclusively to writing. He died at St. Petersburg, April 19th, 1885. His poetical works, which were written in the Little Russian dialect under the *nom de plume* of Jeremiah Halka, were published collectively at Odessa, 1875. Some of them have been translated into German. As an historian Kostomarov occupies a very high place in Russian literature. His work has assumed the form of monographs, owing to his idea that Russian history cannot be understood without an exhaustive study of the numerous ethnological elements and the separate territorial divisions of which the Russian empire is composed. In his own words, "the Russian empire represents an integration of parts that once led an independent existence, and for a considerable time after unification the life of the parts expressed itself in separate tendencies within the general political structure. To discover and disclose these peculiarities of national life in the divisions that make up the Russian empire was the problem I set before myself in my historical labours." The justification of this view lies in the comparative recency of the Russian empire, its weakness in the assumption that the national or provincial character is unchangeable and immobile. Kostomarov had at his command a vigorous, dramatic style and a lively imagination, and his books contributed greatly toward the popularisation of historical studies in Russia : but he was also possessed in a high degree of the critical faculty, and more than one historical legend has been demolished in his pages. His "Russian History in Biographies" was translated into German and published at Leipsic, 1886-1889.

**Kovalevski,** M., Modern Customs and Ancient Laws of Russia, London, 1891 ; Le Régime économique de la Russie, Paris, 1896 ; L'Agriculture en Russie, Paris, 1897 ; Russian Political Institutions, Chicago, 1902.

*Maxim Kovalevski* was born at Kharkov in 1851, of a rich and noble family that is remarkable for the number of men—and one woman—of science it has given to Russia. He studied at Berlin, Paris, and London, and in 1877-1887 he was professor of comparative law at the university of Moscow. Owing to his liberal views he was compelled to give up his position. Since then he has settled at Paris, where he has collected a valuable library, and lectured at various seats of learning in Europe and America—Stockholm, Oxford, Brussels, Chicago. He has written numerous and important works on the history of Russia, France, England, the Caucasus, etc., and is a recognised authority in the departments of pre-history, public and private law, and economic history.

**Koyalovitch,** M. I., Dnyevnik poslyednyavo pokhoda Stefana Batorya na Rossiyu, 1581-1582. Osada Pskova (A diary of the last campaign of Stephen Batory against Russia in 1581-1582. The siege of Pskov), St. Petersburg, 1867 ; Tchtenya po istorii zapadnoi Rossii (Lectures on the history of Southern Russia), St. Petersburg, 1884. — **Kravchinski,** S. M., (Stepniak). The Russian Peasantry : Their Origin, Condition, Social Life and Religion, London, 1888, 2 vols. — **Kropotkin,** P. A., Memoirs of a Revolutionist, Boston, 1899. — **Kulish,** P. A., Istorya vozsoedinenya Rusi (A history of the unification of Russia), St. Petersburg, 1874. — **Kunik,** E., Die Berufung der schwedischen Rodsen durch die Finnen und Slawen, St. Petersburg, 1844-1845. — **Kuropatkin,** Gen. A. N., Les confins anglo-russe, translated by G. Le Marchand, Paris, 1879 ; Kashgaria, translated by Col. W. E. Gore, Calcutta, 1882 ; Kritische Rückblicke auf den russisch-türkischen Krieg 1877-1878, Berlin, 1885-1890, 3 vols.

*Alexei Nikolaievitch Kuropatkin* was born March 29, 1848. In 1866 he joined the army of Turkestan as a lieutenant, served with distinction in the expedition of General Kaufman in 1867-1868, was sent at the head of a diplomatic-military mission to the emir of Kashgar, and studied in 1872-1874 at the academy of the general staff. He joined the French army in Algeria as a volunteer, was active on his return in Turkestan, and then became chief of the Asiatic section of the general staff. In 1877-1878 he was chief of General Skobelev's staff, under whom he also served in the campaign against the Akhal-Tekke Turkomans, 1880-1881. In 1890 he became a lieutenant-general and governor of the Transcaspian territory, and later minister of war.

He is the author of two important works on the last Russo-Turkish War, which have been translated into French and German, and of a book of travels on Kashgar.

**Labensky,** A., A Russian's Reply to the Marquis de Custine's "Russia in 1839," London, 1844. — **Laferté,** V., Alexander II : Détails inédits sur sa vie intime et sa mort, Paris, 1882. — **Lamartine,** A. de, Histoire de la Russie, Paris, 1855, 2 vols. — **Lansdell,** H., Russian Central Asia, including Kuldja, Bokhara, Khiva and Merv, Boston, 1885. — **Latham,** R. G., Native Races of the Russian Empire, London, 1854 ; Russian and Turk, from a Geographical, Ethnological and Historical Point of View, London, 1878. — **Latimer,** Mrs. W. E., Russia and Turkey in the Nineteenth Century, Chicago, 1893. — **Leger,** L., Cyrille et Méthode, étude historique sur la conversion de Slaves au christianisme, Paris, 1868 ; De Nestore rerum russicarum scriptore, Paris, 1868 ; Traduction de la chronique de Nestor, Paris, 1884. — **Lehmann,** C. and **Parvus** (pseud.), Das hungernde Russland, Stuttgart, 1900. — **Lemke,** M., Otcherki po istorii tsenzuri (Studies in the History of the Russian Censorship), in "Russkoe Bogatstvo," 1903. — **Leonov,** R., Documents secrets de la politique russe en Orient (1888-1890), Berlin, 1893. — **Leroy-Beaulieu,** A., L'empire des Tsars et les Russes, Paris, 1881-1889, 3 vols. ; Un homme d'état russe : Nicolas Milutin, Paris, 1884 ; La France, La Russie et l'Europe, Paris, 1888 ; Israël chez les nations, Paris, 1893.

*Anatole Leroy-Beaulieu* was born in 1842 at Lisieux. Since 1881 he has been professor of modern history at the *école libre de sciences politiques* in Paris. His chief work, "*L'empire des Tsars et les Russes,*" is one of the most important works on Russia ever published in western Europe. The first two volumes treat of the geography, ethnology, and the economic and political institutions, while the third is devoted to a study of the Russian church and the sects.

**Leroy-Beaulieu,** P., The Awakening of the East : Siberia, Japan, China, New York, 1900. — **Lestrade,** Combes de, La Russie économique et sociale, Paris, 1896. — **Lessar,** P., La Russie et l'Angleterre dans l'Asie centrale, Paris, 1886. — **Lévesque,** P. C., Histoire de Russie, Yverdun, 1782, 8 vols., Paris, 1812, 4 vols. — **Livov,** G., Michel Katkoff et son époque : quelque pages d'histoire contemporaine en Russie (1855-1887), Paris, 1897. — **Loris-Melikov,** M. T. T., Konstitutsya grafa Lorisa-Melikova (The Constitution of Count Loris-Melikov), London, 1893. — **Lyaskoronski,** V., Istorya Pereyaslovskoi zemli s drevneyshikh vremyon do polovinny XIII stolyetya (A History of Pereyaslavl from the earliest times to the middle of the thirteenth century), Kiev, 1897.

**Maggiolo,** A. de, France et Russie ; Pozzo di Borgo, 1764-1842, Paris, 1890. — **Maltsev,** A., Die russische Kirche, Berlin, 1893. — **Manstein,** Baron de, Memoirs of Russia 1727-1744, translated from the original manuscript, London, 1773. — **Martens,** F. F., Étude historique sur la politique russe dans la question d'Orient, Gand, 1877 ; Recueil de traités et conventions conclus par la Russie avec les puissances étrangères, St. Petersburg, 1878-1889, 10 vols. ; Russia and England in Central Asia, London, 1879. — **Martin,** H., Histoire de France depuis 1789 jusqu'à nos jours, Paris, 2nd edition, 1878-1885, 8 vols. — **Marvin,** C., The Eye Witnesses' Account of the Disastrous Russian Campaign against the Akhal-Tekke Turkomans, London, 1880 ; The Russian Advance Towards India : conversations with Skobelev, Ignatiev, and other distinguished Russian generals and statesmen, London, 1882 ; The Russians at **Merv** and Herat and their Power of Invading India, London, 1883 ; The Russians at the Gates of Herat, London and New York, 1885. — **Marx,** F., The Pacific and the Amoor: Naval, military, and diplomatic operations from 1855 to 1861, London, 1861. — **Marx,** K., The Eastern Question : a reprint of letters written 1853–1856 dealing with the events of the Crimean War, London, 1897 ; Secret Diplomatic History of the Eighteenth Century, London, 1899 ; Lord Palmerston, London, 1899. — **Massa,** Isaac de Harlem, Histoire des guerres de Moscovie 1601–1611, Brussels, 1876 ; Skazanya Massy i Herkmana o smutnom vremeni v Rossii (The Accounts of Massa and Herkmann of the Troublous Period in Russia), St. Petersburg, 1874. — **Masson,** C. F. P., Mémoires secrets sur la Russie pendant les regnes de Catherine II et de Paul I, (in Bibliothèque des mémoires relatifs à l'histoire de France pendant le 18e siècle, vol. 22), Paris, 1859. — **Maxwell,** J. S., The Czar, his Court and People, New York, 1849. — **Mechlin,** R., Das Staatsrecht des Grossfürstenthums Finland, Freiburg, 1889. — **Mérimée,** P., Les faux Démetrius, Paris, 1852 ; Épisode de l'histoire de Russie, Paris, 1854 ; Les cosaques d'autrefois, Paris, 1865 ; Mélanges historiques et littéraires, Paris, 1867 ; Portraits historiques et littéraires, Paris, 1874. — **Michelin,** L. H. S., Finland in the Nineteenth Century, Helsingfors, 1894. — **Milukov,** P. N., Glavnyia tetchenya russkoi istoritcheskoi mysli (The Main Currents of Russian Historical Thought), Moscow, 1898 ; Skizzen russischer Kulturgeschichte. Deutsche vom Verfasser durchgesehene Ausgabe von E. Davidson, Leipsic, 1898–1901, 2 vols.

*Milukov* was born in 1859. From 1886 to 1895 he taught at the university of Moscow. But like so many other Russian professors of history and social science, he came in conflict with the government, and accepted a professorship at the university of Sofia, Bulgaria. He is one of the ablest of the younger generation of Russian historians, his method being the realistic or economic. During several years he was a regular contributor of reviews on Russian literature to the London *Athenæum.*

**Milutin,** D. A., Istorya voiny Rossii s Frantsieu v tsarstvovanie imperatora Pavla I v 1799 g. (A History of the War Between Russia and France During the Reign of the Emperor Paul I in the Year 1799), St. Petersburg, 1852–1853, 5 vols.

*Dmitri Alexeievitch Milutin* was born July 10, 1816, at Moscow. In 1833 he entered the army as lieutenant, then served in the army of the Caucasus, in which he advanced in 1843 to the post of chief of the commissariat department, and in 1856 to that of chief of the general staff. In 1860 he became first adjutant to the war minister, and in 1862 war minister. In this capacity he devoted himself toward reorganising the army on a modern basis, and in 1874 he introduced universal military service. The campaigns of 1877–1878 showed the shortcomings as well as the improvements of the army under his administration. In 1878 the title of count was conferred on him. In 1881 he was dismissed by Alexander III owing to his expressed dissatisfaction with the reactionary, strictly absolutist manifesto of May 11 of that year. He was the author of a number of works on military history and science, and his history of Souvorov's campaign in Italy appeared in a German translation, at Munich, 1856–1858.

**Moltke,** H. C. B., The Russians in Bulgaria, in 1828–1829, London, 1854. — **Monteith,** W., Kars and Erzeroum : with the campaigns of Prince Paskiewitch, London, 1856. — **Morane,** P., Finlande et Caucase, Paris, 1900. — **Morfill,** W. R., Russia (Story of the Nations series), New York, 1891 ; A History of Russia from the Birth of Peter the Great to Nicholas II., New York, 1902. — **Motley,** J. L., Peter the Great, London, 1887. — **Munro,** H. H., Rise of the Russian Empire, Boston, 1900.

**Nagasee,** H., Die Entwicklung der russischen und englischen Politik Persien und Afghanistan betreffend bis 1838, Halle A. S. 1894. — **Nestor,** Prepodobnavo Nestora rossiski lyetopisets (Holy Nestor's Russian Chronicle), St. Petersburg, 1767 ; La chronique de Nestor, translation by Louis Paris, Paris, 1834, 2 vols. — **Neuburger,** F., Russland unter Kaiser Alexander III., Berlin, 1895.— **Nicolai,** on (pseud. of Danielson) Histoire de développment économique de la Russie depuis l'abolition du servage, Paris, 1899 ; Die Volkswirthschaft in Russland nach der Bauernemancipation. Autorisierte Übersetzung aus dem russischen von Dr. G. Polansky, Munich, 1899. — **Nikitin,** P., Istorya goroda Smolenska, (History of the City of Smolensk), Moscow, 1848. — **Nikitski,** A*., Otcherk vnutrennei istorii Pskova (Outline of the Internal History of Pskov), St. Petersburg, 1873. — **Noble,** E., The Russian Revolt : its causes, condition and prospects, Boston, 1885 ; Russia and the Russians, Boston, 1901. — **Norman,** H., All the Russias : travels and studies in contemporary European Russia, Finland, Siberia, New York, 1902. — **Novikov,** Mme. O. K., Skobelev and the Slavonic Cause, London, 1883 ; Russia and England from 1876 to 1880 : a protest and an appeal : with a preface by J. A. Froude, London, 1880.

**O'Donovan,** E., The Merv Oasis, London, 1882. — **Ordega,**V., Die Gewerbepolitik Russlands von Peter I bis Katharina II, Tübingen, 1885. — **Oxley,** T. L., Character and Reign of Alexander II, London, 1881.

**Palmer,** F. H. E., Russian Life in Town and Country, New York, 1901. — **Parmele,** M. P., A Short History of Russia, New York, 1900. — **Pavlov,** N. M., Russkaya istorya ot drevneyskikh vremyon (Russian History from the Earliest Times, 862–1362), Moscow, 1896–1899, 2 vols. — **Pekarski,** P. P., Nauka i literatura v Rossii pri Petrye Velikom (Science and Literature in Russia at the Time of Peter the Great), St. Petersburg, 1862, 2 vols. — **Pember,** A., Ivan the Terrible, London, 1895. — **Pfuel,** E. von, Der Rückzug der Franzosen aus Russland, Berlin, 1867. — **Pierling,** P., Rome et Démétrius, Paris, 1878 ; La Sorbonne et la Russie, Paris, 1882 ; Un Nonce du pape en Moscovie : préliminaires de la trêve de 1582, Paris, 1884 ; La Saint-Siège, la Pologne et Moscou (1582–1587), Paris, 1885 ; Bathory et Possevino, Paris, 1887 ; Papes et Tsars (1547–1597), Paris, 1890 ; La Russie et l'Orient : marriage d'un Tsar au Vatican, Ivan III et Sophie Paléologue, Paris, 1891 ; L'Italie et la Russie au XVI siècle, Paris, 1892. — **Pingaud,** L., Les Français en Russie et les Russes en France, Paris, 1886. — **Pogodin,** M. P., Izslyedovanya, zamyetchanya i lektsii o russkoi istorii (Researches, Comments and Lectures on Russian History), Moscow, 1846–1857, 7 vols.; Nestor : eine historisch-kritische Untersuchung über den Anfang der russischen Chroniken. Übersetzt von F. Loewe, (Beiträge zur Kenntniss des russischen Reiches. vol. 10), St. Petersburg, 1884. — **Popowski,** J., The Rival Powers in Central Asia, London, 1893. — **Porter,** R. K., Narrative of the Campaign in Russia During the Year 1812, London, 1814. — **Possevino,** A., Antonii Possevini missio moscovitica ex annuis litteris Societatis Jesu excerpta et adnotationibus illustrata curante P. Pierling, Paris, 1882. — **Pozzo Di Borgo,** Ch., Correspondance diplomatique du comte Pozzo di Borgo, Paris, 1891. — **Pyzyrewsky,** A., Der polnisch-russische Krieg von 1831, Wien, 1892–1893, 3 vols.

**Rafn,** K. C., Antiquités Russes, Copenhagen, 1850–1854, 3 vols. — **Ralston,** W. R. S., The Songs of the Russian People, London, 1872 ; Russian Folk-tales, London, 1873 ; Early Russian History, London, 1876. — **Rambaud,** La Russie épique, Paris, 1876 ; Souvorof, (conférances de Saint-Cyr), Paris, 1889 ; Français et Russes, Moscou et Sevastopol, Paris, 1892 ; L'armée du tsar Alexandre III, in la Revue Bleue, November 10, 1894 ; Histoire de la Russie, Paris, 1900 ; The Expansion of Russia : Problems of the East and of the Far East, New York, 1904.

*Alfred Nicolas Rambaud* was born July 21st, 1842 at Besançon. Appointed in 1864 a teacher at the lyceum of Nancy, he advanced steadily until his appointment to a professorship in the university of Paris in 1882. In 1896 he was minister of education in the Méline cabinet. He is the author of many works on the history of France, and in conjunction with Lavisse he is editing the "Histoire générale du IVᵉ siecle jusqu'à nos jours." His "History of Russia" is regarded as the best of its kind that has ever been written by a West-European.

**Ravenstein,** E. G., The Russians on the Amur ; its discovery, conquest, and colonisation and personal accounts of Russian travellers, London, 1861. — **Rawlinson,** H. C., England and Russia in the East ; a series of papers on the political and geographical condition of Central Asia, London, 1875. — **Reinholdt,** A. von, Geschichte der russischen Litteratur von ihren Anfängen bis auf die neueste Zeit, in Geschichte der Weltlitteratur in Einzeldarstellungen, vol. 7, Leipsic, 1886. — **Reinsch,** P. S., World Politics at the End of the Nineteenth Century, New York, 1900. — **Rivière,** Ch. de la, Catherine II et la révolution française, Paris, 1895. **Rocca,** F. de, Les assemblées politiques dans la Russie ancienne, Paris, 1899. — **Rozhkov,** N., Gorod i derevnia v russkoi istorii : kratki otcherk ekonomitcheskoi istorrii Rossii (City and village in Russian history ; a rapid survey of Russian economical history), in "Mir Bozhi," 1902 ; Obzor russkoi istorii s sotsiologitcheskoi totchki zryenya. Tchast pervaya : Kievskaya Rus (A survey of Russian history from the sociological point of view Part first : Kievan Russia), in "Mir Bozhi", 1903. — **Rulhière,** C. C. de, Révolution de Pologne, Paris, 1862, 3 vols.

**Saraw,** Chr. von, Die Feldzüge Karl's XII, Leipsic, 1881. — **Schiemann,** Th., Russland, Polen, und Livland bis im XVII. Jahrhundert, in Oncken's Allgemeine Geschichte in Einzeldarstellungen, Berlin, 1886–1887, 2 vols.; Die Ermordung Pauls und die Thronbesteigung Nikolaus I : neue Materialien veröffentlicht und eingeleitet, Berlin, 1902. — **Schlözer,** K. von, Russlands älteste Beziehungen zu Skandinavien und Konstantinopel, Berlin, 1847. — **Schmucker,** S. M., Memoirs of the Court and Reign of Catherine the Second, New York, 1855. — **Schnitzler,** J. H., Geheime Geschichte Russlands unter den Kaisern Alexander und Nikolaus, unter besonderer Berücksichtigung der Krisis von 1825, Grimma, 1847, 2 vols., English translation, Secret History of the Court and Government of Russia Under the Emperors Alexander and Nicholas, London, 1847, 2 vols. ; L'Empire des Tsars au point actuél de la science, Paris, 1856–1869, 4 vols.; La Russie en 1812, Rostopchine et Koutouzof, Paris, 1863 ; Les institutions de la Russie depuis les réformes de l'empereur Alexander II, Paris, 1866, 2 vols.; Geschichte des russischen Reiches von der ältesten Zeit bis zum Tode des Kaisers Nikolaus, Leipsic, 1874. — **Schuyler,** E., Turkistan. Notes of a Journey in Russian Turkistan, Khokand, Bokhara, and Kuldja, London and New York, 1876, 2 vols.; Peter the Great, London and New York, 1884. 2 vols. — **Ségur,** P. P. Comte de, History of Russia and Peter the Great, London, 1829. — **Semyovski,** V. I., Gornozavodskie krestyane v vtoroi polovinye 18vo vyeka (The Peasants in Metallurgic Works During the Second Half of the Eighteenth Century), in "Russkaya Mysl," 1900. — **Sergeevitch,** V. I., Vetche i knyaz : russkoe gosudarstvennoe ustroistvo i upravlyenie vo vremena knyazei rurikovitchei (Folkmote and Prince : the Russian Political System in the Days of the Rurik Princes), Moscow, 1867. — **Shilder,** N. K., Imperator Alexandr I (The Emperor Alexander I), St. Petersburg, 1897, 4 vols.; Tsarstvovanie imperatora Nikolaya I

(The Reign of Emperor Nicholas I), St. Petersburg, 1901. — **Shoemaker**, M. M., The Great Siberian Railway, New York, 1903. — **Shpilevski**, S. M., Drevnie goroda i drugie bulgarsko-tatarskie pamyatniki v Kazanskoi gubernii (Ancient Cities and Other Bulgaro-Tatar Monuments in the Government of Kazan), Kazan, 1877. — **Shtchebalsky**, P., La régence de la tzarewna Sophie : épisode de l'histoire de Russie, 1682–1689, translation by Prince S. Galitzine, Carlsruhe, 1857 ; Tchtenie iz russkoi istorii (Readings from Russian History), Moscow, 1861, 6 vols. — **Shumakr**, A. A., Tsar-Osvoboditel (The Czar Liberator), St. Petersburg, 1901. — **Skrine**, F. H., The Expansion of Russia, 1815–1900, Cambridge, 1903. — **Soloviov**, S. M., Istorya Rossii s drevneyshikh vremyon (History of Russia from the Earliest Times), Moscow, 1863–1875, 29 vols.

Sergei Mikhailovitch Soloviov was born May 17th, 1820. In 1850 he became a professor at the university of Moscow. In 1877 he came into conflict with the reactionary policy of the government toward the universities, and demanded and obtained his dismissal. He died October 16th, 1879. Besides his monumental History of Russia he was the author of numerous monographs. The Relations Between the Russian Princes of the House of Rurik was of epoch-making importance in Russian historical literature. His History of the Fall of Poland has become the standard work on the subject and was translated into German (Gotha, 1865). But all his other works are cast into the shade by his stupendous History of Russia from the Earliest Times, in which he proposed to himself a task excelling, perhaps, the power of any single human being—the presentation of the entire history of his country, based exclusively on original research. The result has, therefore, been not wholly successful, and the later volumes present the appearance of a mere aggregation of materials hastily arranged. But the material is of the finest quality and will serve as a rich quarry for all future historians. Soloviov's method of presentation is calm and dispassionate, his style tranquil and somewhat dry, but admirably clear. From Karamzin to Soloviov the gulf is wide indeed, and perhaps it will be well to present a few of the latter's ideas in order to show the indebtedness that all modern historians of Russia owe to him. Russian society, like all primitive society, was in its origin tribal and based on kinship. The introduction of Varangian rule represents the beginnings of the dissolution of that society and the introduction of political society, based on territory. But society was still in a transitional stage. The warlike followers of the princes were free to renounce their allegiance to one master and to choose another in his stead, and the principle of kinship was still dominant within the house of Rurik itself, thus counteracting the separatist tendencies of the appanages. It was the colonisation of the north and east and the removal of the center of Russian life to the Volga, that first makes possible, as well as necessary, the centralisation of power : for the colonists settle on land that belongs to the prince and in cities founded by him, while the colonists themselves come from different parts of Russia and are unconnected by the bond of kinship. In the struggle that follows between the prince and the refractory, unsubmissive elements—whether of the common people or of the noble followers—the prince is victorious and the irreconcileables flee to the forests of the north or to the steppes of the south. Thus we have the origin of the robber bands, and of the Cossacks—another name for the same thing. But the removal of the centre to the Volga also implies the estrangement of Russia from European influences, and the Tatar rule plays in this only a subordinate and external part. The grand princes of Moscow in the fourteenth and fifteenth centuries are thus seen to be the continuators of the policy of the grand princes of Suzdal in the twelfth and thirteenth centuries, while the episode of the period of confusion represents an abortive attempt at the establishment of a milder rule by the Cossacks. Ivan III and Ivan IV, in their struggle with the foreigner, begin to appreciate the superior potency of European civilisation, and are the precursors of Peter the Great. But the new tendencies work with unceasing force during the intervening period, and those who resist the new tendencies become the nonconformists or Raskolniki (Old Ritualists). This tendency finds its parallel in Western Europe, where the task had been accomplished two centuries earlier ; but not so the effort to reach the sea, which is a peculiar Russian phenomenon. Soloviov's work reaches down to 1774.

**Sorel**, A., Histoire du traité de Paris, Paris, 1873 ; La question d'Orient au XVIII. siècle, Paris, 1889. — **Stepniak**, S. (pseudonym of Kravtchinski, S. M.), Underground Russia, New York, 1883 ; Russia under the Tsars. Rendered into English by W. Westall, New York, 1885 ; King Log and King Stork, a Study of Modern Russia, London, 1896.

Stepniak, whose real name was Sergius Mikhailovitch Kravtchinski, was born in South Russia, in 1852, of a noble family. When he left school he became an officer in the artillery, but his sympathy with the peasants soon led him into the revolutionary agitation, and he became identified with the terrorist party. In 1880 he was obliged to leave Russia, and after a few years' stay in Switzerland and Italy he came to London, where he lived until 1895, when he was killed by a railway engine at a level crossing at Bedford Park, Chiswick. He was the author of numerous works on contemporary Russia, dealing chiefly with the revolutionary agitation and the condition of the peasantry.

**Strahl**, P. and E. **Hermann**, Geschichte des Russischen Staates, Hamburg, and Gotha, 1832–1866, 7 vols. — **Stevens**, W. B., Through Famine-Stricken Russia, London, 1892. — **Stumm**, H., Russia in Central Asia, London, 1885. — **Sugenheim**, S., Russlands Einfluss auf und Beziehungen zu Deutschland (1689–1855), Frankfort on Main, 1856, 2 vols.; Geschichte der Aufhebung der Leibeigenschaft, St. Petersburg, 1861.

**Tatishtchev,** V. N., Istorya Rossii s samykh drevnyeishikh vremyon (History of Russia from the very Earliest Times), Moscow, 1768. — **Tchitchagov,** L'Admiral, Mémoires de (1767-1849), Leipsic, 1862. — **Tchitcherin,** N., Oblastnyia utchrezhdenya Rossii v 17 vyeke (The Provincial Institutions of Russia in the Seventeenth Century), Moscow, 1856. — **Thun,** A., Geschichte der revolutionären Bewegungen in Russland, Leipsic, 1883; Landwirthschaft und Gewerbe in Mittelrussland, in Schmoller's Staats-und Sozialwissenschaftliche Forschungen, Leipsic, 1880. — **Thomson,** V. L. P., The Relation Between Ancient Russia and Scandinavia, and the Origin of the Russian State, London, 1877. — **Tilly,** H. A., Eastern Europe and Western Asia, London, 1864. — **Tissot,** V., Russians and Germans: translated from the French by S. L. Simon, London, 1882; La Russie et les Russes, Paris, 1884; Russes et Allemands, New York, 1888. — **Tikhomirov,** L., Russia, Political and Social, translated from the French by E. Aveling, London, 1888, 2 vols. — **Tolstoi,** L. N., La Famine, Paris, 1893. — **Tooke,** W., Russia; or a Complete Historical Account of all the Nations which Comprise the Russian Empire, London, 1780-1783, 4 vols.; The Life of Catherine II, London, 1800, 3 vols.; A History of Russia from A. D. 862 to 1762, London, 1806, 2 vols. — **Turgeniev,** N., La Russie et les Russes, Paris, 1847, 3 vols. — **Tugan-Baranovski,** M., Russkaya fabrika v proshlom i nastoyashtchem (The Russian Factory, Past and Present), St. Petersburg, 1898. — **Tyrrell,** H., History of the (Crimean) War with Russia, London, n. d. 4 vols.

**Ustrialov,** N., Skazanya knyazya Kurbskavo (The Accounts of Prince Kurbski), St. Petersburg, 1868.

**Valikhanov, Veniukov** and others, The Russians in Central Asia, translated from the Russian by J. and R. Mitchell, London, 1865. — **Vambery,** A., Central Asia and the Anglo-Russian Frontier Question, London, 1874. — **Vannovski,** P. S., Doklad po povodu studentcheskikh bezporyadkov 1899 g. (Report on the Students' Disorders in the Year 1899), Publication of the "Rabotchnoe znamya," 1900. — **Vereshtchagin,** V., "1812," Napoleon in Russia, London, 1899. — **Viniarski,** L., Les finances russes (1867-1894), Geneva, 1894. — "**Vladimir,**" (pseud.), Russia on the Pacific and the Siberian Railway, London, 1899. — **Vogüé,** E. de, La revolte de Pugatchef (Revue des Deux Mondes, 1879; Spectacles contemporains (Loris-Melikof; Lettres d'Asie), Paris, 1891. — **Voltaire,** F. M. A. de, Histoire de l'empire de Russie, sous Pierre le Grand, Paris, 1809.

**Waliszewski,** K., Peter the Great, London, 1897, 2 vols.; A History of Russian Literature, London and New York, 1900. (Short History of the Literature of the World, vol. 8); L'héritage de Pierre le Grand : règne de femmes, gouvernments des favoris (1725-1741), Paris, 1900. — **Wallace,** D. M., Russia, London, 1877, 2 vols.
*Donald Mackenzie Wallace* was born November 11th, 1841. Studied at the universities of Edinburgh, Berlin, Heidelberg, and the École de Droit de Paris. Resided and travelled in various foreign countries, chiefly in France, Germany, Russia, and Turkey, during the years 1863-1884. From 1884 to 1889 he was private secretary to Lords Dufferin and Lansdowne while they were viceroys of India, and during 1890-1891 he accompanied the czarevitch during his tour in India and Ceylon. In 1883 he published a work on "Egypt and the Egyptian Question." His work on "Russia" is universally regarded as the best book on that country that has ever been issued from the pen of an Englishman.
**Westlaender,** A., Russland vor einen Regime-Wechsel : politische und wirthschaftliche Zustände im heutigen Russland, Stuttgart, 1894. — **Wilson,** R., Brief Remarks on the Character and Composition of the Russian Army, and a Sketch of the Campaigns in Poland in 1806 and 1807, London, 1810. — **Winckler,** A., Die deutsche Hansa in Russland, Berlin, 1886. — **Windt,** H. de, The New Siberia, London, 1896. — **Witte,** S. J., Samoderzhavie i zemstvo (Autocracy and Local Representative Government. A Confidential Communication by the Minister of Finance, S. J. Witte, in 1899), Stuttgart, 1901. — **Wolkonski,** Prince S., Pictures of Russian History and Russian Literature, Boston, 1897. — **Wright,** G. F., Asiatic Russia, New York, 1902, 2 vols.

**Yozefovitch,** T., Dogovori Rossii s Vostokom, polititcheskie i torgovye (The Commercial and Political Treaties of Russia with the East), St. Petersburg, 1869.

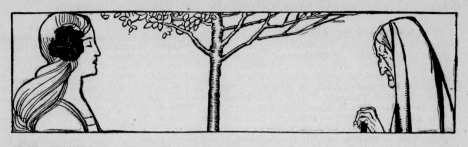

# A CHRONOLOGICAL SUMMARY OF THE HISTORY OF RUSSIA

862 The Varangian chieftains **Rurik,** Sineus, and Truvor settle at Ladoga, Bielo-ozero and Izborsk. This date is purely conventional.

865 Askold and Dir, two Varangian chieftains who had settled at Kiev, lead an unsuccessful expedition against Constantinople.

879 Rurik dies, leaving the regency of the principality and the guardianship of his son Igor to **Oleg.**

882 Oleg takes possession of Kiev after killing Askold and Dir, and makes that city his capital.

907 Oleg leads an expedition consisting of eighty thousand men and two thousand boats against Constantinople. A treaty of peace and commerce is concluded.

911 Oleg renews the treaty with the emperor of Constantinople securing valuable trading privileges for the Russians.

913 Oleg dies, and is succeeded by **Igor.**

941 Igor leads an expedition against Constantinople. His ships are destroyed by the Greek fire, and with great difficulty he brings his troops back to Kiev.

944 Igor leads a second expedition against Constantinople. The Byzantines rid themselves of the barbarians by renewing the treaty that had been made with Oleg and also paying a ransom. The treaty is given in full by Nestor. Of the fifty names attached to it three are Slavonic and the rest Norse, which shows that the two races, the conquerors and the conquered, are beginning to be fused.

945 Igor is killed by the Drevlians, a Slavonic tribe. His wife Olga assumes the regency during the minority of his son Sviatoslav.

955 Olga embraces Greek Christianity. Her subjects, however, remain on the whole pagans.

964 **Sviatoslav** assumes the rule. He is the first of the Varangians to bear a Slavonic name.

968 Sviatoslav, in the pay of the Byzantine emperor Nicephoros, leads an army of 60,000 men against the Bulgarians of the Danube.

970 Sviatoslav, after dividing the country among his three sons, again marches to Bulgaria, this time on his own account.

972 Sviatoslav is defeated at Silistria and compelled to evacuate the Balkan peninsula.

973 On his retreat, Sviatoslav is surprised and killed by the Petchenegs of the Dnieper.

977 Rout of Oleg by Iaropolk and his death.

980 **Vladimir,** after killing Iaropolk, becomes sole ruler.

988 Vladimir is baptized and makes Greek Christianity the state religion. On the day of his baptism he marries a daughter of the Byzantine emperor Romanos II.

1015 Vladimir dies and the country is divided among his eight sons and a nephew.

1019 **Iaroslav,** prince of Novgorod and the youngest son of Vladimir, finally becomes grand prince, and removes his capital to Kiev.

1054 Iaroslav dies. The country is divided among his five sons, one of whom, Iziaslav, is recognised as grand prince of Kiev. The custom, first introduced by Sviatoslav of breaking up the country into appanages, has now reached its full fruition. Russia has become an extremely loose federation of principalities. The central authority has been reduced to a nullity, and the period is filled with wars among the petty princes. This, of course, weakened the power of Russia for resisting foreign invaders, and made it an easy prey to the eastern nomadic tribes, from the Polovtsi to the Tatars. The chief events during this period are the foundation of Moscow (1147), the rise of Suzdal in Vladimir, and the pillaging of Kiev (1169) by Prince Andrew Bogoliubski of Suzdal. The hegemony of Kiev comes to an end for all time. The principal figures during this period are those of Vladimir II, surnamed Monomakh (1113-1125), and of Andrew Bogoliubski (1157-1175), who strove to re-establish some sort of unity and was assassinated by his nobles.

1068 The people of Kiev liberate Vseslav and make him grand prince.
1069 Iziaslav is restored by Boleslaw the Bold of Poland.
1073 Iziaslav is again expelled from Kiev by his brothers Sviatoslav and Vsevolod. **Sviatoslav** becomes grand prince.
1076 Death of Sviatoslav. He is succeeded by Vsevolod.
1077 Iziaslav is again restored to the grand princedom.
1078 Iziaslav dies and is succeeded by **Vsevolod.**
1084 Failure of Vsevolod's attempt to conquer Tmoutorakan (Tmutarakan).
1093 Death of Vsevolod and accession of **Sviatopolk,** the second son of Iziaslav. The Polovtsi defeat the Russians in the battle of Tripole.
1097 The congress of princes at Lubetz.
1100 The congress of princes at Uvetitchi.
1111 Defeat of the Polovtsi on the Sula.
1113 Death of Sviatopolk and accession of **Vladimir Monomakh.**
1125 Death of Monomakh.
1147 Legendary date for the foundation of Moscow.
1157 Andrew Bogoliubski becomes prince of Suzdal.
1169 Kiev is captured and plundered by Andrew Bogoliubski.
1175 Andrew Bogoliubski is assassinated.
1221 Nijni-Novgorod is founded by Iuri, grand prince of Suzdal.
1223 First invasion of Russia by the Mongols under Jenghiz Khan. The Russians are defeated on the banks of the Kalka, near where it flows into the Sea of Azov and adjoining the present site of the town of Mariupol.
1237-38 The Mongols, under Jenghiz Khan's grandson, Batu, invade northern Russia, burn Moscow, defeat twice the army of Suzdal (at Kolomna on the Oku and on the Sit), and plunder Riazan, Suzdal, Iaroslavl, and Tver. But Novgorod is spared.
1239-40 The Mongols ravage southern Russia, burn Tchernigov and Kiev, and extend their conquests as far west as Volhinia and Galicia. All Russia is now under the yoke of the Mongols, except the territory of Novgorod.
1240 Alexander, prince of Novgorod, defeats the Swedes on the Neva; whence his surname Nevski.
1242 Batu establishes the Golden Horde of Kiptchak, with Sarai, on one of the mouths of the Volga, as its capital. It constituted one of the five divisions of the great empire of Jenghiz Khan.
1245 Alexander Nevski defeats the German Sword-bearing Knights on Lake Peipus, in the "battle of the ice."
1260 Novgorod submits to the Mongols and consents to pay tribute.
1263 Death of Alexander Nevski.
1303 Death of **Daniel Alexandrovitch,** founder of the Moscow dynasty.
1320 Prince Michael of Tver is executed by order of the khan.
1321 Vladimir in Volhinia is conquered by the Lithuanians. Kiev and all west Russia soon become Lithuanian.
1404 Smolensk is annexed to Lithuania. A son of Alexander Nevski, named Daniel, was the founder of the principality of Moscow, to which he added the cities of Kolomna and Pereiaslavl. He was succeeded by his son **Iuri Danilovitch** (1303-1325), who annexed Mozhaisk. In 1313 he marries a sister of Usbek Khan. In 1320 he is appointed grand prince in place of his murdered rival, Michael of Tver. Iuri is the initiator of the Muscovite policy to dominate Russia with the aid of the Tatars, for whom the Muscovite princes henceforth act as tax collectors. In 1325 he was assassinated by Dmitri, son of Michael of Tver, and **Alexander,** Michael's second son is appointed grand prince. But the grand princedom soon reverts to Moscow, and Alexander is executed in 1329. Iuri is succeeded by his brother **Ivan Kalita** (1328-1340), who receives from Usbek Khan Vladimir and Novgorod together with the grand princedom, and who also adds Tver to his dominions. He assures the pre-eminence of Moscow in the Russian church by inducing the metropolitan to reside there, thereby also securing the alliance of the all-powerful church in the realisation of his political schemes. **Simeon the Proud,** son of Kalita (1340-1353), **Ivan II,** (1353-1359), brother of Simeon, and **Dmitri Donskoi** (1359-1389), son of Ivan II, continue the policy of dominating Russia with the aid of the Tatars,

whom they conciliate with Russian gold, while they gain the support of the nobles by enhancing their power at the expense of the princes of appanages. Towards the end of his reign Dmitri feels himself strong enough to resist the Tatars, whom he defeats in the battle of Kulikovo (1380); but two years later the Mongol general, Toktamish, invades Russia, burns Moscow and puts to death a great number of the inhabitants. Dmitri was succeeded by his son **Vasili** (1389-1425). On the death of the latter, first his brother, and then his brother's son, laid claim to the succession; but the direct lineal succession triumphed twice in the person of Vasili's son, known as **Vasili the Blind** (1425-1462).

## THE FIFTEENTH CENTURY

1407 The river Ugra is made the boundary between Moscow and Lithuania.

1408 Invasion of Moscow by the Tatars, who burn many towns and villages, but fail to capture the Kremlin.

1412 Vasili Dmitrievitch goes to the Horde, pays tribute, and the khan confirms to him the grand princedom.

1435 Vasili Vasilievitch blinds his cousin Vasili Kossoi.

1446 Vasili Vasilievitch is blinded by Dmitri Shemiaka of Galicia.

1448 The archbishop Jonas is elected metropolitan by an assembly of the Russian bishops, without regard to the patriarch of Constantinople.

1453 Dmitri Shemiaka is poisoned.

1462 **Ivan III,** son of Vasili ascends the throne. He assumes the title *gossudar* (lord, autocrat), and is regarded as the founder of autocracy.

1463 The princes of Iaroslav cede their domain to Moscow.

1464 Ivan gives the hand of his sister to Vasili, prince of Riazan, thus making sure of the approximate annexation of that appanage.

1469 The khanate of Kazan becomes a dependency of Moscow.

1472 Ivan conquers Perm. Marries the Byzantine princess Sophia, niece of the last emperor of Constantinople, Constantine Palæologus. Assumes the title of czar and adopts the two-headed eagle as the symbol of his authority. In consequence of this marriage many Greeks come to Moscow, bringing with them Byzantine culture.

1474 The princes of Rostov sell their domain to Moscow.

1478 The republic of Novgorod is annexed. The principal citizens are brought prisoners to Moscow, their property is confiscated, the possessions of the clergy serve to endow the boyar followers of Ivan. Ahmed, khan of the Golden Horde, sends ambassadors demanding homage. Ivan puts the envoys to death, except one, who was to take back the news to his master. The reply of Ahmed to this outrage is a declaration of war.

1479 Ivan issues Sudebnik, or Books of Laws, second Russian code after the Russkaia Pravda of Iaroslav. A comparison of two codes shows how much the Russian character was lowered by Mongol domination; it is in the reign of Ivan that we first hear of the use of the knout.

1480 The Mongols invade Russia. The two armies meet on the banks of the Oka and flee from each other in mutual fear. On his retreat Ahmed is killed and his army is annihilated by the Nogai Tatars.

1482 Cannon is used for first time at the siege of Fellin in Livonia. It was founded by the architect and engineer Aristotle Fioraventi of Bologna, the builder of the Kremlin.

1485 The principality of Tver is annexed to Moscow.

1485 The last prince of Vereya leaves his domains by will to Ivan.

1489 Viatka, a daughter of the city of Novgorod and Pskov, and like them a republic, is annexed.

1489 Poppel comes to Moscow as the first German ambassador.

1491 Mines of Petchora discovered. For first time silver and copper money is coined at Moscow from produce of Russian mines.

1492-1503 A large part of Little Russia is reconquered from Lithuanians.

1494 Alexander of Lithuania marries Ivan's daughter Helen.

1495 Ivan, considering himself to have been insulted by a Hanseatic city, orders all merchants of all the cities of that union at Novgorod to be put in chains and their property confiscated. This marks the end of Novgorod's commercial greatness.

1499 The princes of Tchernigov and Novgorod-Seversk come over to Moscow.

## THE SIXTEENTH CENTURY

1501 Russians routed in the battle of the Siritza, near Izborsk, by the grand-master of the Teutonic order, Hermann von Plettenberg.

1503 A treaty is concluded with Lithuania. Moscow retains all her conquests, and Ivan is granted the title of sovereign of all Russia.

1505 Death of Ivan. **Vasili,** second son of Ivan, succeeds him.

1508 The Russian army is defeated by the revolted people of Kazan. The victors unite with the Tatars of the Crimea, invade Russia and carry their ravages up to the gates of Moscow. Vasili pays a large ransom for the safety of his capital, and signs a treaty by which he engages to become tributary to the khan. Thirty thousand prisoners are carried off by the invaders, and sold at Kaffa to the Turks.

1510 Pskov, last Slavonic republic, annexed.

1514 Smolensk is taken from the Lithuanians after being held by them for 110 years. But in the same year the Lithuanians defeat the Russian force at Orsha, on left bank of the Dnieper. Thirty thousand Russians are said to have fallen in battle.

1521 Riazan and Novgorod-Seversk, the last independent principalities, are annexed. Crimean Tatars devastate the country.

1523 A second expedition against Kazan, consisting of 150,000 men, fails of its object; one of its two divisions is almost annihilated.

1530 Third expedition against Kazan. The city is surprised by night and 60,000 inhabitants are massacred. But the Russian commander, bribed, it is said, by the remaining Kazanians, enters into a treaty of peace with them.

1533 Vasili dies. Regency of his wife, Helena Glinska, 1533-37. Supremacy of the Shuiski, 1537-43. Ivan is under the influence of the Glinski till 1547, when they were torn in pieces by the infuriated Moscow populace. Such was the youth of Ivan the Terrible.

1547 **Ivan** is crowned and takes the title of Czar.

1550 The Sudebnik of his grandfather Ivan III is revised.

1551 The Stoglav, or Book of the Hundred Chapters, by which the affairs of the church were regulated, is issued.

1552 Kazan, which had freed itself during his father's reign, is annexed.

1553 Chancellor arrives at Archangel and proceeds to Moscow. The English secure great trading privileges and establish factories in the country.

1556 Astrakhan is annexed. The power of the Mongols is now almost completely broken.

1558 Treaty with Elizabeth of England. A Russian army invades Livonia and takes several towns. The Teutonic Order thereupon makes an alliance with Poland.

1564 Ivan, with a few personal friends, retires to Alexandrovskoe, near Moscow, and does not return until after repeated supplications by his nobles. A printing press established at Moscow.

1571 The Mongols of Crimea invade Russia, burn Moscow, drag 100,000 Russians into slavery. Next year they make another raid, but are defeated.

1580 Conquest of Siberia by the Cossack Iermak as far as the Irtish river.

1581 Ivan kills his eldest son in a fit of fury.

1582 Peace of Sapolye. Ivan is forced to surrender to Stephen Bathori (Battori) king of Poland all his conquests in Livonia. The attempt to open for Russia a passage in the Baltic fails for the present.

1584 Death of Ivan. **Feodor,** his weak-minded son, succeeds Ivan. Boris Godunov, Feodor's brother-in-law, is the real ruler.

1587 A company of Parisian merchants obtains trading privileges.

1590 War with Sweden.

1591 Dmitri, the younger brother of Feodor (Ivan's son by his seventh wife), and the only obstacle to Godunov's ambition, dies at Uglitch. The khan of Crimea makes one of his periodical raids against Moscow, but is repulsed with great slaughter.

1592 Godunov issues a ukase (edict) binding the peasant to the soil, thus reducing him to unmitigated serfdom. As a result, peasants emigrate in large numbers to the Cossacks in order to preserve their freedom.

1597 An edict is issued prescribing the most vigorous measures for the recovery of fugitive serfs.

1598 Death of Feodor, last of the Ruriks. **Boris Godunov** is elected to succeed him, first by the Council of Boyars (douma) and then by a General Assembly (Sobór).

## THE SEVENTEENTH CENTURY

1601 A terrible famine, accompanied by pestilence, devastates Russia. Boris causes immense quantities of provisions to be distributed in Moscow, whither multitudes flock from all the provinces. Five hundred thousand are said to have perished in Moscow alone, which had become a city of cannibals.

**1604** Dmitri the Impostor invades Russia and is victorious on the Desna.

**1605** Dmitri is defeated on the plain of Dobrinitchi, not far from Ord. Godunov dies. His son **Feodor** is proclaimed his successor. Basmanov, commander of the army, proclaims Dmitri. Feodor and his mother are strangled and Dmitri enters Moscow.

**1606** A rebellion breaks out under Vasili Shuiski. Dmitri is killed. **Shuiski** is proclaimed emperor.

**1608** A second false Dmitri defeats Shuiski's army near Volkhov, but fails in an attack on the Troitsa monastery, near Moscow. He is murdered by one of his followers in 1610.

**1609** The Poles invade Russia and lay siege to Smolensk.

**1610** Shuiski is defeated at Klushino and **Wladislaw,** son of the Polish king, is crowned czar.

**1611** Revolt of the patriots led by Minin and Prince Pojarski.

**1612** The Poles are driven out of Moscow.

**1613** **Michael Romanov** is chosen czar.

**1617** Wladislaw appears with an army under the walls of Moscow, but is repulsed. The Treaty of Stolbovna is brought about by the mediation of England and Holland: the Russians give up Kexholm, Karelia and Ingria to Sweden, and receive in return Novgorod, which was lost during the Troublous Period.

**1618** Wladislaw consents to abandon his claim to the Russian throne, the czar gives up his claims to Livonia, Tchernigov and Smolensk, and an armistice is concluded for fourteen years.

**1619** Philarete, the father of Czar Michael, comes back from the Polish captivity, is elected patriarch, and becomes his son's associate in the government of the country.

**1627** The Cossacks of the Don conquer Azov, which they offer to the czar. After convoking a sobor, which shows little enthusiasm for the enterprise, the czar orders the Cossacks to evacuate it.

**1633** War with Lithuania.

**1634** Peace of Polianovka: the czar surrenders all claims to Livonia and all the country that once belonged to the Order, as well as to Smolensk, Tchernigov and Seversk. The Polish king abandons his claim to the Russian throne.

**1645** Death of Michael. He is succeeded by **Alexis.**

**1648** Revolt at Moscow against misgovernment of the czar's favorites, particularly Morosov, and depreciation of the coinage. This revolt led to a new codification of the laws (the Ulozhenie), which was based on the preceding codes of Ivan III and IV, and was sanctioned by a sobor convoked at Moscow. A new police institution, the "chamber of secret affairs," is created for the prevention and suppression of popular uprisings. The Cossacks of the Ukraine revolt from Poland under the leadership of Bogdan Chmielnicki.

**1649-50** Khabarov occupies the course of the Amur.

**1654** The Ukraine becomes a Russian protectorate. War with Poland.

**1655** Outbreak of war between Sweden and Poland. The Russians occupy Vilna and join the Swedes in their march upon Warsaw.

**1656** Truce with Poland. The Russian arms are turned against Sweden. At first they were successful, and Narva, Dorpat and other places in Esthonia were taken, Livonia was conquered, but Riga was besieged in vain, and after many losses all the conquests are restored.

**1655-56** The patriarch Nicon calls two councils of the church for the purpose of revising the Bible and service-books. In consequence of this change a great schism takes place in the Russian church. The adherents of the old books are known as Raskolniki, and are to this day subjects of persecution.

**1667** Peace of Andrussov with Poland: Little Russia east of the Dnieper, including Smolensk, Kiev, Seversk, Vitebsk, and Polotsk, is acquired by Russia. Thus the territory which had been taken by the Lithuanians and annexed to Poland by Treaty of Lublin (1569) became Russian again.

**1670** Rebellion of Stenka Radzin. He takes Tzaritzin, Astrakhan, Saratov, Samara, Nijni-Novgorod, Tambov, and Penza.

**1671** Stenka Radzin is defeated near Simbirsk and executed at Moscow.

**1676** Death of Alexis. He is succeeded by his eldest son, **Feodor.** During his reign the books of pedigrees (*razviadnie Knigi*), which determines the rank of each family and the office to which it was entitled (*mestnichestvo*), were destroyed.

**1682** Death of Feodor. After a sanguinary outbreak of the Strelitz, which lasted three days, **Ivan** and **Peter** were declared joint sovereigns, and their sister Sophia was to act as regent during their minority.

**1689** Treaty of Nertchinsk: the fertile region of the Amur, conquered by a handful of Cossacks, is restored to the Chinese, and the fortress Albazin is rased.

1696 Peter takes from the Turks the fort of Azov, situated at the mouth of the Don, and converts it into a naval port. In its vicinity he commences the building of the new town of Taganrog.

1697-98 Peter makes his first journey through Europe.

1698 The Strelitz break out into open revolt, which is suppressed with great bloodshed. Their corps is dissolved.

1699 Peter forms a coalition with Poland and Denmark against Sweden.

1700 Beginning of the Northern War. The Russian forces sustain a severe defeat at Narva. The beginning of the new Russian year is changed from the first of September to the first of January.

## THE EIGHTEENTH CENTURY

1703 Peter begins the building of St. Petersburg.

1706 The Cossacks of the Don revolt.

1707 The secret marriage of Peter with Catherine takes place.

1709 Mazeppa, hetman of the Little-Russian Cossacks, revolts. Battle of Pultowa.

1710 Turkey declares war against Russia.

1711 The old supreme council of boyars (*douma*) is replaced by the senate, into which merit and service might obtain admission independently of noble origin. By the terms of the Treaty of the Pruth Peter surrenders to the Turks his artillery, gives back Azov, and undertakes to rase Taganrog.

1714 The Russians gain over the Swedes the important naval victory of Åland or Hankül. Peter becomes master of Finland.

1717 Peter makes a second tour through Europe. A general police, modelled on that of France, is instituted.

1718 Peter's eldest son, Alexis, is executed. The old prikaz is replaced by colleges for foreign affairs, finance, justice, and commerce.

1719 The Russians ravage Sweden almost up to the gates of Stockholm.

1720 The Russians renew their devastation of Sweden, notwithstanding the presence of an English fleet.

1721 Treaty of Nystad with Sweden: Peter is left master of Livonia, Esthonia, Ingria, and the districts of Viborg and Kexholm in Finland. Peter promulgates an ukase (afterwards abrogated by Paul) that the sovereign has the right of naming his successor. The Patriarchate is abolished and its income united to the public revenue. In its place the holy synod is established for the supreme direction of church affairs.

1722 The *tchin* is established: whoever enters the service of that state becomes a gentleman. The exporting of merchandise through Archangel is prohibited in favour of St. Petersburg.

1722-24 War with Persia. The provinces of Ghilan, Mazandaran, and Astrabad (Astarabath) are annexed to Russia.

1725 Death of Peter. He is succeeded by his second wife, **Catherine.**

1726-27 The St. Petersburg Academy of Science founded.

1727 Death of Catherine. She is succeeded by **Peter II,** son of Alexis. Menshikov, who was the real ruler of Russia under Catherine, is banished to Siberia.

1730 Death of Peter II. **Anna,** daughter of Ivan, the brother of Peter the Great, is chosen his successor after submitting to the terms dictated by the great nobles—terms intended to convert the government into an oligarchy.

1733-35 War of the Polish Succession: Russia intervenes on behalf of the elector of Saxony, Augustine III, and defeats the French attempt to replace Stanislaus Leszczynski on the throne of Poland.

1735 Russia surrenders her Persian possessions in return for extensive trading privileges to Russian merchants.

1735-39 War with Turkey, in conjunction with Austria. The Russians conquer Otchakov at the mouth of the Dnieper and the important fortress of Khotin on the same river. But at the peace of Belgrade, hastily concluded by the Austrians, they retain only Azov.

1740 Death of Anna. **Ivan VI,** her grand-nephew, succeeds her, with Biron, duke of Courland, as regent during his minority.

1741 A coup d'etat, led by Field-marshal Münich, deposed Biron and raises Princess Anna, mother of Ivan, to th regency. But Münich is the real ruler. A palace revolution deposes Ivan, sends Münich to Siberia, and raises to the throne **Elizabeth,** a daughter of Peter the Great by Catherine. Sweden, urged on by France, declares war. The Swedes are defeated at Vilmanstrand.

1742 Seventeen thousand Swedes surrender at Helsingfors. The Armenian churches in both capitals are suppressed by order of the holy synod.

1743 Treaty of Åbo with Sweden; Russia acquires the southern part of Finland as far as the river Kymmene.

1753 The custom-houses of the interior, as well as many toll duties, are suppressed.

1755 The first Russian university is founded at Moscow.

1756 The first Russian public theatre is established at St. Petersburg. Three years later another theatre is established at Moscow.

1757 The Russians under Apraxin defeat at Jägerndorf the Prussians under Lewald.

1758 The Russians under Fermor are defeated by Frederick the Great at Zorndorf. The Academy of Fine Arts is established at St. Petersburg.

1759 Saltikov defeats Frederick at Kunersdorf.

1760 The Russians plunder Berlin.

1762 Death of Elizabeth. She is succeeded by her nephew, **Peter III,** son of her sister Anna. He makes peace with Frederick, restores to him east Prussia, which was entirely in the hands of the Russians, and orders his army to aid Frederick against the Austrians. Peter issues an ukase freeing the nobility from the obligation of entering upon some state employment; is assassinated and is succeeded by his wife, **Catherine.** Catherine recalls the Russian armies from Prussia.

1764 Assassination of Prince Ivan. Resumption of the ecclesiastical lands with their one million serfs by the state.

1766-68 A great *sobor* is convened, first at Moscow and then at St. Petersburg, for the compilation of a new code. It fails of its object.

1767 An ukaze forbids serfs to bring complaints against their masters, who were authorised to send them at will to Siberia or to force them into the army.

1767-74 War with Turkey.

1768 Massacre of Jews at Uman, in the Government of Kiev, under the leadership of the Cossack Gonta.

1769 The Russians under Galitzin take Khotin.

1770 Rumiantzev is victorious over the Tatars on the banks of the Larga and over the grand vizir at Kagul. Three hundred thousand Kalmucks, with their wives and children, their cattle and their tents, flee from Russia to China.

1771 Conquest of the Crimea by Dolgoruki. Annihilation of the Turkish fleet at Tchesme.

1772 The Congress of Fokshani fails to bring about peace and the war is renewed. First division of Poland. Russia acquires White Russia, including Polotsk, Vitebsk, Orsha, Mohilev, Mstislavl, Gomel.

1773-74 Pugatchev's revolt.

1774 Peace of Kutchuk-Kainardji: the sultan acknowledges the independence of the Tatars of the Crimea, the Bug and the Kuban, and cedes to Russia Azov on the Don, Kinburn at the mouth of the Dnieper, and all the fortified places of the Crimea.

1775 The Zaparog military republic of the Cossacks is dissolved. The empire is reorganized. Instead of fifteen provinces there are created fifty governments subdivided into districts.

1783 Formal annexation of the Crimea and the country of the Kuban.

1787-92 Second war with Turkey in conjunction with Austria.

1788-89 War with Sweden. The Peace of Varela restores the *status quo ante bellum.*

1788 The storming of Otchakov by Potemkin, accompanied by an indiscrimate massacre.

1789 Suvarov wins the battles of Fokshani and Rimnik. Potemkin takes Bender.

1790 Suvarov takes Ismail. The Austrians sign the Peace of Sistova, but the Russians continue the war. Repnin defeats the grand vizir at Matchin.

1792 Treaty of Jassy. The Russians retain only Otchakov and the seaboard between the Bug and the Dniester.

1793 Second division of Poland. Russia obtains an enormous extension of territory in Lithuania and absorbs the rest of Volhinia, Podolia, and Ukraine.

1794 Kosciuszko is defeated by Fersen at Maciejowice and Suvarov storms Praga, a suburb of Warsaw.

1795 Third division of Poland. Russia obtains the rest of Lithuania, besides other territories which at one time had been Russian, while Poland proper is divided between Austria and Prussia. The former power also obtains Galicia or Red Russia. Courland is annexed by Russia. Its last duke, Peter Biron, voluntarily renounces it in return for a yearly revenue.

1796 Death of Catherine. Accession of her son **Paul.**

1798 Paul promulgates the line of succession according to primogeniture, with precedence in the male line. Russia joins the second coalition against France, with England, Austria, Naples and Turkey.

1799 Suvarov defeats Moreau on the Adda, Macdonald on the Trebbia, and Joubert at Novi. Korsakov is defeated by Massena at Zurich, and Suvarov is forced to make his memorable retreat across the Alps.

1800 Reconciliation with France, chiefly owing to the English occupation of Malta.

## THE NINETEENTH CENTURY

1801 Assassination of Paul. His son **Alexander** succeeds him. The new emperor concludes treaties of peace with England, France, and Spain. Georgia, or Grusia, is formally annexed, and a war with Persia follows in consequence.

1802 Eight ministries are established in place of the colleges founded by Peter the Great.

1804 The Persians are defeated at Etchmiadzin.

1805 Alexander joins the third coalition with Austria and England. Battle of Austerlitz.

1806 Conquest of the Persian province of Shirvan, and the taking of Derbent.

1806 War with Turkey. Alexander joins fourth coalition, of which Prussia is also a member. Battles of Pultusk and Golymin.

1807 Battles of Eylau and Friedland. Peace of Tilsit. Russia acquires Bielostok, a part of Prussian Poland.

1808 War with Sweden. Finland is overrun by a Russian army.

1809 By the Treaty of Fredrikshamn Sweden surrenders Finland. The Finns are allowed complete autonomy, the czar being its grand duke. War with Turkey. The Russians are defeated at Silistria.

1810 The Russians are victorious over the Turks at Batyen on the Danube.

1811 The Russians are victorious at Rustchuk. Twenty thousand Turks surrender at Giurgevo.

1812 By the Treaty of Bukharest Russia acquires Bessarabia and a large part of Moldavia, with the fortresses of Khotin and Bender. The Pruth becomes its boundary. The district of Viborg, which was acquired from Sweden in 1744, is added to Finland. Count Speranski, leader of the liberal party, is dismissed. Later he was exiled to Peru. Invasion of Russia by Napoleon. Battles of Smolensk and Borodino. Firing of Moscow. Napoleon orders a retreat (October 18). Battle of Malojaroslavetz compels Napoleon to retreat by his old route. The Beresina crossed (November 26th-29th).

1813 By the Treaty of Kalish Alexander engages not to lay down his arms until Prussia had recovered all its lost territories. The Russians and Prussians are defeated at Lützen and Bautzen. The allies are repulsed before Dresden. Battle of Leipsic. Peace of Gulistan with Persia. Russia obtains Baku and the western shore of the Caspian.

1814 The Russians invade France together with the allies. At the congress of Vienna Alexander insists on the creation of a kingdom of Poland under his rule.

1815 By the Treaty of Vienna Alexander obtains all of Poland, except Galicia, Cracow, and Posen. Conclusion of the Holy Alliance.

1816 Abolition of serfdom in Esthonia.

1817 Abolition of serfdom in Courland.

1818 Abolition of serfdom in Livonia. In all Baltic provinces the emancipated peasants receive no portion of the land, which remains in possession of the nobles. A constitution and separate administration are granted to the Polish kingdom.

1819 Establishment of military colonies in the border provinces of the north, west and south.

1825 Death of Alexander. His brother **Nicholas I** succeeds him. Revolt of the Dekabrists.

1826 War with Persia.

1827 War with Turkey. The Turkish fleet is destroyed at Navarino by the combined fleets of England, France, and Russia.

1828 Peace of Turkmanchai. Persia cedes the provinces of Erivan and Nakhitchevan, pays a war indemnity, and grants important trading privileges. The Russians invade the Danubian principalities and take Varna. Paskievitch takes Kars.

1829 Diebitsch defeats the Turks at Kluvetchi, takes Silistria, crosses the Balkans, and takes Adrianople. Peace of Adrianople. Russia gets control of the mouths of the Danube, of a portion of Armenia including Erzerum, and receives a war indemnity.

1830 The new code, a complete collection of the laws of the Russian Empire, is promulgated. Polish insurection. The Russians are compelled to evacuate the country.

1831 Paskievitch takes Warsaw. The building of new Roman Catholic churches in Poland is prohibited.

1832 Poland is incorporated with Russia. The constitution granted by Alexander is annulled, and Poland is divided into five governments.

1833 By the Treaty of Unkiar-Skelessi Russia obtains additional rights to meddle in the internal affairs of Turkey.

1839 A Russian expedition to the khanate of Khiva is compelled to return.

1849 A Russian army is sent into Hungary. Capitulation of Görgei at Villagos.

1853 The Crimean War. The Russians occupy the Danubian principalities. Destruction of the Turkish fleet at Sinope.

**1854** France and England join Turkey. Battle of the Alma. Siege of Sebastopol. Fall of Bomarsund.

**1855** Sardinia joins the allies. Battles of Balaklava, Inkerman, and Tchernaia. Fall of Sebastopol. Bombardment of Sveaborg. The Russians take Kars. Nicholas I dies. His son **Alexander II** succeeds him.

**1856** Treaty of Paris. Russia relinquishes the mouths of the Danube and a portion of Bessarabia, restores Kars, gives up the protectorate over the Oriental Christians and the Danubian principalities, and agrees to have no war vessels in the Black Sea.

**1858** General Muraviev signs, the treaty of Aigun with the Chinese, by which Russia acquires the entire left bank of the Amur.

**1859** Capture of Schamyl.

**1861** Emancipation of the serfs.

**1863** Polish insurrection.

**1864** Final pacification of the Caucasus. Reforms in judicial administration. Institution of representative assemblies (zemstvos) for governments and districts. By ukase, Polish peasants are given in fee-simple the lands which they had cultivated as tenants-at-will.

**1865** Tashkend taken from the emir of Bokhara; organisation of the province of Turkestan.

**1866** Karakozov fires at the emperor at St. Petersburg.

**1867** Governor-generalship of Turkestan created. Sale of Alaska to the United States. A Slavophil congress is held at Moscow. The prince of Mingrelia relinquishes his sovereign rights for one million rubles. Russian is substituted for German as the official language of Livonia, Esthonia, and Courland. Peasants are given the ownership of the lands which they occupied as tenants.

**1868** Samarkand taken from Bokhara.

**1870** Khiva is stormed by General Kauffman.

**1871** The Pontus Conference, held at London, abolishes paragraph 11 of the **Paris** treaty delimiting Russian fortifications and naval forces on the Black Sea.

**1873** The right bank of the Amu Daria (Jaxartes) is annexed and the rest of Khiva becomes a vassal state.

**1874** Universal compulsory military service is introduced. The vice-royalty of Poland is abolished, and its administrative fusion with Russia becomes complete.

**1875** Russia cedes to Japan the Kurile islands. Japan gives up its claims to the southern part of Sakhalin.

**1876** The khanate of Khokand is absorbed and transformed into the province of Ferghana.

**1877** War with Turkey. The Russian advance is beaten back in Europe and in Asia. The Shipka pass alone remains in Russian hands. Three defeats before Plevna, which is besieged and forced to capitulate with 40,000 men. Kars is taken.

**1878** The Russians cross the Balkans. The Shipka army is captured, Adrianople taken, the last Turkish army is almost annihilated, and the Russians reach the Sea of Marmora. Treaty of San Stefano: Treaty of Berlin. Assassination of General Trepov at St. Petersburg, and acquittal of Vera Zassulitch. Assassination of General Mezentsev, chief of gendarmerie.

**1879** Soloviov fires six shots at the emperor. An attempt is made to wreck the train by which the czar was travelling from Moscow to St. Petersburg.

**1880** An attempt is made to blow up the Winter Palace. Loris-Melikov is placed at the head of a commission with dictatorial powers.

**1881** Assassination of the emperor. The Tekke-Turkomans are subjected by Skobelev. Anti-Jewish riots in southern Russia.

**1882** The " May laws " of Ignatiev issued against the Jews. Agrarian disturbances in the Baltic provinces give the government a welcome pretext for additional measures of russification.

**1883** **Alexander III** is crowned at Moscow.

**1884** The Turkomans of the Merv oasis make submission to Russia. The emperors of Russia, Germany and Austria meet at Skierniewice, where they form the Three Emperors' League for the term of three years.

**1885** The Afghans are defeated by General Komarov at Penjdeh. The Trans-Caspian railway is begun.

**1886** Contrary to Article 59 of the Treaty of Berlin, Batum is transformed into a fortified naval port.

**1887** A convention between England and Russia is signed for the delimitation of the Russo-Afghan frontier. The Russian advance in the direction of Herat is stopped.

**1888** An army officer named Timoviev makes an attempt on the czar's life. The Trans-Caspian railway is completed. Samarkand is linked with the Caspian. The imperial train is derailed at Borki. The czar and his family escape injury.

1890 Three commissions are appointed to prepare plans for assimilating the Finnish postal, monetary, and fiscal systems with those of the empire.

1891 A French squadron under Admiral Gervais visits Kronstadt. A succession of famines begins. An ukase is issued directing the construction of a railway line which should connect the European system with the Pacific coast. Work is commenced on seven sections simultaneously.

1893 A Russian squadron under Admiral Avelan visits Toulon.

1894 A military convention, arranged by the military authorities of Russia and France, is ratified. Death of Alexander III and accession of **Nicholas II.**

1895 An Anglo-Russian convention is signed settling the disputes as to the Pamirs. Russia, in conjunction with Germany and France, forces Japan to revise the terms of the Treaty of Shimonoseki by giving up the Liao-tung peninsula. Russia obtains the right to carry the Siberian railway across Chinese territory from Stretensk to Vladivostok, thus avoiding a long detour, besides getting control of North Manchuria.

1896 Coronation of the czar at Moscow. Catastrophe on the Khodinski plain. The emperor visits Germany, Austria, England, and France.

1897 President Faure makes an official visit to St. Petersburg, and the term "alliance" is for the first time used in the complimentary speeches. Specie payment is established.

1898 Russia leases Port Arthur and Talienwan, and obtains leave to carry a branch of the Trans-Siberian line through Manchuria to the sea. An imperial decree declares that the powers of the Finnish diet are to be limited to matters of strictly local, not imperial, concern. General Bobrikov is appointed Governor-general of Finland.

1899 During the Boxer uprising the Chinese authorities in Manchuria declare war against Russia. The Russian authorities retaliate with the massacre of Blagovestchensk. Russia assumes the civil and military administration of Manchuria. Peace Conference held at the Hague.

1900 The Bank of Persian Loans is founded by the Russian government.


## THE TWENTIETH CENTURY

1901 The state monopoly in the manufacture and sale of spirits is extended to the whole empire.

1903 Vice-Admiral Alexiev appointed as first Russian viceroy of the Far East.

1904 Outbreak of the Russo-Japanese war.

1906 Revolt put down. First duma opened by Czar. Dissolved in July by Imperial Ukase. Political crisis. Duma meets in Finland. Revolutionary movements and disorders throughout the Empire.

1907 Second duma opened in March; dissolved in June; socialist deputies arrested. Revolutionary movements continue. Treaties with Great Britain and Japan. Third duma opened in November.

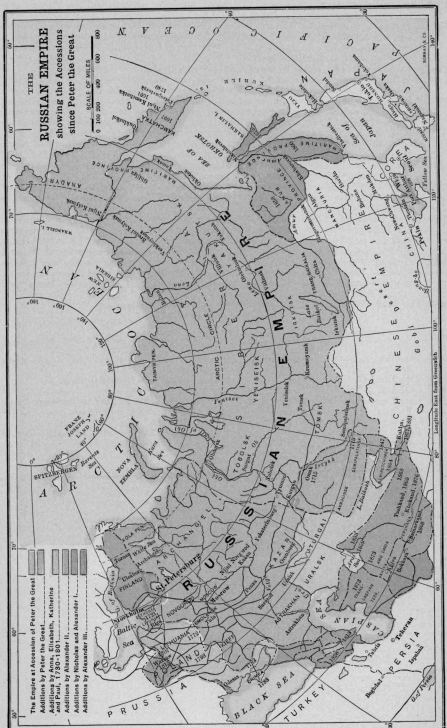

THE
RUSSIAN EMPIRE
showing the Accessions
since Peter the Great.

SCALE OF MILES
0   200   400   600   800

The Empire at Accession of Peter the Great.
Additions by Peter the Great.
Additions by Anna, Elisabeth, Katherine and Paul, 1730–1801.
Additions by Alexander II.
Additions by Nicholas and Alexander I.
Additions by Alexander III.